Best Poems of 1995

BEST POEMS OF 1995

The National Library of Poetry

Editors
Cynthia Stevens
Caroline Sullivan

Associate Editors
Joy Esterby
Nicole Walstrum

Best Poems of 1995

Library of Congress
Cataloging in Publication Data

ISBN 1-56167-260-2

Manufactured in The United States of America by
Watermark Press
11419 Cronridge Dr., Suite 10
Owings Mills, MD 21117

Editor's Note

The *Best Poems of 1995* is an impressive collection of artistry from our most outstanding contributors of past anthologies. This volume holds a vast array of delightful poems that touch our senses with more than mere words. As one of the editors and judges of the contributing entries, I had the rewarding opportunity to review and ponder the many pieces presented within this anthology. As always there are several poems I wish to honor with special recognition.

George W. Crampton was awarded the Grand Prize for his composition "Coral Reef" (p. 1). Using a wide spectrum of colorful descriptions, Crampton takes us underwater into a beautiful deep-sea paradise. Although some of the oceanic terminology may be esoteric (such as lichen, goatfish, or wrasses), you will still find the structure of the verse captivates you by sound alone. Crampton composed a melody of language which flows with wonderful rhythm and alliteration:

Trumpet fishes standing tall, tails straining to the sky,
Mute relays for sweet seraphs call to angel fishes shy.
Placid goatfish grazing low, in fields of grass and stone --
A brief bucolic cameo adorning Neptune's throne.

Throughout the poem the coral reef is presented as harboring a place of supreme delight -- a heavenly place of purity:

Stone fingers standing, interlac'd and loc'd in placid prayer --
Both temple and a trysting place for creatures in its care.

and

Enchantment in Elysian Fields, in Eden's wat'ry earth --
The coral, in renewal, yields the promise of its birth.

I urge you to dive into this verse for a lucid journey into the hidden treasures of the "Coral Reef."

Another intensely imaginative piece is "An Eddy of Thought," by Oscar Perkins Jr. (p. 429). Perkins speaks of the obstacles a writer may face in his or her own thinking process when trying to create:

Writers rummage round the memory bin,
Dowsing for dreams, with their bag lady shrew
Dribbling, drivelings, barking at them,
For things they did and things they did not do.

Perkins uses several metaphors for how a writer may be in torment for being stuck in writer's block and for not producing any worthwhile writing:

Let 'em [the writers] *kneel before Mnemosyne now,*
In livid choler for the muse to view;

and

Declare that he [the writer] *should full of wonder be,*
To languish forever in lawful woe;

Perkins follows with the concept that when stunted with writer's block, the writer cannot function with normal day-to-day living:

Can't remember how to season his eggs,
How much milk to put in his cereal;
Could it be because he's steeped in old age,
Could it be because he is ethereal?

The writer, according to Perkins, is merely caught in "an eddy of thought" -- a whirlpool of ideas in which not one will surface. Although some may view this as a normal process of writing, others believe it a hindrance, or failure:

Mayhaps he's caught in an eddy of thought,
That some deem as right and others deem naught.

A wonderfully vivacious work of art is "The Filly Finished First" by George T. McWhorter (p. 7). You are bound to race through this poem which delightfully keeps you moving from one line to the next.

"Autumn Relic," by Eric Noel Perez (p. 426), is an enchanting piece implicating the concept of life and death with forever changing seasons.

Fed from the strums of virgin's lips I exhale the
ash of an innocent's pyre and call the requiem my
atmosphere, watching the dead fade to crimson.

With unique connotations Perez implies he is in the autumn of his own life:

I dance with childhood friends whose voices have
grown wooden, sing of acorn theories that stay
mysterious beneath the orange static of leaves,

Life goes on while he continues to hunger for the past, his summer.

Also revealing the pains and pleasures of reminiscing are: "My Youth" by Daniel G. Baker (p. 427); "The Stronghold" by Grace Roberson Hicks (p. 432); and "Windmill Memory" by Julie A. Rapose (p. 187).

Several other prominent poems you won't want to miss are: "The Fool" by Kerry Jo Lee (p. 265); "The Nature of My Homeless Man" by Caroline Todd (p. 347); and Penny Weeks' "American Urban Hymn 1994" (p. 151).

Although I do not have the time or space to individually critique every eminent poem appearing within ***Best Poems of 1995,*** you will notice that each piece of artistry is an admirable contribution. May all of the artists within this anthology be renowned for their talents and efforts in creative writing.

I sincerely hope that you enjoy reading the ***Best Poems of 1995.***

Cynthia A. Stevens,
Senior Editor

Acknowledgements

The publication ***Best Poems of 1995*** is a culmination of the efforts of many individuals. Judges, editors, assistant editors, graphic artists, layout artists and office administrators have all brought their respective talents to bear on this project. The editors are grateful for the contribution of these fine people:

Elizabeth Barnes, Jeffrey Bryan, Chris Bussey, Kim Cohn, Amy Dezseran, Joy Esterby, Aundrea Felder, Ardie L. Freeman, Hope Freeman, Kathy Hudson-Frey, Paula Jones, Steve Miksek, Diane Mills, Eric Mueck, Lamont Robinson, Rich Schaub, Michelle Shavitz, Jacqueline Spiwak, Caroline Sullivan, Nicole Walstrum, Ira Westreich, Tiffany Wilson, and Diana Zeiger.

Howard Ely,
Managing Editor

Winners of the *Best Poems of 1995* Contest

Grand Prize

George W. Crampton / Bath, NC

Second Prize

Daniel G. Baker / Santa Monica, CA
Grace Roberson Hicks / Corsicana, TX
Kerry Jo Lee / Rancho Palos Verdes, CA
George T. McWhorter / Louisville, KY
Eric Noel Perez / Port Jefferson Station, NY
O. E. Perkins Jr. / Wylie, TX
Julie A. Rapose / Plymouth, MA
Vivian Schulte / New York, NY
Caroline Todd / Flemington, NJ
Penny Weeks / Houston, TX

Third Prize

Monique Adam / Oakland, CA
Arthur Byrd Adams / Detroit, MI
Cheryl L. Ahner / Oak Lawn, IL
Muriel W. Alexander / Rochester, NY
Barbara Barnes / Elkhart, IN
Clyde Beakley / Waldport, OR
Michael Craig Berg / Tamarac, FL
Donald L. Biesecker Jr. / Waynesboro, PA
Joan Boyes / La Lucia Natal South Africa
Josette Reboul Brogan / Washington, DC
Dorothy Brooks / Ardmore, TN
Earline Brunt / Logansport, IN
Erika Bruesewitz / Appleton, WI
Ron Busbee / Valparaiso, FL
Tom Carey / Flushing, NY
Elizabeth Cartwright-Hignett / Wiltshire, England
Lewis I. Chace / Brewster, NY
Louise Wilkerson Conn / Hazlehurst, MS
Phebe E. Davidson / Aiken, SC
John C. Flores / Angleton, TX
R. Arlin Genzoli / Fortuna, CA
Seamus Gorrell / Donegal, Republic of Ireland
L. S. Thompson Greuling / Duncanville, TX
Christopher W. Hanson / Delavan, WI
Connie Hess / Lexington, OH
Rose Mary Hooper / Bovey Tracey Devon, England
Grace Hyland / Westbury, NY
Piera Incitti / Kingsville, ON Canada
Callixtus E. Ita / South River, NJ
Christopher R. Jennings / Las Vegas, NV
Anne Kaye / Digby, NS Canada
Carin Kontner / Redondo Beach, CA
Bud Lipscomb / Ellettsville, IN
Martanne Louthan / Bartlesville, OK
Darlene A. Lytle / Hubbard, OH
Shauna MacKintosh / Kearns, UT
R. J. Matheson / Middlesex, England
Cara McCafferty / Cherry Hill, NJ
Michael J. McCune / Chevy Chase, MD
Harriet Mishkoff / New Rochelle, NY
Cavin T. F. Mooers / Fort Bragg, NC
Jean Manning / Decatur, GA
Barry W. North / Boutte, LA
Karl Oleksak / Phoenix, AZ
Jan Olson / Torrance, CA
Valerie J. Palmer / Peace River, AB Canada
Richard Paul / Bergenfield, NJ
Helen Platt / Winter Park, FL
Elisabeth Richards / Burlington, ON Canada
Erin Riddell / Appleton, WI
George E. Schmauch Jr. / Macungie, PA
Vicki Schrieber / Mesa, AZ
Marie Scott / Kamloops, BC Canada
J. C. Smith / Roswell, GA
William T. Smith / Sacramento, CA
V. L. Steward / Grand Rapids, MI
Ann Marie Stoltz / Saint Louis, MO
Gene W. Taylor / Los Alamos, NM
Marcia Waldbillig / Spring, TX

Congratulations also to all semi-finalists.

Grand Prize Winner

Coral Reef

The coral castle rises sheer from bottom sand's pure white,
Its lofty turrets reaching near the azure surface light.
Stone fingers standing, interlac'd and lock'd in placid prayer —
Both temple and a trysting place for creatures in its care.

Elkhorn coral's shadows soar o'er convoluted boulders
A-jumbled on the ocean floor, bedecked with lichen shoulders.
Sea fans test the current's gage, defending sacred spaces —
Sheltered lees in pristine cage of ocean's warm embraces.

Trumpet fishes standing tall, tails straining to the sky,
Mute relays for sweet seraphs call to angel fishes shy.
Placid goatfish grazing low, in fields of grass and stone —
A brief bucolic cameo adorning Neptune's throne.

Brilliant, dainty wrasses flash their chevrons blue and gold,
Darting swift to guard their cache, as sunbeams they enfold.
Squads of soldier fish enrolled by sergeant majors bright,
Wheeling, leading charges bold against intruders might.

Kaleidoscope of color found in ocean's depths of blue,
Encircling the ramparts 'round the castle's varied hue.
Enchantment in Elysian Fields, in Eden's wat'ry earth —
The coral, in renewal, yields the promise of its birth.

George W. Crampton

The Wall

They walked
Slowly, silently, hesitatingly
Along the black wall honoring their dead.
The wall grew before them in numberless inscriptions,
Thousands of stark names imprinted on black granite sand.
Their loss was real again and they cried unashamedly to each other
And finally the hawks and doves of long lost years
Spread their worn wings together
To share their love for the lost
And become one
Once more.

John F. Gardiner

Bryant Park, NYC 1994

A SOPHISTICATED plateau like a lady, ERECT,
Walking freely and elegantly, Breezily...
In her very high-heeled, forest-green, open leafy-laced shoes...
Amidst the cascading REFLECTIVES, ENCLAVES toward the skies.
* * * BRILLIANT SUNLIGHT * * *
- - - Mirrored - - -
- - - Down - - -
- - - Waterfalls - - -
Submerse the landscape in a pleasantry, Rollicking Muffle,
Not swampy; Verd Antique.
A soothed Parisian Refreshment,
Bench marked by filtered darkened and lightened lime-sun.
Flanked, Sectioned, by a Caesarean Library; "Et tu Brute?"
- - - - CHAMPAGNED - - - -
To pour smooth the cobbly Kilometers and Miles.
Where the VIOLA VIENNESES, WALTZES, MY EXISTENCE.
Where the TUBA SOUSAS UP A MARCH, SO PATRIOTIC,
GRANITE AND STEEL CRY A GAMUT OF EMOTIONS.
SO LIKE NIAGARA, YET OFF - - - TO AN UNRUSHED PACE AND STATE.
DEW-DROPLETS SETTLE, NOURISH, AN INNER GREEN OF MY LIFE!

John Laffey

Winter Skeletons

Tired eyes alight on brittle branches,
a cold reflection of a common fate;
Winter skeletons alike on desert plains,
longing for indifference.

In the quiet of this frozen waste
are locked the lonely echoes of the lost -
and yet
too lonely to be lost,
too chained to be adrift,
Like empty dreams that scratch the shattered panes,
to unleash forgotten truths.

Tired ears awaken in the stillness -
a symphony of fragile chimes:
icicles against an angry wind
that strips the branches bare.

Debra Kraft

The River

The quiet river flowing smoothly in the dark
A duck lying by the river bed.
Listening to the river's music is so beautiful
The river makes a lovely sound
Sing away, sing away, sing me to sleep
Oh sing, sing, sing me to sleep

Alicia Virg-In

Firefighters

Snap hook to wire, jump into wild fire
Chute opens twelve feet, five seconds real feat

Smoking trees coming fast, then just go past
Land hard on rocks, jars body to socks

Join up with team, ground full of steam
Fight inferno red hot, trees explode go pop

Trade tools shovel pick, fire tries to lick
Inaccessible spots they go, fire breaks hurriedly hoe

No time to talk, job is to block
Keep starting new line, sweat makes face shine

Self contained all day, team effort little say
Live in sauna clothes, never have water hose

Relief tumbles from sky, passes then right by
Wind shifts watch out, spread word all shout

Fire envelopes they're trapped, hardly time get wrapped
Oxygen gone from air, blast removes clothes hair

Death is very quick, like candle snuffed wick
God takes them 'way, not fight another day

Incredible people property save, so few that brave
But their families' pain, not worth our gain

Fred Small

Molded Clay

God didn't ask me if I wanted to be
Black, white, or yellow.
God didn't ask me where I wanted to be
Hill, sea or meadow.

He molded clay, tints concert symphony
Beast, plant and person.
Light cycle, God's Image live harmony
Mid tide and season.

God's order: Love, Cherish, Share, Amity.
Keep faith for power.
Greed, hate and war threatens world's destiny.
Heed God, my brother.

Doris Snyder

The Gift

Give of yourself this Christmas Day, for Christ-filled love has come your way

May your heart sing gladly in prayer, rejoice in the Lord everywhere

Dream a little, laugh a little, hum to the tune of a fiddle

Dance in delight around the tree, of God's blessings for you and me

A Savior is born to teach all, the Art of forgiveness your call

Surrounded with Angels galore, may a peace arise from your core

In awe of the promise Christ brings, may you blossom on Angels' wings

The birth of Immanuel reigns, His love will be strengthening veins

Share the greatest joy ever known, in a lifetime solely your own

In remembrance of his glory, speak of the world's greatest story

Give of yourself this Christmas Day, for Christ-filled love has come your way

Beverly Withee

1458

6 One day is innocent and zero, you bleed don't procrastinate 1
18 Two by two, eons or seconds, beheaded, 1458 1
32 Three worlds from now who will know, care, try, manslaughter or 1
procreate
38 Dark moments, bright hopes 1
46 Dark flesh, bright clothes 1
54 Dark rooms, bright quotes 1
60 One night I checked, you'd have to know why 1
68 Too sad to laugh, too surprised to cry 1
80 Three feet away I couldn't look you in the eye 1
86 The distance to the sun 1
92 Is the only greater sum 1
102 You're closing fast on infinity 1
108 All the dirt makes land 1
116 But your total is quicksand 1
128 A numerical monstrosity 1
132 Knock knock; who's there? 1
140 2000; 2000 who? 1
152 2000 is coming and there's not a thing you can do about it 1

1458 Even Quitters Use A Little Something 1

David Rojas

How Have You Been

"Implanted Mind - eyes deceitful - fermented thinking - second opinion Dominion doubted — awaited reunion — Mind, Soul, and Body. Four-score wacks and death — awaited stay — may come this way soon Painted moon, she sets a missing plate, one less — a mess. Indecision — fate decided — decisive ruining — reunion complete. Death so sweet! Too late — fate awaits, waiting — change, I must deceive! Receive the sign — this is mine, so true — how blue. The blood, running slow — the life blood's flow, blue — I miss you; 'so do I!' I could die, maybe — Someday; awake thee — see Life go on without — within these walls... Deceitful eyes, Satan — reflected — tumorous Mind — Soul betrayed, allayed. May, the summer month — sandals for thee — remedy, failure; little left of her within — Soul in ruin — the Beast prevailing — Body's failing 'posure — lifeless babe, maiden, fair — fair the sentence — guilty, guilty Hell! Swells the tumor. Beastly rumor true! Pallid hue, portrayal — betrayal, pricking thorns — November's storm abrew. Never more than you. Such sweet sorrow that Tomorrow — Death! Good-bye, Farewell, Auf Wiedersehen! We'll meet - we'll meet again — what sad end!"
— Your Friend

Billy Bowden

Recipe For The Future (Ingredients)

1 1/2 c...of...AMBITION
1 1/4 c...of...ENCOURAGEMENT
FAITH IN CHRIST
2 1/4 c...of...HOPE
3 1/4 c...of...BRAVERY
(but a lot when needed)

Mix AMBITION with ENCOURAGEMENT.
When mixed well, you get willpower. The willpower to adventure out into the world.
If the first road you take is closed, and detours are necessary, you may get lost.
Don't get discouraged. Just have FAITH in CHRIST. He'll get you there!!
Try another road and HOPE it's the right one.
If not, show your BRAVERY and keep trying.
When these INGREDIENTS are used together throughout the years of life, success will be yours.

Jan Fillinger

Recipe For A "Tasteful Poem"

What you will need:
1 pad of paper (large size)
1 1/2 boxes of pencils (with erasers)
1 desk and chair (can substitute table)
2 reading lamps (include extra bulbs)

DIRECTIONS:
Slowly pour appropriate words onto paper.
Add several thoughts, plus a few tidbits.
Pick out any negatives, while adding positives.
Begin to condense, adding only necessary
words to complete.
When properly assembled, entire mixture
will congeal.

Temperature:
Try to keep yours at 98.6.
Time to complete:
As long as necessary (check often for doneness).
Expected Results:
Possibly a prize winning "GOODIE".

Eve Westaby

Ahoy There!

We sail with roaring tide tonight,
A cargo of precious pearls on board
To add to the fierce old dragon's hoard.

He'll churn up the sand in his fiendish glee
And rattle his scales and roar with delight
When we lay at his feet our pearls of the night!

Together we'll celebrate our success
With mountains of food and gallons of wine
And music and dancing and many a rhyme.

Then, during the night, he'll fill up our ship
With fireworks made from the stars up above...
That magical stuff we all of us love.

He now has his pearls and we're headed for home!
Oh, the lighter the load, the faster we'll go
And the sooner we'll be there, m'lads, you know,

And the fireworks show every night of the year,
Thanks to our mythical monster friend,
Ought to never never ever ever come to an end!

Joan M. Jones

The Touch Of Memories

She sat down by the fireplace,
a chilled bottle of wine and two glasses.
The fire seemed to warm the room
and the shadows grew warmer.

She gazed at his picture on the wall.
His eyes seemed alive with feeling and passion for her even now.
She stirred the ashes, and the shadow grew closer
almost holding her, embracing her.

She poured the wine into the glasses
and a faint wind stirred the flame.
To you my love.
The wine felt like a long passionate kiss on her lips.
She felt the touch of a tear at the thought of those sweet memories.

The shadows would comfort her
like they had done so many times in the past.
The picture seemed to move with the flicker of the burning logs
and the stillness of the room seemed to be filled with his presence.

Time passed and evening disappeared
leaving two empty wine glasses flickering in the morning light.

David C. Reffert

Vivid Embrace

The granddaughter recalls with vivid embrace
A classy, aged woman, a distinctive worn face
A long legged woman, with red patent shoes
And definite talents to charm and amuse
Crossing her legs, as she sat in her chair
Transfixed with the way, she spoke of her hair
Dark and exotic, she could sit on the strands
Weaving her story with knuckled old hands
Grandmother's remembered in vivid embrace
Gone now for years, yet still able to trace
Her life through her stories, which time can't erase
A life full of color and vivid embrace

Jeanne Roberts Maertens

What Is Prejudice?

What is prejudice?
A dark and unknown bias,
that wears an ignorant face,
to which we hope few will ascribe,
and that none will let it replace,
the cherished hours you can pass with friends,
when you no longer see the color of their skin,
nor see their differences as a barrier,
but see only the harmony that they bring,
don't listen to an ugly voice,
that speaks nothing but hate,
listen to your friend who brings you harmony and bliss,
so when someone asks you
what is prejudice?
just say it's something ugly,
and you can't be a part of it.

Celine Rose Mariotti

Living The Dash

The saga began when a cry was heard
A date appeared but not a word
Yet a dash emerged amid guarded glee
To await the trials of destiny.

Growth is nurtured at time of birth,
And knowledge accrues during time on earth.
Knowledge is unfounded if we fail to care
For those in wait for an equal share.

A share of an existence, transient in scope
Filled with success, failure and hope.
Our being continues with a meager breath
While we strive for perfection as our lone bequeath.

A dash is our being whatever its worth
Depending, of course, our time on this earth.
It's a transitional state as we should know
But in spite of all we continue to grow.

Grow in contentment to finish the race—
Filled with awareness of love, peace and grace.
Then God with his chisel can complete the slate...
"He lived on this earth: Date Dash Date."

George Larkin

A Falling Rose

A rose,
all alone and thirsty, gasping for air.
Its roots,
dry and dead, feeling its life being torn away.
Its petals,
crumbling and breaking off, falling from their life.
Its thorns,
no longer sharp and deadly, now they are dull and smooth.
A rose,
it screams for life, but is silent as it crumbles to its death.

Jolyn Hecht

The Evergreen Pine

What kinds of trees are found in the line?
A fir, sycamore, juniper, or pine.
The trees all stand so stately and fine.
My favorite of all is the ever tall pine.

People during the holiday season stand in line.
To pick out their own special pine.
That one is yours or is it mine.
Oh really how sad to cut all the pines.

So regal and glorious, oh how fine.
The mountains so full of the evergreen pine.
Up hill and down they stand in line.
What fun to walk in the woods through the pines.

Candice M. Myer

The Little Frog

A little frog sat on a lily pad
A gazing up at the sky.
He turned his head and winked his eye
And stuck out his tongue and caught a fly.

A wily snake came slithering by
His dinner he did see the itty, bitty, frog said,
"Today it won't be me."

He slid down from the lily pad
Into the water very deep
And dug down into the mud
and tried to go to sleep.

But a noise kept bothering him
It was a belly deep, belly deep
So back up to the top he went
To try and take a peek.

With one eye in and one eye out
He looked around and all about.
And spied a big frog when his head did cock.
Out there sitting on a rock
Croaking "Rebbit, Rebbit, Rebbit."

Billy L. Walker

The Gift

A gift of love, a gift of joy,
a gift for more than one to enjoy.

She came wrapped in pink and white,
a gift of happiness and new life.

A gift of love so few will know,
a seed from one that will not be known.

One mother takes her gift of life and passes it beyond her sight.
For on that night she gives her daughter a new life.

From trembling hands to trembling hearts
passes a life and a new start.

As one's life returns to normal,
a new family starts.

Adoption, the breaking and making
of families and new starts.

Jeannette McCain

God's Gift

The world of God ... the abode of man.
A gift God-given .. without deed.
A universe dedicated to God's earthly plan
To meet mankind's need ... not selfish greed.

We are the keepers of a fertile earth,
The recipients of God's priceless gift,
Served by His bounty from the day of our birth,
And led by His spirit ... our souls to uplift.

The world is a haven with wonders untold,
Where man can stand on hallowed sod,
Counts his blessings ... not his gold -
Raises his eyes and speaks to God.

Burl P. Stead

Precious Miracle

Angelic voices heard on high
a glorious morn after the nigh,
a savior born and the world rejoices
listening once again to heavenly voices;

A peace so calm across the land
the king has arrived with power grand,
a sign of hope unto the world today
for in his manger Jesus lay;

Our most precious miracle filled with grace
as wise men gaze upon his face,
a sign to all that our God reigns
to rid the world of sin and stains;

His glory shown both far and wide
He came to love and teach and guide,
He was born to live so he could die
to make a way for you and I.

Carol Lee Grainger

Sorry, Botticelli

No Aphrodite here, born in the seafoam,
a half-shell to surfboard ashore.
Once-turquoise waves from the bright ocean rocking
tug at her ankles as she slogs her way to the beach.

No flowing golden hair strategically and gracefully placed.
A bandana this morning collected and still holds breasts
while swimming trunks provide other modesty.

She drops to her hands and knees, stretches flat on her belly,
then rolls over. She wriggles her buttocks into the cool underneath
sand and presses the small of her back against a rolled towel.

Waves of heat pulse over her. Sweat beads on her upper lip
and among hairs of underarm stubble, puddles on her chest,
and glistens behind her knees.

Enough. She stands and puts on a hat to shade
the sun-crisp sunburn on her face and shoulders.
Rubber sandals slap across the hot sand
before she wades into the water waist high.

Waves pat her bare midriff.
Hands on hips, she looks around, smiles.
No demure stance affected, not on this beach.

Adrienne Davis

Family

F is for faith, friendship and fun
A is for all, altogether for one
M is for members, each forming a chain
I is for Ideals we share with our name
L is for lives with love together sewn
Y is for you and your place in the home
Each letter is needed to spell Family
From the home comes the seedling of all society
It's the nursery and class room
of each generation
There is no substitution
For its life long foundation
If the family is happy
and all well adjusted
If they've prayed together
and in God they have trusted
If they've learned in the hard times
To all stick together
Then in the whirl winds of living
They can master the weather

Doris Cornett

The Seven Angels

A touch of your hand; a twinkle of an eye
A kind word as you're passing by
They went to the door with joy in their heart
They knew their journey was soon to start
For each trip you make may be your last
But many a shadow and memory you've cast
For many a child with their eyes to the sky
Pray for your safety as the minutes go by
For in your hand part of our history will lie
So as you fly on to answer your call remember
on earth you stand tall to all
For life must go on as we are always told
But there always will be the memory of the seven so bold
I know as I sat and looked toward the heaven
There appeared new stars exactly seven
So tomorrow we'll start on another mission to go
Cause we're all on the river of life, on the flow
But there will always be the touch of your hand,
A twinkle of your eye, a kind word as you were passing by

Clara Tearpak

The Knight With His Armor On

Through the streets walks a great knight,
a knight with his armor on.
Never does he disrobe.
He walks gracefully with his armor on.
An armor that shines more than silver.
His hands are led to weld a great sword.
The knight moves in the center of a battle;
he comes to save lives for this Lord.
He smiles as he cuts off Evil's hands,
and takes greater delight
in giving the humbled to his King.
This one is sought out and attacked,
but his offense is too strong.
For he carries with him an awesome shield.

As the battle ends he walks into the sun
as a true hero might.
He walks with his armor on.
He is the greatest of warriors under the King,
and his servants call him "Christ."

Chad Swift

What Stems Motherhood?

A story starts with just a word,
 A life a cry that's newly heard.
To fill the void and slake the thirst
 with lungs a'filling forth we burst.
The world admits, with patient nod,
 a newborn soul, with mother awed
by pain's great lesson, surely so,
 and new adventures yet to know.
Dare we to take of Life's full measure?
 We'd find that misery's Life's great pleasure.
In absence, yes, but past the pain
 and guided by our love again.
From day to day and dawn to dawn
 how can it be relied upon
To calm the fears and soothe the tears,
 the broken hearts all through the years.
And if it seems we've played the fool
 Forget us not this cardinal rule -
That which eludes ourselves in history
 keeps us a'yearning Life's great mystery.

John D. Wilson

Our Garden Of Eden

This lovely house so proud and tall
 A life of happiness fond urge to call
Its rooms so warm... serenity do shower
 A chimney tall... as a mighty flower
Hearth blazing merrily so warm and bright
 happy family merry in its glowing light
Blending of chatter and smiles at passing of day
 a blending of thoughts... all cares at bay
May it ever remain a cozy domain of content
 with blessings abounding... closeness cement
This haven and family with warm image so grand
 must surely be planned by God's Holy Hand

Anne Porter Boucher

Youth, My Fickle Friend

Youth is but a fickle friend
A mood, a song, a trend
Hope and love stay by her side
And when she's gone
They run and hide.

I knew a day when youth was near
Her friends and I were very dear
Together with him, our days were fun
Of walking in fields and running in the sun
And two hearts that beat as one.

But then one day, youth was gone
And her two friends tagged along
And he? Oh yes, he's gone too
Though I still see his yes of blue
Memories are all that's left of what we knew.

Oh youth, my fickle friend and me
Have parted now as you can see
But the mood, the song, the trend
Blow through my soul like winter's wind
Stored deep within my heart for keeps.

Ethel S. Butler

The Old House

High in the cliffs with rain and hail
 A night of blowing winds
Creaky house stood with creaky floors
 and wind blowing at the doors

A squeaky mouse lived in this house
This old house with many rooms of old paint peeling off
and a fence half down
With all the animals sneaking in

All the animals ran into the old house
 in different directions

Sparkle the crow flew to the open cupboard
Bandit the raccoon ran into large room, jumped into old chair

Snappy the turtle walked into small dark room
Squeezy the squeaky mouse ran through the narrow hall
 to the stairway
Up he went to the attic and found all his friends

What a night, so much rain and blowing winds the animals fell sleep
The night passed and morning light shone
What a beautiful day, all the animals were happy
And each one went its way.

Dorothy C. Guterman

"Camelot Regained"

Paradise, my boy.
A place where the best can rest enjoy.
Where you silently realize that life was no toy
And that for plenty of space there is no alloy.

Though after a fashion your dreams were once torn,
You never forgot that this town could be born.
Were clouds but to part with the dawn of the day,
You would still be so safe in the place where you stay.

The Word may yet go forth though looking unforlorn;
And a gladder but a simpler boy you would awake in morn.

John White Westmoreland

The Filly Finished First

On Derby day, the third of May, in an old Kentucky town
A race was run in beaming sun that brought the bleachers down!

The Derby picks for the "One-O-Six" were thirteen thoroughbreds:
A dozen males to tip the scales and a mare to turn their heads.

The odds were set on a NICKEL bet as the "darling" of the race,
While the KLUGMAN gray and a local bay were sure to show or place.

When the RUMBO black came on the track with canter bold and brisk
His rating soared on the betting board, and down came GENUINE RISK!

Like thunderbolts a dozen colts shot forward to the race,
While in the pack and holding back, the filly kept her pace.

The turn was made, the jockeys played their reins to gain position;
The leaders tugged, the NICKLE plugged, and stayed in this condition.

RISK hit her stride and pulled inside, the bluegrass bay close by;
The KLUGMAN gray then made his play in a burst of "do-or die!"

With bold attack the RUMBO black put wings upon his feet
And closed outside the actor's pride to challenge in a heat!

Three thoroughbreds spun out the threads of destiny that day...
The filly's speed kept up her lead, the black nosed out the gray.

The crowd went wild as fortune smiled and all the odds reversed;
The race was done, the Derby won, the filly finished first!

George T. McWhorter

A Rose

God gave me a rose, in my garden of life,
A rose more precious than gold.
A rose whose beauty will never die,
And a smile that will never grow old.

God gave me a rose to have and to hold,
To treasure my whole life through,
The love that she gave, each day she lived,
Was a love so precious and true.

Someone who cared, someone who shared,
All of my heart aches and joys each day.
Only God could bless such tenderness
That she shared along life's way.

One day from Heaven, an angel came down
And took her to Heaven, where all angels are found.
Someday I'll see her, the rose of my life.
That wonderful rose was my darling my wife.

Clay Perry Sr.

Peace Images

Guernsey cows rest beneath shade trees on
a Sabbath morn.

Kittens, cuddled at their mother's side, bask
in the autumn sun.

Cypress trees look at their profiles
in still waters.
A gentle breeze creeps across ripe wheat fields.

A gold and orange sun sets on gold and orange
marigolds.

Mockingbirds, in concert, shatter the quiet
of twilight, and

A weatherboarded meetinghouse keeps vigil in a
nave of pine trees.

Carlton W. Rountree

Quiet Things

A walk along the shore,
A simple dance across the floor,
That familiar step outside my door,
Are the quiet things
That give my heart its glow.

The happy planting of a marigold,
Watching a fire die to an amber glow,
Music in twilight, bubble baths by candlelight,
Are the quiet things
That give my heart its glow.

Perfect petals on a blooming rose,
The words from my soul called prose,
Lying with you, holding you close,
Are the quiet things
That give my heart its glow.

If you walk out my door,
The quiet things will be no more,
In their place my heart will implore,
And the wind that blows
Will then extinguish my heart's glow.

Donna L. Blackhall

The Rocking Chair

She's thinking of a song her mother taught her,
A soft hum coming form her lips.
The pain in her chest grows more intense
As her chair moves forward, then back it tips.

Still she hums that old folk song
The creak of the wooden chair keeping the beat.
She smiles, her grin breaking the make-up,
A strange response to life's final defeat.

But she's not afraid of the eternal rest,
She's seen her life reflected in her grandchildren eyes.
And that life was filled with love and hope.
No, she would never die.

So with these thoughts kept in her heart
She raises her eyes and smiles sweetly.
She reaches out and takes the Lords hand.
The chair slows, then stops completely.

Danielle LeDeoux

Dreams Of Summer

The day is cold and raw on this cloudy January morn.
A sparrow looks for food on a ground no longer warm.

Christmas has come and gone like so many in years passed on.
The happy and decorated season leaves me sad and feeling alone.

Everything looks so bleak now. The colors, so pretty, are gone.
The beauty of Summer's showcase no longer can be shown.

Hay is hauled for the cattle. The grass has all turned brown.
They look for a place protected, the cold wind blows all around.

Oh, for the sun to touch my face and warm earth beneath my feet.
To watch the flowers growing, with their nectar, for the bees, so
sweet.

Bears have the right idea, to sleep right through it all,
to wake with Springtime glistening, not remembering what
followed Fall.

On days like these so cold and damp, my mind would rather rest,
to dream of Summer days again, the season I love best.

Irma Catherine Lowery

Our Mighty Mississippi River

Ah, the wonders of the Mississippi River at its source,
A stream of lively waters on a destined course!
Its source comes from a spill of Minnesota's Lake Itasca;
It flows and grows like winter magic up in Alaska.
Tourists choose time to wade across twenty feet of cool sparkling
waters, for refreshment in contrast to this far-away down-stream
that's hotter.
From where did early explorers get this big river's name?
Yes, Itasca's Indian neighbors is from where it came.
Tallest red and white pines, and beaver ponds adorn the area of its
source, with a deep primitive .
Woodland stillness awaiting will bird's chorus.
This adventurous baby stream, after its source departure, first turns
North, then South, growing wider, slower, and older - crawling two
thousand miles to its mouth.
The Upper River wanders and winds to flow between the Twin Cities -
St. Paul to its left, Minneapolis on right; close, like twin kitties.
The Mississippi became historic for farmers, travel, fishing, and
even wars.
Giving motive to pioneer's Western Movement toward Pacific Shores.
Mississippi and Minneapolis, both names from the Indian Red Man,
Have earned importance for geography and history students to scan.
Have you found your way to the wondrous Mississippi Region?
It can give you freeness, wonder, and tourist views in legion.

Charles W. Miller

In My Mind's Eye

My life renewed with dawn's first light,
A victory won, a valiant fight.
The mighty foe stood straight and tall,
As would a king before his fall.

This villain loved to taunt and sneer,
Which filled my heart with dread and fear.
A stronger match I'd never known:
This fiend upon a golden throne.

I'd been reduced to just a shell,
This empty feeling I knew well.
I had to fight or all was lost,
I had to win, spare not the cost.

For what seemed an eternity,
I fought this beast which haunted me.
And finally, standing toe to toe,
I dealt the beast a fatal blow.

I cried aloud with all my might,
'Twas love, not hate that won this fight.
In my mind's eye I clearly see,
I was my own worst enemy.

Deborah L. Hite

Shared Perfection

A dream.
A vision of perfection,
Elegantly placed together, piece by piece.
Satin and soft lace embellished with pearls,
A touch of rose as trim.
Skilled hands shape my future, my honor - her dream.

Longing nervously for the moment to fulfill my purpose.
To finally be in her presence,
To witness her legendary beauty and grace.
Patiently I wait.
Suddenly she appears.
Gentle laughter fills the room.

Slowly my veil is lifted.
Her beauty is beyond compare.
Love, joy, happiness, excitement, overwhelming emotion.
She gently slips into my arms.
I embrace her soft, elegant being.
She turns and glances at our reflection - The Vision Of Perfection.

Gwendolene Kidwell

Valley Of The Clouds

I flew one day away up high
Across the broad wide open sky
A glimpse of heaven came in view
As I looked out into the blue

When I looked down into the clouds
My heart was pounding oh! So loud
I wanted to capture this beautiful scene
To know it's real and not a dream

The sun was shining oh! So bright
The clouds so beautiful so fluffy and white
God gave me this moment for which I'm proud
To view from the heavens the Valley of the Clouds.

Frances Roberson Deaver

A Sea Gull Means Home To Both Of Us

Watching a sea gull in graceful, silent flight
Against a sky of blue dotted with a cloud or two
Brings us a sense of peace; pleasures much the sight.
We could be at home or in a land far away and new.

Restful are both our spirits as we watch that sea gull.
One of us come from the West; the other from the East.
We both feel safe at home and everything seems peaceful.
The sea gull, is it over California or a Maine lobster feast?

John C. Calhoun III

Spring

Nature is awakening from a deep winter's sleep
  All around you see the promise of spring.
Little birds busy building their nests.
  And looking for twigs and string.

Soft breezes carry the fragrance of flowers
  As you see trees dressed in pink and white
You lift your eyes toward heaven,
  And give thanks for this beautiful sight.

The mountains towering high above
  The shade trees turning green
The crooked old river rolling on
  It is the prettiest spring you've seen

Have there been others so special,
  And you've been too busy to care?
How God's beautiful promise
  Is always everywhere

Take time to look and listen
  To the sounds and beauty of Spring
Your heart will be so gladdened
  You will lift your soul to sing.

Boots Billings

Just One

He took a sip, he said, "It's just one"
All he wanted was to have some fun
One became two then three, four, and five
He soon looked like he was barely alive
He managed to pull himself off of the floor
He started to head for the front door
He found his car and jumped inside
He decided he wanted to go for a ride
He didn't think he would hurt anyone
All he wanted was to have some fun.
He gunned his car to 80 miles per hour
And hit an on coming car with tremendous force and power
They both died instantly at the scene
They didn't even have time to let out a scream
He didn't think he would hurt anyone
All he wanted was to have some fun.

Jennifer Peltz

Blessed

As the sun comes up each morning,
And another day begins
I marvel in the glory of every living thing.
Then I realize just how blessed I am
With your love and you beside me
My life has been complete.
Now that we've reached our golden years
I look back to what has been,
And give thanks to the Almighty
For the wonderful life he's given me.

Erasmia Cacciola

Almost Christmas

It was almost Christmas, but in our house,
all our stomachs were growling, from not eating enough.
Dad got laid off at the factory this year.
Mother's new baby was almost here.
Brother fixed our radio so we could hear,
Christmas carols played over the air.
Little sister made cards from her coloring book.
While mother made Christmas decorations, from scraps she saved.
Dad fixed our toys making them like new,
I helped them all the best I could.
Hanging the decorations mother made and wrapping toys daddy
had fixed.
Little sister had a ball making cards,
there was so much joy it spread to our yard,
with all we were doing with our hearts.
No one would know we were almost starved.
Come Christmas morning I knew we would be,
holding hands in a circle where a tree should be.
Singing a few songs of cheer Christmas brings.
Then taking time to say a few prayers, each of us thanking God in
our own way, for the things we had and for the love that he gave.

Felix Bourree

Master Painter

As I sit here and think about
all the hues of life I've felt,
All the blues, and greens, and yellows,
all the colors seem to melt—-
Into one hue of life, and love,
given me from God above.

The orange of passion, the reds of hate,
Blues of serenity and greens of hope—-
of things to come.
And the grays, with which I cannot cope,
melt into one, a canvas.

His palette, with the sweeping stroke
the blending of His color,
None could paint this life I live so well, not any other.

When God completes His concept of my life, with colors varied,
And all His values blend into this life I've led,
Please, let it be a masterpiece—-
with the perspective right,
As I feel His gentle brush,
when I fall asleep, tonight.

Charlene W. Kohoutek

Love So Deep

It's amazing for me to be able to know
All the love this one man can constantly hold

The sound of His name sends chills up my spine
And tears always fall whenever He comes to mind

Talking to Him makes my days so much brighter
As my heavy burdens suddenly become so much lighter

The love I have for this man is so unmistakably strong
When I think of the pain He willingly suffered for so long

He is more than a friend - He is my beloved Savior
And I wish somehow I could return all His sweet favors

But for now I'll live this wonderful life He created for me
Till I can say to His face, "Dear Lord does thou know how much I
love Thee?"

He won't need to answer - not one word He'll speak
I'll know by the tear falling down on His cheek.

Aimee R. Moore

Traitor

Here we are again.
Alone.
Discussing life, the universe, death and taxes.
Again.
Sorting out our lives and trying to salvage
what little is left...
of us.
Too blind with love to see it was
over long ago.
I love you still.
I think.
I must have, because I put up with
your mood swings, and insults.
I'm glad you moved on first.
It makes things so much easier on me.
For I'm one who needs comfort;
you don't.
So, come back when you can't stay so long.
Goodbye my darling, dearest
Traitor.

Jennifer Smyder

"Pictures Of Time"

Through the many years
Along with many tears
Turning pages for happy hours
Looking from faces to colorful flowers
The pleasures and joy now appears
With the coming of the little dears
Adding new pages for our picture book
Time now to have second look
Watching changes in their stages grow
With each holiday more memories to show
One day for their smaller eyes to see
The love and fun married life can be
And knowing they shared a large part
Of life we live turning pages in their heart.

Dorothy I. Brown

Sonnet of Sadness (Sepulcrum Cordis)

This dark tomb of long forgotten essence—
An ancient gate fades into misty air—
Granite stones forever melting presence,
Long winter rows so brief they disappear
Under snowfalls of fading memories;
Ice crystals reflect in each placid mirror
Watching a sunset world of secret dreams,
Disturbed by slowly falling frozen tears.
Sleep with the echoed pools of cool moonlight,
Delusions floating through the drifting days
Despondent as the never-ending night—
Eternal thoughts like soft white silent waves.
Cold endless blanket hide my empty grave,
This lonely, broken heart and ceaseless pain.

Jay F. Manning

The Blue Sea Rolls

The blue sea rolls; the grey gulls sound,
And fishes flaunt their souls.
The waves are all of eiderdown;
The blue sea rolls.

The brown sand creeps; the brown sand folds.
The man-o-war's aground;
To the beach it firmly holds,
Huddled in a purple round.
A lone beachcomber now beholds
An ice-pink shell he's found.
The blue sea rolls.

Barbara R. Reid

Vagrants Of My Mind

As white, warm sunlight pours through the west window,
an instinctive command occurs. I run away with vagrants
of my mind.
Ambling fields of dry weeds, I kick cans and cattails.
I grab a stick and stab ground or slash a filmy pond.
Roaming railroad tracks, I confront hobos who live
just for today or clowns with grins that fool. Following
aroma of singed, pink cotton, hot popcorn and hearing
bellowed organ music, pumping into the sultry air,
I am drawn as if charmed by the piper. Barking voices,
ringing bells, clicking and whir of armature stirs excitement.
Upon a silver, sprinting pony, I fly away for always or
hop a train moving toward infinity.
Then, slowly sliding back to reality, dusk begins
This is how I find what was lost so long ago
.........a child.

Irene E. Senkiw

Caroline

dedicated to my daughter "Caroline"
When twilight falls across the sky,
And all the world is still,
I gather my thoughts again,
In tenor of refrain.
For the sweetness of a tender word,
To warm your very heart.
A pleasant word or two,
That floats as does a silver cloud,
And clings like morning dew,
A fond hello or how are you,
Can brighten your day,
And lead us from a darkened path,
Toward a lighter way, that's cheerful with tenderness,
I think about the things to come,
When morning light breaks through,
And starlight dots the blue.
No poet can relate what is in my heart,
I love you every second.
Whether near or far apart.
For you are woven tightly; in the corner of my heart.

Henry Camacho

The Maple Tree

In my childhood, there was a maple tree
And as I climbed from limb to limb,
I thrust aside the dull weight of reality,
The prodding stick of responsibility
That goaded me on and on.

The green jeweled bough
Gently touched my brow
And nurtured me.

My child, an adult before its time,
Long before its prime
Found in the tree
Quiet strength and peace
The essence of identity.

Now grown up, mature, in state of retrospection
I have recaptured my maple tree
The tightly-furled buds of introspection,
The cutting apart of past from present in dissection,
The far-reaching branches of reflection
I know the secret of my identity.

Barbara Carr

A Rose To Give

I'm sitting here and thinking dear, your birthday's coming soon.
And as I think, it's very clear, why I love this month of June.

It has your warmth, your gaiety, your sparkle, and your smile.
It has your sense of humor, your beauty, and grand style.

The evening has your fragrance, the breezes sing your tune,
And last night shining bright on high, I knew it was your moon.

And so I wondered what to buy to bring you happiness?
Shall it be a pair of gloves, and apron, or a dress?

Then I recalled another time - it was just a year ago.
Now let me see, what did I do to give you that special glow?

I took some paper and a pen, the words just seemed to flow.
So now I'm trying once again, the verses grow and grow.

It seems so easy to write it down and tell you of my love.
And my appreciation to our God who is above.

I know now why he chose this month, it could have been no other.
He had a special rose to give, it was you my darling mother.

Jean Deason

Karron's Mirror

My once and always love stepped to the glass
And believed the lies
Saw time and care where once was rose and blush
Then turned away
To grieve for things long lost or cast aside
And await the night
So sure the thief still marked her every move
To exact his price
But what for her was hidden I found most clear
Not diminished or worn
A face that calmed my baby's fears and stirred my soul
In times of need
Gentle movements and angles and shapes I trust
Because they're hers
A part of me in ways I no longer question
But accept as blessing
This graceful warming image I hold most dear
Still ripe with promise
Would that she joined me to share in the beauty
Mirrored in my eyes

Dana M. Jolie

Domestic Paradise

I start each day with good morning kisses
And big bowls of strawberry oatmeal
Packed lunches and tied shoelaces
Then kisses goodbye
A whirlwind of neatly tucked sheets
And Eiffel Towers of dishes
Peanut Butter handprints
Jack-in-the-Box and baby rocked to sleep
Soft voice of my husband calling just to say "Hi"
Dinner at six
Little man pushing fire trucks with sirens blaring
An angel in pink laughing, wildly chasing kittys
Bath time and bubbles and giggles
It's story time and sleepy eyes
I snuggle up with my lover
And thank the Lord for my "Domestic Paradise"

Angela D. Wilson

Daddy's Vacant Chair

When we gather around the family table.
And bow our heads in silent prayer;
For all our blessings, sent from God above,
Then we look up, and, see a vacant chair.

It's the chair that daddy always sat in,
At the head of the table at each meal,
Oh can't you still see him sitting there;
With his tender smile, and his old hands.

Though he is gone, he will never leave us;
We have his love all around us to share;
To help us in our troubled times of need;
But daddy we sure miss you,
when we see your vacant chair.

His face was worn, and wrinkled with pain:
There was silver hair on his head;
But you will always live in our memory,
We are so lonely, when we see your vacant chair,
God Bless daddy and that old chair.

Iva Mae Swinford

The Veteran

Have you ever looked into the face of an old vet
And could see the pain from the past and yet,
He stands with pride, his head held high
This veteran of a war gone by?

Do you think of the price he's paid
Standing by a buddy laying ready for the grave?
His eyes are a mirror to the scars of the mind
As he walked away, he said, "We'll meet again sometime."

He fought for our freedom as he his country served.
We should honor him the way that he deserves.
Let's pay homage to all vets, don't forget what they've done.
They are the real heroes, each and everyone.

Frances Lunn Odom

Disconsolate

When dreams have all forsaken you,
And day is only a veiled sun;
Life seems to lose its rosy hue
Even when twilight says, "Day is done."

When hearts let discontentment inward creep,
And the bad in you sullen words repeat
Home loses peacefulness in the deeps;
Love bids bitterness "God speed" as she retreats.

Oh could our lives be always heav'n filled!
No harsh words, tears, or broken lives;
Then even so, we'd repine still,
For we have natures nothing satisfies

Dorothy Dickson

True Friendship

True friendship means so very much,
And friends should always keep in touch.

To have a friend who's always true
Is like a gift from him to you.

It's something one can't touch or hold,
But worth much more, my friend, than gold.

The naked eye can't even see
How much true friendship means to me.

Carrie Knowles

Looking In

I've embraced my dreams in my subconscious,
And filled my heart with hope.

I've stretched my mind to great lengths,
Yet never quite far enough.

I've spoken to my soul,
And have found how strong I have become.

I've held my spirit in my hands,
And have smiled at all of the prosperity.

I've taken each breath with each memory,
And regained sweet remembrances.

I've reviewed my morals,
And was pleased with most results.

And I have looked into my heart,
And have found a place reserved for only you.

Claire W. Odoms

Nostalgia For Old St. Croix

For sunrise, like molten gold spread on, Christiansted harbor,
And foaming waves splashing, vigorously, against the nearby reefs.

For acres of cotton, with snowy pods, glistening in the sunshine,
And vast fields of sugarcane, with mauve tassels, waving in the breeze.

For the sweet scent of frangipani with the rose-essence of oleander,
And the aroma of hot sling, blown into grains of crystal sugar.

For trees with glossy, green and yellow fruit, and rows of coconut palms,
And a blue, translucent veil, spread over lush, green fields.

For the flaming, red flamboyant, vying with the pink and emerald skies,
And the blue and green Caribbean, unblighted by sails of white.

For the wide horizon, like a curtain, drawn against the sky, and sea.
And canaries chirping a symphony, in the brief, tropical twilight

For sunset, spreading colorful radiance, over land and sea expanse,
And glorious moonlight silhouetting palms against hills and valleys.

For stars that hang like meteors, lightning their dome to silver,
And trade-winds that cool the heat of day, and delight the tropical night.

James Latimer

"Thank You, Lord!"

Father, we thank you for this day,
And for your love, you send our way.
We thank you for all the blessings you give,
To make our lives happier, and easier to live.
Thank you for family both far and near,
And keeping us healthy through another year.
Lord, we thank you for shelter and food,
And everything that is perfect and good.
We pray for all the pain in the world,
For all the hungry boys and girls.
We ask for a miracle to come their way,
Giving them a brighter, happier day.
For all the homeless of our earth,
Renew their minds, and give them new birth.
Help each one of us to do what we can,
To make our great country a better land.
We pray for all our leaders today,
That you will show them a better way,
To ease the pain and suffering now,
Lord, we just pray you'll show them how.

Elsie B. Gentry

My Best Friends

My best friends are miles away
and, I can't see them every day.

They're always there to lend me a hand
when and if I give the command.

They listen to me talk and give advice
even when I'm not very nice.

Sometimes I'm cross and not worth a dime
but they will still give me their time.

I think it's good that we're far apart
because I'd be mothering from daylight till dark.

If you're wondering why these friends are special to me
It's because they're my daughter's one, two, and three.

There's still one more
a granddaughter whom I love and adore.

Barbara Grant

"Sometimes I May Seem A Little Frustrated"

Sometimes I may seem a little frustrated
And I can't stand to anticipate
But it doesn't mean that I am angry with
You or anyone else
But I get a little tired sometimes under so
Much stress and strain
For I am only human—you know
With any human limitation
I never mean to hurt anyone or make
Anyone feel bad
But there are times I do not know what
Kind of expressions my face shows
But you can rest assured my friends
It wasn't because of you
So please don't judge me by my frown
My face still holds frustration's
Trace.

Annie Hopkins

First Love

You entered my world when I needed someone new
And I could see in your eyes that you needed someone too

It seems I learn more about you with every passing day
And my love for you gets stronger in each and every way

You are in my thoughts each day and in my dreams each night
And I know the feelings I have for you could only be right

You opened up my soul and brought out the woman in me
How was I to know that it was you who had the key

You have shown me things that I have never seen
You have taken me places I have never been

You are a lover, a companion and a friend to me
You brought joy to my life and showed me just how happy I can be

Everything you say and do shows me that you really care
And when I need you, I know that you will always be there

I want to say "Thank You" for coming into my life and my heart
And I pray that our hearts and souls will never ever part

Dawn Frohlich

Red, White, And Blue

I live in a country of red, white, and blue
And I know all of which this country's gone through
Buckets of blood that have spilled in its name,
The thousands of souls that died, not in vain.
The farmer who lived by the sweat of his brow,
Only to die by the edge of his plow.

A distinguished brave soldier justifiably proud
Waved a white flag...wiped a tear; his head bowed.
Waving a flag clandestinely white,
To end a Civil War he no longer could fight.

Working at night 'til the sky turns bright blue,
An inventor fiddles 'til things do come true.
Ingenuity cries out; loudly once more,
Pick up your feet and open the door.

Years of struggle and torment indeed
Meant only to defend; great moments...great deeds.
Red by the blood of which it has spilled
White by the bravery of which it's instilled
And blue by the work carried on until dawn.
To pick up the fight....look up....and march on.

Jesse C. Griggs

A Sunset's Goodbye

The end of another day has arrived,
And I rush outside to see.
For each sunset that unfolds across the sky,
Holds wonder and beauty for me.

I never tire of sunsets,
And the beauty of their flame.
Life and sunsets have much in common,
For neither is ever the same.

Tonight the sunset brings sadness,
For a friend has passed away,
And the sun for her will never rise,
On a new and sparkling day.

So I savor and remember,
As I watch the glorious sky-
No tribute could be more eloquent,
No better way to say, "Goodbye".

Life is such a fragile thing.
It shines but for an instant in space,
Like a sunset glows in magnificence,
Before it vanishes in the night's embrace.

Cassandra Fitzkee Moss

Days Of Old

I watch her now as she grows old
and I still remember the days of old

When laughter and joy was the way of life
for this wonderful mother and wife

How she could dance to the music of old
and move her feet to the rhythm and beat

She made life look like a fairy tale book
but the pages are worn - and her life has been torn

Now what do I see?
A woman who doesn't even recognize me

Who just sits in her chair - looking blank into the air
Watching life pass by - with a now and then sigh

So how do I cope? I blanket her with Gods love and hope
So she won't feel cold - and tell her
I love her more than those days of old

Dorothy Iken-Mendler

My Only Sunshine

Not so very long ago I had dark thoughts,
and I walked in gloomy shadows.
There was little, or no light in my life.
And then, not so long ago I began to see more clearly.
The clouds slowly rolled away,
and beams of light began to shine all around me.
I am not exactly sure when it happened....
Perhaps, it came in a dream?
Because of you, I finally woke up and said,
"I don't want to walk in the shadows anymore...
I've been there for too long!"
Because of you, I decided to change and enhance my life,
and make it bright as day once again.
Because of you, my love-light burns brighter now!
Because of you, there is hope a brighter tomorrow.
Because of you, and your friendship,
and most of all.... YOUR LOVE!
You are.... My Only Sunshine!

Edward F. Willett

Jonnie And The Moon

When I looked up at the moon tonight, I thought I saw your face
And it brought back all the memories, that time cannot erase
I see your little finger prints, everywhere I look
And all your little traces in all your story books
I see your toys everywhere, although they're put away
I think it will always be this way, until my dying day
I look out and see our rocker, where I held you to my heart
I wish we could have found a way, that we never had to part
You're off to Florida with Mom and Dad, I wish you didn't have to go
Grandma wants you to never forget, that I'll always love you so
You are this special little guy, who stole my heart away
You did it from the very start, you did it your first day
I'm always thinking of you, I've shed a million tears
and I know I'll always miss you, through all the coming years
Though sometimes life is just meant to be, as sure as night follows noon
I know I'll always see your face, each time I look at the moon

Ann Kiddoo

That Which Endures

I've always heard it
And I've even said it
Life just ain't fair

A good deed can turn into your worst nightmare
And your dreams never seem to be realized
The lazy succeed
Yet the harder you work the less you're appreciated

But there are days that life is nothing but fair
When the ambulance passes you by
And the car stranded by the road doesn't belong to you
Your laughter is uncontrollable
And the skies are blue
The things you hold dear are so near

The fairness of life seems a mystery
Always between what we think we deserve and what we don't deserve
But during the worst times there are elements of our best times
Our tears don't last forever
It is all fleeting
Yet it is the good times that endure

Cheryl Witman

Compassion

Oh to have the power to understand
and know what other minds contain.
So we could try to help mankind
as flowers are helped by sun and rain.

To understand and say the spoken word
or gently reach out the helping hand,
That gives the comfort, touches the heart
for those whose problems seem too much to stand.

Many of us want to help another.
We have dedicated our lives toward this aim.
When we can find no way to help
we feel their desperate need, their pain.

So often our efforts seem so worthless
but let us not give in to strife!
Perhaps some day we will learn the skill
that's needed to fill the vacant spot in life.

Alice Rogers

Portrait

A mother's love is like an old famous painting whose brilliance and luster is hardly fainting
From times of infancy she gently stroked the brush as things spilled and caused a fuss
For there is only one original and none other will be quite the same whether it possesses the same name
Her love is special and you will remember her cooking like an artist whose name and style you will be booking
For her character might paint a flamboyant color scheme so bright and shiny as it gleams
For her background of love might progress into the forefront from years past
For it has built a strong relationship and made love last
For upon this easel is a simile of you
The colors you show for the things you do

Curtis Clay, Jr.

Rite Of Passage

Off he went to New Orleans,
and made his way to Bourbon Street.
The brothel lay on a darkened lane
with ivy vines hiding the windows.
Slowly he walked up to the door,
then paused, sweating, pale.
About to knock he stopped unsure,
not really knowing what to do.
The door creaked open; a girl stepped out,
clad only in a black negligee.
"Come young man, spend your money here."
Temptation screamed against reserve.
He backed down the crumbling steps.
The proving would await another time.

Brent Webber

Lost Love

As I sit on this cliff overlooking the open sea, I think of you and me and the sadness that seems to be. How heavy the days are, like the clouds hanging on these hills. My heart like the ocean feels rough, cold and chilled. A sense of hopelessness has come over me. Life has become a burden and the future a way to death. I sit here trying to let go of our love, watching it blow away like a flower in the wind. As I watched you walk away to your new love, I felt my desires, pride, joy and my soul drain out of me. So unsure of what will happen to me. You were what made life worth living and to you I still keep giving love, forgiveness and a wish that some day you feel all that I feel and that our love will become very real.

Joan Fernandez-Douglas

Have A Nice Day

Excuse me for staring but you resemble a good friend
And maybe your heart is soft just like your skin
You're short but I think you're sweet
And maybe you have pretty feet
This is a message that was meant for you
I'd like to be your friend if it's alright with you
When nature made sunshine
Something beautiful was born within time
And my eyes had the pleasure to behold
The lovely sight from your parents' soul
It's a nice treat just to hear you speak
And you shouldn't eat candy because you're already sweet
I didn't need a reason to write this part
Because what is absent in my eyes is within your heart
I felt I had to tell in a friendly way
Please respond to this if you like what I have to say
I try to think of more than just myself
And give a friendly message to someone else
So as you walk with grace at a gentle pace
Take care of yourself and get home safely every day

Bobby Lawson

Without You Nothing Is Left

No one compares with the beauty you possess outside and in
And merely thinking of you makes me smile time and again
One look in your warm brown eyes and I feel so secure
My heart aches to be with you; it needs you I'm sure
I see in you a purity and joy stronger than any I have known
Beauty's true power lies within; in that regard you stand alone
A beauty, to the world's fortune, reflected by your lovely appearance
Not masked by it but enhanced by it without interference
Kings would have killed for so majestic a queen
Simple man that I am you love me only in my dreams
If only I could make those dreams come true
Love would not be denied; life would not seem so cruel
Oh the agony of being without you is killing me inside
Viciously tearing out my heart and casting it aside
Even heaven longs to hold all the happiness you give
You bring joy to my heart; you make me want to live
Only you can fulfill me; I have known it from the start
Until eternity has ended I will love you with all the strength in my heart

Aaron Carlson

Human Destiny

The shroud of night is lifted.
And morning dawn comes on the hills,
Where hangs the fate of nations and the world.
The people stir once more from nightmare sleep,
And with courage dare to stand erect and speak.

The long awaited days have come at last.
The Berlin wall no longer divides.
Fear of silent rocket bombs subside.
Again, the common man has hopes of tranquility,
Happiness on his wide world below.

A restored faith, to redeem the human mind from error.
Where the word Democracy takes on a new meaning.
Yet, people still do not sleep so well at night.
Grim nightmares haunt their working thoughts.
The powers released, can they be yet controlled?

What threats still exist in the worlds domain?
The perils not yet unleashed, man has mold to destroy.
The genie will not sneak back into his flask.
And man must learn to cope with him, to rule him well,
Lest mankind prove too wise to live.

Fern M. Evans

Because I Love You-For John

Not so long ago, we gave this thing a start,
and not long after that, to you I gave my heart.
We started to get to know each other, both a little shy,
you showed me I could trust you, and that you're a special guy.
On you, I knew I could always depend,
and it seemed like it could never end.
Together, we spent all of our time,
there was never a moment when you weren't on my mind.
You held the key to my loving heart,
and I couldn't imagine us ever to part.
With you, I can always be the real me,
And I have lived that way happily.
Lately, our relationship has been rather strange,
I guess because our feelings have changed.
You really are the first love of my life,
and for that alone, I'm willing to fight.
But no matter what happens between me and you,
I'll always be here for you.
And I'll always be your friend,
because I love you.

Hope Mier

A Parent's Story

I have reached my golden years and think of all the happiness and not the tears.

I have had a grand and wonderful life, with all of my family, friends, and especially my wife!

There were times when we didn't know where to turn, and things looked really bad.

We turned to our faith in God which held us together, and he showed us happiness and joy so we were never sad.
We raised five children, three girls and two boys.

They are the gems of our lives and have brought us much and many joys.

As a parent you will always say, "I should tell my children how much I love them, oh yes I will some day."

But, it seems that you never find time to tell them, and the days turn into years.
Now it's late in life and you try to tell them through your tears.
Our lives are too short to argue and fight.

Because we should not be bitter and harbor harsh feelings, when we turn off the light.
Who knows when our life will end, it could be this night.

Albert M. Pirolli

Mid-Night

Ah, the luxury of waking up in the middle of the night.

Yesterday is gone, locked forever in the past
and nothing can be done to alter it.

Tomorrow is waiting in the wings, but untouchable.

There is only the dark and silent NOW, though not
completely dark nor silent.

The mind fills it with the glow of a thought,
as fleeting as the flight of a butterfly
acknowledged but gone in a flash.

Colorful ribbons of anticipations swirl about,
and perhaps a dark thread of care
still connected to yesterday.

But the present NOW is the only reality,
and it too will disappear
as sleep again draws the curtain of oblivion over it.

Oh, the middle of the night is truly a wondrous time!

Elaine V. Mead

Today

Outside my window, a new day I see,
and only I can determine
What kind of day it will be,
It can be busy and sunny, laughing and gay,
Or it can be boring and cold, unhappy and grey,
My own state of mind is the determining key,
For I am the only person I let myself be.
I can be thoughtful and do all I can to help,
Or be selfish and think just of myself.
I can enjoy what I do and make it seem fun,
Or gripe and complain and make it hard on someone else.
I can be patient with those who may not understand,
or be little and hurt them as much as I can.
But I have faith in myself, and believe what I say,
And I personally intend to make the best of each day.

Betty L. Redlin

Sight

I have sat on the shores of iniquity
And pitied myself

I have moaned alone sorrowfully
and pitied myself

I have hidden myself deep within a shell,
Never desiring to emerge
And pitied myself

I have looked in my own eyes
But was locked out from seeing my inner self
And I pitied myself

Then!

It became clear one day..as clear as the message a newborn baby's eyes relays as it looks into the mother's eyes and says...I need you now... More than I ever will. Clear, that I and only I, may allow iniquities and moans to consume my life causing a shell to cover me.

Why?

Because I control me...regardless of outside influences.

Because, I, have the power to continue to hide, or, I have the power to break from the inner darkness to emerge free.

I can see...me...now

Clover D. Hamilton

To Sleep

Sleep, you thief who steals away one third of my time
And purloins precious hours when I would work or rhyme,
How I deplore the excess of your crime
And wish to retrieve moments of my prime!

And yet, by countless folks I know that you are blest.
To them, old Robin Hood, you are a welcomed guest.
For, when a poor soul's weary of its quest
If it but turns to you, you offer rest.

Since you are gentle, sleep, perhaps you will agree
To listen to a tired dreamer's ardent plea.
If you'll return some flashes of my youth to me,
Before long I shall give you my eternity.

John J. Mollick

I Am Only Six Going On Seven

Don't yell and jump and stamp your feet
And shake me 'til my head is like a whirligig
That I can't see nor think nor speak.

I am only six going on seven
It's hard to act like a grown-up man.

I was terrified, I thought I would die
Each time you held my feet and let me dangle
Upside down two stories from the ground.

I am only six going on seven
It's hard to act like a grown-up man.

When you tied me on the bonnet of your car
So tight! I cried! No one saw me cry.
After driving back and forth you set me free.

Mom, I am scared!
Mom, why does your friend
Do these things to me?
I try so hard to please.

I love you mom.
I am only six going on seven.

Alessandra A. Poles

The Departure

He poised neatly on the chair, regarding nothing,
and she across, a statue might have been.
But you could hear the shadows on the ceiling.
And the troops and troops of silence moving in.

And you could hear the twinkling of the dishes
a kind of rustling in the willow ware,
and rows and rows of glasses sparkling loudly
and tones of quiet carpet on the stair.

When he arose and closed the door behind him,
sounds of stirring was the room becoming cold.
And if you listened closely in the hush of twilight,
you could hear her, in the gloaming, growing old.

Helen Platt

"Turned His Face In Love"

He could have looked away
And sought a greater servant,
He might have found a more precious love
In someone else's heart;
Still, He looked down through the years for one-
The one...me...whom He chose.

He turned His face in love
And rescued me from my weakness;
Tenderly He whispered,
"I claim you as my own!"
He saw my heart and yet, He did not turn away.
Instead, He held out His hand,
Took a strong grasp of my life
And led me to the radiance of His love.

He daily longs for me
To turn my face to His gaze
This awesome God...in grace...sought and found me.
Amid the haziness of my fears
Was the warmth of His face
That turned in love...and saved my shivering soul...

Dianna Bell

Spring Walk

I walked through the woods to the stream bank
And stood by the old holly tree.
And there in the woods in the springtime,
Beloved, I heard you call me.
I caught my breath in the silence
That followed the sound of my name.
I held my breath in the silence
In hopes you would call again,
Then swift came the realization
That never again could you be
There in the woods in the springtime,
There in the springtime with me.
It's been so many years, beloved,
But time doesn't set me free.
Sometimes in the woods in the springtime,
I still hear you call to me.

Charlotte M. Johnson

The Good Times Keep Coming

Sometimes we are blind
and the good times keep coming.
We see only what we want— what we think.

Sometimes I am up and I can't get down.
Flying all over. I dream that I am awake.

On the road of our dreams
we run forever—never to tire.
Escaping to the world of our choice,
we consume irrelevance—never to satisfy.

Moving closer to the truth
as I move away from you.
The world is spinning round.
It's time to start again.

I look for you.
I stare into the mirror.
Nothing to grasp, nothing to see.
Everyplace I go I look for you.

Everything I know and nothing true.
Songs of our existence.
There is a power sleeping that no one knows.

John Horoszewski

My Childhood Home

The gravel roads crooked, dusty and hot
And the mailbox - about to fall down
The shutter it hangs by a rusty old hinge
At the edge of this old one horse town.

The house of my Childhood, of so long ago
Has seen years of abuse and neglect
But the memories rekindled as I drive by
Can bring laughter or tears of regret.

Laughter for times that were happy and warm
Of a childhood so filled up with love
That the memories still linger inside of my heart
And soar high on the wings of a dove.

Tears of regret - for the lost years of my youth
And the carefree summer days as a child
Where we ran and we played in an innocent way
When the weather outside had turned mild.

But the years slip away in a flurry of time
That speeds faster and faster each day
But the memories we cling to will help see us through
As the years of our lives speed away.

Juanita Loonan

"Finding Contentment Of Personal Success In Life..."

The foundation occurs...

From the imprints of childhood,
And the moments of past life experienced.
Cherished, savored blocked or forgotten,
Filled with memories of pleasures or nightmares.

The needs originate...

From the solidification of past core roots implanted within,
With attempts of solving personal difficulties.
The striving for self-satisfaction in life,
The craving for personal security and well-being.

The goals form...

From the acceptance and coping of self-imperfections.
Seeking fulfillment of life through maximum abilities,
By planning, exerting willpower, and enforcing determination,
Upon the execution and completion of planned tasks.

The results reveal...

Obtaining a positive, satisfactory outcome,
Developing responsibility, self-assessment, and self-worth,
Achieving self-fulfillment in personal accomplishment, and
Finally experiencing contentment of personal success in life.

Charlene D. Chan

Crimson

The color that makes the line
And the rose that grows in spring,
The tale of the crimson hunter
And what the cross on his sword will bring.

The last words ever spoken
Dying souls that cry at night,
The hand that reaches to touch
The moon when it's touched by the light.

Beauty as the sun leaves the sky
And a touch on a shimmering face,
With elegance on the sands of time
And the mood when an orchestra plays.

The rose petals fall with time
As the hunter with the gods has flown,
The crying souls find time to sleep
But this crimson heart has a story of its own.

Dan Green

Late Again

The snooze goes off, I'm late once more
And the school bus is coming as I rush out the door.
I'm freezing and numb on this cold winter's day
In my warm cozy bed I wish I could stay.
I go to my locker and open the door,
But silly ole me drops a book on the floor.
So I bend down to pick it up,
When oh my God this is just my luck.
They're fuzzy and brown and huge to see,
My teddy bear slippers are staring at me.
I forgot to take them off in my rush
I look around me and start to blush.
To my gym locker I'm off to find
No tennis shoes there, I left them behind.
Laughs and giggles and stares all day,
My teddy bear slippers are here to stay.
Don't laugh at this, the story is true
It happened to me, it could happen to you.
So if you're in a rush, please check your shoes
And make sure teddy bears aren't staring at you.

Dawn M. Kilgore

Jesus

He spread out his arms and cried
and then it ended, he died.
I used to always question his reasons, why?
How could he just make the choice and die?

He could have chosen not to go,
he could have turned his back, said no.
He suffered through so much pain,
what was he hoping, wanting to gain?

He prayed for me from the depths of his soul.
My sins must have been such a terrible toll.
What kind of man would lay down his life,
and go through so much torment and strife.

Why is all I wanted to know,
Why did he chose to go?
Every time I stared at the cross
I cried for the useless loss.

One day I realized the reason for all his pain,
It was then I knew, his suffering wasn't in vain,
Because when he spread out his arms and cried
It was for you and me that he died.

Christina M. Ward

We Must Take Care Of Mother

She's old, still strong and steady, she still has a job to do,
and tho' she's done the nurturing she must be nurtured too.

We've enjoyed her pleasures - the quiet times and walks
among her flowering gardens, her lessons and her talks,
the music of the bird song, the shade and comfort of her trees,
and her majestic mountain sights bring us to our knees.
We scurry for safe haven when her winds pick up their force
and dread the wrongs we've done for the anger in her voice.
And we've shuttered at the fury she thunders from above....
with childlike anticipation await reassuring love.

She may be the one so quickly to forgive
but every little wrong we do is one day less she'll live,
for the sun will shine tomorrow and the moon will shine tonight -
the sun perhaps through hazy mists, the moon not quite so bright.
By wastefulness and unconcern for this our precious land
are we telling God His gifts fall to unappreciative hands?

We must learn what she teaches, we must treasure her great worth,
we must take care of Mother - our precious Mother Earth.

Charlotte Eichfeld Reinicker (Mikki)

Poets

To create, communicate, associate
and to anticipate.
As poets, we desire to emulate
a passion, feelings, or thoughts to stimulate.
We assume to paint a picture,
with our pens and imagination.
For the world to assort our potential
with consideration.
They must see our hearts, minds, and sufferings
so crystal clear
With these words we write
on this paper we hold so dear
We are the life blood of the world
each poet, man, woman, boy or girl.

Bonnie Morris Munoz

The Earth Provides

On mother earth we live and build
And tread her precious ground
With all the things that man has made
Engineered so strong and sound

The busses, trains and all the planes
Transport us with their power
The bridges, streets and freeways
With a million cars each hour

From the tallest structures in the world
To the smallest of all chips
And sophisticated energy
That propel the greatest ships

As we make our ways through life's deep maze
In many a different profession
We shall not waste to suit our taste
But always use discretion

For it seems almost impossible
As we travel far around
That man and all the things he's wrought
Come directly from the ground!

Julius L. Denning

The Good Old Days

Do you remember the good old days when trains and street cars ran?
And we had no super-highways we could ride.
Most all of us were passengers, whether child, woman or man
Going to school or work be it indoors or outside.
Times were not as hectic then, wherever we had to go.
We relaxed and we enjoyed life day by day.
A nice thing 'bout those times was all the friends we got to know,
For being friendly to everyone sure did pay.
Wouldn't it be nice if we could go back to those years
And the happy, simple pleasures that we knew.
When I think about them, it's not easy to hold back my tears
I long for the old times and friends who were ever true.

Floyd Edward White

The Simple Things In Life

The simple pleasures found in life are often hard to see;
and we never stop to realize that the best is always free.
The silver and gold of voices in song brings a warmth and
peace to the heart.
The sound of laughter as it echoes through time lifts a
veil from the dark.
The understanding of a friend when the soul has been
wounded within;
the special treasure of a smile when things are looking dim.
The gentle breeze that softly falls upon the lovely rose;
the sparkle of a single star as day draws to a close.
The happiness of two old friends when perchance they meet—
A child's delight when someone gives an unexpected treat.
If money could buy the treasures of hearts, of what
value would our love be?
For of the simple pleasures that are found in life
the best are always free.

Donna M. Wright

Black Birds Game

The sun at dusk throws a red arm down a leaf strewn path
and wraps around my feet, begs The Game begin.
From its humble barb-wired perch, the knightly tour proceeds.

A blue-blackened cloak has lost my shoulders; wings become,
twitch upon recognition to propel the lift.
A proud vehicle to a soul's freedom journey;
heartbeats.., eyes quicken..,
to drench the owner's purposed flight.

Trees waving, smiling at the joyous dance,
unencumbered flesh without needs soars by.
Any goals the goal you chose; any dream your dreams allowed.
Always winners of the dreamer's fancy, goals succeed.

The satiated spirit's proud power, freedom nourished,
recollects an earthly cage, its gifted professor.
As joyous as the flights began, a childish game,
to its adult the pleasure gained. Perspective cured and
all is well, as the grateful host returns to its grandeur perch.

Cynthia H. Delgado

Think Yourself Happy

If for some reason each day brings trials anew,
And you get so frustrated you don't know what to do
Think yourself happy
If the sun seems to meet the dawn
And you are all bogged down
Because there's not enough time to get things done
Think yourself happy
If you're tired and need some rest
And at your work you've given your best
Still there's not enough money to go around
Think yourself happy
If your marriage isn't what it used to be
And you and your mate need to give each other more T.L.C.
Think yourself happy
If depression starts to get you down
And you would like to smile but all you can do is frown
Remember there is always someone worse off than you
Think yourself happy

Helen Brown Dunlap

Difference Of Religions

We have so many religions
And you hate Mine
Though I've gone to bask in your fire
Several times!
What is it you hate of my religion
Don't we believe in the same God!
Or do you pray to the Devil,
And call it God?

I can notice in your eyes you don't
Why, I think God
Shall forgive whatever your conscience does!
Yet, if you kill men,
What He has already commanded you
Not to do,
To stay forever away from,
You will die! Perish!

Caesar Porttelo

Gifts Of Life

As you travel down life's highways
and you look all about.

You wonder if things would have been better,
if you had gone a different route.

But, as you raise your head and gaze into the sky,
you know that God has guided you.
Even though you know now why?

You take the gifts he has given you,
and thank him with a prayer.

Then you continue on Life's highways
even though you know not where.

George L. Hall

Angels

Look into the eyes of an angel
  And you'll never be the same again
They change our lives forever
  As they walk among men
They stand with us and guide us
  Along life's rocky way
Angels walk this earth quietly
  Dispensing hope along the way
Some say they are mysterious messengers
  There is no mystery at all
For they are here to be at his beck and call
Some say they are messengers of the light
Always standing for what is good and what is right
Angels will go where others fear to trod
For there is nothing to fear in the light of God
Just look around and you are sure to find
An angel could be your friend or possibly mine
So someday we can go onto a higher plain
When our work is through here on earth
  In His Holy name

Cansada R. Lanosz

Another Year

Another year goes by My Love.
Another day to fill with dreams.
To hold you for another night,
And learn what happiness truly means.

Tomorrow starts another thought;
Begins a memory not yet known.
I leave behind my silly doubts,
And all the uncertainty I've shown.

I wake up in the morning's hush.
And feel peace in the Love I see.
I become a child when I look in your eyes,
And find the person I wish to be.

So another year goes by My Love,
Of showing I Love You till we're old and gray.
Of filling our hearts with the Laughter and Love,
That we found in each other from the very first day.

Celeste A. Giovannetti

Fuzzi

I watched you creep like a baby.
As you began to stroll, I still looked at you.
Across the floor you went—
Slow, quick, slow, quick.
As an adult you flew through the air
like a basketball star and landed in my pocket.

Jennifer Eibach

A Broken Branch

Another branch broken off the tree
Another troubled soul set free
Trouble followed this soul from the West Coast to the East
Now, at last, it has found everlasting peace.

This branch once had leaves that were colorful and bright
And flowers with an aroma that sweetened the night
Then a poisonous substance from the form of a snake
Spilled on this branch and caused it to break.

But this branch held on as long as it could
For it came from a tree that produced solid wood
And then late one mid-summer night
The branch gave up and lost the fight.

Now as the branch lies dead on the ground
The tree stands tall but its head hangs down
Flowing with the breeze of day and weeping at night
Thinking of the branch that once was colorful and bright.

Betty J. Hugley

The Anniversary

The years we've had together
are a mere prelude of the many ahead.
The shared laughter, few tears,
all the beautiful moments since that day we wed.

The romantic that I married
so many years ago this day,
Still thinks of me as his bride,
yet not seeing the age, the lines, the hair of gray.

This love will ever be a lifetime guest
and treated with tenderness,
To give unconditionally, unfailing,
but never to strongly possess.

Our togetherness has meant caring, sincerity,
a blessing from above.
We are no longer young in age,
but will remain forever young in love.

Adoration knows no age, no time limit,
but to be shared deeply and true.
You have made that so easy, my darling,
for me to give to you.

Jeanne Hire

The Wall

I am really here at the wall. Words cannot explain the feelings that are in the very air in this place. This tribute to the veterans of Vietnam came so late, after so much struggle. Is this the reason for its impact?

Or is it the names that make these young men real? These are not the nameless, faceless dead. These are the sons of parents, they are someone's little boys. They are lost husbands, lost lovers, who will be forever young. What of their children who will never know the fathers who were part of their creation?

None of these survivors came home from the war together to be welcomed
back by cheering crowds who thanked them for a job well done. Their return was solitary, lonely, to an unforgiving and divided people who didn't want to hear about their war.

These veterans who come today to etch in gold the names of friends they lost, do not hesitate to cry, to feel. Perhaps this will in some way help to heal their wounds which can't be seen.

No black reflecting wall with names starkly etched upon its surface can ever change what happened. But it gives a place to come to for all who would remember. A place which says, at last, "We give you honor and respect that you so rightly earned."

Ashley J. Woods

Kaleidoscope

The colors of the kaleidoscope
Are like the moments of life
A turn to the left or a turn to the right,
— May bring joy or strife.

Like a turn of the lovely kaleidoscope
A golden color disappears;
The colors change with another turn
As the black and grey stones appear;

So it is with our life's journey,
For just around the bend,
The sunshine of life may fade away
As the black clouds of stress life sends.

But if you just keep walking,
Blue skies will once more come;
Like blue chips of color in the kaleidoscope,
With another turn, the golden sun.

So keep turning the lovely colors;
As they change with each new turn.
Your life will become a kaleidoscope
Of wisdom from which to learn.

Joyce Murphy

"Peace"

Forever looking for you!
Are you near
or far away?
When I experience a touch,
Is it a whisper or just the wind speaking
As I try to listen with my heart
My thoughts get in the way.
I must be quiet, and wait—
It seems like such a long time
To feel you near.
I yearn for your touch, if only for
a moment. Please come close once more.
And you will fill my heart with your presence.
Then I will feel the peace that only you can give.

Howard G. Roberts

Island Living

With skies of blue and forests' green and water all
around the scene; To contemplate eternity, an island is
the place to be. I've lived the life myself, you see,
and so am an authority to speak upon this topic.
A place where seeds however scant spring up into fine
hardy plants; And where the sea will furnish food for anyone
who seeks her brood. There are drawbacks since you
insist: You are an isolationist and mostly out of current trends
and late to get the newest fad. Although that is not all that
bad when viewed from time and distance. What of the other
island heights? A gusty wind to fly all kites. Perhaps a
lighthouse is a gift and precious pools wherein the drift
from all the world comes with the tide and often stays there
to abide. You may not want to stay forever in an
island life endeavor; But if you will enjoy its hue it will
weave fond memories for you. And you can brag in party haunts,
Yes, I lived on an island, once.

Gene Petersen

My Ship Amid The Storm

On today's journey to the edge of the dock
As I anticipate the arrival of my ship,
The rain from the storm beats down on my soul
With a raging evil lashing like a whip.

The pure silver of raindrops meets with my eyes
As I seek to understand
The grayness of the skies touches the solitude of my heart,
Feeling the grasp of life's clutching hands.

I tremble from the cold, as does a rose,
Unsophisticated in its first bloom
Captivated by the emptiness, imprisoned by the darkness
Awaiting only the light of the moon.

As the Eve grows near, it becomes eminently clear
The bitter thoughts of disappointment transpose
With wounded spirit, the whirlwinds of heaven
Descend upon my soul.

Blinded for awhile, yet, when I look again
The sound of beauty emanates from the sky
Lifting my spirits gracefully,
As an eagle spreads her wings to fly.

Barbara M. Ward

Three Loves Of My Life

I get a softness in my eye..my heart beats rapidly,
As I see my lovely mare searching out..where I may be.

She stands transformed..then knickers..as she sees me looking, too,
"Come be with me..play with me and brush me..I am missing you."

Then, dear old "Freight Train" woo's me in 'goose talk'..
Beats his wings and waddles close beside me as we talk.

His brown eyes tell me sadly..how he's lost without his mate,
Then bows his neck and thanks me for the bread that tasted great.

"Shonee" is a sheltie dog..as faithful as they come,
She keeps chicks and crows from the yard and varmints on the run.

Happiness is the conditions of the heart..
With caring..togetherness..protective, in love they play a part.

Joyce E. Savok

The Steam Engine

Looking up at the railroad, I let out a sigh
As I watch the Am Trak go whizzing by
The passing train makes my thoughts run wild
I think back to the days when I was a child
I know I must be a romantic dreamer
But nothing replaces the glorious old steamer
The blowing of the whistles and the exhausting of steam
Were very much a part of this little boy's dreams
Many loaded trains were passing each day
I always looked up when I was at play
The rhythm of the rails would always let me know
Whether the train was going fast or slow
I always wondered, and I still can't equate
How one steam engine could pull so much weight
Now the steamer is gone, and the diesel takes its place
But I have memories time will never erase
The rails are all welded, and there's no clickety-clack
Sometimes I wish the old days were back

When life was simple, and I was a care-free guy
And I'd sit and watch the trains go by

John R. Jensen

"Seen A Miracle Or Two"

Seen a miracle or two
As I'm sure so have you
It's a special thing to see
When good prevails suddenly
Know a man who got a heart transplant
He never accepted the word can't
His jubilance endures today
In a unique and special way
A lady stricken with cancer
While doctors had no answer
Given only six months to live
After three years she still has a lot of love to give
There are miracles everywhere
If we take the time to care
Some love, hope, and prayer
Will get us all there
Have you seen a miracle today?

Galoris Brownley

Whistle Of A Train

A far-away train sounds its mournful wail,
As it blows its whistle and rides the rail.
I hear the plaintive, haunting sound
And muse where it comes from and where it's bound.

Around green summits and majestic peaks,
Past billowing fields of grain it streaks.
Echoing through canyons deep,
Rushing along with a schedule to keep.

Hurtling across a river's trestle,
Winding through dales where villages nestle,
A silver blur on a western plain
With the melancholy hooting of a train.

Announcing its warning as it ambles through town,
Rumbling and roaring as it goes around,
Clickety-clack go its wheels on the track,
It heads out of town as its sounds fade back.

That plaintive call seems to beckon me.
What an adventure it would be
To get on board and ride and ride
Viewing the beautiful countryside.

Janice Moore

Seasons Of The Heart

Will you love me in the spring time
As leaves all turn to green,
When the dew is upon my skin
And our world is filled with dreams?

Will you want me in the summer time
As flowers wilt and thunder rolls,
When the bloom of youth no longer shines
As it did so many years ago?

Will you like me in the autumn time
As leaves fall and orange pumpkins grow,
When streaks of white and laugh lines show
Years flying fast, no longer slow?

Will you know me in the winter time
As the lands laid bare and the harsh winds blow,
When I am bent with time, ever so frail and old,
Will I remember you?

Jessie L. Parker

The Coyote Cries

Bulldozers clearing the land for new neighborhoods
As little animals scurry away, to find new woods
Off in the distance the coyote cries
The older animal lies down and dies
No more bush, no more trees
Who are we trying to please?
We build these homes one, two, three
Then we come back and plant more trees
Why not just clear the land for each home?
It'd give the animals a place to roam
I wouldn't mind having a raccoon for a neighbor
I'd feel like I was doing nature a favor
But we don't do that, we kill them, or leave them homeless
It all sounds cruel and senseless
We destroy nature with more of our lies
And off in the distance the coyote cries

Alan Conway

The Hand

The delicacy of the human hand can only be experienced as one studies it.

The tool of which we depend, is also an exquisitely designed piece of art.

The hand directs, guides, opens and closes so one can grasp the smallest of things.

Think how it can cast a shadow, be a welcome warmth of greeting—even more—-

To experience the total expression of feeling when gently entwined, caressed and held by another's.

Ann L. Fitzgerald

Stand An' Fight, We're Americans

The times of war are at hand
As proud Americans we shall make our stand
God bless the men an' women who defend
If they should die, to God they shall descend
Stand an' fight, we're Americans

Besides our battle afar
There are Americans, whose memories will be marred
History of Vietnam, Korea, an' others
Loss of fellow sisters an' brothers
Stand an' fight, we're Americans

But here on our homefront we find
A battle of a different kind
Drugs, alcohol, racism, shootin's
These people need a good bootin'
Stand an' fight, we're Americans

Whate'er happened to love thy neighbor with all thine heart
This American pride of ours is torn apart
God bless Haiti an' our fighting men an' women
Bring them back alive, so we can be at peace again
Stand an' fight, we're Americans

Bud Mann

The Currents

My heart is despondent to the day's call. My soul has withered away to the sweet smell of budding clover. My nights run the same over and over. I go into the bevy of my withered soul. I find a lone icicle ready to fall into the cave of shattered dreams. As it falls into a river of unhappy days, it is washed into the currents forever.

Dahn Sweet

Spring's Reawakening

The sun and the rain warm up the earth,
As she makes ready for nature's birth,
Awakening from their long wintery sleep,
Beautiful flowers peek out of the deep.

The spirit of springtime is felt all around,
Its splendor and elegance is quite profound,
A fragrant perfume seems to fill the air,
As the magic of spring is cast everywhere.

A gentle breeze hums a springtime lullaby,
As it rocks a Robins' nest way up high,
The streams frozen dead by winter's grip,
Now flow freely on their downward trip.

Woodlands dormant through the bleak winter long,
Become alive again with birds and their song,
Spring's reawakening is refreshing and sweet,
Filling our hearts with a joyful beat.

Edith Madge

Woman

Who is this woman who lives down the street?
As she walks, every man watches her hips sway with a beat.
Don't you recognize her — with skin so soft and smooth?
One touch of her hand the wildest beast she can sooth.

Who is this woman whose beauty brightens the day?
When men look into her eyes, it's there they want to stay.
Surely you know who she is — because you've seen her before.
They say to be held by her a man couldn't ask for more.

Who is this woman with a heart as pure as gold?
Her love a man has to earn, it cannot be bought or sold.
You know who she is — when she passes, people stop and stare.
To be in her presence, you always want to be there.

Who is this woman? It's not a mystery.
An African queen so regal, a part of the world's history.
Her being exudes an aura so serene it can calm an angry sea.
Look closely now — can't you see? This woman is me.

Denise S. Lloyd

"Topsy"

She was so little, but not intimidated,
As she wound her way through the big Labs
That occupied her space
In the County Animal Shelter.
She had been there twenty-eight days.
She had only two days left before
She'd join the fate of countless others.

I hated to choose,
But she was so young,
Surely she deserved something better.
I took a deep breath and said "I'll take her."

I could see the helpers were glad.
"She's just a puppy, what will you name her?"
They asked in unison.
"Topsy", I replied as the small yellow and white
Benjie-type bundle wiggled in my arms and licked my face.
"It's time for her to just grow and enjoy a topsy-turvy life."
She has!
And the rewards to me have been - endless!

Julia M. Phillips

The Old Admonitions

The old admonitions are as useless to me
As the big bellied wind in the tree,
The difference between what is taught and learned
Is the difference between butter bought and churned.

"Look before you leap," they say,
Seems logical, I say "amen,"
But "He who hesitates is lost,"
You see I'm all confused again.

"Birds of a feather flock together."
That's an undisputed fact,
But we've been told again and again
That only opposites attract.

Absence makes the heart grow fond,"
Dreaming of you, that seems true,
But "out of sight is out of mind,"
Now who am I going to listen to?

"Two heads are better than one."
But that's not true in poetry,
"Too many cooks spoil the broth,"
Those wise old rules just don't agree.

John W. Harold

Quenched Flame

Turn back in time when the flame burned bright,
as the image of love was there in sight;
Who was to know as the fire burned fast,
stricken by fate and could not last.

Cast aside in such grievous pain,
as flooding tears fall like rain;
That numbs the heart in disbelief,
for only those - that know such grief.

To see love's castle - crumbling down,
the broken remnants on the ground;
Within this hour of discontent,
the broken heart so mortally spent.

Where went wrong and did disclaim,
the fateful hand that quenched the flame;
Who was to know there would emerge,
from love's sweet song a funeral dirge.

John Philip Bolar

The Pleasures Of Autumn

Time to sit back, time to relax.
As the leaves begin to fall
Faster, faster, swirling they go.
As the autumn winds begin to blow,
The leaves form into tiny whirlpools as they hit the ground.
While the breezes go from tree to tree with a whispering sound.
Reds, golds, browns and shades of greens,
The leaves flitter and flutter,
As they dance merrily to nature's beat.
We kick through the leaves,
Crunching them under our feet.
Then we rake them away, but their moments we will keep,
For it's time to prepare, for a long winter sleep,
As the Autumn breezes cool us from the summer heat.
Take my hand and enjoy this time with me,
While we run through the beautiful piles of leaves.
This is the time to remember, how wonderful life can be.
Autumn is the season, to put away our summer dreams.
To enjoy the coming of winter.
For this is how the wonders of nature, are meant to be............

Connie S. Elliott

Untitled

Who are they? that gave these people features -
As the pied pipers, 'er politicians;
Was it some philosophical preacher,
Or merely a wand-waving magician?

Who is it then, that schools them in their thought,
To ruse with rhetorical deception?
Ah! maybe from alchemy are they wrought!
Or, did it begin - at their inception?

What transformation charged them to use guile?
To never answer - with straight-forward words;
Are they, per chance in the sophist guild -
Meandering through the sea's fjords?

Ah - professors in the collegiate schools.
Hastens to - fashioning and forming minds.
No matter whether they be wise, or fools;
Whence then comes, the politicians - we find!

Having mighty egos - with lots of time -
To tout by mouth - with no reason or rhyme.

Bill Standridge

Untitled

My heart longs for us to unite once in a way
As two colors submerge and become ONE.
Sky is so full of noise, crimson all over
As if god's have gone to war with each other.
I breathe it's true, but such state I sense
That all my limbs are simply pasted to my human trunk.
In my ears two voices resound even now
Some head is cut down, some bangles break.
My dreams - they all died in my tearful eyes
Like helpless kites drenched in a rain.
So secret filled is each masked face today
Like the two meaning word suha - depicting red color and spy.
Not even himself a person can take care of self
As your Kang has been taking care of you.

Harjinder Kang

"Queen Of Our Home"

A truer wife there'll never be,
As you my love, have been to me;
As roses strut their beauty deep,
Even at night they still are sweet;
Is you my love, my one alone,
Mother of my children, "Queen" of our home.

Fourteen short years we'll soon be wed,
Never enough kindness has been said;
I can't express feelings like others do,
But "oh" Sweetheart if it's the same to you;
I go on trying to be "Dad" of the home,
But you must be the "Queen" on the throne.

So throw back your head, keep your chin high,
Don't even droop or stop to sigh;
You have nothing to loose, but all to gain,
So watch for the sunshine, ignore the rain;
We'll walk together, never alone,
Mother of my children, "Queen" of our home.

Robert V. Brown

Though You Would Never Know

My eyes began to tear,
As you walked into the nights darkness...
Forever.

Our hearts still longed to be together,
Though it wasn't allowed.
Having you hold me in your arms,
Urging to feel your touch again.
The way you would kiss my lips.
Never forgetting the scent you left behind.
Being swept away in the cold wind,
Along with my heart.

Until that day,
When you would walk back into my life.
But was it to break my heart all over again?

And my mind full with clutter, I wonder.
Though my heart longed for you,
And I could not push you away.

To need you by my side,
To have your touch up against mine,
Though you would never know.

Jennifer Shadeed

Why, Is A Child's Favorite Word

Why, is a child's favorite word, seeking more truth each day.
Asking all who will listen and then running off to play.
Their minds are like supple sponges, soaking up all they hear.
Marveling at the little things, that they will hold most dear.

They love without questioning, seeing beauty in the plain.
Seeing our best and our worst, they will still never complain.
Why do clouds look like popcorn, why does the sky look so blue?
A child wants to share your mind, they want to be part of you.

Why is mommy's tummy so big, she let me take a peek.
Why do fish live in the water, can we play hide and seek?
A child is full of questions, be patient in your answers.
Can the reindeer really fly, have you ever seen prancer?

A child's universe is endless, their spirits dwell in love.
For they were with God, you know, like gentle spiritual doves.
Reach out with love to a child, even when they still ask why.
Together you will dwell in love, you only need to try.

Donald Hixon

Redemption

We are searching for death
at a strange hour
When the world is still
and infinity is hidden from us
by the pale ghost of fear
As the children cry
for the instinct of loss
Small fingers reaching into the mind of darkness
Frightened eyes longing for recognition
Trembling hands opened to comfort
When none is found
Do not speak to me
of false specters clad in black
Waiting to take my soul
in a white hand hidden in innocence
For death makes spirits of us all
and gives us the freedom to finally live

Justin Behrens

Pal, Partner, And Friend

I finally found my pal, partner, and friend
at a time when I thought my heart would not mend.
He was shy and quiet, a big teddy bear,
and I knew right away, his life I would share.

We were cautious, yet steady, afraid of the woe.
Third marriage for each, we had to go slow.
The children — unsure — did not make it easy.
On our wedding day, our stomachs were queasy.

Though one went here, the other there;
no matter what, I knew he cared.
Through thick and thin, together we've been.
His children, mine — couldn't think for the din.

When I was down, he was always around
to pick me up without making a sound.
When I was upset, he knew what to do:
a hug, a kiss, never let me be blue.

The children are grown now and out on their own.
Looking back, we often shake our heads and groan.
"How did we manage?" we ask one another.
We made the time to talk and love each other.

Joan E. Hric

Marital Mending

The modern bride always cries
at hubby's remarks that tantalize,
Too much salt ruins a cake
all her messes were hard to take.
Mother came to hold the fort -
Saved daughter's marriage from divorce court,
Home cooked food make meals a whiz -
A happier, healthier family — that is.

Eldora Harlow

Thinking On Rainbows

With palette pale or sometimes bright, a master hand creates an awesome sight. As each fine color clearly appears, a joy begins that quiets the fears. I welcome the calm and remember.... So close my sisters and I would snuggle on the sofa, sitting side by side, waiting.....and watching the elements raging forever outside. In truth, the storm had come quickly and just as quickly passed. Now it was time to catch the rainbow and wonder how long it would last. We were sad at its fading, but in our memories it would stay; alas, we had other treasures to find on that damp, but sunny day. We were caught in a dimension that only a passing shower brings where colors are brighter and air is purer and a gloss lay on all things. Wherever we looked the world was reflected in pools — some clear, some oiled. At that moment everything was enchanted; nothing in nature was spoiled. We poked a finger or stepped quite boldly into those mirrors of water. We watched intently and were quite amazed as the world began to alter quickly at first, then slower until all was the same again.
I'm still enchanted with a rain-touched world sparkling in the sun;
and I smile when I see children stepping in puddles just for fun.
I'm stepping with them. Always I am awed by the rainbow —
God's sign.
Always I welcome the calm and remember.....

Anna Shearer

"Cherished Memories"

Your eyes lit up every time you'd smile, and your laughter could be heard by every man, woman and child.
Your voice had a lilt, a sound all its own it carried
a warmth, that made our house a home.
I'll always remember your beautiful, white hair and the way a breeze could move it across your face, so fair.
The songs that you sang made it seem like you hadn't a care.
For you sang from your heart; a heart made for love, to give and to share.

Joyce Virginia Hetzel

People Portraits: Girl Child

Slender girl child of ivory fair,
Bathed in timidity and simpleness,
Pale as the puffy pastel sky,
Baptized in clear colored waters.

Spirit bubbly and buoyant, light and airy,
Fleeting aimlessly to new heights,
Wild and free spirited like a runaway mare.
Filled with innocence and promise.

Laughing in whimsical melodies,
Simplistic childlike pleasures,
Jumping and frolicking in toad-like play,
Boxed sand shimmering in illumination.

Dancing in free spirited prances,
No cares to burden her lightness,
The cool spring breeze caressing her face.
Winsome and lofty, floating in timeless motion.

Estelle Isbitski

Youth Day A Visit From The Pope

The pilgrimage day was one sent from above,
beautiful blue skies, filled solely with love.
From Springfield, across the flooded Mississippi they came,
all of one mind, but hardly the same.
Youth had come from various parts of the world,
and flags from all nations in the breezes unfurled.
The arduous journey from "Celebration Park",
thousands of blankets passed out in the dark.
Waiting for the program to get underway,
you could feel one to another the grandeur of this day.
Testimonials from across the globe were shared,
as a group of youth showed "Five Points" they cared.
The pope condemned violence, weaving a web of nonviolent change,
with 250,000 attendees, he addressed the Front Range.
Emotionally pored youth, soaking up every word,
quieting the crowd so the pope could be heard.
Our lifeline to the future today would embrace,
an understanding of determination, world peace, and grace.
Tears freely flowing, with a burning since of hope,
forever to have been touched by a visit from the pope.

Andrea Burrell

What Beauty Is To Me

Beauty is the feeling of the fall and winter air, beauty is the sweet aromatic smell of perfume that a female wears; beauty is a smile that radiates on a young woman's face, beauty is the sun showing on all the plant and human race.

Beautiful are the memories we all somehow treasure, beautiful are the special moments we wish would last forever, and wouldn't let go. Beauty is the rain that falls to make the plant life grow and quench their thirst, or beauty is the snowfall that covers and blankets the earth.

Beauty is a fine young woman who's the "apple" of a man's eyes, having all her surpassing beauty by his side, making him have tears of joy on the inside with a smile of happiness on his face telling her she's the most beautiful of her female race. So as I said to thee, this is what beauty is... To me.

Cleveland Adams

Beauty Is

Beauty is a bird, singing at dawn,
Beauty is the vision of a new born fawn.
Beauty may be a budding plant, or a tree,
Or even a ship, sailing the wide open sea.

Beauty may be, in the form of an art,
Or possibly in the people, at a shopping mart.
Beauty is hard to define; and often our words let us down,
'Cause beauty may even be captured, inside a frown.

Beauty is born where it is least expected,
And on many occasions it is rejected.
Beauty can be anywhere, at any given time,
Beauty is left open for you to define.

Darlene Schnackenberg

The Big Apple

New York a big state not in size but in fame
Because one of its cities copied its name

New York City with several
Names it adopted
Opted for Manhattan

Manhattan is the core of the Apple
It has a shiny red rind
Don't peel it, that's not kind

You just let loose, jump in and enjoy the juice
of that tasty Big Apple

Now, there's an off-shoot of the apple named
Greenwich Village
In the old days, no pillage

Rents weren't high
You could even view the sky
What a haven for up-coming
Poets, writers and actors

When some reached their mark they didn't park at the village
On to the core of the Big Apple where there were seeds for success
And in time happiness.

Joy E. Stone

Two Hearts

Two hearts breaking apart
because there is no love left
to hold the two of them together

The lonely nights
when no one is happy
when all of our feelings are held inside

The empty space
where I sit
all alone in the darkness of the night

When my family acts as if there is nothing wrong
when really
they are crying inside

When there is a war between all the love and the hate
and at this moment
the hate is winning

And when everything is wrong
and there is no hope for anything to return
back to the way it used to be.

Danielle Jodie Kohn

A Prayer For The Lonely

Oh dear Lord please help me, I feel that I may die
Because when I think of love I just break down and cry
Please help me to find someone to fill this empty hole
One who'll mend my broken heart and ease my troubled soul

I'm feeling I've been chosen to live life without love
And am slowly losing faith, please help dear God above
Bring somebody to me so that I may try again
And help to open up my heart so I can let them in

I'm floating, lonely, on love's sea and I just may drown
Because love escapes me when I see it all around
So dear Lord please help me so that I may try
Because when I think of love I just break down and cry

It's really very simple when all is said and told
Please dear God I pray to you give me someone to hold
Just someone who will love me, this is all I ask
I know for you dear God, this is no great task

I plead, dear God that you will take away the stress
Because all I want in life is love and happiness
Change the way I see life through these lonely eyes
So that when I think of love, you won't hear my cries

Gerald Reed

Journey

Silently I journey through the sturdy gate.
Before me lies a world of calm,
A world of green, of stillness.

I wander quietly through the lush fields of clover,
Inhaling the scent unleashed by each pressing step,
Leaving behind a trail of limp, lifeless buds.

Alone, I rest by the cool rambling creek.
Its gurgling waters glisten in the waning sunlight,
Tranquilizing the body of my mind.

The wind gently caresses my being,
As it softly folds itself around my body's shadow
Only to pass on, never to return.

Startled, I awake, and rise from my lowly perch
As a sudden chill begins to fill the air around,
And sharp bolts illuminate the gathering billows above.

I turn and race back over the limp trail of buds.
Trembling, I pass safely through the sturdy gate
Silently escaping my lonely journey.

Barbara J. Wegge

Ode To O. J.

You did someone wrong, but it didn't take long
Before you got caught.
You will soon be gone, and as you live on
You can give this some thought:

You were well respected, until you got arrested
Now you've lost all your "cool"
Guess you feel rejected, but what had you expected?
Man, you're such a fool!

You said the truth was bent, you claim you're innocent
But you didn't convince the judge.
And now, as to jail you're sent, you'll have many years to repent
Do you think you'll hold a grudge?

I hope it feels like hell, all alone there in your cell
Nicole and Ronald never had a chance, I swear.
So now, as you lie in silence, think of all that violence
And just be glad you didn't get the chair!

Henry J. Nunez

About Dawn - And Love

Come with me, in the early morning quiet
Beyond where brick and chimneys split the view
To a place where dawn comes softly, pure and lovely
Diaphanously veiled, in rainbow's hue.

Come, where we may see the dawn as promise
Filling the heavens, and singing of pure bliss
Believe, if you can, that promise, so impassioned
For noon can bring no light as pure as this.

Our days are fraught with care, dull and prosaic
Dawn's joy is fleeting, and was meant to share
Come with me, if you will, and steal the moment
One lovely dream, so fleeting, and so rare.

My love is like the morning, fresh and sparkling
Bedewed with colors - still an ardent plea
Come with me. Take my hand and watch the dawn break
A promise for this day, and days to be.

Hazel F. Lindquist

Big Red Mountain

Big red mountain, whoa high
Big red mountain, touch the sky
Soaring spirit, eagles glide, far below the buffalo dies

River strong, torrent wide, Mother earth, heaven high
Laughing spirit, freedom cry, touch the earth, touch the sky

Virgin forest, silver stream, golden meadow all agleam
Big red mountain whoa high, big red mountain do not cry

Crack the ground, crash the spear, start of rage, start of fear
Broken carcass on the valley floor, the buffalo dies the eagles soar

Of what was then, is not now
Buffalo once was, now the plow
Agony reigned far and wide, Indian blood, Indians died

Silence waits on the valley floor, charge of calvary is no more
Tribes and warriors of yesterday
Have disappeared and lost their way

Why this carnage had to be, I must admit perplexes me
Whoa mountain, mountain high
Whoa mountain tell me why
O big red mountain, do not cry

Gene Evers

"Apocalypse"

Chaos, anarchies, cataclysm, are caused by egotism.
Bigotry, prejudices, are the tools of schism.
Invented by those seeking to rule us all.
Their false divine rights, will surely fall.

The social fabric, by them is torn to shreds.
We live in their dyslectic, deceiving beds.
They divide the world, by race and creed,
Enhanced by genocidal words and deeds.

Their fabric of earth is torn open wide,
By fears, doubts, hates of ridiculous pride.
There is destruction around us everywhere,
With poisoned land, the sea and air.

The worse of all, we always find,
The chaotic thoughts placed within our mind.
The rulers with their chaotic derision,
Cause mental confusion and indecision.

With greed they kill, and plunder earth.
They pollute each mind in every birth.
Apocalypse is near, disease, death is our plight.
Is it too late, to try to make things right?

Ervin H. Chase

Early Ev'ning

In the early ev'ning when the sun is down.
birds begin to murmur, and to slip around.
One last sip of water, one last bill and coo;
the evening breeze caress the trees
another day is through.

Children scream and scuttle playing hide and seek
as the shadows deepen along the trickling creek.
The glow of flood/lights grow along the walk.
Two lovers talk and plan.
Some fish/wife hammers on a pan.

Traffic noise is climbing along the far high road.
Diesel engines grind and roar soft'd by trees,
And distance like sorrow's dull abode.
Con/trails cross the ev'ning sky like
Lizard's tracks upon the sand;
Cirrus crystals drawn so high as if not made by man.
As long as earth remains the summer's eve
will stir the prose, and love its old refrains.

Floyd E. Davis II

The Birthday

Birthday, a day of age, a day of grace.
Birthstone, gemstone, why don't we get stoned?
In the month you was born, with love for you birthstone.
Flower blossom, flower blooms and flowers grows on the moon,
on this the day you were born. A birthday that is sunshine bright,
a happy heart, that's warm and light. Make's a year that suits you
right, with friends to keep you nice and right. Good things to
share, fun things to do, these things are wished today for you,
on this, your birthday delight.

A life time filled with joy and pride, a peaceful feeling deep
inside. With each day bringing a never ending day, birthday's
with parents are the beginning. Finest and dearest, they're the
best. Always listening, always caring, always giving and always
sharing. I regret, that I may or might be the first to go, to
leave you, the parents here alive and alone, without me, your
birthday child. Your eyes to see, the breaking of the day, your
eyes to see the setting of the sun, on this the day you were born,
on this the day of our lives, this is your day, this your birthday,
a day that will long live, in our birthday child.

James E. Williams

Stream Of Consciousness

Twisted, knotted,
Bleeding, clotted —
A swaying, fraying, graying rope.

Curled, unfurled,
The end of the world —
Still mundane, blood-stained, fingers grope.

Swimming, spinning,
A neck that's grinning—
It slips right through the skin like dough.

Arresting, protesting,
The mind still digesting,
The poker-chip droplets from ballet toes.

Cynthia Walker

Momma Got To See The Christmas Tree

Momma got to see the Christmas Tree
But not the way that you and I see...
For 'neath the Christmas tree's celestial light...
We placed her urned cremated remains this night.
Yes, Momma got to see the Christmas tree.

Jean B. Hoogstad

"Taken For Granted"

The birds how they sing,
Breeze gently blows,
The calm of today is like a gem when it glows.
No humans in sight,
Wildlife all alone.
This begins a new day; that to us is unknown.

Butterflies awake the flowers,
While the bees enjoy annoying them for hours.
Deer find delight in frolicking among the grass,
They all wish this pleasure would forever last.

But as all great things must come to an end
This life of joy is destroyed, by us, my friend.
With our highways and malls, our condos and cars,
We banish this beautiful world only leaving a few scars.

But for now what is left we must care for and love,
for we only live once in this world,
So we must now preserve this beautiful gift..
Given to us from above!

Courtney L. Stallings

Golden Dreams

Fall is the weaver of golden dreams
Bringing out colors, reds, yellows, and greens
It's a beautiful time of the year
With keeping of a beautiful memory, so dear
Flocking to football games and having fun
Seeing new life as it forms before our eyes
Through the birds and young wildlife, we see
The turning of golden leaves
As the corn tops ripen in the fields, wearing of a golden hat
Hoping "Jack Frost" will stay away
For us to have more time to play
Knowing soon will be Thanksgiving Day
Thanks for all the many prayers we say
With the grooming of our tables we share
Turkey and dressing, also pumpkin pie
"O do we dare"
Gathering of our churches, and special groups
Giving God our Blessings, and of our fruits,
Soon will be the basking of pure white
Our beautiful snows are so bright.

Bertha Duff

As The Night Falls

In the west the sun sinks low,
Bronzing the sky with a golden glow.
The silence seems to close in,
Another day has come to an end.

Dusk falls slowly all around,
You can barely see the green lawn.
Quietude falls over the marsh,
Then the tree toads start their nightly chorus.

As you lift your eyes up high.
You behold a star studded sky,
Placed by God to give us light.
They twinkle and sparkle all through the night.

Slowly the moon begins to rise,
To wend its way across the skies.
Marvelous beauty all around.
As the night objects abound.

What a mighty God have we.
Who created the Heavens and the seas.

Helen Bowers Pierson

A Great Golden Gift

My elderly eyes reflect years of wear,
But emit love as vivid as daylight
The dark thick glory that once graced my head,
Is now a vision catching snowflake white.

Robot knee joints have retarded my stride
To a graceful slower uniformed pace.
Aches apparent during the golden years,
Rarely appear on my youth exempted face.

An alertness to my blessed world has waned,
Still, I possess a lucid thinking mind.
Chores are done during infrequent work moods,
And I never fret if I fall behind.

Acute hearing is now yesterday's skill,
Still, I converse well enough to appease.
Often sleep intrudes on my daylight hours,
Yet, the intrusion never fails to please.

My golden years are a high golden time,
For I have earnestly learned to perceive,
My body changes as a great golden gift
That the Father has blessed me to receive.

Cora Wells

The Twin

You should have been given a chance to live,
but fate denied you that chance. I feel
responsible for that and I hope you forgive me.
I see you every so often in dreams, and I weep
for the world which never had the chance to know
you. I believe that, if you had lived, your life
would have far exceeded mine. I am troubled by
the fact that I am still here and you never were.
You always have been, and always will be, a part
of me, and I will dedicate my life to your memory.

Deanna J. Benoit

Travelling With My Little Friend

We can travel the hour and he'll not make a move
but finally nature calls and there's nothing I can do
so off the road I pull and out the door he's gone
this is very important stuff as ritual he'll prolong

He thinks he's a mighty hunter and will probably point a grouse
generally it's just a stinky bug and once in a while a mouse
as my patience starts to wear thin there's one more clump to nose
and thankfully—at last—he lifts his leg and goes

James H. Freeburn

The Finished Work Of Calvary

Someone asked, "How did God you find?"
But God was not lost, it was I that was blind
Through His love and grace He let me see
The finished work of Calvary.

Now and forever I shall give Him praise
To The Father, The Son, The Ancient of Days
To the Holy Spirit for revealing to me
The finished work of Calvary.

For He loved me first, when I was dead in sin
And He raised me up from where I had been
That a child of God I now may be
Thanks to the finished work of Calvary.

Carl V. Sundquist

You And Me

I was just three and you weren't even one
But I already dreamed of good times and fun.
Checking on you from time to time,
I'd teach you new games and nursery rhymes.

School would start soon and we'd be on our way,
Learning more and more every passing day.
But what I learned most, I learned from you:
Sharing, caring, and hard lessons too.

We've always been close, sharing secrets and dreams
Oh, how time flies, so quickly it seems.
Today is not an ending, but a brand new start
And I'll always be there, I close my heart.

You'll go your way and I'll go mine
We'll always have each other and be just fine.
And when you get lonely, just think of the past,
Of the times we shared and memories that last.

Now you're older but I'll always look after you
Even if I have to look up an inch or two.
I love you sis, only the best you deserve
Cause you've got what it takes - brains and nerve.

Angela Condra

My Mystical Someone

I am not sure where you are from,
but I know of how you come to me

I know nothing of what you are like,
but yet I've known you an eternity

Although I've never seen your face,
I know how you must look
Although I have not yet touched your cheek,
I know how you must feel.

I know we have not yet to share many memories,
but a future together I promise you

To my baby Gage or Sierrah
I'm looking forward to meeting you.

Janice J. Champine

The Mountain Man

I did not know the Mountain Man,
But I know people who knew him well.
I heard their words when they spoke of him
and his story they can tell.

He walked in beauty and in grace.
There was love in his heart for everyone.
God shone through in the smile on his face
Like a blazing Texas sun.

Nature bowed and wept that day.
It would miss this Mountain Man.
He loved it all - the woods - the hills,
The arrowheads clasped in his hands.

What better place for him to rest
Than God's own earthly Beulah Land;
Where in our youth God smiled on us
And took us by the hand.

I wish I'd walked a mile with him,
Or saw his smile or clasped his hand.
I feel a loss in heart and soul.
I did not know the Mountain Man.

Hilda Kirchman

Walking With God In The Dark

They say there's light at the end of the tunnel,
But in order to see that light-
We must first find ourselves in the tunnel,
Where nothing is light or bright.
There's darkness all around us and every where we look,
We see trouble, problems and heartache in every cranny and nook.

As we look around to make matters worse,
We find we're alone to deal with this curse.
In desperation we cry out to God,
Why does my burden have to be so hard?
As I continue to stare at the light out there,
I begin to realize that someone does care.
I feel a strong presence very near to me,
And as it grows stronger I begin to see,
That I was not alone for God was there,
Showing me his love and tender care.
I put my hand in his and from then until now,
I walk beside him as He shows me how.
When he has finished his work with me, he'll lift
the darkness and I will be free.

Elsie Gillette

Let It Show

There's a lot that's been written...Much more that's been said!
But most of it after they're gone....Then it's read.

What great folks they were!....How you miss them so bad,
And you look at each other...with hearts heavy and sad!

Why didn't you tell them,....how you felt long before?...
While they were still here?....So now I implore...

Listen carefully while I say to you...
Honor your parents while time permits you!...

Don't discount the old!,... I beg of you!...
The day is coming,....when you'll be old too!...

And your heart will cry out for your children to see,...
The need in your heart .....Love and respect me!

Yes they're old and they're tired.... But,... it's worth it all!
If you pick up the phone and GIVE THEM A CALL!

Just to know you love them, ... AND NEED THEM EACH DAY!
They're one of a kind .... YOU'RE HAPPY TO SAY!

They don't ask you for much .... JUST THE NEED TO KNOW!
They're important to you! ..... WHY NOT LET IT SHOW?

Betty Blanton

"Thoughts"

In our lives, there is no prose, poem or poetry,

And the love letters were never written,
but most thought of in,

The "Winter" winds in summer skies, the aroma of,
"burnt" Autumn.

Summer, three quarters of the way gone
already,

August's shorter days begin, waiting September's
embrace,

To run in "December snow", then, sit in the
fire's glow,

The "winter winds" in summer's sky blow.

Charles A. Millard

Beyond Good And Bad

As I walk, dirt covers my feet,
But my shoes leave no impressions.
I lift my head and glance
At the faint stone buildings
Around me.
Having absorbed the sun
They now veil me in merciless heat.
Their wooden shutters are closed,
But one allows my eyes beyond the dream;
I squint and sense the contours of a woman
Dressed in black.
A heavy book rests in her lap,
And her wrinkled face is framed by snow-white hair.
She returns my gaze
And I see my reflection
In her pale blue eyes.
I kneel down and water the flowers
On my grandmother's grave.

Christina Hoffenbacker

Listen

The wind blows
but no one hears,

No one hears it calling,
screaming for attention;

They withdraw from it
making it search.

Its search ends
as it comes upon a listener,

A soul with love and empathy for
everything near and far.

The wind slowly calms
as it shares its anger with a loving one;

All is calm for now,
but one day the listener will also withdraw

And the wind will not be heard.

Amy Mara Johnson

Silent Cries

Her cries are endless,
but no one sees,
Not the wind,
not the birds,
nor the leaves on the trees.

Not moonlight,
or stardust,
or the dew on the lawn,
Nor the sun breaking through with the first light of dawn.

Not the warmth of the rays on a bright spring day,
Or the blooming of flowers in the month of May.

Not the lake,
or the waves beating on the shore.
Her cries never heard,
only grow more.

Beth Bader

Autumn

There are twelve months in the year, each has a character of its own
But October seems to be, one of the loveliest I've known.

The love of life is in the air, the Autumn colors glowing
Every branch seems so clear, the refreshing wind is blowing.

The heat of the summer behind us, winter is yet to arrive
The vivid color of leaves on the trees, sing "It's good to be alive!"

They've had the drying sun, and soon, the branches know
The coming months ahead, will bring the chilling snow.

But now they stand there proudly, not looking back or ahead
For us to take in their beauty, of yellows, orange and red.

So take a few moments today, for soon it will be too late
They'll be wearing their winter coats, for they change at a rapid rate

Absorb that glorious beauty, be grateful that you may see
That special touch of life, that nature grants to a tree!

Beverly A. Ralph

Where Have All The Fathers Gone?

A question, which mother cannot answer,
but only to a father.
What am I to do, I have no father; I ask mother,
where is dad? She tells me that father has
left us, found happiness elsewhere.
How am I to grow up without a father? I don't
even know how to fish, or hunt, I don't even
know what a man is supposed to do.
My question is very personal, I need to talk
to a father and I could talk to a father next
door, but that boy has no father either.
What am I to do, who will answer my question?

Jesse Centeno

America's Crossroads

The cold war is past;
but, remains to exist,
with a deficit too large as a post war task;
as great as it is, we must not resist.
But, a solution to seek to balance the budget
that was created by so much waste.
The CROSSROADS is here, we must not forget.
So, as a nation let's realize this is the case!
As a nation UNDER GOD, we claim to be;
Surely time to get back to the God we've shamed,
and to take our stand that other nations may see,
that in Him WE TRUST and our fame will remain.
Our children we raised without a prayer;
The crimes they commit prove this omission,
and we all must admit that this isn't fair,
to children and God; so let's get back to our commission:
"IN GOD WE TRUST, by FAMILY, COUNTRY,
and GOVERNMENT of the PEOPLE
and for GOD'S SAKE by the PEOPLE!"

James E. Kirkland

The Bond

When I'm at home and she has left the house
But will come back within an hour or so,
I always take the chair that's nearest to
The door through which she will return to me.

And when she does I take her in my arms
And feel a little thrill that she is back.
I want for her to know the very same,
That every time we meet we reaffirm
The bond of love that's forty four years old.

Adrian M. Ostfeld

Love In His Shadow

The road we travel is o' so rough,
But sometimes we pick the smoother path.
The right way is not always the easy way.
Time slips by and the waiting is worth the love
I feel.
I feel the power of His unseeing love,
In His eyes we have no flaws.
The Almighty is not just a name,
It is the ultimate pleasure of all mankind.
Love in His shadow is greater than any I've
ever known.
To walk in His shadow is better than
shining above everyone else in the darkness
of evil.

Amy R. Murphy

Tears Of Happiness

The tears you see drifting down are not tears of sorrow,
But tears of happiness for our hopes and dreams of tomorrow.
The tears I cry will fade away,
And the love I have for you
Will continue to grow with each passing day.
You make me happier than any one from my past,
That's how I know our love will last.
Think back to our promise of honesty -
Now when I have pain, joy, or sorrow you'll be the first to see.
For now, let's enjoy the happiness we share
And when we run into problems, let's find comfort in knowing
the other is there.
Before long we'll both have eyes filled with happiness for
our wedding day,
Until then there's one last thing I want to say:
Dale Lee Barnes I love you with all my heart and soul
And you always bring happiness into my lifelike I've never known

Amy Sculley Barnes

Uncertainty

"Take one day at a time" I always hear,
But that's easier said than done I fear.
My companions lately have been stress and confusion,
And try as I might to end this intrusion
I find my confidence shaken and this pain in my back
Trying my best to get back on track,
Yes uncertain times have got me down and out,
But I know I'll be up soon I have no doubt.
There are times when we all have to face,
Those inevitable stumbling blocks that will slow our pace.
But you can find rest in this knowledge my friend,
There are no losers we are all winners in the end.

Carmen Robinson

Tis So Sweet

Tis so sweet to hear thy name
called amongst the crowded room

Tis so sweet to speak the words
and be heard by thy patience

Tis so sweet to touch thy skin
which is smooth and irresistible to mine eyes

Tis so sweet to kiss thy lips
that are moist and tender to mine

Tis so sweet to go about life
Knowing you are mine.

April Moore

The Deep Deep South

I was born in the busy City, Oh, so many, many, years ago
But the Country born in me, just would not let go, yes,
I was born in the City, and I loved to watch things grow anywhere
I found a piece of the rich good earth, I would find a seed to sow
My Mom and Dad were born in opposite directions
This would cause problems — too many to mention

Mom loved the hustle and bustle of a big crowded City
And Dad — Do I have to say it? — Yep, he loved the deep, deep South
Neither of them wanted to leave their birth place — What A Pity!
He really loved the deep, deep South, Yes, — he truly loved the
beautiful, deep South. War was declared and Dad was stationed up North
Finally they met, it was meant to be, or the blame could be
put on "Fate" — "of a sort"

I was one of their children, I was one of six
And my blood ratio was one-fourth City and three-fourths Country
Yes, my blood was certainly mixed
Yep, I was born in the big, bustling City, but the deep, old
South won out! I'm Country, through and throughout
Oh Yes! I'm Country, the deep, deep South won out!
I might even quote an old Southern saying —— "Well Shut My Mouth!"

Gloria Margaret (Clinedinst) Wode

Brother Fred

Once we had a preacher, just a small man in size.
But when he preached God's Holy word,
it often brought tears to our eyes.

For he preached with all his heart and soul,
to try and save the lost.
He always made it more than clear,
that God had paid the cost.

He'd say, listen now, listen to what I say,
and we'd all be a whole lot wiser,
when we left the church that day.

We only knew him for such a little while, but we'll
never forget his words, nor his pleasant smile.

We'll miss you brother Fred and we're sorry you had to
part, but you'll always be with us,
because you're engraved upon our hearts.

Chris Kannmacher

Bethlehem

Sublimely sound the vibrant cords of arcanum harp
By quick gratitude of the lover's deep human heart,
Burnt by tenderness rising by inner beauty
Of expressions and by the fullness of power-light
Above the ancient miraculous Bethlehem's holy night.

Stupors circumvent. The cosmos, transformed
By the glimmer of the stars,
The regal splendor of the sun,
The luminous flux-silver of the moon,
The intense fragrance of the gardens,
The azure breathing of the sea,
The harmonious waters of the rivers,
The high snowy crests of the mountains,
The soft rotundity of the hills,
The green oasis of the forests, the immense plains
Of all the nature are in festival and merriment
Because of an immortal charming event, that continues,
At Christmas holy day to astonish the space
And the season among the growing humanity,
All the souls in love are shuddering placably!

Franco Buono

A Mother's Heart

A Mother's heart is often torn
By the thistles and the thorns
That grow amongst the garden of love,
Yet it's mended by God's grace from above.

She often shed tears through rays of hope
Wondering how much the heart can cope,
When it bends beneath the weight of care
Only God knows how much more it can bare.

A mother's heart is fertile soil
Tilled by pain, sorrow and enduring love
Weeding out the times of doubt and fear
With prayer, faith, and His sustaining grace.

Trusting in a more powerful hand
Quietly and reverently she takes her stand,
Against the blows that wound the heart
Piercing deeply sometimes never to depart.

Yet the pulsating force of her love
Filters through with strength and compassion
Because it is ruled by the Master's Hand
With a forgiveness and cleansing no one understands.

Bertha Garrett

Me Too

Little Me Too standing at the gate.
Calling, "Granddaddy! Wait, wait—
Take me too,
I want to be with you."

Granddaddy slowly turns and smiles—
"Come on little Me Too, we will play awhile."
Blond hair flying in the wind,
She catches up again!

"Can I feed the baby lambs today?
I really don't want to play,
I want to help you all I can.
Want me to put the feed in the pan?"

"Go swing for awhile,"
Granddaddy said with a smile.
"Let me do the work today.
You really need to run and play."

Off she goes to another chore,
Calling, "Granddaddy, I want to help more."
Little Me Too so happy and free,
She's growing up, you see!

Corene Luedecke Draper

Nameless

You say I got a problem personality
'cause I don't want to live in your reality
well take a look at your society
all the followers missing your hypocrisy
caught up in a dog eat dog mentality

It's either conform or die
punch the clock and live a lie

So I choose to live in my dreams
where things are what they seem

And for now I'm going to be me
and never will say sorry
for wanting to be free.

Brian Brown

Alone

ALONE ... the mere mention of the word
can bring forth a chill to one's innermost being;
or serve as a touch of fresh mountain air.

ALONE ... for whatever reason:
the death of a loved one;
the death of a marriage;
the empty nest as children depart.

ALONE ... a state of dread or desire:
dread if one has only self to daily face;
desire if contemplating the deep mysteries of life.

ALONE ... The silence welcomed while pondering
and searching for seemingly elusive answers
amidst the clamor of a world gone wild.

ALONE ... the answer finally makes itself known,
not in the wisdom and folly of men,
but in the Person of God's only Son.

ALONE ... no more is this to be
as the winding paths of life are trod;
Abide in Jesus - He is the True Vine,
And you'll never be alone again!

Gale L. Player

Career Boost

You begin with, I think I can! I think I
can! I think I can!... As along comes that
little train of thought... a trickling through
your brain... so off you go to the station
(in life) to get on board.... (or a plank)
which ever is available, to hitch onto
the other career you already have, your
engine,... and with all your strength you
...boost...and poosh and poosh yourself
along until the rubber band of life is
stretched as far as it can be and
you feel it almost ready to snap!... to
send you into oblivion... then along comes
the little train of thought... I know I can!
I know I can! I know I can!... And off
eases the tension and you are held in
suspension as over the crest of the hill of
career you careen and go flying down the other side of thought...
to deed done... singing and yelling at the top of your voice...
I knew I could! I knew I could! I knew I could! Pheew!

Evelyn H. Cardwell

Words of a Blind Man

Amazing how so many things in the world
can make someone cold
A breeze on wet skin and northern wind
Snow-covered shoes and midnight stillness
Nothing ever seemed this cold before
Somehow now it chills me more

Strange the noises some voices can make
inside someone's head
Echoes of crying spirits in between the
living and the dead
Sadness in the voices sorrow in their pain
The echo unlike changing winds or snow
forever will remain

Brilliant images flash before someone's eyes
scaring, enchanting, engulfing them
holding up a perfect picture once in awhile
And nothing had ever seemed that perfect to me
These are the images that I can no longer see

Joanie Corn

Hypocrisy

Sham of Dignity - You counterfeit impostors.
Canting with pointed fingers your syllables of deception.
As proverbs decree, "They who beareth false
witness against their neighbor are a maul,
and a sword, and a sharp arrow."

Smug in your pious surety, Far beyond Transgression,
Content with selves, too blind to your own inequity.
Strike, - Cast the stones of Personal Destruction,
then with squared shoulders, boast your victory.
Destroy he or she-you see as thee-thus shroud your Hypocrisy.

The Fangs of Words wound deep, oft' times
Never to heal, only to fester and bleed with agony.
What reward do malefactors reap
as their victims sink in defeat?
Sanctimony can only be but skin deep.

Go your way Pharisees... Content and Triumphant,
Yet Fools, only to be one day foiled by your own deeds.
Beyond this time is Judgment for all.
Then will the gavel of truth prevail.
Beware forked tongued libelants... Justice is FINAL!

James M. E. Bower

Love Of Country

Love fly through air, as gentle winds blow.
Carry it to Americans, who wish to know
Blow gentle wind, whistle and sing,
With the spread of an Eagle's wings.

Everyone loves to see our flag on high
March to freedom, as our colors pass by
Everyone knows folks listen, for that thing
With the spread of an Eagle's wings.

Love of America, our friendship we share.
Even if our paths never cross, on earth
Lift love to windswept summit, then wan.
With the spread of an Eagle's wings.

Day is gone, shadows fall before night.
Feathers wafer down from doves in flight,
Your friends, love them as Queen or King,
With the spread of an Eagle's wings.

Irene E. Robertson

Thoughts Of A Middle-Aged Failure While Driving On A Freeway

Blow wind
Carry the ache
The gripping hunger of unfulfilled dreams
As my long hair blowing behind me
Let what cannot be
Be forgotten
I will look ahead where the sun
Of unconcern soothes my empty soul
A sedative please
To ease the caring
Until I care no more

Eilene Meadors

Untitled

Watching the day go by. Whispers of clouds fill the
endless sky. The roar of thunder echoes with all its
might. As weeping rain caresses below ever so slight.
My form takes vision of these events. To the day's
end, leaves a delightful scent.

Alice Jeanne Web

The Outsider

I am the outsider
Cast out by lack of love and care
I live alone
Depend on no one but myself, and filled with fear.

No one to hold and cry to
No one to complain and lie to
My feelings and problems matter to no one but me
I stand alone in times of horror and war
I know living like this, my life will not go far.

No one hear's my cry for help
No one see's the pain my eyes tell
I must admit I hide it well.

So I wait until the day, when I will be free
And I stand erect and head bowed to the ground
Waiting for the undertaker to make his rounds.

And I shall go peacefully without a sound, knowing I won't be missed
I, the outsider goes leaving a shredded body on the ground
And a soul that will never be found.

Dandrea Churaman

Fencing

In the friendly fencing match of
casual conversation,
often we forget to blunt our verbal blades:
we probe each other's weak points,
thrust and parry with
half-laughing insults;
but joking jabs meant to tickle
sometimes wound.
And so we wince behind our fencing
masks,
and hide our feelings, smiling while we bleed,
denying that we've been run through
the heart.
Oh, must we always wear protective masks?
May we not drop our foils and bare our souls?
Must conversation always cut and sound uncaring?
Must I, when speaking, ever be en garde?

Jerome Van Kuiken

Amber

Her name sweet on thy lips, tender in thy heart,
sweet in thy sound.

My love for thee is as true as the sun rises and sets,
and as pure as water runs down a brook.

Again and again, a hunger inside bothers me all day,
but it is not a hunger for food but a hunger for her love.

She has something special about her, it is different than other girls,
I am not sure what it is, but my heart is yearning to find out what it is.

Her name strikes love into my heart,
her smile can brighten the darkest day,
her laugh can make you feel good all over.
Her name is AMBER, and I am in love.

AMBER, AMBER,
I say it again and again, meaning it more so than the first.
With love in thy heart and love on thy mind,
I think of you all the time.

Chad Michael Smith

"The Child In Us In The Fall"

The sun is shining over head, leaves are
changing color, corn turning brown and
looking out my window it reminds me of
snow coming down, it's only the beautiful
leaves in yellow, red and gold falling
to the ground;

It's autumn there, isn't anything to compare
of tramping through the golden leaves that's
scattered everywhere;
Oh, never let me grow old, make me a child
once again, when we feel the miracles of fall,
arriving across the land;

In the soft sweet smelling haze of fall,
a maple stands alone;
A blaze of color stirring memories of rustic
lanes and golden trees, no joy so simple,
none so rare as the mounds of leaves in
red, yellow and gold everywhere;

Erna M. Sawyers

Untitled

Bitter rain washes the memories,
Cleansing the past, the present,
The future

As the mighty river of love swirls with fury,
Its blinding, endless heat
Captures and enfolds the beckoning dawn,
Staining the moon,
Silencing the weeping stars

Upon hearing the echoing cries of the night
Struggling in suppressed pain,
The ocean spirit releases,
Letting go
With a final sigh

As the storm abides,
The rain ceases
And the river,
Parched and barren,
Flows no more

Heather Heitfield

Our Planets

To All Astrologers of the World
Mercury is the smallest planet and
closest to the sun.

Venus is the second planet from the sun.

The Earth is the third planet from the
sun on which we live,

Mars travels very slowly -

Jupiter is the largest of the planets
and Saturn is the second largest.

Uranus and Neptune are both larger than
the Earth.

AND...

Pluto is so far away it only can be detected
by photos of the heavens.

Thus looking into an optical instrument
in a room with a dome, these planets
can be seen.

Evangeline Katranis

My Thoughts

Sometimes, some days, my thoughts are as the rain—
cold, dark, and crying.
Sometimes, some days, my thoughts are as the sun—
glistening, happy, and shining.
Sometimes, some days, my feelings are as a lion cub—
restlessly unable to sleep because of troubles.
Sometimes, some days, my feelings are as a pet—
faithful and happy in his place.
Sometimes, some days, I feel just like dirt—
unwanted, downtrodden.
Sometimes, some days, I feel like a rainbow—
loved, like someone cares.
Sometimes, some days, my thoughts and feelings
make me wish I were gone.
Sometimes, some days, my thoughts and feelings
make me happier than ever, it seems.
But I know, however I feel, there's always someone,
somewhere, who cares, even if we're apart.

Julie Anne Burbridge

Detroit By The River

There rolls a river
Cold, dark, lining the city
Sport's arenas, clubs, newspapers, restaurants to go
Marinas, hotels, monuments, music, and festivals
City buildings tall
A wide river flows
Big business, a Motor City
The river bold
The Big City Detroit
With Ambassador Bridge that reaches over Detroit's river to
Windsor
To understand, how busy Detroit has been by the river
All the while, still growing

Jack T. Armstrong

"Communicate"

Communicate! Communicate!
Communication is a 2-way street.
Listen well! Think it through!
Choose your words most carefully!

Articulate your sounds;
Enunciate your words.
It's not always easy, but well worth the effort;
And you will be successful—-
You'll hear and be heard.

Elaine M. Uonelli

The Robber

Without any warning, the robber came in
Destruction and chaos was about to begin
He first took her energy and made her feel weak
It was even an effort, to eat or to speak
She fought back, with all that she had
This robber was relentless, and so very bad
Her struggle was slowly ebbing her strength away
Treatments were given almost every day
Prayers were offered and support from family and friends
The outcome is unknown, where will it end
We ask why and nobody knows, where the robber comes from, or
Where he goes
He has a name you all know quite well
He is called cancer and to know him is hell

June Ann Johnson

The Soul Of Man

A bird in a cage flying around,
Confined by the structure in which it is bound,

Breathes in the air and sings its sweet songs,
Relying on the owner to which it belongs.

The soul of man is like the bird in a cage,
Connected to a body for its work on this stage,

Moving around in the world of creation,
Dependent on others for its growth and elevation.

Yet independent and free man's spirit remains,
Unaffected by change in this worldly domain.

For if one should lose a limb of his body,
His spirit stays whole and undivided.

He still thinks and dreams and plans ahead,
His soul is alive though a limb may be dead.

Reflect on the dream in which you see and move,
Though your body be still and your eyes be closed.

The dream is a mystery, a clue to man's soul,
That matter is not everything, our life has a goal.

For each person is a seed meant to give forth fruit,
To give happiness to others and glorify his spiritual root.

Jeanette Hedayati

Love

How do I love thee let me count the ways
Could a poet express my feelings from countless bygone days
For 'twas it not the highest mountain to depths so far below
How did he knew how I love thee, how did that poet know

Could he tell my arms were aching to hold you once again
Did he know the deepest longing and feel the endless pain
Did he feel the spark of pleasure share the highs and then the lows
How did he know how I love thee, how did that poet know.

When I tremble with desire did he experience that too
Were his thoughts just filled with magic like my fondest thoughts of you
Could he slay the mighty dragon when the sweet love juices flow
Did he feel as soft as a kitten then how did that poet know

Just three little words I love you will be there till the end of my days
But they can never express my feelings when this poet counts the ways
For I love you with a purpose that grows with each new day
My love has a special meaning it's lived out in a special way

So when I say I love you and my love just grows and grows
It comes from my deepest feelings and only this poet knows.

Jean Croft

Faces

Perhaps there is no way to know the faces that are real.
Could the soft, sweet smile, the glistening eyes for sympathy appeal?
Sometimes the frown, the lip-curled sneer, the arrogant, haughty mien
Conceal a real concern and care for the troubles you have seen.
Some faces are but social form, required but not revealing.
And others are but masks to hide a depth of tender feeling.

I like the look of real concern, the face of love and sharing.
It could be that the smooth clear look belies the depth of caring.
I like the quiet display of peace, the light of selfless giving.
I like the faces that reflect the true response to living.
I like the sparkle in the eyes alight with joy or fun.
I like to see the solemn pride when our country's song is sung.
Masks these may also be it's true, but I am firmly sure
Those faces I like best must be the faces that endure.

Doris Barton

River Of Truth

I cry the tears for the dreams shattered,
for the countless lies you've spoken,
for this loneliness in my heart.

I cry the tears for your lack of devotion,
for the fears I know so well,
for the endless promises on hold,
for the coldness blaring from within your eyes.

I cry the tears for the real love I had for you-
for my innocent heart you mangled
and tossed so harshly aside.

I cry the tears to soothe my open wounds,
to end these very blues that wallop in my soul.

I cry the tears for the truth I've come to terms with
acknowledging your way of love was so very wrong. I've
become merely your possession-your prisoner of love.

I cry the tears to end this awful state,
this hurt that bleeds inside.

River of my eyes please run dry,
I want of this no more.

Hope Januszewski

"Seasons Of Time And Mind"

In my mind I see snow - so pristine and white,
Covering trees - all the ground - fallen gently through the night.
Nothing has stirred - no imprint of tracks to behold,
It is winter - just "thinking" it makes me feel - oh - so cold!

Within minutes I change time - imagine some cool, green grass,
The budding of trees - warm, gentle breezes that soon come to pass.
Flowers showing their colors, we have an awakening of spring
And I know all the goodness this "Mother Earth" can bring!

But the days grow hot - I feel summer is quite near,
Fierce thunderstorms and wild fires bring thoughts generating fear!
Some storms do bring rain for farmers' life-saving grain
And I hope this world's people will be fed once again!

But the most beautiful season soon appears in my mind
Glorious autumn - a kaleidoscope of colors, the most brilliant kind!
The days are turning "cool" - there's a "nip" in the air!
Children visit pumpkin patches - frolicking gaily here and there!

I feel rejuvenated - I look ahead to all the seasons -
Being happy I am here - sometimes wondering the reasons
For the changes that are wrought, each and every day
Then peace invades my soul - "His" love comes my way!

Agnes M. Dobias

Widows Lament

Billowy clouds drift slowly away as dusk gently
covers the bright light of day,
the hours draw near for my dreams to unfold,
My mirage, my fantasy, hidden desire grows bold,
your essence flows through my soul on timeless wings,
I dream sweet, secret, intimate things,
Adrift in this deep sleep with only these misty
raptures to keep,
images so vivid, they seer my brain,
whispered endearments ease reality's pain,
waking is a wasteland barren and cold,
I am thrust into this sterile lonely mold,
Why were you destined to die before we grew old,
As the years pass, it's become clear the
messenger from eternity soon will appear,
In a forever garden, there is a promise divine
love and happiness again will be mine.

Donna McFrancis

"Entwined"

A famous welder was creating one day
Creating, for that is what he does best
So he put his torch to the test
As the sheet metal dissolved under the sweltering torch,
The metal was conforming to its master's wishes,
Or was it?

Slowly, very slowly things began to happen
He and the metal were so in tune like synchronized dancers.
Then the metal bent... He bent.

After all was said and done, neither could be found.
They will be forever entwined.

Jodie Webster

Little One

Walk with me to an unknown place where prophets and angels
cry tears like falling raindrops, hearts bleeding
as they cry out. "Why you might ask of me?" I say unto
you they are watching the babes of the Universe hungry
for love, hungry for shelter, but most of all hungry for
food and drink to quench their thirst.

Thou wonders where they are and to whom they shall go.

Drape thyself in colors of pink and blues rise to a new
beginning where the Nations unite to end the pain and hunger
granting the babes of the world peaceful but not forgotten
slumber.

Does thou the nations of the world not remember how it
is to be kissed by those tiny lips and hugged by those
tiny little arms, while the babes of the world cry out to
humanity.

Deborah Mae Post

"Ash Wednesday"

Yesterday,
  dark clouds to the West tried to block the sun
Sunset's light streaked to the East, illuminating acres
  of Pistachio Valley almond trees.
Spring's excessive abundance of purple blossoms, so thick,
  and the canopy you could walk on.

Today,
  from behind pin-held bundle of black hair
Pigeons are scratching facial cracks to her lips
  as the warning sings of impending age.
Ancient wisdom, perhaps, (nonsense too!) flashing smiles, bright
  and able to talk words lighter than air.

Forever,
  deaf and blind to religious service cries
We confess self-indulgent appetites and ways.
  Living separate lives, I cannot see these changes
Passing daily, only in timely fashions
  and when, metaphorically, from ashes we arise.

Donald P. Chvatal

"Destiny And Fate"

Destiny awaits the willing soul, the one without fear.
Destiny controls the one, the one to fulfill the dreams.
Destiny awaits the time, the time when the heart is prepared.
Destiny fulfills its promise, the promise of everlasting unity.
Fate has guided the light, let the darkness rule no more.
Fate has fulfill the dreams, let passion control the heart.
Fate has provided destiny, destiny has led to fate.
Fate has joined the unity, fate has brought you to love.

Danny R. Steward

A Little Boy's Prayer

With tiny hands clasped in prayer, Johnny prayed by his bed each night,
"Dear God, I'm asking you, please for a little sister to love always.
I'll take care of her, dear God. You don't have to worry."
Such was the prayer uttered every night for two years.
Finally, on August 9, 1931, one terribly hot summer Sunday,
the grandfather,
A precious doctor, brought forth a beautiful little girl, his granddaughter.
The little boy was called from play and told his sister had arrived.
Sweaty and dirty from playing in the heat, he hurriedly wiped his
hands and face on his coveralls before rushing into the room to greet her.
"Perhaps I can — just maybe — touch her — and tell her I love her."
At the tiny crib he wiped his hands again, reached gently into the crib,
Touched her beautifully dressed little body, with tenderness and love.
Turning to his father he said: "Daddy, she's mine. I prayed for her.
But you and mother will have to take care of her for awhile.
Then I'll take care of her all the rest of my life." And so he did.
Proudly he watched as she grew up, as he taught her piano and voice.
He played the violin and cello - she the piano, and sang beautifully.
They sang together at home, special functions, and played in concerts.
Home was vibrant with music, fun and love until God called
Johnny home,
On August 10, 1988. He had kept his promise to God and his
sister Babs.

Florence Bryant

Open Life's Pages

Searching the plans of God from the past.
Devoted to learn and wisdom to last.
The unknown meaning to open all eyes.
Untouched are his words, by no way of disguise.

To comprehend the old ways of life lived,
Leads to the true meaning of new to give.
Depending upon the feelings of the heart,
Tells the story in which is to part.

As the pages are opened for all to see,
Each chapter tells of what is to be.
Of the beginning, to the end of time,
God's word tells all, for the world to find.

Catherine M. Ayers

I Never Could Have Thought of That

Did you ever see a rainbow curving across the sky?
Did you ever, ever watch a butterfly go shimmering by?
Did you ever wonder how these things could come to be?
If you've wondered about these things you're just like me.

Did you ever see a bud become a full-blown flower?
Did you ever see a four-o'clock patiently waiting for just the right hour?
Did you ever hold your face up to catch a snowflake's kiss?

I know I never would have thought of this.
Have you ever spent an evening list'ning to a whippoorwill's calls?
Have you ever known the wonder of rippling streams and waterfalls?
Have you ever been delighted by shady places under trees?
I know I never could have thought of these.

A rainbow high! I never would have thought of that!
A butterfly! I never would have thought of that!
Do you think it all came out of a magician's hat?
I know I never could have thought of that!

Helen Gildersleeve

Do It Now

If you would say for me one prayer,
Do it now - filled with care.
Softly, softly - as the air.

If you would light a candle in my name,
Do it now - while I may see the flame,
Flicker and wane - then grow strong again.

If you would take my hand and feel its touch
Do it now - while it still means so much.
Just like a caring, gentle clutch.

If you would smooth the pillows for my head,
And ever smooth the covers of my bed,
Do it now..............before I'm dead,

And can no longer sea
All the things you did for me.

Joan E. Conroy

"To Love Deeply"

"Hold Carefully" they say,
"Do not cast your heart away indiscriminately!"
I answer them, "My heart meets on this road of life many others"
Should I close the doors, turn away,
What then, could my heart say?
"Guard Well" they say.
I reply, "What if one asks?"
"Should I refuse the heart that needs,
And send him on his way?"
"Survive," they say.
I reply..."Surely, it's better to give freely, as
life be in the giving,
Than to die unproductively."
"Take Care," they say.
I reply, "I cannot close my loving Soul to the one who passes by."

Charlotte Bruce

Final End

What in the final end,
Do we really hope to gain?
Love, happiness and a friend,
All of this and no pain?

We all know in our heart
It is wrong to hate.

We must all walk our own path,
In the end we choose our own fate.

How do we know where to begin?
Which is the right path to choose?
We all just want to win,
No one ever wants to lose.

With our minds cluttered in fear,
We see that our destiny is near,
So, we put on a smile and with love in our heart,
We start off on the journey to make a new start.

Cheryl L. Becker-Wiech

Untitled

Behind a smile, I try to hide my battle scars
from so many fights. But my black and blued eyes gives
all my secrets a way. Like how your punches crack my
bones. And how, my blood runs like rivers from my mouth
and nose. Your mean words brake my heart. Tho I stand strong
before you, underneath I am falling a part.

Even tho, no one sees, in the after math I am left crippled
and alone. There's no ones shoulder to cry on. Or anyone
to call on the phone. I wipe my blood and tears a way
praying that this hell will change. That I will find a way.

Helen Sherman

"Accept Me, As I Am"

I am, what I am,
Doing the best, that I can.

You could be my ray of sunshine,
Helping me to make it on down the line.

Come, walk with me, through this world, searching to find,
Day to day, freedom, with peace of mind.

Sharing together, this beautiful land,
With God as our guide, walking together, hand and hand.

Even though we may again see hard times,
We can accept this, with the sound of chimes.

Accept me as I am, until death do we part,
I will always carry you in my heart.

I will accept you, as you are, looking not at your past,
Hoping and trusting that our friendship and love will always last.

Let us look forward to a new tomorrow,
Will it be of happiness, or of sorrow?

Be it of sorrow, your eyes flowing with tears,
I will hold you, easing your fears.

May it be of happiness as we travel along our way,
Let us join as one, until our last and final day.

Bobby Clark

Field Trials, 1880

The shock of steels bore echoes across conquered
Domains, as a volley of powder and thunder sounds
The victory of the moment for the world's kindred
To rejoice in a spectral warrior's accurate flame.

Phantoms of the heavens throng in the clouds to
Praise the arrival of the banner of triumph, while
A plenitude of souls examines the glorious pageant
Of dress soldiers shooting at field's still target.

The ground of day's honor tread by man's feet lay
Before troops, as riflemen stride to band's music,
And the shouts of roaring cannon firing across the
Green parade common of the hour's splendid festival.

Preluded by the demonic marshal array of a small
Formation of marksmen, the clash of guns' discharge
Vibrates over the land, while the convivial crowd
Of many spectators awaits the winning test advance.

The clap of hands on rifles breaks the quietude of
The field trials, to sound victory for a magical man
To receive a high prize for an arduous match shot
Won by steadfast struggle and an accordant spirit.

Donald M. McIntyre

On Doing

Don't tell me what you'll do for me to help me in my plight.
Don't draw for me a blueprint of how you'll make things right.

Don't sing me songs of deeds to be or dragons that you'll slay.
Don't form a "planning committee" to just get in the way.

Don't legislate, or order, don't promise or assume
These only cause a waste of time and lead hope to its doom.

But bring to me the bright sharp edge of a keen and active mind.
The strong arm of a "Doer" who leaves promises behind.

Tell me instead of what you've DONE, of why you did it thus
Strike square the nail upon its head. Leave the hammer's swing to trust.

To trust in self and experience to pride in a job well done
To be there after all is PASSED and realize you've won!

Alta I. Adamson

Memories

As I sit alone in the twilight
Dreaming dreams of yesteryear
I think of you dear husband
And wish that you were here.

Yes, I'm alone, sometimes lonely
But memories they are so dear
I can live again the pleasant times
And feel that you are near.

As the strains of soft music comes drifting
Upon the evening's fragment air
I smell once more the lilacs
We grew with tender care.

If only I could will it
And turn back the pages of time
How sweet it would be my darling
To see you one more time.

Eunice Crume

A Melody Of Love For You

One night as silvered sequins
Drifted down like thistle down
Upon the world and all around
And fairy nymphs danced on the ground
And wound the silvered sequins of the blue
Into a melody of love for you
Silvered sequins from the blue
Came drifting down like silver dew
Into the dark sweet silence there for you
And love fairies wound them round
My heart for there I found
A melody of love for you!

Annie Ruth Forrester

Untitled

In the dense woods of Saratoga
during the dry August days
we sweat the passion of curious youth
whose realities were still a haze

In the tree's rising shadows
we sensed a chill forcing us to feel
that the days of youth would pass by
and "us" would no longer be real

So we clung to the afternoons
and huddled through the nights
giving memories to married lovers
by our vulnerable sight

And as autumn left its trace
a calloused breeze pierced our hearts
reminding us that fairy tales are for the young
and in time people move apart

Early September days are here
spent studying for college degrees
keeping one's mind occupied
from those intimate redwood trees

Jean Coggiano

Am I Or Am I Not?

Walking out my dog I enjoy the quietness of the
early morning hours.

I am happy. In the backyard the trees are still
alive balanced softly by the refreshing breeze.
The birds are gracefully fluttering and chatting.

My dog and I are distrustfully observed by other
survivors of massacre, hunger and sickness.
Finally we are accepted by seven exotic, brave
and smart little cats...or, are they lions?
Do they see me a human being...or, as a monkey?

Motherhood is our link. I decided to feed them every
day with no-effort-food. Do I well? Will they
loose their freedom and hunting ability?

By my "Intuition Reel" I have the feeling that
I am coming as a human being directly from Eden
and, during my temporary stay, to survive I must
adapt myself to the Modern Timing Time.

Carmen Bustamante-Just

Water's Edge

Sitting on the damp sand
embraced with heaven's tears
the lingering mist surrounds my soul
each wave breaks along this desolate beach
trying to outrace the increasing wind
cries of sea gulls fill the air as they look for shelter
I sit never so aware of nature's beauty
wind grows angrier as if warding off
those who wish to intrude in her dance.

Sitting on the damp sand
unafraid I feel safe in the arms of the ocean's mist
the cool tears of heaven cling to my face
unable to move enchanted by nature's glory
the tears stop falling
heaven's light gently moves between the clouds
the wind slows her dance
breaking waves depart slowly to the sand
heaven's light dances about my face
the mist gave one last embrace and returned to the sea.

Gloria M. Giblin

The Night

And then the bent time of midnight closing like shutters the day's
end
Then hand in hand the unpeopled strands of living dissolve and
disperse separately
Climbing down perspectives of infinity to warrens of hiding from
night's terror
The dark bearing down like lids and lonesomeness
The dark stretching out to screaming nothingness
Tier on tier of tunneled living escaping the night the loving night
the vast and peaceful night
Phalanxes of city lights in squares and cubes and pyramids of
necklaced shine
March this night of phantomed being
Canyons of stone engulf some small and faraway footsteps hurrying
like frightened deer
This forest of staring glass and ponderous steel
But two by two the cubicled secret sharing holds back the odds
Imposed by fearsome aeons of waiting in this same night
The silent folding shine of night's embrace
Covers those victors of tomorrow with today's redress

Glenn Stuart Pearce

Make Peace Profitable

Let us pay the sums for peace
Equal to or far above
What is paid for war
Let us bait the brilliant mind
for boosters of economies
for longer warless periods.
Let us fund research for peace to reap a paradise on earth
More tangible than futures earned
In some unknown eternity.
Let us still the sabre clang of pointed rhetoric and acts
That prune our lives well in their prime
That mires ideals in swamps of death.
Let this be a world endeavor to right the wrongs that do exist,
To weld us into happy peoples,
Though ideologies, language vary,
Though faiths have many different faces.
Let the goal be ever present to ease the struggle of the living;
To stifle hate, not generate it,
Not make of peace the aftermath.
Of devastating war and grief.

Florence K. Wiener

World In My Eyes

I gaze out my window into your world
Escaping the darkest depth of my sea
Thoughts of us climbing our highest mountain
Invade my mind, stuck in my memory
Where is the cure for my depressing thoughts
How can I look at the world in your eyes
Let me reveal my devotion to you
Succumb into my existing darkness

Angela Hicks

"What Christmas Is All About?"

Christmas is fun for little children,
Especially for the ones who open their first toy,
Yet, Christmas is for the young and old alike,
Yes, for you, me and everyone to enjoy!
Everyone knows that religious impact it gives;
But what about the traditional value it does unfold?
The many Christmases long ago, but the difference now is,
The gifts of today are more expensive to behold.
There is also the sentimental side of Christmas,
Even for those people who don't believe,
Because if anyone has a heart like mine,
They'd rather give instead of receive.
Christmas is also very special to newlyweds,
A chance for romance around an open fire,
to enrich each others' love and devotion,
To share with their family, with whom they desire.
But, what Christmas should mean to one and all,
Is for all fighting to cease and world peace and tranquility,
For if man would take time to stop and think "Why are we
fighting?"
Then maybe, we could lay down our arms, and live in perfect
harmony.

James A. Pionke

Something That Will Never Go Away

Sometimes a broken heart will never mend
Especially when the person lost is not only a lover, but a friend
Their absence is seemingly impossible to fill
Leaving you feeling as hollow as a porcupine quill.

The void they leave you with is immense
You try to fill it with anything, even false pretense
But the pain is as persistent as the air you breathe
As you cling to fading hope, never willing to concede.

Jason Calabrese

The Crying Rose

Snowflakes fall all around me
Even on the rough brick steps
That Support my weight

Tears stream down my cheeks
As I remember the troubles I had today
The one I love ran out on me

Teardrops
Fall onto a patch of snow just below my arm
I realize that in a few months I'll be right
here, again.

Spring arrives and again I'm here
Wondering if I should just give up
I look to the sky and ask for a sign

A moment later rain begins to fall
I look over my shoulder
To see a red rose stretched toward heaven.

Jennifer L. Moore

An Angelic Song

Like flipped pages many years have rolled by,
Events, voices passed with the whip of wind
But an angelic song held in my mind
Indelible for its flawless, fluid tune
From crescendo to its hushed dying strain
With pianissimo, forte, and trebles.
It discloses an empyreal isle
Of pearl-studded gates and paved golden streets
Where hunger, distress, and death dissipate
Where all taintless hearts and spirits abide
The uranic chorale of winged angels
Proclaims this far-off supernal Eden,
Distinct in memory, the harmony
Floods with beauty flowing into my soul,
So encompassing, it dispels dark thoughts
Lifting me to the dais of the holy;
I rise with pure euphoric elation
Higher than he plane of my mortal self,
Soaring in delightful glorious moments
With the song never muted by time.

Herminia P. Marapao

"I Love You"

Dedicated To My True Love, Timothy Brown

If I could say "I love you"
Every minute of day and night,
It still wouldn't be enough
To let you know how I feel inside.

I would have to say those words for many centuries
To let you know the true extent of what I feel,
For the love I share with you,
Is o' so very real.

So my love, my darling, my dear
Please hear my words out,
For you're the one in my life
That I can't live without.

I've built my world around you,
In the hope we'd never part,
For I knew we were meant to be together
Right from the very start.

Crystal Lada

A Portrait In The Darkness

Every day that she's alive ... she's dead;
Every smile that she smiles turns sad;
Her days are like canvases, obscure, faded,
Of an artist who, alas, never made it ....

A blossom withered by inclement winds of fate,
And caught in a seesaw of love and hate -
She waits alone night after night,
With not a silver lining in sight ....

Caged in kismet, how can she ever break away
From the dictates that hold her under sway? -
Instead, she sleepwalks through life undaunted -
In spite of being unfulfilled and unwanted ....

Feroza Abbasi

'Emotions Of War'

With the cold war just beginning,
Everybody is now departing.
The old town's brave soldier.
He is trying to act much bolder.

Trying to hold back endless tears,
Trying to escape their newly found fears,
Their misted, teary eyes,
And they don't want to keep their goodbyes.

And as the lonely months go by,
With them slowly fade away warm goodbyes.
Free-flowing spirits zoom,
That the sad, killer war might end soon.

Many men and women have died.
Taking with them their dignity and pride.
Hoping they all come back,
Although the long days look dark and black.

And now that the war has ended,
The tired soldiers dream to be mended,
And come home cold and wet,
But wanting to get out of this net.

Dana Hedin

Reconciliation

Somewhere in time, ancient memories.
Evoked from the great beyond, revealing,

The heart of Heaven, a hidden life force,
awaiting the sacred moment of awakening.

Embraced in a frozen dream, haunted
by unfulfillment, on the stained altar of Eden.

Holy are those sacrificed, in their
quest, to wipe the tears of Heaven.

Hear the prayer of forgiveness and reconciliation,
receive the word, carried by angel wings, the voice of Time.

See the enlightenment of rebirth, the marriage
of Heaven and Earth. The gate is Open.

Benny Andersson

Rock 'N Roll

Rock 'n roll is like a dream, far away into the night they scream.
Far away from everything that is just so very plain.
They scream the words of truth, love, and pain,
Forever for rock 'n roll to remain.

Legend metal gleam Holiday, Zeplin, or even Hendrix to make plain.
To seem so plain in a purple haze, forever Holiday to sounds of
stairway,
Forever rock 'n roll to remain

Joy Hope Toler

A Country Respite

My first night in a country town was still as still could be
except for the continuous hum of a million crickets.
I lay quietly in bed, intently listening, for more of nature's sounds,
as my ears were only accustomed to the sounds of the city.

First, I heard the clear, plaintive call of a night bird, unknown to
me, but with a sound so sweet, it seemingly hung suspended in the
night air. An answering call rang out in the stillness, as pure and
sweet as the first. How dear the bird songs are to my ear.

Then the blare of a two-tone automobile horn sounded, a city
sound like I knew back home, where freeway traffic, airplane engines,
the plaintive whistle of a freight train, augmented on its approach,
diminishing as it departs, the high-pitched police sirens are the city.

Country sounds, so soothing by comparison, do lull us into blessed
relaxation, refreshing our souls. For us who drive miles from the
city, a get-away weekend in the country can be as precious to us as
the bustle and excitement of the city might be to the country visitor.

Edith Doyle

Autumn Pathways

We met and walked in the park.
Exchanging thoughts and feelings, that's' all.
We talked, we listened, we cared.
The leaves were turning, it was early fall.

Winter came, we were both still listening.
Yet, the walking and talking had changed to more.
We were touching and holding-bodies moulding
Still we were friends, but not like before.

The leaves will change and float to the ground.
The paths in the park will not hear the sound
Of our eyes and thoughts as they meet and touch
Our wants, our hopes, our desires and such.
Or the snow that now caresses the waiting land,
Like our eyes holding love, as I hold your hand.

David F. Marik

New Rider On The Light Rail

Sitting across, one on one, glances don't meet.
Eyes stare, lips don't move, no sound comes from closed teeth.
Standing quickly to get off before the door
Closes on my sleeve, watching feet, down lower

Step to red brick sidewalk. Wait at the signal.
Blonde fat woman in a blue pin-stripe suit talks:
"Beats driving, I'm going home to a cold brew."
"I think it's worth trying. See you tomorrow."

Street power line gets broken. We're put a bus.
Driver takes us right down train tracks, 'til the trestle stops her.
We squeeze down an alley, get bottomed out.
Can't move until people exit.

Strong black athlete sings rap as we get started.
Black Security Guard raps, "Need your ticket."
Eyes meet, say, "I was going to go to Med School.
I didn't have the money I needed."

Riding Light Rail, saving the ozone layer,
Reading on the rails about the Stealth Bomber.
Talking, sleeping, people watching, thinking hard;
Taking Light Rail beats driving my white Ford car.

Geraldine Sawyer Coomes

When All Else Fails

When all else fails, you can lift your
eyes unto the hills from whence cometh
your help. Your help cometh from the Lord
who made heaven and earth.

When all else fails, you can sing songs
in your heart to the most high above. And
he'll give you happy tunes. To praise and
worship him in all things we do. So lift
your head up high and look to GOD for all
and everything you need.

When all else fails, count it all joy when we
fall into temptations and escape, GOD will
see us through, as we trust in him with all
our heart and lean not on our own understanding,
He'll direct our path, IF WE LET HIM,
WHEN ALL ESLE FAILS.

Catherine Winfield

Friendship

Walking through the garden of life, our memories are filled with;
Family, friends and enemies,
Happiness and tears.
Each person that makes our acquaintance adds a chapter to our
book of life.
Every enemy writes a tale of darkness,
Each love a tale of the heart,
And each friend writes the memories we continue to cherish
until the end.
Some people we know all our lives,
But don't hold any special memories.
Some we know only for a day can change our lives forever.
Whenever you feel low pull out that book of memories,
And turn to this chapter;
No matter how short,
No matter the bittersweet feeling it sends to your heart.
Read what our friendship has written on those pages;
And know true friendship like ours will forever fill your book.

Julia Lee Doss

The Seasons Of Your Life

The seasons of your life
Correspond to the pages of a novel,
Each filled with different emotions, experiences
that run like a river through the years.
There is a time for all changes,
And as with all changes come the bitter sweet
Along with the sweet;
A time when you can clearly see the path,
The sunshine so bright it's blinding,
The spirit free, the heart full;
A time when the light is clouded, but the road
is straight and you walk the distance, content
just to have made it through; a time of acknowledgement
When there are no set rules, just the purpose of fulfillment;
A time for discovery of ourselves, then to discover others;
to see the good within so to be able to discern
the good in others; a time to take a partner to travel the by ways-
to challenge, strengthen, comfort, accept the other
each time has its purpose-come hold my hand friend,
the seasons are waiting

Eileen M. Haviland

"All Is Not Gone"

I walk into the room and I see you sitting in your favorite chair by the window.
I see a man who has lived a long life and seen many things.
Do you remember though?
Has that dark shadow in your mind clouded over all those memories?
Birthdays, anniversaries, holidays and graduations.
Where have they all gone?
Some days I look at you and I want to ask,
"Are they really all gone?"
Will you look at me standing here and catch a fleeting memory from the past?
Then you slowly look up at me and I can see for a moment that familiar glint in your eyes.
You may have forgotten something but, deep inside I know all is not gone.....
ALL IS NOT GONE.

Danielle N. Reed

"Shades Of Autumn"

Rain rocks the night damp, dark pools,
fear fills fading eyes deep gleaming jewels.
Visions vie to invade my mind, so intrusive,
making moments of inner peace, so exclusive.

Laboring limbs ache restless for the light,
seeking solace in starshine, a comfort in the night.
Waking worries wane at the first rays of dawn,
fleeting flurries of fantasy asleep, but not all gone.

Time twisted trees dance in the dark days sky,
winds whistle howling tunes, the words are mine to cry.
Sun sifts through clouds, so it's seldom told,
my hopes wilt, wither and die like the fallen autumn gold.

Denise Profumo

Wanting A Partner

My meditation takes me deep.
Few could understand the love I keep.
My strength is in my heart and in my soul.
To learn and live the love of Christ is my goal.
My love is simple as is my life.
Yet insecurity cuts at me like a razor sharp knife.
To the world...to show your emotions is weak.
But, those who shall inherit the earth are the meek.
Love of nature, love of peace
Is part of me till my heart does cease.
Concern for those close becomes strong.
Love of this kind just can't be wrong.
Meditation brings to surface my inner thoughts.
Loneliness seems to be one of my biggest faults.
There's so much love I have stored, ready to share, ready to give.
Without a companion it's so tough to live.
My faith is strong, I will have a wife, a companion.
If it's His will, My Father will bring me out of this famine.
For now I survive, I plan and I hope.
I am lucky, I've learned how to cope.

Bill Flynn

Heart Smile

When I think of you my heart gets a smile
Getting to know you has made my life worthwhile
You came into my life when I needed you the most
I was so lost till I found you my heavenly host
My life has always been hard and I know that when I pray
Your loving guidance will lead me the right way;
The best way to make it an incredible day
Is to stop, listen to my heart and pray

Christina Thomas

Journey With Me

Go out from the city, walk into the woods,
find a spot that just looks good.

Sit on a stump or lean against a tree,
just close your eyes and journey with me.

Listen to the rush of the stream near by,
the call of the hawk flying high.

There's a squirrel on a limb talking in chatter,
we look around to see what's the matter.

Nothing wrong here, no reason for concern,
simply a deer feeding on ferns.

Birds flutter by from trees to the ground,
Searching for seed and eating insects they've found.

The whisper of the wind, the sudden slight chill,
we open our eyes as if by God's will.

Still here in His garden we feel the beauty and peace,
what a great place for stress release.

Return we must to our everyday lives,
to the demands of success, to our husbands and wives.

But remember this place, it's not very far,
just close your eyes wherever you are.

Glenn R. Sweet

The Wounded Warrior - (An Ode to the VA)

Reach out to this warrior "O" Lord of peace and truth
Find my heart in the darkness....
I have killed;.....I know not who.
My brothers and I are lost, we are so alone at times.
Our souls have been taken....
By a legal crime______
The justice is in the system....
The system does not work...
Our lives are in the hands of others,
Who cannot feel our hurt.
We struggle to go on______
Our brothers die each day...
The system it goes on, with the games it likes to play.
Reach out "O" Lord; with a healing hand...
Heal this warrior Lord....
Who has fought for this land....

James M. Cowan

Battle Of Youth

Torn between an evil desire to create and destroy.
Finding things you sought after to be lacking in joy.
Feeling stranded within the walls of a world without love.
Seeing that your ridiculous dream is all you can think of.

Noticing the emptiness of the glass that lies upon the table.
Making up your life as if it were nothing but a fable.
Getting lost between reality and what you believe is true.
Fighting a hopeless battle, 'Tis the battle of youth.

Bleeding dry tears for what you do not know.
Trying to feed a hunger that by the instant, it just grows.
Finding only that wrongs are rights and we're running in a maze.
Trying with everything to be happy when the sadness only stays.

Learning how to kill your brother for just a crust of bread.
Then, remorselessly saying that he was better off dead.
You can hear the battle cry, "We know not what we do!"
But deep down your heart just tells you,
"This is the battle of youth."

Catherine Klotsche

Twilight In Valholl

It was twilight when we reached the hill;
Flying bullets, I can hear them still!
They came from a German outpost nearby,
Where Lieutenant Conner was soon to die!

Dark and handsome, and tall was he;
How young he was, to cease to be!
He poured out his sweet, red wine of life,
A hapless victim of a deadly strife.

He gave up his years to stay forever young;
Now may his valor be forever sung!
May this meadow stay hallowed ground,
For here was once a martyr crowned.

It is a meadow fair and promising,
Just waiting for the flowers of spring.
Perhaps a barefoot shepherdess
May someday skip across its grass.

This is where Lieutenant Conner died,
And this is where my thoughts of him abide;
Here in this valley of the slain,
Always a somber twilight must remain.

Benjamin Franklin Mickey

Untitled

For I'm a flowing river,
For I'm a rolling stone,
For I'm a burning fire,
And only good Lord gives me strength to carry on.

I've done a lot of living,
Did the things of every sort,
But I get the funny feeling
That my life is in the songs that I have written.

I used to run,
I used to stumble,
I used to climb,
I used to fall
Oh, I was getting close to the bottle,
But instead I wrote this old-fashioned song.

I love old-fashioned music,
I love the stars at night,
I love to think you love me,
'Cause you stand behind the songs that I write

David Blokh

Master Of Dreams

Master of dreams don't take away my sleep
For love is waiting for me in that place so deep
When I dream, she holds me, and kisses me sweet
If it wasn't for the night we'd never meet

Master of dreams do you know my lover
The one who's nestled beneath my cover
I know not her name, only her face
My wish is simply to visit that place

Master of dreams does she speak of me to
That mortal young man who's love is so true
Does she also curse the boundaries we must obey
And long for the end of the agonizing day

Master of Dreams when you come to lift my strife
Can I stay in your world for the rest of my life
I know you see how our love for each other grows
And I must be with her always, not just when my eyes close

Eric Christopher Pendery

Sun Life

I can see God's love shining in the living sun
For miles and miles and miles and miles
As he smiled flowers grew wild
For miles and miles and miles and miles
Birds flew in harmonious skies
For miles and miles and miles and miles
In weather warm sweet and mild
As fish swim in perfect file
For miles and miles, miles and miles
His smile a style to last a while
For miles and miles and miles of smiles
He styled a smile of living tile
To live life in his profile
For miles and miles and miles of smiles
I can see God's love shining in the living sun
And it keeps on shining finding and giving one to the living sun
All the people and animals knew
Love from the living sun
All the plants and things drew
Life from the living sun

Bufar Palk

He Gave His Life For Me

Forgive me Lord Jesus is what I asked today
For my life's busy schedule is what kept me away
Please close your eyes tight and imagine with me
What the pearly gates in heaven must surely be
As we go there on our journey our final call to rest
Oh how they must shine and look their very best
I wonder who keeps them up and brings them their shine
Hope I'm not asked to as I may not have the time
I am sure there is many more to do the job right
The Lord won't mind this one oversight
He knows how busy I am doing all the other things
Wonder if he'll mind all the extra work I have to bring
To volunteer my time just isn't meant to be
Oh by the way thanks Jesus for dying on the cross for me
What a sight we just seen in our minds eye
Wonder how many more missed it due to no time

Debora Dodge

Patiently Waiting

Don't put me off, my darling
for there is another woman lurking in the shadows.
I love you so, you are my life,
but it has been so long since we have been close.
And oh, how I have hungered for you...

I do not want to betray you,
but my body dances and throbs and aches with desire.
And oh, there she is everyday,
smiling - laughing - touching - making me feel wonderful.
And oh, how I have hungered for you...

Those lonely days, those lonely nights,
day after day, I've lain wanting you, I've lain dreaming of you.
Never a thought of going astray,
when you've been so preoccupied and absorbed by everything else but me.
And oh, how I have hungered for you...

I've tried to understand, I've tried to be patient,
I've even helped tackling the obstacles that got in the way.
Positive your energy would quickly be freed,
only to be disappointed in you always finding so much more.
And oh, how I have hungered for you...

Judith A. Bond

Consolation

Be not dismayed when troubles descend,
For they come to us all some day,
Just be sure you're right and hold you're head high,
And go to God often to pray.

'Twas Paul who so often had troubles galore,
With churches in the early days,
He stood his ground and continued on,
Preaching and giving God praise.

Be patient and kind in the face of adversity,
Long suffering as Paul was then,
You'll finally win the faithful and true,
And never regret the stand you've planned.

It takes courage and strength to be a preacher,
And carry God's Word everywhere,
You need all the strength that Christians can give you,
And the greatest strength is in prayer.

Be not discouraged, it will not last,
It is only a passing wave,
The thunder is only a warning sign,
But the sunshine shall appear, to save.

Edna Rush

A Dream Of Christmas

Twas the day before Christmas with shopping to do,
For Tommy, Jimmy, and Elizabeth too.
There will be lots of surprises
With big and small packages in all different sizes
There would be whispers, secrets all kinds of giggles
With little white kittens with whiskers and who wiggles
While the doors in halls hangs mistletoe
We watch the little brown puppy run and roll
Popcorn balls in the big Christmas tree
Even stop lights on the streets of red and green
With snow flakes falling on the ground
We fall on the ground like Angels all around
While Mom in the kitchen, makes pies, cakes, and cookies
Dad checks in the oven on big tom turkey
Grandmas sits in her rocker telling us stories
Grandpa is down in the basement sitting and snoring
Santa's at the North Pole checking on Elves reindeer and toys
For all the big and little girls and boys

June Parks

Poetry Born

Poems spill from me,
Geysers impatient to sniff
The air, to spout, and live,
Needing the form of words to tell their tales
To contain their images, to form their rivers.
Only life holds the form
Poetry craves.
Poems belong to the living,
The songs of mankind
Created and sung by bards,
Telling of man's plight,
Man's flight,
Man's sights.
Death nor eternity
Hums the tunes
Man needs to sing
Poetry alone fills
Man's need to link
The species to
The Godhead.

Carol A. S. Tiernan

"The Poet's Corner"

Tis the poet's corner to which we do read!
For we are surely a dying breed!
Tis the poets of the world, we do have a strong need!
For we are surely a thinning and dying breed!
Of our brothers and sisters, we surely have a need to read!
Tis the world we call our home, and its air we do breath!
Tis the greed and wars our poets' words do strongly fight!
For the world's health we'll join our combined might!
Tis our children who are in a terrible plight!
Tis the evils of this world our words do send into flight!
Our combined words and might, tis for
our children and Earth we do shed light!

John W. Jackson, Jr.

Good-bye

The say it's not fair, but yet it is
For we only have a short time to live
And when it's over the time has come
The last words are spoken, and all is done
But sometimes your life is cut short, before you can really live
All you had was sixteen years to give
It must have been wrongly timed
For you left a world of family and friends behind
We'll never get the chance to find out why
And you never got the chance to say good-bye
If only we knew, why it had to be you
Then things would be a little less confused
And if we had the answers to why
Then we wouldn't have to cry
And all would be set aside
And we'd know you said good-bye

Bree Mick

The Place That I Know

I have no doubt there's a loving Maker from Whom all beauty flows,
For without a caring Creator, whither the garden, whither the rose?

Just to think of Life is to think of God. How can the two be apart?
From the tender, devoted Almighty comes the Power that pumps each heart.

But constant awareness of life's fleeting pace makes me worry about The Last Day
When God will announce that The Hour has come. O what will I think of to say?

I steadfastly cling to familiar scenes in this world that's so filled with woe.
It's Heaven I seek as Eternal Home, but Earth is the place that I know!

How fearful and fragile and feeble I feel, though devoted to God's Perfection.
I plead for His mercy, for understanding, for judgment in loving reflection.

May the Author of all that ever was made humor my trembling qualms,
And shower me with His healing Touch, give me a blessing that calms.

Majestic, marvelous, powerful, pure, Protector and Patron of all,
He leads us kindly by His Light to banish each frightening wall.

Now by His strength may I be helped in doing all I can
To live each day with hope and trust, and then yield to His Holy Plan.

Helen Willis

On Language

Metaphoric consciousness shapes one's soul to the earth and fosters a love in one's mind for everlasting truth.

Little is known about why and when this awareness is created, and for what reason and the like.

It defines love and hate at the same time, but still hinders us in dealing with many facets of what is and what is not.

Many words we gather, possess, and use in our lifetime, though we do not understand the deep meaning of what we say.

Beauty can be created with great emotions that touch our very essence; the beauty penetrates many realities but hides its own function.

Visual creations are formed and shaped that make us see the world in many complex ways, and at the same time attempt to simplify what is and what could be.

A Chomsky, a Whorf, and others will use language to explain it, thinking that objectivity has been accomplished.

The poet will smile and continue on in the exploration.
Language, I still do not know what it is.

Antonio Simoes

"Freckles"

Freckles, Freckles, everywhere;
Freckles, Freckles, "who put you there?"
Was it the food we ate and did not know
Or was it the people around us they made them grow.

As I get older you continue to be made known;
Sometimes you get bigger because you have grown.
You are strange and not well known,
Sometimes people think you come from something I have sown.

Freckles, Freckles, what will I do,
You won't go away, you keep coming through,
This can be lovely for others, but you make me blue
I plan to remove you, and that's so true.

Freckles, Freckles, you used to be so cute
but now with all these age spots you made a repute.
A repute that gives me a nickname.
One that will not put me to shame.

Alice M. Roberts

Rhythms Of Life

Life orchestrates our rhythm while on this earth we dwell
From "Rock-A-Bye My Baby" to the tolling of death's bell.

The rhythm of the lullaby shifts to hop, skip, and run.
Nursery rhymes and game playing are childhood songs of fun.

Rock, Pop, rap and loud music blast rhythms of the teens.
Youth seems to be in presto seeking thrills from any means.

Melodies of love start playing and we hear a rhapsody.
Two hearts that beat together will create intensity.

Love songs slow down to largo as the organ starts to play.
A mellow sound—a wedding march—we take our vows this day..

Life whirls in crescendos spinning in life's learning lane.
The tempo sometimes quickens—speeding up to make a gain.

Life's trials beat shaky rhythm—chanting blues in the night.
Hymns harmonize our stresses when life's chords are not played right.

We waltz into the "Golden Years," too tired to do the swing.
Sweet memories of life's melodies will ease the aging sting.

The grand finale is closing in, of this there is no doubt;
There will be silence in our rhythm when our song of life plays out.

Joyce Johnson Merryweather

Friends

Friends are people you can trust, who will not go out on you.
Friends are people who never rust and love the things you do.
Friends are people who care about you, and you care about them, too.
Friends are people you can laugh with and talk a ton with, too.
Friends are people you can spend time with and always be a helping hand.
Friends are people who can also help you if you don't understand.
Friends are people who listen to you and what you have to say.
Friends are people who will always be close to you until your dying day.
Friends are people who will stick with you and always hear you say,
"That's what friends are for, and that's how it will stay."
Friends are true and loving to you, and they will cheer you up if you are feeling blue.
Friends will love you for the rest of your life and will try not to cause you any strife.
Friends should be true friends, and that's what this is about;
because if they are true friends, there should be no doubt.

Janet Barksdale

Life

Life is just what we make it
From dawn 'til setting of sun;
Each thing we do is good or bad
In life as this race we run.

If we choose to do the things that are right,
Though we're tempted to do the wrong;
As we battle with our soul
The winner is always the strong.

Some take the high road to travel,
Some are satisfied with the low;
Still others are seeking rich rewards
As they journey to and fro.

We have a challenge each new day
Without it life would be vain;
But with courage and determination
Our goals can be attained.

There are many who might have won this race
If a little harder they had striven;
If they'd thought more of others and not just self
Of their time and talents given.

Edith Cox Turner

The Summons

Not so very long ago, my friend heard death's call
from far away and yet within, he held her in his claws.

The summons was so discreet, she knew not what caused the pain,
but only if there was enough she'd never feel it again.

Beyond her conscious mind, the lure was placed carefully there,
eerily drifting in her head, inviting her from her cares.

Silently death stepped in, so insistent was his call,
that she wasn't sure how to resist or that she could at all.

As she lay there, still and spent, breathing sluggish, shallow breaths
her heart slowed beat by beat closing down into death.

Death grinned a mirthless grin, for it seemed, one more, he'd claim.
This night his quest would be easy for she had nothing left to gain.

But one who had the faith stood within the room
and begged and pleaded for the life that death dragged into doom.

The Lord heard that humble cry and knew that faith was there.
The prayer He heard was from the heart, and He answered swift and clear.

From the door that death held open, she turned and came away,
For God opened the door to life and invited her to stay.

Debra S. Robertson

The Earth As We Know It

The earth as we know it won't stay the same,
From the babbling brooks to the wide-open plains.

The rivers and rain forests destroyed by our hands,
The senseless fires raging throughout our lands.

Pollution and smog everywhere that we go,
What's to become of our earth; well, we all really know.

Our children's children will have no more trees,
No more lakes, no more rivers and soon no more seas.

The animals will die and that leaves only land,
Earth as we knew it, destroyed by human hands.

Jessica A. Graham

Man's Inherent Light

To bring about man's true freedom,
Fulfillment, and profound experience of joy,
It would seem folly to have a way
To put any other man down.
In true freedom and fulfillment of soul,
Man cannot look down in such a way,
For a frown he could not get rid of,
And so to be able to step with a natural, inherent lightness,
And be rid of all burdens upon him
In life he would otherwise meet along his way.
It seems time to let true individuality flourish;
Each wonderful man a world unto his own,
Of all shades, hues, subtleties, complexities,
Wonders of creations for him to realize
Deep from within his untamed spirit.
For all not to rely on one another to beat the opponent down,
And each to grow with freedom all around.
To grow in and see places that have never been found.
Where wondrous light lights a new profound world,
And awakening, a new and joyous experience, can abound!

James Frye

My Life's Dream

(boy) You're the girl I've been seeing in my Dreams
(girl) Just hold me Darling I know what you mean
(boy) I fell asleep many nights praying for someone like you
(girl) And I prayed many nights for someone to love me too.

(together) My life's dream was to have someone like you are
(together) To find each other we traveled so very far
(together) Even after all the things we had to go through
(together) It was worth it to find someone like you.

(boy) Darling tell me you'll never find someone new
(girl) How could I when there's no sweeter guy than you
(boy) I saw so many others let their love grow cold
(girl) I know I'll still love you when I grow old.

Jay Osborne

Tears Do Not Lie

I'll never forget the look on his face
for him it was out of context, it was
just out of place
Then he grabbed me by the hand in hopes what
he had to say would help me understand
I looked again into his face, and his tears
began to flow
he didn't need to tell me he loved me, his
tears had told me so,
I think of that day often, and yes it makes
me cry.
for I know he truly loves me, cause tears do
not lie

Connie L. Beers

Ambiguity Plus Rapid Eye Movement

Well, well, well, walk along the beach, walk along,
glasses without, within, can't you see that well?
what clouds your vision? elemental,
are these artificial suppositions not supportive
enough for your eyes? detrimental,
constantly, change, switch the lights on and off, and on again,
won't see me any better in either case,
your hair is long, or short, both at once depending
on necessity or whatever, moines cing, don't bite me,
commercial style voids them both out;
words bubbling out of mouths that
would better serve some perversion,
take a stroll on the wild side;
these words will be mine, talk about it, friend,
I spend my soul with these strange currencies;
he imagines the notes as he drums out the beat,
the notes of smoke are towed in line by the beat,
the song is as if it were really there;
the laugh, the grate, the great, the mighty,
the smile, 'dunno, wide, takes up the face.

Adrian Loder

The Promise

The story tells of a promise, the coming of a son,
God has chosen a woman to
Bring forth this blessed one!

Soldiers were ordered to find and destroy
this little Jewish King;
And yet the angels sing, glory to the newborn King!

A star shone in the sky, extremely bright that night;
Shepherds were frightened when they saw
the sky's radiant light.

The star led three Kings from the Orient to a stable.
There they saw a babe wrapped in rags,
In a manger bed padded with straw.

This babe had a glow of no baby they had ever seen.
He smiled as if to say, I will give the world
a special love.
A love for all humankind to know!

Gracie Sanderson Hill

Comfort

We search God's Book, a treasure store,
God's message is clear, we can't add more.
To bring true peace to those we love,
Our only source, from God above.

In our weary times, God has reached out;
And freed our minds from stressful doubt.
We were assured that God was there;
Our anxieties were removed by prayer.

Stay close to God, all your life through,
To handle the load life's given you.
So when your neighbor is put to the test,
You can tell him how you've been blessed

I am depressed, perplexed, solutions rare,
I'll search God's Word and find Him there.
God's promises give me the greatest strength;
And guide me through my cares at length.

"Come unto me," His message clear,
What comfort, knowing God will hear!
It's when I've been lifted by God's grace,
I can see the hurt that others face.

Claire Vomhof

Going Home

Daddy, I know you're going home today;
God's sending an angel to take you away.
I know I've been selfish for a few weeks or so,
For asking God to spare you,
When I knew you must go.
So now I have accepted His plans for you,
And have asked Him to stop the suffering
That you've been going through.
He won't let you suffer anymore.
He's taking you home now, through Heaven's Door.
I know you can hear me - everything that I say,
So please listen to me, before you go away,
I love you so much, and the others do too,
But now we just want what's best for you.
God's taking you home now to take good care of you;
The pain will be gone; your life will be new.
You're just taking a trip that we will all take someday
So, we will see you in Heaven, when
God shows us the way.
Going Home.

Chester E. Hembree

The Paintings

Memories exist as picture perfect paintings.
Golden fire of the sun's endless rays caress skies,
Windows of opportunity open to catch a glimpse of life,
A world of fortune. Laughter rings out wild; I dream of you
Your face in my memory. They come and go, visions they tease.
My heart cries to you, just an image in my mind.
Cloaked in shadow of morning's dark hours you stole away my heart
As the golden eye of dawn kissed your face my heart leapt;
Calling to memories of you, dreams come and play, you are there.
The sun brings life to a sleepy world,
Lighting impressions of happiness that might be.

Come the images wild and free, tempting my heart, sweet whisperings
Voices they call in the heat of day, visiting dreams in still night
My heart bleeds, longing for one more day to touch your heart.
I wish you to stay a living memory, in my heart always to be,
As summer nights recall the moments lived together wild and free.
Knowing all I wish to be, love and life sail hand in hand
There we will be, just you and I, drawn into the paintings of life,
Memories brushed by the artistry of heart
Upon a canvas of love that will never tear apart.

Casey T. Whiting

Mother's Day

Here's to the mothers of the days
Gone past they gave us wisdom
that will last and last.

They played the board of education to the seat of
knowledge and gave us wisdom you can't get in any college.

Whose same dear hands without
discreation brought us through the great depression.
We still need them for the future is gained from the past.

They gave up their sons by the
score when our country was in the last big war.
They gave us the mothers of
its present with their smiles
so sweet and pleasant who have the task
to guide this nation in this fast
world of this now generation.

To the mothers yet to be for they are the
hope of the future and glory of the past.
God will bless them and we do too for without them.
What would we ever do.

Jacob W. Van Wyk

Gone With The Wind

In loving memory of my son, Paul Fusco

It has been five years since I have been
gone. The memory of me has just gone with
the wind. My face has faded from your mind,
and my name you never speak. It is like I
never lived you see. I have just gone with the wind.

I wait for you my friend to come and visit
me. To put just one small flower on my grave,
to say you cared for me. From where I am, I
see it all and remember all we shared. But
in the end, it is all just gone with the wind.

I did not ask for you to grieve for me until
the end of time. I only wanted for you to
remember some of the good times. They have
just gone with the wind.

If you loved me, you would have remembered
me. I would have remembered you, but yesterday
is forever just gone with the wind.

It is all right, my friend, you see I
understand, because I know someday you too
will just be gone with the wind.

Diane Fusco

To My Children

Oh precious extension of mine,
Happy am I that you have grown up so fine;
So caring and generous all of you,
"'Twould be my prayer that you live that way all the years through!"
The universe is made up of different individuals, that is true,
Some good, some bad, but all with postage due;
For when God calls us up to Him, He'll ask us one and all,
"What good works did you do for your fellow man, and where
did you fall?"
Children of mine live each day as if it may be your last,
Feed the hungry, clothe the naked, and forgive each other's sins past!
I know in my heart that you will be granted passage
through the Pearly Gate,
Because you have a lot of your Dad and me in you,
and it's never too late;
So someday in Heaven we'll meet again, wait and see,
It's up to you, and it's up to me!

Love,
Mom

Isabel Kent

Lake Okeechobee's Song

The morning sunlight danced upon the clear blue of the lake.
Hark! Cacophonous chirping of the birds as they awake
A slumbering world deep in sleep. A state of calm repose,
A state near death; how does God manage THAT, do you suppose?
Silver fish leap through the air...blue gills, wide-mouthed bass.
Leaving ever-widening circles upon this sea of glass.
A mallard dives beneath the surface, searching for a bite.
It isn't long before he has a juicy fish in sight.
The campers have their bacon sizzling along the peaceful shore.
Some say this is as close as you can get to Heaven's door.
This is a land of sugar cane, of gators, lizards, snakes.
But peaceful times await upon the shores of this vast lake.
The wild life and raw nature here puts one in touch with God,
And really all you need to have is your cane fishing rod
To rest your mind and body; let it soothe your every care.
A peaceful sanctuary in this world today....that's rare.
Egrets, sea gulls, turtles, fish and near-extinct manatees
Grace the waters and the shores of Lake Okeechobee.
So cast your caution to the wind! Come and sit awhile
Upon the shores of our tranquil lake and leave here with a smile.

Cathy L. Mohney

Harbingers

Harbingers - We are harbingers; we foreshadow what is to come.
Harmonious - We will exhibit accord in feeling and action.
Activators - We will set in motion a proactive life-style.
Revealing - We will divulge or show a portion of ourselves in relationships that here-to-fore we have for our most private projects.
Beautiful - Because we enjoy conscious use of our five senses; seeing, hearing, smelling, tasting and feeling, we perceive ourselves to be what our minds allow our emotions to absorb.
Innovative - We will begin to renew the dormant creativity that exists and try to be refreshing by being refreshed.
Negotiators - We are effective negotiators; we set goals, not limits.
Generating - We practice living within the known bounds of nature; thus, generating new energy for each new day, month, year, etc.
Empowered - We are strengthened by our faith in God and intangible gifts shared with friends as well as the obvious rewards of labor.
Responsible - When we accept responsibility, we are accountable to ourselves and to our commitments.
Stratum - The commonalty we share with others at SENIOR'S JOY is that we wish to facilitate the passing of time and spread joy amongst ourselves and reach out to others.

Gwendolyn A. Roberts

Normal Nineteen

The myth of Ms. Dickinson as Virgin Spinster
Has caused some writers to paint Her—Lesbian
Too outrageous—claims about lady lovers yet
When gentlemen—*fact*—made Her youth "normal"

Letter 30—Normal Nineteen—1850—"sleigh ride
Party of ten—New Year's—frolic—charades—
Music—home at two—no worse next morning—
Cozy sociables—*universale* at Sydney Adams"

February—George Gould invited Ms. Dickinson
To a "Candy Pulling!!" at friend's "this evening"
"Payson—gone to Ohio—sorry to have him go"
Letter 35—"The voice of *love* I heeded, tho'

Seeming not to"—"I have dared to do strange
Things—bold things—heeded beautiful tempters
Mr Spencer—he may go 'where he listeth'—never
A bit care I—something—helped me forget *that*"

Letter 36—"A friend I love *so* dearly—asked
Me to ride in the woods—I wanted to exceedingly
He wanted me very much—tears came to my eyes
Struggled with great temptation—much of denial."

Bill Arnold

Christmas Night

A little child was born on Christmas Day,
He came to earth to show us the way.
The shepherds and wise men went out to seek,
The little Savior who was so meek.

They were so happy, for them bells did ring,
They hoped to find the Savior, Christ the King.
All around was peace, happiness and joy,
For they knew He was Christ, the Baby Boy.

Sheep, animals and camels roamed around free,
They shared the shelter under the tree.
The stars shown so high and bright,
This was our first Christmas Night.

Children awoke in their beds.
Visions of Angels danced in their heads.
What great wonder could this be?
It is the Christ Child, can't you see.

Gloria Spitzfaden Fourroux

Rainbow Of Two Colors

The rainbow that we built once colorful and bright
Has now begun to fade and turn to black and white
When you left you took away all the colors that made it shine
But now it's only two arcs separated by one line.

You took away the red
Which were the roses I gave with love
You took away the blue
That once were the skies above.

You took away the green
Which were the stars I wished upon every night
And you took away the yellow
Which was the sun that used to shine so bright.

But purple is the color I miss the most
Because it represents the pain in my heart
It was wounded in the last battle we had
That eventually caused us to part.

For now I'll walk this earth alone
Hoping someday we'll reunite
But it sure is going to be lonesome
Just me and my rainbow of black and white.

John C. Stringer

Holocaust At Home

Drugs. Crime. Children with guns.
Hate. Violence. Man against man.
What has happened? What has gone wrong?
Why are we so torn?

My God, my God, we have forsaken Thee;
We have left our children forlorn!
Once a bright and hopeful nation,
We turned away from Thee
Now we stand bereft, as only the lost can be.

Our redemption; our hope;
Gone...as our children take dope.
We are to blame; it is our shame!
Father forgive us, for we know not
What we've done!

Joanna Heitmann

Tragic Day

If had but known, thou would not
hath sow'n thy love of life beyond
the unknown.
Burn not rod an scepter waver
right from wrong darken'd so yet
shone, thine eyes see'eth but thy
senses flee'eth.
Swept to bone thy brain draw'eth thy
breath in pain, the sirens blast
thy brain hath cast into oblivious mask.
Bolt of lightning, thunder struck way -
out some-where come'eth rain?
The black cloud shift'eth but not for
gain thy mind grabbl'd in sea of pain.
God, alone see'eth an know'eth why so tragic day?
Gone is thy ocean of memories
sweetly stored on the shore -
Swiftly swept away as though
there were no yesterdays.

Elizabeth Tracy

Like You

Oh yea who critique everything I do,
Have never once attempted to walk inside my shoes,
as you laugh and scorn the things I am about,
Oh you perfect people why don't you help me out.

Help me to be unblemished like you,
so you can never notice the "bad" things that I do,
because I realize the world around you spin,
for being not like you I'm guilty of that sin.

To be scourged and stoned is what I am worth of,
I seem to have forgot who made you God above,
your insults are the salt that burn inside the sore,
I guess I should die so I bother you no more.

Please forgive me master for the stupid things I do,
you know I live my life so I can be like you!

Jamie A. House

The Eucharist

Because I cannot reach up to Him unaided and alone
He comes to me
In the outward and visible forms of bread and wine.
Once again, the cycle renewed
Love, tormented and rounded, and raised up for me
showing forth the new dimension of love.
Dimly, I see out of the outward and visible forms
A ladder rising
A rope flung down
To keep me from falling
To help steady me
Up the treacherous ascent
Of life's implacable mountain.

Judith Beliveau

God The Artist

God held out His hand and said, let there be.
He divided the earth into the land and sea.
He drew the stars and the moon in the sky.
God is now preparing a heaven for you and I.

He never held a brush or a pencil in his hand
Yet there appeared trees and flowers through the land.
He runs the greatest picture that was ever drawn.
He created every tree, every flower on the lawn.

He said let there be darkness let there be light
He divided the time into day and night.
He divided the seasons into winter summer and fall.
He never drew a picture, yet he's the artist of all.

Freida Lucas

A Father

What is a father?
He is there when you want to talk
Or if for no reason at all
You want to go for a walk.

When you were little he gave you a hug and a kiss
And a birthday was something he would never miss
He worried about you in your teenage years
And was always around to dry your tears.

And as you grew older and moved away
He gave his blessing but would have liked you to stay
You miss him very much each day
And remember him each night as you pray

Now he has gone to his home above
He is happy and safe in our God's love
We all miss him but we are not sad
For we remember him as our Great Dad.

Gwen Douglas

Immortal Dream Teams

Our all-star Olympian, who holds all records, created the Universe.
He gave Adam and Eve Dream Team Almighty, His glory to fame
coupled with His Eternal knowledge and wisdom of all games.
Included were the gifts of His powerful might and insight, to be
dispersed.

Our commissioners' original team violated His rules, causing a
flagrant foul, to no longer be disguised. The uniforms were
stripped and their franchise. They were banned from his League
of Trust and covered by His radiance.

Two immortal forwards, with no time-outs, were drafted to act as
guards for their rookies training camp years. Boundary lines were
written on His clay seal. Banished, were broken contracts, fines,
technical fouls, draft choices, nor deals. The game plan of speed,
accuracy, team-play and hoops, was a bench of Love with no steals.
Faith, the big center's full court press, was their basket of goals to
score rewards.

Our Hall-of-Fame Coach, the timeless referee of all chosen Olympian
games; the highest scorer and Captain of all dream teams and
Keeper of all our winners' dreams, whose scoreboard of flame will
always glow from the top of His Olympic Throne; gave us all our
Three-Pointers from down-towns on loan, in the name of the
Father, The Son, and The Holy Ghost. These are our trophies for
our final game and tournament of life, our home team, His Host!

Are we mortals double-dribbling, goal tending, and jumping to pass
though His portals to score? Immortal Dream Teams? Will the numbers
on our jerseys be recorded with our Olympian forevermore?

Betty Sue Lowe

My Little Dog Bruno

I have a little Dog named Bruno,
He is above all dogs, you know.
He barks when you leave the house,
He barks when you return.
He even barks when you turn off the lights,
He barks when you walk in front of him.
He barks when you cross his path,
He even barks when you walk around him.
He is my little Dog Bruno,
He is a joy of have around.

I love my little Dog Bruno,
He's the best watch dog, I ever had.
He doesn't eat or drink at all,
He doesn't go out for a walk.
He is my electronic eye dog,
Who sits and waits for a sound.
But, when some one looks at him,
And brushes a hand across his eyes,
It triggers a light sensor, and he barks, loud.
Then, I know someone's around.

Catherine M. Karpiak

Untitled

The unrepentant sins of the
fathers,
Living vicariously through their children's
souls.
Searching for the realism of
life;
and the mysticism of
love.
Cascading through time like a
waterfall;
Reaching the sole in a pool of
nothingness.

Brenda Amman

Happy Father's Day

A Father is so wonderful so much love he has to share,
He is so understanding, it's so good to know he's there,
A Father shows his caring in all that he will do,
His love grows stronger everyday, because of me and you,

He's a very caring person you know, because he is our Dad,
He let us do a lot of things, the best friend we ever had,
A Father's love is wonderful to have, so very nice to see,
And in his heart it overflows with love for you and me,

He really works so very hard, to clothe and feed each one,
He must be so awful tired each day when all his work is done,
a Father is so proud of his children, be a girl or a boy,
We all get together, play some games it really is a joy,

Dad is always there with you going through thick and thin,
If there was a medal given out, our Dad would surely win,
Dad is really a lovable person, he's jolly and happy to,
All wrapped up in one loving bundle, just for me and you,

Tell him that you love him for all things that he has done,
Because he is your Father make him know he's the special one,
Take time to sit and talk a spell, and have a laugh or two,
About the fun you've had together, just your Dad and you.

Janice Robinson

My Darling Daddy

I remember the first time I met him. We were playing hide and seek.
He said, "come here I'll save you," and he accomplished that feat.
He was someone special I knew right off. I could see in his kind brown eyes.
His smile, it was magnificent, it surely lit the sky!

He took us in and raised us, as though we were his own.
As an outsider looking in, you would have never known.
We were small when he married mom, he helped us grow together.
He was special, rare indeed, I'll love him forever and ever.

I cannot begin to tell you, the kind of person my father was.
Loving, caring, gentle, kind, he was sent from heaven above!
I miss him so, he left a hole in my heart you see.
I was one of the lucky ones, my daddy really loved me.

On the day of my 34th birthday he whispered softly, "I love you sweetheart."
Three days later God took him. He gave daddy a brand new start.
As surely as there are angels in heaven my father is smiling above.
His halo is shining upon his face, the wonderful man who in life,
knew how to love.

Jackie Klipfel

My Blessings

Her smile - a shimmering ray of morning sun
Her love - it binds two searching souls in one
Like mighty oaken roots her firm resolve
Yet her gentle heart all anger would dissolve
Her voice - a melody of harps together strummed
Her courage - a march to battle ever drummed
Her eyes - a brightly shining venus put to shame
The red of her lips no ruby e'er could claim
Her breath as fresh as morning dew on emerald leaves
Her faith as sure as ivy reaching for the eaves
Her companionship as full as combs with honey filled
A living dream where I forever would be thrilled
To dwell in the ecstasy of the lilt in her laughter
That lingers in my very soul long thereafter
She - herself a piece of poetry - frames her rhyming schemes
Of life and death and family love her touching themes
Her touch as soft as eyelids closing on the eyes
Then a blessed reminiscence, when all this about her dies

Henry R. David

My Son Is A Soldier

My son is a soldier and proud of him am I.
He serves his country and his flag wherever it may fly.
He prepares himself for readiness so when the call-to-arms doth come,
And obeys the orders he is given...and never thinks to run.

My son is a soldier and wants America free,
Yet with some of the orders given him he does not always agree.
But in his heart he knows he has a job to do...
To guard against the enemy...to protect both me and you.

My son is a soldier and the orders did arrive
To prepare for their departure and possible battle lines.
He said, "Mom don't you worry. I'll surely be all right.
I won't be in any danger...I won't have to fight."

The pictures flashed within my mind of my tiny baby boy
And all the things which he had done that brought me so much joy.
I thought of his baptism and his cub scout uniform,
Of all the cherished moments and his love so true and warm.

The tears streamed down my cheerless face, and I tried to be so bold;
To God above I prayed...my petitions to Him I told.
My prayers were answered by God alone...for He knew what was best.
With praise and thanksgiving in my heart...Once again I am blessed!

Doris Dunn Smith, Ph.D.

For Me

Christ died for me, on Calvary
He shed his blood, He bore it all for me
He's my friend when times are tough
He did more than enough; more than enough for me

I'm a soldier of the cross; 'cause Christ
He paid the cost; He suffered pain for me
He washed each sin away; He holds my hand each day
No one else has done as much for me

I'll serve Him till the end; He's my friend
With Him this world holds nothing for me
With Him I have no doubts; can't wait till the trumpet shouts
He's got a mansion, He's built for me

As I stand before His throne, I'll bear all the deeds I own
I pray He'll say those words to me
Yes child enter in, you lived a life; avoided sin
A robe and a crown He'll have for me

So my friend it's not too late, you see
Jesus died for you and for me; heed His word and obey
He'll wash your sins away; I know He will
Cause He did it for me; thank you Jesus, you did it for me

Carl Emanual Bailey Jr.

Suddenly Home

Oh! God! I've been so richly blest right
here.... but, show me other quiet places
in your vast domain...where love, and
kindness, and respect, are equally made
plain...Lord, come and quickly lead me
to a lighted hearth, so blest...felt in
tender loving, sharing with all dear
hearts as guests...my own strong heart
is bent, but does no crying...it repeats,
"home is where the heart is"—Lord, with
thee desiring...then suddenly, I found
it, Lord, right where I left it—seems so
many eons ago...Your Holy Spirit ever-
watching, ever-guiding, in this vast planet
earth, below...so, with newly-opened eyes,
I'll just let old rhythms flow... 'till all
is at peace, at rest, and slow...I will know.

Corrine Esther Buckingham Glass

My Son

He was my little sailor boy, in coat of navy blue,
He stood with a tiny boat in hand, and he was only two.
School displaced the special toy, by the time his age was seven.
And soon he was playing the drums quite well, when he was just eleven.

And then his eyes turned another way, new interests to this youth.
Cars and girls had his attention, yet he was aimless and uncouth.
As a teen, he was belligerent, full of anger and resentment,
To him the world was crazy, and his life had no contentment.

Then, sitting bored in church one day, the Lord to him did call,
"I want you to be a minister, son, and that's a job not small."
So he gave himself to the Master, his existence now had meaning.
At twenty-five, he reached his goal, his ordination found him beaming.

Ten years of service as Pastor, and having a wife and children, too,
Again, he heard God's voice so clear, "Be a Chaplain is what to do."
At thirty-five, he joined the Navy, as a Chaplain for the boys,
And, serving God and Country, proved to be one of his joys.

He's now a Lieutenant Commander, he obeyed what he'd been told.
He's dedicated to family and ministry, and he's forty-seven years old.
"You've grown up and away, my son, our years together—too fast and few.
But, I'll see you always, with boat in hand, at the permanent age of.....two!"

Dawn M. Hagerty

Last In The Lighthouse

The fog obscured the view beyond the shoals.
He touched the windowpane, so slick with mist
As in his breast, arose a crying pain
Not to be what he was, but to be whole
In overpow'ring spirit.
Small and dark, the rocks were lost in spume
As sparrows robbed of hope, plummet down...
Death meets death.
The man cries
For to his tired, beleaguered eyes
There is no hope.....!!
The storm moves in.
Finality, her final lance
Grips to his heart
As through the distant grey, so far unfolding
A ceaseless, senseless tolling reaches through...
Blanketed by more fog.

Clara Tse Hertlein

Memories Of Love

A lone figure on a deserted street
Holding a bouquet of roses, special for tonight.
A tall fellow with a ragged coat
Wondering which way to turn.
Recalling joyous times he has shared
With the one he's on his way to see:

A smile and a twinkle in her eyes
When he first came to her door
With a look she'd never forget.
The first kiss shared beneath an old oak tree.
The whispered "I love you" from her sweet, red lips
And the "I do" that soon followed.
The sweet little baby in the cradle
And the same darling going off to school.

As he thinks about her love,
A tear slides down his cheek
And a ghost of a smile passes over his face
As he lays the flowers softly on her grave.

Candice Murray

"Dad"

Slick back hair and groomed to a tee.
He was a sight for all women to see.
Tall as a giant, big and strong.
In my eyes, he could do no wrong.
His hair has become grey-white.
Still the same man, shining bright.
When you're down and out, he can pick you up,
And make you laugh and shout.
Love's pulling a trick on someone,
And you know no harm's done.
We all have idols and heroes
Guess everyone knows the one I chose.
Dad I love you with all my heart and soul.
And this I promise will never grow old.

Diana Beaver

Destined Course

Jesus gave his life to save us all
He was perfect in every way.
He never turned from his destined course
but quite often he would pray.

Father please forgive them
As they know not what they do
For the sins of many, they fall on me
The one whom you did choose.

I take this destined course of life
to free men from their sins
I do not come this time to judge, but with my blood to cleanse.

Let every ear just listen and every heart obey
For every eye will see him
When he comes on judgement day.

There will be no more excuses of why we disobeyed
We'll wish we would have listened, obeyed and even prayed.

The first time he did come to us
to serve and save and love.
The second coming will be to serve
the great wrath from God above.

Gwen M. Young

Dear Church Member

It was a miracle and surprise I must say
Here is how it happened to me that day.
When I went to get my mail, I met the postman there
I know he must get requests from everywhere.
I told him not to leave bills that I have to pay
But only those that pay me would be OK.
I gathered up my stack of mail and went to see
If what he brought would make me sad or fill me with glee.

I opened them all and the very last one was from the church,
which gave me a good chance that it might have won.
And don't you know it was a $100 check to help me pay for the trip
To the Poetry Convention in San Francisco and help my cost to whip.
It really surprised me and brought on some tears from me and I hope
you might have some miracles to make you happy as you can be.

I did not get my trophy there as they had predicted
Because the lady who was to present it to me was heart attack afflicted.
I'm waiting now for my trophy from the parcel post
To be delivered to me from the Western Coast.
God Bless the member who sent me the check
I love and thank you for a surprise I didn't expect!

Helen M. Dearduff

Messiah

In the villages and hillsides and Galilee
Healer, gifted teacher ad preacher man be
Proclaiming the kingdom of God is at hand
Spoken with authority and wit around the land
Curious crowds would gather to witness his deeds
To hear His teachings as He plants a seed
God's anointed one or pretender and troublemaker
Which could he be?

Arrested in Jerusalem
Executed on a Roman Cross
This man from Nazareth paid that cost
Testimony of others, He arose from death
"He's the living word" that's what some said,
The Son of God is not dead."

Jean-Philippe Quietstorm

My Prayer to the Father

When I dream of his eyes of blue
help me to rather think of you,
when I cry because I want to be loved;
send me your ultimate comfort from heaven above.
When I fail to hear your direction or your plans,
hold me like a child and guide me with your hands.
When I sin and when I lie,
please forgive me so I'll be pure in your eyes.
When I worry of tomorrow, the next day, and on,
take away my anxious thoughts so they're completely gone.
Lord, send me a girlfriend so I can grow in you,
and deliver my old ones so they can praise you too.
Tomorrow when I go out in this world of sin,
guide me to where you want your works to begin.
When I'm confronted and when I'm shot down,
may my strength be in you as I stand firm ground.
Thank you for knowing my plans and my dreams;
let your love flow from me like a human sunshine beam;
thank you also for tomorrow, when I can start new.
I will keep all my heart, soul, and mind focused on you.

Aimee Jo Fish

Aenigma: Basic Training, 1994

Oh, Christ, film-specled in photo-eucharist
hemmed, homed wrapped in warmwood, glassed
over: more life like than old lore veil
passed by veronica to you, outcast,
for wide imprinting each wearied whips-wale...

Oh, Christ, O here-treasured prize, blood-priced
more than old relic or any such souvenir
of moments momentous, portentous and precious,
please, my prayers' pleas wide-world sphere,
before world, war, the wilers enmesh us...

Oh, Christ, ceiled, sealed in this thin photo-trust,
no quicksilver, o beggar, backs black bleeder
to mirror us both. Yet, ah, this divine.
proud poverty, fairly, reflects, heart-heeder,
my (faintly) eyes there in yours-mine!

Oh, Christ, framed in enfeebled flesh, disguised,
not skin-surfaced, nor in daguerreotype,
but, sensitive, still as soul-hid negative
needing but raylets of light; not stereotype
but alive: God, full-in-me, Christ-live!

George H. Gardiner

The Fated Heifer

The diaphanous corpulent heifer is sated with greed
Her insatiable desires and sins doth run amok
The bloated girth hath diminished her vitality
Thwarts the capacity to rejuvenate herself
She opines not of the morrow
Her zeal is rampant and un-controlled
The doom of a pre-mature demise is imminent
Looms much too early in her short life
The remaining carcass will reflect many facets
Bare-bones truths of a wanton life
The frivolous excesses of ennui
The knell of a once great heifer
Though fated to falter and wither
After decades to be re-born anew
There shall arise a great leader
One anointed in the Wisdom of the Lord.

Herbert Lathan Carter

"Old Man Winter"

"Old Man Winter" is so considerate.
He's not like autumn which sneaks up from behind and pounces on us.
He lays subtle hints at our feet
And howls in our ears on the breath of the North Wind.
The nights will grow colder and light become scarce.
If we're paying attention we'll see him staring us in the face.
After Autumn has destroyed things and turned them all to brown,
We'll awake one morning to a lovely coat of white upon the ground.
And awake we must to be sure all our outside treasures have been found
For "Old Man Winter" has arrived in town
And before we know it, we could be snow bound.
But, this time it was just a visit and it will melt away.
Don't be fooled for too long though,
For he'll soon be back to stay.

Bonny Christensen

The Creator

God, the creator, of all living things.
He's the masterful artist of earth.
The greatest of great, the king of all kings.
Holds the power of life, death, and birth.
God knows the second each baby is born.
He knows when each man breathes his last,
God knows when we're joyous, he knows when we mourn.
He knows the present, the future, the past.

God, the creator of the heavens above.
Of the moon, the stars, and the sun.
Brings joy to our hearts, for God is love.
And is with us, as life's race we run.
God made the mountains, the rivers, the seas.
The valleys and meadows, so green.
The beautiful flowers, and all of the trees.
The Almighty God, reigns supreme.

James W. Dodd

Your Life Depends on God's Good Trees

Dedicated to my father Joseph and wife Marian
Your life depends on God's good trees
He made these plants so you could breathe
You want to live and so do they
So let them live in their own good way
They stand in the forest from morn to night
They do no harm but everything right
Life like yours flows beneath their back
They work and build in light and dark
So keep in mind words like these
Your life depends upon God's good trees

George M. Knipper

The Little Children

With the birth of an infant comes the miracle of life as the Mother holds the precious child to her bosom,
With love and compassion to fulfill her life dreams.

The dreams of the Father are beyond imagination as he gazes at his newborn with wonderment and love. The child feels that miracles are happening hour by hour, day by day, with the soft rain caressing the window pane and the warm breeze blowing through the mighty pines.

The universe is in full adorn as the aspens and the maples color the landscape with a blanket of beauty. Miracles never cease with a pure white cover of snow purifying this great land with its blessing.

Children are in a universe of dreams for they know not what is beyond the childhood of their dreams. Each day the child recognizes the love and the attention that is bestowed on him. With a deep feeling the child becomes part of this great evolution of life.

Now the child begins to unravel the great mysteries that surround this vast universe. It's a theater in full display every day that goes by with the darkness, the light, the sun, and the moon. Where does it all come from, the mysteries of this great planet are so revealing day by day.

Sleep on dear child and dream, for the creation of this universe lies ahead, with sorrow and joy to complete your future and mysterious cycle of life.

Armand N. Bouley

Tribute To Grandma

Raised on a farm; faithful dog at her side,
Home from a dance, horse and buggy would ride.
A beautiful young lady, old photos reveal,
Hearts of several young men, she often did steal.

The story of her life, not like any other,
Widowed three times; bore a daughter — my mother.
Alone to raise a child, Great Depression the time,
Worked long days in the factory trying to save up a dime.

The house tidy and clean were truly her wishes,
Especially the windows and surely the dishes.
Flowers brought joy; ninety-three years of her life,
Helping erase all the tears, the pain and the strife.

She always looked gracious whether home or away,
Her clothes neatly ironed, her hair not a stray.
All dressed up for church wearing necklace and pin,
To forget bracelet and rings, an unthinkable sin.

Many memories of her I've recalled now for weeks,
That special face powder and rouge on her cheeks.
Her smile and laughter; she liked to have fun,
Today she would have been one hundred and one.

Joan H. Kruse

The Being Of Love

Love: The eternal infinite lamb of God
How can you refuse its intention
.....its purpose.
The wholeness of wholeness
How can you refuse its objective
Love,
Sacrificed in its benevolent influences..
Love:
Loyalty, bondage, calor humanistico;
Universal linage;
Infinite chain of constancy
Fruta de la fruta
Ripen fruit.
Love, like no other desire, cosmic libation,
Knows nothing else but its priority...
Loves and hopes to love.
Solo loving loves.

Joseph Raphael Dante

Lonely (Where's Tomorrow)

As today slowly fades into yesterday and tomorrow is on the horizon, I end each day just as the other, thinking of you, gazing into your lovely brown eyes and wishing that all is as it was, you and I were friends and lovers sharing special things with each other, wishing for time for midnight rendezvous, intimate walks, private holidays for romance but colder are my nights as I am hopelessly alone, with reminders of our separation biting and cutting me down to my very bone. A love so hot and burns so bright is the love that I yearn for every night, I pray to the good Lord above to send you my special love, a love that burns as brightly as the woman you are. With each night comes a dream of loving, holding, kissing and caressing your body only to awake and find myself alone. With each passing day, I find myself looking at my future, I look to tomorrow because today I'm lonely, how many todays must fade away before tomorrow finally comes and brings you to me, I don't know, I only know that yesterday left me dreaming of you, today left me without you, will this finally be the day, tomorrow.

David Phyllep Andrews

Levee

The more I drank, the more it rained,
hostilities flowed, while I numbed my brain;
I saw my children kneelin' and prayin',
but I wasn't listenin' to what they were sayin'.

Then one day the Levee broke,
I didn't even have anything to smoke;
along came a friend (of which she spoke),
and pulled my family into his boat.

Washed away and swirled around,
I finally made it to drier ground;
the more I looked, the more I found,
that my family was not around.

And so I sit, with my peers,
watching the time, counting the years;
feeling my feelings, fearing my fears,
watching for my children, through my lonely tears.

So don't you let the Levee break,
there's no telling, what it will take;
so keep on guard, for goodness sake,
don't let the Levee break, don't let the Levee break!

Dennis A. Burke

Nature's Forecast

Ah! Me lad, I foresee a winter,.. bitter cold...
How do you know, ye man of old...
Er,...Sir?

That's all right, me lad.
Old that I am, and glad.
Know by its fur! Its fur?

Aye, a fuzzy caterpillar, the Wooly Bear!
Black as coal, this year.
By its fur, I know..

No coloring of cream, orange or brown,
Only black and bigger all around...
Means a long, hard winter, lots of snow.

Just by the Wooly Bear's fur, you can tell?
Aye, and the bark on trees, the thicker nut shell.
Squirrels not eating, no shell bits on the ground. Duty,...

Busy storing nuts for eating when the cold wind bloweth a spell;
Planting 'em, replacing trees, snow-laden branches may fell
During winter's snow...Nature's foretold blizzard of woe and beauty!

Frances Snyder Keith

Feelings?

What are feelings?
How does one feel feelings?
How does one teach someone to feel feelings?
Are we born with feelings or are they learned?
Are feelings empty, dead or alive or any one of these combinations?
Why is it easier for others to feel and others it is hard?
Is a feeling something mental or physical or both?
Is it healthy not to feel at times or should you feel all the time?
What is the importance of a feeling or feelings?

Feelings, I know can be scary, or you are not sure now to feel them
Or there isn't a feeling at all.
Could your feelings be stifled as a little child by such
Statements as "you should not feel that way" or "stop your crying," etc...

Why do we have to have feelings?
How do you deal with feelings?
When you do feel, is it easy to describe or is it hard?
Are there really words to describe all feelings?
Why are we afraid to feel?
What actually lurks beyond that feeling?

Carol-Ann Swatling

Do You Ever

Do you ever stop to consider
How I feel, what I feel or that I have feelings?

Do you ever wonder,
What I think, what I may need, what I'm doing?

Do you ever feel the pain,
I have endured, I have accepted, I put to rest?

Do you ever ask yourself,
Why it started, why it continued, why it stopped?

Do you ever imagine,
What could have been, what dreams have been broken, what the future holds.

Do you ever ask myself,
How could I hurt her so deeply?
Do you ever want to see me happy?

Donna G. Sutherland

"Nobility Of Alaska"

Across the diamond-studded land, a sled of power drawn by a team,
Husky and Malamute dogs pull with all their might.
A full moon and northern lights shadow the silhouettes
emphasize their impressive sight.
Through the centuries; service they gave to a harsh
almost impossible land this wolf-like breed.
The nobility of Alaskan territories the progress,
the northern dogs lead.

You pulled man burdens, played and warmed their
children from the snow and cold.
Been helpful companions of the weak and old.
A pat on the head, a warm fire, a fish now and then,
couldn't have measured up to what you have give.
This nobility of Alaska, you so strongly gave
your life, without question, so others might live.

After the days' chores are over and everybody has
settled for a good night's sleep, surely the thoughts of the wild
distant howls sometimes creep.
When the wolves bay at the moon, on cold winter
nights, darkened images, gather for a hunt to take place soon.
The wolf-like dog, the nobility of Alaska, drifts
off to sleep for he knows his place.
This regal animal, who for sure, is the most
wonderful breed of his race.

Barb Saveley

To Those Who Inspire

Why it happens, no one will ever really understand,
How one person can inspire another to be all that they can.
You have done that for me; my dreams I will expand
Wherever they may lead, I'll always be your biggest fan.

You have made me see that my dreams aren't so far away,
But even if they don't all come true, I just had to say
Thank-you, because you gave me the strength to do it my way.
I'll never forget you, even when I'm old and gray.

I hope that someday, I can be like you.
To inspire another, to make their dreams come true
To believe in themselves enough to follow them through,
To know I made a difference in someone else's life, like you

If this puts a smile on your face, then I'm right on cue,
Because that's what I am really trying to do.
For all the hope you have given to me, all the way through,
I just wanted to give a little something back, from me to you.

Jean L. Barney

Marionette

Fresh painted face, rosy red lips, sparkling blue eyes
how pretty he looks
Dancing with the pull of each string the children
laugh and clap with glee
Each wanting their chance to touch, feel, and hold
the beautiful doll
But time passes, paint starts to crack, blue eyes lose
some sparkle, rosy lips not so rosy
the marionette lays slumped in the corner
face tucked to the chin as the strings surround his body
Maybe he is not as pretty, but he still can dance
if only someone would pull the strings
Where have the children gone?

Joan S. Parker

A Teenage Poet's Anguish

Take me and wave me aloft like a banner on high.
I am nothing.
Crucified for a cause that no one believes in,
I die from within.
Am I merely a sacrifice to the gods of blind popularity?
Can it be that you too
Will fade and become grey like the others?
No soul and so I cannot have a soul.
Thoughtless, you call for my death.
Do my ears deceive me
Or is your voice grown harsh and indistinguishable
From all around you?
You are gone.
You nothing,
As you would have me be nothing
The taste stings bitter in my mouth,
Sweet balm to misery.

Jessica Meyer

View Of Death

Watch of constant, that is thee.
Hoping to meet one like me.
Thy hand is old, and mine is cold.
Thy smile unvailed, and mine is failed.
Now we go, where? ... For only you know.
I do not ask; for I am the task.
You are the guide and my time is past.
Your sickle, the tool used to reap.
Harvest is ready, my life complete.
Take me and do as you wish.
For you have granted me my wish.....

Ross Daniels

I Am The Poet

Thou art the inspiration.....
I am the interpretation....Thou art the voice within
I am the writer's pen!

Soul...speak your peace....from without....then from within
Getting in touch with him! Feeling his hand so intertwined
with mine... Thou art the voice....I am the poet

Ah world! There're people out there Gathering.......
Wandering...Hoping....Gaining...Hurting....Losing.....Wasting.....
Spending gathering it all. Into a tiny little ball - called LIFE

Hear you, the rumblings? Strange!
Unmeasured...resounding as if the drum, drum, drummings then
The rumblings as of a sad heart.
There it is again! Then the new dawn breaks

People! Ordinary people.
Rushing out into it! No fear is there with....Him
There's humanity everywhere.. Real human beings with real human
feelings....Asking one little chance....

At it? Yes, of life! I can help! You and I! We're one!
- Thou givest life...I live life! Thou art the creator...
I am the poet

Bertha L. Marshall

Teach Me

I pleaded with you to teach me, I wanted so to learn new things,
I asked you to teach me about love, wanting, needing,
I wanted to know about loving and not receiving,
I asked you to be my teacher - I knew I could learn so much from you.
And you taught me so much-hard lessons for me,
About wanting what isn't yours-what never will be.
About needing, reaching out in the air-finding nothing there.
About lonely days-where there is no one to share with.
About changing ways-to accept and walk away head held high.
About stone faced emotions-you taught me not to let them see me cry.
About never letting them know what is coming next -
Don't ever do what they expect.
About the pure ecstasy that can come from two friends-
Who became lovers.
About two lovers who can still be friends.
About how love is to end.
But I don't understand, how to forget you-the love we
share. How will you let it all go?
Once again I ask you to teach me.
I plead; how do I let you go??

Cassandra N. Decker

Nature's Forecast

Ah! Me lad, I foresee a winter,.. bitter cold...
How do you know, ye man of old...
Er,...Sir?

That's all right, me lad.
Old that I am, and glad.
Know by its fur! Its fur?

Aye, a fuzzy caterpillar, the Wooly Bear!
Black as coal, this year.
By its fur, I know..

No coloring of cream, orange or brown,
Only black and bigger all around...
Means a long, hard winter, lots of snow.

Just by the Wooly Bear's fur, you can tell?
Aye, and the bark on trees, the thicker nut shell.
Squirrels not eating, no shell bits on the ground. Duty,...

Busy storing nuts for eating when the cold wind bloweth a spell;
Planting 'em, replacing trees, snow-laden branches may fell
During winter's snow...Nature's foretold blizzard of woe and beauty!

Frances Snyder Keith

I Believe

I believe in our Father who is up above,
I believe he is with us and sends us his love.
I believe he created the heaven and earth,
I believe he is master and gives us our worth.
I believe he created the flowers and trees,
I believe he saw beauty and that he was pleased.
I believe he created the birds in the sky,
I believe he was happy and taught them to fly.
I believe he created the grass on the hill,
I believe he watered it gently till it had its fill.
I believe he created the sand on the beach,
I believe he sifted it softly till it was in reach,
I believe he created the stars that we see,
I believe he made them to show us we're free.
I believe he created all this and more,
I believe he was happy with his final score.
I believe he was ready with his well made plan,
I believe he did this, then he made man.

Della Miller

On The Other Side Of My Rainbow

I feel your hand in mine
I close my eyes
I see a white bird
Spread his wings to fly

I listen to the song of the ocean
I hear the sea gulls cry
Perfect nature, perfect soul
I can see your eyes

I think of what was, I feel no pain
The wind is caressing my face
The sun just smiles
I almost know who it is

Waiting for me on the other side of my rainbow

Dora Silvia Krannig

"Anita"

Heavenly Father, It's me again calling on your name.
I come before you and a world of uncertainties,
I come Lord because It's your power and a spiritual path I
wish to follow.

My life hungers for the love of a woman, my heart intoxicated with
her beauty, I ask you my God to make us one in love and direction,
shackle my love to her, and her to mine make our love strong like
the mighty oak, and as true as a mother's love. Lord let all
temptations vanish like the stars at beginning of light, let our
love fall softly like snow flakes on a cold winter's night.

My God in my confusion forgive me, in my ignorance teach me, build
me up to be worthy, direct my life in understanding. I wish to be
all that I must, Lord I beg of you, direct her heart to love me
just as much. I want to love her with all my heart, I want to be
with her until my days depart.

Master, take me out of this loneliness let my heart suffer no
more, let this dream be of sunshine not of cold winds. My father
God, it is with prayer that I come to you, it is with trust I know
my life is now new, it is with love that let's me know of your
greatness, and the beauty of the rose that has captured my forever
faithfulness.

Alton D. Britt

Daddy

My Dad is so strong, my Dad is so brave
I could hide behind him and always be saved.

If only I could stay so young and so fair
So, I could stay by Daddy
He'll always be there

My Dad can be relied on
He'll never let you down
He'd come home every night
He's nice to have around

Whenever I got frightened
I'd say, "Daddy, I am scared."
He'd say, "Don't you worry darling, Daddy always will be here.

I'd feel so safe and cozy
I'd feel so good inside
I'd feel secure and happy, to have him by my side.

Oh, if only I could stay so young and so fair
And didn't have to grow up and didn't have to care
And have my Daddy leave me and let me stand on my own
And never be replaced
The Dad I call my own.

Agnes Thacker

Get Thee Well Quickly

A very wise and ancient physician once said,
"I could prescribe a wagon load of love and
never change a scowl to good cheer."
"Yet with the nicer of my patients a lesser
container was all that was needed, and the smile
and bloom of good health would appear."

So will you please accept this thimble filled
with love, surely enough to share with someone
else if they're as nice as you.

Claire Joseph Phelan

I Heard A Voice

I'm proud to be a Christian, as proud as I can be
I crossed the road to Jesus, as he died and rose
For me.
I took my time arriving, the world controlled me so.
Yet I heard a voice so clearly, seek me - and then
You'll know.

And now each night before my light goes out, I read
Upon his word then pray, Dear Lord, forgive me for my
Sins, they've mounted up today.
Indeed I go to Church on Sunday, and choose to
Praise His name, I meet with other people, no longer
I'm the same.

Fill me God with your word, it's so hard in the
World I'm in, there are those who question my
Relationship to you, it now hurts me
From within.
I'm proud to be a Christian, I'm proud as I can be
You too can have this knowledge. It's not meant for
Only me.

Alice Makla

"I Was"

I lived for only a little while, within my mothers womb.
I didn't even get to cry, because there was no room.
My mother cried, my Father cried for I could not live.
My sisters and brother cried, for the things I never did.
But God knows best, He called me home,
To wait for them where I'll never roam.
For parents to decide a baby's fate
Is more heartbreaking to relate.

Joyce Giblin

Transformation

Thought I would tell a short fish story
I doubt that you find it the least bit gory
'Twas a cute little fish, had a bad fate
It would up flat, right on my plate

This poor fish slid forward and back
As I spun the plate, ready to attack
The fish couldn't tell me exactly his weight
Someone took his scales, before he hit the plate

The fish, apparently was not too smart
He lost his head, right at the start
The poor fish even lost his fin
That's why he looked so terribly thin

Out of sympathy, I offered him a deal
If he'd consent, he could be my meal
That would combine our flesh you see
But, would I become fishy, or still be me

How do you suppose I would react
If that fish took over my life, intact
Should you desire an answer, would be fine
If I am away, just "Drop me a line"

Bud Smith

Falling Into Darkness

Uncontrollably,
I fall into the unknown world below,
Where dark and mysterious creatures roam.
Keeping the troublesome lives of people going in the wrong direction,
Laughing at their discomfort,
Causing the most dreadful fears of mankind to come true,
Underrating the hopes and love of the people,
Their ways mysterious to their victims.
Only in the end are they struck with the knowledge,
That these are creatures of imagination.
When people stop believing in them,
They will perish.
In their place will be the freedom to believe,
In themselves and in their dreams.
Hearts will be whole, and peace will fill their souls.
And finally they will have reached,
The Ultimate Goal.

Barbara Austin

Walking And Serving Thee

When I walk and serve Thee:
I feel greatest joy and peace inside of me;
Thy presence is the strongest in me.

How many ways do I love Thee?

All I want is to become an instrument for Thee.

Even when I am scared, I keep walking forward with Thee

As my life keeps flowing through, how do I serve Thee?

I need to trust so much in Thee,
that I keep walking down the Lord's path,
even when I don't know exactly what You want me to do.

My trust and faith needs to be so great
that I can allow myself to be molded in Thy image.

All I want is to spread Thy word and to serve Thee.

Elizabeth M. Putnam

My Special Friend

My friend has a sensitive compassionate heart.
I feel her love even when we are apart.
She is never weary of giving her all,
If I need her she gladly answers my call.

She plunges right in and can take charge,
Of many tasks whether small or large.
Her spirit seems to soar above,
When she is helping or doing for love.

She never thinks of money for what she is giving.
She wants only the best and encourages living.
Above the mundane or simplistic few,
She has a happy way of uplifting you.

I never knew anyone so happy in giving.
It's just her way of exemplified living.
She loves God's words and Jesus' teaching,
Can give one good advice without preaching.

She is as rare as a many faceted jewel.
Her spirit is sparkling with unending fuel.
She writes her own music, sings her own songs,
Her name with the greats truly belongs.

Estelle Custer

"I'm Coming, My Darling"

I'm coming to join you, after so long
I feel more content, in my heart is a song.

We shared so much, for so many years,
It couldn't be wiped away, like our tears.

Life without you has been so strong
It made me cranky - had!
Try as I might, I could not change.
I hurt our children, made them sad.

With all the love around, they couldn't understand
I only needed you, holding my hand.

Now, the smile on my face says see?
I'm happy now as happy can be.
Together will smile, from up above
Shining our love, on the ones we love!

I'm coming my Darling, I'll soon arrive -
How happy we'll he standing side by side

Corrinne Adamski

Precious Savior

Precious Savior in heaven above
I feel your caring and constant love
As raindrops softly caress my face
I remember your free and wonderful grace
How you died on the cross to save me from sin
When I started to believe I felt new life begin
I feel your touch in the soft breeze
And comfort in the shade of your trees
As the quiet evening shadows fall at night
I'm secure and know everything's all right.
As waves roll against the shore
I see your power even more
When the wind rages before a storm
Your love keeps me safe and warm
Thanks to God who gave his Son
I give my praise to the living one
His blessings I hold tight in my heart
What feeling I cherished from the start
At life's end His guiding hand will lead me home
So now I'm never lost or alone

Alice L. Abrams

"Moral Hunger"

As I read, hear, see my fellow-men- these days -
I find a coarseness I did not read, hear or see before...
I am saddened: such a beautiful nation! such a diversity of people!

We are God-given: Generous, kind-thoughtful of other nations...
But 'why' is it that at home these days we're torn
among ourselves as if we're at each other's throats...

Our agricultural products are in excess - we eat well! dear God!
I read, I hear, I see - the pain I feel is not the lack of bread...
It is moral hunger our beautiful nation is suffering.

I feel, I desperately feel! a moral hunger - the lack of
moral sustenance in my beautiful adopted land!
America, the U.S.A., the beautiful!
Note: There is that old adage: "Man does not live by bread alone."
some thoughts regarding my adopted country.

Carmen Maria Alvarez-Babin

Forest Chapel: Christmas Eve

The hibernal wind moans constantly and in these woods
I find sanctuary, in the distance sleeps the village tonight,
in silent slumber behind shutters tight.
Where lemon light seeps through the cracks,
and children's dreams are of Santa's sack.
Here I marvel without fear, there is a special solace here.
The kind that few men ever find,
serenity that quells the muddled mind.
Alone soft steps I gently tread, on the crystal cover
of the forest bed, beneath the boughs of cathedral trees
that press their rafters to the stars,
where heaven's harmony comes strong and clear,
the wind choir of angel vespers from afar.
The moon's milky magic gently spills
my blue shadow like a stain across the snow,
leaving me frozen in pensive thought,
here purity reigns in this splendor sought,
and as I gaze into the galaxy,
the northern orb still points the way
as the ebony curtain parts for Christmas Day.

Davan James Dodrill

December Song

In the winter of my years
I find summer in your charms,
And bask in the warm embrace
Of your tender loving arms.
I harken to an earlier time
When the world was fresh and new,
And the meadow grass stood lush and green
Sparkling with morning dew.
I feel your sensuous heart beat
Pulsating through your veins,
Sparking the embers within me
Into flashing rapturous flames.
Then a quiet peace comes o'er me
That bids my heart to rest,
And dream the dreams young lovers dream
With my cheek upon your breast.
And the burden of my years
Slip their bonds and fall away.
In the ecstasy of our bliss,
I am become youth, and the time is May.

Anthony J. Daniels

"A Stick In The Stream"

I am a stick in the stream of life-
I float on God's big river-
Giving the glory to Him in all I say and do.
As long as I don't take myself out of the stream-
Which is His care and protection-
And the flow of the Holy Spirit-
And I willingly live in Jesus Christ-
I am that stick in the stream- pressing on to know Jesus-
And I go where God leads me.
I do not turn to the right or to the left-
But I look straight ahead- following Jesus Christ.
I shall complete my mission on earth as I praise
My Lord and Savior Jesus Christ.
I shall give to others the opportunity to know my wonderful
Lord and Savior and my Friend.
A stick in the stream of life- that's following my Lord-
Like a stick goes down the stream riding on a wave-
So shall I follow Jesus Christ.
Nothing in this life compares to Him-
For Jesus Christ loves us so deeply and tenderly!

Jan Barnes

Remembrance

In remembrance of a long ago time I stole your heart and
I gave you mine we spent warm sunny days as we strolled on the sand,
You promised me true love as you held my hand.

Then you kissed me goodbye and went away -
You said you'd be back some future day,
I have waited and watched as my poor heart does yearn
Just waiting the day of your return.

The summer has passed and winter's coming on- I'll greet each day
with a sad autumn song, I'll cozy up by the fire's amber glow,
And watch for winter's first fall of snow.

I'll wait for return through the long winter's cold the summer's
precious memories in my heart I will hold I hope you will return in
the lovely spring time, and bring hope and joy to this lonely heart
of mine.

We will stroll through the meadow in the warm summer sun- and
plan our future as our dreams are spun, we'll dream of a little
cottage setting high on a hill- and look down on the world, so
peaceful and still.

We'll live out our lives in this lovely little home- I hope and pray
that you will never more roam, we'll count our blessings at the end
of each day and enjoy all the pleasures that God sends our way.

Delia Mays

Ages Of Time

With cloudbursts of sunshine alighting on the roof,
How could any poet dare remain aloof?
These things, and more, make a great combination
To invest in my soul-inspiring great vibrations!

Long rays of light shine down through the trees,
With mystic bits of rhythm -voices drifting on the breeze.
And murmurs of a brook trickling down through the ravine
All take me back to where it's time to sit and dream.

Glory is drifting through the trees of time—
Invented forests, and events sublime,
From imaginative memories going back in ages,
Encapsulating with dust, the words of ancient sages.

Wake me not, oh, voices of contemporary existence.
Remind me not that there's a question of subsistence.
I'll stay as I am until the ages of time
Take away my ability to make a verse rhyme.

Eva McLelland

As I Watch The Clouds Go By

As I watch the clouds go by,
I gaze at the ever changing sky.

An airplane, a jet liner, no less,
Is descending through the clouds to rest.

Airplanes and sky writers put in their time,
Helicopters help the ill hospitals to find.

Birds, butterflies and insects, too, seem to know
Just where the changing clouds are going to go.

Now the clouds are gathering again,
I hope we get that much needed rain!

In the West the setting sun filters through,
Streams of light, auras, changing colors, too.
Become a part of this enchanting view.

From white to melon, orange, red, purple then gray,
Color brings a glimpse of the ending of day.

The night descends, and breezes blow,
The moon peeks through the mounds of "snow"

As I watch the clouds go by.

Frances Juanice Fox

Pretty Flower

Of the many flowers in this vast and wonderful garden,
I have found one which I truly admire.
Her strength and beauty alone create the radiance of a
brightly burning fire.
Her strong will and determination allows her to withstand
the winds of seasons change.
The fact that her name is associated with beauty and
love does not seem strange.
Of the many flowers in this vast and wonderful garden that
becomes more ravishing as it grows, there is no flower as
beautiful or wondrous as the Rose.

Courtney Sherrod Calhoun

"Evil Passions"

I know what you have done.
I heard your primal screams of lust.
I heard your fists beat in fury.
My mind ponders upon the betrayal
you might have in store for me.
I try to erase these thoughts,
But they linger forevermore.
An obsession you might say,
Paranoia
Call it what you wish,
But inside I can still feel the fire you left burning
The night you abandoned me desperate and lonely.
An excruciating lust for you was left behind.
Your disillusion fills my nightmares.
Your insanity cleanses my superfluous need for love.
I can still recall every woe,
Every sense of anguish,
Every moment you disengaged my animosity.
I despise you in a way not capable of being perceived by mankind.
But yet I love you more than anything else.

Dorie Gutsch

Precious One

You are so small, I find myself fighting hard not to care
I hold you close, I touch your hair, how can any mother not care
Your little fingers, your little toes, God protect you from future foes
I look into your shining eyes, I can't help the way my heart just dies
I know our time is drawing near, the nurses' steps I can hear
Come to take my life away, this will be my dying day
No matter when I am buried deep, my heart will continue to always weep
Will you know? Will you understand?
I did not even know that man
What he did, it was a crime; can you see the fault was not mine
I know you are the one who must pay, to be created in such a way
Come in search of me one day, I will tell you in my own way
Our time is gone, the nurse has come, I must give up my precious one
It was in my heart, from the very start
To give you to someone who will love you so, and never ever let you go
Blessed be the ones you find, may they be generous, caring, and kind
I hold you close one last time
I hold you close for never again will you be mine

Heather Lynn Coffman

The Final Blow

When life has finally got me down
I just stand up and look around
To find the places where there's some good
To heal my heart like it should.
I have to search hard, even deep within my soul
To find a middle and set a goal.
The harder I work, the more I find
It's not so hard to ease my mind.
And soon my heart follows along
My thoughts have earned a better song.
Then I find myself right back where I'd begun.
By just putting one step in front of one
The storm has passed, the calm set in
For the healing has started deep within.
So when I'm ready to fall and feeling real blue
I just stand up, look around and begin anew.

Diana Irish

Robin Of Albuquerque

You are beautiful, oh Robin, dear
I love you so, and I am sincere

Wide emerald eyes, warm ruby lips
Dark flowing hair, graceful curved hips

After forty long years, a friendship revived
You slammed into my arms, when my plane arrived

We toured Bandelier, a leisure walk
Los Alamos, Inscription Rock

The Grand Little Church, we tightly held hands
God, it was fun, with you to make plans

The little raccoons, silly Ovaltine
Hot Toddy Coffee, my first olive, green

You poured the wine, White Zinfandel
The Raffinée, would cast a magic spell

We saw Neal McCoy, watched him sing Wink
The traveling roses, one red, one soft pink

Tranquil, serene, so contented my soul
I've never felt so at peace, so alive and so whole

I've nearly loved you forever, and will 'til my death
And I'll whisper your name, as I—breathe my last breath

Arley M. Bischoff

"Finis"

I cannot dismiss the image.
I knew it was the end.
There goes my sweetheart.
There goes my friend.

I watched you as you walked away.
That smooth fast stride.
I wanted to be with you, walking at your side.

You did not wave, you did not turn around.
Your mind was on your destination.
To someone else, you were bound.

That beautiful cord between us,
is no longer connected.
You broke it without warning.
It was so unexpected.

Just as happiness is never here to stay,
hopefully the unacceptable,
will also pass away.

Betty E. Kraus

Heart's Illusion

I thought it was love
I know I was mistaken
I was living in my fantasy world
My world of beautiful false images and half-truths
A world of elegant glass figures
Carved with care and detail
"God!" when they fall down shattering to the ground
Manna mutates to mold
My heart filled with tenderness and passion...
I was blinded by my own hands
I couldn't grasp the double-edged sword of truth
Its shining brilliance twisting deep into me
My world, melted away
My fantasy life of perfection and romance gone
Life - blood flows from me, forming a pool at my feet
I gaze into the darkness of reality
Cold and emptiness all around me
Time stops in endless silence
Now when I wish I was blinded
I cannot turn my eyes away

Ann Marie Hurst

Under The Oaks

Under the oaks in my granddaddy's yard
I learned a few lessons which life couldn't mar.
When I asked for a dollar for a bit of my time,
Instead of a dollar granddad gave me a dime.

And later in life when I asked him for snuff
Granddad smiled and obliged knowing once was enough.

Granddad's hammock enticing in the cool summer air
And that's where I'd be when he wasn't there.
He would sit in the yard watching spiders spin silk
And grandma would bring him some cornbread and milk.

When he hitched up the mule, I would ask him to plow
So he taught me to "Gee-Haw" and now I know how.
We would walk in his pastures; I would trace in his steps
And the moments like these were the memories kept.
Granddaddy and I are plain, southern folks
And his memory lingers somewhere under the oaks.

James D. Hodges

Crickets Chirp, Frogs Croak, And Grown Men Cry

With my windows open,
I lie upon this lonely-without-you bed,
on my back, naked,
with my hands clasped together behind my head,
staring into the emptiness
of the dark,
of my heart,
listening to the lonely critters of the woods
singing their mating calls
to anyone who'll hear their cry and respond,
and,
I wonder . . .
do you hear mine?
How foolish of me . . .
tears
rolling
down
cheeks
onto a pillow
make no sound!

Bo Wring

In Retrospect, D-Day 1944-1994

I long to hear true praise of America.
I long to see Old Glory furled with joy!
I long to feel us all pull together
Uniting hearts and souls; each girl and boy.

I long for strength to care for the aged.
I long for support of MISTER PRESIDENT.
I long for strong respect and honor
For an office born from strife and confidence.

I long for the kindness of my childhood.
I long for plain politeness now and then.
I long for farmer's smiles in the city.
And that uncaring ways forever end.

I long for Kate Smith's "God Bless America".
I long for flags flown at every home.
We must grow steadfast and enduring hope
In our hearts for this dear country— Our Own.

Jimmie Nell Bush Sutton

"No-One Ever Told Me"

No-one ever told me, it was stormin' in the night, but when
I looked outside my window there it was alright, so many
times when I'd stop to think about the things you do the things
you think.
I wish you could only understand that there's love still here
to be given from my hand. No-one ever told me it was
stormin' in the night, but when I looked outside my window
there it was alright.
I see you standing there in the shadows of the night, just to
wish I was by your side. So many times I wish you were there,
"to hold me and scold me", as if you were mine. Your kiss so
sweet your looks so fine, the heartbeat of two, yours and mine.

Denice L. Glover Cordova

"Friends Are Not Forever"

Friends are not forever, so whoever told you so is wrong.
I found that out the other day,
When my best friend kind of slipped away.
I didn't realize what happened
until it was too late.

Now that I stop and think about it.
Our lives are like a rose at first.
We bloom and then we start dying out.
We bloom again in just a matter of time.

Aethena C. Watkins

To Little Charlotte Ann

When I tiptoe into the nursery and peek at your sleeping figure,
I marvel at life's miracles.

When your brown eyes sparkle and you softly say, "hi",
I glow with tearful pride.

When you tug at my glasses and laugh delicately,
I join in the laughter, too.

You smear birthday cake all over your chubby cheeks,
And my camera catches each gooey moment.

How totally precious are you, my very first granddaughter.
When I became your paternal grandmother, I inherited the wisdom
of all those who preceded me.

I became the carrier of our family's culture, its faith and traditions.
What lies ahead of you in the twenty-first century?
What will be your hopes and dreams, plans and directions?
Daddy and Mommy will always be there for you, wisely and lovingly.
So, too, will I.
If your dreams are dashed, goals detoured or honors bestowed,
I'll be there for you with counsel or congratulations,
And a soothing cup of tea.
I love you dearly.

Janet Marks

Klabu

It's so elementary.
I miss you in the morning.
I miss you at night.
I miss you most at dusk,
when daylight takes flight.
I miss you when Poppa Cardinal feeds his gal.
I miss you when the Chicadee takes his bath
I look and "ah" alone and can't call you.
When the butterflies are on the terrace,
Could you be watching too?

I miss you when it's thundering
and the rain is pouring down.
I listen to the radio to have a voice around.
Meals alone, with no one to share and enjoy.
It's been four years today.
It's not the same, my dearest.
It hurts and it's empty since you've gone,
For all I knew of love and laughter
has followed after.

Helen D. Dunn

Don't Push Me Away

Don't push me away, don't lock your heart,
I need time before we part,
I need to tell you of my love,
That is all I have to give,
I pray that God will let you live,
And take me away instead, life is so empty without you,
If only you could love me too.

Don't push me away because you're changed,
Don't lock your heart and cause more pain,
Appearances don't change the man,
Not the one with courage to stand, just as long as you live,
What matters most is how you feel within,
All the feelings in your heart,
I so wish I could know...
because darling...
In my heart "I love you so",
You know I care—but it's so much more,
I've never felt like this before,
Why does this cause such fear?
I'd give my life to have you near!

Hazel Froemming

I'll Miss You

You will never know how much you meant to me.
I never knew I could love someone the way
that I love you.
Even though I know I'll see you again,
Just getting through the endless days
before I do will be hard.
You taught me so much, and you made it fun,
I'll miss you.

Christie Conrad

On My Way

On my way
I passed by the gateway
leading to your orchard.
The fruits behind the gate arched
with flowers, greeted me
from tree to tree,
rich, ripe, and inviting.
I slowed down, wandering. And
waiting it might be.
Beyond the gateway covered by moss and dew,
you smiled at me,
rich, ripe, and inviting, too.
But it was locked, the gate,
guarding the treasures in many a tree.

Dailin Gao Williams

What About Tomorrow

Glancing over my shoulder at the past
I realize all the memories I've made to last
My life is like a roller coaster ride
Some memories surface while others just hide
We never know what tomorrow may hold
Only thing for certain is what we've been told
We can glance over our shoulder at things in the past
But it's all our tomorrows we must make to last
There's no going back to change yesterday
It's a memory now and behind it must stay
So make each tomorrow bright and new
You never know how many's left; there would be just a few
Do the very best you can with your tomorrow
And remember it's only time that you borrowed

Donna Schmitzer

Quietude

Whilst sitting by my window observing the unfolding view,
I realize it was the Great Creator who
Hast seemingly reserved this especially for me,
In my private cocktail hour sanctum where I'm free.
The bird feeder arrangement of my design
From two joined crossed posts a la clothesline;
So that six feeders could be arranged
To accommodate so many — none short-changed.
What a story of integration!
It completely startles the imagination.
Instead of the different species fighting for domination
They have solved their own problem of amalgamation.
Each group from each breed
Voluntarily choose a different time to feed.
The finch, doves, cardinals, blue-jay's, and blackbirds all
Eat from the same feeding place and no conflicts befall.
What a wonderful world this would be,
If we used this same method to be free
From prejudice, vanity, and ignorant bliss,
Maybe all God's creation could find happiness.

Clyde Nelon

In The Mountain's Shadow

As I stood on draper mountain when the sun was sinking low,
I saw a little city in its shadow far below
The shadow shimmered brightly as far as I could see,
And the city seemed to glisten like jewels on a tree.

It nestled in a valley among the trees and sky,
A town of friendly people that is home you and I.
And as we walk together we want this town to be,
A city that will prosper and live for you and me.

We want to raise our children in this city that we love,
In the shadow of the mountain with sky and clouds above.
So let's provide a reason to keep the children here,
To build a lasting future in this town we love so dear.

A place we can be proud of, a place where all can see,
The face of happy children and pride from you and me.
We must plan a future, a future that is here,
We have no more tomorrows that fact is very clear.

So if we act together we can surely make it know,
In the shadow of the mountain why we truly feel its home.
So let us all move forward to dawn, and leave the night,
And remove the mountains shadow and bathe our town with light.

Charles Don Crispin

Turmoil

Looking through the windows of my soul
I see a world that is anything but whole...
Nations fighting far apart, striving without heart,
to best all people and be God of all.

What makes them rant and rave, being anything but brave,
without thought for human love and life?
Despair deranging minds, unmoved by starving people,
without pity for man or animal alike.

What makes man or woman fight for their imagined Eden
pushing them beyond the limits of historic heathen?

...Judas who sold the Lord...
...Lot's wife who had no faith...

...Nothing's changed in ageless centuries;
fear and greed still drive men to hate.
The world spins; the wars continue still.
Just make sure you're on the winning hill.

...Looking through these windows once again
I see little hope for this world of men.
No lasting peace...no great Messiah here...
...only the world upon its own funereal bier.

Janet I. Broad

"Just Like His Daddy"

With his overalls on and a wrench in his hand.
He'll tinker with the car.
"Just like his Daddy."

"Going fishing I see," I'll ask,
as he walks away with his fishing pole.
"Just like his Daddy."

"I love you," he'll say in too deep of a voice,
as he tries to sound,
"Just like his Daddy."

But if I had one wish, that I knew
would be granted, it would be to know
that he will always be,
"Just like his Daddy."

Joyce L. Campbell

"What Ever Happened To The Wooden Bat"

I look back to a time long ago, to what now seems like a dream.
I see myself as a young boy, and for a dime two scoops of ice cream.

On a hot summer's day we would cool ourselves
with the renderings from a garden hose, at night
be entertained by a hard fought battle in a game call dominoes.

Yes times were simple then when we gathered at an old vacant lot,
With a time worn ball, a leather glove, a wooden bat—our worries
were soon forgot.

But time moves on and progress is good or so they tell me,
After all, there are video games, fake leather gloves,
Aluminum bats, and of course don't forget TV.

What happened to the nights of fireflies in a jar,
The swing on the porch in a cool summer's night,
A bowl of popcorn, a game of "Old Maid,"
And on the radio a championship fight.

My thoughts come back and I look at this boy who sits upon my knee,
He calls me Gramps, a tear comes to my eye because he's only three.

I take him in arm and on his back lay a warm loving pat,
To think there will be a time when he will never hear the crack, that
wonderful sound, that beautiful sound, when a ball meets a wooden bat.

Allen L. "Oh" Kelly

The Mirror

Time after time I look deep into those eyes.
I see so much pain, that you cannot hide.
A pain so strong that cannot be put aside.
A pain that eyes should never have to show or see.
A pain that has grown for quite some time.
Looking for hope they could not find.
Because of love this pain grows strong not
knowing how to right the wrong.
Hoping and praying it will all go away.
Wishing that I didn't see my eyes in the mirror today.

Erika Bumgarner

"My Place In This World"

"Looking out my window, watching the falling rain,
I see the faces of the world crying out in pain;
People standing in the shadows, running from each
other, always living their lives undercover;
Thinking of the way things used to be, I truly begin
to see the yesterdays and tomorrows that may never be;
Can I look to borrow, every tomorrow, so I can
save a piece of today, or is my place in this world just fading away."

"Nothing lasts forever, I know this is true
Is life worth saving, if there's no meaning inside of you;
Maybe I'm a dreamer or maybe I'm a fool,
why are there so many people in this world
so careless and so cruel;
And though I try to remain so strong even
when everything in life seems to be going wrong,
I wonder is this their time to hold on, and just how long;
So where is my place in this world, where
all my dreams have come unfurled, is it
hopeless as it seems or am I just
dancing through my dreams."

Joseph Geralis

Looking Back

The contemplation of days past can either haunt man,
Or fill him with joy, depending on one's will.
Yet either way, in it lies wisdom,
With it, all of our tomorrows,
Are better than our yesterdays.

Daniel M. Shattuck

"Blessings From Above"

As I watch this sweet young lady, who stands before my eyes,
I see you looking down at her, from through the vast blue skies.

You see the sparkle in her eyes, as I have done with you,
You smile with pride and happiness, at all she's learned to do.

You look at each accomplishment, she's made throughout the years,
Your heart just swells with pleasure, as the course of life she steers.

For you laid a good foundation, for her to build upon,
And so she goes, from step to step, as life swiftly moves along.

She continues to be your sweetest prize, and strong she'll always stand,
Because she has the will within, that makes her know she can.

Her Mom and Stepdad treat her well, and have guided her with care,
I see you nod approval, of that I'm well aware.

For you have left her in their care, they shape her life each day,
They've made this home, abound with love, where she thrives every day.

I feel you send your blessings, as you smile down from above,
And wish the best, for everyone, in the home they built with love.

Helen Kelsey Morgan

Fields of Green

From forest's fringe
  I see your lovely form
Come consort with me!
  In nature's unsullied scene
Lie with me
  Upon fields of green
Caress earth's soft loam
  Whence springs forth life's delicate flower
And partake with butterfly's flight
  The flutter of heart's joyful beat

Tranquility of senses
  Together in sweet caress
Now race forth
  In joining of hands
Through fields we run
  Then pause to press wild flowers'
Nectar sweet to lips
  Joined in love's embrace
Thence once more to dream
  Our return to Fields of Green.

Gareth Thorne

Archangel

One day it should happen for sure!
I should have to go to a hospital!
And there in ten days I will find a cure ...
To my selfishness, my pride, and everything at all!

Dressed in a uniform IMMACULATE WHITE ...
Available to work hard even around the clock ...
To offenses she usually reacts with a smile always bright ...
And nothing else her brain should block!

Her place of work I should name house of sorrow!
Keeping her own head and those of many patients cool ...
Is only part of her day-by-day in that place I call horror!
But she would never panic or act like a fool!

Now comes the epilogue, the GREATEST!
The WONDERS of the ancient world are SEVEN!
But I will ADD the number eight WONDER, the BRIGHTEST ...
NURSE - FALLEN ARCHANGEL FROM HEAVEN!

Henrique de Paula

The Journey

Standing at the edge of consciousness
I stare blindly out into time and space
My mind's eye revealing
The hidden secrets of tomorrow's past
And yesterdays yet to come
I fall forward into nothingness
And touch down on a cloud of being

Outside of existence and within us all
Lies the truth I seek
Not so easily discovered is this treasure
But the search must continue

Travelling across fertile plains of imagination
Resounding with the hollow echoes of despair
Pausing to quench my thirst with all too infrequent
Draughts of happiness, I continue on

Answers flow less freely than lies and half-truths,
Ours is a world of mists
What once was, may never be again
But that is the nature of the journey
And from this flows life

Jason Babin

The Rose

As billows of tears fall from my eyes,
I think of how much I miss you.
Wishing you didn't have to go so soon.
"Everything beautiful must die," you
once told me. But I didn't even get to say
good-bye. When I come to the place where
I'm told you lie, I place a rose knowing
how much you loved them.
Months later when I return, the flower is dead.
As I leave I remember your weak voice
saying. "Everything beautiful must die."
But why?

Heather Battles

The Joys We Shared

When I recall my teaching days,
I think of my first grade classes,
And all the years I was privileged to spend,
With little lads and lasses.

And do you know what I loved best
About those bygone days?
It was the magic of Storyland
We found in our classroom plays.

In the big wide world of historic events,
Came a War that followed a Depression;
But we had Peace, and we had Joy,
In our world of Creative Expression.

Where are you now, dear children,
Now that you are grown?
What are the lessons you have learned,
Through years so swiftly flown?

What roles you play I cannot guess,
But in my heart I know
We were enriched by the joys we shared,
In Storyland long ago.

Dorothy S. Handler

Friends Remembered

I've been to many far places, known many friends and seen many things.
I traveled light; my only souvenirs are friends and memories I
collected along the way.
I took few pictures for they were lifeless, capturing only an instant
of a friendship or a place.
The ease with which I can recall the majesty of a mountain or an ocean
is a measure of the impact of the wonder I beheld.
The ease with which I can recall the warmth, laughter or tears of a
friend is a measure of how dear to my heart I held them.
It will be easy to call you back from memory, for you rest close to my
heart and gentle on my mind.

George R. Burkam

Teacher

Out the window, I hear the noises of the inner city.
I turn my glance to the figure, softly speaking at the front
of the room.
I stare upon that face, as so many before.
Inquiring, listening, loving, needing.
I can see it all upon that face.
The joy, the hope, the pain, the fury.
Those eyes stare upon my face, as they have so many before.
Needing, lost, ignorant, forgotten.
Through the years, the many innocent, the many young.
In pain, that face has witnessed, those eyes have seen;
Evil overcome innocence.

Jessica Nagy

My Jesus, My All

When I am in trouble or deep despair
I turn to Jesus, He's always there.
To lift me up when waves crash high
I have His promise He'll always be nigh.
To see me through life's troubled sea
My Lifeboat, My Anchor, He hears my plea.

My soul in turmoil, no peace or rest.
He says "my child, just lean on my breast."
And when I am tired, it seems, near the end,
His strength is my lifeline, on Him I depend.
My Sword, my Shield, my Propitiation,
the One I can turn to in my desperation.

I will not say He means the world to me.
This world can't compare with His worth, you see.
He means so much more than this world's array,
with its riches and pleasures that soon pass away.
He whispers sweet peace to my weary soul,
my Rock, my Fortress, my Jesus, my All.

Bernice Sloan

When Time Has Flown

There was a time when life was full of dreams.
I was a child such a long time it seems.
A year or two ago.

Then came the day my heart was filled with joy.
When that young man, who was really a boy, appeared
A month or two ago.

A child was born, such happiness to share.
Then he was grown with someone else to care
A day or two ago.

Now I am old and where have they all fled,
Those years that seemed to stretch so far ahead
An hour or two ago.

Ann Richards

Like Eagles We'll Fly

A voice called me-while I was in a dream.
I was deep in sleep-walking by a stream.
Somewhere in a world-filled in peaceful bliss.
When I heard these words-so sweet insist.

Come follow me and we'll ride the wind,
Come follow me and we'll walk the sea.
My day has come-why don't you run?-
Don't hesitate and follow me.

I followed the words-to a mountain high,
Reached out my hand and touched the sky.
I lift my feet-like an eagle to flight
And soared to a land-where there is no night.

And when I arrived-what a beautiful sight.
I saw a city bathed-in pure crystalline light.
With streets of gold and gates of pearl,
I knew this was home and this is my world.

Come follow me and we'll ride the wind,
Come follow me and we'll walk on the sea.
Come follow me and we'll climb a mountain high,
Come follow me and like eagles we'll fly.

Edward E. LaMay Sr.

Forgotten Souls

I wandered through a cemetery one day.
I was not surprised to see a couple
of graves -
names illegible and molding with time's decay.
Who are these people? I thought.
Do they know that they are forgot?
We should respect life
as it comes and goes
it is precious as everyone knows.
But still it puzzled me to see
a few unmarked graves
cold and empty as can be.

It bothered me to wonder
when I lay six feet under,
with my tombstone molding with time's decay
would people stand around and question
Who was that person who lived one day?

Hillary Laurent

Ode To Daughter II

You arrived... Without pain.
I was prepared to do what was required...
To be awakened while others slept,
To wheedle, to cajole, to reassure.

But you did not find the world a hostile place.
Your infant rhythms were in tune with your surroundings,
Your nights were filled with dreams, not nightmares.
Your palate was receptive to food of every flavor.

Possible trauma....A tonsillectomy is scheduled.
I was prepared to do what was required,
But you succumbed to the anesthetic with a trusting smile.

The school play is being cast...The heroine is the Pink Fairy.
You were chosen, naturally.

We put you in the lake... You swam.
We squeezed together in the club chair for the wondrous
revelations of the birds and the bees...
You were comfortable with the facts of life.

The letter said "You are hereby elected to Phi Beta Kappa..."
Another offering added to the riches I have already received.
And so little was required of me.

Clarice Hoffer

Don't Worry My Brother

Don't worry my brother that you cannot see,
I will be the eyes for you and me.
Don't worry my brother about things that go bump in the night,
We've already been blessed by a heavenly light.

Don't worry my brother about what people say,
You and I will make it all the way.
We have our bond and our family,
And we have determination no one can break.

Don't worry my brother about the future,
Mom will see to it we always are nurtured.
Don't worry my twin about one little thing,
Your life and mine are virtually the same.

Don't worry brother when we feud and fight,
Everything will work out right.
Don't worry my brother that you visually cannot see,
Most importantly you see the love between you and me.

Alice Apperson

Somebody

Am I "somebody" that nobody loves?
I wonder why?

Lifted upon a doorstep of a strange abandoned place.
No milk, just nothing...in my suitcase.

As I cried out, from under the garbage bag that hid
my tiny body from plain view,

I was discovered by "somebody," who I thought
had nobody too.

As he picked me up, and gently placed me,
right next to his heart.

It felt warm and comforting.
And at that very moment,
I thought that I heard an angel sing;

As I slowly opened my eyes, above
his head was a brightly lit ring.
Right then I knew that he was the great "God," Almighty King.
Who had came to take me back home with him.

So my little life would never be cloudy - for today,
I am loved and I am "Somebody"...

Morganna

Trusting Him

To trust in God, Oh, how we fail sometimes.
I wonder why? So easy it should be to do.
For, who more can we trust, than our Redeemer,
The man who died, to give us life anew.

God has a perfect plan for our lives,
But, lovingly He let's us go our own byway.
If we would trust Him to guide our path,
Less heartaches we'd have on life's highway.

But, we struggle along as if left orphans,
Though He says, "Give me all your cares".
He longs to help carry our burdens,
He only wants our trust with our prayers.

We find peace and know His deep abiding love,
When our trust in Him we give,
And, as we cast our burdens upon Him,
In faith and trust we learn to live.

A more faithful friend, we could never find,
Than Jesus, Our Savior, Our precious Lord.
So, let us give Him our trust completely,
And know He will guide us to our reward.

Gayleen Lucas

Why Do People Hate?

In a world that is going to demolish soon,
I wonder, why we hate?
If we can send people to the moon,
Why can't people relate?

I am black, my neighbor is white,
I consider us good friends.
We talk politics, but never fight.
I hope our friendship will never end.

Lets say we all went blind,
None of us could see,
Would there still be racist people,
If you had to depend on me.

What is the purpose of racism,
'Cause it has nothing to do with pride.
It has nothing to do with patriotism,
Because over it many Americans died.

Can we ever live together,
Or is it to late?
Will we get through the stormy weather?
Why do people hate?

Amber Gray

My Mistake

As my tears fall, with no one to wipe them away, I wonder why you left. I had only done what you wanted. But now you've left me, when I needed you the most. I really wasn't ready, but somehow you didn't hear my protest. You had convinced me that it was okay. Because you loved me, and with love it was okay. But now that I'm pregnant, you're nowhere to be found. My mother wanted me to get an abortion, because I am so young. But even though I know that what I did was wrong, I won't go against what I believe again. I've decided to give my child to another, so that they may give my child a life. And pray to God, and ask for FORGIVENESS.

Jessica Snider

Your Bath Water

If I were the water of your bath.....
I would surround you in mellow warmth, like liquid love.
As a playful, childish wave against a sandy shore
I could dash and break upon your firm body.
I would engulf you, moistening the places in my dreams.

If I were the water of your bath.....
I would caress each and every muscle.
Your indentations would be filled with me.
I could take your shape, mold myself against your curves.
I would lie on, roll over and slide on your skin.

If I were the water of your bath.....
Part of me would be sent to the hollow of your navel
To move when you move. Inherit your temperature.
I could frolic, sloshing against your thighs.
I would become intimate with your nature.

If I were the water of your bath.....
I would be as my ancestors before me and cleanse you.
Your desire to have me puts you in control of when I am here.
I could be taken without hesitation.
I would always be waiting for your decided naked return.

Giovanna Burleigh

Where Are My Rose Buds

I would pick a petal from a rosebud
I would say to the rosebud, you are a pretty flower
And I would say, he loves me.

He loves me, he loves me not
My first love of my life loved me for sixteen years.
We had our own house, we had four children too.

My love of my life died of a heart-attack.
My loved-one is gone, but not from my heart
I picked three more flower buds

God gave me a second chance in love
My second love gave me everything too
We traveled thirty-six states in a motor home
We saw so much, and did different things, too
The adventure to the both of us made us happy

With my two loves, we did everything together
Now I have lost my rosebuds
There are no more petals to pick.

Fannie Thomas

Nocturnal Thoughts

In this fragile slumber of secrets and silence,
icicle whispers fall from your lips.
The dying melancholy of this ending day sleeps in your dreams,
Until the next moment of light, awakens them to life once again.

From the depths of your mind, regrettable sadness seeps slowly in,
And a black velvety embrace covers the earth.

This lingering denial gives birth to despair.
- But clear away the ruins and burn the ashes of grief.
Lay roses so red on the pain instead, for eternity.

Caroline Cho

A Tribute To My Wife

If you'll give me just a moment of your time
I'd like to expound on someone who is mine, all mine.
She's gentle as a kitten most the time,
but a bad day at the office can have her roaring like a lion!
On these days, I know just what to do.
I'll fire up that ole John Deere and split a log, or maybe two.
But on the good days, when it's safe to be around,
the tractor stays under the shed, and we might even go to town.
I love her very dearly, and I know it's not all her fault,
'cause when she went shopping for a husband, just look at what she caught!

Joe Ogletree

The Picture

There is a way to do things, and a way to not.
If you want something to happen,
Give it all you've got!
In my lifetime, there could be no slacking,
Every hour was go full bore!
From up in the morning to the bed at night.
From leaving the home to evening coming in the door.
This surely sounds familiar to most people,
How can we cope with such nonsense?
Within the memories you are building,
You will see a picture of many accomplishments,
It's rewarding, exhilarating with many pluses,
Like the lifetime friendships that are made,
Learning about the "tickings" of different people,
Feeling the needs, and caring about those beginning to fade,
This is a word picture of a dedicated Volunteer!

Evelyn J. Brent

The Storm

The seaman grasped the boat's tiller as a wave broke over its bow.
'I'd pray to you God, if only I knew how'!
Lightning flashed while the wind roared with such cynical mirth
Would this be the seaman's last day on earth?

He closed his eyes while his mind whispered, in a small voice
'Pray even if you've never prayed before. Maybe God will hear you
and guide this boat to shore.
He said to himself, 'What's to lose, it's my only choice'.

His words seemed strange, he didn't know what to say.
He stumbled as he tried to form the words, 'Dear God'.
Even his lips wouldn't help him, he found to his dismay.
As a wave broke over the boat, he heard himself utter, 'Save me!
Let me live, I pray!'

He felt a sudden jerk. He opened up his eyes. Something had grasped
the boat's painter and was swimming for the distant shore. As they
flew toward the foreign shore, a small voice seemed to say, 'wake up,
My Son, TOMORROW'S ANOTHER DAY!'

Edwin L. Spight

Don't Judge The Way I Am

Don't judge the way I am,
if I walk away from your outstretched hand,
Unless you have experienced my pain,
you cannot understand.

Don't judge my different moods,
and talk about what I should do.
Unless you have experienced my pain,
you and I are not the same.

Don't judge my tears so harshly,
and say I am not strong,
For if you walked in my shoes,
you would see that you are wrong.

Don't judge my everyday actions
and say I am unkind,
Unless you experience the pain I bare,
you and I have nothing to share.

So please don't judge the way I am,
because you cannot understand.

Carolyn J. Richter

Promise Me

...And the last kiss - romantic as the first...
I'll love you after I'm dead, but promise
You'll throw a red rose on my grave surrounded
By 364 black roses to show the world
How our love should be portrayed

Love in the midst of pain

After the ground has settled   Promise me
You'll visit weekly with eleven black roses and one red rose
Signifying the love you feel and the pain that won't let go
Kiss the grave with your lips, feel my pain

Of having died in your arms. Of living in death alone.

And on the last full moon of May when you visit
Bring the roses and the gun
Lay naked on top of me, kiss me and shoot yourself
Letting the world see the deep seeded love
And pain we've shared in life as well as death

As you lay in the plot next to mine
I will dream of holding your hand
Thenceforth we shall turn to dust — with the

Red and black roses...

Gregory T. Appeldorn

Reminiscence

Looking back on all my years and how they've been spent;
I'm astounded and pleased with the blessings I've been sent.
The first was my family - one that really cared
Happiness or sadness, everything we shared.
All the wonderful teachers I could never repay
For their guidance and examples of how to live each day.
The day I met my husband was a special one in my life.
And another happy one was the day I became his wife.
In a few short years, our house echoed
With the laughter of little ones.
We welcomed one sweet daughter and four great sons.
There were exciting trips to London, Dublin and Rome
Soon we decided there's really no place like home.
Some sorrow along the way I was able to bear
Because my family and friends were there.
I think of the years ahead and things I'd like to accomplish.
To be able to do even half of them is my fervent wish.
My life on the earth has been happy-regrets very few.
If I could live it over, very little different I'd do!

Frances B. Kelleher

Our Second Anniversary

I hope our marriage lasts a life time;
I'm happy knowing I'm yours and you are mine.

I know there's a time or two that I've made a mistake;
And I know each time your heart has begun to break.

Maybe someday I will become the man you want me to be;
I hope you love me enough to wait and see.

The last two years have been the best years of my life;
Because I have the most loving, most caring,
and most beautiful wife.

I haven't been that good of a husband, this I know;
But please never leave me; never let our love go.

There's nobody in the world; no matter what they might say;
That could be happier than you make me every day.

Happy anniversary and I love you with all my heart
May all your dreams come true when we're together and when
we're apart.

Joey Hotchkiss

Ewe Lamb To Shepherd

You are so important;
I'm only a grain of sand
Still, I love you dearly,
Can you understand?
My heart doesn't know
The difference in your stand and mine.
It is really far behind in knowledge, but I'm glad.
Love is something uncontrolled.
I wouldn't want to try,
Because if you didn't love me,
I'd have reason to cry.

Frances Adams

Tiffany

The Sun sparkles on her soft golden hair.
In her eyes I am lost in love.
From morning till night she is present in my mind.
From day to day she is the true meaning of love.
A day with her is a day of true joy.
Now she has left me.
Yes I know she will return, but when is still a mystery.

Frank B. Cowan

The Child - The Beauty - The Woman: Happy Birthday, Mary

Mary, today is your special time
I'm writing these words, hoping they will rhyme

Arriving on a cold March snowy morn
You—the darling little girl with the black hair—were born

You always helped children that were poor
In your small way, hoping to give them more

Charlie Brown was who you really liked
Troy and Sherri didn't always share your delight

You have become a loving lady with a tender heart—
My small share and God's huge part

Betty Baker

Soul Mate

I have left my remains on distant shores
In nameless ages, fighting nameless wars
I have traveled often through Death's doors
But I always returned to you

The faces I've worn are as clouds in the skies
Though changing, you see through my misty disguise
You'll know me once more by my kiss and my eyes
When again I return to you

When the years wear away these trappings I bear
And again I ascend Death's timeless stair
I will come back soon with a new love to share
I will always return to you

Dave Vahlberg

Paragon's Words

Love as a topic, glides through our language
in sonnets, poems and prose.
As a twining vine seeks sunlight's rays
So this emotion continues to grow.

Stated with elegance or whispered in secret
Read, acted, televised or sung.
Perpetual waves of resounding voices
Speaking in every tongue.

Invisible cords bind my inner thoughts
holding my words in check.
When feeling moments keep passing by
And I stand mute before your eye
....magic, deposits my perfect words in a net-
and yet-

If I could release these imprisoned jewels
Sweep away the enchanted web
Then astonishing words would flow forth
Polished gems, that have not been said.

D'dee Lanier

A Peaceful Place

The most peaceful place for me to be,
is at the beach, looking out to sea.
I love to watch the sea gulls dance and play;
on a lazy, sunshiny day.
A man and woman, hand in hand;
walking through the sifting sand.
The sound of the waves as they crash to shore.
It touches me to the very core.
There's a calmness that comes over me;
when I'm at the beach, looking out to sea.

Jane Morgan

Another Trick

Up, up and away went morals
In the anything goes nation
Warped from the hill-top to the gutter deep
Like roving birds, puberty keeps moving
Drifting higher, higher
In the cloud of legislated evils
Free doctors honor the card, do not stop STD.
It bars no territory.
Hormones in overdrive get condoms, free
And little girls get pills,
And shot, free
And arm-patched.
Abused and neglected babies are beautiful
In the anything goes nation
The month's stamps half pay mom's crack supplier
Hungry little boys help themselves at Arab stores
And deal to the gutter or gun shots
Social workers weep, and
Taxpayers curse loud and angry
Politician! You turned another trick.

Augie M. Lehmann

The Candle

Last night I looked for your birthday candle
  in the blinking heavens, hoping to glimpse your silhouette
  beyond the mountain you stood on before they took you home.
  I remembered voiceless Love (like an orphaned crocus
  shivering between rocks in cold, Dakota winds)
  asking you to sing His song... while your timorous arms
  stretched — placing a stitch in God's tapestry.
  (Frail hands make big stitches; maybe that's why
  God gave you such beautiful colors!)

Again, I watched upward hands on the kitchen clock
  folding in prayer — viewed from Limbo-torture
  your breath (kindly, but slowly) leaving to follow you
  — parting worlds setting pain free
  and Love (like a gentle mother wrapping her child)
  coming down to claim His own! When joy was too full,

I saw you moving in ecstasy toward
  raptured throngs singing your name — and
    I had to let go so you would dance! ...while
      God lit your star — when
        you brushed His smile.

Floyd Hansen

Freedom

A spark of life
In the depth of a soul.
No treasure will purchase it
Only insight discover it
Faith nurture it.
No boundaries confine it
For it is borne on the wings of hope
Possessed by those who set it free.
No legislation can dictate it
Only love of a human heart guide
And the bond of brotherhood hold it steadfast.
Choosing life
And living that choice.
Free
To see
To touch
To know
A hint of darkness
A hint of light
Before it's time to go.

Jane Winkler O. Carm

Community Friendship

The black orchid is usually found
in the dark regions of the amazon
where there is hardly no sun
giant trees stand firmly in the black earth
on its branches rare birds perch
in these beautiful jungles of great realization
believe me there is a civilization

In this great community of ours
friendship is not like the rare and precious flowers
compassion is at the mission door
where we readily feed the poor
when people say we have a certain knack
success is a major fact

On the exotic ocean floor you will find black pearls
things that will make your head swirl
better than precious gems their motto is care
community loyalty a special ingredient no fear
one is always welcome there
our community will always give a helping hand
for human rights it stands

Carmelita T. Cass

Morning Waves Of Memories

The sun rises as the gentle waves collide.
In the distance, beautiful creatures flip
 through the sun's warm path.
They continually crescent over the water with endless patterns.
Blossoming on the water
 is a rose of light.
The animated animals collide with the eternal waves.
 sprinkling life upon a
  world which watches with watery eyes.
Gray, heavenly mammals advance
 magnified by songs of everlasting shrills.
Eyes filled with ecstasy vanish beneath the surface.
Like children, they frolic around the boat.
One suddenly bursts from the sea
 over the boat like a rainbow
  as it sprays smiles across our faces.
Rocking the boat and bobbing the waves, the creatures swim away,
 leaving the waves to expire.
This day of remembrance of the dolphin species,
 as it disappears from sight, FOREVER!

Barbara Little

A Private Walk

A large black buzzard feather lay
in weeds, beside the path awaiting me.
This random fluke boon I stuck into
my graying hair, so that I might wear
the faux sign of a Lakota brave.

This feather, a simple trick of nonchalance
which hides any evidence of pain, fear or plight,
just like my father taught me so very long ago
by his frequent stern command, "Son, be a man."

As I journey on with my private walk today,
a passerby will be distracted if they see
this jaunty feather, perched image of bravery.
A disguise for a small boy I still carry
deep inside, who once again wants to cry.

Hiding now, tears for my father, my dad,
who only yesterday lost yet another ability.
His eyesight is gone, no more reading or tv
as age advances to rip away, again and again,
thread from his cloak of worn out dignity.

Jim Burneo

Precious Jewel A Child Is Born

There came some news from far away, through the star that shone
in the sky that night.
Its brilliance falls on a sweet baby named "JESUS CHRIST," that
spreads its glory to us all.
 ALLELUIA! ALLELUIA, the angels sing,
His holiness slipped into our hearts.
Shepherds and many of God's creatures came and adored with joy.
Immanuel they say our King of Kings.
Glory to God our King did come.
We glorify His presence and adore him. His blessed mightiness
we keep in our hearts, forever then through all the world,
every creature man of every kind.
Blessed is the day of Christmas, its spirit thrills
our heart with joy.

Angela M. Palacio

Life Works

Life works on all people
In very much the same way.
Some lives are straight and tall like a steeple
And others change from day-to-day.

Life works on all people
Its pilgrimage to work out.
Often we hear only a ripple
In that small stream of the devout.

Life works for all people;
They have much accomplishment.
Those who claim to be worthless stubble
Are among God's heartfelt want.

Life works for all people
As given to us by the Lord.
And God helps us in all trouble
Filling our hearts with peace and accord.

James H. Duke, Jr.

A Tribute To A Great Man The Rev. Dr. Martin Luther King Jr.

This man of love, this man of peace, he had a constant dream.
In which all contention ceased, and all men were supreme.
One he could share, inspire, and make aware, the people of this nation
People from every walk of life, every creed and every station.

He never asked for very much, only to love your brother,
He knew if you could do that, then you could learn to love one another
This man of peace, who knew no fear or shame.
Who would bear his soul to all who would hear and take whatever came.

He could walk and talk with anyone in a manner to stir and move you.
For a cause that was righteous, a cause that was just, he would see
 it through
This man of faith, who hoped to change men's hearts,
with whatever he had to give.
So he gave his strength, his heart and soul, a life few men can live.

This man of grace, the light of love and the Grace of God,
are the things of which he was made, and he used these gifts until
the last and with his life he paid. But his words ring true on the
ears of men who would seek their own selfish stand.
For today they know the worth of a great and God-sent man.

Gloria E. Thomas

The Vicious Mind

The cosmic mind created the Universe;
Innocence flowing as rivers, with many a verse
born as Vedas, Bible and Koran; to nurse
the baby mind to wake up in the path of coarse
knowledge and energy, to ride on the horse,
"a better life" to hold the gold in the purse,
and shoulder upon him, the world's biggest curse.

Between the births of "A" and "Z"
many zees came rolling, pages after pages
through the pen of the child of the creator
and here he comes our beloved writer
to mold the world into a nice theater
holding the hands of an orator.

The pen and tongue of these traitors
sharper than the sword of the cold murderer,
the child is not kind as his father, the creator
who gave pen and tongue to knead the creation much better

Ha! No! O Mind!
Destroy not the garden of Adam and Eve
into a miserable hell.

Jayashree Rajaram

The Beauty Of Nature

On a bright summer's morning
Inspired by the melodic timbre of birds,
I cheerfully stroll the countryside.

As the wind quietly embraces the trees,
Invigorating is the constant breeze
And the sweet essence of honeysuckle fills the virgin air.

High aloft spans the infinite sky,
A celestial canopy in disguise;
Clouds softly hover beneath like disheveled wreaths.

As I gaze at the magnificent dawning sun
Rising from behind mountains beyond,
The lofty trees appear to kneel in reverence to this wonder.

The wildflowers freely imbue the hills
While the Morning Glory stands sublimely poised
As if to serenade her amenable peers.

In the midst of these fields
with meadows green and wide,
The beauty of nature is truly revealed.

Bernice W. Wilson

Fort Lamy

I thought I'd find a desert nude and dry
instead I came upon a castle and a sky
so clear, so blue, so filled with stars
that it must make my wounds turn into scars.

I thought the desert would be mine to cry
with no one there to live for or to die...
instead I found a prince with golden hair
whose deep voice drowns out all despair.

I thought that castles, tales and Lorelei
were lost, that princes all now buried lie —
but here are you outshining all that's bright
creating splendors lovelier than light
and filling all of me with new delight.

Christina D. Lebworth

Daughter

Face first into the Winter storm,
Into the cold dark night that engulfs my life,
To die in its blustery isolation.
In desolation I endure the cold
Blame of his eye.
The hard edge of his words
Reigns strong,
Gripping my brain in an iron fist.
The harshness of his holy commandments
The headstrong dominance
Of his fatherly ways.
How I loathe control,
Like a jew in a German Camp, confined.
I stand again
Before each man,
As white as a newly washed lamb.

Chastity R. Penfold

Forgetful

As I look out the window,
into the dark cold sky,
I think of his face.

The sky melts shades of dark blue,
quietly it reminds me of an emotion,
but I don't remember which one.

As I step outside into the wind,
the swaying trees remind me of a person,
a time, that I can't recall.
The wind blows a feeling through me, one of serenity,
but when I've felt it before, escapes me.

As the wind rushes through my hair,
it seems to whisper to me,
but I cannot hear it.

Thinking back, I remember a time,
when someone held me,
but my mind has erased their face.

And as I breath in the air to taste the rain
that approaches, I swear I could place it,
but the taste, is unknown.

Carmen Pardel

Color Me Humble

The person humbled from within
Is filled with peace and bows to God;
Then spirit soars to heights unknown
In rainbow hues created there
Within the natural shell of life;
Like butterflies released from grey cocoons.

A wisp of light, ethereal grace,
A breath of freedom in our soul;
Ungrasped, yet overflowing there
Beneath Magnolia Ridge Chateau,
In Berchman's touch at Grand Coteau,
From saints to men...Chi Rho!

The person humbled from without
Is like a tiny grain of sand
Forced into grey and dismal shell;
A lonely imprisoned solitaire, reformed in layered pearl,
Obscured until the shapeless mass
Is opened and gouged loose to die;
And God is life.

Frances-Faith Tretton

Concerto

I rode into the blue of the mountain
into the velvet slate blueness of the mountain.
My dreams and the music took me there
as I nestled against your coat.
Then the violins began to play.
I closed my eyes and followed their voices
to a river surrounded by reeds
where we danced and laughed in the shadows
beneath a cobalt blue sky.
I saw my life in the ripples on the water,
my soul in the pulse of the current
as natural and free as
a fawn or a willow or a single reed
in a deep and intimate place
that only the music could reach.

Janet C. Green

Childhood's End

The end of childhood is near.
Into the world we step without fear.
We walk proud and stand tall.
No longer children our dreams will soon fall.
Like shining stars to the earth far below.
Reality kills them but somehow they'll glow.
In the eyes of our children and their children too.
Maybe someday someone's dreams will come true.
Maybe not yours and maybe not mine.
But someday somehow like stars we will shine.
In our own special way each and every one.
Because childhood is over and life's just begun.

Dawn J. Marks

1954 - An Army Brat's Return

Home from an island speck in the South Pacific, Virginia
is a culture shock. A young teen tries to enter the peer
Mystic, a cloak of dreams about her head... she cannot blend.

Four months pass in school classes of shy silence, walking
the halls alone, ashamed to be lost, projecting her mind
To other places, the interminable wait to escape. Living

The agony of exile in her own country teaches her that life
abroad is better, that the family of five is her only true
Reflection. A transfer to Turkey, following Dad wherever he

Goes. Probing the minds of many cultures is the lifestyle
she understands, growing in tolerance of diversity, unaware
Of the new breed she represents. Goodbye Liberty, harbor

Lights fading fast, echoes of other trips on military ships.
A page of poetry flutters under her cabin door from a
Baptist boy bound for Tripoli service. Blueberry Hill finds

A thrill in the Common Room and the girl learns to dance
on a leaning floor, sliding to the waves, finding friends
On the fly and looking for letters with SWAK on the back.

BB Ensor

I Miss You, Shanghai

It's the raining season again, dear Shanghai
Is grandma's strawberry already red
Is mom already making those spring cookies
Is there another little girl
who likes to walk in the drizzle?
Does she wear a long pink shirt?
Does she sing "Yesterday Once More?"
Does she have a big dream?
If she leaves you for her dream someday
Will you be raining the whole season?

Bianca Yongrong Bao

My Grandson Raphael

My grandson Raphael
is named as an archangel.
Looking at me with adoration,
with his clear eyes full of passion.
So young and so dear, so near God
And so far from the world.
He just left, he's only three years old!
I am his "grandmaman."
He speaks to me in French,
But he knows all languages
When he reaches to me and gives me a big hug
with his bewitching smile.
He knows the language of love,
This young "Taurus," as soft as a dove,
Tiny hands and feet but so strong already.
He's the world of tomorrow, our hope
And joy on this earth,
With so many like him, of his age,
They will beautifully manage
To bring to our worlds a magnificent PEACE...

Claudette L. Clerin

Horses Of Course!

The beauty of a horse's muscle in action
Is something special to behold
He lifts his head, arched high in splendor
With those huge brown eyes that are so bold.

"Cheyenne," a quarter horse, runs forcefully through the woods
His muscles strain; THAT HORSE is really in control!
Oft times he speeds forthright to the three-bay stall
Majestically down the path he goes, barely missing a pole.

Winnings from horse races, bought this fine horse
And two others, with bridles and saddles, too.
We seven were ecstatic and gleefully proud
For unexpected gifts from Dad, to us completely new.

"Pitta Pat," gentle with spindly legs was for Liz
While big-footed "Peaches 'n Cream" carried Dad.
What great family times together we spent -
Magical hours most families do not have.

We bought fifteen acres on which the horses could run.
We cleaned equipment, saw their blankets were aired;
After rides, we brushed them down, even manes and tails.
Oh what joy and pleasure - God's creatures entrusted to our care.

Elsie J. Staska

The Wings Of An Angel

To ride upon the wings of an angel
Is something that would set most people's heart and soul aglow
But to ride upon the wings of an angel
We should live a good life in the world below.

Most people are sure they have a guardian angel
Watching over them from up in the sky
Because we have lived through so many sicknesses and injuries
There seems to be no other reason why.

When we have crossed that shining water
And our time on earth shall be no more
There we will meet our guardian angel
Waiting for us on the other shore.

Maybe then we will be a guardian angel
And watch over someone from up in the sky
Always ready to reach out and help them
And never letting them know the reason why.

Herbert H. Smith

Wanted Heart

To find, love someone like you,
is to find someone to love me too.
To keep, share those happy days,
is to share them in many ways.
To feel your lovin' arms around me,
is to feel the love that surrounds me.
To miss you so when we are apart,
is to miss your warmth within my heart.
To be lonely when we're not together,
is to love you more, more forever.
To wipe away the tears I've wept,
is to show the love inside I keep.
To really think, finally know,
is to be sure of the love you'll truly show.
To want, love someone like you,
is to want someone to love me too.

Florence L. Hemple

The Ultimate Dream

The light from the moon
is what leads me to you.
I know it's now morning
because there's dew on my shoes.
I awake...lost...in a field...a field of dreams
where everything is made
like candy land,
there are no names
or no name brands
everyone is equal, treated the same
there are no racists or rapists
or murder games
kids run free without any worries
no pollution or litter bugs
everything's clean
animals run wild
ones I've never seen
it would be great weather everyday
... HEY YOU ... WAKE ... UP...
I heard someone say.

Jamie L. Despathy

Honesty, Truth And Integrity

Why do people have to put on false faces, what happened to the truth?
Isn't truth couth anymore, why must people play games?
Not say what is in their heart, when did political correctness start?

I will not play games or put on a false face to be accepted by you.
Honesty, truth and integrity always win and will come through.

It may be old fashioned, some of us like the old ways.
How it was in the old days of great men like Washington and our fathers.
When men were real men, when being unfaithful, lying and
cheating was sin.

I have to inform you Brother and Sister they still are.
With honesty, truth and integrity you can go far.
You will be a role model for those who follow you.
So let's all get our act together.
Let honesty, truth and integrity shine through.

Joyce K. Nielsen

Rainbows

A little crystal hangs in my kitchen window,
Just waiting for the sun, and a gentle breeze to blow.
It makes the most beautiful colors all over the room.
This fills my heart with glee,
It was a special gift, my grandchildren gave to me.
Thank you Matthew and Renee.

Esther Stolz

Suicide Funeral

Why is not a word - propped up - on legs of its own...
It cannot stand - to bear the weight - of sorrows.

Standing by a casket full - of flowers - and compressed human soil
looking down at some terribly bad waxwork caricature joke
of a missing human soul...

Why - has no taste in my mouth...

When pain cannot hurt enough - and numbness no longer cares to fake
the exquisite agonies.. why do we - harden ourselves?
Why are we cold? And arranged by others in their choice of box?
Softly implying the lying of family and friends floundering
nearby...

Why moves among us - and through us - it doesn't seem to care
Which - of us.
"But one of us says no - says now - and isn't kidding, anymore!"
NOW DO YOU UNDERSTAND?!

She just wanted us to know that she was dead - on the outside - as well

Why stumbles - against family members, out-of-season...
and while I may get out the door
WHY will never leave her side: She cannot make HIM go.
Ever.

George Roland Wills

"I About Died; They Told Me"

"I About Died; They Told Me" in a wreck; I don't remember; you see
It could have happened to you just as it happened to me.
I guess it wasn't my time to leave this world for sure,
'Cause as long as I believe in the "man" above, there ain't no cure.

"I About Died; They Told Me;" I awoke in a hospital bed,
Flashbacks of yesterday going all through my head.
They had to cut me out the car; it took an hour or so.
There is one thing I want everyone to know:

Stay in tune with life and believe in yourself and the "man" up above,
Who will show no hate, but a whole lotta "love."
Hold fast to dreams, 'cause you can make them come true.
I am me, and you are you.

"I About Died; They Told Me;" I looked at the car I was in.
When I looked at it, tears were about to begin,
'Cause I have dreams I know will come true;
My family, friends, and kin will never ever have to feel blue.

Danny Wouten

No Chance

There once was a tree that stood in my courtyard.
It did not stand alone for it was fragile and weak.
It needed support, but it wasn't taken care of.
Unimportant to most — it was just another tree.
But to me it was special.
I watched it grow every day, with pleasure.
In the Winter, it fought hard against the cold wind.
Springtime - it came back to life.
Summertime - its beautiful green leaves provided shade.
But this summer the leaves turned brown too early.
No one came to care for it.
I kept telling myself - it will come back to life.
IT WILL COME BACK TO LIFE!
But it wasn't given the chance.
Today, they cut down my tree rather than care for it.
There once was a tree in my courtyard;
It gave me so much pleasure.
Now there's just a bare spot,
Reminding me of what was once there.

Jeanette Strianese

I Remember You...

I can remember the day when I heard the news of your death,
It flashed all over the television you were dead, it just took my breath,
I can remember hearing the way your fellow neighbors treated you,
I can remember seeing the pain the nasty disease put you through,
You were treated like an outsider, like a person of a different kind,
All it was, was a bunch of people misinformed about your disease,
they wouldn't listen to reason they had made up their mind,
I never knew you, but I felt like I could feel your hurt,
My heart just ached when I saw how cruel children could be, it hurt,
It wasn't just children a lot of adults rejected you too,
If I could've met you I would have wanted to say, you were brave
and I wish everyone could be brave like you,
The disease was Aids and the brave kid was Ryan White,
He fought the disease, he didn't let it get him down, you might think
he did but he always would say I am gonna fight,
In a lot of ways he won,
I just wish people weren't so misinformed and dumb,
But you know these days people judge you for what they hear,
not for you,
I wish people would wake up and see,
People with Aids aren't any different than you and me...

Christi James

Windows Of Time

Life is like a window
It gives us a view
Of all that we can see and things we must do.

Life is the growing of two hearts to one,
It carries great freedom to those who do come.

Life is knowing you are not alone,
Of sharing and caring for all who we love,
Making a family and a good home.

Life is like panes of a window in time,
Showing us all it has to offer with no reason or rhyme.

Gloria McDonald

My Secret Place

In my heart there is a place that no one knows about.
It holds a lot of little things, like hurts and pain and doubt.

I wondered sometimes, if anyone knew about these things inside.
To take the time to look in there and see these things I hide.

Then there you were, so much like me, the loving caring kind.
Someone who took the time to look and get into my mind.

You opened up my secret place with a key you kept inside
your own secret hiding place. A place where you often cried.

I asked, "How could you unlock this?" "No key was made before,
to enter in this secret place and open up this door."

And then I knew, what happened then. Why you had set me free.
God had made our doors the same, and given you the key.

Allen Mitchell

People

People today have a hard time,
Life is not what they had in mind.
We live as animals and not as humans,
They fight and kill, and steal from each other.
When will they learn that God made us all sisters and brothers.
This world is not long as people may think,
The drugs, alcohol and guns will make everyone extinct.
I hope that everyone will stop and listen to what God has to say,
And apply it to their lives and put all those terrible things away.
Let us all live as sisters and brothers,
And learn to love and respect each other.

Gloristine Brown

"The Cradle Of Time"

The cradle of time rocks ever so slowly,
It keeps the same time for the high and the lowly...
It sings lullabies for those who will listen,
And with the SIGHING WIND, man can be christened
IMMORTAL CREATURE OF GOD...

While talking with a little flower,
I asked it, "Why do people grow SOUR?
And why it was so bright and happy?"
And it said, "I have the warm sunshine to embrace me,
And I love the whole flowery race of me...
I even love the thistle as much as the ROSE...
And my petals thank the wind that blows...
So sweetly across the meadows green...
I thank GOD for my few hours of joy and bliss...
For the DAWN'S EARLY KISS,
AND THE RAINBOW'S SMILE...
I THANK GOD ALL THE WHILE...
Everything is radiant in my life...
BECAUSE, I JUST CAN'T GROW IN STRIFE...

Fred Daulton

Clean Air

The city air is such a haze
It nearly puts me in a daze
Let's use less gas, the air to clear
No more pollution, then, to fear

The country air is like a breeze
That's fresh and blowing through the trees
With fragrant flowers all around
From clean rain falling on the ground

Let's take a hike or climb a hill
Forget the city for a spell
When we return we'll be refreshed
With new ideas for the rest

A bike could go so fast and far
More fun and cheaper than a car
Help keep me sharp for any test
Help keep in shape to do my best

Anita Alexander

Comparison

When I see a tall beautiful oak tree,
It reminds me of my wonderful family.
My hubby is the trunk so strong, tall and wise
And I am the firmest limb that grows from his side.
Our children are the branches that spring forth from me,
Each with different shapes, sizes and personalities.
We stand tall together, each of us filled with care
Having confidence that love and support is always there.
Oh! What a sight to behold, the beautiful oak tree
And what a blessing to receive, my wonderful family.

Janice Halsell Simmons

Enigma

Deep in the heart of every soul
lies a shadow, dark and frightening.
A secret of the past, it sleeps restlessly.
Finally, when the moment arrives that you believe
it to be hidden, it awakens and crawls
wickedly back to haunt your conscience.
Frantically you try to conceal it, denying
its presence. It is likened to the
water beneath a sinking ship in
the night; it seizes hold and sucks
you down into the darkness and
a watery grave. Agonizingly it lingers until
the destruction of your heart, soul and mind.

Elexia Ruth Patterson

Duty

If you have a duty in this human time,
It revolves around pain.

There is so very much of it
Crying out, crying out for you to join

"It's all around us," voices wail.
"It's in us all," disciples despair.

But, if you have a duty in this human time,

It is to find....
the pebble of joy in your shoe
the pilot light of your soul
To welcome the burning search for air as laughter overcomes you.

Nurture these. Nurture these without regard for pain.
If pain is a part of the All,
It's only a stepping stone meant to be visited for a moment.

The foot only need touch it gingerly, and balance for a brief moment—before moving toward the horizon.

Pain is not a pinnacle, but the sharpening of clarity.
If you have a duty in this human time,
It revolves around the clouds; not the sod.
Look upward...Into Your Destiny.

Debra D. Romine

A Human Reflection Of The World

There is place not far from here,
It runs deep feelings through my soul, feelings of deep compassion...
It controls my being. This thing called love...
That lingers in my heart....

I walk through the dark, wet, forest;
The tallest of trees overprotect me
and the perfume of nature brings the beauty
only one can reflect upon as we respect each other...

Human compassion, roams the world everyday,
Undescribable, mystical feelings,
That only music of great mystery can fulfill.
Hear the music and reach out...

Sadness, loneliness, depression;
Despair now, but let go and take my hand soon,
Look towards the spaces between the night and day
Hope is only what you make of it...

The world is only one, and we each live a mystifying life,
But one thing we share, and it lives within each of us.
Is the soul of nature, the endless compassion of the human heart,
and the hope we can bring for the world because of what it gives to us

Jean H. Oshiro

Love *** Of The Intensive Kind

I've been in Intensive Care all my life.
It started out that way the day I was born.
No, I was not ill nor did I look forlorn.
My Mother just wanted to take care of me —
And she did just that as you will see.

Every time I'd leave the house she'd say:
"Button up your overcoat and wear your mittens —
Don't forget to slip on your galoshes, or
Your toes could be smitten".

Today my nose is stuffed — my throat is sore —
I didn't heed those rules of yore.
The ringing in my ears keeps singing ——

"Wherezzzzz your mittens and your boots?"
You'd think a girl of forty-nine
Would watch her health and GIVE A HOOT!!

Helen Bole

Mother

Where has all the years and time gone MOTHER?
It seemed like only yesterday that I was a little girl myself.
Now I have children of my own that I answer MOTHER, too.
Mom, GOD gave to me the greatest gift of all whenever he gave me, YOU, for my MOTHER.
I couldn't have asked for a more precious gem than YOU as my shining star. Yes, to guide me throughout the bad times and the good times.
Mother, you taught me how to stand on my own two feet;
Because of that I've become a much better and stronger person for it.
With You as my bright shining star I couldn't go wrong.
You taught me first you've got to be honest with ourselves.
With your Prayers and Guidance I'm very proud of what I've done with my life.
MOTHER, I hope I've showed you in some small way either by what I've said or what I've done over the years to let you know just how I feel. Nobody can ever take these precious MEMORIES away from me.
I'll always have them to hold on to for the rest of my life;
How lucky I've been to be able to take this JOURNEY with you.
Please know that your love will sustain me over the years.
MOTHER, I LOVE YOU, with all my Heart forever and always never to depart.

Dorothy J. Miller

Saint Patrick

He drove the snakes from Ireland,
It was a goodly deed,
Then he began to fill
A more important need.
The peasants gathered 'round him,
He plucked a shamrock from the grass
Let a moment pass, then pointed to the leaves,
"This is a sign that there is a God,
Who wants you all to know
That though you cannot see Him
He is close to you as clover—
God and Son and Holy Ghost!
He made us all
So now we must all thank Him
For reminding us this way,
And we must worship Three-in One."

Ireland became a Holy Place
With Patrick, leader of the race,
And God in Heaven must rejoice
That the peasants listened to Patrick's voice.

Alice Whiteside Jorg

Laudations

For one mad, manic moment
it was one hell of an ego trip.
I feel therefore I am, I am,
I write, I say something.

Elected I belong. Mail remuneration,
flattered to amortize my laurels.
Interviews, name in print, "local poet,"
"gifted person," oh negated neurosis.

Megalomania, be thou ever so...
bitter, prodigal, wasteful.
Swaggering down the avenue,
daring the world not to touch.

Venturing into the library
to taste what those other "gifted personae"
have to say, feel if they are alive.
They are, I am small, hide under my humility.

Roethke, Giovanni, Bishop, Benedikt, Bell,
Kavanaugh, Williams, Sexton, Lowell,
Oh Satan I will sell my soul,
when E. P. Dutton prints me whole.

Amy Foley Gustafson

In Your Memory

When we were young
It was so simple
The world was so small
It never existed beyond the playground.
My friends and I lived each day,
Not searching or planning just living.
Life was a bowl of fruit
Not knowing where we fit in
But we did not care.
Life was nothing, and reality, it never existed.

Now that we are older
It is not so simple
The world is so big,
Now our playground is no longer there.
My friends and I still live each day,
Now searching, and planning for each and every day.
Life is still a bowl of fruit
But now, unfortunately, we know where we fit in
We are nothing but an old discarded pit that no one cares about.
Life really sucks, and reality, it's a bitch.

Craig Beck

"Cottage To Mansion"

There was a cottage at the end of the lane.
It was tattered and worn, from all of the rain.
Its shutters were hanging by the edge of a nail.
and the windows were dusty - and soiled as well.

As we were walking one morning, in early May
We came upon the cottage that was in dismay.
We stopped in our tracks - and made a decision.
We would buy this cottage and make it a mansion.

So we paid for the cottage and started to work.
To make it a mansion we washed off the dirt.
We painted and washed and repaired all the panes.
Rehung the shutters and put them in place.

We planted some flowers, and covered the walls
to make it look homey and ready for all.
But it was our love that finished it all.

No it wasn't big and it wasn't tall
But with our love it was a mansion small.

Esther S. Kinder

Devil In A Bottle

Don't under estimate its power.
It'll take your heart, and cause you pain.
With time you will find
It was really just a waste of time
Only he has something to gain.
With nothing better to do, it'll turn you really blue.
It'll turn a good man bad.
And make a young woman sad.
That devil in that bottle has a real attitude.
Inside that bottle trying to forget the pain.
No more self pity, you know it'll drive you insane.
Be a man and make that stand, put it down or it'll make you drown!!
No matter what his shape.
Your fate he'll take, don't make that big mistake!
Hard to shake, hit your knees and pray
Lucifer's his name, trickery's his game.
He'll pick you then he'll trick you.
It'll make you lazy, make things hazy, even drive you a little crazy.

Carolyn Abbott

River Of Love

The river of love comes flowing down,
It's all around, it doesn't make a sound.
When you jump in, it will carry you along,
You have to sing its beautiful song.
You cannot hate or trade wrong for wrong.

You have to forgive if you want love to live
Anytime you pass by a friend in need,
You're expected to do a wonderful deed.
You cannot hide in love's strong tide,
In kindness and peace, you must abide.

For if you do not, you can't go on
The river will stop because something is wrong.
But the song will still be heard, it will be sung by a friendly bird.

If you want the river to flow,
You must join in and think good thoughts
For love is something that can't be bought.

The river of love flows all around,
You just have to find it, though there is no sound.
But you'll be able to hear with your heart and mind
Whenever you do or think something warm and kind.

Doris Jean Owen

"Jen My Dearest Friend"

I await the night, the night is mysteriously comforting to me,
Its cool air filling my lungs, at the same time its hot adrenalin fills my blood.
I'm safe in its darkness from the piercing glances of day.
I'm strong at night, my senses are unmatched. You can't see me in its shadows, footfalls are unnoticed, my scent is never close enough.
Tonight I left the light on, directly overhead, now we are reversed I am in your world and you mine.
I feel so naked.
My action is completed, do you embrace me or cut me? The voices
in my head fighting a losing battle, I listen to my voice because they are weak and predictable.
Tiny fingers pierce the waters surface.
I release my dreams to those with purpose.

Edward Heisey Jr.

The Dream Of The Rhino

A rhino slept in the hot summer sun amongst the dirt
its ear flickered to an occasional fly that tickled it so.
The rhino slept and dreamed.
The rhino saw itself as a butterfly fluttering along with gentility and grace, with the beauty of its wings full of color and life, as the rhino-turned butterfly dreamt this life.
The butterfly was like the gentle breeze that cooled the summer's heat
The dream made the rhino forget that its waking existence was encased in a bulky leather skinned body
whose only grace was being alive.
The rhino awoke to see on its horn a cocoon there
that some worm had formed.
The rhino cared for this creature being sure not to disturb it
until it bloomed like a flower of beauty into a butterfly.
The rhino remembered its place in life among the strong
and the brave and also knew now why the rhino is that way,
the rhino is to give worth to the dainty butterfly
by contrast alone, the two were beautiful together.

James G. Sides

My Heart

My heart is in pain, it's hurting so,
Its pressure is low.
It's laden and heavy.
My heart longs to be free.
For the burden that it carries makes it very weary.
My heart, it talks to me,
My heart I can see.
It's black and blue and bruised,
From everything it's been through.
My heart can endure a lot.
I know from all the battles it's fought,
And still keeps on ticking,
No matter what the extreme.
My heart needs to be free,
To sigh and breathe.
My heart, my emotional, sensitive caring part.,
That knows how I think and feel,
My heart, it will heal,
For it's strong, and it's real!

Gayle Burchett

Nature's Secrets

I, too, remember the garden -
its soft sense of peace, its calmness,
its gentle touch, and its love.

I walk the garden often these days
just hoping to relive its beauty, to
feel the wind upon my face, the sun
as it warms my soul, and to see
the birds as they, too, share its secrets.

As I move through the garden, I, too,
feel as one with its hidden secrets.
I feel its internal peace as if it was
only a breath away.

Like two souls coming together as one,
I see the trees touch one another in
such a way as to say I, too, know its secrets.

The sun is going down now, and I must go;
but as children do play here now, I know
that the secrets this garden holds will once
again live, for it is not set in memories,
but in that eternal place we call the heart.

Clarence David Jones

Life Of A Single Mom

Children are such a joy
I've been blessed with a girl and a boy
Times have not been easy for us
Due to the fact there's only the three of us
I hold down a full time job
I finally got rid of the drunken slob
Their father is a dead beat dad
And for the children I feel extremely sad
Money is tight, but I know I'll win this fight
My family has stood by my side
On this long and bumpy ride
The children are the most important thing
We love to laugh and love to sing
Happiness is now our main goal
And for this I would sell my soul
He said I could not do it alone
But without him we have grown
We love and respect each other
And I am very proud to be their mother
With love to my kids D. J. and Brittany

Barbara J. Strong

"My Last Poem"

Dear Ones,
I've been thinking lately, that the Lord may call me home.
My last words to my family, will be this final poem.
My sincere wish will be that you will call on Him,
for comfort and assurance that I'll be there with Him.
God has prepared my home in Heaven, and I will be safe there.
I'll be expecting you, my children, will you meet me there?
Accept Jesus as your Savior and live for Him each day.
He is there to hear and answer. Don't forget to pray.
My greatest blessing has been my joy in pleasing the Lord.
May you love Him, serve Him, and live according to His word.
God bless you, each one and know that I've loved you,
for I won't be completely happy if you're not all there too.

Your loving mother and grandmother.

Hazel A. Barnhart

The Broken Hearted Victim

I was once in love at one time. Now that my heart is broken,
I've come to seek my lost lover that did this crime.
I'm what one would call the broken hearted victim,
trapped in a world of loneliness.
Oh, how I wish that I had never gotten into this mess!
I thought that as much I love him, his love for me would be the same.
But when it came to the end of our relationship,
I became another victim of his, caught in a dirty mind game.
This mind game was cruel. At the end, I turned out to be the fool.
"That's o.k.", I said to myself, as I was writing his final letter.
Because I can find someone better,
Ladies, I give my advice to you to please really study him
and don't become another broken hearted victim.

Felicia Renee Lee

Joy

What is joy to you?
Joy to me would be knowing that your love is true
You think I know what your feelings are,
Oh how I wish I did. I have before wished on a star;
It didn't work of course. The only way
It could work would be if you told me,
For you are the only source.
Why can't you come out and say it?
You just don't have enough wit.
If you would say it just one time,
I would never doubt you again
If you would say it just once then you would win,
Win my heart forever
If you said I love you,
I would jump for joy!

Amanda Ramos

Unstoppable

All these little injuries getting in my way
Keep me from being less than me every blacking day
Sure it's a conspiracy to keep me from staying hard
Keep the wolf from the sucking sheep in the unprotected yard

You cannot scare me as I'm not afraid to die
My brand of indestructibility always starts with I
You cannot weaken me if I refuse to lose
You cannot crack my discipline with sex, pills, or booze

Your subliminal messages scrambled by a healthy dose of rage
For now I am nobody but I can see you from my cage
You destroyed my identity
You started this inner war
I am your future, motherf—er
Look at what's in store.

Frank Stepnowski

"Kiss Me"

Kiss me in the morning and in the moonlit night.
Kiss me when I say I love you and when I hold you tight.
Kiss me when you're unhappy and even when you're sad.
Kiss me if you're angry and feeling a little mad.
Kiss me because you love me and always want me there.
Kiss me because we are happy and such a lucky pair.

Eleanor Carrillo

Homage

Silken stream slipping from the new marsh that
lately slept beneath comforter of white,
touching with soft lips each shore.
Nurturing glacier milk feeding thirsty earth,
infant moss and tiny trees.

Whispering hush of leaves from sheltering trees
softens the air and the sun changes shapes
in shadows cast upon the murmuring vein,
innocent earthly clean life-giving stream.

Nothing stays it unless it be another
earthly element naturally
but wins a way around
in unworried immortality;
treasures endless moisture for the gathering
of precious rain.
I love the endless circle of sovereignty.

Estelle Jones Langston

The Legend Of The Pioneers

For you and me it was to be just a page in history called the Legend of the Early Pioneers.
They fought their way, they came to stay, to work and build, to kneel and pray, it's in the Legend of the Early Pioneers.

The chosen place for them was unknown but by the legend they knew they would be shown and when they'd reached their place of peace they'd hear it whispered in the trees it's in the Legend of the early pioneers.

In their search for the peace the pioneer placed trust beyond recall in a person they knew as an Augur they placed the greatest trust of all for as they pushed on into the wilderness to a home they knew not where, to the Augur they looked for guidance only he could lead them there. They often saw him pause and listen as they moved along their way there was a whispering in the forest, he must hear what it had to say. To others it was only a murmur but to him the bode was clear and the words through faith was guiding every pioneer.

That's how they learned of worthy guidance when the voice in nature spoke. Why they obeyed like ancient Greeks who obeyed the Dodona Oak. Why they pushed on through the valley and spread out across the land they knew whose voice was guiding them each word a just command.

Arnold Ditmer

Fall

Colorful flowers are fluttering and FALLing
In the brisk morning breeze
Autumn is fully flourishing
On this bountiful Pacific Isle.

Impressive sights attract attention
Like an unexpected FALLing Star
Or a timeless vision
Of a cascading waterFALL.

Memorable is the Enemy's FALL
Putting conflict and war to rest
As peace and calm spread over all
Life resumes triumphantly.
Have a thankful! FALL season!

Fumi Migimoto

Wisdom They Say

Look before you cross
Lend no money, have no loss
And never, never
Talk back to your boss

wisdom, they say
Let status quo be
Cover your eyes, no evil see
And always, always kneel to get eternity

wisdom, they say
Comfort, oh comfort, please, more reality convey!
Darkness gives way as sun will rise
With winsome whispers, "Let's truly be wise,
Open the ears, see with the eyes
Allow heart to maximize
Faith is a free fall, Joy has no wall
And Hope will probably smile through it all
Now, without delay, register:

WISDOM, they'll say

Judy Ann Masters

An American's Prayer

Let the trumpet of God sound out, America, for which you were founded.
Let her misfortunes not be counted for it is now midsummer.
Let her set forth renewed goals, not whispers in the distance.
Let her live in co-existence with all of her neighbors.
Let America reach out her hands of intervention through the land.
Let her not be sentenced because of her means of self-defense.
Let her be a voice of comment'ry to shout for a cause she understands.
Let her seas and shores be protected by God's merciful hand.
Let her not be deceived by those who walk in unbelief.
Let her sincerely be a place of endearment for all who have a yearning.
Let there not be a disappearance of her many dreams of reconciliations.
Let her grow strong a country with many moralizations.
Let America be a place of admiration; make the people proud of
her dedication.
Let her be a nation strong and rooted with great expectations.
Let her move, henceforth, to defend all who live within her splendor.
Let her days be lengthened; all who look upon her be strengthened.
Let her pour wisdom out upon her youth, giving them new dedications.
And like delicious fine wine let her be an individualist.

Diane M. Bernardy

On Wings Of Love

Come and fly with me.
Let me take you to that place, that will not be.
High, high, and high we will go.
Places and things we will know.
Love is you, love is me.
Love is like planting a tree,
Love is up, love is down.
Love is red yellow, green, white, black and brown.
Love is hurt, love is suffering, love is pain.
And that's the way we all came.
Charity, peace, and hope we all know.
Love is the only way to go.
As this fight is about to end. Try love try love
again and again.
It's the spirit everyday that give us these things to do.
On wings of love he will take us, and love we will to you.
On wings of love there are no laws, only grace.
So until the next fight, don't be late.

Harry H. Johnson Sr.

Greed

Greed - the destroyer of mankind,
Let us not teach it.
Greed - riding with the Four Horsemen
Bringing unhappiness, misery and death.
Greed - beginning in childhood with desire for another's toy
In men, for another's land and way of life.
Greed - let us not teach it.
Let us destroy it,
By the greatest rule of mankind:
Love - for each, for all.
The Golden Rule - given so long ago by the Greatest Teacher
Let us teach it,
Let us live it,
That Greed may be destroyed.

Julianne S. Hamilton

Rainbow For You

There's a rainbow for you in dreamland
Let's go there and find all the gold,
Your eyelids are heavy with dew drops
Too heavy for you to hold.

So close your eyes, it's dream time
As we climb up through the stars,
We'll find that pretty rainbow
And play up there for hours.

When we're through just playing
We'll slide down both the ends,
We'll find all the gold our pockets can hold
And bring back some to our friends.

There's a rainbow for you in dreamland
It's time that you were there,
So close your eyes, it's dream time
A smile will be your fare.

Joseph H. Saling

The Colossus Restored

Silent Guardian of sea and shore
Lift your flaming torch once more.
Cast open wide that Golden Gate
To the downtrodden, the homeless,
The persecuted, longing to escape,
Bid them enter the now empty
  Ellis Island stalls
Once the refuge of the poor,
  The weary and forlorn.
Together they again will blaze the trail
  And join the masses journeying
To a land of wheat and plains
Cottage or cabin built on hill
  or prairie sod
Blessed forever by "One Nation Under God."

Claire McTavish

Nite Eyes

NITE EYES-I saw them crying in the rain
NITE EYES-they never are the same
NITE EYES-they affect your body and your brain
NITE EYES-they look at you and stare
NITE EYES-are sometimes big and bold
NITE EYES-are sometimes piercing and cold
NITE EYES-they need a rest-some say they are over-blessed
NITE EYES-they seem to be the norm
When is the last time you saw a pair that are caring and warm?

Donald Edward Heitmiller

"Undying Love"

Sunlight glistens through my window, shining like a ray of hope,
Like a ballet dancer dancing, its gentle movements help me cope.
Soft lit shadows pass before me, rest upon my face so light,
That had I not been watching closely,
I should have missed his awesome flight.
I shall always bare remembrance of his sweet and gentle touch,
Of the way he'd hold and warm me, and other things I loved so much.
Was it yesterday you warmed me, 'twas it then the day before.
Old man winter now upon me,
he chills the warmth you once instilled,
Can he be so blind and stupid,
To think your warmth I cannot feel.
Tho' his icy fingers touch me,
frosting up my outer shell,
The fire within me burns as brightly,
As the fires that burn in hell.
I shall love you now and ever,
Until the sun doth leave the sky,
Until the last of dying embers,
Until the sun within me dies.

Brenda Sue Fredline

Vacant Building

Vacant building with boarded windows,
Like blinded eyes looking only inward,
What do you see in the realm of memories?
What scenes do you create from dust and darkness?
Or do they really inhabit your scared, faded walls?
Are hopes, and dreams, and strong emotions
Somehow captured in your empty rooms?
Do you relive them and laugh and weep,
As they replay themselves over and over
As you wait to know your fate;
Be it wrecking ball or interior designer,
Annihilation or rebirth?
How like man you are.
As the string of his years runs out
He looks within, remembers
and waits.

John M. Doyle

Lamentation

Shadows now move through my mind's attic
  Like dusty winds through an empty house

Where have all the hours gone

The wet faces and the laughter
  and the soft contemplative voices
In quiet coffee shops at midnight

Time boasted and endless skein
  of mornings and twilights
And then etched its deceit
  in the gray of my temples

Where have all the hours gone

The throaty smell of musky rooms
  where mystery lived like incense
And the rustle of pseudo-silk
  was an intrigue within itself

Mornings now come
  like cold hands
And rub themselves
  into creaky twilights

Where have all the hours gone...

David C. Gaines

The War Introvert

The anger swells
Like Hiroshima that fateful day,
Where all the kindred of that initial domain
Are consumed in the fires of frustration.

The residual decay
Is in truth, a moral calamity
Like a contagion of bacilli,
Which imbues a dangerous impotence.

Now I attempt to smote this most molten of emotion
With Sylvan-Conscious and Urbane-Rational,
But the rage is more than any past altercation.

Yet I know if I chose
The cooling shade of blindness,
The cancer would decay with blase tones
And reduce my emotions to molecular dust,
(themselves ever subject to inconstant winds.)

So eventually calm sweeps away ember and ash,
Ensuring no cinder flares back to life;
And neutralizes all that irradiated grit,
(again at peace with the virtue of self.)

Cavin T. F. Mooers

Vision Of Loveliness

I feel the moon shining in my eyes
like rays from the sun, lighting up the sky.

I behold the happiness of life in my heart
of that special day, when you and I had our start.

I inhale the moments of love in my hands
where the scent is like your perfume, pleasant in the air

I savor the presence of you in my room
like a lover's concerto playing all the right tunes.

To all of your loveliness,
essence and flair,

I am thankful to GOD,
because He made you with care.

danny williams

Meditations Of The Leaves

It's September! And it seems
like spring was only yesterday
When we danced and swayed in the gentle breeze,
We were so young and gay.

I remember the time young lovers
paused in the shade 'neath our tree
To steal a kiss and softly whisper
words not intended for me.

Little by little our summer coats
have changed to bright red and gold,
And our sleepy heads feel a little heavy,
Could it be we're growing old?

The time is getting near at hand
When we will flutter down
And make a golden carpet
To cover all the ground.

But there is a season for everything,
One to be born and one to die,
The earth below is soft and warm,
It's September! Let's laugh and not cry.

Berniece Cover

Feelings Of Nature

I feel the gentle breeze blowing in my face,
like the golden sunrise shines through white lace.
I've seen white doves high up in the sky
and sit here and watch them as they go by.
The ocean is so blue and clear as can be.
Like the waves hit the rocks and the sounds of the sea.
This poem I'm writing is to tell you how I feel.
About this certain someone that is quite real.
The clouds are slowly moving in.
There's a storm coming but I don't know when.
Even the wind is picking up quickly and fast.
I hope this storm will not last.
Oh no! Here it comes, it's time to leave.
Right now it's not the best place to be.
The thunder is rolling, the lightning is flashing bright.
You know it's a scary and strange sight.
Finally the storm is now passing through.
And see the rainbow and the misty dew.
Now everything smell's so clean and fresh.
So now it's time to say goodbye in the flesh.

Gail E. Taylor

Now

This moment
Like the last
Like the next
Contains the universe
In all its splendor
Its every essence
Like a drop is ocean
A seed a tree
This moment holds eternity
All its time
All its truth
Now is the result and source of all moments
Give this moment what you want to give all the rest
Protect it
Expand to it
Embrace and love it
Now in this very moment
All past is honored
All future glorified

Ginger Cobain

Rushing Of The Water

I hear a beautiful sound.
Like the sound of rushing water.
I try to get closer to hear, I try a little harder.
I look up way up high, the tallest mountain.
I see water coming down like from a thousand fountains.
I stand amazed at the sight.
Sparkling water, rushing sparkling like neon lights.
All adorned like angels in satin white
It is an awesome sight to behold in my mind,
all the thing God created I can see.
I feel so insignificant and small.
I clasp my hands and look toward Heaven.
Thank you God for giving your all.

Alini Frier

Christ Is Born

Awe-stricken shepherds, tending restless sheep
on Judean plains,
Sensed the wonder of a miracle happening
and knelt in humble adoration
At the Christ Child's birth!

Jo Burford

Ice Storm Of 1994

Sitting on the porch, wrapped in a warm blanket, listening to the lullaby of the soft rain on the lawn, I heard the sound change from soft melody to sharp static. Nature's orchestra was growing louder; rain changing to sleet gave a sharper note to the melody. Cold crept under the blanket, chill invaded the bones, ears listened sharply to the change of nature's song. Ice formed on power lines, tree limbs, shrub, and in less than an hour the lullaby of soft rain changed to the awesome, magnificent, frightening sound of nature's overture. Transformers boomed as they blew, yellow, green, red and blue lights brightened the skies, showing diamond power lines, glassy trees and limbs. Crash go the tree limbs as they splinter to the night sounds of nature's music. You stand, watch, listen, wait, afraid you'll miss the finality of the last crescendo as you witness the wonder, awe, splendor, and yes destruction, of the great ice storm of 1994.

Brownie Lawler

Cincinnati Skyline

What a wonderful view to behold.
Living near there was my goal.
Ohio River divides Ohio and Kentucky at this point.
North Licking and Ohio Rivers here also join.

Living on Northern Kentucky hillside for best view,
This panoramic sight always looks new.
With barge and train traffic increasing daily
Over bridges auto and trucks speed loudly.

In summer, pleasure boats cruise along,
Paddle wheel boats' calliope plays a song.
They dock here, at times, from many states,
To walk through them or cruise on one is great.

Sunrises and sunsets, to the right and left of you,
One never has time to feel very blue.
Here you feel part of the busy world,
To share this sight sometimes, with a pretty girl.

At night, this view is more spectacular,
Suspension Bridge and tall buildings lit dramatically.
Skyline of Cincinnati and Northern Kentucky, to be specific,
Has an hour long fireworks display in September, that's terrific.

Curtis A. Cook

Waiting

It's the middle of winter as I
  look out my window
The sun barely shines and the clouds
  are grey and low,
The temperature hovers between ten degrees
  and zero-
Trees are stark naked, branches black,
  brown and old-
They have nowhere to hide from the
  bleak winter's cold-

The wind whips and tears at them yet
  they bend and stand tall
They'll survive the winter like they
  did the fall
Green leaves that turned colors and
  were taken away
Impossible to hold them, they
  couldn't stay
No time for weeping so they wait in anticipation
For the spring and the warmth a brand new creation.

Carolyn Conway

"Look At What I See"

Look there at what I see, isn't that a lovely tree?
Look over at that stream, it is just as lovely as a dream.
Well would you look over there, what a gentle looking bear.
Hey look over here, isn't that a beautiful deer?
Look up into the sky, just look how high that eagle can fly.

Yet with water that isn't safe to drink, not even
the water from our kitchen sink.
And forest burning everyday, I see nothing in my way.
With all of the animals close to gone, how can I carry on.
The sun is burning everything that is known, because of the
rockets burning up our ozone.
So now how can what I see be, yet through my thoughts,
but still, look at what I see.

Would you look at what I see, I see things which were meant
to be.
I see not the evil in this place, only a need
for change in the behavior of the human race.
Don't you see the things I see? I see things that can still be.
So change most definitely must be, if you want to look at what
I see.

James A. Newbolds

Panther's Stepping Lightly

There!
Look there!
Behind the green!
Black sleek night,
Eyes glimmering emeralds.
Stealthily moving
one paw...then another...
A growl of pleasure,
The panther's stepping lightly
causes no disturbing action.
He slinks through the darkness
matching the night...just a pair of
moving eyes through the wild grasses...
Mice scurry into their burrows, they sense him,
they can feel... The panther's stepping lightly.
Larger beasts seem not to hear... The panther's stepping lightly
causes an animal to die under his paw.
Devouring his kill, he secretively continues on...
The panther's stepping lightly...
is heard by no one.

Cinsearae Santiago

Empty Soles

dedicated to The Silent March 9-20-94

In memory of Marie McGowen and Melissa Cavender
There were so many that you couldn't count them all.
Loved ones came to put them on the steps of city hall.

In the midst of thousands, I saw ballerina shoes.
I could imagine a little girl, with eyes of blue.

The satin wasn't shiny, and the ribbons were tied.
These shoes never dance, because their owner died.

I saw a pair that belonged to a mother and son.
For eternity, they'll be tied together as one.

There was a pair of old boots belonging to a man.
His wife brought them, hoping to make us understand.

That each pair tells a story about suffering and pain,
And about lives that will never be the same.

She hopes when they look, and see this tragic sight,
That Congress opens their eyes, and sees the light.

That these empty shoes belong to murdered souls,
And to broken families that will never be whole.

Cheryl Hopper

Within

Looking past the outside, I see a heart, soul, and mind.
Looking past the skin, I see someone generous and kind.
Looking deep into their soul, past their religion and color.
I see a person inside no different from another.
Paying no attention to what I see with my deceiving eyes.
I notice what really matters and ignore the racist lies.
We separate ourselves from them because we aren't the same.
We criticize who they are and call them meaningless names.
Looking past the black and beyond the white lies a person
just like me.
Searching for opportunities, fairness, and equality.
I admire this person greatly for never giving in.
This person is the same as you and me, if looked upon from
within.

Julie Michelle Bryan

The Greatest Of Gifts

Love is a gamble and love is a risk
Love can make you happy and love can make you sick
Love is free but love can cost
Love can be won but love can be lost
Love can be pure and love can be sound
Love can be elusive but love can be found
Love can be true and love can be faked
Love is too important when all is staked
Love is for the young and love is for the aged
Love cannot be harnessed nor can it be caged
Love grows with nourishment and withers with neglect
Love is hard work and requires respect
Love is for a boy and his dog and a man and his wife
Love is for everyone in all walks of life
Love is the greatest of gifts that one may share
Love is the answer to many a prayer!

Dennis Michael Wells

How Quiet, It Is

Soft rolling hills of snow,
listening to the wind blow,
how quiet, it is.

Fiery ball of sun perched low in the sky,
watching the crows wing by,
how quiet, it is.

And, there she stood, drinking this beauty in,
hoping to pierce the tree line within,
how quiet, it is.

And now, the footprints are slight,
once again in the early morning light,
how quiet, it is.

Glen R. Anderson

Whispers In The Morning

We said it was forever, and we meant it from our hearts.
Little did we know we'd grow so far apart.
When we said good-by, tears fell from my eyes,
I was no longer by your side.
Words to express my sadness, I could not find.

I missed the whispers in the morning.
I missed the way you'd hold me and say everything is all right.
I missed your annoying little ways, and the silly things you'd say.
I missed the kiss goodnight.

We said it was forever, and we meant it from our hearts.
When you said forever it was not to be forgot!
Now we're back together, not knowing what the future holds,
And together we'll stay until lead turns to gold.

Christina Gregg

The Chaplains

Lt. Alexander D. Goode, 31, Brooklyn, NY, Rabbi
Lt. Clark V. Poling, 32, NY, Dutch Ref. Minister
Lt. John P. Washington, 34, Kearny, NJ, Catholic Priest
Lt. George L. Fox, 42, Altoona, PA, Methodist

Four chaplains, two Protestants, a Catholic and a Jew
calm frightened men and distribute life jackets.
They give their own to those without.
On slanting deck, arms linked together
and heads prayer-bowed, they slip into the fired sea.
Fifty years later I see their pictures posted together
like a carnival backdrop with face holes cut in.
Separate snaps you'd send to your mom, change your face
for his if you dare. Push away winter clouds with sunshine.
Raise the Dorchester, warm the waterlogged chill from their faith,
dry their mother's tears, bring them back and expose patches
of stringy hair growing five decades in brine
Boned faces with teeth set in lipless mouths.
Don't test them again.

Herb Reich

Star Space ... Beyond Diamonds

Myriads of stars — we've gazed at them before,
lush trees, a breeze...
Science detracts from the true magic and mystery
of the place,
Many light years, these tiny candles of the moon,
are away from us,
We've measured and studied,
yet the romance of them remains...
The tiny beings here can only marvel and
stand high in awe of the glowing tapestry above.
Absence of light ... bright pinholes in the satin
darkness...
Falling stars ... star gazed streamers across a
subtle velvet sky...
Blankets of stars - laid at the creator's feet
Be at peace, and retreat into fields of
Beyond diamonds.

Jillann Brizzi

"Small Shadow"

She walked alone because it's all that she knew,
madly in love, but with who?
It was only an image, a fool's shadow.
She thought it was real, but what did she know.

He left her without even a glance,
She walks alone with the burden of a sour romance.
There is no hope in sight and she doesn't seem to care,
no more burdens of life running through her hair.

The lingering summer breeze brings her out of her daze.
She no longer walks alone, for, a smaller shadow now walks
beside her through the summer haze.

Julie F. Wilson

Skater's Reverie

The whir of blades on a moonlit night
Go gliding swiftly o'er the ice,
Never resting, never ending,
Torso tense, limbs extending.
Every skirr of skate forbidding
Thoughts of blissful carefree living.

Pleasant memories of the past
Stop the speeding stride at last.
Slower, ever slower skating,
Sparkling ice illuminating
Inner peace and harmony.

Ann Marie Stoltz

Relight The Flame

Relight the flame within your soul,
Make yourself fulfilled, and made whole.
Be useful, gainful, while on this earth,
To care about your deeds, and what they are worth.

Sew the seams of wisdom, you have gained,
Broaden your ability of knowledge you have retained.
Patchwork and color scheme, will surely be seen,
That is a sure sign your heart is clean.

Remnant of fabric left over unused,
Choose a bouquet to not be refused.
No more leaving our work undone,
The day for salvation, is soon to come.

Through the storm, through the night,
At the end of the storm, came the light.
Be perfectly sure of any blame,
Open your heart, and relight the flame.

Florence Daughtry

"Shadows"

A shadow upon my heart
makes me step into the light,
to dissipate my tension
into the oncoming night,
I wonder at the activity,
marvelling at the fear
of people running to their cars
far away from here,
Homeless people, runaways,
walking in the street
no clothes on their backs,
no shoes on their feet
We treat them like shadows we have but we ignore,
unless we're a part of the family
that's lying on the floor,
like shadows of people
they once used to be
we look with our eyes
but we refuse to see.

Julie M. Baker

Yesterday's Sunshine

Many stars have shone before us
Many winds have rustled leaves
Many times they've told their stories
Under the cool shade of the trees.

And with each passing tale I wonder
What they have lived and done and seen
That makes the silence or the thunder
That breaks the image of the dream.

It must be yesterday's sunshine they're spewing
Along with some old tattered yarn
In the end adventure brewing
Made of bold words, free from harm.

Onward to tomorrow now
It's easier to face the day
When each performer takes his bow
And the past is safely put away.

Still the brightest moments linger
To live without the tragic side
A world with style they do not hinder
Over miles of sleep we do abide.

Janice Barancyk

Life's Road

Life is but a road we travel as we journey through this world.
Matters not if it is short or long; what matters most is that
We do no wrong.
How you live it is the key. Do you live for self to please
Only thee?
Or do you try your very best to help those in need whom you see?

The road is wide and winding through steep mountains hill and vale.
You stumble, fall, then rise again to meet our Saviour's call.
Now the road to heaven is narrow. Few travel on its paths.
The going's tough, things get rough; it seems we can't get past.

But do we stop and take the wide road and follow earthly man?
Or do we continue the struggle to reach that golden strand,
And stand before our Saviour, a saved and honest man,
And wear the crown of glory, for we obeyed His command.

So as you journey through your life, which road will you be taking?
Think long, think hard and no mistake be making.
Plant your feet firmly on the road of service to our king.
Walk boldly on your journey, let no one stand between.

For Jesus will walk with you, if you but ask Him to.
Just place your trust in Jesus; He's the only one for you.

Fay Ward Hillberry

Mighty Men Of Valor

Oh, mighty men of valor who stood so big and strong,
Mighty men of valor who seemingly could do no wrong.

When weaker men had fallen or were overcome,
These mighty men of valor refused to succumb.

By the thousands, mighty men of valor slew their ancient foes,
Swinging sticks, clubs, and swords, they struck their mighty blows.

Where are these mighty men now who seemingly could do no wrong,
And where are their mighty deeds acclaimed for so long?

Why, these mighty men of valor all lie within their graves,
Surrounded by lesser men who used to be their slaves.

In death there is no fortune, fame, or glory,
Except through the living who embellish every story.

The true heroes, you see, are not those unafraid to die,
But those paralyzed by fear, yet brave enough to try.

Harry E. Butts

Misery

The up has fallen, all is down.
Misery scars the lives of all. Nothing has priority over conformity.
The sadness goes unnoticed. The rush into depression is considered
good.
The anti-enlightenment is not seen as such. The past comes forth once
again. There is no end, one questions why they fight.
Why? There are no decent answers.
They don't even realize there's anything wrong.
They think conformity is good. They don't care that conformity
stifles creativity.
They don't care as they bring forth weapons; the slaughter continues.
The different, people or actions, are bleached.
Colors remaining. Briefly. A fire burns, materials thrown.
Trash, worse; hide. They hide. So many hide.
Another minority is destroyed before their cause is taken up.
Another minority, one of twenty, survives; laughter.
So untrue. They hide while society destroys them, unseen.
All different are denied entry into history; never existed.
All has fallen. All is dying.
We live, possibly fight, fall over and again, age; and ultimately die.
All is down. Misery.

Edward Joseph Jonas

"My Writing Souls"

Writers seem to have a certain rhythm in their heart, and soul and mind, it's always of a certain meaning, real words of a meaningful kind.
And as we grow older, our thoughts deepen through the years, our thinking takes away the fear, and gives life new meaning in every year.
Writing should be a treasured thing-no matter what subject we think of and write, it's a pleasant experience to read a new poem, and very much cherished to read it in "type."
When our writings are published on the Poets page, it makes a smile come to my face, and I know others value my ideas too, my thoughts I have shared with all of you.
Though some people don't understand we "writers' plight" we even get up and write in the night. It's so peaceful then to find the right words and they are precious in our sight.

Charlotte Marie LaPeer

Foreboding

"Come back! There is a tale to tell.
Moonlight's exposure of life in its spell.
Carrion's smudge upon the earth trying to fawn.
Principles wrestle back, their whited breaths gone."

I turn upon my bed and punch my pillow.
I will not listen to desolate voices filled with woe.
I turn again,
And again.
They keep calling and demanding, beneath a muddy sky.
A fragile comet hits hard; the mountain is too high.
Light bursts wide open upon my face.
I want to run from this place.
Kicking and biting mentally, I reach for the bed railing.
I rub perspiration from my eyes and they are still seeing.
Not in an orange room where white roses belong.
Up high upon a mountain where wolves are slinking along.
Like finished music, I know the forms that maul.
They are coming in a rush toward me, and I fall.
I lie upon the floor with a bang, that wakes me up.
I stumble to the kitchen for coffee, from the largest cup.

Audrie M. Fiskaali

"To Eternal Lover"

A shira to Eternal Lover
Most found tribute to Faithful King
My Beloved who dwells in chamber of heart
Forever my Rachel, may I seek after Thee
But, can one be finally found
Pursuit of eternities will forever lead to thee
To know more of the Goddess of You
Blessed sovereign of my every moment
Ruler supreme of the gift of my breath
That You and I, Sweet Bride might cleave in passion
For this, my quest, does this man live

Barry Rubel

May

May our tomorrows be free of sorrow and full of joy.
May our yesterdays simply be in our memories.

May our todays keep coming one day at a time until we can
 say we have learned all we need to learn and lived
 our lives full and carefree with no regrets of
 yesterdays gone by.
May we find love and our destinies in each enjoyable step.

May our days be filled with sunshine and rainbows, but also
 with moonbeams and sparkling stars.
May we learn to enjoy today, release our yesterdays and let
 our tomorrows be forgotten.
May we learn to love today, tomorrow and forever...

Jessica L. Bur

Modern Music

The buzz of the alarm sounds the battle hymn.
Morning has broken.
The glory of the sunrise is forgotten as
The distant fanfare of rush hour traffic greets the brand-new day.
The ticking of a clock keeps the beat.
Coffee pots and slamming drawers strike up the melody,
while the dripping of a faucet hurriedly turned off tinks softly underneath.
The polished mumble of newscasters carries the baseline broken by
the clicking of stiletto heels on the cheap linoleum floor.
The beeping of a microwave answers and the horns return.

Recitativo.
The fast-paced whirlwind of piping keypad numbers and the swish
of fabric against the door — SLAM.

Finale.

Heatherlynn Waldo

My Darling Wife

My darling wife, the pride of my life
 Mother of my children you see
I will take this time to write a short line
 To thank you dear, for being just mine.

The years have gone by so swiftly
 So many my dear and so soon
Why it seems to me only months you see
 Since we wed on a rainy afternoon.

Some rain fell on us too my darling
 Oh the times I've broken your heart
But you would forgive then we'd start to live
 Dear I pray that we'll never part.

We both now have Christ as our master
 His love does dwell in our hearts
 I'm unable to say it on paper
How my love dear has grown from the start.

I know my Lord God will guide us
 He'll lead us on through life's way
Now darling lets bow our heads quietly
 And just thank God for this day.

Charles Everett Scroggins Sr.

The Yellow Rose

It beckons me
Must I heed the call?
Out of despair and pain comes the most sincere inspiration
For the yellow rose
A simple flower that speaks a lifetime of verse
A simple flower that can make the difference 'tween life and death
Just as a broken cup can hold no water, a broken heart hold[illegible]
love
Is that my destiny?
To wander without aim through life without purpose, di[illegible]
 no calling...and no love?
Is it?
IS IT?
I cannot believe that I could be forsaken this way-
 to be left in pain until the flower fades away
Can it be so?
If I will never be a poet until I have hurt enough
 -if that is all I lack-
I shall throw away my pen!
For no art is worth this pain-
Thorns of the yellow rose

Christopher L. Paul

Amiss The Skies

Your eyes kiss me beauty, my dear.
My eyes grace and find your fingers;
Your wise face lingers in my mind.

Your hands give me feeling, Ellen.
The tips of your nails rouse my soul;
You the goal, ships thousand set sail.

Caress me, be host of my dreams.
Throw cold-blooded thought down below;
Let golden floods flow through my drought.

Oh let me consume you dear heart.
Yes, I will us together, forever, my dear;
Yet I fear that together we never will be.

Andrew Mitchell

My Grandpa Carrison

My Grandpa Carrison is always full of love for everyone to see.
My Grandpa Carrison will always have love for everyone, even me.

My Grandpa Carrison has a smile that's as big as the glowing sun.
My Grandpa Carrison is just like a kid who always has fun.

My Grandpa Carrison has lots of love in his heart.
My Grandpa Carrison loves each of us and he will never part.

My Grandpa Carrison is like a man sent from God above.
My Grandpa Carrison is like a very special friend who is full of love.
My Grandpa Carrison

Jennifer Lynn Carrison

Findings

As the moon shines over the horizon,
My heart begins to shatter.
The noise I hear rumbles in the depths of my soul,
Reaching for my heart, it shows no mercy.
The thumping is unbearable
And I hold back my scream.
I wait patiently for the break of night...
For the darkness to brighten.
But night defies me
For it remains motionless.
The sun is long gone, far from my reach.
And I hope to myself for sight
But I look and find nothing.
Soon enough my soul will devour,
my heart will rebirth,
and I shall renew.
For there is hope,
As the moon shines over the horizon.

Christina Scalise

Waste Land

From all around one can see,
miles and miles clear to the sea,
Tons of sand covering what was once our society,
Here there across this land,
Are the remnants of what was once built by man,
Nothing now remains but wasteland,
In man's insatiable rush, upon his very hands lies,
What is now us, from where I stand, with only human eyes to see,
Nothing will survive here, for an eternity,
Man in his rush to conquer and consume, wakens the monster of
his doom,
Into the bowels of the hell that he made, good intentions lead us into
Greed and despair, our darkest hour, waited somewhere,
Now our worst nightmares unfold, seems like fairy tales of old,
See what we have become, dust in the heat of a burning sun,
Wasteland.

Frederick J. Newman

Empty Faces

I see the empty faces, I see there are no smiles.
My heart goes out to them - if I could comfort them awhile.
I can almost feel their little tears, I can see their wounded hearts,
I can almost hear them crying somewhere in the dark.

Little lives filled with storms - their days are filled with rain,
Their bodies bruised and broken, gray clouds surrounding them.
Yesterdays have long been gone, todays are yet to be,
Tomorrows to overcome, their future - what will it be?

My heart is aching, I cry for them, Lord,
All the little children who are hurting in this world.
Lonely and lost, so many know their pain,
How do we put love back in their lives again?

I would kiss their empty faces, I would give them all my smiles,
I would mend their wounded hearts and dry their teary eyes.
I would give them each a rainbow, fill it with their dreams,
Put my arms around them and show them what love means.

And if I had only but one miracle to give,
I would gladly give it to them for the way their lives have been.
There would be no more shattered lives, no more tears in their eyes,
Just a world filled with songs and special...wings to fly.

Gloria Trudeau

A Glimpse Of A Dream

My life is but a passing dream.
My heart is full of joy.
My mind is of another set.
I know not what to expect.
The yesterdays have come and gone
And left me with impressions
Of wounds that left their memories to bear
All healed by a laughing heart which guides
Me through each lesson.
Tomorrow is a brighter day
I know not what it brings
As life unfolds its wondrous events
I shall coil around the inevitable.

Christine French

Not Handicapped

Thought I walk in darkness,
My heart sees what two eyes would.

My fingers touch and feel beauty
In everything my heart sees.

My ears are like magnets.
They don't miss the tiniest sound.

And seemingly as if being led by an invisible hand,
My feet wander away from dangerous paths.

I am not hindered by my eyes being closed.
I behold every beautiful thing.

My nose tells me the fragrance of flowers,
The freshly mowed grass and the fresh smell of raindrops.

My hands are as a mediator,
Assisting me with all things.
So readily I accept my life as it is
And being thankful for all things,
Makes it much easier.

Corinne Brown

Renewal Of The Heart

On that first day we met,
My heart was as cold as a wintry day.
It hadn't been touched by you, yet!

I gazed into your beautiful, dark eyes;
Their warmth enveloped me and melted the ice.

The sun began to shine bright.
My heart was in flight.
How quickly it flew,
As if it were brand new.

It was like the first day of spring:
Life renewing itself as the robins sing.

Carrie Taylor

Innermost Thoughts

As I look to the horizon - though we are miles apart,
My innermost thoughts are of you, sweetheart.

Our hearts are drawn closer day by day,
As our web of romantic intrigue will display.

Darling it is not mine to ask why........
But to reply.

My courage is under pressure...I am vested,
Good men and women my country has requested.

There is but one USA...my native land,
For which I proudly stand!

Its honor I will universally uphold,
With loyalty and patience our love will enfold.

A straight line isn't the shortest distance between two hearts,
It's our reasons for loving each other, sweetheart.

For every mile I travel around this earth,
My loving you is given a new birth.

Darling, in my life you are a very special person.
I await...our future in unison.

Juanita Farrar

The Regret

I see her face so sweet and kind, with blood all over in my mind. I see her again in pain thou is, I see her saying again "Stop let go" again, and again.

She was so innocent to hold, until she left him, he smite like old, again and again it repeated itself, in his mind she was so kind, yet again and he abused her so, yet he loved her, oh.... how he loved her, thou saying again "Stop, let go" again and again.

The outline of his fist against thou's face, the contour shape which showed his haste. Again it repeated itself, it ended up affecting her health. Saying again, "Stop, let go". Again and again.

This is what most call hate, but it is which of love to thou and yes he shall call her name in agony, with her repeating, "Stop let go" again and again.

He recalls when he trust his fist to the deceased temple, thou falling down the flight of stairs, her body covered in blood. He now sits in regret to be left alone hearing, "stop let go," again and again.

Jacqueline Riedel

"Without You"

In my eyes I will always see you, in
my mind I will always think of you, in
my heart I will always miss you, and in
all of me, I will always love you.

Today I sit without you watching the
Ocean rushing the shore, peacefully above
me the sea gulls soar, children playing in the
Sand, lovers walking hand in hand.

This was our favorite place to be, you
loved the sun, the water and the warm
Ocean breeze, but what I loved the most, was
You loving me.

I'll not say goodbye and I'll not ask why, as
in time I know we'll be together again, the
hardest part is not knowing when.

Carolyn Selvoski Reedy

A lost love

His face is fading now
my mind is going blank
his face is fading now
an outline of him I can hardly make

My tears are frequent
my memories are few
his face is fast fading
his voice has disappeared too

They say he was great
they say I loved him dear
but it appears my affection came too late
for him and most of his memories are no longer here

His face is fading
the light is growing dark
his face is fading now
I don't remember his last remarks

I know soon the light will go out
the sound is long since gone
his face is fading now
the light will not be here long

Brandy Mohr

My Mother

My mother is a lady who cares
My mother is a lady who can help with my fears
My mother is a lady who will never leave me
My mother is a lady who made me see
All the hardships in the world
Really don't have to be!

My mother is a lady who will do anything
To bring my sister and I a special surprise
My mother brings her love which helps us rise
When the neighborhood is low
My mother needs to know
That I love her so
And I will never let her go!

Charron Simmons

"My Name"

As a cloud full of rain Jesus came down and called
my name. Now there are no chains on me for
Jesus has the keys. He keeps them over there by
the ocean, where I heard the whisper. Past the sadness
and sorrow next to the son under the spirit of the palm
tree, and I arrived and was raised from the dust and
trust is a must. Then my sins were cast to the
winds and I was free at last. Glory be, glory be,
free at last, free at last, my God set me free at last.
Now today I am an itinerant preacher that the Lord
Rose from the dust, for it is the Lord that I trust.
I go from place to place telling His name, it's
still the same—Jesus, Lord of Lords, King of Kings,
the rock that doesn't roll! Messiah, and
the word became flesh and dwelt among us. The Lamb
told the way and was led to slaughter and won the
victory. Then rose as He said He would. Truly
you are! "I Am!" He said, "Peace be still."
And the wind stops. Who is this man?
You are I Am.

James R. Arns

A Happening

When in the desolation of my spirit
my pleas evoke no answering solution,
I cast about in anguished thought
for alternate plans of action.

I see the problem narrowly...
as blind men touch the tusk and see an elephant...
just partially.

I choose the field to be experienced...
I stay indoors and shut the world out;
I scan the sky and miss the squalor at my feet.

Four windows face in diametric opposition...
I turn to one, rejecting all the rest.

I view the light emitted by the stars and sun
reflected from the edges and the surfaces.
The patched and patterned illumination
becomes a happening
my eyes interpret to my soul.

My prayers indeed are not unanswered.
Solution lies within my channeled vision;
My eyes must see as others do.

Barbara Purtle

Untitled

At times like this I close my eyes and dream of death and dying,
My soul escapes its prison, as my body is left lying,
On the ice cold earth of sand and soil that leaves my passions
burning,
As I exhale my heart of turmoil of which I am still learning,
I release my pain and anguish which chains my emotions inside,
In hope to fill the void and cause the engulfing sorrow to subside,
I cannot start all over or try to begin my life anew,
I can only dream to wipe the slate clean and forever forget you,
When my past is past forgotten, and my future not too late,
Then there is room for the present life, in which I control my fate,
I open my eyes to find a world as dismal as before,
The difference is the glow inside, that helps me go on once more,
When my heart is not a captive of some other loveless soul,
I grasp the reigns of destiny and steer them to a new goal,
Along the path through pain and sorrow without a lamp to lead,
But with You by my side I know, in the end I will succeed...

Gregorio Cesar Israel Climaco

Growing

The first time we met was strange and new
No matter how hard she worked, it was better for you
'To Just' know you!
Like the seasons of the year, your thoughts change and become
clear.
It's not like the first time you met, for now it's good to be here.
Day after day answers are sought, to the questions you've hidden,
Why you and your mother fought?
You judge yourself - wrong and right,
With gentle persuasion, your friend sets your sight.
To find that young girl who once was so gay,
Before growing-up sent her scurrying away.
While on the next journey through young womanhood,
You discover more clearly,
Why you were misunderstood.
It will take hard work, laughter and tears
To find the best of all these years.
But, when my teacher and I are through,
Together we'll find what's true.
My heart, My soul will then be free,
Again to be the very best of me.

Emily B. Moffett

When I Come To The End Of My Road

When I come to the end of my road,
No more sorrow there will be,
For I will be resting peacefully.
When I come to the end of my road,
My soul will be blessed, with peace and happiness.
When I come to the end of my road,
No more sickness there will be.
When I come to the end of my road,
No more sickness there will be,
When my Saviour's face I see.
When I come to the end of my road,
My work on earth will be done,
Then my new life has begun.
When I come to the end of my road,
No more death there will be, for
I will be living with "Christ" eternally.
When I come to the end of my road,
I will join the angels band in that happy, happy land.
When I come to the end of my road.

Fordyce Green

This War Machine

Lost in a prism of insanity, Burning inside
No, not insane, it's all very logical, it's destiny
Despair masks these days which I wearily stagger through.
Pain is a virtue which the weak claim in defiance of true emotion.
Real emotion is not pain.
Pain is what we must learn to love.
Rage and hate: Disgust and meaningless existence,
These are what the love of pain creates.
The blackness of indifference loves company,
As does misery, and though it can't rain all the time,
I love that it does.
Does this show you enough?
Can you see inside of this fined tuned wrecking machine of war
Closing in on the misery of myself.
An arm outstretched, reaching for all that which hides
in the dark, wet corners of despair: or rage and hate.
It reaches for all that nightmares are made of!
Loneliness is a peace, It is contempt and contentment.
So on grinds the ruthless machine of forgotten battles,
and the ones it shall still face.

Daniel Hall

Once Upon

Once upon a dream,
no one said they loved me, friends or family.

Once upon a discussion,
I let my feelings arise, but it didn't matter.

Once upon a feeling,
I was left alone in a world, dark and dreary

But now, upon a vision
my dear wipes away a tear, holds me
close, and loves me.

Jennifer Forshey

God Is My Hope!

God in all His majesty, is my God in Heaven above.
No other will I worship, no other will I love,

I like to read the stories of my Savior and my Lord,
How He teaches love and kindness throughout His precious word.

In the Bible is His promise of the truth, the way, the light,
To gain entrance to His kingdom some wonderful day or night.

So I pray thy daily guidance as I walk the righteous path,
So on the day of judgement I will escape God's hostile wrath.

Please help me walk beside Thee holding tightly your nail scarred hand,
For I want to live eternally with my Lord in His glorious land.

Agnes L. King

Happy Hooper Day

This is for all us Hoopers
None of us are really party poopers
Carry on with gambling, cards, dice, and bingo
Just don't forget all our foolish lingo
So, get out your nickles, dimes, and quarters
Time to put your best foot forward
We don't have enough of these family dinners
But we are all Hoopers and all of us winners
Now hurry and past the veggies and the meat
So we can eat these fattening treats
And see which one of us can't be beat
Come on and go Hoopers
So we won't be seen on TV's
Family Bloopers!

Donna Kaye Hooper Foster

Understanding

These words are for you - our first-born, our joy,
Now grown to manhood - no longer a boy.
Oh how special you were, and will always be
Deep in the hearts of your Daddy and me.

You came to us as a gift from above,
A blessing bestowed on our young love.
We couldn't explain, though we wanted to,
Just how we loved you - mere words wouldn't do.

Now time and love, moving hand in hand,
Have spoken for us, you can understand.
Now you can whisper "My Son, My Son"
As in years gone by your father has done.

And feel in your heart the surging joy,
The wondrous love for this tiny boy!
And finally know, so clear and true,
The nature and depth of our love for you.

Betty J. Kiener

I Watched

I watched you lay there
Not so long ago - so helplessly
Remembering the things you taught me.
I dreamed you had something to say
- I got the vision on the next day
Knowing it wasn't your fault
I was being pushed away.
I watched you twitch with pain
And cry out for God's mercy in vain!
I watched you
take your last breath so peacefully...
I closed your eyes with my own fingertips
After the angels had come and taken you away
I sat by you and held your hand
even though it had turned ice cold
And I knew you were gone...forever.

Christina Zak

When The Boy Becomes A Man

His life begins - he let's the whole world in; Letting out his cries of confusion. And soon he knows his hunger grows, Reaching out to what's all around him. Traveling down a one-way street on the wagon of success - Standing up for all his dreams, he'll always drive his best. Meeting many people along the way - He's gonna make it someday.

Another stage - one of sufferage; the drags of Life have crept behind him! He starts to think, and he starts to drink; Still letting out his cries of confusion. And there's sudden change and it's mostly for the good, He'll start to realize what he can't and what he should. Then he'll remember the man he tries to be - His eyes will open, you'll see.

And in the End, he'll lay upon bed, His wife and children stand beside his head. And though his dying lips have tried to form a song, He closed his eyes and never told anyone, that he was proud to live the life he lead. He looked at his son, and this is what he said:

When the boy becomes a man, It isn't hard to understand;
He'll change the song he plays, but he's always with the band;
When the boy becomes a man.

Archie R. Pairadee III

Kaleidoscope

Cushioned on a bed
of crinkling, cuddling leaves
I look up lulled by the lullaby
of fluttering leaves, whispering winds.

The spell of autumn magic
tantalizing, seductive
captivates my restless spirit
stills swirling thoughts
of thousand unfinished tasks
spirals my body deep inside
to birthing place of wonder
awe and delight.

Christa Henrich

One Thing

One fulfillment, to be heard
One goal, peace of mind
One commitment, to be understood
One reward, to be loved
One regret, the past
One hope, the future
One relationship, myself
One constant, truth
One thing, oneself's uncompromised integrity.

Collin E. Brown

The Gift

The sun is setting behind the mountain, the shadow
of darkness is drawing near, the moon is rising
majestically beyond the horizon and reflecting
brilliant lights of color off the new fallen snow.

What is that sound? Do you hear it? It sounds like
the wind gently teasing the silvery icicles twinkling
in the moonlight.

Listen...there's a soft, mellow sound, touching ever
so softly the mountain and flowing down to the snowy
valley below and returning again to the peaks of white
to play its magical song over again.

Did you see it? It passed so swiftly - the swirling snow
encircling my hair with a crown of sparkling flakes of ice.
Breathless and bewildered, I look to the sky...There!

A wave of an arm and a flick of a whip, the image is gone
just as quick and I knew at that moment that I had been
given a special gift.

As I turned my misting eyes to the East and gazed upon
The Eastern Star, I thanked the Lord for this wintry night
and letting me behold such a wondrous sight!

Carolyn Grider

Flattened Automobiles

A truckload
Of flattened automobiles passed me as I walked down the road.
The cars were once the star of the show;
And the road.
They were placed on a pedestal for all to see and admire in the show
Room when they were new.
Now off to the scrap yard they go—
Not much to see
Now!
The same happens to us!
When we are (born)
New, everyone admires us
And makes a big fuss.
Then we get old and worn
And then off to the
Cemetery
We
Are
Borne.

Glenna Weber

Heroes Among Us

Think if you will in your daily career
of heroes among us, bold against fear.
They call from inside the strength to stand
when others sit with folded hand.

We seldom wonder when chance to meet
the volunteer medic from down the street,
exactly what makes him act
when others simply turn their back?

A colonel charged with pilot command,
in '68 he took a stand.
In a Skyraider near Dong Hoi,
he risked it all to save a boy.

The Medal of Honor sung in a drawer,
now sirens howl as he bolts for the door.
Donning a jacket with the Star of Life,
he quickly kisses his honored wife.

Racing again into the breech
his actions have much to teach.
For America to be the freedom land
heroes among us must take a stand.

D. Thomas Lang

Reflections

Days pass slowly in monitored moments
of layered time; a caged world within
a world, frantic, furtive, filled with
ancient echoes, sad as old ruins.

Nights pass lonely in stretched hours of
dark fantasies and illusions, sleep fitful,
haunted by specters of splintered lives
and dreams unfulfilled.

Years pass in age old ritual, each step
circumscribed. Yesterday is a memory woven of
tears, tomorrow lost in a mirror image of today;
a jungle dance seen in a silvered glass.

Jean B. Finley

As The Clothes Line Flows

I stroll down the walk where the clothes line grows,
of many faces you've come to know.
You've seen them on the front page news,
these are the women with no choices to choose.
Murdered before there loved ones eyes,
mothers, children, and passerby's.
Why couldn't the lawyers and judges see,
the lies, the games, as the life that couldn't be.
Look at the line to see the faces,
Warm smiles and love, these mommies..no one replaces.
Support the cause of changing laws giving them there rights,
so they don't have to go under ground, nor hide in the
the gloom of nights.
Spread the world to heal the wounds of children who are
orphaned by there fathers' gun,
who did away with his own life, not to face his son...
why did he leave me motherless, in a rage he went wild,
in grief I am alone, I am an only child.
Now my grandparents are raising me they try to ease the pain,
as I see the clothes line grow the tears mount as rain.

Geri LaVeglia

Springtime

Bring back the memory and the scent
Of meadow lands with dew at sunrise.
Oh, bring back again to my heart's content
The warmth of spring and pleasures of summer tides.

Spring is with us at last, again
With blooming buds and flowers.
We have missed you, as a long lost friend
Yes, springtime gives us fragrant hours.

As the aroma of flowers in bloom emanate the season,
It's realized there is a time for all things.
Our seasons give no promise of return, or reason,
Without us willing it, they come and pass by with wings.

Suddenly the summer burns,
But sadly at sunset, the winter returns.

Elizabeth Joyce

Untitled

God paints the sky with exquisite artistry
Not for just a day, but for eternity.

He created a world of beauty;
He created man and set him free.
How can I doubt His plans for me?

How can we express our gratitude?
By believing in faith
which does elude.

By thanking Him for His Son
Who for us forgiveness won.

Betty E. Stisser

Amidst The Jaded Woods

The stillness of the virgin dawn, stirred only by the mist-laced veil of morning rain, and the ebony crows' wake-up cawing through the crisp, chilled air, echoes the birth of yet another new day.

I sit here nestled in the warmth of his living room,
drawn by the panoramic view the windows invite.
I stand in awe of the dense, towering pines, all dressed in shades of green refreshment with boughs outstretched before the heavens.
I can almost hear their voices lilting endless praises
to the One on High...thankful for being among His Grandeur, and the freedom of movement in which they delight.

The rays of platinum sunlight slowly spread to warm the dew-kissed grass of his nearby lawn, and choose not to ignore an earthen bed that boasts the softly scented petals of magenta beauty...as those of Michael's Rose.

The stately giants have endured ages past, shedding light to "living life to its fullest;" this wisdom they seem longing to impart, for even amidst the jaded words, a little life continues...that of Michael's Rose.

Each new day that unfolds renews my faith in how real my Lord reveals Himself; I need only open my eyes and heart to see His Supreme Artistry, thus feel His Presence.

Faith T. Irving

That Lucky Old Sun

I am solemnly reminded
Of one of Louis Armstrong's songs
Describing the sun as having nothing to do,
But rolled along all day
While he worked his troubles away on his jazz.

I wonder if Armstrong really knew
It was the very sun's rays
That gave him the energy to move about
Or which made plants grow
To provide food for him and the world.

Whether Armstrong seriously wrote
Those lyrics or in jest
Americans are facing similar irony today
In denying credit to our sitting President
For his accomplishments at home and abroad.

As sad as it is, Bill Clinton has opened
A new Chapter in American Foreign Policy
For the first time transforming a Nation
Without bullets nor human destruction
And only historians can give him his due.

Anthony Kofie

Listen

Listen, a still quiet voice, it is speaking - it speaks
of peace, it speaks of joy

If we would pause just for a moment, stop all of our fussing-
stop all of our fighting, put a stop to all the killing, and
violence just for a moment then we could hear and receive
this sweet message this voice is sending forth.

Listen! It's in the air everywhere
Listen! It's giving instruction,
Listen! It's giving warnings of swift destruction that's to
come, can you hear it?

Listen! It's not loud,
Listen! It's so sweet, it's so soft
Listen! It comes with power all mighty, Power from on high.

Are you tuned in to listen, to hear what this powerful
message will be?

Turn and listen to what will come forth.

Elizabeth A. Harrison

City At Night

Evening comes to the city last rays of sun shining through clouds of pink then grey in the fading, lingering, lights soft glow.
A city outlined in deep shadow is suddenly transformed by lights soft glow.
A city outlined in deep shadow is suddenly bright with street lights soft glow.
Cars hurry along with headlights ablaze unaware of the splendor of of the suns last rays. Buildings like a child's pile of playing bricks light up with the coming of light turning the city into a fairy land.

At the edge of the city stands a cathedral dark and tall. Its former beauty diminished by the coming night. Soft lights coming on hidden in the facade of the cathedral welcomes life as grandly and solemnly in its beauty it stands.

Inside sitting on the steps of the great altar with head bowed low hands clasped tightly about bended knees praying silently sat a young woman in the altar lights soft glow. The bustling noise of the city so near yet so far is lost in the peace of the cathedral and the one sitting on the steps of the great altar lost in prayer.

Enid Jo Williams

I Consider Myself Lucky

Tired of living a silly charade,
Of playing dress-up and pretend,
I want you to know how much I care,
Before our friendship is to end,
I'm not saying that it's over,
Or that I want our friendship to die,
I just want you to know how much it hurts,
When I have to say good-bye,
The feelings I have for you are strong,
Stronger than any man alive,
A friendship like ours is hard to work at,
But for you I will strive,
I consider myself lucky,
To have found a friend in you,
A friend who gives me hope, strength, and courage,
Along with a love so true.

David John Koon

"The Author Of It All"

He worked in the darkness, towards a light that only he could see...
Of the deep inner beauty revealed in many faces
And then, he left this treasure of love for posterity,
To recall that which was found in unexpected places.

The laughter of a child, loved in his mother's embrace...
The contentment of a husband, blessed with a loyal wife,
The joy he found just being with her, nothing could replace...
She made the day and she made the night radiate with life.

He continued on what he knew just one day had to be,
Often the ideals of the weak perish before they die...
Enough if but one a part of this beauty he could see,
The Author of it all spoke from the cross for you and I.

Bob Wangler

Deadly Times

In the darkest months of the deadly days
One would be killed for the love of one
Until the next will come
For it has come for the hate of hurt
For which the trail of death has come for you
Death has come but not as one,
But as two has been killed by the gun
The gun is down for now
For death has gone down for now
In a hell inside us
But be sure it will rise again

Billy Richter

Waiting To Die

You come into this world unaware and unsure,
Of the everyday struggles you'll have to endure.

An innocent baby lays peaceful, asleep,
Along comes a stranger and takes it to keep.

An innocent child walks one block to school,
Along comes a stranger, fatally cruel.

An innocent woman at the bank getting cash,
On the way to her car, strangled with her own sash.

An innocent man on the job doing work,
Crushed by equipment by some careless jerk.

An innocent mother about to give birth,
Complications arise, she's leaving this earth.

Is anyone ready? Does anyone know?
When it is "their time", where will they go?

You live in this world unaware and unsure,
Will today be the day you find out if you're "pure?"

Debbie Lynn Saltiban III

Another Lost Love

I had the most wonderful dream last night
Of you and I by the fire's light.
Not a care in the world as you held me in your arms so tight.
A full moon, stars above, the crashing of the waves upon the shore
And being with the one I love, I could not have asked for more.

You looked deep into my eyes of blue,
Our hearts were racing and our words were few.
All doubt was suddenly erased and I knew our love was true.
Your kiss was so sweet and tender by the fire's glow,
The time was right to let emotions show.

Gently you reached out for my hand to hold
And placed upon it a diamond on a band of gold.
It was more wonderful than any fairy tale ever told!
Then you softly whispered...
Together...life was a sweet as heaven above.
Unfortunately it was only a dream of another lost love.

Debra A. Swearingen

The Challenger's Corner

Enter the challenger, proud and bold to meet his fate,
On a chance to list his name with those who are great.

Born into a world where high expectations reside,
And the price paid for failure is cheers on the other side.

But the challenger persists with confidence in each move,
For those who lose are forgotten with little left to prove.

With his fury unleashed and a KO in sight,
The challenger does battle and shows the world his might.

For life is a battlefield with victories the goal,
To succeed is a virtue but losses take their toll.

Then enters the champ, beaming in his winning ways,
His successes are proven for all of his days.

What is it that champs have that challengers must,
In order to succeed and win mankind's trust.

Is it persistence or timing or creativity or money or such,
Or is it a flame deep within burning hot to the touch.

The champs are mere mortals, the challengers are too,
But a distinction exists since the champ has come through.

With a shrug and a groan the challenger returns,
To the corner of dreams for to win he still yearns.

Joel Greenman

Echoes

Friends' voices still to hear,
often times sounding so near.
Chasing away the midnight fear,
so frequently through the year.

Music, laughter, conversational sound,
noise that is constantly around.
More friends to be found,
breaking the stillness that will surround.

The feelings that are left in these walls,
echo throughout the halls.
All to be left behind,
carried only in my mind.

All echoes that now ring true,
this chapter in my life is through.
As I close the door,
to hear no more.

Charles A. McAninch

Retirement No Fun

In the spring of 1975 we sold all our cattle
Oh! How I miss spring time for calving.
Picking rocks, raking, hauling bales, cultivating corn
The alarm would go off at four thirty each morn.

In August of 1975 a tornado hit our area
Thanks be to God no lives were taken.
Prayers and fellowship were a combination
Not once was faith in community shaken.

Retirement finally had to come in 1984
Alvin's health failing more and more.
With heart problems, Alzheimer's, Colostomy, too
I thank God daily for the great health He's given me.

In April 1987 had our farm sale
Friends said I looked sad and even was pale.
People came from afar to bid and look
Knew we must let all go... The last chapter in our book.

I love to bake and remember the lonely
While Alvin tries to enjoy his big brown chair.
I'd rather be sitting down by the creek
Pulling in fish, sometimes loosing gear.

Betty Lou Pollestad

Autumn Aspens And Apples

Listen to the quaking aspen
On a crisp autumn day;
Gaze upon their shimmering golden leaves,
Gently moving in the breeze.

Take a walk out to the old orchard,
Gather red and yellow apples;
Off the twisted antique trees.
Think about making tasty apple pies,
Applesauce and apple butter.

Watch squirrels and chipmunks scurry about,
Dashing up and down the trees and
White tail deer leaping through the woods.
See how the white firs blend with the
Gold tamaracks and purple oregon grapes.

Then know God's touch in both the aspens,
Apples and in the woods.
Thank Him who bestowed,
These beautiful autumn gifts.

Anne Shirley Linden

The Soldier

There are hundreds and hundreds of men of fame.
Oh! I really couldn't say them all by name.
There were Washington, MacArthur, Grant and Lee.
They served their country for liberty!
But the best of all was he who climbed up a hill-
Not a man of fame but an ordinary Bill,
Joe, John or Jim.
Did they win fame?
They didn't give their lives for some old game.
They went to serve their country true,
But they smiled;
For they died for the Red, White, and Blue!

Gerald Bloss

Patrick Daly

Patrick Daly, Patrick Daly, did you die in vain?
Oh, Patrick Daly, children's keeper, pray you made some gain.
Your love of children was unsurpassed, tho they were not your kin.
Patrick Daly, Patrick Daly, your death was more than sin.

For death snuffed out a helper, a true and trusted friend.
Who cared and loved the children, who went to any end-
To make them feel important, that life was not a waste.
You always had the time for them, you never talked in haste.

How could this happen to you, you savior of the child?
Who cared enough to love them, kept them from running wild.
Who tried to give some meaning to their worth and life on earth.
We have to believe at this time of year, and reflect upon His birth.

We must believe your time was up, you served and made your mark.
But those who took your life from you, had better listen-HARK!
For you were loved by everyone-both parents and their kids!
As keeper of those children, yourself you never hid.

You loved each one and nurtured them as if they were your own.
Whoever gunned you down like that has got a heart of stone.
That was so cold and ruthless, but it can't fan out the flame.
You'll live within their hearts and souls, they'll never forget your name-PATRICK DALY!

Judith Bienfang

Wish You Were Here

I can see you sitting by the window
on a dark and rainy day;
perhaps sometimes thinking of me
or of the things I didn't say.

...and I wish you were here - or I were there
for just a little while,
I'd hold you in my arms, say nothing and make you smile.

There's an aura about you
that turns my night to day,
and paper isn't enough
for what it is I'd like to say.

I can see you so alone,
perhaps sometimes thinking of me,
of the times of long ago
or of the times that aren't to be.

I can see there's a loneliness
that fills your empty heart,
and if I could tell you how I feel,
I fear I wouldn't know where to start.

I can see you so alone
lying awake in bed;
perhaps sometimes thinking of me
-or cursing my memory instead.

But still...I wish you were here, I'd not let you go again.

Dean Huffstutler III

The Mighty Ocean

The mighty ocean reveals its strength
On a stormy day, so well seen
That it shows its power.
At times the ocean can seem mean.

When there is a storm
The ocean turns gray
To reflect that hue of the sky
That is so like a jay.

The swirling waves go this way and that
It has the motion of an erratic dance.
Now, one has much respect for the ocean
That has been created by the Power that is God.

Elaine M. Horvath

Nightwalk The Highland Keep

I caught the sweeping silence but briefly
On the rising wind,
As the secluded valley unfolded
Just beyond the bend.

My only audience, the whispering juniper
Cloistered upon the meadowed hill,
And somber spruce looming tall and still
Like monks robed in silent grace and benediction.

Fireflies flickered on whirring wings,
And quivered the air with luminous glows,
As the tendrils of whispering current sings
Through grasses that respond in rhythmic trembles.

A glitter of stars cloaked in bright new twinkles
Assembled like unexpected guests,
To share with me
The humble vespers of the gathering night.

Raindrops brailled their secret message
Across the surface of the tranquil pond,
And applauded themselves on decomposed leaves,
Thusly, ending my nocturnal walk through the Highland Keep.

Doye Ford

Under A Spell Of Tranquility

It is a far better thing I do not rely
On the superstitions that blind my mind
  Break free from the evil of unwanted lust
  And shatter my confining sarcophagus

For I believe in beauty and being true
Yet something haunts me inside my refuge
  Over the course is an everlasting thought
  That maybe there's something more that I want

This reaction utters such a strange aroma
To wake my feelings from their coma
  But by being locked up, waiting for some answer
  A spell breaks with the power to enchant her

Such pleasures and pains do we receive
In an erotic torture that helps deliver me
  On adventures that make things seem so hilarious
  Have now begun to spin me until I'm delirious

So anxious without fear, that we're not dreaming
You are all that I'm seeing
  For there's no crypt on earth that can seal me in
  Like I've been captured by your vision

James M. Jones

Farewell, Farewell My Beloved One

As God awakes you on the break of Sun, He has chosen you to carry on until you've reached your destination. And as a close friend and relative, I feel I should say farewell, farewell my beloved one.

Though we had our misfortunes just like every other, the outcome became astronomical because we wound up caring more for one another. However your sweetness, kindness, bitterness and laughter will always remain within my heart, mind and soul until the very end. And as you prepare yourself for departure, for now the time has come, I feel I should say with warmth and joy, "farewell, farewell my beloved one."

Andrew Cannon Winstead

The Storm

As the lightning flashes and the thunder rolls,
Once again, I'm left all alone.
Since you left, many hours have passed.
I don't know how long this storm will last.

Here in my mind, lie a million doubts,
I no longer know what you're all about.
You no longer laugh, you no longer cry.
All emotions in your heart have long since died.

So here in silence, I motionlessly sit,
Wondering where in your heart do I still fit?
Just another question that's floating in my mind.
One of these questions where answers are hard to find.

Heidi Wilkinson

"Down Under"

I wrap myself in all these wonders the Great
One has given to us here down under.
I look about these tree's on this mountain side
the beauty that is hidden to us; lies here deep
inside.
Let the wisdom of the Great One touch your soul
see the beauty and he will fill you with love
untold.
Come Autumn while everything is still green
the beauty shall unfold in colors of yellow
and gold; it shall be there for all to behold.
Listen while music made from branches above the
rustling of leaves birds of different breeds
how they sing so wonderful.
As I look to the sky an ocean of blue unfolds
before my eyes.
I wrap myself in all these wonders the Great
One has given to us here down under....

Jesse L. Rea..

Choices

Two trees stand side by side,
One is straight and tall
And the other is twisted and bent.
Each tree had the same choices,
One chose to live and the other to die.
The strong one reached out to neighboring trees,
The weak one pulled back its branches and bowed its head in defeat.
The strong tree became stronger
By overcoming the trials of the life in the forest.
The weak one became bitter.
As the months passed by
The roots grew deeper beneath the strong tree
And its trunk grew straight and tall.
The roots under the weak tree are shallow
And its trunk is all twisted and bent.
Many years have passed by
And they are still standing side by side.
The strong tree is looking to the future,
The weak tree is waiting to die.

Anna M. Farrow

New Direction

Along many paths straying in opposite directions
One searches for answers amidst past reflections
Wandering in wonder with a far off stare
Blind to reality, cursed by a near-sighted stare
A dreamer of dreams, an oddity to the norm
Continuously growing and searching, weathering every storm
Ignoring all obstacles on this quest of unknown reason
Pondering not only the questions, but the reason for the season
No longer with a boy's sensitivity not yet with a man's affection
Hoping to find answers and happiness along this path of new
direction

David Case

Their Love

When we know God, the saviour of our souls,
only by knowing Jesus, will we be made whole.
The dark clouds of our life then roll away,
we will be with them on high, on that glorious day.

Our souls always searching for some sort of sign,
can cease the endless search...they are there all the time.
We've done it to ourselves, when we become lost,
they give us their love...at no extra cost.

God and Jesus knew us before we were born,
if you know them, you are not lost nor forlorn.
Peace abounds, their love comes from above.
because of their gift, there is no greater love.

Johnnye Kleckner

The True Hero

I did nothing wrong so to say.
Only I was different in another way.
I was imprisoned for believing all men are equal.

Now freedom is just another word-
Off and gone like a bird.
I was happy and free until that day,
Until I was captured and led away.

Now here I am in jail.
I wasn't offered a trial, not even bail.
I have fought nor resisted violence solves nothing;
I just hope I'm not forgotten.

David Capozza

Life As A Painting

We are born on this earth in a space frame called time.
Our actions are like a painter's brush stroke,
Or a poet's thought written in rhyme.
Childhood's desires and frustration are sketches
On life's canvas to create a scene.
Throughout lifetime colors are added to express
Our moods and show to the world what we mean.

Green is for the envy we have for those who have a lot.
Blue is for the sadness in our heart for things that we have not.
Black or dark is for despair we feel on some trying days.
Shades of gray are for indecision on our part to find better ways.
Red is for the passion or hate we have for our fellow man,
And to experience life's pleasure and adventures in any way we can.

Light colors show our optimism, happiness, and days of sunshine.
And to let others know we are doing just fine.
When our days on earth are finished and they lower us to the grave,
In the space frame of time will be our painting,
To show what we have taken from mankind, and what we gave.

Joe Dylik

Manna

If peace ruled
Only once - and
Clouded minds were cleansed
Hearts would grow and the seeds we'd sow
Could tame the warring winds. We cannot
Remain at odds. - Time's chains are not
Unfettered. Though wanton souls ache to grow,
What matters is not the latter.
Wondrous things await for
Souls who strive to be what
Mortals could and
Would - if they only wish to
Be.

Gary Bennett

On Tolerance

The sands of the earth are beneath your feet;
open your heart and from hatred abstain;
give naught unto malice, none to deceit—
leave not the souls of others cleft in twain.
This world of ours is not for the taking;
destroy the vices of warfare and strife—
the whole of our time fashioned for making
our thoughts and our senses enriching for life.
One may be "heathen", or just plain knave,
yet a creature of God, as me and thee;
lay down thy weapons, be forthright and brave,
and fight for rights in the land of the free.
Eternities united, hand in hand,
for the future good...the future's demand.

Jason Winter

Libraries

Who knows how high the mind can soar——-
Or what depth it can explore——-
Who, but he whose pen is thrust——
Into his yearning, burning thirst.

It is he who gleans your words and phrases——
To build of them rocks-of-ages——-
Where honey drips and earth-biles flow—-
Where the lamps of knowledge glow.

It is here the feast of man is set——
Where all the minds of man are met——
It is from here our brothers call——
Who dared climb high enough to fall.

Flora Spears

"Slipping By?"

Don't let life slip you by
Or you will wake up one day and wonder why
You will wonder what could have become
If you had only stuck to your guns
So you can't give up, and you can't give in
You must not let the evil win
So follow your heart and stay free,
Only yourself is holding the key
The key to happiness, the key to success,
Is to stop, look, listen, and rest
Whatever your task is that you want to do
It can only be reached with faith from you
So believe in yourself if you want to succeed
And to believe in the Lord is all you need
Face up to your problems, think positive
With help from above, you will live and live
So live a happy life, don't live a lie
Or you will wake up thinking life is slipping you by!

Jeffery Grant Amsden

What Lonely Is...

They came for him today and binding him to the litter,
orders were given in a foreign language,
falling on the frailty of late Autumn,
rustling sounds of Winter approaching.
Time moving as pages and leaves turn in the dim light,
the figure lies quietly alone,
drugged and forgotten,
glass blue eyes staring at an unseen ceiling where a bug buzzes.
They took him to a place he used to visit far away from home,
a place where he would be safe from harm.
He could not speak. He could not walk.
The weather was cold and his face was shaven.
Let mine be an understanding heart.

Catherine Berra Bleem

Thank You

People always appreciate what
other people do for them.
Some people say "Thank You" but
some people don't say anything at all.
When people are kind and caring it
touches other people's hearts.
When people do things without being
asked it makes people happy.
When people say encouraging and
uplifting things it makes people have hope.
When people show their love it helps change
other people and their hearts.
People sometimes give other people things as
a way of saying "Thank You"
We should all try to have these characteristics
all the time.

Desiree Crawford

Home

Home is where you can take
Off your mask and shoes, relax and be yourself.
It is a place where you speak freely to your
Family, not having to weigh your words.
Although sometimes we hurt those we love most.
Home is where you can forget the day, collecting your
Thoughts and solving your own problems.
One's home is characteristic of the folks that make this place
Called home, such as books, pictures, plants, pets, hobbies.
Home is your corner of the world where you climb into bed
At night, where peace and love entwine.
You awake in the morning
Regenerated to begin a new day in this world again!

Grace Porter

"Sweet Dream"

Sweet dream I adore you
My life with all I have to live is for you
My heart can't ignore you
You are the fragrant light that fills my soul

When night wraps her tender arms around me
Then once again
I'll feel the soft embracing of your charm as it surrounds me
Till slumber has found me
Where I can touch the fragile dream that we are one

If you could but caress me
Then and only then would true love bless me
Hold me and press me
Into your endless warmth for I am cold.

Damon Leigh

The Lonely Walk

The lonely walk to Calvary
Our Lord took it for you and me.

He was mocked and whipped time and time again.
He was denied and left alone by disciples and friends.

He was scorned and called a blasphemous Jew
As He took the lonely walk to Calvary for me and you.

Two thieves hung with Him that day.
One cursed Him the other one prayed.

The day grew dark, the end was near
And our Lord cried out in fear.

"Oh heavenly Father, why has thou forsaken me
On this lonely walk to Calvary?"

Three days later He arose again
A new life to begin.

You and I are totally free
Because of the lonely walk the Lord took to Calvary.

Elizabeth Hansen

Where Did The Little Boy Go?

Where did the little boy go?
Out back in the Cherry tree-a favorite spot - you see
Now to the front on a summer sled - a card board box -
lemonade for a fee.
Where did the little boy go?
Down to the brook where the big kids go - a Tarzan's swing
on a dare,
Foraging the dump for a treasure - ah! a big rat's lair.
Where did the little boy go?
Hopped a ride on the milk wagon - cool ice for a summer treat
No nickel for a Crown Cola to beat the heat.
But - Where did the little boy go? Down to the school yard -
Big fight - might blow - Little boys do that, sometimes - you
know.
Where is the little boy - Where did the little boy go?
To the river - a friend - quiet times - to fish - to pray.
Would that it could always be that way.
Where did the little boy go? To war in a far off place - he's a man
His country called - an embrace.
Did the little boy go? The little boy has gone -
Gone to the sunset in the Great Green Forest.

Ernest A. Botti

Treasured Friends

Some friends I've had, I merely outgrew
Others were there for one reason or another;
Some in life are there for convenience
Others are true and blue like dear mother.

But there's one other kind of friend I have
That only my Lord could send my way.
He plants this person at the edge of my life,
As I'm oblivious to what they do or say.

Time slowly passes and I become aware
Of this beautiful Christian rose growing in my garden.
Just waiting on me to discover its treasure,
And when I do, I feel I've received such a bargain.

Only God could give a gift to someone so unworthy,
A gift that is precious and fragile and treasured.
He has entrusted to me our special friendship
One filled with love, and fun and pleasure.

Thank you for being where God wants you to be
To love and to nurture and to old-fashionably care.
Thanks for all the listening and sharing and encouraging
Thanks for so plainly...just being there!

Judy Archbold

Our World Becomes

dedicated to Molly Peterman
Meadows where green grass grows,
Out of our cities, far from our homes,
Lakes where fresh water flows,
Long journey to travel to reach this world,
Yards full of grass turn to stone,
Place life in the ground and let grow,
Extermination, exhausts our soul,
Time will come when we will grow old,
Enjoying a world so barren and cold,
Right next to us our children, our souls,
Moonlight reflecting off of stone,
A thank you from those young, to their peers old, (for)
Neglecting nature, burying it below.

Fran Murnaghan

To My Wife: Norma Comin Carranza

Never have I met a woman like you:
Outspoken, strong but sensitive too.
Roses worth giving once a week or two, but
Money I spend for a gem or for a show
Are only worldly things to you.

Children are truly a happiness to you,
Or to your husband who loves them too.
Maybe I'm wrong to judge you, yet
I sometimes feel like I'm losing you,
Not to any man but to the boys
who are dear to you.

Coming home late at night makes me worry,
And on the phone you've never tried to say sorry;
Reaching our goals we strive and work together,
Remembering what is best for Kevin and Kyle's future.
Awe! for a five-year marriage, to my dear beloved wife,
Now, what we can ask more from God than a longer life.
Zestful world! we've never been that far,
And where could we go without a dollar.
(I LOVE YOU Norma Comin Carranza)

Efren P. Carranza

Lady Of Liberty

The meadows are green, birds fly far and high.
Pearls of smiles shine from the sky
Reflecting colors in our eyes
Listening to the ocean tides.

Sands sparkling in sunlight of silent sounds
Memories on our lips peaceful and profound.

Stars shine where I fly on a free bird of time
In a country of art, music, poets of perfect rhyme.
Where heavens shine through windows of our mind.
Lady of Liberty with you I float on a rainbow
Where the seasons in our souls can flow.

The pianos play, people free to pray
What even their religion tries to say.
Theaters filled where stars are born
Playing patriotic songs.
Dawn lights the sky, I'm glad to be alive
And see your eyes in the skyline.
Lady, Lady of Liberty,
Where lovers can love, singers can sing
And dreamers can dream.

Frederick Jay Leitzes

Falling Star

I was watching the sky one hot summer night;
peering into the heavens at the stars soft light.
It was clear, no clouds were around to see.
There were many stars there shinning for me.

All of a sudden, as I stared with delight;
I saw a star falling out of my sight.
A bright streak of light went across the sky,
and I knew I should make a wish that night.

So I wished upon that falling star,
to be a great poet, famous, renowned.
As I imagined it, I had to sit down.
I could see my name up in lights,
and people would know me and get my name right.
I would be wordly and have much success,
and sign autographs, no less.

But when I came down to earth,
the star had faded and fallen away;
and I knew that I would have to wait for that day,
and remain now an unknown poet to all;
giving my love in the words that I call.

Debi Hensley Moeckel

Wild Violets

I can remember a little girl
picking wild violets with her mother on a warm spring day.
The little girl was stooping over
to grasp a fresh purple violet
with her tiny childlike hands,
while her mother also gathered the
wild violets that carpeted the yard in amethyst and emerald splendor.
The little girl proudly handed a fist full of
wilting violet to her mother, who
marveled at the wondrous gift, which inspired the little girl.
How I would like to return to that time,
and to that little girl who had
no cares in the world, except to
run through the fields, pick wildflowers, and be
held in the security of her mother's arms.

Heather Lynn Hart

Canute's Tide

The Norseman's wind keens through the sedge,
Pine laden—with old stories of the sea.
The distant cry of a wheeling tern
Splits wide the silence.
While boats lie sleeping, sea-abandoned,
On their sides—aweary.
Waiting the next coursing tide to work anew.
The wrested land will dare the sea at flood again
As on this self-same sand before
A Danish king did dare—nine hundred years gone by.
"Stay back, ye waves! Stay back!" he bade,
To no avail—till men of Orange came
To curb the sea and steal her land—
Bank high the dykes and drain with skill
To claim new land.
As always—though—the sea can wait
and wait
And quietly win all back again.

Hubert W. Dean

What If?

When far in the future my thoughts seem to stray,
Fear grips my heart, soon I'm carried away.

Tangled in sticky webs of confusion,
Struggling hard in tomorrow's illusions.

Race through the next day, the weeks or the years,
Find it so difficult holding back tears.

Events that might happen, disasters befall,
Can I withstand these calamities all?

Is there no end to what might or could be?
Panic and dread seem to overcome me.

Then silently tugging, I feel in my heart,
My Lord seems to say, "Take one day as you ought.

My Grace sufficient for this moment alone,
With Worry and Fret PEACE will never be known.

Tomorrow's My burden, be not carried away.
Have faith in My promise, and live in today!"

Michele Carr

A Tribute To Greg And Dino

Dino was a special friend, so loyal and so true
He came when you were small, and he grew up with you
A closer friend you never had, with Dino by your side
You'll never forget the love you saw, when you looked into his eyes.

He followed you through life, like a shadow, always there
He fought for you, protected you, because he knew you cared
As years went by and he got old, you didn't let him down
You gently carried your faithful friend, when he couldn't get around.

You had 15 years together, Dino always by your side
And then too soon the day arrived, you had to say goodbye
I watched you as you struggled, to stop the flow of tears
With all your friends around you, that you've known throughout the years.
They came to say goodbye to him, sadness showing on each face
As they watched you gently carry him to his final resting place.

Sharon Welch

Andalusian Song

A solitary castanet on a Spanish eve
Heard amidst the wheat and given reprieve
By the tumbling, trembling twitter of a guitar
A ghostly cancion for a fallen star

No bell rang, no word was heard
No bird sang, no soul was stirred
No one aware of the silent serenade
Asleep, they dreamed of stars that fade

Ghost bards have such icy hands
Playing ghost songs in icy lands,
While dying stars and shed waning years
Star songs hearken their failing gears

He was her sun, he shone all bright
Now he is done, and so is her light
She sleeps alone, no kiss or caress
Can stifle the tone, or undo her dress

As turbid castles in the terraced cloudscapes
Do float so emptily in fields of night,
The unseen scents of ardor's airy escapes
Rouse dreamsongs of forlorn orbs torn from their height

Marvin I. Guymon

In You, In Me

In you I see
A beautiful soul
One that's kind and sweet
Pure and whole

In me I see
A destructive past
One that's destroyed
Your house of glass

In you I see
You're no longer the same
For hard is your heart
And I am to blame

In me I see
A will to turn
No more do I want
Those bridges to burn

In us I see
A beautiful thing
It'll bring smiles to our faces
And make all hearts sing

Stephanie Hillen

Mother's Love

In your eyes I see
a beauty like no other
Grace and charm that
is yours alone
Wisdom that only
living life can bring
In your eyes I see
all I hope to achieve.

In your eyes I see
all I hope to be
Patient and caring toward
others
Proud in who I am and
worthy of your pride
In your eyes I see
a mother's love

LaNae M. Roe

Where Are My Wings?

Where are my wings?
A bee, a moth, a butterfly,
A lark that sings,
An eagle in the sky have wings,
But none have I!

See! See! The glint of sun
Shines and delights on Wings; I run
In search of sights; the sun
Gives wings those lights;

I am alarmed
Because I cannot fly;
Am I deformed?
Unfinished wings can't fly unformed!
No wings have I!

Sweet Nature, fair,
Each to her own she brings
Breath from the air, the song it sings; but
where,
Where are my wings?

Sandra Wallraven Stone

The Dim Lit Room

A chance it was that room was there,
A chance I sat in just that chair,
A chance his eyes could not refrain,
Not pierce my soul and chase my brain
From walls of the dim lit room.

How I'm held in such a fashion
By his unrelenting passion.
And how I've come to love this thing
Since fate made way my heart to sing
That night in the dim lit room.

I should not love that man I found
In those four walls to which I'm bound
And should not pray that fate might play
So fair a game to let him stay
With me in the dim lit room.

Peggy Jo Mason

Unappreciated Life

Tiny, almost obsolete circles
a circus of rings, different shapes
gathered together in confusion
to be joined by others
catching speed, while being tossed,
into a tunnel of nowhere
Stepped on, splashed, splattered
tormented, like a tired boys eyes
spent crying in time
such as these, helpless drops,
from a thundering cloud
of pain
and loneliness

Melissa Kowalski

A Peace Disturbance

Sitting on the grass,
A cool windy breeze
came by. The willow trees
waving side to side
as a little bird sings
its tune.
Later, walking down a
path I hear a roaring
waterfall getting closer and
closer. Then "Boom!"
a storm has begun. Running,
Running through the forest
as fast as I can
to beat the hard wind
and rain.
Soon, all went calm and
fell to a sleep.

Mary Drach

Possessor

Locked. Imprisoned.
A slave to my dark desires.
Bound and gagged, I own you.
You are what I say you are.
Slave.
Your mind, your body, your soul
Mine for the taking.
You are an extension of my will,
pawn.
You are nothing without me.
Am I nothing without you?
Who is master? Who is slave?
Why am I afraid?

Mike Ursu

A Memorial Day

A day of remembering
A day of pain
A day of honoring
For all who came.

Some survived
Some did not
Some lost forever
None forgot.

A day of memories
A day of sorrow
A day that'll last
For many a tomorrow.

They gave their lives
They gave their arm
They gave their strength
To protect freedom from harm.

Some survived
Some did not
Some lost forever
None forgot.

Theresa Flesher

Out My Window

I see outside my window
a figure of you and me
being together happily

And I say to myself
is this really true?
Are you and me two?

But I do believe
this is true, that I don't
have you, don't have me.

Because it's all a dream
in my greatest fantasy
that will never be
because you don't even know me

Sherrie Hauser

Reflection

Past the gilded mirror
a glimpse of a silhouette,
A look into yesterday
of raven hair, smiling eyes.
Naivete of youth spent
replaced by gray sadness
from hard lessons learned.
Inside the young girl
lives, laughs, loves.
The world sees only gray . . .
but she sees raven.

Sandra K. Day

The One Before

We both have loved one before,
a love we will never forget,
I have let go with mine,
I wish you would yours.

The love you have for me is not
in your heart, you have not let go with
the love you had before.

It's hard to understand how you
can love her, even though she's no longer
your love, somehow you did.

Sandra Stroup

"Love Takes A Holiday!"

What would happen if love were to take
A holiday?
Would your world crumble?
Would you feel betrayed?
Would you feel forsaken?
Or would you be outraged?
Would you understand and know God
Is in command, and that his word must
Stand, in this sinful land of man!
Would you apologize for not keeping
His commandments and the misuse of
His names?
Would you try to talk with God about
The promises you had made?
Would you not defend yourself if
He were to ask?...
Give him love and heed his word,
is all he ever asks...
Now tell me what would you do if love
took a holiday from you?

Roxann Lewiel

Untitled

"A mouse is mightier than
a lion" I said to him
and he laughed in my face.

He said I know nothing
and I should open my eyes.
But I noticed the mouse
did he not?
He who finds the lion?

I found the pain in the
lion's hear - which made
him weak, he only
saw the ferocious behavior.

I saw a mouse who believed
in himself and saw the
pain in a beast.

Sometimes I feel I must
be a mouse to him - the lion.

Sometimes I feel a mouse
is mightier than a lion.

E. Corey Downey

"My Wife"

Have you ever felt
A love that's new
A love so deep
Like a sea of blue.

It pulls at your soul
And plays with your heart
And sometimes you think
I can't do my part.

But if you give in
You'll find you're content
If your love is returned
You'll wonder where the sadness went.

Twenty three years ago
We became husband and wife
You may not understand
But that's when I started my life.

My life is wonderful
I wouldn't change a thing
So please stay with me
See what the next 23 will bring.

William Dryden

Autumn Odyssey

Walking down a country lane,
A nip in autumn breeze,
Floating to the earth floor
Unnumbered, multicolored leaves.

Goldenrods sway to a tune
Made by the whistling wind
Leaves dance a little two step,
Chase each other round the bend.

Mocking bird sings, summer's gone
Wild berries hang galore
For the birds and bees and squirrels
Bountiful is their winter store.

Babbling Brook flows lazily
To places far, far away
As a raindrop they promise
They will return some day.

Puffy clouds bounce gently
Rainbows arch I see
Isn't it just wonderful
What God shows you and me.

Lily May Yarbrough

Shaun

A bolt of energy shooting by
A scritch and scratch going on the fly
Over the sun chairs, across the lawn
Goes little boy by the name of Shaun
Into the telly games for adventure
Quickly and bold and his hand is sure
No video bully is his match
He will shoot them all with hot dispatch
Nothing is too hard for him to climb
Nor is this action controlled by time
He'll climb the slide or your arm instead
Even climb when he should be in bed
A good little boy everyone loves
Except for the times his luck he shoves
Mother and father he will defy
With look and demeanor that is sly
To bed at the end of day he's told
Cuddle and charm, they try to be cold
He snuggles and woos them with his wiles
Then they wind up a bundle of smiles

Seth Marshall

God's Delight

My mind is raising abstract thought
All aimed at God's delight
I can't imagine any less
When finally in my sight

I clearly see it in my dreams
The place I know is dear
Finding friends of truest kind
Where secrets have no fear

To share with them my endless thoughts
To speak out free means quite a lot
For here on earth I hide my feelings
lost in poems - not for revealing

For judgment on the earth is painful
Loneliness is less a rainfall
Facing God is not my problem
It's facing earth and all its goblins

So I will hide them in a case
Printed nice and wrapped in lace
Only viewed at my request
Secrets hidden from the rest

Michele Curry

I Could Still

She seems to have
A stronger personality
And be more self-assured
Than I'll ever be,
But I could still
Fall in love with Theresa.

She gets along with children
Much more easily
And has traveled to more places
Than I'll ever see,
But I could still
Fall in love with Theresa.

Though we both are interested
In computers, we appear
to be as different
In the way we live
As Earth from Jupiter.

But, even though
I can see all that,
I must admit
To all of you, in fact,
that I could still
Fall in love with Theresa.

Robert P. McKendall

Riverside

The bear has become our Mascot
A symbol of strength from Above,
And when transformed to a "Teddy"
Reminds us of comfort and love.

We've chosen red and yellow
The most vibrant colors on earth,
To stand for the bright potential
All children are given at birth.

We believe in complete devotion
To the tasks at hand each day,
As our quest is to help our children
Grow in every possible way.

We're committed to sharing knowledge
With the students attending school
Since we know life's future development
Will depend on the minds we rule.

We can never say we've completed
The job we've set out to do,
As the world in its infinite wonders
Forever brings forth something new.

Nancy Jo Rockwell

Coiled

Ah! The snake
A theological rake
Lying low - listening
Leering, eyes glistening
The Head of all, snaps and bites
Changing wrongs into rights.

A tiny nibble, devoured, eaten
Fighting, thrashing, never beaten
A tale unfurled, a tail is taken
The teeth move on though quite mistaken
A little, a lot, not counting the score
One last bite ... the snake's no more.

Moral: He who judges make no mistake
Thy judgment may thyself o'ertake.

Rhonda Russell

When Two Hearts Are One

There was a time we shared;
A time when we both cared.
It was a mystical time;
A time of special magic,
void of all things tragic.
You were You and I was Me,
We laughed, we vented
our anger, we cried;
We talked of things world wide.
We shared some things from deep
within;
And when we were done,
Our minds were at peace,
and our two hearts were one.

Richard Gute

Pretty Lady

Small and petite, how blonde is she!
A tiny little lady with hair so thin
So thin and shiny it sparkles like stars,
Sparkles when the sun hits it;
Even the moon.
You think she'd be happy,
Instead she's always in a gloom.
Why? Who knows why she never smiles
She always seems to smirk.
And it's not just a smirk when spoken to,
She always looks that way!
Be happy you are small and petite;
With hair so blonde.
Or are you in a gloom because,
Because you know it won't last long?

Robyn D. Martin

At Days End

As we walk along the seaside I think about the different things that were said and done. As the day comes to an end all these special thoughts come to mind. Each and everyday different thoughts come to mind as the day ends.

Kathryn Otis

"Precious Are Our Children"

I hear people talking
About the way things are today
It is mostly about our children
And how they run astray.

With both parents working-on the job
They spend little time at home
While our children need attention
So they won't feel alone.

When our children need attention
If we turn ourselves away
Why should we wonder-what went wrong
When they turn bad someday?

Is our job all this important
If we shut our children out?
We should take time to listen
To what our children talk about.

For-what good is all the labor
If it cost a child his soul?
A child brought up to walk with God
Is more precious than the gold.

Shirley C. Spurling

Winds Of Change

The winds of change are blowing
  Across life's troubled sea.
We can no longer enjoy
  Things as they used to be.
Man's relentless ambition
  To make a better life
By means of technology,
  Has resulted in more strife.
Now, slaves to the system
  Of high-tech society,
We create more problems
  From which we long to be free.
We can't turn back the tide,
  Yet there is a remedy.
We can by faith abide
  In our changeless Creator
Who is the anchor of the soul.
  We can weather the storm
And reach our eternal goal.

Mona Broadus Nolf

Sailing The Sky

To sail the wind
Across the sky
Like the eagle
Flying so high

Oh to be free
No attached strings
Just gracing the wind
With feathered wings

But spectator I am
Patiently awaiting delight
When I close my eyes
And dream tonight

Timothy A. Peters

Childhood

The clouds gently roll
across the springtime sky,
and it brings back memories
of days gone by.

Days so long, it seemed
they would never end.
Every day an adventure,
Every day a new friend.

Dreaming childhood dreams
under an endless sky,
trying new things only
a child would try.

Knowing in few weeks
school would be out.
Not knowing or caring
what life was about.

Richard L. Proudfoot

Watching You

Watching you for so long,
afraid to get close.
Hoping that you'd realize who
loved you the most.
But unless you open your eyes to the
one who will always care,
You'll never ever realize that I'm the
one who will always be there.

Rebecca Westman

Autumn Leaves

The autumn leaves are falling
All around me as I stare
At the gray and gloomy sky
That once was clear and fair.

What good these fallen missiles are
Is hard to comprehend,
They will not disappear from view
Even if I play "pretend."

They crunch beneath my slippery feet
And blow around at will,
I think they plan to stay around
Till winter's frosty chill.

It seems I hear them laughing
As they spiral down, down, down,
And cover every grassy place
Until not a blade is found.

The splendor of their colors
Is over for this year,
But by the next great Autumn
I'll see them - I have no fear.

Mary J. DePrez Barron

To A Song Bird (Mine)

In the spring, when birds
  all sing their mating calls,
I think of thee.

I'll never hear your
  voice again,
For it has gone from me
Back to the dust from
  which it came, and
  for me can never be the same

I heard your mating call
  and answered with my heart
I stayed within your arms
  and thought we'd never part.

Fate was the ruler here not love,
God took you to be with him above,
And left this lonely little bird
Without a song to sing,
Life's harmony takes two,
To make the song so sweet,
I wait in vain to hear your call.

My Song is incomplete.

Lee Reynolds

Savored Moments

She was always
Always busy
Taking care
Of all of us.
So, I felt so
Very special when
She'd beckon me,
"Come sit."
Then she'd read
To me the stories
"See Dick, see Jane run."
Oh! I remember when.
In all the years
That followed and
There never were enough,
I never felt as
Close to Mom again,
As then.

Kate Campbell

My Prayer For Help

I come before you
and beg to be freed
from all of the things
that suffocate me
my brokenness
formed by their deeds
has finally brought me
to my knees
my weakened body
scarred by their lies
their form of love
was hate disguised
I yearn for you
to take my hand
and help this child in me
to stand.

Wendy Walters

Why Do You Want This?

It grows towards the sky,
And breaks through to the heavens.
It lies on the ground,
And burrows deep into the earth.
It sits on that limb,
Trying to reach the next tree,
But it never actually touches that tree,
Or sees the end of the heavens,
Or reaches the middle of the earth.
All it does is try,
And goes against its destiny.

Kendra Leyda

Into The Light

I stood alone in darkness
And called out to the night.
You heard my voice and called me back,
Much to my delight.

For all my life, I will recall
How we met one night,
When we dispelled the shadows
With our smiles so bright.

My eyes were used to shadows
Before I saw your light.
Now I look, and look again
Upon this lovely sight.

Before my life goes dim,
I would love you, if I might.
When we are together,
This warm glow feels so right.

If you will be my lady,
I'll be your shining knight.
As one we can face the world
And walk into the light.

Mike Miller

Husband

Small things, they make a homeside.
A light, a husband, a child,
But they track you across a Continent,
And follow you into the wild.
They reach and beckon, and draw you,
Holding you all the while,
For Home is in a Baby's prattle,
and the light of a Daddy's smile.

Rose Milligan Tschantz

Like A Favorite Easy Chair

Comfortable,
and comforting.
Restful,
and revitalizing.
Dependable,
and trustworthy.

A place for ideas to come to mind,
and strength to form.
A place to quietly hide,
from which we can't be torn.

The one space where we can feel good,
where we need no obscure hood.
The one space were the world's not curt.
and where we can contentedly stay.

Our love will e'er be this way . . .
A place where we can contentedly stay.
From where we'll not want to stray . . .
Like a favorite easy chair.

Kelly Gohm

In Memory Of A Dear Friend

God saw you growing tired.
And cure was not, to be
So he placed his arms around you
And whispered "Come to me"!
With tearful eyes, he watched you
And was there, when you passed away
Although, he loved you dearly
He was unable, to make you stay
Your golden heart, stopped beating
Hard working hands, now rest
God broke our hearts, to prove one thing
That he only, takes the best.

Peter R. O'Dell

Conquering Light

In this world of mounting perplexity,
And days so full of uncertainty,
Where tempestuous winds of evil blow,
And deception comes from evil foe,
Where it seems that only evil prevails,
And right and good is to no avail;
Where raging waves of hatred roar,
And depraved injustice seems to soar;
Within this dark's world's erie night,
Breaks forth a Shining Conquering Light.
A Conquering Light that rids the night,
A Conquering Light that shineth bright.
A Light that conquers every foe,
A Light that calms the winds that blow.
A Light that burns away the gloom,
A light that takes away the doom.
Righteousness and justice it will bestow,
This Light that all will come to know.

Madelyn Yanchyshyn

Heart's Resolve

I would not choose the cynic's route
And doubt Our Lord made man.
I'll take His Way and someday find
His precious Promised Land.

The other route I once did run
I tried it long and well.
A dead end road is all it was -
A highway bound for hell.

Sam Worthington

Desire/Fear

I want to rise on the wings of a dove
And fly through clouds beyond stars
and the moon.
I want to reach the pearly gates,
And have St. Peter invite me in
To my heavenly home.
I want to wear a starry crown,
And join the angels in a heavenly choir.
I want to walk the streets of gold,
And live in a bright mansion above.
I want to meet my Savior and King,
And see my God seated on His throne.
Yes, I want to enjoy eternal life,
But I'm afraid to make the journey.

Roberta E. Howell

Ingrimo

Caught between dreams of yesteryears
and hopes for tomorrow
I wander
through an oblivious present

Occasionally I linger
hoping to catch
an itinerant emotion
but all is to no avail

My thoughts echo
Through the chambers of my being
From the apex of my aspirations
To the nadir of my neuroses

Now my aimless limbs fail me
Dangling about my tangled trunk
Numb and rootless I stumble
Nurtured solely on wanton whims

Though surrounded by many
I'm but one of the few
are there no kindred spirits left
To soothe my solitary soul?

Robert Levin

The Sound Of Your Voice

The sound of your voice echoes within;
And I grasp at the sound.
As if I could capture you
And keep you bound
To me - for all time.

But my hands enclose on - air.
Your voice slips past closing fingers,
Floating free, just beyond my reach
But the memory still lingers,
And will - for all time.

Pamela B. Moore

"Love You"

I love you,
And I know you love me too,
So what to do,
Run off and get married with you,
Maybe we could do that too,
But no matter what, I love you,
You love me too,
Right,
Yeah, let's do it tonight.

Latonya Landers

She Was Falling

I was walking through the garden
And I saw her standing there
On a bed of liquid roses
I thought to call but didn't dare.

I heard the mumbles of her life
As I heard a cold voice calling
And I looked at her and saw the tears
And I knew that she was falling

The icy wind engrossed me now
The sky was black and crying
I heard the fear as she reassured me
But I knew that she was falling

Her rising fire burned me now
The earth beneath her crumbling
And I saw a smile touch her lips,
For she knew that she was falling

Her ice blue eyes shared my tears
And I found I knew her suffering
And I saw all of who I am in her,
And then I knew that I was falling.

Natalie Wolc

Untitled

Let me always open my eyes
And let the sunshine in
And have a smile in
My heart for a lovely day
With our love
We show God's love to others
Who pass our way

Ruth H. Martinez

No Distance

If you could understand what I say
And listen to what you hear,
There would be no distance
Between us far or near.
When there is fear
There often comes tears.
But there is no distance
Between us far or near.
when your heart tears,
Mine tears, too.
But most often there is no distance
Between us far or near.
But there is no distance
When you are here with me!

Mary Johnson

Purple Berries

What are they, so ripe
and mellow,
tempting the eyes to ask?
Once were greenish
or a shade yellow,
Now to ripen...
Such an easy task.
Not edible unless you
wish to fly
far from this garden
and from my eye.
Just purple berries delighting
our vision
hanging from a tree
in such precision.

Sarah Ayers

Memories

Those things you always remember,
And never forget.
The things you did,
The people you met.
The summer walks,
And the winter talks.
The pain you bared,
The love you shared.
The tears, the fears,
The joy though the years.
Memories,
Those things gone by, but will never die.
That's what you are to me
An everlasting memory.

ReGina Crawford-Martin

Inspiration

One flower is not a garden
and one person is not the world.
There are many opinions
that are not like yours,
just like there will be choices
you will make on your own.

Many people will try to make you believe
what they believe and try to discourage
your dreams and say, "it can never be."

Just be faithful to your dreams
never giving up, always with your head up.
The fire is burning in your heart;
never let it die.

Sergio C. Silva

One Last Farewell

One last farewell before I go
And please, hold back the tears.
Remember all the good times
We shared throughout the years.

The many times we talked 'til dawn
How we laughed until we cried,
Oh, my Dear One, I can say
I call you friend with pride.

So, as I sadly take my leave
I do so with a heavy heart,
Please remember, Dear One
I love you 'though we are apart.

Ruth C. Rupert

Life Living

All the while you love life.
All the while you fear death.
All the while you may never die.
All the while life continue ever.

Pervading to all creation.
Animating all moving creatures.
Bestowed on all earthly races.
Is this thing called life.

Descending in unbroken line,
From parent to off spring,
Through out the span of time.
Life that is forever living.

Life living before the creation.
Life living before humanity.
Life living after the destruction.
Life living through out eternity.

Marvin B. Wingfield

Taking A Chance

I look at myself in the mirror
And see a life of pain and sorrow.
I close my eyes and try to think
If it will be better tomorrow;
Wondering if I'll be hurt
If I take that chance again.
Remembering how it ended
When I was with you then.
You told me that you loved me
Then I discovered you had lied.
I acted like I didn't care,
But the truth is that I died.
It took me a while to get over you
And now you're finally gone.
Now I've met the person
That I've waited for so long.
I'm not quite sure if I should let him know
Remembering what happened back then.
Wondering if I'll get hurt
If I take that chance again.

Nicole Zmuda

Now And Always

I look into her trusting eyes
And see how much she needs me.
Today she looks to me for guidance,
But one day she will be grown and
Leave the safety of my arms.
I will always provide her with
My support and understanding.
No matter where life leads her,
I will be here when she needs love.

Lori D. Johnson

Nightmares

Broken glass cuts so deep,
and sends me into endless sleep.
Lonely dreams keep me from wake,
day by night life slowly breaks.
Eagles flying through the air,
their empty eyes filled with despair.
Windows shatter in a spiders web,
the lost puppy is dead.
Dream through dream my mind goes in,
I don't care to see the end.
Life drips from my every pour,
Am trapped here for ever more?
I hear the sound of deadly tears,
before me flash those secret fears.

Theodore W. Duncan

Blessed Be The Godchild

Dance upon the hearts of man,
An angel in our midst,
Never asking much of others,
Image of what we've yet to be,
Effective in your silence,
Learning from our past.

Where is all our hope, perhaps,
Abiding in your heart?
Yet can we unlock its doors,
Not knowing what's the key,
Explore our inner souls.

Bless all the little children,
Living as you have,
Inspirational is your example,
Stalwart as you are,
Sanctify the one I call Godchild.

Roman Perez Jr.

My Mother's Legacy

My mother was the best of cooks
And she taught me long ago,
If I wanted bread to turn out right
To add lovin' to the dough.

Now when you make a pie she said
Add a pinch of faith and trust,
And add this to the shortening
For a flakey tender crust.

Stir in love and understanding
In the batter of a cake.
It makes it come out light and fluffy
Just the finest you can make.

But these things could not be purchased
At any store I say
But mother kept them in her heart
And used them every day.

Ruby F. Rippy

Autumn

Leaves are falling,
And snow will soon.
Lovers gazing,
At a bright harvest moon.

Flowers fading,
So are our dreams.
Floating away,
On our life's silver stream.

Swift is the tide,
As years fly by.
Fifty in all,
I've walked by your side.

Golden those years,
We've spent as one.
Without you, Love,
I would have had no sun.

Opal L. Wright

Lonely Streets

I walk on unfamiliar streets
And stare into strangers' faces,
Knowing only my own two feet
In this strangest of all places.

I am a stranger in this town,
I seek the familiar and dear-
In search of smiles, I wear a frown.
I will reach out for I have to-
Into the night, for the sweet known,
Into the earth, kissed by the dew-
Into the wind, from which I was blown,
In search of a twig to hang on to.

Shirley Longnecker

Without You

Without you I'm lost,
And I'll never be found.
Without you I'm deaf.
I can't hear a sound.
Without you I'm blind,
And can't see.
Without you I'm locked.
Only you have the key.
Without you I'm a bird
That can't fly.
Without you I'll just
Say good-bye.

Sandra Hull

Untitled

Thank you, dear Mom
And thank you, dear Dad;
A lovelier wedding
No girl ever had.

I'm not good at speeches
(Some write words of art);
I just want to tell you
What is here in my heart.

It takes more than ribbons
And satin and lace
To form precious memories
That time can't erase

I'll always remember
The sight of you there,
Your smiles that reflected
The closeness we share.

You both did so much - which
Was proof that you care,
But what meant the most was
Just having you there.

Lisa L. Wood

I Dreamed My Dreams Had Come Mature

I dreamed my dreams had come mature
And that your love I did procure.
As heaven filled my lonesome soul,
The looks of you bestowed me bold.

The dream was wrought in colors blue
And showed your worth and beauty too,
And from your body came a spark
That flew out from your generous heart.

Your face was ever in my sight,
While shining in the darkest night.
I dreamed my dreams had come mature
And that your love I did procure.

Your eyes of love outshone the sky
And caused it to just wonder why
You could outstrip the likes of it
In color and unusual wit.

I saw your feet in beauty walk,
And heard your tongue's fancy talk
And was amazed beyond belief
Then hung my heart upon your wreath.

Reagan Murff

Day Dream

Close your eyes
And imagine this
A relationship free from lies
And warmed by a kiss.

Close your eyes
And imagine a day
When no one denies
Or holds you at bay.

Close your eyes
And imagine a star
That somehow applies
To the essence of who you are.

Close your eyes
And imagine a world
That never dies
And has no grief to unfurl.

Pearlie Robinson Garner

Rain

As I look out my window
And the rain is coming down
I think of all the things it brings
As it has come to town

To a farmer if the rain is right
It means his crops will grow
Or else it means the ground is ready
In which his crops to sow

To the builder it brings hardship
It means one less day of pay
Tonight when he gets on his knees
He will pray for a sunny day

To a mother is means muddy boots
And extra work as well
As for this moisture God sends down
There is a lot to tell

We have to taste the bitter
If we are to enjoy the sweet
And to be honest, we must admit
A good rain can't be beat.

Violet Bennin

Your Presence

I see the sparkle in your eyes
And the smile upon your lips.
I feel the touch of your hand
And the caress of your fingertips.

At every glance, at every touch
Something stirs inside of me.
At every hour, on every day
I know how happy you make me be.

Over mountains and over seas
And through every whispering breeze.
My love for you shall never fail—
Only Fate can choose who to please.

When I'm with you
Nothing will hurt me.

Kristine Olsen

Mourning

The day was sullen
and the wind
sang a silent song.
The soft sound of footsteps
treading lightly
as if afraid to be heard
threatened to break the silence.
A man walked alone.
Tears filled his eyes,
Eyes that pleaded for understanding
The forlorn figure stopped and fell
gently to his knees.
His hands folded in prayer.
The pain-filled eyes
shut tightly
and only a whisper could be heard
among the gravestones.

Linda K. Daugherty

First Love

We fell in love so long ago
And then we had to part,
You lived your life and I lived mine,
But you lingered in my heart.

Now there is joy for me in the morning
As I look upon your face,
And see the love still in your eyes
That time could not erase.

Each day is very special now
Since you've come back to me,
We will live the dreams we had back then
For the best is yet to be.

Linda Riley

Hold Me

I want someone to hold me
And treat me right.
To show me true love
And cuddle all night.

I want someone to hold me
And keep me warm.
To always be there
And keep me from harm.

I want someone to hold me
And surprise me with flowers.
To do silly things
And dance in April showers.

I want someone to hold me
And listen to my dream.
To hear my every thought
And work together as a team.

I want someone to hold me
And love me tenderly.
To look deep into my soul
And take good care of me.

Wendy Luehmann

Can't Let Go

You took my heart
  and tore it apart.
You said that you cared
  You'd always be there.
I trusted you so,
  Now I can't let you go.
I thought you were a man
  but you took my heart and ran.
I waited for you to call,
  Then thought I got over that all.
So I tried to move on.
  But you're still on my mind.
I can't let you go.

Theresa A. Ungerecht

Reality

How can we look directly
at it,
Yet never know it's there?
How can we stand face to
face with it
And not look in its eyes?
Why is it so hard to accept?
Why are we so afraid to shake
its hand
And say "Hello"?
And we afraid it will answer
Us?

Michele Marie Dunagan

The Weeper's Hill

Far above the city lights,
And up above the lowland,
I spend my lonely nights,
At the place where I was summoned.

It is a place where I can see
The wrongs brought to this world.
The only place where I can be
Free of evils being hurled.

A place called The Weeper's Hill,
A place that I alone know,
Where I observe, sitting still,
Watching everyone else dying slow.

This hill is my sole place of peace.
I sit there and keep wondering why,
Why won't this chaos decease?
Why must the human race die?

I'm awaiting the day I will know,
As I watch but another man kill.
All of my life I have watched them die
slow,
Up atop, on The Weeper's Hill.

Stephen Alexander Thompson

My First Grandchild

Times are hard
  And very trying
Why is my first
  Grandchild dying

Paul and Toni
  Are so much in love
Is this just
  Some test from above

I'm not bitter
  Or am I lying
Why is my first
  Grandchild dying

For my son
  I will try to be strong
But the death of a baby
  I feel is all wrong

For Toni my heart
  Will always be crying
Why is my first
  Grandchild dying

Karen L. Paynter

The Hand

Where Spring waters flow
And fruit trees grow
I dare to dream - of
Something spiritually free
Dancing in my dream.

Of the face, the body
I cannot see -
Only the hand itself
So tiny and thin, but
White as a sheet - danced
About, waving at me....

And in my dream
It sings to me
Its heavenly voice
So gentle and sweet
Gave me a message -
From heaven above.

Mary Stevenson

April In Dakota

When it's April in Dakota,
  And Winter once more flees,
Spring is creeping o'er the prairies,
  I can feel it in the breeze.

The crows are flying northward,
  We can see them in the dawn;
All the little roots are waking
  Before the snow is gone.

Little icy snowbanks linger,
  As if they'd like to stay
To see the summer's magic,
  But they slowly melt away.

The big buttes in the distance
  Take on a color grand;
It makes me love Dakota
  When Spring creeps across the land.

Then the breeze is fresh and balmy,
  And the birds begin to nest.
Ah, there's nothing has such beauty
  As a Springtime in the West!

Prarie Maid

This Woman

With de anachronism of a goddess
and with a twentieth century in her gaze,
this woman modernized my song
and planted my shores with emeralds.

There are hybrid notes in this woman
from a piano a violin that intertwine,
because a musical mixture scatters
in the trilling of her white laughter.

This woman neutralizes my heaven
when she paints the stars that I lack,
and with her philanthropic caresses
she implants a pacemaker in my soul.

This woman populates me with horizons
on a dawn of winds and wings,
and the tyrannical goad of her stimulus
voids my daily sloths.

This woman is the firm presence
of my God, my muse and my homeland.
Vital vitality for the poet.
This woman loves me.

Luis Mario

Tattered Woman

They always laughed at her
Because she didn't
Look like
Smoke like
Drink like
Gossip like
They did
They called her names
Because she did what
She set out to do
And didn't make excuses
She carried on
She was fully clothed
With dignity
Glowing with pride
Perhaps if you think about it
She was actually the best looking
Of all who talked about her
Even tattered she had it all

Meeka Muse

Life

It all begins with birth,
And you living on this earth.

The first step is being a child,
And acting quite wild.

The second step is being a teen,
Some try to be mean.

The third step is being a adult,
With no assurance of the ending results.

Life is hard,
It's not as easy as the bending of a card.

Life includes danger,
Possibly for a child in a manager.

People getting abused,
And feeling used.

There may be a time in life,
That you get stabbed with a knife.

In the end there comes a time,
That time is death.

Tonya Hall Bonyea

I Believe

I know not why men won't believe
Angels sang on Christmas eve;
Wise men's gifts and shepherd's light,
Glory crowned that holy night.

I know not why men won't believe
Jesus walked through Galilee;
With heaven's manna the throng he fed,
Healed the sick and raised the dead.

I know not why men won't believe
The Savior died on Calvary's tree;
The Lord of glory was crucified,
For mankind's sin he bled and died.

I know not why men won't believe
He will return in ecstasy;
Declare us saints on heaven's shore,
With loved ones who have gone before.

I only know since I believed
My living Lord meets all my need;
Doubts and fears his power erase,
By faith I'm saved through wondrous grace.

Lloyd F. Brownback

Just Friends, My Love

I may not kiss your hand, madam,
As others lightly do.
I may not hold your arm, my dear,
Though others do that too.
For I would kiss your lips, my sweet,
And I would hold you tight.
But we must be just friends, my love,
And smile and say goodnight.

In dreams it seems that I'm with you,
That we will never part,
That space and time have vanished
And you are mine, sweetheart.
Then comes the dawn, comes the light,
I wake to realize
That we must be just friends, my love,
And tears come in my eyes.

Robert A. Van Nordstrand

The Day Has Dawned

Oh my! the day has dawned;
Another day the Lord has loaned.
"This is the day the Lord has made."
I thank Him for the plan He laid.

"I will rejoice and be glad in it;"
Learn His word as I walk or sit.
The flowers must be tended,
And all the fences mended.

Repent for wrongs that I did.
Be ready for the things He bid.
The plenteous harvest ready to reap
I pray for wisdom, His word to keep.

Praise God, for blessings wrought,
For sunshine and rain He brought,
Learn the fear of the Lord to know,
And strive to do His will as I go.

Yesterday has gone from me.
Tomorrow may never be.
Today is the day to be used.
May today never be abused.

Martha P. Porter

To The Poet

What makes a poet noted,
apart from all the rest?
The rugged path now traveled,
how you passed the test?

Or are words all written,
in even lengthened lines,
with an easy flowing cadence,
and every other rhymes?

No, more than single words,
with which you say your say,
it is the pure emotion,
that those words portray!

And so we bid the poet,
"Write not just to fill the shelf,
but scribe your pain or passion,
with words that please yourself!"

That we may grasp your insight,
as we journey down life's road,
and draw upon your wisdom,
to help us bear our load!

V. R. Merritt

Untitled

As I look into your eyes
and touch your skin
I've often wondered
if I reached out
and touched a star
would a dream come true
The dreams I have would be
only of loving you
If you were a flower
I would water you
and let your love grow
If you were the sun
I would let you shine
If you were by my side
I would love only you
till the end of time

Richard Vasquez

Prairie Winds

Prairie winds
Are calling me,
Calling me away.
They are leading me
To the hill top.
"Listen," they murmur.
"Listen, to the whispers
Of the flowing grass
Dancing with the breeze.
Listen to the secrets
That only the prairie
Knows, only the prairie
Remembers, of people,
Of places, of things.
We will tell you,
We will tell you all.
We will take you away."
Prairie winds are calling.
Wait for me
Prairie winds.

Lillia Gajewski

Mulled Wine

When rain is amber, seas
are damson promises.

The moon rises mauve across a sky
that pollutes sane young minds.
The dandy vends his love
in quantities of plastic violets.

When rain is silver, seas
are lilac promises.

The victor picks his plum
and runs. We drink the wine
though grapes are bad this year.
The whims of summer fly
to peak with purple gulls.

When rain has rusted, seas
are royal promises.

The amethysts of time
are ever bound to lyrics
and dallied old men sing;
the coward gathers laurels,
and the prince has mastered rhyme.

Mara Squar

"Precious Little Breath"

Little child so young,
Beautiful and bright.
You're so small but
You're growing everyday
Full of excitement, laughter, and joy.
You make me happy when
I am sad and I hope
To do the same for you
You fill my heart with delight.
Oh precious little breath
Which proves you are alive
It brings a tear to my eye
As I strive not to cry.
Your innocent words and
Actions make me remember
When...and they make
Me hope that one day I
Shall have a little child

Scarlet Dee Reny

A Poet Has To Rhyme (Sometimes)

Sometimes the poet's lines
are insidious and dark
like heavy curling smoke
that hides the kindred spark.

He weaves into his musings,
admitting in his rhymes,
familiar fears and doubts
of our unsettled times.

And sees a spider's web
across a windowpane,
finds in it some ancient art
repeated once again.

Wonders how the swallows
count the days and nights
to keep the perfect rhythm
of their migratory flights.

Sometimes his words are like
a sunrise through the rain
a rosary to bless the hours
just to dream again.

B. Margaret Greifenstein

How Can I Help But Love You?

How can I help but love you?
Are there the words I can say,
Is there a poem I can write you,
Is there a song on the way?

Is there a book in the making?
I know what the title would be:
HOW CAN I HELP BUT LOVE YOU?
The question is: Do you love me?

Yes, there's a book in the making,
Yes, there's a poem to write,
There is a play to be written,
There is a song in the night.

This is the poem I write you,
This is the play I will start,
This is the book I'm beginning,
This is a song from my heart.

How can I help but love you?
Much more to the story there'll be,
For "How can I help but love you?"
Are the words you've just spoken to me.

Margaret Evans Wright

Sincerely I Say Unto You

Love one another
as God loves you

This I Sincerely say
Unto you ...

Believing and knowing
in God's Holy Word

Will give you passage
to Eternal birth ...

Dwelling forever
in God's universe ...

Surrounded by His
Almighty Grace

Could you imagine
a better resting place
then to let your Soul
walk through the Golden
Gate of Heaven not Hell ...

Nancy Lee Sudziarski

"The Judgement Of Mankind"

It has long since been written,
as has it endlessly been told.
Down through the legends of the ages
and stories that are very-very old.

That the most infinite of judgements,
of all the expanse of humanity;
be not left to the narrowness of mind,
on the edge of total insanity.

For as the immortal gods well knew,
in their great wisdom and sight:
that it would be as if to tell
mortal man not to fight.

Knowing mortal judgements do depend,
on who they believe wrong or right.
Deciding this most arrogant of questions
through the pretext of the most forcible
might.

For mankind has not yet seen to evolve,
beyond the oldest of his doctrine.
That what he cannot fully understand or
control,
he condemns for not being Christian.

Lorilee J. Wood

The Lamb Of God

The lamb was content to rest in her care
as he snuggled close to his mother.
The love that encircled them there
was more wonderful than any other.

They were joined together at the heart
by the same God they both served.
She knew that one day He would part
to go out into the reaches of the world.

The Lamb's wool was darkened bright
as he bore the stains of our sin.
The day became like the deepest night
when He went where He'd never been.

The third day after the Lamb had died
He proved His love for you and for me.
In our guilt and shame we were blind;
But in His grace, we now can see.

Why did the Lamb have to die that way?
Why didn't the Father take him in?
He chose to pay the price for us that day;
If there'd been one, he'd have done it
again.

R. Kay Buchanan

God Bless You Eileen

God blessed the world when you were born,
As Angels sang that misty morn.
The brilliant sun then kissed the earth,
In celebration of this special birth.

the gift of Love was yours to keep,
You shared it all with strong and weak.
Pure of heart for young and old,
All Gods' creatures are in your fold.

A glowing star in the darkest night,
There always for your mystical light.
Every night I say a prayer,
To thank you God that she is there.

Sunny Santry

Dreams

Here I am
as I make my stand.
Upon this hand
set a better man.
Who am I to say
what is a dream?

But hold on
to these dreams
the best you can,
for dreams are meant,
to come true for any man.

While I pray
for every step of the way
these are words I say
Dreams will never slip away
and I hope and I pray that someday
our dreams are here to stay.

Robert Byers

The Farm

Their eyes graze across the field
as the cowbell rings in the morning dew.
Whispering voices from afar
the crickets are saying ado.
The day has opened, business begun.

Their hands are stained
from the fruits of their conviction.
As hay bales fly and children cry
the morning work catches up with the son.
The day has opened, business begun.

Their work clothes are soiled
from the labor of their bounty.
As the mule gears up for his midday run
the flowers shuffle in the sun.
The day has opened, business begun.

Eighty years they've worked the land
sun up till sun went down.
Their boots now rest
near the smoldering ash.
The day has closed, peace at last.

Kevin Whattam

Illumination

A light in the darkness-
Beaming for all to see-
A brilliant delight-
GLOWING - s-i-l-e-n-t-l-y!

Sending out hope-
For those in distress-
A beacon of light-
In a foggy abyss!

Leading lost ones-
Navigating home-
Sentry of darkness-
N-E-V-E-R alone!

Strength for the traveler-
On a black filled night-
A rock of Gibraltar
Always in sight!

A LIGHTHOUSE brings hope-
On nights filled with dread-
Ships may proceed-
With safety a-h-e-a-d!

Rosetta Ewing Schemenauer

Thirteen

I went and joined some cowboys
at the age of thirteen, not
knowing what it meant to be so
far from home out on the prairie.
My first day seemed so long.
Then came the sunset; the herd all
bedded down, and then they built
a camp fire just before nightfall
and those drifting cowboys all
gathered around the fire singing and
playing with their old guitars, oh
how those cowboys sang, and I won't
forget them or the age of thirteen.

Kodiak E. Johnson

Prayer For Strength

Sitting alone in the twilight
At the close of a summer day
And the silence brings recollections
Of a day long passed away.

Far off in the distance
I hear a plaintive whip - or - will
And continue in my dreaming
Where all is peaceful and still.

And the ripple of the water
Is a soothing lullaby
With it's clear reflected beauty
Of a moon high up in the sky.

And as the twilight deepens
Silver star appears one by one
To twinkle in the heavens
Until the night is done.

As I sit in calm reflection
On some job that day begun
Give me strength for each tomorrow
And the tasks that must be done.

Mary Elizabeth Chapman

It Matters Not A Wondrous Why

To Marianne
If butterflies' unheard song
Be colorfully, wistful goodbyes
And silent sunset hues belong
To breezes of the skies...
To one grand season
Present a fate:
A Heart's soul may glisten
Ever to a lilting gait
As the winds
It Listens.

Rita Vaughan

The Storm

A radio played in the background
As the heavens opened up
Dark clouds loomed above
A lone figure sat by the window
Pellets of rain hit the earth
Lightning cracked through the sky
Answered only by thunder
A sudden flash of light
And then there was darkness
The figure cried out
But no one answered

Lisa Schreiber

The Arrow

Youth's perfume has faded.
Beauty will fail.
The robbed and invaded
Have stories to tell.

Temper and error
Loaded the bow.
Which strung in the fervor
That levied the blow.

Sharper than sword
He fjorded the notch.
All of this discord
Was marked by the "Watch."

His dart had no charity!
It bore through the core.
Then pieces of matrimony
Fell to the floor.

Mad bowman of error,
My senses you've torn.
You've landed your temper,
My name is reborn.

Patricia Florida Penick

Who Will Inherit The Sea?

Who will inherit the sea?
Becoming sunset glow.
Tidal moonbeams, slowly dancing,
crested waves below.

Who will inherit the sea?
Its bounty on the shore.
Bounty mixed with scattered fossils,
spills and nets and more.

Sea life measured, man's dilemma,
constant shifting sand.
Beaches left with scattered moonbeams,
sea life on the land.

Who will inherit the sea?
Dolphin afterglow.
Tidal moonbeams dancing slowly,
crested waves below.

Marlene Stanford-Cox

She And I

Has our love song ended
Before it's even begun
Did we dream of sunbursts
Before we saw the sun
Did our stairway to the stars
Falter in its anxious climb
As each breath with the promise of love
Can be lost in the mist of time
Where do we turn for memories
Vanished before they've transpired
How do we answer those heartbeats
When no answers in fact are required
What do we say to our feelings
That encouraged this warm inner glow
Turning our backs on reality
Yet fearful of the time to let go
Surely you know I could love you
And beg you to be present, not past
Why were there love songs and sunbursts
If they weren't meant to last

Richard A. Diem

Building Our Monument

We each build our own monument
before the setting
of our sun.

We built it with the deeds
that, in this world,
we've done.

I want mine to be a lighthouse
that will stand
forevermore.

To guide the weary footsteps of
others to my Father's
door.

We already have the foundation,
the Rock of Ages, you see.

But the building of the monument
He's left to you
and me.

Stanley Evans Griggs

Endless Lines

Through endless lines a poem does oft
Begin one's sad lament.

Did time in hours control the sadness
Felt through days long spent?

Can pain be measured in coined terms of
Hours, months or years?

Can tears and hurt be balanced
By the depth of ones own fears?

Could poets in their metered phrase
Put time in timely note,

To ease the suffering one has felt
While reading words one wrote?

To say, uncloaked, one's naked thoughts
Of sorrow, grief and pain,

How do the endless lines explain
The search from whence we came?

Susan Bonnette

I Saw The Sun Now Setting

I saw the sun now setting
Behind a tree;
Another day was ending,
Tranquilly.

The swelling orb fell gently,
Through denser air,
Its face flushed orange-red
And summery fair.

It cast a parting glance
Upon the glade,
Which soon retired from light
To deeper shade.

And then I felt regret,
As day took flight,
As if I'd been marooned
Upon the night.

I saw the sun go setting,
But smiled to see,
It kindly left me stars
For company.

Mark Julevich

Surrender

Behold
Beloved enemy
The tender white hills
Of my defenselessness
Rose-sentried
Before your cannonading gaze.

And I would beg
This hour
The mercy
Of deep-thrust
Damascan blade
Scimitar-curving
Seeking steel
Bearing a shuddering
Breath's span of
Death,
Love's coup de grace.

Mary Peat McDonald

The Final Dive

-As the diver descends
below the surface of cessation,
submerging in a vast sea
of lifeless wonder,
breathing in eternity
from the tanks of immortality,
wrapped oh so tightly
in a wet suit of enduring blackness,
he weightlessly slithers
between the tombstone reefs
to enter the cave mouth
of the mystical hereafter.

Passing into endless bliss
with calmingly numb reluctance-
slowly rising bubbles waltz upward,
stagnant chill of isolation vanishes,
erasing a wretched existence-
glow like a pearl forever.

Michael Kuzmitz

Paradise Crossed

Luscious ecstasy born
beneath rustling green canopies
encouraging limitless escape
from toxic urban atmospheres

Shrouded in these magic confines
naturally occurring tranquility
blanketed in humid silence
liberated our stifled imaginations

Greedhead developers crowd the horizon
conspiring with lurking outcasts
to perversely lacerate
these once evergreen stage curtains

Now our walking-distance retreats
are doomed to a painful fog of memory
because of insatiably vile patrons
who infiltrated these treasured hiding-places

Reams and bolts of irreplaceably stolen
fabric
are being consumed by these undeserving
trespassers
and they do not choke...as we'd hoped
and rapidly we become naked

Rick Vigenski

Broken Arrow

Broken arrow cracked
Beneath the rock of stone
The pounding of the hoofs
Of the spotted ponies
Snapped its tip into pieces

Ancestral blood ran down
The feathered arrow sheath
Bleaching it into time
Once sturdy and strong
Now hidden under the Sun God

Gone to yesterday in sadness
Weep by the big rock
Where the lizard and crow
Feast on the orgy of blood
Sun hurts their eyes uncovered

Fall winds change to the north
Today a wild flower seeds
Blowing across the rock of stone
Dark grey clouds meander by
Bringing the gentle raindrops

Randee Sky

A Menopausal Leaf

A point
between parallel lines
a manifested moon
a cycle shined

My home
the place of heredity
the symptoms the assumptions
my maturity a reality

The heat
coming toward me
exploding from
within

Particles melting
chilling me down
cooling my mind
the seed is free

Marilyn Sinnette

To My Sister On Her 77th

I never had a brother,
But my sister sure will do,
Like the flowers of her garden,
She graces all in view.

Pulls the weeds and rakes them,
Prunes the bush and vine,
Trims around the edges,
Keeps the homestead looking fine.

Feeds the birds and squirrels,
Watches for the deer,
Burns out tent caterpillars,
Without any fear.

Helps her friends and neighbors,
And whosoever comes
Upon her pilgrim pathway
Into the promised realm.

The family they all love her,
Let the admiration swell
For the Great Aunt Helen
Who does everything so well.

Marvin B. Gardner Jr.

Eyeless In Gaza

I am in Gaza
blinded by apathy,
Philistines surrounding me,

no jawbone of an ass
for fighting my way free,
nor temple columns near
to bring down upon me,

chained to the grist mill
grinding down the grain,
cut away from poetry;

What drove me was the passion
and the imagery of flight,
the diving down at night
into burning worlds
from foxes with flames
tied to their tails.

Blindness now grown;
no words to make
the world my own.

William H. Lloyd

"Iris"

I'm a forgotten iris,
Blooming a virus.
My future is bleak,
With soul petals so weak.
I remain sane,
As defense mechanisms wane,
To the last bud,
Where repressed emotions flood.
My tamest roots have grown wild.
Forgotten iris, tangled fire child.
Always wanting to soar,
Yet I am stripped to the core.
Health's withering reject,
I'm so pale from constant neglect.
Once amazingly immune,
My iris shriveled too soon.
So defeated I can't ask why
I've been cultivated only to die.

Melissa Kozlowski

October Song Bird

Still singing in October bright
blue weather
a tiny song bird enjoys the
coolness of the morning
He knows there will come a
time to fly away.
Yet he provides a lilt
and joy to my October heart.

Norma L. Vancil

Closer To Thee My Lord

There's something I am searching for,
But like the blind I seem to be
Fumbling in the dark for something
something that will bring me, Lord
closer to Thee.....

The more I see, the more I pray —
The more I learn, the more I want
The more I love - the more I long
Long to come, my dearest Lord
closer to Thee.....

Regina Noell Service

Twilight

Blue,
Bright blue
Then periwinkle blue,
A slowly drifting rainbow.

Lavender,
With a pinkish hew,
Then a faded indigo,
The colors are flowing.

Grey,
With a dusting of white,
And a gleaming yellow disk,
The heaven's are rising.

Blue,
Dark blue,
A deep dark sea,
The twilight has ended.

Shannon Eileen Mitchell

The Storm

Big boom
Bright flash
Shadows of the storm
Beating of rain
On the stone pavement below

Another boom
It gets closer
The rain gets harder
It passes over

Flashes lighter
Booms softer
Complete silence

Sun comes up
Birds start chirping
Flowers start blooming

Scampering of little feet
On the stone pavement below
Children playing
Adults praying

For This Is The Miracle Of Life

Laura L. Voytek

The Boo Boo

Black + white = brown sometimes
Brown + little = hurt sometimes

When two squirming bits of brown beauty
visited my aunt one Christmas,
she began pouring on balm
before she saw the wound.
They forgot she was a stranger -
she reminded them of someone.....
"Our grandmother doesn't like us,"
one blurted out.
"I'll be your grandma," she soothed.
"She'll be sorry one day.
She doesn't know what she's missing."

Kisses + hugs = bandages sometimes
Oranges + cookies = healing sometimes

Emmanuel.
God with us.

Marjorie A. DeAngelis

Homo Imperfectus

Jungle thoughts, like Tiger eyes,
Burning in the darkness -
In the deep and hidden
Caverns of ourselves.
Who among us have not felt
These rumblings - risings -
Then self reproved,
Reached inward to squelch them
With our "civilized" mind,
Or bury them deeper
From society's probing sight?
We are too recent
From our Jungle Beginnings
To proclaim perfection,
Our fangs and claws
Concealed
By Laws we make,
Less honest than the Jungle Law -
And call ourselves
Superior.

Paula Patterson

Joined At The Lips

Joined at the lips with a kiss
Burns their souls and brings bliss
A love for all time is at hand
Forever a promise they demand

Joined at the hands with a ring
Love's become a material thing
Promises words they just say
To make it through life, day to day

No longer joined by their hearts
Their love's broken in pieces and parts
Too soon, they gave up on faith
And let their love slip away

Lindsey M. Wilborn

Life-Long

It started with a simple hello,
But as time passed we
Started talking more and more,
Learning a little each time.
You listened to all my feelings...
And I learned about yours,
Not knowing then how
Close we would become.
Now through our talks
We not only learn
How much we have in common,
But also that we'll be there
For each other
ALWAYS.

Melissa Tracy

Criminal Urge

I would like to be a robber,
A breaker of the law,
And hold up each passing day
To loot the beauty that I saw.

Love, laughter and happiness
I would steal in my foray,
And hoard them all for the coming time
When there would be no wealthy day.

W. A. Read

Untitled

They say nothing lasts,
But can we change that?
They say nothing's forever,
Can we change that, too?

What would I do without you?
You're there for me through everything,
No matter what it is.

The ups, the downs
The bad times, and the good times.

You're so much more than me,
I don't deserve you,
So why is it we're together?

I guess it was meant to be.
I remember how it all started
And still I don't find it true,
What I did, but it's for the best.

We're together now,
And we'll always be,
Hopefully.
I love you Billy.

Michelle Nacht

Remember Me

When I am gone, remember me
But not with tears or longing,
For my Heavenly Father called me
To where those gone before are thronging.

Forgive yourself for things undone
And do them for the living,
Though time be past for both of us
Don't spend it now in grieving.

The hands of God will lift you up
And take sorrow's burden too,
For Jesus died that we might live
To give us joy forever, true.

Remember me just long enough
That a smile replace the tears;
And thank your Heavenly Father,
He allowed you, us, these many years.

Rita Warntjes

Emotions

Love is free,
But you still have to pay
for it,
Sadness isn't natural,
But you don't wait all day
for it,
Joy what is it,
Nobody knows,
Beauty is within you,
and you shouldn't have to
pose.

Samantha Macdonald

Sanctuary

I thought I'd found it in a dream,
But, waking, you were there....
And over on the other shore
I saw the golden stair:
But rivers are forbidding,
And so I turned and found
False sanctuary in the dream,
My feet on solid ground....

Nell B. Tucker

Untitled

Slowly being eaten away
By problems unneeded.
The terrors of the darkness
Wrap around the body,
Screaming for help.
Not a single sound is heard.
The rages inside want out,
Longing to be let free in the world;
Yet, they only seem to get worse.
As the demons continue to destroy,
Anguish of the good is caused by the evil.
Nothing is left of the body,
For it has been too long.
The screams were never heard,
The rages never let out.
A spirit rises to the sky
Of a body that no longer is.

Michelle Evasew

The Oxygen Machine

Electricity keep on running, please
Can I still hear that humming?
Keep that water coming
Just for my oxygen machine.

Make my troubled breathing
A little easier today.
My influenza tires me so
But my dear machine is listening.

It is there just for me.
It hums softly in the night
Its air is there for me to know
It can help my plight

At 85 I should not care
It worries me to leave my wife
Don't fail us, oxygen machine.
To leave her side, I cannot bare.

I glance at my reflection
Thin, gray, frail, and old
Then the realization
The oxygen machine cries tears for me so cold.

Sheila Love Nicholson

A Friendship

How important is a friendship?
Can you live without one?
Is it really that important,
Just to have a little fun.

Is it better to be alone,
And having no one at your side?
Is it really that important,
To share a secret that you must hide?

How important is a friend,
Do you really need one?
Is it really that important,
To share your feelings with someone?

It is important to have a friend,
It is important to confide in someone,
Because without one,
You're no one!

Kristy Armas Oliveira

Violence

Look around,
can you see the sound?

Look toward the sea,
can you hear their deeds?

Look into the light,
can you engulf the sight?

Look into the sky,
can you fly, way high?

Look through my chest,
can you hear it rest?

Look past my soul,
can you smell the coal?

Look into my eye,
can you feel me die?

Look among the wild,
can you find it mild?

Sarah L. Tikalsky

As One

Please don't cry my child
'Cause I am here to stay
And all the pain you feel
Will slowly fade away
I'll teach you the powers of love
Tomorrow will be a better day
Cause we will fly so high tonight
That we will find a better way

So don't you fear my love
'Cause love is here to stay
And you'll know when I hold you
That there will be a better day
Be strong like your magic
Feel proud like the sun
To shine upon the world
So we can be as one

Michael John Miller

Christie

Christie, Christie image of love
Christie, Christie image of love
Oh! What have you been thinking of?
The pain, the hope, the truth to know,
that I may know which way to go.
Just to gently caress your hand
Then, perhaps, I will understand,
Why Christie seems so heaven sent.
It's because her soul is diff'rent.
Christie, Christie image of love
Tell me what are you thinking of?

Paul F. Ernst

James

He does not see as you and I,
But far beyond the human eye.
He hears the wind roar its sound,
And rocks that tumble around.
He feels the warm sun and cold moon,
And knows that both are in tune.
He tastes the ocean's spray,
And laughs his cares away.
He smells the clean fresh air,
And walks with grace and care.
For James is blind, you see,
Maybe, not as much as you and me.

Mildred Pumroy

Penny

Stored in jars
collecting for my rainy days.
Found on streets
increasing luck,
increasing superstitions.

Put in a shoe,
flattened on railroad tracks,
to make exact change,
for ash trays.

Exchanged for a wish
when dropped down a
wishing well.
Exchanged for candy
in country stores.

When the lowest currency
brings so much joy,
Whoever said money
cannot buy happiness?

Sarah E. Peterson

Goodnight

(a lullaby for my children)

It's time for bed, Mommy said.
Come and close your eyes.
And while I sing a lullaby,
The sandman waits nearby.
He'll help you fall asleep he will,
And this is what he'll do:
He'll sprinkle sand upon your eyes,
Then sigh a tale or two.
And now that you are fast asleep,
He'll leave you to your dreams.
You'll dream of all the pleasant things
Which only sandman brings!

Rita E. Deleurme

Eternally Bound

How sweet the
comfort you offer.
  So alone.
How loving the look
in your eyes.
  So missed.
How gentle the touch
of your hand.
  So yearned for.
How cherished the sound
of your voice.
  Forever gone.
Your love will always be with me
every moment of my life...until
we reunite, alone no more.

Wendy Walter

The Endless Summer

"Cigarette," says he;
"Fire," says she;
He, of noble stature,
She, of flesh and earth.
Intertwining smoke of ages
Makes clear the night's solemn hue
In nether-light reflections
Of fading sensibility.
He stands exposed,
The noble savage,
Submersed in white light
Of flesh and earth and fire.

Kris Curtis

Listen

She wanted to scream,
cough up that clot of emotion
that swelled under her larynx,
pressed against the lining of her throat.

But would her cry,
like the tree that fell in the forest,
make a sound
if no one was there to hear?

Or would her vocal chords
simply vibrate,
move the air into waves
that struck nothing, then went flat?

What noise could she make
to alert someone
that a foundation was crumbling,
a facade about to collapse?
If not her voice,
what instrument of alarm?

The shot was heard by her neighbor;
the siren, by her entire town.

Katherine Lind

The Starving Cry

So many times I wonder,
Could all the world be fed
From plates we've over loaded
And scraps of leaven bread?
Those little extra portions
We scrape from bowls and pans;
Could they have been diverted
And placed in starving hands?
The ice cream cone that melted,
The pudding left to dry,
The sandwich someone nibbled
Of Swiss Cheese, Ham and Rye,
Could our misguided judgment
Our lack of self-control
Replenish someone's cupboard
Or a hungry child's bowl?
So many times I wonder
When in my bed I lie,
If God, so many worship,
Can hear The Starving Cry?

Violet D. Stout

Home

Log burning in the fireplace,
Country music on T.V.,
A book, another trip to take,
And a quiet time just for me.

Pictures hanging on the walls,
A Bible on the table,
Rocking chair beside the hearth,
Baby in the cradle.

I love to watch the firelight
As it dances on the wall,
And listen to the thunder
As it rolls on like a ball.

Rain beats against the windows,
The winds makes lonesome sounds.
This is where I'd rather be
Than anyplace around.

Opal E. Watkins

Winding Roads

Many different pathways
Crossing through our lives
Ever changing patterns
Kaleidoscope the mind
Terrain seeming strange and new
To fear and yet to go
Traveling so fast it seems
Down roads we do not know
Exploring hill and valley
Our thoughts are kept adrift
So beautiful yet daring
We fear we may soon slip
The passage ever varied
As seasons to unfold
The journey of a lifetime
On ever winding roads

R. Dean Passmore

Cruelty

Cruel is your laughter
Cruel are your words
Cruel are my tears that are never heard.

Uncaring snickers burn in my ears,
as drops of water drench my cheeks.
I glance around this blurry room.
My whole body is weak.

Seeking a corner to hide away.
I just want to find a small space,
some where I can decay in silence.
My brain can take no more of this violence.

Reality is lost, far back in my mind.
A place I hope to never find again.

Patricia Davis

Act Of Apollo

His are eyes that mesmerize
Crystal pools in rainbowed arc;
Screening rays for dawns to come,
Arcturus wading in the dark.

His are hands that tranquilize
Silken skeins in tendrils tight;
Tempering tears to rein the rays,
Aurora racing toward the light.

His are strains that synchronize,
Lashing lenses to the beam
Hailing humors well composed,
Apollo airing Nature's theme.

His the eyes that spanned the arc,
His the hands that cleared the pane,
Mine the heart that all day sings,
"How good to see the dawn again!"

Miriam R. Kossman

The Gift Of Motherhood

Innocent laughter, trusting smile
Eyes, blue like the sea
Hands, so small and curious
Reach out to hold onto me

A child so loving and giving
So bright and full of life
Who takes pleasure in the simple things
And teaches me the gift of life.

Mary L. Earls

Darkside

Liar!
Deceiver!
You hide the truth.

Jealousy!
Envy!
You despise what you can't possess.

Loathing!
Hate!
You cannot love.

Sinner!
Blasphemer!
You destroy my faith.

Greed! Avarice!
You corrupt my soul.

Away from prying eyes.
Immune to my cries.
Within the blackest recesses of my being.
It is there that you hide.
My other self.
My Darkside.

Mike Versocki

Peace Offering

Don't you know? I'm hurtin' so,
Deep within I feel so low,
With a love afraid to grow
I'm hiding this from you,

Foolish pride, kept locked inside,
Feelings I'd be left denied,
Fears that pain, that you'll decide,
To tear my heart in two,

Been so bad? Just don't be sad,
You're the only joy I've had,
Call me friend, and I'll be glad,
And treat you fair, and true,

You can see the friend in me,
If you let your heart go free,
Like branches in a big oak tree,
There's room enough, for two.

Steven Price Turner

What's In A Smile

What's in a smile - it all depends
Did you give it to make amends
Or give it to a downcast stranger
To keep him from further danger
Or to a friend who loves you so
Just to keep them on the go
Or to give a child some hope that life
Isn't always filled with strife
Or to give hope to a senior person
Who's afraid life will only worsen
Or a challenged one striving bravely on
Wishing his infirmities be gone
For all of these, your smiles intent
To show your love was what you meant
To everyone in every way
Your smile will brighten up their day!

Stanley Byers

The Night's Magic

Do you believe in the night's magic?
Do you believe what it holds?

It holds your deepest secrets
And all the passions you possess inside.

It holds the love you crave
And the hate you live with.

It lets you fly to the heavens
And fall crashing to the earth.

It magnifies your fears
And makes you relive the pain.

It believes in you
And it urges you on.

It lets you be who you want to be
And not what everyone believes you are.

It helps you escape
And it lets you feel alive.

It holds the beauty
And the understanding that only your eyes see.

There is no beginning to the night's magic
And there is no end.

Sharon Ida

The Circle Of Secrecy

Have you heard about - - - but
don't tell a soul.
I was sworn to secrecy, the day
I was told.
I was also told tales about this
and that,
And, I swore to keep them
under my hat.
But, you can be trusted - - I
know you well.
So, promise me that not one
soul will you tell.
But, promises mean nothing - -
Sooner or later they're broken,
And, to some close friend those
secret words will be spoken.
The only true secret is kept inside,
And, to not one soul must I confide,
For, confidence is breached - friend to friend,
And, just one breach is the secret's end.

Stanley N. Harrison

With God's Blessing

Look inside
down upon your knees
call on Him as you pray.

If you've given him all
your love
don't think about
what formal thing to say.

He wants to be your
Sovereign Lord
don't grieve at being led

He doesn't need a whipping boy.
Lean on him instead
I'm telling you the truth
satan's lie — there is no proof.
But, Jesus really died for you.

Kimberly Loignon

Love's Harvest

Leaf fall, leaf fall
down on mossy green waters
filled with minerals,
those that heal.

Cattails waive
hello and good-bye
and I leave, but
my heart stays.
Please let him come soon

For my arms
need to hug him
and I
to laugh and giggle and cry.
Oh my, oh my,

How time makes the soul
so friendly,
As the leaves
turn golden and peach and brown.

Karen A. Ziegler

Thanksgiving

November rain
Drums a staccato refrain
Against the roof;
Snow will fly,
Curtaining a slated sky
Remote, aloof.

Murmured grace
Blesses each expectant face
Around this room;
Savory feast
Greets the appetites released
By its perfume.

Not to name
Are the sparks from which a flame
Ignites a mood—
Familiar things,
And the radiant spirit sings
Its gratitude.

Sari J. Fisher

Sunrise

Sunrise: Fair skies often disguise
faint cries beyond which lies
the hope of the ages
of princess and pages,

Sunrise: Swiftly gilding my lawn
I see the dawn as a fawn
relishes the idea
of the cornfield near.

Sunrise: Brilliant sparks of love
shining as dew from above
as bits of smiles
scatter across the miles.

Sunrise: A new dream, a new hope,
a new life, a new soul
emerge from darkness
a spirit whole.

Sunrise: A new day, new chores,
new friends, new shores;
lasting peace, new lore,
sun sets no more.

Rosie Branch Gay

Growing

Down this hole I fall in
each time I want to hide
Forever being young can't be
as I hide it in my pride,
Let these flowers blossom
each and every day
so I can see the beauty
where growing old will pay.
With every wrinkle covering
each scar upon my soul
a list of sins and resentments
that's scratched into life's scroll.
And child of mine before me
I'll be leaving you to your lone
Remembering how life once was
as it aches my fragile bone.

Kathleen Jennings

Together

Let me not wander this
earth alone
With no one to love and
call my own.

With no hand to hold
as I walk in the park.
No one to lie close
to me in the dark.

Let me hear laughter
as I walk through the door
and someone to greet me
as I walk across the floor.

Let us share together
the hurts and the pains.
Someone to rock with
when my hair has turned to gray.
Don't let me walk this earth alone.

Thelma Gilpatrick

Winter Into Violet

Snowflakes tumble
Echoing around your dance.
Thighs of blue glass
Stretch across my own
Creating drifts,
That are drifting still.
Spotted winter panthers
Crawl over crystal fields,
Searching for spring caverns
Where we have abandoned
Trickles of our laughter,
And crimson drops of pain.
Footfalls composed of electric frost
Imprint our bantering trail,
That mystic cats will pursue
Deep inside this unborn wood.
They will chase us, panting,
From secure tree-spirit branches
From winter, into violet.

Melanie M. Ellis

Tired

Tired of the sun's
ever bright smile,
I turn to the moon
to escape for awhile.

Stephanie M. Wiegel

Angels

Three angels God has sent to me
Entrusting me to guide and see
That they are loved and cared for.

Faces three to scrub and kiss
Where dimples come and go or miss
And light where lips curl upward.

Three mouths to eat and praise my cooking
Three pairs of eyes to be a-looking
at loving tasks my hands may do.

Three blessings - tender are my boys
Filling me with constant joys:
Three angels God has sent me!

Nancy Fay West

The Old Eskimos Ways

Today
Eternity...
The day fades
The past is gone
voices go still
no more talk

My life was full
I gave life
it takes my place,
they will remember
I ran my race.

The spirits have spoken
I heard the talk.
My space is gone,
I go my way
I go alone.
TODAY...
I take a walk.

Marvin Fuhs

The Puzzle

Every day, every minute,
every person, every situation
Is a part of the puzzle.

And as the years go by,
the pieces come together.

In the end, the final picture
may not be apparent

But every piece will have
been cherished along the way.

Victoria Bruun

Forever

He is here, with us
Each night, and day.
Our troubles, with sorrow;
He shares, in every way.

The Lord is here.
Through winter, and our fall.
But most happy of all,
Through summer, and our spring.

With blessings galore.
He is right here, at our door.
If we just open the way,
Each day!

Kimly Shurvinton

King Of The Tower (Race of Worries II)

King of the tower, King of the tower
Everyone wants a piece of the power.
Where one man's fall is another's gain
And we all rejoice in his pain.

King of the tower, King of the tower
Soldiers stomp upon every flower.
Where the battle never ends
Man kills his family and friends.

King of the tower, King of the tower
The gain is only but sour.
For once you reach the very top
Someone comes to knock you off.

Shannon Bray Belonie

Memories

My memories seem to be
Excerpts from a reading book;
Close enough to grasp,
But too far into my past.
Feelings I cannot conjure up
Unless the book is read again.

And, unfortunately,
Memories are a book
Read only once
Yet, for some reason
Kept forever.

Nicolina Marra

Hopes And Dreams

As I look into my child's
eyes I see my hopes and dreams

As years go by and my child
grows again I look into their
eyes and see their hopes and dreams

Again as years have passed I
look into their eyes and now
I realize I have my hopes
And dreams come true

Karen G. Heitman

Untitled

Just when I have my
face all arranged, a hiccough
shatters my facade

Voni Yerkes

Does She

Does Tammy still fall in love
Did Tammy grow up wise and strong
Does Tammy still sing that love song

Does her heart still fall
in love so easily

Will Tammy always stand by her man.
Or will she ever learn you
Love to follow your heart

Or does Tammy know what
She knows is true-that
Tammy is in-love.

Kathy Garrett

Wind And I Howl

Wind and I howl
Facing each other
gusting fronts
Refusing to crouch
behind wearying rocks
seemingly so strong

Wind and I howl
Marching army of black clouds
Begging for a shield
but knocked to the ground
A ceaseless force
hurling from hiding

Wind and I howl
Deep and sudden
a new found strength
Now silent, a life recovered
Standing once again
as Wind and I howl

Melinda Huisingh

Rain

Rain....
Fall gentle on me....
Wet and cool....
Peacefully bring life....
To all in need....

Pools form....
As you drip off the roof....
Reflecting all around you....

Air sweet and pure....
Your cleansing on all seen....
I marvel at your simplicity...

Lord....
Come to us as rain....
Bring to all....
Life so free...

Lord....
Bring Your rain.

Larry Holmack

Tempus Fugit

Cobwebs
fill the shadows of the room
They stick like glue
Like certain memories
Better to be washed away
Than held on to.

Blue and white rice bowls
Porcelain figurines
The black and gold Chinese furniture..
These are the new - the old can go.

Chaos -
Newspapers
Never finished projects
Goals not met
Dreams wasted.

Confusion...
The clock keeps ticking...time passes...I
waste it.

Forgive me...
Forgive me...

Phyllis Teitelbaum

Unwanted

It was left alone for a long time,
Finally moved to the attic for storage,
Forgotten for awhile, it just sat there,
Collecting dust and rotting,
Then she was going away to college,
And she wanted it,
In the attic, it had sat-
For too long,
Brought down into the light,
It was found shabby and unusable,
She returned it to the attic,
Thinking to repair it someday -
And got some cheap plastic thing,
To use for now,
After she finished college,
She came back for it,
The repairman whom she showed it to-
Had said, "Might have saved it 4 to 5 years ago,
but it's sat too long."
They threw it away.

Lynnae Triebenbach

The Unanticipated Sensation

A gentle brushing as you pass,
Fingertips spray igniting fire
Unsettled feelings for oneness with...

Your touch.

A responsiveness awakens within me,
Creating heightened senses with
Uncontrolled spreading of warmth by...

Your touch.

The confusion of frenzied emotions,
Caused by your sensual caress
Unsatisfied with just nearness and...

Your touch.

The rushing wave of heat,
Throughout my body for the
Unspoken pleasures declared by...

Your touch.

Awareness of your closeness,
With the soft grazing of fingers
Unnoticed is the effect you have

Only with...Your touch.

Patricia A. Perras

Old Friends

The image of far off friends,
Flashes across one's inner eye
As summer's lightning flashes
Across a dark, rain-swept sky.

And the sound of friendly voices falls
Like soft and distant thunder,
Down memories canyon walls.
We pause in awe and wonder.

One asks, "Where has time gone,
The hazy dreams, — the spent years?"
Yet, memory brings it back again,
The smile, or sometimes, the tears.

Eva Darrington-Rule

Reality

Delusions-
Floating,
Now gently
Through my mind-
Create
Illusions-
Of reality.
A reality-
Much like
Mirages,
There-
Yet just
Beyond-
My grasp.
Shimmering-
Fuzzy-
And then,
Gone!

Roland L. Crosby

Life

A single feather, one, alone,
floats along the heavens
its path not known.

Aimlessly the feather moves as
it sits on a little breeze,
Is this the place the feather belongs,
Is this the moment it shall seize?

Who's to say, who's to know,
For once again the feather is on the go.

When it's low, many things dictate
the way,
But once it's high, so high it's free,
it's the feather's say.

Stacy Pagac

Butterflies

Wispy rainbow bits of light
Flutter in the sunshine bright
Bringing magic, smiles, delight.
What a lovely, lovely sight!

Morning until still of night
Flower castles they alight.
Waked to splendor, now my quite
Joyous heart with them takes flight.

Theresa Chiaravalloti

Footprints

In winter when the lovely snow
Falls on the ground so white
The full moon shining overhead
Makes glistening snow at night.

And with the dawn a new day comes
'Tis then we walk around
Out in the white and drifted snow
Our footprints on the ground.

And when the sun shines out so bright
Our footprints melt away
But these are just the ones in snow
Our footprints here will stay.

And by these prints we will be judged
In days that lie ahead
Be careful of the prints my friend
Since others too may tread.

Myrtle C. Stanley

Flying Down Hudson With Marie

Pilot flying airplane, sky hawk,
Flying down Hudson with Marie.
She is steering sky plane, don't hawk,
Hudson River time so merry.

Ms. Marie Louisa on 2
Half wheel of 2 sky hawk, oh she
Turn to 2 right, what a glad sight,
Excellent steering and nice height.

Shopper restaurant seen below,
Superior food "Escargot."
That in English means Gourmet Snails;
Use to bring them in by the Pails.

Smart people snails for breakfast gums;
Those eating snails from New York comes.
Their interest it never fails,
We hope they don't ration the snails.

See the New City College site
And Alpenstock Mounts white cliff heights
Sighted by the high S. Teamed Dean.
You know that we R Human Beans.

Stephen B. Paddock

"The Mystical Black Butterfly"

A mystical black butterfly always
follows me in the city or the country
or wherever I may be!

It's beautiful and magical,
and mystically laced as it flies
and glides with such hypnotic grace.

Its beauty is flawless as it flies
through the trees and it shifts
direction in the soft summer breeze.

It appears mysteriously with no pattern
to its flight and before you know it -
it's disappeared from your sight!

This mystical black butterfly that always
follows me is a lesson from God
that I'm being shown you see,
that no matter where I am,
I'm never alone, and whenever God
wills it he'll make it known!

Theresa V. Wilson

Crocodile Tears

I could cry
For lost hopes,
For vanquished dreams,
For vanished loves
And nocturnal screams.

I could cry
For all that was,
For what might have been,
For music recalling
Where and when.

I could cry
For opportunities missed,
For the fleeing years,
For memories merging
Into midnight fears.

So go your way,
You know who.
You doubt, you scorn,
That I'd weep for you?
I shouldn't. Really. But I do.

Rolle Rand

A New Christian Cry

So many months I've waited
for God to send me a friend -
One that I could share my dreams
You know, deep thoughts within -

I've tried to talk with many
whom I thought would guide my way -
They made me feel rejected
having nothing much to say -

You see God saved me this year
and I'm thirsty for much more -
I don't know who to talk to
when so many shut their door -

I truly sense a burden
for new Christians everywhere -
Let me be a shining light
to those who are in despair -

I want to be a true friend
A listener and a guide -
Bringing hope to those in need
Let me not just walk on by -

Patty VanSlambrouck

Our Grandson, Our Joy

Jason came to our house to stay
For the night and the next day.
Tinker toys all over the floor
From the kitchen to the front door.

While happy at play, a joy to see
Playing race cars with shouts of glee.
A garage made under Grandpa's chair,
Pulling it off with a superior air.

Playing stops when the cartoons come on
Watching 'til all the good guys won.
Now, wash your face, you've hair to comb
For here comes Mother to take you home.

Winifred Jones

Be Calm

Many people are restless
For they are hunting success
If they slow down to look at the sky
Enjoy the birds, flowers and why

Be patient never go with the flow
It's better to be calm and not go
For if we stop along the way
We can hear what God has to say

Slow down and talk to the bees
They enjoy your voice you see
If we sit down let our mind be calm
And enjoy the whisper of the palm

You may overlook success
By rushing from East to West
Many times we let success slip by
Without knowing when and why

God made this beautiful world
It has become a rushing twirl
He made it for you, me and all to be
Rely as you calmly sit in the shade of a tree

Ola Varnell

Faith

I have a knot in my heart
Fork can't loosen
It drips salty within
Preserved by frozen thought
Safe from sharp points
And heat of night
Functions as living
Morbid in countenance
Old and strong
An enabler, a rock
Poignant ins and outs
Come to well-secured ends
Extracts the precious
From the worthless
Bound together
Wisdom is its seal
Desire, the strain

Suzanne Moffat Brooks

Love

Love is pale and pink,
fragile, like a rose.
It is a warm embrace
that lingers in your memory.
It is as soft
as a spring day
and as tender
as a gentle kiss.
It is the one flower
left after the frost has gone,
lingering and growing
until it falls away
to come again another spring.
Love is pale and pink;
delicate, like a rose.
The wind carries it away
to bless another soul
with its warm embrace,
its soft spring days
and its gentle kiss.

Melissa Bailey

New Horizons

Her long fair tresses
Frame a face, so angelic
A grooms loving hand, timidly caresses
Poses... a painters dream relic

Now, a white veil lifted
As one, they stroll the aisle
Onward, unknown valleys and rifts
Well-wishers awed with beguile

A tailored carriage awaits
Garnished with aromatic florals
Fresh pathways ahead, the day late
Trotting hoofs, echo the terrestrials

A mother strains dried eyes
Catches a glimpse, fading away
Waving a hand, with a sign
Ponders a new vista, sprouted today...

Mary Margaret Konz

The Insects' Song

I hear your voice
From out of the night,
A joyous sound not heard
In the light—of day.

Is it sheer joy of living
That makes you sing?
Or the pleasure to my heart
You bring.

Perhaps for a lover
You labor for hours.
Hoping for favor above
All the others.

Whatever the reason
Sing on little one—
I hear you and feel
Not so all alone.

Nancy A. Butt

Alive Again

As melting ice from rooftops
Furrows its way into welcoming earth,
Mr. heavily burdened Winter
Opens his gripping hands
In welcome to Miss comely Forsythia.

Ash-colored, cracking limbs break easily
For storage in Christmas fireplaces
For future family gatherings.
Greener, sister trees
Ready themselves with bushels of buds
For Easter finery.

Tentative warbling of song sparrows
Causes the morning air
To risk warming her breath
That all nature may respond
With familiar fertileness.

Now happy hearts in bodies free
To hug, to bless, to boat the sea,
For ice has dripped down on the earth,
And all creation welcomes birth

Millie Shaver

Death Rattle

Endless battle,
Gasped death rattle,
Quaking, aching,
Lungs keep shaking.

Pondering deliria,
Contagious hysteria,
Today, tomorrow,
Morbid sorrow.

Craving carnage,
Tangled harness,
Lies, deceit,
The frayed ends meet.

The kiss of curse,
The blessed hearse,
Behavior, savior,
My soul is braver.

Reddened sun,
Evil one,
Laughter, after,
Burn in hell, faster.

Renee Porrett

Halloween

The simple frights:
Ghouls, goblins, sprites
Must be conquered by maturity
But alas with age,
Some often trade the simplicity
Of Halloween's ghosts
For a host
Of mindless fears
That wisdom's years
Should dissipate.
And so
We did bargain bogus
Treats and hollow tricks
To contrive a life of delusions!
So with the price paid
We ponder our predicament,
And as reality eludes us
We long for those simpler days
Of jack-o'-lantern illusions.

Peter H. Kaufman

Friends

When friends are happy we are
glad to hear,
But when they're sorrowful we share
the burden they bear.
It seems to lighten our very own load
As we travel along life's busy road,
Just to help where the way seems long,
Maybe we hum a cheerful song.
What else can we do but answer a need?
If you're Catholic, Protestant or some
little known creed.

Mary L. Peterson

Last One On Earth

Under the blazing red of a sky
Glaring on a vast, parched world,
Stood one thin shadow of desolate cries,
Knee-deep in bones and objects hurled
To the ground by its own race,
Who in destructive madhouse rage
And dark, foreboding, dead disgrace,
Maimed their planet, their only life.
A quest for power
Lead only to strife...
And of course, to certain death.
So now, this shadow, dying alone,
Raw and bloody and rotten breath,
Falls among the scattered bones.
Years ahead its screaming birth
Its last words echo all alone:
"So, is this what we did to Earth?

Kristin Fry

Spring, The Beginning Again

The ground is cold and unfed
Gray skies overhead
Suddenly, the sun emerges
To cast its warmth upon the sod,
Revealing the handiwork of God.
As under the wet leaves and snow
Touches of green, are beginning to show,
To start new growth again.
The birds migrate, the robins sing
A song of joy, it's spring.

Mary Muello

Tell It Like It Is!

Words can make the difference
Go on now and speak up...
Don't settle for just weeds
When you can have a buttercup!

Words hold so much meaning
So let the heart confess
Convey truth to all mankind
We should do no less!

Words make the world go 'round
Please tell me how you feel
Then I will answer in reply
"This goodness is so real!"

Words may change our lives
Oh! Say it!...Don't hold back
Don't fail to express your love
It takes no special knack!

Martha Duncan-Echelson

The Path Of Time

He came about with a
God given plan.
'thought he might better
his fellow man.
Teeming with passion unfulfilled,
he'll take his revenge
in the blood they spilled.
Now we're wandering down
the path of time.
One breadth removed from
the ultimate crime.
Will your life be well spent,
or had you better repent?

Roman Dolny

Untitled

Look at the wonderful things
God has put on this earth.
The flowers, the trees, and don't
forget, he has given us birth.
His son, he did send,
Through Joseph and Mary,
So through God's son, our burdens
are carried,
He loves us so, and how do I
know?
Because of his word, I believe in
Him, for us to serve.
And when I leave this troubled
world,
I will go to Heaven, where my
Lord has ruled!

Lucretia Vallecorsa

My Love

My heart belongs to he
He who does not know
Was this love meant to be
This love that I cannot show
I feel empty without him near
And I cry my sadness away
For he has another he loves dear
For this is why I do not say
What my heart desires.

Mary Rebecca Tedder

God's Tiniest Angel

As the world slept,
God's tiniest angel wept.
An angel that never
experienced life.
Yet, felt the pain of death.
In the mist,
In the sky,
The tiniest angel flies,
with wings so small,
as if those of a sparrow.
And sometimes among the
roar of thunder,
This little one wanders,
surrounded by clouds,
As if still in the womb,
of its mother.

Mary Anne Crowe

Amidst A Thousand Heartbeats

On the cliff we stand,
Grandfather and I,
Overlooking the tumultuous water
A thousand heartbeats, it sounds like
The spirits of lives past

"Listen," Grandfather says.
I press my ear to his chest.
His beat is sure and strong,
Like that of the spirits.
"That is life."

That autumn,
As the leaves turned red
And the flowers withered in the cold
Grandfather's heartbeat weakened
And the sleep of forever claimed him.

On the cliff I stand,
Alone,
Overlooking the tumultuous water.
There are a thousand heartbeats.
But I am here to listen for only one.

Linda Adams

The Glint Of Gold Is Sorrow-Dark'd

The glint of gold is sorrow-dark'd,
Guilt-glided scarlet stain —
Exacting payment Satan mark'd;
Years of exquisite pain.

We kneel in reparation
And repentance for these deaths.
Our Nation's hedonism stalks
New life that God has blessed.

Our moral aberrations are
What steals each baby's breath.
Such vile permutations:
Politics' permissive death.

Tears were shed for precious dead
Which sin put in the ground;
While laws protecting human life
Man's highest Court struck down.

All these small, sad corpses here
Shed tears in which we'll drown;
And babies bled of promised years
Will one day wear a crown.

Kay Trudell

The Destination

This lost lady
has found herself,
in his arms...

He who has held her,
while she recovered
from the pain of her past.

He who has understood
such intense pain,
having lived through his own.

Weathering the years
with dignity,
always navigating his own destiny;

The sea of fear
has never conquered
this captain.

And so she has come home,
to a new love,
a new life- to hope eternal.

B. J. Brackin

My Cowboy

I once knew a cowboy so tall and burley
He had cold brown hair that was curly
He was nice, kind and polite
He made me feel like I was somebody
not just a voice in the night.

He sings as he goes through the day
Everyone waits to hear what he says
as they go on their way
If you listen to the words carefully
you hear the melody of days old
Listen carefully you can hear
the stories he has told.

My cowboy has become a recluse
and wants to stay home
If he was again that cowboy he would roam
The cowboy is still in him barely
as he sings his songs merrily
Come July he will turn fifty
but I still think he is nifty.

Marion Brakel

He Lifts Me Up

When I feel blue
He lifts me up.
He shows me the way
To have a better day.

When my mind is deeply troubled
When I don't know what to do
I get down on my knees
I pray.
He lifts me up.

When I stumble, and fall,
With mercy, and kindness
He lifts me up.
Off the floor
I stand strong.
I stand tall.

When I get lost
When I lose my sight
He lifts me up.
He shines his light.
I find my way back home.

Karen Frazell

Duo Of Love

They romp and play down on the floor
He screams and squeals then begs for more

Little hands so strong and stout
Reach out to find her still about

She lifts the child upon her knee
And whispers to him lovingly

Brushing lollipop from windblown hair
She finds him something clean to wear

Eyes of blue meet a gaze so tender
As he seeks her out before surrender

Scattered toys soon forgotten
Little boy cares seem to lighten

He lays his head upon her chest
And finally does consent to rest

His dreams drift on without alarm
Because he lays in Mommy's arms

Silvia Walker

The Norseman

He is kind, he is clever;
He tries always to do good,
To win at every game he plays,
And do the things he should.

We like his cheerful intellect,
Loyalty and all.
But most of all, his great strong arms,
That would not let me fall.

He gathers in his car,
The elderly and lame;
Takes them all to church,
And brings them home again.

With gentleness, he helps us
As we come and go.
With Christian love and tenderness,
And patience when we're slow.

An angel in disguise?
An angel he is not.
He is a Norseman from Wisconsin,
And we love him quite a lot!

Martha Alden

My Dear Child:

Alone I sit
hearing you breathe
watching you squirm,
wondering if you'll wake.
Alone I sit needing to hold you.
Needing to tell you
oh how much, "I love you."
Alone I sit
hearing you cry.
Knowing you need
to feel security from me.
Alone I sit tears in my eyes.
Your cries I hear
within my heart.
I sit alone
haunted by free choice.
Wondering how you'd
feel in my arms.
I sit alone hearing your cries,
knowing a part of me has died.

Trisha Renee Lund

Cheremie

No longer stands the little girl,
Her eyes ablaze with wonder,
She stands with dreams within her heart
And goals for her to ponder.

She gazes at the endless sky
While winds caress her fears,
And ease those uncertainties
That cause her silent tears.

Much like the butterfly in flight
With beauty, strength and grace
She brings to those her gifts of joy
Like lilies on white lace.

Her paths will cross with many
The choices are her own
She'll learn of truth and honesty,
And wisdom through her soul.

The Lord will be her candle,
Her rainbow in the sky,
The song that whispers in the wind
The light within her eyes.

Lisa Ann Noelani Brown Barretto

Eagle Wings

To fly like an eagle,
High up in the air,
Feeling so feather light,
Without a single care.

I would soar up above,
and look down below,
and not be sorry I left,
All my troubles and woes.

To feel so free,
and full of peace,
My worries and concerns
would surely cease.

But that is just a dream,
not reality,
then a verse in Isaiah,
Comes running back to me:

"But they that wait upon the
Lord shall renew their strength,
they shall mount up with wings as
eagles...."

Sandra Jean Maynard

Ho! Ho! Ho!

I believe in Santa Claus
Ho! Ho! Ho! Ho! Ho! Ho!-
I believe in Santa Claus
I want you all to know-
'Cause I remember yesterday
But-it-was-many years ago-
When all I got on Christmas morn'
Was the fresh new fallin' snow,
Ah-h! But there were many other times
Good fortune smiled on me-
Then I found all the things
I could wish for
Underneath my Christmas tree-
So-o-I believe in Santa Claus
Ho! Ho! Ho! Ho! Ho! Ho!-
I believe in Santa Claus
And - I love him so-
Ho! Ho! Ho! Ho! Ho! Ho! Ho!-
Yes - I still love him so-
Merry Christmas everybody

Lucille Planz

Secrets

The china doll sits
high upon the shelf
appearing so delicate
and far above fear.

Her secrets are guarded
beneath her painted face
and heavy gown,
guarded so well that
she feels they may exist
in her mind alone.

But if someone were
to take her down
and remove the paint from her face,
they would find many cracks
in the once-solid facade.
Then the secrets would come out
amidst her many tears.

If only someone
would dare to ask her
about the secrets beneath her gown.

Pamela C. Benedict

Nature

This sight that often goes unseen
Holds a place in the heart of man,
For only by taking time to look
At this beauty will we understand -

The sunrise that holds a sight
Of crispness the sharpest bestowed,
The frosty grass glistening
Holds beauty for young and old -

Can we hold these four seasons
To sharpen our love of this view,
Or does beauty pass in anguish
No longer bringing happiness due -

Let us revisit this beauty
More often than four times a year,
Spring and summer are beautiful
And in winter this beauty is clear -

But in autumn this beauty is breathless
With a multitude of colors to see,
In this beautiful country we live in
This land holds an ecstasy -

LanaJo Watson-Hansen

The River Jordan

I scrub my head.

I sit in this river
Hollering to the heavens.
Begging him to cleanse
My soul.
Trying to remove the white wash
From the picket fence.
Asking him to help rid
My indoctrination into sin.
I don't seek knowledge
But The Truth.

So I scrub harder.

Phillip L. Hampton

"The Battle"

Evil unravels its wings.
Hope runs and hovers in fear,
The armageddon rises growing off
of sins,
Things cherished are no longer
held dear.
Through the clouds creation shines
upon the day,
That God's Leviathan goes forth
to play.
Death returns to its evil crypt,
As the last tear falls with
nowhere to hit.

Kristina Klippert

Oh Child Of Mine

Oh child of mine, so small and frail
How can I make you see.
The dangers lurking everywhere
As if this was to be.
Do not give into this unrest.
Your peers will put you to a test
Remember inner strength is one to rule.
Not race or creed,
This is the rule.
So hold on sweet child of mine.
The truth will be here soon.
You'll understand these words I say.
To hold them dear both night and day.
And you'll be grown on that fine day.

Patricia Ekonomidis

On And On

Aging men still holding their guitars
how much they tell us at their task
We wish their lives could be ours
themselves giving without any mask
on and on

Unheard messages for years and years
but the melodies still persist
We can never know their tears
the stories are ours we insist
on and on

Still only a child in a fading body
trying to tell us what they know
Attempting to teach the hard lesson
the ones they are trying to show
on and on

Suddenly awakened from our sleep
their message becomes very clear
And we pray our souls to keep
so our memories remain forever here
on and on

Richard Kaufenberg

Our Son

He lived this life in a few short days.
His life on earth we can only praise.
Why he was taken God knows alone.
He is with him in that immortal home.
Though his hands I cannot see.
They will always beckon and reach for me.
To meet him on that beautiful shore.
Where we will meet and part no more.
Though it breaks my heart with pain.
Although we miss him just the same.
Our earthly loss is heaven's gain.

Mamie Tefertiller

I Cannot Find The Words

I cannot find the words to say
How much you mean to me.
Please remember that the wind is cold
And the winter is bare
Like the mantle of the hungry tramp
Who stares blindly
Out of a Manhattan bistro.

I wish that we could dance with the wit
That Shakespeare knew
And it would comfort me—-
So rare the mind he had.
I wish that you were here
To cast away the darkness.

Smile as you do
And the world cannot help but bow.
Love and you are shod in silver shoes.
They run together in the swiftest manner
And never grow tired
Of the maddening dance of life.

Spencer Knox Kendig

And The World Came Tumbling Down

Like Humpty Dumpty all in pieces
Hurt and pain never ceases...
Sweep the floor, make the bed,
Wash dishes as tears are shed,
The whole world falling apart...
Not even one knows where to start.
A child in the barrens losing hope,
Another in a city trying to cope...
Starvation and fear....common friends,
Their futures on our present depends.
Do we choose to end the race
To self-destruction and disgrace
Or make for all an early grave...
Too late this world of ours to save?

B. J. McKee

My Daughter

The sweetest person that I know,
Hustles, bustles, always on the go.
This young lady, with children three,
I'm proud that she's a part of me.

The sweetest person in the world,
Always there brave and bold.
This young lady, I hold dear,
Ever close, always near.

The sweetest person, dear to my heart,
Through life forever, we'll never part.
I hold her dear, above all others,
For this young lady is MY DAUGHTER.

Margaret A. Fife

Without You

I cannot cry
I feel I could die
without you here
my world is full of fear.
I sit alone and scared
my feelings unprepared
not knowing what to do
the next time I see you.
Will I receive a kiss,
filling my world with bliss
or will you push me away
and make me wait another day,
Another day without you.

Tricia Bouchard

"Think Of Me"

Think of me and know that
I am thinking of you-
"Feel my love my nearness!"
It's there! - It's all around you.
You are always on my mind,
and forever in my heart.
That special place that belongs
to only you.
Glory in this good feeling,
just as I will.
And know deep in your
heart how much I love you and
miss you.
"How much I will always love you."
Long as there's life left within
me, you will be a part of me.
For nothing last's forever
we live, we love, we die,
and meet again in Heaven.

Virginia Raymond

The Man Who Cared...dedicated to Richard C. Wade M.D.

It was back in 75
I called the office,
Of the Best Doctor Alive!

As the years did come and go,
He took good care of this
patient from head to toe.

We had many laughs,
He helped me through many a cry,

Before his time came
And God called him to rest,
I told him Dr. Wade
You're the best
You can't leave us,
Now to go to heaven on high
(We're selfish you see)
Who'll care for us if you die?!

God gave his answer
Richard you've done your best,
Now come home my son
Come home to rest.

Sarah Porter Reese

Nasturtium Seeds

I have thrown
Nasturtium seeds
on poor soil
Near the window
to cover
the memories
of past houses
and my gardens
Of long ago.

The enraged lice
that cling and drink
and suck the juice
of their green leaves
Will not defeat
My purpose - no!
For still
I will
on the debris
grow nasturtiums
By my window.

Josette Reboul Brogan

Mother

Of all the ways I love you dear
I can't begin to tell,
Because you've always stood close by
When I was sick or well.

The little things you've done for me
In many countless ways,
You deserve the best in life
Today and all your days.

If I should try to write a book
And in that book reveal,
I could not begin to try to express
The love for you I feel.

In our rush of daily living
I all too seldom mention,
My love for you dear Mother
For your love and kind attention.

But should your years on earth be few
And I am left behind,
Your precious love will be my guide
Dearest Mother of mine.

Margaret Jones

If You Believe

Last night I saw your face, and
I could have sworn you were here,
I thought my eyes deceived me,
but, your image was so clear.
You came to me, kissed me, and held
me tight,
The love we feel for each other
filled my room last night.
You gently caressed me as your image
began to go,
You held my hand so tight, and
said it's time I know.
We may not always be together
and yes, it is hard to leave,
but, we will always be together
in spirit... IF YOU BELIEVE.

Sharon E. Sherry

My Grandma

I came home from school that day
I didn't want to talk or even play
my Grandma had passed away.

As I flew back to Mass.
I thought about the past
I knew I should have said my last
I love you

It was the day of the funeral
Everybody was in tears
No one could bear, to think she
was really gone

Some people say it was God's way.
That's why my Grandma passed away

Marigold Scott

Autumn Song

The wind conducts a symphony with trees
In radiant shimmering colors.
Twirling leaves drift above like notes
From a crimson crescendo.
In finale that fades with the last cooing dove,
October becomes a whisper.

Carin Kontner

Awakening

As I stand at your grave and weep,
I hear a whispering voice upon the wind,
I am not here, I do not sleep.

I am the summer breezes that blow,
I am winter's fresh fallen snow.

I am the sky of white and blue.
I am the early morning mist, you call dew.

I am the day which brings you light,
I am the stars that shine for you at night.

I forever live in your heart,
For in your life, I played a part.

Do not stand at my grave and cry,
I am not here, I did not die.

Marjorie J. Carroll

Ode To My Love

Weekdays when I rise,
I hear music in my chest,
It is happiness in disguise,
It is me feeling my best.

You are my sweet inspiration,
The one who keeps me dreaming,
Blessed imagination, exciting
Anticipation,
You are my reason for living.

I love you so much,
It's driving me crazy,
I long for your touch,
Don't ever stop being my baby.

Pablo J. Agrio

Missing Trees

It is quite ironic
To watch subdivisions grow
Prospective homeowners contract
With reputable builders who know

What the market will bear
The value of each plot
Removing every tree in sight
Visually enlarging every lot

Foundation, bricks and mortar
Walls framed with lumbered wood
Reaching up two stories tall
Where once dense forest stood

Wood shingles for roof aesthetics
Sapling planted on boundary line
Tree growth will take many years
On this new street named Shady Pine

Marcia Waldbillig

Soweto

I saw trembling hand
leading a cane
to a box of dreams,
drenched in blood and
hopes.
I saw a man, tall
in his unspoiled pride.
I saw a people walking
to their freedom through
unfailing strength,
I saw a nation
bowing to its truth.

Monique Adam

"We... Find"

I dreamt ... one night
I held truth ... in hand
While the other held
Epitome of man

And ... sewn between
This wreath of time
The epoch search
To what we find

Watch echoes passing
Of scenes ... to dream
Closing the circle
With reason ... for being

Embryo's of time
Conceived ... in space womb
Lay postulate soul
Seeded to ... take hold

For ... We Are ... The Beginning
That threads a time
As We ... Are the End
To what ... We find

Nathan T. Sharpe

Tears

See my face,
I hide my tears.
My smile fades,
I hide my tears.

Loneliness is known,
I hide my tears.
No warmth is shown,
I hide my tears.

No laughter near,
I hide my tears.
I often fear,
I hide my tears.

I hide my tears,
I hide my tears,
I hide my tears.

Linda S. Thompson

Bring Back My Heart

When first we met, I fell in love.
  I know you loved me too.
Right from the start I knew that I
  Would give my heart to you.
The time we spent together
  Was the happiest I knew,
And we both told each other
  That always we'd be true.
Then the day you went away
  And left me sad and blue,
Not only did you take my love
  You took my heart with you.
I cannot love another,
  For that would never do.
Come back to me someday my love
  And bring my heart with you.
And when you come I'll welcome you
  With open arms, it's true.
You'll bring my heart back to me
  So I can give it back to you.

Marion M. Peterson

Memories

As we walked across the old mill bridge
I looked into your smiling face
And touched your warm, soft hand
"Don't cry - school is fun," you said.

All day you'd clean and cook and mend
While singing songs of praise and joy
At night you'd read and talk and pray
And teach me how to think and live.

When winter came and I was ill
You sat long hours beside my bed
And sponged my feverish brow.

When you were ill your other child and I
Didn't stop our game of hide and seek
Till Papa said, "She's dead."

Martha Belle Wright

My Boyfriend

My boyfriend is so special,
I LOVE him so so much
I don't know what I'd do without him
'Cause I'm oh so much in LOVE
Some people say I'm crazy
for going out with him
But as you can tell, I don't really care.
If it wasn't for him
and of course my favorite cousin
I don't know where I'd be today
For I'm glad I found him first.
This is truly the first person
I've ever really LOVED
I don't know what I'd do without him
Cause I'm oh so much in LOVE
My boyfriend will always be, that very
special one
And I pray to God that we will never part
'Cause I'm sure it'll break my heart
I just want my boyfriend to know that
I LOVE HIM WITH ALL MY HEART.

Yvette Valdez

Aftermath

With terror in my heart
I rambles.
Over the dissolute land,
Where once rich fertile
soil lay.
Untouched by human hand.
When suddenly, without warning,
From the darkness of the night.
Legions of warriors came
On wings, in flight.
Roaring of their engines,
Made a thunder like sound.
Rendering noises fulled the air.
Death and destruction,
seemed to be everywhere.
The quiet calmness,
Surround the earth
and sky.
There I stood alone,
Afraid.

Margaret Grzyll

Life's Generations

So many years, so long ago
I reached back in time
Your Bible, Mother, came to me
as I sat quietly aside

Little X's marking words
Finding reference for your needs
I followed your life's journey
as if I were at your knee

I saw your struggles, felt your pain
understanding you more today
Not just Mother but the woman inside
So much you had to say

I couldn't set the Bible down
Excitement filled my being
HIS HOLY SPIRIT entered in
This was the time for seeing

I saw life that must go on
through generations of the years
The Hope, Peace, Joy and Love
will cast out doubts and fears

Loraine Wojtysiak

Tribulation Or Clouds Of Glory?

When I look at the heavenly blue sky.
I realize we will meet Jesus up there
In the sweet by and by.
And then we will never have anymore
Heartaches or worry.
When god gathers his children up in
The clouds of glory.
Then those we have tried to warn but
They wouldn't hear.
Would be left to go through all that
Terrible tribulation and fear.
God doesn't want you to be left for
He loves you so be aware.
And let's be ready and waiting so he
can gather us all up there.

Nellie Mingus Roberts

My First Best Friend

The day I was born,
  I respected and loved you.
I spoke my first word
  to prove that I adored you.

The first day of kindergarten,
  you were there because you cared.
As long as you were beside me,
  I never once felt scared.

Years passed on, I grew up,
  and along came many problems.
You understood me through them all,
  and tried to help me solve them.

Now I'm older and I realize
  what a special person you are,
We made it through all the bad times,
  no problem too big or too small.

I love you, Mom, you are the
  best friend I have ever had!

Leigh Stephens

Untitled

As I watched the crowd
I saw you there
You looked very proud
All I could do was stare.

Then you saw me
I shyly smiled to you
And it was returned quickly
I then knew what it meant to you.

Though we never met
I knew you would see
You could never forget
A kind person like me.

Victoria H. East

When...

When I look into your eyes
I see someone who cares.
When I stand by your side
I know you will always be there.

When people ask I say
Yes he is mine,
He makes me feel happy
And leaves a warm feeling
inside

When I think of you
I see a smile on your face
and know you'll be there with
every embrace.

When I think of us
we are growing as one...
This is not over we have yet to begun

Kathleen McFadden

Music

As I dance,
I think of you.
The music.
My passion.
Touching my heart,
you make me feel.
A desire...
I still don't understand.
My heart,
full of peace.
I move to the music.
Beautiful music.
And I can feel it,
yes...
In every inch of my body
and soul.
I can feel it.
My feet
no longer on the ground.
I can fly...

Marci Guglielmetti

Gypsy Moth

A Gypsy moth
In Gypsy cloth
Clothed in satin
And sheer silk chiffon
With a bodice
Of brocade and lace.

Matt T. Maki

No Where To Go

Lost and deserted,
I walk down this road,
Miles and miles I walk,
with no where to go.
So many turns, that could be wrong,
should I try one, or just move on?
I'm so confused, "Oh, what should I do?"
Should I keep walking until the
skies are blue?
Where am I going? Where does it end?
Where will it take me?
What will it begin?

Shannon Ortiz

Do You?

I need you, do you need me?
I want you and I might even love you.
Do you feel the same?
I want to be a part of your life.
Do you want to be a part of mine?
Do you dream of me as I dream of you?
Is it only my desire that you exist?
Or do you?
I believe that we were made for each other
From the beginning of time.
I think you are my destiny.
Do you believe you are mine?
I pray for you every night.
Do you?
I've wished upon stars for you.
Do you do the same for me.
Do you?

Tawnya Crossland

Undying Love

If only tomorrow were today
I would ride the winds of change
To bring back all my dreams
that have gone with yesterday.
To say goodbye
I've found so hard
But in my heart
you will always be
a true friend who has come to part
from a world so unserene.
And in the days that are to follow
Many tears
I will have cried.
Your love will always be with me.
For within each day
a little sun will shine.

Timothy S. Swan

Yearning

Drifting through divine winds,
Her awe filled beauty I'd love to win.
Spinning hearts, twist through the air,
Her crying soul just sits there.
She dislikes to see the love that's there,
Her bleeding heart rests in despair.
When alas, there is another soul,
Which bleeds and cries, so full of woe.
He yearns to meet the one who's there,
But he just sits in his despair.
None-the-less the winds shall change.
The hearts shall meet and be the same.
As joy and laughter echo on,
Spinning hearts drift through the dawn.

Russell George Robardey

If I Were Younger

If I were just a little younger
I'd rid the world of all the hunger
Dive for Pearls in the Indian Ocean
Go to Paris, if I had the notion
I'd climb Pikes Peak and get to the top
and ski down a slope, I wouldn't stop

I'd walk over hot coals in my bare feet
never, never feel the heat
Write a best seller you can bet
Autograph seekers I would get
I'd sing in the opera and gain acclaim
Everyone would know my name

If I were a little younger!

I'd go the moon in a rocket ship
Travel at a terrific clip
Ride a horse at Arlington Park
I'd even skinny dip in the dark

I know you believe all I say
I'd like to do these things today

If I were just a little younger!

William J. Formusa

Dear Mother

If only I could just look in on you,
I'd see your happy face.
For some of those who loved you,
Were waiting in that place.

There's a father and a mother,
A little brother too.
All waiting there with open arms
Just to welcome you.

Your loveliness outstanding,
On those streets of golden sand.
A little boy from long ago,
Now holds his Grandma's hand.

These thoughts give us peace,
But mother we miss you so.
Our lives go on without you,
But our hearts with you, you know.

Z. Louis Howard

If I Were A Spider

If I were a spider
I'd spin my web.
Then weave diamonds and
gold into my bed;
I'd spin in the morning,
and late at night.
I'd catch my prey with a
silken thread;
I'd dream of feathers
tiptoeing through my head.
Then after my work was done,
I'll marry me a spider
and we'd rest in the sun;
We'd play in the shadows,
and dance in the heat.
We'd dream of tidbits,
and good things to eat.

Nethelia Osgood

My Prayer

Thy love constraineth me.
If anger in my soul doth ride
Resentment to stealthily hide
Their ugly heads must fall and flee
Lord thy gentle love constraineth me
If stay deceit and worldly pride
Should seek rendezvous at my side
Cleaned of these I must be
Thy gentle love constraineth me!
If love of a person my life does surmount
To possess me, lure my from thy fount
Thy perfect self be first my plea
Thy gentle love constraineth me.
If death as a mighty choir should sound
Or decent adept, silent I to be found
Lord hold me fast thy face to see
Thy gentle love enfoldeth me!

Vilma Jean Ake

Hope!

Dear Heavenly Father-
If I could have one wish tonight,
And granted it could be-
I'd wish that every soul that lived
Would choose to follow Thee.
That peace would reign and love abound,
From coast to coast the whole world round.
That everyone, on bended knee
Would turn wholeheartedly to Thee;
And all the Halls of Heaven abound
With praise symphonies of sound.
Oh Father! what a joyful day
The world would know if I could say
"The prayerful hopes of grateful men
Have been fulfilled" -not might have been!

Rosemary E. Helmer

Mirror

If I do not look into my mirror,
If I do not look into your eyes,
I am not old.
My mind and spirit range,
Free in time and space.
I am still that child, who
Looked upon the world
With wonder in her eyes.
If I do not look into my mirror
If I do not look into your eyes.

Verle Nichols Higgs

Homage

Living on existence
Between the stained glass and the sea
She pays her homage only
To this ragged majesty ...

Who knows her name?

Her precious breath
Falls beneath the soul's intensity
For the child left unknown
To a broken legacy ...
Who knows the shame?

Twisting and turning
Red and gold the leaves are shed
"I give life to you, someone else's
Child."
She gently bows her head ...
In homage.

Kelly K. Herman

Feel With Me

If you are tired of life,
If you have had enough,
Just look into my eyes
and feel what you see.

If you are torn apart,
if pain feels your heart,
just look into my eyes
And feel what you see.

If you are sick of disguise
and of constant lies,
just look into my eyes
and feel what you see.

There is love in my eyes.
There is strength for both of us.
Just take a good look
and feel with me.

Miriam Gotlib

The Walk

I'm going out to take a walk,
I'll only stop when my feet hurt
And wait for a breeze to come
As well as you - my friend.

I'm going out for some spring air
That comes once a year
It's warm breeze going through my hair
I shouldn't be long, come join me.

Michele Harwood

Dreams Of Hope

Put a cloud in my hands!
I'll touch the silver drops,
I'll paint vast fields and meadows
with green and golden crops.

Put a sunray in my hands!
I'll warm your hearts and melt the ice,
I'll wipe the tears of yesterday
and fill with songs and lullabies.

Put a bread crumb in my hands!
I'll let the hungry feel its taste
as they regain their veins of life
and melt their footsteps in world's haste.

Put a dream in my hands!
I'll make it real, believe it's true,
I'll climb the mountains, sail the seas -
I am your hope - a lifetime friend for you.

Ona Bauzys

Age Or Not

I declare!
I'm beginning to wear!
My heart works just fine?
I find that I recline- a lot.
The prostate reciprocates,
And my kidneys hibernate.
I have to coax my mouth to articulate,
And boot up my mind to calculate.
It really is scary I know,
But I am crazy enough to keep right on
Living and loving just like
Any young fool.

Richard J. Thomson

Magnificent Mustangs Of Las Colinas

Wild Freedom Frozen
In a marble oasis
Reveals sacred bonds
Between art and history.
Magnificent grace
Propels enshrined mustang braves
From dusty mirage
Through civilizing decades;
Mute splendor halted
Between instinct and spirit.
Once radiant flesh
Now silent, shouts ecstasy;
Sculpted reminders
of unbridled courage, faith.

Kathryn Burns Ernst

Marriage Without Love

There was a time
In days of old,
For man to give
His love is told.

Payment of sums
In gold or fur,
Part of his wealth
Of value for her.

Chosen for what
She can provide,
Visions of love
Are set aside.

Marriage prevails
Doth love disdained,
Foolish man's bad
Bargain ordains.

Rose Leiterman

Autumn's Nocturne

Mystery shrouds Autumn
in her paradise
of golden lanterns
and amber lights.
Haunting melodies echo,
melancholy fills the air.
The voice of the trumpet
is muted.
Wind of Destiny
dances with Autumn
a fantasia of bolero.
Artists are enchanted
and then, a silent note.
Heaven's tears
console Mother Earth
Autumn
bids farewell.

Marian Lackey

Telling You

Telling you "I Love You"
Is easy to do,
Telling you "I Need You"
Is very easy too.

When I say "I Want You,"
And that I love you true,
Believe me when I say it,
Because I really do.

Shirley Downs

Keeping America Beautiful

America is so beautiful
In many, many ways.
I've found this out, as I traveled through
These great United States.

Each state has a different thing
That distinguishes it from the rest.
And, of course, everyone likes
Their home state the best.

Mine was South Dakota
With their Presidential shrine.
Their Black Hills and Bad Lands
Are favorites of mine.

All of God's creations
Are in one or another state.
The mountains, the desserts, the canyons,
The oceans and Great Lakes.

But most of all, God created us.
We're part of America, too.
So let us keep it beautiful,
By things we say and do.

Karen Olson Brinkman

Esther - "My Wife"

Who is important,
In my life—
That's easy to answer,
Of course, it's my "wife"...

She is the one,
Who looks after me—
Not only loving,
She is my "key"...

She always ignores,
Her own precious health—
Always doing for others,
And not for "herself"...

But, now it's time,
To slow down my "Dear"—
There's always tomorrow,
So have no fear...

Yet, there's one thing more,
I want you to hear—
That, "I Love You" dearly,
Each day in the year...

Bill Johnson

The Rhapsody Within

In my heart,
in my soul,
Music is composed.
In my heart,
in my soul,
The music stays.
The message,
the lyrics,
Contain no words at all.

The tempo,
the beat,
Create no rhythm.
In my heart,
in my soul,
This unique music plays.
In my heart,
in my soul,
This silent language speaks.

Shari McLean

Come With Me

Come with me,
In my world of misty green mansions,
Where there is only quietness,
Where the only roof over my head is the majestic giants of trees,
We will run through the magic endless beauty,
Where unheard of peace exists,
Where time has no measure,
With the wind laughing in your ears.
Where the birds sing endless melodies,
While the sunlight trips magically through the trees.
Come with me, on this endless journey,
Through countless moments, minutes, and hours,
While your heart and mind seem to travel through the span of time.
COME WITH ME.

Rosemarie Jackson

Still?

Is there love
In our age
Whose voice
Dispels rage?
Are there souls
In our day
Whose calls
Answer, I pray?
Is there truth
In our time
Whose demands
Punish all crime?
Are there morals
In our hour
Whose stature
Does not cower?
Is there justice
In our epoch
Whose strength
Makes the lame to walk?

Wade J. Bove

Monastic Elderhostel

We leave the stress that takes its toll
In search of sun and peace;
To contemplate our inner soul
And give new life a lease.

The monks in silence supplicate,
Incense and robes refine,
With chant the canon celebrate
To live out God's design.

We Elders meet to meditate
'Mid Holy Cross and shrine:
A hymn to sing, a verse create
A stroll 'neath scented pine.

All this beside a mighty stream;
Rainbow - Creation's sign,
A bell tolls on to end our dream,
At peace, we wine and dine.

Renewed, refreshed, restored to health
For most our tasks confine
Us to our worldly search for wealth
Less thought of things divine.

Wilbur Harold Wright

The Firing Squad Of Time

The hearts of men beat slowly there
In single rooms paid by the week
For loneliness is hard to share
With no one there no need to speak

Their faces sharply lined confide
With eloquence a last lament
Of silent rage that burns inside
A fireproof building of cement

Defiantly they wait to fall
"No blindfold" angry eyes declare
Like heroes up against the wall
They wear the darkness of despair

With next to nothin' but regret
No sweetness save a sip of wine
Small comfort in a cigarette
They face the firing squad of time

Tony Gorman

Sister Mine

Sister, oh my sister
in the dark
I can hear you whisper
Alisa - lis - alisa
such a little girl
with a head full of curls
sister, little sister
I look at your picture
and want to go back in time
to hug you, little sister mine.
Film caught for eternity
a slender child
bright-eyed and hopeful.

and I want to whisper yesterday
sister, sister
do you want to play?

Marilyn B. Robinson

The Leaves Of August

When birds begin to gather
In the distant northern sky
And breezes, soft, are chilled
By autumn's early sigh...
I note the Leaves of August
Have a lessening of green
And my feelings of nostalgia
Overwhelm my very being.
It's not the Rite of Passage...
The inevitable flight of summer..
That makes me feel so sad,
But, rather, the measure of youth
Each of us has had..
Faded gently from the start..
Forever precious in our heart.

Mary Ann Sannita

Untitled

The moon fills my heart
in white feathers
trembling gathers through my fingers
weights my eyes
falls like stars
north and south, east and west
astride her breast
escaped aureoles of silk and satin
in heavens in between
spent down

Norm Sedelmaide

Shadows Dancing On The Wall

Shadows dancing on the wall, caught up
  in the golden sun
Laughter and joy at last, sadness and
  sorrow gone
Filling my heart with joy, the joys of
  his love
The beauty of his presence here;
Thoughts bring us back again, reflections
  of our past
Shadows dancing on the wall, caught up
  in time.
It seems like yesterday, how quickly we
  forget
As I reach the ending of
  my life.

Lawrence I. Deutsch

In the Middle of the Moment

In the middle of a street I stood,
In the middle of a neighborhood,
In a place where I grew up and learned,
In a place I thought I understood.

In the middle of a yard I stared,
At a place that was no longer there.
Where the children, on a sunny day,
Played their games without a care.

In the middle of my life I knew,
That I would no longer be with you,
Because the game they played that day,
Took the middle of my heart away.

Don't they feel? Don't they care?
Don't they see? Don't they hear?
Can they no longer shed a tear?

In the middle of the world we've made,
In the midst of hope for a better way,
In the middle of my yesterday,
In the middle of today.

Susan A. Rife

"Ode To My Mentor"

Your boundless energy
  In the quest for truth
To right the wrong
  Was your constant pursuit.

The hours spent
  When no one cared
You gave me hope
  In my despair.

The sky was dark
  Shedding an ominous light
My dream was crushed
  And out of sight.

The darkest of tunnels
  Before me laid
Your hand reached out
  To guide my way.

My faith is restored
  In all of mankind
I can look towards tomorrow
  Knowing once again, the sun will shine.

Katherine Kalanta

Rainy Thursday

Where do all the birds go
  in the rain?

There my happy thoughts go,
  leaving pain.

When the sun shines,
  I can fly.

Tears on my window
  make me cry.

Mary Ellen Petty

"Wolf"

They eat carcasses rotting
In the road.

They drink stagnant water polluted
With trash.

They sneak around in the dark hours
Of night.

They are weak without the company
Of a pack.

They often bleed to death with a
Leg mangled in a trap.

They mate with only one for life.
I wish I were a wolf.

Robin Suzanne King

Who Am

In the park
in the spring
nobody knows how to sing.

I am who am
the one that is
carry me through
my loneliness.

Thoughts of a new day
dreams of one gone
give me the strength to carry on.

How long is forever
just till the end
stop trying to finish
and try to begin.

Robert Casarez Jr.

Smiles

You can find smiles
In trees
On Cheshire cats
With fleas
They can also be found
On airline stewardesses
Who never frown
Or on a half toothless face
Of some kid
Who just stole second base
And if you see me coming
You'll notice me humming
For I found love today
In a different place
See the smile
On my face

Richard A. Garcia

Household

My house holds two octogenarians
in various stages of decay
and, their widowed daughter
in the youth of old age.
Sometimes the three laugh
at some old memory
or some present hilarity.
Often they show the strain
of sixty years together,
moving around each other
like days end shadows.

Loretta V. Swisher

Untitled

Truth is unchanging,
Indestructible, some may
Seek to conceal it

Lusting for power
They may destroy each other,
This nation, this world

Then truth will be found
Standing freely and alone
Still immutable, indestructible

Leah A. Jones

Get Out Of The Rain

We will come out of the rain
  into sunshine
And watch the daffodils bloom
  And we will forget our sadness
And say goodbye to the gloom
  They say the grass is greener
On the other side of the street
  Not so if you look at your side
And value the friends you meet
  I think I will stay on my side
And be a friend to man
  If I can only find my way
According to our Master's Plan.

Minnie McMahan La Pointe

Every Moment With You

Every second with you,
Is a second,
  That goes too fast.

Every minute with you,
Is a minute,
  That wants to go back.

Every hour with you,
Is an hour,
  That doesn't want to pass.

Every day with you,
Is a day,
  That is forever cherished.

Val Blakely

Time In Life

Alll the time inn life too spend.
Knot a fog doo I fend.
Never think about thee end.
Time to prepare,
life to endur
hazy blr
frtilizr

Sara Kaden

The Pathway To Heaven

The pathway up to heaven
Is steep and hard to climb,
But if we ask our Savior
He will help us every time.

For life has its sorrow
And life has its joy
But we will get to heaven
If God's graces we employ

If we see another person
Who needs a helping hand
And we extend ours gladly
Because we understand

God will bless us greatly
With a love so deep and pure
Any faults or sins we have
His gentle love will cure

He will take our souls to heaven,
Where he wants us all to be
Yes, he will take us all to heaven
And there will set us free.

Magdalene R. Maynard

"Dreams Of You"

To dream a dream come true
is to dream a dream of you,
Loving thoughts of beauty seem
so blue, if I only knew what
kind of dream you'd be...
I would feel a life content in me.
You're the only dream for me...
The only one that's in harmony...
Let there be feelings of colors
matching yours, (for you're the dream
come true)...
Blue to match the sky
and green to catch the grass,
Telling me...you're the love
in my dreams....

Tina Louise Rastrelli

Heart Break

I have tried to love another.
It is so hard to do.
All my thoughts and feelings,
Are wrapped up in you.
I have tried to do without you,
But it cannot be,
I have loved you such a long time,
You are a part of me.
I only have but one heart,
And giving it to you,
Surely was the sad start,
Of breaking it in two.

Lavina Gamper

Fade To Black

Love is like a burned-out star.
It keeps shining despite its dying,
for the light takes forever to reach me.
I never knew the star had died.
But, alas, it did.
Its light still shone brightly,
for the source of that loving light
was lost to me, but memories—
They only fade from view,
like the light of a dying star.

Karri Emly

My Unjust World

In a newspaper that I had read
It seemed so wrong to me
That an innocent man had been killed
And the guilty one walked free.
When people are hurt every day
For the color of their skin,
When a person's thoughts cannot be heard
They must be kept within,
Where politics rule our lives
Our written rights are burned,
When men in suits can take and spend
Every penny earned,
Where drugs are common on the streets
And guns are sold to kids,
Where cocaine rots the future's mind
Another secret hid.
This unjust world it seems to me
We live it every day.
The only thing that we can do
Is close our eyes and pray...

Tremayne Harer

Questions

Oh what is our world coming to,
it seems to be such a mess;
With riots, killings, racial wars,
we are living under great stress;
Whatever happened to our heritages,
where everyone got along;
When people spent time dancing,
and crooning sweet little songs;
Let us hope we come down to earth again,
and make our lives more worthwhile;
Greeting our neighbors happily,
with a handshake and a smile;

Patsy K. Mathis

The Dance Of Time

The dance lady danced.
He liked to watch.

The dance lady talked.
He liked to listen.

She called out his name.
He went to her.

She spoke of her years.
He suddenly stopped.

When the dance lady dances,
He does not watch.

Rosemarie McDonough

Never Said Goodbye

I see his face
it's remembered well,
but the way he smiled,
and the way he laughed
have left my mind.
Protecting me from evil
I feel his spirit near,
holding my hands through
the rough times
I know I love him
but does he?
Why has death taken him
from me,
'cause I never got to say goodbye.

Kelley J. Edwards

The Tide At Night

When the tide comes in at night,
It takes a long and narrow flight
When it takes this narrow flight
It is, a cold dark night.

When the tide comes in at night.
It's set on, a course just right,
In it comes, flows up and down,
As it heads for higher ground.

When the tide comes in at night,
It runs under, the bright moon light,
On it sloshes, all around.
Maybe, there will be, a calm.

When the tide comes in at night
On it goes 'til morning light.
Once it reaches, its own main,
Then, it starts all over again.

Ruth E. Albro

My Husband, My Love

Fourteen years in December
It would have been for us
Oh why did God have to take him
I guess he knew he must

My heart is so broken
I wonder will it mend
He was everything in the world to me
He was even my best friend

My days are filled with sorrow
The nights are oh so long
The tears I shed are many
I pray God will make me strong

I am very thankful
That we got to share our love
And I know he's very happy
With God in heaven above.

Linda Widner

The Passage

There was a storm inside my soul
Its eye left a pain in my heart,
And there remained an emptiness
And a life slowly falling apart.

I searched for what I did not know
And blindly walked the days,
I looked most everywhere for answers
With a last resort - to pray!

Then pain became but a memory
Giving way to a new life so dear,
Now when I sit alone in nothingness
It's a place I no longer fear.

I've learned that this was but a passage
To a world so new and so bold,
I respect the peace of my solitude
And the faith in my life that unfolds.

Madeline Arlotta-Cupo

Grandpa's Little Girl

I know it's wishful thinking,
Just as wishful as can be,
Still I wish that I was young again,
and sitting on his knee.
One tearful day I moved away,
but Grandpa had a plan-
He wrote for me bright poetry,
(I was his favorite fan!)
His plan was interrupted
by a greater plan above-
God carried him to heaven
where I sent him all my love.
The years were sad and lonely
after Grandpa went away,
but as I grew, I treasured more
his kind and loving way.
When adversities upset me
and my thoughts are in a whirl,
a knight in shining armor,
rescues Grandpa's little girl.

Virginia Roossien

The Time Of Waiting

As I set mine eyes toward heaven
knowing the one above.
I consecrate my life
as sure as God is love.

The path of life is hard.
There is no easy way.
Rough and rocky is the road,
with many a curve and sway.

Will this have been in vain
or success around the corner,
still, seasons shall continue
for all should be in order.

The Master cometh quickly
as the Bible does specify
Let us cease from our raging
so that no one should needless die.

Farther down the Road,
no longer a muffled sigh.
The answer will always be there,
as for the Lord we try.

Randall D. Wheeler

Grave Descent

November's shroud descends
Lamenting shrunken days
Whose brevity of light depicts
Time's swiftly tilting passages

Elastic days depart
Escorted by stretches of darkness
That demonstrate
November's somber consort

Elemental, stark,
"No moon—no sun—no stars"
November hosts
The weather's harsh arousal

In fits and starts
Casting dismal shadows
That illustrate
November's razor-sharp embrace
Of time's relentless orbit
Of the grave.

P. Marguerite Forcier

"Night Watch"

Heard a diesel engine
last night around
about 10 o'clock

Stopped at my corner
then took a left and
chugged on down
the block.

I didn't get up and take a look
didn't want to press
my luck,

Cause I like to think you
guard my nights
in that shiny
big red truck.

Patricia F. Law

My Prayer

Dear God, hear me when I pray
lead me on the narrow way.
Be a light that shows me how
to tread the road I'm walking now.
A better friend I cannot know
to help me in this world below.
Without God life is not complete
whether it is bitter or mostly sweet.
I try to live my life each day,
to please you, God, let come what may.
I want to live some day with you
when this old earth has been made new.

Vivian Gower

Pocahontas' Plea

Papa no!
It's so unfair
He needs our love
You have to care

What has he done
I beg of you
This man who cares
Whose heart is true

Let him go
Set him free
Don't kill this man
Listen to me

Who is this man
What has he done
It's so unfair
He is but one

Laurie Stevens

The Virgin's Chamber

Light be at my window
Love be at my door
Shadows dissipate soundlessly
Into petals lying dead on the floor

Innocence cover my roof
Maiden Pride adorn my walls
Knowledge flood the interior
When resistance softly falls

Passion provide my foundation
Modesty thrive in my room
Keys will unlock the secrets
That left in darkness loom

Stacy Greathouse

He Was There

When I was born I had
Just one special wonderful dad...
He was there when I was small
He was there when I grew tall...
He was there when I was a child
He was very gentle and mild...
His lap was my favorite place to be
While he sang his songs and rocked me...
He was there when I needed a friend
He was always there to the end...
He was there when I needed him so
He rarely ever told me no...
He was there at night
He was there even when it was bright...
My dad Louis Dufek was always very near
I am thankful he was, he was so dear...

Yvonne Dufek-Hogue Welbor

The Vampire's Kiss

Fleeting moments -
Lifetimes lived in the
Passing of days. Passions
Shared, desires quenched
Needs awakened.

Fleeting moments -
Life's abundant cup
Taken, by one, from many
Memories, happiness, ultimate
Sorrow, absolute pain.

Fleeting moments -
Lifetimes of hope
Lived in darkness.
Loving, wanting, touching...
Eternity of night.

Fleeting moments.
Lived in a lover's
Last breath...
Eternity alone.

Sandra Bergen Cook

Individuality

Why make your feet
March to the beat
Of someone else's Drum?

Why let the defeatist attitudes
And platitudes of some
Dim the light of your Rainbow?

Let your Spirit fly.
Control your life.
Choose a Path and follow your dream
To Somewhere.

Myrtle Cox

Expectations

I thought you would,
But you didn't.
I hoped you'd see the need,
But you couldn't.
I wanted you to be there,
But you weren't.
I expected you to understand.
But how could you?
I never told you what I wanted,
needed or expected.

Debbie Haney

The Cross

CHRIST
Son of God
Alpha and Omega
Jesus gave his Life - in our place - to gave us
And give us Victory over sin and death
The Spirit of Adoption we can call him Abba
Trust the Lord
and obey
Inheritance of
eternal life
Obtain peace and
joy
Never cease to
praise him for
his blessings
without
Number!
How precious the gift of SALVATION.
Ask him into your life TODAY.

Lorrie K. Bowers

The River Of Forgotten Souls

The River of Forgotten Souls has hungrily greeted the doorsteps of those
Who are weak and defenseless.
It knows how to break those who are strong
And those who are courageous.
Primarily, it feeds upon those who have been broken for so long
And have already been forgotten. Is it they themselves
Who have forgotten how to live,
Or is it that life has forgotten them?

Whatever the case may be, it is saddening to look upon
The River which has taken so many souls, but yet hungers, never
to be satisfied.
Those who once had pride are stripped down, revealing to the world
The shame and mock they have become.
It is the world, its people, who allow The River to exist.
Their ignorance, prejudice, and stupidity have created this
Corrupted and unrelenting sewer of thought. The River will
always exist,
Simply because people are too frightened
And refuse to stop and ponder...
To look inside these Forgotten Souls...
Only to find themselves.

Magali Olivencia

Outside My Window

The hawks outside my window take to flight, spinning their tale of love
And stretch their wings to catch the light,
in the brilliant blue above

The slender trees stand defiantly, tall and proud
Their silver leaves shimmering,
Arching in boughs to the ground

The stream sputters and bubbles, taunting the willows while it laughs
And the wind picks up the leaves, turning them into pixies
Who dance across the grass

The long warm fingers of the sun, caress the sleepy day
Which sighs and turns over to the night
More protective, but less gay

A night owl shakes its head, its yellow eyes mirroring the moon
And a screech from a darting mouse below
Seals its fate of doom

A coyote, its hackles raised, howls a note pure and sweet
Which reaches my soul, and touches my heart
Mingling with its beat.

Kyla Mader

The Bad Best

Democracy is the worst form of government...
except all those other forms that have been tried.—
Winston Churchill

People mumbling.
Workers grumbling.
Cities crumbling.
Solons fumbling.
President stumbling.
Law courts bumbling.
Masses rumbling.
Media jumbling.
Humbling, humbling,
status tumbling...

But even still,
I'll buy Churchill.
Democracy gives you range
to make things change.

Ray Davis

"Windy" - Hunter

Windy, Windy I been thinking, what a grand world this would be,
if all the tales that you've been telling, would all jive, from a-to-z.
That big catfish in coal river, a good eight inches between the eyes,
afraid to gig the dirty rascal, 'cause your boat may capsize.

That big "Red squirrel" up the hollow climbed that tree without a sound
A good six feet up from the bottom, while his tail, still touched
the ground.
That big buck, I saw last winter, just below the river locks.
Was so big when I first saw him that I thought he was Paul
Bunyon's Ox.

"Boon and Crockett" would have new records, in their books! Right to
this day
If I'd have fell that slippery scoundrel, and he hadn't got away.
Mark my word, now come next winter, that big "buck" is gonna die,
cause I scouted every angle, and I never tell a lie.

Zeddie Gillenwater

Destiny Falling

Stars fell from hot August skies
Fresh, humid winds blew up from canyon's black rim
We stood at its craggy edge, seeing no yellow moonrise
White-hot, molten metal streaks, each a winged seraphim...

Two lives there touching became destiny's star-struck
Predestined each to hold and love the other
Looking deep within each soul, to each awestruck
By what each knew speechlessly, was their lover...

Astronomically tangled, their spirits to bond, to entwine
Twisted together forever, endlessly woven within each other
Spiraled tightly, connected by flaming stars in steep decline
On this stargazer's night, never alone again to suffer...

God's showers of burning banners bright
Heavensent to stir love's first passionate breath
Exchanged in sparks between touching fingertips that night
Fate's connection, timeless tangle, forever without death...

In meteoric splendor love was born, Heaven guided, angel-cast
Sealed by melted meteor dust, annealed in astral fire
Our love entanglement, a soul-tied knot will forever last
A fate-filled August summer's night under Heaven's burning
pyre...

Gene W. Taylor

To The End Of Counting

"How long will you love me?", he asked with a smile, as he gingerly touched her sweet face
"I'll love you forever" she quickly replied, "With a love that time can't erase."
"Ah, I've been told that before, by many a lass, who sought my affection to win."
"But, have you ever been told, by a woman so bold, how she's loved you since creation began?
been told by a woman so bold how she's loved you since creation began?

From the very start of this beating heart; from the moment I drew my first breath. I knew even then that a love without end I would give Thee unto my death. A love that was true, I harbored for you, when first our eyes chanced to meet. I knew, at a glance, my heart stood not a chance as it tumbled down at your feet.

Oh, we were so young; but yet even then, we both knew we were part of some plan. A plan not of our own, but from the Heavenly throne, God ordained for woman and man. Our love burned so strong, but our time was not long, and what had come quickly soon fled. And you left me one day for a land far away; with hopes that some day we'd wed.

Like an eagle you soared straight into my life; on the wings of an eagle you left, you left with a part of my broken heart, and you left my soul bereft. And I felt so helpless; I loved you so much. My soul ached as you flew away. But somehow I knew, beyond reason and truth, that one day you'd be back to stay.

You're back...My Love! My Endless Love! How I've longed all my life for this day. And God has ordained it, so nothing on earth can ever take my Baby away. To the "End of Counting"...and beyond...My Love;
never doubt how long I'll love Thee. And, if that can't impart the love in my heart, added words cannot make you see."

Linda D. Finlay

A Special Moment

A fading memory,
A forgotten place,
A picture you remember,
An expression on a face.
A very small moment, that is captured in time.
It stays in your heart, but fades from your mind.
An emotion you felt, a story recalled,
A moment of happiness, a person you saw.
They'll stay with you now,
They stayed with you then,
You'll never forget how, where, and when.

Kelly McCluskey

Impressive Journey

Embarking on numerous journeys,
a horrendous anguish constantly tormenting us,
arduously searching through innumerable paths,
erroneous paths leading us to empty roads.
Claiming for delusive gods,
delusive gods that make us prisoners,
prisoners behind our own bars,
tormented by our own equivocal desires:
wealth, power, fame, praise, possessions,
appetite, pleasures, pride, passion, lust...
Expending our life searching for an answer to our quest...!

The grandiose cosmos dispersing its profound knowledge...!
Letting go of our poisonous desires,
returning from our journey,
and landing on the most subtle petal
of the most beautiful, lovable rose
that'll transport us
to the aspired road of inner peace,
the only attainable happiness
in our baffled terrain.

Nelly Linares

Lace...

There are images; intricate like a fine piece of antique lace.
Untouched, but held sacred. Folded gently, perfectly divine. I miss your face.
Precious and enchanting, your innocent smile. He had a treasured look.
Unique, as the autumn's fallen leaves...and as Indian wind strum through his blessed hair; sounds of celestial harps rained through the air.

A silent beauty-a creature so captivating, whose Aura embodied a linked

eternity
band...and sang in the melodic music of the ocean's mermaid dance.
Above, our Luna glistens with silver tears. Listen, serenely while Angelika holds you dear-
The memory of her tattooed upon your flesh appears before me-guiding me magically.

Yet my heart races to the thought of your features fading away...But,

then awaken
suddenly in the middle of a snow-filled sky with your stare vividly fascinating me. Leaving me to wonder and hope: will it take one more day...

One more week...

One more month...

One more year...

One more lifetime...

The candle flickers...

I hold you and miss you in a delicate and soulful embrace. Keeping

your
spirit alive meshed in this piece of lace.

Marie Agozzino

The Power

Many people believe in God, and that's as far as it goes.
We know deep down in our hearts he is the power that grows.
Through the Christ within we find a treasure of happiness and peace,
Where every need is met, and a love that will never cease.
Tune in to God, be still and know you are his beloved child.
He knows, he shows believe in Him, and go the extra mile.
The will of God is the highest and best to which we can aspire.
Centered in God in feeling and tho't fulfills our every desire.
Make us a fitting instrument O Lord for this our shining hour,
That God may fill us full of Himself, the only presence of power.
God our hope of glory, our temples an inner light that shines,
Believe with all your hearts and souls, God is wisdom, God is divine.

Alice Stewart Wilson

A Helping Hand

You're the story of my life
You're the one who got me through the night
You're the one who was always around
And you're the one who wouldn't let me down
You're the story of my life
You're the one who would pick me up when I'd fall
You're the one who was always there when
I'd call
You're the story of my life
You're the one who walked me through the
Pain
And you're the one who showed me
What's to gain.
You're the story of my life

Shanna L. Immings

Serene

To understand, a foretoken of truth
A barren heart, the corruption of youth
Though endearment and indifference seem never to end
The words of illusion are always a friend
And time with its clock face sings out of tune
Reminds us forever, vituperation came soon
What of the troubles hath man brought to me
Question your heart for then you will see
Opinions are dubious, the pilot of life
The fusion of nations, a political knife
Wisdom ignites jealousy and pain
Stand in the courtyard, pray for the rain
Season of violence, anguish, and grief
Actions are critical, make known your belief
Hateful, unpleasant, and easily seen
But we are the wretched, a loathsome serene....

Laura Wright

SHADOWS ARE CONTAINERS

As I look from my picture window,
A beautiful lake I can see,
With its water of crystal gray
Lying still and peaceful as can be.

Pines, sweetgum, cypress and oaks
Tower tall along its banks;
They circle into a wooden fence
With exposed trunks as standing planks.

As autumn reaches its peak,
A color picture I now see.
With mixed colors of red, yellow and orange,
It is a gift given only by a tree.

The water's surface becomes a pallet
As the shadows fall on its face.
Rippling waves mix and splash the colors
Into a blending, close embrace.

The shadows are nature's containers
Of orange and lemon ades and wine.
Floating leaves top off the drink
With flavored twists on which artists can dine.

M. Elizabeth Lucas

"Nature's Presents"

The sunset with its tinge of orange and yellow
A glow in its promiscuous astonishing setting
So glorious to behold like a song by a singing cello
And nary a thought of ever, ever, forgetting
Even the stars glittering brightly in the Heaven's above
Showering tiny dots on this beloved earth in the dark horizon
Brings forth the inner beauty of nature's way of love
With its ultimate apparel of sheer sizing
The rabbits and the squirrels scurrying about from dark till dawn
Feeling the freedom this world has given them
As they revel from lawn to lawn
Like that of a beautiful exquisite form of a life-like fawn

The measure of philosophical nature's animals
Are in essence experiencing worldly things which are absolutely free
And we as mortals can pave the way to these channels
For all the wide, wide, world to see.

Myra Seideman

Cry Of The Wolf

A stark silhouette against the pale full moon,
A great lonely wolf cries its mournful tune.
Does he cry for his mate, is she gone is she dead?
Listen to that cry, feel the pain, feel the dread.
And as your spine does tingle and your hair stands on end,
Listen with your heart the message he does send.
For times were not so long ago that wolf and man did share
A common land of beauty, a place of love and care.
But now we speak with guns, with poison and the snare.
Could it be that mournful howl is but a plaintive prayer?

Mary Ann Tripp

The Ducks

The ducks were coming in for
A landing on a lake and you could
Tell that they were going to land there
Because their feet and wings were just right.

A peninsula that these ducks were flying over
And losing altitude over to get to
The lake had green grass and green trees
While the majority of the trees were a dark green.

You could tell that it was near sundown
Because not only were the clouds reflecting
The sun's rays but the other clouds were
Also reflecting the sun's rays as well.

The majority of the lake beyond the peninsula
Made a person just guess what it looked like
But the ducks were going to land where
The water looked deep.

Michael Swartwood

My Son Brought Me A Butterfly

My son brought me a butterfly,
  a lovely, delicate thing
With shining eyes, a blue-black body
  and a slightly crumpled wing.

"Look," he said "isn't he pretty.
  "See the spots on his wings right here?"
"Can I keep him, Mom, to look at him,
  to always have him near?"

Perhaps God explained to the little creature
  in His silent, understanding way
Why it had to die to teach a boy the beauty,
  the wonder of life, I couldn't say.

But I do know this, dear God above,
He brought me your butterfly,
  the closer to see, the closer to love.

Marjorie J. Olson

Untitled

Spring is here.
A season to share with warm sunshine.
Spring is a poem waiting to be written.
Spring is a new song that we must sing,
A time to enjoy sports like tennis and baseball.
Picnics and fun are on the weekend agenda.
Spring enters and temperatures are warm.
Flowers are growing,
And life is beautiful.

Mary-Ann Hromoko

A Call

There was a place so long ago, across the ocean wide,
A man of leprosy would call, unclean, unclean am I,
Down the street and country side, wherever he did go,
You could almost see him cry,
I wonder now if wise we would be,
If to others we would call, unclean, unclean am I!
Because of Aids I am unclean,
To love one another as thyself,
And help our neighbors all we can,
To keep them healthy and wise,
Shouldn't that be our goal for this day and time?
So be a pal to one and all, and tell us true,
Are you unclean, unclean because of Aids?
If to others you would be true,
Your love for all will grow,
Even after we are all gone —

Ruth Lewis

Useless Reflections

Meaningless words evolve from my mind,
A myriad of emotions that have no essence,
I search deep for the expression that will leave behind
Dreams of purpose and an artificial confidence.

From an ancient tome comes the mandates of wisdom,
A multitude of abstract ideas that hold truth for a select few,
False promises of an eternal kingdom,
An ancient deception that cannot be true.

There can be no forgiveness in the minds of the bitter
For the charge is heavily weighed against a desecrated trust,
An angry intellect mocks the toils of the pure
And savagely scatters to the wind an acrid dust.

Memories reveal in the darkest night,
Useless reflections traveling on a turbulent sea,
Soaring onward in deadly flight,
Aloft on wings that eclipse all that can be.

William G. Bernand, Sr.

The Thinking People

Each day — more clearly
A picture forms.
The balance of the thinking people
In a world ruled by majority,
Where the thinking people
Are a minority small,
One good speaker sways a crowd.
Right or wrong he sways the crowd.
A Prophet — in God's truth,
Is crucified by majority.
A tiny minority is martyred.

Conjure a new picture.
A multitude stilled by
An abominable desolation.
A still small voice breaking the silence —
The majority knowing it has blundered.
The thinking people — the minority
Have a plan and speak.
The others listen and follow —
Led by the thinking people.

Natalie Norris

"Book Of Rhuenell"

Dedicated to My Mom
Restoring a gift so precious in truth-
a petal of a rose, a sign of you.

Hours of joy, a part of life's games-
a portrait of spectrum, not fully framed.

Understanding the grace, between each written line-
is a token of faith, a remembrance of time.

Energy of hope, a room filled with cheer-
a portion of warmth, for all to hear.

Nothing takes shape, in the absence there's pain-
yet a bold reminder, an inner restraint.

Every cloud that roams our precious skies-
wipes the tears of our lost one's cries.

Losing them, leaving us, a family token toss,
a mirror image of a dear old rugged cross.

Loved one's dreams are our presents of time-
yet sharing our faith, their memories will always shine.

Randy J. Wilke

For My Special Son David

Sunny skies, butterflies
A rainbow now and then
They're all a part of this
Great earth, the free world we live in.
So let us count our blessings for each
And every day, and be so ever thankful, to
Have just one more day, to sit down and remember,
To thank the "Lord" above, for giving us his prayers,
And his undying love, He is the life, he is the love,
He has a kind, warm hand, so if you ever need a friend
You'll find one in that man; He'll bless you and He'll
Guide you, He'll be there to see you through, so never,
Ever be afraid to tell Him "I love you."

Marletta Barrick

My Rainbow

I saw a rainbow today!
A rainbow that offered hope
In a world that has at times
Been dark and dreary and full of pain.

A friend that had been lost to me
Came back into my life,
Bringing comfort and reassurance
That my life has worth
And my friendship has value.

Friendship is indeed a wonderful thing!
It has a way of holding dear
The memories of a lifetime ago
That helped shape our lives,
When living was new and exciting
And pain was a cut finger or a bad hair day.

My rainbow was very real
And I can stand a little straighter
Because it brought me hope.

Ollie Sutherland

Oklahoma Cowboy's Lament

"I had plans for the future, living with a beauty,
a rose of perfection. I thought it my duty
to love her and keep her in a style we both like
but I hadn't counted on betrayal or my own dislike
of wasting money I'd earned on a drink she poured with malice
down my arm, saying, "take that you two-timing, long-legged
Oklahoma cowboy!" and walked out and spurned
my efforts to explain that I wasn't untrue. Perhaps I had yearned?
"An arm around another beauty? Is that reason to rue
seven long years of living with her in a "menage a deux?"
A bit of Scotch and ice water poured down shirt collar and arm
by this dove who always before had been faithful and true,
but she mistook flirtation for being false and untrue.
"Oh, misery is mine. I cannot make her relent—
Just think of the money I wasted!! She spent
my hard-earned money—two dollars and change—
taking revenge—and walked out of the bar with two escorts
in that strange and fascinating stride she has.
She says we're still friends. Was I always asleep?"
Next time he will swing lariat in a wide loop, a cowgirl to keep!!

Veda Nylene Steadman

"At Calvary"

One day long ago at Calvary,
A Saviour went up to die for you and me.
There on that dark Golgotha tree,
My Saviour died instead of me.
'Twas my sin and shame He bore that day,
And for me He did the penalty pay
Oh JESUS, sweet JESUS my heart now would break;
To think sweet HOLY ONE, that THOU didst take
The whip and the beating, the nails and the cross.
That I, wretched sinner should not suffer loss!
YOU did it all gladly, my soul for to save.
YOU sacrificed all to save me from a grave.
What more could I ask, what more could YOU do
To show YOUR great love —-
For this whole wide world too.!!

Margaret Ann Dwyer

A Sculpture—Small Pieces

After selecting the finest material and tools
A sculptor started to carve
Putting all his knowledge and skills into his creation
Chiseling and forming
Striving for perfection
After years of hard and tedious work
It was finally completed
The masterpiece was put on display
People came and pondered, but could only find flaws
This doesn't look right they said
Something is wrong with this and that, they would say
As they gathered and continued to criticize the carving
A strange thing occurred
Hardly noticeable at first
Bits of the sculpture started crumbling
Eventually leaving a pile of small pieces

Leola Waeckerle

Both Sides Of The Looking Glass

I looked into the mirror and I saw a stranger there.
A slightly overweight older man with thin and graying hair.
What happened to the young man I asked this old gent.
He was here just a short times ago where has the young man went.

And say, there was another man I often used to see.
He'd sometimes hold his children up so they could talk to me.
The old man looked right back at me; but he uttered not a sound.
And as my eyes searched behind him, I could see no one else around.

So I advanced up to the mirror—likewise the old man drew near.
As I looked into his tired old eyes, I saw him shed a tear.
For the younger men they are no more; and, as we wait for the time
to pass
The old man and I will keep a watch on both sides of the looking
glass.

Norman R. English

Beautiful Noise

Somewhere in the night I hear your voice,
A sound that I remember, spoken words.
Sometimes as I walk the empty streets
An echo fills my mind with sounds unheard.

The clatter of the day returns the joy
Of other days when only you and I,
With silence, danced the dance of love at will,
And breached the vast expanse we call the sky.

There was a time, there was a happy day
When just we two could scan the world and know,
No solitary sound could spoil our time
Or untold millions cause our bond to go.

The rushing wind, the rains that kiss the grass,
Creating sounds that set my mind afire,
Recalls to me your ever gentle voice,
Resplendent sounds to lade me with desire.

The stillness of this dark and empty room
Creates a sound, a silence and a tear.
And as I wander through this thunderous day,
The silence now is only mine to hear.

Robert P. Clayton

Our Legacy

To See: Snow capped mountain peaks, at dawn
A sunset - when day is done
Hill-sides covered with spring flowers, a butterfly:
An eagle soaring, in the sky
To Hear: The wailing wind, in tall pine trees
A babble-ing brook
The song of a mocking bird, in early morn
The rumble of thunder, in a storm.
To Feel: The warmth of the summer sun
A cool evening breeze
Wet sand on the beach, with bare feet
A babies breath, against your cheek.
To Smell: Fresh, pine scented mountain air
A field of new mown hay
Honey-suckle in bloom, lilacs in the rain.
To Taste: The salt in an ocean spray
The sweetness of fruit
And I dare say-
These are only but a few - of the earth's glories
And they are free! God's gift to us - our LEGACY!

Sandy Cron

Southern Pride

The South had her own gracious, grandiose world;
A tale of pride and preservation unfurled.
One plantation had an all white ballroom,
which showed off rainbow colored ball gowns, which Southern Belles wore.
Dancing couples gaily waltzed and whirled across the floor;
but, a way of life was about to meet its doom.
Our country became divided against itself because of slavery;
Every person has the right to be free.
Southern states seceded from the Union, one by one.
The first shot was fired from Fort Sumter! The battle had begun!
Many battles were fought before the final Civil War battle was done.
Cemeteries held Confederate soldiers buried on one side;
Still divided, even in death, from Union soldiers, buried on the opposite hillside.
Wives and Mothers from both the North and South looked on and cried.
The North won the war for which both sides had bravely fought and died.
Both generals, Grant and Lee, signed the peace treaty.
Our country, again, became united, as it should be.
The South rebuilt her cities and plantations, far and wide,
And kept her fine old traditions and southern pride.

Leah Jeannine Charles

God's Gifts

The gift of life, a body strong;
a temple of the living God.
The gift of supply for our every need to
continually enrich, bless and prosper us.
The gift of love, the all encompassing love
of the Father above.
The gift of pride within our hearts to
always share.
The gift of power to do and be all that we
long to do and be.
The gift of faith which God has implanted
in each heart.

The gift of wisdom, the indwelling of the Holy Spirit
within each of us.
These are the marvelous gifts that God has given to you and me.

Vera E. Brinck

Influence

You have given me a purpose for my being -
A tenderness for my remorse
Instead of the bitter pain of regret.
You have given me a hunger to seek for beauty
That lies hidden - beyond the point of grasp -
And you have shown me the way
To a quiet solitude for my own thinking;
A confirmation for my own beliefs,
And a sanctuary for my tired body.
You have taken me by the hand
And led me to God.
You have taken my heart
Into your own keeping,
Leaving me - just as you designed it -
The heart of you
That you always wanted me to keep,
But in my haste, I left behind.
I need you more now than ever before,
And, God willing, I'll need you more -
Even after death!

Katrine F. Stone

Sacred Ground

Majestic mountains rugged and timeless
A valley stirred by the breeze
The quiet, reverent soul can feel
Ghostly shadows in the trees.

Early dawning when day is new
The lacy mist rolls in
Above the drifting sounds of life
Are whispered voices in the wind.
The sunlight warms this honored place
Stately pine trees tower high
Amongst the swirling clouds there are
Spirits dancing in the sky.
Reflecting colors of endless sunsets
Ageless laughs and hopes and fears
The mountains resound with life everlasting
And echoes of thousands of years.

On sacred ground the darkness falls
Softly wrapped in silver moonlight
The forest sways in rhythm to
Haunting music of the night.

Lenee Bendio

Requiem Of Summer

Shards of silvery sunlight slash across
A veil of alabaster clouds and sapphire skies
to illuminate the crimson, bronze, and amethyst leaves
Like fragile stained-glass windows
Hanging perilously from towering sylvan shrines.
Summer's last breaths hang on the sturdy limbs
Until their fingers grow numb from cold and fatigue
And then fall in their colorful languishing splendor
With their ruddy faces gasping one final time
As they join the other ghostly remnants of summer.
Tired, thirsty twigs lay beneath the mottled autumn carpet
Hiding from the cool, crisp snips and snarls of the wind.
Their refuge almost secret until the unforgiving leaves
Betray them with their crackling whispers.
The swift wind pricks his ears, then chases the leaves off so
The knobby skeletal twigs lay abandoned on the damp ground.
The wind laughs and howls-then cocks his head
And sets his dark eyes on a flock of birds above a russet-tipped maple.
The birds sing a somber requiem -
of summer days that have gone by.

Pamella A. Cunningham

Beyond The Blue

Not a brilliant blue capturing a man's soul,
A wintery mist turning his heart icy and cold.
Blue like the well-spring of humanity's tears,
Asking to turn to grey, a color all too near.
Blue like the lonely waves of a northern sea,
Of the melting icebergs, the glaciers, reminding me.
Blue like a fall afternoon's cloud-powdered sky,
The tint of worn, faded denim beckons; tell me why.
Blue shows as if once warm but strength now wanes,
The sadness of a hollow shell left to be explained.
I can see it within you without much of a try,
Your soul, deep within, hidden by reflective, blue eyes.
Blue absorbing what is happy and all that shines,
Showing of it none, storing away what little you find.
You recognize the feelings, admit that they are true,
I have felt the same, though without eyes of blue.

Mark A. Gunter

The Victim

I sit and ponder
About life's little wonders.

Is there fear in the things I say?
Is there a reason for me to go the other way?

Is it fear in your face?
Is it something you've done, do you feel disgrace?

Did I have any choice as a kid?
Did you treat me as an adult, so you could do what you did?

I am in fear of what I may find
Because I am going on a search of my mind.

In order to help myself
I must face these feelings, so that I may gain wealth.

I am looking for all of the facts
And not wanting to ever look back.

But, back I must go
So that I may know this was truly so.

A life of pain and fear
Because you wanted to be too near.

Persefanie Nowakowski

"Centurion's Confession"

It is a ballad sung for everyone,
Across a reddened land, freedom shall flow,
Father, mother, please do not cry,
Today, I feel will be a good day to die,
Freedom so precious, so dear,
Bought with spilled blood which drops as silently as a tear,
Time honoured tradition of the noble centurion,
A true confession,
Whose freedom am I or are we defending anyway?
Mine, ours, theirs, does anybody know or even care?
Only the silent sand/shoreline knows the winning score,
And this I know is no game.

M. L. Frey

God's Beautiful World

Tonight I'm gazing out the window
Admiring the sparkle in the fast falling snow,
As it swirls round and round in circles
When the cold north wind begins to blow.

The dead hydrangea flowers, are rolling
Like tumbleweed to and fro.
Then they abruptly change direction
And off up the street they go.

The world I live in is now a white-out.
My neighbor's house I scarcely can see.
The wild winter storm goes raging on
While I cozily relax with a cup of tea.

Some of my friends go south for the winter
To avoid our winters cold and long.
A few left behind are thinking of spring
When the earth bursts forth into song.

But when I look out on God's beautiful world
I wouldn't dream of changing a thing.
Let's put on our warm coats, mittens and boots,
Relax, enjoy the beauty, rejoice and sing.

Mildred V. Oleson

Alone And Afraid?

Separated between fact and fiction I stand
afraid and alone before another choice,
the choice of two paths,
I ran through my mind the choice of fiction,
Where reality has no stand in my dreams, ideas, or hopes.
To be my own person, and to have my own say,
Oh how great it would be to just take that one step,
That one choice that could change my entire life around,
that could rid me of my worries, and that could rid me
of being afraid to make the right choice to help me.

I choose the other path, and once again I stand
afraid and alone,

When you come to that two-way path, be opened-eyed, not afraid,
or you too will stand alone.

Krystal Lee Whaley

Goldwood's Ms Candifection

Glowing and fresh as the morning sun
after a springtime shower.
Energy radiating a rainbow
of northern lights.
Incandescent as a Japanese lantern
filled with fireflies on a summer's eve.
Sparkling with the effervescence
of a glass of golden Champaign.
Happy as a babbling brook rushing merrily
over the rocks, always on the way to somewhere.
A riot of fourth of July firecrackers
igniting the midnight sky.
You are bigger than life itself.
Happy first birthday Candi,
Love surrounds you.

Katie Ward

As I Look At You

You left me there helpless,
All alone.
Not one problem to be solved.
I looked at you see the truth.
I looked at you to see the wisdom,
You need me.
I need you.
Do you need me? I need you.
I looked at you.
What I saw could never amount to what you are.
I was there for you.
I gave you truth, I gave you wisdom
You gave me a broken heart.
When you said you cared no longer,
I figured why should I.
I must not care, I must not feel.
I will never be hurt.

Lori Orti

Soft Spring Absence

A shadow cast upon the earth,
prepared for a new birth.
A mother in pain lies in the shade,
there she was, and there she laid.
A leaf falls from a heavenly sky,
the child awaits, not to see, but to cry.
A lonely wind whispers in her ear,
SILENT but living comes a tear.
And she realizes she is now a mother.

April Maurer

How I Learned To Love

Though I never met you
I've known you all my life.
You taught me all I know about
Life, love, family, and faith.
All through my mother's eyes.
Your daughter,
My greatest supporter.
Although you passed on before my birth,
We share a bond so strong that
words cannot convey.
I feel it when the days and
nights drag on.
I often wish I had gotten to know you.
Thanks to pictures, stories, and
your guidance,
I do.

Melinda L. Castilloz

Christmas Is A Sad, Sad Season For The Lonely

When people wish you "Merry Christmas" while in your heart you're all alone. When they call you up and tell you that their kids are coming home. And they tell you what they're having for their Christmas dinner too. While they never seem to notice that inside you're feeling blue.

They never seem to notice that you'd rather be alone or that you never have a Christmas tree or decorate your home. They never even notice that your windows all are bare. And they don't know that the reason is not that you don't care.

No one seems to notice that you stay inside for lunch while very deep inside your heart you'd like to join the bunch. The Christmas songs they sing that fills their hearts with Christmas cheer only fills yours with an emptiness you wish would not be there

No one even knows of how you wish this time would pass so that Christmas would be over and spring could come at last. Then the heart that feels so empty won't feel half as empty then. At least not for a little while until Christmas comes again.

Michele D. Fancher

Grandpa's Heart

A little girl stood crying at the grave.
All around her loved ones were near.
What had caused this small one such pain?
A Grandfather's love so dear.
How had his life touched one so small?
Why did his life matter at all?
He never met a stranger
Always loving, everyone he met, visitors, friends and family
He loved them all can't you see?
You could see him in many places
Watching excitement on different faces
Football, baseball, softball and fishing too
We're many of Grandpa's favorite things to do.
The little girl remembered when it became hard for Gramps to breathe
Couldn't someone give him a reprieve?
Keep trying he seemed to say if I can do it so can you.
Keep trying each and every day.
The little girl now cries no more.
In her heart will Grandpa's love always be
It is there for her to share with you and me.

Melissa Kruzich

Listen To The Trees

Am I not pretty, said the big fir tree,
All covered with snow, and cold as can be-
As icicles form on each tiny tip
Sparkle like diamonds from every drip.

But my arms are tired with so much weight,
I can't lift them up as I have of late;
I do hope the sun will soon be my friend
And this heavy burden bring to an end.

I, too, am ladened with ice and with snow,
Replied the maple tree just down the row;
My branches are thinner than yours, that's true,
But that's hardly cause for you to be blue.

That nearby pine tree lost some limbs today,
And power has been out, I've heard folks say;
So we really shouldn't complain at all-
We're dressed for winter and having a ball.

For we three trees, with so many more,
Have combined with nature, from each back door,
To show our artistry to folks first hand
In this white and cold "Winter Wonderland".

Kathleen Blaisdell

Alleluia

Alleluia, alleluia, let's praise His Holy name!
Alleluia, alleluia, it's time for
The King of Glory to come into your life!
Alleluia, alleluia, it's time for you to change your mind!
Alleluia, alleluia, let the King of Glory come into your life!
Alleluia, alleluia, you must confess
and believe in God's word!
Alleluia, alleluia, you must be baptized,
and filled with fire, and filled with the Holy Ghost!
Alleluia, alleluia, you must be born again to enter God's kingdom

Alleluia, alleluia, it's time to work
in God's Kingdom!
Alleluia, alleluia, let us sing praises unto God!

Alleluia, alleluia, God's word shall
stand forever and forever!

Alleluia, alleluia, God shall return someday!
Alleluia, alleluia, will you be ready when God returns?
Alleluia, alleluia, you must be born again, to enter God's Kingdom!
Alleluia, alleluia, will your name be written in the book of lamb?
Alleluia, alleluia, God shall return someday!

Suzette Fulce

Science And Religion

Science without religion is blind
Although its purpose is to help mankind
Seeking out how the universe was designed
But that would not be the greatest of find
But to discover what God had on his mind
That he created us to be of his kind
And that should make us feel sublimed
As for religion without science being lame
That should not put us to shame
More importantly is the reason why we came
Rather than knowledge of the scientific game
But no one could put us to blame
For adhering to God's holy name
And that my friends is the greatest of fame

Nicholas J. Kayganich

My Road, My Cross

The Lord Jesus wore his crown of thorns
Am I not his child, you gaze upon,
You call the hardship of my life, bad luck, misfortune, strife
Can you not see, it is my beautiful cross, he gave me to bare

Do I not carry it, everywhere I go
So that it may bring relief to others, also suffering
My cross is of no burden to me
Do not save me from my cross, with your tears

You weep because my body is broken and weary
Yet, your sympathies are misplaced, my dear, dear friend
For the soul within is shining for his glory
With heaven waiting for me, just around the bend

Lillian Heigle Ridlen

A Walking Stalk Of Corn

In stalking jungle, the full-fogged moon, he sees
an invader from ants' lookout leaf, he

trips over a huge piece of last year's manure, saying
"I'd love to be like the corn."

Gigantic human computer [5 ft. 10 in.] in lotus
posture computes nearby, breaking
up the "vibration" so that
he can distinguish between
ants, corn, himself.

Tanha waves cut through empty cut husks
seeking the right recipe
to hear from a different ear.

Hand-me-down concepts only capable
of contradiction,
they upset the equilibrium of the leaf

with nothing left to cling to, it topples
and...and crash...
his six-shoed feet walk new path
——a walking stalk of corn.

Mark S. Dranchek

Side By Side

I consider myself fortunate, more fortunate than most
And about this treasure I feel I must proudly boast
When dreary days seem endless and I can no longer cope
It's in my sister's infinite love that I always find hope

I don't think she realizes the pride that I feel
Her ability for compassion, her heart so real
On this earth walks no other whose soul is as kind
I know for a fact the worlds greatest sister is mine.

Pam, I'd never trade you; for you're worth your weight in gold
Our unbreakable bond to my heart I will forever hold
You are a beautiful gift sent from the Lord up above
Never doubt that you're his child, so full of his love

When life gets you down and your clear skies turn grey
I'm here when you need me; I'll listen, I'll pray
Know that I love you, never doubt that I care
For you my dear sister, there's no risk I wouldn't dare

I love you big Sis, more than you can conceive
I'm your friend for life; that, you must always believe
There's no need to worry, we'll take each step in stride
You and I forever together, walking side by side.

Maria Lyn Cepeda

When I Go

When I leave this place I call home,
And all the friends I've ever known,
There is still one thought that haunts thee,
When I go, will you miss me?
Many tears fall from my weary eyes,
For the treasures and memories that are held inside,
And all the days that I wondered,
When I go, will you miss me?
I shall look back only once,
Remembering the joy and pain,
And when I asked you,
When I go, will you miss me?
I leave this place with thoughts of the past,
Thoughts of friends that in memory last,
Thoughts of when I say goodbye,
Thoughts of when I do,
I will say,
When I go, I will miss you.

Suzanne Myers

A Mother's Prayer

I look at the war machines moving
And ask the world what are you proving
The mother's tears that will soon be shed
Do you realize what you carry on your head

My grandchildren who could have been born
With their lives look what you have done
The boys whose love means so much to me
May soon be gone never again to be

Don't take my children away to die
They are my love my joy my pride
Through them my life will continue on
Even when from this world I am gone

Please let them taste the joy I have known
When they have children of their own
Don't take from them the right of living
Don't take from them the joy of giving

Don't do away with the good they can do
The chances they have left are very few
Men of the world please get together. Let's do away with war forever.

Please listen world to a mother cry. To live in peace let us all try.

Nilsa Broughton

My Marigold Children

As waning days of Summer fade,
And autumn—once again—is near—-
Its scents stir memories within my heart,
Transcends me to that yesteryear.

Although my children are now grown-up,
With families of their own—-
It seems that only yesterday
Their laughter made this house a home.

I merely have to close my eyes,
And I see them now—as then—-
Waiting impatiently on the big front porch,
For the old school bus to round the bend.

So, in the Autumn of the year,
When leaves begin to fall—-
Midst pungent scents of Marigolds—-
I miss them most of all.

Mary S. Chevalier

God's Carpet

I have a new carpet on my front lawn.
And brilliant and lovely are the colors thereon!

They range from bright yellow to a deep, crimson wine,
With golds, browns and greens - even black intertwined.

As I walk to my mailbox, I must stop - both ways
Just to pick up a leaf, on its beauty to gaze!

Ah, Friend, if you're raking YOUR "carpet" today -
STOP, I beg you. ENJOY it, ere you cart it away.

Those leaves that, in summer, gave comfort - in shade,
Now - remind us of the promise the good Lord has made.

"For as long as the world stands, there'll be SEASONS - Yes, all -
WINTER and SUMMER and SPRINGTIME and FALL!"

As the "Rainbow" reminds - "He'll not destroy us with rain",
So the LEAF CARPET tells us - there WILL BE Summer again!

Thank you God, for MY carpet; and were it "my call" -
I would proclaim Autumn - LOVELIEST SEASON of all!!!

Pat Reidelberger

Frustration

When my daughter was a little girl
And came to me in sorrow
I'd pat her saying, "I'm sorry dear,
It will be better tomorrow."

I'd put a lollypop in her hand
And place a kiss upon her brow.
Then through her tears she'd smile at me,
"I feel better now."

But now she has grown and comes in tears,
Her heartbreak too great to bear.
My heart breaks, too. There's nothing to do
To let her know I care.

Kisses and lollipops for a little girl
To ease a hurt or pain.
But a way to ease young heartbreak
I endlessly search in vain.

Lola E. Grant

Seasons Of Change (Free As The Wind)

Even though Winter may have some inclement weather
And cause me to have frostbite,

It's still a joy to see the children playing in the snow—
Reminds me of the child inside me and I can be free—
Free as the wind.

Standing outside, I feel the cool breeze of Spring
Wrapping comfort all around me.

I am content with the way things are,
Fabulous, Fine and
Free as the wind.

As I walk along the beach in the Summer air
I feel the warm sun beaming down upon me
And I am relaxed and
Free as the wind.

As I look at the beautiful changing colors of Fall,
I am reminded that everything must change.

Now is the season to shed the old and prepare to put on the new
So I can be....
FREE AS THE WIND.

Paula Lynette Neal

To Remember Again

Scattered thoughts and broken words,
and dreams worn and shattered;
locked inside from long ago on pages torn and tattered.
The secrets that are told,
the questions that are found,
the answers that are lost.
Inside a tiny child comes alive,
her voice speaks in pages black and white;
entrapped in words still searching for some light.
All this, for me alone,
to remember again,
that child within;
to feel again,
those memories;
to see again,
who I was;
to find again,
myself,
the me that nobody knows;
moving quickly through life's joys and woes.

Michelle Kleine

Untitled

It's been so long since I've given love,
and even longer since I've received love.
That may help to explain my apprehensive nature.
Please don't misread this fear I have of becoming close and losing
someone as a sign of mistrust in you as an individual;
Please don't see it as disinterest in the love you offer.
My skepticism is deep-seeded and not intended for you.
It's this awful, heart wrenching memory that haunts me sometimes,
but somehow you make it easy for me to accept you,
to come out from behind my wall.
I want to always feel like I do when we're together;
somehow you help me to find happiness, and I thank you.
You're what my heart's been aching for, and it seems unbelievable-
that you should want only what I can offer.
Perhaps someday I'll be able to offer my heart as a whole, rather
than testing the waters and showing you one fragment at a time.
All I ask is that you be patient with me; it's been so long since
I've given my heart away, and even longer since I've received one.

Paula A. Dabney

Grandpa's Rocking Chair

In the old rocking chair, he smiled his pain away;
And every time we'd visit him, the others would all say,
"Come on... tell him a joke, a story, anything you care.
Go on over for he's sitting in the old rocking chair."
So I'd use imagination, and weave a story from thin air
Intending just to please the man in the old rocking chair.
I always had his attention, and back then I didn't know why,
But each time I'd tell a story, he looked so pleased,
he'd near cry.
Now, many years have passed since then, and things have changed
so much.
I have grown older, and he's out of my own touch;
For the man that I have loved with all that I am worth
Has gone on toward Heaven: one whose life has gifted Earth.
Now Grandpa's rocking chair does not rock anymore.
It is sitting motionless behind his closet door.
But I know he's now at peace within God's Gracious Care,
For I am sure he shall be seated in a Golden Rocking Chair!

Timothy Ole Fugleberg

The Big Trail Drive

The old cowhand sat at the end of the day
and gazed across the yesterday.
Through dim misty eyes he saw the big herd,
cattle as far as the eye could see.
Once more the herd would cross the streams
and we trailed that herd to the final stop.

As the old cowhand sat and dreamed.
There in plain view were some of the boys he once knew.
Ben, Dan, Tom and Joe. They were so real he whispered hello
as he slowly rocked to and fro.

Thou it had been many years ago.
There would be a reunion by and by
somewhere in the western sky.
A tear filled his misty old eyes.
As the herd slowly drifted out of sight.
Twilight descends into night, once again
he rode in the big trail drive.

Leoma Cardwell Allen

Alone

As the lonely sea gull sits upon his perch
And gazes across the ocean blue
I ponder over my solitary life
And the closeness I longed to ensue

I wish I could have found a person to love and care for
At that very moment, the gull began to soar

High, high above the sea
Away from people's touch
The bird is a symbol
Which resembles me very much

I am all alone,
Nobody will understand
Until that far away day
When the lonely sea gull lands

And as that day approaches, people slowly begin to see
I was not so bad, I was only being me

As I drift towards my afterlife
The lonely sea gull flies away
It will relive this journey
Forever and a day

Killarney H. J. Suniga

Pacific Grove

The sun rises
and gives battle with the clouds
for the morning sky —
resulting in a continuous explosion
of ever-changing vibrant colors
encircling the rain-filled clouds passing by.

Sea gulls briefly take flight to swirl the cliffs,
returning to alight on the rocks,
awaiting morning, and the tide it brings.

Otters frolic in the surf
before starting their search for food;
swimming amid the waves,
playfully arcing and diving
through the breaking wave crest, which falls
into foam around the jutting rocks
on the way to the shore.

While the sea's majesty is ever beckoning,
the rhythmic pounding of the surf
soothes the beast in man,
smoothing rough edges, settling jangled nerves.

Marilyn Fielder

Mother Nature And Father Time

They are meeting in space this morning to observe through the smog and grime
And they're hoping we'll take their Warning-Mother Nature and father time
They have found no appreciation of this world that was once sublime
They're remembering the great creation-Mother Nature and Father time.
They ask what have they done to the water? What have they done to the trees?
What have they done to the atmosphere? There's pollution in every breeze.
If we work we can make amends now and atone for this shameful crime
And together they'll show us just how-Mother Nature and Father time

We are making a plan to clean up all our cities of smog and grime
In our forests there'll be a green up - Mother Nature and Father time
Soon there'll be an appreciation of this world that was once sublime
We'll remember the great creation-Mother Nature and Father time
We will have to clean up all the water. We will have to replant all the trees
And then look for the reason the atmosphere has pollution in every breeze.
With this effort we'll find the good earth will forgive us this shameful crime
And then soon there will be a rebirth-Mother Nature and Father time

Mary Bruss

"If God Can"

If God can come a tiny babe and walk the earth a man,
and hang a million twinkling stars and count each grain of sand,
If he can take a little dust and make a form to stand,
then breathe the breath of life within and call this thing a man,
if He can build a mountain high around a shimmering sea,
and by His power, grow yonder flower,
Then He can handle me!

If He can cause a fish to swim and set a bird in flight,
and from a seed grow all we need and change the day to night,
If this is truth, then why can't I let Him my future hold?
for He who died and lives again, is surely in control.

I see no reason I can't trust the One who sees all need
with all my life, my hopes, and dreams, for He Created Me.

Mary Pittman James

An Abiding Soul

Once the journey comes to an end,
and having taken leave of my fate,
Untried and left alone to attend,
laurels written on a permanent slate.
Behind me, the life of one's coping,
From all of the troubles and sorrows
Beyond the summit, there's no groping.
Without hope, there are no tomorrows.

Return to dust, where time stays
physically worn, tarnished and old,
And not as youthful, as the yesterdays,
No more will the soul still abode.
But lay me down once and forever,
for a life more leisure than this.
Traveling where heartaches shall sever
Where the yearnings of heaven exist.

As spiritual gates spring wide, at my knock
From across the firmament, that I might see.
Friends and loved ones alike, come to flock,
Where all celestial angels welcome me.
Goodbye to the world which is still embedded
Loosened by the cutting edge of strife,
As death should not be denied or dreaded
For it's just the beginning of a new life.

Richard E. Cox

One Snowy Spring Morning

It is different for me now as I sit in my pillowed corner
and hold my eyes to the winged life I see on the branches
outside my window.

OH, CEDAR WAX WINGS! What a total delight you are for me this day, as you pause and perch on the snow piled branches. Your wings flutter and clumps of snow drop, fall, change.

Do you nestle there as I nestle here to come in touch with who you are as bird, as I come in touch with who I am as Ruth?

OH, STOP! Do not shatter your beautiful self against the reflective pane. Please do not let me find you lifeless in the courtyard...though, even in that, there is such stillness and feathered gentleness that I can only say,
YOU ARE BEAUTIFUL!
Ah yes, there now, it takes ever so little to lay you to rest-
the small garden shovel to turn the hard earth.

No doubt, the flock has missed you by now, and here I am treasuring these last moments of presence, struggling in letting go into absence, to full presence again.

YES, I AM DIFFERENT NOW!

Ruth Coleman

Rumination

My soul is a pyramidic crystal
And I am a child
I study the rainbows, systematically scattered
Seeking to discover the secrets to the world
Seeking to discover the enigmas of my self
I gaze into the crystal as if into a seer's ball
Trying to glimpse my future in its obscurity
Yet all I see is my perennial reflection back again
Like a red rubber handball off the garage door
The holy light refracts to the trees, the seas, to heaven
But they are a blur to me as obstinately I concentrate
On the solemn "realm of answers"
And then a leaf drifts to rest upon my shoulder
Perfumed with dirt and sun and wind
It crackles in my ear and scratches my cheek
Glowing in the russet awe of this fresh season
I gaze up at the oak, one tree, of life
And I set my pyramid down
I study the grass, and earth, and sky
And I choose, to live

Melissa Z. Savlov

The Sea

I stand poised on the brink of the world
and I am overwhelmed by the vastness of the beauty my eyes see,
it reaches to the far horizons of eternity;
I lift my face to be kissed by the warmth of the new day,
and watch as the morning sun sends it's golden ray to dance along
the water, and I listen to the laughter of the waves that's
carried back to me by the breeze; and feel its cooling touch as
it softly brushes fevered skin and runs its playful fingers
carelessly through my hair, still yet to muffle the raucous cries
of the birds that fill the air;
I walk along this corridor, the sand warm beneath my feet, and
feel the cool refreshing touch where the sand and water meet; I
gaze into the depths of this living, breathing thing they call
the sea, and as the tide comes rushing in, the sand shifts
beneath my feet, and suddenly I'm reminded of the insignificance
of me; as I stoop to retrieve the treasure left behind on
shifting sand, this restless, faithless beauty rushes back to
take it from my helpless hand............

Shirley Ping

God's Beautiful World

I awoke this morning to a beautiful sunrise,
And I thanked God for the most gorgeous skies.
Colorful leaves were gently falling from trees.
They covered the ground with their beautiful leaves.
Only God could make these colors so bright,
And give us the magnificent sunlight.
Soon the leaves will blow away,
Then winter will be here to stay.
Be not dismayed by the thought of the cold,
As the snow will be a beautiful sight to behold.
The trees and bushes will glisten to bright,
When we awake from the restful sleep of night.
God gave us these splendid things to enjoy,
So we should be happy and give Him the glory.

Tressie Hammer

Missing You....

To know that you touched my life,
and I was touching yours,
profoundly changing us,

Though you are gone,
you live forever in my life,
your words of wisdom, laughter and anger,
for all of you is precious,

You live through my life,
and every life mine touches,
until the end of time itself,

But through it all we will miss you,
even those never fortunate to know you by face,
for they met you through me,

Great loss that I feel,
realization of your love,
longing for memories not yet real,
knowledge that we are no more,

my soul knows that yours has moved,
pain felt now is conscience that your past felt love,
will not be doubled by your missing presence.

Kenneth Kurtiland Brown

Amnesia Victim

I heard her screaming far down the long hall,
and I wondered if she were in pain.
As I approached her, the nurse softly said,
"it's just the old woman again.

She awoke from a nap and didn't know
who she was or where she might be.
There was nothing here she could recognize -
not the view, not the room, not me".

I pondered awhile what the nurse had said,
and I wondered if I could cope
with a world filled with strangers all the while;
would I ever feel any hope.

To awake at dawn and be unaware
of what was a dream and what real.
Was there any way to step in her shoes,
and her fear and terror could feel?

I approached her bed for it was my job
to comfort her and heal the scar.
She fell in a peaceful sleep when I said,
"don't despair, God knows who you are".

Ruth Warner

Songs Of Old

Guess I'll sit me down this morning
And I'll wile away the time
As I play the old piano
With familiar chord and chime.

With each tune I see a picture
As I gently touch the keys;
I am back in days of bygone
While I play the ivories.

Each loved song tugs at my heartstrings;
'Smiling Through' brings 'most a tear...
As I linger at piano
Playing songs of yesteryear's.

I can sit for hours a-playing
Melodies like 'Old Refrain'
Seems I hear the boys in khaki
Whistling 'Til We Meet Again'.

Olden melodies e'er haunt me...
Each recalls a place...a face;
Reminiscing at piano...
Memories time can't erase.

Ree Shaver

Your Love

Today you look forward to your new beginnings,
And look back at where you have come from.
You have left parts of your heart behind,
But you have gained a love of a new kind.
A love that grows each and every day,
A love that means to give and forgive.
It means caring, sharing, and compromising,
A love that can be shared in many ways.
Begin looking into tomorrow with great expectations,
And with the both of you begin weaving your dreams.
Hold onto the seed deep in your heart that carries
this precious love.
For this love can never be found again.
In the back of your heart always remember those vows you once
said: I will comfort you, I will honor you,
and love you for as long as you shall live.

Sandy Dechant

Dakota Winds

Dakota winds, blow gently on my love
And, Lord, watch over him -

A new job beckoned in South Dakota
Hundreds of miles due west of our present home -
Perhaps a couple of weeks separation?
"No problem," I said, "For only that long."

So my love accepted the offer,
And off he drove to start -
His new job in South Dakota
Hundreds of miles due west of my aching heart.

Though almost thirty years of marriage have passed,
My heart still skips at the sound of his voice -
But as "two weeks" continues to stretch,
His passionate embrace is not a choice.

As I long for his strong arms around me,
And the tears cascade like a rain -
I remember, that when he talks of his work
There's a long-absent bounce in his voice once again.

So Lord, grant me patience as to join him I wait,
And, please, Dakota winds, blow gently on my mate.

Linda I. Crow

Nostalgia

I sit on a moss-upholstered stone,
And meander back through memory-lane.
Primroses bright-colored in profusion glad
Lie couched contented 'neath the great oak tree,
And a laughing world throbs with exultant joy.
Blackbird and thrush chant their endless songs,
Larks' sweet anthems soar in cerulean skies.
The cuckoo's call echoes from distant woods,
Pollen-stained bees buzz in clover's sweet depths,
And a glad, young world inhales the fresh evening breeze
Children's sweet laughter floats on joyous wings,
Lowing cows pad to their milking stalls.
Farmers bent, heavy-stepped, fatigue-laden
Wend their way home to fresh-brewed tea.
And a dazzling sun sinks in a ball of fire-filled glee.
But the wings of fancy melt in dismal moist wrapped in grey clouds
inky black. A city mantled in brick, mortar stark, and my heart,
heavy and suddenly grey, longs for the days of pollen-stained bees.

Sister Laura McDermott

The Bitter Winter

Tis a beautiful winter day on this wondrous earth,
And nature rejoices as if to see a new birth.
But be still, be quiet, a sudden change is to occur;
Its severity is unknown, its destiny unsure.

The rays of sunshine quickly hide behind the clouds,
As if they know a danger enshrouds.
A mysterious calm descends upon the land,
Like the eeriness of a storm at the snap of a hand.

All at once a gloomy darkness prevails,
A breeze rustles the leaves, as a ship on the waves it sails.
Then an outburst of snow hurriedly crashes down,
Now a white blanket covers all, like the face of a clown.

This destructive force, so powerful, so vast,
Has abolished most life where a keen eye is cast.
Still there is a major struggle that continues on,
From a single little root that contends until dawn.

It is this one stem of life conquering through the day,
That makes even the bitter winter surprisingly fade away.
And a glorious hope lies in store for everything anew;
There's no time to waste, for there's much ahead for you.

Pamela S. Weaver

The Thinking People

Each day — more clearly
A picture forms
The balance of the thinking people
In a world ruled by majority,
Where the thinking people
Are a minority small,
One good speaker sways a crowd.
Right or wrong he sways the crowd.
A Prophet — in God's truth,
Is crucified by majority.
A tiny minority is martyred.

Conjure a new picture,
A multitude stilled by
An abominable desolation.
A still small voice breaking the silence —
The majority knowing it has blundered.
The thinking people — the minority
Have a plan and speak.
The others listen and follow —
Led by the thinking people.

Natalie Norris

No Words

I've heard the line "No words can tell,"
And now at last I understand
That things can be so large or small -
So far beyond the scope of man

That he can only sense them there -
He cannot write, nor paint, nor say
The things that trouble all his night
And ride his inner mind by day:

The utter chaos of a world at war,
Concern for home and people far away,
The boundless spaces of the ocean's deep,
The shade of Death which follows night and day.

And though these things are with me every hour -
They follow close - on silent wings, like birds -
I cannot write them down for you to see -
Such things are far beyond the realm of words.

Ray Winslett

God's Seasons Of Love

He dipped His brush from the Heavens on high
And painted the trees against the sky.
With browns, yellows, greens, scarlet and gold
The approach of the winter season they told.
These leaves will soon be blown to the ground
And on the trees only snow will be found.
Then the earth will rest for yet a short while
Till God awakes the world with a smile.
Decking the Spring with many a hue
He covers the ground with blossoms anew.
To bloom in splendor for many a day
Till the suns of Summer chase the flowers away.
And the warmth of these days will come and go
Till again brilliant leaves will herald the snow.
And while we as God's children share these gifts from above
Let's remember to thank Him for His wonders and love.

Kathy Womack

The Key To The Quest

Then did he grasp the sturdy axe
And raised it high above his head for all to see
That the sun shone reflected by the blade
And he would respond to no man's plea.
Beyond the door he knew she stood
Who was the object of his lust.
Could she scorn him now
Who had been the object of his trust?
He tolerated no barrier that shielded her
And with a cry that rolled across the clouds he smote the door.
Though its strength was great.
His strength was more.
He reveled in the flying splinters
And cared not for the wrought iron frame.
The axe's blade sent sparks like meteors
Soaring skyward and heralding his fame.
At last she stood before him calm, undaunted
With tremulous voice she did complain
You are a dummy.
Have you lost your key again?

Michael A. Lea

The Butterfly Tree

A child was playing on a wooded hill
And saw a sight which gave him a thrill.
Butterflies on the limbs just hanging free
Fluttering just like leaves. A butterfly tree!

He looked and looked just filled with awe
At this miraculous sight that he saw.
Parents and science explained the thing
as migrating butterflies on the wing.

But his heart of hearts let him know
What grown-ups often forget, and so
He truly knew what he did see
A wonderful, beautiful butterfly tree!

Martha E. Brown

The Rose

I look upon a rose bush so fair
And see the lovely roses there.
Their blossoms are so rich and red,
Nestled there in the flower bed.
They stand among the petunias white
And catch the morning dew and light.
A drop of dew on each velvet petal,
Shining like some precious metal. The center yellow,
The flower red, to the bumblebee, its pollen shed,
It gives the bee its food of life,
Then faded away in the evening light.
But its fragrance lingers through the night,
Like a haunting melody lost in flight.
Its color is gone when the moon is high,
But it lingers there for the morning sky.
And once again, when the sun appears,
It's laden with the dew's sweet tears.
And once again, its beauty is shown to those who look.
Let it be known that the rose's blossom can only be
One of nature's gifts for us to see.

Walter M. Yesia

Cherished

There is only one you, and for that I am grateful,
and so happy that I am the one who has you,
you are mine, forever

You are in my every thought,
for you are always there
in ways that no one else has ever been

You have made me realize
what life is all about,
There is no way that I
could turn back now

For me to express what love is
would only take one word,
you,
you are love
so dearly to be cherished

Held in my heart,
for all times
you, are all I want

Michelle Tidwell

Tiger

A tiger went a-walking, on a Summer day
And stopped to sniff a flower, that happened on its way;

The muscles of his body rippled as he plodded on,
His coat, so sleek and shiny, glistened in the sun;

From time-to-time he stopped and turned and listened on his way,
To feel, or hear, or see a sign to guide him to some prey;

He wasn't in a hurry, but leisurely strolled along,
There was even time to listen to a jungle bird's odd song;

The sun was nearing mid-day, 'twas late for hunting food,
But, somehow, strolling through the brush, he wasn't in the mood;

Instead, he went to fish nearby, the river was quiet and serene;
Who said, he mused, a tiger - must always act so mean?

Raymond H. Fowler, Jr.

Out Of Winter Into Spring

Between the cold of winter...
And the dawning of Spring,
Time has come to visit the civic center.
While some would rather spend time in a swing,
Watching birds, zooming...
high into the sky.
Wild flowers blooming...
by the roadside,
Where the air is brisk and cool.
And a multitude of colors...
Can be seen far and wide,
While swimming in the pool.
The sun is all aglow,
Portraying the beauty of the land.
Keeping us all on the go...
walking hand in hand.
Trying to live out our dreams,
While we're feeling the magic.
And while the whole world gleams.

Martha L. Herrin

Trust

When I look up at the morning sun,
And the fleecy clouds of blue,
And feel the breath of a gentle breeze
That caresses me and you,
I think, "There must be a God."

When I look up at the sky at night
With myriads of stars twinkling down,
And the silvery moon riding high
Casts an eerie glow on our quiet town,
I think, "There has to be a God."

When I look into the faces
Of the ones I hold so dear,
And feel the warmth of their constant love,
It fills my heart with cheer.
"I know there is a God."

Winifred Hesser Leicy

Who Decides

The rain drops shed the child's tears,
And the wind caresses the child's laughter.
The thunder screams the child's pain,
And the dew remembers the child's sweetness.
The river shows us the child's blood,
And the earth can see the child's innocence.
The birds whisper the child's fear,
And the child asks is this life or death,
And humanity wonders who decides.

Michell S. Redfoot

Doubts

The pen connects to the paper
And the ink begins to form words
As thoughts of you are filled with suspicion and doubt.
My love, I know I should have faith in you
But a feeling, a feeling too strong to turn away,
Burns deep in the very pit of my soul.
Where are you now my love?
Where have you gone; what are you doing?
Questions, questions which are left unanswered.
Images appear out of subconscious thoughts-
A wagon with a broken wheel, a bottle with an
untwisted cap,
Memories of days before on moonlit nights.
Oh, these thoughts I should dismiss
But the love I feel stands in the way.
How I long for the ringing of the phone, to answer
and hear your voice,
Full of reassurance and hope bringing a sigh of
relief which runs all along my body.
Knowing then, my love, the questions can be answered.

Sherry Bocook

One Day Rainbows Will Fail

One day the sun shall fail
and the mystique of winter will roll in.
To place whites over greens, and grays upon blues,
until the earth is shrouded by cold,
and night overshadows the day.
In the deepness of December's song,
we may turn a thought to the robins,
for they are the messengers of spring.

One day rainbows will fail
and the darkness of depression will seep in.
To drink from our waters of happiness, and blow away our
dreams.
On you, on me, like an eternity
it drains us, and sucks out our soul,
to fling our shatter hopes, on bitter snows,
until the perception of life is so twisted, and people seem cold.
It is not that the world is evil, nor innocently cruel,
it's just a winter that has appeared.
And in our hardest sorrow, we will have to anticipate.
Love can renew its growth, if we open our hearts
and let life usher in the spring.

Richard Allen

Mendocino Headlands

The moon was a soft comma in the sky
And the night a long quartet of lovemaking,
Silence, playful chatter, and quiet talk.

We spent the morning hiking along the Headlands
Breathing in the scent of wild roses mixed with pine
Watching sparrows fly in playful circles
With no scheduled takeoffs or landings.
We shared our food with blackbirds
And tried to forget our scheduled weeks ahead.

I thought about the easiness of our friendship
mixed with passion
Of the space we give each other
For both serious and playful flights.

In this moment we are happy
Sharing small pleasures and quiet talk
A small miracle of exchange
In our busy lives.

Kathleen Rampton

Pain

A sense of rage and hurt,
and then you feel like dirt.
A loss of forgiveness, a change of times,
the pain will heal, as time goes by.
To feel a mixture of anguish and love,
it only hurts from someone you trust.
The need to cry, someone to comfort,
you feel this way once your feelings have been shattered.
What would it take to get rid of this pain?
You're starting to think you're going insane.
Your emotions run wild, you can't get a grip,
it's frustrating to deal with so much conflict.
People who hurt others,
Acting out of ignorance or spite, are
Incapable of many feelings, and one is
Not caring for others' lives.

Keisha Outerbridge

The First Zoo

After many hard years of labors...
And time spent preaching to his neighbors
Noah finished the job God meant him to do...
Went about gathering animals...two by two...

He didn't get just one...he needed a pair...
Of elephants...tigers...even the hare...
Monkeys...gorillas...and ugly baboons...
Possums...squirrels and masked raccoons...

Goats and lambs...and horses and mules...
And kitty cats (just people were fools)
Cows and pigs and dogs with a bark...
Happily strolled...into the Ark....

Rhinoceros...bears...and big hippos....
Alligators and crocodiles...I suppose
...That even Mr. and Mrs. Kangaroo....
Helped Noah fill the very first zoo!

M. Kaylor Williams

Mom And Dad

They were there to share in my joy,
And to try to help lessen my pain.
When I didn't understand their reasoning,
They loved me enough to explain.

Sometimes parenthood is a thankless job,
And they may have wanted to resign.
Every child needs positive role models,
And my parents have always been mine.

They didn't always know they were teaching,
But I learned things from them anyway,
From the great examples they set for me
By the way they lived life every day.

I loved my life growing up with them,
And I often look back and reflect
On how they enjoyed friends and family,
And treated everyone with respect.

I will always treasure the memories
Of the good times we have had.
They were always there for me,
My wonderful Mom and Dad.

Patty White

"How Glory Sings"

Why has the doubter's breath, O world, breathed upon me;
And tuned my heart and soul to such higher melodies,
Illuminating my words with joy, my soul with trust,
Inspiring my ear like a solitary sweet thrust
  'til there is but a universal twilight hush?
Then in the storm and with head erect I sing:
Though all the poet brothers and sisters lend not their force,
To my strong caring for everything,
My verse will still ring, and beautify all in its course:
For with studious mind I grope,
Snatching from the heart, the slippery child of wit,
With knowledge superior to pagan hope,
Most anxiously speed forward love, not bending backward it;
Making the UNIVERSE'S divine music a lasting hit
Until every mortal soul is finally lit;
Then will the verse bear;
God cannot bend the line - not one - that
  this atheist poet has writ:
So I timelessly live, who lived but for Death once,
And truth discern, who knew but Superstition's lore.

Lonnie Bailey

Missouri Just Waitin' For Me

As I travel the highways and byways, and as I tramp the hills and wade the streams in Missouri, I sometimes stop and look around me and I think "All of this, just waitin' for me."

As I hunt and fish in Missouri, I remember all of the ambitious people who have restored, cultivated, and preserved all the wildlife, and it is just waitin' for me.

Each change of season brings something anew in the fall as in October when the forest leaves change to a blaze of a thousand colors, I say, "All of this, just waitin' for me."

I should hope when we, the older generation, turn the reins of Missouri over to a younger generation, that they too will work, educate, cultivate and preserve Missouri so their children can also, with pride and deep admiration, say, "All of this, just waitin' for me."

When I have come to my journey's end and have climbed the golden stairs and am standing face to face with the Master, may I be heard to proudly say, "Master, in this vast place called heaven, don't you have just a little place like Missouri, just waitin' for me?"

Russell Heindselman

Dawn With Dianne

It was in late Summer, when I first met Dianne
And we held hands at the Frontier days, in Beautiful Cheyenne
Then we danced the night away on the Hotel lawn
And I got my first glimpse of Dianne at Dawn

Dawn with Dianne, is an ultimate sight to behold
Dawn with Dianne, is more precious than any gold
And there's no better view in this whole land
than when I awake at dawn and focus on Dianne

they say capture memories, while you have the chance
And I've seen Dawns in Boston and over in Paris, France
But none can compare to Dawn with Dianne
and the morning when we first met in Cheyenne

New Dawns will always come and always go
but the best dawn happened to me, a long time ago
In the Misty Morning, in good old Cheyenne
When I first met my love, my Beautiful Dianne

Dawn with Dianne
Dawn with Dianne

Lindo M. Sullivan

Perfection Delight

A perfect will, a perfect hill, a perfect house.
And what comes by, a perfect louse.

A skunk with a perfect smile, a perfect smell
On a cold night, with perfect sight,
With a perfect will filled the hill,
Filled the house with His Perfect Delight.

Yes, dear God, he shot his gun.
The air is on, it is no fun.
Here comes the sun but his damage is done.
Mr. Skunk has won.

Perfectly warm, perfectly shorn with his smile
He has torn back into the night
Without a fight, but left his perfume
PERFECTION DELIGHT.

Perhaps he will resume to see
If we really like his Perfect Perfume.

Oh, God! With your might, deliver us from His Delight.
On our next cold night just send us your light
The moon, but not His Smell, we promise not to tell
We dislike His Delight.

Mary Bullock

The Vanishing Countryside

We moved to the country
and what did we find
But that the city we had left behind
is closely following by.

The oak trees spreading their branches wide
The pine trees reaching to the sky
The cattle grazing on the hills
The horses romping on the land.
All are giving way
Like the city on the bay.

We used to sit and watch
With awe and delight
The sunsets at night.

Already I can see
The trees crashing down around me
Giving way to homes, apartments,
Office buildings and shopping malls
Changing my beloved countryside.

Lillian Berman

Maybe Someday

Our world is made up of multimillion opportunities,
and yet lacks the ability
to let the young learn from the old.
Old tales and talents left unspoken,
for fears of laughter in this day and age.
Yes, lost as a rolling gem, in a roaring river,
memories will fade and grow cold in time.
as do talents from the past fade away.
A kindle of a spark of hope from the past,
could generate a fury of dreams for the future.
A dream once held so tenderly by age,
as a falling star from above,
could travel one's future lifetime again,
by only passing from knowledge to new seeds,
like a dandelion feather floating in the breeze.
MAYBE JUST MAYBE SOMEDAY
unspoken words and dreams will burst out,
and gently, tenderly, engulf our young again.

Loreen E. Beeman

The Measure Of Success

If you think this life is all that God is giving,
and you break his laws to make your mark while here.
You have sacrificed your greatest gift from heaven,
an eternal life of joy, for success in your earthly years.

Life is not just a simple test of manhood,
or gathering of riches while we are here.
But rather, a proving of our worth to God in heaven,
judged in this life by helping others we have paid.

For to God and man the measure of success is different,
for God counts not the earthly gains which we have made.
He looks within for truth, and love, and goodness,
and at the price for helping others we have paid.

For one day we shall gather at the river,
and be rewarded for the things we did or did not do.
Some shall live with Christ and God forever,
for some, eternal death in hell shall be their due.

So weigh upon the righteous scales of heaven,
the things in life which you frantically pursue.
Do they warrant the gift which God has offered,
or is eternal death the final payment due.

Kenneth C. Boyer Sr.

"Hot Pot And Hot Pot Retort"

Oh, please lady please, you're obviously a hot pot,
And, you see me as the cook, but let me tell ya' —
In your pot, I will not look nor will I cook.
In fact, my apron has already been hung in your kitchen
And, the mere fact that you imagined it there in the first place
was just your smelling my gourmet food passing your door.
In my journey to reach, look, and cook —
in the hot pot down the street.

Oh, just like a man, typically, a broiler as you sure most are.
You broil before you know and know before you ask.
Hot pots are always to blame, while broilers retire to a bar.
Why? 'cause while one of us is a hot pot the other is the task.
The broiler's task to find the hot pot that's hotter,
but, at the same time — find the one who doesn't matter.
And, in this short world — who needs that!

Kevin L. Little

"Valleys"

When you're down in the valley
And you think there's no way out
Think of all your blessings and praise God with a shout.
Lift your eyes toward heaven, and say to God thank you.
And you will find that you're no longer blue.
So here's a recipe for happiness start counting all your blessings,
Name them one by one
and you will find that your blues will be on the run.
So remember, when you get down in the valley
Just take time to look up
And say thank you to God, and he will fill your cup
And then you will be able to tell others what to do.
When they get down in the valley and feel so blue,
To just take the time to look around and
See what God has done
and they too, can put their blues on the run.
So I guess valley's can't be all bad
When they make us realize all the blessings we have had.

Martha Samples

Being A Friend

You're a special friend who shows love by the things you do,
and you're someone I really enjoy talking to.

You're an understanding friend who gives such good advice,
and having you for a friend is so very nice.

You're a reliable friend who encourages when times are hard,
and you're always sincere in expressing regard.

You're an important friend who's generous, and so willing to share,
and I can easily see how you really do care.

You're a loving friend who's loyal and a friend forever.
And to be a help is what you always endeavor.

You're a real friend who serves, and continually gives,
and you're a friend to God, and in you Christ lives.

You're a close friend who is kind, and by faith you stand,
and the beauty in you is so very grand.

You're a dear friend who's wonderful, and there is no doubt,
that you exemplify what being a friend is about.

Stephen Hervey

Anger

Anger is an emotion as well as a feeling
Anger can make you go right through the ceiling
Anger can make you feel really bad
Anger sometimes makes you twice as mad
Anger can be turned on just like a light
Anger will surely cause you to fight
Anger will cause you to break up your stuff
Anger will deceive you and make you think you're tough
Anger comes disguised in many ways
Anger knows that it's you who pays
Anger causes you to push and shove
Anger also makes you hurt the ones you love
Anger can cause all sorts of pain
Anger will drive you totally insane
Anger will make you yell and shout
Anger will destroy you without a doubt
Anger can really tear you apart
Anger is very hard to stop once it starts
Anger isn't very difficult to see
Anger, please don't get the best of me

Sharon Neibert

The Telephone Never Rings

From the bowels of the earth came a foul taste,
Another soul falls into this land of waste,
In hope my heavy heart clings,
But the light begins to grow dim as the telephone never rings,

A piece of my soul is gone, far departed,
As sorrow grows stronger, sitting lonely hearted,
I wait, even as the bluebird sings,
Enveloped by denial that begins to fade as the telephone never rings,

All day and all night I wait,
As the hour grows late,
Coming ever closer to face the unveiled reality, how it stings,
As the day passes, and the telephone never rings,

The black hand of death has stolen another life,
With a cold bullet and a jagged razor sharp knife,
All that is left is reminiscing over sentimental things,
Only memories emblazoned upon my heart remain, for the
telephone never
rings.

Ronald E. Maples

Destiny

Parallels of Life
Are surprisingly real
Shadows reflecting, images shared
Neither know, much less care
Chances are the dreams were yours and not mine
Yet the visions are lived through both our lives
You made yours for glory and mine is a sad story
It's very compelling to just stand and start yelling
The judge will rap the banister
Bringing all to an order
We will be judged on our merits
Even while we cross Destiny's borders.

Tawnya Keller

A Divine Wish

Heroes of the battlefield
Arise from the graves!!!
And the world will celebrate —
With great parade!!!

And angels will sing —
And church bells will ring —
And children will dance in the street —
It is our fathers, we are going to meet...

And thunder will be heard —
And walls will crush...
And music will accompany
This phenomenal march!

And a rainbow will appear —
Long and bright in the sky,
The symbol of peace —
Like in biblical times!

Heroes of the battlefield
Arise from the graves!!!
And the world will celebrate —
With great parade!!!

Ruth Peretz Epstein

Kurt's Operation, Ode To My Six Year Old Son, A True Story

They "gassed" me was his comment
As from surgery he came
Complaining with a vigor
To put a healthy man to shame.

"I wanna go home," he told us
With big-brown - glassy eyes.
"I don't feel sick at all," he said
Then "threw up" in surprise.

"We think you'll have to stay the day,"
We haltingly did venture -
And the answer that he gave us,
Must die within the censor.

So goes the story of his day,
We made one good discovery.
For such a disposition,
He must be near recovery!

Nancy Foley

Creature Of The Night

I want to lick your salty tears.
As I calm all your fears.
I want to drink your blood.
As I pick you up from the mud.
I want to hold you tight.
As I tell you it's all right.
You turned me into a creature of the night.
Now I can smell your bitter fright.
As I let you go.
My fangs start to grow.
You are now in my sight.
You will now feel my bite.
As I look into your eyes.
I see all your lies.
The moon turns me into a beast.
Your bitter sweet blood is my only feast.
You I don't want to kill.
But your blood I want to spill.
I want to taste your heart.
As I rip you apart.

Natasha DeServio

The Majesty Of It All

My eyes see thy glory in these hills O Lord -
As I raise them high to reach the sky above -
And the silence hangs like mist -
Broken only by the sigh of the wind -
Gently blowing through the pines -
And the call of birds - muted by the majesty of it all -
Seem the only living thing -
My heart roams to the lofty peaks -
And the wondrous beauty takes my breath away -
I stand in awe and dare not breathe -
For fear the living splendor of it all -
Will fade away and be only a dream.

Shirley Squire

Agony

Tears spring to life and consume me
as I watch my mother strain against
four point restraints in a monument
to her former self - so proud and free.

Yet there is no freedom or pride left for
her; she is instead like the gallant
shell of a great tortoise, destroyed
by the ravages of time and land.

This Alzheimer patient pleads in her
moments of lucidity for peaceful
death, and she hurls agonizing
pleas with piercing eyes and clutching
hands.

I curse the world's insanity, and my
religion that keeps her so imprisoned,
and I weep oceans for her and all
those like her...

Then I weep rampaging rivers for
such a helpless me as I wretchedly
ask, "GOD, do you no longer hear or see?"

Mary Lee Stanley

Dear Emily

Why do you write of death so sweet
As if life were a damning thing.
Your poems, your letters, your private thoughts
Of death you do cling.

A mentor, a friend, a prized possession,
You have wrapped yourself in its vial of depression
With death as an author's constant obsession.

You've lived it, you've loved it,
You've ate it, you've breathed it,
And you've felt its infinite sting.

What would you tell us now about death
Since you have passed through its door?
Would it be what you expected in life?
Or is it much, much more?

L. M. Moores

"Dark Land Of Magic"

The land was dark that summer night,
As its people came from their homes to fight;
Black silhouettes rose from the ground
And advanced toward the defenseless little town.

Armed only with sticks and bricks and stone,
The townspeople faced the frightening unknown;
The skies clouded over, rained a vicious storm,
As a merciless army of goblins took form.

The elfin queen looked at her people in fear;
What could they be looking for here?
The elves had no jewels or gold,
Only people, who were loyal and bold.

In the end came total devastation,
Both people's destruction and annihilation;
The evening sky was crimson red,
Foul with the odor of the dead.

And nothing came of the senseless fight
But the further darkening of the dark night.

Patricia Noyes

A Gift Of Love

There's nothing as special in this old world
As one of these gifts of love,
A sweet and gentle, trusting child
Given to us from God above.

What warms a heart faster than a little hand
Placed there within our own
As two little feet strive to keep up
With ours that are full-grown?

And, oh, the joy that bubbles from within
And the laughter that tumbles out
As a fun time is shared with one who is "old"
By one who is just "a sprout",

How precious is the beauty of that head as it bows
And those two little hands are clasped to pray
As the Lord is asked to "bless and keep"
His child at the end of the day.

Phyllis Seifrid

Gentle Breeze That Will Please

The young girl swings way up high,
As she dreams of Sweet Williams in which to lie,
The breeze sweeps her hair from side to side,
As she thinks of a young pony on which she'd like to ride,
She thinks of sweet, soft songs,
So sweet, so gentle, she has to sing along,
She stops the swing so swift and light,
Oh, look it is the coming of a hot, summer night,
The young fresh dew on the grass,
It has finally come at last,
The wet grass tickles her toes,
The sweet fragrance of the last of the flowers fills her nose,
She thinks of how it is and will be,
The way things are and will be under the old oak tree,
She is so lucky, she is, she is,
How lucky is she to be a happy, contented, young miss,
The crickets begin to serenade the beautiful, young lass,
She feels the wind in her face slowly pass,
She curls up under the old oak tree,
There she lies so very fast asleep.

Kelly Jo Cooper

No Talents

"I have no talents," a lady said,
As she gently stroked a little head.
"I cannot sing, nor yet even write,
If I tried to draw, 'twould be a sight."

"I have no talents," she said and sighed,
As she soothed the little girl that cried.
She dried the tears, also tied a shoe
And then straightened bows of ribbons blue.

I watched her hands that were quick and strong
As she guided little feet along.
I heard her answer, 'twas no small task,
All the many questions children ask.

I saw her smile, her whole face alight,
Into eager eyes so shining bright.
She baked some cookies, turned a hem
And she sang and worked and cared for them.

I thought, "no talents!" Oh, don't you know
That the things you build will grow and grow.
God bless your efforts from day to day,
For you are molding living clay.

Lillie G. Monter

Killing Me

How could I miss, it was just one kiss!
As strangers we met on a cold winter night.
The smile that was just right.
The twinkle of his brown eyes that took
my breath away.
I knew I had to have him the very next day.
He had a love for quiet sometime, but I knew
that someday he would be mine.
It seems he let her go,
for why he does not know.
I think he cares, I think he loves
Until he puts his past behind,
he will only be loving me blind!

Rose Cammarata

Danny

In the silent beauty of twilight
as the first stars begin to brighten the heavens
I let my mind float freely back to all the yesterdays
we shared together in love, in laughter, and in play-
but all too soon reality draws me back
to the suddenness of your death
that's when the loneliness creeps in about me
like the fog kissing the dawn of yet another endless day
while I struggle on
trying to calm
the restless seasons
that I am-

Stephanie Aldrich-Krachinski

A Reason To Cry

A dark, lonely soul - crying out for help.
As the pain increases - you let out a sudden yelp.
The tears now fall freely - as you no longer try to hide
All the pain and suffering - from way down deep inside.
First you took just one drink - then another, and another,
It seems to be the only way - to cause the pain to smother.
After a short while - your life seemed so much better,
But wait! 'Cause suddenly it's all red-letter?
Everything was so wrong - as it had been for so long.
But, you just didn't notice - your life was no longer pure bliss.
'Cause, when you were drunk - you turned your life to junk -
But now it's too late - you're doomed, call it fate...
But you know the truth - you acted uncouth,
And now you must live with this life
That you've created for yourself.
So, you just ended up - with yet another Reason to cry.

Marie J. Mack

Donna Marie Nee' Evans

From the sea of Coronado you came,
as the rising Moon of Bogard
spraying opals upon the earth with
twinkling luminescence until the blind could see.

Your laughter burst our heart
in all flooding and undiluted joys
and we sang thanks to you
for ending our years of wishes.

All knew our day had come,
for your smile dazzled the mountains
into beaming emerald spring birth
and our nights were bathed in radiant happiness
of such softness world never knew.

The little ones who had cried for bread
wove garlands of magnolia blossoms and danced around you
in mirth and gratitude for the feast now, once denied;
Fountains sprung again, elixiring us in the salubrity of the
ever-wending, never-ending path; and new words were invented
for defining Love as Donna Marie nee' Evans,
and we were borne out of you to Paradise in your New World.

Thomas R. O'Neill

In Your Memory

When the sun melts into the sea
  and the moon is bashful behind the clouds
your eyes...
  lighten up the worlds
  burst life into the hearts
  fire up the colors

I beg you,
  do not take this magic away
  and stay... till the end of the journey

Mamoun Ahram

Sundown

An autumn wind whistles in my brain
As the scent of stale rain squirms inside my pores
My eyelids are heavy and my spine threatens
To curl into a little ball
A shriek reverberates in my ears—"Fear!"
It is my heart, wailing that I cannot sleep now
And I agree, becoming feverish
What if, what if I do not awaken?
Terror rises in my throat, sickening me
What if I do not awaken?
What if the night stays forever beneath my skin
As stars fill my eyes, my mind, my soul with...
With—

Regina Braidotti

The Night

The wind howls around me
As the world shatters beneath my feet
I find myself in a darkened land
Where shadows reach for me like a Demon's hands
Eerie voices ring out from the darkness
Begging to be released from their plight
While aspen leaves whirl in an autumn dance
Twirling in the moonlight.
The trees look on mockingly as, with
No one to catch me, I stumble and fall
Down to the red depths of the nightmare that plagues us all.
Blood runs in mighty rivers, cries echo through the night
I see faces that haunt my dreams, as ghostly hands beckon me
I run toward a distant light,
Thorns catch at my clothes slowing my escape,
Wispy fingers mar my skin tightly holding my skin
The hellish light is all around me, invading the depths of my mind
Molding it to their will, with evil intent
As the lightning flashes, the thunder rolls
And the leaves weave their dance of death around my soul.

Lacy Scarborough

The First Easter

Mary, His Mother, was standing nearby
as they hanged him to Calvary's tree;
No fault they could find, and yet he must die—
That brave, strong soldier of Galilee.

They mocked, spit on Him, crowned Him with thorns;
Yet never a harsh word He spoke;
He prayed out of love, "Father, please forgive,"
While His tormentors jeered and joked.

He promised His friends, "I'll rise again,
To bring new hope and new life."
His enemies pretended they didn't believe,
Though they guarded His tomb each night.

Mary began weeping, and a stranger approached
asking her troubles and cares.
"The body of Jesus was stolen, she sobbed,
"From the tomb just over there!"

"Mary," said the stranger, and she recognized Him
By the voice she so dearly loved;
"Jesus!" she whispered, and fell at His feet,
While a light shone from Heaven above.

Mabel Fuller

Crystal Clear!

The crystal clear light show at early day,
As to chase the dreary darkness of night away;

My mind was cloudy-unsure of the, "Right!"
Until the daylight peeped his head through the night.

Now I can see vividly crystal and clear,
My priorities are straight, and I know
What is dear;

So listen very carefully my peer
Treasure what is precious and always hold it near.

Mary C. Kelly

Dante's Dream

Leaves of many colors paint the countryside,
As trees of every kind in harmony abide.
Living together they create this masterpiece.
For if only one kind, this beauty would cease.

Faces of many colors paint our wonderful world,
As the dream to live in harmony is constantly unfurled.
Living together we create this masterpiece.
For if only one kind, this beauty would cease.

Patricia Byther

Endangered Species

She quietly confessed she was a Mermaid,
As we sprawled upon the blanket, in the sand.
The half-moon hid behind the darkened clouds
But, I could feel the band upon her hand.

Soft, warm kisses, from sweet moistened lips,
Enhanced the swollen nugget in my hand.
I could feel heavy breathing on my shoulder
And the warm metal band upon her hand.

I had already sinned within my heart,
Huge sins, about as big as any man;
While I felt the fever throughout my being,
And pressure of the band upon her hand.

I could read the slow movements of her body,
Revealing each tiny thought at her command;
Wet moving fingers crawled up my thighs
But, I could feel the band upon her hand.

Oh! There is guilt, where once contentment,
When I feel cold water slash upon the sand;
And my broken dreams are haunted nightly,
By the Mermaid, with the band upon her hand.

I. J. Evans

Solar Powered

The sun, it warms me
and makes me want to weep
It's drawing me to the surface of my body,
so I am near the skin.

All a-tingle, the sensation tells me
I'm alive
The heat expands me and generates
the passion of my heart.

I am hiding now, from the revolution of the earth,
On the run with the rays of my star power of warmth -
Endless light to remind me I'm here
Casts a spell of sunflowered prayer.

Leslie Engel

Jesus' Love

How brave you were, JESUS,
As you turned the other cheek.
Politely you sought to answer their mocking lies,
Even Peter three times denied.
Love for us you showed, grace you bestowed.
Your anguished heart breaking deep within,
Shedding blood for our sin,
Redemption you gave, hoping to save.

Do you think you had lost as you walked to the cross?
What did you feel when your robe they did steal?
As they sought to cast their lots,
Little did they realize as you were crucified,
Your love without measure is greater than any treasure.

As you cried, "My God, why hast Thou forsaken me?"
You then died upon the tree.
As the veil was rent, God's wrath he sent
Thundering across the sky
Telling man, THIS WAS NO LIE!

"It is finished! It is done!"
My JESUS, YOU now have won!

Karen Nikkel

"So Late In Life"

We met so late in life, well after the hair had turned grey
at temple, and brow.
We met so late in life, but our steps are still firm,
only slower by a fraction.
We still find our pleasures, but, in the smaller things,
and in quieter places.

We met so late in life, but life is still so very sweet,
and we sip the nectar in smaller portions, from a smaller glass,
savoring each drop, and making it last for a longer time.
We met so late in life, and now I know what really counts, much
more than storing up "things" to be left behind.
We met so late in life, when the road ahead is far shorter than
the path already tread.
But, however long or short, or whatever the time
there is, this lesson of life has been well learned.
Life cannot be happily lived, whether young, or old,
without a hand to hold, a soft caress,
or a smile to warm the heart, and lastly,
a sweet kiss to end the day!

Olen C. Fuller

The Meaning Of Life

On a misty morning
at the start of another day,
The sun rises again
to stretch its great rays.

It throws onto the world
whatever color is may hold,
A magnificent hue
of orange, yellow, and gold.

And as the dawn breaks through the darkness
the songbird will rise soon,
To sing to the world again
another enchanting tune.

I don't ask for the meaning
and don't look for the reason,
Of why these things just happen
for season after season.

For everywhere you look
from places near and far,
There these things are beautiful
and there they are.

Willy Yu

Spirit Lady

I can cry, I can laugh,
At the time, if at the worst.
In my dream the blessed return,
And she realizes what a swindler she was,
How long the executioner hands held her.
I seize her face and encourage confidence,
How she can keep faith with her love,
Under the spirit clothes.
She didn't sob, only lived in my dreams,
But I sob, when she fears in the bad hands.
She trembles in my soul's deep nook,
And shouts in my brain.
Don't give there nobody for nothing!
Shouting already me too,
Because the pain pushes me in the bad hands.
From the sweaty bed kicks out the awe.
I did laughing, because on my neck,
There was nothing of rope,
But I bewail the spirit lady,
Who may come back never-more.

Laszlo Szuromi

Way Down There, Somewhere?

We've sent you our son, way down there
Away from home, we hardly know where
He's tall and strong, alert and straight
Whistling a tune, often with gait
We've guided, nurtured him along the way
Protected him best we could each day.
Fun watching him play those boyish toys
"Bang, bang, shoot 'em up," such gleeful boys.
They're only games, frisky wee tiger be
Surely rejoicing in muscles strong, brave young he.
Always preparing him for what, we didn't know
All we knew was, "stay healthy son, as you grow."
Remembering well," Spinach is good, dear. Brush your teeth."
Look, he's that handsome one, his name is Keith!
When you see that super son of ours
Does he rank with pride, polish and shine?
We're LENDING you our gift of love, that precious
son so fine.

Priscilla L. Carter

Ulva

Good news travels on speedy wings.
Bad news sometimes waits.
Births cause fast phone calls at any hour.
Deaths pause like rusty gates.

Obituary pages show
Dear ones day after day.
I scan to see anyone I know
And learn what loved ones say.

Then on a week I ignored all news,
She appeared on B5.
Her angel face, there in black and white,
No longer smiles alive.

She whose strong hands could dispel my pains
And those of many more
Rests now, at peace. All that remains
Are lessons she taught before.

I loved her. I miss her. I needed her.
Her strength was divinity.
How could she leave Earth and me behind
When she was just eighty-three?

Linda C. Brittain

The Derelict

Like a bit of wreckage washed ashore,
Battered, bruised by battle with the tide,
Tattered, weary, worn by circumstance,
Faith and hope destroyed, he lingers on.
A band of boys, in search of fun,
Fling taunts at him, unmindful that
One day they too perhaps might be
A replica of what they jeered at —
In chorus unified and shrill,
Jeered at — until the creature crept away,
Seeking in some sheltered spot to stay.

Lusty lads, in their gaiety,
Blinded by their momentary glee,
Saw not the tears that rose and welled
And streaked a weather beaten cheek;
Saw not the eyes, once clear, now dimmed
By year on countless year
Of drifting, dragging through a world
Too smug for lifting up a shell
To make of it a man again.

Mori Fremon

Friendship, With Love

When the line gets too thin while you're walking through life's battlefield I will be there for you to lean on, always hold on to your notions for believing in yourself is an obligation to you, as you sort through your frustrations trying to understand the meaning don't be afraid to speak openly and honestly of all true feelings for they are your salvation.

In this mad world it seems were constantly struggling to grasp onto some reality trying not to confuse what's real and what's not, when you're standing on an edge and you feel yourself slipping from the grips of sanity all you'll need to do is reach out, I will always have an extended hand waiting to help pull you back.

In this puzzling society filled with uncertain wonder there's many times the direction is repeated as you keep choosing the same piece of concern while questioning the truth, before entering a comfort zone we need to unite our day to day experiences for then we can acquire an interlocking circle of knowledge together which will gradually give us the ability to appreciate a complete sense of peace.

If you want someone to talk to I'll be here to listen, if you just need me silent but in body, I'll be there...right beside you, I shall be here for you in all ways for I am your friend in mind w/Love at heart.

Sally Newell

Thank You God

Thank You God for all your lovely creatures of
beauty here on earth
Thank You God for the warmth of the sun and the
quietness of the moon
Thank You God for the waters that refresh our
being
Thank You God for your smile on us that
saturates our whole self
Thank You God for your never ending
love and care
Thank You God for your greatness and
magnitude and all the beauties of the earth
Thank You God for holding me
under your wing
Thank You God for my loved ones and
pets
Thank You God for shaping my
mind to write this poem

Susan Smeltzer

Forever Young

Her only words to me were, "too bad you can't remember."
Because there used to be a time when he couldn't have loved you
more.
But you were just a young one, and your memory not yet formed.
It's all too bad and all too sad that those moments you can't
remember.
I can still see you in his arms, showered with love and affection,
He vowed never to let you go and no one would ever hurt you.
You were the pride and joy of his life and it's something you
should always treasure.
But it's a shame that the happiest moments are the one's you can't
remember.
I don't know if there's anything that I can say to help you try
to understand.
And I don't know if anyone will ever figure out what went wrong.
But I hope my words are a comfort to you, and you use them to your
advantage.
And you try to find a place in time where you can see him without
any anger.

Michelle L. Anderson

Renaissance

A spark effulgent that glistened for moments divine
Before it vanished into the awesome stillness of the velvet night
Was that your love writ large across the sky
That fugaciously into the sea of eternity did blend.

Ne'er for a moment did your love unfamiliar seem
'Twas as if revived in its fullness from a distant dream
A love I had known well in another sphere and frame
That had returned my dormant yearning to fulfill.

And after the majestic galleon of an ancient love reborn
Was shipwrecked by your lack of perception in a storm
My soul mortally wounded by the arrow of that remorseless hunter Fate
In the depths of the forest did healing and solace seek.

Until greater wisdom did your heart inspire
To right all wrongs and the flame of love rekindle
To burn more ardently with the passion of romantic desire
And row my ailing heart back to streams more tranquil.

Vasantha Khublall

The Mermaid

She sits on a rock surrounded by a quiet blue sea.
Behind her the sun is setting,
and the water is gold about her.
She is a black silhouette against the fading day.

She sits with hands clasping tail;
gentle light touches her shoulders.
Her head is raised: thoughts of love occupy her.
She is thinking of someone
whose caresses are all she lives for;
Or of someone
who once held her, but no more;
Or perhaps of someone
who kisses her only in her dreams,
a phantom whom she must find.
Yes, I think it is that Someone
of whom she is thinking,
for whom she is wishing.
I am he.
Can I count the twilights that I have sat likewise
and thought of her?

Shane Pitkin

Black Child Of A Lesser God

Black child of a lesser God, Trying to find somewhere to belong, searching through the world of the strong, looking for a place called home, living life on the edge of a sharp cold stone.

Black Child of a lesser God, Heal the pain of my forgotten soul, the hypocrite is a member of my own, traveling on an unstable mighty throne, looking for a place called home.

Black Child of a lesser God, Comfort me as I venture into the unknown, lifting my spirit above the spacious dome, Looking for a place called home.

Black Child of a lesser God, Proclaim your glory among those who doubt, giving them the wisdom to rise up and gain clout, looking for a place called home.

Black child of a lesser God, Hear my prayer and seek me out, Devour the innocence of my bright light which has lost its might.

Black Child of a lesser God, rise above the gods who have forgotten this Black Child.

Black Child of a lesser God, Trying to find somewhere to belong, looking for a place called home.

Tamika McIntosh

Magic Rendezvous

Where blue waters wash the clean white sand
Beneath an azure sky, it blends the magic
Of many things unseen, and matches
In perfect harmony a combination
Unique in time and space-
And wears a dream of days to come
Just as, at last, the brilliant sun
Slips out where shining islands lie
Scattered like jewels within the Western Sea
So that, when in proper time and place,
That which should be so may be -
Then, to this pledged trust I must be true.
I shall not fail this magic rendezvous.

Norma J. Nemec

Golden Light

Yonder lays my golden light,
Beneath the green garden.
Down my cheeks my fallen tears emerge,
like a river that's ever flowing.
My heart broken like a wing of a bird.
The wind is cold against my soul.
Without his arms to hold me the moon is just a
shallow light that falls upon my window.

Pamela L. Crews

The Pendulum Swings

How lucky we are to live in a land that is free
But crime and turmoil all around us we see
Our hearts still flutter as a band marches by
We raise our hand to salute as the flag waves high
But crime and greed are tearing us apart
We seek for an answer, how did it all start?
What can we do to reverse this trend?
We love our country, when will it end?
The pendulum swings just so far I hear
A feeling within tells me the turn is near
Then again we will salute our flag with great pride
Thankful we live in a country where goodness,
justice and mercy abide.

Thelma Marsh

Evergreen Square

On the banks of babbling Hay Creek
Beneath the pines of Evergreen Square
Were the trails of chief Fukarwee
Where all creatures knew him there.

He stalked these woods for food and game
He strolled them for his pleasure
He knew every rock or limb and knoll in any kind of weather.

Fukarwee lived his entire life here
With memories both sad and fond
He raised a family and lead his braves
Now he's gone to the Great Beyond.

The whippoorwills call at twilight
The warning cry of the Jay, the lonely hoot of the wise old owl.
All seem to have something to say.

The grey squirrel's chatter from his high perch,
The red squirrel's endless sassing, the crow that's cawing from atop a birch, all seem to mourn his passing.

For us human creatures who miss him most, a replacement can never be found; we can only pray there's an Evergreen Square in the Happy Hunting Ground.

Vernon H. Tarbox

The Littlest Hurricane

A hurricane is coming; it's on the way
Better get ready or a price we'll pay!
Stow the treasures and batten down the hatches
Close all doors and secure the latches

Nothing should be left unattended
Hurricanes can be worse than portended.

The devil hath no fury like this storm
It leaves everything tossed, turned and forlorn
Its power will be used to full measure
Doesn't ever know what's trash or treasure.

It will take some time to set things aright
But this won't likely be life's greatest plight

So not to worry and not to fret
It is the littlest hurricane yet
Moving through quickly, it will soon be gone
It's just a visit by our tiny grandson!

Ora S. Lewis

The Cowboy Way

Eventide beckons a gradual, ever so smooth exchange
Between buzzing honey bees pollinating wild flowers.
And the robust coyote reminds him from the ridge,
Of ceaseless ranch work and family moments fleeting.

Yet, cowboys toil and sweat with scarred hands.
Few things compare to the rewards of hard labor.
Daily we respect nature's bounty from mother earth.
Our love for this Land drives us to our knees.

GIVING TO LIFE HIS BEST.
THAT'S THE COWBOY WAY!

Riding the range by horseback makes us cowboys strong.
Barking dogs herding sheep or cattle excite stillness.
Kids helping mend fences, feed chickens or milk cows
Are the cement that binds family ranch life even more.

A cowboy is a rare breed with uncommon love.
He dares not take caring neighbors for granted.
The real cowboy opens his heart and home to share.
United, with God, he will achieve America's Dream.

GIVING, NOT MERE TAKING;
THAT'S THE COWBOY WAY!

C. Ray Tucker

The Voice From Flanders Fields

No more in Flanders fields do poppies bloom
Between the crosses, row on row - there is no room.
Where setting sun sinks crimson overhead,
Reflection from the earth bathed hotly red,
Unseeing eyes are skyward turned to God,
And lifeless hands dig deep the blood-soaked sod.
There long-stilled voices raise one last appeal
To loved ones left, - their grief to heal.

"O, mourn ye not at this our sacrifice
Lest madmen doom all man to slavery,
But rather think the end is worth the price
That none shall live and not know Liberty!"

Muriel S. Duncan

How Will I Know Love

Your thoughts
blocked and blinded from me
How will I know
when your whole world
is me
Your heart
opening slowly and in one giant burst
how will I know
when your whole world
is me
When your eyes burn me and your gentle touch
creates quiet words and blank thoughts
and an exploding jumble
of knowing and unknowing and wonder and fulfillment
a burn that is deep and scars me
wonderfully forever
when your whole world is me!

Mary Brown

Lake Pend Oreille In The Morning

The silver ripples,
  Blow towards the shore;
The green Pine Islands,
  The mountains, and more.

A mountain lake is hard to beat
  With its steep treed edges,
The Picture is complete.

The sun's warm rays
  Bring the world to life.
All kinds of song birds
  The woods are rife!

There is nothing nicer than spending a Day
  With family and friends on Lake Pend Oreille.

Marion Knott Powers

An Ode To My Sisters

I was never blessed with a brother,
But sisters? I had five.
We had a wonderful childhood.
There are three of us still alive.
We're all of us now over eighty,
'Tis sure we won't all be here long.
Thus, we're living our lives to the fullest
Since health-wise we're still rather strong.
We enjoy going places together,
Have journeyed both near and quite far.
Have flown overseas three different times,
While in the states, mostly travel by car.
It's so great to have wonderful sisters,
I'm glad that God gave them to me.
And I'm glad that He's always there with us,
That's why we can travel, you see.

Lois Kahl Davis

Seasons

Leaves, briskly swingin'
Branches bendin', trunk swayin'
Heavily laden in pourin' rain
The tree, outlasts the hurricane.

Drops of water wildly sprinklin'.
Blades of grass, below lies.
Will spring back, but in
Winter, packed with snow dies.

People, like fields of grass, sway in
Are crushed, by this holocaust we call livin'.
The tree battles the storm and survives.
We, try to better our lives

Workin', playin', lovin' and schemin'.
All, will pass on, to return in
Another season.

Thomas A. Phelan

Untitled

A glimpse of light, out of desire
Breaks through the clouds, and lights a fire
So it burns, amongst the rest
And surely it, will be put to the test
Here comes the wind, westward bound
Along with rain, thunder pounds
And through it all, if it still gives
Then we know, this love will live

Keith Nitsch

In Revolutionary Days

It was she who appeared, first in costume
breath of fresh air in the drowned city
where few saw beneath her glass
there on the street, where I walked and lived

The revolutionaries cried anarchist tears
and thanked our God for making her
I recognized her, child of Atlantic
my special friend

Whence again, she appeared, out of costume
on the street where we lived
I thought, it is she
Is it you?
It is you
And my own God's radiance drew to hers, majestic
on the steps in the drowned city

Michelle Suzette Patènte

River Inside My Mind

Softly the wind blew, I could feel the
breeze.
Quietly the river ran, past the trees.
I listen for the silence, so I can think
clear. Hoping today all my problems will
disappear.
I walk along the trail, suddenly I
start to cry. Hoping that all this beauty
is not just another lie.
The sun went down, the moon
appeared in front of me.
It's so beautiful, how could this be?
Suddenly, I forget about the pain inside,
the loneliness, I no longer need to hide.
I cross the river, inside my mind.
Now I know what I will find.
Always, here in this place,
until the end of time.

Kimberly Bridwell

Walls

These walls have become the death of me.
Brick by brick, moment to moment.
These are the walls that I've created.
They've only left me bitter and jaded.
All of my happiness has been abated.
For so many years I've kept the curtains drawn.
Covering my pain in a shroud.
So soon does silence turn to broken veins.
I only have myself to tie to the blame.
I built these walls to keep me from the storm,
But grief is found rather than being forlorn.
I've created my own private hell,
To which I am the prisoner and my body is the cell.
What is there left to protect?
When there's nothing to be gained.
Open wounds are all there are to be claimed.
Seldom have these walls done me just.
They've only filled me with insecurity and mistrust.

Steve Belcher

Blues Preacher

Acoustic (music) night at the local book store
Brought thumb-snapping poems and songs about war
Copper-kettles; first kisses/Mighty-Mouse on T.V.
Could never compare to what we heard (outside) in the street

A crowd gathered 'round as The Blues Preacher stood
That foot kept on tappin': man, it was good!
To feel that eclectic-mix audience clappin'
In the southern night air: electricity happened

The sky opened and the sod-earth shook
As the blues riffs spun magic like in records and books
But commercialized compact discs could never match
The spontaneous combustion of sound...what a gas! What a blast!

Listeners mesmerized by a rainbow of notes
Nostalgic songs sung by inspired poets
The wind and the rain were all part of the flow
And too soon, it was time: we had to go
Guitar cases closed on a welcome surprise
Inside of the cases in front of our eyes
Tens and twenties/coins tossed by readers and teachers
Showered by love of The Music/Blues Preacher

lynn alyson fields

Silhouette Wheels

Rays of sunlight hit routined rotating spokes
bursting into a gigantic black shadow
hovering my motivated spirit,
an alien to my attention.

The rush of endorphins fills my being
overflowing growth rising
like a fire nurtured by the wind,
an invisible peaceful strength.

Rounding lush green curves alive fragrantly
touching my nose, tires groan,
my heart keeping cadence
to lyrical pumping peddles.

Stretched out beside my movement
coaching me on
my empowering celestial shadow
flying ahead pulling me uphill.

Downhill picking up confident momentum
my shadow retreats.
Gifted I soar
immersed in the salty sweat of success.

Linda Hansen Anderson

The Road We've Walked Together

The road we've walked together has been filled with twists and turns,
But as we come to part our ways, for you my whole being yearns.

The way has not been easy, a path with highs and lows,
Through which we both have stumbled and struggled with our souls.

At times the road's run smoothly, paved with happy memories,
The path's been straight and clear and wide, cooled with
life-sustaining breeze.

Although we've come to parting, this road is part of me,
It's all I was and am today, and all that I will be.

And as I travel now alone, without you as my guide,
Your duties you have well-fulfilled; you've made my pathway wide.

You've kept me firmly grounded; accept your due reward;
I give you back your guiding hand to guide you to the Lord.

Paul F. Hernandez

Future Beyond Reality

We search for the soul that belongs to our body
But everyday seems to be an endless battle.
Sure of what we want, but
Unable to assimilate desire with reality.
Will the two ever unite?
Or do they just grow further apart?
A desire so strong... stopped by an evil reality.
You ask what is this evil reality?
I answer the world.
The world of materialists.
The world of perfection.
The more we have the more perfect our lives will be.
Is this not true?
Or is it a fallacy of the rich,...
An assumption of the greedy?
The weak in spirit believe these ideas,
But the strong will deny this kind of logic.
I foresee my union of desire and reality.
Do you?

Mary Ellen K. Aduleit Nestor

The Past Time Gone Waste Time

They claim to act, for the good of the game,
But I tell you for sure, it isn't the same,
In the midst of it all, they cast it asunder,
and slammed their doors, like claps of thunder.

They cared not a whit, that their loyal fans,
Had little to do, but sit on their hands,
They just battled each other, these players and owners,
What an arrogant lot, of moaners and groaners.

Remember how great, were long ago days,
When heroes abounded, such as Mantle and Mays,
Or Murderers Row, and the Boys of Summer,
The Gas House Gang, or Bob Feller's hummer.

Jocko was an umpire, and what in the heck,
One of the owners, was old' Bill Veeck,
And we followed intently, knew all the stats,
But can't get excited, over today's fat cats.

They're taken the heart, from the grand old game,
And likely as not, it will never be the same,
With their strikes and shut downs, it's a vast crime,
What their greed has done, to our national past time.

Darby O'Toole

hear i'm blind

i can not see
but I want to hear what you're showing me
truth be it in words
so they fly like mocking birds
standing on a wire
burning with the fire
trying to get the feel
but I'm blind so I can't grip the steering wheel
just put an ear on the wall
and put me on hold with my call
see in the dark with glowing eyes
but never to hear your moaning cries
if I could only hear the picture you hold
it would make my blindness o so very bold
then I could finally paint
my deafness in colors of faint
and I would hold the final key
to hear I am in this sightful sea
april 26 of ninety three

sven lars loebler rafferty

Tired And True

I'm just an old chair,
But I've had a lots of fun
Being a rocker for the old and the young.

My rockers are wobbly, my back almost broke,
My velvet covered seat smells just like smoke.
I'm all full of holes, rips and tares too,
I've had very rough usage, since I was new.

How old am I? You're asking Me?
I can't quite remember, but it's plain to see,
I am up in age, about 73.

All of my usage is a long time gone,
Among the ancient is where I belong.
For my lumps, and my bumps, my kicks and my thumps,
I've been a pretty good chair after all.
To have many children crawl over me,
and never once did they fall.

So now I am old, worn out with care,
I'll just bow out with the memories I share.
In hopes you'll never forget,
I was a good old chair.

Mary Baker Watts

Words

There are no words in heaven.
But look what words do here.
They come to bless us, come to haunt us;
Come to love us, and to damn us.
Words, some chosen with thought.
Others fly out with unexpected swiftness.
Words can calm the most tormented soul.
Words that one mind can touch with another.
Some words bring with them the joy of the morning.
Others close the day with darkness and foreboding.
Which ones will come out of my mouth?
Ones that come from the heart?
Ones that will become as blessings on wings;
That bring love and happiness
And, one day, wisdom.

Merry Battles

The Contumely Of Life

The wife who says ok if you must-
but make it fast.
The lover who says forget those sex manual prelims -
hop in here.
The lightning that strikes me, rolls my eyes back -
and spares two nearby companions.
The traffic death of a health nut-
by a drunken driver.
The wedding postponed forever by a-
blood test showing AIDS.
A family reunion starts in an outdoor picnic area.
A thunderstorm forces them into cramped indoor quarters.
Ancient feuds turn fixed politeness into acerbic bickering.
A sudden shot. The number of family members is reduced.
It was a memorable family reunion.
The husband who has feared fire all his life -
is cremated by his widow.
the exalted winner of a Ten Million Dollar Sweepstakes
30 annual payments of $333,333.00 each -
is a Death Row inmate. Execution IMMINENT.

Raymond G. Doersam

The Cries Of A Clown

Greasepaint, galoshes a bright shiny nose....
But the heart of a clown, nobody knows.
Hidden away by a bright red grin;
Are you laughing or crying my friend?

Pulling out flowers from under your hat,
Rolling and tumbling, this way and that;
What are you hiding away with false glee?
Why can't you be honest with me?

I know your heart's breaking, behind your bright smile
And you can't be you for even awhile,
There never has been a more wrenching sound;
Than the cries of a clown, when there's nobody around.

When the mask of grease-paint is all streaked with tears,
And the costume is off, and you must face your fears......
The laughter is empty, you strain at the sound,
Of the cries of a clown, when there's no one around

Are you really too tired to put back your mask?
And pretend that you're fine; it's all that we ask?
Just tell us a joke; make us smile, bring a token
Ignorance is bliss when a clown's heart is broken.

Patricia Middaugh McGillivray

Until

Until you came to me, I wasn't very strong
But then you gave me hope and I keep holding on.
Just help some one and you will see—
That it can bring joy and victory
If everyone would give a smile
To some one on this day
You never know what good you do-
Just like my life was made a new.
You will be so happy, when you do the best you can.
That you have helped your fellow man
We can do so much in the world
To make it a better place
And then you will get your reward
When you meet God face to face.

Mary Reynolds

Excerpt From My Dad

He was the bestest friend I ever had;
But where is he now? My Dad.

My Dad just packed up and left me,
Said he didn't want to be here no more.
I heard him and Mom a fussin',
And he slammed out the door.

He said he'd be here at noon;
But it will be dinner time soon.
Night time has come - the lites are on;
But I'll wait, I'll wait till it's dawn

He said he still loves me, and that didn't change,
But if he really meant it,
Why is he gone? My Dad.

I think of the times we went fishin';
Just my Dad and me. We were best buddies.
He taught me to climb a tree.
Now who will he do these things with.
Why can't it be me, My Dad?
Now he won't be my best buddy. He won't be here when I'm sad.
He won't be here at bedtime, will he still be, My Dad?

Mary Jo Piatt

Unknown Heritage

The search for our heritage seems so strong
but why do we look so extremely long.
Let the past stay asleep in peace
It will bring a great release.
The earth itself holds secrets dear
Open your eyes, listen and hear.
Time will pass and we too will go
That is called HERITAGE as we should know.

Virginia Cornelius

Rain Must Fall

Into each life, some rain must fall,
But why does it have to be a thunderstorm?
Everyday, the clouds roll in,
The sunshine never seems to win,
Although it's raining, the sun still tries.
Look up, there is the rainbow,
The sun still trying to shine,
The dark clouds roll on.
One day your sun will break through,
Then, the sky will be bright blue.
So keep looking up, never down,
So we can see the sun through the clouds.

Rosalie M. McKim

Flyin'

Can you see me, am I real?
Can you tell me how I feel?
The night is dark, though the moon rises high
One more hit and I'll start to fly
Fly away, fly away into the sky
Reach for the moon
Reach for the darkness
Grab the demons beyond the earth
I feel myself as giving birth
The black hole is endless, there's no way out
Scream, scream, scream and run about
"Let me out" "Let me out"
I'm coming down from the night
I hit once more and I'm back in flight
Can you see me, am I real?
Can you tell me how I feel?

Meggan S. Brault

Is There a Mother Out There?

Is there a Mother out there, whose heart was ever broken,
By a daughter's cruel actions, and dreadful words she's spoken?
A daughter who is selfish, who forgot what she was taught.
Full of sin and hate, and "self indulgent" thought.

A daughter who is prayed for, to "change herself," some day.
Before it gets too late, and her child treats her "that way."
A daughter who was raised, by "decent folks," and love.
And Sunday School, and Church, and "Guidance from above."

I'm sure the Lord above, is watching us on earth.
And surely knows by now, what "this child of his is worth."
Please have faith "Dear Mother," for things that went so wrong.
And make your daily prayer, "Dear God, please make me strong."

And when you're "hurting," "Mother," because you've worked so hard,
And never got much thanks, and did not receive a card;
Just "hang in there," "Mother," and be glad for blessings given.
And if there's any justice, you'll get your Thanks in Heaven.

Norma Dragon

The Color Purple

The maddened Sorcerer's robe is ravished
by one color.
The center of his dancing inferno sparkles
of one color.
Wondering eyes search the darkening horizon and see
one color.
Rushing feet without cover, trample the brilliant buds
kissed with one color.
Thundering clouds expel their tears
shadowed by one color.
Crashing waves of the hungry sea are tainted by one
mysteriously luscious color....
the color purple.

Laura Larson

Trust Gone

Once there was nothing written among friends;
by your word and name you were bound.
When trust goes, friendliness ends
and reasons to hate are found.

They say a man's bond is his word;
never to break.
Between friends I've heard
it only takes a handshake.

Boys once learned that to break a trust
brought with it shame;
and knew as men they must
honor each trust forget with their name.

Now finding a true friend is rare;
and trust is a forgotten trait.
It seems we've lost our ability to care;
and we're drowning in a sea of hate.

Larry W. Cook Sr.

Will God Do?

No matter the question, the thought, the action—nothing
compared to WILL GOD DO?

All other words/sentences left the mind. Each passing
moment of time re-emphasizes the words WILL GOD DO?
When all is said and done, the question remains: WILL GOD DO?

Somewhere deep inside something rumbles upwards, finally
breaking through to the surface;
When asked again, WILL GOD DO?
Somehow I know the answer is a RESOUNDING YES!
GOD WILL DO!!

Terri Sue Meister

Farewell To Brittney

Today, Wednesday January 5th 1994 at about 6:30 p.m., God called our precious Brittney into his fold
To sing, laugh and play free of pain for Him to hug and hold

He let this family borrow her for a short while
To know a little baby girl's beautiful smile.

To experience courage, togetherness and love
The way we hear and know things are up above.

As we write the final page of our miracle child, now an angel in the sky
We won't close the book because we know we will be with her by and by.

Lying here in this pretty pink dress of satin and lace
It looks as if she were just peacefully sleeping with a smile on her angel face.

Pat Wheeler

Violence Of Silence

If truth be told what unspeakable things might reveal!
Can we afford not to seek what once we dare not ever speak

If truth be told, what unspeakable things might reveal!
Hidden deep and trapped within are memories that keep us bound
and when ignored remain unfound.

If truth be told what unspeakable things might reveal!
Broken places lie in wait for us to own our rage, our hate.

If truth be told what unspeakable things might reveal!
Silence bears false witness of self and others.
Will its presence ever lead us to discover the unspeakable?

If heaven ever waged hells war within it was unspeakable.
If hell were ever well defined, it's SILENCE.
If truth be heaven ever it must be shared
and blame, its game is famous!

I have a voice now,
gave to me from violent struggles deep within
and when it surfaced I knew fear,
then, I knew me.

Linda Ledsworth

Untitled

I've lost my teddy bear
Can you help me find it?
I have to find my teddy bear(!)
Or did I give it away to somebody?
No, I wouldn't have given it away
Oh God, why would anyone take him?
It's just an old teddy bear
No one wants it
I have to find it
Sh__
Sh__
I remember where he is, he's in the
shower, I had to wash him off, he was
dirty, he smelled ugly
I scrubbed him so hard, it wouldn't come off
Oh, I can't get him clean, what will I do?
My teddy bear, my teddy bear
Dirt, smell, torn, ouch, no leave him alone
My teddy bear needs a doctor, please someone help
I left him in the shower

Lynne M. Drew

Hurry Sundown

Star of day with descent so slow,
Carries fallen hopes to a hidden quest.
Edge of light in search to know,
Embraced by a horizon with promised rest.
The day's demise leaves remains behind,
Portrayal of colors upon canvassed sky.
A tranquil hush deepens viewer's find,
Twilight conceived another day shall die.
Shield of darkness envelopes far and near,
Suspend shades of black so plights may hide.
Inspiration procured from poet's celestial sphere,
Shine wishing stars tending a lunar guide.
Comfort in solitude another world lurks through,
Hurry Sundown, as night awaits for you.

N. B. Schlepp

American Urban Hymn 1994

She sours like old cream
caught in time's clutch and pinch
the rope of sorrow taut with hope
day breaks in her monastic bed
the morning ritual a solitude of mirrors
fidgets in the vestibule of the world
fluttering against that litany of work
until the cloak of dusk purls
all silent all sequestered, a nun's abandon
cat in the crook of her knee
stripling light harvest moon
a dappled quilt of silver solace
pale steps silent in the hall
outside her window the licorice whip night
its squat of feline human heart
tires yodel on the shiver of road
whining moving sobbing singing bane
quell of homeless squat, cough and sputter
a broken muffled lullaby, some choke of night bird
some loss, some hairball twisted twine of night.

Penny Weeks

"Today"

Today is the time to start your life anew,
By starting a new hobby you've put off, but always wanted to,
Make a new friend, spend quiet time with God,
Let something go inside, and work in the yard.

Today is the day to clean up the clutter,
So you don't have to make excuses, or mutter,
Today is yours, so take a little of it for yourself,
Then do something important, with what's left.

Like witness to a lost person, and lend a helping hand,
Think about what you expect from life, and your fellow man,
It does you good, to spend a few minutes alone,
To realize what you want to accomplish, and make a happy home.

Today can be a drudge, or the best one you've known,
If you give it your best and some tenderness you've shown,
We work hard on our jobs, and it's important to work on today,
By being careful with each minute, and wise in what we say.

Today can affect, how you spend the rest of your life,
So take time to do something nice for your child, husband, or wife,
Today is a precious gift, nurture it, and grow,
Yesterday's gone, tomorrow hasn't come, today is all there is to sow.

Louise Blakey

Love Pulls Us Together

Dreams of passion radiate on the horizon
Chasing after love in the direction up
What a feeling
It penetrates the human heart

The single thread of love pulls together
Intertwined throughout the universe infinite
The pattern intricate but definite

The tapestry, woven by His loving hands
Where we are enveloped
Bound in the family of God

In pursuit -
To embrace the sacred heart of Jesus
The center
Interwoven through our lives forever
Where heaven is the limit

Marianna Cimarrusti

The Huddle

In textile mills,
Children change bobbins on sewing machines
Spinning at a fast rate.
In meat packing plants,
Blood from frozen carcasses of meat
Sticks to welt shoes
Only to float on satin robes;
Robes that wash plaster hands with decadence.
Mankind will stretch its bold neck
For a golden seed driven by mangled limbs
That stagger along blister roads.

A sanctified decorum consumes passionate winds;
The executioner stands alone in a grotesque dream,
A vision filled with hungry cobwebs
That cling to ceramic minds.
Humble tombstones etched by novice swordsmen
Who take the long way down chowder mountains,
The way that brings them to a plighted crossroads.
Angry trees set forth godly moans
That drown out correlated flutes.

Kiki Stamatiou

The Sea

A canvas of black for miles around;
clouds loom above, no sight, just sound.
The clapping of the thunder and the pelting of the rain
intermix with the ocean, the fountain of pain.

The waves are stirred and crash to shore;
in the distance are cries, blocked out by the roar
of the mighty king, the one called the "Sea",
from its stifling grasp, no one may flee.

The salt air spray stings the wounds,
of souls who forever sing cacophonous tunes.
Their hopes and dreams washed away like the waves,
imprisoning their victims, making them slaves.

But wait, what is that? A streak do I see
enveloping the darkness. Almighty, hear my plea.
Chase away the dark of doom and despair
with your light, disperse this dungeonous lair.

Then, a ray shot, out, like a glimpse of hope
filling me with purpose, a reason to cope.
As I looked out and saw the wonders of the sea,
I saw my reflection looking back. It was me.

Lena Kasahara

My Paradise

Use your imagination now to take a little trip.
Come now, don't be afraid; we'll ride in a magic ship.
We'll catch flying fish and cross enchanted seas;
And wave to the dancing moon in the land of humming honey bees.

Look now towards the silvery stars
At an island made of chocolate bars;
A land of marshmallow mountains and strawberry streams,
A place free of worries so it seems.

Close your eyes and stretch your mind
To a mirage made for even the blind;
To a breeze that will blow away death,
And bring new life in a single breath.

Tell me, now, if you can imagine
Life without this magical land.
It is a place where the people are so nice.
Yes, this is my paradise.

Lindsey N. Baker

Come Unto Me Little Children

Come unto me little children,
Come unto me young and old.
For I have been waiting so long.
To gather you in from the cold.
Be diligent in all that you do,
Be more diligent, when I'm calling you.
You shall see, all your loved ones on the other side,
But you must serve Christ, while in this Earth you abide.
They are here with arms outstretched,
Coming soon his loved one's to fetch.
Be ready when I come for you,
For heavens promise you don't want to lose.
Call on me and I'll be there,
Call on me for I really do care.
I'm ready for you all to come home,
But there's still so much work to be done.
Hasten to do your chores,
For you're not far from heavens doors.
Help to save souls, every last one.
Then when their saved, your work will be done.

Millie Krobel

To Kill A Whale

"There she blows," a cry
comes from the crows' nest upon high.
"Lower away" calls the Captain;
A whaleboat drops into the ocean main.

"Give it to him," shouts the Mate.
Two harpoons driven home to incapacitate.
In agony the whale wept,
sounding into the sea depth.
The bowchuck smokes as the line is swept.

It then surfaces pulling the men and boat
as they jump wavetops and try to stay afloat.
The men pull and pull on the harpoon line.
Alongside with a lance of sharp steel design
puncture a vital spot the harpooner defined.

Blood shoots from the blowhole.
Its final gasp a violent shaking soul.
Now dead and on its side it did roll.
The tail fin rising from the sea
telling all it will no longer be.

Roy A. Parker

The King Is Coming

Blessed is he that hungers and thirsts after God Rightness.
Confess and repent of sin, let it be blotted out.
Jesus said, come unto him, Jesus can save.
It is the time to seek and save those who are lost.
Jesus is the True Messiah, he has love for all.
Follow God's commandments, Love one another, and read God's word.
All Jesus promised is true. He speaks the word and it shall be done.
Jesus is the redeemer of my life.
Like a bright and morning star, Jesus give's us love, joy and peace.
God made the beautiful rainbows and sunsets.
Lead me in the way of Salvation, Oh Lord.
Jesus will shield you with is covenant.
Blessed is the King, that cometh in the name of the Lord.
The King is coming for the bride.

Louise Allen

Distant Daughter

As conception progresses—I'm certain your gender—Mommy's faith has confirmed. Obsession regresses—Arrives blessed splendor—unconditional love affirmed. Endeavors fueled—parturiency my favor—spiritual bonding compromised. Accomplishments loom—the victory savored—our closeness for now minimized.

Carnal desires—the essence of time—priorities are misdirected. Your beginnings require—the absolute mind—cognizant of perfection. Daddy regrets—the provisional condition—to fulfill what's been elusive. Society's affects—achievement admissions—the academic prize conducive.

My ambitions spawn—the distance between us—our communication amiss. Inundated is dawn—of obstacles that screen us—from our prenatal bliss. Approval ratings—my preoccupation—long an abysmal quest. Still private settings—in contemplation—bring moments picturesque.

My sanity tried—remains intact—asperity fills duration. Turbulent miles—a juggling act—like balancing tribulation. Vexation lessens—resounding laughter—iniquities on decline. My covenant begins—my Distant Daughter—with distance being denied.

Though at times—the spirit's fruit—of patience was not received. I stayed in line—and thoughts of You—showed graces in Your being. Steadfast living—of my Creator—perseverance my reward. Unworthily I'm given—by my Sweet Savior—humility onward.

Reginald D. Tarver

Confusion

What? Where? When? How? Why?
Confusion circles my brain
and tangles itself in a web of questions.
I am dizzy.
Slowly spinning like a top beginning to fall,
my wobbliness is unsure of the direction I am to take.
I am lost.
My questions are unanswered like a child's prayer to God,
waiting in silence for a sign to direct me towards my future.
I am scared.
I'm in a frenzied fury to answer my questions
much like a shark feeding in blood infested waters.
I take a bite at my thoughts.
Bit by bit
my questions are gone. I am at peace.
Next year. Next month. Next week. Tomorrow. Tonight.
My future is closing in,
silently stalking me like a predator
ready to pounce on its prey.
I am ready.

Kimberly A. Kohn

Romantic Buddha

Fortunate is time that escapes indignation
Conquering ill-will harbor, and hearts of aggression.
A staple of existence, calling upon duty and survival.
And demanding its place among the noble elite.

Fortunate is light which shines upon truth.
Despondent of lies upon its waking paths.
A shadow of ancestry, claiming a right of divinity,
Insisting upon recognition, of our humble defeat.

Fortunate is space which controls its place.
Allowing fantasy and truth a common existence.
In token response to the dictates of science.
Towards cowardice - assuming - a casual friend.

Fortunate is time that escapes indignation,
That regretfully parts, to seek retaliation.
To bargain an attempt,......to gain......
To alchemize the living into regent domain.

Zen Hishynsky

That Is The Question

(The Rime Of A Modern Quandary)

Several years together, no vows to bind —
Countless life strands intertwined.
"Can happiness like this endure?"
They are not so sure.

They are long on love and communication.
Both have chalked up education.
He views with approval her career.
With the Olympics, his calling is clear.

It is plain to see
How many ways their wants and needs agree.
Both like freedom, home and song —
Have positive views of right and wrong.

They like stimulating conversation.
Both think style is a botheration.
Against being "copy-cats;" "put-ons" they deplore.
Both like roses growing by the door.

Siding with each other — pure delight.
Like me, you'll likely deem as right
Their decision to be married.
He is black. She is white.

Ruth Garms Terry

Snow Fall In London

Would love to see snow fall in London some day
Clinging to cathedrals; that's where it would stay
Hear angels who sing to the glory of God
And play on the harps with the fairies of Nod

Would love to study music with the masters of France
To fly through the wind, to learn how to dance
To say "merci beaucoup, il est mon plaisir"
To run in the sun, paint a picture of tears

That might fall from my cheeks if I don't get a chance
To do all of my dreams in England of France
Wherever life takes me I'm eager to go
I just can't stand hearing that awful word "No"

Would love to see snow fall in London some day
Clinging to cathedrals; that's where it would stay

Susan Lynn Martin

Fun In The Sky

So often on high in the vibrant blue sky
Countless whipped cream clouds float lazily by
Things of beauty nature lovers agree
And a closer look let's one readily see.

There's a perky little poodle with a wooly lamb
And a giant fish swimming away from land
A pointed torpedo next looms into view
Skirting between mountains made of puff clouds too.

A profile comes in focus of an aged man
Gazing afar across the billowy white sand
Near the rugged face of an Indian Brave
Surveying the land that he's fought to save.

Soon appears a bird gracefully soaring in flight
Looking for a place to rest within sight
And a cluster of balloons floats across his way
Released by a child who is out to play.

Lo and behold appears a plump roasted chicken
Make believe food good for finger lickin'
Ah, yes, imagination is a challenging thing
Providing much fun in the beautiful Spring.

Virginia M. Plaia

First Snow

A blanket of beauty fell overnight
covering everything a pure, pure white

A blanket of beauty for all to see
the wonders of nature are amazing to me

A blanket of beauty upon the ground
not a footprint of anything to be found

This blanket of beauty will meet its fate
as soon as the day begins to break

The sun, the wind, and creatures like me
will ruffle this blanket for eternity

So before this blanket changes its shape
I will cherish every moment that it will take

Ronald R. Peets

The Life Of Flanders Fields

Within these fields the poppies sway:
Covering the memories of yesterday.
White crosses pay homage to the men;
That stood for honor, love, and land.
Now lying sleeping souls lament:
From Flanders Fields a message's spent.

We took the oath and faced the doom;
We lived then died in anguished gloom.
We spilled our blood and lost our limbs;
We carried that torch of freedom's spin.
At last at peace: with God we're healed,
We've come home to rest in Flanders Fields.

Passed on to others the torch still burns;
The elixir of strength in courage's turn.
We remain at peace in this field of red...
The poppies move gently above our heads.
The messages of duty and valor live on;
Giving still a life to those who've gone...
To rest in Flanders Fields.

Ruth E. Duffina Lake

Mothers

Mothers are a gift from God,
Created special by His hand,
From Adam's rib and earthen sod.
By Adam's side she came to stand.

From Eve the human race has come.
She is the mother of us all.
Through sin they lost their garden home,
When Satan tempted them to fall.

But Mary bore the Lord of Life.
Through Christ redemption's plan was born.
Her heart was pierced as by a knife,
When Jesus died for us alone.

Her mother's love had suffered loss.
We thank her for the part she played,
When Jesus died upon the cross.
Our debt of sin for us He paid.

Our mothers too have played a part,
In who we are and hope to be.
We oft as well, broke mother's heart.
She gave us love, forgiveness free.

G. George Ens

Who Am I...

I am a spirit — a soul ____ a creature of GOD's
CREATION. I AM ALL THINGS IN MY SPIRIT __________
A star at the furthest corner of the universe — A wild
flower, in a deep forest, a twirling leaf on a tall tree on some
cool bank of a flowing stream. I am the water, that sparkles
like a million diamonds, during a spring shower————-
The soft aromatic floor of a sweet virgin forest————
I am the wind that tastes and smells————-
and gazes at all God's creation — I am an Indian mother.

P. Simmons

Imagination

Butterflies fly over valleys and streams
dancers they dance and dreamers will dream...
Dream over stars that soar through the sky
spirits that skate so free that they fly.

Magicians that make lovers connect
for voices don't sing unless they project...
Babies are carried by storks overnight
when they come down to earth, what a fantastic flight.

Crickets that hop from strand to strand,
fireflies glow across the warm beach sand...
Fairies that kiss each and every dream true,
unicorns that prance their way unto you.

They fly past your heart and into your soul
to capture your thought and your mind to enroll...
Enroll into endless fields of wonder and fun,
stars overhead you may wish on but one.

Where is this happening this wild new creation?
It's something we call Imagination...
This does sound wonderful, you have to admit,
just close your eyes and partake in it.

Nicole Barbara Castelino

bluelove

slips	(like)	between		ice blue
dances		upon	(silk)	angles
flows		within		the ancient
rides	(high)	on		edges
curving		toward		tomorrow
shining		in		today
finding		this		(time)
		again		

Sharon Shepherd

Untitled

She wasn't searching for the answers - she was just looking for a friend
dancing through her darkness - until the moon touched down again
She wasn't asking for the world- she just wanted something special to love
some kindness to help her make it through - when her storm comes rolling round
She just sat there in her silence - a cool breeze blew through her hair
she needed a longtime companion - and when she turned no one was there
She cherished all the little things - that no one else could see and
when she cries her saddest tears - I'll help her make it through
because she needs a helping hand - and because I need her too
I was looking for the answers - that no one else could give
and when I reached down deep inside - I found a child there
Nobody had held her - in so many years
that when I reached out for her - she shed a million tears
I told her I'd protect her - though I wasn't sure I could
I watched her soulful eyes - sparkle in the deepest blue
I felt a tiny hand - reach up and clasp onto mine
it was then I knew I cared- and we would make it through in time

Stephanie Hemphill

Nature's Surprise

Nature is a wonderful thing, changing from
day to day.
You never are sure what will come, for it
will surprise you in many ways.

One day you'll look for sunshine, to only
find the rain.
Then again there'll be another surprise.
each day is never the same!

And don't forget the night time, when you
see the moon and stars.
The night has a way of drawing you in...
No matter where... you are!

Patti Rose Tracy

Derivation

With little patience, the turbulent clouds
cast violent showers amongst the relentless winds.
The enveloped landscape accepts the nature in
times maturity, and drinks with gentle composure.
The skies submit in eventual haste, to the
brilliant blaze being born upon the horizon.
The landscape absorbs the adolescent warmth
of the penetrating sunlight. While the leaves
of the trees in their wisdom, have positioned
themselves to meet this outcome with welcome.
Embrace the wisdom of the leaves as an
unselfish truth. Any outcome may be
awaited in patient anticipation, for in
its conception your wait is its own reward.

William L. Janes, Jr.

Something For The Head

Pretty eyes, once again
deceived me of love.
Soft lips, upon my heart, made me
dance with the song of love for you.
Just something for the head,
to chase the blues away.
Try to comprehend the show, if you can.
Friends, and lovers, sometimes come and go.
Some shine happiness, and some rain sorrows.
Some bring pleasures, some bring pain, and all
I do is work, create, and play.
Just something for the head,
Pretty eyes, once again, lead me astray,
curious of what the love's all about.
Just something for the head,
A taste of warmth, made me sing, and play
the blues of a true poet.

Stephanie D. Wilson

flying games

those playing the game experience
departures and arrivals of thought before the fact
which summon a certain breathlessness
a certain flush in the cheeks
a certain rapping of fingernails on terminally stationed plastic chairs
a certain false wall of outer confidence
so entirely concrete and stolid to anonymous masses
entwined in a web of to and fro, back and forth
ascending and descending
in everyday order
with short day impatience
inside an oppressing entrancement brought on by the vagueness of high
ceilings and vast corridors filled with hum and holler
only to be crashed down with an inkling of omen barely noticed
but altogether present diffusing into individual peripheral senses
and perching them directly on the edge of common reasoning
slowly teetering toward an opening in the dense air
where the players carry on the only way they know how
but end up losing all ground, and the game, anyway

Shaunna Morrison

Dreamers

Can you create a dreamer without knowing the secret,
depths of the soul, is it akin to setting,
then reaching a goal?

Can you teach a bird to sing
if you don't know his song?
Is it instinct, knowing which magic lasts
only moments, or which is prolonged?

Can a dreamer see the dawns of tomorrows,
is there a greater vision of mind
healing their sorrows?

How do they know, anything they can envision,
they can nurture and grow?

How do they see, what most never sense,
or know there to be?

Dreamers teach dreamers, you teach what you know,
freeing the imagination, letting dreams flow.

Dreamers throw off the chains of logic,
to wander and seek, dreaming impossible dreams,
creating new realities,
that's what makes dreamers unique.

Nancy L. Wilson

The Monkey's Disgrace

Three Monkeys sat in a coconut tree,
Discussing things as they were said to be.
Said one to the others "Now listen you two,"
There's a rumor going around that just can't be true.
That man descended from our noble race,
The very idea is a terrible disgrace!
You never knew a mother monkey to leave
her babies with others to bunk,
Or pass them on from one to another
Till they scarcely know who is their mother
Here's another thing a monkey won't do,
Stay out all night and get on a stew.
Or take a gun, a club or a knife
And take another monkeys life.
Yes man descended, the ornery cuss,
But brother he sure didn't descend
from us

Robert C. Lawton

To A Special Lady

What kind of love do you have in your life?
Does it make you feel good all the time?
Is the person who loves you concerned how you feel?
Does he try to assuage all your pain?
Does he help you to grow - to spread out your wings
Will your spirit be able to fly?
It should be that way - true love should help
Your spirit soar high in the sky

We've talked at great length about matters of heart
I've explained how I feel deep inside
To make you happy - that's what I dream
Will you give me a chance in your life?
There's so much to do and to share as we live
To treat you as a queen - yes, I would
You'd be first in my life - I'd be almost your slave
How happy I'd be - if I could

R. M. Miller

Timing Stoplights

I was sitting in the grass the other day,
doing nothing but think of you.
I could see the cars zip back and forth,
hurrying to someplace important.
I think about you a lot. Don't really know why.
I wonder what you're doing at thins very second.
Maybe I'll see you fly along the street in your car.
Maybe if I'm lucky you'll miss the light,
and I'll have a chance to see you for eight seconds.
That's how long the cars stopped for. Eight seconds.
But to me that could be a lifetime. Eight seconds
to just glimpse your profile; to possibly catch your eyes;
to see you one more time before I leave.

I'm here. Whenever here is. I'm lonely.
My husband is off in another country; he's not around much.
There's nothing to do but sit in the coffee shop and watch
the people on the street. I was timing the stoplight yesterday.
You missed the light. For eight seconds you smiled at your wife.
Eight seconds is longer than eternity.

Martha J. Carr

"An Instant Millionaire"

I don't need a lottery to play here
Don't need a lot of money to be rich here
But I will have the best of anywhere
I'm gonna be an instant millionaire.

Folks don't think a lot of me way down here
Don't need a lot of money to be rich here
But I don't have one care I can declare
I'm gonna be an instant millionaire.

And I don't mean money piled up high
Let the greedy have it stacked up to their thighs
I don't need but one thing to make me a rich guy
It's not money, Honey, but makes rich men sigh.

Oh don't think I'm not very rich out here
Don't need a lot of money to be rich here
Oh dog gone my love has just come in here
She's just made me an instant millionaire
Each time I am an instant millionaire.

Sam J. Alcorn

Do Not Forsake Me

Do not forsake me, now that I'm old and grey.
Don't turn your back on me, my hurt won't go away.
See me as a person that stood straight and tall.
Don't make me feel I'm helpless, that I might stumble and fall.

I watch when we are together,
All the laughter and funny sneers,
Was it something I had said or done
Now that I'm up in years.

Oh, I remember what it was like
To see my grandma at her best.
She cut out paper dolls for me
and made my first dance dress.

She got too old and feeble
and couldn't get around.
Her mind failed with her age
so we just never went around.

I kinda feel like her I guess
I see the children less each day.
Maybe it turns into months or years
But that's how time slips away.

Rita Joyce Offineer

Skydiver

Jump!
Downwards I fall
Soaring
The gush of wind slows me
Free fall
I see the curved horizon
Vision of the men who thought the world round
Downwards I soar, fondling the rush
Arms embracing the sky, legs straddling Mother Earth
As I kiss the sunrise and drink to its beauty
I can fly, yes I can
I need not wings, I need not a craft
Pull the string! No, I want to fly forever!
A tug brings me back, yearning
Gently, slowly drifting
Reluctantly spiraling downwards
A human cloud plucked from the sky
By Earth's magnetic grasp
Quiver, Quaver, wig-wag
Touchdown

Robert A. DeMovic

Eccentric-Am I?

Cause and effect open our eyes and help us to accept dreams as dreams.
Reality sets in.
The blood is red and the cut really hurts.
Who said writing was difficult?
It is only knotty for those with no gray matter.
Who could that be?
Everyone thinks, everyone feels, and everyone writes, if only in their minds.
If I had one wish, it would be for an extra sense called Mental Telepathy.
I could peruse your mind and write your story.
No more guessing or wondering.
The blood is red and that cut really does hurt.
I didn't imagine it and neither did you.
You know how I know?
You told me and you didn't say a word.

Toni Hodgins

Honestly Among Us

Rest assured far left of doubt, I won't immobile romantically a long duration
same as card houses on sand our times together will blow over if we're not guarding
when the purist drum-dums with raging fists will you also dissolve to scathing?
Chutes and ladders, low man on the totem pole, how ever do we keep
Grace she's within her own star player gone for lengthy seasons,
I'm no homologous embodiment of splendor here like once flourished
a promise of no monstrous inclusions, a refusal of reduction to a curtseying midge
not speaking honestly among us is a diminished offering to anyone
I love the man, like to have his family, let's start willingly again
from nowhere established the ponderous salt-tanged surf disinfects on contact all that's not desired leaving only earthtones and nudes to consider, leave the room all hers for Grace
I'll thwart with spirits who mean no harm, why eradicate the woman who gave this child legacy?
A mother's daughter reluctant to move a new one in, crackling debris is discounted but honestly!
Among us is a buttress of garish window-dressing.

Noel K. Johnson

"What Money Can't Buy"

Years ago, I left school-friends, and home
Eager to "make it" on my own.
Each week I buy the hometown press,
Comparing peaks and valleys as our lives progress.
To reminisce with my chum, Jim, I yearn
And save hard for my return.
Yesterday, through the rain, the far-off whistle of a train
Recalled to mind that day, in Kindergarten,
When brave Jim and I had run away.
They found us at the train depot waiting to depart
Even then, wanderlust was in my heart.
Today, I read, to my dismay, that Jim had passed away!
"Head injuries from a bicycle fall" it said.
The money is saved for my return, but the time is spent; Jim is gone.
I ponder all the things I hope to do
And wonder if I will live to see them through.
Life is as it is, and intended to be, a span of unpredictability.
Is it wise to postpone dreams until tomorrow?
Do I have the time?
Do you?

Maxine Sue Feller

Life Is Here And Gone

Life is like a vapor being exposed to the
elements of time. It will evaporate leaving
only signs, letting us know life was here but
passed on. We always put off projects, people
for the next day, next week, next month and
next year. Time ticks away we think we can
beat it until one day time stops! No more life
you see, the friend or the relative we were supposed
to see left without saying that final good-by.
Our minds race for answers in our heads, this
should not be. We thought we had time to see
them before they took their final journey home.
Life is a vapor; it is only here for a while.
The elements of life will evaporate as the clock
of time ticks by. Life disappears without written
notice. No one can prepare for it, it just happens.
Value life to its fullness, do not put off what you
can do today. When life leaves it is final, no tracing
back or turning back the hands of time.

Tesha Johnson

A Letter To Someone Lost In Sadness

Dear you,

I try to see you but you always seem to be somewhere
else, and somehow I feel you're avoiding me.

I try to ask you what's wrong and try to help, but
you act like you don't hear me...

I want to say I love you and want us to be close
but it doesn't matter because you just don't care
anymore.

I know you're sad, I know you're hurt, and I know you cry
but so do I.

I can try and try but no matter what I say,
No matter what I do, the choice of love and friendship
is all up to you.

Susan Stetson

Confusion

Jumbled thoughts mixing together
Emotions being where they don't mean to be
Mazes of what is right and what is wrong
And things that don't matter at all
Confusion and chaos are in my head
Blocking the clear path that leads the way
Leaving behind faint glimpses of what happened
That don't connect, don't make sense
No patterns, no clues
Just feelings that mean nothing-
An unbreakable code.

Rachel Helfrick

Enter

Enter into My Kingdom.
Enter into My Heart.
Enter the meek and humble to start.
Enter the weak, enter the strong.
Enter. Come near. Share in My Love with joy.

Come to me surrounded in light.
Come through the shadow of darkness,
that I will make bright.
Come shed the misery and pain.
Come feel the healing and joyous refrain.
My Child has come home in love and light.

Phyllis Burns

One Week

Crystal moondrops shimmer and gleam,
Essence of a midnight dream.
Flickering starlight, diamond dust,
Gently sweep the sky in gusts.
A path of light beckons to me.
Open your heart and let it be.
A tingling sensation fills my soul.
Harmonic rhythm rocks and rolls.
Angels gather above my head,
If I follow, I'll be dead.
The choice is mine, give me one week,
As my mission here is incomplete.
That dream occurred many years ago
And as each week passed, I was ready to go.
We never know when our mission's complete,
Until all of a sudden, it has been one week.
Time has always been an illusion
And a midnight dream my conclusion.

Linda Caray Halpern

Untitled

Carved from the winds of time, long ago
etched deeply into its present
a sudden winding curve, somehow straightened and stopped
Kissed by the sun, places the eye may never see
A wondrous flow of energy and life
unyielding to demands whose shouts were never heard
Stories of the past and reminders of yesterday's mistakes
go unnoticed
having fallen on deafened ears
A willow may weep
a heart may bleed
Our mistakes may cost the children
the earth they need
It is ours for this moment
and though time may one day stand still
what we take from our Mother
time can never refill
Honor your Mother
cherish Her children.

Raven Douglas Criss

My Beloved

I met you in the Winter of my life
Even though I was considered youth in bloom
You picked up the pieces of my life
Holding them like tender rose petals.

I cherish you like a precious sunrise
The one that warms my heart each day
How little you cherish yourself sometimes
How ultimately grand I cherish your heart.

The beautiful buds of my heart only grow
Because of you, your smile like raindrops
On my skin, early summer morning.
And you loved me, always truly deeply.

You've been the fondest memory of my life,
The only memory my heart ever made.
Your laughter warms my soul
With love I never knew existed.

I find great delight in your wit
Much like the first flowers of Spring
Knowing like them, I survived the Winter
And you were the Spring flowers of my life.

Leslie Nunamaker Sawyer

Balance

Wild and wooly expectations fade into the afterglow of the evening's loud chattering, telling of the simple times of cleaving to only one Rock.

Timely messages, tied with bows of vivid colors, to be opened at will.

Splendors amassed in a visionary panorama of highs and lows, seemingly put together by a palette of varying hues, in need of a home.

All is free, all is good, all is in harmony, to be enjoyed, envisioned, released, broadcasted to those who will receive.

Fantasies, ecstasies, eulogies, marches, arias, staccato similitudes, ranging in lights and darks, make their ways in and out of life.

Mushrooming romances, closely held delights, a simple smile, a far away glance, delving restraint, tittering responses, falls of laughter,

Warmth untold, coldness unbearable, silence both maddening and healing;

Telestars of glistening highlights that weave their way in all lives, must to the Maker return for balance.

Patricia A. Gail

Tears Of A Child

A beautiful tree loses its leaves
every winter every year.
A beautiful star falls from the sky
a child crying you will hear.

A heart being broken, feeling all alone
parents are supposed to be loving and kind.
But tears fall from a beautiful child
as parents love is being left behind.

They don't understand why they're treated that way
they try their hardest to do things right.
But things do not go as they had wished
instead it is a dreadful fight.

See what exactly is troubling the child
listen to their little hearts and minds.
Children do have feelings of their own
don't ignore the soft tears they cry.

Natalie Duncan

Fear

The unknown.
Everything seems different
Although, the only thing that has changed is you.
Starting over is the hardest part of it all
In a world where you once saw through naked eyes,
You must now see through other senses.
Adjusting to the darkness,
A feeling of aloneness sweeps over you,
Setting you apart from all others.
A silent barrier begins to form between you and the world
One that will keep you from feeling any pain,
From daring to dream.
Until, there is no more hope left in you,
All life has died.

Sherilin Jennings

If Not Born Free

It is rewarding just to sit and ponder,
examine nature aimlessly, explore and wonder,

The first seed planted for this tree,
the first flower kissed by a bumblebee,

Melodious sounds made high above,
by a delicate bird known as a dove,

Multitudinous shades of forest green,
a beautiful sight that I have just seen,

Watching the river's water rushing by,
etching layers of history does make me sigh,

What nature bestows, I am allowed to see,
I would miss it all, if not born free.....

Sharon Nelson

Sure Dwellings And Quiet Resting Places....

A state of uncertainty—Security is always unsure
Exhorting yourself of stability—Mindful acceptance to allure
Convincing to be one complete—Heart and thoughts you Seduce
Distorting good senses of discernment—A lifestyle of steady abuse
Rejecting sound words understood—Striving about what is true
Hypocrisy growing so rapid—Wrong is wrong and wrong is right too
Wrong battle so forcefully fighting—Draining your high standard thought
The imbalance began to take over making room for furthering sought
Starting over going back to the simple—Moving away from all the complex
Not bothering with strivings and wonders—That leaves the heart heed to vex
Acceptance and faith came along—For sound words came hunger and thirst
Beginning to fulfill yourself fully—Because wisely you took first things first
Knowing of the Gift you were Promised—Finally understanding what Grace is Forever to abide in True peace—"Sure Dwellings And Quiet Resting Places"

Mark Russell

"See The Happiness This Brings"

I want to help the young in school.
Explain to them, be careful, it's easy to become a fool.
Go out, and have fun, while you are young.
Pick your company, be mindful of another's tongue.
Build character, and reputation; without it you'll end in a bad situation.
Think first, honesty is the best policy, use your insight.
You are never wrong in doing what is right.
Have good thoughts, and you do good things.
Your mind controls you, try this and see the happiness it brings.

Virginia D. Waters

Wisdom

Wisdom hides amid false conceptions,
Camouflaged with obscurities,
Watching unsuspecting misconclusions,
So close...yet...related only remotely.

Smartness struts, so vain and pretentious,
Reciting facts and memorabilia,
Impressing some with empty theories,
Missing truth, though, in every area.

Hindsight often spotlights true wisdom,
Too late to avail, instilling only regret.
Then, foresight compels us to focus onward,
Our hearts soon harden, again we forget.

Timothy D. Miller

Generation X

I have left my words upon the page
Expression, my crime
my sin.
You have touched my hidden soul
but don't think you have tamed me.
Taking meaning like bread
to sustain you.
Know in your heart that I too am searching.
We have watched Presidential assassinations
replayed for detail and effect.
A shuttle that explodes in the sky
intimate with strangers as they die.
Look out your window— you might see me.
I am your alternate thought
Incarnate.
But for now, I have left my words upon the page
for illiterate eyes
Expression
my natural crime.

Rebecca L. Newbrey

Tomorrow

I stood atop the majestic hill
Facing the wind and all its will
I turn my face upward to the dusty blue sky
Feeling the freedom of years gone by

I feel like the great eagle in freedoms flight,
not like the timid deer running with fright
I sense and feel the great master is near
Taking away all my doubts and fears

He cleanses me, body and soul with the sun and air
Warming my face and tossing my hair
I close my eyes and enter into a place of peace and serenity
A world still with its virginity

A world not yet destroyed by human hands
A world not filled with countless demands
A world with our hate, war and lust
A world full of honesty, love and trust

Karen Minler

Rage

A shattered glass bleeds red wine across the kitchen floor
A rose drowns in this pool, this pool of hate
Scraps of paper, of someone's heart, drift aimlessly, going nowhere
Eyes unfocused, stare, emotions clash, nothing can take control
A mute scream erupts from within, then silence
A shaken hand reaches out to erase,
Erase the evidence of chaos
Too late; hate seeped into the cracks, under the floor boards
Only to remain, until the next explosion.

A chalk-drawn figure decorates the alley floor
A foot steps around it, careful not to smear the shell of what was
Wide-eyed children stare from behind yellow plastic strips
No hopscotch today; lets go home; but they stay to see, to understand
Untold secrets fight unfulfilled dreams, battling forever inside
Inside society, society's masterpiece unfinished, unexplainable, yet unforgotten

A frosted window hide two eyes, peering to the deserted street tiny hands create melted prints on its icy glass, leaving two peepholes innocent fingers stretch toward the tarnished doorknob longing to explore the wonders of the cracked cement lawn -- a locked door, meant to let no harm in, lets no one out to the real world, a world too angry to live in

Cara McCafferty

Sentry

Silent sentinel it stands
Faithfully keeping vigil over ashes of yesterday.
Broken promises, crushed dreams,
As shards of scattered glass—
Reflecting distant sun rays or silver moonlight.
Day—night; summer—winter; fair weather—foul.
Staunch, never wavering, always watchful—remembering.
Raindrops, as tears, coursing down
Past the armor-protected heart.
Sunshine as fire, passionately searing again.

A portrait among the ruins! —Cherished smile,
Hands clasping a single rose—
Simple words upon a nearby stone, "Here lies —."

Secrets hidden, locked forever in silence,
Within the fortress of this sentinel.
All is sacred —nothing shared—memories—.
A single brick chimney —
Protector of a golden yesterday.

Maurece W. Lloyd

The Summers Of My Life

Leaves of Autumn
fall upon the children
at play in the yard
where the grass
is already brown
except in spots of green
that remind me of my yesterdays

The screens need replacing
and in my mind's eye
I see tomorrow's winter's snow
fall upon the children
at play in the yard
where the grass is already white
except in the spots of brown
that remind me of my yesterday's yesterdays —
The summer of my life

Robert A. Mills

The Noble Eagle Flies Again

The noble eagle flies again
Far above sea or friend

He takes with him an independent heart,
Though gentle, kind and giving
Soaring to untold heights above the clouds
Far from the tumultuous living

Always seeking the true core of life's mystery
Trusting the answer lies within his own life's history

Determination and resolve are his constant companions
One is his left wing the other is his right
Without them he would never attempt a flight

Each piece of life's puzzle he will duly solve
And put in its proper place above the cirrus cloud

Swooping down from time to time
To intermingle and make some rhyme

Get too close and he is gone again
Far above sea or friend

Wanda Simpson

The Way Home

Dancing gracefully across the shore, the glorious teal ocean
feeds its milk of foam to the sand bathing in elegant beauty.
The ocean with its varied hues of blue creates in me a
lonely longing for a touch of gentle bliss.
Gentle dusk silently bids me farewell.
Refreshing the sun floats into the ocean's floor,
telling me to rest well.
Gliding gently, the ocean bathes itself within my every step.
The warmth of the new hidden sky seems to linger in the breeze.
My longing within me is for a new heavenly touch of life.
A caring and passionate breeze is sent from heaven,
refreshing my spirit and giving me a renewed joy and peace.
My steps seem to float away into the heavens
and lead me to a place unseen by earthly eyes.
As my eyes gaze upward, I see divinely placed stepping stones
that are perfect in every way.
They reveal a beautiful pathway of a new reality.
This path is my gentle bliss, given to me as an open gift.
All I have to do is be willing to follow and I will find
my way home.

Saralyn V. Smith

Hope

Problems in life come along...
Feelings of despair cause me to wonder where I belong,
It's true, others have worse disasters than mine
And I don't want to be unthankful or unkind.

What can I do to help my situation get better,
Should I put forth effort... does it matter?
Then I think of my creator...
The one true God, who sent me a Saviour.

When I say a prayer I know God hears.
For He is never too busy to calm my fears.
God sent this Saviour for me and for you also
This Saviour gives freedom to one's soul.

Karen L. Rucker

Narcotic Images

I have fallen from the sky
From a cloudburst passing by
Pain and pleasure - words used to measure
Points in a game ... both the same
The door opens and the figure comes into view
Who is it looking for, me or you?
An expanse of time, of presence,
Strange cities with no warmth
Outcasts in our own society.
A long black ribbon outstretched before us
Challenging us, compelling us to travel its course
Play if you dare, but promise not to care

Michael A. Westerback

Anne

How does one make death poetic?
Death is a poetry in and unto itself.
It sneaks up on us with a wonder
and awe of unknowing's.
Discarding all earthly spirits
and possessions.

Knowledge of death is our life long companion,
the spirit of things to come,
our yearning
being in the presence of the master,
our goal.

Mary DiPaola

The Wish

Dedicated to Patrick McElroy
I wish that I could change your world - your thoughts and feelings too.
I'd make you believe in me, as much as I do you.

I'd keep a smile upon your face,
I'd find that smile you couldn't replace.

I'd make you laugh until you could no more,
I'd make you laugh until you were sore.

I'd make you as happy as happiness can be,
I'd let you know you will find it with me.

I'd build your dreams and let them soar,
I'd make you strive for more and more.

I'd make you secure enough to bare it all,
I'd let you know you can tell me things, and never fall.

I'd give you strength to find some hope,
I'd give you courage and help you cope.

I'd let you know you are the one,
I'd let you know you are my only, bright and shimmering sun.

But most of all I'd show you what dwells inside my heart,
I'd show you that I love you lots and never want us to part.

Tanya R. Schueller

Chameleon

There on the fence one day out by the pool I saw a little fellow who should have been in school.

He wasn't being bad, or doing anything, just sitting motionless enjoying all of spring.

I looked around and saw the flowers, with colors of all kinds. Then I knew why he sat here silent and sublime.

What a lovely place to think, so luscious and serene, even for a tiny lizard who is completely green.

I've seen him in the Spring and Summer and I've seen him in the Fall, but I never see him in the Winter, no....I never do at all.

I bet he lives on our back porch and his family lives there too, and that he can change his color from green to maybe blue.

Chameleon learn this lesson early and people take a while to change for the better will always bring a smile.

Margaret L. Goodrich

Christopher Columbus

From King Ferdinand and Queen Isabella of Spain,
Financial support Christopher Columbus finally did gain
To set out on his journey to sail
With men who had rather go with him than go to jail,
Over five hundred years ago they began their navigation
Seeking to fulfill his expectation—
The three vessels: Santa Maria, Pinta and Niña were small ships
That they were using for their trips;
This voyage became a long and tiresome one,
But they were on for exploration and not for fun,
Often the men became threatening to him,
And he eventually was forced to deceive them.
Then one midnight they saw a light—at last they could boast,
For they were about to reach the coast;
After landing on October 12, 1492,
He felt that his dreams were coming true—
He and the crew stepped ashore, and with them
He looked upward thanking God for helping him.

Ruby L. Stephenson

Youthful Presence

The twilight of life has come to call. It has seen fit to remind, to define its all.
It has made us weary to judge our friends. It has also seen fit to disrupt the messages that our mind defends.
Our thoughts race feverishly like youths' playful presence as our bodies' flexibility slowly fades with destiny's reverence.
Being around the very young leaves patience somewhat in the past. As the presence of the elderly makes reality's dye all cast.
Memory is the catalyst that beckons our spirit to make so uneasy our heart. It is the humorous attitude that initiates each inspirational new daily start.
So where is forever Lord, is it behind the tree? Is it some place where my thoughts can be heard by only thee?
Somewhere beyond the breeze just resting where time has stood still. Way beyond tomorrow where your presence renews my whole being in an instant, spiritual fill.

Phyllis J. Cardassi

Phantoms Of The Night

Phantoms drift in dream-time sequence,
Floating on the edge of night.
Echoes of forgotten memories
Entombed by daylight — lost from sight.

Hidden secrets rise to taunt us
As day's guardians loose their hold,
Darkling shapes burst forth from prisons
To speak aloud what can't be told.

Come — Saving Spirit! Angel voices
Sing your song in vibrant hues.
Alone — we cannot find the entrance
Or travel freely where we choose.

Asleep, we wander through dream's doorways
That open into misty halls,
Melting into deeper visions,
We slowly fade through timeless walls.

Searching, listening, waiting, hoping,
Reaching out a trembling hand
To touch a shining strand of knowing
Granting us the Sacred Power to understand!

Marlyn H. Perkins

The Gift

The first rose,
Flushed red as his newborn face on the morning we first embraced.
When did it bud?
How boldly it has thrust into full bloom!
Nurtured in fertile soil, weeds uprooted—How it's thrived,
Green stems strong and striving for the sun!
Like water through my fingers, all the time
I did not notice.
Who is that dancing? Elusive shadows splash the garden wall.
How deliberately I pruned against the winter —
I was careless to forget the threats of spring.
Snatched by the mountain breeze, its heady scent infects the wind.
How odd I should be captured by surprise?
In answer to his shy request, my trembling fingers pluck it. The petals caress like velvet: my heart is pricked by the thorny stem.
How quick the hug, the token kiss. How suddenly he's gone.
I brush aside the tears that hide behind a mother's pride.
What better gift to give his love,
Flushed red as her pretty face on the morning they first embraced
Than this first rose?

Lois Jennison Tribble

Unconditional Love

In the gentle waters you gave me breath, my life I gained from you.
For nine long months you gave me shelter without a penny's rent come due.
Though I knew not who I was or who I'd someday be, I felt sure that
I was loved and that you cared for me.
And when that day came when I was born, you had to set me free,
into a world of many harms from which you protected me.
Though now by body no longer joined our bond will always last,
it seems in fact that it's grown stronger with each year that has passed.
As now I stand before you, a child grown to a man, I still find
strength within your wisdom that helps me see I can.
So I'll carry you inside my heart like you once did for me,
and through this love we'll never part, my mother you will always be!

R. Mark Woodall

Sweet Peace

Thank you Lord
For sparing me pain
And reminding me, in your care to remain.
Thank you Lord
For tender loving care
And family members here to share!
Thank you Lord
For eighty two years
Memories of laughter, mixed with tears.
Thank you Lord
For prayers and song
That paved the way (so very long!)
Thank you Lord
For earthly release - quality of life gone
But now - sweet peace!

Ruth V. Marshall

Untitled

I guess I would do anything
For that I can't comprehend myself
Even as a tangled specie I raise my sword
Piercing through the wasted skin
None of the times passed had I sensed myself
Listened to preachers and popes
Charming charity spokesmen
Leading the thoughts to dust
The golden crown I see on the top of the hill
Anticipating
Up there hiding behind the throne
Enjoying the everlasting thrill
Unable to reach it
Until this lovely rainy day
I'll do all that I possibly can
Run and burn to block the way
And knock the pirate down.

Lucy Teichmann

"Green Is A Forest"

Green is a forest on a mid-spring day,
Green is up in the mountains with the birds chirping away.
Green is a lily pad with a frog,
Leaping around from pad to pad, bog to bog.
Green seems like a river, slowly flowing by.
Green tastes like a fresh bundle of herbs,
And has a sweet smell that no one disturbs.
Green feels like a soft, fluffy mat of grass,
Which spreads so far over a mountain pass.
Green sounds like some rustling leaves,
So gently swaying in the breeze.
You can smell green in a sunny cascade,
Toward the end of winter when a ground hog sees his shade.

Mike Urban

Autumn

Despair-
for the warm, fruitful passage of the sun
falls low today...stay
but no-its work is done.
Darkened skies give birth to the rain
which washes the warm away.
The rain forces the leaves to the ground leaving...
color.
Many beautiful colors leaping from tree to tree
displaying each other's beauty, absent of fear.
Not for everyone though; this is a time for death.
Even for the beautiful leaves, who have just gained
the courage to show their magnificence.
Difference.
Death-on schedule or random, surely will come.
Wind and rain slowly rape the branches of their color
leaving behind,
colorless
naked
souls.

Michael W. Hartnett

Something Special

He was writing something special to end the fighting
For their life together had ceased to be exciting
Dullness had crept in to spoil the joy
Like a kid playing with an old old toy
Days seemed long and awful tough
And so many things made it rough
There wasn't much said while they were eating
And some of the food needed reheating
All through the house things lost their glamour
And—afraid—their son would stammer
One morning he left the letter for his wife to read
And it was one of those letters—the kind that met the need
When she read the letter a lovely change took place—right then
For he started with: Sweetheart,
Do you remember when...

Wood M. Campbell

Fast Friends

We met in the bathroom, a likely place
For two women new to the company.
And in that first meeting both of us knew
We were destined to become fast friends.
Both animal lovers,
Both manic-depressive,
Both extremely outspoken,
Both honest to a fault,
Both readers,
Both writers,
We finished one another's sentences.

As quickly as we became fast friends
Opportunity struck,
And you moved away from our old stomping grounds.
Our letters can give no inflection,
No giggles,
No mimicry,
No banter,
No presence.
These are the things I miss most.

E. Talley Brown

Friend

No one could ask for a better
friend than I have in you;
you have been with me
through thick and thin.

You are a part of my family
we have shared in so many things

You have brightened my world;
you have touched and always
will be in my heart.

You have shared and so many
times you have cared;
You are a part of my life
and I hope that our
friendship will last forever

You and I have many memories
and will probably have many
more; you are very special;

No one could ask for a better friend;
I thank God above for the friend I have in you!

Lora Albright

Song Of Tendresse, Of Sorrow

To J. and R. Ballou's toddler, self-styled "Joe Blue."
April's sun - bright days call
From the elm's tight buds, the exquisite, green wings of spring:
Too soon rollicking
In leafy cascades with the hollow winds,
Too soon following
The lure of freedom's feigning flight - to Earth.
Fall's brilliant skies will cloud on noting the bright death.
O leaflings, from our hardened hearts, call
songs of clear delight.
And you, darling toddler, beloved child,
Will you, too, be enthralled by frenzied motion?
Will you, also, be allured by autumnal splendor?
Acclaim will lead a foray on tomorrow's grace.
Weary wayfarers, we follow the echoing call from the sunny isle
of your smiles;
We have longed for the rock-based land of your perfect faith;
We yearn for the singing fellowship of your guilelessness.
Oh vanishing younglings of youth, of spring, call;
Oh poignant loveliness of the Lord God's largesse
Recall us to the garden whence you come.

N. M. Walsh

The Whale

Jumping out gracefully into the shimmering sun,
from the glassy diamond of ocean.
The whale breaches into the air, as though she had
practiced hard to be so graceful.
A crown of bubbles forms around her head, as she
dives down deep into the mass of blue sea.
She sings, of freedom as she continues her journey
through the endless ocean.

Rachel Billos

The Jungle

The calmness in this jungle, it is an eerie thing,
for even after a fire fight, the birds return to sing.
The dead and wounded lay all about, waiting for
choppers to pull them out.
Men struggle here, lose or gain, yet...
the eerie calmness of the jungle remains
the same.

Paul Roberts

Begotten Freedoms

They see my tribe
From the shade I wear
None will circumscribe
The rejection I bear

Between black and white
Instead of gray, I'm all for democracy
For white isn't all wrong, nor the other
And I reject any pigmentocracy
But the tribe which lost me to Africa, real mother
Needs a language, a caste, a village
Otherwise I must remain "Other"

Different! Not quite white;
Nor black enough!
Destined to roam day and night
For a drink at a familiar trough

Color is a political myth
I remain Asian for the educated
I've never been there, forsooth
All must have a tribe, or be assigned it.

Neil SookDeo

Joy

Adults cavorting as children those days—
From the Snow Angels so perfect
To our uncritical eyes;
Then on to the swings
Demanding to go
"Higher, yes, Higher"—
Just to try to touch the sky.

Never considering how ridiculous
We probably appeared
To those perhaps questioning:
"Will they ever act their age?"

Lord, I pray not—

For Life with its problems, sorrows, and pain
Must always be bubbling, sparkling, effervescent—
Shot with sunshine, shining with Light
Always and forever trying to touch
The
Sky.

Laurel Joan Paisley

Walk With Self

We divorce ourselves everyday
From those who did not say
Exactly what we wished to hear
We did not listen and only understood our fear

We burn our bridges
And walk our ridges
In hopes that one day we will find
All we distrust have fallen on their behinds

What a very dispirited way of living
Unable to accept all that have been given
To graciously hold or discard
All of which are truly avant-garde

Choice is forever ours to make
To infinitely remain or to separate
Only one can decide for oneself
Whether to run from, or walk with oneself

Vanessa Hart

Tribute

Women are the weaker sex. At least, that's what we're told.
From watching and observing though, that simply doesn't hold.
Though man has struggled long and hard to reach his goal in life,
The driving force that spurs him on is the woman in his life!
When things get tough and doubts set in, and no one seems to care,
He heads for home with a joyful heart for he knows that she'll be there.

She welcomes him with open arms, and asks about his day.
He knows she asks because she cares; it's there he longs to stay.
Within the confines of these walls, the worries of the day
When put into their proper place just seem to melt away.
No longer does he need to prove he's worthy of his time.
He's met with love, a home-cooked meal, some candlelight and wine.
So, if you know a successful man, dependable and steady,
Be sure all this was brought about by a very special lady!

Max Sorge

"The Incredible Flight"

For the seven brave men and women, who sacrificed their lives to fulfill a dream.
It was a cold winter morning, the crowd tense as the air stills,
From beyond this fence we waited for the moment when she would go up.
Never knowing what was about to disrupt.
As the count declines, the adrenalin starts to flow.
First ten, then five, now two and one,
The count is over, the lift is done,
The incredible mission had just begun.
We stood and watched as she slowly left the ground,
Rumbling and roaring with a shattering sound.
Faster and faster, higher she went,
On this magical day the incredible mission was sent.
"OH MY GOD." Something's has gone wrong,
What's going on, what's taking so long.
There's too much smoke, the fire's too bright,
Where did she go, she's gone out of sight.
This disaster had happened to the challenger flight,
Good-bye my friends, rest in peace and sleep tight....

Michael Lane

My New Best Friend

There was a time within my life I'd lost sight of my soul
Giving in to all my doubts, all pride I had let go
It seemed that I had nothing left, my hopes and dreams had fled
While sitting down, with face in hands, my body filled with dread

Then suddenly I met someone who thought that I was great
She knew I could do anything, it never is too late
I'd have to start a brand new life, take one day at a time
For only then could I begin to live my life in rhyme

This person does believe in me
She brought my soul back home
She helped me find the road to peace
I'm no longer alone

To think, I met her just by chance
She took me by surprise
When she said, there's something I must see
If I am to survive

Her hand in mine, she led the way
Through her eyes I could see
Within the looking glass, I found
My new best friend was me

Marcella Anna Bacon

Slay The Dragon

Far away, far away, the clouds begin to gather,
The quiet rumble of the drums are ever growing louder,

They do not hear, they will not hear, the
Threat of storm and strife,
The monsters growing stronger and blotting
Out the light.

The time is growing shorter, the days are growing grim,
The drums are growing louder, the Monsters
Closing in,
Wake up! Wake up! my people, the time is very
Late!
Rise up and slay the Dragon, that's storming
at our gates!

Marion C. Drappo

Audrey Of Spring

Such a soft spring breeze
gently brushed my cheek
today, fresh and sweet,
bright and new, and fragrant as a forest.

You are Spring and a spring breeze,
gentle and sweet, new and bright!
The fragrance of your being
(you're just a child, like me)
is of The One, who made you
so beautiful to see, so precious, inwardly.

Your eyes are spring skies,
clear and clean and blue;
the strands of sunshine 'round your face,
a golden crown that God has given you.

Jesus is The Poet;
you are His special poem.
When, in your heart, you know it,
you'll be home. Spring will be
forever, and so will you!
Jesus is God. It's true. It's true!

Reginald Murphy

The Poet's Pen

The Poet's pen forever writes
From a brilliant mind, both day and night
An imagination, vivid and strong
With his pen, he writes on and on

Always there's a pen in his hands
He listens within, as his consciousness expands
Hearing an inner voice, he begins to write
Putting impressions together, with all his might

His awareness is keen, his perception's sharp
Just keep on writing, seem to never stop
Writing of things in far away lands
Giving descriptions, the best he can

His Poetic thoughts are precious and dear
His beautiful writings, make heaven seem near
Sharing his dreams, with every one
Expression through poetry is part of his fun

He writes of the past, the future too
He writes of his happiness, writes when he's blue
He writes about people, the things they do
But never, ever, does he seem to get through with the Poet's Pen.

Vernell Black

A Great Grandma's Prayer

After checking in his "Books of Records"
God noticed that little ones were missing in our world
So, in his wisdom and infinite mercy
He added a fourth generation to our family

Two beautiful little angels arrived, both prematurely
Impatient, no doubt, to join their anxious family
Sensing the expectations and loving care awaiting them
They just couldn't wait till the end

A great big welcome home Caroline and Andrew
Our world is richer today because of you
May God bless you, my precious little treasures
And fill every day of your life with happiness
beyond measure.

Lilianne B. Nadeau

I Feel So Sad

I saw a dog die the other day,
Got hit by a car and it didn't even stop.
I ran to see what I could do.
The dog looked at me with pain filled eyes;
It whimpered a little and I hugged it tight.
It died in my arms and I cried for the dog.
No one stopped, no one cared
Just another dead dog on the side of the road.
I carried the dog up a hill and dug it a grave.
I put up an old wooden cross,
But I didn't know if the dog had a name.
It had no tags or a nice leather collar.
I laid down some flowers and said a prayer.
I wonder if someone misses the dog.
I feel so sad.

Karen Curcio

Cousin George

Cousin George and I were in our early teens. One day, we had an argument. He said, "A man lives only to eat." And I said, "A man eats only to live."

Cousin George and I met in our forties. He was a rich man, and I was a poor college teacher.

Cousin George and I met in our fifties. He had a criminal record, but he was still rich. And I was the dean of the college, but I was still poor.

Cousin George and I met again in our sixties. He was in a wheelchair struggling to survive, and I was yet writing to live.

Roy M. Seoh

Cheerful Neighbor

Supple as a sapling the clean-limbed youth
Hands in pockets, enjoying May,
Does not tax his mind with morals or truth
Though he will consider them another day.

Let him whistle and sing and laugh and shout
And soar through space while his heart is free.
Too soon must he ponder what life is about
And feel bound to solve its mystery.

Now he decorates earth with his innocent face
Prime production of the human race.

Too soon will our systems stifle and bind him
And hard-wrought decisions furrow his brow.
Tomorrow we'll not be able to find him
As cheerful a neighbor as he is now.

Thurston John Lewis

Reach For Your Own Source

In the face of the child the future doth live
Happiness and hope in the smiles he gives
Will he keep smiling when he grows old
And lives in a society that has grown cold
They've turned their back on their Mother who has given them life
Think they know what's better and technology is right
They worship Gods from the past, who no longer live
Or pray to the future they've named technology
Look out the window, see the grass and the trees
Witness our Mother, the only living deity
Our Mother, The Earth, The Sun and the Moon
They've given us our lives that we seek to ruin
We've raped our Mother, now we seek to confine
We have saddled Her with chains, we call them time
We want everything now, there can be no delay
We hasten the coming of Mother's death day
Her body lies torn, Her body lies bleeding
Pockmarked by the presence of Her parasitical children
Our Mother is bleeding, We feed off Her blood
Is murder the reward for our Mother's love

Michael Mascitti

The Talented Teacher

Standing at the blackboard the teacher
has a winning way. She's a petite
young lady, her chestnut hair flowing
to her waist. There's a comradery
in the classroom when the teacher shares
her talent. When she opens her bag
of tricks her students are delighted.
The teacher tells them stories about
"Leo the Late Bloomer" and the magic
of numbers. She brings in menus to
help them calculate their math. Her
ninth graders think she owes them chocolate
chip cookies because they found out
her second period had donuts for a treat.
The teacher loves radiating colors.
She's the only one in her school with
rose colored curtains!

Martha Adesso

Bouquets or Laurels

If someone you know, and meet every day
Has influenced your life, in some special way
Do you ever tell them? Do you let them know?
Or, do you take for granted your love will show?

Has there been someone who lived long ago
Whose life was a blessing, when you needed it so
Whose memory lingers, and blesses you still
Whose place, in your life, no one else can fill

Scatter some bouquets, of praise, in the way
Of those who still live, and are struggling today
Or, some laurels and of thanksgiving, today, you may send
To God, in remembrance of that special friend

The bouquets may give them the strength to go on
At a time when their courage is all but gone
The laurels may become precious jewels, up there
In the crown, which the Father will give them to wear

Lillian M. Kirby

Song Of Sorrow

The times we've spent together
Have meant too much to me.
In my heart I'd hoped it would never end.
It hurts me to think that this is the end
For you and me.
Together we made such happiness.
The others could not see
How much you meant to me
But my life and my world
Are centered around you.
No one else can see that we were meant to be together, FOREVER.
Yes, just you and me.
In this world comes sorrow,
That cuts right to the bone.
And my sorrow is here,
Because the only thing that hurts me
Is living my life WITHOUT YOU.
I need you here.
Oh, can't you see?
Because without you, there is no me!

Pam Baisden

Spring's Voice

Glancing out my kitchen window
Having heard a fluttering rustle
I saw tender green leaves
Fluttering in the breeze.
A dip of a branch to a love-bound pair
To make a nest, lay eggs there
And two darting redbirds
Accepting the place
What a wonderful Spring
When Nature accepts the God-given urge -
And continues creation once begun,
Another time I saw two busy redbirds
With twigs and grass
Forming their home for five tiny eggs
Then behold one May day a tiny one ready to fly - leaving
Where the pair had prepared a safe haven
To begin again the natural creation
Of objects of beauty and proof of God's Love.

Mattie Belle Barber

Take Time

Parents, your children are a precious gift from the FATHER on high;
HE gave them to you, to teach and to guide.

GOD wants you to discipline your girls and boys;
that doesn't mean to give them all those toys.

HE gave you ears to listen and a mind to decide;
if you are doing right in the way you should guide.

Take time to listen to that little voice;
Take time to pray, then make the right choice.

Read to that little one, a good little book;
Take time to let them help you, even as you cook.

Oh, dear parents, they grow up so fast;
Take time to make a relationship that will last.

Teach them to do right and not to do wrong;
They grow so fast, and then they are gone.

They're only young once, so take this time;
Teach them to love, to be good and to be kind.

The LORD, will look down from HIS HEAVENLY THRONG;
A smile HE will give you, as HE makes your family strong.

Trust in the LORD, and you will have no regrets;
Trust in the LORD and your needs will be met.

Patricia P. Mize

The Prisoner

Contemplating the cell,
He looks out at the world.
Oh, how he longs to be free!
Free like the trees swaying in the breeze
and the birds who soar unhindered above the land and sea.
But he is trapped.
Trapped by something he cannot see,
but which keeps him from freedom
like a leash on a dog.
He sits poised at the barrier,
rubbing his palms together as if thinking:
Now how did I get myself into this predicament?
He takes a flying leap at the obstruction,
trying again and again in vain
to free himself from the clutches of most certain death
from starvation and loneliness.
A swoosh and a thunderous clap assault the prisoner like a tidal wave,
smashing him against the window.
"What was that?" asks the woman.
"Just a fly on the wall."

Sabrina Hanelt

The Road To Life

To My Brother Leiland Donaldson, With Love

When God gave us life
he made two roads long;
The road that leads to righteousness
and the road that leads to wrong.

What will your life be?
well that all depends;
On which road you take
and who you choose for friends.

If you choose the wrong road
bad friends you will meet;
Wind up on drugs and alcohol
and find yourself on a dead-end street.

You'll know if the right road
is the right one for you;
For good things will come your way
and God will see you through.

I don't mean to preach
but these words are very true;
For your life and happiness
depends solely on you.

Robbin Westcott

Reflections

When I look back upon my life, and ask, "Why am I here Lord,"
He answers because you were meant to do good for others and
never be bored.

When I ask, "Why did you let me be abused as a child, why weren't
you there to help me?"
He answered, "It was I who kept you from giving up, don't you see?"

When I asked, "Lord, why won't you make my life easier and let me
be happy all the time?"
He answered, "If life was always easy, and you were happy all the
time, you might never have discovered you had the talent to
write this little rhyme."

Now that I have been through the worst - sexual abuse, physical
abuse and a divorce after 39 years of marriage, I finally see
the rainbow ahead,
I'm going to college to get my degree and I'm happy most of the
time - I have you Lord, to thank for giving me the courage and
the strength to carry on - from the time I wake up until the
time I go to bed.

Pauline Davalos

Orphaned

Kitten peaked out from under my car; 'li'l' kitty sat.
He was in the pouring rain, and had no cap.
A brown, orphaned kitten had no home.
He had a buttoned nosed, face; under my car, li'l kitty sat.

I coaxed, 'li'l' kitty, but he would not budge.
I offered him food, but he would only meow.
I offered him milk; he got the hint.
He got some accrued courage!

Kitten ran in the house; he drank and stayed.
He was not abandoned; I guess he just strayed.
He's mine; he walks and meows, a friendly cat.
'Li'l' kitty on my chair, at the fireplace, he sat.
He's only months old, but quite a cat!

Marie Haas

In Silence We Can Find Him

In silence we can find him, if we listen to our
hearts; each beat we hear, brings him near,
we know serenity starts.

In silence we can find him, no matter the time
of day; only be still and let him in, he
will show us the way.

In silence we can find him, when we call we know
He's there; we need only reach out, to reach
within and receive our share.

In silence we can find him, no matter what we're
feeling; we need only ask, and he'll remove
our fears and hurts, refill us with his healing.

In silence we can find him, in that place deep within
the soul; take in the light, open up, and he will
make us whole.

Shawn H. Bonnett

Peaceful Acceptance

I saw an old woman living out on the street
Her hair was in combs, her ragged clothes neat

She sipped her tea from a cracked china cup
She folded her napkin, then she stood up

She shook out her crumbs and rinsed out her dish
The birds flocked about her and then I did wish

That all human kindness could witness this act
A pure simple gesture no denying the fact

Here's truly a lady of elegance and grace
The eyes of years knowing-this angel misplaced

Vicki Kohl

Jeremy

I love him so,
He has eyes of blue.
He's there when I don't need him
And never when I do.

But I can't force him to come back
I am not his owner.
I cry over him and sometimes I scream.
Still it does no good.

He isn't my boyfriend
He isn't my father.
But those are two things that can't compare
To a brother named Jeremy.

Katie Stonebarger

Trees

The trees were waving at me today.
"Hello, how are you?" as if to say.
They were so full, pretty, and green.
They would bow and then they would lean.
They seem to be happy that spring has begun.
Enjoying the breeze and the wonderful sun.
Not so long ago they didn't wave at all.
They were sad and bare as their leaves would fall.
They were naked, standing in the freezing rain.
Stripped of their pride and not so vain.
As if once they were dying, but come back to live.
Their beauty and shade to us they give.
They seem so glad just to be alive.
The warm air and the sun makes them thrive.
Nothing to do, but stand and wave.
So a wave back to them I gave.

Teresa Walker

Lord Help Me

Lord help me through the moments that I am dismayed.
Help me through the troubles, the sorrows, the pain.
Help me to live a good Christian Life,
and help me to be a good husband to my wife.
Help me to be that special loving Dad,
and help me with my family, I'm glad that I have.
Help me to teach my children about you.
Lord, help me in raising them as good Christians too.
Help me in my Christian walk each day,
and help me Lord not to go astray.
Help me Lord not to fall into sin,
and help me be strong from Temptations within.
For all I want is to be there with You
when my time on Earth here is through.

Michael Curtis Johnson

Woman Is To Man

Man is conceived in woman.
Her womb clutches and protects him.
His time is spent among women.
Matronly bosoms smother and comfort him.
He is praised and punished by them.
Their feminine voices soothe and scold him.
Their outstretched arms cage and caress him.
He is unable to be free from women.
His desires pursue him to their company.

He chooses just one as his own.
She delights and yet deprives him.
He attempts to satisfy her.
She forever tantalizes and torments him.
Wounds, inflicted over a lifetime, infect him
Her taunts and tears seal and stain his casket.
She buries him with efforts to better him.
Man is born of woman. He lives for woman.
And dies from the living.

R. W. Reynolds

"Even Though You're Gone"

Tear drops like falling rain.
Holding to ease the pain, crying to the
moon as it leaves the sky, looking in the
mirror just wondering why?
Holding your picture close to my heart,
knowing our love has fallen apart.
Wanting to have you whole night through,
because even though you're gone "I still love you"

Vicky Stamatovic

Fair Lady

In the cool mist laying, over the moors of Glengarry,
Herald the hounds betraying, the gypsies silent wayfaring.
My Percheron stands stolid, yet ears seem pricked,
As mine eyes are quite keen, are my senses then tricked?
I stand emptied of service, my mind's sanity wrung,
A simple chevalier, thy dexter far flung.
Distraught in decision, devoid of thane,
Clad only in lineage, my own humble name.
I await by the lakes silver face, in yon twilights lieu,
To descry the face of an angel, only once hastily gleaned.
Astute fascination desirous of dreams,
I spy deep in the shadows a shimmering view.
Looming, a troupe comes burbling, cloaked in harmonious lading,
Harken the night! the young ladies in waiting.
Doth soon suffer a royal fulminate,
Averring the aberration of a candle promenade.
Oh Joy! how melodious the night!,
As the fair Lady Blackstone comes into sight.
The promissory was mine, all of the while,
As my fears are soon crushed by the array of her smile.

Stephen J. Williams

Dearest Amanda

Sometimes I don't believe you know how much I love you,
Here's something I'm saying because I want to:
You were the first baby I ever had,
When I first saw you I was very glad.
When I pulled you close to me that day,
Tears in my eyes I wiped away,
You were the little girl I had always dreamed of,
Sent to me from God above.
Now my baby is getting so big,
Putting on Mommy's high heels, lipstick and wig,
Silly things you do every day,
How I love to watch you play!
Roses to me you always bring,
Little songs you often sing,
My life you have turned completely around,
Since your love I have found.
There's one thing I want you to see,
Amanda dear, You're precious to me!
Remember you are more precious than any other,
I truly mean it.

Robin Hill

Untitled

Long ago God gifted us with Christ Jesus' birth,
His own Son, our Saviour, sent to men on earth.
Sent to show us how to live according to God's plan,
Sent to die - yet rise again - salvation He gave man!

We give gifts to those we love at Christmas time each year,
But what can we give to Jesus who gave His life so dear?
God has placed within our reach gifts for each to share,
To tell the world of Jesus, Lord, give us hearts that care!

Give us eyes to see the hurt in a lost and lonely world.
Give us ears to hear His call and a mouth to speak His love.
Give us hands to soothe a wound, willing feet to go where He leads,
Fill our hearts with compassion to meet another's needs.

And in giving to another may we our Father please,
For we give unto our Saviour when we serve the least of these!
"...In as much as ye have done it unto one of the
least of these my brethren, ye have done it unto me."

Peggy Hamrick

"Turning Away"

The old man walks away in agony, in tears
His shredded and well worn clothes are scarcely
enough to keep him warm from the cold night.
A little money for food is all he asks,
Yet we turn this man away;
We turn our backs.
We look away when someone needs us most.
He is a human with a heart, with a soul.
We care nothing about his feelings.
We show little interest for his life.
What kind of world exists that will laugh in
The face of a man who has nothing?
The streets are his only friend,
Yet even the streets are unkind.
We go back to our warm home satisfied
after a large meal,
While the man sits on the cold street, hungry and alone.

Molly Elam

As A Person Thinks

As a person thinks, so shall he be..
His thoughts are shaping his Destiny!
You can't escape what your thoughts will bring..
But you can dwell on the better things.

As a person thinks...Make no mistake!
His thoughts direct each step that he takes;
Each deed is born, at first, in thought...
The direct result of what thoughts have wrought.

As a person thinks, he may shrink or grow..
To be caught in the tide, or the undertow;
Whatever you think...be sure it's your best,
For you'll reap what your thoughts have manifest!

As a person thinks...each burning desire
Becomes a powerful hidden fire;
Whether it's great... or wise... or tall..
Or whether it's mean... and faulty.. and small.

As a person thinks, it will show in his face
As a glow of goodness.. or frown of disgrace;
You are today what your thoughts have wrought...
So begin right now to control your thoughts.

Madeline F. Sewell

The Second Commandment

The man was an alcoholic. Life's agonies had overwhelmed him!
His young children were "legally" seized - never seen again;
Voluntary return from AWOL was finalized in Leavenworth;
Unproven charges of arson resulted in jail time.

As in baseball, life throws fast-balls, hard-balls and curves.
Being highly sensitive and with minimal coping skills,
Leon deeply buried his agonies, drowning the pain in liquor —
His life resembled a small barque on a stormy sea...

Alone and ill, in the final hours of his anguishing journey
Came this pencilled confession:
For a lifetime "feeling" could be achieved only by
Hurting himself and those he loved.

With the burden lifted came unconditional recognition
Of a Higher Power and surrender to it.
The power of AA's steps I and II
Had brilliantly illuminated his path.

Surrender completed, he shaved and dressed for departure;
When found, serenity and peace attested to the gentle terminus.
How like the Christ's last minute forgiveness of the thief!
LOVE THY NEIGHBOR AS THYSELF!!

G. Calvin Tooker

Ship Of Life

Brand new ship and its crew,
Hoists its sails into the blue,
Catches the wind and rides the waves,
As they start their lives as man and wife.

Satin pillows with frilly lace,
Caresses curls of red that kiss its face,
Islands of bluish green sit in a sea of pure rich cream,
Lips of molten rock will scorch your mind at the thought.

Satin sheets of snowy white,
Cover peaches and cream that flow beneath,
As she sails beneath my beams,
We surrender to our dreams.

Like a ship of long ago, I fill my sails with all her love.
As our journey nears its end, I thank God for His gift,
A lady's love, for our children's hugs,
For all the years we sailed this ship.

Larry L. Tuttle

Heart And Soul

A single heart, struggling to live
Holding the love it's yearning to give.
So much to offer that no one will take
How much longer before it finally breaks?

Caught up in circles, around and around
Searching for something that cannot be found
Longing for answers, needing to learn
But stuck in the maze with nowhere to turn.

Waiting for just one small glimpse of light
Propelled by refusal to give up the fight.
Tearing the chains by which it is bound
Finally, finally, true love is found.

Suzanne Drinnon

The Hunger Within

The answer to a prayer
Hooks on the heavy walls of hope.
Every infant in a stare
Harks the harvest stalls like noosed rope.
Under his cracked lips without life's sweet scent
Now, his throat abandoned, homeless, is the prisoner of malcontent.
Granted the rope - a nasty caress,
Extremely tender, one starves the distress,
Rising upon the chin's weak marrow,
Wanting to rides on the wings of a sparrow
In black and brown like the earth that gives them life
Today they return in marriage as its wife.
Hold out a responsible hand
In which we might lose the grains of sand; but,
Now we care, somehow awakened by the glare.

Todd Davis

Baby Whitney's Love Poem

She is like a special angel from the sky
Our love for Whitney will never die
She may be tiny and she may be weak
But our love for her we will always keep

Although she's sick and cannot cry
My love for her will never die
Even though she can't feel our loving touch
We want Whitney to know we
Miss and love her very much!

Anne M. Barto

Vent Song

Gonna change my name, leave my home,
Hop on a train, 'cause everything's gone.
Little girl married, left me alone,
With some damyankee she's up and gone.

A choppin' the cotton, a hoein' the corn,
A cussin' the day that I was born.
Once in the city, once on the farm,
Now everything I own a hangin' on my arm.

A strummin' my fiddle, a thumpin' my bow,
Singin' little songs everybody knows.
A singin' little songs, and I ain't a gonna stop,
'Cause the ground I'm a standin' is too danged hot.

A runnin' and a shootin' from the house and barn,
Gotta reach the river away from the harm.
Shot in the middle and shot in the head,
A runnin' and a screamin' till I fell down dead.

Trudy Van Ripe

A Blind Man Talks To God

Man: Wilt Thou give me grace and praise?
God: Is this how thou wouldst spend thy days,
With grace and praise?
Man: Wilt Thou let me do Thy will?
God: When thou hast no more tears to spill,
Wilt thou do My will?
Man: Wilt Thou give and let me love?
God: Who art thou thinking of,
To give and let thee love?
Man: What shall I say?
God: That thou dost pray
My will be done.
Open up thy star-filled eyes,
Put away thy mournful cries,
And be My son.

Thomas Motika

Truth When Crushed Shall Rise Again

Truth when crushed shall rise again, like returning from south, the robin or wren; when winter comes they all disappear, but are sure to return here, year after year.

Truth like the grass may be trampled on the ground but sproutings seem everywhere to abound; for Truth will be found in people's heart, and only in Truth will integrity impart.

Truth is knowledge, honesty and veracity, it is agreement with order and reality. Truth is knowledge that makes men free, containing principles of law in society.

Truth is what one believes to be right; it causes individuals to stand up and fight; it shall always when crushed continued to rise, - and shall never - no never fade with demise.

Truth is the individual's way life, and aids in encountering this world of strife; it is necessary in this world of turmoil, where there's disturbance on sea and nearly every soil.

For Truth can never, ever really be crushed, nor can it ever, ever really be hushed; for it stood the test of centuries, influencing countries in their histories.

So rejoice when you seem to be bruised or crushed, and you've been forced in your thinking to be hushed; remember—Truth, when crushed shall rise again, for crushing will rebuild and character regain.

But Jesus Christ is the way the Truth and the life the remedy for this world of chaos and strife; for Christ, the Son of the living God-is the Truth that was crushed and rose again.

Josephine T. Braddock

Only A Prayer Away

If you're feeling downhearted and blue-
Pleasant memories are just the thing for you,
If they don't bring a brighter day-
God is just a prayer away.

When you're feeling you are at a loss-
Remember Jesus died on a cross,
And everything doesn't go your way-
God is only a prayer away.

When your heart is heavy, filled with despair-
And you think no one around, to care,
You would like to make this a fruitful day-
Remember God is only a prayer away.

Through troubles and woes, you feel alone-
Remember, they're only a stepping stone,
On the path of life, you feel astray-
God is only a prayer away.

For on this short journey of life
When trials and troubles bring dismay,
There is always a promise of hope-
Knowing God is only a prayer away.

Ed Keller

Costumes

Ernie's mask, flanked by flapping, double-sided
pony tails, as on to trick or treat you pranced.

Brown-felted palms and soles,
(size six the tiger pattern said)
later served in back yard play.

Next, upon request, you became the stripèd-tail
raccoon which (you pointed out) displayed
a set of supernumerary black rings.

In close succession came the harlequin clown,
the tu-tued ballerina, and later on, a green
silk-clad, and pom-pommed young cheerleader.

It is as though each year you grew, my
needle and my machine performed, accepting
your growth, and splendid act of childhood.

And then it happened. The day arrived, and
the parade of costumes in my mind made
eyes well up each time I reminisced.

It leaves no doubt. I see my glorious
grandchild metamorphosing before my eyes,
with each increasing pattern size.

Clarajane Browning

Shipwreck

Roll and roar, roll and roar,
Pound on the ship that will sail no more,
Scatter it over the ocean's floor.
Leave but a lonely spar or mast
For the hull of the ship could not last.

Were there souls on board that shattered wreck
Praying to their Lord on the sinking deck?
Was rescue near on that stormy night
With bonfires glowing, a welcome sight?
Or were they alone in their hopeless plight
While the breakers roared through the long dark night?

Did the gale that blew in from the West
Tear at the ship and lay it to rest?
The hulk that drifted up on land
Lies buried deep 'neath shifting sand.
Nothing is seen but the boom and a spar
Forever pointing toward the far North star.

Josephine O. Ritchie

Peace

All we need is to live in peace
Preserve all of man's fine qualities
We've got to understand war won't win it
Not with all of God's children in it.

The only way that man can succeed
Is try to live together in harmony
We've got to stop bearing those arms
Selling those drugs-stealing kid's hearts.

We've got to think about where we're headed
Remember the Kennedy's and Martin Luther said it
Keep a happy home-love one another
Or there's no way we can be brothers.

Man has the power in his hand
To destroy all mankind or take a stand
He can send up a rocket to the moon
But a rocket with a warhead means only doom.

Man knows life is very short and sweet
So he better wake up or wind up six feet deep
Love and peace should be on our minds
For the good of the world and all of mankind.

Darrow Kennedy

God Bless Our President

While the whole nation is weeping,
President Clinton keeps on sleeping.
And his "get-up-and-go" just got up and went.
Oh, what the heck, God bless our president.

Thinking about the national debt really makes me blue,
But Clinton says, "Don't worry, I'll write another I.O.U."
Some of us are "broke," others are "badly bent."
Oh, what the heck, God bless our president.

Is "Dollar bill" trickier than "Tricky Dick?"
I don't know, but his Health Care Plan makes me sick.
All of the atheists think that Clinton's "heaven sent."
Oh, what the heck, God bless our president.

All of the odd-ball people think that Clinton's "quite a gem."
Which causes me to wonder, is he one of us, or one of them.
The prostitutes are working overtime to pay the rent.
Oh, what the heck, God bless our president.

Clinton's just a draft dodger, not a deserter,
But his Crime Bill makes me want to commit murder.
Now that I've vented all the anger I can vent,
Oh, what the heck, God bless our president.

Carl L. Paulun

The Quest

I searched the world for unique treasure,
Riches beyond all possible measure,
I wanted rare diamonds that glistened in the sun,
Carmine rubies, creamy pearls, pure gold by the ton,
I lusted for expensive cars, like those of movie stars,
I traveled far and wide, my greed I couldn't hide.
Yet there remained a strange yearning, a deep burning
That couldn't be quelled, life was over, turning,
In a dream the Master said "You've lost your way,
On this globe we are truly not meant to stay,
Only the simple things will do, free from rot and decay,"
The Lord, on earth, found a quiet place to wash his feet,
His disciples too, and such a spot will be my retreat,
Soak my feet, utterly relax and calmly repose,
Perfume my nose with fragrance of a beauteous rose.
Happiness is so serene and nice, there is no worldly price.

Elvira C. Schnabel

Alone

I sit alone, entranced by morning rays
Projecting strange particulate displays
Of hazy sunlight through a window pane,
Becalming some——my melancholic vein.

The stillness of the early morning air
Conjures the dust to float as if a prayer
Or some lost thought, out searching for its brain
And some kind soul to bring it home again.

My wandering thoughts list to a somber mood,
Remembering home and all my noisy brood—-
I ask why I've been doomed to this duress
Of unrelenting, cursed loneliness. . .

But no one answers from the stillness there
Among the specters dancing in the air.
And no one hears my woeful, silent cry;
And no one sees my anguished, tearful eye.

The silence of the room begins to pound—-
Each heartbeat magnifies the pulsing sound,
Like denizens consigned to share my woe
Entombed within this marble breast of Poe. . .

A prisoner of one I live, till when
The phone—your voice—and I am home again.

Harvey Joseph Dockstader

The Crucifixion

I was a minor, so they gave me the shaft,
Punched in the stomach, and then in the aft;
They tugged at my hair, and stepped on my toes,
Just why they did this, nobody knows.

Perhaps they are angry, and filled with frustration,
At the sad state of affairs across our vast nation;
The high cost of living, the huge population,
The deficit spending, and excessive inflation.

There is a way how we can solve all our troubles,
Our problems would vanish like so many bubbles;
Increase Federal Taxes, and decrease our spending,
Over a twenty year period, eliminate lending.

The U.S.S.R. and the U.S.A. should cut the expense,
Of the extravagant amount they spend on defense.
If we could save yearly a full ten percent,
Our income, without working, would drop twenty percent.

James A. Cannon, Jr.

Thoughts At Altitude

The sun condoning with the clouds
Pursued its normal course
And in its setting
Drew across the layered rolling mass of wool
Chords of glory
Evening music, purple fading into grey.

And I, turned alien to all earthly things,
Was caught,
Submerged in heartsong,
Centered in a gold circumference.

What perverted genius comes to men
That they should direct brain
Toward the ultimate destruction of their like?
Yet to the human envoy of their will
Their brainchild brings down heaven to the earth.

Above the sun's sonata to the cloud
I carried death to others of my kind.
As I looked down from its free element
The purple disappeared......to leave the grey.

Anthony John Hemelik

A Chapter's End

G uest of honor, adorned in robe,
R ejoice this day in ceremonial bliss.
A las! Enough i's are dotted and t's crossed
D etermined by educators, a chapter has ended.
U nbeknown to others, and between each line,
A re lifetime memories filled with love and wisdom
T o guide you each dawning day with a radiant path of
E verlasting peace and exhilarating happiness today, and ever after.

Judith A. Baker

In This Land "America"

In this land of ours, there stands the Great Lady Liberty,
reaching out her flaming torch, to all those people who want to be free.

For in this land of ours, we are free to soar like an eagle,
and to offer our help to those people, where freedom is illegal.

In this land of ours, where we think and speak without any harm,
let those people believe in peace and freedom without sounding an alarm.

In this land of ours, where the red, white and blue waves ever so proudly, let those people who are suppressed, hear our voices loudly.

In this land of ours, where we reach out and share,
to let those people feel our warmth and love because we care.

In this land of ours, where many brave men and women have died,
because they let those people know we were always on their side.

In this land of ours, where we have long since come out of the caves,
to band together as a nation and to free those people who had been slaves.

For in this land of ours, may the spirit of freedom be felt all over the world, so the visions within those people shall never decay or spoil.

Freedom, freedom, hear our voices raise; we sing to America, we all give you praise, freedom, freedom, give us the strength to be free; for in this land, America, that's where I want to be.

Jeffrey Kelley

Emergence Of Women In Ancient Athens

Athena, Goddess of Wisdom, and Patroness of Arts and Crafts, keynoted RELIGIOUS THOUGHT and ARTISTIC ACHIEVEMENT for Athens.
Citizens of Athens believed their Goddess made their City Imperial.
A spirit of competition was nearly as important as religion in the building of the ACROPOLIS.
Artists transmuted Periclean ideals into works of enduring beauty.
The Chief Business of the State: help create wiser, more virtuous, and happier citizens.
Athens observed 60 official holidays; perfect occasions to present their matchless theatre FREE to the populace.
c.445 B.C. Aspasia established a hetaira (school) for married women.
The hetaira flourished: girls of good families studied; husbands brought their wives; men attended her lectures.
Aspasia set an example in freedom. To participate in cultural life she lived as Pericles' mistress in unlicensed union.
Aspasia transformed Pericles' home into a "French Enlightenment" salon where art, science, literature and philosophy came together.
Married women rejected the seclusion that society prescribed DURING THE GOLDEN AGE OF GREECE.

Clara S. Dick

Surrender

Remember what it used to be like?
Remember when you could look her in the eye
and she'd know exactly the way you felt?
She knew what you were thinking before you ever did.
What ever happened to that life?
Where did those days go?
You were so close to her,
but now you're so far away.
Surrender yourself to this life.
Forget all the hurt and the pain.
Live for this day.
As it's said, "Out with Old, in with the New."
Let yourself forget how you felt.
Surrender yourself to the others and let them enter your life.
Let them cease your tears.
Let them help you sleep again and forget your pain.

Jeannie Roseberry

Walk, Do Not Run

Walk past the gate, past the late great's
residence, past fields, flowers, bougainvillea
bowers; walk, do not run; the sun is yet high,
and the sky will not weep. Walk past the tavern
where dreams are drowned, friends found, hopes lost
with ragged remnants of losing lottery tickets.

Walk past the shell drive alive with wings that
thrive on bugs, slugs, the wide-eyed scaly fruit of
a rolling, restless sea. Walk past the pier where
last night's lovers left promises carved in pine,
where pelicans perch, fishermen search, reeling in
dark and dripping weed. Walk past twinkling harbor

Lights; for night draws near; children hear supper
calls; cats prowl, dogs howl, beg for bones. Walk
home; day is done; be swift, do not roam. Shadows
lengthen, distant sirens wail; follow the trail
of drake and gander; careful now, do not wander.
Enter and shut shadows far from view.

Dixie J. LeDoux

My Son

It's hard to imagine this little guy having to carry such a responsibility.
Growing up too fast, and becoming a man without pleasures you knew as a child.
You try to help mold a greater person than you had been, but want him to take a smoother path with fewer hardships.
You try to answer question that have not been asked, yet expect perfection from one so young.
If you could only share with him the experiences it took you a life-time to achieve.
But stop and consider that these dreams are what make a boy become a man.
They shape and mold his character and give him responsibility no father can tell him about.
Your function is to help guide, counsel, discipline, love and be his best friend.
Let him determine his own destiny that his mind has chosen.
Be the gardener that plants a rose and does not take credit for its perfection and beauty.
He knows the planting of the seed and the loving care is what makes a miracle come true.

Danny Haynes

Books

The treasure shines from out the world of men,
Riches of winged thought the mind to glean;
In drawing from the ancient and the new,
The essence of all things so vast and true.

The romance and flavor a book contains,
Fashioning soils of dreams for terrains;
And silver seas are there to ease the way
To prospects fine that gleam and cold that day.

Books, good in their spreading power to show
An ever deeper stream to see and know;
Volumes, wonders to grasp that lay revealed;
The lamb glow rising, as to light the world.

Amebi Doombadfe

The Cadre

I hear the sounds of discipline
Ringing in my ears
Discipline that molded the soldier
Into a victorious fighting machine

Forward march, right, left, right, in cadence count.
Hut two three four, tramp, tramp of marching feet
The boom of cannons, the steady crack of rifle fire.
Load, ready, aim, fire at will.

My thoughts mix with these sounds of discipline
As I travel along life's memory trail
Remembering all the soldiers that were trained
Then shipped off to battle.

Some sent off to battle did return
To ticker tape parades and cheers
From all those who did not get their turn
To fight and die for their country

We must always remember and celebrate the victories
Of that fighting machine
But let us also salute the cadres
With no purple hearts or ribbons, just service stripes

Arthur L. Johnston

Home Again

Ozark home...so humbly beautiful,
Rocky old hills blanketed with lush green trees
That fill the horizon and quiet creeks go bubbling o'er rocks,
Flowing to that place where
Silent humid air hangs
Over misty rivers and fireflies light up the sky.

On top of the hill sits a house...weathered and gray.
'Hollyhocks grow bumblebees fly,
Two people stand, rocky as the hills,
Open arms reaching, welcoming,
Swing in the swing,
Ride the mules,
Run on these hills.

Then
Leaving it far behind...forgotten
Returning once again to this place in my heart,
Quietly making it my own,
With open arms welcoming...the deep cool well of refreshment,
Love filtering down,
Cultivating...enriching...ripening...my love for life.

Betty Borcher

Mother Nature's Beauty

The sun lies low in the horizon, the violet and
rose-pink hues breathtaking at the very least.
It sinks slowly, leaving a fluorescent blur on the
eyes as it retreats to the other side.
And night is here.
And one by one, the stars peep out from underneath
the dark cover of night and twinkle timidly, sending
messages of morse code to the lovers and
dreamers on earth, the stargazers.
And upon them, too, is cast the heavenly glow of
the moon, whose kind face watches all.
And as the stars grow tired of their game of hide-
and-seek, and the man in the moon grows
sleepy, they too, like the sun, retreat under the
cover of sky, to return again tomorrow night.
And the sky grows lighter, slowly, slowly, until that
one blessed moment, that magical moment, when the
sun kisses the earth and the dew covered grass.
And a new day has begun.

Angie Krysiak

1935

The rails are thrumming, she's coming, boy
Round the bend there she is old No. 7002.
Steam striving, smoke blowing, cinders flying,
She's got the ties dancing and the ballast prancing.
Black steel shining, stoker frying, coal flying,
Flames roaring, pressure building, throttle open wide.
Drives wheels churning, with a flashing thunder
She's pounding those rails with fists of steel.
She's coming not stopping here just flying through.
Wave to the engineer, boy.
Whistle blowing fading, fading
Box cars passing, wheels clacking, clacking.
New York Central, B and O, Pennsy, Norfolk Southern
Names of roads across the land passing, passing by.
Doors open hoboes waving, bundles stashed on the floor,
She's dead heading that's for sure.
Must be doing 70 now, won't be stopping for many a mile.
Here comes the caboose, clacking, clacking, flagman waving.
What a joy! Whistle blowing, fading, fading.
You won't forget, boy.

Dale Williams

A Childhood Dream

A fairy Princess I became, to
rule the World like a Queen.
With gentleness I touched each strand,
that went before my wand in hand,
and there before my eyes did fall,
a land transformed again for all
The rough was made so smooth and soft,
I could not view the prints aloft.
The aged became so young at heart,
portraying great examples and teachers of Art.
The beggar there I saw no more, for
he had plenty and some to store.
The lame so straightly walked erect,
for here he received a host of respect.
The rich he too was made the same for
him there was no earthly fame.
No harsh words spoken could rule this land
only kindness and gentleness were in demand.
I stood in awe as I viewed this scene,
what majesty in a Childhood dream.

Elisabelle Greenhaw

"Going Nowhere"

Time is without end, and end has no time
Rusty iron rails, going nowhere
On rotting ties, and broken bridges
The rusty iron rails, sticking out over space
The wind cries here, a mournful sound
As in the sobbing, of a far away child
My feet crunch, the rocky road bed
As a cold rain begins to fall
This, I thought, could be a portrait of my soul
A copy of sadness, and despair
Rusty dreams, broken schemes of love
A trail of empty, space and time
I am weary, but I may not stop to rest
My soul weeps, at the lonely sound of the gulls
Soon the land will reclaim, this ancient roadbed
And time too, will turn my empty life to dust

Cleve Whitmore II

The Poet's Salt

That's no fool wind knocking at your door, no lonely ghost
salt grass sways to its own swooning
sea mist has harbored her home in these relic dwellings
for an eternity or more salt soaks into this old wood pier
sandpipers scurry to safety as that same fool wind bend us
a haunting sleepy spell covers these streets
stars emit crystal light shrouded in white magic
the Row can kindle old flames
tonight I listen here in this musty cafe to these wild poets'
words and dreams fly from voices in color
salt tipped notes sing music, dance like ghost set free

I can feel the salt grass swooning me I feel a drawing upon my soul
cradled in this entrancing hub lullabies cry out from the sea
drowning me, taking me a pulling towards the current's ebb
in this ghost of a night still embers burn, we are poets then not
lost in salt spirit lives on
caught in the poetry the Steinbeck is here
in this still porthole of time where the heart will dance to the wind
and the soul can taste the poet's salt.

Julia Lee Cerepak

My Mom

My mom is so very special to me
She is the greatest Mom on earth you see
My Mom has been through a lot
Things that would make other people hot

My Mom never relaxed on her butt
Things that she endured took a lot of guts
My Mom didn't have the easiest of life
From childhood on there was misery and strife

My Mom raised us as best as she could
She never ever let us do things that weren't good
My Mom is the best Mom that there is
I knew that more and more down through the years

My Mom instilled in us the manners of time with words like
Thank you, excuse me, and you're welcome and words of that kind
My Mom is the greatest Mom to know
She is always in my heart wherever I may go

My Mom is purely a real rare kind
I never knew her to partake of liquor, beer or wine
My Mom is divine as can be how glad I am
That God chose her as a Mom for me

Barbara K. Bynum

"Jamie Lee's Warning To Grandma"

Dedicated to Jamie and Katie and Brock Ryan Veenhuis
Grandpa and Grandma and Jamie Lee
Sang Christmas Carols on Christmas Eve.
Jamie Lee and Grandpa sang quite well
But Grandma messed up Jingle Bells
Grandpa said nothing, Grandma he feared
But Jamie Lee cried and said, Grandma dear
You either shape up and get it in gear
Or you can't sing Christmas songs next year.
Grandma looked somewhat perturbed,
But she uttered not an angry word.
Instead to the kitchen she quickly fled
And baked three batches of ginger bread,
One for Grandpa, and one for Jamie Lee
And one that she shared with my sister Kate and me.

James C. Price

The Green Eyed Monster

Bellowing through the dark night,
screaming in the bright sunlight.
Frustration in every thought,
unaware that all's for naught.

The monster comes in many a disguise,
tormenting and abusing the poor unwise.
Foolish ones with so little self-esteem.
look within yourself for the beautiful dream.

For within your soul lies your true worth,
given to you at the onset of your birth.
Say to yourself each wonderful morn,
I am worthy to have been born.

Put the monster to bed, and so to sleep,
remove his green eyes from your soul so deep.
Focus instead on the kindness and love,
bestowed upon us from our blessed God above.

Dorothy Morris-Dillon

Untitled

Oh my love when death slips silently inside,
Searching for a soul to take away,
I'm frightened, I try to hide,
I whisper not yet, I must stay.

I cannot leave you yet and go alone,
I cannot bear the absence of your touch,
With wonderful harmony our spirits have flown
Hearts touching and loving so very much.

I pray God will bid death wait awhile,
Until you are ready to go with me.
Together we'll greet death with a smile,
Hand in hand for all eternity,

Audrey L. Ray

Lonely 'Til You

Up there-look up there.
See that star-that all by itself.
Lonely-floating so high, but yet, all alone.
Over there-look over there.
See the homeless-strangers forced together.
Lonely-having so much to offer, but no chance.
Right there-look right there.
See the blind-those who are so naive.
Lonely-thinking, but yet, not knowing.
My eyes-look into my eyes.
See the tears-the tears in my eyes.
The tears, that until you, were those of sadness.

Angela Lothridge Bentley

"The Secret"

Secrets within,
Secrets withheld
The Spirit knows them,
Although it wasn't told...
...and we long for that person,
who we can tell,
All of our secrets,
that we hide so well.
When the day comes,
that the Light surrounds...
the darkness and closets that open...
...ourselves to reveal,
there is nothing to hide...anymore.
He said it Himself - His name is the door.
And when I reside (in green pastures)
And nowhere to hide; I'll rock myself...(Selah)
To rest, in the palm of His hand,
Thankful to live, in the Light of the land.

Alice K. Marko

No Words

No words can say how the heart feels but to
see the external actions is just a little glimpse
See just the slight mention of his name;
There's that glow
When he walks into a room;
There's that smile
Nights you sit and think about him;
There's that spark
Even the times it seems like confusion
There's even a tear
The glow, smile, spark, and the tear is coming from within
like a fire that can not stop burning and it
burns a hole trough your heart
So you don't have to speak words because
I already know how the heart feels and it
is saying "I love you."
So don't just stand there keep fighting and
believing is what you know in your heart is true
And I promise that dream and Desire will come
true for you.

Crystal Gayle Reece

Cindee

My dear little friend has gone away,
She will not see another day.
Her many illnesses she could not transcend,
Her life is over, it has come to an end.

The first time I saw her she was just three weeks old,
A feisty little runt, yet brave and bold.
At six weeks of age we brought her home,
She took right over as through the house she'd roam.

She'd follow me from here to there
And nip my heels if my feet were bare.
A spirited little gal was she
And she meant so very much to me.

Through the years she was so faithful,
A companion to behold.
At ten the years began to show on her,
It was clear she was growing old.

At thirteen years a matriarch was she,
But time had taken its toll on her, that was very plain to see.

And now her life is over, it has suddenly come to an end.
But I shall never forget her, my Cindee, my canine friend.

Colleen A. Gehr

Big Bend

Space! Deep vastness beyond the horizon —
Seeping to the edges of eternity!
Scorching hot; choking dry; desert mirages tease the
Fickle road. No sounds but silence. Two wary eyes emerge:
Abruptly are destroyed, like stealthy winds which
Gnaw away the land. SUDDENLY: Thrusting raging
Fists, tearing constricting bonds, clawing selves
From far within the earth — MOUNTAINS!
They DARE to mock the nothingness of time!
Alone, they offer refuge.
Scrubby trees, pinion pines, prickly cactus:
Snag root-holds in the rocks.
Profusion swallows self.
Rattlers keep the check.
Deluging rains smother mountains in primeval fog:
Gnashing stone away — disembodying all!
Lightning smashes crags!
GONE.
Fiery sunset corrodes the storm.
Window to majesty!

Frances E. Ballard

This Is Pepper

I have a friend, and she's a pup.
She has long ears with a tail curled up.

Running wild, hair in her eyes;
happy is she chasing butterflies.

She goes everywhere with me;
puppy excitement for me to see.

Prancing, dancing, jumping for my attention;
being my friend when there is dissension.

Puppy eyes looking at me adoring;
tail wagging and expectation soaring.

She's my friend, you see, a darling pup.
She has long ears with a tail curled up.

Why did she come to me, this friend,
when another one it could have been?

This dog is special, she's happy as can be,
and only this one belongs to me.

Charlene Fuhlendorf

Footprints In The Sands Of Time

Somewhere it's said that all mankind
Shall pass this way but once
And that each precious moment spent is ours to wisely use,
So I must always try my best
To diligently seek
The path of wisdom that I know is mine to freely choose.

For I alone know I am given
The choice of my own path,
So I'll waste not a moment in my lifelong journey here
To touch another's life and make
A better world for all
And take advantage of each chance to bring another cheer.

And when I die, those lives I've touched
I hope some day will say
Their lives were changed because I gave, through poetry and rhyme,
A laugh, a smile, a ray of sun
And love that lifts the heart
And that my life reflects my footprints in the sands of time.

Jane Marie Long

"My Little Girl"...dedicated to Richelle Jolly Dean

I only have one little girl, to me
She means the world,
She is like having a real live doll,
I've really enjoyed her so far.
She has long blond hair and
blue eyes you see, she's always been
beautiful to me.
She's such a little softie to hug and to
touch, I love her very much.
Sometimes she doesn't act like a lady,
likes to fish and play ball with the boys,
She can beat them if she half way tries,
She's good at catching baseball flies.
She goes fast on her bicycle and gets hurt,
then she does something very sweet like
singing in church.
I'm thankful that out of the whole world,
God gave me this little girl.

Bonnie Watson Jolly

"Love"

Sometimes it feels so right,
sharing pictures of you, walks in the setting sun,
you're a sweet thing, love at first sight,
It's a love story just begun,
come out of the cold, out of the driving rain,
our lives together about to unfold,
other reasons aren't to explain,
I'd look after you, find the right thing to do,
nothing can make our love and times more unsung,
sometimes it feels so right,
In my heart you're number one,
you're a sweet thing, love at first sight,
It's a love story just begun,
sharing pictures of you, walks in the setting sun,
right or wrong, this day is our first love song,
we'll never drift apart, our love will
always be for long-as it will always be so strong

Frank C. Chludzinski

The Editor's Harp

I met an editor once
She thought she was very very smart
And every word she spoke was
Straight from Heaven's Golden Harp
Time after time, line after line
Her B-I-G R-E-D P-E-N-C-I-L flew across each line
God! What power pulsed though her veins
How she loved this critique game..
How she would make those writers toe the line
She would improve each and every line.

She knew she was sharp
Every word from her vocabulary
Was, straight from Heaven's Golden Harp
The writers?..They could swim or sink
You heard right,..Let them drown in their own ink!

She was just too smart..She thought..
Her wisdom was straight from Heaven's Golden Harp.

Arthur R. Morrison

My Mom

My Mom was a lady with strong family ties
She was a hard worker no one can deny
My mom had beautiful powder blue eyes
So soft with love for my dad, brothers and I

My mom would cure my toothaches in time
Just by letting me climb in bed with her
So she could hug her warm cheek to mine
I knew her great love and warmth was the cure

My mom was my friend she was my rock
She was a great lady and so very precious to me
She is a sweet memory in my heart forever locked
How blessed it would be if only I could again see
My Mom! I Love You

Dorothy Cain

The Mask

You wear so well as you so poignantly deceive,
Shielding the world from reality as you reflect untruthful images.
You do not wish to be exposed, for fear of your true identity,
So you fabricate a facade to conceal your illusive personality.

You boast in your insidious gambits as you aim to tempt
and lure the minds of the innocent into evil enchantments.
With unrivaled hypocrisy you polish lies,
As you exude the finesse of a gentlemanly stranger.

Oh Mask, strip your hollow visage and look into the mirror of truth.
Let your heart be healed as you bury your arsenal of weapons.
For only the sun in its scorching heat can melt your mold,
Which have encased and rendered you a player in life's masquerade.

Frances E. Bellot

Grandpa

He was a small man,
short and bald in the center of his head, with gray, white
thin hairs on the side. His eyes, big, brown and round and shiny
like a ruby. He often wore khaki pants with the hem of each leg
rolled above his ankles. He rose early each morning to cook
breakfast, rolling and baking biscuits from scratch or flipping flapjacks
or stirring steamy, bubbling grits, or turning crisp sizzling bacon.
A big wide smile always shone on his face and he'd sang his favorite
hymn: "WHAT A FRIEND WE HAVE IN JESUS. ALL OUR
SINS AND GRIEF TO BEAR..."
His voice, smooth and low like a baritone. He loved reading the
morning paper. Sometimes he'd smoke a cigar, blowing blue and white
circles toward the ceiling. He loved doing math, and especially
reading history; and always had a tale or two to tell.

Alfred L. Huntington

Hurt

I have faced the fact that I may never
see you again, it has been the way that
I have made it.
You were once here and then you were there
Now you have forever gone your way without me
You have left with me thinking about you
You were to blame for the way I have been
For the way I am now
Never have I said a word
to let you know that you were
Breaking my spirit till I had none left
I gave till I couldn't give any more
And not once did you care to give
A kind word of gratitude or a hug
To let me know that you were sorry

George Cox

Adriatic Bondage

The whispering music is still in my ears
since early childhood
of your gentle waves caressing white and rugged shores
memories of sun and color;
The most azure of all seas in the vast Kingdom of Poseidon

The rage of your storms
made me fearless, romantic, wise and strong
mirror peace of your summer morning lulls
made me forgiving, loving and Christian believing.

The nostalgia for you is curved in my heart
Baptism is performed long ago,
The bond is like that of Salmon,
in the last swim upstream, the known river
For me this is coming home, on thy shores
just for that one last time
Sail off to the Island of Proizd
to catch my daily meals
I am thankful for your blessings
because you taught me never to steal,
to respect each other is part of our deal.

Ivan Mirosevic

In Memory - Last Flight

Fifty years have come and gone,
Since you left our humble home;
To serve your country -The U.S.A
Every night and every day.

At that time you were brave and young,
In fact, you were only twenty-one;
When you got geared-up, leaving at night,
Little did you realize it would be your
last flight.

As you soared off into the "wild blue
yonder",
Little did you realize your plane
would be torn asunder;
but you willingly gave your all,
That our "good ole U.S.A." might not fall.

And now in closing, let me say,
you're in a land of constant day;
Where all is happiness, joy, and laughter,
That's what we all are striving after.

Agnes Greene

"Peace On Earth"

Peace flows from the sweet song of the blue bird,
singing gaily in the apple tree.

Peace dwells in the beauty of the garden, kissed
tenderly by the honeybee.

Peace lies in the heart of the little man, making
mud pies by a friendly stream

Peace rest in the glow of our fireside, alone with
our thoughts to drowse and day-dream.

Peace is not a creative element, that materialized
from man's design.

Peace comes from the humble depth of our hearts,
of all creeds and race and faith combined.

Ginny Fretz

If I Could Fly To Heaven

Sewing in the bedroom, crocheting in the front room,
Sitting on the porch swing, sipping your ice tea,
Out in the garden, working like no other, these are my
fond memories of my dear, sweet mother.

If I could fly to heaven, I bet that I could see,
My mother sitting on the swing, and making things for me.

Things would be changed, now that we're worlds apart.
But one thing would remain the same, and that's the love
that's in our heart.

The swing is solid pearl, and the chains are made of gold.
Bluebirds fly overhead to bring the thread you hold.

If I could fly to heaven, I bet that I could see,
My mother sitting on the swing, and making things for me!

Dianna Feece

"A Man-Made World"

Choking on the man-made figurine is only proof.
Skeletons rising above the black ocean are from the former sea monsters.
Masks of death cover the mouths of the no longer innocent children.
At noon is when the cloud sky is of a colored cloud.
Claws and fangs are fashions of man.
Bitter aromas fill the endangered lilacs.
Planes that release gases with a surreptitious plan to kill.
Agreements to abolish religions of purity is in man's mind.
Trains run on the uneasiness of tortured life that wishes to hear the
tones of sweet voices.
Evening out this disaster that man loves and lives for will be
virtually impossible.
Too much was destroyed that only the hope of the most desperate can
figure out what's left to figure out.
What's left that exists.

Alpana Choudhury

"Droplets Of Time"

Photographs capturing "Droplets of Time"
slipping through fingers
Treasured memories, their warmth to linger
Nurturing body and soul with
reason and rhyme
To fill the journey of one's span of time
Like a clock ticking "Droplets of Time"
seconds minute filling the hourglass of life
To reach God's home above all strife.

Barbara Lee Cody

Memories Of The Past

Life is filled with memories of the past
Some that you hold onto with a firm tight grasp
Never wanting to lose those memories that
are a strong part of your life
Like those of a loving husband or a wife
A special memory of a grandma or grandpa
Whose love seemed to never die, and
even though they maybe gone,
their memory will live on
Or a radiant sunrise peaking over
the crashing waves of the seashore
Which you had never seen before
All those special times
with your parents will last
And when your friends
were there for you in the past
No matter now insignificant they maybe
Memories make you what you are today,
Don't you agree?

Carrie Taylor

Reflection

Walking west, uptight and full of defenses
Snow weaves its opaque cloak
Over foot-trodden concavities of earth.
Nothing rings so true, as silence, or snow
Falling on a cold winter's night.

Crossing Broadway, wrung out like a towel -
I recall the party coming from
Where someone sang the blues.
Who was it looking for Paradise.
Found a street of broken dreams instead?

Waiting for the subway train, I saw
My life versus a still undiscovered
Journey which I must still traverse.
There is no turning back,
No choice, but to move in time.

Knowing as I ride the train
That somewhere on the other side-
This, then is the place; this is the time
In my heart's dream of sure, safe destiny
Towards the unknown of my inner self.

Gloria M. White-Epstein

Weeping Willows

Weeping willows with your large bouquets of green,
So bounteously your twig-like branches lean.
Clad so generously full with rustling leaves,
Dancing entwined, like a waltz in the breeze.
While the soft wind creates its musical notes,
A vision, of a beautiful crinoline floats.

Banks lush with moss, like emeralds so mellow,
Draped by weeping, lacy leaves of the willow.
Thirsty roots reaching out to the brook below,
Quenching a ravenous thirst to make it grow.
For minus the water, earth, sun and the sky,
This gorgeous creation would surely die.

Eileen G. Snyder

Always Today

The tomorrow of today is forever tomorrow
So chase race the days we spend and now borrow
Time to wish, wait, walk, wonder or ponder, on a path so narrow
We delay then decay under an ordered ordeal of sorrow

Yesterday's tomorrow is today, always today
For you and me to see, to be, to feel, be real and say
I am, I can, I will or won't, or might or may
Build up, tear down, put off, put on, and display

The glory of tomorrow's yesterday, this today we now know
How time takes our youth in concerned yearnings flow
The expected events lose an anticipated glow
And maybe we mature in our reflections of long ago

Jonathan D. Lipson

How Can You Not Believe

How can you not believe and see the rising of the sun,
Soft white clouds drifting slowly by in that blue eternal sky.
How can you not believe while viewing flowers, all unique,
Formed and fashioned beyond belief.
How can you not believe and hear the birds in spring,
A raucous melody they sing, racing about on colored wing.
How can you not believe and walk a wooded path
In the shade of low hung trees, or fish a silver stream.
How can you not believe while holding a tiny baby close,
Feelings of wonder, joyous mirth, a bit of heaven, come down to earth.
How can you not believe? Impossible, I find.
You cannot escape that loving hand. He makes for us, a life so grand.

Helen Mowery Boyer

A Piece Of Bread

A piece of bread -
So common, yet so holy,
He touched it
And the commonness is gone,
A piece of bread -
Short nourishment for bodies,
But for the soul, a banquet has been spread.

A piece of bread -
Enough for all the ages,
And all the lives who come to Him in prayer,
A piece of bread -
His holy hand has touched it,
And we eat glory as with him we share.

Grace M. Weaver

A Ghazl's Shadowed Tale

Ah, black thunder drums the soul of time's grace,
So dancing ghosts of sorrow your honor will embrace.

An eagle flies to greet the flaming dawn of time,
To reclaim spiritual trust which enlightens disgrace.

A crystal river still runs to touch salty tears,
As its cataracts weep all along its ancient race.

Squirrels gather up corn, fruit, seeds, and nuts
As they store shadow hearts to nurture their birthplace.

Watch the wild wind as it kisses the mystic graves,
That cherish the sacred bones of every Indian race.

Deborah Ann Bruce

Sea, Wind And Sky

We leave this life to seek a better world,
So do not gaze in sadness at the sea,
My earthly form may lie beneath the waves,
My spirit lives and knows where I shall be.

I live with the colorful, sparkling sunbeams,
Reflecting from an ocean wave,
I join in the mystic sounds of the sea,
Like enchanting music great orchestras play.

I sail the seas with the silent sailboats,
Silhouetted against a moonlit sky,
I fly with the long-winged ocean birds
That soar so gracefully on high.

I travel the world with the wild west wind,
Storming across the oceans deep,
I flow with the gentle breeze on summer nights,
That cools the air and helps you sleep.

I am thrilled at the sight of the blazing comets,
Streaking across the midnight skies,
But I follow the light that shines forever,
I live the life that never dies.

Henry O'Grady

God's People

Strange that God made
so many kinds of faces,
if only one race and color
is the correct one.
I do not think it was
trial and error,
but Divine intention
to make all mankind learn
appreciation of each other's gifts and talents,
and, someday, to become
the One People He envisioned at
the moment of creation.

Eileen Overbye

A Tired Railroader

Well, I'm getting tired of a railroader's life
So I think I'll retire and just work for my wife.
I know I'll have many more rivers to cross
But I'll be very happy for I'll have a good boss.
I've worked many years with no pleasure at all
So now I'll go out and have me a ball,
And do what I please, and love it-you bet
for I won't have no foreman to look down my neck.
Come on you railroaders, I hope you will stay
And keep the trains running while I'm out making hay
and while you're all out on a dirty old wreck
I'll just wait for the postman to bring me my check.
So good-bye my old buddies, it's now time to go
To join Pete and Bill and others I know
My fishing fever is high and the way that I feel
I'm heading right out with my rod and my reel.

Charlie E. Ellis

Love In Poetry

Because my darling you fail to see
So I wrote my love for you in poetry
I do not know it if you have the
slightest notion
Darling but for your love I would
swim from ocean to ocean
and I would climb the highest mountain
And build you the biggest fountain
If only you will tell me that you care
Then together a perfect love we can share
I would sing you the sweetest love songs
I would do you all the rights and no wrongs
And if you can prove my poetry of love is untrue
Then my darling I'm not deserving of you

Anthony Mercorelli

True Lies

So many lies in the world,
So much pain felt when the truth is known.
The liar never can tell how much pain is given,
They care only for pains of their own.
The receiver may love one only for their lies,
And when the truth is known,
Their heart drops like a stone.
It is hard to be on my own,
Nobody to help me,
Always being alone.
Please, I need your help
For without help, I cannot carry the stone,
May the gods help me
For I am all alone.

Ehren Manning

Seeing

They stood on either side of her
So as to gently guide
Warm sand underfoot, caressing
Insistent, making her smile
She stopped for a moment to savor
Salt dipped fingers of wind
That delighted her nose
And the summer sun's warmth on her arms
Down into the water they led her
Till it reached to her bony knees and
The breeze played games with her wispy white hair
Those on the beach who were sighted
Saw the wonder on her face
Knowing they were truly the blind
For she saw the hand of God

Alwyn D. Lewis

Grief And Hope

When we lose a loved one dear
So precious in our heart
Our grief can go so deeply,
That we can't bear with them to part.

Our grieving never can remove
The pain that goes so deep within;
We have to slowly move on through the day,
And let another painful phase begin.

We have to look beyond ourselves
And search for that glimmering light,
Our trust in God must be our strength
To guide us through the lonely night.

We must lift our tear-filled eyes,
And look into the heart of others grieving too,
To let them see that we can our faith impart,
That God alone can safely see us through.

Curtis B. Tabor

Alex

An angel of God who passed through here
so small but perfect and oh, so dear.
The little boy I barely knew
I rocked you to sleep when you were brand new.

We can't understand why you were taken away
Maybe there was a shortage of angels that day.
Or why you were chosen to be the one
Someday it will all be clear to us, right Son?

You left behind a brother and a little sister too,
We know you will watch over them, won't you.
And your mom and dad; they miss you so.
But there is a heaven we all know.

You almost made it to the first day of school
But God in His wisdom had different plans for you.
We know you are in a much greater place
For one day like you we will see His marvelous face.

Here on earth you live through others
What a generous gift to your sisters and brothers.
At your funeral we cried and leaned on each other
As we gave you back to our Heavenly Father.

Mrs. John M. Elliott

"Suicide To Step Aside"

He stood six feet tall in only his fifteenth year with hands
so strong you thought you would buckle under his hand shake
yet his soul and heart were one of tenderness and the shoe
that once fit in my palm now extended to my elbow...

The strong scent of Right Guard told me he had grown too
fast and sprinkles of chin hairs cleaned from his razor on
the bathroom sink reminded me of his blossoming manhood and
the ache of knowing he would be gone before it was desirable

The Bills monument that engulfed his room was to be exchanged
for a uniform of his own as he fell into rank as a high school
athlete and I was in awe of his determination and courage
for he had brought himself so far in a small measure of time

Laundry, dishes or cooking were not a bother to him and he
could build the most complicated projects without hesitation
He always took a moment to ask how you were or to comfort
and understand, the honor student has found his place

He stands alone as one of the few survivors of divorce and
rejection and he has in turn become my hero as I watch him
grow with strength and sensitivity, with so many battles my
son has come from suicide to step aside to leave his mark...

Carol Sorge-Kokinda

The Closed Door

Nature surrounds us with an abundance of things
So we can live in luxury and feel like kings.
She gave us ten fingers to serve our needs
No two prints are alike that record our deeds.

Neither are any two snow flakes exactly alike
Although they are so delightfully white.
What a beautiful model to use for our soul
To make it snow white should be our goal.

But to meet that goal we must travel alone
No one can help us to reach our new home.
No matter how famous, how rich or how poor
Tis only God in heaven who can open that door.

Eugene Douville

Persian Gulf Prayer

May the war cease,
So we can live in peace.
Lift our hearts in song and spirit
For all to hear it.
We pray for those on land, sea, and air,
Display yellow ribbons to show we care.
They are heroes, brave, with courage, to save you and me,
To make our country free.
Let's remember those in the Persian Gulf,
Where it's tough to be away
From the U.S.A.
Bring our loved ones safely home,
From war and strife with great aplomb.
Amen.

Claudine W. Larson

Birth

It is dark and moist and warm
Soft and sheltered from all harm
Without warning pressure and fright
The darkness changing to glaring light.

Emergence from the haven is frantic
Twisting, pulling screaming and panic.
There is no return, my fate is sealed-
Mind, body and soul revealed.

I am born - unique like no other.
Different from sister - different from brother,
And with the birth a mournful sigh
Given life, I must surely die:
I am afraid.

Edward A. Pascucci

Blessings

Our blessings are many, we must agree.
Some are in nature for us to see.

The birds and flowers near a mountain brook,
Combine their beauty for a contented look.

A deer grazing under a blue sky,
While squirrels chatter and play near by.

The trees and leaves and whispering breeze.
We thank our God for all of these.

The world's creation comes from above
And shows the way of his true love.

Heavenly Father to one and all.
He's always there to hear our call.

Janis B. Drinnon

Voices

On evenings when I cannot sleep
Some disembodied voices creep
Into my world.

Their muted voices fill the air
Much like a medieval prayer.
Out of this world!

Could be my covers rustle so,
my rhythmic breathing sets the flow.
What in the world!

Or could it be that voices past
Stayed in the ether, holding fast from ancient world?

So many voices rent the air,
some cries of pain, some of despair.
O troubled world.

Could we but tune in at the Fount
Of Jesus' Sermon on the Mount! O blissful world!

Should we be mindful what we say
To fill the void, and make each day a different world?

Such witless babble fills our mind!
Perhaps we should give humankind a joyful world.

Irene P. De Baun

I Can't See...

Dedicated to God

I can't see courage, but I know it's there when someone recites something in front of an audience.

I can't see pain, but I know it's there when your friend dies.

I can't see frustration, but I know it's there when you feel you've done everything wrong.

I can't see excitement, but I know it's there when you've just won the lottery.

I can't see fear, but I know it's there when your country is at war.

I can't see love, but I know it's there when my dog comes up to me and licks my face.

I can't see pride, but I know it's there when I've just won a contest.

I can't see happiness, but I know it's there when your mom says "I love you."

I can't see sadness, but I know it's there when your friend says I hate you.

A. J. Leffew

Lost Playmate

With russet hair, Autumn is sometimes shy,
Sometimes bold. She tosses her vibrant head
And leaves in tawny hues of gold and red
Drift down across the fields where sky larks fly.

Her air is sometimes somber, often sweet
As she prepares for Winter's heavy tread.
For he, in boots, tramps down her verdant bed
Then covers her dwelling with snow and sleet.

And I, with tearful eyes, am sad to see
Her go away with him to lands of snow.
She cannot come again for months, you know
But lives where frigid bluffs border the sea.

Oh, how dreary the wint'ry days will be
For I am Summer, and she played with me.

Elise Bills Rumford

Ode To Alan

You are my soul mate and now you're gone.
Sometimes I feel so lost and very much alone.

I know it was time for you to go away.
And I can't help myself...I think of you every day.

I know there wasn't enough happiness in your life.
Now you are happy and safe with no more pain, hurt or strife.

An illness was the enemy that parted us forever.
Going on without you has been a hard endeavor.

We shared so much that I smile when I reminisce.
Laughing together over old memories is very much missed.

You knew me in ways that no one else could.
A word, a look, a gesture; only you and I understood.

Peace and love have finally found you.
This makes me happy for I know it's true.

It's not easy without your specialness.
The hole in my life will be there forever...I guess.

Someday together again we will be.
Until then I know you will watch over me.

I know you look down on me from Heaven above.
And I'm looking back, my cheeks streaked with love.

Deborah E. Angell

The Eagle And The Wolf

The eagle soars in a big blue sky,
Sometimes I sit on a hill and ask him why
What's it like to be free, for we will never see.

The wolf runs by the shinny moonlight
The howling, the hunting,
The pray that just can not get away.

For the eagle is the ruler of the sky.
For the wolf is ruler of the land;
For someday we shall hope they will walk off hand in hand.

Irene Hazel Coureges Lindsay

Sometimes When I Pray

I pray to my Lord and Savior several times a day.
Sometimes when I'm talking to Him, I'm so emotional I don't know what to say.
When I think I have all the words planned in my heart.
I go down on my knees or bow my head; then I don't know where to start.
I want to thank Him for all His blessings; He has been so good to me.
He has kept all of His promises; He hasn't let me down, I know He loves me.
Even when I get all mixed up on the words, and take a round-about way,
He is there to say, it's O.K. my child, I know exactly what you're trying to say.
Anything I have asked for, I ask for in His name.
If I don't receive them when I think I should, I still love Him just the same.

Joan M. Brewer

Music

Sounds emitting celestial radiance sweep our being.
Like water clear as crystal, runs its way unto the sea.
As the wind that stirs the trees, music's dream
of bitterness and rapture, sways our hearts.
O music sublime, lifting our souls in mystic wonder;
As the spires of flame rise heavenward in a sunset blaze.

Amelie Doombadze

Madness

Oh, this dark and lonely place I dwell,
Somewhere between heaven, earth and hell.
My madness beckons me to yell!

Taken from me the love of my wife,
It was at night by my brother's knife.
I've not the will to live nor the courage to die.
How can I tell her my last good-by?

The days and nights are long and endless.
The wine has made me utterly senseless.
Roaming about both naked and wailing,
The markings of madness are unveiling.

The forest calls clear the sound of my name.
Is it she or is it a game?
Shall I look or remain the same?
Desperate to know rather than ponder,
I searched in vain like rumbling thunder.

Shall I discover my lover or my brother?
Could there be any other?
Could destiny be that I should wander?
I must be mad that I should wonder.

Deborah Lum Purviance

"Born In Silence"

Although Mother language is pregnant again,
Sorrow may kill her before new words are born.
Looking into the vacant eyes of her ancient children
She chokes with remorse at their tragic evolution.

Expression, her offspring, has become a cult of laziness,
A shifting and drifting shapeless mass, chanting in boredom,
While sacrificing itself on a meaningless altar
To a deity of nothingness.

As consolation, I speak to her of love, dreams, hope, etc.,
While denouncing mediocrity in a hateful curse.
Touching her swollen stomach, she softly sighs,
And remarks that the constant misuse of powerful words,
As a means of quick gratification, has crushed
Her beautiful family into an empty echo of an abstract cave.

O.K. I apologize. Now I understand the price. Shall I speak anymore?
I can't stop. Worthless phrases continue to spill out of my mouth.
Should I cut out my tongue? Life is collapsing inside this brain.
Dust on mud with rust and blood, my thoughts are wreckage,
Wounded animals, crawling in pain,
Dying in the grass along a stretch of directionless road.

Damon Moss

The Native American

Once we stood proud upon the face of our land.
Spirit unbroken even the wild mustang
yielding to our command.

Gazing into the heavens, great spirit our Father.
Elements of survival, passed down through generations
of wisdom.

The mighty buffalo, our friend, provided food,
clothing, shelter to all.
Taking only what we needed, waste wasn't known.
We offended no man, but befriended many.
The white man came, a different word, a new way.

Driven from our lands, battles fought,
History recorded glory, honor, and fame.
Blood spilled, hearts broken, are they different today?
Still they push and shove.
We are confined in a world that once we owned.

Irma J. Martin

Woodstock!

The rains came in torrents as twenty-five years before...
splashing colorless beads that mingled with the Earth
creating mud slides, mud people, and pacifism in frolic
as instrumentation beamed its instilling message
on those who braved the crowds and inconveniences
but would be numbered as the hallowed who gathered
to reactivate WOODSTOCK in their souls...and
for the world to see...sporting tee shirts of many faces
in the rain forest temperatures of August in upper state New York
...an integration of ages, minds and addictions of all kinds...
hundreds of thousands in harmony with signs that said "Music/Peace"
And the love children, flower children, hippies were gone...replaced
by themselves and their offspring in times different—yet same—
as the radical summer of '69 when the spirit of free love prevailed
in a time of uncertainty that anyone would survive to flock
to Woodstock '94!...But those who made it as Baby Boomers
in numbers far fewer than Generation X were thankful for survival
as Santana and Cocker...Crosby, Stills and Nash must have been...
...But the music that spoke in everlasting colors of the rainbow
targeted Youth in selective promise of yet another WOODSTOCK
Reunion.

Bianca Mihalik

For Two Dear Friends

May 6, 1930 at the First English Lutheran Church Forest and Violet
spoke their wedding vows.
Ever since it has been Mr. and Mrs. Lotridge and I'm sure everyone
here knows this anyhow.
After 64 years of married life these two still have a lot of zip,
You will see them on about every senior citizen trip.
Violet was a homemaker all of her life while Forest worked for a
streetcar line for a time.
But working as a meat cutter for Werners Market was his real line.
They have lived at 711 W. Auglaize for as long as I can recall
and to walk by there was always a treat,
They always keep their home looking so very neat.
Sometimes you can see them walking to church on Sunday,
Especially if the weather is nice that day.
We want to say congratulations to them and wish them the very best,
Also to let them know we hope they have many more years together left.

Eldon L. Stolzenburg

The Choice Of A Lifetime

Open your eyes and close the door,
Spread your wings, it's time to soar,
Hide your emotions and try to peak,
The search for reality is what you seek,
The questions are there for you to ask,
But the answers are hidden behind a mask,
The future will come in due time,
As yesterday falls further behind,
Tough times will put you in misery,
Making the good ones hard to see,
Happiness does not come for nothing,
You're going to pay the price for something,
Sitting all alone, you think you're a "dead duck,"
Be patient because there's time for good luck,
To get things done you have to try hard,
Because every deck has a wild card,
The earth is going to turn and spin,
The only choice is to go for the win,
There is only one way that you can lose,
Being undecided and deciding not to choose.

Dennis J. Johnson Jr.

Beastly Angel

Twilight tickled away the night,
spreading sunlight across the land.
A Beastly Angel descended.

Its very presence disrupted the earth. It began
by ripping up the dirt. On a path of blatant
destruction, killing first plants, bugs then rodents.

Wanting to see it. To stop its calamity,
before it worked its way to humanity,
But it escaped my futile attempts, by skidding far from me.

It submerged itself into the sea. There this beastly Angel
caused debris, to annihilated creatures of the deep.

Floating out of the water, it sat high upon the sky.
Shooting weapons of all kings, killing people rapidly,

This beastly Angel turned to me, smiling most beautifully.
It sprayed chemicals from a cloud.
That stinking cloud stretched for miles.

Then it came to me! I recognized its face!
Now I pray it's not too late.
For this Beastly Angel you see
has our face. It is We!

June N. Engles

Seasons

Just before winter softly closes her eyes, she nudges her cousin spring and tells him it's time to wake up. As he rises sleepily, blinks his eyes, thus causing color to be expanded to trees and flowers. He calls his nephews robin and blue jay and tells them get in touch with their friends so they can all have a get together. It didn't take long. The next day, spring, his nephews, robin and blue jay and all their relatives and friends threw a big bash and it could be heard and seen all around. Robin and blue jay formed a choir. The others painted the canvas with brightness and colors. They decided everyone was having such a good time they would continue with this until spring's brother, summer gets in town and then he can take over. He's good at getting everyone motivated into activities. He keeps things going until his uncle, fall comes to town. He usually comes the same time each year, thus bringing all fun a cool down. Fall then breathes and cools us all off - he paints too, painting the canvas with warm neutral colors. He tells his friends to shed their leaves and get ready to take a nap, because his friend winter will be back soon.

Delores Sikes

First Garden

Grass is gone - dirt is turned - seeds in hand

April 14 - ready
  Squash - make 3 hills
  Tomato - celebrity - must be a star
  Cucumber - bush - President?

April 21 - Oh my! Life - only tears
  There are no words

Weed it - feed it
  Loosen the soil - roots go deep

May 24 - Grilled chicken
    Mashed potatoes
    Stewed squash
Thank you - sweet Jesus

Diane B. Dull

What Was Dad Thinking?

Clad in overalls and blue shirt
Standing in the barn one foot propped on a board
Forearms on the sill and gazing out the window
I can remember wondering, what was he thinking?

Sunday afternoons there was no work
Spent listening to news reports on the couch one arm out stretched
As I lay down beside him his arm became my pillow
I can remember wondering, what was he thinking?

Sitting on a bar stool at the local tavern
Drinking liquor and seven with only half a jigger
I took up the stool beside him as he was visiting with our reverend
I can remember wondering, what was he thinking?

Lying on the couch naked as a jay bird
Years of lying on his back made him a muscleless figure
I took up wash cloth and shave cream and cleaned all of his body
I can remember wondering, what was he thinking?

Lying in his casket his soul looking down upon us
A pin could be heard in the silence, the ceremony was gorgeous
As I asked our Lord, "why did he have to leave us?"
I can remember wondering, what was he thinking?

Donna D. Davison

Footprints

Hard, worn face of a man at the window
staring in at me. Window oiled
and sprinkled with dust of the past.
Uneven panes of glass
with soft cloud patterns traced
along his moist breath; fog turning
the translucent face into a misty gray.
I'll stare at him until the years
melt away and reality becomes clear.
The clock stops and crickets in the loft
won't chirp as he beckons me with his eyes.
Piercing eyes, soft with emotion.
Yet I know he'll vanish if I get too close,
leaving only footprints in the grass.

Jan F. Herold

Untitled

if I could, i would make the world
stop spinning;
i would suspend time.
i would silence humankind for just one day,
to mourn your passing.
no wind, no movement, no sound.
just an awesome, horrific silence.
instead I shed my tears quietly, and
silence the world within myself and
scream into the void, NO!!
  No!
    No......

Denise Duncan

Untitled

The gleam in her eye
The glitter in her smile
The way she laughs, with the sly little grin
The hurried little run when Daddy gets home
The many times she says Momma when in need
The glow of joy in completing a new feat
The excitement on her face when big sister strolls by
The sleepy little angel when bedtime is near
Elizabeth

Amy Schwarz

Double Meaning

When I first saw you it was raining, and I was lonely. A constant stream of water dripped from my head and hair onto my face, its icy fingers piercing my skin and blurring my vision. When I saw you, the space where you stood brightened, and it stopped raining, like a beam cascading down from heaven. You took me under your light and sheltered me from the bitterness and rain. We skipped along, hand in hand, oblivious to any pain or suffering of anyone. All we saw was each other. We continued to be happy, until you jumped in a puddle and splashed me. The cold water hit my face like a slap, and I let go of you to put a hand to my stinging face. I felt you slipping away, but I was too aware of my own pain to reach out to you. That was the last time I saw you. It started to rain again, and I was lonely. The rain was pouring down now, intense and enduring. In the midst of all the disarray, I looked to the sky and saw a small gleam of light, a rainbow.

Christina Marie Hager

Tribute To Mother

When I look in your eyes, I see the
strength of the earth
And when you smile, the meaning of
life is being continually revealed to me.
I always remember the purpose of my
journey whenever you hold my hand;
And your kindness is like a rock in shifting sand.
Your unwavering love saw me through
my darkest days and most frightening nights;
Against these demons you taught me how to fight.
Being there for me was all I needed to know.
And the joy I feel in knowing you,
can only equal the pain I sometimes feel
in knowing you may one day have to go.
There has to be a heaven, even if I did
not believe in one before;
And a part of me you'll take with you when
you enter through its open door.

John Morgan

I Cannot Survive

I am a dead valley nestled between barren hills
Stripped of their timber and eroded of soil.
I am a dark thundercloud filled with acid rain
Rolling across the great dusty prairie
Blowing away the top soil and flooding the plain.
I am a conifer forest trying to survive
A thousand chain saws and deadly rain.
I am the wasted river winding through the tortured land
Carrying tons of pollutants and a few sick fish.
I am the great lake lying turbid in the hazy sun
Dying slowly surely for a cesspool I have become.
I am the mighty ocean, Mother and Father of all,
But mercury and lead have rendered me sterile.
I am the environment, but I cannot survive
The thoughtless greedy hand of senseless man.

Edward Hartman

Lord Take Thee

Oh LORD:

TAKE my hand and lead me in the right direction
TAKE my feet and walk beside me through troubled times
TAKE my mind and fill it with happy thoughts
TAKE my mouth so good and kind words will be said
TAKE my ears so I might hear only the good in the world
TAKE my eyes so I might see the beauty you have provided
TAKE my lips that I may always turn frowns into smiles
TAKE my heart and fill it with love so I might spread joy
TAKE my body, and put these ingredients inside,
that my light might shine on someone less fortunate.

Betty Whitehead

The Beginning

Darkness, haze, matter spinning
Substance in an aimless churning
Chaos rules; the world beginning

Shapes appear, the movement slowing
Shafts of light flicker through the curling
Patterns sensed are growing, growing

Shades of gray now appearing
Haze and mist soon departing
Particles attracted, now expanding

Forming shapes start circling, circling
A scheme in sensed, slowly flowing
There's rhythm to the universe unfolding

Darkness rescinding, grays ascending
Now color born as light increasing
Planets and stars, their forms are shape

Motion has slowed, the universe awaiting
A creature unique, man soon appearing
Will he be worthy of this wondrous creating

Jerry Martin

Yonder

Big Country sky, deep blue and clear,
Sunshine that's endless 'most all the year,
Acres of cactus filled prairies to wander,
And miles of the unknown out yonder.

Heavens so dark with the stars hangin' down,
Seems like they're near touchin' the ground,
All natures beauty to soak up and ponder
'Bout the mysterious secrets out yonder.

Storm clouds so huge like mountains piled high,
Suspended in space between earth and sky,
Barbs of hot lightnin' and long rollin' thunder,
Billow from dark caverns out yonder.

Days spent roamin' hot hills and plains,
Evenings refreshed by the cool, gentle rains,
After mile upon mile, a rest and to wonder,
Is there an end to the depths out yonder?

Harry W. Bowers

The Tides Of Sicily

The sun shines down in beams of crystal glory,
Surrounding you in loving warmth as a mother's sweet caress.
In the early morning mist, all that is green
Has been kissed by lips of dew.
The Island awakes in mighty splendor.
Gentle ocean breezes sweep away smoky nocturnal clouds,
Leaving the sky naked in its pale blue skin.
The first cock crows into the new day's promise,
Initiating the faint stirs of life.

Enveloped by the vast sea, your land has been touched
By a potpourri of ancient cultures,
Leaving behind remains of their day.
Battle scars from the past serve as silent reminders of your
History, bequeathing skeletal remains of old abandoned
Houses and sanctuaries.

Strong hands work your soil gently, as a sculptor's hands
Create a masterpiece.
Through this union is created the fruits of plenty.
Sicily, the pillar of past and present.
May your land of wildflowers continue to grow.

Anza Lo Presti Myers

Autumn Dancers

Little Autumn dancers, dancing in the wind.
Swirling from the air above them to the ground again.
They scuttle low against the grass and fly above the trees.
Dancing freely in the wind, dancing as they please.
They're dressed in brown and yellow suits,
They're dressed for a fall day.
They catch a gust of wind, and then
They're off to play.
They play until a winter day and
Then it's time to go.
Time to leave till once again the
Autumn wind does blow.
Then our little dancers will
Put on another show.

Jessica Robinson

Dear Teacher

Oh dear teacher,
take my child by the hand.
See in him the future, see him as only I can.
He has dreams and aspirations
I never dared to dream.
He views the world with celebration,
and holds it with great esteem.
Show him that he has the power
to choose to do what is right.
He is my delicate flower,
teach him with love, not might.
Help him to see life's wonders,
teach him all that you know.
Give him new things to ponder,
help this child to grow.
Teach him with love and understanding.
Give him your soul if you can,
for this is the future
you're handling.
Please lead my child by the hand.

Colleen E. Hudson

In The Tub

As we were lying together in the bath tub
talking by candlelight
Her back against my chest
the water was warm and calm
scented of lilac, baptizing our union
Soft beads of sweat on my face and hers
she looks up at me and says
"temptation is a very powerful thing"

Our sex is beautiful
we are beautiful together
Her movement has disturbed the calm waters
it beats upon us like tiny waves on a shore
I feel her hair
damp and cool against my skin
I kiss her forehead and wrap my arms around her
and hold her closely
Her body, warmed by the water
her body becomes one with mine.

Bryan Schroat

People

People are like the flakes of snow. Each and everyone is different.
Some young, some old, some good, some bad. Yet they are all the
same. They're all flowers in God's garden. Some are cultivated
and grow into pretty bouquets. While others wither and die
and have to be weeded out so others may grow strong.
Yet they all have one thing in common. They all have souls.

James G. Jones

The Power Of Poetry

I had departed long ago, you chanced upon a poem of mine,
Tears are running down your cheeks as you read it line by line.

The story of the poem is a mirror image of your own,
You thought you had closed it inside you,
By none would it be ever known.

I had departed long ago, a poem falls into your hands,
This one will give your tired soul
New freshness and new cheerfulness.

It is the story of two lovers:
Life had drawn the two apart,
Yet, at the end their love triumphed
Because they were innocent at heart.

Reading it your lips are smiling,
Your face is beaming, no longer stern,
At this moment I shall be with you
From non-being I shall return.

The spirit that has moved me prompted and inspired me
Will link our two souls together by the power of poetry.

George G. Strem

Being Present

She took my hands and looked into my eyes and said,
"Tell me what's in your heart."
I couldn't answer so she repeated, gently,
"Tell me what's in your heart."

Tears came as I peered inside.
There they were: fears, dreams, hopes, wishes.
She listened, and after each response, said,
"Tell me what's in your heart."

Then it was my turn.
I took her hands and looked directly into her eyes and said,
"Tell me what's in your heart."
And she did.
I heard and felt it all.
No judging, no agenda.

For a few minutes, we were two souls connected.
No space or time.
No labels or separation.
We experienced Being Present.

Etta Jean Smith

Social

Swaying in the breeze is the silvery bough of
Temptation
Calling in its sly silvery tone of
Tintinnabulation
What does it call to me, what does it say?
It wills me to go places far away
From my comfortable home.
Quiet, dead stillness ushers in night
And the social fireflies begin to
Take flight.
Fly, fly away, I say, into the
Night
Only slightly hoping their flight will
Fly right.
Light fades away and shadows begin
I am all but silenced by the deafening
Din
As butterflies and starlets emerge from cocoons
While non-social butterflies stay
in their rooms.

Candee Lindsay

An Open Letter To God The Father In Heaven

Dear God,
Thank you for this gift of life, which you have leased to me
Thank you for giving me wonderful parents,
Who allowed me to be in this complex world today.

I'm scared to even think of the fact that my parents had their choice
To snap my fragile life right from the start,
But instead, they chose to accept me as a precious gift from you.

How wonderful this world could be
If all parents were responsible enough
To accept every gift of life, fruit of their mutual love for one another
Rather than fear of their inability to support us, their kids?

Why Lord, can't they trust you enough
That if you could take care of every sparrow
And clothe every fragile flower in the field
You can also give them the wisdom and courage
To feed every child that they bring forth into this world?

Help us Father, we need you!
Stop them Father, before they abort every child they consider a burden!

You're a lucky child to be born into this world.

Aquino Tubola Trasga

Thanksgiving 1992

Thank you Lord for your mercy and grace
That allows me to still live at the old homeplace.
About sixty-five years I've been here today
Thank you Dear Lord, for letting me stay.

Some of the road has been rocky and rough,
But character is built on that kind of stuff.
New hope I see in each shining face
When we meet every time at the old homeplace.

Thanks for those who came long ago
And built cabins to hold in love and keep out snow;
They have left us a heritage in time and space,
That we still may all meet at the old homeplace.

Thanks Dear Lord, for those here today
Lead and guide us on our way.
May our thanks to You and our love interlace
Today as we meet at the old homeplace.

And when our work here on earth is done,
As we pass beyond the setting sun,
When that last venture we embrace,
May we all meet together in that new Homeplace.

Eugenia L. Elliott

Snow

I love the fresh, white and clean snow-
That fell and deceived my world today.
Shadows prostrated on the snow-
Conjure up images I do not know!
Here on my little niche of world below.
The obstructed snow covered trees, bushes, buildings and signs.
All appear to be a figment of my mind.
I have the privilege to look at my surroundings with a fresh new eye.
I shall not pry the illusion away.
The familiar is hidden under the fresh, white and clean snow:
This I know!
This is my time and excuse to wait
And to hibernate.
I can feel free to dream
And snuggle in my nest and rest.
If I please!
And let nature have her fun to tease.

Joanne J. Saunders

The Rose Still Blooms

She was like a Rose,
That green were all could see,

She sheltered us beside her bosom wall,
for us to spread our branches straight and tall,

One day a bream of light shone through,
A crevice that had opened wide —

The rose bent gently toward its warmth,
then passed beyond to the other side.

Now, we deeply feel its loss —
Be comforted — the rose blooms there,

Its beauty even greater now,
Natured by God's loving care.

Carolyn Wilkes

Alex

Right from the beginning he seemed so alert that people remarked that he must be a very old soul who had been here before. He arrived at a time when his innocent wisdom was really needed.

When things got too serious for those close to him, he always seemed to sense in his own gentle way the right thing to say or do to lighten the mood.

By the time he was three years old, he was already a hit with Grandpa and his friends—strolling with them at their pace, hands in his pockets and absorbing their talk about cars. They referred to him as "the little old man."

It seems like only yesterday we left him on his first day of kindergarten with tears running down his little cheeks as he reached out with both arms pleading with us not to leave him.

Now he strides confidently into school with his backpack slung over his right shoulder, his thumb hooked around the strap, as he looks around for his friends. He waves once briefly and is gone.

He is so grown up now—not wanting to be called by terms of endearment—brushing them off as little boy names. After all, he has turned six years old and is in the first grade.

Eleanor Foland

"The Daughter Of My Dreams"

Daughter, there's something I want you to know
That I am so proud of you and do love you so
For you see, you are the daughter of my dreams
And it was only yesterday that it seems
I lay my hand down on my pillow at night
I dreamed that dream, ah! Oh! What a beautiful sight
I was walking down busy Chillocothe street
And by my side a little black-hair girl, so neat
She so beautiful, perfect in every way
And I could feel my pride as I walked with her that day
When I awoke I began at once, to make plans
For the day I would hold you in my hands
For you see God had already planned the seed
And how I thank Him, for that wonderful deed
That would bring me, you, my beautiful dark-eyed child
Such a wonderful child, though sometimes quite wild
You are all grown up now, quite a success
A wife, a mother, and a teacher no less
You are certainly a wonderful dream come true
I want you to know, I love you and I am so proud of you.

Janet Van Bibber

My Fullest Potential And Then Some

I awoke this morning with a persistent idea
That kept running amok through my brain.
As I lay there I wondered where time had gone
While I governed the U.S. terrain.

In the blink of an eye my grandson appeared.
"You play with me today," he commanded.
He led and I followed. He won and I lost.
"And you were the President?" he demanded.

His comical question sent me back to my thoughts;
While I wandered the house, all alone.
My wife was away on a charitable cause; and
My family, well me- they had outgrown.

I thought of my critics who said this and that.
Then I dwelled on my own achievements cache.
Suddenly, an echo loomed out of the past.
My childhood ambition came to mind in a flash.

Instantly I knew, I had ways to go and some
Mountains to climb. I'll find a low one.
For success can be lonely at the end of the goal.
The fun is in the doing and not when it's done.

Ethna M. Burns

Ask Not When The End Time Shall Come

Somewhere not far away, but yet very close, there is one
that knows when the earth shall end.
He knows the name of everyone that will parish at the first
and everyone that shall survive longer than that by a small time.
Yet with all this that he knows, he has not tongue that we
may hear, at least for now.
You know his name but not his face, for he is Christ the son
of God!
Seek him out for guidance and understanding of life and seek
him not for the date of the end time!
Everyone who has lived and is yet to live have and shall
encounter him, but shall not know him unless he is let to be known.
Then on the day when all who know him and all that do not hear
his mighty tongue, then shall be the date that the end time
shall come!

Coty Lynn Whitlow

Rendezvous

Those men that dared to seek out the hidden places, that are treasure
that was hidden from the faint of heart.
They went out to explore the great AMERICAN DESERT.
There they found mountains that rose to the sky, rivers that watered
the land valleys that were places of beauty.
Large prairies of grass that went on for miles, trees that reached for
sky, animals that covered the ground like rain.
Instead of a desert they found a land just waiting for people
Beauty undreamed of, peace that touched the soul'

Death was all around them, danger was everywhere.
They loved the land and enjoyed the challenge of living.
They learned from the land, a new kind of life.
They had there animals and there guns, it was a lonely but excitement
of keeping alive was a daring challenge.
They enjoyed life with others of there kind, they made up that great
AMERICAN heritage called RENDEZVOUS.
Today others in memory of the past, have captures the joy of the
RENDEZVOUS.
And band together to live the simple life that is part of their heritage.
And join others in the joy that is RENDEZVOUS.

Harold Olsen

The Bond

Your knitted brow betrays the worry in your bosom
That long-ache and suffering known only to those who love,
Truly love someone so deeply that emotion takes
Physical form in your body.
I see that you know there are no strings here.
Even if there were, no tether could ever,
Ever hold us here.
So what is it that does? Can you hear, feel, smell it?

Yet, we each know
Beyond knowing
It is there.
Yes, just as we are here.
It is like a sedative that
We know is there, not by feeling its power,
But rather the pain that is no longer.

Joseph McCauley

No Matter What

No matter what situations or problems
That may come by
Though you may feel as if your laughter
Has turned into a sigh
And in your mind you question or wonder
Why?
Always remember that the Lord is on your side.

No matter what worries or frustrations
That may come your way
Trust in the Lord to be your guide
In whatever you do or say
Don't let go and fall into
Lust, pleasure, and pride
Always remember that the Lord is on your side.

Akilah Freeny

Summer's End

It starts with hope, or even a dream
That might be.
I hear a child cry in the breeze.
And I lie back and think of when life was new.
The games I played.
The people I knew.
The notes I passed in school.
The first time I kissed and held her hand.
Even the first job I had.

Now dawn is fast approaching.
I can feel the chill in the air.
And my fall years are coming, I feel them drawing near.
My dreams have yet to be answered, no hope of that changing.
But, in my fall I'll have it all with the love of a few friends and family.

Gary Lee Hayworth

Just Drifting

I picked up a piece of drift-wood,
that was between my feet.
Was it from a local boat?,
or from a distant fleet?
If this piece of wood could give it's message-
I wished that could be so.
It might have told of its long journey-
from down where the cocoa-nuts grow.
How long it had been a-drift,
riding on the waves.
It might have come from an ancient pirate ship,
or a galley that had been transporting slaves.
I left the drift-wood there upon the sand.
I'll never know its story,
and if it came from a distant land.

George Long

Windmill Memory

It may have been the tube in my arm,
that reminded me of the five in yours,
and that June day, and the windmill cookies.

I relished their spice flavor,
my new hat and the sun.
You relished simply, your cookie
chewing mouth,
- the only orifice vacant -
of plastic, gauze, and adhesive tape.

Or, perhaps it was the cartoon lipsticked woman.
Her offerings of magazines from
a waiting room coffee table - empty -
Evoked a memory of you
searching the kitchen freezer, for battle clothes.
"The Civil War begins at dawn," you
commanded in a drug-strong voice.

But, I think it was the doctor,
starch-stiffened and serious, pen
poised and interviewing: "Age of father?"
"Deceased," I said.

Julie A. Rapose

The Ones Who Pay

I wonder what has happened to
That self-reliant point of view
That gives each traveler the strength
To walk his road of life full length.

Has it been lost as parents give
All things, that children better live
Without requiring that they earn
A single priv'lege in return?

And in the process, have we taught
There's not a thing that must be bought,
For simply wanting pays the price
And there's no need for sacrifice?

So then we hear the whining voice
That blames another for the choice
That ought to carry an expense
But seeks to sidestep consequence.

And then at last, with no one left,
We engineer our final theft.
Our government must save our day.
But really, we're the ones who pay.

Don F. Johnson

Dreams Come True

I look out my window and what do I see
The beautiful St. Lawrence flowing to the sea
This was the dream many years ago for you and me
That one day we might live here when we retire
And then go south when we needed a fire.
As we lounge in the yard under the maple tree
The birch and the pine we also see.
We watch the fishing boats and the lakers go
Wondering what they carry as cargo
From what foreign port they came and where they'll go.
We hear many kinds of birds as they sing and flit to and fro,
The robins, the wren and then others we see.
This year a pair of scarlet tangers out in a tree.
We watch for the cedar waxwing to appear
As he always comes by every year.
There is so much beauty around us to see
Help us Dear God always to remember and thankful be.

Elizabeth Peters

Imagine

Sometimes I imagine
that the garden is huge and I am very small.
What would it be like in that giant paradise
where the whole world is fragrant and green?

Sometimes I imagine that the hillside,
soft and golden extends as far
as the eye can see..
and I could run through the fields endlessly.

Sometimes I imagine
that the stars in the sky
are really tiny cutout holes
in a black velvet cloak.
What light so bright could be shining
so far away on the other side?

Sometimes I wish
that I never had to sleep..
What would it be like
to have all the hours -
day and night -
to explore, imagine, and dream?

Dana Tanner Kunze

"Friends"

Friends are special people, who understand and know
That we have great potential, and want to help us grow.
A friend will always listen to what we have to say,
Then set a good example by showing us the way.
A friend is always waiting to lend a helping hand,
Is quick to see our special needs and help us understand.
A friend is one who's willing to help in every way;
And often has the sweetest smile, to brighten up our day.
So dear friends we love you, we want you all to know...
"You'll be forever in our hearts, no matter where we go."

Barbara Z. Williams

The Passage Of Time

How precious is the time
that we spend on this land.
Each moment of each day
disappearing ... slipping away.
With a blink of an eye,
a decade passes us by.
As we journey through the memories of our past
clutching, hoping they will forever last.
We must take seriously
each moment of each day,
and in a new and vivid way.
For in the morning it shall come to pass,
that today simply did not last.

Diana Gerlick

Nature (World Of Wonder)

There is a crystal blue stream
That winds around little fairy homes, trees in the woods
And if you sit and dangle your feet and wait
Cool breezes, deer and squirrels and little birds
Will come and take you to a dream world of wonder
Where flowers and sunshine, fairies and birds
Hope and happiness, deer and bunnies talk

This magic place wraps you with warmth and comfort
And makes you welcome and special
It's called nature

Cornelia Smith

Did You See

Did you see the mighty river
that you passed a few miles back
Did you see the sprawling valley far below
Did you see the distant mountain
in the twilight turning black
Did you see the sun begin to lose its glow

Did you see the eagle soaring
in the wind that soon will die
Did you see the beaver glide across the lake
Did you see the fleeting nighthawk
as it streaked across the sky
Did you see the moon's first light that it would make

Did you see me in your deepest thoughts,
and in your dreams at night
Did you see a vision vanish in the air
Did you see a dreadful wrong in life,
and try to make it right
Did you see a child, and make it know you care

Did you see these things in the dark of night
Did you see these things, - but not with sight

Charley Jones

Morning After

Turning my head unconsciously, a faint scent rocks me
That's of you! The heart gulps and the blood reels.
Is it in a fingernail, or on my cheek, or in my mind?
(Dear muse, my pen has wakened to a scream of sensibility!)
I knew I'd plumb the void, this solar plexus weightlessness,
This drifting through distraction's daze. A haze
Of Lithuanian blue cools down your forehead's blazing rays
And laughs at my bemused astonishment.
Our feet patrol the sidewalk from St. James; our fingers
Touch, entwine - so soon such seas between,
Sans scent, sans swans, sans you, sans everything!
Sweet Lady of the Wayside, guide our feet...

The toast twitches teasingly, tumbling to the smiling floor -
C'est bon voyage encore, mon appétit!

James A. Donaldson

Inside My Heart

Inside my heart a flower blooms.
The beginning of hope. A soul flees the ruins.
Old petals and leaves fall to the ground.
Blossoms begin to open. New seeds are found.

Waters of life drop on each radiant leaf.
The Son shines down giving rise to belief.
Life restored through the essence of love,
brought to fruition by the One from above.

The wonder is not lost on the waters and seas.
Praises of His grace are exclaimed by the trees.
The mountains leap to the heavens, acknowledging Him,
and the grass sways in laughter giving reply to the wind.

In a moment, in a twinkling He changes the heart.
The necessary transformation of the malevolent part.
His love permeates every essence of my being,
producing the seed to the flower foreseeing.

The corruption that surrounds the life within,
shrivels up in the light and glory of Him.
The hope of the flower bestowed upon the seed
originates from His fragrance to the human need.

Cheryl A. Lavender

Ra

Through the endless fires of eternal night
The ancient god of Egypt has spoken
White fire black night
The winds of change have blown in Egypt
Ivory dust and endless wind the Nile
flows through the sands of time
White fire black night
The winds of change have blown in Egypt

Ebony fire upon the endless sands of Luxor
No ancient gods are dead
The ancient god of Egypt has spoken
O Ra, your time is now as well as long ago
From the ancient fires of night eternity has spoken
Through the tongue of a god
Alabaster breath upon the Nile
No season is over forever
White fire black night
The winds of change have blown in Egypt
And will forever in the eye of a god

Antoinette Voget

Seven Days

God made His world in seven days, the earth, the sky, the seas
The animals, the flowers, the rivers and the trees
He made the sun to light the day, the moon to grace the night
And then He looked upon his work and saw that it was right.

Still, there was something missing and so needed in his plan
Someone to love and share these things, so God created man
In his own image we were made and, fearful lest we stray,
He gave us rules to live by and His son to show the way.

How sad that gifts in love bestowed to fill our every need
Should be abused by humans through destruction, war and greed
Will the beauty He created disappear like drifting sand
Or will we make it flourish with the power we command

Will deeds of mortal man endure, be worthy in His sight
Can He still look upon His world and know that it is right
God's work, complete in seven days, has stood the test of time
Should we, with all our days not ask, what have I done with mine?

Charlotte B. Thomas

Small Pleasures

Small pleasures are like
the bricks with which a strong wall is built!

They are the units which lay the foundation of delights!
It's a pleasure to watch the house plants grow
even if they only have leaves, no flowers!

I have begonia and gardenia plants growing side by side, one pink
the other white, both equally lovely!

Believe it or not a sparrow often stops by
and sits on the window sill.
It is my good friend, and starts to sing!
Do you know a sparrow can be such a song-bird?

I believe only male sparrows
can sing - they sing to serenade
their mates; it's quite a romantic scene.
For all these pleasures, no matter
how small, the perpetual giver
is God! It is He who understands the meaning
of this and teaches man the true meaning of SMALL PLEASURES

Oh, dear small pleasures, I love you all!
Let's pull together and have a ball!

Harry Wang

Ode To Nature

I am drowning in my sea of turbulent emotions,
the beauty of nature my only salvation;
the freshness of the air reviving my peace.
Oh, to have the sweetness of yonder blossom
or the wings of swift dragonfly!
To have a single moment so rare,
to feel the sensation of soaring over the negative.
The creek babbling gently rocks my soul to sleep,
releasing my spiritual tension.
I dream of wondrous flight,
carrying away the thunder of the stormy world.
Nature, infinitely powerful and healing,
gives the strength to surpass the harshest obstacles
yet is sadly often ignored.
The subtle power rests in the rustling wind,
which brings scent of forthcoming seasons
while restoring my shattered peace.

Jennifer Nakatsuka

Peace

The sun shines bright with its radiant light.
The birds sing their song as the day grows long.
The trees move and bend in time with the wind
And all is peaceful.

The grass grows green to complete the scene.
The clouds are fluffy white floating with great height.
Rainbows appear making happiness near.
And all is peaceful.

The day comes to an end, the sun descends.
The moon softly glows, the starlight shows.
A midnight sky, the crickets' cry.
And all is peaceful.

The morning rays showing bright new days.
A gentle breeze that moves the trees.
You sit and stare, you whisper a prayer.
And all is peaceful.

Andrea Smith

Steel Spirit

The cold heartless steel is frightful yet enchanting,
The blade of my sword seems to have a life of its own,
Its razor edge is animated to serve its master,
Apart we are two but together we become one,
It's not just a man before you wielding steel,
This Katana is a part of me and I am a part of it,
My spirit is the soul of this ancient blade,
Because like this shimmering blade I am just a piece of steel,
Long ago how poetic the sound of sword play,
Two men, two blades.... One walks away,
Sing with me the song of steel, and dance with me the dance of death,
I am steel forged in the fires of life's tests and temptations,
Hammered down to hardness by failures and despair,
Cooled down in the soothing waters of old age,
Then sharpened by the stone of wisdom,
I will be polished and shine with life's memories and
accomplishments; then when I have at last become like the refined
razor edge of this Katana,
At last I will know truth,
At last I will have become a man...

John D. Allen III "The Dragon"

And Indian Gives Thanks

Thank you Great White Father for
the blessings you have bestowed on us.
For the great wide space you have reserved
for our use where nothing grows on bald mountains.
For the once - wet washes now naked and parched,
the buffalo who are no more, the songbirds who have grown silent,
the deer who fled for food, the fish who drowned in dry air,
the burned-out brush to shade our shacks,
the endless days of nothing to do but sit and watch
a foreign world fly by on whirling wheels.
Once proud and fearless leaders of men,
we are humble and eternally grateful for these gifts.
By your infinite example you have shown us the waste
of war - like ways. Our pain of conquest now dimmed but
damned.
Broken promises almost forgotten. Our needs are few.
You are generous, you are good.

Ida T. Morris

No One Hears The Cries

Who saw the bruising or tears in their eyes,
the blood stained coats or heard their cries?

A small body beaten each day,
or molested by a family member who will have his or her way.

Why is it the public can't see or won't tell,
did you really think again that he or she fell?

Who can they run to, talk with or confide in?
About all they can do, is look for a place to hide in.

It is no longer unheard of, but rather common place,
just ask any social worker and she'll know of a case.

These children cry out, but no one hears,
no one to hold them or calm their fears.

A kinder gentler nation our president's aim,
but what does this mean to the children in pain?

Only when we hear another child died,
will we remember that we did indeed hear the cries but we just
stood by.

Arden K. Carpenter

The Ring

I wear in my finger a jade green ring
That you put there one day,
Whenever I see it my heart will sing
Joyful, that friendship will stay.

The jade green ring, that you gave me my friend,
makes my heart grow happy and light,
I like to sing to the ring on my hand
and the tune of love is bright.

The jade green ring gives me courage for now
The strength to forget the past,
And faith in this world, for always somehow
Friendship and love will last.

Hedy Richfield

Lost Memories

Lost are the memories we once had.
The memories of us together.
The memories that will combine.
The memories that were yours and not mine.
Lost are the memories I want to keep.
Lost are the memories I wish to seek.
Lost are the memories you take to heart.
Lost are the memories that led us to a new start.

Jermaine C. Bailey

Arms Of War

Dirt impregnated, cracked and dry,
The calloused hand of a Midwest farmer
Wipes a tear from his facial furrows,
So proud this man who cannot cry.

Whose babe has he who knows not mom?
Whose tiny hands have only once touched
Its mother's face before she answered
To the cry to end Iraq's Saddam.

Once soft, her hands are dry and sore.
With pink nails her hands are clinched to fight.
With grips that once held her child tight,
They hold now... the arms of war.

Calvin E. Hubbard

Those Kansas City Chiefs

Triumphant as champs, from whence they came,
The Dallas Texans, ultra - ferocious and untamed
They drifted into K. C. with a mission in sight,
Creating tremors and havoc, flexing their might

And little did this midwestern city know
This team would win the fourth super bowl
Hysteric hopes rung high, in a grotto of red
"Was this the year?" the fanatic fans all said.

Ageless Joe Montana was leading the pack
Could the Chiefs bring that 'ole glory back?
Constant agony of defeats left a bitter taste
Would all this razzle - dazzle, fizzle into waste?

For games were won and lost on the field
But what took so long for the Chiefs to rebuild?
And those griddon Gods, could they not see?
The beloved Chiefs had an invitation with destiny

Then Arrowhead Stadium would thunder galore
Would it be another twenty-five years... or more?
But the football experts, with their negative beliefs,
How could they doubt those Kansas City Chiefs?

Grover J. Garrett Jr.

The Little Glass Case On Blue

He asked if I remember the day when first we met
The day he said these words: "you are a beautiful girl."
Yes, I wore blue velvet and I'll never forget -
Yes, his lovely wife's aware he thinks of me.

She says he ne'er forgets and often speaks of me
That once he had an argument, lasting far in the night
With some man who claimed his girl a beautiful girl -
So he argued for me, the most beautiful in the world.

It's gallant for a man to take a stand for a lady
But, you see, this lady's just a girl in his dreams.
I think he placed her high in a little glass case on blue
Just for them to look at and to show to a few.

I don't think that I have really turned to stone
For I am like white marble that is warmed by the sun.
I know that I am only an icon for that one -
That he has given it my name and appearance, too
Like a marble statue, or some other treasure -
What difference is it whether it be me or you?
If I should die tomorrow he can keep the vision
Where he placed it high in the little glass case on blue.

Frances Carnahan Ebaugh

Happiness

There once was a flower who sat hour after hour watching the days go by.
It would talk to the sky to ask the sky why she felt like she was going to cry.
The sky was so smart that he said from his heart to use one of his clouds as a pillow.
Because he knew the true reason why she was so sad was because she was under the willow.
The willow would weep day in and day out making everyone around him feel sad.
But the sky knew if the flower would dream a small dream that it would make her feel glad.

Jackie Biggers

Twilight Years

I cry for my youth
the days of everything being possible.
Frightened as my life is coming to an end.
Years passed so quickly
seemingly faster these days.
Time has become an enemy-no longer a friend.
I love living
worlds left to visit-vastly more to see.
I need countless years yet in which to be.
I'm terrified of dying
my sun is setting and I am afraid.
Joyous life-you are leaving me!

Dorothy C. Lobel

Rage Of Our Age

Long as I can remember, my life is as September,
the days of summer pass, and the memories never last.
With spring never to follow, I am empty and hollow,
but in the winter dead cold, it was you I did hold.

With passion and care it's life that we share,
not caring the season, but believing our reason.
So young and alive, you brought me the way,
but I'm old they will tell you, and it's good-bye you must say.

With rage of our age, no hope for us they hold,
all they will tell you is just turn the page.
With love in my heart why don't they know,
back in to time I cannot go, and oh what a shame,
that you cannot grow.

The difference of years is followed by tears,
not that it matters, it's their foolish fears.
If pages are turned my love will still burn,
and like April showers, I'll remember you as a young flower.

John Pulver

For The Love Of God

A praise to my lover
The destiny of my pursuit
What name can contain her
How can I express her.
She who knoweth no end,
But with trembling awe of utter fascination
The Goddess, be ever more real to me, my furious lover
I am an eternal desire, for my bride
O divine, I pursue her, in my heart
In the purity of my deed, I worship her
In the nobility of my intention, I serve her
I am wild, in adoration, for my divine lover
"I am my beloved's, and my beloved is for me"
Cleaving together for eternity with Heaven's help

Barry Rubel

Suicidal Insanity

Despondency runs inside my blood
The dreaded hour seeps into my soul
Embracing the fears of the night
Wishing I could rush into flight
Away from the memories of bygone years
The memories of blood falling
Dripping down so slowly one moment
To pour faster and faster the next
To feel myself go quietly and deeply insane
For a few hours, minutes, moments of time
To see the color red glaze my eyes from normality.
Until I can no longer see anything but death
Mine's not to know why, only that it's happening!
My head is growing worse and worse
Only a few more minutes or seconds of sanity are left
Helpless am I to control it
I am so much a failure at anything,
everything I try.

Juli Miller

Snow

The moment of conception came not as an explosion from the bowels of the earth but as a whispered thought between secret lovers

Then, as with any embryo, grew at a preordained pace until finally entering the birth canal was pushed away from the security of the womb

Gravity pulled this squalling infant down onto her bosom

Born today - a colorless child capable of creating rainbows simply as an afterthought with a touch so cold as to burn away flesh

Born today - an eyeless, heartless babe, the delight of other children, an infant so powerful as to create and destroy mountains

But later - as the child sleeps, a glow emanates from the very flesh which just hours before devastated a countryside

Almost dead - this infant mourns the loss of life and draws tighter its blanket of security creating an atmosphere of solidarity whose heart is cold as ice

But still capable of creating rainbows merely as an afterthought

Carolyn Jean Custer

True Love - A Flame That Always Burns

In the dead of night, a candle burns,
The hands of time silently turn

A crackling fire in an old fireplace,
Casts its light on her old time scarred face.

A tear stained photograph of a tall, slender man
She clutches in her old wrinkled hand.

She's all alone with a love in her heart
that's burned for many years.
A love that burns so deep and true
through all the nights of tears.

She could never love another
so she lives in the past.
Her memories, a photograph are all that's left,
of a love that couldn't last.

She knew she would always be lonely and alone.
He had to always leave her side
for someone else at home.

This love she carries deep in her heart,
Will still live on even when in death do they part.

Glenda Hodson

Honesty

Honesty is the night....
The ever-faithful, unchanged night...
It embraces all hurt, all pain and assimilates it.
It steals the pain from me,
It is calm.
It is passive.
The hellish, hectic day is dead.
The harsh biting of the light which
Penetrates, beats, berates
Lashes at us to be what we are not,
Cold and unforgiving!!!
The day is relentless.
The night is peaceful.
People are their true selves at night.

Cathy Loveland

Who Am I

I looked in the mirror
The face I saw was not mine
I turned away, stared in space,
Did someone take my place
Who am I, I don't know
I'm lost can't find my way
Tell me, is it night, is it day
Am I a child, I felt my face, arms and legs.
I feel strange in a daze
I am alive.
A voice said, don't worry
I looked in the mirror, smiled
And said who am I.

Clara M. Holland

Commencement

The time of preparation now is past.
The fruits of labor wait upon your call.
The beacon now is ready for the mast.
And e'en the short are suddenly grown tall.
The way ahead may not, as yet be clear.
Give pause, the way will, in its time, emerge.
Success was never sudden, ever dear.
It comes but slowly, never does it surge.
What will it mean? Why you alone can say
An anxious feet upon the threshold rest.
To what commitment will you lend your sway
In seeking yet the better yet the best?
Seize this hour nor its import disdain.
This time of life will never come again.

James M. Buckley

Sea Of Leaves

Just this morning, as I walked by,
the brown leaves of the White and Pin Oak

layered the grass. A placid sea of brown.
I wanted to dive in and stroke across,

to touch my finger tips on the pavement
on the other side. Brown between my clove

colored nails. To smell their slow decay, to taste
the months of summer sun and autumn rain.

To feel the leaves in my hair, russet
mixed with the brown. Swirling around

in an earth-tone tapestry. The memory of apples
tickles my tongue, a core, browning, gnawed

to the stem. The seeds hidden in the leaves.

Colette L. Huxford

A Haunting Vision

I see that spirit who always is just outside my reach,
The haunting vision of a personality who held my place before.
I need you to come to me and be real for just a time.
Can you feel my heart breaking for your sadness?
I wish you only peace, new hope and love.
What once brought life into your dreams now fills mine.
I would give up the song my heart sings if
You would make that song your own and forget the pain
That you have chosen to carry within.
Come closer, close enough to become the beat of my heart.
Feel the sadness of your shadow as it darkens me.
Come closer still. Still closer.
Let that joyful fire burning within my soul swallow you.
My heat and your sadness have the same source.
Where you once stood I now stand.
Come close enough that we stand together.
Let my joy from his love fill the sadness of your loss.
Let me hold you within my heart until you feel my peace.
My essence aches to embrace your tender spirit and find
Grace through the gentle release of your sorrow.

Florence Dilworth

Heroes

From the very beginning The Divine Plan was to create
the heavens, the earth, the universe and then man
That God did and with unmatched empathy He endowed each
man with a certain equality. With thoughts for the future,
he set aside a concept man could live with, emulate, and abide —
Men with special abilities in which all could take pride.
From David who slew the terrible Goliath with unmatched skill
To Moses who freed the slaves from the evil reign of the
Pharaoh in Egypt according to God's Will.
Yes, trials of heroes God left behind, we hear of them everyday
Like the tragic hero Othello who was a great general of the
battlefield until he was finally led astray. Then there was Hannibal
who crossed the treacherous Alps in his struggle against the Romans
who plundered every land, killing its people,
laying hands on its prizes and claiming the rights of every man.
Then the pleas of the great leader Martin L. King "freedom
for every man despite his religion, race or creed."
Heroes lighting the basketball courts the football field, the Olympics
and we have not even begun to name all the heroes God left behind
Whose greatness will always stand to help shape our hearts and minds.

Dorothy Maria Wingo

Forgiveness

Eyes will become red and the tears flow
The ill will we feel are the bad seeds that we sow
While bitterness remains deep in the heart
Persons who maliciously, spitefully, use us
If we are not strong in prayer, we can become a curse
Miserable, self-centered, unforgiving to the core
Forgiving is good, the best word there is

Learning this from Jesus - he forgave the thief on the cross
Jesus will not forgive you if you cannot forgive
So love again be ready to take his advice
Be a born-again Christian, there's nothing to lose
You gain some self worth, help save a soul

So we live by His word, it's your choice to choose
Being forgiving - Joy comes forth shedding her light
The happiness and Gods' Love brings
A new surge of Life

Jessie S. Cobb

Like A Gentle Breeze

Today I forgot to close the gates
The invisible gates of my heart;
In a fragile moment you walked in
Like a welcome, warm gentle breeze
Bringing back the memories of you
That I treasure -keeping them ever close to me.
Remembering is painful but how does one

Not remember
Do leaves forget the summer,
Do birds forget to fly,
Or seas forget to roll?
So you see I will not be forgetting you
Or how we lived for each other those many years
Not always in complete balance but as strong
As lichen on a rock - welded together
Remember me where you are
You a traveller of Eternity - me of earth.

Evelyn Kimball Blake

Home Again

They say you can't go home again but that's not always true
The land is just as fertile and the sky is always blue
I saw the hills we played on as we drove down the lane
I remembered my first home with a touch of pain

The big front porch beckons, come and sit a spell
If it could only talk, the stories it would tell
I look up at the window to the room where I was born and used to play
And the freshly painted farm house welcomed me to stay

We drove around and saw my grammar school sitting on a hill
It brought back memories of teachers who cared and always will

Those were the days you took care of you own when they were old
You held them and listened to their stories

You didn't have to be told what to do and it didn't bother you
I was dancing on my Grandpa's bed the day he died
And didn't realize he was gone 'till later, then I cried

Our parents had a big family so we worked hard for a living
But they taught us to be loving and giving

So don't say you can't go home again you might be surprised
It will make you realize
It seems like only yesterday when you went away.

June R. Howard

Albumblatt (For Memories Shared Over Old Photographs)

Leaf by lovely leaf you hand to me
The life-imprinted relics of each fall,
Calligraphic treasury of all
The waving generations up your tree
In hectic gold profusion massing there -
Mounting the silver sky up the thick stalk
Your sturdy ancestry of Linden walk.
And from a nodding bough a sheaf you tear
Of tassel days, the hue of palest straw,
Laughter like flax in sunlight streaking down -
Then sullen sadness mottling a thrust-brown
This spring of blighted leaves mocked by a thaw,
Its dark-bruised golden apples oozing mead
To proffer what oblivion we need.

Alice Costantini

The Night

A mournful shriek encircles the globe:
(THE LIGHT IS COMING. THE LIGHT IS COMING.)
Ah, flee, flee! It is too much; it is too much.
Naked I stand above a wounded city of snarling traffic and snarled lives.
Watching the mingled masses of humanity murdering each other.
My soul screams: "Why do they kill each other so? Why will they die?"
At my side I hear a compelling voice: "Ah, flee, flee. Flee the cities."
(THE LIGHT IS COMING. THE LIGHT IS COMING.)
Flee to the hills where you can pause in the stillness of nature
To listen to the voice of God.
As the voice of the sundrops dappling the brook;
As the voice of the moon glow silvering each grassy glade;
As the voice of the sunbeams; sifting, filtering, fleeting
Through the leaves of the trees.
Ah, do you not hear the voice of God so softly saying,
"Turn, turn again. Turn to the light.
That it may flow through you, too." Turn to the Light
To lighten your burden, to enlighten your soul.
OH, SHALL WE BE BUT FOOLISH SHADOWS UPON THE CRUMBLING WALL OF LIFE
WHICH FADE AND DISAPPEAR BECAUSE THE LIGHT COULD NOT PASS THROUGH US?

Donna D. Conant

Time Passes On

The days they come and then they go
The lines in my face tell me so
My hair is white, my eyes are dim
Seems I'm waiting just for him
To arrive one day and take me home
Then I'll no longer be alone -

I'm happy here with Pat and Dave
But seems there is something else I crave
To touch again his work worn hands
To tell me that he understands
He knows I love him and always will
Until my breath leaves me and I'm silent and still

Forgive me my dearest one if I ever treated you wrong
For my love for you lives on and on-

Bennie J. Humphries

Porch Of Homage

She cast a lusterless gleam across the swollen streets
the longing in her eyes had long since left her face

Life for her was sleeping near the shading willow trees
stowing under an old etched stone bench
abandoned in a vacant park

I tried to trace the lines of her face beneath her tattered scarf
but much was hidden by barren threads and the silver in her hair

I'd bet the grey that shadowed her brow, used to enjoy the sunlight
when youth tarried by her side and walked with hands entwined

Oh to embrace the beggar's hand and assure her of a bright day to come
But who am I to offer what fate has since denied?
I have to sit and ponder as the years remain a passerby
What path must one avoid to end in such demise?
How will I know which road to trod and which to step aside?

The blue in her eyes that used to dance with hope, in vain searches
now, fumbles through a vagrant's cart, now her porch of homage.

Carmen Wright

Awakening

All you too blind to see,
the loving creature that was me.
What could have been, lost in hurt.
Knocked to the ground, laying in the dirt.

All you too blind to see,
the lovable creature that was me.
In love and pain I reached for your hand,
deny your heart, cover me in sand.

Beneath the sand - a beautiful flower.
Waiting, waiting, for the desert shower.
I have blossomed for all to behold.
I cry for you. Your heart is still cold!

All the hopes and all the dreams
compressed into moments it seems.
The hurt and pain of so many years,
finally washed away by salty tears.

A shattered mind yearning to be free,
Opened the door to who was really me.
All the love I found inside
is worth every tear ever cried!

Calgary B. Jones

The Gang

Dear Friends at Stanford Hospital;

I want to thank you for your support,
the loving thoughts you sent for me to court,
the angelic friends you sent my way,
to lift me up through my day.

A beautiful plant reminds me of you all,
the help that you gave me when I did call,
and your loving help when I did fall.
Your positive words would help me stand tall.
Each flower reminds me of the beauty in each one of you,
the unity of your work in each day anew.

A greater desire to wish you the best,
and the end of your day you would receive peace and rest.
Thank you again for showing you care.
Thank you again for being there.

Jeanne M. Snyder

Everything Is Beautiful

Our beautiful summer is at an end,
The many lovely flowers start to bend.
Leaves are turning red and gold,
While nights become longer and cold.

The children are back in school
And their parents cover the swimming pool.
Now the games are football and basketball,
As the roller skates and bats stay in the hall.

Going shopping shows a big change.
Instead of cottons, there are woolen things.
Shorts and swim suits are put away
And sweaters and slacks are worn all day.

We crave hot soups and such,
Instead of cold dishes for lunch.
The oven is turned on for baking
And cakes and pies are for the taking.

Soon we will be planning our holidays,
Snow will fall and ice will glaze.
We really are blessed with beautiful days
And should be thankful in so many ways.

Joyce Peck

In My Dreamscape

The sky is as blue as sapphire, and it shines like a jewel
The moon inspires us and holds mystic powers
In my dreamscape.

My most secret wishes all come true
The world is strange and exciting
In my dreamscape.

Everywhere there is mystery and beauty
All lives are filled with laughter
In my dreamscape.

I have a place where no one else can go
My own very special universe
In my dreamscape.

My wildest fantasies all come to pass
Life is always wonderful
In my dreamscape.

I wish that I could live there forever
But I am only a visitor
In my dreamscape.

Amanda M. Hayes

Where Did It Go?

That glow in your eyes that told me you loved me.
The one I always used to see.
It used to tell me how much you cared.
The one that kept strong the love we shared.
At one point it grew so bright.
That's how I knew our love was right.
That look that gave me so much hope.
With my problems it helped me cope.
So, where did it go?
All of a sudden it disappeared,
and you were no longer near.
You drifted away day by day,
but I couldn't turn the other way.
I believed in our love and I believed in you.
Will you please say you believe in me too?
Once again I will find that glow.
The only question is, "Where did it go?"

Julianna Perez

Hebron Massacre/Argentina Bombing

The path of terror never deviates.
The pain of terror never alleviates.
Current political arguments do not persuade
And memories of past massacres do not fade.
This in itself is another phase
Of an attitude problem in the Middle East maze.

There is a definite character deformity
When anger and violence reaches such enormity.
Be it in Hebron, Rwanda or the United States
The decay of the goodness of humanity's soul
Is in a threatening non-objective state.

Mankind's inability to forgive perpetuates a militancy
To only be relived. Time to get off the never ending binge
Of pathetic unproductive revenge. Instead of attacking
Each other, attack the vicious disease. The mental illness
Addiction of: terrorism, reprisals, threats, power struggles,
Tease, never ending, mind bending, paranoid discrepancies.

Peace cannot be determined by a couple of hand shakes
If the hearts are false and the smiles are fake.
We have to address the hate.

Barbara Bloom

One Year More

One year more Lord, to love and to serve,
The poor, the sick, and the lonely.
One more year, to search God's Word
For what He willed I should be.

One more year to test myself
If what's been done's my best.
Sheltering homeless, caring for their needs
Regards to both, races and creeds.

At my End of Time, how great it will be
To hear God say, "Well done! Gee Gee"
As love in my heart, bursts into joy
With my fearless pass to Eternity.

Grace Guthrie

The Golden Days Of Autumn

The days of autumn are coming to an end,
The pumpkins are in the field,
The harvest all gathered in.

We remember the golden days,
And the fun we had, we acted as though we were
Still young girl and lad.

We romped over fields and strolled
By the stream,
There was laughter and sunshine
And many daydreams.

Winter will find us
Sitting by the fire,
Rocking away in our favorite chair.

We will dream of the golden days
That have passed, dream of an autumn
That did not last.

I put gingerbread into the oven to bake,
Its golden color reminds me of autumn.
And I can hardly wait,
Hurry and return autumn, for my sake.

Anita Heard

Abused

Fright, runs through my mind.
The night turns black and cold.

I sit and stare endless at the face in
front of me.

A warm tear falls down my red-hot
face and I can feel the pain that had
been struck upon my eyes and mouth.

I notice a bruised limb and some torn
flesh.

But these bruises and scars don't hurt
as bad as my heart that feels torn in
pieces, 'cause it knows you hit with force.

Isolated,
I can't get out, no matter how many times
I look at the face that was once beautiful,
Now disgraced with a bruise or two, I
just can't seem to leave. The man I
love hurts me, but not as much as I hurt
myself by not leaving.

A'Lesha Markee

The River Of Hope, And Dreams

The water flows rapidly as it beats against the rusted rocks.
The river, as pure as the heavens above.
The water is crystal clear.
If you look closely you can see your reflection staring at you;
It glistens off the sun beams.
The sounds of rushing water echoes through my mind.
It talks to me, each rhyme; sounds describe hope, and dreams beyond another world. A different dimension.
My anxiety draws me closer, as the forces push me slowly.
I anticipate a new beginning, a fresh start.
Or no one will hear my cry.

Caroline Okantey

"The Girl With The Hoe"

The warming sun was bright upon the dusty field.
The rows were long with growing cotton,
The New green stalks of Spring.
There seems to be no end she thought,
As row by row she thinned the crop,
And cut the weeds.
Her swinging hoe in rhythm to her thoughts
Of life beyond these cotton fields.
She had her dreams of better things,
A home, and clothes and books.
Her special dream was of books to educate
her mind.
She hoped in future years to fulfill
that dream,
This Sharecropper's daughter.

Beulah Langston Porter

Sonnet For November

Gold and silver is the chill November day;
The scarlet leaves have left the gnarled bough.
Blue sky is hidden by a pearly gray;
Green ocean turned to leaden now.
Far in the west a splendid stream of gold
Is spilling on the bright quick silver sea;
Would God there were a wondrous magic mold
To capture evermore this alchemy!
Silver and gold November has to spend
To purchase stillness for the restive soul,
And surcease from the summer's hectic trend
To make a broken, troubled spirit whole.
Silver and gold November has to buy
Peace, a grateful heart to fortify.

Evelyn Sampson Valentine

The Dark Side

I've seen the dark side....
The side that evades the light
And cowers in shadows
That are too vague to comprehend.
I've seen the ugly multi-faceted dimensions
Of hate, of violence, of disease, and death
And I've walked circles around the sun
Forever without its healing rays.
I've seen the dark side of life where no life grows,
Where sun only shines in shadow.
I've seen the bitterness, strife, anger, pain
And madness of mankind
As they blot out all else.
I've seen the sun eclipse itself
In the brightness of noon.
I've seen the darkened veil of void
In the absence of light and room.
I've seen the dark side of people,
The dark side of the moon.

Heather Noelle Seifert

The Beauty Of Autumn

On a brisk autumn morning,
the sky is a radiant spectrum of colors
Each a perfect hue in the cloudless sea above
The leaves, now a brilliant rainbow
of deep, rich shades of reds, yellows and oranges,
fall aimlessly, yet miraculously, from the tree above,
and flutter toward earth.

A sweet, rainy essence calmly floats
about in the gentle breeze
All is quiet, all is still
Yet in that monotonous silence, I hear a single leaf abandon
its slightly swaying branch and tumble to the ground,
landing among the growing pile
of fresh scented leaves.

Elisa Goldade

Purity

I love a cold, white wintery morning,
The snow so pure, noble, quietly adorning.
Everything glistening with this new crystal scheme,
No trace of impurity can e'er be seen;

Old junk cars look brand new, a lying in a heap,
Even shacks become castles, their powdery edges steep.
Shimmering in early morning dawn,
It makes a heart to soar,
Oh, to mar this beauty is to be
Innocent no more.

The shining flakes piled high
With rounded corners soft,
Seldom are such bright icy
glimpses caught;
But our Dear Lord in great wisdom
Surely must know,
That sometimes His children need
To see the Purity of The SNOW:

Alice R. Roberts

The Night

The night is full of ambience which daylight seldom knows.
The songbirds are now silent, and see how the street lamp glows.
Now fearful unseen voices are heard through the thick grey fog.
The city, so quiet by day, at night is all agog.

I like to take the risk of walking solo through this town,
Through the dark, dirty streets of Detroit city, up and down.
To go into a club and see a wild punk rock band play,
Or to a Greektown taverna where belly dancers sway.

The Irish pub's band plays well, and the Guinness freely flows.
Outside, the streets are cool and damp, feel how the west wind blows.
But the time rapidly runs out for nighttime's dark domain,
And then the daylight comes and things are quiet once again.

John P. Danko

God

The Creator.
The Master.
He loves us unconditionally.
He asks no questions or favors.
He put each one of us on this earth
for a special purpose,
and even though we may not know what it is,
God knows that we are able to do what He wants us too.
But, if for some reason we can't,
and we have tried our best,
and He knows that we have, he will always forgive us.
For we are all His children.

Jennie Holmes

To An Old Rocking Chair

If only I had means to see
The stories that you hold,
The sorrows, joys and comforts
Which were yours in days of old.
I'm sure there hides within your folds
A very special tale.
A tale of life and faith and love
And all that did prevail.
For rocking chairs are faithful friends,
They bring us peace of mind,
And, there, a person's being blends
With everything sublime.
He finds a solace sitting there
Rocking cares away
Or gives his thanks that he can share
A faithful love each day.
I wish that I could purchase you
And take you to my home.
But, rocking chair, that would not do-
I have one of my own!

Donald B. Stevenson

Wondrous World

The earth gives us foundation the sky to cover and delight
The sun to give us warmth and shine the birds in flight
The trees so spiny in winter time, bearing fruit and leaves
in summer like the romance that blooms in a lover's heart
in spring. Hills and valleys and mountains, facial features
of our globe, symbolic of the wrinkles of time kissed
with wisdom and beauty Grass that tickles my toes
air to keep me alive and the wind to remind me of my
freedom the thunder to remember God and the rain to
fall coolly upon my skin, to refresh my soul and to
remind me of the tears that fall from angel's eyes the
rainbows to keep me wishing. A sunny day to brighten
my heart a dip in the lake to revitalize my falling
spirits. These are the wonders of this great earth
our planet our giver of live I salute you, green
and blue.

Claudette L. Hudson

"Sometimes, I Have To Close My Eyes To See"

Sometimes, I have to close my eyes to see,
the true beauty that lies before me.
A sincere heart and loving favor,
though often overlooked,
is what my soul really savors.
Sometimes,
blinded by what I see with my eyes,
external beauty with no treasure inside.
What appears to be desirable,
or even a work of art,
may seek to destroy me,
and shatter my heart.
So while tempting, it may be,
and an intense struggle on my part,
I must first ponder,
the intent of the heart.
Is it blessings or curses,
though beautifully wrapped it maybe,
I must be discreet and consider:
"WHAT MY EYES DON'T SEE!"

Alfred J. Jenkins Jr.

Can't Go On

i watch her rock back and forth as she cries.
The tears are streaming from her eyes.
i try to comfort her but the pain is getting to me,
The hurt she feels, so blinding she can barely see.
She sits in the darkness and stares into space.
What evil could take him from her loving embrace?
Now all she has are sweet memories.
The pictures she grasps are all that she sees.
She bears them closely to her heart,
Hoping it will never let them part.
She's shaking and trembling frantically,
Muttering to herself quietly.
It's too late to say goodbye, now he's gone,
And to her it seems she can't go on.
For no two people could love one another
As much as a baby and its mother.

Brandishea Christian Nott

The Class Of 1989

The Delight class of 1989, how happy you must be. You've stood the test and done your best. You have the stepping stones to become anyone you want to be, but remember responsibility is the key. You've had good times and bad along the way, all of these necessary as you worked and played from day to day. Your lives were shaped by your parents, teachers, leaders of your nation, and friends you knew at school, because it was through them you learned how to set your own rules. Education is a life long process learning something new every day. The mind is like a computer storing knowledge that is ready for replay. Remember your career is one thing you can depend on when all others let you down. A positive attitude is essential for setting goals and turning them into reality. To be the best we can be, that is our destiny. Go forth and accomplish what you may remembering always that today is the day.

Diane Burton

Untitled

The path that I travelled wasn't easy
The time that it took seemed too long
But the rewards that I've reaped in the process
Have sustained me and made me strong.

The gifts which I have received
From the struggle that I've been through
Include character, strength and compassion
Just to name a few.

The scars have fully healed
The pain has dissipated
The spirit has finally mended
The soul rejuvenated.

More struggles await me in the future
I'm sure I'll get through them alright
The knowledge and wisdom inside me
Will be my shelter and guiding light.

Dana L. McCuen

Guardian:

A small green village closes its eyes.
The face on the clock watches as time fly's
Tick Tock, Tick Tock, Tick Tock
Beats the heart of the lonely clock.
The sky is bleak and expels tears of rain
onto the cobblestone where the homeless once had lain.
Dampening the ground with unending sounds
as the arms of the clock spin round and round.
Tiny wooden roofs keep the children safe and dry.
The Grandfather looks on with a watchful eye,
wishing he could be one of them
a hard steel guardian.

Heather Ann Hobbs

Waiting Under A Starry Night

The sky was the color of Venus.
The trees shook their heads in the wind
and there I stood, once again, waiting -
waiting for her eyes to open,
waiting for her kiss to melt in my mouth,
like rice paper
under a gently falling rain.
I have grown older and wiser, I remind myself,
I am ready for her to return to me
and all that I have become
then the wind dies.
My heart floats back down to the ground,
joining all the other balloons,
and as I stand there,
staring up at her
deep into the clear blue nothingness,
I can still see the light from her eyes
shining back down on me,
like a star that no longer exists.

David J. Parrish

Beloved Mother

This is my beloved mother
The very life and breath of me.
She with gentle hands
Who tended me so carefully, who looked with loving eyes
upon her child each day
And guided me along
The safe and righteous way.
She lived her life
Just as she wanted me to do
And was a beacon in my world
Her whole life through.
And when I slipped a little from the path
That she was leading me along
She never once condemned me
Only said" I know you meant no wrong."
And gave me extra love
To make me strong.
In her old age I tended her with loving care
And now I pray that God
Will keep her safe for me up there!

Ada Jones Bergren

Voices On The Wind

"Come with me,"
The voices echo in my head.
"Come with me,"
The sounds tremble from the painted cliffs.
Ghost figures dance in the shadows of the rocks,
and their voices softly whisper,
"Come with me."

In the cry of the eagle overhead,
In the sigh of the wind in the canyon below,
The voices pull at my mind, my heart, my soul—
"Come with me."

Spirits from times long past,
Ghosts from battles long forgotten,
Riding on the wings of the wind—
I hear your voices;
I come.

Janet F. Whiteaker

Paper Wall

Imagine yourself in a tunnel, with only one way out,
the way is blocked by a brick wall, impenetrable, no doubt.

You're walking towards the wall, useless as it appears,
you're convinced it's a dead-end, as the barrier grows near.

But you will not stop, you're determined to try,
holding on to your hope, and trying not to cry.

When you reach the wall, it's not brick of which it's made.
it's merely paper and paint, your apprehensions quickly fade.

The tunnel is your life, and the barriers, only perceived,
when a wall makes you stop, perhaps you've been deceived.

Brick walls are often paper, so not to stop is the key,
meet the obstacle head on, and you will see what you will see.

Chris Maxey

"Three Elm Trees In The North Are Shining More Than Gold"*

**Dashdorjyn Natsagdorj*

Past the three martyrs of elm, sweet elision in
the whispering speech of their leaves in the prospering
sun, through those palisades of honor into the wide
heaven's music you winged. Now, ember-eyes of new
countrymen film this time you abandoned: your land's
awakening memory, my journey. Beijing: I wake as a
night's lanterns flicker out on stalled longing, the summer
of light settles in on the rimming mountains to focus
my hostage view northward; twenty floors toward
the sky, forty borders of memory. Your birth
beyond that high horizon beckons: I will ride
toward a fate I remember. Far west of dreaming the elms
of the clan signaled: strong as dying, meridians
to the ribboning paradise promised where leaves
for healing shine. In the time of great lightscapes, the grace
of audacity, I sang you the Name; then, westward a last sojourn, you
stood shadow in elm shadow in the slipping summer. I hear the singling
melody lit between distance and distance now, trees
in garments of praise, in the north, gold as torches.

Geraldine Gobi Greig

Observations

How short the summer is!
  The winter, long.
How slow the pain of memories;
  The happiness—a turtle's song.

How high the summer skies!
  In winter, low.
How glad a girl's warm inward sighs;
  The shy sadness—a purple glow.

How warm the June-night eyes!
  In winter, cold.
How soon on top the youth who tries!
  The slide on down—the man less bold.

How high the stack of things undone!
  The 'complished, low.
How late the time has got—it's won!
  The seeds of life too old to sow.

How then for me to stay the call
  For it to pass me by?
How quick, how slow depends on Fall
  When leaves of gold smite my plans awry!

Albert J. Calandra

My Inner Sadness

There's a little girl inside me, who sat down and began to weep,
The wound she feels inside her heart, the years have made so deep.
The child inside me tries to reason, why over the years she feels so sad,
But this child knows the answer, she only wants a loving dad.

Her father doesn't truly love her, yes she knows that for sure,
The sadness she feels inside her, she feels she cannot endure.
Her father shows no love since the divorce, but she is willing to forgive,
She has tried to love her father, but how much more can she give?

The little girl inside me knows
For a loving father she must wait,
But this little girl also tries so hard,
not to give into sadness or hate.

The sad little girl inside me is weeping,
But her father, he cannot hear,
But the young adult inside me, comforts the child,
And wipes away her tears.

Diane Roosa

The Voice of the Children

Out of my pen flows words in rhyme.
Their meaning far too deep for the mortal mind.
The river of thought, information, and such
Isn't something I asked for. It came in a rush.

If you look on the surface you might catch a clue.
The true message however may overcome you.
It's nestled between line and verse.
Be very brave. I'm here to help you.

I heard God calling one day in my youth.
His voice was no more than a whispered hush.
He said "little girl stand straight and tall."
"Don't be afraid, I won't let you fall."

Look to the heavens. Be proud of who you are.
Running through fields with flowers in you hair.
That day as we talked God gave me a gift,
It's the voice of the children, oh please listen
To them.

Andreia Catherine Wade

Release

Red, brown, and gold the leaves come tumbling down.
Their Mother Earth receives them as with afterthought
since turning she had set the dial on "cold,"
and to this end her yearly plans had wrought.

Red leaf that first withdrew tree's hold
was glad to take the hero's leap;
then brothers, sisters in tumultuous game
whirled down, their rendezvous to keep.

The last brown leaf fell softly to the ground -
was loath to weaken tie from parent grasp.
Now brothers, sisters in their silent joy
their patchwork quilt around him clasped.

The wind whined cold and lifted each
to scatter over field and snowy hill.
This brown and gold of autumn's store
must bend to lash of winter's will.

As softly thus the years have floated down
like autumn leaves from maple tree.
This clasp of years must soon release
and whirl me flying fast and free.

Erma Wingham

A Rose For Tara

If beauty is a rose,
Then how can I compare you?
With velvet skin,
Soft as a petal covered with early morning dew.
A fragrance so seductively shy,
Lingering lustfully as you walk by.
Dazzling brown eyes,
As if stars had fallen from heavenly skies.
Deliberately sharp as a thorn in your ways,
As gentle and innocent in your gaze.
And your smile, a smile so pure,
Making life's rain easier to endure.
Mere thoughts of you intoxicate my soul,
Giving new meaning to religious whole.
So if beauty is to be compared to a rose,
When asked, I would insist,
The most beautiful of roses be compared to you!

Christopher Reed

Memories Of Lost Loves

Upon the clouds of a clear blue moon.
There was life in full bloom.
Filled with wondrous memories,
Filled with sadness that makes us weep.
With in the sadness, I can see your eyes.
Which brings tear drops with in my sigh.
That we will never share another tomorrow,
We can never weep together in sorrow.
To where you perished, and I remained.
In one motion I have lost, and I have gained.
Lost my loved one, and gained the ability to let go.
Does it ever get easier? Will anyone ever know?
The pain you carry with in your heart and soul?
Which can not be seen, so how could anyone ever know?

Dina G. Munro

"Tiny" The Christmas Angel

A long time ago in the heavens above
There were many angels, all full of love
All angels have beautiful long, wavy hair
And wings that carry them through the air.

When combing and brushing their hair and wings
Their halos stood out like bright golden rings.

The honor to be with the King of all men
Would soon be chosen from one of them.

Tiny, the angel, the smallest of all
Kept praying that God would give Tiny the call.

The Good Lord listened and heard Tiny's plea
And called to the little one, "Come here to me."

All the angels in heaven were pleased to know
That Tiny was the one called to go.

As Tiny flew very fast through the skies
Teardrops streamed out of her eyes.

The trail Tiny left was very clear
The wise men followed with nothing to fear.

It was then all the angels knew that Tiny's prayers had come true.
She was the star, the light that shone so bright
When Jesus was born on that first Christmas night.

Joseph R. Tomaino

"My Dad"

In Memory of Alfred C. Lynn
He was one of a kind, the best and
there will be no other
He touched the lives of the young and
old and our lives were changed forever
His accomplishments were many because
he had curiosity and ambition to know
He knew so much about anything, that
he could take care of anything
He was your friend, if you've met him one time
To be honest, loyal and dependable were his virtues
Busy as he was he had time or made
time for your concerns
Your interest he shared and added
to make it whole
He gave love and love he received
in return from many
My admiration for him is untold
and he will always be my hero
My dad, how could I have been so
lucky to have had you

Clarence N. Dennison

Autumn Has Come To The Ozarks

Autumn has come to the Ozarks.
There's a chill in the air.
Why are you there chill in the air?
Because God decreed that I be there.

Autumn has come to the Ozarks.
Trees are arrayed with red and gold.
Why do you wear colors of red and gold?
Because God has made us thus, so we are told.

Autumn has come to the Ozarks.
The pumpkin has frost in his hair.
Why do you have frost in your hair?
Because God in His wisdom has put it there.

Autumn has come to the Ozarks.
Hummingbirds to the south have flown.
Why fly south small bird? I'd like to know.
Because winter is coming, and God will send snow.

Autumn has come to the Ozarks for winter all people prepare.
The wood stoves are glowing. Smell the smoke in the air?
The woods are peaceful, and nestled in God's care.
Yes, Autumn has come to the Ozarks.

Joyce Ward

Earthquake!

Land masses rumble and shake,
There's no mistakin' a big Earthquake.
It first begins... (You recognize,)
The doors start to swaying, the floors seem to rise.
You bounce out of bed, (it doesn't stop!)
So under a table you're forced to drop.
The longer it lasts the more you fear -
"Oh God... What damage it's doing out there!"
You turn to feel it's finally calm, it's Sunday, 4:58 at dawn,
You turn on the tube to find out more,
Reports confirmed, "it's a 7.4!"
Your world has been so rudely awakened,
By a shifting earth and a whole lot of shakin'.
Bridges fall and cars are flipped,
Destroying homes, foundations stripped.
People injured, lives are lost,
"Oh Lord...God, will it ever stop?"

Bunni Koblentz

I Went Searching

Looking back on all the years,
There's a time in my life that always brings me cheer.
It's the time when we first became friends,
When I was knocking, and you let me in.
We were two different people, with one common flaw.
We both needed a friendship that wouldn't fall.
As time progressed, it soon became clear,
That with you around I could always find cheer
You were always there for me, you never left my side
And with you I was always myself, I had nothing to hide.
I remember times when I cried, you never discouraged my tears.
You just comforted me with gentle words, and let me explain my fears.
You were always there to help me stand; you gave me something to
believe.
So no matter what things the world hurls at me, I'll always face them
on my feet.
And I'll always have a smile on my face, because you never taught me
to frown.
And no matter how hard life seems to be, I'll never let you down.
I went searching to find a special friend. You are what
I found.

Christina Boorse

"Chocolate Bear Mountain"

The world is peaceful on Chocolate Bear Mountain,
there's plenty to eat for all who live here,
but of all who live here, up on Chocolate,
there is none quite as nice as Semi-sweet Bear.

When he's not collecting Choc-o-late Berries,
exploring the depths of Chocolate Chip Cave,
he drinks from pools at Peppermint Fountain,
tells funny stories, of his milk chocolate days.

One day when Semi-sweet went out for berries,
to see if they turned a choc-o-late brown,
he met an old friend he had grown up with,
Chocolate Moose was his name, but he lived in town!

Then Semi asked Chocolate, "is town still the same,
full of Man creatures who know you by name,
who hold you tightly and open their mouths,
put you in a dark place, where you can't get out?"

Chocolate Moose just smiled and said, "Hasn't changed.
In fact, that is why I've come home again;
I miss my friends, and I don't want to be
dessert on a menu, but here ... running free!"

George Michael Dile

Our Hearts

In bright sunshine - always we feel fine
the world is like a treasure chest - in which we choose best
that we are on earth a guest - is true in east and west
family life is everybody's shrine - your's and mine
love is in our hearts divine - hope is like sweet wine
around us birds sing in every nest - without rest
with the silver-hairy crest - we pass each life's test
our star is a good sign - for ever with happiness in line
good thoughts we must ever keep - in our souls very deep
progress is not a steep hill - ocean's waves never be still
have futuristic dreams in sleep - never for the past weep
be smart - for better everywhere is a good start
to reach a goal we do not need special skill - only will
because we are from humanity a part - each with GOLDEN HEART

Frank Z. Glinski

Moonrays

A cool and gentle night, I silently reflect
These past five years I ponder, fond memories I protect

We started out unstable, we shared once three now five
Our precious little family we lovingly derive

It isn't always easy, together we move on
No one knows the future, one day these five be gone

While all together at this time, these moments we shall cherish
For what takes place at present, these thoughts shall never perish

The worlds flow now so smoothly, at times hard to convey
But always first upon my mind, goodwill for mine I pray

These years oh how so precious the joys you six have brought
Though still somewhat a novice, life's lessons you have taught

As we begin our second five commitment is premiere
Soon young adults and on their own, our young soon be our peer

Through it all keep uppermost respect for you my sweet
I love you from my deepest root no feeling can compete

Now I retire, though moon still bright
My special thoughts, of you tonight

Brian Dolan

The Trumpets Are Sounding

As I was praying one day
These words to me did come,
It was Jesus as I heard Him say
"It's time to come home, my son."

I looked up as the sky did split
Jesus and his angels were on their way,
Even Satan himself would have to admit
It was a beautiful and glorious day.

As I looked around me, all I could see
Multitudes of angels coming from the sky,
The people all around me falling to their knees
For it was Jesus returning from his home on high.

His word tells us that it won't be long
And I know it is getting closer to that day,
We will be singing a brand new song
For the angels with their trumpets are on the way.

I can hear the trumpets now sounding
They are coming from the Eastern sky,
Oh, how my heart is pounding
For now I will meet Him eye to eye.

James D. Alcorn

Being Mom

Being Mom means my children are not an interruption.
They are part of my every day living.
Not to compete with, not to match wits with.
Being Mom means being the heart of it all.
The earth you stand on, the solid ground on which all you do
reflects the love of life and the joys of being a family together.
Being Mom is maybe being best at making apple pie or being
best at sharing it.
Being Mom isn't the money put in a card and being dropped off at
your convenience.
It's not the gift at all.
It's being there and the time that you share.
Being Mom is a happy time when you know your children are all
getting along, and family history's not repeating itself.
Being Mom is accepting it and knowing, maybe you did
something right after all.

Jody Whalen

The Silent Language

Hands can express, communicate and direct.
They are means of expression, kindness and respect.
They emphasize an idea, sentiment or attitude.
They express feelings, pleasant or rude.

By dropping hands or lifting them high,
They tell of discouragement in a silent reply.
Shaking hands... in friendship, meeting or a fond farewell.
Hands over mouth... "Hush"... a secret, don't tell.

Clapping hands... attention, anger or a time to rejoice.
Hands back of head... defeat... gesturing, a silent voice.
Hands over eyes... thinking, resting, pain, pressure or stress.
Hands on hips... an act of authority, it means business.

Hands in the pocket... for warmth or to rest for the day.
Palms together... extended to God... clasped to pray.
Hands speak for the deaf, they see for the blind.
They express many thoughts that are on the mind.

Not the sound of a voice, but the sensation of touch.
Warm, harsh, gentle or quick... can express so much...
Sorrow, excitement, fear, or happy events.
Gestures... the language of hands... The language of silence

Jane Luciene Nowak

"Our Home"

A home of their own, once was a dream for two,
They are now sharing the reality of that coming true.

Unpacking will seem like an unending task you'll have to face,
Putting everything away means choosing the right shelf or closet space.

A home requires inside and outside chores to be done,
Two sharing the work will accomplish more than one.

Your investment of time, labor and money eventually will be known,
As these assets will increase the value of your home.

Changes and improvements have already been accomplished by you two,
Your other plans will be seen in the near future too.

God Bless your home and all those whom dwell within,
May it be a happy place shared with friends and kin.

As the years pass you'll relate to the memories each one recalls,
Of those get togethers and holidays that took place within these walls.

Anne Devine

Victim Of Child Abuse

She sits watching out the window at the kids playing in the street. They are so naive, she thinks. They know nothing about the evil in this world. As for the girl, she lives in a world of fear. Her monster is more real than the creature under the bed or in the closet; it is her dad. He shows his love by the bruises on her arms, legs and the blood stains on the sheets. He comes into her room after her mom has gone to work and says he is punishing her for whatever reason he has now. However, his beating goes beyond just punishment. Then he leaves as her nightmare begins, bruises start to appear but sooner or later they disappear, however the scars they leave behind go beyond mere skin and hurt, far worse than any belt or hand. Then comes the excuses, I slipped and fell or I ran into the door. And then continual apologizing from her dad, "I will never do it again, I promise. Please do not tell Mommy." And he will stop for awhile, until something triggers, triggers the monster within. She does not breathe a word hoping this time will be the last. She starts to wonder when this hell will end and the love begin. The next time you feel the urge to hit your child, think of these few lines. Thousands of children, like your own, die every day when punishment leads to death. Don't kill the love that you are crushing in your hand.

Jennifer A. Davis

Waves Upon The Sand

They wrote silly notes upon the wet sand;
They built mighty sand castles there,
But the waves came along and soon they were gone
To the ocean so blue and so fair.
Just kids having fun on the wet beach
And laughing at what the notes said,
But the surge to the shore took them forever more
From the beach where they once had been made.
Those castles they saw as they walked on the sand
Till the waves swept and washed them away,
Then the castles so tall did crumble and fall
In the surge of the great ocean's spray.
Now the shore is all bare of the castles and words,
And the kids, they have quit games they played.
And nobody but they know that once on that day
Were some words and some castles they'd made.

Clarence E. Billheimer

"Mothers"

Mothers are like lilies that grow in the glen
They cure our ills, our broken hearts mend
They listen to our troubles, whether large of small
How we failed our exams, or how we played ball
Mothers are like soft winds that blow
Never seems to tire, always on the go
She is Doctor, Nurse, Bookkeeper, Cook
Finds time to read from your storybook
First to rise in the morning.
Last to bed at night
Puts out the cat, turns out the light.
Mothers are like raindrops from heaven sent
But we must remember, she is only lent.
So treat her with tender loving care
For she won't always be so near.
Mothers are a great work of art.
Without her our world would fall apart
How could we do without Mothers, you ask a thousand times a day
So give her a rose, tell her you love her
Make every day Mother's Day.

Alta M. Martin

You Are A Gentleman

You are a gentleman, and I a lady
There are so few around
Why does it take a gentleman
to make a lady feel like a lady?

It's more than opening doors
It's the pride and the respect
With which you introduced me to your friends
You are a gentleman, and I a lady.

It's the gentleness you showed
As you carefully touched my lips with yours
Not demanding more, just giving a promise
You are a gentleman and I a lady.

I've run from men who refused to see
the lady that I am
But you only drew me closer when you showed me
You are a gentleman and I a lady.

You are a gentleman and I a lady
And I want you to see that my response
Is one you can trust and depend on.
It takes a gentleman to make a lady want to be a real lady.

Charlotte M. Peiler

Food for Thought

Autumn leaves are colored yellow, orange 'n red.
They fly, like little birds, in the sky overhead
until they are gathered in a bag or a pile,
and trees that once wore leaves are naked, for a while.
But trees are never cold whatever the weather,
Whether they stand alone or they stand together,
for the sap within them keeps them warm 'til spring
when their leaves shall return and they, like birds, shall sing,

So let us, like the trees, enjoy winter's weather
whether we stand alone or we stand together.
Let us, like the trees, be so thankful every day
that all things that are old shall, someday, pass away.
And let us, like the trees, look forward to the day
When all things shall be new just as the Scriptures say....
when the Holy Spirit, just as sap does a tree,
shall keep us warm as toast throughout eternity.

Beatrice Sykes

Windows

Oh beautiful eyes of night....
They follow me through the darkness of
dreams to haunt me in my sleep

They ramble through the day to torture
me in my consciousness

They cloak all emotion so none can be found,
yet they know all I feel and all I fear

They love so tenderly and loathe so brutally
they urge me to tell all, but I falter and cannot

They are timid and shy, yet audacious and daring
They are genuine, but unfeeling
they are full of joy and sorrow

They seem so unreal to me, yet
everyday they stare back at me
in the mirror.

Amber Forland

"As I See Them"

Poets are a strange lot.
They know what they've got.
And want to share it with the world.

In moments of despair, they
want to share. A common bond with his fellow man.
They are altruistic rather than egotistic.
I have a feeling of fellowship when I am among them.
They may be a little off "The Beaten Path"
But I am so honored to be a member of it.
He is in a shell where he is most comfortable
Part of the time yet, when he burst into the open
he is so gregarious.

His idiosyncrasies about life in general is unique,
He likes to dissect the meaning of his existence in prose.
and thereby arrive at the conclusion of the
axiom "am I my brothers keeper?"
Sharing his thoughts and innermost feelings
with his fellow man are his greatest assets.
He is in full command of his faculties and in the
center of his being. "Bravo"

John B. Cruz

Himspiration

I am inspired by men, as I approach the 21st century
They, like hymnspiration, soothe many women's souls.
Some men are like righteous and some are brassy and bold.
Many have little conscience, so seek shelter in holes.

I am inspired by men, who stand as leaders of what's right.
They are symbols of honesty, commitment, peace and love.
So, I call upon these men, who are my himspiration
To treat women with respect, using wisdom from above.

Hymnspiration includes words and music of praise.
It brings out natural beauties of hope and joy!
Himspiration includes comforting words and support
To increase women's confidence, with any man or boy.

Music is my hymnspiration!
Men are my himspiration!

Eunice Paddio-Johnson

Visions

Man is dogged (or blessed) by visions that the lesser beings lack
They may lead him to enchantment or put his soul to rack
Remorse may cloud his conscience and the visions he'd disown
And welcome crude companions when he fears to be alone
He may move in drab precision where the influential lead
Or live, a slavish victim to a vice, his work, or creed
But, freed of encumbrances that handicap the mind,
Man enters mystic realms the creator has designed.
Native of the living earth, he feels the lure for things beyond
And something deep within his psyche struggles to respond
He walks upon the mountain with the moonlight in his face
And, startled, stops to marvel at the magnitude of Space
'Mid the moonlight and shadows he feels the breeze with incense cloyed
Is rustling through the grasses from out a timeless void
He sees the stars as lustrous pilots, ringed by hosts of unseen spheres
That guide their spinning legions through the vortex of the years
At sea or on a distant shore—wherever he may dwell
Man may sense creation's glory when the visions cast their spell.

George A. Hymer

Letting Go

Many times I have cried, letting the tears go;
They say time heals all wounds, but time moves so slow.
I've let go of so many in my life I have loved;
Not even looking out for me, when push come to shove.
Is it possible for anyone to return my love so freely?
To give, and to care, and to love so completely?
No, not always, for many have left me to cry;
Left me to drown in my tears while my heart cries out, "Why?"
How can this be done, have they no eyes to see;
All that they've done and are doing to me?
The tears often come and I let them go;
But my heart is breaking, more than they'll know.
A heart may be broken, but it beats just the same;
As each day we wander through new kinds of pain.
Through the thick fogs of my memories;
And through my teary eyes like stormy seas;
Pain or no pain, we all do what we must;
To walk hand in hand, and to slowly build trust.
Though the pain and the sorrow burn more than we'll show;
The best part of crying and hurting, is that of letting go.

Cory Jean Watters

Goodbye

I have bid these farewell words one last time,
They sound so much like a rhyme.
Goodbye...

We've bid these words to our loved ones in the past,
Their journey is now over, heaven at last.
Goodbye...

We've all said a special prayer,
And asked God to please take care.
Goodbye...

We view the body just once more,
Then forever shut is the casket door.
Goodbye...

We stand here as it is lowered in the ground,
Then it is covered with a huge dirt mound.
Goodbye...

Goodbye we say,
On this saddening day,
Goodbye...
Written in memory of Myrtle Klick

Gina R. Schmitz

Prayer Of A Firefighter's Wife

There's an angry fire that's raging through a mountainside tonight.
They've called for everyone to help, for now all districts will unite.
The news is stating the inferno was started by a passer-by.
It is amazing how disaster can flare up with a wink of an eye.
My husband was called along with his crew to help control the blaze.
This all could have been prevented in so many simple ways.
There are a lot of men and women whose lives depend on the others.
Some are fathers, husbands, some are sons, daughters, wives and mothers.
I pray to you, dear Lord, please protect all the men and women at that fire.
I pray they receive the manpower and equipment they need to acquire.
Please help them to protect all the homes and structures in the fire's deadly way.
Please, please bring my husband home to me so I can tell him all I need to say.
Please give him strength and power to drag that heavy line and hose.
Please give his crew all it takes to draw this to a close.
I pray to you to protect every firefighter's life,
and please return my husband to his forever loving wife.

Jacki J. Boone

Inspirations Of My Life

As I enter my senior years of life,
Things come to my mind of happiness and strife.
I started my life as one of three.
My sister and brother are dear to me.
My parents I lost a few years ago.
And I truly do miss them so.
I married and had a family of six.
Of whom we lost one due to fate's sad tricks.
But my life has been inspired by
family and friends dear.
I would not trade them, Oh! have no fear!
They have stood beside me, my troubles to share.
To back me or help me because they care.
My troubles have been many, through loss of those dear.
But my family has been there with kindness and cheer.
When I am gone, I hope they'll know
How much I have loved their concerns so.
Life's inspirations mean much to me.
And I pray God will bless my family.

Betty Orender

Think Of Me

When you think of me
Think of a stately forest tree
One not easily felled by fate
Unless it's the final date
that no one can foresee.
Think of me bending with the wind
But never quite touching the ground
Think of me listening to every sound
Absorbing into my very being
Everything around me I'm hearing and seeing
And my leaves quivering with the forces shaking me
And from which I can never ever flee.
Think of me - the stately forest tree.

Catherine A. Cahill

Autumn Will Come Again

The years are piling up as I reach that milestone,
thirty something or just plain thirty
whatever you call it I call it young yet old,
Or should I say young enough not to be old.
So I'll continue one day at a time, each day getting older still
till the day comes when I'll be too old to be young.
So time will continue, then autumn will come again.
The leaves will turn color and drop to the ground.
Just as the winter of life comes on.
My joints will stiffen, my hair will gray and autumn will come again.
Then when I am laid to rest and all but forgotten,
Decaying in the ground, the beautiful leaves of autumn
will fall once more.
My spirit's joy will be that autumn truly will come again.
Only now my great great grand children shall enjoy autumn in the
spring of their life.

John E. Anderson

Lynn's Flower

Each day, when the sun heats through
this clenched green casing,
and I feel it warming the cool darkness —
Each day, I trust these rays a little more,
and dream of my blossom's softness,
and brave shape, and vivid hues that
change in dreams from night purples to
fuchsias to blood red.

Will you remember the fragrance after
petals scatter in the wind?

I am a flower in Lynn's garden, rooted
firm in blessed earth. And summer storms
have bent this stalk, tearing leaves on
jagged rocks, but I stayed clench until
I felt the warmth and light return.
And now soft petals may unfurl safely.

The gardener lets no one pick her blossoms
to complement the vase in the hall,
so wild winds can carry these seeds,
far beyond the beauty of this place.

Jacqueline Raznik Shapo

Three Precious Gifts

Our life, our love, our children
These three are most special to me,
For without these things the world would not be.

God gives us these precious gifts
We should cherish every moment we have,
And never let them go.

For we may never have this chance again.

Beverly Van Zandt

The Storm Inside

As a storm tosses a ship as of whim
This control or lack of rages inside
Feeling and thought reeling about
Question and worry threaten to capsize
The brink of destruction all too near
Fleeting moments lined up in sequence
Life perceived as such all too often
Solitary confinement of sorts by choice
Precious thoughts kept in secret knowing
A whirlwind of activity paralyzes the brain
The escape desired found in pages
Body bound to earth mind free to soar
Written worlds self-created or otherwise
Words and sentences create visions of wonder
Hope once more restored to heart
Freedom to exist as one yet again
Chaos which threatened avoided another time
The storm inside finds momentary peace
The ship sails on placid seas once more.

Jamie Simpson

Dawn

That smoking shadow in the mirror awakens me again
this time I stare long enough and see the pot burnt black
smoldering with my love left on your back burner
evaporated to a distinctly memorable shape
a charred outline of many attempts:
A face scalded by sad smiles
a scarred tongue
torn licking the ragged rim
inside my begging cup
taking only the state of tin to bed.

Now, beginning at the end
I untravel the trail
which has led me to this clearing:
thickets no longer prick my arms
no snapping branches whip my eyes
and you no longer cover my face
with your blinding kisses
I am free of your memory
although I will never forget
the sweet taste of our lives led together.

Alexander D. Bingham

Villanelle Anyone?

A thing there is, to speak of which I'm keen
Tho' what it is I've no idea at all
A state like this has kept me ever mean.

It came to me a languid, pale spalpeen
And o'er my life it spread a grisly pall.
A thing there is, to speak of which I'm keen.

A cosmic post 'gainst which The Fears may lean?
A rogue archetype or th' Angelic Fall?
A state like this has kept me ever mean.

A past from where, in fact, I've never been?
"La Belle Dame Sans Merci" hath me in thrall?
A thing there is, to speak of which I'm keen.

A place the heart hath felt but eyes not seen?
The ultra metaphysical catchall?
A state like this has kept me ever mean.

The echo of our song, mayhap, Eileen?
The memory erased by grief beyond recall.
A thing there is, to speak of which I'm keen.
A state like this has kept me ever mean.

John Devine

Snowy Mountain Snowflakes

Away up in the Heavens reaching toward the sky,
Those beautiful covered mountains, look so very high.
The blue of the tree covered mountain, is pretty as can be
But the white of those snowy peaks, look pretty to me.
Now I wonder what those snowflakes, that fell throughout the night
Could tell us of the country, that they saw throughout their flight.
Oh you beautiful little snowflakes, if you could talk to me
You could tell a great big story of things that you did see
As you floated round the earth, away up in the sky.
You have seen a lot of scenery, as you were passing by
The winds I'm sure have brought you many times this way,
Then turned around and blown you back again next day.
Now you are a snowflake, shining nice and white
You came to earth so gently, falling through the night.
And though you cannot talk to me, I know that it is true
You have seen a lot more country, than I can ever do.

Clinton Hassett

Phenomenons

A phenomenon is very much like a dream,
Though a dream makes inroads while you doze.
A phenomenon strikes like rapids in a stream,
And a dream more like where calm water flows.

From a bud a blossom begins to swell,
Nature's grandest phenomenon of all.
The bees are attracted by that heavenly smell,
'Till the petals at last they must fall.

How very much like that blossom, is love,
Suitors drawn to it in a parade.
Then reality strikes, no longer a white dove,
And that beautiful blossom will fade.

That robust blossom now strikes me as odd,
Having survived many a windy squall.
A departed love, like an act of God,
Is what causes those petals to fall.

Jack Stevenson

Heartbreak Of Mt. Maurice

Mt. Maurice broods o'er the town
Thoughtlessly flung at her feet.
Once it was a star in her crown
Its streets so straight and neat.

The homes gleamed new and bright,
The yards with flowers all aglow,
Kept by hearts gay and light;
Then depression laid them low.

The houses were deserted, one by one
Paint peeled and fences fell down.
Sightless windows stared at the sun
As the yards turned bare and brown.

Mt. Maurice watches in silence and in sorrow,
Her listless people no longer hope.
They have given up their plans for tomorrow
With the future they are unable to cope.

Her sadness deepens as the days go by
And in the quiet pines you hear her sigh.
As she reaches forlornly to the sky,
You can feel the echo of her broken cry.

Inez Mahan Wagner

"An Old Apple Orchard"

Did you ever go walking on a warm spring morn,
Through an old apple orchard where new things are born?

Majestically and proud—in rows they stand,
Yet change with each season to enhance the land.

The white profusion-has a brush stroke of rose,
The perfume travels—as the wind gently blows.

The drifting petals make a curtain of white,
Then float and sway to the grass where they light.

Stand under these trees and see a blue sky,
The beauty is so great—it will make you cry.

The bees are busy and visit each tree,
This is a sight every person should see.

These petals are so light—and paper thin,
You can barely feel their touch on your skin.

Birds are busy—with babes in their nest,
But after awhile—they sit down to rest.

Before you're too old—go—take the time,
See an old orchard—like I do mine..........

Janey B. Johnson

Buzzards

They float along with the raging wind,
Through days unnumbered, without an end.

They have not beauty, but unfailing grace,
And fly together as if running a race.

They get higher and higher, almost touching the sky.
And then they almost forget to fly.

They circle around, again and again,
Giving the pretense they have nothing to win.

Suddenly they drop, with talons outstretched,
To an unsuspecting victim, that's made a good catch.

They glutton their catch, then invite one or two,
Too pick the remains, in the darkening hue.

Then they fly up high, with an upsurge of wind,
To the days unnumbered where there is no end.

Deborah H. Erby

Reflections

In His eyes she brings happiness.
Through my eyes she brings sorrow.
In His eyes she is both sweet and beautiful.
Through my eyes she is ordinary and plain.
In His eyes every day with her is a pleasure.
Through my eyes every day becomes a struggle.
His eyes came to me today, asking to give her a chance.
To search deep inside my heart.
The time was now....
Standing face to face, our eyes met.
"What do His eyes see that mine can't?"
"I want to feel the happiness."
"I want to see with opened eyes."
"I want to believe in all of His words."
Tears began to flow.
As I gently wiped her tears, my hand touched the mirror.

Bonnie L. Swanson

Father

He lost his way,
Through the side streets and alley ways.
He was just a drop of water in a raging sea,
of lost souls and foolish foes.

Yet he still walks within my soul.
Like waves crashing upon the shore.
Covering my pimples and persuading my pain.
And cresting but again with the past.

His pounding presence upon my mother,
as he searched for his
manhood and respect.
Each lost with every blow repelled

But singing Jolson tunes,
Whilst coming home to the
Aroma of luscious cuisine.
And crying upon my lap for Frank's departure

Father
He was hopelessly human,
Which is but a joyous diary of deeds,
which we must all digest.

John F. Tozzi

The Widow

I see the widow standing there with her head
thrown back in rage,
She can't believe her husband died, it's like a
book without a page.
She shadows her mourning all around, as she sits
by the fire with her head hanging down.
I hear the crackling fire as it tries to comfort her.
But this feeling will never leave her cold and
blackened soul.
I feel the anger coming on, because we know
this isn't fair.
For the widow to be standing with the wind
blowing through her hair.
She stands beside his grave, and tries to
feel like someone strong and brave.
But without him, she'll never be the same.
I see the widow standing there with
her head thrown back in rage.

Ashley E. Taylor

The Search

This pursuit, this relentless drive in quest for truth
Through the jungle of jargons pretentious, ungainly, uncouth;
The tracks defined by complex dimensions of space and time,
Leave the mind puzzled in quandary, sans grace, sans rhyme.
A sense uncanny, overshadowing commitment to precious objective -
Pride, prejudice, or passion, could have pitiful, pejorative
Reflection on trusted companions, whose love and compassion
Life's essential raison d'etre, existential sine qua non!
The seductive serenity and charming magic of a starry night,
Or the dazzling daze of a marvelous morning bright,
Or the stupendous glamour of a gorgeous, beautiful ballet
Could have befuddled the vision through an ominous, mendacious melee!
Malicious intrigues, mutilated thoughts of the misanthropes;
Debilitating destiny, deranged mind, direly devoid of hopes;
Harrowing exorcism, slaughtered souls and sacrificed sanity;
Conscience, courage, creed, and credence rendered to vanity!
A grieving heart, groping in the dark, in muted motion;
Despite faults, foibles, failures, commotion of compunction,
Switching to redundant dreams in a totally obscure trance;
No exuberance nor cynicism, searching for truth, for deliverance.

Jerry Chowdhury

Quest Of The Quill

Shall rushing din of dawn repeat??..
..Thus, barren parchment my defeat!?

Hath Frosted echoes not been caught?..
..And tear-blurred Browning??...all for naught???...

Shall not this mind and pen be one?!...
- No conquered verse remain undone!

Will not this heart, this brain, this hand - succumb?!..
to soul-inked, desk-stilettoes - flung!?

Shall, retrieved, blue-bleeding, fingered lance lay down
not one posteritic volume - bound??

Shall not melodic ethos - soon revered - spew forth;
to alter distant poet's course?..

Shall moon-fought Battle of the Pen
ooze words - forgotten - at my End?

Hath this lust for language - painted - so deceived..
Thy composition; yet bequeathed??

....Should all these fears befall - at Thy Behest;
as Ever Known: Thy wondrous Gift - of sculpted word -

..I, did so truly quest!....

John Willard DuVall

Ghost Of Respect

My country called; I packed to go
To a foreign place I didn't know
I was young and having fun
Then taught to fight, and use a gun

Was dodging bullets and running fast
Then tumbled back from the blast
Was sent back home before I was well
And welcomed by a go to Hell!

I thought this is the country I went to defend?
I lost my eye, my hand, my friend?
A friend who wrote this and knows me as Ghost?
Said listen, my friend; I admire you most

You could have run and hid when you went
And in 30 years been President
And for those who told you to GO TO HELL
Obviously don't think very well

They voted for one who didn't go
Who didn't inhale, and never did blow
If asked who I respect the most?
It won't be hard to say my friend Ghost

Grover C. Walker III

Salvation

You said you wanted to heal my wounds,
To dry my tears, to touch my soul,
And to love me unconditionally.

I've been fed with all the countless lies.
Trust shattered like glass on pavement.
Why should I let you be my Savior?

But I'm soothed by your tender words,
Caressed by the look in your eyes,
And reassured by your faith in me.

I long to reach out and touch you
Before you fade away
Like so many other opaque dreams.

Choo H. Oh

The City And You

So often I have tried to find the words
to explain just what you are,
But they always seemed to escape me,
till now in the darkness with the noise
of the city - my thoughts are of you.

Like the tall buildings of steel and glass,
your heart so cold and hard.

Beware my love before it is too late
and the city claims you forever.
Open your heart and let the love grow.
Beware my love of a day to come
when you wake to a cloud of smoke,
and the beat of an empty heart.

Janet Gordon-Lee

God's Will

O God every gift given us is thine,
To help us achieve thy great design.
We should dedicate all earthly treasures,
time, and skill,
In order that we may always do thy will.

All our days from early youth,
We should surely use to spread thy truth,
Where ever we work in office or mill,
Your word we should use to do thy will.

Whatever strength you give our arms or hands,
We should always dedicate to run thy lands,
If we just run a home or nurse the ill,
We should be found trying to do thy will.

If we try to be leaders or make a great speech,
To be great singers or do our best to teach,
We should dedicate all the places
we try to fill,
In order that the results may be thy will.

Elva King

"Come With Me, Listen To The Sea"

Have you ever been where you could listen to the seas?
To just lean back, close your eyes, and feel the breeze.

If not, then come along and do some daydreaming with me,
Find your favorite place to relax, be comfortable, feel free.

Now, hear the thunder of the waves as they come near the shore,
See them coming in, when they arrive, just hear the mighty roar.

Can you feel the power of God's hand, and feel His presence everywhere,
As he moves the wind and water and pushes them up into the air.

See the white caps forming as the wind gathers in the wave,
Then it's gone, only its beauty in our minds we will have to save.

Look at the sand there on the beach, can you see it glisten?
Do you feel someone there telling us to stop, look, and listen.

Hear the many sea gulls cry as they soar in the wind,
Searching for the food from the last wave that came in.

Can you hear the wind whistling through the tall grasses,
As we sit there enjoying the sea and beach as time passes.

It seems to be telling us to enjoy what we have witnessed today.
And to give our thanks to God as we travel down life's highway.

So fold your hands and thank God with your prayer,
Even though you didn't have to leave your rockin' chair.

george gurney

Progress!!!

They say we can't stop progress, but why can't we slow the race?
To level the land, cut down trees, and build strip malls all over the
place.
I've noticed that many of these strip malls aren't even filled.
But still they continue to build and build and build.
Will these speculators be around when they board up the store
windows in town?
The old timers who've lived here for ages
Some were born here and here hoped to die.
Are becoming really frightened, at property taxes rising so high.
Is this the price of progress? There must be a better way
Than putting old folks out of their homes
What a terrible price to pay.

Elsie Veno

To Have A Dog

Have you ever had a dog? If not I bet you wish you had.
To live and grow up without a dog is sad.

There are all kinds, short, fat, long and tall.
Some with short hair, short tails, or no tail at all.

There will be times of complete frustration,
There may come a time for castration.

The agony you feel when one is lost.
You would do any thing to have it back whatever the cost.

Of all the love you seek,
None is more rewarding than the lick on the cheek.

You will miss the toss and
Fetch with the stick whenever your dog is sick.

You will miss the friendly bark when you return after dark.
You will miss the muffled whining when it comes time
for the evening dining.

So while you are young and with plenty of time,
Go out and find a loving canine.

James C. Fletcher

The Sand Dollar

The day at the beach is a treat for me.
To look and search for a special treasure.
Many are looking to find their delight,
But the sand dollar to me is without measure.

The sand dollar has a Poinsettia representing
The birth of a child who is so dear,
The crucifix on the opposite side telling
He died on the cross for me without fear.

He gave His life for you and me
Because of His great love for us, you see.
He was obedient to God our Father
And laid down His life on that old tree.

He arose from the dead and became our Savior.
We can place our faith and trust in Him
Knowing He'll always be there.
Peace and trust and love for all men.

So I look for sand dollars far and wide
They are great reminders, these little shells,
Take the symbols and hold them dear,
Abide by them and it will keep you out of hell.

Hazel Sturgeon

"Brownie"

Moving slow and crooked down my cabinet door, seeming
To look with eyes, as if to explore.

His surroundings are vast, but his world is small, and
He moves with such swiftness, although just a crawl.

Even though he cannot hear, his antennae is far more
Superior than a human ear, when he falls on his back, and
Seems to squeak, during this time, he's a lot more weak,
And if you're there, try not scare, the little brownie
To death.

Although he is intolerable, and absolutely venerable,
There are facts that should be considered. Today diseases
Are prevalent, though we are sometimes benevolent, people
Are dying, and pestilence is rising, and brownies are
High in protein—!

Now let this be understood, especially to those who are
Prude, this may suddenly change your mood, that someday soon
It may be our thoughts for food!

Ijaaz L. Givens

Sin

I'm sin, I've come to set-up shop upon the earth
To make humans act their worst

I can lure your mind and veins with poison
Take you off the course you've chosen

I'm sin, I've come to set-up shop upon the earth

I can make a woman sell her soul
Give up the birth she wants to hold

I can make a man smile until he cracks his lips from enticement
Then cool his mouth with the wet sip of excitement

I can make you hit, kill, destroy the friend-nurturer-companion
You sift to know - and make their spirit cease to grow

Am I evil, destructive, or bad
I can make the human race mad

How do I multiply and breed
I existed since mankind was a seed

I'm sin, I've come to set-up shop upon the earth
I've grown so much, please measure my girth

I've been here once before so please do not search
Only this time
I've come to set up on the four corners of the earth

Grace Elaine Stewart

The Flower

The flowers once bloomed so bright and fair.
They filled the air with fragrance everywhere.
As you strolled the walk on the garden path
You plucked them off as you passed.

These beautiful flowers that grew each day.
Gently faded as time passed away.
But the pedals soon faded day by day.
Leaving their foot prints here to stay.

Each day God looked down, on his flowers.
Watching them fade from his beautiful tower.
When the time has come for me to pluck.
I'll pick these flowers to put in my book.

There's a name to match these beautiful flowers.
God gathered these flowers to put around his throne.
So look for them there when, you get home.

Addie Combs

Our Country

We piled into our car to drive this land
To see these beauties we salute by our flag
In New York we drove over bridges so high
We could almost reach out and touch the sky.
Further on South we crossed a bridge
We were driving so low we could almost reach out and touch fish
Over hills over dales the beauties are breathless
Marking each entrance and all exits too
Each state seems to have its invisible bounds.
Then on to the West with its mountains so high
Then dropping to deserts ever so dry.
The trees of our nation too numerous to name
Maples, Apples, Peaches, and Pine
Redwoods so big they boggle the mind.
Beauty abounds in this land of ours
But settled by humans thoughtless and unkind
Trying to destroy this land of ours
With garbage strewn highways and pollution run wild.
Please Dear God help us reclaim our land
This beauty You gave us - this beautiful land

Helen L. Casavant

Golden Pond

If there were such a thing as a golden pond
To seek faces that smile upon you
To see or to believe in the black pond,
  hearing the evil behind his frown
Looking deep into the eyes that are
  staring back at you
No words are needed to be said
Feeling your eyes gazing beyond the
  imaginations of our minds
Hearing your brain talk without a single
  movement of the mouth
Searching for your soul with your eyes closed
You will not find it without knowledge
Wisdom is the key to knowledge to find
  your soul
Believing, when your mind talks in silence
Having faith in your actions to receive
  fulfillment in your life
If there were such a thing as a...
"Golden Pond"

Dana Hess

Mother's Words To The Children

Your family and friends have come today,
  to share together, your wedding day.

We have watched you grow throughout these years,
  sharing your happiness and wiping your tears.

Today you will be united as one, may God Bless
  your lives with daughters and sons.

Life together will be a give and take,
  along the way, there will be many mistakes.

If you can keep Love and Faith in your life,
  the rest will come easy, with very little strife.

We wish you happiness with all our hearts,
  and give you our blessings, for a prosperous start.

Janice P. Kern

"Prophesy Of Soul mates"

A heart's spreading quivering wings,
to soar and fly,
unfettered, no cages
Graying wisdom reaches into my soul,
caressing me gently
Hands and gold-kissed hair entwined,
my neck exposed and tingles spread
like beads of fire
Trembling fingers trace, the outline of my face,
soul mates,
lovers of the ancient and the middle ages
Haunting strains of Enya, fill my ears and chest
vibrations of the soul laid bare,
I kneel exposed
Wisdom cautiously guides,
passion like sweet wine
and I
the leaping light of inexperience

Janell Marie Reyes

School

We need prayer in school
To take us through the day.
Don't listen to the devil,
And say we don't need to pray
My friend, if we don't pray it's a sin.

We can't get along without God.
God is the beginning and He is the end.
God gave his son Jesus, and Jesus is the way.
Who woke us up this morning to start another day?
Jesus does it every day.

Who woke us up this morning? Jesus did.
Who put food on our table? Jesus did.
Who carried us to school to study? Jesus did.
Who gave you a healthy mind? Jesus did.
Who gave us a mind to do right? Jesus did.

There are many reasons people in school should pray.
It's a God given right, and it will teach you to obey the right.
You will get your lessons better day by day.
The Lord will lead you the right way.
And you won't have any desire to fight.

Hattie McDonald

Anticipation Of The Storm

Slowly my head rises
to the distant rumble of the skies
as the wind becomes nonexistent
behind the layered darkness' disguise

Questions bubble in my head
like butterflies on a summer's day
long since died with tears I've shed

What is to be washed away
to a land far beyond?
Who's to say what eyes shall open
to see another day?

The breeze now seeps from darkness' veil
now the pattering of drops and leaves fill the land
while winds now fill a blackened sail

The rains are now set here firm
and trees yield to the westerly wind
the clouds now wet the surface of the earth
and wash pure the ones who admit they've sinned

Andrew C. Ross

Reunion In The Sky

I am sending out my invitations
To the Reunion In The Sky,
On that day, in the sweet by and by.
We shall greet our friends and neighbors
With a smile, and how are you?
The clouds will part, to reveal a heavenly view
The Saviour shall rise in all His Glory,
To welcome us with open arms,
A gentle peace will surround us,
Protecting us from all harm,
This will be the greatest reunion, we shall ever attend,
It will be in honor of our Saviour,
When He shall come again.
The trumpet will sound in great crescendo,
Announcing the arrival of "The King"
The Heavenly Chorus shall sing,
"The King is coming, the King is coming"
Praise God, "He's coming again."
Please accept my invitation, "To The Reunion In The Sky"
We shall live forever, in the sweet by and by.

Almeda Lou Utterback

To Thee Utmost Jesus Saves

To thee utmost Jesus saves
To thee utmost Jesus saves
To thee utmost Jesus saves

He'll pick you up and he'll turn you around
He'll plant your feet on higher ground
To thee utmost Jesus saves
He saved my soul and he made me whole
He helped me reach my goal

To thee utmost Jesus saves
He is a burden bearer
He'll lift your heavy load
Because Jesus save, Jesus saves
To thee utmost Jesus save
He heal my body
He saved my soul
He set me free
And now I can agree
That Jesus saves to these utmost

Edna E. Lewis

I Give Thee "Thanks"

From those of us that push the pen...
To those of you -who read- to search within.

I give thee thanks for taking time...
To read and remember my little rhyme.

I'm not so trained, to write a book...
But my eyes are trained to take a look.

At the world which does surround...
to hear the delightful little sounds
to see the beauty within our gaze.

Through the sunshine on special days
or through the misty morning maze.

To give thanks for memories
To smell the flowers and look at trees
To feel the earth, beneath my feet.
For food on hand, of which to eat.

The ability to survive - I thank thee
Lord for being alive.

I thank you friend, for reading on,...
Maybe, within your heart...
I've put a song.

Barbara Driggers

Wounded

Crouched in wait, the moment will come
To unleash the fury, taste the blood he so much craves.

Time's a friend, every heartbeat brings closer the moment
He'll relish terror, agony in the eyes of his enemy.

Neither are thirst and hunger foes.
Nourished by the smell of revenge growing stronger
each moment.

He alone knows of his presence in the jungle
he hides in ambush.

Pain is great, borne is silence.
Roar of rage remains within
Ever deepening his lust for mayhem.

Heart once warm, now cold, hard,
Love overwhelmed by hate.

Fire of vengeance raging,
Patiently . . . he waits.

Joe Wackler

We Poets Must Take A Stand Against Our Critics

Well we're people from all walks of life who come together to celebrate one thing which is poetry for a lot of reasons, because we read and write for season to season. Therefore we can't let others stop us from dreaming, because we don't know what life will surely bring. While we can't be ashamed of our cause it's something that we enjoy doing with ourselves that's why we choose to share it with the rest of the world instead of leaving it on the shelves. No matter what we go through our faith will keep our heads up real high mainly that we as poets can't let opportunity pass us by. Most of the time if we listen to others we will no accomplish nothing in this business and our goals will be a big old mess. Why should we just sat back and waste out talent, because of fear it's something inside of us that don't need to be, and every day we don't have to listen what others have to say. If we don't show that we have some backbone, our profession will not get no where, because we will give others the impression that we don't care. So as we experience failures and success to prove our cause is fulfilling means to do our very best. Why should we let the world make our decision, because we poets has our own visions.

Donnie Vale McAllister

Darlin' I Wanna Be Your Only Love

This story has a beautiful beginning but I'm not
too sure about the ending
You're not free to love me and I'm sure someone
will be hurt and so afraid that someone will be me.
Darlin' I wanna be your only love can't you see
Don't you know how much you already mean to me?
I want all your caresses and kisses for me
and if you're holding someone too
I want to be that someone held close to you.
I don't wanna be the one waiting and
waiting for just a glimpse of you
Darlin' I wanna be the happy one not
the one cryin' all alone when you leave
and go back to your home.
You say not to worry things will be alright
that one day you'll stay with me for more than just a night.
Just tell me over and over again that your love belongs to me today
Darlin' I wanna be your only love for always.

Della Hurn

The Whale Watch

We quiver on the breech of swells tormented.
Tossed and churned by Neptune's fork unseen.
White winged scavengers soar and wonder why
My cry of joy at a school of silver bream.
Neophyte eyes intently searching whitecaps
Are shaded, by hands to curb the silvan glare,
As we leap from trough to trough like dolphin playing,
Plowing the sea to finbacks spouting there.
Your presence stands beside me silent...waiting;
Watchful and refreshed by frothing spume.
This will be a very "special happening".
I thank the Master everything's in tune.
All around warm spouts from blowholes shower.
Are these giants laughing at our laborious way?
Are they calling us to join them in their playground
Deep beneath us in the cold Atlantic bay?
Brothers of the deep salute we must your freedom.
My brother of the earth, deep thanks are given you
For the gift.....a moment of realization
Of things I dared not dream of coming true.

Christel B. Ellis

Angel Wings

I tiptoed into her shadowy bedroom and knelt beside her bed. I touched her hand; she grasped mine. "Thank God you're here," she said. "Just rest, let the Lord take over," was all that I could say. She nodded too weak to answer; I bowed my head to pray. "Dear Father in Heaven, just touch her...we know you can do all things." And then in the shadows, I thought I could see the shape of "Angel Wings."

When next I tiptoed into her room, I held her hand as she slept. My fervent prayer was: "Touch her, Lord," and I bowed my head and wept. "Just touch her, Lord, relieve the pain, let her rest," was my silent plea. "We know you hear and answer prayer, 'That she may walk with Thee,' we give you the praise in Jesus' name for all these many things," and I was sure I heard the silent flutter of "Angel Wings."

Again I tiptoed into her room, just to touch her hand and see her precious face. Then I knew at last, she rested within the Father's saving grace. Yes, God reached down and touched her, gave her rest, relieved the pain. I hope someday I'll hear "Mom" say, "Thank God you're here."...again. I know God looked down and beckoned her to come where the angels sing. He lifted her up, up to heaven on a pair of "Angel Wings."

Judith Wooldridge

Loneliness

Loneliness is a complete starvation
To hold someone close in the dark;
Or, to run and laugh in the park.
It's a need to explore and talk;
To make a journey out of a short walk.
Loneliness is an island forbidden.
Being alone, barren, hidden.
It's needs and desires pushed so far inside,
All emotions become too numb for sighs.
Total emptiness - is this how a soul dies?
I forget even the warmth of tears;
That too, is lost in paralyzing fear.
Loneliness is needing to feel - to care.
Reaching out
Only to find
That no one is there...

Anna Frances

Emotions

Emotions,
Trapped inside a heart-shaped jewelry box.
Emotions of anger,
Hurt,
Humiliation,
Regrets.

Destructive emotions,
That can eat you up.
Like a time bomb waiting to explode.

Emotions,
Locked-up in the heart-shaped jewelry box,
Hurting too much for it to get out into the open,
For everyone to see.

Every day,
Each second,
The emotions eats up the heart-shaped jewelry box,
Destroying it,
Ready to explode any second.

And one day it does explode,
Leaving nothing but broken pieces of the heart-shaped jewelry box.

Elisha Ouano

The Ride

Thick black ice, high revving engine
trees, sky, ground spinning into the night
Twenty miles away in bed
I sit up with a fright!
The vision unfolding in my mind
as if I were standing there
My loves last wish granted
is the last moment we would share.

Now wretched, sitting, looking,
fingers tangled in chain link fence
Glazed over eyes, lost sanity,
really, nothing makes much sense
Self tormented beyond repair
in my mind nowhere to hide
If only I'd done like I was asked
and went along for the ride.

Jack Robert Olson

"The Secret Of Love"

A love that most never find .... a meeting of souls,
truly one of a kind.

A love where dreams put reality to the test,
and leaves the imagination without place to rest.

A love where the inner self is complete and refine....
rising up to meet God's mate of design ....

To love we must give ... all that we can, putting
first in our life ... one woman... one man...

My prayer is for you, waste no more of your life...
but share them together, as husband and wife.

Carol Osborn

The Path of Life

As we wander down the path of life, through many twists and turns, challenges and struggles are met yet never to return.

Every hurdle overtaken shapes who we will become, each memory stored deep within our souls for centuries yet to come. Until one day when one must say my traveling is done, and the memories will stay stored far away from those we had once loved.

Barbara Pease

Power Struggle

Power struggle perceived in all walks of life
Trying to destroy with contention and strife
The earth is so beautiful God's own creation
But why are so many in such devastation

First it is mild works like a real charm
No hurt or distress but later brings harm
Why is there not a place betwixt or between
Where things wouldn't be so confusing and mean

Power acclaimed in many conversations
Not only in bad but also good relations
Its struggle and pull then push and shove
Ending some of the very best kind of love

How good it would be to just meet halfway
Instead of one saying I shall have my way
One always gives while the other one takes
Cause usually one things I make no mistakes

Are we fooling ourselves or others its plain
Deep down we know but it is hard to explain
Why can't we both take and both also give
Then life would be so much easier to live

Eleanor Hunt

Your Smile

You bid me bye the other day with your smile—gay,
'Twas a surprise that certain hour for my calm eyes,
The vividness of your smile carried miles away,
Recessed into my mind—sublime, comforting sighs.

Your smile is vivid, with red lips of true perfection,
And those white teeth, all surround with,
Soft complexion, fragile face of sweet confection,
Encompassed by hair fair, all-backgrounding width.

I was encouraged to receive your happy radiance—bestowed,
My soul was spirited, my madness calmed from sorrow,
Relieved sadness, instilled mirth and worth—untold,
Etched my memory, lifted my hopes—longing for morrow.

John C. Flores

A Journey

Silent one who lies there as still as a tree trunk that has fallen upon the ground motionless though it seems, does it still breathe? His complexion paler than before, a tint of yellow glow surrounds him as if to protect him on his travels. His lips parted as if to say "Good-bye, Farewell, I will see you soon."
His hair flowed like a stream each strand following the other so smoothly in place.
His face, calm and pleasant, a sigh of relaxation after a long day.
He wore a fancy black suit as if to celebrate a wonderful event.
A mournful sound came from a short distance away like a pack of wolves using unearthly voices. His vision gone, he grew weak and tired from his fixation to focus on the surrounding sounds that began to become eerie and sent chills through him.
He laid there still and tranquility began to settle upon him.
He thought of his family and all the things he knew and loved, slowly they flourished before they began to fade away.
His soul opened up and heart embraced them so he could take their spirits with him on his travels.
All was done and it was time for him to leave.
The rectangular wooden object soon became his ship, set to sail as it was lowered down slowly with care to insure no damage would come to his vessel. He then released his anchor and set sail his ship as his navigator guided him on a journey of mystery.....

Heather Matthews

The Veil

Beneath her veil all I see
Two perfect lips to smother me
Hands to cook, to clean, to mend
A lucky lass the king does send
How thankful for me I know she must be.

I'm her knight, hooray! Hooray!
Down from the village to take her away.
For loyalty to sovereign to neighbor to kin
I'm no longer a pauper, can raise my chin
Oh, princess, what a glorious day!

Beneath her veil is something more
An impending chaos that opens doors
To anger, selfishness, and self-doubt
Unheard voices that rebel and shout
Craving vanity that was hers before.

Carmen Lusignan

"My Most Wanted Gift"

If you wake up on Christmas morning,
Underneath my Christmas tree,
I want you to know that Santa Claus
Brought my most wanted gift to me.

You know you might be awakened
To something that could be shocking.
You see that old Santa Claus
Might stuff you in my stocking.

It's not how or where I find you.
It's just important to find you there.
It's also important for you to know
How much I really care.

Now I don't know what you want for Christmas.
But with me you can't go wrong.
In time you'll see that here with me
Is right where you belong.

Frank Gilmore

Morning Blues

It was just another early morning,
Until the alarm-clock jangled clues
Rending sandman's grip from sleepy eyelids;
And rose-colored dreams to sluggish blues!

Half awake, he ambled to the window,
As the morning's sun came into view.
The mind still tired, remained a sleeping;
Missing sight...of a pretty patch of blue.

The maples stood tall ...like sentinels;
The grass, a carpet adorned with dew,
The scene as seen, was.... well, normal;
Sleepy-eyes missed ...that little patch of blue.

His half-awake mind suggested breakfast
Enticed by an aromatic brew;
But then, eye and mind were dazzled,
Sun's rays...found that tiny patch of blue.

In that single, unexpected moment,
With eyes fixed on the sun-filled view;
"Bluets" transformed the listless morning
And his heart...to a pleasing rosy hue!

Bernard W. O'Day

If I Had Wings

If I had wings, I would take to flight,
Up and away, and out of sight.
Up where my face, could touch the sun.
Floating gently, till day was done.

If I had wings, I would greet each day,
With the hope that God would show me the way,
To carry life's burdens, when the road is long,
Giving me courage, making me strong.

If I had wings, I would spread them wide,
Offering shelter and warmth inside
To those whose souls are tired and broken,
Giving them solace, peace and hope.

If I had wings, I would let them fold,
Around the world, let the story be told,
That men must learn to love each other,
That each man is the other's brother.

Joyce Lawrence

Stone Gathering

Loved ones past and present reunite this day
Upon rugged stones with paid respects
The angels among stare with mystic eyes
As this day marks the casting of all fossils

Of the world alone

For this is the death of awaited time
Comprehended by the flocking of spirits beyond mortals
The earth is a shadow from a distance
As a kingdom is yet to be roamed

From the world alone

The voyagers of life we have always been
Upon a stone cloud within the universe
Governed by the hands of time
Balanced by the scales of fate

Through the world alone

The sun decorated the days
The moon feathered the nights
Glory shined among a gathering
Heaven is now home

And the world is alone

James Hodges

Silver Tin Ben

Colorful leaves are falling from trees.
Watch out for the stinging bees,
The village house lit with bright lights
Brilliant hues that sparkle in the night.

Soon Mom will be yelling get ready,
Dress warm for the day.
The bus has passed-by, aghast
Crank up silver tin Ben fast.

Gracious Ben is always sleek,
Look ahead and take a peep -
Ride it far with elation
Thankful for a service station.

Teachers and lawyers gathering at holiday time
The clock ticking away with a chime.
People chattering away in the den
Who will inherit old Ben?

Village people along the highway
Children like to play!
Life can trail on many levels
Old Ben is mine now forever.

Della Reeves

"As Night Drifts Yonder"

Atop the waters - so I shall forth cast - one rose for only - Andy.

One rose - one red rose - that I thus treasure deep - I shall cast
upon the ripples of cascading blue - I shall toss a blossom
of love for only you!

Gentle tears from an angel's eye - shall guard my rose - so
deep love shall never die!

Atop the waves that kiss tender against the morning shore -
clung to each tatter'd thorn shall pain be no more!

A thousand tears from mine heart shall be - a bloom that
enchants my soul with poetry.

O'er! O'er! For the rose shall drift - 'pon the clutch of
the water's hold.

Against the insecure wind - such a rose shall drift - so
it can lie in the taint'd aura of moonlight gold.

Atop the waters - so I shall forth cast - one beautiful rose
for thee - at last!

Upon each delicate petal - I shall ever deeply ponder?

As night drifts yonder - to lace mine dreams with the elegant
beauty of you. One lovely rose - a lone rose of red - I long to
pass unto you - from the essence unsaid.

George D. Kovach

Father

How sleep you now, my father? Beneath a square of marble and the sod
upon the shoulder bare of ocean hills where fog pours in through
seaward pines along the mounds of Indians by the shore who once walked
upright just as you - in mist from off the vastness of the sea which
hides within its deep the ancient ships, and onward bore above
three sons and you

A written page before me spread in your fast moving easy hand tells
me of care and thought with you and me twenty years and more ago

Both in a distant place from home
Both with need to see and know the sickness in the world, and hope -
The pain of fear and hate - and longing to be free

Would that I could have shared your pain
As well as warmth and care you gave -
To know you closer, see you clear -
My memory dims of past beyond the grave

Tonight I put my three young boys to rest
Give love and warmth in blanket, hands and voice -
How can I tell you, little sons, how full with tears
I feel the nevermore and yet-to-be - across the misty years.

Drayton S. Bryant

Oceans Of Tears

Sadness appears, weeping...
Using her handkerchief to wipe away tears,
She overtakes me, threatening to swallow me up.
I could wander forever in sadness, crying oceans of salty tears.
Waves of hurt wash over me like the surf of an ocean.
In and out, back and forth, with rhythmic force,
Wearing away at my resistance,
Eroding my judgement, and washing away my hopes,
Through my SADNESS, the death of a child appears,
The child stands, desperately clinging to herself:
A child so forsaken, so forlorn...so unloved.
My eyes are red with tears for this child.
My arms outstretched, and I motion for her.
"Come dear child, let me hold and comfort you."
As the child comes to me, my sadness disappears.
The child know she is loved by me, by someone.
"I love you, child within"

Cynthia Nemec

A Child's Memory

She rests on the Hill of Tomorrow.
Views the Valley of Yesterday.
A small face without an expression,
A young voice with nothing to say.
There's a house in the valley she watches
Through eyes overflowing with tears.
One would think she'd be tired of seeing the past
But the child has been there for years.
She longs to be back in the old house.
To stand in the light that was cast
From the window that meant her security
In that home that belongs to the past.
That house represents all her past dreams,
Her plans and her hopes from within.
Now that house stands abandoned and icy
Swept clean by time's arctic wind.
Now the child has grown much older
Her past is familiar to me
For engraved in the heart of the child
Is her name - my memory.

Debbie Szetela

Heat Wave

I sat on the porch and looked
waiting quietly for something incredible to happen
as the heavy haze lingered.

Suddenly a burst of wind destroyed the silence
gusting through the sizzling heat
banging shutters and hurling dry leaves.

Then the rain hit the earth
as thunderous sparks threatened to strike and burn
the drought stricken land.

Dry streams began to flow through the dust
which covered the spongy soil
as the rain slowed to only a light sprinkle.

The sun began to shine
and a transparent rainbow beamed in the clearing sky
as the heat wave returned.

Barbara L. Darlington

There Is A Cottage Somewhere

There is a cottage for us somewhere
Waiting to be found.
It could be in a flower-strewn meadow
Or on the sandy shore of a sound.

Perhaps it's where lofty mountain peaks
Tower to the sky
Or even beneath a mighty oak's bough
From which robins lift to fly.

Maybe it's in the depths of a forest,
So dark no one hardly sees,
Amidst lush green fern on moist brown soil
Where sprang sky-high redwood trees.

It could even be in the City
High atop a hill
Where the busy din of city-life
Is muffled by fog-shrouded still.

I'm not going to search for it:
My quest ended where it got its start.
Because, as you may suspect,
It started in my heart...

Bill Hoover

The Deep

In that dark deep standing
Waiting to be realized, actualized,
Anticipating an enlightenment
I stand ready

And I know it will not happen
Because it will be what is unexpected, unrecognized,
With results and changes unimagined
For the imagination is a shifting shape
In existences of shapes shifting

Ellen Browning

"Angels Without Wings"

Descendants from youth like tightly woven yarn
waiting to be unraveled to a new world.

Celestial acrobats dance under gothic clouds
watching endless lines of humanity
march to strange sounds; echoes from distant dead.
Stumbling through grey gardens

Old statues with solemn faces lean eerily over me.
I wonder, will ancient flowers bloom again?
Scorched skin, broken spirit, the crowd pushes on.
Stringless puppets, with severed limbs, blemished souls,

Monsters without faces, somehow familiar.
Feeling alienated, I walk by slowly.
Black shadows cast in unusual places fade quietly,
dense darkness changes the look of things.

The path not yet worn, uncharted,
beckons new light of another day.

Gary Thomas Pniewski

Argonauta

In this light coracle,
Waiting to leave,
We've finished duties well - cradled serene.

What strings to duty tie?
What bonds do bind?
None whatsoever - freedom to find!

Freedom of nautilus?
Leave shell for sea?
Overcome feelings of uncertainty?

Can mid-aged argonauts
Shed bonds and ties?
What Golden Fleece waits for us to find?

Imagination - a chartless sea!
Extension of love; creativity;
Personal growth; wisdom; sensitivity.

Perceptive awareness, spent reveries,
Search for completeness,
Gifts from the sea.

Janet M. Franklin

Reflections

I look in the mirror,
Waiting to see.
What is my future,
And where will I be?
What is my purpose,
Down here on earth?
What should I do,
And where will I go?
Some people live lives of happiness and cheer,
Others live lives of gloominess and fear.
Where do I fit in between all these people,
And where will I be in fifty years?

Erin Fitzgerald

"A Father"

I just want a father who will show me love. I just want a father who cares. I want a father who will hold my hand and give me a hug when I need someone. I want a father who kisses me good night and tells me it will be okay when I am scared. I want a father who will wish me happy birthday and he'll remember what day it's on. I want a father who will say thank you and maybe I love you once in awhile. I want a father who will help me when I'm hurt and not just say good for you. I want a father who will go to my games and other special events and not just make an excuse why he can't go. I want a father who will call me his daughter not because he feels guilty but because he wants me to be his daughter.

Danielle Marquis

Empty Dreams

Walking along the road,
was a figure,
his head bent,
his face tear stained.
In his hand was a box;
it held his hope, dreams, and love.
Trying to give it away,
It was rejected.
Now standing facing the luminous setting sun,
thinking back to when that fiery mass gave him peace,
knowing that peace was forever gone,
all he had was his empty box of hopeless dreams.

Amanda Poff

The Plaque On The Wall

In a beautiful farm house on the kitchen wall
Was a plaque that told it all.
Read these words and take heed,
Follow this saying whenever in need,
"When you are out of sort and feeling blue
Flirt with nature, she's tried and true."

Take a walk and you will see
Happy birds singing in a tree.
The joy of their song and beauty of each feather
Will enlighten your day in any kind of weather.
Stroll through the woods some sunny day
Smell the wild flowers as you continue on your way.
If possible, go catch a fish.
Enjoy the beauty and make a wish.
Nature is beautiful and will help you calm down
So get out there, away from home and town.

Eileen McCollum

The Sea

The Sea has always beckoned me, to come share its serenity.
The crashing waves are such a balm, as are the gently swaying palms.
It's difficult to understand - as I stroll out across the sand,
How anyone could fail to see - Our Maker's hand upon the Sea!

The gentle squirrels on the shore, call to me to feed them more.
The seals are napping tranquilly and squinting up at me to see,
If I can understand their barks or only want to share their park.
Gulls swoop down amid shrill calls - and challenge me to ride the squalls.
Otters frisk among the kelp, making people laugh and yelp.

Divers enter the foamy surf and vanish quickly from the curse,
Of hectic noise above the waves to escape thy neighbor for a day.
My Maker's voice is in the air, "I made it all for you to share."
All my troubles seem so small - when hearing the Seas' siren call.

Debrina Peek

When The Family Acts As A Whole

A young strapping Father whose color was of any human hue
Was briskly walking on the sidewalk of the street,
Herding his five sons forward, all clean and youthful, and without much ado,
While they rapidly proceeded in unison, avoiding his rhythmic feet.

Ahead of them was their Mother,
In white jacket and raspberry pants.
carefully checking signal lights and traffic,
And her children, with many a watchful glance

Across the street was the movie house,
Undoubtedly, their particular goal,
And you knew there was hope for America
When the family acts as a whole.

The friends of your children should be carefully watched,
And caution be taken lest all lives be scotched,
Parents and friends should team up, and cover the neighborhood rubble,
The hangouts and bad spots, and get rid of potential trouble.

No matter one's color, culture or creed
Nor how hard it is to raise your breed,
By loving and sharing, and teaching and caring
The lives of your family, can be wholesome, not wearing.

Herman N. Rabson

So What!

You have tried, you have failed. So what! Try again!
Was Rome built in a day? Do you think the Master Plan
took just a spurt of ingenuity, without a great mind and hand?
Every song written, or great work of art, must pass a test
of strong desire, before the world is set on fire.
A maestro must practice time and time again
before the keys he's looking for fall into rhythm
making the "sound of thousand tongues of music sublime".
Ask the man upon the street who built that grand
architectural dome? Did he aspire to do it?
Or just sit at home. The artillery of guns in
battle, great ships that ride the sea,
were they not created by men like you and me?
So don't give up trying when the answer's on its way,
turn to him who'll gladly help you, if you'll come to him and pray.
Put all your heart, soul, mind, and strength
to the goal that you pursue. Sit and ponder if you must,
but don't forget to do. There's never been a man that's failed,
who just would not stop, but climbed the steep and shocked the clock
to do the work he knew was in the plan of God for him to do!

Iva Midkiff

Soul

As the body sleeps,
the soul speaks to the mind.
As the stars cast their light,
many lives entwine.

As day breaks the message of dreams forgotten.
The whisper of salvation unheard.
Hurrying into sunlight, cursing the frustration of existence.
Running head on into the traffic of survival.

Looking not back, to the realm of the soul.
Heeding not, the voice that could guide.
Seeking not, the age old answers.
Learning not, the meaning of life.

Cheryll Hallmark

The Way Of The Winds

Prints in the sand unlike etchings of time
Wash away by the touch of swirling winds,
Leaving a dune with slopes settled and smooth
While beneath is unfazed by the outer trends.

The winds are free of time's ways and demands;
They can bring ruin or enhance the surrounds;
They can comfort and aid to journey's end;
They can move the living within their bounds.

Time yields to the winds in clearing the sands,
Not changing the beauty my eyes behold,
Yet hovers gently while seeking a path
To engrave such traces that life foretold.

The winds protect her from these stains of time,
Whisking away that which is undesired,
Unveiling the flower that fills my life
With a joy that only her love inspired.

When the winds become calm my love prevails
To shield the image only my heart sees
And yearns for this day to return again
While her life with me continues to please.

Gene Brock

The Bluff

We sat on the bluff in summer darkness
watching tugs pushing barges
up and down the river,
casting their lights from side to side.
We spoke softly, admiring the sight.

Then a train, we were not sure at first,
came along the river, doing the same:
great rays of light flashing up the banks
now on one side, then the other.

The only way we knew it
was by its giant arcs of light.
Sound coming first went unnoticed,
muted by the bluff we sat on ...
Three people, enfolded in the cocoon of the night,
Watching, listening, and liking each other.

Elaine N. Taylor

Short Stuff

SIMPLE THINGS
The simple things in life, I love—-
A letter, card, or book,
The sound of crickets, birds and rain
And frogs beside the brook.

RISKS
Some risks I've taken in my life
Turned out to be no fun,
But the greatest risks I've taken yet
Are the risks I haven't run.

HUH?
In bed, he whispers sweet nothings so softly in my ear.
My hearing aid is not in place,
So sweet nothing is what I hear!

FOOD?
I see the meals stretch back in time
And ones that lie ahead—
The lakes of soup, the hills of meat,
The highways filled with bread;
But in all this there is a lack of food to fill my head.

Betty Webster Bishop

Leaf Cutting Ants

They just wanted to move her
The queen they loved so much.
Workers were all about her,
The Queen they carefully touched.
They were just going to move her
A short space away, but the head
Was caught in a very awkward way.
Her neck was snapped, and she did not live.
The workers were beside themselves
For the Queen was not there to give.
They knew she was so important
To them and their life was not to be.
So in a few months they will die for
Lack of their Queen you see.

Anna Lou Bozeman

Storm

Thunder rumbled, the earth shuddered,
With the powerful force of the darkening sky,
She trembled from the passionate onslaught,
Sweat poured from the burning blue above,
Quenching the parched soil beneath,
A savage wind caressed her dampened fields,
She quaked from within,
She shook from the final thrust of the raging storm,
A flash of lightening bared her dampened plains,
and swollen rivers,
A cool, calming breeze whisked away ominous clouds,
Drying her tearing eyes,
The sun peeked out of hiding,
Casting an array of colors upon the cleansed world,
The sky held the earth in his arms,
Warming her soul,
Teaching her of a love untold.

Louise Lepage

Reality

The nightmares that seem so real
trapped in a world of immortals
seeing them everywhere
watching you touching you
feeling into your mind
knowing your every footstep
more and more immortals attacking you
hitting you until you become black and blue
Black is the last color you will see
The funeral hall is dim
Your coffin beside the bewildered people
You look to see your face
Lying there defenseless
Wanting more from life

Jen Blenner

A Rose

Wondrous in color and beauty
Petals so silky and soft in nature,
That even to touch is a sin
Hence, the treacherous thorns to pertrude
the skin at an invasion of such tranquility
Caring, love, and peacefulness
Such emotions from one little flower
To receive such a gift of beauty is unreal
But then again, its maker has such beauty within,
What else should one expect, but GREATNESS.

Kathy L. McBroom

Beyond The Gate

To Paul G. Yommer: My love for you is constant, and forever.
Thank you for making this journey with me.

You give me strength, when I have none of my own,
You have given true love, that I had never been shown.
You live deep, within the heart of me,
As an intricate part, of the soul of me.

When the pressures of life, seem just too great,
Trouble and confusion weigh me down,
You breathe new life, into my soul,
Your love reaches far, beyond the gate.

When I am tired, and my strength is gone,
When I have not, a smile of my own,
You give of yourself completely,
Today, I have a love of my own.

Time, space, and distance mean nothing,
For the circle will always be unbroken,
Together as one, interwoven hearts,
The sum of the pieces, the whole of the parts.

Forever and always, two halves of a heart,
Reaching past the normal, to the center of the core.
Giving encouragement, never too late,
I will love you always, even beyond the gate

Carol M. Bell

Farewell Fair River

Farewell fair river in the spring
Your new leaves, ever green
New life gives birth
the robin sings.

Farewell fair river in the summer
Take care muskrat, beaver and dragonfly
For the news has come
I must say good-bye.

Farewell fair river in the fall
Your leaves are bare, your trees stand tall
Your strength and sparkle
I miss most of all.

Farewell fair river in the winter
Farewell to a good friend
Blanket of ice, hidden below someday,
to the river I will go...

Margaret Brunea Falker

Anna To Gurov, 1994

Like wine in my blood
your warmth floods my veins,
erases the rigid agenda in my brain
then recedes, leaving heaviness, stupor,
a hangover I don't want to get over.

You play me like a violin straining to the peak
of that painful crescendo in the Liebestod
when the longing builds, and seems never to reach
what it grasps for; then crashes, dies
in a slowly receding cry.

You are like a black and white movie
where cigarette smoke, rain and fog obscure
something secret, dangerous, desirable, where lovers
throw lives away for passion, throw passion away for
honor, or everybody dies. Or maybe all three, and we

Have to pick the ending. And friend,
we could spend
a lifetime in this denouement.

Natalie McKnight

Sagittarian

Bow string taut, inner voice badgers
'Let it fly fail where it will'
Struggle to live with the consequences
Or deal with the pain of not
Knowing how the target would be struck
If the arrow never feels the air.
Hoofs rooted in the dirt
Bow raised and arrow aching for the sun.
Take the chance. Let it fly.
Patterns of dynamics creating the destiny
Born in the constellation of the Archer
Endless pursuit to ultimate truth
Found only as the arrow gains release.
Bow string taunt, the voice badgers
'Let us fly.'
Choice is made, the arrow obtains momen-
tum.

G. S. Huggard

On Writing

Why do I write,
Let me count the reasons.
I write of all my days and years -
For all my times and seasons.

I write to give expression
To the feelings I often hide.
The hungry yearning and burning
Kept hidden deep inside.

I write as vapor rises
From a kettle as water boils.
As sun bursts seeds into life
Warming damp and fertile soil.

Words are the waters that flow -
From the rivers of my mind;
Anticipation of things hoped for,
Recollections of those left behind.

Words have often given flight
To the winged emotions I feel;
Sometimes sorrow, often joy,
Always profound and real.

Marj Strickland

"Grief"...dedicated to Betty Nelson

Let me rant,
Let me rave,
But kindly grant
Me time to be brave.

The wound in my heart
So deep and real,
Is surely a part
Of all that I feel.

Give me time to learn
To live life through;
The comfort I'll earn
Will bring relief too.

I'll find my way
As time goes by,
To deal each day
With pain I'll try.

My loved one so dear
Left me here alone;
Still I know God is near,
His comfort's my own.

Mary Delaney Pope

"Upon A Wall"

When a man is forever laid to rest,
Let us believe he tried his best.
Place his honors upon his chest,
for all to know he passed the test.

The casket passes, salute with pride,
as a hero takes his final ride.
A wife and children teary eyed,
now the Lord will be his guide.

Once with strength he answered a call,
to the beat of the drum he marched tall.
Who could know that he should fall,
then they carved his name upon a wall.

J. F. Yergan

"My Poppy"

I love my poppy,
Like he loves me.
From the time I was born,
To now that I'm 3,
He is big, and he's tough
As people can see.
And loving, and kind,
That's the way I want to be
When he walks down the street
With me by his side
I try to be like him
By keeping the stride
But my legs are to short,
To keep up the pace
But I smile when I see
The look in his face
He's proud to be with his grandson,
That's me!
And that's my poppy,
The way I want to be.

Louis S. Iannicelli

Revelation On The Shenandoah

The river flows
Like life goes.

Some rough spots.
Who calls the shots?

Man supposes.
God disposes.

No end in sight.
I'll do what's right.

For me, seems best.
Glory be...I've passed the test!

Sheila Brown

Memories

Recollections of the past
Like reflections on the pond

Evoked by a simple word
Like a pebble thrown

Memory following memory
Like ripples on the water

Spread through the mind
Like the circles growing wider

Robbie Davis

Mind's Eye

People come close,
Listen to what I say.
There is something you must do,
When you find the perfect day.

Close your eyes
And look around.
There are wonderful ways to see,
Ways that I have found.

I could close my eyes right now,
And let my mind roam;
I see the view of Yosemite
I saw from the top of Half-Dome.

So have a seat
And look around.
Close your eyes
Don't make a sound.

Go back to somewhere
You have seen before.
See it once again,
Be sure to enjoy it even more.

Tara M. Carr

"Sir Damla Deniz Yapiyor"

I haven't time to worry about
Little things today.
I'm really in a hurry to get
Big things underway.
But wait! - don't I remember
That old, familiar tale,
Of a rider, a battle, a kingdom, lost,
"For want of a horseshoe nail"?

I had a turkish student once
Who did calligraphy.
Once project that she lettered was
So beautiful to see!
At first I couldn't read it, but,
Quiet seen I got the notion
That what it said was simply this,
"A Raindrop Makes an Ocean."

Martha M. Caldwell

Empty Desperation

Desperate for companionship.
Longing for love.
I fight and cling to hold on.
I feel myself falling, slowly slipping.
Gasping for every painful breath.

I cry salty, bitter tears.
My head spins, my chest aches.
I shiver with pain.
I want, I need someone to hold me.

My dreams.
They're haunting my subconscious.
Dreams of living,
And then dying alone.

The fear.
The overwhelming, intense fear
That I will never find someone to love.
And even greater is the fear
That I am unworthy of love.
I've never felt so empty and so alone.
So very alone.

Libbie Henley

On Counsel

If we were to, perhaps, one day
  Look just beyond our mind
We may then see inside ourselves
  What others sometimes find

No one of us is perfect now
  Nor in the future, too
And should we hold ourselves aloof
  Believing heart is true

It's real that some perceive much more
  Than we do see within
The actions that we do in life
  With comprehension, thin

So let us our opinion join
  With counsel others give
Enhancement of the very soul
  Is gained, as on, we live

No Island must we be, is writ
  Within fine writing, past
In joining those who complement
  Will much achievement last

Ronald W. Mealing

To Be Alone

Looking within and feeling sad,
Looking back to what I had,

Reaching out to open space,
Finding none to take your place,

Your face is held within my mind,
With smile upon my heart did shine,

Your touch was tender upon my hand,
To guide me to an unknown land,

This land is love, I run away,
For fear that I may want to stay,

Instead, I pick the lonely road,
That brings me here all alone,

A man is strong and rough to be,
He charges forward for all to see,

Knowing not where he will lie,
Until death knolls and he does die,

I will know this land of love,
The guide to you is from above,

This story ends with happy glee,
And I'll no longer alone to be.

Samuel S. Fulginiti

Who Am I Lord?

Sometimes I sit and wonder
LORD who am I?
Do you feel my pain Lord
DO you hear me when I cry?

You said I am the first part
Of your special plan
You gave your life at calvary
Help me understand
You promise I'll be with you
in a home far away
but help me please here Lord
to make it through THIS DAY
I feel like such a small part
I'm hardly here at all
AND yet I know I am
Because I hear you call

Ruthenne Oerly

Love Or Hatred

Love or hatred, which will win?
Love, if we love Christ, hate sin,
Hate, if from Christ many stray -
The end time when they fall away.

Peace or war, which will it be?
Peace should last eternally.
War should soon become extinct -
Hell alone the Devil's precinct.

Myth or fact, does logic help?
Myth produces flim-flam whelps.
Fact can logic understand;
Enlightenment is in God's hand.

Christ or satan, which will rule?
Christ will head peacemakers school.
Satan his few will take to Hell.
I'll live for Christ. Will you as well?

Katherine Shelton

Dead And Dying Butterflies

Dead and dying butterflies
lying in the road,
committed insect suicide
before they got too old.

And no one ever cries,
because no one ever cares;
no one ever notices
when an insect isn't there.

Pretty thing, the butterfly,
with wings of black and gold,
committing insect suicide
before it gets too old.

Katherine Durham

Ultimate Goal

God took a rib from Adam
Make a likeness of me,
Not good that he should be alone,
'Twas plain for Him to see.

In love he put us on this earth,
A man and his mate;
To build a home around them
To block out earthly hate.

To rear a loving family,
Through sickness, health and strife;
To set up morals for their young,
To last them all their life.

Kind words, love and patience
Are virtues of the soul;
And families that radiate them
Will reach their ultimate goal.

Velma Ruppel Gish

Moods

As good as gold,
melancholy blue,
or envy green,
mask the chameleons
of the world.

Who stage life,
like the melodrama
of a soap opera,
lest they are revealed.

Shirley Bailey-Jones

Thank You

Thank you for loving me,
Making me feel all things
Like a brush of an eyelash.
A wisp of a touch
You've made me aware of
sight and sound.
I'm alive no longer to hide
my hurt and despair.
That's in the past
your brush strokes soft colors
then so bold
Put all together I feel
as one with you.

Mary C. McBride

Me

Me, I can no other be,
Me, I am, as you can see.
Me, always busy as a bee,
Me, sometimes I'm very lazy.
Me, with others I don't always agree,
Me, but most times I go along amicably.
Me, strong and stalwart as an oak tree,
Me, oft times fragile as a pea.
Me, showing signs of jealousy,
Me, which is a part of my humanity.
Me, upset over some peculiarity,
Me, but then so full of levity.
Me, looking seriously at reality,
Me, a downright mystery!

Laura S. Woods

"Coming Of The Death Season"

Sunrises, in the East,
Melt down, in the sky.
It's time, for the beast.
Hear, the angels cry.
It's another revolution,
Another holy war.
A stand against the mighty dragon,
Battling till there's no more.
On the ground, lie the dead ones,
Of those who tired to win,
Destroyed by the demons,
Perished but never repent.
Mangled and out of place,
Their bodies badly torn,
Shattered, amazing grace,
For no-one's left to mourn.
Coming of the death season,
No truce to be called.
To plan for a peace offering,
On the day we take the fall.

Tina Menser

Untitled, Undated

Some things never come again
Moments,
  Like this.
And people who, in passing
Touch us
  And stay
  Forever, in the Heart.
Or who are
Always in the shadows
  Hoping
  For a friend
To share the night
For the warmth.

Timothy S. Petsch

Astral Experience

One night long ago I had a wish,
merely a wish.
That was all and nothing more.
'Twas misty below.
Huge white mounds, shadowy under night,
glowing eerily of the moon above.
Wind Upon my being, brisk and hard.
Ah, what wonders I beheld.
To float across the eons, to touch nothing
yet feel all.
Just existing, briefly forever.
Inner goodness and peace all about,
beauty beyond words.
To dive into clouds.
Moisture upon my lips.
From the lightning to the unknown,
everything was mine and mine alone.
All long ago, merely a wish, merely a
dream and nothing more.
Nothing more.

Rick Isaacs

A Joyful Heart

My heart overflows with joy,
Morning sunrise brings warmth aglow,
Birds awaken singing,
Butterflies fluttering by my path,
Squirrels scuttering up the trees.

My heart overflows with joy,
Evening sunset leaves rainbows,
Dazzling stars lighting up the skies,
Crickets and frogs harmonizing in song.

My heart overflows with joy,
Walking barefoot on grass aglaze with dew,
Wildflowers sprawling across the lawn,

For all this beauty in my own back yard,
My heart overflows with joy.

Paula Levin

Family

Grandmother, Grandfather
Mother, Father
Sister, Brother
Aunt, Uncle
Niece, Nephew
Or Cousin
A special group of people
Related to one another.

Whether related by blood
Or by marriage
All are kin.

Part of the past
Sharing the present
Making the future.

Good times are always remembered
Bad times hard to forget
Yet to come times mystifying.

All related as one group
All loved as individuals
All together as one Family.

Victoria J. Broekhuizen

My Dear Children

As you go along your way, learn from
Mother Nature, she has something to say:

The hummingbird's quick, but stops for
a while. . .
To witness the flowers growing in style.

The caterpillar fools the impatient viewer.
For time turns the cocoon into something
spectacular.

When night time is upon us and darkness
prevails.
Don't be scared, for the moon and the
stars will brighten the air.

The cow looks so meaningless as it grazes
the grass.
But the benefits of milk, may never come
to pass.

So my dear children, always remember to
pay attention.
For Mother Nature is ready to teach you
a lesson.

Mary Jo Navarijo

My American Dream

In my dream of dreams
my American dream 'tis no more.
Did someone come within
my dream of dreams
and steal it away?
For I have asked
what was, what is,
and most of all,
for where is my dream of dreams?
For I have listened,
I have watched,
and most of all,
I search this land.
Who can tell me this:
for where did,
my American dream go?

Karen E. Hamlett

Thank You Lord

Once in time, I could not see
My eyes been open to reality
His word, His truth, His light
The love He has that shines so bright
Thank you Lord.

I no more walk in darkness
He gave me life and happiness
He is love and He is kind
He will give you peace of mind
Thank you Lord.

He put life back in my soul
Once again I've been made whole
He give my joy, He gives me peace
He keeps me calm, my souls at ease
Thank you Lord.

When He holds me by the hand
I can walk with Him throughout the land
I know my Lord, Oh how sweet
He is one I want to meet
Thank you Lord.

Regina Boggus

Walking At Dawn

With staff in my hand and hat on
my head,
I set forth in the morning, wonder
led.
While the sun's peeking over the rim
of the earth
And bringing the new day closer to
birth;
The birds warble joyfully deep in the
woods;
The breeze tosses trees just as it
should;
The crows caw forlornly over the
hill;
The cows munch quietly eating their
fill;
The mist hangs low down over the
lake;
And everything waits for the day to
awake.

Vera B. King

His Love

I struggled on an uphill road
My heart filled with despair
I prayed for strength to reach my goal
And found Him waiting there

I wandered a dark valley
Alone, I could not see
But when the darkness lifted
He was there leading me

I trembled 'neath a heavy load
Of care impatiently
I stumbled and cried out in pain
And His arms lifted me

I longed and searched for happiness
And fulfillment desperately
I failed until I looked within
And found His love in me.

Mildred Verhelle

No More

A day so golden
My mood so dull
Besets this moment
Into a lull

My thoughts will wander
And I'll reflect
Upon another golden day
I recollect

A day at the beach
Watching wave displays
And specks of snails
Covering tidal ways

Of tufts of grass
And sand and sky
And The Golden Girl
That I passed by

Bejeweled Jewel
Wearing a pearl
I had to know
This Golden Girl ...

Umberto A. Aversa

Losing Sight

Such a peaceful countryside,
My heart is my only guide;
And it leads me back here,
To the precious sounds I hear;
This beautiful land,
That God created by his very
Own hand;
When I'm here I can see,
What life means to me;
We often lose sight,
Of the things that are right,
Looking only at the bad,
We grow weary and sad;
So hold your dreams tight,
And no matter how hard it
Seems don't lose sight.

Kimberly Eldridge

Christ Is Everything To Me

CHRIST is everything to me.
My husband, my family,
HE provided me.

CHRIST is everything to me.
My Church, my friends, my home,
HE provided me.

CHRIST is everything to me.
Even the breath I breathe alone,
HE provided me.

CHRIST is everything to me.
This poem I write to be
published you see,
This, CHRIST provided me.

CHRIST is everything to me.
The Eternal Life I have,
HE provided me.

CHRIST is everything to me.
For me HE provided
HIMSELF, you see.

Marjorie Roberts

July 4, 1976 America's Bicentennial Cairo, Egypt

He waves a flag proudly,
my little blond boy -
to celebrate the birthday
of a Nation that he only knows
from pictures in bedtime stories
read lovingly at night.

Apple pie and baseball games,
picket fences, ice cream cones;
the pages of these worn books
provide a basis of a distant world
that in memory seems so far away -
as I pass the little donkey carts

and the dirty, rumpled soldiers
who stare at me with nasty eyes
and point their rusty weapons
and laugh - because they sense
I understand and fear - that my freedoms
do not exist - in this place.

Patricia Duncan

Abuse Truth

The anger and disgust burning
My mind and soul, turning
Every living cell into ashes
I have let my life choices
Strip away my dreams pride
And self respect
Yet I must stay to keep
Another mother and child well
And safe, even if it is myself
I waste
Someday the pain is more overwhelming
Than acid rain
Then I look into the faces of my
Special people that I must shelter
I am again dragged down in shame
For I myself will never be enough
To fulfill their needs

Maureen Cordell

Open Your Heart

God is watching me from heaven,
my mother used to say;
But every time she mentioned God
I would always turn away.
I grew up praying to my Lord,
only times that there was need;
And if something in life went wrong,
I'd be upset at Him and me.
Now I realize what I've done,
I was hiding from God's love.
I hope you don't follow my mistakes,
so I can see you in Heaven above.

Monica Carrion

Stones

As I walk life's wondrous path
my shoes are full of stones
the little stones which bruise the feet
and irritate the sole.

I stop to shake the stones away
but as I travel on,
I find the stones are back again
just when I thought they'd gone.

I spend my time removing shoes
to shake the stones away,
instead of looking up the path
of which I'm on today.

The beauty of life's path is lost
with each stone I feel and toss,
My mind is on the stones, you see,
not on the beauty surrounding me.

Mary J. Lewellyn

Appalling

Paul, the tall pallbearer,
Met me at the door.
We get our pallbearers.
At the tall-pallbearer store.

We had a short pallbearer,
But he ain't here no more.
He had to bend,
And dropped a friend,

Much to the poor man's horror!

Norma Hamlin

Evolution?

I'm not the off-spring of an ape
My soul will live again.
Our Heavenly Father would not make
His promises in vain.

In His won image, he made man;
My Father is a king
We're heirs and joint-heirs by His hand
And not a 'lesser' thing!

He's God and Father, God the Son,
The Spirit and all three
We praise and worship them as one
Blessed Trinity.

The beast and creeping things of earth
Were MADE, we understand (Genesis 1:26)
The crowning acts of all His works;
When He created Man.

Yes man is from the dust, we're told
In Genesis two and seven
Then God made him a living soul;
There're no animals in heaven!

Valerie B. Howell

Reflections

Like quicksilver,
My spirit lies
Trembling in your hand.
If your fingers
Were to close
My soul would shatter
Into bits,
(A shining look here,
A bright word there,)
Too many pieces
To be graspable,
Escaping into air.

Now,
Being held lightly,
It is still
As a sterling moon
Upon your palm.
It is a mini-mirror,
Reflecting just
Your smile.

Mary Louise S. Hardin

As We Are One

When I hold you in my arms,
my thoughts and my dreams become
reality, and so my clear never leave
me, never forget me. The wind the
rain and the fears my come, but
as long as we are one nothing matters
at all. Love me with all your heart
and we will never part. Remember
if you are ever sad or feel so all alone,
I will be there to hold you in my
arms, and brush those tears away
as we are one.

Robert M. Williams

Always

When—-
My time has come
For sad goodbyes
To spring and summer

When—-
I've grown too old
To dream and wish
Of Spring's sweet madness
And Summer's glories

Then—-
I'll be content with memories
Of you and me
In life's long journey.

Us—
Together or apart
Yet always forever
Within each other's heart!

Paulina C. Cabral

Love Renewed

A face appears,
Mysterious,
Then becoming clear.

A handsome face,
Almost forgotten,
But still remembered.

A voice speaks,
Barely audible,
Then growing stronger.

A caring voice,
Filled with love,
And understanding.

Hands reach out,
Cautiously,
Then giving in.

Gentle hands,
Longing to hold,
A love lost.

Michelle Lowery

Giving Thanks

My life is filled with myriads
of blessings, great and small.
The Lord has given many things.
It's hard to count them all.
So I take opportunity
to thank the Lord each day,
although I'm not a superstar,
my pockets aren't filled with pay.
It's the little blessings that He gives
to brighten up my day:
The songbird's waking call each morn,
the friends met on the way.
The breath of life He gives so sweet,
the comfort of a smile,
the elder's confident advice,
the laughter of a child.
I never know from day to day
what blessings He might give,
but this I know, that with His peace
I'm able, now, to live.

Rebekah S. Brown

Something Is Missing

Where did all the children go?
Nary a one to be seen or heard, just so.

Great big houses sitting all in a row
in all their loveliness.
And yet, what is missing?
Where did all the children go?

Mature and responsible people can be
seen as they come and go,
running here and running there.

Everything must be in order.

No time to waste on trivial matters.
No time to waste on the past.

Onward we must go,
Where did all the children go?

Yvonne G. Engel Davis

Friendship Is Like A Flower

Friends are two people who
never force any doubt of each other
Red is the color of the flower it's
gentle to fall upon
I'm a flower who never let go
a flower as close as we are
Identity means forever we are
forever friends
Now and upon we never break
this promise till we will died with anger
Dare or not we will never drift
apart.
I call her the flower, flower
of love and friendship.

Tracy Tuazon

Homage To Little Red

You never flinched from my touch,
never learned when climbing my
pants leg that your claws might
bite too deep. But you would
be held, actually cradled like
a baby, loving your throat stroked:
contentment in your homely little
face and peerless the liquid amber
of your eyes and how like the
look and feel of suede your russet
ears. And days when I would
reach the backside of the hill
and see you coming in home a
far speck in the fields moving
more rapidly when you saw me
how could I help but marvel
at the way you ate the distance.
Once, a slender russet-red tiger cat,
whom I couldn't keep from dining
on the wind. . . .

William R. Johnson

Now

We see our life begin
on this day again.
Each moment precious,
to be savored.
The future and past do not exist,
except in each mind's abyss.
Now is the only true time.
So from your past,
your future you'll find.

Peter Gundunas

Lost

Lost is gone forever.
Never to be found again.
I never thought it could be over.
But here I am.
Alone.
In a world filled with people.
No soul touches mine.
Yours was the only one.
Lost is gone forever.
The sun comes up every morning.
The seasons come in their time.
New buds in spring.
New hope of change.
But here I am alone.
No soul touches mine.
Lost is gone forever.

Shirley May

Doll Cat

My mistress says I'm her doll cat
Next thing'll be bonnet and dress
Riding bye-bye in a baby buggy
Oh I'll love that—I do confess

Little old ladies looking in
Going cootchy-coo little kitty
Pretty face and great big eyes
What a precious itty bitty

Susan Rose/Gail Fraser

Curmudgeon To Tree

How young and smooth your skin,
No blemish or canker rude.
Vigorous juices flow within,
To nurture well thy leaflet brood.
Upstart, strong and straight,
No thought of flicker or wood bore,
I caution thee, take heed for great
Wind storms and fire are in store.
Once too, I stood straight and strong,
With vigorous mind and patient smile.
The fires of striving, living wrong,
Hath burned within a nature vile.
Take heed young thing, nature's call,
Age will mar and you will fall.

Robert Galen Genoway

Anger

A million thoughts storming my mind,
no peace or calm anywhere to find.
Words strike the target - now I pay.
Anger is having his way.

The body tense, the head pounding,
hands are shaking, the battles mounting.
Love has vanished beneath the fray.
Anger is having his way.

How many times must I defeat this foe,
before he is bound forever more!
Must he lurk in my shadow night and day.
Anger is having his way.

Help me Lord to grow in Your Love.
Keep me humble, gentle like the dove.
Remove from my spirit this rotting decay,
so anger no longer can have his way!

Marilyn Louise Barling

A Crack In The Cement

She grew up in the city
No room for pity
Noise in her culture
Act like a vulture
Such a race, blurs a face

Blows came swiftly
Innocence fled
Head held high, such pain
You could die
Pride fierce, blood red

Courage
And lack of fear
Sustained her life
As her time drew near

The quiet of evening
The song of the bird
A snow flake passing
She soon heard.

Renee Roll

"Our Last Walk"

"When mother took me out -
no thought my life would be in doubt.

Until I was struck by a car,
as mother looked on.
Saddened by an aching heart,
the thought of losing her only son.

A day to enjoy
became brief
When a thought of pleasure
turned into grief.

My life was fading fast
with the thought of fear
as God was giving me a call
I could barely hear.

With mother's final touch
when she came near
wanted to take me home,
but took only tears."

Lloyd H. Roy

Within

If I could be my poem,
Not just write the rhyme.
If I could show the world myself
Let the light begin to shine.

To show the world my true self,
Have the courage to let it out.
But I know I wouldn't do too well,
Too much hatred all about

So I think this other me,
Wouldn't want to hang around.
Where the world's general feeling,
Is to tear another down.

So I guess that lonely person,
Will stay locked within the cage.
And touch no one around him,
Till the jailer dies of age.

That's why I'm not afraid to die,
It's just a freedom day.
When the jailer drops the keys of life,
And the real me flies away.

Roy F. McWilliams

The Homeless

I have no roof to shelter me,
no walls to mute the cold—
I am the young with somber eyes,
the sick, the very old.
I watch the rain on city streets
from doorways where I lie
or sleep on benches in sprawling parks
as joggers pass me by.
I am statistics that you read,
the pleas that you resist
and if I die some lonely night,
by whom would I be missed?

Wanda Weiskopf

Darkness To The Extreme

I've lived my life invisible,
nothing to me is real.
I merely seem to exist,
my heart, it cannot feel.

Dead it lies within me,
useless as can be.
No matter how I fight it,
my heart won't set me free.

For all the things I've longed for,
have died with the fire.
And ashes are all that's left,
nothing more for me to aspire.

This is the long night,
my life without any dreams.
Invisible, and without heart,
Darkness to the extreme.

Katrina Whittington

"Affection"

Dear World's Grandchildren,
Nothing with this soul
to hand you on the 25th of December,
except affection.

Mind heart and eyes
make me to understand:
To hand children, precious present
is nothing but affectionate vision.

Alphabets are away from me.
However, I have learnt:
Polished words
never create affection.

It flows only from:
magnanimous mind,
humanitarian heart
and vast vision.

Let me pray:
God! Inscribe word affection
in my mind, heart and vision.
And help me to dedicate it,
to world's grandchildren
before I lose vision.

P. B. Patel-Das

Our Horses

Wild, they run and are free,
Now they cannot, because of me,
They once ran together,
Now they walk in the heather.
People now take them as pets,
Then they ride them, swift as jets,
Cowboys ride into the sun,
Quickly as the horses can run.
They rope one, then two,
Until they have enough for me and you,
They bring them in on that day,
And on our ranches they shall stay.

Tiffany Arciszewski

Circus Trumpets

When circus trumpets trill and sing
Of circus horses in the ring,
They imitate the brassy style
Of circus horses frolicking.

The horses thunder down the aisle,
The trumpets shout a bugle smile;
The horses dash and toss the mane
And leap the water hazard stile.

The tempo lifts, the trebles reign,
The horses wheel, then leap again
A flaming wall — a perfect pair —
And sprays of bright glissandos rain.

The thudding hooves, the flashy blare,
Earth, fire, water, air:
Circus trumpets at the Fair!
Circus trumpets at the Fair!

Richard Everson

Deliberation

Is homosexuality of man an act
of free expression of uninhibited
love or a distorted sense of
misdirected emotions?
Does it not have a tendency to
enslave, maddening homogeneous to
the obsession of the heterosexual?

Its origin from creation, adversity,
liberation, or inclination?
If all, then insanity, and why?
Perhaps, gentlemen.....
Just a misunderstood complication of life,
or twisted lust born of an unbalanced mind
with diabolical proclivities.

R. F. Caldwell

No Cure

She tells me of the end to come.
My heart grows cold, then only numb.

There is no warmth in endless night.
So ready to give up the fight.

Wishing I could shield the stares.
Is it only me who cares?

Foolish laughter, foolish pride,
Disease she can no longer hide.

Trying to soothe her darkest fears.
Still my shoulder's wet with tears.

My worthless soul I'd freely give,
If my friend could only live.

Melanie Bunger

Forgotten Is Their Name

Forgotten, those sons and daughters
of liberty,
who dared to brave fierce waters
just to be free.

They left their loved ones and their home,
with what was on their back,
for promises we made to them,
awhile back.

They left in rafts, in tiny boats,
in anything afloat,
with just one thought, that ninety miles,
would fill their dreams, their hope.

Ill from the sun, and thirst, and hunger,
still they came,
the young, the old, with babies,
Forgotten, is their name.

So many dead, in waters deep,
and they will never know,
that those who lived were fated as,
The Cubans of Guantanamo.

Stella V. Balandran

Too Late To Be Recalled

Golden moments
of my life
have flown,
in flurries
of December snows.
Each moment, passing
as wings upon the night
Until at last
it's flown
far from the hands
that bind the earth;
too late to be recalled!
But memories blown
by gentle rains,
I live them all again
and bitter winds;
of disappointment, and of doubt...
Fade as dying embers
in the Healing fires of Life.

Will Jones

"The Security Blanket"

What became I often wonder
Of that sad little lass
The only child of color in my
all white class
In that school in the North in 1924
Clinging desperately in loneliness
To the knob of the big school door
Never included in the recess play
How could the teacher have allowed
that to happen day after day
No white hand in hers as we filed
hand in hand, two by two
Into the school as we were taught to do
She never returned after that first year
But I knew that her loving mother
Comforted her and wiped away her tears
She has been in a kinder world
Dear God, I pray, and may that no
Child of color ever again be treated
In that heartbreakingly cruel, cruel way

Marie M. Grant

Motions Of Love

My heart can feel the movement
Of the love you have for me
With each and every move you make
True love is there to see.
Your arms they hold me tightly
And you make my heart melt fast
With you I have no memories
Of lost loves in the past.

You hold my hand, I feel so faint
My heart begins to pound
The love we share is thrilling
Without even making a sound.
Your eyes they shine like diamonds
When I look into your face
And when you speak to me it's done
With caring and such grace.

Our bodies intertwine into one
Our hearts are blended too
For all that we both feel inside,
Shows in everything we do.

Michelle D. Rogahn

Ascension

O Warrior Son:

From the ancient breast
Of the rocks risen,
You have passed the crest
And, by Time driven,
Now seek thy bed;

Since battles end
When the slain who bled,
To the Lord commend
Their souls in peace—
To the earth their bones.

And above:
The fleece clouds, circling thrones,
Now wreathe a shroud;
While, Heavenly choired,
The Warrior proud,
From earth expired,

Now honoured—to the Temple borne—
Is laid in state, as anthems rise
To greet the resurrection morn.

Ricardo Martel

Home

I'd like a place with a little yard
On a little street
Not a big boulevard
A house of wood and glass
Where I could live
And tend the grass
Oh, and a garden too
That I'd work and weed
'til the veggies grew
Then I'd share the feed
With all I knew
And save some seed
From the things I grew

A little house with warmth and light
Secure and cozy even at night
Not a palace of royal beauty bright
But
A little house with warmth and light

Mary Wheeler

All For Love

The hooves ring out
On the stones of the courtyard.
As the great black steed enters,
Mane flowing, nostrils flaring.

Upon his back, a knight,
Dressed in silver armour,
Something powerful, regal,
An aura of strength.

Slowly he removes his helmet,
Blonde hair flows to his shoulders,
A ruggedly handsome man,
Strong jaw, dark eyes guarded.

He comes to win her love,
For she was promised to him.
A pact made at birth.
Yet he wants her heart.

Of all the many battles,
The long journeys, endless sieges,
This will be the hardest won.
All for love.

Marketa Cornwall

Love Is The Soul

When your beauty is a reflection
on the water of the lake, you
look like a mist from the
heavens above.

When your eyes sparkle in the
moonlight, they show all meanings
of love that couldn't be described
in words.

When your arms are around me,
I feel so precious to be
a part of you.

When your heart beats with mine,
I know heaven is not far away.

When our bodies are joined as one,
I know we were meant to be
together as one.

When God gave us love, he blessed
us with the nature of special love,
that is so very hard to find.

Marquita Goins

A Dark Encounter

Dark eyes; Dark heart;
No tenderness to meet...
Only the cold Dark...
To freeze the stark!

I sought to probe the Dark;
But lost heart.
It consumes in emptiness...
That which is filled with lovingness.

Love is replaced
By something cold placed...
Cannot penetrate....
Such evil prostrate!
It seethes and wreathes...
As evil lives.
Is evil given life?

LeRoy Kruse

Katherina

She came into our lives
One crisp autumn day-
A moment we'll cherish
For e'er and always.

With her washed-denim eyes
And her wrinkled-nose grin
You can't help but wonder
What mischief she's in.

As we watch her grow daily,
What a wonder is she!
Oh, the things you can learn
From a child of just three!

She's all laughter, all bounce;
She's all ginger and sass;
She's the joy of our lives,
Our sweet bit of a lass.

She's a light-hearted fairy,
A joy-burst of mirth;
Our God-send from Heaven—
An Angel on Earth!

Karen McFarland

My Rose, My Love

Intimate thoughts
only of you,
Crossing my mind
the whole day through.
Your love is sweeter
Than a rose,
Which in my heart
deeply grows.
If you shall wilt,
I won't throw away,
For you will bloom
again someday.
Intimate thoughts
fully in bloom,
I love your essence
in the room.
Growing deeper
a love so true,
You are my rose...
and I Love You!

Mia Smith

Don't Break My Heart

I open my heart and let love in...
Only to get it broken again...
They're all the same lines and
false emotions...
Tell me what happened to true
devotion...
Is it something gone in the past...
Is it one of those things that just
couldn't last...
Love was meant to be safe and
secure...
Another broken heart I cannot
endure...
Please tell me you're not like all
the rest...
And I'll love you forever the
way I know best.

Kristy Tumey

L 'homme

This is for no holiday
or special occasion,
it is meant for you.
When you are in your
most comfortable abode,
and, body and soul have
found solace...
Close your eyes and let
The mind wonder 'till consciousness
of the distant sound permeates you...
Then, take a sip and toast the one
who may love or hate you!

Ramona Therese Dolega

"Gone With The Wind"

A love that went away
Or the death of a friend
Like leaves on a fall day
They are gone with the wind
You wanted them to stay
Everything comes to an end
Like snowflakes on a winter day
They are gone with the wind
Life is always changing
Love will come and go
Some things you can't change
You just have to let go
With the cards life deals you
You have to play your hand
With the cards you receive
You do the best you can
Everything has a beginning
Everything has an end
For in time everything
Will be gone with the wind

Michael Kendrick

Untitled

So we travel
our minds our souls
we root, stem, and leave
one another alone
seeking sanctuary
in habitual decay.

In sleep the toil
of fertile thoughts
and each waking moment
a reminder found
in such tender touch
your skin our pages
of past significance.

Laurence E. Paverd

The Worth Of A Little Love

Like a treasure in a gilded chest
Of rubies, pearls and gold,
The ransom for a kingdom
Within one's grasp, to hold.
The strength within a father's love
For those he holds so dear
And the calming of a mother's voice
To drive away the fear.
The riches of the world to see
Are lighted from above
And reflected in a child's eyes,
From just a little love.

Mabel Langworthy

Ye Olde Curiosity Shoppe

In the city of Seattle where the
Pacific laps its shores
Stands a shop packed full of wonders
Of odds and curios

Where folks are always welcomed
Through a door that's opened wide
And a feast for the eyes is certain
As you gaze toward either side

Where nature has provided
A variety and host -
Decisions are difficult to make
For the ones you'd treasure most

Fashioned into beauty by the heart
The mind and hand
These curios and wonders from out
This and every land

So whether you be curious
For curios or not
A pleasure really awaits you at
"Ye Olde Curiosity Shoppe."

Truea Margaret Lerch

Battle Cry

Into the battle, he ran head on
Pain in his heart, on his lips, a song
Singing to God, for the gift of his love
Praying for wisdom and strength from
above

He fell many times and his blood ran
But he got up, screaming I can!
Blow after blow, made him take heed
Feeling the end, seeing his need

His life in pieces, scattered around
He cried for answers, not yet found
A lifetime of tears, left to the rear
Still he fought bravely, facing his fear

Maybe someday...he can rest
Maybe someday...there won't be a test
But for now, the battle rages strong
And maybe that someday...will come
before long.

Mike Kimzey

Pith'ecan-Thro'pus

Blond hair...blue eyes
pale skin fair
Dark hair...brown eyes
ebony skin
Neither rare
It is so unfair
to measure one by this
or discriminate because
of clothing he wears.
Beauty is as Beauty does,
this the time worn them.
For men to search deeper
is my fondest dream.
Cancel out the prejudice,
relinquish all the hate,
Determine contents
of heart, mind and deed
No longer to prejudge
by color or creed.

Marilynn J. Eagan

Whatever

Everyone is scrambling for their
Piece of the pie
In a protean universe
Where what's in becomes
What has been in rapid flashes

Hands reaching out of necessity
To snatch forever before it's gone

And me? I move at a snail's pace
Watching the human collage
Through the kaleidoscopic eyes
Of a chameleon
Blending into the milieu of life

Suddenly I make a cameo appearance
As the kinetic stops at inertia
And then some catalyst starts
The process again and I'm gone

Marylin Reed

Embrace The Journey

A heart can shatter many times
pieces melting in the dew
The mind may say you'll never mend
it need not be true for you
When you think the rainbow ends
look beyond the clouds
Close your eyes and feel the hues
embrace the journey at the bends
There may not be a pot of gold
to make your dreams come true
through it all you will discover
the survivor's spirit within you

Karen Belle

Untitled

Tell me you're sorry
Please help me understand,
Why you needed
To raise your hands.

Why do you keep hurting me
over and over again,
Can you tell me why
Cause I do not understand.

I needed to be praised
just once,
but you never gave me that
not even an ounce.

Why do I love you
I must be confused,
I'm still trying to please you
And all I'm getting is abuse.

I need your support
In whatever I do,
I need to know you love me
and hear the words "I LOVE YOU"

Kay Renee Nash

Selene

The moon is spying high,
Queen of the darkened stage sky.
She has shed her shadowed skin,
To be reborn again;
Light in eternal darkness.

Ryan M. Hickey

Not Quite Golden

"You hold that box so tightly, dear.
Please let me put it down for you."
"Oh, no, it comforts me, my boy.
Just get us there. Keep driving, do!"
Her trembling fingers smoothed the box—
Her shoulders straight, concealing gloom.
"You'll like your little garden there —
And crafts and hobbies near your room."
A garden two by three she knew.
"You'll make new friends —"
She hugged her box.
"Tiresome memory always mends."
He glanced at her. "What's in that box?"
"No matter, son. Just little things."
A baby shoe, a lock of hair, yellowed lace,
And some old rings.
"Well, here we are!" her son enthused.
"Green rolling lawns and paneled halls!"
She nodded then and clutched the box,
And saw strange faces — closing walls.

Lois Ijams Hartman

Away Back Then

Around my knee they gathered,
Pressing close to me.
"Tell us a story, Grandma
Tell us a story, please."

"Tell 'bout when you were little
Playing with your friends.
Tell about your school days,
About way back then."

I told about my school days,
Days of long ago.
Told about my little friends,
Things they wanted to know.

Little faces looked up at me,
Drinking it all in.
Oh, it seemed like yesterday
That I was young as them.

These precious little children
Bringing joy to me,
Are writing their own stories
Oh how it used to be.

Wilda Louise Carriker

"Hour Glass"

Reflections in store front windows
seem to frame a vagueness
within our souls,
as images rush for tomorrow
shadows steal easily, the value of today.
Steadily sun and moon pull at the tide
always keeping time,
and though this hour glass we try to hold
already, grains have slipped away.
Here lost sand castles resemble
life's material riches swirling in
crumpled dreams.
Look back and see,
we are mere impressions
left briefly on the shore.
Listen to the breaking waves
and heed the sea gulls cry,
for in the misty light of day
we are left to stand alone
our footprints, washed away.

Vicki Vilsmeyer

Fallen Angel

Their shame untold,
Pride is not sold,
'Tis the pleasure of flesh and money,

But as the time passes,
The toll is taken,
Secluded, alone, and feeling forsaken,

Their hearts reach out,
But must say goodbye,
Fallen angels never lose their wings,
Only their will to fly.

Peter Mancuso

The Dancer

Music comes to me
Pulls me
Moves me
Rocks my hips

Move I must and follow its beat.

Music
Presses against my body
Lifts me up to whirl around.
Twists my heart and makes me cry

O let me dance until I die.

Rita G. Eshuis

October

Beautiful October
queen of autumn's court
dressed in swaying yellow
she grandly holds the fort.

Stately trees of every color
mark the paths that people tread.
The splendor of paradise;
blue of blues stretched overhead.

Listen to the soft twitter
of the birds in early dawn
Do they whisper to each other
God makes all October morns?

Nell Johnson

Panes

He stands at the window
Rain slides down the panes.
Another day his field
remains unplanted.
Flood waters rise before
his eyes.

"It's a risk he took,"
say high-ground farmers.
"The drought is over,"
joke the townspeople,
Covering their own fears
of the effects of a crop-less year
on their livelihoods.

He looks at the stack
of unpaid bills.
A tear, like the rain,
Glides down the pane of his cheek.

He reaches for the gun.

Pam Von Hagel

"Into The Peace"

The time you put toward wisdom
Reaps many rewards, as life
levels off into the smooth patterns
You See for the first time as
the truth of Him permeates the Soul.
Always there, Always simple. The
Walls are down...Life is up!
You gather together the Real
meaning. You look just One Way!
Feeling like the first time...Every
time. You're into the only pattern.
The pattern that brings you
"Into the Peace"

Michel J. Priadka

Street People

Enduring people
refuse to break,
Oak falls but
palms shake

Relentless people
become wind
rippling flags,
raising skin

Upright people
grace our day
advancing truth,
point the way

People generous
warm as sun,
nourish many,
shading none

Shawn M. Bland

Fragile Child

Satisfaction is where it's at
said the blind rat to the cat
Say your prayers before
you sleep, are your dreams
dark and deep
Cross the edges of your mind
Find a reason to survive
Fragile child lost and scared
All alone, no place to go
Find yourself before they do
don't ever let them change
you and follow your own advice
But curiosity is where it's
at, the blind rat ate the cat
and upset stomach brought it back.

Richard W. Peterson

Freedom To Fly

I am the blue Latex balloon
sailing...soaring...
chased by the child
who shall ground my direction
and cling
to my string handle
hesitant am I
as my helium soul lusts after
freedom...air, and space...
room to explore the sky
above the land of expectation.

Tasha Witkowski

Creaky Old House

With holes in the roof, out in a field,
sat a lonely old creaky house,
Nobody lives there anymore,
it's scarcely fit for a mouse.
Spiders in the corner,
crickets clinging to the walls,
Thankful for a dry place to be,
when the cold rain falls.
Screech owl,
thinking the house was a barn,
landed on a window sill,
It perched there for so long of a time,
as it was raining still.
A lizard on the old splintered porch,
crawled up the post to the eaves,
The ragged curtain, hanging at the window,
flapped in the morning breeze.
In a field on a deserted road,
sat a lonely creaky house.

Peggy Cruise

Eventide

Cascading colors erupt in profusion:
Scarlet, yellow, orange, and burgundy
Mingle with azure hues
And dance over emerald seas
As the vibrancy of God's day
Recedes into night.

Day's death throes
Transform into night reborn;
Twilight concludes,
Night emerges.
Resplendent ebony
Illuminated extravagantly by stars
Who exult and consort with the angels.
God's vespers conclude.

Melinda K. Blade

My Angel

I'm sure she was an angel,
sent down on loan to me.
To teach a valued lesson,
on what life is meant to be.

Celebrate life with joy,
right from the very start,
Share with others daily,
the love that warms your heart.

Wake and rise with courage,
at the dawn of each new day,
Face each challenge with new hope,
whatever comes your way.

Appreciate the gift of life,
for its value can't be measured,
Take each day one at a time,
each memory must be treasured.

You cannot always choose in life,
The outcome of each test,
Have faith and trust in God above,
for He knows what is best.

Teresa Foster

An Angel Walks Before Me

An angel walks before me
sent from Heaven above
to open doors before me
that others may hear of His love;
to know the joy of salvation
which only Christ can give.

Above and all around me
are those who are lost in sin.
A little at a time, Lord,
may blinded eyes come to see
their need of Jesus Christ
and assurance of Eternity.

Thank You, Abba Father,
for love that set us free;
for your moment by moment leading
that has opened doors for me
to speak to those about me,
of your grace which to all is free.

Mary Alice Montgomery

Newcastle, Wyoming

Evening rolls on
Shades of brown
Fields and posts
Another day's ghost

Into the sunset
Radiant visions west
Ward of the moon
Light bears Coyote's croon

Silence drums the dark
In my breast my heart
Holds still one breath
Each step next to death
And morning 'gain awakes
Arid thirst never slaked

Thro' Spirit draught come alive

Renew all ... approaching twilight

Timothy Mitchell

The Road To Love

Oh guiding hand of destiny
So full of life and light
Roads unwalked and those to come
A choice is all you give to me

Oh gilded wings of fate
That flow unchecked by time
The way is always clear and true
To those who choose to wait

Oh glowing star from heaven
That glitters from afar
A beacon shining through the night
To show where I have been

Oh gracious dame of fortune
Your luck is mine tonight
A stranger comes across my path
Beneath the shining moon

Oh gleaming dove of white
An omen from my heart
My love has come and taken me
Away into the night

Lisa Anne Behrendt

A Mother

She wipes away my tears.
She calms my fears.
She listens when I'm down.
She clears away the frowns.
She's there when I feel alone.
She even buys me ice cream cones.
She supports me when I'm right.
She sometimes makes me see the light.
She admits it when she's wrong.
She always helps me along.
I thank the God above
For giving me this mom to love.

Katherine Sears

The Song Of Rising

Lo, lo...how does the song go?
She contemplates the single step
And never once looks up
To view the endless flight ahead
Steps, steps in the mists of unknowing

With lowered eyes she stumbles through
Bewildered years of childhood
Saying yes when taught it's right
And no because they said to
Sad, sad in the ground of her being

In breezy colors comes the day
A question blossoms from her heart
Poised and paused, she lifts her eyes
To find there is a higher step
Yes, yes to her restless longing

The mists are pierced by golden rays
Which lead her feet in finding
The way, her eyes to clearly see
The ease of steps ascending
Lo, lo...how does the song go?

Lily Gebhart

And Then There Was One

Josie ate the apple core,
she shoved it in her mouth.
She took another one or more,
and ate them facing south.

She went into the garden then,
and stood awhile there.
And then she started up again,
now eating cores in pairs.

She walked down by the river side,
and sat down with the geese.
The rippling of the river's tide,
helped her sit at peace.

I met her at the school one day,
I found her in the yard.
I found she had a lot to say,
though she found it hard.

She ate the apple cores she said,
that's where the life was found.
And then she said her soul was fed,
and comfort there abound.

Trista Morgan

A Beautiful Person

A beautiful person I do see,
She has a heart of gold and
always an open mind and ear continually.
A beautiful person that you are,
you're always near and never far.
A beautiful person I do treasure,
always to be my friend forever.
A beautiful person is you, because
you make me feel beautiful too.
A beautiful person I do see,
her name is Annie, and her
friendship means so much
to me.

Midge Spaulding

"Sleepless Night"

Waiting
She lies awake
looking out the
window at a
moonlit sky
listening for
Familiar footsteps,
listening for the
faint sound of
a key turning
in a lock,
listening for that
sound of her
husband climbing
into the bed
beside her,
knowing he is
safe so she can
sleep.

Theresa Barrow

On Playing Debussy's 'Clair De Lune'

Silver-cool moon silver
Slipping down the sky
Softly spilling liquid light
Into dream-dark pools of night.

Silver-cool moon silver
Filtering through the trees
Forming fragile lace work
Out of sleeping leaves.

Silver-cool moon silver
Mist-wraith of the years,
Yielding still, white loneliness
Immutable through tears.

Mary L. Lopez

Waiting Love

A thousand tears I've cried
Since you've gone away.
I know I can't see you now,
But I will someday.
Wait for me on the other side
Until it is my turn to die.
Save me a pair of wings and
All those heavenly things.
If my name's not marked on
A golden stair,
I'll know you're not there.
To show the love I feel is true,
I'll go to hell to stay with you!

Kelly Edgar

Anniversary

He looked in her eyes
she smiled through the tears
Just another turning point
after more than fifty years

They told them to prepare
for hard times were yet to come
They must learn to live
without, they said
security and home

Years have passed, she sits alone
in a room where time stands still
She glances out the window
Reflections dance at will

Memories have kept her strong
though one has laid to rest
One heart, one mind, one soul survives
to carry on as best

Kathleen Bock

I Cried

Death dances at my window
She taps a happy tune
calling me to come and play
forever leave this room.
She needs to come inside you see
to keep my Daddy off of me.
I only have to let her in
and then I would be free.
She is my friend my only choice
the safest place to hide.
I couldn't lift the window.
I tried. I tried. I tried.
I call to her to take me now.
My Daddy's almost here.
He's coming up the stairs for me.
I hear his breathing near.
I want to run. There is no place.
I cried. I cried. I cried.
He's coming up the stairs for me.
To have his nightly ride.

Robin O. Dorrbecker

The Greatest Person I Never Knew

She was born dead
so doctors had said.

She was lying down
with little tubes to her head.

We are asked
How is she doing doc?

He said come with me
I went into shock.

For hours we watched the clock
and awaited the return of the doc!

For when he returned
it was them I knew

I had lost
the greatest person I never knew.

*(In loving memory of my sister
Kaitlin La'mour Armstrong-Beverly
Born Aug 6, Died Aug 7 1994)*

Tonya Richie

Solace

Ah atrabilious tree
shorn by Autumn winds
yet still.
Taciturn.
Solitary veg astray from forest rule.
Sway not,
for gavel has condemned me.
Culled.
Bow only to sweep
me in mire that I
may be saved from hanging branch
and rest in comfort,
of irrigation
root.

Rachel Blue McDonnell

Uncertainty

If there is a flicker of hope,
should you reach out and grab it,
or
should you wait?
If there is a glimmer of faith,
should you believe,
or
should you remain detached?
If your heart is pounding in apprehension,
should you speak your mind,
or
should you just keep it at bay?
Uncertainty,
Leave us clutching at hope
Trying to hold on to something,
That wants to be free.

Sonya Ann Keserica

Truth

A smile so radiant,
One to knock out a crowd,
Rosy Cheeks,
Glowing eyes,
All of it a mask of identity,
A mask to cover the truth.
It's there out of fear,
Shame.
A mask made by peers,
Family,
Society,
The real smile, so non-existent,
One of deep depression and pity.
Pale skin,
Sad eyes.
Underneath the mask is the pitiful truth.

Terez Fraser

Untitled

Someday you will find
Someone who is kind

Someday you will meet
Someone who is neat

Someday you will see
Someone who will flee

Someday you will hear
Someone shedding a tear

Someday you will feel
Someone's love is real.

Katrina Ragon

Sing To Me Forever

Sing to me of life, love, and adventures
Sing to me that we will always be friends
Sing to me of your dreams and our future
Sing to me forever
Will you sing to me forever?
Sing to make me happy
Sing to me when you are sad
Sing to me of beauty and of gloom
Sing to me forever
Sing a song to me from heart
Sing to me about our love
Sing to me forever

Margaret Rodriguez

Wissahickon's Willow Weep

From the winter bones of sleep,
Sleep, willow, sleep.
In the hollow valley's keep
Keep, willow, keep.
Where the leaf mould thaws to steep
Steep, willow, steep.
From the earth, a pressure deep,
Deep, willow, deep.
Through the shivered branches creep
Creep, willow, creep.
Furry tears of spring buds peep.
Peep, willow, peep.
With a green and yellow sweep
Sweep, willow, sweep.
In a slivered fountain leap
Leap, willow, leap!

On the sprays of willow weep
Weep, willow, weep.

E. Chipman Higgins

Sunrise At Midnight

In a half-lit bar
Smoke and whispers
Fill every soul
With a dying melody;
Shadows move,
Back and forth,
Like ghosts
Gliding around
The rocks of ancient tombs;
Music in the air,
Gun fire not too far away,
Timeless ruins
Bringing beauty
Through centuries of death;
In a moonlight night
History weeping
In the death march of tomorrow,
And hopes of yesterday
Once more melting
In the foamy cups of today.

William K. Yakoubian

Mad Horses

The belly of my soul
Swells for the birth of new song.
All night the tide has ebbed.
But now it turns...
And words...mad words...
Come galloping on mad horses...
Riding furiously o'er the
Mud flats of my mind.

Robert W. Mather

My Little Persephone

My little Persephone,
So gentle and sweet.
She sleeps and she plays,
And follows by my feet.

But when she's rambunctious,
She seldom is around.
Off on an adventure,
No where to be found.

And when she comes home,
Everyone knows it.
She's often in mischief,
There's no doubt about it.

My little Persephone,
Her own in her ways.
Up like the sun,
As bright as its rays.

Miranda Kleschuk

"Blurred Vision"

I can't seem to find the words
So I can speak gently to you
Speak for all that has heard
That my love for you is true

I can't make myself sweet
So that I can comfort your heart
No love can be beat
But hearts torn apart

My love is strong
But vision is blurred
Something went wrong
None have heard

I guess I'm crazy
For not seeing okay
But isn't that the way to be
In the world we have today

Sean Ian Cassidy

Visionary

One silhouette,
Shrouded in darkness,
Wingless,
Yet struggling to rise,
Hearing only what nature gave to hear,
Moved by breath of a nightingale,
Sharing a dream's fleeting destiny,
Revealing glory's song of sacrifice,
Wingless,
Within unbridled shadows,
Desirous to betray their realm,
Inflame a fragile voice,
Beyond the breath of lies,
Awaken innocent imagining,
Within a dispirited mind,
One silhouette,
Longing to embrace approaching wind,
Evolving toward uncovering
Boundless light.

Linda Marlene Cory

This Old House

Here stands a building
so pretty and sweet,
Until you peek through
the windows and you see an
awful sight you seek.
Long years of memories,
hang on and about,
you would be surprised of
how things turned out.
Oh how the smiles came
and went, the laughter
lived and died.
The pain came to stay and
hang on for dear life.
Oh how this old house
deserves better,
To live in vain with no
Shame and no more pain to gain.
As I sleep in this old house.

Teressa M. Land

Soft

Soft are the voices that call,
Soft are the tears that fall,

Soft are the hands that hold,
Soft is your heart, now cold,
Soft and tender is my heart,
Softly you tore me apart,

Softly you said goodbye, and
Softly I did die

Softly you realized you lost a friend,
Softly my heart you tried to mend,

Softly you realized I was gone,
Softly you wonder what you did wrong

Softly in the night's breeze,
Softly flowing through the trees,

Softly I whispered it's not the end,
Softly and forever I'll be your friend!

Lisa Roper

To The Future

Here's a toast to the future!
Some give it limited scope,
Yet just what else can offer
More fulfillment and good hope?

Some say that it's not real,
That it is pie in the sky;
A problem with today is
You can't keep it if you try.

Living only for today
Just gives hope no place to go:
Today gives no incentive
To attend school or to grow.

Some think they may die too soon,
Or that their future will fall flat;
That's, of course, quite possible,
But who can be sure of that?

Today may be quite prosaic;
Why not steer clear of sorrow,
By weaving today's loose threads
In fabrics for tomorrow?

William A. Paff

Spring

Seasons come and seasons go,
Some bring sunshine, some bring snow.
My favorite season of the year
Is spring, which I hold dear.

Robins come and build their nest
So they have a place to rest.
Purple, yellow, and white crocus bloom,
Dispelling all despair and gloom.

Picnics in the park, reunions too;
School lets out, trips to the zoo.
Vacations to some faraway places,
Happy smiles upon all faces.

It makes me want to shout and sing
Of my favorite season, spring.

Shirley Anne Gorman

It Is.....

Some say it is a miracle.
Some say it is a gift.
Some say it is unreachable.
But I believe it is...
The window to your heart.
A search to find your soul.
To create that inner strength
I know I can't control.
Some say it is a magic.
Some say it is a thought.
Some say it is an evil,
But I believe it's not.
I say that it is love.
I say that it is true.
I say that it is everything,
I say that it is you!

Stephanie L. Ziemba

Hope

A world full of disaster
spinning out of control-
Everyone's moving faster
Ignoring the toll.

A divine whisper
blows through the trees
Is it a message...
Or only the breeze?

Listen close and hear
It's time to slow down
By now, crystal clear
The way has been shown.

At the end of your rope?
Open your mind and heart
Believe me, there's hope-
Don't be afraid to start!

Kelly Rumler Barson

Passing Showers

The sunset, yet, may promise joy,
Though dawn and I knew grief,
Our countenances well concealed
Neath sodden handkerchief.

The midday sky has dried her eye;
My weeping, too, is o'er.
But, dears, my tears have not transformed
Parched gardens - green once more!

Kathleen R. Brumage

Despair

He looks so lonely sitting there,
staring at her empty chair,
his grief so difficult to bear.
He's filled with longing and despair.

God took his wife to be with Him
and now he's all alone.
It's left him filled with emptiness,
and memories of his own.

Together for so many years,
his aching heart is filled with tears.
I wish that I could ease his fear
and give him back his love, so dear.

I want to take away his pain,
I feel such empathy.
For he's my loving father,
and she was "mom" to me.

Sandi Chaussée

Spirit Dance

By the light of the moon, with the
stars as its guide,
your soul came searching
and finally found mine.
Like the waves of the ocean, as
they sweep 'cross the sand,
our bodies crashed together
and our spirits danced.
The winds of the east, with the
angels of sky,
whispered of love's passion
and our hearts replied.
Like the glow of the sunset,
as it burns down the sky,
our lips flamed with fire
and our souls combined.
The rhythm of the earth, with
the thundering tide,
spoke love everlasting
and peace to our minds.

Sharon K. Wohlers

You Are So Real To Me

You are so kind my Lord to me.
Thank you Lord for loving me.
My Lord, you are so real to me.

The days around me are so bright.
The nights above me are just right.
My Lord, you are so real to me.

I wonder what I might have been
if my Lord you had not been.

O Lord, the days around me would
be dark, the nights above me would
bring fright.

But praise the Lord, no despair
for all around me You are there.
My Lord you are so real to me.

My hopes and prayers I send to Thee,
That day by day I might go Thy way
so that I might hear You say, my
child you are so real to Me.

J. W. Matlock, Sr.

Autumn

Shaded hollow passages
strewn with animated hues
brittle, curled and crunchy
beneath ginger footfall
Scarlet, Amber, Sienna
floating and gliding softly downward
gently catching the last balmy breeze
as winter chill looms near
The Sun: strong, penetrating -
yet ever-yielding to the supremacy of
nature's dominion -
begins to ebb
conceding the immanent change
as dusk's subtle coolness
sweeps across a silent, shadowy
October landscape.

Veronica Timpanelli-Dempsey

In The Hour Before The Dawn

Ghost-dog chasin' late summer moon
Strides across a grave
Barking orders to the shadows
Not even prayers can save

Wander upon mist-broken pool
Pale one caught by silver
Rings threaten pixies unseen shore
Secrets run for cover

Star-message flashed on jungle eyes
She blinds the trusted beast
Heads turn to catch a golden glow
That dragon in the east

Timothy W. Grebiner

The Soul Of Nature

The beauty of nature is in itself,
swiftly, falling from wind.

It holds the creation of all,
in the depth of its soul.

Cannot let go of who it is,
the secret must not be past.

The warmth of its calmness,
is known not at all,

Only to whom the greatest is,
and that is nature itself.

Kira Alvarez

Little Boy

A small fist in the palm of my hand
takes me away to another land

A land of sunshine and rainbows
where love will always grow

And at this place I will show to thee
how much love grows on our family tree

Happy smiles and funny days
make all our worries go away

To watch you learn and grow
there is so much more for you to know

But for now you play with your toys
for you are such a wonderful little boy

Patricia D. Henkel

Counterpart

True love is blind,
Takes the scales, ignores the rind.
Water shifting...into wine

True love takes time,
Reach the core, and read the sign.
Through your eyes...the knot unties.

COUNTERPART...TATTOO MY
HEART

First loves burn deep,
Shapes the core, for us to keep.
Skin that haunts me...memory

New love EXCITES!
First kiss, the sheets ignite
We tune into...appetite.

COUNTERPART...TATTOO MY
HEART

Paul Llew-Williams

Untitled

You have a hold of my heart
Taking it from the first sight
Of you
Then your grip grew tighter
As we followed the steps
Of knowing the other
More and more
Even now my heart sparkles
With just a remembrance of you
But now we've gone through the steps
And made it home
Making it harder to pull away
Cause now I know
What's missing
And your grip on my heart
Has reached its max
For now
I know
I'm in love with you
I love you, xoxoxox.....

Teri Ann Otto

Soft Power

Tingles down my back
Tears in my eyes.
Peace in my heart.
Clouds vanished from the sky.
Love replaces bitter hate.
My mind is clear
Is this a miraculous fate?
How can it be possible
To loose the darkness inside?
Replaced by love and pity
For one my heart despised.
God must've known somehow
That eternity rides in one choice.
Only he has power to remove pride
With the powerful softness of his voice
That stills my festering
And melts these hard eyes;
A spiritual softening.
Potential molded by one on high.

Valerie P. Stephens

I Alien I

I alien I
tempest rages
internal see
foreign invaders
imaging me
looking glass scene

I alien I
piercing sight
striking mind's I
crashing waves
I undertow
inward see

I alien I
striking image
viewing me
reflecting self
turmoil see
consuming me

Mirror tempest
I alien me

Robert E. Reber

Consume Me

Consume me with Your spirit, Lord
That a beacon I might be
Reveal to me the things of self
That I might shine for Thee
My faults and failures I confess
Are known full well by Thee
I know that I must daily die
That You may live through me
A vessel in Your keeping, Lord
For Your purpose set apart
Cleansed both from without, within
Your mercy to impart
Lord, grant to me the power
In the calling meant for me
To greatly magnify Your name
As I hide myself in Thee.

Martha Champion Lewis

Beautiful

All of the holy grace,
that belongs to the dove,
has fallen upon you,
with unending love.

The beauty of the rose,
is nothing to compare,
to the beauty of your soul,
and the love you hold there.

As I gently stare,
deep into your eyes,
I see a shine so bright,
the sun has learned to despise.

The beauty all around us,
should be hiding in disgrace.
For there is nothing so beautiful,
than the smile on your face.

ShariLynn Wrezinski

Spring

You need not say the magic word
That fills our hearts with gladness
The new life growth that can be heard
Making our feelings both joy and sadness.

Oh this one thing that can make us sing
Yet can make us sad
Is no other than the new born spring
Last winter the Mother, summer it's Dad.

Peoples of it's many races
Enjoy its new born green
The blind show it on their faces
Although they've never seen.

God gave us the seasons
About which we all sing
We named them all with reason
The most loved one is spring.

Thomas R. Bloom

Today

Today, I started down a path
that had no footsteps in;
Not knowing of events in store
but trusting God to win.

Today, at dawn, new life began,
never, yet, been viewed;
Exciting, full of trust and love
in a world so brash and rude.

Today, Savior, be my guide
to face the hours ahead.
While whispering, "Use me, my Lord,"
life's challenge I'll not dread.

Today, when fearful of what lies before,
on You I rest those fears.
You, Keeper of today,
Keeper of the years.

Shirley Jackson

A Special House

The old house stands deserted now;
That house which once was ours.
The house was filled with voices then;
With music and with flowers.

The paint upon its weathered sides
Is peeling in the sun.
The memories haunt my reveries;
They come back one by one.

There's Grampa in his rocking chair
And Papa's reading news,
While Mama at her Kimball plays
The classics and the blues.

The house was often full of folks;
The children numbered five.
Now, most who crossed the threshold then
No longer are alive.

It saddens me to see the house
Forsaken and forlorn.
I have a special feeling for
The house where I was born.

Lillian Houchen

Theological Virtues

Faith is a spiritual safety pin
That keeps soul and body together
It fortifies your resistance to sin
Till your passport time forever.

Hope is the soul's special telescope
Keeping you focused on what is ahead
Guiding you now so your spirit will cope
When it's time for your body to shed.

Charity is the flowing grace of love
Supreme forgiveness from the Almighty
We should accept what comes from above
And show that we are insightful.

For the day will come when we must go
And we should prepare to be ready
Sowing the seeds that we should sow
For our harvest in heaven be steady.

Marion M. Hayden

Feelings

If I could expunge the love from me
that makes my inner being burn,
This I would gladly do for you
and ask nothing in return.

If I could purge the pain from you
and take it unto me,
This I would gladly do for you
so you would be forever free.

If I could give of myself to you
and help you through every turn,
This I would gladly do for you
and expect nothing in return.

If I could express my love for you
in each and every way,
This I would gladly do for you
through each and every day.

If you remember nothing else,
please remember me!
For I shall always remember you
And the happiness you gave to me.

Rebecca Liner Sheriff

Fait Accompli

The clean washed walls
Surround me trapping me
in their sanctuary the air
smells of bleach and death
and the only faces I can see
are distorted versions of my
own the voices I hear are
disguised and the words
they utter are meaningless
on and on they drone
the bodies around me
are multiplying their breath
on my face is hot and
smells of old age
and senility
my eyes tear open and
I lie in my bed gasping
for life while their
promise echoes
in my ears...

Sabrina Rocheleau

The Idiot

There's a part of me
That not all can see.
For usually I hide it -
The idiot in me.

But now and then
He sneaks up on me.
He makes my life hard -
The idiot in me.

He hurts those I care for.
Which, in turn, hurts me.
He's stupidly cruel -
The idiot in me.

I wish to dispel him,
To drive him from me.
I want to get rid of -
The idiot in me.

This may be impossible,
As you probably see.
For to my great shame -
The idiot is me.

Ronald DeMille

My Master's Hands On Mine

It was my master's hand that touched
The blind man and he was made to see

And yes, it was my master's hands
That made and fashioned me

I've placed my life in his hands
I lie waiting and I lie still

For in his hands, I find refuge
And there I'm ever in his will

With my hands I'll lift high
And in adoration, I'll ever raise

Holy hands to worship him
As I utter words of praise

With my hands I'll work the vineyard
My master has no hands but mine

Lord, my hands had no purpose
Till they had been touched by thine

Ruby Jones Dickson

Moon Path

Soft, silver - coated autumn night.
The bright air crisp, yet calm and hushed.
Coin moon, intensely glowing, white;
Brush-stroking woods in silver wash.

A moonlight path lay just ahead,
Enticing three to walk along.
She, longing to explore the way,
Beseeched them both to follow her.

But he who prized her pristine grace,
Disdained to try enchanted roads.
And he who prized her questing soul
Now turned to walk a different path.

Alas, alone! Her heart despaired.
Will no one choose enchantment's way!
And thus it was that ever more
She traveled moonlight paths alone.

Mary Parsons Stokes

Blindness Is Bliss?

Open your eyes
the Cancer Moon is full
Can you see your way?
It's twisted
Watch for falling
bricks

Where are you going?
Where are you going?
The corridors are empty
There is no center prize
The entrance is no exit

Look at the box
the same
different paint
different view

Open the box
Open your eyes
they all fall down

Trevor Wilson

Winged Rainbow

Red, yellow, brown, and gold;
The colors flutter by,
These heavenly hues all rolled
Into the tiny wings of this butterfly.
A winged rainbow
Adrift on a summer's breeze,
Traveling by at a pace so slow,
Moving with God's grace and ease.
Its delicate innocence so evident
As it moves from flower to flower,
Enjoying the fragrant scents.
Drinking sweet nectar for its power.
Suddenly, it catches another soft breeze
To journey to all new lands,
Doing its sacred job to release
A piece of heaven into another's hands.

Steven Kidd

My Sleeping Child

I spied upon my child around
the corner of her bedroom door;
And discovered her safely guarded
By a stuffed menagerie on the floor.

My precious girl lay curled
Upon her bed throughout the night
While she slept and dreamed
In the glow of pale moonlight.

Her angelic face was streaked
By strands of tousled hair.
The clothes of a princess
Draped neatly upon a chair.

In the blue light of the moon her
Old rag doll sat slumped upon the sill.
Shadows softly silhouetted the yard,
And crickets chirped at will.

I recalled the song of her laughter
As she frolicked throughout the day;
And gratefully counted my blessings
As I knelt beside her to pray.

Karen S. Granato

February Second

Today's the day when he comes out.
The crowds are standing all about.
"I must say, to look at him,
He is looking rather slim"
A trim little ground hog
In the rain,
Maybe he ran out of grain.
The weather is so dark and sloppy,
I think that it would make good copy.
"No shadow seen about today,
Sky and world all light gray."
The ground hog takes another nap,
The people look for trees to tap,
In four more weeks the buds will swell.
No shadow seen in how you tell.

Mary L. Fogg

Birthday Thoughts

Today's the day we celebrate
The day you came to be
The first step of your journey
That brought you here to me.

From the first breath you took
And the first time you cried
Destiny started leading you
To be here by my side.

This day is one of many
That together we will spend
For we will be together
Until the very end.

And one day we will celebrate
Another start in life
As we start a family
When we are man and wife.

So happy birthday little one
With my endless love
That God sent for us to share
From Heaven up above.

D. Ferguson

Kilimanjaro

A colossus on the roof of Africa.
The ice-crater towering above my African
sky-line.
Kilimanjaro,
The 'white' mountain,
Africa's mightiest highland.
Your crown of ice creates a land
More Alaska than Africa.
Yet the rising of my tropical sun
Drives melted water, clear and crystal
Down the slopes of your soaring summit.

Over your slopes, it is Winter every night
And summer every day.

O! slumbering giant of Africa,
They now say you are worn with age,

Yet I know,
You may still rise above your ashes,
for at your heart,
The crater still breathes.
For now,
My sleeping elephant bids its time!

Lui O. Akwuruoha

Enigma

I rearrange the books and plates
The knick-knacks that I treasure
I always seem to find a place
For things that give me pleasure;
A picture that I love so well
Must have a lot of thought,
It has to have a special place
Or its impact will be naught;
A chair is placed with loving care
With a table close beside it;
And if something old has lost its glow
Deep in a drawer I'll hide it.
But, as I stoop to make some room
For one more "used-to-be"
I ask myself in retrospect...
Where do you hide a memory?

Mary Jo Wiman

Wild Turkey

He came from
The leafy green woods
Dark with early morning shadows
And damp with the mists of a foggy night.
Onto the sunlit road.
  Where he posed and spread
  And preened that great fan
  Of iridescent plumes.
The bright vermilion wattle
Hung trembling from his neck,
A brilliant exclamation point
Against the ruffling rows
Of feathers.
  Then ready for the day
  He strutted off.

N. Edith Barnett

Untitled

Silvered Mine
the mirror-shadowed eyes
belie the smile that echoes
in rasping gasping breath-caught sighs
Panicked asking if it's true
we can/can we will ourselves to die?

Have I let your jeerings
jested/tested love
your apathy, your ignorance
your gender shackles
your defiance
your pretended self-reliance
Slay me daily

Have your words cut Bone?
Do I bait the cycle
cheer on the decay
dance the dance your aberrated way
as you stalk me Hear you mock me
is it true we can will ourselves to die
INSIDE?

Victoria Sebanz

Searching Butterfly

Though butterflies are not forever,
The Monarch's moment is quickly spent.
Awareness of a searching passage,
Laments tragedy on their ascent.

Though butterflies are not forever,
Nature's great appetite must be fed.
The path they leave for those that follow,
Is the shooting star who's gone to bed.

Though butterflies are not forever,
We ignore the signals that they speak.
Their common presence we acknowledge,
Accepting only that they are weak.

Though butterflies are not forever,
Our memories warm in their reflection.
The mystery they spin abounds with love,
Their weakness lies in our perception.

Mary Moline

Untitled

The sun in the water
The moon in the water
They both look the same
But the sun it seems so fierce
And the moon it seems so tame
The land is harbors both
They go round and round
The sun, the man of yelling
The moon, the women of no sound
In the day the land sees everything
But at night its eyes are dim
The man of yelling has quieted
And let the women in

Sara MontBlanc

Friend

To the one I respect
the most.

You're the one who listens,
the one who cares, the one
I need in times of fear.

You support me and
lead me, and give me advice.

You are the one who receives love
and gives it back in return.

Yes. You're the one I
respect, and I'm glad to
call you a Friend.

Virginia Jackson-Flach

A Mother's Love

A Mother
So warm and true
To be there for me,
And for you.

You give us hope,
I have to say;
For without you,
There'd be no day.

There is no other,
Like you, our dear mother,
Your love is rare,
Just like the time we share.

Lynn Ferris-Dunn

Asking For More

Can you hear my prayer tonight? —
The one I have prayed before?
"Lord, help me get through tomorrow,
And I will not ask for anything more."

But every night has a tomorrow
That I must face again;
And I need your strength beside me
As another day is about to begin.

I do not understand your reason
For taking him away.
It was in your very presence
I promised to love, honor, and obey.

The promise was to be forever —
Until death do us part;
But death came much too early
Leaving me with this aching heart.

I know you hear and answer prayers
For, I made it through another day.
So now I am going to ask for more —
"Lord, please take this pain away."

Norma Atherton

Angel Wings

Beneath the wings of angels lies
The peace within my soul,
For angels guide me through my day
And guard me, so I'm told.
I feel that I've been touched by God
As most good people do;
He gives an angel to each of us;
If blessed, you may get two.
But I've got five from up above
To see me through each day,
To love and guide and lead me
So that I'll never stray.
Angel one is Kimberly;
She was my dearest friend.
Rose and Lorita are two and three,
Both mothers and, oh, so grand.
Ernest and Lance, who died so young,
Are the last of my angel crew.
So now you know "I believe in angels."
Some day you may, too!

Kathie Guidry Doucet

Firenze Notte (Florence Night)

Walk
The moon will follow
Under ancient arches
Down cobblestone streets.

Walk
Night will move you
Along the silver Arno
Across the Ponte Vecchio.

These steps are worn
Dante was here
Galileo, too
And Michelangelo. . .

Walk
Through antiquity
With a modern gait:
We are all here.

Luce

True Spirit Of Christmas

Let us remember as Christmas nears
The reason for this special day
A Babe was born beneath the star
He was born to lead the way.

Yes, He was born on Christmas day
The world should all rejoice
This babe born in a manger
By necessity, not by choice.

JESUS was born on Christmas day
And we celebrate His birth
We do the things the Good Book says
And try to prove our worth.

So enjoy the family and the friends
And enjoy the gifts and such
But remember, GOD sacrificed His only Son
He loved each of us this much.

Remember this day is His birthday
Not just for gifts and fun
The greatest gift we ever had
Was JESUS, GOD'S only Son.

Rex H. Marks

The Beaten Path

On this beaten path I walk,
The road has come to a Y.
So to my future I say hello,
To my past I say goodbye.
The only question in my head,
Is which turn do I take
If there's such a thing as fate
I couldn't make a mistake
So I guess I'll simply flip a coin,
Let Mr. Lincoln make my choice
And when I get to the end of the path
I'll look back, and I'll rejoice
'Cause I know I'd have done all I could
To be the best person I could be,
On this beaten path I walk
Where many walk with me

Susen Kraft

Passé

The Sun has lost its luster
The Rose its fragrance
The Stars their brilliance
The Sea its reflection
The Woods their singing
Where has it gone?

It went with you, Sweet Child
The Day your time with us was lost
The Day, the Predator
Disguised as a Man
His hands on your delicate throat
Extinguished your Light for ever.

For us, those who loved you
In our Heart lies a deep wound
We cry out in pain and anger
How could you, so trusting and loving
Have fallen Prey to this Monster?
Justice rendered, Verdict "GUILTY," so
little comfort!

Yvonne Ross

Ghost Town Theater

I sang by Shieffelin Hall and found
the splendor of its concert stage;
the silver echoes still rebound
from singers of another age.

They tell me sound is never lost;
it drifts around a cosmic world,
a caroler in Winter frost...
a bard when Spring's baton is twirled.

Now, doors are locked against the wind,
the dust lays still upon the floor
and yet the singing voices blend
with mine, for I am troubadour.

Vivian Way Bonine

Let Us Feast At The Mesa Of Mount Moriah

In the twinkling of a cock's eye,
the sun begins to shiver with cold
Could there then be warmth and healing
from this once precious gift of gold?

The darkened woods are filled
with startled deer.
They hear the ancient sounds
and the threat of changing gears.
It is no longer the "spy box"
and guns that they fear. . .
Before them and being devoured
is the sly, red fox—
Everywhere there are powdered ashes and
smoldering red hot rocks.

I'm no quiz master, not I;
but, can we not go again to Mount
Moriah
and seek the reason for our fate?
Caring and pity holds the key; moreover,
only here can we circumnavigate
our future finis and keyless prison gate.

Maxine Graham Frank

Death In The Fields

Born to work at the stick of the land,
The sun now drying my flesh.
Dreading long days, even longer nights,
I've lived a life unblessed.

Terror the sight of me to some,
For that is the reason I'm here.
But now the rain has rot my bones,
With death so ever-near.

Please let me relieve my post
In a less gruesome way,
Falling apart at weather's content,
A body of neglect and dismay.

Laughter only comes to me still,
From the crows' old foolish mistake.
All these years they feared me so,
But soon they realize I'm a fake.
Scarecrow!

W. G. Williams

Pastel Shades

Have you ever watched a setting sun?

Just as the last rays of day kiss
the twilight goodbye.

With vivid flashes of color riding
along the evening sky,

and pastel shades interlacing as
if painted by an artist's brush.

Who but God could make such a work
of art?

Showing us a world of canvas full
of the master's touch.

Giving us a private view of

pastel shades at evening dusk

Pamela Sears Mitchell

"Hope"

It was he who built this foundation
The very one I stand upon.
My tears mix with his blood
To form a binding bond.

Sometimes I am in such despair,
And fear dominates my mind.
I lie flat on the ground dear Lord
Clinging to your merciful vine.

Please don't depart from me dear Father,
And leave me struggling so.
No, it's not you who moved
But I in rebellion go.

Ruth Ann Piccola

Is There Something Peculiar About Georgia?

The streets are white;
The walks are white;
The houses are white;
The bricks are white;
The clothes are white;
The cars are white;
The people are white;
The buildings are white;
The flowers are white;
The trees are white;
The beaches are white;
The ice creams are white.

Yes, there is something
Peculiar about Georgia.
More than half
Has not been seen!

Milton F. V. Glock Sr.

Autumn Leaves

Autumn leaves spiral to the sky,
Then fall again, a rhapsody of
color on nature's restless
earth do lie.
Lingering thoughts our minds do
shed,
For summer in its glory past,
Earth's beauty covered,
The bleak and lustful winter
lies ahead.

Melvin Fridh

The Water Falls

From the high hinterland
the water comes
over quartz and feldspar
it splashes, hums,
a tune from glitches gleaned
off glist'ning stone
show'ring list'ning lichen
splotched and bestrewn

Zigzagging further down,
filling fuller,
the lath'ring foam end cliffs
and flows over
down, where the thunder rings
the water falls
through a nebulous mist
the hinter calls

I sit, watching, dreaming,
o'er smooth water
with a lone dragonfly
for a swatter

Mark Stahley

My Walk

I walked down to the sea one day
The waters were calm and still
I offered a prayer to Jesus, my Lord
To keep me, ever, in His will.

Another day I walked to the sea
The waters were rough and wild
He seemed to whisper these words of love
"Come unto me, my child."

So when the days grow long and weary
The tasks of the day burden me
It seems that to find peace for my soul
I must take a walk to the sea.

Margaret Lawhorn

Call The Hero

Call the hero within you.
The wise
the divine in you
call them.
They are an inner side of yourself
prompt to fight for you.

But have no doubt on your call.
There is also the coward, the shy,
the foolish, the sinful,
the opposite side compelled to appear.

Sometimes we are heroes
sometimes cowards.
Bring in the hero within you.

Bring in the bold, the learned,
the good.
Bring in love.
Call the hero, the wise,
the sacred within you.
Summon them in confident belief.
They are prepared to be yourself.

J. Austin Cordova

Nothing Is Impossible

With God nothing's impossible
The word does not exist
Just take your problems to the Lord
He's happy to assist.

When problems do overwhelm you
And start to cloud your days
Know that God is beside you
And He'll show you the way.

Soon you'll see possibilities
You've never seen before
What really made you feel anxious
Won't be there anymore.

This may seem too good to be true
But God is always there
And if you need to talk to Him
He can be reached with prayer.

So never doubt what God can do
Because He cares for you
For when you put your trust in Him
He'll be there to help you.

Melanie Smith

The Ship Not Wrecked

The cold wind blows and the sails billow
The yardarms sway and creak like a heavy rusty barn door
The skipper shouts, "Pull in that jib — it's going to storm — with rain and wind, thunder like sinned, on and on till morn."
They pulled the jib and set the mainsail before it would be torn.
The crew worked hard to follow the bard, every man up high on the yard.
The storm hit soon, blotted out the moon, and the skipper knew he was right,
For the good ship weathered, made port and tethered,
So she could sail again next night.

Moritz E. Pape

"Mirrors Of The Soul"

If eyes are mirrors of the soul
Then what is it I see?
Among that misty morning dew,
What message might there be?

If I were blind, would I not know,
A lie from such sincerity.
Alas! 'Tis I who would still count
On your integrity.

Yet sacrifices must be made,
And hearts once broken cannot break.
Choices made so long ago
Reflect the life we make.

But sweeter love I've never known,
Two hearts, two bodies but one soul.
And at death's doorstep I will smile,
Where I see it was all worthwhile.

So when your life seems very grey,
Don't think that you're alone.
Just look upon the brightest star,
And think of it my home.

Regina Jones

Hour Of Truth

Somewhere in the secret chamber of night
There is an hour when the mind
Sees clearly and accepts no lies,
Even when it desperately wants to.

It's the time when sleep withdraws
The veil from dormant brows, and
Whispers unrest to the soul,
Stirring a cauldron of anxious thoughts.

Heartbeat syncopates itself,
Matching rhythms to the clock;
Eyes plumb the depths of darkness,
Seeking the keys to locked dilemmas.

Doubts and fears surround the bed
Leaning down to steal one's breath,
Plucking nerves taut as piano wire,
Giggling at the twitch it brings.

Truth comes in with indisputable tread,
Stands at the foot and, without a word,
We recognize in the dark what we refuse to see
In the daylight as we're running away.

Kathleen Moore Joiner

Unpardonable

When in my heart
There is no flower,
No birdie's song
Or April shower:
No skies to hide
The darker clouds,
No children's laughter
Sweet and loud.
No hope, no faith,
No love, no friends,
I'm guilty of
UNPARDONABLE sin....

Martine Hovis Huckeba

First Love

Mother Earth is a drunk,
There she turns around and around.
Brother Cloud is a drunk,
So he flies all over the sky.
And I,
Running after you,
Day and night,
Perhaps,
I am a drunk, too
Of your innocent eyes,
Of your virgin breaths.
Yes,
You are my first love...
Now you know,
So?

Thanh Nguyen

Last Dance

Just toss my ashes to the wind
Watch them swirl and dance around,
They may blow all to pieces
Or they may float to the ground.
Just toss my ashes to the wind
Far better place to be,
Than underneath the cold, dark earth
For all eternity.

Maribelle Cooper Ash

Life Is Profound

You have given me a pad
Therein I'm glad
A small abode, where I can sup
Elixir from a cup

You have given me your time
Therein I find
Those inventorial treasures of the heart
Serenity's counterpart

You have given me your heart
A place and part
And in this bond together I have found
Life is profound.

Myrtle Mercer

Our Commander-In-Chief President Bush

They said he could not do it.
They said his plans would fail.
They said the world would view it
With scorn and condemnation
But he refused to change his plans.
He said he knew it could be done
If he could just pursue it.
Due to his determination
The Battle of Desert Storm was won
And the stature of our nation
Was raised on high once more.

Mary M. Coughlin

Reflections

A woven thread, to make secure
This life of trials, we must endure
With our mind, we learn and teach
A perfect world, just out of reach

A kitten lapping up his milk
This Chinese girl, all dressed in silk.
A storm in progress, fallen trees
An agile bird flies in the breeze

An early sunrise, in the east
A pretty sunset, a hearty feast
Of all these scenes, to me it seems
I saw them all, in last night's dreams

J. B. Pendleton

The Ol' Home Place

He got into his pick up truck
this morning;
He hit the road doing fifty-five.
He was headed back to the ol' home place
And was thankful to be alive.
He'd lost his father a few years back,
Now his mother had passed away;
He was on his way home to his
Only sister,
To help put things in order today.
He pulled into the driveway, an auction
Was taking place:
The bidding had already started,
There were memories he was
Trying to erase,
The last bid came in, it was high
And it meant wealth;
But he said, "I'll bid a dollar more,
And buy this ol' home place for myself".

Shirley Salyer

The Path

I dare not guess how far we'll walk
This path we share together,
For no path that we ever take
Will travel on forever.

But walk with me a little way.
Let's talk and get to know,
What goals we share, what paths we seek
And where we'd like to go.

From time to time the road may fork
and then we must decide
If we should go off on our own
Or go on side by side.

For now I choose to walk with you
And hope you'll walk with me.
Choose only that and leave the rest
In the hands of destiny.

Michael J. Lewis

Apple Tree

For many years she stood there
This stately tree I know
Her knurled branches clearly tell
Of winter rains, and snow.

I used to lie beneath and listen
To the tales she had to tell.
Her leaves with soft light glistened
From each bud an apple fell.

They said that she was getting old
And bade me go and cut her down.
I took my axe, firm was my hold,
She whispered, this is hallowed ground.

Would you but take this life from me
I've treasured all these years,
And with a stroke, cut down a tree
That brings to Nature, sorrows tears?

Some other tree I'd have to fell
And leave this one to rest.
To wait for Nature's sounded knell
To call her back onto her breast.

Ted H. Runyon

I Can't Find It!

Try as I might, I can't find it
Though it was here just a minute ago
I only know I must find it
Now where the heck did it go?

I know it was there on the table
Or fell on the floor in the hall
I can't believe I can't find it
It's driving me straight up the wall

Could it be on the shelf in the closet?
But how could it get up in there?
I've looked in the strangest of places
I swear that I've looked everywhere

By now I think it's been stolen
But no one would want it but me
Why, then, oh why can't I find it?
Just where the hell could it be?

Retracing my steps in a panic,
What was it I did that I've missed?
I just know that I'll never..find..it..
What! oh my God, there it is!!!

Kathy Rossell

He's Gone...

"Dave is dead"...
Though words come out,
Full meaning isn't there,
Not yet...

It's so hard to believe
Beyond reluctant doubt,
That he's really gone -
His sun has set...

Memories flood my mind,
Things he said and did;
I'll always have those.
I won't forget...

For now, I must accept;
And release my sorrow,
Setting his long life free,
With regret...

B. B. Watkins

A Ma Chere Amie

You are the sun that lights me on
Through life's dark dismal way,
Your smiles to me are morning's dawn
That speaks a lovely day;
Your eyes, the stars that ever guide
My footsteps out of night,
And lead me to the sunny side
Where everything is bright.

You are my first thought in the morn,
The last that night can reap;

Your image in my heart is worn,
In daytime, and in sleep;
You are the pulse that life doth give,
My everlasting goal,
The joy for which I long to live,
The heaven of my soul.

Joseph Augustine Signaigo

God's Blessings

Fleecy clouds that float on high
Through the beautiful blue sky
Little birds that sing and fly
God made them, do you know why?

Mellow moonlight oh, so still
Verdant trees upon the hill
Rippling water of the rill
All of these He made at will.

Scarlet roses 'round the door
Welcome mat upon the floor
Faithful friends we just adore
These He gave and so much more.

Butterflies with gauzy wings
Sun and rain and all good things
Besides these, His love He brings
So we crown Him, King of Kings.

Marjorie Miller

Journey

Your running sends me on a journey
through the most beautiful parts of
fantasia. I want to sing to you
the Creator of such beautiful music.
It sends me dancing among willows
unknown, all graceful, loving, maternal.

Swiftness brings me to attention,
it cries to me as it settles
into a sleep deceived by flurries
of your wanting
It starts again the dance to which
my song goes.

He must be insane, they all cried
in their own festering looniness.
If only they knew your emotions,
Knew that you felt only like they did.
Would they have immortalized you,
blaming you for benevolence.

Tracy Steele

Times

Times of change, times of life,
Times for moving on.
Times to leave the past behind.
Times for a new song.
Times to let the sunshine in.
Times to feel the rain.
Times to let down all the walls.
Times to loose the pain.
Times to look ahead, not back.
Times to accept the now.
Times not to question with what if.
Times not to ask the how.
Times to spread the wings again.
Times to fly away.
Times to run with pleasures joy.
Times to stop and stay.
Times for laying bare the soul.
Times to open up.
Times to once again be whole.
Times to fill the cup.

Rae Nell Causseaux

The Roads I've Walked

I walked a road
To a point in life,
Called the end....
At that Point,
I turned at a bend
In the Road
Called the beginning....

And still I walked.

I saw on that road nothing old,
All was new and unfamiliar......
Occasionally a faint memory stirred;
A road familiar? Yet all was new...
I stopped in the road and rested a while,
Then all was old.....
I renewed the journey, amidst the familiar.

And still I walked.

The Roads I've walked
In old, and in present, and
Yet the future, all are one.

And still I walked.

Leon Rogers, Sr.

The Challenge

Each new day is a challenge
To improve what has gone before,
To deepen your footprints in history,
Show your love for those you adore.

Too often we waste precious hours
Postponing those things we should do,
While we dream of a wonderful future
Not helping to make it come true.

It's easy to feel in those early years
That many tomorrows remain,
"There's plenty of time to chart my course,
Doesn't sunshine follow the rain?"

Although a very sobering thought,
But, at times along the way,
Perhaps you should pose this question,
What if this is my final day?

Would you be satisfied with your progress?
That at least you had done your best
In meeting the challenge of each new day
And know your conscience can rest???

Marlon M. Rosenberger

It All Begins With I Love You

Love in dreams is what we choose
Within my heart some might come true
So pretty girl hear things I say
That find a way into your soul
I adore our yesterdays
The sky with music won't disappear
Who sings our song should make us long
I see your face within my mind
I want your love that just reminds
That I live you
A kiss remembered is like spring
Resisting dreams won't bring new things
Just wish our nights won't fade away
So longer nights won't go away
Let us light those stars above
That do not know we're so in love
Words I love must never die
That I unwind within my mind
To set a goal within my soul
It all begins with I love you

Pete Barrow

Visitations

He drinks because it is today,
To make it melt and float away,
To soften skin and toughen bone,
To liquefy the falling stone...
Fill the glass for yesterday.

I pressed my nose against
A winter window
When the snow was piled higher than
A six year old boy.

Sometimes I get a glimpse
Of what could be,
A place that I don't live in
Come to visit me.
Sometimes I get a glimpse
Of what could be...

Lawrence Wolf

The Veil

Crust by karats is kissed
To quilt all nature's mystery
maturing still underneath
An unknown wondrous imagery.

Mary Patania

Stir This Heart

You stir my blood,
To run hot, in the evening
You stir my soul
To a warm and tender feeling
In your arms each night
So listen, my love
To my heart, as it's telling you
How much I love thee
Within these old and golden,
Days and nights of ours
Sweet tender lips
As they touch mine
In our long and lingering
Kisses of passion
Tender body next to mine
As you warm my blood
To run hot for thee
Lover be mine tonight
As you stir this heart
To love you forever

Phillip W. Haywood

Courtney

To hear the lovely laughter
To see the smiling eyes
The never ending pursuance
All the canning tries
Tanned toes curled
'Round slightly worn pedals
Brightly colored streamers flow
From faded pink metals
Never to be as tough as the boys
Who ramp the hill
Add her judgment eyes
Thus creates the thrill

Valerie Jeanne Ridgeway Martin

My Gift

If the only way for me
to shower you with gifts
is through the words I write
then even the ones left
unspoken are yours.

If the thoughts I hold inside
my mind
Are the only things I can share
You are who I'll express them to.

If my emotions can bring you
happiness and all the riches
you dream of
some way you'll feel just as
a millionaire might
Because I will forever overflow
your heart with love.

Maybe it's not much
and they can never compare
to the gifts you've given;
right now it's all I have and it's yours.

Karre L. Nieto

Time

Tomorrow became today
To soon become one more yesterday
Time blending on and on
With no hint of stopping
Not slowing nor halting.

Life's balance as we move
With this ever ebbing flow
Sits precarious within our will
Will we hear and follow Jesus
Or will we wait to know only death.

Time does not wait
Death peaks its loathsome head
To catch us alone
Away from the love and protection
Of knowing and following Christ.

Tomorrow became today
To soon become one more yesterday
Time blending on and on
With no hint of stopping
Not slowing nor halting.

Sherlene Berry

"A Woman Clothed With The Sun"

Only She can suffer peace
to sorely stressed Middle East,
and sweep hubris from Son's own bed
that rays may crown His glorious head.

Only She can lighten soil,
and heal the earth of bloody spoils,
then raising hearts on sea of gold
unveil man's eternal soul.

Only She can pen 'new' tale,
or, turn the page on past travail,
so every nation under God
may know Her mercy in His rod.

Marie C. Andrea

One Hour (The Cost Of A Prostitute)

"What's the matter?" She whispers
to the complimentary coffee,
to the stiff pillowcase,
to the lipstick smears on my cheek.

"Nothing," staggers through my teeth;
we kiss like a drag off a cigarette
from the seventh box.

She rocks on my carcass
waiting for manhood to kick in;
there's soap in her sweat,
sweating in the ebb of lust,
the smell of a dirty sponge.

Stockings roll back on
rewind into high heels and a smile.
She pinches a tear onto my cheek,
stained with lipstick;
another carcass on a box spring.

She leaves the sexless freak
staring at the stucco,
more alone than an attic.

Martin A. Cohen

"Mirrors of the Past"

Take me back, take me back,
To the mirrors of the past,
Be it unbearable or be it sweet,
To find my love, my love, at last,
In triumph or in defeat.

Take me to another time,
Of unforgotten memories,
The same that haunt me still,
That have stricken my heart with maladies,
That have made my brain so ill.

Take me to a time before,
Where life was vain and death did fade,
So I may find all the lost,
That my destiny betrayed,
That now dance about like shadow ghosts.

Take me back, take me back,
To the mirrors of the past,
Where the spirits shall be freed,
And my soul no longer overcast,
By the demons that have bound me.

Linda Lee Ervin

We're Back Here Again

We're back here again
To where it hurts the most.
Again you made a scene
And then disappeared like a ghost.

I sat up all night
Wondering where I went wrong.
Can't really argue or fight,
Take my weakness for I'm not that strong.

So we're back here again!
You controlling my senses.
You've made me schizophrenic.
A need for great panic.

I've lost my smile,
My inspiration and motivation.
Too many days I have cried
For my happiness has died.

So we're back here again
To where it hurts the most.
Mental illness you are the fiend
For once let me be the host.

Lisa Baker

That Special Kind Of Friend

Do you have that special kind of friend
that no matter what you do
that no matter where you go
they're always there for you

With reassuring words they raise
your confidence
your mood
your spirit

They have been there through the years
through the joys
through the trials and triumphs
through the heartache

So if you have that special friend
tell them how much you care
tell them thank - you
for always being there

Katie Gospodarek

True Love

Together we walk along in the sand.
together us two hand in hand.
The waves crash upon the shore
they're the color of your blue eyes
I so much adore.
When we hold each other tight
I know everything will be alright.
I will go with you wherever
for true love lasts forever.

Renee Benedict

If I Could Only

If I could only
touch your heart, feel your heart
beat next to mine,
If I could only
fill your love with the happiness
sent from above,
Now this chance has
come to me, and I can
hardly believe that my dream has
become reality.

Kelly Jacobson

My Mother

Her warm, kind, serene blue eyes
Touched by a kiss of sunshine
Her rosy cheeks filled with
Hope, joy, and a love of life
Her full curved up lips
Producing laughter and strength
A few wrinkles imprinted
In just the right places
For each worry or decision
She so carefully made
Her warm, tender, caring hands
Soft as a rose petal
Her arms open wide
Waiting to give
Her abundant love to others
My mother, my friend,
God's gift to the world!

Margie Cohen

My Dearest David

The kindness of your heart
touched me deeply inside.
As I see the warmth and tenderness
that is mirrored in your big eyes,
I know I have to be cautious
with all I do and say,
Because your heart is so fragile,
I fear it to break.
Your inner most emotion
have been so long repressed.
The trust that you have placed in me
leaves me feeling blessed.
I long for times I can hold you
so tightly in my arms.
And shield away all worry
that may cause you any harm
There is a lot of risk
to place your heart into my big hands.
I will try to guard and pamper it
as well as I possibly can.

Karla Hubbert

The Family Of God!

The world revolves around the sun,
True source of all its life;
So, too, the core of peace on earth
Is family love, not strife.

The child's the center of that love
And, like the sun, sheds light
That gives us strength to face each cross
And overcome each plight.

When we children of God become,
Honest, candid, and fair,
We can expect true peace on earth,
Which is today so rare.

The poor and needy we must serve
As our community,
It must be done with grave concern
And sincere charity.

The world is all one family,
Held firmly in God's palm;
We'll find gold at the rainbow's end
If we but live His Psalm.

Mary E. Murray

The Beauty Of Poetry

When regards you wish to send
Try poetry.
Rhyming words do magic lend
Most certainly.
Since your thoughts they can display
And express without delay
Words of comfort while you pray
Through poetry.

Nature's beauty's best portrayed
In poetry.
Words of healing are conveyed
To set you free.
For by it you can address
What your heart wants to express
Thereby, bringing great success
Artistically.

Use it then to bring you peace
As emotions you release.
Serenity, will then increase,
Through poetry.

Mary Marcy Baldys

On Bended Knee

Honestly, God, do you think I'd lie?
Try to hoodwink the whole sky?
Oh, no, God, not me.
If you can't believe the things you see,
Ask any fellow in the block
How much they pay around the dock;
If it'uz only that, I'd not complain,
But my wife's been put to lots of pain,
And if she'uz well, she'ud need new teeth,
and things you can't get off Relief;
I hate to mention it again,
But we've tried hard to keep from sin:
I've worked my fingers to the bone..
This beat-up truck is all we own.
A feller just gets tuckered out,
Especially if he's none too stout,
And I'm not feeling well this time:
Really, can't you spare a dime?

Labelle Gillespie

Division

Fusion

Balance

Confusion

On a daily basis
Trying to provide HARMONY
Actions of LOVE
Reactions of FEAR
Too many hats to wear
On my head
My shoulders can't bear
As a single mother
Missing the laughter
Of the passing years

Sandi L. Cohen

Untitled

All that I touch
Turns to dust
All that I feel
I cannot trust
All that I see
Is deceiving
All that I know
In my heart is leaving
Nothing I do
Can fix my mistake
Everything I say
Is completely fake
I hide behind a wall
So very high
There is hope
No, that's a lie
So down I draw
Myself within
Dying for love
And living for sin

Susan Cesler

The Mating

Traced upon a winter's sky
Two charcoal skeletons of trees
Naked where the land rose high
Thrust heavenward their filigrees
Of branches that were sharply limned
So strangely formed they have not dimmed.

One grew with perfect symmetry
Its form unmarred, its balance whole.
One crippled by proximity
Accepting, bowed. And from its bole
No branch thrust out to override
The other's fullness on that side.

Close as lovers near were they,
Though separate in every part,
Delineate in such a way
The questing mind withstood a start.
For recognizance of their stance
Shone too clear, too true for chance.

Lillian C. Curry

Untitled

You've given me a rainbow;
You've given me some sun;
You've given me love
When I thought there was
None...

Richard A. Kustra

A Perfect Day

The wind rushing

The windows rolled down,

Two loves sharing the quiet
Unbelievable—not a sound.
The countryside dotted with pines galore—
The trees in different shades and hues—
The countryside in its splendor—
So fantastic was this tranquility.
Lonely roads—yet not lonely—
Nature—intimate—whispering—
The magic of the day—
The bigness of the sun
As it slowly sinks at the day's end
And I ask myself—where did it all go?
The day had hardly begun.
But I felt relieved, relaxed, refreshed
And I am ready to go home.
My lover sensed my mood.
Without a word—we were in accord.
So ended a perfect day.

Zadie L. Andre

Spoiled Angel

You were an angel
until you slipped
and broke your wings.
In my eyes you will
never fly again. You
went down in vain
and felt no pain.
You went for nothing
and had nothing to gain.
Now each time you try
to fly the petals from
your wings will fall.
There will be no greatness,
their will be only wasted
sorrow and tears.
The trust is broken
and the anger is felt.
You shattered my dream
and made me see that
angels are only in heaven!!

William Henry Modglin

Knighted Silhouette

Lightening strikes
upon
my window sill.
My eyes are
unfurled.
MY thoughts
drift
to that day
beneath
the warm
wind, and
a delicate
shroud
drapes my
worn perception,
unfolding
a flawless
envelop,
where tattered
edges have no animation.

Laura Wright

The Time Master

And by chance I gazed
upward, and stood
transfixed by the
heavy lidded moon,

Submissive to its
scrutiny, yet desiring
the anonymity of its
ageless searching.

Becircled and silent,
whisps of fog obscured
its vision, yet I
remained basking in
the wake of its
tranquility.

Marlene Corrigan

Shaping Romanticism

In skies of lethargy, an evening's
vase is romantically shaping Buddha's
tattoo through the extending vivid
constellation.

Under them, shaded hills are
arranged over gray intellectual people
reciting original haiku.
Each swallows a blue berry in love
by picture-like green meadows
meditating a higher level of revelation.
Self-consciously they mate, soaking
this black and white starving
Monday, living their sunny Sundays
mimicking harmony.
After emotions have aesthetically
reached divinity, talk aloud, for there
will be nothing here when we're gone
from our community's flowery bouquet.

Scott Buster

"Ghost"

Your name is always on my lips,
waiting to slowly escape me in
the dead of my sleep.

Inside I am dying a slow,
painful death because I know
that no amount of love will
bring you back to me.

Your very essence silently surrounds
me now and tries to smother me.

Everywhere I look I see
something you have touched or
talked about and I cringe inside.

I am a person only in body,
my spirit remains with you always.

You took a part of me that I
will never get back.
My soul is in torment.

Please set me free.
The only time I felt alive
was when you once loved me.

Shonda L. Rigsby

Treasures In The Evening

Treasures in the evening,
Waking up at night;

Passing by a window,
Making everything right.

Peeking through a door,
Find a babe asleep;

Cuddling tight a bear,
Enough to make you weep.

Gliding down the hallway,
Hear a ghoulish sound;

Peek around the corner,
There's nothing to be found.

Walk into the kitchen,
For a bite to eat;

Sitting at the table,
Your husband's who you meet.

Pour a glass of milk,
Drink it with a sigh;

Back we go to bed,
Honey, you and I.

Robin Engberg-Maluvac

Rise With Him

I heard a quiet voice say,
"Walk with ME
I AM the way
Walk with ME
Come, take my hand
Walk with ME
Throughout this land.
Walk with ME
Among the stars
Rise above circumstances
And scars
For with ME
You can go far.
Without ME your works
Are dead
How can they
Be otherwise
Without My Head?

Mary June Foster

That Old Road

We all walk on that same old road
We take our time to see the view
With hills and slopes and rocky ridges
Ten million miles between me and you.
Our love is true and its hold is tight
We try to keep this bond
With all our might.
But the path you take is heading East
Too far to see, to say the least.
My direction is West
God whispers in my ear
"It's for the best."
And in my heart a grin peeps through
I take my time and absorb the view.
Making memories and laughing in the wind
Is all good and well
Because in the end-
Our paths will join and meet
When our journey is through.
Together for always Me and You.

Michelle P. Jamison

Laura's Gold

She gently rocks by the window
Watching the waning sun's glow...
Nodding and smiling as she recalls,
A love they shared so long ago.

A "bonnie lass" she was then,
With laughter that fluted the air,
As he swung her high, swung her low,
And tousled her golden hair.

(And always through the passing years,
laughter silenced all their fears)

They filled their home with treasures,
But they are such fragile things,
They treasured mostly the laughter
Their tender love could bring.

Alone now, she sits there dreaming,
Of the gold in the sunset sky,
And hears the song of laughter
They shared in days gone by.

(Laughter rather than tears it seems,
Is the precious gold of all love's dreams)

Lillian H. Porter

Untitled

Water by the molecule
Water by the drop
Water by the spoonful
Water for the mop
Water by the pail
Water by the stream
Water in the sea for the ships to sail
Water in the bath tub
Water in the sink
Water in the pitcher for a cooling drink
Water in the glacier shining in the sun
Water in the iceberg
Water in the dam
Water in the river for the Salmon run
Water in a song cool and clear
Water in the church to purify the soul
Water in the snow pack for the skier's fun
Water in the leaves that you gather for a
bed
Water in your veins to keep your blood
from clotting
Water in every living thing for without it all
is dead

R. J. Worcester

Leaves Of Autumn

Leaves that dance for Mother Nature,
to the sweet music of the wind,
wearied so, they start to fall.
Resting on the soil below,
a hue of orange, brown, and red,
adorn our splendid earth.
Scattered fiercely by winter's gale,
the leaves will be no more,
until the warmth of the summer sun,
and the sweet tears of cotton clouds,
will trim the trees again.
For Autumn will quickly come,
bringing the sweet music of the wind,
and once again the leaves will dance.

Sharon Reisch Cherry

Fifty Years - The Class Of '44

Fifty years can it really be
We still feel so young and so free,
We want to dance throughout the night
And oh we do feel very bright.

Yes, we are so brilliant and wise
And we have no need to disguise,
We know all about diversity
And there is nothing we can't see.

Our hearing is the best of all
There's nothing that we can't recall,
And how we love to tell the tale
The 'Class of '44' now goes to Yale!

Luetta G. Werner

"Words Spoken"

So caressed and carried away
we took our sleep beyond silence.
For many moments will we wake
together for the first time.
Early morning dew drops falling
to splendor are but the moments
captured in this love.

These words spoken, not from my
breath but from my heart.
Hold my heart in your hands
or hold me not.

For I love you, not for
what you do in your life,
but for what you do to my life.

Steven Richardson

Goodnight

Sitting by the window,
weary as a thousand men.
Puddles forming everywhere,
drip, drop, drip, drip, drop.
Sitting by the window,
sun shines through.
Suddenly shaken and
as wake as can be.
Run outside,
play for hours.
Sitting by the window,
weary more this time.
Stars come out,
moon is full and bright.
Goodnight to the day,
goodnight to the world.
Goodnight,
goodnight,
goodnight.

Stacey Hughesman

Ode To Elston - (The Violin Man)

Through the village up and down
Weary traveler weathered brown
Companioned with a violin
And an ever - secret grin
Charming folks along the way
As they stop to hear him play
Haunting tunes of yesterday
Although somewhat torn and tattered
Never matter, Never matter
Beauty follows where you go
Little tattered maestro

Nieves Redfern

Walking

I said I wanted to take a trip today.
Well, I certainly have.
An inward journey to self-land,
where the core resides.
I am "an unwelcome visitor,"
says my inhospitable host.
But, I shall stay awhile and smoke,
because we need to communicate.

Thomas O'Neill

Lettuce In A Mayonnaise Jar

The sound of a humming string;
what a dainty whim - little ditty.
humming string(s)?
white legs curve down to a point;
half-moons painted
on a tawny sky...line.
whistle to the cowboys, Lazygirl;
maybe they'll come to you-
lazygirl(s)?
did you pull a meaty muscle.
oh-just a little sprain, Babybruise
Umbrella the sidewalk pictures.
they wash... wash
away in the rain-
Hurricane?

Kerry Porter

What Do I See?

When I look in the mirror,
What do I see?
I see a broken-hearted girl
Could that be me?
I see the tears
Roll down my face
My soul I know
I can't replace
There was a day
When I could see
A smile filled with laughter
And a face filled with glee
When I look in the mirror
I know now what I see
I see a broken-hearted girl
Yes, that's me.

Kimberly Coleman

Slow Down

Slow down!
What have you got to lose?
There's so many ways to choose,
Just what you must do,
Relax, have some fun,
With what you enjoy doing,
Stop and think where are you going?

Tell a joke once in awhile,
Learn to laugh and be jovial sometimes,
Don't get so busy
You forget what you set out to accomplish,
Loosen up,
Slow down!
Relax, let's see that smile,
It sure looks good on you once in awhile.

It's a crazy world,
We need a change of pace,
Think how to change it if you could,
Make this world a happier place,
Put a smile upon that face.

Shirley Nielsen

If

I'm sitting here thinking,
what it would have been like,
if she didn't go to that party,
or if she hadn't got her drink spiked.

The last thing I knew,
we were laughing alone,
just her and I,
talking on the phone.

But when we hung up,
something must have happened,
for the next day,
no one was laughing.

Her mother called me,
and said that she was dead,
"It happened last-night,
after the party" she said.

Since that day,
I have just been thinking,
what would have happened,
if she hadn't been drinking.

Rhonda T. Dingman

Time Was

There was a time,
when all the world was gay:
birds were messengers of hope;
angels slept upon the clouds;
stars were ships for dreams;
oceans were emotions rare.

Yes, there was a time,
when I saw the dew sparkle;
Jack Frost was a painter;
the hummingbird was marvelous;
wheat performed a ballet;
the moon was platinum.

There was a time. But,
time has passed, and it's no longer true.
All is shiny, but not so lovely.
Things are soft, but not so tender.
Life is real, but not so happy.
No longer do things appear poetic.

For you are gone. And so,
my dear, is the magic.

Sandra R. Smith

Spices My Life As Perfumes!

Each brick on my patio
snuggles close to another
Just like a wee little child
snuggles close to its Mother.
Foot long Bleeding - Heart stems
flutter in a gentle breeze,
As a child's long golden curls
flutter with a breezy tease.
Many blue Creeping Phlox flowers
are slowly carpeting rocks,
Just like children's belongings
carpet a floor - toys, books, socks!
Working in my rockery
among its plants and their blooms
Is like a young child's laughter -
Spices my Life as Perfumes!

Lucille Brubaker

An Angel's Kiss

My heart was in a lonely place
When an angel came and kissed my face.
I sensed the brush of wings so light;
I felt a warm and new delight.

The angel whispered in my ear
And wiped away the ling' ring tear
Of sadness that coursed down my cheek
That seemed to mirror visions bleak.

This angel's whisp'rings gave me hope
To not despair and not to mope
With sorrow mean and downcast heart
That channels joy to be apart

From God's great universe of love
And cuts the ties to Grace above.
"Lift up your heart," the angel said,
"Fear not to strive and forge ahead.

"Seize now the opportunity
To live and shape your destiny.
Renew your inner Sacred Vow;
All of heaven's with you now!"

Laurel Mae Matthews

Miss You

We didn't have a chance to say goodbye,
When angels came on silent wings
To carry you up to the sky,
Much had been left undone
And many things not been told
But memories linger on and on
Most precious far than gold
Of you as a happy, carefree Lass
Ever steadfast, ever true
You stormed the barriers of my heart
And captured all my love for you
Now love has lost its charm
Friends silent are long gone
There is no laughter and no song
Someday I will scale the well of mystery
That lies between your world and mine
Keep a place for me by your side

Rose Harkins

Sweethearts In Heaven

I know the day will come
When hand in hand they'll meet.
The pain will be worse for some
But in his hand hers will greet.

They've known each other a long time
Sweethearts since first grade.
Some of the years weren't kind
Some I'm sure they'd trade.

Someday I know he'll reach
For her hand he'll ask again.
She'll stretch to meet that reach
And time will turn again.

Sweethearts for so long
One not without the other.
One of them now gone;
One looking for the other.

Sweethearts on earth we see
A girl beside her raven.
I know they'll someday be
Sweethearts in heaven!!!

Shirley Stewart Roberts

Chimes

It happens maybe once a year
When I relax with wind bells near,
And hear the close harmonic notes,
And watch a cloud dance as it floats,
Without a forethought in my mind,
Or thoughts that stalk me from behind,
I only hear the chimed relief
However brief, however brief.

Mark J. Haefele

"Did You"

"Did you ever wish for happiness
When it seemed so far away
That when you received it
Life was bright as day?"

"Did you ever want something
And want it oh; so bad!
You waited long for it,
Then got it, and was glad!"

"Did you ever feel downhearted,
Sad, and some what blue
When suddenly life was good
When some one cared for you!"

"Did you ever go out shopping
Of course all by yourself
And when you tried to buy a thing
Your purse was on the shelf?
"What odd things will happen
To all us human folks
It really is surprising
Life plays such funny jokes!

Minnie E. Cates

Remember

Those sad and lonely days
When life was almost lost,
I was your bridge...
You gave me strength
Entwined as one - yet separate.
Tread softly through the caverns
of my mind,
Lest you become entangled
in a web of dreams
Embrace each moments pleasure
For together, we will see the
seasons change
Dawn of the rising sun
Another day begun

Sonia Moodie

Soul of an Era

Wind swept mention of an era gone by
When men were men and women reveled
in as much

Alas the past, though not so long ago
We loved them with passion and resolve

Gale force emotion romantics abound
Professing mended spirits

Perhaps there is time this Century still
To recapture the era of the conscience.

LoLetia C. Williams

When Once

When once I fell in love with you
When once you said you cared
When once I knew you were the one
When once your dreams we shared

When once you held me close to you
When once our love declared
When once we lived here as one
Then once my soul I bared

But now I know my heart has died
now I know it's true
When once the emptiness in me
was filled with thoughts of you

When once I was a frightened child
So scared and all alone
When once I felt I needed you
Now I stand alone

Now I know I'm not to blame
Now I know I'm free
and all the emptiness I felt
I've filled with dreams for me

Robin Wilcox

Someday Our Souls Shall Soar

The time is soon to come
When one of us must part
And leave naught but love
To soothe an aching heart.

Should I go first, my dear
What would you miss of me?
My hand held fast in yours
Sweet names spoken softly
Sounds of joyful laughter
Cherished in memory.

Should it be you, my dear
What would I ever do
Without your silent strength
Each day to see me through
To crave your tender touch
While waiting to join you.

So 'til our souls shall soar
Let us embrace each day
With true and heartfelt care
To see us on our way.

Maureen Murr Kidwell

An Autumn Night

Midnight autumn sky so clear
When sun is gone and stars appear,
The land is quiet and serene
Where only darkness can be seen.
Wind whispers in the autumn night
When the owl comes out to take flight;
He flies to the east and then the west
Looking for a silent place to rest.
Leaves falling from the dying trees
As birds fly south toward the seas;
Time flies by in the night
As noises flow from nowhere in sight.
The sun breaks in towards the park
As the light fights against the dark.

Robert S. Bowker

Twinkling Of The Blades

I remember ——gray November
When the brooks were filled with rain
And there came a cold December
So the frost returned again
Here the brook down in the meadow
Turned at night to silver white
And we skated in the shadows
Of a moon so round and bright
Down the ice we went a - flying
Coat tails flapping in the breeze
And the winter was a - whistling
Through the stillness of the trees
All our cheeks were red like roses
On that night so long ago
And Jack Frost nipped at our noses
As we scattered to and fro
But our hearts they were a - singing
Through the frozen meadow glades
And we set the night a - ringing
To the twinkling of the blades.

Phebe Anne Boyle

Questions

What did you do today
When trouble came your way?
Did you crumble when things got rough,
Or are you made of sterner stuff?

Did the opinion of others sting and chafe,
Or was it accepted with manly grace?
Being criticized when you were wrong,
Did you hold a grudge for very long?

In defeat, did you throw in the towel,
Or finish the fight never crying foul?
When judged, did you knuckle-down,
Or grin and bear it with nary a sound?

Did you wallow in the dregs of self-pity,
Or learn to deal with the nitty-gritty?
Did what you discover have real meaning,
Or fade with the twilight's last gleaming?

Did you master your lessons well,
So when next you hear the bell,
Believing that you are right,
Will you stand up and fight?

Merle R. Zeschke

Unforgettable

The time will fly,
  when we say, "Goodbye!"
To all our friends,
  and their memorable trends.
Once by once,
  each day is done.
For we will be there,
  with some time to spare.
Trying to hold on,
  while looking toward a new dawn.
Together we stand,
  to give each other a hand.
Everything starts to flow,
  but not in slo-mo'.
It's going a bit fast,
  and the parties will be a blast.
The time will fly,
  and we'll say, "Goodbye!"

Thomas R. Chi

There Was A Time

There was a time
When we walked
Together in the sun.

There was a time -
When we talked;
There was a glad tomorrow.

Now I wait
For I know not what -
A dark abyss before me.

I gave my gift-
A gentle heart
That ever will adore thee.

Once, "Someday" had
The ring of hope
And then my heart was glad.

I've come now
To the end of me;
My heart is sealed and sad.

Michael A. Riolo

Paradise

Paradise is any place,
where happiness reigns supreme,
a place of sweet perfection,
of which we often dream.

Some call it Heaven,
where angels spread their wings,
and every heart in chorus,
lifts it's voice to sing.

Like no other place on earth,
Paradise is provident,
supplying every human need,
and that is evident.

The eye is filled with wonder,
wherever it may look,
absorbing the beauty everywhere,
which time has not forsook.

There is love in Paradise,
which none would dare amend,
perhaps someday we find it,
at the rainbows end.

Luke N. Baxter

Rolling Stream

Where do you go.
Where is your destiny
Where do you flow
From where was yesterday's flight
And what is tomorrow's plight
your rippling waves dance
in the sun
you move and roll and your
Restless way

Laughing for fun (dance)
As you laugh and dance and
play
To flow in your uncertain way
You know in your heart
that you know - not the way
But still
you go on and on and on.

William

Silent World

We live in a silent world,
Where nobody
Really speaks to anyone openly.
We're all trapped!
Trapped to solve our own problems
And deal with our own disappointments.
It feels like everyone's alone
And everyone keeps to themselves.
Only the people who love each other
Actually share feelings.
Somehow, someway,
We have to find something
That will break all silentness
And bring us back to the way
We should be
Out of the Silent World!

Melissa Lord

If Only For Awhile

In the depths of each
Where "Self" is quite well hidden
Within reach
Often forbidden

The foundation laid
The fortress stands
The price paid
Guards given commands

So cold and cruel
Lacking in trust
A constant duel
Survival a must

There must be a time
When all can cease
Feeling sublime
Truly at peace

This time can be
If only for awhile
Between you and me
Sharing a smile

Lynne Montz

Bridge

Life is a bridge
Which arches
From now
To next.

That arch
Becomes a rainbow
If you'll just
Flow the colors!

Ralph E. Grimes

Future

Wantonly burning a path
through the thick underbrush.
Careless of trapped animals
crying out in pain.

One cage shutting quietly
greedily tempting man.
Separating humanity from
its empty soul.

Lost in a raging hell
fighting for life.
A shimmering rainbow
the only sign of hope.

Kathleen A. Muja

"Innocence Of Youth"

Crying and laughing simultaneously,
While a myriad of tears
Rush down my cheek.
The anxiety of my fears
Turns my joys into weep.

I remember vividly
The innocence of youth.
Living wild and free...
A lifestyle purely uncouth.
Unfortunately though,
Like every child born,
My tarnished soul
Has been made to conform
To live in accordance
With society's norms;
Turning a soul,
Once-filled with life's simplicities,
Into a begotten one
Corrupted by the world's complexities.

Rick Pino

Observation

Quietly I sit and watch,
While children are playing about.
Their innocence so refreshing,
Awakens a life of self doubt.

Children sense each day as new,
Uncluttered by yesterdays,
Eagerly testing all they see,
Regardless of their taught ways.

At what age will they refuse
To preserve this inner being,
Holding on to experience,
Comparing the days with reason?

Will they reminisce as I,
Of the wondrous days anew,
Lost amid surface enigmas,
Disjointed, beyond any view?

Children see the universe,
For them it is full of treasure,
I see satiated faces,
Knowledge has stolen my pleasure.

Margaret Tardiff

Friends

It's really nice to have friends
who care
Through good times and bad times
they will always be there
So long as you're honest and never
lie
They will always be there to stand
by your side

So I thank my friends who have
hung around
They will be the ones who put me
in the ground
I'll always think back at the times
we had
But only the good and rarely the bad

Mark Silva

The Kiss Of The Deer At Font De Gaume

The magnificent Cro-Magnon
Who carved a kiss of deer upon
The fissured walls of a dark cave,
Strove not to see it, nor to save
Its tenderness for us to see.
But to release his agony

That magnificent Cro-Magnon,
Who hunted early, struggled on
His rocked stone scaffold in the bleak
Recesses of his cave - to speak
With hammers, till the darkness thrilled,
The beauty of the thing he killed.

Mary Matosiah Morabito

Maxwell

Stonyhills baby horse,
who just completed the course;

Boy he's swell,
Sensitive as well;

A character who's adorable as you
can well tell.

Kelly Brings

Modern Observations

Does it matter
Who we are
When we're alone

Pain
deep within
a moment's notice

I can enjoy
the depression
after a long sigh

Soliloquy
to the living and dead
one hugh breath

Freshly baked
cutting into the crust
on the wood board
oh what pretense

Martin Cohen

The Graduates

Black-robed they rise up
shake out their wings
flock and scatter
unwounded.
No lawn KEEP-OFF them.
Fortuitously armored
with invisible shotgun repellent,
they come and go
wink on and off at will.
They light on any twig they choose
and eat up all the berries.

O fortunate they
who have their statements signed
on everlasting parchment
by The President.

Mary Hutton

W Questions

Why do some flowers smell so sweet?
Why do some make me sneeze?
Why when the air moves gently
Is it called a breeze?

Where does time go when it passes?
Where goes the tide at sea?
Where is the end of the rainbow?
Please tell the answers to me?

What way is up when I'm upside down?
What songs do the robins sing?
What will make me a happy child?
What is a pleasant thing?

When will I be a grown-up?
When does the night turn to day?
When is a smile an adequate gift?
When do words mean what they say?

Who's in charge of everything?
Who will succeed if all try?
Who turns on the stars at night?
Who are you and who am I?

Martha W. Brock

Long Distance Call

Calling a distant tomorrow
Will any human be there?
I'm in and of a time
When your chances we may spare
We are waking to the limits
That our tiny world can stand
Though it is no certainty
We won't foul it with our own hand
So that's why I'm calling an age
When I don't know if you will be
For I want you there to read this
As it matters much to me.

Richard M. Kane

Dance In Genesis

Watercolor whispers dancing
With a passive tone
Penetrating gliding
Trust brings closer
To the flame of subtle words

Simple themes covet simple textures
This gesture
Is our embrace
The gate to silence
I come in
She follows
I know
We know...

Lucas Polowczyk

Like A Butterfly

Like the butterfly, we find
We can no longer stay behind
Self-made walls of
Protection.

We struggle to be free,
Breaking the bonds of the self we see,
To soar in a new
Dimension.

Nancy Ferraro

Forever Young

I wish that we could live forever
With all our hopes and all our dreams
Life should go on for eternity

Even though one day we'll die
Our time will come
Our hearts will stop
We'll never be forever young

Through all our joys
And all our sorrows
We'll live through it all
Until one day
We're no longer
Forever young

Lisa Brown

Hope In The Kuwaiti Desert

Out in the sand and stifling sun
With bayonet and long line gun
Stands a soldier, desert clad,
Away from home, and feeling sad.

His buddy in the same attire
Cocks his gun as if to fire
At an enemy yet unseen
By the searching eyes, still keen.

Before they lift a gun once more,
May peace come knocking at their door;
Thus bringing joy to friend and foe.
From there to here the soldiers go.

Lord, bring my loved ones back to me
In good health and good mind
And grant us knowledge thus to see
Each person on earth as great as we.

Vincenne A. Waxwood

Auctioneer's Cry

This is America
With freedom aplenty
What do I hear for
The price of the chance
To destroy yourself freely
Wheat is the substance
On the shelf seedy
Going, going
Coming
To here
One dollar
Does no good
Baseball
Competition our cheer
Shores at either end
'Tween is the blood to defend
Of nations thrown
Into media wide as
Rivers, mountains, plantations.
Sold.

Mary Verrill

Sometimes

Sometimes
when the rain falls
I can hear
all the voices of friendship
huddled together
having a good time.

Mary E. Phillips

The Anniversary Gift

You are the Golden Oak Clock
with its warm gentle chime
resounding to those who are near
a glorious life and time

You are the pendulum shining
with its slow steady sway
giving comfort and wisdom
to all who pass your way

You are the face that can teach
with a smile or a frown
straight hands maintain a forward reach
whether pointed up or pointed down

You are the Golden Oak Clock
standing solid in its encasement
fulfilling a special need
always there in its placement

You are the twelve numbers gathered
to celebrate a family complete
blessed for sixty-five years
your love chimes gracious and sweet.

Marty H. Wells

On Immortality

Like a shy princess
With jewels in her hair,
My maple tree has golden leaves
Just anywhere.

The fields are tan and orange
Now the harvest's done.
The cat-tails are all fluffing out
Underneath the sun.

Whatever we remember,
Whatever we forget,
We've seen the end of summer.
Perhaps we should regret.

There is a new life before us,
A new life, a new light -
How shall we maintain our ways
In the new world of white?

Marie I. McHenry

The Will Of God.......

Alone since you have gone,
With life to rearrange,
How strange that life goes on,
As tho' there's been no change;
Why did I feel that this
Could never happen here,
That life would be all bliss,
You were so very dear;
Why wasn't I prepared
So I could brave the pain,
And why have I been spared
To tread life's path again;
Forgive my damning the day
When you and I had met,
I'm hurt, God's will was this way;
Still I have no regret;
Alone now, grateful for the past
Where our hearts were one;
Life we know cannot ever last;
Here: God's will was done......

Sarina Sue Stans

A Retrospective City

The capital city beckons
With such an eye catching appeal.
For what city offers so much
To the mind's imagination.
A lengthy, cool, reflecting pool
Stands between two great monuments.
One marvels at the construction
Of the artisans' renderings.
Seekers search for clues of the men,
Who helped set up democracy
In America years ago.
Tourists find other attractions
By Pennsylvania Avenue.
The Presidents' grand columned house
Welcomes visitors far and near.
The splendid historical rooms
Capture visitors' staring eyes.
The furnishings of bygone years
Help the sightseer envision
Dwelling places of yesteryears.

Pat Cruzan

Moving Wind

Chimes are playing their tune in time
with the whistling wind.

Clouds race across the sun, as it becomes
bright, then suddenly dim.

Dew sparkling on each blade of grass.
Somber then light, the darkness is past.

Long needles of the pines, shimmering
in the light. The swaying branches
lifting, then dipping from their height.

In a sudden gust, the wind is cool upon
my face, then warm again as the Sun
demands its place.

Nylah Weldin

People Who Care

I sit at night
With things on my mind
trying to understand
Why people are so kind.

They do things for me
I've never asked them to do
and they always make me smile
When something has made me blue.

It doesn't matter where I am
or even where I go
They have shown me I have a friend
to walk beside down the long hard road.

Shannon Gostiaux

Alone

Where is she
who holds
my future?

In darkness dreams
all there is
is nothingness.

There are no tomorrows
I wish to live
lonely.

Sean M. Taylor

Dandelion

A garden is no garden
without ME!
I glow like the SUN
My fluff when blown
IS A LOT OF FUN!

Some call me useless
undesired pest.
Spoiling coveted carpet
of green grass, YET!

Nature's unique gift
is ME. . .unloved
I GROW, I GLOW
There is no end to ME!

WHY DO THEY CALL ME
A WEED?

Philomena Christie

Too Late

We all have loving
words and messages to say.
We can quickly forget them,
say these words today.
There is a wealth of
love in our hearts
that is rarely even spent.
The loving words not spoken,
the letter never sent,
For these things, someone
will always wait,
Let's tell them that we
care for them, before
it is too late.

Lili Dracopoulos

Random Thoughts

we
worship icons having clay feet
fight battles solving nothing
use terms demeaning others
discard people growing older
neglect families seeking shelter
ignore babies going hungry
slay others citing Jesus
condone children killing children
heed voices spewing hatred
yet
we are not so different
than those who passed before
but
we must curb the frailties
bringing bleakness to our lives
and
emphasize our commonness
lest we become extinct

Kay Gary

"Together"

Your eyes shine bright,
You blind my sight.
When I look in your eyes,
I see the sun begin to rise.
I don't know what to say,
Except I long for our next day.
I love you in so many ways,
Just don't be afraid,
For when I said forever,
I meant we would be together.

Tammy Garland

If

If everyone in the world
would take the time to say
A kind word to someone new
each and every day.

If everyone in the world
would take the time to do
Something special for someone
or to try something new.

If everyone in the world
would take the time to hear
A bird chirp, a child sing
or a voice filled with fear.

If everyone in the world
would take the time to understand
That sometimes a smile is all it takes
or to just reach out a helping hand.

If everyone in the world
would take the time to see
That compassion and courtesy
may be all that we need.

Nicole K. Titus

A Brother And A Friend

God called him home several
years ago
And now his soul is free.
Left with memories I hold dear,
His smiling face I see.

Like a brother through
the years
Though short a life he gave,
Every one he seemed to know
And a road of love he paved.

Never selfish
He gave his all
Nor a stranger did he meet,
His life he lived and conquered best
Not meeting with defeat.

Now I praise our Lord
On high,
For his life will never end
God choose him as a special one,
My brother Ron, my friend.

Melva Blakley

Stormy Weather

You could see the clouds
You could feel the cold
It seemed so loud on this rocky road
You could see the lightning
You can feel the rain
It seems so frightening
There's so much pain
The wind is blowing
Gloom makes it dark
True colors are showing
You can hear a dog bark
The rain turns to drizzle
The clouds break apart
The sadness starts to fizzle
What comes together is your heart
You see a little sunshine
You start to feel fine
What has been lost? A couple of feathers
But you survived
The stormy weather

Sef Garcia

"Heaps To The Stars"

Acceptance by merit.
Yielding to the spirit,
Of the artist within.
Creation begins;
Birthing, personified heaps
Humanity's notable leaps
Beauty of diversity shines.
Tapping into the sublime.
As a tightroper, walking the line.
Assisted by guides and judges.
Withstanding a few envious grudges.
Audiences; receive, as waves upon a coast.
Recognition, allows yet another to boast.
Competitions create wins:
Palms go to chins,
Elbows rest on thighs,
While entertaining thoughts of pie in the sky.
Leaving history to date;
A new awareness or Fate.
"Artist" revolutionary star.

Lydia R. (Bowers) Watson

Tribute To Mr Hellar

Everybody has their troubles
You are not the only one
They have been around forever
Since the rising of the sun;

Why this must be is a mystery
But it is so obviously so
We must have faith and do our best
To make all our troubles go.

If we don't give in and we don't sin
Just to show Him our defiance
God will show us we were right
To place in Him all our reliance.

Everybody has their troubles
Said the kindly man who saw me there
Depressed and sad, tears in my eyes
He helped me find faith in my despair.

Winifred Byers

The Tide

I'm not certain when
you entered me
though now, I cannot be
without you.

for it's you
who stirs the leaves
against the oak
and light upon water.

I stand silently
on the bank beside you,
notice everything,
the smallest leaf

spiraling onto sand;
the tiniest hair
curling at
the nape of your neck.

I need no stars
or galaxies this time;
only your current
whirling through me.

Kathleen Bevacqua

Birth of Righteousness

On this magical day of birth
You fell to this mystical earth
changing things around you
Life has awakened
It will astound you!
The sun kisses the moon
And the moon in turn smiles upon the land
While the stars reach out a hand
to welcome in
THE KING OF MAN!
Morning Glory sings his-story
Angels dancing in a glen of laurel
Under a flaming sky
darkness is swept aside
There is no need to cry
whispers the watchful eye
Arise and Behold
The dawning of a new way!

Karin Ruf

Nowhere To Go

Through all the years and all the tears
You have been there for me.
I loved you and looked up to you.
Without you, where would I be?

Everything I ever wanted,
I have found in you.
You showed me things I've never seen
You made my dreams come true.

I wish you hadn't left me
With nowhere to go
I'll never be able to forget you
And now my tears do flow.

My tears made up an ocean
You're gone; I'm left behind
I search all over looking
For something I'll never find.

Toni Marie Marotta

Tonight I Lost My Innocence...

As I cried aloud a sigh
You hear this from the shadows
As dreams begin to die

A man can drown his sorrows
But can never turn his back
While he worries 'bout tomorrows
His soul begins to crack

Yeah, tonight I lost my innocence...
Like the silky whisper
Of a sweat-soaked sheet

Or the ill-fated boy
Towards the beckoning street
It's the tainted virtue
Of the drunken virgin
It's the suicide-blues
As you put the words in
Tonight I lost my innocence...
I Awake!

Rick Grijalva

Forever

When I ask you for forever
You say you'll never go.
But deep inside your heart and soul,
Do you really know?
When I say "forever"
You should know it's true.
With every breath I give or take,
My heart belongs to you.
I give you everything I have
And you know how I feel.
You should never have to ask,
"Is this love for real?"
I love you more each passing day
And I want you to know,
That when I say "forever,"
I mean I won't let you go.

Lori Jean Strader

December

Sagittarius, tall and lean,
You turn your face to the sun,
With your soul still touched by Orion,
Hanging low in the winter sky.
But the warm sea rises beneath you,
And the tide runs fair and free.
Fellow Sagittarian,
.......Wait for me!

Shirley Dykman

Street Kid

It wasn't that wall
you wanted to write upon, was it?
It wasn't even the words.
The wall was the venture
a stand that you took.

The wall itself;
just another uncaring person,
not listening.
The paint; your way to express
words you have never told anyone.

Unspoken feelings do that, you know,
they long to be expressed
acted upon, comforted, acknowledged.
The wall is like a few uncaring people
cold, aloof, non-expressive.

It wasn't the wall, then, was it?
Just a question,
How do I speak the emotions I feel?
Who will listen and not deem me strange?
Street kid, find a friend bearing no wall.

Rebecca Ginn

An Apology

We're grown now.
You with your children and
long, thick hair.

I wronged you badly
with my indifference!
A past we could not share.

I give you this
with all my love,
I'll wrap it gently.

Theresa Sheridan

"Treat Me"

Treat me like silver,
  you'll be my gold.
As for our love,
  it will never get old.

Treat me like fuel,
  you'll be my fire.
Through each day,
  our love will get higher.

Treat me like dusk,
  you'll be my dawn.
Our love for each other,
  will be so strong.

Treat me like day,
  you'll be my night.
For heavens sake,
  let's never fight.

Kenneth S. Geller

Untitled

Oh mother, dad, why can't you tell
Your babe, your child, your growing youth
The ever feared, deep hidden truth.
The truth and knowledge build on years.
Years of pain and dissolution.
Yet they arrive at their own conclusions
Their worlds so fresh, so free of doubt;
But soon they see what you have known.
Yet to your age they must have grown.
They try in vain to tell their child
Who listens not at all
Just as you once shunned the truth,
Once when you were in your youth.

Susan Shields

Love

  Sweeter than wine are
your lips that I kiss.
  Food for the soul, with
each hug and squeeze.
  I live for tomorrow
just to see your sweet face.
  It's really so simple,
this love with its grace.
  I really can't help it,
this love goes so deep.
  It touches my soul
and invades my sleep
  This love that I have,
just can't be all wrong.
  It's clean and it's true
and so very strong.

Martha Hale Carlile

Colors Of Life

Our lives are like paintings,
With colors of many hues
Of vibrant reds and purples
Violets, pinks and blues.

We live our lives in color
Be it bright or more subdued.
We find them oh so varied
With soft pastels endued!

The vivid ones reflect our joys,
Drabber shades, our sorrows.
The softer shades speak peace
And hope for all of our tomorrows!

Mary G. Burlingame

Rose Gathering

I saw a rose today,
And so I thought of you.
Who could have guessed that
The rarest of roses
Would be cut down so soon?

As you embraced the sun and rain,
You unfolded before us.
You scented our world
With joy and hope
Of brighter tomorrows.

But God longed to bring you closer,
My rose. So you were
Plucked away from us—
Budded on earth
To bloom in heaven.

Diana Picknell

Friendship Pact

You and I should make a pact
  - a solemn promise
    - a vow, to bring salvation back
      - friendship that,
          like love, will last forever.

Remember. . .
  Wherever you are
    - whenever you need me
      - just call my name
  - I'll be there
    - anytime.

You and our friendship
  mean just that much to me.
- That's a promise you can depend upon,
  My Friend.

Debbie Peterman Swick

Untitled

My spirit breathes free
and floats with the clouds.
The trees bend with my presence
and the leaves softly rustle.

The rays of sunlight
give warmth to my soul
And the birds of happiness
tread softly on my wings.

As summer turns to autumn
and winter yields to spring,
I will always be alive
for my spirit breathes free.

Heather D. Wilcox

Trust

I love you but I don't trust you
And love without trust can't work
If I give you my trust again
Would you give me your love back
If we could just talk
I'm sure we could work things out
It could be so easy
You are the only one I want to love
But if you don't love me
I'll have to forget my love
And remember my distrust

Bridget Kruger

The Drug War

Clever, deceiving and destructive, invade bodies, minds
hopes, dreams and homes.

Convincing is the way-man it's the way, it's where it's
at, it's what's happening.

Man don't be no fool, don't be in the dark, don't be ignorant.
Man come into the light. Come on, take a bite of
the coke, heroin, the weed, crack and the ice. Pop a pill
man, your eyes will come open, wide open; you can see the light.
The real world, it's the way.
No more cloudy visions, no more shadows or clouds, thinking
will be cleaner.
Peace within yourself, no more wars, wars of any kind.
Man, make up your mind stop your hesitating, come on and
take your bite. Once you take your bite, your wars and
troubles will be over. Bite man bite.

Mary Coffey-Watkins

How Much Do I Love You, Darling?

How much do I love you, darling?
How can I answer this?
Can we measure the sweetness and passion
Of a lover's kiss?

Can we measure the dewy beauty
Of a fragrant summer rose,
Or the raindrops in the ocean-
And the depths of its repose?

Can we capture the song of the nightingale,
Or the moonbeam's silver light?
Can we capture the mystic wonder
Of a cloudless, windswept night?

Can we measure the length of laughter,
Or the sorrow when we part?
Can we define the anguish
Of another's broken heart?

How much do I love you, darling?
The volume, I must confess,
Cannot be found in earth or heaven-
My love is ... measureless.

Valeria Jane Thomas

The Right One

The passion you feel for the new love you meet
How can you know it will last?

How can you know that this is the one
With whom you should share your life.

The answer my friend is not what you feel
The answer is who you are!

Are you the one who always will give
Your love to the person you love?

Are you the one who will forgive
When words are said that were not meant to be said?

When sadness and hunger give you and your loved one pain
Are you the one who gives hope and faith?

When you know that your love is strong
So strong that you never want to be with anyone else.

Then my friend you can be sure,
You are the right one...

S. Ingemar C. Olsson

The Search

Where to begin this long trying search?
How can I find what I have yearned to find?
I've looked near and far, everywhere I know.
Though the trails are many, they become dead ends.
What seemed to be a street of shiny gold,
turned once again to damp, cold cobblestone.
Warm summer breezes filled with scent of lilac
become iced winter winds and storms of ice.
A finely written symphony, soothing and sweet
turns bitter and sour, clunking and out of tune.
I find myself, feet on clouds above the ground
only to topple back to earth, scuffing my pride.
My search has taken me to the highest peaks
but has deserted me in the lowest crevices.
What is this wondrous treasure I've searched for
so long?
It is merely happiness.

Penny M. Green

How Can I Tell

How can I tell when the snow has gone and the spring has come
How can I tell when the day has come and still the dark is here
How can I tell when it's cold outside and the sun shines so bright
How can I tell
When will the birds sing their song and let me know that spring is
here
When will the soil in the ground show the sign of flowers growing
through
When will I be able to say that spring is here
How can I tell
Now that the spring has come and the day is light, I know not how to
take it
Now that the flowers has grown within the soil, I have no time to pick
them
Now that the sun shines and it's warm outside, I have no time to enjoy it
Still, how can I tell

Shirley Shuler

"Not A Minus But A Plus"

The world right now is in such distress
How can we solve things and change this mess
It will take all of us together to work for peace
To get back our schools, jobs and see that
crime will cease.

We must help our children who are the future
generation
Turn back again to a once great Nation
Be proud that together we belong here and the
world is "US"
To start over and meld together is the only
way a "PLUS"

Lorraine F. Buchanan

Yellow Rose

I have fallen and it is deep and dark.
I am in a pit because of life's fall.
I feel the depressing blue that encircles the top of the pit.
I grasp and reach high to the circle of blue sky above.
I can smell a yellow rose bush growing in the green grass.
It flutters in the warm breeze of the sun up above.
Buzzing bees pollinate the rose making it prosper.
I am filled with the hope of salvation from this fall.
Remembrance of the fragrant rose will help me out of the deep dark.
Life's change will help me climb into the brightness,
smell the fragrance,
hear the song.

Phyllis Southwell

All Is Destiny

The little tree asked the big tree
"How come I'm small and you're so tall?"
The big tree replied
"Because you're young and haven't grown yet your all."
The rose asked the butterfly
"Why it had wings and it did not,"
The butterfly said
"Cause I could not be happy in a pot."
The bird asked the wind
"How come you can be felt but not seen?"
The wind replied
"Because that's just me."
The sky asked the clouds
"Why am I blue and you white?"
The clouds said
"Because light is day and dark is night."
One heart asked another heart
"Why did you choose to so love me?"
And the other heart replied
"Because all is destiny."

Tina Bennett

Mysteries

How does the sunflower know to face the sun?
How does the grass know just which way to run
To find the water it must have to grow?
These are things we surely would like to know.

We see the birds have learned to flap their wings
And fly through the air. We hear them sing
And thus they recognize their own
And find the nesting place which is their home.

We know the air we breath is made of many things,
And various elements which cause the odors it brings,
But exactly how our nose knows what it smells
Is something that my old nose never tells!

Just so, Lou Ellen, when my eyes light on you
There is another mystery that is ever new.
The world lights up! It does it every time!
Sweetheart, will you be my valentine?

Richard G. Harvey, "The Napkin Poet"

Shadowed Lands

When the day is black
How much darker is the night

When the sand is wet and cold
And the sun hides behind its mask of clouds
How the shore seems deserted and forgotten.

Walking on the beach in winter
My life is encapsulated and summarized succinctly
By a lonely summer resort
Deprived of its pleasure, there is no happiness.

I put my soul into a cardboard sign
Hanging from the dusty window of an empty bar

"Closed for the season" (Going Nowhere Gone to Nothingland)

I can turn a shoulder and walk away from sadness

I know that summer follows winter
Night turns to day, the cold gray ocean
Is a home for brightly colored life
And even God has bad days.

But my mind whispers in shadows still

Whole huge worlds of wasted words
Who will listen to my song? Who will sing along?

Kerrie Holton Tainter

The Margin

Look, my love, and see with me
How the row of trees along our road
Yields its glory to the ground
And goes uncrowned into Winter

Granted I have grown old
Though I recall the Fall of our first meeting
The paired passion and sweet grief
Of our two hearts rising up and out to give all
Was fleeting
It could not stay
(Yes, but it was everything)

Agreed, but now you see there is our falling away
Our retreat to single pulses and the interrupted
Play of late day board games
(I seem to recall your calling out my name)

Each year I find time leaves me standing on this narrow tract
This place of rising forward and falling back
Looking for what is always unfound
Enduring griefs, lost beats and pulses
(Yes, though finding leaf and ground)

Steven S. Richmond

Wonders Of The Sea

Did you ever wonder, about the mysteries of the sea,
How tireless or endless it might be?
Have you ever sailed from here to there,
And felt you weren't getting anywhere?

Have you ever watched the dolphins and whales
As they graceful swim past all of the sails?
Seems like the sea is far off, as a star
And yet as close as your neighbors are.

There is something foreboding about the sea
Yet when I get near, its magic hits me.
I love the breeze, coming softly across the waves,
Tis like an early morning coffee, after a man shaves.

You may watch a ship, as it sails by,
Until it sails out of sight of the eye,
Or watch them sail in past barrier and rock,
Till at last they come to rest at the dock.

The sea is large and it is grand,
And it encompasses all the land.
So if you ever go down to the sea,
Look out across the water and be proud as you can be.

Robert D. Barber

I Love You Mom

Speaking with my Mom on the phone.
I can tell she feels somewhat alone
The pouring out of her gentle forgiving heart.
Of something she can't seem to dart-
The choices that seem to bother her in our past
And for her, my true devotion will always last
I get choked up, with not much to say
She is a breath of sunshine on a rainy day.
She has been such an inspiration for my days
Always so supportive of my many ways
Without her my life has no meaning
Always there when the world starts beating
She apologizes for the ways it came to be
Wishing she could have provided the best for me
She has always given everything she had
Yet today she feels a little sad
As I write this poem and feel
My love for my mother is so real
She is always the passion in my heart
For my life, she is the biggest part.

Randy Plummer

Special One

There are no words to describe
How you make me feel inside
You are very special to me
You left a lasting impression on my memory.

In everyone's life people come and go
But the special ones are few
And my special one is you
These fond memories will last forever

But you can call it a wish or call it a fantasy
I can tell you this; it is plain to see
If our timing had been better
I could have loved you forever

You made me feel alive; when you held me
Your touch was so warm and caring.
It's a feeling I'll never forget
Or be able to describe.

But from the start, any fool could see
You had an invisible hold on my heart.
We were kindred spirits; you will always be
Very special to me...

Owen Oakes

Silence

Life dwindles on in a daze of insanity.
Humanity has lot its touch, while the children sleep.
Dreams linger in minds of creativity while the pain of emptiness lingers in mine. My soul is void of decision as I sit numbly staring into oblivion. An infinity of problems stretch throughout my meaningless life. Passions lie heavily in my heart, as I scream to the heavens in confusion and vulnerability. Reality has lost is grip on my mind. Only insanity can heal my pain and bring my soul peace. The moon has stolen my tears and given them to the stars.
Society marks me as an outsider, believing that my thought and touch are poisoned. They shiver in revulsion at the sight of me, and scuttle into the sunlight to escape my dark gaze. An outsider I am marked; and in solitude I shall perish.

Nichole Lynne Alons

Temptation

Into a trance I have fallen
hypnotized in a moment he stole
not breathing, not moving; hesitation
trying to shatter his supernatural control

Feeling the hurt, the need, I close my eyes
turning slightly in the direction of you
seeing reality but still wanting the dream
a dream, one with no chance of coming true

Anger quickly makes its presence
trying to convince me to stand and be free
but my honor, my word, my promise
are the shackles that keep binding me

I feel you though we've never touched
tasting you though we've never kissed
alone to drown in my own river of shame
yearning desperately for a chance I have missed

Release my soul I beg of him
For I'm not strong enough to master his hold
The hunger, the irony, the impulsion
Desperate to shatter his supernatural control

Rebecca L. Gulley

Someone Stole My Childhood

Someone stole my childhood, and no one is aware.
I am rushed and pushed from here to there, and no one seems to care.

No time to lie upon the lawn, and watch the clouds go by.
No time to dig deep in the dirt, and wonder where and why.

I must conform, and join the team, and fit into the mold.
Don't wish don't dream, just do as you are told.

Grown up cares, and woes are forced for me to bear.
It's too soon. I am not ready. I am not yet aware.

As time goes by you'll notice, life's comfort eludes me.
The reasons deeply hidden, and difficult to see.

Just look around for the blame to share.
Someone stole my childhood, and left me nothing there.

Victoria A. McGhee

Kindness

What is real good!
I asked in a musing mood,
Order said the law court;
Knowledge said the school;
Ruth said the wise man;
Pleasure said the fool;
Love said a maiden;
Beauty said the page;
Freedom said the dreamer;
Home said the soul;
Fame said the soldier;
Equity said the seer;
Spake my heart is not here,
The answer is not here.
Then within my bosom softy this I heard;
Each heart holds the secret, kindness is the word.

Marion Honson

Legend (A Book Discloses)

I am a sensual beast.
I can feel your warmth through the sheet of your skin.
I savor the tang of your lifeblood on my lips.
The seductive rhythm as you breathe life into me.
The raging of your heartbeat as you believe in me.
I am in the shadows that surround your light.
I would have your eyes slice me open,
your mind unearth my force.
I could shred your heart,
  rape your soul,
    but no.
I will caress you with my breath,
kiss you with my company,
guard your illusions,
and collect your every tear.
I will make you mine.

Vicki E. Bryant

"Earth"

What happened to the flowers
I don't see any anywhere,
Did the earth suck them all up
Or did they wither and die away.

Is the earth going to suck me up like it did the flowers
Or is the earth going to suck up the evil,
Is the earth going to keep all purity
Or is it going to keep impurity.

I wish I knew all the answers
For what evil is going to come to me or my family,
For we need the earth
And the earth and everything on it needs us.

Katina Rice

Beyond The Rape

There is the sound of sweeping:
I can hear the broom,
Notice the a cappella weeping:
I can hear the doom,
Cry and rattle,
Of a wound being born.
Mine is redemption's battle;
A white wing that's been torn.

Was it wind sheer or pilot error?
Here are my tears, the fledgling steps from terror.

Inside the lung of free will and destiny,
I have felt shame.
So invasive, it almost killed me,
I have crossed my name
Off the innocent's moan and sweep,
Toward the freedom of a white wing's repair.
Beyond where I (shattered) groan and weep,
One more time I fly into the night air.

Vicki Schrieber

New Games

I can wait; and there is no intolerance in waiting
I can trust
I can dream; and toil to make the dream come true
I can start anew

I can confront; and do whatever I choose to do
I can communicate
I can walk and there is no pain in moving
I can win

I can play many games; more and more the ones I choose
I can lose
I can be quiet and serene; or shout at the devil and the stars

I can bring order
I can grant rightness to others; without forfeiting my own

I can let chaos be
I can laugh with the crowd; or alone
I can create

There is no scarcity
Now I understand

There is no death
I LIVE

Katie Botha

The Cliff Called Life

Without your wisdom everyday, Lord,
I cannot live

I cannot draw a breath
unless you say I may.

I need your love,
your presence all the time
around me,
lest I fall from this high cliff called life.

It is a perilous place,
but, breathtaking in its beauty.

The birds fly round its face.
Flowers cling to its rocky crags,
most beauteous though largely unseen.

I reach to the skies and let the winds flow round me
knowing you will hold me fast upon its heights...
and I will feel the joy I could not know alone-
without you,
and your love.

Mary Sacauskis

Water Melons

When I was young and in my teens, no farmer's life for me.
I didn't want to work that hard, it brought no revelry.
Along would come a holiday with all the special eats.
And after dinner we'd save room for all the special treats.

Most times it was a melon, iced cold in our spring house.
My mom had bought it at the store, she was the ideal spouse.
No matter how they plugged them it was really hard to find,
A totally sweet melon, clear down to the rind.

While riding through the country with my pals one sunny day,
We came upon a farmer with a wagon load of hay.
We asked if he grew melons. He said no but his neighbor did.
He said, they're out there by the road and his house was kind of hid.

We thanked him for his help and then proceeded down the lane.
We came upon the melon patch, our thoughts were all the same.
We stopped the car, hoped out and grabbed the biggest one of all,
And took it to our club house and devoured it, one and all.

The chance we took was worth it, not just for saving money.
We could have bought one any place but this one reeked of honey.
I've bought many watermelons, large, medium and small.
But that stolen watermelon was the sweetest of them all.

Lambert T. Jones

"Fond Memories Of 'Uncle' Roman"

You're gone, I'll never understand why.
I don't know how to let go, I refuse to say good-bye.
You meant so much to me, and you always knew what to say.
I need you here now and you're so far away.
You understood me and always heard me out
But you also let me learn for myself what
life is all about.
Life...what a strange word. It was here for you and
too soon it's gone. But my fond memories of you
will forever carry on.
Although hearing your voice and laugh will be missed,
in the back of my mind, they will always exist.
Our interest in poetry will always be shared. This is
for you - you know how much I cared.

Vicki Lynn Wright

The Drive

Gripping to the wheel with whitened knuckles
I drive without a thought of time or space,
Drifting now my mind moves into high gear
to a mystical, yet spiritual place.

The rush of traffic fades into the background,
Intruding horns simply disappear,
I breathe in a feeling of contentment,
as tear drops softly wash away fears.

My fingers loosen hold of raging anger
The wheels and engine hum in harmony,
The beating of my heart picks up the rhythm
And my spirit directs the symphony.

The sprinkling of a few stars call for nighttime,
and I shift back home with appreciation
for I've been given a feeling of vitality
from the drive that had no destination.

Lenora M. Bell

Today

Today, I awakened and looked at my sleeping husband.
I felt contentment and love.
Today, A friend dropped by for breakfast, unexpectedly.
Her presence pleased me.
Today, My friend took me to see baby birds in their nest.
I looked with wonderment.
Today, I watched the humming birds as they
fought for the sweets in the feeder on the deck.
I watched and smiled.
Today, I looked from my window and saw the
mountains through the haze.
I felt at peace.
Today, I tried to count the shades of green
in the trees as spring arrives.
It was impossible.
Today, I am appreciating all of the beauty
and love with which God surrounds me daily -
And wish I could share it.

Marjorie Steeves

Homeless

How could it start
I guess some families just fall apart,

Not being able to call a place home
Having no one to care if you let out a groan,

Having no clothes to wear
Maybe some rags but the rest would be
bare,

Who would care if it's your birthday or not
Having not one send a thought,

What would you do all day
Sit and wonder if it was April or May,

Just one person out of the mob
Would know you needed a job,

Being with out a bed
laying on concrete from toe to head,

You would not understand the pain of being
homeless
Unless it happened to you-oh would you be
a mess,

Kristin Martino

Lost

I woke up this morning to a beautiful day ahead of me.
I had this urge to thrust myself into the unknown,
But I felt trapped as if I was in a large invisible cage.

As I fought to open the door, I found myself losing the battle.
I stood looking beyond. I longed to venture out,
To see new sights that I had waited so long to see.

As the bright sunlight beamed down on me,
This day beckoned and tugged at me with tremendous force
As it wrapped itself around me encasing me in rapture and awe.

I tried to step forward, but something was holding me back.
Was my fantasy world holding me or can reality make itself real?
I was caught again in desperation.

I began to float. Everything grew hazy.
I found myself looking down at what I thought was reality.
I am truly puzzled. I felt so weightless, so calm.

I awake to find myself in my room again wrapped in loneliness,
In isolation, in utter chaos, in a mass upheaval.
This is insane. This is a beautiful day.

Louise Waltrip

Confused

I do not know if I am coming or going,
I have been sitting down on this buoying.
I am confused about everything
and I do not know what this year will bring.
I look around and I see people running,
I guess the devil is really coming.

I guess I am messed up and confused
because I do not know the road I have used
to get this place on my mind,
where I will find myself in no time.
This place may be real paradise
or just something I have to rise.

I do not know what all this means,
but I am confused about all my sins.
I do not know if I am coming or going,
but I am still sitting down on this big buoying.
Maybe the plane ride is over for me,
but, I know, I just want to be free.

Nestor L. Perez

Emotions Within

I have eyes with which to see, your broken heart filled with misery. I have ears with which to hear, all that is said from one so dear. I have arms that will reach out to hold, pull you close and keep you near as we grow old. I have hands for you to grasp, as we walk beside one another, while our love lasts. I also have a heart that's filled with love and I would gladly give it to you as long as it's wanted. 'Cuz saying "I Love You," never sounded funny in my ears; loving you took away all my fears. I still feel you warm and tender embrace; I still see the wonderful smile upon your face. Those are some of the things I'll never forget; my life with you; well, there are no regrets. You always my dreams seem real; just some of the ways you made me feel. I know that saying I'm sorry can't take away the pain, and those words can't shelter you from the rain. They can't mend your broken heart; for too many angry words tore us apart. Though some words were said, not all were spoken; a lot of promises were made, quite a few were broken. I know that we both said we'd change, but from neither one of us were any made. Those changes came after we parted; still some time and ways to mend a broken heart. I'll always remember the wonderful moments we shared; because until you no one else cared. My love for you is still strong; please believe that, even though some time has passed. I still need you, admire you, adore you, and you are still my hearts desire; the flame of love no longer just burns, it has turned into a raging fire. The feel of your touch slightly on my skin; still stirs sleeping Emotions Within.

Norma Knapp

Inner Thoughts And Discussion

Fifteen years have passed and still I stand alone.
I have friends, but they only count for a small portion of my
emotion.
Without a companion to share my experiences,
Still, I sit in my bedroom with nothing to do but cry,
Because I realize that these four walls
that I've hidden behind have been the only
'companion' to see me through my trials and tribulations.
Alone. All alone.
My mind wanders over all the sorrow I've been through,
Alone,
Have I spent my life in a world of fantasy and seclusion?
Have I imagined my happiness?
I ask only these questions.
But only I hold the answers,
Alone within my vast mind.

Rebecca Douglas

The Vigil

Have you seen her there?
I have seen her many times.

She rocks and she waits...

Heart full of sadness...pregnant with memory,
She feeds upon dreams of the past.
Curtains rise and fall upon scenes of long ago.
Weddings and dances, children and birth,
Plantings and harvest, and dinners for all,
Joyous full life, needed and loved,
Now all gone, gone, gone.

She rocks and she waits...
Pathetically eager to talk to someone,
In quavering voice...for someone to call.
She waves as we pass, she smiles and nods,
And watches after us with stilled and bated breath,
Lest she hasten our departure.

Night falls; with short and tottering steps, she enters her house.
Mortally wounded, she lies on her bed.
Bewildered...afraid and alone,
With eyes open wide, she stares...into the past, as she waits.

Mima White-Harrison

My Sonnet To Nature's Harmonies

No raucous city noises dulled my ears.
I heard the sounds of nature - wind and rain
And crashing thunder that inspired fears.
The sweeter songs of birds I hear again:
the red-wing black bird singing "okalee"
That Beethoven used in his symphony;
The myriad songs the mocker trills with glee;
The songs of warblers joined in harmony.
There is a calming of my restless mind
By nightly murmurings of birds at dusk
And robins loud "good night" called from their nests.
As fading twilight stills the sleepy birds
And brings release from tensions of the day
My soul finds peace in Nature's harmonies.

Mildred Walters

Lean On Me

While sitting quietly in meditation the other day,
I heard the voice of my Lord Jesus pleadingly say,
When you have problems, the solution you can't see,
Come to Me in prayer, turn to Me, you can lean on Me.

When life becomes too hard for you to be able to cope,
Come to Me in prayer, I will give you unending hope.
If your heart is broken, do not despair, for I am here.
I will mend your broken heart, with threads of cheer.

If you have a loved one, and they are tired and ill,
Bring them to Me in prayer, I can always make them well.
When the world is pressing in on you in a financial way,
Call on Me in prayer, I promise you I will save the day.

Whatever your needs, I know about them even before you do.
So if you ask Me in prayer, believing, I will give them to you.
Just trust Me to do it My way...it may not be the way you choose,
But believe Me, if you love Me, and lean on Me, you can't lose.

I said it to my Father, as I died on the cross that day for you,
I pleaded, "Father, forgive them, they know not what they do."
Through my death and resurrection, from sin you are now free.
Love Me, trust Me, give me your problems, you can lean on Me.

Winifred A. Cartwright

I Knew True Love

I knew a love so good and true.
I knew a love that came from you.
I knew true love.

You came to me so filled with love.
The love that came from God above.
True love I knew.

Then one day you came and said,
"This love I had for you is dead."
That love I knew.

My heart was burdened with a heavy load.
Sorrow and torture in my soul did abode.
Without the love I knew.

Then one day I recaptured the light.
I met someone I knew was right.
Beneath the umbrella, encased with tender care
I again knew love was there.
This love that came from God above.
I knew and know true love.

Martha Thompson

Today

Ever since the day I first laid eyes on you
I knew you were the one to make my dreams come true
We've been together now for quite some time
I must admit you've made my life quite divine
The way you drag me to every football game
Making sure I know each player's position and name
The way you let me drive when you want to take a nap
Or when there's not enough room let me sit on your lap
When you fall asleep ten minutes into a movie
Then wake up at the end and smile at me
When you give me a hug for no reason at all
The day you showed me how to use a goose call
The look in your eyes with the birth of a calf
All the ways you make me smile and laugh
The love I see when I look at your face
The warmth I feel from your embrace
All these and more have filled a hole in my life
Which is why today we become husband and wife
To share with each other the things we have done
To live the rest of our life together as one

Stacy Malsam

I Know—You Know

I know that you know what I know.
I know that you know that I know
  what you know.
I know that you know that I love.
I know that you know that I know that you love.

I know that you know
  my hope is trembling.
I know that you know that I know
  that your hope is trembling.
I know that you know that my heart is broken.

I know that you know that I know
  that your heart is broken.
I know that you know my courage is gone.
I know that you know that I know
  that your courage is gone.
I know that you know that my love is dying.

I know that you know that I know
  that your love is dying.
I know that you know what I know.
I know that you know that I know what you know.

Paul Pascal

Nothing But Life

I lie here with nothing...nothing but life.
I may be alive...but I'm dead outside.
I can't feel Mommy or Daddy next to me.
But somehow...
Someway...
I know they are there,
Giving me the strength and hope
I can't give myself.
"Mommy... please forgive me?"
"Daddy... please don't hate me?"
I don't want this life I'm living!
I'll never feel the coldness of ice,
or the warmth of his eyes.
I'll never taste the sweetness of honey,
or see the color of money.
All I can do ...
All I'll ever do ...
is lie here forever: feeling nothing but life.

J. Knowles

The Pretty Girl

As I was walking down the street.
I met a girl, she looked so sweet.
Her eyes were blue, her hair was red
The sun made a halo around her head
Her belt was white. Her dress was green.
She was the prettiest girl I had ever seen.
Her feet were small. Her stride was free.
Her every movement appealed to me
With figure fine and head held high,
She looked the world right in the eye.
I'd give my soul, if I could meet
The girl I saw coming down the street.
I'd like to hold her in my arms, and tell
Her of her many charms, and kiss the lips
That are so fair, while fingering ringlets in
Her hair.
I'd give my soul, if I could meet,
The girl I saw, coming down the street.

Samuel Preston Fields

Autumn

I sat beneath the old maple tree,
I fancied to see a bright yellow leaf.
I noticed the leaves were changing quickly,
I thought by winter it should look quite sickly.
I wandered around seeing all sorts of colors,
Not one looked like any of the others.
Someday winter shall fall upon us,
Nobody will bother to make a fuss.
Withering away, falling to the ground,
The leaves shall die without sound.
And so after that I shall leave,
I will no longer sit beneath the old maple tree.

Kelly Gilby

My Plea To Daddy

Daddy, let me grow up and be my own person.
I can make my own decisions and stand up for myself.
I can be more of a person than you could ever know.

I want to tell you my opinions, not just falsely agree with yours.
I want to make my ideas and dreams reality, not just tell you.
I want to live and be my own person, not hide behind your shadow.
I want to experience my own mistakes, not just hear about yours.

I am not going to be a whole new person, Daddy.
I will still be your little girl, I just won't need your help when I fall.
Daddy, please step behind me, arms wide open so you can let me go
But especially so I will know that I can always come back home.

Maria Jeanne Kachel

Rose Garden

While sitting in the backyard,
I noticed that the roses are blooming.
Watching the roses in bloom
reminded me of you and the first time we met.
You gave me a yellow rosebud during the introductions.
As it bloomed with time,
our friendship bloomed with it.
When it died,
our friendship did not, but merely moved up to another level
with a pink rosebud from you.
Over time that rosebud bloomed
as well as our relationship
flowering into a beautiful red rose,
which will never die
for it is still blooming
deep within our hearts.

Kim Hashberger

Sometimes

Sometimes, in the chilly radiance,
I pause to reflect what the landscape would be like
if you had not retired into its shadows.
How this moment would internally mimic the morning's glow
rather than be the mirror by which the past's failure
is once again revealed.

Sometimes, stationed in the warmth,
I halt to think what a dissimilar man
I could be.
Full of confidence and verve, I could recall
without recoil and re-live without
cloaking reality.

Sometimes, looking into the darkness,
I ponder those splendidly surreal moments
with you in my days.
Wondering what it would be like to battle
furiously for the future rather than
think ponderously of your flight.

T. D. Spiker

To Cindy

When I hear talk of the end of time
I pray it can't be so.
My angel's eyes deserve much more
than famine, waste, and woe.
A daughter's trust, a daughter's love;
Can it be too late?
Her hopes, her dreams, her wants, her needs;
Can't we defy our fate?
Another chance; the gods must wait
Give us more time, they must!
She needs clean air and a safe milieu;
I'll not betray her trust.
It's not for me I plead a stay;
I've had my fun and more.
It's for her I bend my knee;
The daughter I adore.
I cannot wait for days to come,
As time throws on each year;
And if my will is all it takes,
Her time will come, no fear.

Lee Patten

Thirty-Nine

Your gentle touch and the way you hold me,
I pray, reflect all the words you've never told me.
Sometimes, it's hard to stop the tears as each day ends,
When I think we can't be more than "special friends."

I'm sorry, last night, for running away;
I pray I can see you later this Christmas Day
(If only to say "I love you"),
But in saying that, I'm so afraid I'll push you away.
[Neil Young is playing from the room next door,
Which only makes me think of you that much more.]

I can't blame you, can I? For not
feeling the same way I do;
But twice you said "Luv You," plus
Your kisses, and roses too.

I'm so confused—I don't know how to act
or what to say.
I can only take second by second, day by day.

I long to hear you say
"I love you" this Christmas Day.

Lynn Effinger

Real Love

I am sorry if I offended you
  I really didn't mean to.
Please let me explain
  So I can take away the pain
  And keep us both from going insane.
You had me put on hold
  I know it's your way of trying to scold.
There is nothing I can do but pout
  But it's the end results that count.
Real love never dies
  It just has its lows and highs.
Time can go on and on and I'll still pine
  And never give up this dream of mine
  To be with you till the end of time.
I know you have it in your heart to forgive
  So we both can go on and live.
I love you with all my heart
  I always have, right from the start.

Ralph Schmitz

The Man In The Street

Yelling to me, "Don't fall down boy."
I listened with disturbed emotion.
He seeks money - while offering
words of wisdom through his scotch flavored breath.
I stood wondering how could this happen?

Through his eyes and motion, I recognized his pain,
a pain that I have felt once before,
and one that will torment him for some time,
although he is too intoxicated to realize that.

Escape, I think, pulling a dollar from my wallet,
I pray for this man in the street, a new beginning.
A hope that this pain covered eyes will soon
look upon himself, instead of the bottle
which entraps every fear that confronts him.

The thankful words again come loudly, "Don't fall down boy,
and if you do - get up - don't look back, and move forward."
I wish him luck, and turn to leave;
stopping in my footsteps, I ask myself,
would this man in the street have done the same for me?

Matthew A. Celso

Arrival

Shaking off the shackles of this earth,
I rise above the mist of sorrow and confusion.
Slain are the cruel task-masters of agony, hate and
deceit.
The rod of strife no longer bears my name.
My heart soars as sunshine breaks new horizons;
Like dazzling jewels, rainbows sprinkle the sky.
Mirth and merriment are a joyous strain.
And angels proclaim a wondrous Name.
Of this new land, I stand in awe;
Bounteous love doth here abide.
A land where ne'er a tear shall fall,
And sad songs shall ne'er refrain.
Peace, be still!
Before my Maker I stand,
And in His bosom is my rest.

Marilyn B. Cooley

Untitled

With excitement pulsating through my veins
I rush to your greeting arms
with our pleasure we fall to the ground
side by side
holding each other
You kiss me so softly that my heart must
beat louder for me to hear I am really alive
holding you
kissing you
enjoying the pleasure of being your love
the sun smiles warmly
the grass laughs and plays around us
and the trees around us whisper.....
that is love.

Sarah Stallings

If Like In Dreams

If like in dreams, I could erase forever
hurtful words I've said to others (to you)
knowingly or not,
Not minding the one's hurled at me.
We go in life spewing out so many
senseless things. Open sepulchres' throats.
We create chaos by letting loose of the
poison asps under our lips.
Once it comes out or let it dominate our souls,
we're doomed.
Looking back to other times,
it seemed so important then, not any more
and now it haunts you to no end;
can't shake it loose.
If I could heal those wounds,
If I only could, I would.

Luis Pomales

Untitled

I have only one sheet of paper so I'm writing this poem as I go.
I really don't want to make a mistake but a mistake I will make
I know
Since this is my one sheet of paper I am doing the best that I can,
to give to you the most of me with every flip of my hand.
I'm somewhat afraid of this paper since this is my only one.
I do not know what will come next and there's so much
I want to get done.
Since this is my only paper, I want to show it to you.
I want to share a great big smile and let my loving shine through.
This is my one sheet of paper and what is written is said.
I keep it deep within my heart and accept it in my head.
Because this is my one sheet of paper.

Kevin Cruz

The Face Of God

I saw the Face of God in a white, puffy cloud drifting overhead.
I saw His face again, in the multi-colored flower bed.
I saw The Face Of God in the innocence of a child,
In cool mountain streams, and in a herd of elk, free and wild.

I've seen The Face of God in the people of this great nation.
And once, they were very proud to be called His creation.
But they must remember that The Face Of God cannot be found
In every piece of junk that's just lying around.

What people need, if I may be so bold,
Is to find The Face of God again, and attach it to their soul.
He isn't so hard to find, you know,
Just say, 'Good Morning, Lord!' and wait for His 'Hello.'

I've seen The Face Of God in my friend's eyes,
It's that indelible quality that only God supplies.
And I want to see His face in you-
In everything you say, and everything you do.

If you think The Face of God is just a thespian's mask,
Then you need to look a little deeper, that's all I ask.
You'll find The Face Of God right there in your own heart,
Waiting to shine forth, if you'll just give it a good start.

Ruby Hopper

Quatrains From A Message From Martin

I have a dream, and I am The Dream,
I see brotherhood as a thoughtful stream
Of each of us knowing who we are,
By our thoughts and kindness, a shining star,
That acts from awareness and thoughtful meaning,
So have I this thought, and am I, this dreaming.

That all men dark or light, are free,
We're truly brothers don't you see,
That's what I stood for when I was here,
Knowing that, I had no fear.

Calm your passions, rule with your mind,
Leave your unruly self behind,
Help one another with reasoned thought,
Bring us to one Nation, as an example wrought.

I am The Dream, I am with you still,
Make of this message what you will,
But I did not lead, and before you preach,
But that I had first made thoughtful speech.
Thus, hold your passion, still your mind,
In silence think, for all mankind.

Wynn Earl Westover

"Mirror Image"

As I look into my mirror,
I see youth that has begun to fade.
As I look into my mirror,
My hair is lighter, a more golden shade.

As I look into my mirror,
I see lines that come with age.
As I look into my mirror,
knowing I have turned onto a different page.

As I look into my mirror,
I see life in a more mature point of view.
As I look into my mirror,
where there is me, there is you.

As I look into my mirror,
there is a face I am not ready to see.
As I look into my mirror,
I see my mother, starting back at me.

Lee Wood

Pieces

As I look into the crowded grandstand
I spotted a girl wearing glasses that are your brand
The beating of my heart is the only sound
My body calls for a breath, none can be found
My eyes catch sight of a girl with your hair
She laughs at me because of the way I stare
I always look for your make of car
I thoroughly inspect the license plate from afar
The scent of your perfume is in the air
I panic and look, you are not there
To hear your name sends chills up my spine
Again I panic, I tell myself I will be fine
Why do they continuously play our favorite song
To torture me with past thoughts is so...wrong
I see two lovers walking holding each other's hand
Memories of us makes tears flow as if by command
Your friends always tell me about your new date
I tell myself to be happy for you, but I curse his fate
Pieces of memories, thoughts and sounds of you drive me insane
But in my heart these pieces of you are all that remain

D. R. Teuscher

My Best Friend

As I lie here an my bed at night,
I stare into the darkness with not a soul in sight,

I lie here thinking about the years,
remembering all the laughs and all the tears.

You have always had an open ear,
to listen to me about any fear.

You gave me a shoulder to cry on,
when I realized, my first true love was gone.

We have had our little fights,
but we always turn our wrongs to rights.

This is our fourth year together,
and I hope this friendship lasts forever.

Through triumph and dismay,
our friendship is still okay.

Here's to the next four,
and all the surprises,
to walk through the door!

dedicated to Leah K. Haluzak

Misty Dawn Collins

You Left Me

Why did you leave me? I hate you! I thought you were my friend,
I thought friends are forever and forever never ends.
Why didn't you share your feelings? You kept them locked inside,
I thought we said they were one thing that friends should never hide.
I have so many questions that I will never know,
Our friendship has ended but I still can't let go. Sure you felt lost
But now I'm lost too, why didn't you talk to me? We could have gotten
through. I thought you were my friend but friends don't betray,
I'm sorry that I blame you for the things that I can't say.
I'll admit one thing you deserve a lot of credit,
You put the gun to your head and I hope you regret it.
I hope you regret everything you put everyone through,
When I first found out, God how I hated you.
I hated you for leaving everyone behind
I hated you for making your family find
Your dead limp body lying on the ground
Having your family pleading for you to make a sound.
Still you just laid there dead as can be, no life left in you
for anyone to see. It doesn't matter now nothing will again,
For yesterday is gone and tomorrow is a sin.

Rachel Leonard

His Promise Fulfilled

Many days I walked through life and never had a care.
I thought I had no need of God and never bowed in prayer.
Then the doctor told me that soon my life would end —
I thought back on my empty life and knew how much I'd sinned.

With contrite heart I knelt right there as tears poured down my face.
"Dear Lord" I cried, "please hear me now - I need to find Your grace.
Lord, please forgive me for all the wrong I've done.
Is it too late for me to know the Father and His Son?"

Then a light brighter than a million suns
Touched my heart and soul and I knew now came God's Son.
"My child," He said, "arise from here - go stand by Heaven's gate.
Because you asked this moment past, you did not come too late."

"For here am I as promised, back to end the world.
Those who've never called My name through Hell fires soon will swirl,
Yet now you're in the number who will meet me in the sky —
There to live forevermore in Gloryland on high."

Rolande Hayner

Unfinished Lives

Thinking back to what happened tonight
I try to think of what went wrong.
Trying to talk to you doesn't seem to help
And it's been so long.

Remember when it was all right,
But that's when we were all carefree.
We used to swing from the tire
That hung so proudly from your tree.

Now that we're growing older,
We are growing apart.
This is true and I don't mean to hurt you
But it's coming straight from the heart.

Since this has happened
Tears keep flowing.
Just like the wind
Never stops blowing.

I've tried to help
And make everything all right.
But it's obvious that
You just don't see the blind light.

Tracy Nason

My Brother, My Enemy

When you first saw me very long ago my presence to you was absurd. I was supposedly another unique creature of the wild, isn't that what you heard? Biologically, my very being is that of you and religiously, as any other. Though for centuries you denied this to be true, are you still so persistent, my brother? In serfdom I silently mocked you without the teachings of your skilled hand. How rampant this silent mocking grew and how vast the yearning for land. Today, the mocking is a shallow mirror of you, with some teachings forced by another, and you can see how well the mocking I do, as you hear the sad story of my brother. Through trial, appanages were granted me as my blood soiled the given land. You laughed at how bad my mocking could be and you laughed at all I demand. Today your laughter, a murmur and still, in contrast to your other. Why continue to challenge what's left of my will, why continue the fight, my brother? Now sadly You are to blame, for every deadly game, a killer I cannot see. Now again I am born, now how quickly you mourn, for my brother, my enemy.

Vaudry B. Clinkscale Jr.

Non-Replaceable And Non-Erasable...

You were so sweet,
I was swept right off my feet.
The feelings I felt for you,
To me, they were so true and so new.
You said you loved me while looking me in the eye,
I never even considered that it might be a lie.
You cuddled me in your powerful arm,
I refused to believe you could do any harm.
With you I did something that before you I had never done.
It meant everything to me, but to you it was just fun.
You took something no one can replace.
You filled my heart with feelings I can't erase.
When it was all over you promised that you would call,
It probably would be better if I could just forget it all.
Without my permission my feelings grew too strong.
My heart is sending love where it never belong.
I am wearing a constant frown.
Because right from the start, I knew you couldn't settle down
It was a terrible mistake; but you were so sweet,
Like a love-starved fool, I let you sweep me off my feet.

Lisa Olah

Untitled

I look over your shoulder, you don't know I'm there
I watch every move you make though you are unaware
My heart aches to hold you but it cannot be
I long to talk to you to tell you I'm free
The pain is gone, the heartaches too
I wait for the time I'm joined by you
I was given my time to be in your life
We will have time in eternity, there will be no strife
Now I set you free to live out your time
I will wait for you with patience and love
Together we will journey to the heavens above

R. Jane Meyer

First Kiss

With sweaty palms and shaky knees.
I close my eyes and pucker my lips.
As he leans in closer I know he sees.
The fright in my eyes as his hands move to
my hips.
He plays some music to make the mood right.
And knows all the right things to say.
My heart beats fast as he's holding me tight.
The jitters slowly fade away.
But it all ends as our lips unlock.
As he walks me to my door.
I look up at the ticking clock.
and remember nothing more.

Lisa Smith Esposito

First Times Are Scary

The barber's chair looked so b-i-g to see
I was frightened to think what would happen to me.
The snips made a noise so close to my ear
'Twas enough to fill a guy with fear.
I wiggled and squirmed, I twisted and turned
That thing on my neck really did burn
I reached out to Mommie to set me free
All she did was try to reassure me.
"It won't be long," her voice was sweet
But it seemed forever 'fore the job was complete.
"You were a good boy," the man said with a smile,
And the pop in my hand made it all worthwhile.

J. Patricia Holohan

Help Me

I stand on the edge of a dark void, I am separated.
I watch with detached emotions, and contemplate.
I am above the violence, and thievery, waiting.
I watch aimlessly, the dashing and running about.
The everlasting struggle, to take what belongs to another.
I am there, and yet I am not, I see, but I do not want to see.
Oh, but to stay forever in this void, to live in my own world.
Having nothing to do with the other.
But wait, my mind cries, someone has to take a stand.
But why me, why me, oh God, why me?
If I wait long enough, the evil will run its course.
Goodness will prevail in the end, want it?
But how many souls will be lost with the waiting.
My mind struggles with the question, and tries desperately to evade the answer.
Suddenly the darkness is stripped away, and a light shines through the void.
I pull myself up from my complacency, determined to do what I can.
And in doing so, set in motion a spark, that will ignite others.
Like a babe, taking its first step into adulthood,
I take my first faltering step, into a place, I know nothing about.
Help me Lord, guide my footsteps, help me.

Lois E. Cook

The End Of The Road

I stood there all alone
I watched you say goodbye
I knew you didn't want to leave me
I know you shouldn't have seen me cry.

I watched them take you away
I watched you tremble with fear
I wanted to be with you and hold you
I wanted you to be near.

I can't stop myself from crying
I can't believe it's done
I can't believe your life is over
There are no more songs to be sung.

It didn't have to end this way
You could've stood by my side
If only you had spoken to me
No one would've said you lied.

It's hard to believe life
It's hard to forget about the past
It's hard to forget the tears in your eyes
It's sad we had to say goodbye so fast.

Manda L. Pierson

If

If you shall ever fall,
I will pick you up.
If ever you should cry,
I will catch every falling tear.
If your heart should break,
I will be the sewing machine that mends it.
If ever you should get scared,
I will be the comforting thought that comes your way.
If a disaster should occur,
I will be that extra helping hand.
If you should ever get into a fight,
I will be the peace maker.
If you shall ever fall and feel that you can't go on,
I will pick you up and carry you the rest of the way.
If you ever take the wrong path,
I will step in and show you the way to the right one.
And if ever you should need a friend,
I will be the one right by your side.

Myranda Susanne

From The Bottom Of My Heart

From the bottom of my heart,
I wish to praise...
All of the brave souls... like you,
Who walk upon this earth.
Sometimes struggling through life,
With limited knowledge,
Of what to do, or where to go.
Sometimes you stumble... then you fall.
When certain obstacles intrude.
Upon the emotions held deep inside...
Clouding your vision, like a blind man;
You flail, hoping to rise,
Above these oftentimes painful situations,
To be the victor, and not the victim of life.
Your strength is your beauty.

Linda Spillan

Peace

I with YOU makes up a WE,
I without YOU is just a ME.
Staying together it is plain to see
That WE will shape our Destiny.

While WE are together, WE may get along fine
Aimless pleasures and fun, all down the line.
But what have WE gained, for true Peace of Mind,
If WE garner no honors, they are all left behind?

No God, No Peace
or
Know God, Know Peace

Join God, with You and Me, to make up the We,
Then guided by his love, it's a calm serenity,
Giving Peace to the Mind, a conscience that's free,
Pure solace to the heart, for all eternity.

So why should We listen to idle dreams,
Pervert the goals of life, with wasted schemes;
When God's plan for man is so complete,
While others all lead to a sure defeat?

Therlow R. Leach

A Place To Go

As I thought I closed my eyes for the very last time
I woke, looking down on the body that was once mine
I could not describe the feeling I had but it was so strong
In a way it had been too powerful for something was wrong
Inside I felt completely immaculate and this felt strange
Outside I felt as if something were wrong; something had changed
I saw a bright and gleaming light and it called out my name
I felt as if it would release me of all my sorrows and pain
But then I heard my family telling me to come back to them
I promised them soon but could not tell them when
I struggled to return to them but the light was so warm
So I tried to fight it, but could not and they began to mourn
I stepped into the light and the glory of Love was there
I had a beautiful feeling that for me it would always care
I looked down again and saw them mourning my new life
I tried to console them that my new life here was nice
Now I know my loved ones will pass on to a beautiful place
And I will be waiting for them with love showing on my face
They have nothing to worry about I wish they could know
I wish I could tell them that they'll always have a place to go.

Marie-Catheline Jean-Francois

I Am

I am afraid and worried
I wonder what the world will be like in years to come
I hear children crying
I see children hungry and alone
I want to help
I am afraid and worried

I pretend that nothing in the world is wrong
I feel like I am not able to help
I touch the fingers of a dying homeless man
I worry for the homeless
I cry because they have no food or shelter
I am afraid and worried

I understand that there are dying homeless people
I say why can't the human race look beyond themselves
  and see that there are those in need
I dream that the world will soon become a better place
I try to think of a way to help
I hope that people appreciate what they have
  because there are some who do not have anything
I am afraid and worried

Lisa N. Marriage

Celtic Dream

as I stared across the room and met those warm blue eyes
i wondered to myself if you were real or just my imagination
i turned around for a second and in an instance you were gone

but somehow as if by fate we were once again face to face
i wanted so desperately to know who and what you were
but my shy nature kept your name a mystery for a while longer

i began keeping a careful eye out and watched you as you grew
more into a kind and gentle man and less of the playful child
but still with your innocence you were able to touch my heart

the day we finally met I thought I would die yet I lived
and saw and touched the one who had always seemed out of reach
and from that day forth nothing could ever be the same

but fate has once again stepped in and made you invisible
my broken heart aches with wonder of what is happening
i desperately need to see your face if just once more

your warm smile and tender heart opened towards me again
for such a gift I'd give you a king's ransom
but for one sweet kiss I'd give you all the more

Sean C. Thomas

Forever In My Memories

I won't see you come through the door,
  I won't hear you laugh anymore.
It's been awhile
  Since I've seen your smile.
It will always and forever be;
  In my memories.

When will this hurt I feel, go away?
  Maybe, just maybe someday.
Then I won't feel the pain,
  Of losing the love that remains;
  Forever in my memories.

How am I supposed to feel,
  Now that you're gone, nothing seems real.
Your kiss, your touch, your warm embrace,
  What I would give to see your face.
It will always and forever be;
  In my memories.

The love we had, our days together,
  They will always and forever be;
  Forever in my memories.

Lorna L. Pool

Wishes

I wish that I could go and visit God,
I would see how the sun shines
And learn about the lightning rod,
I could sit down and talk with
  The angels,
And learn why on this earth
  we trod,
I could visit with Jesus and get
  To know my God.

I could learn all the Bible
  Stories,
I would like to know how those writers wrote,
I could visit the holy land and
  See the colors of Joseph's coat,
I could lean on my Savior's arm,
And see his glorious face.

I could see so many things
There in his heavenly place,
Oh, how I long to go there
After I have run my race.

Sarah Langley

I Vow

I vow that once again I will learn to reconcile.
I'll even find a way to hide my feelings with a smile.
My heart like stone has grown from the sadness I possess,
And from the pain that rages on deep inside my chest.

I'll hide my heart from reality and live in a world of make believe,
And never again will I be found wearing my heart upon my sleeve.
I vow to never trust another or even myself again.
Lest I become the victim of a cheating lover like him.

I will not concern my mind with any but myself.
A shield of armor I will wear to protect my heart and health.
I'll steel myself against my pain, a smile I'll always wear,
And when your new love passes by, I'll say that I don't care.

I'll be content to know that I will never love again,
And accept the fact I'd be better off to leave this world I'm in.
To be alone is my destination, never to know love in this life.
So I'll pass the hours day after day, awaiting my time to die.

Vera Mayfield

Prayer?

Remember when people used to say,
"I'll see ya in church come this Sunday!"
I wonder what's happened since then to now,
Has time changed that much or do we no longer need prayer?
Society dictates that we don't need a church
That God should be put last on our list...not first.
The homeless, child abuse, homosexuality
Have all become such a prevalent reality.
Drug abuse is rampant on every hand...
Needless slaying because of it throughout our land.
Old age once was deemed golden...in it wisdom did abound.
Today, little to no respect for the elderly is found.
Malachi gives the formula upon which this society must stand
When he tells us to enter the storehouse with tithes in hand.
He says the Lord will bless those who this message believe
By pouring out heaven's blessings too numerous to receive.
Yes, prayer is the key that unlocks the door
To heaven's rich blessings and so much more.
So, to those who say we don't need prayer
Let them take a look at our world...from then to now.

Mary Wyatt Byers

Through The Years

Through the years we've been,
I'm glad to say I'd do it again.
Through the years we're in, we can only win.
Cause our love is true, baby it's me and you.
Through the days to come, I'll bring you total
happiness and then some.
Through the days and minutes we share, let's hold
each other close and show we really do care.
Through the hard times and sorrow, strength from
each other we will borrow.
Through the times of joy and laughter, let it
always be there before and after.
Through the times we're apart, always know
you're in my heart.
Always longing for you to be close, which can't
always be, which hurts the most.
Through all the times we're side by side, let not one
minute pass by, that you won't know I'll be
right here through all the years.
It's true, it's true, baby, I only want and love you.

Sue Wheeler

Abe

I carve. It's just a hobby although
I'm really pretty good. I carve
One subject only once and that's enough:
An elephant, and Indian brave, old
Winston Churchill (that baby's face was tough).
My last piece I'm carving now.
It's Abraham Lincoln,
Whose history I know well.
But now I see that history in
The sad and lonely face.
I'm carving on the eyebrows
And the eyes that looked at
Gettysburg, at young Tad Lincoln's
Face. I carve the ears that heard his
Early generals say why they couldn't fight and
Listened to Mary Todd's unhappiness.
His brow is tired, but I try to show the
Strength that saved our country and
History in a face.

Roy Patterson

The Next Darkness

As I ponder the fate which awaits me today
I'm surprised by the courage which stays
With a man who is dying not quickly, but slow
From the battle to which I must go

The dew of the morning lies thick as it fell
While we wait for the order to fight
There are no smiling faces on men who know well
That the next darkness comes won't be night

Are the answers to questions eluding our best
While we settle our problems with wars
Is there reason to search for a way to fight less
Is it built in society's mores

We are marching to drums that are ordered to beat
By commanders who watch from the hill
From the heights they can see all the damage they'll mete
As their soldiers are ordered to kill

The dew of the morning lay thick as it fell
We awaited the order to fight
There were no smiling faces on men who knew well
That the next darkness to come wouldn't be night

Rick L. Hubbard

Images

I see images day and night,
images that often give me fright.
These images are often in my mind,
always strange and very unkind.

These images distract me when I'm
sitting alone,
Half of them will chuckle, the other half
will groan.

Some of them are dark, and always faded out.
Others are clear as day, and stand right out.
They stand there starring, and they never look away.
But, then they disappear as I reach for them and say:

"I know this is my mind, just pulling another stunt.
But, who are you, and what do you want?

Steven D. L. Hardin

Imagination

If the day is cloudy, overcast and grey
Imagine the Master with His giant brush
Just streaked the early skies of morning
With tints of red, yellow and rose so gay!
Perhaps a huge arching rainbow with colors lush.
Now doesn't that start your spirits soaring?
Have you taken time to watch clouds as would a child
Seeing dogs, dragons or maybe a ship in full sail?
Just lay quietly in the shade on a hot summer afternoon
And let your imagination run a bit wild.
Any hazy early morn or eve is an ethereal veil,
But eerie goblins hide in hazy midnight without a moon.
While in misty moonlight, one can easily imagine a wooded ring
With shimmering fairies dancing about their tiny queen.
To indulge in such fancies, you're never too old!
Reasonably you may believe, it can even help you young to stay.
So let the imagination flow and really reign bold.
Oh!..Could that be a leprechaun behind that stack of hay?

Mary E. Gravlin

An Early Morning Encounter

Walking down the ward one day, early in the morn',
in a dirty white gown I looked like a silly clown.
After having spent a sleepless night
saving many sick people that otherwise may have died.
I longed for coffee and a pillow or whatever I could find
to quench my thirst, to rest my mind,
instead, I encountered a lady of a different kind.
Her eyes were blue as the sea, her hair was black as the night,
her body was made for Gods to see.
I asked her who she was! I asked her what she wanted!
Was she sick, did she need an MD.?
She stared at me without an answer.
There was silence between us broken by overhead pages
summoning doctors to codes or places.
It was as if we where there for eternity!
And then, I felt her hand in mine and heard her whisper,
"I loved you, I loved you, when I saw you for a brief while
one day, somewhere, sometime."
She was someone else's woman whose wounds I had mended
someplace, sometime, onetime.

J. Anthony Gomes

Threads Of Gold

Tiny stitches are made through time
in and out as we go day to day
creating the pattern of our lives
each one different in his own way

The stitches are started from the day of our birth
as we are taught, as we learn, as we grow
testing and proving, our confidence building
our pattern beginning to show

As a child our character begins to take form
we learn to share and to give
though the threads are not orderly, the stitches are many
as we are still learning how we should live

The stitching may be long with graceful lines
when life has been gentle and kind
but the threads can become crooked and short
when troubles take over the mind

When we've reached the twilight of our years
and the pattern is worn and old
we give it to God with its luster so faded
and God turns the threads into gold.

Netta Shannon

Candle Ceremony

By offering this bright and shining candle,
In honor of souls that are gone.
Their passing has been hard to handle,
I know they have found a far better home.

The candle I'm offering for lighting,
Representing my care and my love.
My final remembrance to you is the flickering,
In the same air that carries a dove.

As a dove glides higher in the sky,
I know that I gave you my best.
I light this candle to say 'Goodbye'
And may your souls be equally at rest.

Lois Driscoll

"A Surprise In Store"

There you were, young, scrupulous a "7-11" clerk going about business
In prompt command, yet with efficient finesse.

After occasional walks I'd stop for cups of "7-11" Irish Cream
Hardly to notice your gentle hello or friendly beam.

However; one day in hot pursuit your presence came into focus
You all but burst into view like a new born crocus.

So startled was I to see you there
Arrayed in the soft glow of morning air

Your face radiant in light shining
Your brisk attentive manner — how exciting!

Then and there an emotional thrill did win me over.
With gusto we did date. Proclaimed friends, to cherish and savor.

Dear Lord is this a dream — can this ecstasy be real -
Sister Time, what secrets will you reveal?

Is there a future - even a fighting chance
For a sexy "7-11" clerk whose heart pants

Wild and bold for the likes of an aging Fair Haired Lady -
A romantic, whimsical yet perky - ME!

Martha Guenther

Silent Strength

Poets' fleeting thoughts are caught
  In quiet chorus of paper and pen
Relieving psyche of its burden
  Pondering mystery within
Quintessential messages sharing passage
From their soul into hearts of those who read,
And apprehend the rationale romantics perceive
Like witnessing:
  Snowflakes breaking limbs off trees
Invisible breeze altering faces of deserts and temper of seas
Woman's love conquering man's foolish pride
Embracing smile melting a child's moment of fright
Tenacious insight displacing doubt, so as to imbue
Our only actions of the year that really count
Today's awareness shaping tomorrow's route

A. J. Wieland

The Only Way

Nicodemus came to Jesus by night
In search of answers that were right,
Be born again - Nicodemus was told
How can this be when a man is old?

Nicodemus learned how to start anew,
Just do the same and you can too,
'Tis the Lord that calls us into the light,
Open his book and search for your plight.

Be born of the spirit from heaven above
Accept the gift from the God of love,
Yes, Jesus paid the price for our sin,
So open the door now, let him come in.

Jesus says, "I am the way, the truth, and the life."
He is calling you now, there is really no strife,
Accept his dear Son, repent of your sin,
That's all that it takes for you to come in.

Martha Ingram Miller

Live Things

It struggled through a crack
in the broken, tipsy sidewalk.
Laying in a puddle of brown rain water,
cigarette butts floating,
old paper bags,
broken styrofoam cups blew about.

In April it climbed slowly
up the chipped broken walls.
Crept over the four letter words of graffiti.
In May it hooked itself on jagged broken windows.
June came.
A profusion of soft pink wild roses
covered all with perfumed beauty.

Winifred J. Osborne

Troth

With abiding faith that erases doubt
I stand and watch the tide go out
That it will come back before day is through
I do not know—and yet, I do.

I see the winter with its icy grip
Cover all with death like a final script
Will spring come again for all to renew
I do not know—and yet, I do.

I see loved ones droop and die
and disappear like the morning dew
Will they rise again our lives to fill
I do not know—and yet, I do.

Ray Johnson

Tuesday Evening Man

Images form, as beads of sweat sliding
in the crevice between my breasts trace
a river path valley of flesh hiding
the lines of your face, my breath embraces
the edge of my lips like a gentle fan
as your lingering kiss of air grows bright,
your fantastic arms those of a real man
enclosing me in my clutch of delight.
My silent whisper puts lust in your voice
as you rough the soft sheets of my mind
with your loud echoes of sexual noise
like an old tape I can't help but rewind.
I try to imagine you with flesh I can see,
but the excitement is just as empty.

Sylvia Booth

In The Darkness

They came and took him away
In the Darkness.
Not a sound did fall
From the lines painted on stone faces,
Nor did eyes glitter in the quiet moonlight
As they swept through the house.
Gathering his belongings,
No tears were shed, but happy thoughts instead.
They promised a dream, excitement,... travel.
Thus, he followed without a fight.
Far from home was he to go.
They said he was much needed
And to come quickly by train (It's so much faster).
Now, he sits in padded seats
Hoping, wishing, dreaming for the journey to begin,
And to catch a glimpse of the world beyond the blinds
Yet to be explored by his eyes.
But, they come with blindfolds,
And there he sits (he now knows why)
In the Darkness.

Liane M. Nishioka

"Point Of View"

It's not enough to say you understand when
in the next breath you invalidate my view,
Or to reach out your hand in gesture to start anew.

It comes down to acceptance of Who I Am and Will Be,
the rejection of temptation to try and change me.

I've been uniquely created as have you,
And that definitely entitles each to his
Point of View!

Maryann Kovilic

I'd Take The Stars Down

I'd take the stars down and make of them a crown
If you could only love me too.
Yes I'd take them down and spread their light around
If I could have your love and you.

I'd take the stars down and never make a sound
If it would bring you to me.
I'd take them down and make a smile from your frown
And light your way for all to see.

I'd take the stars down, in your eyes they would be found.
My light is found in your eyes, your touch.
Yes I'd take them down and place them on the ground
Just because, I love you so much.

Pat Drummond

Praha Opium

In a drunken dream and glossy eyes
In the night a shadow flies, back and forth and side to side
It flew real low, I tried to hide; in my house I hear a sound
Opened my door and guess what I found
A scary looking creature 'bout four feet tall
with hair and teeth and wings and all
we talked for a while through the window screen
By now you're asking what I've seen
His name was Pete, he was a bat
Came in, drank coffee, and this and that
With proper English and a way cool grin
Pete talked, I listened, then he talked again
Said he never bit a person that he liked
But he scared the hell out of me that night
So when it's cold outside and it's looking rough
Leave your window open, but that's not enough
Have a hot pot of coffee, and a nice warm chair
And you'll never know who'll show up there
He's the grooviest creature and the coolest cat
His name is Peter, the way cool bat.

Peyton W. Chitty

My Dad

I got to know him the very best,
In the winter of his life, at rest.
My Dad and I could share by then,
We'd not done this since I don't know when.

He wasn't well, and could hardly hear,
But all that mattered was my being near.
He so much missed being able to work,
But he still tried; he'd never shirk.

He loved his family, his home and his horse,
His garden and truck, and much more of course.
But life was ending and this he well knew.
I knew too, but there was nothing I could do.

I knew we didn't have a whole lot of time.
So I'd try my best to make his life fine.
Then one night he left us as we watched on.
One last breath, a shudder, and he was gone.

I'd said goodbye in my own way.
I'd told him I loved him just that day.
I'll miss him now and later too, I fear,
But I'm so grateful for that one last year.

Shirlene R. Pierce

Ode To Mother Dear

There's a special time, that comes once a year;
In which appreciation is given to someone dear.
The person may be young or even old;
Her love-full giving is considered gold.
She gave to us our human life!!
Taught us how deal with strife.
She showed us how to love and be loved,
So we can be like God above.
We are very lucky to have someone
To put our trust and hope in.
This will bring happiness from start to end.
In every life, she is placed above all others
So let's be thankful for our Dear Ole Mother.
So let's all say, "Happy!! Happy!! Mother's Day!!"

Tony S. Garner

"The Nightmare"

Violent dreams, a soul cries.....
Inspiration lost, spirits die.

Memories of the past gone but not forgotten.
A hatred, sore, painful, awful, and rotten.

Torment in the shadowy night,
of childhood dreams and horrific fright.

Generation to generation the cycle unbroken.
It is a secret kept quiet, and always unspoken.

Sherry Kitts

Lissa

When Lissa was born our world fell apart.
Instead of happiness, we were sick at heart.
"She's not normal," the physicians said.
Our hearts and souls were filled with dread.
"Retarded," "Special education," we were finally told.
"We have no idea what her future will hold."

A child like Lissa has exceptional needs, and,
God has a purpose when He plants "special" seeds.
Lissa brings joy with her lamb-like smile.
Having her and loving her is enriching and worthwhile.
We need patience and perseverance, and God's guidance from above.

From a child like Lissa, we learn unaffected love...

Pat Huffman

Untitled

Lying in your bed alone, the night is dark as you wait by your phone. The crow screams out his lonely cry like the young virgin waiting to die. Dark shadows fill and cloud your mind, searching, searching for your soul. Come on now play the game, once you do you'll never be the same. Crawl back deeper inside your brain, search your soul and find your pain. Release it now and set it free and see just how beautiful things may be.

Nicole Depew

"Diamond Eight"

It's a magical place to be, with a mystical porch for me;
It allows my imagination to see...My life - in poetry.

I always wanted a place like this,
Since I was steadily on "The Roam" -
Somewhere that I could truly rest,
That enabled me to write a good poem -
So I bought this land and built a cabin,
And now I call it my home.

It's the only one I ever owned,
Miles away from civilization -
And so delightfully conducive,
To the welcomed inspiration -
And even if I work all day,
It's still living meditation.

Up here, writing comes so easily;
Upon my daily reflection -
My verse, comes so pleasingly;
Upon my every inspection -
And my thoughts become increasingly,
Finer interjections...into the physical world.

Michael J. Grant

Friendship

What is the meaning of a friend?
Is it the leaning in times of needing
Is it the caring of the sharing
Is it the joking or the provoking
Is it the tiffs or the gifts
Is it the teasing for our pleasing
Just maybe a friend is:
The love from the heart when you're miles apart
The touch of the smile when you're running a mile
The little nudge to keep you from the fudge
The quiet unspoken talk when you're out for a walk
The reading of your mind that lets you unwind
This all combined has always been a friend of mine

Lawrence E. O'Brien

The Apple In The Room

A small, shiny, dark, red apple
Is laying alone helpless, on a small, shiny, glass table
In a room filled with an eerie silence.

All of a sudden, there are footsteps growing louder and louder.
Finally, the sound of footsteps overpowers the room
Where the apple is laying.
Suddenly, the sound of footsteps stops.
A small, chubby hand tightly grasps the apple
And slowly picks it up.

Suddenly, a loud crunching sound pierces the room—
Over and over again.
Suddenly, the room is quiet.
Then the sound of footsteps fills the room.
Quickly, the sound fades away—
Leaving the room with an eerie silence.

Sharon D. Person

A Day With The Deaf

The world of the hearing impaired,
Is like entering a different country.
One feels like a foreigner
who cannot speak the language,
An outsider, an uninvited guest,
An atmosphere absent of sound,
writing would be best.

Not entirely absent of sound,
Some do speak an awkward noise,
But they would rather sign,
And use the language of the body,
Than the complex and complexing language of oration.
Instead of pity, one stands in admiration.

One admires the heart and fortitude,
Of people society deemed less fortunate,
They have overcome the silence,
To graceful movements of another language
Where communications are like unfettered clefs,
Only in the mind of the deaf.

Richard Inniss

White Mask

It was a white film that covered my face on that hazy day
I tried to breathe but the fluid covered my entire being.
A mouth peering through the flowing mask
I tried to break from this mold that cast me into silence.
As I sat and watched, I tried to pull myself from this venture
But, I laid in terror and fright from an unwillingness to believe the truth.
For, it was on that day that my troubles began,
and it was on that day that my troubles never ended...

Laura Bruni

To The One I Call Father

The one I call father
is not the one who raised me.
The biological one, well he just couldn't see.
So to say and mean father, I really didn't bother.
A father's love should be something so strong
that it is capable of shooting you to the moon
or should be like key verses in a song
that are connected by a lovely tune.
I didn't see this in my mother's first one.
It was the second go around
that I truly found
the one, and then my search was done.
Some call him Lee
but for me, why bother?
If people could just see what I see
then they too would just call him father.

Kristie D. Moore

About Nothin'

To have something to do when there is nothing to do
is the oddest of things that there is to do!
To do nothin' is somethin' but nothin' is nothin' so
nothin' as good as can do!

So here's nothin' of somethin' yet really it's nothin' but
that's the point of this all!

Just keep on a pushin' at somethin' and tryin' for
nothin' and maybe that's somethin' to do!

Now when you are through, you've had somethin' to do
so you see nothin' is somethin' to do!

Mary Jane Linder

Abortion: Think About It

Pro-choice or Pro-life, which decision will you make?
Is the right of a woman so important a life you must take?
When you look in the mirror, what do you see?
What if your mom had decided your life was to no longer be?
What if it was your life they wanted to take?
Ever thought of what decision you'd want them to make?
If my birth mother had felt it was her right to take my life away,
I wouldn't be standing in front of you today!
To most it's just a mistake,
To me it's a life God meant to make.

Tari L. Waldrop

A Woman Of Valor

It was predestined first within her brain.
Its aura fit the glove of her remark
And by her word the cancer flamed the dark.
And off was cut her breast in shameless pain.
The monster could hold no more than just her name

For she had long the battle been prepared.
This was no sniffled capitulating prey.
Not by lack of courage would it stay
Nor would it be for reoccurrence spared.
I've never seen her beauty thusly faired.

I've held the cups of vomit in my hand,
And watched her writhing body then convulse.
And all the world of fury's bursting pulse
Would not she bow a trace to its demand.—
She would turn the hourglass to build more sand.

I know what love will do for testing love:
There cannot be a heart of greater grace.
I take between my hands her lovely face
And kiss the lips that spake the cancer of,
And strive to fit my hand within her glove.

E. L. Elias

Untitled

For what is love?
Is to be loved the reason we are put on this earth?
I hate love for it always brings hurt and
lots of it.
It makes you bend over backwards and lower
your standards.
I hate when it's stolen away and given
to another more pretty, or kinder, or richer
than I.
I hate love for all that comes from love
is madness and unkind words.
Friends who question their friendship and
love as their love.
People who question their worth and people
who ask "Who am I?"
That's how I feel about love, even if I
hunger for it as if it were my last
meal and there was no one to feed me.

Kimberly Griffith

Beautiful October

Sunlight, filtering through thinning leaves
is warm and inviting and in taking your ease
you long to escape and to follow your moods
be it traveling far or a walk in the woods.

In October the beauty of Autumn engulfs you,
the brilliance of colors in the various trees-
the haunting last fling of Indian Summer-
the tang in the air from the very first freeze.

As Nature prepares for the winter ahead,
so man must harvest his crops to store;
the northern birds head for a warmer clime
and the noisome insects will be no more.

October is indeed a time to rejoice
in the goodness of the Lord and the fullness thereof-
worthy of praise in unceasing voice
we must hasten to tell of His wonderful Love!

Marie Marks

Dad And I

Years ago the words weren't there
It almost seemed as if we didn't care
Trying to communicate was so very hard
For you my heart had an empty void

Finding ways to work things out
Left my head full of doubts
Doing things to make you proud
Caused arguments, making our voices loud

Shouting, screaming, and a couple of fights
Left many regretful, and sleepless nights
Giving all I got to work through this
Vowing never again to use my fist

For you and I to talk to each other
Puts a big smile on the face of my mother
"JACKIE" also has to do her part
For all of this to reach momma's heart

We can't take her death in vain
But communication will eliminate the pain
With momma gone we have to try
To close this gap before we die

Paula Marie Angelle

Martin Luther King

His voice is like magic as it reaches my ears.
It drifts through the air over the huge listening crowd.
The words are so strong.
They pound with my heart, my soul, and my dreams.
I listen so closely, drawn to the words.
He speaks of justice, peace, and life.
The man is so mystical and such an honorable man.
Indeed he is true to the American dream.
This man is my hero.
His name is Martin Luther King.

Michelle Canales

My Home

'Twas the home of a mother and children
It encompassed all in its care,
Lowly, meager, bereft of beauty
Love and compassion were there.

The children played happily and safely
'Neath apple tree, lilac and pine.
Cherry trees challenged bare footers
With red luscious fruit so fine.

The seasons followed each in their order
Cold winter, spring, summer, and fall,
Blizzards, showers, hail and hazes
An omnipotent eye watching all.

The old house a few steps from the windmill
Shared scenes of sorrow and joys,
Homespun games were their pastime,
Mumbletypeg and cat's cradle their toys.

But there's never a home so plain, I've found
When the time comes to leave it behind,
A part of one's heart still clings there
With only fond memories entwined.

Violet V. Clausen

Games Of The Heart

Confusion - once again - here I am
in between what's right, what's wrong
I know what I can have, don't know what I want
Yet Curiosity - always seems to get the best of me
And sooner or later, I'll have to play my cards.
Once again - I was dealt the wrong hand
once more - I have played the fool for
Another no name someone, who
I thought was going to make us a pair
Who will be next? A joker without a deck,
or...a lover without a heart. Confused?
I'm just waiting for a new dealer to
deal his selfish games and I, as I always do
will bet it all and lose
Someday, maybe I will get an Ace,
or maybe win with a wildcard
instead of always being bluffed!

Sherry Lee Oldham

Reality

Is all vain, that the vision is lost?
Is the hope within only a memory in thought?
Does the carousel of life bring one to emptiness?
Has the desire to try again been stayed forever?
Can one arise from the plight of mere existence-
to shine forth in radiance as a light of usefulness?
Can a stirring from within bring renewal of spirit?
Lord, let fulfillment of life's purpose—in reality—
reach ministering heights.

Nancy Wilson

The Sun

I see the sun above each day, it follows me through life
It followed me when I was young and when I took a wife
It warmed my soul and gave me strength and led me on my way
And though it dimmed and left each night, it returned again each day
It lets me know that all is well and brings a lot of cheer
It bleaches out the darkened days and helps me deal with fear
Its path is steady straight and true, its mass high in the sky
It's really me that turns you see, this makes the time go by
As days go by I wander down life's long enchanted road
The sun will still be here for you when I am growing old
It helps us through the coming years and lights up every day
So wonderful this big old star to watch us till we're gray
And still to come for others at each early dawn
We know the sun will still be here when all else is gone

Robert L. Rustenholtz, Sr.

A Saintly Stage

I face the twilight properly now.
It is neither distanced nor forlorn.
It brings not regret, but peace
and a sensation of early morn. . . . .
For to forget is not the contract;
My self-will no longer dominates.
Rather, I'm held captive by the Creator;
His purposes planned, thus my fate.

A revelation disclosed, my doubts erased,
Acceptance comes only through a Greater Grace!
A gift of Life, eternal, bright and fair,
supersedes worldly wealth and earthly cares.
Could I but transfer this glimpse of glory;
tell others the true meaning of HIS story?

No, it's the Master's decision
to bless a chosen few. . . .
"Draw nigh unto me," says HE,
and I'll draw nigh unto you."

Kathy Arnold Pellegrin

The Legacy

You came into my life on a lovely summer's day
It must have been an omen, for in your gentle way
You smiled, and suddenly the day was filled with happiness
It seemed a common thread had joined us, one I'll always bless
I gathered you into my heart, basking in your glow
I felt a peaceful feeling, only special people know
I was so very honored, for with your heart sincere
You welcomed me to be a part of life that you held dear
The countless hours we sat and talked, are memories I treasure
The lives of everyone you touched, are richer beyond measure
Now you are gone, a void exists, that only time will heal
The legacy you left behind, can only make me feel
That God in his great wisdom, made our paths to cross
So I could see, that legacy, was full of hope, not loss.

Margaret C. Miranda

Your Memory

The world has changed so since you left
It's lonely, and cold, and heartless.
Life can only be more peaceful where you are.
I remember that first and last kiss
Beneath that tree that stands so tall and strong.

I miss you sometimes, and
I need you sometimes.
Now you're gone, and now you're free,
But I'll never forget you...
Because that old tree will forever hold your memory.

Laura L. Weaver

Moonlight Is Still Not Brighter

Though dim, the Moon is still in loveliness
It shines upon children in lantern procession on narrow alleys.
Advances to reign but in shyness
Hardly giving out yellowish and cool rays.

On Mid-Autumn of this year, it is lightly cloudy
So, the Moon is covered partly,
Shooting stars follow falling stars descending into a child's
tiny hands,
Holding a star's lantern, the child proudly sings: "It's here my fan!"

In the year of the Tiger, the ferocious animal devoured the Moon,
So that it was raining intermittently on the Full Moon.
Now, it's the Cat who is coming, He will hang up the Silver Moon
lantern
And enjoy with a multitude of children playing shooting at stars.

Welcome the Mid-Autumn Festival, although the electricity has been
cut off
We still have gentle moonlight on top of the world
While wave after wave tap against the boats on the way to the unknown
We are sending greetings of Peace to the Full Moon.

CUOI, the liar, has deceived this world in years
You, Cheater, get out of here and go back to where you belong,
the sky is your destination
Let out children's lanterns be brighter,
Without stars, we don't give a damn, the Moon would be enough
for our people.

Mac Ly Tao - Ly Dai Nguyen

The Leaf

A leaf fluttered softly to the ground
Its color had changed from gold to brown.
The mighty oak stood proud and tall,
Not knowing the rest of its leaves must fall.

Strong winds blew both night and day
Each leaf tried very hard to stay;
But soon turned loose and fell to the earth,
A cycle had ended that started with birth.

The proud oak stood bare limbs to the sky
If you listened real close you could hear it sigh,
"I'll sleep through the cold winter winds and snow,"
"When springtime comes new leaves will grow."

So the oak stood bare the whole winter through
'til spring did arrive bringing leaves brand new.
Nature was revealed, I watched splendor unfold,
Knowing in time, the new leaves would turn gold.

For life must go on from one cycle to another
New beginnings and miracles, each starting with mothers.
'til the seasons of life are all part of the past,
And we see out great Creator where new things will last.

Martha C. Page

Heaven

Heaven is pictured as such a beautiful place to be,
Its equal on earth, no one will ever see.
God's own Son died in order to lead us there,
To the mansions He said He would go to prepare.

The image of heaven that fills the mind,
Is beyond comparison of any worldly kind.
Such contentment and peace as none can tell,
Will never be known 'till we go there to dwell.

It's only through a turning away from sin,
And putting our faith and trust in Him,
The One who is mankind's Saviour and Lord,
That heaven's reality will become a final reward.

Nalda Morris

Ordeals

This ordeal is over, my life has begun
It's hard to decipher, what victory is won
It's all now behind me, no more to remind me
Now nothing confines me, it's all said and done.

It's hard to relinquish what I know in my heart
And I have to distinguish what never will part
I fight to extinguish and refuse to contend
What's so ugly and frightful, I just cannot mend.

And I'm left with a knowing-that same inner-glowing
That fuels me all through the day
It continues to spur me, no more will deter me
As life's many tricks come my way.

It's not that I'm hardened, no more left to pardon
It's just that I've reaped, what I've worked so to keep
And refuse to be slaughtered, along with the sheep.

When I lie in repose-with my life down in prose
What's finally decided, only God really knows
But I must keep depending, what my heart's really rendering
Is there's more than just what seems to be and I know in a glance -
when my heart takes its stance, I must follow and be true to me.

Susan Estelle Caldwell Jeffre

The Dentist

"I don't want to hurt you."
It's like a flag of truce.
"Open wide. Wider."
The hinge only goes so far.
"Now, if you feel any pain, let me know.
Any pain at all."
How can I do that? Will you see it in my
closed eyes or notice white-knuckled fingers
sealed to the arms of the chair?
"Just a little longer and we'll be through."
Through what? We've already been through
Eternity.
("This is harder for me than it is for you.")
"I don't want to hurt you."
I know. I know. But you're a healer, and
sometimes that's what it takes.
"O.K., all finished. You were great."
You, too

Carmeline

The Fool

Slender of limb and slight in frame, yet larger than he seems
He's agile like the alley cat balancing 'tween the dreams
His shoes of velvet purple cloth with curled and pointed ends
A bell atop the tip of each which somehow ne'er unbends
Your eyes run 'long his leather pants; knees bent out in stance
Quivering legs set ready for motion; spins or leaps — a dance
Then you see his velvet tunic; identical in hue
Loose and flowing such freedom portrayed; a freedom doubly ensued
For upon a study of countenance fair reveals his ultimate blessing
Conferred upon him by a kinder god than He who hears my confessing
His eyes the prize a wise man seeks for vacant and empty they stare
Although they dance with illusion of light-in reality nothing lies there
The very jaunt of his jester's cap upon his tilted head
Suggests he has no worries, no fears, disillusions beyond him...dead
The bells the sound of careless abandon — a silly bow, raised brow
One hand around his waist — he smiles; the other one reaches out
His footing is on the firm ground of innocence — you in urbanity wallow
He beckons once more — you wish you could travel the foggy path
he follows
Disappears in the mist of nothing at all — blessed be the fool.

Kerry Jo Lee

Protect The Child

Guard this miracle called life, it needs no explanation -
It's mankind's greatest treasure, of which there is no measure.
Humans, great and kind, weak and strong, humble too -
Protect the innocence of a child.
We, the stewards of the ship of life, who have traveled here before -
From the wind-blown desert sand, to the utter-most distant land,
Stop! there are voices to be heard -
Weak ones, like the flutter of translucent wings upon the air -
Struggling, stumbling, where first they fell -
Not knowing life, nor love, just a living hell,
The abused and battered little child.
Come back! little ones, we will try again -
The sighing winds are being told -
Your sorrowful tales they will unfold.
Is this an imitation of life, the greatest of which is but a mime -
Rolling along on a playful mind!
Sweet radiance of youth, to whom life is but a spoof -
Flowering amidst the pain and crime, try again, we still have time.
Sublime, these visions cross our minds -
Protect the innocence of a child.

Sophie Chubrich

Miscellaneous Poems On Lake Biwa

Atop Stone Mountain stands stone monastery,
Its pagoda and bell tower renowned since
olden times.
Who are these men of ambition? As for me, I am
wearied and resigned—
Would that this sacred charm ward off the
evils in my life!

Beyond the stream at Seta extends an endless
vista—
On a silk handkerchief, warm and fragrant, a tiny
hand plies the needle.
I cannot help longing for my native country;
In the embroidered picture there is a Chinese-
style bridge.

By the flower-moon pavilion, I stop my
carriage for a while
To stroll under thatched eaves that overlook the waters.
The master painter, dotting with his brush,
habitually forgets his hunger-
He feeds himself on the mountain hues and the lake's gleam.

Wu-Chi Lu

Sitting Beside Myself

I step outside of my all-so-long worn body and sit down by its side. My eyes focus on who is beside me, why it's me! I wonder if I've died. Hair that was once so shiny and smooth, is now coarse and gray. A face which overtime has changed and slowly decayed. The hands, lazily dropped in the lap, are nothing but bones and skin. Without a touch or a sound, I remember what it feels like to be me again. The sun which shone through the window above has already disappeared. The time has surely moved and what came next - I feared. The me I watched finally closed its eyes. Not my body, but something else began to rise. My heart, my soul, they both joined in. When all darkness went away the bright light shined within. I turned and looked down at the other me. But found that which I could no longer see. A presence, so warm, welcomed and showed me the way. Through a passage, a door, and I knew I wanted to stay. I felt so alive, like never before. I felt like a child and wanted to see more. I'm glad I stepped outside myself and sat down by its side. I know you miss me, but I'm always there; last night I saw you cried.

Rae Ann Willingham

Space Race

There's a new race that's engulfed earth's face.
It's the conquest of outer space.
But, the race for space, is it the best place to race?
Could we not concern our better efforts here?
Improving the human race more clear.
With costly amounts, that escalate accounts.
Risks that exceed a million, to the budget of a trillion.
Shall the cosmonauts take-over the space race?
Or will the astronauts out-race them in outer space?
Now other nations want in the space race.
This would lead you to believe it's becoming commonplace.
Can they make the test to space race with the rest?
Can't we help the pauper, instead or orbiting to top her?
With highly a technical crash, we would need an aerospace
M.A.S.H.
Does the struggle of the human race
Need a space race?
Shooting rockets and shuttles up in dollars and cents,
Seems unsafe anymore for the lack of common sense.
We might think of all the rest
Before the space race be placed under arrest!

Mark Mattax

Our Precious Time

Like a masked, well armed thief, it steals through each day.
Jaunty with no care of tomorrow, through the night it slips away.
No matter how we try to possess it, we never score.
We can't keep it as a treasure, although we would like some to store.
We know it was only entrusted to us, not ours to cling or bind.
God gave us each a portion of this, our precious time.
Some wasted their allotment, never taking time to think,
Someone might enjoy their thoughts, if jotted down in ink.
Think of all the happiness wasted, a gift for young and old,
If their time was not squander, and their story had been told
Invisible as the winds it travels leaving its path a clean sweep.
It's gone, yet it leaves its mark of joy, or regrets for us to keep.
Don't be bashful, rude, or selfish, please do not decline,
Relinquish to others, a portion of your precious time.

Maurine Chlovis Johnson

What Life Is All About?

Life is about loving the creator and creating
Joy for ourselves and for others.
Respecting the supernatural omnipresence;
Ever permeating the external eternal world.

Life means to exude love, compassion and forgiveness,
To experience total emotional and spiritual growth;
To reach the highest level of consciousness for
Its timeless gift of inspiration and inner strength.

Life is about the utmost expression of transcending;
Attaining the ultimate union of tranquility;
Assimilating its nourishing power eternal, feeling
The essence that fills all living creations.

The power of life is inherent in all of us; Not one
Is exempted from the clutch that binds the universe;
There is no need to suffer the void that torments us,
For, we only have to remember that we are not alone.

Orovelia Lao Jones

Faith

Faith is the unswerving trust in the unprovable.
It requires occasional affirmation.

To know the unprovable is not faith,
but knowledge of a certainty so steadfast that it becomes unimportant.

A. H. Reed

Yards Of Harmony

Slide down a rainbow,
Jump along the stars,
Fly to all the planets,
Live in peaceful yards of harmony.
Play with all the animals,
Talk with all the bees,
Don't be afraid —-
Because you know they will not sting.
Slither with the snakes;
Slither on top of rocks,
Wait to hear the conversation
When the sun and moon shall talk.
Steadily rotating and revolving around,
The earth is living life - on solid ground.
What is in the sky at night?
How do bird's wings enable their flight?
Angels are a peaceful reassurance
Of life behind the scenes.
Now, the single question lies...
When will we get our wings?

Kristen Klauer

Our Inner Sounds

Words projected into space find their place,
Just voice your opinion and write with taste.
Life isn't all song and dance and romance -
Sometime you wish you were a rock
Like the poem "sitting on a hill!"
But can we in good conscience sit still?
Our inner sounds know no bounds;
We live to love and give, and give to love and live.
What is life but to share, to care?
To dare to be wheat and not a tare?
Our forefathers long under the sod
Taught us well about love, life, death and God!
We cannot be consumed by no, not or never -
Not "nattering nabobs of negativism" that sever.
But gentle persuasion and words like "kind"
Are more of what we had in mind.
Enduring to the end my friend,
Not counting years or days or months -
Listen well - for the bells toll only once!

Lucille Smallwood Wall

A Dream In My Heart

Long nights spent with a dream in my heart
Knowing this love could never be
I grasped at love's last ember and found it lost to me
Gone were the passions of yesteryear,
Leaving my heart longing for a love that
could never be
Driven by the pangs of youth, were this love and I
There were no limits 'neath earth or sky
Time was like a vast ocean span
Reaching ever reaching to the worlds unknown
Crushing to us our little world - our own.
All too soon 'twas ended, time ceased to be
For I stood at the waters edge and
saw the ship take my love from me.
All that remains of our love now
Are the long nights I spend with a
dream in my heart.

Vicki Brown

Knight

He is far away, yet he feels near
Known him for a short period but seemed a very long time
His love and friendship are offered through his kindness and
generosity
His care for others binds him to them through tears and laughter
He boldly weeps revealing his deepest emotion without shame
He laughs not like any other man who held little sentiment
But like one who cherishes every moment of it
He is not lavishly desired for he is unlike the typical
"tall, dark and handsome"
But he contains a certain charm that can make him to be
"The Knight In Shining Armor"
Just his smile can sweep a damsel in distress off her feet
Just a wink of his eyes can make anyone forgive his ills
And the wonder lies - where can this charming Knight be found
It is within a woman's heart to find and hold
what she sees through his eyes
For then she will discover
the Knight
has been in his soul all along

Teresa Chu-Sit

Mite Or Mighty

Moments in time engraved upon our lives, happy, sad, traumatic leaving scars, visibly healed or still painfully, invisibly concealed within.

Laughter, tears, excruciating pain, sweet ecstasy to cradle upon the breast a newborn life.

A loved one lost, too soon, yet did you not have much in your time together?

Now, apart, the love you shared has new and ever deeper value.

Even in the cold, bleak winter, there is beauty in solitude.

The soft pure snow gently falls enfolding the earth and broken hearts as well.

What is this strange rush of warmth filling the spirit within?

Now, missing those joyous times is but standing in the eye of the Hurricane of life.

We must look for the quiet pool at the bottom of the falls.

From fear and loneliness to bravery and courage ever mindful of great and glorious blessings bestowed upon us.

Perhaps it is not what we as tiny mites accomplish in our lives, but how mighty we become as we live it day by day.

Peggy Newton

Crown And Conc

Mommy cried cause I broke her heart
Leaving the family splitting slowly apart
But, I felt grown, doing what I wanted to
And not the things that she said to do

I could help Mommy as she helped me
Rather than turning my back so as to be free
I don't mean to treat my family, unloving, unkind, unfair
Giving others the impression that I do not care

But when you're nineteen and trying to be grown
And according to the law, you can be on your own
Against good judgement your 'want of heart' soars
As you forsake family needs caring only for yours

Yes, the 'teen transition' causes many Moms to cry
They'll love us in our foolishness until the day they die
But deep in my heart, I know, I only fooled myself
For, I denounced wisdom in the manner that I left.

However, between you and me, I just want you to know
I miss my Mom very much, and I love her so
It's hard for me to make amends; the manly thing to do
But one thing I'm learning is to self always be true

Mary Lee Aldridge

Journey

Year after year we stood by each other
Lent a shoulder to cry on and an ear to listen
Joined the laughter and the tears
And backed up each other's hopes and dreams

Here, today, a new light breaks
And as we journey forth
Farther and farther from each other
I shall not forget
The smiles, the laughs, the talks and the hugs
From those of you who I believe to be
Angels from above

I truly hope,
You think that too,
As I wish you the best of luck
For the JOURNEY you will take!

Sabeen Edwin

"Let America Be America For Me"

Let America be America for me, I'm black Lord but please let it be.
Let America be America for me, I'm in bondage Lord but
I wanna be free.

Lord just look now and your eyes will behold, poor black children
Lord with bodies all a waste. There's sickness and poverty among
people of our race, we would already be gone Lord,
if it wasn't for your grace.

Lord, I know you care for us, and in you I have no doubts,
please reach down and help us Lord, so we can calm the riots.
Now we don't mean to rush you Lord but we've been begging for
so long.
Do try now to help us Lord, and we'll lay down the arms.

If America becomes America Lord, for all people alike.
We can say within our hearts, at last we see the light.
That will lead us out of darkness Lord, hardships, sufferings, wrongs.
Just look down, smile Lord and say come on, we are sure to come along.

Naomi C. Moore

Rain

Mother of love, father of light,
let him rain with all his might. Rains
that pour and bring forth life to this
desolate and lonely place... My heart.
Fear has gripped me with an iron
fist, will I ever be free? Let the
rapids wash over me and cleanse me of
my sorrows. Let my heart be filled instead
with love and light, let me be free. Let
him be brought forth who can fill my
heart as freely as free can be. At
long last I have been loved, I am free.

Nantanit Smith

Calliope

The evidence of the sail,
Leading us to the horizon,
Is my spirit, unyielding but pliant
The wind sings.

Therefore, tonight, I rejoice in mind and heart.
Could it be that even I,
Drunk with music and the harp,
Can dance upon the swaying decks?

Golden moon, that changes the sea to liquid gold,
God has me by the tunic
And has jerked me up so high
That even I can breathe the wind.

L. H. A. Wright

With The Quickness

With the flash of an eye,
Let me get up and have my being.
Motivate my slowness to the quickest,
That each movement may be fluent.
Moving rhythmically with the quickness,
That no opportunity should be amiss.

Make me outrun myself to my destination.
For I will have gathered strength aforetime.
Not to put off for tomorrow,
What could have been done today.
Lord I pray!
Stop me from procrastinating!

Enable me to see ahead,
Facets of tomorrow.
Let me plant the seed today.
So when tomorrow peaks forth,
I will reap my rewards.
Because when tomorrow does come,
It comes with the quickness!

Tony Harris

Out On My Patio

To whom I may concern
Let not the candles burn
Keep your lamps and light jars
Mine, the moonlight and stars to light up my patio

All around me at evening
Hush! The music you bring
Second-hand orchestration
Records, tapes, cassettes - things played out by artists
Of contemporary fame but please, not on my patio

Breezes set the leaves dancing
And music entrancing is filtered wind song
As it ruffles the leaves
How it pleases, pacifies, soothes and relieves
Cares and concerns of all the day long

Oh to stay so enchanted - in my romantic tryst
Evening moonlight, first starlight, by soft breezes kissed
I'm in love with the evening - please don't ask for my mingleness!
No lover intrusions - spare concern for my singleness!

Blissful romance I find
Out on my patio, love's not deaf or blind

Phyllis J. Morgan

Circumstantial Outcome

In the field of freedom,
  Lie the trails of humanity.
Walk on them, follow them,
  And find out what life is all about.

Peace your way down and take your time.
Enjoy the glory,
  Because for some it won't last long.

The trail will split in three.
Force will make you choose.
Rich, wealthy, or poor?
Each choice is as good as the other.

Freedom is given to you.
It will prevail - if you choose to be rich.
It will prevail - if you choose to be wealthy.
It will prevail - if you choose to be poor.

Come now and choose your fate.
Enjoy the freedoms of humanity.
Live the life of an individual.
Feel the prestige, the wealth, the freedom.
The freedom of life.

Mike Burmeister

From Life's Highway To The By-Way

Often, when we least expect it,
Life will take a crooked turn,
Throws us off the route intended,
Jolts us far across the berm.

Stone-filled gullies, muddy marshes,
Bruise our hearts and bog our minds,
Through the thickets, scratched and bleeding,
We survive the testing times.

From life's highway to the by-way,
Oh, the beauty waiting there!
Seems as though God knows what's needed;
Quiet times can be too rare!

There, beside a winding pathway,
Breathe the roses' sweet perfume,
Wander through His lovely garden,
Make of it an upper room.

Soon the weariness will vanish,
Perfect peace will fill the soul
From the blessings of communion
With the Master in control.

Roxie E. Stahl

Thanks To My Sister

I knew that when our Daddy died, my
Life would never be the same.
I knew that there would be emptiness,
Combined with tremendous pain.
I never thought there would be anything
That would make me smile once more, or
Something that would make me see what
Life was worth living for.
Then just when I thought nothing would
Ever change, let me tell you what happened then.
God sent a gift through both of you, that
Gave my eyes light again
So let me say thanks to both of you, for
the gift that came to be.
Because, through you both, God gave back,
a part of my daddy to me.

Tommy Long

Masterpiece

My masterpiece has shattered,
like dust on a tabletop.
There's nothing I can do now,
except blow the pieces away and never stop.
Last night I was sitting on the beach,
the ocean looked like my masterpiece
it was so out of reach.
Then I heard the ocean speak to me.
It told me that life is more
than broken masterpieces.
It's about Love, Trust, and Understanding,
And that I shouldn't put my life on cease.
So I'll put some sand in my pocket,
so my masterpiece will be with me always.
And now when the waves crash on a beach,
I know they're saying to go day by day.
Don't let the world get you down.
Reach for your star,
And you shall have it.
That is your destiny.

Natasha Cronen

Tropical Thunder Storms

As waves come crashing down and thunder rolls around, I see lightning flash across the purple sky.

I can hear and feel the wind, whipping through the palm trees and swirling up the sand, like majestical sand gods dancing across the beach.

I see the rain as little, tiny water daggers aiming deadly at the beach below.

These are elements of a vigorous, emotional, violent, almost deadly Tropical Storm.

Melissa Britton

Desire, The Shadow

Desire, always with me
Like a shadow, follows along.
Never be able to expunge,
Possess me as I am alone.
The sun, which creates the shadow
Is you, making me lust.
No control over the sun, what a sorrow.
As you stay beside me, the shadow exists.
Burden, that is unlimited desire
Will squash me like a squirrel
Under your Convertible's tire.
Too heavy for me to quarrel.
Please, if you ever hear me crumbled,
Just laugh at me ever trying to scramble.

Yukihiro Naito

Weeping Willow

Can I ask you weeping willow, why do you cry
Like me did you carelessly let your love die
Why must your branches hang so low
Don't you know true love is always slow
That's why I weep willow, mine went away too fast
And willow, this was the one that was supposed to last
Tree, why do people lie and say they'll love you to the end
When in a few short months you have to settle for only friends
And why does love have to hurt so bad
When in the beginning, willow, you're happy but end up sad
Tell me weeping willow, are you knowledgeable enough
to answer my questions?
Or are they blown to an untouchable deeper dimension?
Willow, I ask this of you because I am still in love
And I wonder if his touches are only thoughtless little shoves
You don't have to answer now as I sit here in your shade
But it's hard to quit thinking of mistakes I've recently made
So willow, as I sit here and sorrowfully watch you weep,
I hope you can forget my troubles for they are not yours to keep.

Sheris Haines

Through Yesterday's Eyes

When I am looking through yesterday's eyes
Long buried thoughts often arise
Of times and people I've loved and lost
And the many bridges I have crossed.
As I look back down the paths I've walked
Visions of friends with whom I've talked
Emerge through the blurry mist of distance
Memories of yesterday to revive and enhance.
Yesterday's eyes have extrasensory sight
Reviving memories of some former delight
What a special rewarding surprise
That I can be looking through yesterday's eyes.

Mary D. Melton

Old Rivers And Tall Trees

Old rivers and tall trees are important to me;
Like puppy dogs and old chain saws —-
And, so are the eagles, with their long, sharp claws.

Butterflies and humming birds are important to me;
Like kitty cats and late summer's tall, green corn —-
And, so is an April snow on my tulips, showing Earth reborn.

Gladiolus and vine-ripened tomatoes are important to me;
Like red-breasted robins and little league baseball —-
And, so is December's frost, falling silently to cover all.

Newborn babies, so wide-eyed with wonder —-
Upon their arrival, dressed in mother-nature's splendor;
—are important to me.

And each evening at dusk, while enjoying a small libation;
My mind's inner-eye gleams, with bright jubilation!
In deep reverence to PROVIDENCE, who guards heaven's hall
That today, I did not see the atomic flash —-
that would end it all.

Larry Transou

Me, A Tree

In this wonder forest of life
like seeds we do grow,
Trees nurtured by sun and rain
until foliage begins to show.

"Our" leaves are green and are fresh and clean
Each hanging on to life.
"Our" summer is gone
We struggle to hold on
As we fight off the wind and its might.

Just as the tree stands straight and strong
after its leaves are blown away,
We trust and we firmly believe
they will come back again someday.

Our faith in Jesus Christ gives us a tighter grip
as we reach up to the sky,
as we grow old
His story ever told
Eternal life is ours by and by.

Marian Fyhrie Guetz

Exercise In Futility

Keeping pace with your changing eyes,
like the sandpiper's water chase,
is an exercise in futility.

The morning light astonishes your irises
into a new dawn as I laugh,
keeping pace with your changing eyes.

The sandpiper, stubborn and bold,
can't let go of her daily routine,
a futile exercise to challenge the tide.

I held on too hard to habits
until you and your summer day nature
and keeping pace with your changing eyes.

Trying to maintain a distance
between your water line and my private beach
has become an exercise in futility.

The sandpiper wearies from the quest
as I dive fiercely into your blue.
Keeping pace with your changing eyes
was an exercise in futility.

Kathleen A. Kremins

Trains

It is the saddest sound I have ever heard
Like the wail of a lonely bird.

I say goodbye to my most special friend
Not knowing if I will ever see her again.

I hold on to her hand so tightly...not wanting to let go
We are separated...I climb up the stairs knowing I must go.

I look out the window to a sea of faces...
I must find her before...then I see her face.

She has such a brave smile on her face...
No she will not see my tears..not even a trace.

I hear the eerie whistle of the train...
In my heart I can feel the rain.

The train pulls away...I see her blow a kiss
I think of how much she will be missed.

I am going out West to the man of my dreams
To start a new life...a new beginning

The train pulls into the station...
I see him waiting.

I let go..I say a silent goodbye to my mother...
I greet my new husband...my lover.

Mary Ellen Malfitana

"To The Little Boy In The Blue Pajamas"

I stand in the doorway watching this
little boy, all damp from his bath with
his hair slicked back,
Sitting in front of the TV in his
over-sized blue pajamas, a baseball cap
perched sideways upon his head.
A teasing grin sprinkled across his face and I think,
Oh God,
Can I be a part of that?
Can I capture a pinch of the laughter and youth?
I feel as old as a crone, but still,
I crawl in on my hands and knees
to join him in front of the TV.
We wrestle and play the games I'd long forgotten.
Perhaps,
There is a child inside of me, an
adult inside of him.
I begin to peel the cocoon from in front of my eyes, and
Lo! I find that the child is me, and the adult is,
The little boy in the blue pajamas.

Marty Pairsh

A Modern-Day Tale Of Woe

Once upon a time in the valley of Cache
Lived a not-so-wise lady who wanted panache.

She asked for new clothes and a fancy hairdo
So the mirror would say, "The fairest is you."

She gave away all that was worn out and old
Then went to the store with her purse and her gold.

But alas—the new styles showed her ugly and fat.
Her colorless hair didn't match her red hat.

A magic wish brought Fairy Godmother near
"Please bring back my clothes that I love so dear."

Then off she went to the Good Will store
Bought back her own treasures for a dollar or more.

Although her prince shed tears of laughter
She and her heirlooms lived happy thereafter.

Marie Fuhriman Olsen

The Empty Nest

As I sit beside my window,
Locked in thoughts of yesteryear,
There is a gentle whispering in my soul
Just loud enough to hear.
The inner voice speaks to me of bygone
Sacrifices not new to me.
Or to any other mother who has rocked a babe
Or three upon her knee.
My basket of four eggs is hatched now.
Fledglings once, but now in flight!
My lonely heart remembers each little bird setting out alone
But, oh, so brave in its delight!
Do I really wish them back now
To the nest that's empty—but for me?
No, I think not — the season's past now for my wings hovering o'er
each sweet breast to protect them in the nest!
Let each young one meet its own challenge
Soaring on wings of God's Grace and Love.
With this in mind, I return to the present and am reminded
My children always have God's Love. I must let go and let God!

Peggy C. Sidden

A Symphony At Dawn

The summer sun, rising so early.
Looking eagerly to greet the day.
The air, moving softly, caressing the skin.
Everything smells so fresh.
Everything is so peaceful.

I want to stay here, absorbing
all the goodness that God has to offer.

Now the birds singing, quietly.
Wanting, so much to lift their praises
In full fledged song, but holding back,
Not wanting to disturb the peaceful stillness.

Now that breeze stirs the trees,
Adding to the quiet symphony.
I'm almost reluctant to move, or breath.
Afraid I'll miss one note of this beautiful symphony.

One day, I pray, this kind of peace,
This heavenly music, will be heard by all mankind.

Raymond M. Wright

That Special Place Called Home

When planning a trip we wait for the day,
Looking forward and preparing for a long stay.
We vision and picture, with joy so sublime
While dreams and imagination work overtime.

The first days are special in all that we do,
And the dreams of our stay are now coming true.
Then suddenly we know, we are staying too long,
And we feel our decisions are turning out wrong.

We start counting the days until our return
To the place we just left - with so little concern.
"Home Sweet Home" fills our heart as never before,
And is missed and desired each day more and more.

Seeing our friends and those close to our heart
Makes traveling and visiting such an integral part
Of life's joyous anticipation and adventure to roam,
But there's no place so sweet, as the one we call HOME.

Rebecca E. Milner

Easter Love

Love for the Savior, who died on the Cross,
Love for the Father who called Him above,
Love for each other when in distress.
Love for thy neighbor as thy self.
The splendor of Easter, exalted, so grand;
The blessed assurance that Christ did arise,
Did ascend into the Heavens to be at God's side.
God's love is shown after Easter passes; through
the flowers that bloom and the birds that sing
and it is Spring!
With God's love for us all and his creative things,
and we remember it so, for 'Tis Jesus, his son
and his magnificent love that guides us through,
each season that he brings, in the years
that have gone and the years yet to come.
HAPPY EASTER SWEET JESUS, AND
HAPPY EASTER TO EVERY ONE.

E. Lucile Eagleton

The Circle Of Life

An infant's first cry
Loving and bonding with family and friends
The Circle of Life begins.

A toddler's first step
Arms outstretched to embrace the world
Perseverance in quest of knowledge.

The teenager's mind
Like a bird in flight
Soaring to unknown heights
Society and peers play integral roles
In their pursuit of dreams and goals.

Adults passing through the maze of life
Each marching to a different drummer
New beginnings, happy and sad endings
Choices are made, prices are paid

Your role on the stage of life is swiftly
leading to the finale
Have you touched the world in a favorable way?
If not, do it today!
You may not have a tomorrow.

Teresa A. Mamunes

Dream Within A Dream

A star faintly meek, loomed silently in my sleep,
.... low and painfully sweet.
Faded memories, ages old, cascade softly,
.... within my soul.
Heavily scented magnolias, roses, honeysuckle, lilac,
.... butterflies, humming birds, bees.
Childhood scenes, echo the laughter,
.... the tears, of all our years.
Moon beams bursting through my thoughts,
.... casting shadows as I dream.
Snow capped mountains, bitter cold,
.... snowman laughing.
Under the star lit sky, a rainbow,
.... melting into the night.
Awaking from my dream, I saw the moon beams still,
.... while rustling leaves swirl,
I saw my dream ....
.... within a dream.

Richard D. Valentine

A Gift Of Hope

My gift to the world would not be,
made of materials you could see.
You could not touch it, but it would be there.
It would be felt and it could be shared.
It could be kept in your heart,
and would be felt whenever you part.
It would put a smile on your face each day,
and cause you to feel good in every way.
Everyone would have a little to spare,
and the world would be a little
easier to bear.
For love is the gift I would hope to give,
for without love one could never live.
In all the pain, strife and hate
the world brings,
Love can conquer all those things.

Stanley F. Buchmiller

Leave At Peace

Heavenly light in sky's dark night
Makes brightest stars with shame hide.
Ghostly shadows of clouds ride by,
'Tween earth and moon - dark and bright.

Warm current of spring come forth,
With moon's rays from sky to earth.
Dancing fairies 'mongst the trees,
Blond tresses blowing in the breeze.

Moon, as you travel 'cross the sky,
Are you happy with the world?
Have you knowledge of things gone by
Which no human can discover?

There's no record upon your face
Of things you've known on this universe.
Men are searching for even a trace
'Mongst rocks and dust from your face.

Will they not leave to quiet and peace
That heav'nly glow of your shores and peaks?
Must they forever stir and trace
Even dark sometimes hidden in your face.

Margaret J. Wilson

The Blessed Peace Of Freedom

The blessed peace of freedom rings for all
Mankind, but only as a dream; a world
Of fantasy where make believe competes
For equal time. We dream of freedom's peace,
But in reality, there is no peace.

The chains of slavery cling fast to our
Subdued reality. Afraid we move
As programmed robots do, unwilling to
Accept that peace and freedom figments are
Of our imagination's roadless dream.

Oh road of freedom's peace, how can we find
Your way? "Look to yourselves", the road will say.
"Don't seek me in the man made maps, but seek
Me in your hearts, the realm of our true Love;
The only hope of man's eventual Peace."

Love is the key to open Freedom's way;
And with it Peace will shine triumphantly.
We, Love must trust, if we will Freedom seek.
The chains will broken be, and Peace will fill
The lives of all Mankind eternally.

Oscar E. Rodriguez

My Father - A Successful Man

What is the measure of a man's success? What qualities must a great man possess?
Is it wealth or wisdom, talent or fame, that makes man a winner at life's earthly game?

I've known a great man for many a year, and slowly his greatness to me became clear.
The world knows not of him, his fame is not broad - but I'm sure that his kindness is known to his God.

His wealth isn't impressive by standards of man, but his heart houses treasures that angles think grand.
It's not what he's gathered while living on earth, but more what he's given that gives this man worth.

He's given to friends and family for years. His humor has made many smiles out of tears.
I've been lucky to know him - to have felt his warm ways, and to know he has loved me from my earliest days.

This man is my father - a rich man in love. He's given it freely like rain from above.
He knows it's a treasure worth more than mere gold. He knows if he gives love, life never grows old.

Success comes in giving, I finally can see. He's made himself happy by giving to me.
He's taught me the secret of success that is real. If I give of myself, life will be most ideal.

Theran Balmain

The Gifts We Gave Each Other

Long ago, as we remember, we gave our love so warm and tender.
Many days of joyous sunshine, silly things that make fun shine.
Days of happiness and laughter, deeper love forever after.

These are the gifts we gave each other.

They years went by, both good and bad, but somehow we made each other glad,
Glad we had each other to share the problems that we had to bear.
A sorrow divided in half the load and easier to travel the stormy road.

These are the gifts we gave each other.

Sometimes, when I felt depressed, I'd look at him knowing I was blessed.
He made me feel that he cared, he let me know my grief was shared.
If sometimes I had to cry he understood the reasons why.

These are the gifts we gave each other.

The years go by so very fast, what now is present soon is past,
But two in love can stand a lot because of strength within the knot
That binds them each to one another, a tie that's stronger than any other.

These are the gifts God gave to us.

Marie F. Endicott

The Boy

Trapped! There was no escaping it!
Loneliness flooded the room.
The boy was without a friend, and rejected by all who could see.
Sadness filled his heart and tears filled his eyes.
"Why!?", he cried, "Why!?" There was no answer. The room was silent and dark once again. All dreams seemed lost. Insanity seemed sane, and the boy was still.
Peace became him as the darkness evolved into light.
The beauty of life up-lifted him.
Thoughts swirled where the room was once empty. Each soaked in joy and purity.
His soul rejoiced in love. Kindness filled his being.
The positives now filled each pocket, and the negatives lived no more.
Confusion had resigned, and life was enthralling for the boy.
Suddenly, a voice called to him, "You seem lonely Boy!"
"I am not lonely," replied the boy. "I am but alone."

Lisa Sorensen

Suicide In Paradise

Surroundings are lovely.
Many old trees, smooth stones, and birds singing sweetly.
Grass so green; it's earth's little paradise.
The river flows soundlessly around her.
The sun so red.
To look at her from where she stands, an angel she may seem.
Though not an angel, she will take flight.
The rocks upon which she stands are smooth, but cold.
She feels the warmth upon her back, the cold beneath her feet.
She lifts her arm with the grace of a swan.
She bends, slightly, her knees and soars off the rocks.
Down she glides as I watch from afar.
Now she lies, silently, at the bottom of her paradise.
As I observe from my lonely place in this world,
I see a hand come down from the sky.
It takes hold of her hand and carries her soul to heaven.
"Peace, at last!" I hear her cry.

Vienta LeDoux

Rainy The Blind Girl

RAINY, her Name, the dark night rain and her house by the Lakeview matchless
Out of her teens, her pink swelling lips, a dreaming, snowy Mount Hood smiling
In the College cafeteria, I bought her a coffee to show a new friendship
"A beautiful day, isn't it?" I said without notice.
A quiet moment nothing echoed back.
Her black glasses and by her side in hidden, the leaning stick
Oh, is it true that she is in the black color, the color of the bottomless?
She is out of the light from the time she didn't have her age
Twenty years, countless days, how can she distinguish Black and White?
Use the tongue, the blue sea is not as the salty taste?
With her ears how can she watch the duck flying?
The beautiful smiling roses, the yellow apples early morning
The tiny ants walk slowly looking for the wandering insect?
Curiously I asked what does she take and her subjects for tomorrow?
"Computers, they're my classes, and to learn how to make a clay image"
Before leaving I asked if she would like to touch my face to see how fat am I?
And remember to make my statue "A man who likes to walk in the rain"
And don't forget to add some more mustaches
Ha ha ha, our voice be in her as the river roared up
on a nice day or on a stormy night!

Paul Le

Your Wedding Day

On your glorious wedding day
May the cloud on which you're gliding,
Stop only at happy places
To gather souvenirs from hiding.
Tuck these happy souvenirs
safely in your heart.
They will strengthen your love,
And give your marriage a completely perfect start.
And, if later on you might feel a tiny bit blue,
Take out those happy souvenirs
And place them in plain view.
And as you look and reminisce
The two of you together,
Your doubts and fears will
Float away as easily as a feather.

Myrtle V. Beck

Maybe In The Next Life

Maybe in the next life she said
Maybe in the next life I can love you
Maybe in the next life I can whisper things in your ear
That I want to say and you want to hear
Maybe in the next life things won't turn out so bad
She said.

That's such a long time I said
That's such a long time I said
But I can wait until then, to see your eyes again
And if you should die before I
I will remember your grave
I will remember these words you say
But it's such a long time
I said.

Maybe in the next life things won't turn out so bad
Maybe in the next life
It just can't be tonight
She said.

Scott Wesley Newsome

Sad Boy

A little boy five years old
me
by a low window
sat
gazing at huge snow flakes
dying as they kissed the earth
Sad boy
wanting to play with the flakes, his friends

but gone
Sad boy
Thanksgiving Day tomorrow

Whee!!
The snow will make it an "Over-the-meadow-

and through-the-woods" kind of Thanksgiving
snow flakes die

Sad boy
no snow
no Thanksgiving?

Sad boy

L. Joseph Lauterbach

A Mirror

I watched a pretty girl pass by,
Look at herself in a mirror nearby
Adjust her clothing her head held high,
Her image forgotten with only a sigh.

In God's holy book, it speaks of a man
Who does not obey God's blessed command.
He hears it or sees it, but never complies —
Just like a bubble in vanity flies.

But a man who looks closely to God's Perfect Law
That sets man free without a flaw,
Who's fully committed, his thoughts confirmed,
Puts into practice the things he has learned.

We must learn, remember, and practice God's Word,
Not ever forgetting the things we have heard.
A life lived daily in Jesus' control,
Reflecting His love is our constant goal.

Willa Eloise Jarrell

On The Day Of The End Of Time

On the eve of the day of the end of time, before the dawn, the muted melody of starlight will dissolve in the darkness. The tumultuous tuning of the instruments of the cosmos will cease. A stillness will abide; the baton will tap; and the embryonic eyes of Earth will turn to the lessening lunar light.

The concert of the universe will begin its unending crescendo.

All of the colors contained in the spectrum will flash to their final intensity. They will fuse to form a new, white light that will dawn on the day of the end of time, caressing the flesh of the Earth forever. A ring, like unto a rainbow, will begin to encircle the world.

The engine in a cloud will rise to his maximum revolutions.

The scent of Heaven and the smoke of Hell will seep through the bound'ries of all their dimensions to meld with the moisture of Earth. The mirror'd walls will fall; the curtains will be cut, recalling the veil at the crucifixion, confirming the letter to Corinth. The fountains of Heaven and the forests of Hell will be seen as the same as the Earth.

The sum of the number of every dimension will be counted as only nine.

At the turn of the Taro card, the mask of the healer will melt, revealing the face, and sealing the fate, of the dealer in death who'll be dealt his own reward. The Cup will be found in the Ark. The Light will eliminate dark. The Earth will be equal to Heaven and Hell. The circle will close with a spark.

The Riddle will run to rhythm and rhyme on the day of the end of time.

Ronald E. Henshaw

Our Yesterdays

Our youthful tomorrows are now yesterdays—
Memories of childhood to remember always.
Some cherished reflections of sweet dreams come true,
With a sprinkle of ashes from a nightmare or two.

But life's pathway is a mixture of setbacks and gain;
Each step of the way—some happiness, some pain.
Yet, who would blot out the hurts of each year
If they couldn't keep memories of things they hold dear.

By living it all, we're more humble and wise—
We look at the world now with understanding eyes.
If only when young, we had the wisdom of age,
Our life's story would have different words on each page.

Ruby Hubbard

To God I Give Thanks

Young man so tall with black hair and eyes of blue,
Met a beautiful woman named Luci and knew what he must do.

Marry me, my love, have my children for me,
Please, don't say no, mostly good times you shall see.

True to his promise, though hard times there were many,
They laughed, they cried, they scrimped and saved their pennies.

Throughout the years they faced pain, death and sorrow,
But continued to hope for a brighter tomorrow.

Good times and bad, their love weathered the storm,
She blessed him with five children, a family they formed.

Wiser man with eyes of blue, but now with hair of gray,
His wife more beautiful to him today, he knows what he must say.

Almighty one, on my knees I give thanks to Thee above,
For giving me this woman and family to love.

Leala Randall Tucker

Why Not Take Dad For A Ride?

Why not take Dad for a ride? Even if it's just for fifteen
minutes or so?
When you bring him home, watch, and see how his face will glow.

Let him know that you still care. For long after he is
gone these things will still be here.

Sometimes we long to help people in a foreign land and
miss the blessing by not ministering to those who
are right in your hand.

He may not know what others may know. But never be ashamed
to let the world know that he's your hero.
Jesus is still our friend. There is nothing that should
destroy that glow.
But when we have really learned to live, it's just about
time to let go.

Rosie Holmes

Poet's Wealth

I'll sing you a song of my treasure,
More precious, by far, than gold;
But unlike a wealth of worldly goods,
It cannot be bought or sold.
It is eyes . . . like the bluest of violets,
Lit up with a mischievous gleam.
And hair like the halo of angels
Seen in a heavenly dream.
It's a smile as bright as the springtime,
Which scatters the deepest gloom.
And laughter, like crystallized sunshine,
That echoes from room to room.
It is fingers as soft as rose petals;
They tug at my hair with glee.
And toes, like the pinkest of sea-shells
That whisper about the sea.
So . . . I hurry home from my labor,
Home, when my day is done,
Like a miser, to fondle my fortune,
. . . To play with my infant son!

Norma Shippy Meuer

Untitled

Dedicated to: Detective Luis Lopez, Manhatten South 3-10-93, And Always In My Heart

My Friend Lu,
More than a cop with a heart of gold, a friend
that would give his soul, while his hardships went untold.
A smile that stretched from his job to his home,
for his friends and his family, and those unknown.
He laughed and he lived to reach out to others,
I have fond memories of our befallen brother.
God says we are brothers, Lopez proved that to
be true, when you needed him he was there for you.
Remembering him makes me smile, that giggle in
his shoulders, "His Style".
He showed compassion and conviction for what he
believed, he strived till the end to keep our streets
clean, clear from danger for you and me, he fought it
head on fearlessly.
One man's courage, his strength, his dreams,
they live in our memories for us to retrieve.
Your Friend Lou, The Vazquez family misses you.

Louise Paolillo

Traces

Slowly we make our way up the coastal
Mountainside, a trail of red taillights
Twisting, like some irradiated snake,
Toward the summit of Loma Prieta,
Where redwoods point ominously upward,
As if suggesting an alternative route.

Etched against a backdrop of Pacific
Haze, these enormous trees diffuse what little
Light remains of the late October day,
Casting it with shadowless gravity
To intertwine with our crimson coils.

Near the summit we pause, momentarily
Transfixed by gyrating bands of blue and red
Light—reflections of primitive dance as wiper
Blades lash at descending droplets of mist.
Ahead, a deer lies thrashing in a pool
Of blood; so we wait impatiently until
Its removal, cursing this impedance
To progress as our tires track the final
Traces of its existence up the mountain.

Richard Thomas Cartoni

"Melting Pot"

Gregorian Chants...still recognizable echoes...,
Mozart's Prague Symphony...distant echoes...,
Beethoven's Fate Symphony...definite tones...,
Dvorak's New World...contemporary tones!

The Hiawatha Song, or, Negro Spirituals...,
Integrated American omnibus, symphonic portrayals,
Many nations' resolutions enhancing representations,
Co-existing in the system of free elections!

A new culture is in its formation,
Melting nationalities in transformation,
Preserving their colorful contribution,
Developing a new historical destination!

How fortunate, in the nuclear age,
Having free elections in a mature stage,
Based on a miraculous "Melting Pot,"
Broadly spread, yet free discussions abound!

May the United States of America
Bring free elections even in caustica,
May all humanity on this planet
Accomplish free elections in the nuclear world!

M. Synek

The Maid

Maggie O'Leary and Molly McCray
went over to visit old Mrs. McShay.
No sooner had they sat down to chat-
When down through the chimney there flew a black bat.
The bat flew about all over the room,
Until the maid scurried in bringing her broom.
The maid wielded her broom this-way-and-that!
Until finally she conquered the frenzied black bat.
The maid picked up the bat and carried it out of the house.
Only to hear Maggie shriek, "There goes a wee mouse!"
The maid picked up her broom, ran back to the house.
Hence, started her chase of the little gray mouse.
The mouse like the bat darted all 'bout the room.
Until the maid gave it, a-whack with her broom.
After all was over the maid served the three tea.
Whilst, they spoke of what happened and chuckled with glee.
But after Maggie and Molly had gone, said the maid,
"For them it might well have been fun."
As for me; "I'm just glad this damn day is done."

Wanda Warrenburg

A Focus On A Storm

The wind outside my window blows
My door is shut, I'll keep it closed

Her feathers wet, the night bird cries
She has to find where her baby lies

A tree branch snaps, on my roof it falls
The storm grows larger and I so small

I hear the rain, its drops flood the earth
Life is washed away, I smile and smirk

I feel safe in here under my floor
I can't ask you in, the world is no more

It's now suddenly quiet, I hear no rain
I have survived, I have the earth to gain

I must make my way to the window in the wall
I can see the night bird, her baby she calls

I have to open my door, I must get outside
Mommy won't look no more, her baby I did hide

He is flying now, back to his nest
I go to my bed in the floor, I too must rest

The window in my wall exists no more
My babe is gone, I go shut my door.

Lisa Chirigos

Summer Reflections

Today I sit in the sun.
My eyes close, my mind wanders.
Nature beckons to me.
The birds chirp, I feel a gentle breeze.
I reflect on a time past,
...Yesterday's memories, are today relived.
I think of you sweet man,
  of how it felt when we held hands.
I can see your face,
  as you slipped on my wedding band.
I can hear you whispering softly,
  like the ocean waves...
as they rush back and forth across the sands.
I can taste your kisses,
  as they caress my lips...tenderly, yet so grand!
I can smell your scent and feel the warmth of our bodies...
  as we touched and made love in the midst of summer.

In my memory, our loving was every bit as beautiful,
  as it would have been, if it were real.

Wendy L. Page

Hidden Love

As I lay here with you by my side,
My feelings for you I try to hide.
I want to tell you just how much,
I grow to love you with every touch.
How would you react if I told you how I feel?
Deep down in my heart my love is so real.
What I feel for you, you just don't know,
What you feel for me you never let show.
I keep asking myself is your love true?
Do you love me as much as I love you?
Our feelings for each other we manage to hide,
It's so hard keeping all this love inside.
Maybe one day our feelings we'll let out,
Until then my mind fills with doubt.
I know you're not at fault, we're both to blame,
Cause we're so much alike, we're both the same.
Just remember this and it's true,
Always and forever, I love you.

Sherrie Isenhart Wilkinson

Remember Always

When I think of you, my dear friend
My heart smiles with countless treasures.
Our years of friendship, oh, where did it begin;
I know its ultimate worth as priceless pleasures.

An entrusted gift from heaven, without measure,
Is what our kindred spirits endlessly share.
Angelic existences keep us safe and together,
A mere thought of your loss, I could not bear.

From the onset, when we spotted each other,
A rare union of loyal soul mates came forth.
The true love shared is that of a mother,
Forever enduring and of invaluable worth.

Forget me not in this lifetime, I implore,
For the resources of our faith are yours and mine.
Chances are, as time goes by, our endearment will explore
And perceive its sincerity of quality sublime.

Our friendship and love, a blessing not to fail,
Remains steadfast, unconditional, and pure from birth.
Through memories everlasting, our relationship shall prevail;
Remember always, God be with you, my special angel on earth.

Nita E. Clemons Pope

My Hero In Blue

Before I met you,
my hero in blue,

There was a void in my life,
an indescribable hole, where love, caring and warmth
had been replaced by pain and sorrow.

A hero in my life had suddenly gone,
and had left me bereft and inconsolable.

I never thought I'd have another special love,
so complete and soul-giving.
My angel was gone; where could I ever find another?

Then one day, very unexpectedly, I met a man in blue,
he showed me unconditional kindness and acceptance,

He became a friend, but evolved into a soul-mate,
I know my special love had found him,
and scheduled for us to meet at that place in time.

My man in blue turned out to be a hero,
not replacing, but enhancing and fortifying the memory,
of one special love, an angel, taken away,
but who lives on,

In my hero in blue.

Robin Fern Adelman

Unconditional Love

My love for you is rare and true
measured in purity, gentleness too.

Counting the moments until we're together
Then you will know my love is forever

My love grows for you with each passing day;
Rooted so deeply, it's here to stay.

I have been in love with you all my life
my hope is that you would be my wife

You alone are my dream come true
no one can ever measure up to you

I know that God has sent from above
The one who deserves my unconditional love

Steve Santos

Eternal Respects

We walked through an old graveyard today,
my little boys and I.
The six year old was daring and bold,
the older one, quiet and shy.

These people are dead, the little one said,
while running from stone to stone.
Only their bodies, I began to explain,
as I noticed how tall he had grown.

My older son read an inscription out loud,
where beautiful flowers were placed.
He was sad that a child had died so young,
so I stroked his warm, freckled face.

I called the little one to come hold my hand,
and we counted the stones we had read.
Four little blue eyes saw everything there,
while voices resounded in the place of the dead.

As we talked about death and love and life,
heaven listened in silence above.
For a moment, the hands of time stood still,
as eternity paid homage to a mother's love.

Lynda C. Walker

The Thornbirds Of April

Life must go on - it matters not how.
My place on earth made its presence known,
Like the Thornbird, as it take its place amongst
Those which are beautiful, though filled with thorns.
Having had my days of glory, now somewhat faded,
Unlike the Thornbird which lingers on, and on,
My heart beats no more!
Sunlit beaches, moonlit skies, heaven or hell, truth or lies -
April appears within the windmills of my mind!
What's left of my heart dies!
To have life but not live - can't anyone see?
A lonely Thornbird I wish not to be!
What good is a heart if there's no you - no me?
Forgive me, for the well has run dry -
Though the unforsaken Thornbird lives on. Why?
Perhaps at peace its thorns will unfold as soft petals
Leading me to cast my fate to the wind, my spirit free!
At last! I smile farewell to the April Thornbirds!
Tomorrow it will be just a memory - like you and me!

Shirley J. Bench

Depletion

Depleting energy as my soul runs away
My tears flow down the fluorescent shelf
As I dance on the smoke-filled floor
Tile strikes my eyes and quickly blinds
Heavy words hang from my soul's pillow
So I cry wooden memories of anguish and sorrow
You tell me to move on, but where do I go?
I've lost all knowledge and self-inclination
Self-control slipped out my window
Pain's doorbell won't stop ringing
The phone is busy, but you keep talking
So I feel insane and you laugh hysterically
It is all jut a game of numbness and pain
But the longer I sit, the sooner my sanity falls
These eyes spill from my face and shatter on the floor
You don't recognize me, my face is dark
And my pain fills my world completely

Kristie Brodfuehrer

"Father, God"

When I awoke this morning,
my thoughts were just of You....
I turned my mind in silent prayer
for strength and life renewed.

My prayer was brief and simple,
for family, friends, and me...
I gave everyone back to You
for safekeeping, and our needs.

Father, make me, hold me, mold me
into what my life should be,
So when others look upon me...
It's not me but YOU they see.
And, when I sing in church,
make the angels sing through me.

Take the work of my profession and use it to your will,
May it meet YOUR requirements for quality and skill.
Hold me, shape me, love me...I surrender all to Thee,
As I go out into the world, may I Your servant be.

Wanda J. Olender, nurse

Among Us

How differently we are the same,
neither with the will to fail nor gain,
no one can separate or save, the master within the slave.
And it be my will be done, that I shall conquer every one,
and they shall be no more.

Enter strength that comes within,
changing things that would have been,
not just to please my self.

To keep my life a simple course, power explodes with mighty force,
taking time to save our weakest ones.
The fire beneath me finally lit, from up out of darkest pit,
I come forth to fight them all.

Rituals from blood of man, whose hourglass turns to sand
that I might cast upon the sea.
To sprinkle stars across the sky, and bow to beckon moon so high,
thus his mighty power favor me.

Hand of dust and hand of ash, upon the winds a spell is cast,
let thy enemies be devoured by the moon.

Misty Gail Akers

When Starlings Long Have Flown

Weep not that the starlings left,
Never to return at their usual spring-mating time.

Fret not at the silence
As you scan the skies, listening for their song of chime.

Always they have come
To feast, to love, to swell
The numbers of their ranks
On riverbanks.

But in the last year of their coming
They perceived the message of your ending.
Gently holding to their bosoms
All your love
As they softly, sadly, for the last time
Flew away.

They will go on, the starlings, in another
Place, another clime
With your love for ballast,
As you change form to greet a different time,
A new dimension.

Phylliss Faircloth Stone

Remembering A Mother

It's over twenty years since she went away,
No goodbyes were said, just ending the day
Watching T.V. as eternal sleep came,
And took her life in a final claim.

Hardship she knew from time of youth,
An unwanted waif, that's the real truth;
Raised by others till age twenty-four
When a handsome lad came to her door.

He whisked her away to Happiness Lane,
And for a brief span, she enjoyed her new name,
But calamity seemed to be her cruel fate,
And happiness ended when she lost her fine mate.

Courage and strength were her virtues true,
Widowed now with much work to do,
Raising four little children by herself alone,
Trying hard to keep the wolf from the home.

She took a fine job in a restaurant near,
And rose above all anguish and fear,
She managed with God with much love in store
To lavish on loved ones till age 84.
No Mother could have done more!

Lucille A. Norwalk

A Broken Heart

But only a minute has passed and my love for you will always last.
No matter how long the time may be.
The memories of you, have endeared my heart forever.

How I yearn for the sound of your voice.
To watch you as you walk down the street.
The majestic rhythm of your body,
like a wave of wheat swaying in the breeze.

How I yearn to feel the warmth of you.
To touch from the inside out,
for us to join as one in heart and soul.

How can I tell you how much I love you,
when you only have broken my heart.

Ralph G. Conant

The Love Bug

Whether you're far or whether you're near
no matter what it may be,
I feel your warmth, your glow, even the touch
of your hand follows me.
Your voice I hear in the song of the wind
as the breeze hums by.
The rays of the sun speak your name, softly they
murmur with a tender sigh.

In the sunlight, moon, stars and ripples of the sea
I see your smiling face.
Even when raindrops tap upon my windowpane
I can feel my heart race.
On corners, streets and avenues as crowds
of people are passing by,
You vividly appear before me, touching my heart
with feelings—something I cannot deny.

At nightfall, when the world is fast asleep, you
walk into the shadows of my room.
I lie awake dreaming of you, humming a love song,
a sweet melody or a soft tune.
And as I slowly drift into a silent slumber
ending the night into another day's start,
I know tomorrow I'll see you again with every footstep I take
for the "Love Bug" is deep within my heart.

Roseanna Napolitano Lackas

A Dream Of Peace

Peace for mankind! The very dream of dreams!
No more conflicts, slaughters or unrest!
A great mantle of love upon the world.
Each human being caring for the rest!

No more barriers nor a stealthy flight
Made by those in peril and despair
In stormy days or through the dark of night.

Oh come you people, you who live in fear
Of deadly raids, prison or disease!
Unite and fight for the utmost aim:
A world of love, of everlasting peace.

Why fight each other for a piece of land,
For power, loot, ambition and the like
When there are demons raging among us
Of wars, deep misery, down-trodden rights?

Let us awake in a surge of hope.
Remember we are brethren, look ahead
And make peace our goal, our dream.
The air we breathe and our daily bread!

Rafaela de Gaona

My Inner Child

Come out and play - she beckons me.
No, no - not today, for I am far too busy with my work, if
I play now, I shall never catch up!
Work, work - What kind of a life is this? We never have any fun!
I continue to work, trying to ignore her, but inevitably,
every now and then she wins.
Not long ago, I was in a gift shop in Vermont, and my inner
child was completely -"out of control." The shop was full
of wind chimes and lovely music boxes. One never heard a
more delightful array of musical tones. We were the center
of attention. I naturally apologized for my inner child
and explained, the shop was so enchanting, she had taken
over and "we were out of control."
Everyone smiled and proceeded to encourage her - so,
"what choice did we have?"
In retrospect, I must confess, I can't remember when I/we
had so much fun. We were in our glory!

K. Waskewicz

A Dream We Forgot

We once had a beautiful love
No one could break the chains
One lonely dream stepped in to unravel the bond we made
We tried to keep it in our minds
Though how love is blind

We've made distance from the world
We just couldn't find
Alone we became, since we left that dream behind

Someone came to renew our hearts
To give us our dream a meaning
A place to bring out the words of kindness and truth

All we've made is an unpeaceful world
A lonely desire to live on

Though we'll make it work
We'll put our hearts together
We will find our dreams
A dream we've left behind
Which is full of love
Yours and mine

Linda Ann Willis

Endings Are Hard

Although endings are a necessary part of life
No one likes for things to be over and done
What we must remember is that first you must have beginnings

Not everything in life has to have an ending
Such as a person's friendship
There are a lot of stages to a friendship
But they never really have to end

You may take different paths in life
And go your separate ways
Not being together everyday
Yet knowing the friendship's still there

Memories keep the beginnings going
They make the endings not so hard...

Linda L. Jett

Masters Of Eternity

Theirs is Youth Eternal,
No withering by age.
Their song, having reached its highest note,
Goes on unfinished,
Unfaltering, forever undiminished.

Theirs is Life Eternal,
No turning of the page.
Their sun always at its zenith in resplendent glory,
Emblazoning forever
Their immortal story.

Theirs is Love Eternal,
God's gift most divine.
It transcends the stars to the Great Infinity,
Where they rest in Peace and Serenity
In the heart of Divinity..

Youth, Life and Love Eternal,
To the end of Time.
Their horizons as far as God can see.
Their Supreme Sacrifice will always be Sublime.
They are Masters of Eternity.

Stephen Grey

"I Can't Imagine Going Without Your Love"

I can't imagine a day without your charming smile or kiss
nor can I justly convey
How much I love your style
I can't imagine going a week
without your warm embrace;
Nor the absence of your pleasing form
that brings back true love, reminds me of the love we share together.
I can't imagine a lifetime without you by my side;
Or without the love I've known we had,
I can't imagine going without your love,
Since the last time I held you in my arms.
But one day of joy will surely come once again
And the torments which we felt before,
will fade away and hurt no more.
I can't imagine going without your love and understanding.
Nor can I imagine going without your tender kisses
I can't imagine sleeping without you,
Nor waking up without you in bed.
I just can't imagine going without you,
I can't imagine going without your love.

Louis James Ford

The Quiet Spring

Spring comes quietly
not knowing when it will show.
But waiting for the bareness...
to sprout some growth.
You wait and look
the signs are slow.
You wait for the blossoms
of things to show.
So quietly it comes
everyday you look.
Silently it grows
you might miss what took.
Then one day
all sprouts grow leaves,
all the flowering trees,
and everything you see blooming is free.
The array of colors
a show of life.
Spring brings
the sun's warmth... and the beginning of life.

Michael Horan, Jr.

Valentine

She gets up in the darkness and performs her noble deeds.
Not once has she neglected any of her family's needs.
A spoon of medicine for that cough, a bottle for the baby,
Let the dog out of the garage, then back to bed, just maybe.

Who is this Angel of the night? How does she operate?
We hear her order, "Tie those shoes!"
And "Don't you dare be late!"

She elbows her husband in the night, so as not to keep him guessing.
It's not that she don't want to go.....
It's HIS turn to receive a blessing!

Reward is great for those who serve.
She knows this deep in her heart.
So on she goes without complaint,
She's diligent to fulfill her part.

THANK YOU LORD for Donna,
This helpmate that I call mine.
She's known to me by many names,
but today it's.....VALENTINE.

Mike A. Davis

Life

Where have they gone, so many years
Not to be brought back, to correct, to change.
Just to live again in memory, the joys, the fears...
The fears gone, taken care of, the tears shed have long since dried.
Three score years, and ten, a lifetime spent.
How lucky for life, I am here, I have not been called.
Another ten years might I have, to correct, to change by chance?
To change years past...no, no a second chance we do not have
We can never go back and try to enhance
A life that is spent in no matter what manner or way.
We can live vicariously, ah yes, in our children, their children...
With no control, feel their joys, their pain...to be happy when I say
How lucky I am, how much to enjoy; in need, to extend my hand.
Thank you so to the powers that be
For making my late years so very grand...
Yes indeed, Grand, as in...grandmother!

Leanora Casey O'Donnell

Three Little Rose-Buds

Three little-rose-buds so lovely and pretty
Now they have grown to full maturity.
Each one in their very own, special way
Became a rose, day by day.
As I watched over and cared for every petal that bloomed,
I treasured each moment, morning, night and noon.
The most precious gifts that were ever given,
Were my three little rose-buds, from "God", in Heaven.
From these three lovely roses, other buds have been born,
To add to the beauty of a bush, though with thorn
In seasons of heat, cold, with bitter and sweet,
Only made their beauty stronger and more complete.
Now, from three little rose-buds, there has come to be,
A family, that's grown, to a beautiful tree.

Nellie L. Evans

Lament

Lie thee there, in thy pale sepulcher,
O dreams. Let the cypress wave
In motion soundless as an angel wing
Above thy silent grave, when softly,
Vagrant breezes steal and wan mists
Shroud me as I kneel. I could not know
That when I laid thee there, all beauty too
Would fade. That skies should lose their blue,
The flowers their souls, and melody
Become but toneless rhapsody...and yet,
In losing loveliness...tis thee I can't forget.
Pale lilies drooping in despondency and care
In thy hands lie dead. Despair
Alone lives on — Despair and I —
Since God decreed it be that thou shouldst die.
So lie thee there, dead dreams, yet not for
long alone...
As Grief must soon make need to carve
Two names upon one stone.

Rex E. Alford

America's Forgotten Minority

Everyone knows the story
of America's forgotten minority.
You have heard of how we lived in America,
long before the white men came
and wiped out all the game.
They looted our villages
killing men, women, and children

We made peace with some,
but others continued to wage war on our people.
We were betrayed by the American government.
They broke their treaties and forced us onto reservations.

Today this has all been forgotten,
and with it the traditions
that made our culture unique.
This is why we, the Native Americans, are
America's Forgotten Minority.

Summer Wesley

David

David, all great men
Name enduring and steadfast
Making sure he never has to be last
Hunger grows as you see a tramp
Again asking for food and a clean place of land
What is it
Now so grand
A home and piece of land
A bed yes, that piece of land

Mary Lou Zamora

"Are All The Children In?"

I think oft times when the night draws nigh,
Of an old house on the hill,
Of a yard all wide and blossom-starred,
Where the children played at will.
And when the night at last came down,
Hushing the merry din,
Mother would look all around and ask, "are all the children in?"

'Tis many and many a year since then,
And the old house on the hill
No longer echoes to childish feet,
And the yard is still, so still.
But I see it all as the shadows creep,
And tho' many the years have been
Since then, I can hear my mother ask, "are all the children in?"

I wonder if, when the shadows fall, on the last short earthly day,
When we say good-bye to the world outside,
All tired with our childish play,
When we meet the lover of boys and girls,
Who died to save them from sin,
Will we hear Him ask as my mother did, "are all the children in?"

Rozel I. Henn

The Inner Circle

In the woods is a circle of trees
of birches, clean and white.
But I see the black on the smooth bark.

A beam of sunlight shines down inside this circle.
And I, searching amongst the shadows,
can never seem to part the leaves,
so thickly are they grown.
The branches lock arms,
away from all others.

I dance around the circle,
hoping to distract the trees
and finally catch a glimpse
of what magic and light they hold, sheltered,
and too dear to share.

But I trip on a long, dark root.
And their leaves dance with delight,
blown by a wind that gently strokes their slender trunks,
yet tangles my hair,
and stings my face with a slap
that only a tear can comfort.

Stephanie Anne Santillo

Animal Crackers

Wild seeds blow off the North Coast, inland, Rite
Of Buffalo Ghosts roam wheat fields by mute moonlight,
Stampeding under bulbous storm clouds, chased
By chastised Poltergeists - knobby-kneed ape legs
Hinged to horses in Apocalyptic Flight. Crazed

Beast Eaters gimp upright scavenging along
The edges of the Slaughterhouse. Market Aisles
Of cello-feigned flesh smother Elsie's denial -
Haunted moans drifting off a stellar spangled prong
Till electrode shock waves end her perennial cries.

Squeals of pork sustenance reverberate
Unto an ebony slate frosted with blank
Stars - eerie sound, hogs hankering not to die.
The Scythe sparkles above glazed eyes widened
With fear - the pigs writhe to their apodictic fate.

Beneath a Midnight Sun sea-pups get skull-bashed.
The Aurora Borealis casts stroboscopic shadows
Of skinned carcasses scattered in the crimson snow.
In the North Land hearts freeze to stone,
Seal tears' rain, then turn to icy paths.

Karl Oleksak

Treasure

We treasure our pursuit
Of gold . . . Of love . . .
We treasure the treasure
Secondary sometimes
Treasure ourselves and our right to be . . .
Could we only know We Are
Could we only Will To Be
Satisfied.

Susan D. Tausch

"Love"

Is respect and good memories that become a part
Of good in an open heart
It's like feeling music in your veins
The sounds we hear in falling rains
A smell of beauty in a rose
Warmth you feel from your head to your toes
A cry of a newborn
Smell of food in the early morn
That little dance, from a little pup
The friends you knew growing up
A special squeeze when absent for awhile
That different look, that special smile
Love is like sunshine, throw in a few stars and
a breath of fresh air.
These things of beauty, you see,
you feel you treasure, will always be there
All things that are free
A love from the man above,
gave to you and me.

Nicholas Kavaya

Life And Love

Life is yours in a beautiful package
  Of gossamer love and bows.
Be humble, rejoice, you give, you receive,
  Watch as in beauty life grows.

Love basks in the light of its own reflection.
  Helps brothers down the line.
Life would be nothing with nothing to love.
  Like a world with no sunshine.

And if from somewhere comes the mercurial,
  Mercenary, haphazard things,
Life can be fleeting as summer in sun,
  Fragile as butterfly wings.

But life grows in strength where love abounds
  And tries in true manner to please.
Creation was formed through the eyes of love.
  Can man not be one of these?

Laura Lyons Martin

"Cherokee Chief"

Among his people, he stands brave and tall.
Mighty and powerful, of them all.
Leader, warrior of his Cherokee tribe.
From no white man will he except a bribe.

His headband full of victorious feathers.
Won from battles in fields of heathers.
Pioneers frightful of his arrow and knife.
They run for shelter to save one's life.

He mourns for his brothers whom are dead.
All from whites who shot with lead.
Forced to move with his Cherokee band.
Walking miles to reservation land.

Sarah M. Sinclair

A Kelly Princess

A Kelly princess, Grace, did crown her brow
Of Highness white, tiara-braid as dawn.
Each strand of hair upon her head is how
Aristocrat becomes the daughter-born.

Her hair, a silken crown of shimmery thread.
The eyes are blue as topaz stone so bright.
A skin of pink pastel and roses bred
And lips with smile of pink and pearls of white.

Bright taffeta of silk and purple sheen
With v-neck deep the length of pearl as gem,
But slips of silk too small they are unseen;
They do not show beneath a heavy hem.

The Kelly child did reign with Rainier, Prince
of Monaco, Serene, her death, we wince.

Sandra A. Merlini

Imprisonment

He sits in the third story window
of his family's house
and he relives days passed
the loud rattle of war
the cries of anguish
his cries of anguish
the chair he sits in
seems to be his liberator
but in reality only a jailor
they are just parasites to him now
they cling to him, burdening him
in every attempt to excel
they used to be his, now he's theirs
the people stare at him with an unbearable look
of sympathy and misunderstanding
his twisted mind can hardly comprehend
he can't use them now
he lost his legs.

Rebecca Husband

A Venus-Lyric

Sing now with the help of Zeus' daughters,
Of Time's inadvertent child born on waters
Of bloodied froth and pulsing waves of foam and unthought gestures
Of sickled fate overthrown, in pieces, of a potency which wrought
Hers.

To She, the source of the poet's "lovely evil" and whispers,
Sentient smiles, delicious deceits of pandoric pleasures: girls'
Fecund advantage unlost by the chthonic castration of Heaven,
Borne by poseidean realm to new patriarchal shores quite barren!
To She, eternal faith in wish-fulfilling falling-stars, cometic ecstasy-
Rent in violence from Her starry source, in blind rage cast carelessly,
Into the shadows, over the shoulder of Time; beyond Sein;
Beyond Zeit; in filial flash of envy and chronic benighting light;
With metaphysical surety and mystically assureable treatise:
The plenipotentiary power of sweet longing. O Aphrodite-
Philommedes!

A Serpentine Seductress, Minoan Mistress of virility and eco-stability:
All paleolithic, thought parthenogenic, progenerative ability-
O Alpha-beginning of the sole significant human act,
Omega-end of all transcendent signifieds, behind Time's back!
Rise as Sign & Authoress, Text & Audience of primal-scene preliterate,
In non-linear (-A or -B), theogonically pure, ontologically sure,
alphabet!

Steven L. Reinhart

Fiftieth Anniversary

Fifty years is not so long when you speak of history.
Of mountains, kings or planets, or things
of mystery.
But fifty years since you have said, with
a nervous voice, "I do"
When you could count on someone dear,
to guide and comfort you.
When you start down life's highway you
think of things as being gay.
Then there are problems to confront us, and
bills we have to pay.
We may try each other's patience, and think
of love each is devoid.
We learn the things we should accept, and
what we should avoid.
But most of all, Oh Lord, we ask forgiving
for us shall be no task.
Just sharing and loving and being there,
Is proof to me that you really care.

Minnie Palmer

My Lover Has Gone

My love was a beautiful symphony
Of orchestral rhythm and harmony.
My love lifted me to heights of ecstasy
A lifetime of supreme joyous, buoyancy.
If only I were a kind, wise teacher
Or a moving, believing - preacher,
I'd be more able to explain the soft touch
The thrill of why it meant so much.
The pat on the back, the smile, the wink
Indicating I was lovelier than I think,
Taking my side when I felt fitful
Ever pronouncing, "You're wise and blissful."
Pretending I was right, even when strong.
Believing in me, making me feel strong.
Love is my game - altho' everyone plays,
To prove there is self worth in our ways.
I loved the kisses and the soft caress.
It warmed my soul, and I was blessed.
I miss my lover; now he has gone,
But memories I cherish - forever long.

Louise Mitchell

All Of Our Yesterdays

The days were full of laughter and love, as we learned
Of rapturous youth, each the other; to search, and feel, of
Thoughts portrayed, that someday we would not seek
Of furtherous adventure, but think upon -
all of our yesterdays!

My passions climbed high, as an ivy walled tower and
Sweet thoughts gave vent to your smile; what careth more that
Work was lost, as dreams were formed of that, yet to come,
And floatatious mists gave way to thoughts of -
all of our yesterdays!

Sunshine fell and hung o'er shimmering brooks, as we
Joked and ate of life's happiness; yet, knowing it was but
A momentary phase and someday we'd have cause to look
Back, and remember of this, and along with -
all of our yesterdays!

Sweet youth gives way to respected age to rock and
Dream and remember all that was, but ne'er can be again, only in
Memories. But, to capture those loves and kisses and moments
of
Ecstasy, we need simply to rest and relax, and close our eyes,
to envision
All that was, and could be again, but only in
all of our yesterdays!

Robert H. Wyatt Sr.

The Robe And Crown

Course. The golden gates are just inside
Of that beautiful home.
That light will be Jesus
When we get to our new home
That light will shine forever
It has the streets of gold
That we can walk up on if we are ready to go.

Jesus has the robe and crown
He is coming back soon to gather up his jewels.
And take them home with him.
Get ready people to receive your robe and crown
We don't want to be left behind
While they go flying through the clouds

Oh what a beautiful sight
Up there in the robes of white.
After we have walked with Jesus and seen the light
The gates of pearl up yonder
We can walk up on and see our loved ones,
Who have made it home.

Truda M. Little

Highland — My Oasis

I stand amid the historic ruins
of the school I dearly loved.

Deserted, lonely, scarred,
a stone building and a church,
half hidden by nature's untrammeled growth,
remain fragments of Highland's former self.

Victim of inevitable change,
Highland felt forced to close its doors.
Gone were the dairy and the farm,
the school and the hospital, too,
And the two dormitories built of wood
soon pillaged by the few.

In this secluded valley framed by Appalachian hills,
the villager's pillage left a ghostly void.

I feel a chill, but old memories bring warmth:

Endowed by Highland's gifts to me sixty years ago;
Inspired by spiritual guidance that here I came to know;

I leave this hallowed place with thanks and unfaltering love,
Remembering that His watchful eyes looked on me
from above.

Ruth V. Fierros

The Joy Of Living

I've had a good life, there's been moments
of trials, hardships and strife;
but overall I've had a good life.

I've had a joyful time, just living and
enjoying this life of mine. There's been
a few stones here and there, but nothing
to mention or cause me to care.

I've found my life to be exciting but yet tamed.
Filled with promises and monetary gain.
But not enough to make me rich or ignore a
simple pain.

I've had a good life, though there's been
some ill health, I've found the joy of living
to be my greatest wealth.

I've had a joyful time, filled with pleasures
that were so divine. I've found the joy of
living and the pleasure is all mine.

Terry A. Harrison

Voice

I heard you in the back of my brain, telling me all those lost secrets
of tomorrow.
Guiding me to where I should've been, instead of where I was.
How the hell you knew everything, I couldn't guess.
But, I heard you in the core of my soul,
Whispering answers to my memorized prayers.
Sharing stories of lost lovers and prophets whose only crime was
desire

How many times have I heard that sweet harmony of merger tempting
and teasing my agony?
So much talk, talk and talk. Wearing me down, wearing me out.
Were you mine or my imagination?

Your voice, promising me all I'm supposed to have. I deserved the
best from you.
You made me want those beautiful rhymes, because I knew they were
designed for me.
Starving. Hungry I am. Thirsty for your poetry of passion in my ear.
Turning me over and under. Turning me on. Driving me past the point
of...

Words. Lead me past compromise.
Climbing worn out rainbows of possibilities.
Explanation. I could do anything.
All because you said so.

Mari DePorres

Reflection

Tonight I heard the distant squall
of waves surging upon rocks
and the call of the mopoke
from the depths of a darkened bush.
I heard the swishing of skis
traversing lonely trails
and the whizz of a fishing line
unfurling from the reel to plop
at random in the lake.

Tonight I watched an old emu
drink beer from the glass of a guest out west
and saw the sun rise over the Port
spreading magnificent rays of amber and rose.
I looked to the horizon and remembered
gipsy life in a caravan by the beach;
cold toes and noses under cover of sleeping bags
and blankets on a rack for a bed.

Tonight I touched a heart on a fine silver chain
and thought I'd feel nothing
so grand again.

Robyn Drake

Unborn Thoughts

It lies there and begins to think,
"Oh boy, I just can't wait to wink."
Its not formed body is curled in a ball,
"Will I be short or very tall?"

"I'll bet she's very pretty, we'll see.
Just like her I hope I'll be."

"This cord connects me to her ya' know?
I just can't wait to play with my toes.
Or feel her soft hands on my tiny nose."

"She may not keep me but I think that's bull.
My love for her is unconditional.
If my lips were developed I think I'd smile.
But I guess for now I'll just rest awhile."

It ends its thoughts and soon after dies.
For the mother was deaf to her unborn child's cries.

Nansi Kelly

Fate

I walked the roads so all alone, overturning many a stone.
Oh the roads so full of holes, all so deep, dark and cold
I've searched for one-one true lead, in faithless times
I'm in need.
No one to give a hand, treacherous faith of unholy land.
Life built trenches with no shroud, a heartless aim can't be proud.
Out of depths from soul's despair, a layered hope could declare.
Came the source of worthy know. Inside my heart I take your soul.
O'er the crevasse so dark and deep, dredge the pit with dare to weep.
An empty heart can't fill a hole, shattered faith can't be bold.
Yet I walk through this land, while my faith's covered in sand.
I falter life of my own, unjust to all; be it known
Alone shall I forever be? Penalties I owe; only me.

Linda Wright

Reflections

Reflections of a time long gone...reflections of an old love song. Reflections of an old lover's kiss shrouded in an April mist.

Reflections of youth now long past...time well used, but never seemed to last. Reflections of family always ready to teach, still a young girl's dreams always just out of reach.

Reflections of people, and times, and deeds... memories where grown from all those seeds.

Sylvia Hendrix

Two Cuban Rafts

I saw them from my car window,
On a warm and sunny day.
Like a monument they stood there,
Those two Cuban rafts.

Once filled with a cargo of people,
To land alone on a beach.
A fish out of water, they seemed to me,
Those two Cuban rafts.

They were a symbol of their mission.
Made of junk, yet standing proud.
It's sad, thinking about the journey of,
Those two Cuban rafts.

"What happened on your voyage?" I asked.
"Where are your weary pilgrims?"
They didn't say, they just stood and stared,
Those two Cuban rafts.

I will never resolve this mystery.
They kept no logs nor journals.
The secret will remain forever, with -
Those two Cuban rafts.

Temple Anne Hughes

Heavenly Highway

Dear Love of Mine, I'm giving you a star for a Valentine!
Not in Hollywood's Walk of Fame where busy feet pass to and fro
o'er some once-remembered name, while dust and trash
the wind does blow 'til time and memory bring decay,
and stars below crumble and pass away.

No! There is a Heavenly Highway in the velvet dome on high,
where morning stars and evening stars forever light the sky.
The brightest star I chose, and gave to it your name.
I shared with it the lovely things you've done,
the honors that you've won, that brought you earthly fame.
Your Star! For you, it seems, ever brighter it gleams!
There, no earthbound feet have trod; only Saints and Angels
walk this ever-lasting Highway, belonging to God.

Zoila Conan

Reflections

As evening falls, I sit alone and ponder
On all the wondrous beauty God has made.
The brilliant glow of red-top in the meadow
The softest green, beneath the maples shade

The age old apple tree with fruit well laden
The golden grain with full heads standing tall
Awaiting for the coming of the reaper
Before the autumn rains begin to fall.

The dark brown cat-tails standing stately by the roadside
Hold black birds as they sing their roundelay
The goldenrod heralds coming of the autumn
To replace the lovely splendor of the May.

The lovely black-eyed Susans nodding
To each and every one who passes by,
The bright blue sky with fleecy white clouds dappled
And I wonder - are there riders in the sky?

And when my normal growth on earth has finished
And my long awaited night is drawing nigh
Will those riders and my loved ones come and meet me
And guide me to those mansions in the sky.

Lula Rud

That Old Detroit

I miss that old Detroit River smell down by the docks
On shiny days where long, proud freighters inched along
Groaning with grain or heavy ore. Squinty-eyed, we tried
To read their names while munching lunch-hour chow.
I miss those far-off fog horns growling their eerie elegy
And the mournful wail of true train whistles deep into
The night - no sissy sounds like now.

I miss that old, stately Belle Isle Bridge and ten-cent
Ferry rides and that gem, Belle Isle, with mounted police
And mammoth statues, the flower house, the fish aquarium,
The band-shell music on summer-soft nights, the Scott
Fountain with dolphins and lions and turtles spouting water
Streams in technicolor at dark. And canoeing the canals
In summer-time and ice skating them come winter.

I miss that old East Grand Boulevard and Mack where I was
Educated at Eastern High on week days and church farther
Down on Sundays with Mom and Grandma and Brother Bill.
No loud smells on East Grand where magnificent magnolia trees in
Rose and white strutted splendidly all along that charming boulevard.
I miss that old Detroit where I cried my primal breath.

Lucy Stevens Toles

Normandy Watch

Did you see the crosses marching
On the coast of Normandy?
Battalions shrouded in white
Winds ripping their ranks
Sentinels marching from the sea
Soldiers in perfect lines of marble symmetry

Did you hear the clicking crosses of bravery?
Brittle bones of stone regiments
Ghostly divisions marking time
From the rain-swept beaches of Normandy
Infantries scaling the shelled vertical cliffs
Bellying across the pock-marked rifts

Did you feel the ground tremble
On the coast of Normandy?
Waves of advancing crosses 1,000 abreast
Relentless comrades in battle
Their stone faces etched in distress
Marching, marching from the West
On eternal vigilance quest.

J. H. Bolton

Where Were You?

Darling, where were you? Where did you go,
On the night that was dismal and filled with snow?
You asked me to meet you by the old oak tree,
You had something important to say to me.

I remember I'd waited for such a long time,
When finally the midnight church bells chimed.
I heard the snapping of twigs on the ground,
Footsteps came closer as I turned around.

The knife was sharp, the steel was cold.
Who is this stranger so vicious and bold?
I whispered your name as darkness closed in,
My life raced before me, I grew dizzy and then...

My spirit was freed the following day,
My soul as restless as hounds at bay.
I went to see you, but you were not there.
All that I found was your room so bare,

Yet, wait! I look upon the bed,
There lies the knife, still stained with red.

P. J. Bruton

Misplaced

It is peculiar to see him here,
on U of L's Belknap campus.
He seems out of place,
with his neon green cap, brown sweater,
and red and black plaid shirt.
It's too warm for a sweater.
Maybe he studied here years ago: political science or biology.
His shopping cart with the blue Kroger's handle
Squeaks as he pushes it by my sunny bench.
White, yellow and brown garbage bags hang from his mobile home,
stuffed so full I fear they might burst
and vomit their unknown contents upon my feet.
Fellow students walk by. Some stare. I stare.
A pregnant woman and her talkative friend stroll by.
They do not even acknowledge his existence.
He stops and looks around.
Seeing nothing of value,
he adjusts his cap and
moves on.

Stacy Diane Elliott

You

I only see you
once in a while,
But in all my dreams
I can see your smile.
Every night as I lay down
and look in the skies,
The sparkling stars remind me
of your gorgeous eyes.
Ever since you left me
on that dreadful day,
I really didn't know if I
could make it that way.
It wasn't your fault you had to go,
But you really thought that I should know.
I'm finally learning to live without you,
Even though you know I don't want to.
One day I hope that you'll come back for me,
I guess I'll just have to wait and see.
But until the day that you finally do,
I want you to know that I really love you.

Kelli Salers

The Final Chess Game

The new dawn has fallen upon us
one of evil, one of hate, one of death.
God send your angels to protect
us for we know not what to do and can't rest.
It is taking control of our minds,
it is a black fog as our eyes can see
Is this a sign, is this the end? Tell us Lord, if we may win.
For now we are on the chess
board one side good, the other evil
How must we fight, we haven't any weapons,
we haven't any lines, my father show us a sign
Their chess pieces are moving faster,
they're coming our way, they have knives,
they have spears, they don't have anything to say.
Our pieces get down on their knees and pray to you Lord.
Then the angels come down from out of the sky,
falling down on us singing sweet lullabies
The evil is now scared for they know not of this; they run
but are caught and now will not be missed
For the evil is dead and the final chess game is over

Virginia Snowden

The Neighbor

"Hi, Neighbor, how are you?"

"O.K., I guess, feeling a little blue."

"Feeling blue on such a day!
One of the most beautiful this month of May."

"Oh, I know. It's not the weather.
A visit or two would make me feel much better.
I have family, you know, but the phone
never rings.
Everybody's too busy with so many things."

Now, Neighbor is gone. She was very nice.
Her family visited once or twice.
She's at the cemetery; a stone marks her grave.
The Lord called her home.
She has the companionship she craved.

"Good-bye, Neighbor, you were nice to know.
This visit is brief...I just have to go!"

Muriel M. Gregor

In His Words

What is a poet if not an interpreter of the soul
One who takes a broken heart and restores it to a whole
Sometimes they take a lonely wretch and make his life complete
With just a simple little verse that is easy to repeat
A poet can take the hurt out of pain and sorrow
If you don't have love of your own, in their words you can find
some to borrow
At times the poet is the loneliest person of all
He can only gather strength from his words you care to recall
You think of him as a romantic, with his words full of rhyme
You think his life is full and happy all of the time
There is much more to a poet than just some words on a page
He is much more than just some actor on a stage
In his life your happiness is his will
Never thinking of his own, his tear is the last to spill
He strives for recognition in every word he writes
Just waiting for your smile in his poetry he recites.....

Luwonna Rae Gates

Traces

Alone in a place we used to call our own. I look in places and only find traces, of happy times now gone.
It takes me to a time of fulfillment, and utter delight. The fire place that burned strong and bright, the feeling of holding you just felt right. Soothing music in the background. Can it be you I see, through my tears? Please dance with me. Traces of your smile, that brightens for miles.
Traces of the smell of your hair, the smell of your skin. But only for a moment, now swept away in the wind. How, when, if ever, will this heart mend? Loneliness surely must be a sin. I close my eyes, and in my dreams I'm sure to win. There we're together again, side by side; so satisfied and full of pride.
Till I wake, I reach for you, you're not there. I lie there and stare. I even swear, DAMN! Why can't it be? Be, me with you, you here with me, please set me free. Lonely hearts, should never have been made to be.

Mary Beasley

An Old Abandoned House

Old House, alone you stand with cherished thoughts tucked away,
Only you and time are left with memories and decay.
How like the aging creaks within your walls,
Resemble child-like steps echoing through the halls.

The door is slightly open elements have sneaked into your realm,
Summer leaves and earth danced in but now there's not a sound.
The rain searched for holes to find a place to rest,
And each new drop upon your floor is met with fond caress.

I stole again at eventide to your world of blissful peace,
A puff of fur was scurrying around his storage to increase.
The light was growing dimmer chimney swallows were overhead,
After a day of playing in the breeze they were tired and went to bed.

The trees are trying to protect you with arms of love extend,
Their leaves like enthusiastic ballerinas are entertaining again.
There is a steady whisper and great laughter of the wind,
Rehearsing old fashion songs that were heard often from within.

Old House, if you could speak what would you like to say?
"I would say, I am happy, I have memories of yesterday".
"But yet, I am seeking for someone sweet and kind",
"With plump little kids to romp and play and stay till the end of time."

Kathleen Purdum-Smith

What You Mean To Me

This is what you mean to me;
Open your heart, mind, and soul, clearly you will see.
With you in my life I am spontaneous and emotionally free,
I truly feel complete as can be.

I have someone who's love is honest and true in my life.
You have broken my defenses, opened my heart, ended my strife.
For our future I do kneel and pray,
That nothing will take our love away.
To fulfill your life, I wish to stay.
Far from your heart nor mind do I wish to stray.

If the worse may happen, and we walk separate ways,
I would be engulfed by sorrow, like a coyote's cry, at the moon he does bay.
My life would be torn, emotions cold again,
Without you I am empty, there is only my heart's pain.

This is what you mean to me;
By your side I need to be.
As my voice does fade, I say to thee;
You are my everything, I hope you do see.

Robert P. Summa Jr.

Unaccepted Attraction

Long hair pulled back in a ponytail,
Or a tuft of hair riding on white sides.
Mysterious tattoos in nearly secret spots.
Unlaced, oversized tennis shoes.
A t-shirt with a message.
A stud
boldly pressed through an earlobe.
Home on a tiny crowded street.
A job without formal education.
Too much religion, not enough religion, no religion.
Rumors taken for truth.
Dysfunctional family.

Nothing of the kindness.
No reverence for the gentle ways.
Not a thought about goals.
Never an opportunity to see or hear.
Never considering her feelings for him.
He glistens like Forbidden Fruit.

Kim M. Grabowski

No Miracles For Me

Unkind moments never appear to fade, stray
Or go away, continue day after day.
Passing into years, initiating fears, adding, subtracting
Multiplying, applying pieces together, unravelling, repeating
Disarranging, arranging, thoughts for perfect order
Achieved by a higher power.
Toiling, waiting for that Miracle which occurs
Perhaps once in one's destiny, without thought
As that unexpected smile, then
Seeing the butterfly, a symbol of hope
Clothed in a white dress, flying gracefully
Performing as a ballerina in the ballet
To and fro, around me and down
Touched my toe, flew to go
Leaving that thought of hope
To capture and hold, standing bold
Keeping a spark in hearts, enough to
Light the wick of a candle.
Miracles can happen, not predicting when
Through known or unknown passage.

Mildred E. Mayberry

Patty Two

I don't recall just how it started,
Or just who was wrong or right.
But judging by all standards,
It was one hell of a fight.

Our words came fast our tempers flared,
Our thoughts we did not mask.
Our voices loud our hate avowed,
And a dish she firmly grasp

With all her might for in her plight,
The only thing to do,
Was to smash this dish,
And gain victory in this fight.

After all our words and their meaning blurred.
She then began to cry.
And just as quick she was in my arms.
Now why we fight now why?

We love each other dearly.
And we sob, and hug, and kiss and mend.
And so we live, and love, and care.
Until we fight again.

Norman Scriven

That Night

Why did you hold me that night on my bed?
or kiss me goodnight when there was nothing
more to be said. Tell me you want me and then
let me go, especially when you knew that
I wanted you so. I don't know how
your mind works, or what your friends said,
but you hurt me so much sometimes I
wish I was dead. But don't you worry
you were not the first one to tell me you care.
Did you think I was dumb? You stole my
heart and ran as fast as you could so
you wouldn't get caught. Now I know you
are not the love I have sought. So just
leave my heart, you once treated with care
and maybe I can rebuild these few feelings
you've spared. But there's still that one question
that runs through my head. As you turn
and walk away - please tell me -
Why did you hold me that night on my bed?

Karen McDonald

We Are Held Accountable

We may not be responsible for the USA
Or the condition the whole world's in
But we are accountable for a portion anyway
We can battle the conditions in our area, and win

I know some of us may be a little blind
We wouldn't know just where to start
I'd like to help you if you don't mind
Work on yourself, that's the first part

Forget about your feelings, do what is right
Submit to God, He knows what to do
You've come out of that dark into the light
When God's in control, He'll see you through

Start with a hello, maybe a little smile
Help sponsor food, clothing, and finances also
Just getting started, you've traveled a mile
Love started with us, and we made it grow

Ruth E. Moore

"De Profundus"

Despair, unshared and nondescript,
Overspreads fragmented hopes
Held in a hiatus, incommode,
'Neath savage stars.

Extant thoughts that grind gray souls,
Disarranged and out of ken,
Importune without emphasis
Delving to an unappeasable involution.

Antipathetic by instinct.
Incorporeal lions roar in savored stillness
Traversing back roads of overborne beliefs
Toward a dark deprecation.

Shadowed by amorphous clouds,
Unleashed heads, with eyes unmoved,
Refuse nepenthe
In the taking of self.

Bleared by unwept tears
Plashing in purposelessness,
Mischancing minds, listening for oracles,
Die-lost to a legacy aloft in phantom's flight.

Kenneth A. Elvin

The U.S.A. Band

You all are wrong!
Our country is not as bad as you say.
We have so much
And all you do is cry and complain.
Stand up for yourself
And do what is right.
Earn what you want.
But don't expect it overnight.
Nobody owes you anything.
Not the government or anyone else.
You are responsible for your own actions,
And you should only get what you deserve.
We live in a place which God made for us;
Full of beautiful blue waters, a sky, and green land.
So stop crying and complaining
And get up and join the band!
Make the best of what you have and receive
Which is still so much more than some have
in other countries of land.

Shannon Minor

Yucca Sky

As twilight falls and cloud's pass by,
our land seem's some how changed.
The mountain's stand with their red and gold,
like sentinel's of the range.
The color's change, the clouds reflect,
the shadows go creeping by, and the desert
plants as we know them here, stand out
against the sky.
When old St. Nick was here today, he did
view this sight and sigh.
As the reindeer pulled his sleigh away,
I could hear just one reply.
"When God created this scenic place,
he was thinking of you and I, so peace
be with you my dear dear friend and enjoy
our Yucca Sky."

Merry Christmas And A Happy New Year

Rock Davidson

Tomorrow?

We stand alone in a raging tempest,
Our memories causing us to bleed.

Our dying souls are swept away
By the arrogance of our mortal needs.

The once bright light of life now shuns us;
Darkness takes the place of sun.

Our eyes now only see destruction;
The damage wrought by man is done.

Frightened cries torn from our lips.
Hearts shedding blood from a thousand whips.

Screams of terror, fire like pain
Would only stop, if the light came again.

But, by the light we've been repelled.
Man now lives on a rocky shell.

Insecticides, pesticides, famine and war.
The green planet is gone. Mother Earth is no more.

Lost and alone, children roaming the land.
Left only with sorrow, the legacy of MAN?

Ronnie J. Fletcher

A Little Prayer

A little prayer you should say today to keep your woes out of the way.
First, you start with something small.
A bright blue sky that surrounds you all.
Then you pray for sunshine and rain.
To let his love grow and knowledge you will gain.
Pray that your family is safe and sound, like a shooting star that kisses the ground.
Last you should do is thank heaven above for all the blessings he gave to you with love.

Theresa Ann Santos

Our World

Let's go walking, look but no talking
Over there do you see
A man dying, a child crying
Drugs she's buying
Bullets are flying
Duck down the alley
Oh my God there's Sally all beaten and broken
Her husband did this she said
It's a wonder she's not dead
Rape and Murders, Hit and Runs
Will nothing be done
Air pollution, is there no solution
Gangs a running, Kidnappers a snatching
Rivers overflowing, Fires a burning
Wake up Humans even the Earth Rebels
Stop the Violence before it's too late and it excels
We made this mess, it's up to us to clean it up
PRAY, show LOVE not hate, HUG not crush and destroy.

Sharon E. Reese

Bag Lady

Poor lonely soul, victim of chance
Passers by, ignore her for
She's worth hardly a glance
What cruelties of life have taken her
Spirits weakened so low
Dark night of pain
Shivers her to the bone
Hope long departed, sick and hungry
She reached out a hand "please help" she said.

Her voice nearly a whisper
No more can she stand
What she once may have been
Now just aging despair
Dying alone for no one cares it seems

Boske D. Varga

Thoughts Of You

In the light of a misty moon,
Past the shoreline glides a lonely loon.
As I realize it's getting late,
I turn to go back through the gate.
The glowing lights from our little cabin,
Seem to beckon me back again,
But the soft breeze on this warm summer night,
Fills my mind with such delight,
That my thoughts seem to drift to another time,
So long ago when you were mine.
As I stand here dreaming of you,
It seems as if it could be true,
That you are here and I'm with you.
But the stars falling from the skies,
Are like teardrops from my eyes,
As I realize I'm here all alone,
With no one waiting for me to come home.

Sam Roskoski

Planet Earth

From space earth looks like a blue multicolored marble so serene,
Peaceful and warm, unlike pictures of other planets I have seen.

Have you ever thought of the mountains, forest, sea or a desert plain?
Have you ever traveled, viewed the beauty uninterrupted from a train?

Do we really think about the earth as we go through our daily chore?
Each day are we just concerned with where to now, life's such a bore.

Think of the mountains with snow capped peaks, lakes and forest green,
The flowers of a meadow and color of leaves when fall is on the scene.

What about the cleaning cycles of the air and water on this earth?
How the earth uses a fallen tree, recycling its debris in a rebirth.

How we use the four seasons, counting on the snow, rain and sun,
With a time to plant, harvest, a time we work and a time for fun.

Think of what man has done to earth, with his pollution year after year,
Tearing up the earth burning, laying waste without conscience or fear.

How long before earth's beauty is wasted by man's destructive pace?
How long before the earth can no longer support us, the human race?

Where would we go when there is no place on earth man can roam?
Will the destruction be stopped in time to save mankind's home?

How hard mankind will work and how quick to fight for a little ground,
Will we work as hard to save earth, and all the beauty which surrounds?

Ray Horton

Living Your Dream

Catch your never ending dream.
People aren't always what they seem.

You're dying to go out and get it!
No matter the obstacle you just won't quit.

It seems so far out of your reach.
So sick of hearing people preach!

When am I going to get there?
Never getting there at all is what I fear.

It seems like it's taking so long.
All's I want to do is sing my song.

Is there anyone who wants to be in my band?
Living the dream and writing songs in the sand.

Being on stage hearing them call your name!
Living your dream and getting fortune and fame.

Kim Listro

Little One

Little one so soft and sweet
Placed by an angel at God's feet

With little hands and legs moving about
The angels give their joyful shout

Then God placed His hand upon this child
Gave a wink and a gentle smile

I will give you a crown of gold
Fashioned from the moon that I hold

Angels will sing You lullabies by night
And my arms will cradle you at the break of light

Your hair will be lit like the noon day sun
And eyes twinkling like stars when day is done

Little one, you are special in Your way
For you have been blessed an angel, this fine day

Nancy Lee Evans

To A Mighty Stallion

O sleek and mighty stallion of the barren
prairie grasslands,
Through the sharp keenness of thine eye I see into
thy inner core,
Sensing the vigorous throbbing of thy heart, knowing
it to be as my own heart,
Perceiving the acute knowledge that leads thee, undeviating.
Thy black, muscular form, robust, undaunted,
galloping with fierce velocity,
Emanating the alacrity of my own
independent soul.
I recognize in thee thy barbarous, perhaps
misunderstood appearance,
Thy coarse, brazen exterior, intangible,
yet mysteriously sublime,
Ever accentuated by thy rampant and solitary nature.
O wild and swarthy prairie steed, I see in thee
multitudes
Of dauntless courage and irrepressible independence,
Echoed throughout my own unvanquished soul.

Nicole M. Dennis

This Mortal Presence

This mortal presence, though finite,
Presses on as if it lives forever,
Undaunted, never deterred
From this, its present endeavor.

From generation to generation, unchanging,
It has wrought from the very earth
Miracles of growth, pleasures unimagined,
From the dreams of its own birth.

The touch of its hand crosses heaven.
It has plumbed the depths of the sea.
The earth has yielded forth her treasures
To the onslaught of this humanity.

Yet the tainted skies are strangely empty.
Fragrant blossoms 'neath the tarmac lie.
The fawn no longer flees before us,
Nor do butterflies freely fly.

From noxious mists we choke.
Oil coats the once pristine shore.
The god Progress has demanded his sacrifice
And we remember Eden no more.

Price D. Golden

"Self-Confidence Quest"

Foretold sacrifice upon success, a waif am I.
Overcoming all, yeah gaining favor not.
Shall there be a forum fostering hope.
Or will determination see thee through.
What is thy source with which endureth I.
Where doth My fountain spring forth,
Thee elite, Oh, Thee Most High,
Almighty God without whom I would die.
And time tells of death once for ye.
Shall it be twice asked of thee,
It depends on whom spake to Me.
God giveth, and taketh away, and giveth again.
Yesterday leaves Me wondering,
if I be a pretender, but an impostor all.
To achieve, be rewarded, then denied.
What to accomplish in the realization of it!
One moment to feel competent, at least adequate,
Next to feel denunciation, rejection; But why?
Today in pursuit, searching to be, to seize the meaning of it for
Me.
Oh! To possess the knowledge of what self-confidence be.

Sherri A. Coffman

Walking In A Trapped World

Walking with the crowd, I aimlessly wander through.

Everybody around me, rushing to get to their own
private destination.

I am alone with my thoughts.

Thinking to myself, I wonder if their destination is
so important that they are not able to enjoy what
really lies around them.

Looking around me, I see such different colors and
beauty surrounding me.

I wonder if life really is passing people by.

People too busy with different things, they forget
what really matters in life.

Is it that people just don't care about what really
does happen.

Or do they just not realize that life is deteriorating
right before their very eyes.

People are so worried about tomorrow, that they cannot
face today without having it rush them by.

Shelby H. S. Yamamura

"Dolorous"

Lightning strikes as a soul falls apart
Rain starts to pour and washes away the heart
that belongs to the love that was once part of your life.
Once it disappears, everything is still cloudy,
until someone sheds sunlight to make everything clearer.
As the sun starts to slowly break through, you
will notice the way you were living.
Living your life as if you were in seclusion,
hiding yourself from all the confusion.
when all that your seeing is just an illusion.
The lightning was your life flashing before your eyes.
The rain is the tears that you cry.
And the heart that washes away sounds like
thunder, cause of the loud, fast beats from being scared.
You start to wonder if the tearful rain will ever
stop as the water is starting to rise, like a flood.
It is not a flood, it is an ocean.
If you look out ahead, you can see a boat.
It is the boat of unhappiness. Come aboard,
cause we're all on it...you're not alone.

Mark T. Daliege

Danny

Over and under, inside and out
our love twists. Never sure
where or when to stop.
Seemingly comfortable until confusion
mounts and towers over my rainbow.
Shadows encloak and take over.
But as it did, the sensations came
rushing back, and my heart
leaped out to you and attached.
Warmth seeped out of me when I
didn't even know it was there to begin with.
Beautiful passion that touches my soul
and warms it as my fear slowly
melts away.

My love isn't twisting anymore.
Now my heart is so sure...

That I love you.

A. Gennetts

Love Is Growing

Love is growing, Because we are showing,
Reach out your hearts, We can make a new start
We'll change the world for a better place
Come join me and celebrate.

The joy you get when you give a helping hand
Rejoice to make this a brand new land,
Come on everybody, let your light shine through
You'll see a change and a brand new you.

I knew the hunger, I felt the pain
I nearly drowned with every drop of rain,
I fell, got cut, the bruises healed
Got back up when all else failed.

Love thy neighbor, Be thyself
Don't be afraid, love will show the way,
Faith will guide you by and by; God is on our side.

When you live to love and love to live
You'll help another know the meaning to give,
Now don't expect things in return, if you do you're sure to get burned.

Now be on your way, bring a smile to a face;
The reward you get will bring a change within you yet.

Margaret DiOttaviano Medina

Mona Lisa Rose

Glowing like an ember-coal, oh so freshly blooming!
Reddest Rose in a bowl, all the room perfuming.
Garden-picked in early morn, the kitchen window to adorn,
she sways with a fragrant grace, dew-drops glistening on her face,
as the misty Morning Air, through the open window there, breathes,
"Fare-well, Reddest Rose! I'm going where the Wild Wind blows!
Wheresoever that may be; but my heart remains with thee.
Only thee forevermore, Reddest Rose, will I adore!"

Even though he longs to stay, with her petals blending,
in a swish he's blown away! To all directions rending.

She bows her rosy head and cries. "I'll soon be wilting anyway,"
she sighs; then in Mona Lisa style gives a fragile little smile.
"If by `forevermore' he meant to say
he'd love me when I'm weary and passé,
not just the joyous bloom of yesterday;
and if he meant that I would be as dear,
even when I'm bent and withered here,
and not forever what he used to see;
then let the Wild Wind blow him back to me."

Nancy McKeen

My Gray Balloons

As a child my balloons were pretty colors. Beautiful blues, greens, reds and yellows. My world was simple, interesting, wonderful. All I did was eat, sleep, play and dream.

As a teen my balloons were still all colored. But purple, fuchsia, aqua and pink were added. My world became confused, but still interesting. Now I had to learn and listen.

As a young adult my balloons remained colored. Adding many and varied different shades. My world became difficult and uncertain. So many ideas, plans and decisions to make.

As an adult my balloons changed very little. The colors seemed brighter and more vivid. My world began to settle and be less confusing. A wonderful husband made my life worthwhile.

As a senior my balloons started to change slightly. The colors no longer seemed as bright. My world began to slow down and became harder. But love and understanding still prevailed.

As a widow my balloons have all changed. The Love I cherished so long is gone, I'm alone. I prepare for my journey to meet my Love on high. Now my balloons are mostly GRAY!

Marie Davis

Candle Light

My candle flickers in the corner
Reflecting its light off the mirror and unto me
I feel the little warmth it gives off upon my face
It is so dark and cold out tonight
As I sit here alone and gaze out into the darkness
With only the light from my candle
To guide me through this empty house
It gives me time to think, to think of what is out there
So much pain and hurt, I myself have caused a lot of it
Why we must hurt others is something I will never understand
We seem to thrive on the pain of our enemies
I want to be forgiven for all I have done wrong
My only hope is that God has a candle flickering in the corner
Reflecting its light off a mirror and unto him
He must feel the little warmth it gives off upon his face
And he must have only that candlelight
To guide him through my empty soul
Then he will realize how bad his forgiveness is needed
For I have sinned

Linda Hines

Remember When

Remember when you said I love you.
Remember when I used to say it too.
Remember when we held each other's hand,
And how we walk along the sand.
And how we kissed in the moonlight,
And how we held each other so tight.

But now the days have passed me by,
And I sit here and wonder why,
Why didn't you believe in me?
Why didn't you care for me?
Why didn't you need me?
Why didn't you even love me?

But now that time has passed me
by and I no longer wonder why.

But remember when we held each other's
hand, and how we walked along the sand.
But remember when we kissed in the
moonlight, and how we held each other so tight.

But remember when you said I love you.
But remember when I used to say it too.

Michael Mykee Paul Randall

Matisse Report

Ambitious Henri exits from post-war Paris,
Renting a room on quai des Etats Unis
In Nice, to strive there in the ambient air
Of the cote d'Azur, to nurture his
Color and light and space vocabulary
With models Henriette and Aicha fair.

Arriving in rain, he hunkers in his room,
Paints his umbrella in the chamber pot,
His suitcase on the floor, himself at work,
Depicting restlessness, his fear of doom—
Kaput, before the children of his thought
Are grown, or born even, to fight the dark.

Matisse moves, changes models, stays in Nice
To paint his figure-scenes of Antoinette,
In ribboned hat of white with ostrich plumes;
Includes his table, daughter Marguerite,
Flowers and chairs with odalisque Lorette
Performing on the stage that is his room.
Matisse's art raised the Baroque inquiry
Of what is form and what's content entirely.

Russ Nash

Untitled

Being alive is pushing off chains that bind the spirit
rising above the weariness of mortal reality
Being alive is not fearing what other men can do to you
but fearing what you can do to yourself
Being alive is appreciating the wonder of every day and
reveling in each and every borrowed moment
Being alive is loving without condition or prejudice knowing
that your reward is in your own ability to love...

Stacia Giunta

Lover

I come to you in the most intimate glades of my heart
Rising like the opal of shell and bone
Polished smooth
Iridescent with longing
Tracing the path to me over the still, quiet pool
I beckon you with all the fragrant offerings of my heart
Yet I dare not lift my voice in song.
You have chosen another to sing to you the infinite
In her the cycle is complete
Broken for me with the shattering rhythm of desire
It is she who gives birth to angels
In the cold, unfurnished towers of your castle.
I lie quiet, dreaming ripples
Starlight my companion
Breezes of what might have been
Stirring sweet breath of ever-blooming lilies
Reflecting gentleness of moonlit night
Visited by your reflection in the pool.

Amy Villarreal

The Perfect Mother

Your mother held you in her arms,
Rocked you and assured you of no harm.
She took your hand and dried your tears,
And woke you from all your fears.
She made you laugh tickle, tickle,
Made you grin and told you,
"No matter what, you'll always win!"
She cleaned you up from every fall
Ran to you with every call,
Then she told you, "You'll always be my little baby"
You looked up to her and said, "I love you Mommy"
So then you realized you had the perfect mother,
But she had always known she had the perfect daughter!

Tara Leigh Joyce

Beyond The Clouds

A turbulence of beauty tumbling through the sky
Rolling the clouds into many shapes and size
Appearing to stack one upon another
Till they make castles far and wide
Then opening up a passage for me to travel -
As I have often done in my fantasy of dreams
Clouds of flowing beauty all feather light
Layers of fluff and puff all snowy white
I have always wondered, what it would be like -
Since as a child I watched with misty eyes
Overwhelmed and overcome by this awesome sight.

Now anticipating with wonder, just what lies beyond
As I have imagined, the handiwork of God
Entering in to the lights in the firmament
Of the heaven giving light upon the earth
Dividing the day from night
Providing a place of peace
In a heaven of rest, never before known.

Nell Blanton Orton

The Mountains

Beautiful, peaceful and serene,
Rolling, tumbling and often green.
Someday's they're surrounded by erie misty clouds
that softly move during the early morning hours.
They sometimes wait for the rains, the downfalls
the showers.
Look to the mountains, there's a message in
its terrain
High and majestic in all its glory
If you look hard they will tell you a story
Come to the mountains and rid yourself of life's daily pain.
Beautiful, peaceful and serene
look at God's wonder the mountains, often green.

Terry Jeter

The Green Of Life

Golden Strands of timothy, surrounded by the sun:
Running carelessly through time: laughter on the run:

Love and love and love and love, is all that can be seen:
No direction cared about, within the field of green

Laughter growing louder, as the paths of green turn brown:
Now, wondering where to go from here, the smile turns to a frown:

Way up in the distance, new foliage jumps out:
Run to me forever! The grass of green does shout:

Please don't frown, my little one, your time has not run out:
I'll always be ahead of you:
And this please never doubt:

Teri Sherwood-Daniel

Night

The night flies by on dark, silent wings,
Rushing towards the early morning sun.
The birds awake, and slowly begin to sing,
As children still dream of upcoming fun.
The world is full of God's beauty, and joy.
Whether it be blue and sunny, or even gray.
Regardless of the weather, every girl and boy,
Can find a pursuit to fit into any day.
Then the sun sinks slowly into the west,
Birds cease their twitter, and go to their nests
As we recall a day that God had blest,
And, again, at night, go to bed - and to rest.

Mary M. Brinkman

"The Misdiagnosis"

They said, with sad faces, that soon I would die
Said my outcome was bleak, that the stakes were too high
Said victims were many, survivors were few
Encouraged early funeral arrangements
Because there was nothing they could do
They had my family mourning, and me already in the grave!
My ignorance to the situation made me feel like their slave
When I asked the name to my dreadful disease
It was a 24 letter word from an aisle in the seven seas!
Further explanation they just did not give
Yet, they say that I only have weeks to live
I went for other opinions to hear what they'd say;
They agreed nothing could be done and sent me away
No O No! I did not cry!
I knew for a fact that I would not die!
In me there was hope, not a barrel of tears!
Because since that 'Misdiagnosis' I've been living for several years!
So if they tell you that soon you will die;
Don't run to the shadows and begin to cry!
Be Strong! Stand Tall! And look life straight in the eye!

Paula S. Wise

Promises

Was it really all that long ago that you
said you loved me.
You really loved me so.
As I sit here all alone, my thoughts drift
back to that very night.
That night you said you loved me,
that I was the only one for you.
You made many promises on that night.
You said you'd love me for all eternity.
You said you'd never go away.
That was many years ago.
You kept your promises through the years,
up until today.
Today was the day we finally said good-bye.
Early this morning you passed on and went to
a better place.
Now I will make one last promise to you
my dear, there will never be another
until we meet again.

Kristy Nicole Morris

It starts as a child.
Santa brings your first.
For years you sleep with it.
As an adult you remember. The safety you felt.
The love and warmth it gave. Every hour and everyday.
You wish and pray you still had it.
For now when the pain comes, you sit and stare.
Oh where in God's name is that
Bear........................
-Teddy-

Lori-Ann Alvino

Saying Goodbye

Saying Goodbye was the hardest thing I ever had to do.
Saying Goodbye to you was Saying Goodbye to my life,
my love, my world.
Saying Goodbye meant tears of pain, tears of sorrow,
fear of the future.
Saying Goodbye is not forever.

Saying Goodbye is the hardest word to say to a true love.
Saying Goodbye took courage, belief, trust.
Saying Goodbye meant to reach into your heart and say a
word that would hurt your inner soul, but
Saying Goodbye is not forever.

Saying Goodbye was only one emotion our of many that will
be felt.
Saying Goodbye brought mixed feelings, confusion, understanding.
Saying Goodbye brought dedication, devotion, honesty.
Saying Goodbye is not forever.
Our love, our relationship, and our unity is.

Kevin Davis

Going Fishing

Walking down a country road,
Puffs of dust curling up between his toes.
Fish pole slung over his shoulder,
Whistling a merry tune
And dreaming dreams of when he gets older.
The sun glistens on the pond between the trees,
Squirrels scurry through the leaves.
It's a beautiful summer day;
School is out and it's time to play.
Going fishing is a lot of fun.
You get to do that when the chores are done.

Verna Powers

Lost In Time

If God would let me, I would walk through time,
Searching for you, I can't get you off my mind.
I believe that once in our life we are given the chance,
to find the one, who our life will enhance.

You were like sunshine, caressing my soul,
making me a total woman, complete and whole.
I was left breathless, floating on air,
stripped of all inhibitions, without a single care.

Enchantment surrounded us, tender passion was everywhere,
the fragrance of love filled the air.
I remember you saying, this could go on forever,
Whispering words of leaving me never.

Taking me higher and higher with every touch, every kiss,
These are the emotions I will always miss.
Sometimes I feel I will go out of my mind,
Knowing you are out there somewhere, lost to me in time.

Patricia Lindsey

Last Wish

A friend, you say, is what you are.
Secretly making a wish upon the first evening star.

Walking by the river, the cool night's breeze.
Holding you indefinitely, the moment I did seize.

Your touch so soft, slowly caressing my finger.
Your lips pressed to mine, the memory does linger.

As my wish is coming true, something stirring in the air.
Telling you just how much I really do care.

Is it too late? Only time can tell.
Tossing a penny into the wishing well.

One last wish before the night shall end —
I need to know — my lover or my friend?

Kim R. Fical

It's Mothers Day Again

I see and go to places where I shop;
seeing Mothers Day decor, I admire but don't stop.

It's been years since Mom
went home to be with the Lord;
to miss her a great deal and also adore.

Mothers are special to remember her today;
but really she deserves to be honored every day.

Where would the church be today
if our mothers weren't Faithful and Kind?;
not very stable, I find.

Christ is the true cornerstone
to keep us strong today;
mothers are to apply His will
to keep going His way.

Therese Marie Tuckness

"From Now On"

Whispering words of sweet silence
Praying for just a spark of guidance
Dancing to the beat of an unsung song
From now on I want to hold you all night long
A dark glimmer of shimmering beauty
Your arms to hold me cradled by candlelight
From now on my life is blessed
When dawn appears my soul will rest
From now on my heart is true
With all the love I store for you

Tiffanny Spears

Prayer For Room 205

Oh! Father be present, in his sick room today.
Send Thy tender mercy, and heal right away.
Hover o'er him so gently, let Thy presence be known.
Be gentle, Dear Father til, his health he regains.

Oh! Spirit e'er near me, please be near to him too,
Oh! Comfort his family, til his strength you renew.
Breath on him so loving, let him waken once more.
For his wife and his children do need him I'm sure.

And after he wakens, and his strength, you renew,
May his life shine so, brightly, be lived just for, you.
May he raise his dear children, with Thy loving care.
Then may, I meet him in heaven, for I know him not here.

Winnie Holloway

"Grandma's Borrowed Angel"

Grandma's little borrowed angel
sent from the heavens above,
To give us all such great love
but the saddest part that breaks my heart,
Is that grandma's borrowed angel
will never learn to walk!!!

And when this little angel
sits on grandma's lap,
It makes me cry when I think of her
as being handicapped.
You hardly ever see her sad
and her smile lights up a room
like a glowing lamp.

Even though she has to be in a wheel chair
and tries to do things I just can't bare,
She knows grandma will always be there
whether its to hold her hand,
or to just wipe away her fears
Cause grandma's borrowed angel knows
grandma will always be near.....

Wanda Wright

Oh Beloved

Oh my Beloved —-
set me as a signet on your hand...
a seal upon your arm...
a pledge upon your heart...
for I am faint with love;
and strong is the netherworld;
But, stronger still our love.
Rivers overflowing its desire.
Passions unending its flames.
Death will not destroy our love.
For love is stronger than the grave.

Oh Beloved....., Beloved.....
yearning for you my heart was crushed.
Crushed with yearning my heart was poured.
Yet if I am crushed, I will be Myrrh.
Sweet savior of love for my beloved.
Poured on your head; running down your hair;
over your robes; poured unto your feet.

Yes..., though I am crushed, let me be myrrh.
sweet savior of love for my beloved.

Pamela A. Nichols

Message Of The Waves

At dawn, we walk hand in hand,
Sharing our dreams on the sandy beach.
Staccato of waves like drummer's band,
Seems to convey a message, to teach.

Great cresting waves all come crashing in.
Their glory spent, they are no more;
They lie at rest in the sand,
Gone too, our footprints on the shore.

As afternoon wanes, the din of waves
Now carry a message veiled in mystery.
Waves of a new generation may erase
All our footprints we made so faithfully.

In the twilight years, I walk alone.
Time passes, I am slowly trudging home;
Distant sounding waves like a forgotten song,
Content, but not willing to become lonesome.

Darkness looms, now I can barely see.
Setting my sight on the true light,
Jesus Christ, whose love sets us free.
Home with Him will be pure delight!

Rachel Stephens

The Queen Of Diamonds

Like a Diamond in the rough,
She enchants the very depths of my soul
Dark, smooth and lovely is she.
a goddess out of the motherland,
Her body is perfect form;
Not one inch out of place.
Her voice is of perfect harmony,
As it pierces through my body
And touches my heart.
And when she looks at me,
I'm caught helplessly in her spell.
Her words of wisdom keep me aware
That her beauty is far more than skin deep.
My Queen is she. Like no one I have ever known.
For no matter where the road takes her
She will always have the key to my heart.
For my love for her will be eternal.

T. H. Nettles

Earth Day 1994

Old Mother Nature's up at dawn, to sprinkle dew upon the lawn.
She gently shakes the trees awake, and sets the oven-sun to bake.
She feeds the plants, the fish and birds,
And hums sweet songs with unheard words.
She dusts the hillsides spotless-clean
And sweeps the valley's grassy green.
So much to do throughout the day,
And all she does is on display.
In heat of day, to please the crowds,
She wrings the rains out of the clouds.
At last she sits and props her feet: Another day, almost complete.
She sends the sun down in the west, for he has surely earned his rest.
She croons a whispered lullaby, and pins the stars up on the sky.
The moon responds to her sweet call,
With changing smiles, 'neath cloud's coy shawl.
She wakes the night-time creatures so
They'll have their turn in her fine show.
She doesn't sleep, but keeps her eye
On everything beneath the sky.
She tries to make us understand: We're all related to the land!

Verna Macbeth

A Rose Of Any Other Age

Howbeit she a peculiar new floweret, heritage of foliage,
She is far more beautiful than those twice her age
For her artless petals possess a certain immaculate luster that
those pristine perennials seem to lust after in the Autumn of their lives.
Still all is—without change—Metamorphosis as only her second
Spring arrives.
So much as others desire her leaves to crumple and fall she
thrives and this small wonder lives on.
Unbending yet leaning towards the radiant sun for life and beauty,
To gain admirers and strength.
While youth and inexperience say that it is beyond her years.

And I say a rose of any other age is still as sweet.

Tunji Sawyer

The Beauty Of Morning

When a woman is most beautiful,
She is pregnant with a child,
To be delivered soon,
Blessed by God.

She walks in beauty like the morning,
Fair, easy steps among the crowd,
Her lovely smile makes her glow,
Then alters with a calmness of motherhood.

The poet can only ponder,
About a creative process,
When life is conceived,
For man has no ending.

Indeed she has self-composure,
For her baby to be born,
Then her happiness is divine,
For man has no ending.

Did I not write about the beauty of twilight,
When the sun faces away and darkness creeps?
But the beauty of morning is different,
For man has no ending.

Rolando L. Boquecosa

Used

There she is with her head filled with doubt
She loves him so much she's not sure if she can stick it out
She's been without him for a while now
Some days she really wonders how
He turned away and really didn't care
She thinks her life isn't fair
She watches him in every way
Especially today
He's in a world of sadness
His other left him with less
His head fills with regret
But, his feelings he won't show yet.
She knows how he feels
Because her heart knows the hurt is real
She takes him back without a thought
But, does she know she's just been bought
With a single sigh
She's back by his side
Being used once again
When will it all come to an end.

Susie Perry

Mother's Day In May

Heaven of heavens, I am sure that is where she is now.
She passed from this life October 28, 1964, at age 92 years.
If there ever was a good mother, wife, and person, it was her.
When a child, she loved her brothers and sisters,
which she had ten.
She loved her parents and obeyed them.
As she grew up she worked as a seamstress helper.
At the age 13 years she worked six months for nothing,
then she was paid three dollars a week.
She did not marry until she was 28 years old,
Had one husband, loved and respected him as head of their
family of eight children.
She was mother, cook, housekeeper, teacher, doctor, preacher,
nurse, bookkeeper, purchasing agent, mediator, and above all
an Angel to each.
As I remember her now, "surely" that is where she is,
In the heaven of heavens with the other angels as herself.
May God bless you, Mother.

C. S. Billings

Sunburst: Chautos' April Miracle

Age seven months
She runs as one with the morning sunrise—
A glowing, flowing form, head held high,
Sculptured from burnished copper in the guise
Of an eager sunburst mounting a grey-blue sky.
Faint sunbeams touch her flying mane,
Glistening with flecks of sparkling gold dust
That fall to earth as morning dew
Before Sol's fingers probe a damp, chill crust.

Marguerite I. Wilkinson

Buffy, The Cat

Buffy, the kitten, had a life of her own.
She was found in an alley that had been her home.
But she often did stray as alley cats do
And followed Alissa; we believe that is true.

Now Alissa, my grandchild, took her one night
As a small kitten to the 4th of July sight
Frightened to death she ran down a hole
What a commotion to save the poor soul!

Now Buffy became Grandmother's pet
Like the book she had read
About the cat in the hat.
Her eyes tell it all
She's sad or she's hap
Grandmother knows all about
Buffy, the cat.

Verna Henningsen

My Pleasure

It's my pleasure to be part of the earth, to be joyful due to so many sights, to partake in so much provided for all. To know so many people throughout your life, all walks of life, all different personalities. It's a pleasure to work and feel rewarded for accomplishing so much. It's a pleasure to learn so much as a child and to absorb in your mind and put it to use. It's a pleasure to breathe in the air, to drink of the water and to eat all the variety of foods. It's a pleasure to feel wanted and needed and to be loved and love in return. It's a good feeling to respect your parents and others. It's a pleasure seeing all the animals and seeing the earth and all it has to offer. It's a pleasure to have fun when excitement is felt. To get it all together and all the meaning it has, it's a pleasure to be alive.

Sally Buscetto

Spinning In Space

God, please don't leave me spinning in space.
Show me the reason,
I've been put in this place.

Help me to trust that you have a design.
When all that I feel,
has no reason or rhyme.

I am out of control, zooming fast in the dark.
I need you to anchor me,
light the dark with a spark.

A spark of your light God is all it would take;
to slow my world down God,
and shake me awake.

All would be calm then,
a sea of tranquility.
My life would have meaning then,
not endless futility.

Karen J. Jones

Lazy

Sit in my room, thinking my thoughts,
Sit in my room because it's boredom I've bought.

Whistle a tune and make up a rhyme,
Sit in the corner and color a dime.

This can't be fun or maybe it is,
What else to do? I'm not a kid wiz.

Turn on the radio and sing a song,
Contemplate everything all night long.

Look at the pen and paper so near,
Make up a poem, this one right here.

Fall asleep watching Letterman near one,
Wake up with my eyelids orange by the sun.

Watch T.V. 'till six then doze away,
Nothing has changed, just another laid back day.

Not very happy, not sulking with sadness,
Please let this be teen life, not just plain madness.

Madness I can't handle because I'd just be crazy,
This is just a day in the life of someone who is lazy.

Nichole Dixon

Camp No. 5 (Pyoktong, North Korea, 1950-51)

I rise up from my hole, grenade in hand,
Slipping, stumbling, on the frozen hillside, I feel the bullets
tear through my body.
Eileen, the Chinese are going to kill me today!
I awake in hell, but there is no fire.
Can you hear me Eileen? I'm alive, I love you.
I scream the words into the arctic winds blowing down from the
Yalu knowing they will not carry my words to you.
I scream out to my tormentors in vain to treat my wounds, "Byongi
natsseyo!" (I am sick!).
But there is no doctor, medicine; I'm crippled now.
"Baegakopumnida!" (I am hungry!)
But there is only water and cracked corn to eat.
The months go by, there is no hope; I have dysentery.
I share my earthen floor with rats who huddle with me at
night to keep us warm.
My diarrhea won't stop; I'm covered with filth and lice.
Comrade Ding tells me to cooperate and soon I will return
home to you.
Eileen, the Chinese are going to kill me today!

Martin J. O'Brien

The Conqueror

Walking on the streets
smallest in the crowd
(pondering dreams)
I thought,
What could I do if I were a giant?
I would probably conquer the world
who could stop me
Melting cars to make my armor
I could use lighting bolts from the clouds
No weapon could stop me
As I walk seeing my enemies driven before me
Whoops! Another one
what a tragedy

I could jump
earthquakes I make
I fall
Are you all right someone asked
Daydreaming I guess
We just had a tremor! Did you feel it?
I... No! I guess not.

Robert E. Medford, Jr.

The Old Wolf Dies

The winter winds were blowing cold, as the
snow began to fall
High on the mountain side, I heard the old wolf call
The mournful sound that drifted down, to
the valley far below
Would soon be stilled by the winter winds
and blowing drifting snow

The old wolf was facing, his last day alone
His old body tortured, by the ravage of the storm.
The pack had left him there to die, and
he knew the end was near
But deep inside his fierce pride, would
not acknowledge fear.

Once he had been a proud young wolf, and
the leader of his band.
But now the time has come, to make
his final stand
So with an eerie howl that could be
heard, through out eternity
The old wolf closed his eyes, and set his spirit free

Melvin G. Cornwell

Mary Steinlicht

A woman.
So full of life's experiences
so young and alive in her mind.
Spinning marvelous tales of the days long ago,
and pulling out shoe boxes of pictures...
from times I could only hope to know.
(My favorite was the one of your and Great-Grandpa's
first house with the lily pond in the backyard.)
If ever a woman I could hope to be,
It would be your likeness I would follow-
elegant and classy,
demure and so refined.
with your delightful social graces
and ever-present charm-
you are everything "woman" means to me.
And though time passes quickly,
I am honored to have the privilege of knowing you
and calling you Great-Grandmother.

Teri L. Shockey

Recognize A Miracle

If time means "memories" and we have
so little of it
It doesn't mean that we've "lost out"
it's what we now "put in it"
If "miracles" come from "Heaven" and we
are granted "one" in our life
then we must use this "Special Blessing"
he's bestowed upon us to "cherish and enlighten."
Miracles; some have many, they happen everyday
Some might say "miracles" they never come my way;
Could it be we just don't recognize or that
we might set our hopes too high to realize a
"blessing" in disguise?
So use this precious time you have
Be all that you can be
I know that there are "Miracles"
He created you and me!

Linda Jopp

We Stand Alike Before The Cold

In passing through the Ozark Hills December last,
So lovely was our summer place, we stayed awhile.
We have no fuel, in case that flurry comes this way.
We've saw and ax. "Twill be fun to do this chore.

The flurry came that midnight. We quickly gathered sticks
In the dark, just off the porch, to start a fire.
Later, hovering closely there, around a flame upon the hearth,
Within that comfort zone, we sensed our spirits commune.

Where's our comfort, luxuries and affluence could well afford?
Now behold! Our common need drove us into the woods
To face that chilling wind that bit us to the bone,
And there we wrought the means that saved our lives.

A tonic? Yes and lesson too, reality taught.
All, great and small, stand alike before the cold.
By this experience we children learned a lot.
Let's form groups to work together for common good.

Tom Holland

Judgment

We sit in Judgment Day today
So powerful in what we say
No matter what you've done
Your verdict is soon to come

Here is my question
I don't need an answer
Are we so quick to judge others
Not asking about our own judgment day?

We may be the jury for some
But remember this.............
After all is said and done
The only reflection you will see, is that of your own

Pamela Lynn Collins

Angel

Dear God in heaven, I need your solemn vow
Someone special is on her way to you now
She has courage and strength, honor and grace
She fought a good battle, but still lost the race
Her mind might be muddled, her eyes not so bright
But give her wings Lord, let her take flight
She's been an angel for a long time, you see
To many on Earth, especially me
And so God I need you to swear
You'll let her fly anytime, anywhere

Tracey Maule

God's Song

The desert is filled with the song of the birds,
Some of the most beautiful anthems I've ever heard;
And I wonder, as I listen in awe each morn
How they sing so sweetly surrounded by thorns.

Then-I look at the lives of people I know
And realize-in their lives this also is so.
Many whose lives have met with great test
Seem to have a song much sweeter than the rest.

So may I remember, as trials come my way-
They're here to improve my life, they're not here to stay;
And though the trials may seem many and long,
May they help my life to be filled with God's song.

Verna Mull

NO GUARANTEES

Life has no guarantees.
Some promises are kept - some broken
God gives us loved ones for a time
Then takes them away as He sees fit

Ungrateful are we if we bemoan
Pity self or despair
Or bear a cross of sadness forevermore
Or become cynical or full of hate

At a fate we deem spiteful or unjust
For none can have it all his way
That is not the scheme of things
For, were every wish fulfilled

No want unmet - no love turned sour
What then would be the meaning of Life?
What measures for heights and depths
And breadth of joy and kindness?

There would be no balance to pit against
The holes of sadness, loneliness, fleeting despair
No struggle of accomplishment
No race run and won - not given, but earned.

Vernon Cox

For Those Who Have Lost Someone

In every part of this City wide,
Some thought of you, there, seems to hide,
And as I pass, flies in to me
And stings my heart with sad Ecstasy.

Down every road and down every street,
A perfume of memory of you, there I meet;
A sweet essence of fragrance invades every hour,
As subtle and sweet as the scent of a flower.

I gave up our home, it was too much to bear,
Its magic was gone, not having you there;
Every corner spoke out telling only of you,
The garden was lovely, but I can't make it through.

O' to be with you again — I need you so much,
To hear your soft voice and feel of your touch;
God grant that I'll see you again, I'll pay any cost,
Because, now, without you, I'm horribly lost.

Roger D. Burgoyne

Life

Life is but a game for all,
some will rise and some will fall.
Some will laugh and some will cry,
some will live and some will die.

God created this wonderful game we live,
he hoped we'd have the love to give.
Many say that love is not a reality,
the wise know that love is but the only key.

Everyone plays the game a different way,
many change roles from day to day.
Some say that games are just for kids,
but the game of life is for he who lives.

Patricia L. Thompson

Friendship

Friendship is a special trait
Something to value and appreciate
A real friend is charitable, warm hearted, and kind
Supportive, caring, and rare to find

There are so many things one can do
To fashion a confidant who's special and true
Congeniality can blossom and flourish
Loyalty and trust expand easily when nourished

A friend is a soul mate who puts you at ease
Who's grateful and anxious in channels that please
Benevolent friends will share sorrows and treasures
Advantageous in times of heartaches beyond measure

I like to count friends as God's blessings on earth
Helping us master pain and be of great worth
I hope you accept this expression or view
As a kindred spirit, loyal and true

Ruth O'Neill Berger

I Just Wanted To Tell You That I Love You

True love.
Something you only read about,
Only dream about.
A feeling that can't be shared between two
people who have never met,
Yet my heart is connected to you.
If this is life without love, my heart is
truly broken.
So, come to me.
Come and make me happy.
Be my warmth, strength, and protector
While I make your dreams come true.
Love is such a strong word, and it's what
I feel.
Please don't neglect the passion burning
deep inside of me.
To do this would be like dousing a fire,
I'm not ready for the warmth and heat
Inside of me
To go out. For someone close to my heart.

Becki Errington

The Meathouse

Through the meathouse window do I see
The place where the bullets suddenly speak
Leaving him swimming in a sea of pain
Mouth gaping like a wound, as if to catch the falling rain
And he lies in the street like a side of beef
As his parents hang themselves on the Tree of Grief
Then life stops speaking, interrupted by Silence
As Death comes to carry off the product of sudden violence.

Yih-Chau Chang

The Loss Of A Loved One

It is never easy to lose someone you love.
Sometimes it takes a shove
To get you through another day.
It is easy to say
That the pain will go.
It happens to be so,
But it will take a while.
Someday you'll be able to smile
When you think of the good times you've had.
There is nothing wrong with feeling glad
For the good memories of your loved one.
Just set your sights of the sun
And be willing to share
Your feelings with those who care,
You'll be alright,
And see that the future can be bright.

Mike Nielson

....Of Angel Gifts

O! Hair of Sunrise Wonder
Soul of Magic Dew:
Please Sparkle 'way my Deepest Woe
With the Marvel that is YOU...

And I beg - my Love - Your Pardon
If I sit and I stare:
For Thou art the Fairest Flower in the Garden....
Sweetest Song of the Air....

Ah, Debra Ann:
You sing to me with Tulip lips:
"God's Nectar: Bob, now Share a Sip?..."
You Hand my Heart a Smoother Trip....
(Forever now)
When I touch You, Heaven is at my finger tips.....

Robert Steve Allison Jr.

The Dust Of My Soul

A hollow opening in the hearts of men are
Souls that have never been touched. See this
Soul wither, see it as it crushes to nothing
But a lifeless form of air...

My soul has death in its path, my soul has
Dust in the pit of its bottom. My soul is
Lonely for a glimpse of a thousand kisses...

The dust of my soul is content to flow and to
Lay still. The dust was so small
That its beauty stood
Out in full....

"Dust to dust" whispers my soul and soon
my soul flies away like a black dove at
Midnight...

Melissa Chris Swallow

Autumn Thoughts

Autumn leaves are falling
Summer's green now gold and red.
Flowers that once burst forth with color
Are now resting in their beds.
Warm winds that brought us showers
In April and in May,
Now grow cool and brisk
With every passing day.
Soon wintry winds will bring us
A soft white blanket of snow
And cover the earth so her "children" may rest-
They'll waken again in the spring, we know.

Nezera Mrozinski

A September Morning

In early morning the heavy dew
sparkled by the sun. Shining
brilliantly in a cloudless sky -
The sunlight reflections on the dew
covered green grass, gave the illusion
of aquamarine stones
Bordering the leaves were evergreens
lilac, bushes, spireas, and other shrubs
were also arranged earth glistening crystal not undone in beauty
Changing color as the sun shore through the leafy branches
A lovely yellow monarch butterfly, flew
even doing its way over to the fading, flower
bed, bedding farmers before retreating
in another farm for cold weather,
a subtle transformation into autumn
with the breath taking closes of the
maples, ash, oak and Linden
The constant unfolding of another season of nature's residue
It's comparable to the four ages of man
Who could interfere, questions or challenge His Divine Power.

Mary B. O'Neill

Don't Judge Me

Friend, don't expect me to live up to your
standard because I'll fall short
every time.
You've probably got a few hang-ups of your
own, so please don't worry about mine.
Now you can say I'm not living right and
that won't make me cry,
but friend, unless your name is Jesus
you're not qualified.
You might have been a Christian for forty
years or more, but yet I truly do not see,
Why should the good Lord tell you my
bad points when all He has to do is tell me.
If you feel you must judge someone then
do what you have to do, go ahead and spend
your time judging me while the
Lord is judging you.

Richard Hardee, A.K.A. The Carolina Poet

Witness A Miracle

Star of beauty wonders
Star of light and hope.
Star bright, o what
a beautiful light.
What a wonderful sight.
I am blessed to see each day as
my morning began
a brand-new-day.
As I look out my front
door, and look straight ahead,
there stands a miracle tree. Hands
did not plant it and money
did not buy it.
This tree is a symbol that represents my mother.
I look to my left, and my eyes behold
a beautiful bright morning star.
I just know, as I witness this beautiful sight,
God is telling me don't worry about your day,
I got it all in control.

Tensie Lee Strange

"The Power Of The Circle"

As we watch from a window,
Staring into the black of night,
Tempt the repressed intellect to go
Into the past to see the light.

Traveling upon this spiritual road,
Flesh and blood is resurrected.
We not only carry the impotent physical load,
But an emotional center remains unprotected.

The spirit walks upon the earth
While another is hidden until found.
An emptiness forms and gives birth,
Before love can be forever bound.

Force not to unmask
The time that now stands done.
If you shall swallow from the flask,
Jealousy will weigh a poisoned ton.

Our future is untold and unbound
And we dream past this realm of darkness.
When we imagine what can be found,
Hope and desire shed tears, pain and happiness...

Matt Bromley

Trees In Winter

Colorful sentries stood a-waiting— among the forests still-
Guard changing had started on the emerald green, golden hill.
Droplets of white slowly floated down,
Covering the reds and golds of the sentries' ground.
The first frost-dew of the morn light,
Reassuring future life of the sentries' long night.
Winter animals beginning to make their rounds,
As the coverlet of white extended through farthest towns.
Summer had departed with the sentries dressed bold,
Now they were dressed in winter's white pristine fires, and cold.
Another year was ending the sentries' task,
Protecting and mothering new life, as the old slowly passed.

Linda Corkins Buchner

Autumn's Visit

Autumn, dressed in a garment gay
Stopped in to greet our town today,
The gown she wore was crimson, bright.
It glistened in the sun's warm light.

With patient care she'd pressed each fold
And trimmed her gown with leaves of gold.
She sent leaves tumbling to the ground.
As she gaily frolicked through our town.

Some of her gifts, were pumpkins gold yellow,
Apple cider for each cellar,
Jell to make, and corn to pop.
Ere cousin Winter makes her stop.

This Autumn's visit will be brief,
For all too soon each colored leaf
Buried 'neath a blanket white
Will slumber through long Winter's night.

Let our eyes not fill with tears.
To mourn her passing for this year.
Let's send her off with a farewell gay.
When Winter comes, Spring will not be far away.

God and Lorraine Umbdenstock

"The Earth I See"

Earthly greed, my heart can see,
Strength the intra heart of me.
Love beyond what eyes can see.

Love the largest mountain, taller than
Thee to the smallest grain of sand,
beneath the sea.

Killing nor pain, can heal grief for me.
Darkness of night, reached for me,
as lights so softly peeped through the trees,
below the mountain knees lay
tombs filled with meaningful lives
died for heroic greed.

Judge not of me, through tears I see,
wars and drugs there will be.
Invisible peace
God gave free to the world,
not just me.

Odies Liddell-Donald

"The Man I Love"...*dedicated to Larry Laster Sr.*

The man I love acts tough and
strong to all you folks out there,
He's tall and big and beautiful
to these eyes of mine.
  I asked God to provide for me
just this kind of man, with a heart
so tender, he's such a loving man.
  His job demands a lot from him,
his fishing and his fun, but
when it comes to loving time I
know where he runs.
  He treats me better than anyone
that I have ever known, I'm
thankful everyday dear God that
he's my very own.
  Now Honey if you read this,
each word I write is true,
for honey I want you to know
I'm so in love with you.

Linda B. Harrell

Sacred Soil

We were filled with excitement starting out for the mountain -
Such beauty in the foothills, at the gateway stood a fountain -
The hillside sloped, I felt my foot slipping and down I went -
Landing amid small men laughing! Not funny to me my legs bent -
Two months later in a doll making class in that distant land -
Sat I long with many friends, but my head was in the sand -
My thoughts were of a different matter, was I or wasn't I? -
Japanese instructor telling us all that we would need to buy -
She noticed my abstraction the bewildered look upon my face -
Very polite people this culture be "please put away your lace" -
In my thoughtless manner and very nervously chewing my nails -
Longing to be free of truth, wishing I could set the sails -
"What seems to be your problem is there anything I can do?" -
Pondered in my mind seven months from now I'll be engulfed in goo -
Inquisitively she asked "have you been to Mt. Fuji lately?" -
"Have you walked upon the sacred soil" and she waited patiently -
Not comprehending, "what has that to do with my condition?" -
"Mt. Fuji has very fertile soil and has honored your affection" -
"Long time ago legend speaks of this, for you it has come true!" -
I not only walked, I slid down the mountain, I dare not be blue! -

Martha L. Chainey

My Love, The Sea

My mistress' sight is nothing like the light that streams from the sun.
'Tis greenish-blue, port-wine to some.
If hairs be wires
She sports ringlets, wavelets upon her top.
If breasts are white
Why then, breasting her is foamy light.
I have seen roses damasked red and white
But only greyish-green do I see in her deep.
And in some perfumes is there more delight
Than in the salty mist that floats like a breeze upon her body's reach.
I know that music in the air sounds sweet —
Yet in her sounds one feels the rapture of the deep.
I grant I never saw a goddess go —
My mistress, when she moves,
Rolls in waves, up and down the beach.
And yet, by heaven, I think my love, the sea
Is rare as any passion on land, or in the sky.

Sheldon Cholst

Follow The Sunset

The joy to see the beauty untold; when a
  sunset unfolds in front of me!

With a body of water so cold and deep when
  it reaches out for me.

To watch the waves come upon my feet with
  peace I receive!

The joy to see a sunset unfold in front of me!

Across the waves a beam of light shines for me and
  a narrow path I walked to meet
  My Savior, On Bended Knees!

Over the horizon a beautiful glow of light I
  did see; from Heaven it seems to be.

From a beam of light on clouds of white;
  Our Savior will descend from
  Heaven for me.

The joy to see a sunset unfold in front of me!

Ruth Ann Mitchem

The Signals Of Life

I stood upon the curb of life and waited there to cross;
The signal flashed a red "hunh uh." I knew to heed the boss.

I stood and watched the world go by—some happy, some in strife.
The signal flashed a green "un huh." I crossed, went on with life.

Lee Fleming Reese

Love Dreams Free

Soaring,
Suddenly, chaos collides with the hazel pools of thy eyes,
Mirrors reflecting great depths of thy soul,

Adrenaline flows from the feeling,
The secret ability to caress the wind beneath my wings,

To view the world through God's eyes,
The earth renews itself as do I,
What an unrivaled sight to behold,

Souls overflowing with the warmth of golden light,

Falling in love, forever,
As peaceful as the Eagle's flight.

Sharleen C. Hutchins

Surrender To The Holy Spirit

O Holy Spirit - God Divine, take my will and grant me Thine
Take my mind and there instill, Faith, Hope and Charity,
by Thy Holy Will
Take my eyes and with understanding let them see,
my Redemption and Salvation on that Holy Tree
Take my ears and make them hear, God's call to me without fear
Take my lips and let them speak, God's Holy Wisdom, but ever so meek
Take my heart, melt it down, mold it, use it, to earn me a heavenly
crown
Take my hands and let them feel, God's Power surging, in Jesus name
to be healed (and in Jesus name to heal)
Take my feet and walk with me, side by side my true friend be
Take my life, transform it, let it be, consecrated Lord,
and in harmony with Thee
Take my soul, heal it well, that at life journey's end,
in the Father's House it may dwell
O Holy Spirit - God Divine, transform my will into Thine

Milli Marks

One Thinking Philosophically

They manipulate and deceive; play with your mind and taunt the soul. What you perceive as reality may be the mere work of a cunning inner artist; creating its own rendition of a practical joke. Look around, feel the solid ground, and hear the wailing hound. You believe solely because of your senses; yet, how often they frolic with your sanity: seeing where you thought there was; hearing when there was no one; reaching for it when it was never there. .You look with your eyes, yet, do you really see? A taste on your tongue, is it true to the buds? Living by your senses, it may only conclude: illusion. Here it is, existence as you sense it; but what is its true form? You depend on your body's functions for survival; yet that skeleton may be a trick of perception; merely illusive. What if you were to use your mind's eye, your mind's view, and experience the actuality of this existence.

Maybe then...life, as we justify this chaotic animation of the senses to be, would actually be worth it.

Nicole J. Buyansky

Throw Away People

We're throw away people in a throw away world.
Tell me, how did all this get started?
We've thrown away lives and we've thrown away love,
And it's sad living life empty-hearted

You can't see truth when fear blocks the way.
It takes all of your courage just to face each new day.
Oh! Just look deep inside you; don't wait to be called.
It's much better to stumble than to never try at all.

Just give me your hand, and I'll show you the way.
Life is good when we're helping each other.
The road may be rocky, but don't lose your faith.
Together it's really no bother.

There's a very good reason to stop all our hate,
And start living our lives as the masters of our fate.
Oh! Just look all around you at this world we know.
If we can't make it work here, then where do we go?

It's time we departed the path we walk now.
Realize we're all in this together.
With the past as our guide, and the future our hope,
There isn't a thing we can't weather.

Tess Wells

Remembering Mother

Mother is a guardian, doctor, nurse,
Teacher and a friend who gives love without pretense.

Her love is gentle, sincere and sweet.
Don't even try, she can't be beat.

Her love is life, which came about
When she gave birth to her first child, no doubt.

God gave us the splendor of the stars in the firmament,
The sun that warms the world,
The moon that shines in the darkness of the night.
He gave us mother whose love is undivided.

I remember her looking at me, and saying,
"Put your head on my shoulder son,
Tomorrow will be a better day."

Let us wish all mothers a "Happy Mother's Day,"
God's blessing and His love,
In a very special way.

Nicholas Cavaleri

Dreams

Tell me why my mind feels crazy
Tell me why my mind feels lost
Then hold me - love me - don't let go.

Pray this world will start to grow
and feel the love I feel right now.
So hold me - love me - don't let go.

And if I'm dreaming, may I never awaken.
For this is the best dream I've ever dreamt.
So hold the dream - love the dream - never let it go.

Tell me why my dreams feel crazy.
Tell me why my dreams feel lost.

Rebecca Essak

Fools' Folly Numbers

Folly is certain in the errant assumption
Ten men on a job with one year existence
Miraculously creates the lofty presumption
The combined equates to ten years of experience.

'Tis more than folly, this assumption they use,
In attributing more to their effort than deserved
It's an absolute fallacy of numbers misused,
For the results are obvious when closely observed.

The proper use of numbers as tools
Proves a truism without error or mistakes,
For the collective minds of a thousand fools
Does not one mastermind make.

Kenneth D. David

Kristy

There's no greater moment that I can remember
Than the first time I held my baby that day in November
My heart filled with such pride, such joy, such love
I knew that Kristy was a precious gift from God above
From the second she was placed in the crook of my arm
I knew I would do all I could to keep her from harm
From that moment on I knew what it meant to be a mother
To care for this small one's life like I would no other
With each passing year as I watch Kristy grow
I experience a feeling of depth only a mother can know
No greater emotion between two people can be more real
Than the bond between mother and child and the love they feel

Theresa Fenton

That Day In July

It was hot, that day in July, when he came into my life.
Tension set the mood, the air heavy, a room drenched in fear.
The fear of not knowing, not knowing how it would begin, or how this story might come to its end.
I was not surprised when he made his presence known.
His face was red, and his energy swallowed the tension, his voice was loud, relieving my fear, the fear of not knowing how it would all begin. He was perfect, that day in July, hands larger than most, no smile would cross his face, only an expression of awe, his body long and lean. And those eyes, cold steel blue, shooting sparks, igniting my heart, an ocean deep, searching, questioning. Seeking the key to our destiny, knowing it would be his, he took my hand, touched my soul, two hearts forever entwined.
He's changed a bit, since that day in July, his stride more sure, laughter so contagious, always asking questions, looking for all the answers. We've grown together, shared our fears, two lives still magically connected. He found the key and stole my heart.
It was hot, that day in July, when he came into my life. Love now sets the mood, a love forever magic, my grandson and I.

Linda M. Jones

goodbye green oaks

thanks for the caring; thanks for you sharing;
thanks for your point of view.

thanks for you giving; thanks for forgiving;
thanks for the loving you.

thanks for your seeing, my reasons for being
so all alone and so blue. we've beaten the demons;
the cries and the screamin's—
that haunted us day to day.

yes, there was pain, but with it came gain.
i finally was given a clue—why i was hurting;

why i kept blurting out words
that weren't even true.

now that i'm leaving, and you may be grieving,
i offer these words to you:

i made some great friends; so this ain't the end
of my friendship—from me to you.

r. e. gatewood

The Unthinkable Wish

Do you ever feel so bad
That all you can do is cry?
Does a little part of you wish over and over
That God would let you die?

The unthinkable wish keeps moving
Steadily through your mind
You feel the only way you could be happy
Is to leave this world behind.

Many people have felt this way
Depression seeks us all
Sometimes it will catch you
Leaving you trapped against a wall

If this feeling of hopelessness engulfs you
Spreading like some untreatable cancer
Call upon the Lord
For He is the only answer.

Tiffany Andrews

Your Eyes

Your eyes are like two crystal flames,
that captivate me with their elusive dance.
They wrap me with the warmth of love,
they caress me with their grace.
Their beauty brings sacrifices of my tears.
I would give everything, for to behold your eyes.
Their cool tint of blue calms me in my turmoil.
Their song tells me of wisdom I have yet to discover.
Their fluid rapture displays all feeling.
All that is consummately lovely,
all that is inconceivably wondrous.
I would give everything, for to behold your eyes.
And Oh! The sun does shine,
for to behold your eyes!
And Oh! The stars do ponder
the wonder of thine eyes!
And Oh! All I have and more I would sacrifice,
For to behold your eyes!

Susan Hassell

"Words"

Words just haven't been written
That could even nearly express
The peaceful life I've been given
By our dear Lord's tender caress

His love truly lights the world!
Sweeter joy could never be found
Each step with my Lord, still unfurled
Plants me deeper on His solid ground.

Can you imagine, the price that His paid
In sheer agony as He bled from the tree?
"Just follow me!" was the cry Jesus made
Oh, blinded eyes, will you still fail to see?

There are so few that love truth,
And these are the ones our Lord seeks
So hear not the false prophets...
Just the words our Messiah speaks.

Oh dear, precious friends, you're missing so much
Because the Lord loves us all
And your heart wants to touch!

Patricia S. Hughes

Silent Tear

Silent tears
that dropped through my face,
are only one reason
for my heart's empty place!

I think of happiness
and you make my heart cry;
because I'll never get there
even if dying, I try.

Oh, silent tears don't show off again;
I don't want the world to know
that my heart will cry till the end!

Let the world think that I'm happy forever!
And that my heart in love
it's hard and clever!

There is nothing more painful than a silent tear!
It comes straight from the heart,
showing what's your big fear.

Oh, silent tears you reveal my sorrow
by letting everyone know,
that like a poet; I'll suffer more tomorrow!

Kathy Jimenez Roldan

"My Love For You"

There simply isn't a "Single Day"
That I don't look for "A Way"
To show you just how much that I do "Truly Love You."
So until that special day, "When I Find The Way"
To show you just how much that I do "Truly Love You,"
I'll just have to try and put it "Into Words."
There just aren't words "To Express All Of My Love"
That I have for you,
So I'll just have to tell you
That I truly do and always will "Love You,"
With my whole "Entire Heart,"
'Cause you stole that "Special Part"
Way down deep in "My Heart."
No one could ever "Fill That Space,"
Or ever take "Your Place."
What I'm really trying "To Tell You"
Is that I truly do "Love You,"
And want "You To Be Mine,"
"Until The End Of All Time....."

Thomas E. Stewart

It's Now...

I'm thankful for waking up to reality
that it's now that really counts;
it's this moment that's truly meaningful.

Past doesn't exist because it's absorbed in present:
Future doesn't exist because it's yet to come:
Yesterday isn't today; neither is tomorrow today.

It's now that we live and love,
that we give and receive,
that we perceive and believe:
It's this moment that we live in eternity
to care and to share,
to flower and mature
by understanding
that eternity has no beginning... no end...
It's a timeless accumulation of now! now! now!
It's true that we suffer in it time and again
but never alone because He is always with us.

So let's not look for heaven beyond the horizon.
For better or for worse this is the garden He created
For us to build our lives and grow into His likeness.

Yuriko Bayu Cottom

Dream's End

Who are these youth of today
That live life in expectation of things to come
Looking beyond the stars for dream's end
Seeking answers to life's questions in the hearts of strangers
Losing themselves in the repetitious beat of surreal song
Enslaving their heart to the liquid passions of drug
Selling their spirit for fleeting moments of acceptance
Listen to the voice of fear as it speaks to them of their past
Running from the realities of today
Awaiting the perceived freedom that comes with the wisdom of age
Looking beyond the stars for dream's end
Not realizing that dream's end stands before them as a faint
image, appearing in a mirror, tainted with the tears of their past
Not in the hearts of strangers, the repetitious beat of surreal
song or the liquid passion of drug, but within themselves
And once the tears of their past have been wiped clean from this
mirror they will see clearly their dream's end
Not beyond the stars, but in their heart, mind and spirit
Love them, respect them, trust them and protect them
For they may well be our dream's end

Richard Beck

By Love Possessed

If ever I could gain your warm ways,
That manifest in my mind
Nurtured through time's everlasting wisdom
Waiting wistfully without despair
Unable to relinquish the gladdened memories
Where conscience was guided by the heart
And lonely tears turned to joy
By the rapture of her smile

Ever protected by a commodious partition of fear
Showcasing only what she wishes to reveal
She subdues all rivals
Through various subtitles of the mind
Enthralled by her ever entrancing bliss
I beckon against time
To synchronize her idealistic necessities
With the emotional grandeur of love's splendor

A never-ending dream - by love possessed

Sal Schifilliti

Our Baby

He has all of the necessary parts
That one must have to live a life,
Two ears so cute, two beautiful eyes,
A mouth (but no teeth), filled with "oodles of sighs."
His cheeks are so rosy, his hands are too—
He has two legs and two arms, toes five times two.
Ten fingers, black hair, a body so firm—
But oh, does he love to wiggle and squirm.

Abundance of laughs and all kinds of sounds,
When he is awake—the household resounds
With squeals and yells,
With joy and delight—-
It is so quiet when he sleeps at night!

He sometimes cries, though not very often,
Just come cuddling and love and his cries will soften.
All this is rolled into one bundle of joy—-
This is our darling, our baby boy.

Sharon Turley

The Runaway Love

We met one night and instantly I knew
That something was going to happen
As we were together I felt something
Something warm, deep within my heart
But I couldn't tell if you felt it too
At times throughout the night
You went your way and I went mine
But at other times we found each other again
And I knew that something was going to happen
Something in the wind and within the reach of sight
When was it going to happen I couldn't wait
But time flew by and still something was coming
Something was urging to become
But the night ended and so did we
Maybe it was the beginning of love destroyed by fate
We went our separate ways
Never to return to each others arms
You found another when I did not
Something will happen for me, but maybe another day
Next time I hope something will happen.

Shannon Ingraham

Why Is The World So Ungrateful

Sometimes I feel so invisible
That the world has forgotten about me.
All I want is to be a part of things
So I lose how great life can be.

Sometimes the world can be so ungrateful,
And I know that this shouldn't be.
Don't you know how hard I am working,
I wish the world would notice me.

I laugh at those thoughts when I realize,
What I've said, who I've been all through these days.
As I gaze from the eyes of my inner child,
Working to make those thoughts go away.

The resentment builds, my patience is gone,
And inside my spirit is crumbling.
The child is out and wants to be heard,
But instead sends everything tumbling.

The crisis is over, the dust starts to settle.
This whole trip was really incredible.
But looking inside it all seems so clear,
It was I who was really ungrateful.

Louis Salvagno Jr.

Questions And Answers

The world has always longed for peace
That wars and hatred will someday cease
But will it ever come to be?
And would utopia make us free?
And how will we know the state we seek?
By being ever so mild and meek?
Is there a power from above
That gives us life and sends us love?
Or are we just here for a time
To act our roles and pantomime?
Each generation searches on
Throughout their lives and then they're gone
Without much changing as they pass
As constant as energy and mass
Is the strife we all must face
To know our minds and find our place
There may not be answers here to find
To the mysterious questions of mankind
But could we not be less defeated
By treating each other as we want to be treated?

Marilyn L. Hutchison

The King And I

The broken bread before me,
—the broken Christ...
He who was Holy and whole, broken for
bruised and fractured humanity.
The fruit of the vine,
—His blood expelled. The crimson
flow, bleaching out the stain on
humanities' soul.
How insolent of me to think,
my own "noble deeds" could atone,
when Jesus lay...shattered and alone,
the Holy One, sacrificed...God's plan!
As I eat this broken bread and drink
the wine, my conquered, surrendered will, kneels
before You, the Christ...
my sole/soul's Redeemer.
I leave Your Presence, trusting in this, Your
Work. I rest in Your Sabbath.
I am forgiven, renewed, and go in peace,
As hurricane winds...tamed to a gentle breeze.

Lil Toomey

Life's Pictures

Life is just a state of mind,
That which you seek your heart will find.

Peace is a picture preconceived -
And happiness is peace achieved.
For sadness we create our fears -
And loneliness just empty tears.
For jealousy we picture loss -
And freedom see a lack of cost.
Love is attraction held within -
And hate attraction turned to sin.

With thoughts, we can make our mind's eye see -
what we create our lives to be.

Lois Katz Stanton

Loving You Dear Heavenly Father

Praise you for being the God that you are
That you said you would never depart
From us Our Eternal Friend,
For you said I am with you always even unto the end

There is a bliss that comes from God's breath
This Holy mist filling us with His love
Each eternal day
Our breath as we go on our way

Without you we could not be,
God of all eternity
It's easy to love one that first loved us and we do
Forever this is true

You are the bright and morning star
shining in our hearts and not from afar
I will pray the Lord's prayer as my days begin
Thank him that nothing can separate us from our Eternal Friend

In you we have love, joy, peace happiness all that is good,
nothing bad and life without end
Our Eternal Friend, descending down from your throne
where sits only pure love down from streets of pure gold
Will come all things new unto your fold.

Mary Browning

What A New Day May Bring Us

The early morning hours are a strange sight.
The dawn caresses a brand new day.
What lies in store for us all is a mystery.
The calm stillness it renders could bring happiness.
But despair and anger could come into the picture also.
It all depends on how we want to view it, in our own minds.
The total aspect of everything depends solely on us!
We need to gather together to make sure it stays beautiful and
full of life! What A New Day May Bring Us.

To smile and say hello to one another,
shows we can trust in our feelings.
Our feelings show our true purpose in life.
And the reasons why we must go on with life, is to show others!
Love and commitment for one another can hold so much meaning
within our lives.
As the day goes on so much happens, world events and plans for
the future can sometimes connect with each other.
This can bring so much feeling within our midst.
Evening then falls so we may rest, the mind is filled with wonder!
What A New Day May Bring Us.

Pamela M. Sprague

Ballad For The Absentee

The afternoon is beautiful, crimson colored,
the afternoon is sumptuous, but he's far away...
the cypress and willow in front of the pond
following my gaze, they seem as if crying.

He's far, far away, and this afternoon
of imposing fire, the soul feels impotent,
crying taciturn: the afternoon's sumptuous
but he's very far, some oceans away!

Closing my eyes, the deep nostalgia
crossing oceans takes me to him;
he's dying without me
and in his sad evening, he can see me weep:

In my side of the world I seem quite afflicted.
With a quiet abysmal rage he says:
The afternoon is beautiful, crimson colored,
the afternoon is sumptuous, but she's far away!

Leonora Acuna De Marmolejo

December

Like a rainbow in the night
The blind without sight
A cry, I remember...a cold day in December.

Awake I keep, my memories for sleep
Alone in the dark, luscious lips leave their mark
Slight caress lingers, the touch of your fingers
Days long ago, before the first snow
Six years of trial, ends in denial
A life gone astray, a long winter's day
Gracious hosts, the others I meet
Alone in the dark, your memory I greet
Smiles and wishes, warm candy kisses
Laughter and romance, a sweet sultry slow dance

Spring, summer, fall
Now that is all
Nothing left, but an ember...a cold day in December.

Terry R. Fujii

A Red Rose

A red rose on white snow,
The blood so red it must show;
The warmth of the blood melts the ground,
A bird sings the only sound;
He sees the rose in the snow,
How to get rid of her he didn't know;
She knew too much, she had to die,
Getting over her, he'd have to try;
His one and only true love,
He falls like a sparrow, he once flew like a dove;
As the snow melts the ground,
Memories of her go round and round.

Mandy Orr

Love

Love is a special gift
That everyone needs
With some it's hard to give
With others it's easy
You can give it with a look
Such as a gentle smile or laugh
And giggle, as something that is worthwhile
It gives us pep and life
When we are in sorrow it will last
a long time like a never-
ending tomorrow

Sara J. Wilson

"37th President"

Once more the mighty guns salute
The bugle sounds its toll.
Once more a name is added to the presidential scroll.
He joins the grand procession our founding fathers took
Treading paths of greatness that forms our history book.
All the deeds of ages are deftly written there
For all the future sages to study and compare.
What shadows of life's failures veil the valor of each man?
Study, study, study, make a judgment if you can.
If judgments were clairvoyant and motives plain to see,
Still noble of the noblest would never perfect be.
Righteous, rogue, or renegade,
Which one must be confessed?
The flaw of all mankind beats strong in each and every breast.
The mercy that we show to these returns to us again.
Place hand on lips and listen to the sounding great "AMEN."

Ruth A. Black

Niagara Falls

The natural beauty, the romantic loneliness;
The dark abyss, and the divine mystery,
Oh, Niagara Falls
The souls will tremble in facing of eternity.

The flood falls, the mist rises;
The plunge goes endless,
The rainbow flickers only one moment
The brink between life and death
Reveals fascination, solitude, violence, and charm.
Oh, Niagara Falls
How to elucidate the similarity of paradise and hell!

The honeymooners possess time, space each other,
The suicides dream another world;
The pilgrims seek faith beyond human,
The wanderers escape from daily life.
Oh, Niagara Falls
You disclose the deep meaning of life
From nothingness returns to nothingness.

Ling Fan Peng

An Ode To "My City At Night"

The mystical sounds of the city at night are unbelievable.
The honking of car horns that fill the night air with all
different sounds;
An occasional backfiring of a car;
The sound of big trucks and motorcycles,
as they speed along the street;
People talking in loud voices and their laughter floating in
the midnight breeze;
All of this as I try to sleep.
In the distance you can hear the shrill sound of an ambulance's
sirens as the truck races down the street.
Suddenly out of the stillness comes the sound of a fire alarm;
As it gets closer and closer the bright lights shine in my
bedroom window;
Having lived in the country for many years, this is a change for me.
Suddenly the stillness of the night is broken by the sound of an
aircraft;
You are relieved when it fades in the distance.
There is one thing missing from the sounds of the night:
Our train no longer comes through town - it is silent forever.
The clock strikes one o'clock and I soon fall asleep.
Thank goodness this doesn't go on every night;
However, many times in the summer when it's especially dry this
happens.
The morning comes soon. Before long the traffic on our street
will begin again.
But this is a world that I'm getting used too!

Zelma Smith

Untitled

As I sat bathed in firelight
The days of my life came to me
And as though a great book were opened
I began to read,
My love for you is that of a hungry lion
The need for love so great
That I would stop at nothing to fulfill my desire
And hold you in my arms until the end of time itself
Wanting nothing more than to bring such pleasure
And carry you far away from this senile world
To a place beyond the stars
Where we could be together for eternity...
A rap at the door brings me back
I open it to find the one I truly love
Standing there with the moonlight accenting her facial beauty
I'm left as helpless as a lamb
With the wolf ready to pounce
Quietly she vanished into the night
And I'm left alone to mourn her tragic death.

Stephen Gerhauser Jr.

The Ending Of Time

The sinking feeling of a loss
The ending of today's entity...
The finished ending of time
Through timeless ability.
Filling you with love, passion
And mostly with inequity.

The space that carried us thus far...
The stolen wish given by a fallen star.
Twinkling in the darkness of a cool
September night.

Was love really worth the effort of giving?
Or was love the only foundation
That torments our living,
Since the beginning of creation.

Fear had created this make shift of thought-
For words once whispered,
And the brain and soul thus far have been taught.
That the ending of time- is really the ending
Of a rhyme.
Whispering like an echo throughout the passages of time.

Terri King

Dawn

From a wound in the breast of night,
The fabric of the firmament rent.
In the softness of the first light
She comes.
Then follow dazzling colors
Crimson, pink, gold and azure, turquoise
Slowly spreading over all,
Clouds resplendent: Tears in God's eyes.
More tears in heaven, more color spreads.
Fractured light the rainbow brings
Until pure gold slits the horizon,
Life born anew.

So the great changes in our lives
Allow us to glimpse tiny visions with heaven's sight.
In birth the womb opens to the light,
At death passes spirit bright,
Heaven's opening to joy or pain.
At the end of night the transit
And broken light the gift
To life renew.

Shirley Samarzia

CHOOSE TODAY

Thundering through his teenaged years,
the fatherless youth could shed no tears.
To others, he would show no pain but it was there -
in his face, in his tumultuous race, in the hurt
he caused those who cared.
He seemed rudderless in a stormy sea
but then, The One who quiets and parts the sea,
brought peace to that troubled heart.
And the "20-something" man stepped through
the door of faith, studying The Word eagerly until
that certain Wednesday night,
a drunken driver ran a red light, and sent him,
his Bible and motorcycle sprawling in the street.
He had no chance there, no moment to repent.
But it was God's will
that earlier, he made the choice - where to spend eternity.
What if he had waited?
What if YOU
wait too late?
CHOOSE TODAY!

Martha Merriken Frimand

Morning Glory

Adrift in the sea of the darkening Night Sky,
the first star of Dust twinkles a jewel,
alive with enticing radiance.
Its beauty is matched by none
as other stars materialize into existence,
while the cool, blue Sky darkens black
This first star dominates the Night;
a beacon for weary travelers,
an object of passion for lovers,
an entity inspiring awe from the innocent.
As Night progresses,
the Moon even loses her title
as the Gem of the Night Sky,
for the sinks below the horizon.
But this star, the first of the Night,
remains, blazing with furious majesty,
even into the early coming of Dawn,
and it achieves Morning Glory.

Malon Edwards

The Flag

We don't answer questions because we do not know.
The flag does not wave because the wind does blow.
God created justice, freedom and liberty.
One thing he did not is the presence of slavery.
We are one nation lying under our Lord.
Taking another for granted will never be ignored.
He created justice, so we could all be free.
And before we went to Heaven He wanted our life to be happy.
Why decide to hate when you can always love?
Why cry out your problems when you are forgiven up above?
Why turn your back when someone needs a friend?
Why hurry through the start when there will always be an end?
Sometimes late at night I hear a weakened song.
That sings of smiling faces where innocence lives on.
When will the dreams come true? When will I no longer have to pray,
Of blacks and whites being more than the color gray?
When will racism stop? When will peace not have to hide?
When will everyone realize that the flag is waving for pride?
And on most days when it struggles with each kill.
It pretends to wave as it stands so still.

Sara Partlow

Beyond The Gate

On a day beyond the sunset, through the eyes of youth she sees
The Gate where pain's forgotten in eternal, joyful peace.
She takes the hands that waited, standing years of vigil true:
"Glad Welcome, Wife and Mother" greet the dearest men she knew.
They guide her last step over and she weeps in their embrace.
At last, farewells are broken she had long bid to erase.
"Come, sit within our circle", spoke the husband to his wife,
"And play for us your harp again that touched us through our life."
So they sit within the Garden, in the presence of their Lord,
While joyously, her music flows in hymn of note and chord.
Then, as the Gate is closing at the ending of her song,
She says "I'd like to wait here for the girls to come along,
Let's stay for grand reunion with each on her own day.
Let the circle be unbroken when the last has found her way."
So her harp, it plays unended just beyond the Heaven's Gate:
With Claude and Wayne and Emerald, in vigil, Fern will wait...

Lynn McMichael

Wrap Me In A Rage

Last night I was wrapped in a rage
The genuine thing
Felt that in my effort to do it all I had failed
to do everything
Now we've talked a little but only by phone
It's still there
And it's still four days till we sit face to face
and get it all clear
In the meantime I'm left reading this book
With a single page
That's full of my own thoughts
Wrap me in a rage
I love you so much it makes me afraid
I want to give you room but I don't want
to lose you
And that conflict wraps me in a rage

Kevin P. Gallagher

Come Home, Now

When I was just a little girl, I'd go outside to play
The happy fun time games of all the young and gay.
Hopscotch, jump the rope and dolls, to name a few.
I'd play all day, laugh time away, under skies of hazy blue.

Then came the evening tide, when the sun was going down,
I could hear my Mother call me, "You all better come home, now,
Put away all of your toys, there's no more time to play,
Just pick them up and come on in, tomorrow's another day."

Now that I've grown older, and my life is slipping away,
In the twilight of early evening, I can still hear my Mother say,
"You all better come home now, put your toys all away,
Just pick them up and come on home, tomorrow's
JUDGEMENT DAY!"

Martha L. Goff

Justice And Liberty

I'm writing you this letter to be opened upon my death.
The fighting is getting closer and there is only a few of us left.
We're not here because we like it, but because it has to be.
We're here so that others in this world can live and remain free.
We're tired and hungry and dirty, and the fighting is really rough.
We all want to get back home but the higher ups won't call enough.
We know the end is coming and the fact that some of us will die.
But our death will be worth if it the American flag can fly.
As long as we are able, we'll fight to keep America free.
If for no other reason than to obtain justice and liberty.
Keep the flag flying folks, raise it high.
It symbolizes freedom and those of us who die.

Shelby Jean Aldridge

The Poet's Ballet

Passion, Passion,
The heartbeat danced away
And every turn
Was but a prayer
Adrift in its own ballet.

Away it went, away it went,
Like a docile virgin bride
Whose flower unfolds
In the shadow
Of a silent candlelight.

The rains poured down, the rains poured down,
And cast the heart into the mire
Where it kissed the dew
Of beauty's feet
And arose in sublime desire.

"Take me now!" "Take me now!"
Whispered the heart's magnificent plea,
When then her breath
Pierced the heart
And came the final symphony.

Phillip Van Every

Yippy Ie

Rapturous cry on an eagle's wing
The heat and dust and wind she'll sing
Coyote howling at the awesome sight
Gunfighting cacti that challenge a moonlit night
Praying lizards in the vestibules
Sidewinding snake finds a rabbit or two
Wild boar dines on a prickly pear
Honey bee buzzing fills the still air...
Hugh castles reach skyward hewn from the sand
Gave birth to adventure when entered by man
Harmony extracted from this wild landscape
Once he found it there was no escape...
That is why today on this restless yet somehow peaceful ground
A man and his horse still can be found...
They call him cowboy!

Mitchell D. Spiros

Eyes Of A Child

Have you ever looked into the eyes of a child.
The innocence that's cast upon you.
The tiny hands that hold defeat.
In the tired child that can only weep.
The glimpse of happiness when you are near.
Arms that hold their security and there is no fear.
With the dependence of your care.
That only love and proudness would ever share.
No worries of life that surrounds them.
With a parent's guard that bounds them.

Sandra Newman

The Present

This is the day God has given us
The present, to love and worship HIM
Use it for the way it was given.
It may be the only day you will live.
Accept GOD's gift, the present, reverently.
yesterday is gone forever, Tomorrow may never be,
The moment now is the present.
Live it gratefully, joyfully, thankfully . .

Virgiinia Stonestreet Bush

Season's Greetings

We wish you and yours...
The JOY of Christmas
As reflected in the eager eyes of tiny tots-
As heard in the joyous voices of carollers-
As felt by people of good will everywhere-

The LOVE of Christmas:
As expressed by sharing and caring
During the season and throughout the year,
As experienced by showing love for all mankind.
As shown by helping someone today and everyday.

The HAPPINESS of the New Year:
As evidenced by new hope, renewed faith and greater love-
As reflected by increased positive thought, word and deed.
As epitomized by dreams realized.

These are our wishes for you and yours
For the holiday season and for the
New Year!!!

H. Blandenah Black

Happy Mother's Day

For you Mom...
The light that made my life easier -

For you Mom...
The one who understands how I always feel -

For you Mom...
I would say it from the top of the world -
"I Love You"

For you Mom...
When your arms' embrace is ever so needed -

For you Mom...
When we laugh and share together -

For you Mom...
For just being a Wonderful and Fantastic -
"Mother All Year Long"

For you Mom...
"Happy Mother's Day" and "I Love You So"

Roy S. Lewis Jr.

Lost Love

The lonely nights all alone,
The missing smell of his sweet cologne.

The love that is nevermore,
Is now locked between closed doors.

The love that was there that held so strong,
Was torn apart and didn't belong.

I love that nights that we shared.
I love the mornings when he cared.

But now it was just all taken away,
By that women he met one day.

He left me with his loving son.
And now he is on the run,

I thought he'd love me until the end,
I thought I was he's special friend.

But now I know the love is gone,
And the love will never be.

I can't believe I cared for him,
And thought he cared for me.

Loni Runge

The Cherokee Strip Run

High in the sky climbs the sun
The morning of September 19, 1893.
This is the day to make the run
Into the strip called Cherokee.

Hordes of Sooners, the land hungry men.
In darkness over the border fly.
The best choice land they hope to win.
As they jump the gun they just might die.

Gathering before noon at the border line,
People of all walks of life are here.
Many modes of travel, some shoddy, some fine.
Eyes of those walking are inclined to show fear.

The sound of the trumpet or gun shot to start
Sends the would be settlers on their stampede
Red dust churns up, quick, as they depart.
Each person on their own as away they speed.

There they go across the far prairie.
This wild land has no sign of a tree.
A homestead or townsite, which will it be?
Their destiny unknown, until the end of the journey.

Mary A. Fry

Renascence

Not that the dead shall rise again to seek
The old, once-cherished dream it cast aside,
Nor dead desire renew the tongue to speak.
But both shall rest as muted as the pride
Which rendered us defenseless in the glow
Of anguished love. Now that the time has lain,
I do not find it quite so hard to go:
Almost, it seems that I can bear the pain.
Thus, marking in the ashes of the past,
And scattering to the winds the fateful dust,
As final as were we unto the last,
We let it crumble there amid the rust
Of tears. But if your love should call today,
My own would rise and follow it away.

L. Martin Courtney II

"True Christmas"

Years ago, a Child was born in a stable,
The only light from a star, no electric was available.

There wasn't a feather or water bed,
But a manger with hay for his head.

No pillow or satin sheets, only woven wool, no cotton,
Now modern days, the child is almost forgotten.

There wasn't ornaments, colored lights, for a Christmas Tree.
The star of Bethlehem was only there to see,

Poor shepherds tending their sheep from afar,
Looked up into the heavens and saw the star.

Three wise men brought gifts, that were given from the heart,
And prayed for the Christ Child for a wonderful start.

At the time the Christ Child was born, peace was found,
Now wars, starvation, and fraud and even baron ground.

Even before Thanksgiving, people start to celebrate,
Advertise and make money at a tremendous rate.

We should beware of the coming of the Lord today,
For it all started in a stable far away.

It's best to stick to the Christmas that's true,
Only the Lord and Christ will get you through.

Paul Skinner

Age Of The Dove

In a puddle of rain, I watched
the outstretched dove.
With a twist of my hand, I grasp what is left;
all the scavenged remains, captured
dwindling like silver strands
of hair, intertwined through
rustic fingertips.
Through faded eyes, forest green
turned pale and thin. A reflection,
of my lost youth. A view
mirrored over and over, across this frail skin
across the lines that disturb my face,
strangling all that was once my strength.
A tap from the window turns my head to look
upon the raven perched as justice; the birth
of the death, of my youth.

Rae Ann Michelle Briggs

February (A Birthright)

I want to go, to someday see
the place in time or mind where steeples gleam
like snow ice
in tear tired, half shut eyes.
Cold blue sky
magnifies storm cloud white
and all confusion dies
little hands in my hands, warm and tight
bound to other hands
thin-fleshed, almost ripped, blind
but they see pure, like water runs
and rain falls
searching stashed life in black dead ground
filthy like blood on me, I scrape and wash
and cut and bleed again.
Don't look at me.
They see and understand
this need to go and someday see
this place in time or mind
where steeples gleam.

L. M. Hill

"Let Me Walk" - In All This Splendor

"O' God" I hear "Thy voice" - in the "Wind."
The "Rushing of water" - and the "Pitter-patter of rain."
This "Great World" of "Thy creation" . . .
Is one of "Beauty to enjoy" — "Enduring some pain."

Let me walk "O' God" - in all "This splendor" -
"Let mine eyes" ever behold the "Rising sun."
And the "Beauty of the red, and purple sunset" -
at "Even-tide" - "When day is done."

Let our "Hearts and hands" - respect the "Things we're given" . .
.
To be "Wise and understanding". . . and to "Atone."
Help us "Learn the lessons" - "Thou hast hidden" -
In every "Leaf on the tree." . . and "Each precious stone."

Help us "Seek strength" "O' God" . . .
"Not to be greater" than our "Brother" -
But to fight our "Greatest Enemy" - ("Within Ourselves") -
That with "Every Blessing Given" - are "Blessings for another."

"May we always be ready" - to come to "Thee" -
With "Conscience clear" - and "Pure of heart and name."
So "When life fades away" - as the "Fading sunset" -
"Our spirit" - may come to "Thee" "Without shame."

Merle Hooper

The Music The Wind Played

No lyric, found its way in the music the wind played
The rustle of the trees Swish, this way and that
The leaves falling downward so gracefully!!
Each one gliding in its own space
Sometimes swirling, movements swift
This quiet beauty, something to behold
The music the wind played
So peaceful, the breath of God blowing
Let your entire being, become embraced
Don't you know?? It's God's gentle blow
The music the wind played
Ohhh!!!! so much more effective
Than someone's meaningless words
Insincerity is of no value
From one being to another
Ahhh!!! but a touch from the Lord
Wind brushing across your face
Gives such calm assurance
You're in your rightful place
Deservedly receiving quiet music, the wind plays.

Martha Jeanne Fanning

At This Time I Was Born

In the year, 1906 what's great about that? The eight day of July, the seventh month, the year 1990-7/8/90. At 34 minutes and 56 seconds after midnight, and again after noon, the time can be expressed this way: 12:34:56-7/8/90, or 1-2-3-4-5-6-7-8-9-0.

Maybe that does not ring a bell for you; after all, it is but a numbers game and appeals only to those interested in trivia. But, it can only happen again the next time in July 8, 2090, 100 years. later!

(It happened in Amsterdam, Netherlands).

My father came home from church with the older children while my mother was attended by some of her sisters. It was Sunday and therefore everyone able went to church, a short walking distance from home. Coming up the stairs Dad said
I hear we have a new boarder come to live with us.
(They heard the cry of a newborn). I've been one of the family ever since. Now numbering 300+.

About twenty years later, another birth took place, in a much larger family; a royal family known as the Kingdom of God.
I became (one-of-them," to remain so eternally. Isn't God Good?

R. van Oosbree

Vertical Hook

The SKY fell Today....
The Silent Speak of Lovers crossed the Gold Horizon
Captured The Tribal Lords in their Rebellious Drumming,
Summoning all the Dream Weavers to Drink fermented Fruits;
Liquor and Long Lingering Visions that Shamans hook on Belts.
Story Ropes that keep their Souls from falling to Earth.

The Night Shows its Soul....
Crimson Snakes Slit the Quiet Seam of Life:
Silver Shadow Brothers of the Wolf in Fire Dance light,
Tall Black Specters, the Rattle of Beads, Dry Seeds
Tumbling in Reeds of Cane, the Waterfall Rush; Rattling
Dark Spirits, fleeing the Serpents that know no Pain...
The Rein of Sky Lords; free falling....falling Free.

Vertical Time....
Time in motion Slow: Quivering, Quakes Rumbling
Chances taken in the Time of Dreams
The Medicine Woman takes the Child to bed
The Fever of Wild Eyed Natives abates as Night Lords
Cast spells to lid their Wild Electric Eyes...
Spell Bound; Earth Bound in Forever Time...

Michael E. Cowne

Fountains

The fountain's water sparkling in the sunlight
The sound of its splashing brings all a delight
It gently cools the air with its soft light mist
And the mind drifts off to places it can't resist
The allure of the water has lasted through time
From ancient fountains now covered with grime
To the modern ones of glass and metal
Which some artists in cities now pedal
But the allure of the water still remains after all
And I hate when they are emptied out in the fall
For fountains are youthful and so full of life
They take our minds far away from our strife
They fill us with such peace as they play in the sun
And as we enjoy their play, we too have some fun

Phillip Alexander Martin Bray

"Our Eyes — The Windows Of Our Soul"

The windows of our soul are our God-given eyes,
The speak so eloquently when filled with love and surprise,
They cry our when disappointment, sadness or illness arise,
Or, they radiate truth or display downright lies!

We're born with two eyes, great wonders we see,
The beauty of our country, from sea to shining sea.
The love of our family and the many friends we share,
When the magic mirrors of our soul are there.

Do you take your eyes for granted when all is going right?
Life can lose its splendor when we lose our precious sight.
So, be thankful every day for the pleasures your eyes can bring,
For to lose one's eyesight is a most distressing thing.

Viola G. LeRoy

Patton

A general who's stalking in his grave,
The 'spit and polish' soldier of his time
Was one who rode with destiny to save
His fabled army struggling in its climb.
This fearless fighter never knew defeat
But, knew the art of winning at its best.
He's watching so no soldiers drag their feet
When warring nations put them to the test.
His fighting spirit wakens man who knows
That he is still among us even now,
To wage again the most destructive blows
To enemies who think that they know how.
Our nation understands the soldier's part,
That's how the Patton legend got its start.

Steven Hardy Humble

Cloud Of Confusion

I feel as if I am lost in a cloud of confusion.
The question marks are all around me.
In front of me, in back of me, on my left, on my right,
in my past, in the present, and for my future.
Why, I asked, is this my life? I want happiness,
but all I feel is sadness. I want my family to
be whole again, but it can't be.
Why, I asked, can't it be? Someone replied, because the poor are
silent, shunned and mocked. I am poor in money,
but rich in heart. Why, I asked, did this happen to me?
There was no reply, only silence bestowed on me,
not a soul could answer me. Why, I asked,
won't anyone help me? One replied, we can't.
We don't know how. We are poor and unimportant
to those who have it all. We are silent, shunned
and mocked, because we are poor. Why, I asked,
are we poor for we have rich hearts?
Again, there was no reply, only silence bestowed
on me, not a soul could answer me.

Sharel Williams

"Broken Heart"

A dark streak of sorrow takes its place in a lonely, empty, heart.
The stallions' head lying gently in my lap, his eyes faintly open.
He dared to take a last breath.
And there death takes his soul into the sky.
His eyes fall shut.
And in my lap is where the stallion dies, and breaks my heart.

Nicole Marsden

Endless Love

I'll love you until
The stars cease to shine,
And the moon will hide herself
Then slip away into nothingness.

I will love you until
The sun stops shining, and
Will not illuminate the early morning sky
The earth will stop turning on its axis.

My love is endless, boundless, and measureless.
I'll love you until
The weeping willow refuses to cry,
Then her branches wither and die.

I'll love you until
The rivers run dry,
And the sand cries out with groans.
Wet me! wet me! once again.

My love is deeper than the ocean
That washes her waves upon the sandy shores.
Then return to try once more.

Mazell Parker

Apocalypse

Evil is ripe throughout the lands.
The stench of death and doom
It fills our nostrils.

Corruption and greed,
These rule in the centers of power.
The neglected, the poor, the wretched
seek solace in drugs,
And their young folk find comfort and affection
in the gangs,
And security in the firepower of guns.
Remember-
Paul preached that in "the last days"
Such could be the case,
But none cared to listen.
Remember too-
That Nostradamus predicted a sudden
and Cataclysmic END to it all.
The survivors will scream to the heavens -
Savior! Oh save us, O Lord.

Kenneth I. E. Macleod

Untitled

Oh river of thoughts, why run you so low?
The seasons long have cried for rain
The dusty paths choked on their need
And still only the threatening rumblings of a few white visitors
If only the cleansing would come and clear away the dead
Then new beginnings might sprout
And a cycle would be complete
But no mourning is allowed yet
The All-Seeing One waits
To let a heart-broken land bear her silent burden
And pray for dust to be licked up
By the hungry pawns above.

Tracy Karas

Untitled

Through the eyes of an eagle shall I see,
The strength of a lion give to me.
For wisdom I seek, yet how shall I find,
Perhaps, through the gates of my chaotic mind.

Open the door and let me see,
Through the powers you have given me.
My soul animal shall show me light,
Through the sorrowful, darkness of night.

Give me strength, oh, give me power,
Let me live through the witching hour.
Guide my body through blackened hollows,
And let me feel the evil that follows.

For I am good, and I am strong,
My hidden power is for what I long.

Lori L. Clark

Untitled

The world as I know it, ended when you left me.
The sun finally set, and the mountains fell into the sea.
A cold wind started, and began to blow.
And that feeling of love, I will never know.
The stars used to shine and twinkle in the sky.
But the sparkle is gone, and the birds cannot fly.
The rose you gave me, I have in my room
Has fallen apart, and will never bloom.
One last teardrop falls, and I will never be.
As I remind myself for the last time, that you left me.

Lori McHenry

Clipper Mills

Through shuttles, bobbins, spools of waterfalls,
the thread ran, spinning voyage, sea-lane, sail
that heeled the village hard, head-over-hills,
to town. "Cast off, all hands!", the foremen bawled.
Machinery strained. The sun took sextant squint
through steeples' needles-eye. Spars' Baptists veered.
The people waved. "Take care!", they cried. Tight-spanned,
full-crowded dream (mills spun when fingers tired),
weighed anchor towards mist-shrouded landfalls struck
whole cloth from cloud. Till wake unraveled tides'
taut canvas, back through brook and fingerprick,
to first silk-sulky warp. "Land ho!" replied
the skimming crows-nests to "Sail ho!" of farms'
St. Elmo's crows. And steam yelled, "Closing time!"

Marvin Solomon

It's Not Worth It

You hear the shots day in and day out.
The bullet hits and you hear the shout.
An eight year old dead,
Shot in the head,
He wore red.

Fists flying in your face.
The bruises sting like mace.
They didn't know you!
If only you knew
Not to wear blue.

He looked at you the other night,
So now it's time to set it right?
But that must be a lie,
Because now you cry;
It was your little brother caught in the drive-by!

Shannon Marshall

The Black Hole And What If

What if: the Hubble telescope's correct and in
the Virgo Galaxy M eight seven,
there swirls a massive black hole for real?

What if: Einstein's theory is correct and this hole
could warp space and also time so we could
go back in time and really change the deal?

What if: we could swirl through its mass of imploding
stars, and back to the Garden of Eden,
the massive Tree of Knowledge to conceal?

What if: it is not too bizarre to think we could
stop the horrible evil of Hitler,
or go to our Lord's trial and appeal?

What if: there exists a world of love and hope
where the children would never go hungry,
be abused, or be killed - is this unreal?

What if: we could really travel the fifty-two
million light years to the great Black Hole and
all live in a world where we could heal?

What if?

Marjory Nierman

Better Off Dead

Rope around my neck and feet on a sled,
the way my life is, I'll be better off dead.
It all started when I met my fake friends,
but now it's because of everything now and then.
In the beginning life was fun and carefree,
a little kid who wanted to be all he could be.
Now I have no one special to brag about,
and loneliness, is all that haunts my house.
I would love to have a special friend,
whether it be a dog, woman or man.
A wish of happiness is easier done then said,
maybe I will be better off dead.
Heartbreaks and heartaches seem all that plague this life,
and it is so hard to tell wrong from right.
Well, you can loosen your collar I will not kill myself today,
no matter how many reasons,
it's too much to pay.
It's only human I heard it once said,
to feel the world would be happier,
if you were better off dead.

Michael B. Davis

Flight 427

The flight was a good one - the day was bright;
The weather for flying had been just right.
The view from the cock-pit was all the way clear.
The folks in the cabin had nothing to fear.
The descent to the airfield would shortly begin,
And soon they'd be welcomed by friend or kin.

All of a sudden - Who can believe? -
A cry of anguish, a jolt, and a heave -
The plane took a nose-dive, straight down was its course -
It hit the ground with incredible force!
It exploded and shattered in a wooded ravine -
Naught was left but fragments to glean.

It reminds us all - how fragile is life,
With its twistings and turnings, its joy and its strife.
The choices we make, oft determine our fate.
We know not, before us, what tidings await.
While life is ours, let's give it our best;
And relish each moment to live it with zest.

Olive I. Clark

Death

Death is a chill off snowy mountain peaks...
The whisper of wind just before dawn...
The etched memory of a beloved face on the eternal rock.

Those who have lived as best they can
have earned the right
to become one with the dark splendor: Death.

Mary Hosmer Lupton

Winded

Whilst I watch thy misty eyes shine,
the wind whistles for you divine
the melody mine heart aches to sing,
the melody mine heart aches to bring.
If I could but touch your rustic cheeks
and feel the flesh beneath me speak
of love that 'tis as strong as mine
of feelings entangled in that twine
that wilt forever bind you to me,
that wilt always ensure you I see
when I arise with morning glare,
when I reach to feel you bare.
And if that day would come to be
when you no longer wanted me
I shall shed an ocean of tears
and fade away throughout the years
whilst the winds around me change their way
to turn back time so I can stay
where I was yours and you were mine
and where we two knew love divine...

Linh Duong

The Crush

When the time comes that we must part,
The world will hear the shattering of my heart,
I know that there is nothing I can say,
That would make you stay,
And hopes I had for us have been smashed,
Almost as if they had crashed,
Into your heart,
And retreated in hopes of getting smart,
Instead they were stabbed dead as with a dart,
That went all the way down to my lonely heart,
I know as long as I have hope,
I will be able to cope,
No matter what you do or say,
I will be here until my very last day,
When it is time to say goodbye,
I want you to know my love for you will never die,
But as assuredly as I must,
I will place in God my trust,
To guide you through,
And always watch over you.

Robert Erney

You Ask - What Is Love?

Love is the feeling of one towards another -
The tone of one's voice - to one's own brother.
It's hope for the present - it's sharing, my dear,
It's a gift from the heart that's precious - sincere.
Love is belief - in a friend so true,
Small secrets shared - between one or two.
Love is a heartbeat, passion for a friend -
An understanding with joy - which ne'er shall end.
This is life - this is love,
Coupled with God's blessings, sent from above.

Louise Davis

Love Has Left You Blind

Love has left you blind, blinded by all
the wrong things he has done
No, this isn't just a poem, and it's definitely
not a song, but since you chose him over your own flesh-n-blood
you have done something completely wrong.
It wasn't worth the pain in which we now acclaim,
it was a total shame.
What will it take for the blinded love to wilt?
Don't you feel at least a little guilt? Or do you even
care? Is there even shame, or am I just the one to blame?
Would you just listen to what I have to say, or must
you keep pushing me away? Why me? What did I do,
besides always love you? Can you tell me why?
Why I cry a tear that longs for you to be near.
But you have pushed me away every time. Why?
I'm not the one who did the crime. If I could I'd
take my life and try to rewind, but I can't,
because that's not for real. Now I think it's
time to reveal, because my life I cannot rewind,
for love has left you blind.

Michelle Pickles

"Class Reunions"

Fifty years... a memorable milestone in our lives,
The years have sped by, we lucky ones still survive,
Hugs and greetings to those far and near,
Many questions and answers to our classmates so dear,
Everyone has changed... beyond belief!
Not me... I see "Me" Often — to my relief.
It's hard to recognize that person over there,
Nametags help clue, but we try not to stare,
So we discreetly inquire if someone knows,
Those distinguished persons in the "grownup" clothes.
Silver-threads and glasses add to the confusion,
Everyone should look the "same" — but what an illusion!
Some classmates more "pudgy"... and others more thin,
But we're all doing great... for the "shape" we are in!!
Conversations are of memories, of school days,
Growing up, meeting our challenges in varied ways.
About our children, and "grands" we do rave,
Showing precious photos we all tote and save,
Again; class pictures are taken, to help us recall,
Just Who is Who...at our next Reunion Ball.

Trudy King

Today Is Mine

Today is mine; the past has swiftly flown;
The yesterdays that I once called my own;
The carefree days of childhood passed away;
And I, a youth, am privileged to faced today.
Today is mine.

Oh, may I not forget the former years!
The days of childhood learning, joys, and tears;
And may I live abundantly today;
For if tomorrow comes, it, too, shall pass away.
Today is mine.

Mine is to choose the purpose I will follow;
If life be rich, or meaningless and hollow.
Oh, may it be when life's last bell shall chime,
My footprints are imprinted in the sands of time!
Today is mine.

Today is real; tomorrow may not be.
'tis but a breath 'twixt now and vast eternity.
This life is like a flower that fades away.
Tomorrow is unsure; I have today.
Today is mine.

Lila C. Knight

A Search For Reality

So many people seem so felicitous and healthy;
Their life of travel, concerts, and bountiful
luncheons, seems to provide them with
a life of bliss day after day.

Then - if you turn on your television,
You see people dying by the millions
of plague, starvation, and disease;
and still others running madly through
the streets; killing any man, woman or
child that happens to be in their way.

At the same moments in time, on
the same planet, how can this possibly be?
Is life a wondrous dream, or a tremendous
nightmare? Can anyone answer this for me?

Many of the 'lower' animals look after
their own, and live in peace and harmony.

Yet, we are constantly told that man
is the highest form of life.
Is this our delusion ——?
Or is this reality?

Tiffany Nicole Tripp

One Night

As they laid and watched the stars
Their lives began to intertwine
For some strange force
Knew they belonged together
He held her so close
She wished they would never part
So many things he wished to tell her
But not one seemed to matter now
All that mattered was that they found each other
And nothing could tear them apart
Their love was so true
Their hearts so locked
They were destined together forever
And yet they only had one night
One night to fall totally in love
And one night was all they needed...

Melissa Cunningham

Dissent

"If you and I do not agree,
Then one of us must be wrong."
But is this necessarily
The reasoning of the strong?

"Learn to live with diversity,"
Our wisest men have said.
"No one has a monopoly
On the ways of heart or head."

Put not your songbird in a cage.
Seek not to quell dissent.
But let us welcome honest rage
As a blessing, heaven sent.

If you and I board up our minds,
We've done a double wrong.
We've locked our thoughts behind closed blinds;
We've shut out another's song.

If you and I do not agree,
Need one of us be wrong?
Or is it possible, can it be
That harmony makes the song?

Marilyn D. Lawrence

Nights Of Fire

Days, weeks, maybe months go by,
then suddenly you are there.
Standing in a ray of sunlight which
beams down upon you so bright, and
within its glow your beauty I do behold.
Frightened and shaken I stare, longing
for you to notice I too am there. Then
I catch your eyes of gray fall upon my
face, as I continue to stare. Frozen in
my tracks, as I know you know, and
my body trembles with desire when I
remember you and I and our many
nights of fire.
My mind screams out, oh passion, passion,
flame and fire, please let him too remember
our many nights of burning desire. Then
hoping you will not move from my sight
for fear my heart shall melt, putting
out the flame of desire, which is needed
to give us just one more night of fire.

Tamie Pucek

Jesus Called

He called me in the early morning hours,
There among the birds and blooming flowers.
I heard Him in the noon time too,
Heard Him say, I have many plans for you.
He spoke to me in the evening time,
I've still so many things in mind.
I heard Him in the night time too,
There's oh so little time for you.
The darkness comes, it's here at last,
The midnight hour is approaching fast.
I listen for His call once more,
He doesn't call, as He called before.
I cried and cried there on my knees,
Oh Lord, my God, you must hear me.
I know you called in the morning dew,
The noon time bright, the evening and night time too.
He answered me there on my knees,
'Tis the midnight hour and you call to me.
But I will take you for my own,
That mansion I've prepared, will be your home.

Mickie Roberts

Generations Everywhere

There are flowers everywhere, and bones.
There are seasons like spring, beginnings with soft petals
and deep colors and there are seasons of winter
when even hope freezes.

I cannot explain the reason why even flowers wither and die
like ideas and hearts or why fire and ash begin and end in each other.

And I cannot reach out to this generation of seed
and retell my own beginning, my own spring
without denying the shade and color, and without denying
the velocity of generation begetting generation begetting
generation - spring, summer, fall, winter.

I am here, but they cannot hear me.
We share the same season but they will not follow my steps and
cannot teach me theirs, will not reach out as I fall,
grasping my heart, dreaming of spring.

Marian S. Musmecci

Father To Me

In a tiny little church in my home town,
There is a man who lays the law down,
Hellfire and brimstone from behind that stand,
Not one in the county can touch that man,
He stands for truth, justice, and love,
His heart is gold; a gift from above,
With a worn-out Bible in his hands,
He leads hearts to Christ throughout the land,
He prays as he goes throughout the day,
Hoping that somehow I'll see the way,
His life is a testimony to all that he's preached,
And I cannot count the souls that he's reached,
He preaches hard and yet gentle is he,
The friend of many and Father to me.

Lisa Gordon

Do You Know?

I am all dried up.
There is nothing left in me.

I can no longer cry, cry for you, anymore;
I can no longer love, love for you, anymore;
I can no longer care, care for you, anymore.

All the tears have stopped running
because I have used every last drop for you.
All the love have stopped giving
because I have given every last beat to you.
All the care has stopped showing
because I have shared every last heart with you.

This is it.
I have given you everything I have and more,
and there is nothing left in me; not even for myself.
I am just an empty shell, lifeless and painless,
searching for a peace and soul.

Pei-Mei Chou

The Smile

The smile seems to have disappeared, from oh so many faces
There isn't a line on the face, no type of telltale traces
Did you ever stop and think, of the power of the smile
Watch the changes in your face, try it for a while
It is so much easier to make a friend, if you smile when first you meet
You can try it anywhere, even walking down the street
We don't take the time, to show we want a friend
Giving them a simple smile, is a great way to begin
A smile is a ray of sunshine, on a dark and cloudy day
It has a way of speaking volumes, when there's not a thing to say
Smiles don't cost any money, and we have lots of them to give
Imagine how we'd get along, how much better we would live
A smile is just like laughter, you feel good in every place
We could give a smile to everyone, every single race

Kathryn Jackson

To Amanda With Love

When walking down the path of life remember what I say
That there are many thorns, that grow along "the way"
The road of life uncertain, its prospects often "bleak"
And so many times along that path we tend to become "weak"
In this life we must all learn, the difference of right and "wrong"
And at times you will find to be weaker or be "strong"
But troubles are but stepping stones and someday you will "see"
That if you are not careful could be "catastrophe"
If only magic spectacles could really make you "see"
As I'm your little "Oma," please take this advice from "me"
Your future is ahead of you, like a clear white path of "snow"
So be careful how you step on it for every mark will "show"
So to this journey we call life, when troubles bring "dismay"
There's always hopes and promises of a clear brighter day.

Rhena Norma Scott

Ellie's Proposal

Somewhere beyond a golden sky
There lies a land of smokeless fire.
A land where flowers live forever;
A place where love is considered a treasure.
A land whose only river flows into a neon sky,
Disappearing into a cloud that's silver lined.

And where this skyfall touches ground,
Amidst fields of ageless roses,
The smokeless fire may be found.
Buried deep beneath the flowers petals,
Dreams of a magical eternity
Always seem to be settled.
If only ye are lucky enough
To lift the right petal.

Kenneth Soileau

Mother

I found her sitting there alone, her eyes a vacant stare.
There was no indication that she felt my presence there.

Her hands lay idly in her lap, withered, wrinkled, rough
and worn. A wedding ring, a thin gold band, one finger did adorn.

Her shoulders stooped as if to say, no more burdens could
they bear. Yet through the past, those many years, they had
carried their fair share.

I slowly knelt beside her, put one of her hands in mine.
Not a single word was spoken, just hushed silence for a time.

I raised my head and looked at her; her eyes, her lips, her
face. Memories began to come to view, a miracle took place.

Her thin lips parted slightly, a feeble smile began to form.
Her eyes did twinkle softly, and her face was sweet and warm.

"I love you", was all I said , my voice choked with emotion.
I thought of how she'd lived her life with tireless devotion.

Her eyes then closed in rest and peace, a calm assurance of
her fate. She had held on tight to life for me, now she waits
at Heaven's gate.

Maxine Taylor Thomas

My Glass Has Run

In the twilight gently glowing, there's a song in my heart;
There's a calling in the music, boding a time to depart;
The words are heard with clarity, though the song just begun;
Seems life only commenced, and now my glass has run.

Time's passing kept me mystified, in life I have not been seen;
The roads have been tilted upward, thwarting all my dreams;
My strides have been quick paced, like the dying, setting sun;
But I am losing life's race, and now my glass has run.

Life's tide is ebbing quickly, the song grows louder still;
Signifying my fated obligation, a debt I must fulfill;
I look upward for the answer, forthcoming there is none;
Time has consumed my allotted moments, and now my glass has run.

The distant calling within me, compels me to trudge on;
While knowing time is fleeting, I must forever heed the song;
My life's journey is about over, too soon I will succumb;
For spiteful time is in a hurry, and now my glass has run.

And when my day is over, the song no longer will be;
The music once within me, will be stilled for eternity;
I will pause before departing, count my blessings one by one,
For time dictates my destiny, and now my glass has run.

Richard H. Leighton

"Somewhere"

Somewhere, there's a someone to love me. Somewhere
there's a someone to care. Somewhere there's a
someone to be with me and God knows my
every need. I know my Jesus cares. He will
never let me down. He knows my every need.
He can take care of me. People and friends sometime
let you down. But Jesus is always there.
He will never let you down. And Jesus will
never leave you. For he is truly my friend.
Whatever may come and go in life, I know He
is always on my side and if I get too lonely,
I know God will send someone to me. But
anyway as life moves on we know only
God and Father Jesus Christ has all
the answers.

Ramona E. Hamric

A Time For Everything

There's a time heal, and a time to mend
There's a time for reality, and a time to pretend
There's a time for peace and a time for war
There's a time to pay attention, and a time just to ignore
There's a time to laugh, and a time to cry
There's a time to say hello, and a time to say goodbye
There's a time for justice, and a time for truth
There's a special time for me, and a special time for you
There's a time to make haste, and a time to slow down
There's a time for a smile, and a time for a frown
There's a time to talk, and a time for silence
There's a time for anger, but no time for violence
There's a time we like to remember, and a time we'd like to forget
There's a time to take a stand, and a time just to sit
There are times that are the worst, and times that are the best
There's a time to be born, and a time to be laid to rest
There's a time for being safe, and a time for danger
There's a time you make for a friend, and time you make for a stranger
There's always time to become a child of God, and to act like one too
Because there once was a time that Jesus died for me and for you.

Nicole Washington

Live Dying

I hate dying, that's not lying. I hate living
there's no forgiving. I hate Kris with the
venom of a kiss. I hate cats, they claw rats.
I hate this and I hate that's.
I hate being here and I hate leaving. Just have
to do something because there's no believing.

I'll die, I'll cry, I'll perish and that's no lie.
Stop this, stop that. Be strong or be wrong,
you've been here too long.
Despite the right you must fight, if I may, if I
might. Passing time in flight, getting out of
sight.

Love is cured, hate is blurred, in between confusion
is stirred. This is neither and not a
fever. You may say a discontinued believer.
Christians chant and Satanists pant. Get up and
fight and all that "Rem Rant". I'm just here until
I can't, leaving behind my grave and slant.

Sherin R. L. Burris

Caret

One st
There'
To on
Just w
Mopi
Think
Starti
As if
Just
But
It's l
Oh

Li

Yo
Th
So
W

You should also get out,
And a lot of the sights around you see;
Take a good look at buildings,
Flowers, the grass, sky and trees.

You should breathe the fresh air around you;
Smile at those you meet;
Care about those less fortunate than you;
And also about everyone you greet.

And, folks, live your lives to the fullest;
For life sometimes ends before long;
And even if you live to be a hundred and ten,
It may still feel as if to soon you were gone.

Sandra Current

Memories

Memories are gone.
They are always a picture from the past.
And yet it seems, as time goes on,
they constantly change.
For today's outcomes change
yesterday's predictions.
People seem to change into destinies
of success or failure.
At the time you smiled,
for the moment seemed right,
but now you weep,
for you remember how quickly the moment ended.
Memories can't be trusted;
They refuse to remain in the past;
And what was yesterday's joy
of what was to come,
Is today's sorrow of what will never come again.

Melissa Elder

My Thorn

Your Scottish purple fur is beauty.
Though your violent thistle stings me.
The pain in my heart will not go unnoticed.

Your handsome burnished velvet petals.
Your manly Irish scent so sweet.
My blood drains from your inflicted wound.

You are my thorn and thistle.
To love you in ecstasy and pain.
Ouch! My blood shall run again.

Rita May Edgar

d.
ead.
side,
ok it in stride.
, on earth

t," gave up the Ghost

n saw what had been done,
knew truly, Jesus was the Son.
mb, what a sight to behold.
of the tomb, the huge stone had been rolled.
re not false, now the people knew.
on had taken place, He died for me and you.
e paid, He did His share.
suffering, no pain shall He bear.

ISE THE LORD!

D. Polasek

See The Lamb

Down the street the mourners pass.
  They hum the song of death.
"My father," I ask, "of whom do they sing?"
  Humming, my father is silent.

Around the corner the mourners walk.
  They prey the silent prayer.
"My father," I ask, "of whom do they prey?"
  Praying, my father is silent.

Up the hill the mourners climb.
  They cry the pain of agony.
"My father," I ask, "of whom do they wee?"
  Weeping, my father is silent.

Surround the cross the mourners stare.
  Their tears flow a river.
"My father..." I began.
  "Hush child, and look at the lamb."

Rebecca Willmore

A Love Letter

As he sat down to write to her, memories of all the moments they spent together started to flood his mind. The memories were so powerful they filled his eyes with tears as if the tears were trying to wash away the memory of things that could never be again. His eyes were so filled with tears he could not see the paper on which he was writing. But his heart was filled with so many things to say; his hand just had to write. As a teardrop fell onto the paper, he began to write:

My dear sweet love:

I just can't believe that I will no longer feel the warmth of your embrace, or see your beautiful face. I just don't believe this is true. How am I supposed to make it without you? I'll never again be able to enjoy the warmth of the sun, now that our life together is done. Now on those cold lonely nights I'll have no one to snuggle up to. Now that I no longer have you. For when I'm sad they'll be no one here to make me laugh. For God has taken you my better half. I just don't understand why God had to take way the light of my life. Why did he have to take you away, my wife?

Well, my love, it's time for me to bid you adieu. But as you rest in peace, remember I'll always love you.

D'lanor

Sisters

Sisters are people of whom you dream.
They mess up your room and make you scream!

They wake you up in the middle of the night.
They say the reason for this is from fright!

But sometimes they can be so sweet.
They act like a little lady, so petite.

And sometimes they can be so cute.
They put on a dress and a pair of high heels, and down the sidewalk they scoot!

But when they get older, they become your best friend.
One with whom your relationship will never end.

Yes, you may quarrel once in a while,
But it always ends with a hug and a smile.

Yes, sister's aren't always pleasing or nice,
But if you say they're awful, you better think twice!

Kristi Danielle Brown

The Tag Sale

The crowd anxiously awaited for the door to open.
They scurried in and rummaged about, carelessly
and feverishly handling the goods.
Then it began, the bickering, the bargaining
and the bartering, all the B's one could
distastefully think of.
Oh wait, there is one more, yes, the "bitching."
Does no one have any regard for the family?
You see, to them these possessions are sentimental
and priceless.
How could you devalue them or call them worthless?
Buy what you want and enjoy, for this bargain will
only increase in value.
You see, what may appear to be junk to someone is
treasure to another.
The only priceless possession is life itself,
no one can argue that price.

Maureen Becker

My Shining Goal

Oh, a sculptor's hands are busy hands
  They're toiling all day long,
Molding, sculpting, carving,
  And on his lips, a song.

Oh, a sculptor's heart is a happy heart
  Full of beauty, and deep inside
Is an urge to use his talents rare
  Which cannot be denied.

Oh, a sculptor's soul like a shining star
  Brings happiness, pure and bright,
Dispelling from our anguished minds
  The darkness of the night.

For a sculptor's hands, and a sculptor's heart,
  And a sculptor's creative soul,
Are all a part of God's Master Plan
  His beauty to extol.

So give me a sculptor's hands and heart,
  And give me a sculptor's soul,
So that I too may, in my humble way
  Reach out, toward a shining goal.

Mary Levet Emery

Lord I Am Weak

Lord, I am weak, I need your strength, I am saddened by the things I see.

The world around is in chaos and war, I'm in a world of my own, lost in myself, forgetting you God, and loving you no more.

I yearn to live in a world of pleasures and games, I seek nothing else, but only what I can gain.

If you give me strength, I can try and do my best to change.
Lord it's hard to change, and do things in different ways.

Lord I love you, you're the one I truly seek, the world is changing, humble me and make me meek.

Help me forget the pleasure of this world, help me change so that I may learn and accept your precious ways.

Make me strong, direct me on your path, enlighten me, put me where I belong.

Lord, so frail am I, I yearn for two ways Lord, help me, why am I so blind.

Lord, I am always confused, I often wonder, why was I placed here, what am I supposed to do? Give me the strength to serve you.

Lord, help me, I'm weak, I'm confused in this world, but I believe in you and it's you who I seek.

Robert W. Schaffrath Jr.

A Bright Spot

Folks hear me talk about Bright Spots almost everyday.
Things that make life more beautiful along life's pathway.
A bright spot could be sunshine on the wall.
Or sunbeams playing peek a boo up and down the hall.
A kind word can be a bright spot when one is down.
Or someone brings an apple pie luscious and golden brown.
A sunbeam starts dancing on the floor,
When a friend stands knocking at my door.
The phone rings, you hear a cheery voice say "Hello."
A bright spot looms, with the query "Where would you like to go?"
A pat on the back and a big bear hug,
Makes a brighter spot than what comes out of a jug.
Encouraging words are needed as we travel life's road.
Especially when you encounter an extra heavy load.
A bright spot is sharing prayer time with another.
It could be a friend, a sister or a brother.
Jesus' bright spot words are always the best.
"Come unto me ye heavy laden, I will give you rest."
So now dear Friend, let me leave a bright spot with you.
Jesus really loves you and I do too.

Pearl C. Pritchard

Thoughts

I am totally alone, lost to ponder on thoughts
Thinking about them till my stomach burns
Hope I am alone. What if I am not?
Then what will I do? One night, while sleeping
I was awakened by thoughts, they sometimes
are about me or you or them.
I was falling through time not knowing
Where I was to go, then finally I came,
Then more thoughts they came.
Thoughts of laughing, crying, hitting, trouble me.
Why did my mind make me relive those thoughts
I had hoped were buried inside?
I am getting annoyed, wishing it would
Stop, but it will not. Why not?
My mind is tired, my body aches, and now
my stomach burns.
TIME TO STOP, THE END, DEAD.

Leah M. Grove

Daisy, Sweet Daisy

We got her at 8 weeks and 2.2 pounds.
This darling little puppy stole my heart.
She was a shy, little lady.
She tried so hard to please.
She got sick; encephalitis.
She went to live with the angels at age 8 months.
Now we talk about her a lot.
And we miss her something fierce.
We will always remember
Our little lady that stayed
A brief moment and
Then, slipped away forever.

Mary Schlotzhauer

A Picture In My Mind

I know it's not a fantasy,
This dream that comes and teases me.
It is a picture in my mind, of long ago and far behind.
An old thatch cottage in the sun,
Green meadows where I loved to run.
Smoke drifting from the chimney pot
Atop the chipped and chewed roof-top.
Lace curtains billow in the breeze
From open windows in the eaves.
The scent of flowers fill the air...
A wishing well... a shedding tear...
A swing hangs from the chestnut tree...
These memories now come back to me
So bright and clear that I can see,
A gentle hand enclosed in mine
That strokes my hair for one last time.
Too young was I to understand
That I would never hold this hand,
Or see that gentle face, no more.
God, softly entered, through the door.

Mary Manisero

Dreams

Dreams are murderers in the end.
They'll sneak up and invade you—
Cajole you and persuade you
To leave dried blood on their altar.
They'll wring the pulse from your heart,
And tear the lining from a soul,
But keep you alive even so.
For they are the very cells
That flow through your veins,
The reason the sun scalds
The sky every day.
They are infinite, impalpable, inevitable and real.
Dreams are wanted in the beginning
but tend to wear out their welcome.

Meredith Debry

Men From Mars

The little men from Mars have landed.
They're two feet tall, green, and three handed.
They say they come in peace,
Funny, they sound like geese.

"Are you here for work or fun?"
"We're here for babes" Answers one.
"What do you want with our chicks?"
Explains the other, "Ours all have ticks!"

So off they go in their pretty little ship,
Along with hundreds of girls, what a gyp.
They got the babes they wanted, too many to tell,
And all I got was this crummy padded cell.

William D. Martin

Forever My Friend

I feel as though I've known you forever,
this friendship of ours I dearly treasure.

You've always been there when I feel down,
you have a special way of turning my day
around.

I've watched you throughout the years,
and with your lust for life has bring out
my biggest fears.

We've had so many chances but let them pass by,
as easily as a cloud in the bluest sky.

You ask me what I'm afraid of,
is it your innocence, or maybe your love.

I enjoy every minute with you,
in my heart I've never felt anything so true.

All I'll ever ask of you is to be my friend,
now, forever and until the end.

Laura J. Alford

Torn

Since these tears have become lies
This hatred has become my eyes

It forbids me to speak
And keeps me warm under its blanket of deceit

I cannot suppress its aggression
Nor can I stow this emotion away

It consumes my tomorrows
And rekindles my yesterdays

This is my voyage
Which cannot be hindered in any way

What has become of this
Which once was me

Mortal forever shall I be
Searching for some kind of fantasy

Wake up you damn fool
In here Jesus rules

Kevin D. Sheehan

The Lesson

She hadn't a toy to be proud of,
This poor little innocent tot-
And she played all day with a twisted spoon
And a top from a beaten old pot.

She hadn't a doll that was pretty,
A Raggedy Ann was her lot -
It near broke your heart to see girl so sweet
Patiently pounding that silly old pot.

So I found her a doll that was lovely -
'Twas a beautiful doll that I brought -
She could laugh, she could sing, she could almost think,
She'll be wild about her, I thought.

I gave her the doll in the morning,
She kissed her and loved her a lot,
But at noon she was back with the twisted spoon
And the beaten up, dirty old pot.

I think this has taught me a lesson -
To be content with my lot -
For beauty is found in the simple, sweet things
Like a spoon and a beaten up pot.

C. M. Odorizzi

A Love Story

Love is a story, that comes from the heart
This story begins, right from the start
Our love child was born, much to our delight
Be you girl or boy, you turned out so right
Loving memories to be cherished, as you were growing
Doing all wondrous things, your love always showing
Loving you, was always so easy to do
The love you imparted, was known by all whom you knew
All the love that you've given, now can be told
Was so much better than receiving the Olympic gold
Where love is overflowing, it has spread so much joy
Our love shall keep on growing, be you girl or boy
As the years quickly roll by, with stories untold
May this true love story, be yours forever to hold

Louis J. Lachapelle

Teardrop

A teardrop I will shed
This teardrop I will offer you
And the reason unknown to you
So I'll explain it
My teardrop comes as an offering
Of the happiness, joy, and pain
I felt when we were together
I might not have expressed my love for you
Or even told you so
But believe me when I say, that I regret it so
I know that it's too late, for
You've found someone new
But I'm determined that if I ever love anew
I'll never make the same mistakes
That I have made with you.

Lisa Devot

Window Of Time

It brushes our hand and kisses our cheek
this thing called time so frail and weak.

Unseen by an eye, unheard by an ear
this invisible window, so far, yet so near.

Mountains do crumple beneath its great strength
as its fingers stretch out and continually rake.

Atoms are harnessed and can be split
yet there is no tube in which time will fit.

We borrow its presence and momentary peak
through this window called time, as of it we do seek.

The direction it travels is distant and cold
irreversibly, mercilessly, this thing does unfold.

Susan Hillsberry

Falling Star

Catch me - I'm a falling star...of lightness and darkness.
Suppressing tender wounds of heartache and lonely thoughts
with long hidden and heavily protected soul-bearing secrets to
confess
Catch me - I'm a falling star...portraying a woman-child,
of strength and wisdom beyond her years.
Critical of life and death, with a heart at times, hard-rock cold
When in truthful reality - this outward show
is tenaciously protecting just a little girl
with deep tender feelings of old

Catch me - I'm a falling star...seeking truth from within
So that I may finally come out
without the fear of never knowing who I've been
Catch me - I'm a falling star.....
Slowly burning out..........

Tiffany K. Tramell

Faith Returns

I love you hon, always and forever. I love you hon. I'll leave you never
Those were the words I once believed those were the dreams you
Deceived White stallion horse great knight upon, he's fallen off, the
magic's gone
The sword he carries won't glisten no more
Fair maiden cries from behind locked doors
Off with his head the king did yell he's no longer a man since he fell
The maiden screams,"daddy please, he'll change, you must believe"
Their heads all turn, their eyes all stare
What is that shine, what is that glare?
The knight bends down, picks up his sword,
looks at the King, "I'll change my Lord"
Never before have they seen such a sight
As that day when the sword glistened back for the knight
There truly is magic within his touch
The maiden then knows, he loves her so much
The day did soon come, when the knight did return
And upon that white stallion horse, with reins held stern
Road away the fair maiden, with his sword shining bright
And her ever so sorry, her true shining knight

Sharon Floyd McCabe

The Gift

On the crystal lake, the swan droops her head.
Though her feathers are white, her heart is stained red.
Her spirit yearns for the gift of flight,
That she may soar above the highest height.

Alone and forsaken, she weeps in the sun
Until the shadows fall and the day is done.
A veil of comfort, a shield from fears,
The darkness comes to mask her tears.

Then far in the mist - a beam of light!
A golden swan comes, piercing the night.
The swan approaches and touches her wings;
Her burden is lifted, and her heart sings.

The clouds depart with the rising sun,
And the loving voice of the Golden One beckons:
Come with me, and in splendor arise.
Spread forth thy wings and take to the skies...
Fly

Tara Guthrie

I Like

I like our "old-Town" Seal Beach—
(Though it's only three blocks long)
From PCH to the end of the Pier
Adding one-half mile for promenade
That reaches out to the end of the world!!
Yes I like to walk Main Street—
I like the people I meet—
I like to drop in the shops
And kibitz with whoever stops.
I like to sit on the Pier and watch the children play—
Or sit on the other side and watch the surfers sway.
Oh yes!! Our surf has long been known
To be the safest surf on this southern sprawl—
From San Gabriel River's mouth
To Anaheim Landing's wall.
But the Navy came and needed this waterway
Now Anaheim is no longer a place to play—-
But the mile long strand is a joy to walk—
To run and play—or just meet and talk!!!

Mildred C. Sprouse

Eyes Of Night And Day

Throughout the night there are eyes of many.
Though sometimes hidden, thou shan't see any.
And on a bright night, countless eyes to see
Are looking down upon and pointing to thee.
But then night becomes day and all eyes become one.
Now all below look toward this one.
But then that one bows before them all
And the eyes of many again grow tall.
Who are the eyes of these
That seem to hide and tease?
Sometimes hidden before all
As if behind a great wall.
But then exposed and set free.
Look beyond the eyes of yours, the eyes from afar,
And then you will see whose eyes these are.

Scott W. Finney

Darkness

Bitter breeze sends a shiver through my soul
Thoughts are scattered, rampant, brief... yet whole
Lunar creatures speak, distant surf replies
Warped illusions dance before my eyes
Straight lines curved and ceiling floor
Manacled child screams no more

Darkness smothers face of fear
Thoughts are twisted, demented, distorted... yet clear
Mind sees all and all see the mind
Demons laugh as it is lost behind
Past is present and future haze
As darkness sets the sheets ablaze

Daylight calls and psyche centered
Thoughts are lost, adrift, forgotten... yet remembered
Sweat drips from troubled brow
Tattered subconscious safe, for now
Life is full, precious and dear
Yet lurking in shadow, daddy always near

Kevin Barnard

Pass The Day

Sometimes when I pass the day to you
Thoughts like fables explore me
Leaves embrace me as fall crumbles upon my mind
Opening the intensity of reality
Blanketed by apathy and truth of man
Can you understand?
Sometimes I pass the day to you.

Ronnie Lee Gordon

My World

Total darkness but for one twinkle of light,
Thoughts of death and destruction but only one of love,
I'm always lost at heart but always found again,
This is my world...

Hostile but caring,
Nervous but calm,
Greedy but generous,
This is my world...

Leave me alone but I need your help,
Go away but I need your company,
I don't want anything but I need your love,
This is my world...
...and I'm so confused.

Michael Ruff

Farewell In The Moonlight

You, you grieved for me last night
Through all my moments of pain and sadness, my last hour with you
was the sweetest
I felt your warm teardrops caressing my still warm body
Though lifeless, I glowed from within, as each soothing touch
of your gentle hand traced patterns in my colorful hair
I could not have wished to be among kinder friends
As I rest peacefully at the foot of that tree, covered with
grains of sand weathered to smoothness by the ages
I felt my spirit guided by the ripples of the silvery water
merging with other rivers in search of the source
you so often allude to
Flow gentle river, flow;
Take with you that which the
moon witnessed tonight
An act of TRUE LOVE

Nadarajen A. Vydelingum

Beloved And Beribboned

Ribbons are unending revelations
throughout the life of woman
mingled with sweet sentiments
pretty wrappings and a lot of love
First, a cuddly baby in a ribboned bassinet
Then, hair ribbons for a sweet little girl.
A ribboned sash for dress of a "Sweet Sixteen"
Beribboned heart-shaped candy for Valentine
Her first dozen red roses with streamers of love
Homecoming corsages flowing with school colors
Soft trim on white graduation books
Love knots tied in violet nosegay
Wedding dress flowing and graceful with ribbon trim
Baby showers mingled in pink and blue
Anniversaries with fond memories year after year
"In Loving Memory" with white satin streamers
Beloved and Beribboned
encircles the life of woman.

Margaret Harrison Kerr

Tintinnabulation

Tintinnabulation is such a lovely sound.
Tintinnabulation seems to make the world go 'round.
Tintinnabulation just makes me want to sing.
Tintinnabulation makes me think of birds on wing.
Tintinnabulation: I wonder what it means?
Tintinnabulation: could it be something obscene?
I really don't believe it's a word reactionary,
So I'll look up "tintinnabulation" in Webster's dictionary
Tintinnabulation is exactly what I thought.
Tintinnabulation is with lovely feelings fraught.
Tintinnabulation is bells ringing to and fro.
Tintinnabulation-it's the only way to go.
So I will swing along with 'tintinnabulation'
And have a wondrous feeling of joy and sweet elation.

Virginia H. Donnelly

Jesus Hero Of Heroes

Jesus came into this world
To try to get people to heaven one day.
He suffered more than anyone of us ever will
And he taught us how to pray.
Some people made fun of Him,
Yet He showed them the way.
The day that a person dies He said,
Their valuables would have to stay.
When He was crucified He knew before hand
That He was going to die that way.

Raymond H. Angell

Death Of An Ant

Tiny pulses of a tiny life
Tiny beating of a still tinier heart
Slowly tiny silences replaces tiny beats
Tiny convulsions even out
A tiny grasp on life has loosened now completely
Remains of a tiny body with an unmoving heart
A small carcass to be forgotten
A small life to be ended
One might not think of such sadness
Murder in its simplest form
A simple creature but not a simple life
Who has such a right to end that tiny life?
Forever beating so stops its heart
Such is the death of an ant

Meredith W. Miller

A Parent's Prayer

Dear Lord, please help me:
To accept my children as they are, and not yearn for perfect
creatures.
To recognize ability, and encourage it;
To understand shortcomings, and make allowance for them;
To work, patiently, for improvement, and not expect too much too
quickly,
To appreciate what my children do right, not just criticize what they
do wrong.
To be slow to anger and hard to discourage;
To have the hide of an elephant, the patience of Job and the Love of
Christ;
In short, Lord, please help me to be a better parent!

Melba Riggs Lamoreaux

Inward Vision

Within my consciousness my soul grieves,
To be absorbed by cosmic consciousness.
To me, emerging from the world's abyss,
Is life triumphant over force that cleaves.
Shaped from an atom of the universe,
And given consciousness, dimensions change;
My life's immensity of Being is range
Of consciousness with which I can converse.

In life's Divine Abyss, I must accept,
With atom consciousness, the cosmic scene.
Love teaches me to seek and grow to court,
And induce another to accept,
My nature, the atom world that lies between,
The Infinite and love as my consort.

Laurence A. Malone

Field Of Dreams

In a great big green meadow
There stands a rose all alone
In a room with no light a candle burns
Your eyes shine like the heavens above

Now let us walk in the meadow together
Stop and smell the beautiful rose
Together, we will shine on forever
Together, we already have beaten the odds

They told me that the rose would never grow
Now it stands tall, proud and all alone
I treasure this flower, that petals are home
So let's share this moment in the sunlight

Hold my hand and never let go
For tomorrow holds our future
I say to my pretty, lovely red rose
I shall love you forever and never let go.

Robert P. McKenzie

Prince Of Peace

A lost sinner sent Jesus to the Cross
To be without love somebody else's loss
The devotion of Jesus to Christians
Brings our love to him for reflections.

The last words of Jesus on the Cross
Were "Father, forgive them for they know not what they do."
For he knows Christians love Him so true
But would not know how to see Him through.

The stone to his grave was rolled away
As he came to your loving day
To arise like a white dove
To ascend in the air above.

Then to go for years thenceforth
From the care of Christians not to be lowereth
They are to know no death
But loving, ascending, and Christianity breadth.

Jesus, we shall always look to you
In your way so true
Go to your glory in Heaven and Earth
For we love your Holy birth.

Marsha Jean Boyd

A Gift From Nature

Snow falls from the heavens above
To cleanse the earth for spring to come
In the forest a fire is made
No one can say by who it was laid

A wolf howls its lonely cry
In search for its mate with golden eyes
No answer heard the wolf moves on
To find the one who shares its bond

In to the forest on silent paws
She catches the scent of human laws
She waits in the clearing where the fire burns bright
As the sun descends with the coming of night

From out of the darkness he stands by her side
Together they will be forever tied
He whispers her name that no one can hear
She changes her shape for the one she holds dear

With the breath of a word and a touch of a hand
They lie together on the snow covered land
The two embrace with silent cries
She has found her mate with golden eyes

Karen Denise Bowers

Love Like A Tree

Your love is like a tree
that branches out to me.
We grow together as one
with every light of the sun.
The tree grows bigger to reach the
heavens above.
It's a symbol of our strength,
a symbol of our love.
Though it may need water, we don't need a thing.
Only our strong relationship is the food to bring.
Never will it die, it will expand each day.
Although limbs may break off,
the trunk will always stay.
That is why wherever you may go,
wherever you may be
Your warmth will be near us and so stands a tree.

Kimberly Klink

A Tribute To A Great Lady
Everybody's Friend And Mother

Always patient, kind, loving and sweet
To everyone that she would meet
Always most thankful, and very appreciative
Never seeking to receive but always ready to give

She was so gracious when receiving
So very generous when giving
Never doubtful but always believing
That she could do something to enhance the living

Always thoughtful, truthful and understanding
Never selfish, dishonest or demanding
Even the flowers, the animals, and especially the birds
Were loved by her too much to express in words

She was everybody's friend and mother
One of a kind, not just like any other
Our loss is heaven's gain, of that we can be sure
But within our hearts,
This great lady will live on forever more

Lois A. Johnson

"The Crying Of The Dove"

She was content to sit and listen, to hear the drum-beat of her heart;
To feel the slow, dark, steady rhythms, as if life alone could start
From this time of self-awareness, when dark shadows fade to gray;
As layer upon layer of her life is stripped away.

Alone in thought she dares to fight for all the dreams now gone.
For pictures yet untaken; for memories left undone.
And the family that will cease to be no matter how she fought;
For time alone will have to heal what life alone has wrought.

If she stills the pounding rhythm of her wildly beating heart,
And calms the fears within her that the memories seem to start,
She will hear the lonely wind that moans a lullaby of love;
As in the dawn the mourning brings...
The crying of the dove.

Lynne F. Scott

I Want To Stroll By The Sea Today

I want to stroll by the sea today
To follow my feet wherever they stray,
To go along in a dreamer's way,
I want to stroll by the sea today.

I want to stroll by the sea today
Where breezes blow and sea gulls play,
As the waves crest high in their rolling spray,
I want to stroll by the sea today.

I want to stroll by the sea today
Alone with its endless rushing sway,
Where old Mother Nature has her say,
My soul wants to join with the sea today.

I want to stroll by the sea today
As the sparkling sun on the waters lay,
And white sails dance on the face of the bay,
I want to stroll by the sea today.

I want to stroll by the sea today
Down the golden chords of the sunset's rays,
Over wet sands and the gloomy quay,
My heart is one with the sea today.

Lucille M. Kroner

Upon My Throne

I sit upon my throne, day after day,
To judge the paltry cases that come my way,
A sovereign I was never asked to be,
Within my blood is where my foul curse lay.

To be born a serf, and not a leader,
Would mean a life most pleasant, though more meager,
To feel the warm, moist earth between my toes,
Instead of cold marble, stone, and cedar.

Or to be a scholar with great wisdom,
Surrounded by texts, instead of a kingdom,
Respected by men without a war to win,
A life of great tomes, librams, and vellum.

Yes. To be a man instead of a king,
Whose divine right has not won him a thing.

Todd Gernert

My Summer Night

To view the mystic of this warm summer night
To me is a wondrous feeling of awe and delight.
Beautiful music all around, it comes from nature's symphony,
They send out their harmony from every nook and tree.
As the stars sparkle on the glittering milky way
Quiet shadows on the ground about me play.
There is a scent of honeysuckle, as a soft breeze brushes my face,
Dew drops on the roses, but only a trace.
Through the velvet mid-night sky silver moon beams thread,
Just to take in the beauty and never a word be said.
The things of this world fade and they become dim,
My mind, it wonders to thoughts of Him
I must be still and know that He is God,
Thousands of years ago on this earth He trod.
I rest here after a long summer day,
I look to the heavens and to God I pray,
Thank you God for these precious moments is my prayer,
For my day has ended perfect, with You in serenity and beauty so rare.

Shirly J. Mundy

"Life's Choice"

Life, how wonderful GOD has created it to be,
To wake each morning and know GOD gave this day to me.

To hear the Birds singing and see the sight of dawn,
Looking out my window knowing a new day has just begun.

Thinking of all the things that I must do today,
Knowing that before I start them I must take time to pray.

One must never take Life lightly or abuse it in any way,
But do our best to use it knowing we don't have long to stay.

JESUS gave to all a new way to seek their path through life,
He doesn't try to change us, but gives his word on how to live it right

Many take life for granted and abuse it all through the day,
Remember GOD gave us life and GOD can take life away.

As a youth I was more neglectful and sometimes didn't pray,
But now that I am older I try to pray each day.

As a senior citizen and my youthful lust finally gone away,
I can't imagine living life without thanking GOD each day.

To those who have lived their lives and never thought to pray,
Remember GOD gave you life, don't let Satan take your life away.

The choice of the way we live through life you see,
Is not up to Satan or GOD, it's up to you and me.

William W. Shores

Serving Jesus

I want to check my life each day
To see if I'm walking in God's way,
Pleasing in His sight. At the setting of the sun
I want to hear Jesus say, "Well done!"

"My child, it has been a wonderful day.
You have finally learned to trust and obey.
You read My Word, kneel to pray,
Walking by faith with Me each day!"

Father, I thank You for this day,
For health and strength, Your loving care,
And all that makes the day so fair,
The sunshine of Your love sent from above.

My loved ones dear I bring to You.
Please keep them in Your care.
For others that don't know You, may
I, with them, Jesus share.

All this, I want to do...
Always serving You.

Mollie Eckart

Midnight Muse

In the voluptuous heat of southern night I lay myself down
to sleep but the sleep faery has forsaken me.
Sliding along the path of the Moonwoman,
riding through the evening sky, my mind soars with
the music of the mockingbird's call.
Crickets chirp in time with this heartbeat rushing swiftly,
eddying in the tidal pull, drawing me to that place in my mind where I
most want and fear to go. The mockingbird jests at my efforts
to sleep, to forget, to dream (there's the rub!) as he tells me the
story of his home and his heaven. I sail with him through the sky,
feeling and loving
the hard caresses of the wind, the thrill of the height, the sultry
embrace of the clouds. I savor each circling of the stars,
searing my eyes with brilliance. The emptiness and chill
of the dusky gloom seep slowly away as the stars claim me for their own.
Not so far away the same lonesome, primal blaze of stars
burns away the night where outside a darkened window
the mockingbird's mate lies dreaming in her arbor home.
She, too, sleeps alone.

Nancy E. Meilahn

Closed Your Door

I closed your door, what happened from there?
This case is a mystery that leaves me to stare-

To stare at a rock with your name printed on,
Not knowing that night you would be gone.

Gone to a place where you would worry no more-
Walking through a gate, that looks like a door.

A door where a new life will start to begin-
A life of happiness, not sorrow nor sin.

But for all of us down here, on this glorious place-
We will never be able to see your beautiful face.

A face gone in a flash, a split second
from the day -
I hope you had no pain, you just went right away.

Away moving on - and you never said goodbye -
'Cause you knew that word would
make me cry.

Cry till I couldn't speak anymore-
Why, oh why, did I close your door?

Laura Kassel

"Home Of Memory"

Ever and ever my thoughts ever turn
to the old farm frame where we were so young,
Two brothers and I, and Mamma and Dad,
and all of the marvelous dreams that we had.

The Oklahoma prairie was spacious and wide,
with pasture and streams farther over beside-
In sunlight and cedar we were shouting and sighing,
Saw "Mammie" on her white horse, silken veil flying!
With greatgrandmere, so precious,
we mourned her brave dying.

There were mocking birds, robins, cardinal and jays,
Mother quail with her babies, squirrels, rabbits at play;
An Eden of love, and a good place to grow,
A haven of peace, with our Saviour to know.

Ola Margaret James

I Don't Want

Dedicated to David, Chris and Ryan

I don't want to push aside the memories of the one you ran to when frightened.

I don't want to replace the love in your heart for all the Hugs and I Love You's that have been said.

I don't want to cast a shadow over another or try to stand in her shadow for your feelings but, I don't want for you to think your feelings don't matter, they do!

Nor should you always hurt for time's changing of two peoples' hearts for each other. The love for you will always be there.
I can't erase a lifetime of feeling, but I do want the chance to be a friend, someone to listen.

I call you a friend.

Rowena Doze

Family Values, The Past, Present, Future

Family life values were established by God in the past.
Today the present values don't last.
The future looks very, very bleak, because
God's Word we failed to seek. The
family life values are very low, back to the
beginning in the Bible we need to go; future
life is growing dimmer more and more. In
the past we were told to use the rod, because
this was the command by God. But today
it is called child abuse, that is true if
it is misused. In the future the way things
are going, the family plight is unknowing.
Let's go back to family life in the past, if we
want the family to last.
Come, Mother, Father and children get
down on your knees and pray, Father, forgive
us for going astray, getting the family
back to where it used to be; it is up to you, and me.

Mamie B. Lymeh

Beauty

Beauty, that I truly see, comes from flowing, harmony
Trust in God, and know He is there, trusting hearts,
do not despair.
Beauty, like fragrant flowers in decorative vases,
innocence of children, happy and hearts, laughter
in their cheerful faces.
Beauty, describes many a thing, the main ingredient
is love, a virtue, a factor, love comes from the
heart, this — is beauty from within!

Mary Elizabeth Groeger

Time To Share

See crowds thronged around in valleys and towns asleep on the ground.
Today they are the concerned in the world because they are around.
Many are ashamed, confused and disguised, do not want to be recognized.
They were once in the mainstream to survive and be stately alive.

Share with the homeless that they may know others are interested in their welfare. Show love, kindness and patience that they will feel no harm. It is different with the change they don't know how to perform. Just be sympathetic and freely share to help meet their needs.

No responsibility perhaps a mind of woe haunts them everywhere they go. Life accomplishments in carts and bags are stored at their feet.
They will cherish and protect them wherever they decide to roam.
Be they friend, stranger, kin or foe, do not turn them away.

They are male and female with no respect to racial identity. They sit or stand and stare with outstretched hands to anyone who comes near. It was known from the beginning they would be with us to the end. God loves them and we are given the challenge to help them live.

Martha K. McHenry

Secret Thoughts

Life is unpredictable how or when one should meet;
too bad for us it came years too late.

I sit here alone toasting my love
thinking of things that were said or done,
cherishing thoughts deep in my heart...
All special moments kept hidden, apart.

To have a love so sweet and true
To have a friend, a friend true blue
Someone to share secret thoughts and future dreams
Someone who won't laugh at a crazy mixed scheme.

Sometimes I think our love should not be
but then I think of life, empty, without you
And I get cold and shiver and become scared
Thinking you may choose your old life anew.

But Thomas, remember, a life without you
would be no life at all.

Marlene Lukacinsky

Time

I sit here crying inside too mad to talk, too scared to say how I feel. I think of how you said good-bye. I try to tell someone but the words I try to say won't come out.

I think of all the fun we had and try to remember your face but, I can't. It seems that the passage of time has driven us farther and farther apart.

The little girl you once knew is gone and I know the man I called father has changed. We've both grown, fought and suffered over the past few years. Through years of misery and through years of joy.

And even though the time has passed and the memories may be fading I know I will be here to open new doors and accomplish new things. So, then maybe one day I will have no reason to cry because you will be here with me as I have always dreamed you would. AS MY FATHER.

KyraLea Cogill

Autumn

Scarlet, orange, red and yellow, the leaves are no longer green,
Trees dressed in rich autumn colors everywhere are seen.
Their brightly colored leaves are falling slowly down,
To join those that lie scattered, in colorful drifts on the ground.

Long splashes of color spill down each mountainside,
Tall daisies, asters, and goldenrod are in bloom far and wide.
The sharp smell of woodsmoke scents the clear clean air,
The squirrels are gathering nuts, there's no time to spare.

In Fall the decorations are such a pretty sight,
The chrysanthemum are glowing in bronze, yellow, mauve and white.
There are lots of bright orange pumpkin in sizes great and small,
And even fat stuffed "people" that sit on big bales of straw.

The first crisp apples of Fall are now ready to eat,
The ice-cold apple cider is so rich and sweet.
Boiled peanuts, or roasted, add to the country fare,
Autumn's sights, smells, and tastes are found everywhere.

Netta Pickering

Friends

Though miles may separate
true friends at times,
they're never far apart,
for thoughts and memories
of times shared will forever be.

No matter how hard your task in life grew,
you remained a sincere friend...gentle...kind...and true.

After all is said and done,
Friends are like rainbows:
They spread beauty in our lives,
guiding us through the days to come.

Let us build around them,
For some day,
We may lend to others
what they have lent to us.

Thank you dear friend,
for letting us be the friend,
you wanted us to be.

Nona B. Ryder

What Age

The old man smiled a feeble smile.
True, he had traveled the well-beaten path.
Dismal at times - at times with a friend.
But always, always, in the aftermath - survival.

A crease along his brow; a notch in the
Belt of his long life.
Kindly, his hand touched mine.
Wisdom emanated and I felt his inner peace.

What is old? But a mere frame of mind.
'Elder' is deemed more fitting.
Truly, the scholars amongst all of mankind.

Mary Asbury

Procession

The procession to the cemetery drew near.
We were soon to lose someone so dear.
In our moment of grief, we looked above for relief.
There for all our eyes to behold-
Three eagles a fly'in, as I was told.
To fly like an eagle proud, strong, and free,
I knew that my Dad was very soon to be.
The pain was great and full of many sorrows.
But now with the Lord for all his tomorrows.

Karrieann Grisa

Memories

There were eight of us: six kids, Mom and Dad.
Two brothers and three sisters is what I had.
The booties I wore were quite large they say,
So Dad said, "We'll call her Boots," and some still do today.
We didn't have TV or a private phone line.
We played games, read books and life was fine!
In the winter we skated on the small river behind town,
Or took the toboggan to the highest hill and rode down.
Once we lived in the country and walked two miles to school
In the rain, snow or sunshine, hot weather or cool.
The school had one room, a wood-burning furnace below.
On its ledge we put potatoes to bake in the glow.
That was our hot lunch in those days long past.
Those days were good and the memories last.
We had the necessities we needed back then.
Most were hand-me-downs, but something new now and again.
New shoes to start school, summer movies in the park,
The popcorn wagon, taffy—what a lark!
But, for this more than anything, I thank God up above,
The most memorable of all was the family's LOVE!

Sylvia Hall

A Choice Of Jewels

In the downtown part of the city, on a chilly autumn day,
Two young women met on a corner, each going a different way,
The one who stood patting her perfect coif wore a jewelled
necklace at her throat,
While the other one turned her attention to the child,
who tugged at the sleeve of her coat.

Then, Candace stepped into a taxi, bringing with her a
hint of essence sweet,
While Bonnie held on to her Jewel's hand, and hurried across
the street.

Since, tonight, she would be attending a party for guests elite,
Candace went to her stylish apartment suite, where she dressed with
the greatest care,
Then she reached for a jewelled necklace, that lay on the bureau
in front of her chair,
While far across the city, in a tenant house, on a dusty street,
In the room on the right, up the stair,
Bonnie sat in the darkness, and heard little Jewel's bedtime prayer.

Again, on this autumn evening, there's a party, and Candace
intends to go,
Though the mercury dropped in late afternoon, and she shouldn't be
getting out in the cold,
So she fastens the clasp, with fingers slow, on the jewelled
necklace she loves to wear,
While far across the city, in the plainest house on Workman's Row,
In the room on the right, up the stair,
Jewel holds up the looking glass,
When she's finished combing Bonnie's silver hair.

Lenora M. Matney

Emotions

If you depend on a casual friend
To perform a special task for you,
What tremendous disappointment
Comes just when he proves he is untrue.

Consider now, there is another
Upon whom you find you can rely.
A dear kind friend whom you've known and loved,
A faltering trust you can defy.

Against a failing relationship
It is so easy to feel disdain.
But for trust, and care, and true friendship,
You praise God that life and friends remain.

Miriam Y. Fanuiel

Water

Mother Nature has endowed our land, with this precious gift to understand.
Infinite in its purity, illustrated throughout the earth.
We take it for granted, not comprehending its worth.
The renaissance of nature, depicted by its touch. The expense so little, its value so much.
The beauty perceived is blinded to conception. An idea so simple, though beyond our perception.
It's the basis of humanity, vital to survive. Without its enrichments we will never thrive.
Why do we poison our foundation of life? Our hope will be the fate of bitter strife.
Why do we destroy the birth of dawn? Its existence will only be an illusion once gone.
Why must the creatures of the sea die? We continue in its agony as it pleads its last cry.
How long can we go on this way? The earth shall prevail, with nothing left to say.
Here today, gone tomorrow. Once a blossoming garden, now a slough of sorrow.
When the waters are sacrificed, mother earth shall weep.
She will dry within misery, her barren pain too deep.
Her mountains will crumble upon its death. As the sky falls
repressing her final breath. She falls within herself and dies alone.
Her sprawling prosperous land never to be known. For the streams and
rivers, a priceless treasure to behold, is washed away, a story once
told. So, remember, if we continue to destroy the waters, my friend:
we will lose what never can be found again

Natalie Carreira

A Mountain

From a distance I regard her breath-taking beauty
unfurled majestically about the land,
Handsomely surrounded by a scenic view
that bravely protects her with out-stretched hands.

In full view she wears a grayish-white necklace
that drifts around her as a sea-less sail,
slowly gliding about her splendor,
riding a-top a sea-less gale.

She expectantly welcomes the soaring eagle
that dares challenge her prominent size
while circling, darting and loftily flying
through the breezy clear blue skies.

I shall skillfully paint her grace on canvas
throughout the world I'll send
so all can behold the wondrous beauty
of what we call a MOUNTAIN.

Tony D. Young

Sympathy/Empathy The Homeless

Please do not say you really understand:
Unless you have actually stood on the street with your only clothes on your back
And all you own is in a dirty sack.

Please do not say you really know:
Unless you really have nothing to eat
And you really sleep on the street.

If you have never been there,
To say you really understand just is not fair.

Virginia Skinner

Untitled

Tears, uncontrollable tears,
unwanted, uncontrollable tears.
Again! And for what?
For what I've lost? No.
For what I've gained.
Love, respect, discipline, warmth, care,
and most importantly Leonor.
I may have lost a mother, father, friends, wealth, position,
but I have her. Dear, sweet, beautiful, Leonor.
Nothing or no one,
could, or would even try to compare.
True it is that with her I have everything I want, need,
but I would easily, happily exchange it just for her.
Brilliant, loving, caring, Leonor.
Filled with hopes, and dreams for her pride, her joy,
Her second chance!
Honest, fun-filled, radiant, glorious.
A miracle!
A treasure of more value to me than life,
My Grandmother Leonor!

Shauna Poete

Flying

Facing fear and death they know, captain and pilot are ready to go.
Up above the earth so high, swiftly streaking through the sky.
Glints of silver in the sun, flashing brightly one by one.
How they turn and dip and flow, as across the sunny skies they go.
Sometimes silently sometimes loud, as they meet each light and fleecy cloud.
Streams of white smoke far behind, still they are sometimes hard to find.
Flying in skies so far above, this is what our pilots love.
Cutting through the wind and rain, then out into the sun again.
Turbulent winds with ice and snow, all these things our pilots know.
Mechanical failures, explosion and fire, things our pilots don't desire.
Planes are tipped and beat around, some dashed and crashed upon the ground.
All brave flyers, in a foreign land, nothing here but desert sand.
Oil wells aflame with fires from hell, this is where the enemy dwells.
Mid fire and blood and screams they fly, some are blasted from the sky.
Sand and dust and fires from hell, DESERT STORM, is where they fell.

Mary H. Ewings

Image Upon My Wall

Thick hair, looks maybe course.
"V" shaped brows, shows maybe anger.
Inset eyes, like something wild.
Large nose, could be flared.
Wide grin, possibly an evil smirk.
Small shoulders, arched downward.
Beard from jaw line to neck, not well kept.

I see this image upon my wall.
He has no body, but yet, seems lanky, and possibly tall.
He appears to be evil, maybe beyond cruel.
Under him he holds a tool. Almost like a round sided "W."
But longer on one side, and sharp at the bottoms.

Could that shape be his arms bent, and the sharp points, his elbows?
If so where are the hands that belong?

Maybe his hair is soft.
"V" shaped brows could be an expression of confusion.
Inset eyes could be joyous.
Large nose could be normal.
Wide grin could be happy. Small shoulders could be relaxed.
Beard could be the shadow of the hands that I do not see.

Shannon Dee Harris

Elemental Unity

Earth pounds on earth past magnolias, tall phlox,
vibrant geraniums on patio steps,
red clematis climbing rock walls, day lilies
by walks, and colorful roses on fences.

Air meets odor as zephyrs' fresh breezes
swish through trees, flowers, and nostrils
while forest birds warble their mating calls
from blooming woodland's cool, scented interior.

Old Sol rises sparkling his red on dewdrops,
sending his eager photosynthesis
to waiting vegetation, trees, flowers,
each anticipating tendril, branch, bud, petal.

Rain hastens to desperate call of earth's children,
counteracts Sol's fierce rays with wet soil
as sap races through every dry vein;
then, rivers of happiness flow through man's world.

Earth-air-fire-water oppose then unite
to bring universal stability.

D. Elaine Stanberry

An Instrument

I am an "INSTRUMENT," for "JESUS!"
Walking through this "HIS" land,
Talking with "HIM" daily
While walking "HAND IN HAND."
"HE" is as close to me as my "BREATH"
Because "HE" lives within my "HEART,"
"JESUS," and I are the "BEST" of "FRIENDS."
We'll never be "APART!"
Even when I close my eyes in "DEATH"
I will always be with "HIM."
Because "HE" promised me "ETERNAL LIFE"
If I would be "BORN AGAIN"
"PLEASE," accept the "MASTER"
As your "PERSONAL SAVIOR" too;
"REPENT" of your "SINS" ask "HIM" into your "HEART,"
All things in your life will become "NEW"
You will be "BORN AGAIN" too.

Marcella C. Lester Foss

Tybee's Warm Sand

Cool salt water lapping around our ankles
Warm sand beneath our feet
Reliving and reminiscing
Casually letting daydreams and reality meet.

Sand castles so precisely built
By youngsters and adults alike
Soon to be washed away to sea
Like a windswept kite.

Wings of the soaring sea gulls
Shining like silver, reflecting the sun's rays
Precious Sand Dollars partially buried in the sand
Bare legends of begone days.

Porpoises surface near a white breaker
As beautiful sea shells hitch a ride
From beyond the horizon to the open beaches
Then left within our reach by the receding tide.

Lying in your arms on Tybee's warm sand
Our daydreams and reality caress each other
As the sands of time continually move.

Roberta Powell Loyd Mizell

Beginnings

Gentle touch, with electric effect,
Warmth and decadent deliciousness
from the stranger,
barely met
hardly known.
Awaking dreams and fantasies
thought to be dead and buried
in their imaginary graves
Now, reawakened and dreamt in daytime dreams.
The spider has cast his web,
a beautiful gossamer thread.
And the fly awaits in a tremulous state.
Wanting to melt in reds and blues
to the darkest purple like the night
surrounded by stars, of orgasmic light

Linda G. Taylor

The Magic Of The Sea

Being born in a city surrounded by the sea
Was an influential factor that shaped my destiny
Many were the days that I stood on its banks up high
And inquisitively watched the swiveling waves go by.

Sometimes after school, we'd race down to the embankment
And watch huge ships carry out the process of embarkment.
Then we'd listen to conversations from passengers and seamen
Tell about far away places where the magic sea had taken them.

At times, into the city, a great panic the sea would throw
As its waters rose higher and threatened to overflow.
And far away, could be heard the roaring of its sounds
While everything would be impelled to spin round and round.

So, I came to think of the sea like a creature of power
Capable of providing joy, but also equipped to devour.
How much like the sea humans are fashioned to be
Sometimes caring and sharing, but mostly like the sea.

Dr. Rebecca Batts Butler

"Bill And Will-I Need You!"

Paternal great-grandfather Bill Gillespie,
Was an innovative school teacher in the mid-eighteen-hundreds era,
Who supplied pupils with basic essentials for the classroom;
So the poor might be enriched with knowledge.
But, teacher, it seems that I've failed to make the grade!

Maternal great-great uncle Will Boyd,
Was a local philanthropist helping the unfortunate.
Among his achievements was the donation of Camp Roland to the youth;
A balm to Gilead; hoping to lighten someone's heavy load.
Uncle, if you were around today-I'd have it made!

Grandpa Bill, I possess no Ivy League diploma;
Uncle Will, I haven't any wealth to scatter about.
Life's been difficult for me in this century,
Endurance thus far has been my only strength.
If I appear to be contented; it's only a charade.

Both of you would probably laugh at the monkeyish Rush Limbaugh,
Boasting about the invincibility of the privileged class.
Too pig-headed to concede that wealth can be uprooted,
Leaving only arrogance to sprout from the worn-out soil.
Virtue will outlive snobbery; which is only a barricade!

(Dedicated to my Mother, Mary Ruth Gillespie,
who died November 11, 1994.)

Patricia G. DePuy

Untitled

"Everything all right?"
Was that a comment or a question
I think to myself as I watch those words
seep from your lips.
"Fine, fine,"
Fine, fine for I don't think you really want to know.
I remember...
But then again, I always did.
In fact, I can't remember a time when I didn't.
I'm sorry, I forgot—
"What? No, I promise, there's nothing wrong"—
I'm supposed to smile.
That's what I'm here for, isn't it?
"Yes, I agree, it was a wonderful movie"
I just don't fit in here. Petty. Boring. Trivial. —
Smile for the people — is it time to go yet?!
"Yes, lovely seeing you, too."
He says with a smile, "They loved you."
"Are you sure the cage bars didn't block their view?"
He is confused. "What?" "Nothing."

Lindsay Kallen

Time

Step out into the world today, experience the winter nights,
watch the stars twinkle bright, snowflakes falling to the ground,
you'll know winter is still around.

Step out, live life, stand up for your banner, watch the earth
replenish itself, in a quiet manner, rays of sunshine,
showers of rain, helps the flowers grow; it's Spring!

Step out to labor and toil, helping mother nature enrich the soil,
sowing the seeds, spreading the grass, listen to the birds whistle,
as they fly pass, whistling an unknown tune, a sign,
summer will be arriving soon.

Step out to harvest the wheat and grain, come work with your hands;
no pain, no need to worry, it's not in vain; fall entered, approaching
quietly, adorning the earth, with toning colors, red, yellow, orange
and brown, spreading a blanket that covered the ground.

Seasons are over, we begin again, step out into a new season,
no time to reason, step out with faith, hold on to hope,
to live with others we have to cope.

Bow down and pray, for God we trust, blessings from God, for
others we must. The earth will always stay the same,
for people it's different, we can make a change.

Ophelia Moore

Makaha

I leave before sunrise to check the surf
watching from the beach I see perfection
offshore winds and no one out
I paddle out to the line up
as the set rolls in I see huge walls
of darkness coming closer each second
I drop in on the first wave
my heart in my throat, spray in my face
every moment more critical than the next
The feeling of stoke running through
my veins, hot like fire
It's something that can't be explained in words
something only a surfer would know
A smile on my face as I look back
and wonder what I did to deserve this
A chance to ride the waves of the ocean
The only thing I live for
The one thing I'd die for

Misty Costa

The Circus Train

I remember when I was young,
watching the circus train pass.

It moved slow and so carefully,
as to not upset the mass.

I could hear the lions and tigers,
purring in unison with the engine.

It was such a soothing sound,
more than you could ever imagine.

What a sight inside the cages that carried,
the bears, gorilla and pretty horses.

Standing so steadily on their feet,
as the tracks changed courses.

Then came along the flat bed cars,
with chains on the elephants.

Swaying strong and proud,
without any circumstance.

At last the caboose is in sight,
as it patiently followed behind.

Oh, the thrill of the circus train,
has never left my mind.

Valerie J. Tweedie

Little Diamonds

Little diamonds sparkling in the sun,
Watching you is so much fun.
Seeing your glittering light
Brings such exquisite delight.
You are more lovely than the midnight star
Whose light shines from galaxies afar.

Where is your home, little diamonds? "It is in the lake,
Which God with his mighty hands did create."
Do you live in the lake isolated, all alone?
"Oh no! We live with the most beautiful things man has ever known.
We live with colorful water lilies and graceful geese and ducks;
Our home gives nourishment to fierce wolves and mighty bucks."

Little diamonds, shimmering in the golden sunlight,
You make all things around you beautiful and bright.
Yours is such beauty to behold;
It pleases the eye and soothes the soul.

Leigh Victoria Strickland

Where Is The Love?

Love cries before hate,
We acknowledge the cactus, but not the rose.
Searching for the most consecrated soul,
No one has the strength to wait that long.
Everyone wants the pot of gold,
Love that's hard to get, love that's hard to hold.

No reason to search for a victory,
Agony is the reason for defeat,
But a tryst with the obedient love is strong.

Kiss a virtuous treasure,
Open the chest of love,
Follow the everlasting pearl,
Not to the seashore, but to the Ocean floor.
Creativity is deepened by a sense of bond,
No one can fall out of the light.

Relay to GOD for a sense of courage,
He can dispense a friend,
One to meet in Heaven, where friendships never end.

Leonard Caston Jr.

The Seeds Of Life

When our children were growing up
We always used to say
How proud and happy we would be
Of all their accomplishments along the way
Well, time went on and as they grew
We watched their transformations
From toddlers to adolescents to becoming adult relations
The trials and tribulations as the years went by
Made our family something really special
The oldest child brought joy to all who knew her
The middle child was delightful beyond belief
The baby learned well, and grew into the man some day we hoped he'd be
We count our blessings every day, for our family has truly grown
The child of joy, married now, has a boy to love of her own
The middle child now has a wife to love and share in his delightful life
The baby who is now a man, has a wedding day to plan
How proud and happy are we now, our job is almost done
We now have a wonderful extended family, children who are all number one.

Karen Lee Kider

"Help The Planet Earth"

Earth is the planet
We call our home
It's the third planet from the sun
Where people, plants and animals roam.

The earth is our mother
Who brings beauty to see
From the water to the land
Where we must live in harmony.

Some people take and destroy
What isn't ours, but the land
Just to bring profit into his pocket
And say, "It's best for the future" as they expand.

Our planet needs our help
Can't anybody see her tears;
Can't we all do our share
Before the end is near?

Earth is our home
It's where we live
Given to us by our mother
To give to our children and their relatives.

Yoshiye Kimura

Four Seasons

We came into life in the spring
We were born, and the birds sang

Our hearts rejoiced, and life was new
The world was our oyster, we knew what to do

Summer came into our lives
and with it came hard work, sorrow and strife
Our youth quickly faded away
for the dreams of the future, to have it our way.

Fall came into our lives
with it came reality and dismay
Life's struggles bigger than we thought
A trade off is what we bought

Winter came to slow us down
memories linger on
Wisdom, now comes with age
too late to help us in our youth

Could we but pass on, what we know
to all the young people before we go.

Nancy R. Binder

The Blue Dog

While down in New Orleans one pleasant day
We encountered a blue dog standing in our way
We got up close and saw she was painted
She looked so real, so completely untainted

The blue dog told stories that touched our heart
We just stared and stared at that work of art
The knowing look in those big yellow eyes
Foretold of a beautiful and pleasant surprise

She sits on the ground near a lady so fair
Who brightens our lives with her golden hair
So we purchased the blue dog and took her with us
To show to our family and for others to fuss

What the blue dog has learned, she shares by the mile
And enriches our lives with her lovely smile
It's amazing that blue dog can create such a feeling
From the tip of your toes straight up through the ceiling

The joy that emanates from this lovely work of art
Would never allow us to let the blue dog depart
She provides to all truly great pleasure
The blue dog's a painting we'll always treasure

Maurice Levy

In Memory Of Randy Stephen Schell... (July 5, 1947/June 18, 1968)

I have a lot of questions, can someone tell me why,
We had a war in Vietnam, and my brother had to die?
What was so important there to sacrifice his life,
Taking him from his family, his baby and his wife?
You see, he wasn't just my brother, but a confidant and friend,
He had so much to live for, why did it have to end?
He wasn't alone when he died, there was so many more,
A lot of lives lost and torn apart, all in the name of "WAR".
So tell me why and tell me how, you think that we have won,
And tell it to the mothers who no longer have their son.
Who are left with only memories and his picture hanging in the hall,
And their only consolation being, his name is on the "WALL".
No, nothing you can tell them could ever ease the pain,
Of knowing he had gone to war and never came home again.

SPC. 4
U.S. 51916672
C.Co. 1st. Bn. 26 Inf.
1st Inf. Div.

Lorena A. Smith

Imaginings (Love Lives On)

We kiss in the moonlight,
We kiss in the rain.
In all kinds of weather —
We are warm; secure
In each other's arms.

The wondrous luster of our love,
Lights the pathways as we roam;
The flowering wilderness of a distant land —
Hand in hand — lost in that wonderland.

My love for you, your love for me,
This love of ours lives on -
For this, our love,
Has no ending —
Just a magical beginning.

Though you are gone and I'm all alone;
Still grieving and forlorn —
In my dreams you are here with me,
Whispering love ——— in my reverie.

Pacita B. Rysanek

Within These Hallowed Walls

Here, within these hallowed walls,
We meet to worship God:
And praises sing to Christ our King,
And seek the Spirit Guide
With all who call Him Lord;
Who seek His face and claim His grace,
And feed upon His word—
BUT IS THAT ALL?
For Jesus said, "Lift up your eyes!
The fields are ripe, but laborers are few!
PRAY THE LORD TO SEND MORE MEN!
And garner in the fields!
God does not dwell in temples made with hands.
These walls are damned,
If all our vision they contain AND BOX GOD IN!
God will not rest as long as some remain
un-sought, un-saved, un-won;
Nor should we rest; for we belong to Him:
His will is ours, and ours is His;
And in His will WE FIND OUR ONLY PEACE.

Oliver N. Hamby

Fragile, Handle With Care

As the sign reads,
We must comply,
Depletion of all the resources that
have ever been,
The human damage and the
proposition for peace,
The orchestration of much destruction,
Prejudicial towards this world
and all its beings,
And we have taken advantage,
There will never be again what
there has been before,
The light will never shine so brightly,
Nothing will be the same,
For we see only black and white,
There is no gray between,
This deceitful world will be no more,
For there is no compromise,
The consequences of our behavior,
Are upon the door and entering,
And we shall soon be as extinct as the others.

Kerstin Tebbe

Shades Of Yesterday

It seems only yesterday
We said goodbye
Although it's been years
It still makes me cry

We were never really close
Yet I still have this void
And shades of yesterday

I've so many questions
Of why you went away
What did I do wrong
Why couldn't you stay

After all these years, I still don't know why
I feel I still need you
I feel I should try

These shades of yesterday, still haunt me so
All I ask is that this time you won't let go

Maybe it was never really meant to be
But I think I'm finally ready
If not for you, well then for me.

Paula C. Baker

Summer Days Are Fading

Summer days are fading fast away,
We see signs of their passing,
All along the way.

The air is getting cooler,
The sun less bright,
And how early day changes to night.

The trees are beginning some color to show,
The grass is getting less green, to let us know,
That summer days are fading away.

The birds are leaving day by day.
We can see them in flight,
Beautiful against the sky, day and night.

The flowers are dying or changing their hue,
But when we see this, we shouldn't feel blue,
For they have had their day, now they must
be on their way, as we must sometime do.

When these signs we behold
We know that it is true,
That another summer has passed, but alas!
Fall with all her glory is just up the path.

Velma Robinson

Gift Or Loan?

Our children, the boys and girls
We treasure more than beautiful pearls.
We, as parents, teach and prepare for life's every zone
But are children a gift, or merely a loan?

One by one, the days are gone
As life's path is etched with every stepping stone.
At first they crawl, then they walk
A few stumbles between and then they talk.

My children are only five and one and a half
Yet, I realize, they are a loan on God's behalf.
Because I did witness their first smile
And memories of my childhood stride, fill the while.

One day, they too, will follow fate
And I will no longer fill their daily plate.
Although I will always be available for my two,
My gift of wonderful memories will have to carry me through...

Vickie Massey

Our World

As we set arm in arm all along
We watch the stars until they are gone
We dream of all the wonderful days
We count our love in many ways
We climb the far away hills
We listen, but everything is still
We smell the wonderful sea
We smile and wonder how it could be
This beautiful world that belongs to you and me.

Wilma Lee Campbell

Visions Of Tomorrow

Visions of Tomorrow are the strength in which I feed upon.
Visions of Tomorrow are the courage that help me fight the battle of life.
Visions of Tomorrow becomes the sight which allows me to see through
that which is dark.
Visions of Tomorrow becomes the heart which pumps my warmth and
compassion.
Visions of Tomorrow are my life,
for without visions of tomorrow
I have nothing.

Lisa Elaine Johnson

Moving On

As we move on into high school,
We'll meet new people, have different
Experiences, and gain more knowledge
That'll help us in the future.

As we gain more knowledge
About Math, Science, History, and Religion,
We are being prepared for the difficult
Challenges after high school and college.

As we experience new things,
We see that the world isn't the
Way we'd imagined. Sometimes it
May be difficult while others are exciting.

As we meet new people,
Some will probably be left behind,
But will always hold a place in our heart,
And all we have left are memories.

These memories may be sad or happy,
Memories that are painful to think about,
Or memories that make us laugh, but
Remember, we're friends forever.

Traci Moenter

I Remember Yesterday

I remember yesterday when the world was different and children weren't afraid to go out to the park to play.
I remember when neighbors looked out for each other everyday.
I remember when the world was filled with honesty and love.
I remember when a hunter never shot and killed a snow-white dove.
I remember when the air was free from smog and pollution; when the world had problems, the leaders found a real solution.
I remember yesterday when everything in life was so easy and laid back; when children hadn't been introduced to the drug called crack.
I remember when men would take a position and stand and not stand on the corner begging for something to be put in their hands.
I sat and wondered about what happened to yesterday's dream and the good times that we once had. Then I looked around, and it made me really sad.
I think about how Jesus died on that old rugged cross to save the world from a state of despair, and now the world doesn't really care.
I know that Jesus's death was not in vain, so why has the world forgotten that he suffered sorrow and pain?
I remember yesterday's dream, and I know the state of the world today. I am so glad that Jesus died and gave us a better way.

Thelma Bryant

Kismet

Why am I here?
What do I do?
Can we ever know what we should have done?
What road, untrod, awaits as yet obscure?

There should be balm,
balm for all the suffering,
all the pain, the pain inside,
whose hurt is worse than any one of flesh.

Are we tokens of exchange
played about by a god on high?
Do we have move-choice?
Or are we pawns hoping for paradise?

I smile, and my wrinkles deepen;
do I care? Hardly a wit.
But save me from the time when hands burden;
when ideas cease to link.

Stay light of reason, muscle strength,
to bake the bread, and till the soil.
Let always pulse a new creative stroke
to brush o'er the canvas of life.

Moira Rankin

Ode To My Husband, Paul

My husband is a rockhound and he likes all kinds of rocks.
We've brought them home for thirty years and put them in a box,
Or on a shelf, or in a case, or even in a pile,
Which kept our little acreage very much in style.

With nature all around us, a tree, a rock, some dirt;
And in the wash sometimes I'd find rock dust upon a shirt.
He polished some, he displayed some, he traded even more
Until the garage was lined with rocks, with room just on the floor.

I never thought I'd see the day, he'd give the rocks away,
But since we're moving out of town he had to find some way
To keep the weight down when the movers came to load
The treasures we have gathered as we traveled down the road.

So he began to sort and pitch and pack and say to friends,
"Please take a rock to remember that our friendship never ends."
Neighbors on the corner hauled yard rock by the pounds.
The University geology club took much right off the grounds.

And rockhounds right and left were delighted with their find,
As they chose the one just right for them, one of another kind.
So even though the piles are less, the boxes not so high,
He'll always like the rocks as much as he does coconut pie.

Margaret Good

A Tribute To A Friend

Robert Hice has been my friend for many many years
We've shared good times and bad times and shed a lot of tears
Tears of joy and laughter tears of grief and pain
And as I look at Robert now my loss is Heaven's gain
He looked for the good in everyone he was privileged to meet
So he now reaps his real reward as he rests at Jesus' feet
Robert's steps were getting slower his heart not functioning well
Just when his final breath would come no earthly man could tell
He touched so many lives here while serving his Lord and master
And yet the day to leave it seemed just kept getting faster and faster
The end came very very quick as God would have his way
But this too was Robert's wish as many heard him say
So please don't weep for Robert he would not like you to
Just meet him where he's resting now that's all he would ask of you.

Mary Mathis

If This Ole House Could Talk

If this ole house could talk.
What a story it could spin.
It could tell of Indian attacks.
When my great, great, grandparents lived within.

It could tell how they worked and fought.
This ole farm to save.
It could tell how many have died here.
When you look at the family graves.

If this ole house could talk.
Of the many life spans spent here.
It could tell of the sons who went to war.
And the mothers and sweethearts tears.

If this ole house could talk.
It would tell how each generation did try.
How they each in turn improved this land.
For a place to live and die.

Virginia F. Felker

"What's Going On"

What's going on in the world today,
What do people mean by the things they say?
Is there a soul in the world who will really care,
Anyone at all who will always be there?

What's going on with the people around,
Nobody's up, everybody's down.
Is there someone you truly love,
Or is that person in Heaven above?

What's going with the way we live,
Why is it always take and never give?
Is there a place for us to hide,
A place where we won't hurt inside?

Kathy S. Rowland

Future

Lying on my bed I wonder,
What is in my future?
Will my future be anything like my past?
Will I like it after I mature?

What is in my future?
I wonder if I will find that special person.
Am I going to have a job that I will enjoy
Will I have a daughter or a son?

Will my future be anything like my past?
Full of disappointments
Sadness every time I turn around
Childhood is supposed to be one of the best moments

In two months I am going to be 18 years old,
Feeling out of touch with people my own age.
Yet, I get along with people older than me.
My childlike, free-spirit is locked in a cage

Milidia Norris

Confusion or Disbelief?

I'm so confused, and it's all over you.
What just happened, Can't be true.
I thought I heard your voice speak out —
"Just forget," and "It won't work out".
How can you say that; or do you resent,
That we never gave it — 100 percent?
Do you remember, when it all began?
Our Love was a virtue and we didn't even plan.
It seems like you're running, away from me.
I wish you would share all your feelings with me.
I know I should have seen,
What was really going on.
But your Love made me blind
And I could see nothing going wrong.

Rose A. Shank

Dreams

To touch the sky
To make the world better
We all ask the question why?
To be under water and be able to breathe
To make all the violence die
Help the people in need
To build with bare hands
People die from being so weak
Trying to stay away from the devil's demands
To walk on water like God
To stop the war
Make yourself better against the odds
To understand what this poem means
Think of the world as it is
Like what I write, these are all dreams

LaNise Broyles

Death Wish

Now that life is hell,
what more can I ask for?
I wish to be hung, burned, or thrown from a bridge.
As I've lived life to its fullest,
there's nothing more to ask for.
There's nothing I can ask for that's more than my death wish.
People always bothering me,
and saying how bad I am.
Assautemy, rape, and child abuse,
not much more for our children to live for.
Thinking about cutting my veins,
slitting my wrists or slitting my neck.
All good ways to kill myself.
The reason: I don't know why?
Just thinking about my life brings me pain,
and suffering that I feel at this moment of time.
No way, I couldn't ever ask for more than my death wish!
GOOD-BYE!

Nicole Jensen

Fountains

My eyes are fountains crying endless tears,
What should have been a joyful awakening,
Is a tearful morning filled with painful regret,
A choice of wisdom has created so much sorrow

My heart aches and the fountains flow,
A stream of sadness over the loss of another day's joy,
Plans well-planned have been set aside,
Love will not cross over my threshold this day.

My heart's desire lies far out of reach,
The need to be touched is overwhelming,
To feel the warmth of tender lips,
And strong embracing arms of comfort.

My body cries out for solace,
What was to be will not be,
This time, this place feel cold and alien,
And home no longer feels like home.

My life seems suspended betwixt and between,
Fountains and streams of both joy and sorrow,
Eternally joined like two sides of a coin,
Flowing towards a future beyond human vision.

Kathy Knight

Inner Peace

What is this inner peace I feel?
  When all around me is confusion, doubt, and even fear?
Thy Mighty Hand, Oh Lord, upholds me lest I fall
  And gives me strength I never knew before.
Oh inner peace, when didst thou enter me?

The peace of soul that dwells within me now
  Is sweeter than the honey from the bee;
A mind like mine can never comprehend
  The marvel of this wondrous gift to me.
Oh peace of soul, when didst thou enter me?

In vain I've searched this earth for peace of mind,
  The kind of peace this world can never give.
Amidst the trials and tribulations of my life,
  Oh Jesus, let me turn to Thee,
Oh Peace of Soul - Oh Peace of Mind.

This inner peace is deeply rooted in my soul,
  And like the gentle breezes on a stormy sea,
Has taken full possession of my life
  Since I, Oh Lord, didst give myself to Thee,
Oh Blessed Peace.

Rose M. Nagle

Cliche Boy

I am the Cliche Boy
When another man has a better suit than I do,
I think, "The grass is always greener on the other side."
When I forget the report that I worked on all night because I was rushing out the door to get to the bus,
I remember, "Haste makes waste."
When a friend of mine is beat up by a boy with a lead pipe,
I know, "Things happen." or "Boys will be boys."
When I am lying in a psychiatric bed,
I inspire, "Things get worse before they get better."

Cliches, wise or inane,
make me who I am
make me what I am today

Tom Clark

The Child Within

When is it time to start acting our age?
When do we finally grow out of this stage?
The questions we ask are always the same,
But the answers keep changing with each passing day.

The constant battle to grow up too soon;
That moment we realize there is too much to lose.
Too old for the freedom we once just ignored;
Too young to be asking what it's all for.

The honesty and truth of a child's young mind,
A heart that's untainted by the passing of time.
Is there still time to recapture our youth...
To bring back the child we so quickly outgrew.

Can we be forgiven for
All our past sins
And reclaim the innocence
Of the child within?

Andrea Leon

Why?

Why did God put us here on Earth; it's sure a big mystery to me
When He could have put us in Heaven to live for all Eternity

Did He put us here to show we love Him by all the prayers we say
Oh that would be too easy to just pray to Him each day

I can't believe this can be so for it's too easy a plot
If this were the case, my friend, He'd have made us each a Robot

Instead He gave us a mind to think with and a heart to use for love
We must remember we're all His children if we're to live with Him above

It's easy to say God I love you; to prove it we must be sincere
Do we pray because we love Him or do we pray to Him out of fear

I feel He put us here on earth to learn the true meaning of love
For if we can't care for each other here, how can we live in harmony above

Because we are all so different our looks and thoughts don't match
To learn to understand each other can certainly be the real catch

To respect another's way of praying; to realize they're trying their best
To live a life that they know how can be another test

So show God that you love Him not only by the prayers you moan
But by the things you do for others and you'll never be alone.

Margie Gale Hermelin

Sad But True

I was moving one day in a graveyard
when I came across a pretty stone
and on it was a picture of a little Boy and Girl
and I know their Mama and Dad felt all alone

I had a lot of strange feelings that day
when I worked all around the pretty stones
sure does get you to thinking of lots of things
'cause some day we all are going to go home

Sometimes everything is beautiful
and then again they are sad
I get to wondering if your feelings aren't like the weather
oh me, I hope they aren't all bad.

I don't think we are supposed to be sad
but when some of your loved ones leave
it puts a hole in your heart
and most of all it hurts so much to grieve

We have to take the bad along with the good
and all of this is true
but I'd rather act silly and have fun
than to be sad and blue

Vada Mae Henderson

"Remember When?"

Remember when times were tough, and we couldn't spare a dime.
When marriages lasted forever, and there wasn't too much crime...

When we had a problem, we had to think it through.
We couldn't just throw it out, and go and buy it new...

Old cars, old homes, old lovers, we took the time to mend.
They weren't just our possessions, we thought of them as friends...

Now times are getting better, we can even spare a dime.
Marriages aren't forever, and the world is filled with crime...

When we have a problem, we don't try to think it through.
We just toss it out, and go and buy it new...

Old cars, old homes, old lovers, are tossed out in the wind.
Things that once were precious, we don't take the time to mend...

Though the world is growing smaller, the people are drifting apart.
Let's put away our wallets, and start thinking with our hearts...

Peggy Wineinger

Meant To Be Shared

The beauty of life is meant to be shared.
When night's too deep and dark for me,
My soul sends out a silent call;
Oh, spare me this interim of inanity,
When many pressures cloud my daily life,
I feel empty, a feeling of a hollow shell.
Down a lonely path I walk, alone, only to myself I talk.
It looks very lonely, up there in the sky.
My transient thought ensues winter's sigh.
May my monologue impress me, may my words flow smoothly,
Among the raging screams of thoughts within.
May you understand my need for companionship.
I still yearn for life to be rewarding.
Sometimes stormy winds might blow; today it blows uncertainly.
Sometimes the sea may toss and flow.
You may wonder and gaze upon its mysterious depths..
Hesitation brings thoughts of vain defeat.
Have you heard the cries of sorrow in the silence of my soul?
I think we each need another to share our thoughts of then and there.
The beauty of Life must be shared.

Ruby Golliher

By The Window

She sits by the window, dreaming of times long ago
When she had no memories and life had a long way to go
When she was still young and quite pretty
And her hair was the color of gold
Now she thinks it's just a pity that she has grown old

She still remembers when Sam claimed her body for his
And though it's been years now she still remembers his kiss
She aches in the night when she's lonely
For Sam has been gone these two years
She never thought she'd be left only a heart full of tears

And her life has no meaning, no meaning at all
No children around her, no good friends to call
Just a roomful of memories as fragile as she
And a window for her company

How did she ever let her life lead to this chair
With a view out a window, when did she cease to care
Was it her mirror's reflection
Or was it when death took her man
And left her life needing protection like hourglass sand

She sits by the window, dreaming of times long ago

Ramona Q. Blackledge

Why?

Why do we hesitate? Why the delay,
When the finger of fate points a warning our way?
When the world needs changing, we choose to complain,
When we should take some action, some justice to gain.

We look at the homeless, and then, turn away.
There are things we could do that would brighten their day.
The aged ones suffer, from endless neglect.
A visit would cheer then, restore self respect.

The sick ones need comfort, when stricken with ills.
A few cheery words would be better than pills.
There's those in the service, far over the sea.
A letter would thank them for keeping us free.

The young ones who hunger, and sleep in the cold,
Need something more precious than silver and gold.
If somebody's life is a tangled up mess,
We can offer them kindness, to soften their stress.

Be a friend to the friendless. To the lost, a kind word
Would mean more than anything they've ever heard.
And those with discomforts, and burdens to bear,
Will be helped quite a lot, if we tell them we care.

Leland L. Conner

Untitled

Thinking back she remembers the time
When their love was so true and so divine

He always made her feel as though she were being loved
Her heart grew and her hopes soared to the skies above

They used to laugh, they used to hug, cuddle and kiss
Their lives were filled with a passionate bliss

Then it seemed the more she needed him, the more he wasn't there
The more she cried, the less he cared

She found out there was another and her heart broke
But when she told him, he laughed it down as though it were a joke

He takes the defense and he does it well
But looking into his eyes, he is lying, she can tell

She loves him and wants him to hug and hold
She wants to be with him until they grow old

Confused and hurt, she doesn't know what to think
Before her eyes her life begins to shrink.

Shana M. Spillers

Winter Angel

An angel came to earth one day,
when winds were cold, and skies were grey,
The snow was swirling all around,
No signs of springtime could be found!

Inside, the gloom was much the same,
But, that was when my angel came;
A little boy, all pink and white-
with chubby fists all clenched up tight!

I looked into his big blue eyes,
and I saw warmth and summer skies;
Rainbows gleaming through the showers-
Butterflies and birds and flowers!

As each day passed, my angel boy
Brought countless hours of love and joy.
But God had bigger plans than we -
And life with us was not to be!

For, on a sunny day in June,
God took my baby-all too soon!
An angel left the earth one day
And summer changed to winter grey!

Pegi Marcotte

Blue Fuzz And Trash

When we are together from dusk till dawn
When we sit with our legs crossed as one
When we think of wondrous days of fun
My memory fills with loving you in the sun!

When I'm alone in the mid-morning glow
When I let my mind's thoughts go
When I think of the troubles of life's hard race
My memory fills with your loving face!

When we joke, laugh and smile
When we sit or walk a mile
When I think of life's hard trials
My memory fills with your love in piles!

When I'm alone late at night
When I let my mind engage in flight
When I think of great times in our past
My memory fills with Blue Fuzz and Trash!

Steve A. Rood

The Hero Of Entebbe: Jonathan Netanyahu, 1976

The tender beauty of this very man
was deeply embedded in a soul of greatest fame.

He fought and he struggled and he felt so very strong
about his land and all our future to come.

Unaware of Death, yet conscious of the Dark,
he was prepared to pour all of his love
right into the ground of that new dawn,

Racing the blazing sands of a desert so near
or travelling forlorn wastelands
of a burning memory.

On his blood and essence our freedom was built,
on striking luster of incredible might.

Never will our hearts stop bleeding for him,
him and the others who walked out of the light,
those, who chose the end to give their children life.

It art thy name, oh Jonathan,
the lion roars on the mountain high,
the eagle screeches endlessly,
man, though, won't weep,
given all the reason to rejoice forevermore.

Pat Hill-Castillo

Ruminating

Do you ever rummage 'mongst your thoughts
  When you are moved to reminiscing mood?
And bits and pieces of your long-gone past
  Come back to mind to haunt you while you brood?

Do you sit and wonder why you did
  The things you did not thought that you were right,
To later learn that you were way off-base,
  But it's too late to rectify or fight?

Well, now in pensive mood, I think I know
  Just what I should have done—it all comes clear;
But is it now too late to rectify
  The blunders when I hurt the ones held dear?

Why am I sitting here, if it's too late
  To ever right the wrongs I must have done?
Why am I reminiscing on the past
  While time remains before my race is run?

Mary A. Fowler

"Where Are You?"

Where are you? for I've searched for you in ever so many faces
Where are you? for I've looked for you in ever so many places
I've dreamed about you so very long and thought about you with each love song
I've always hoped you'd be somewhere but haven't found you anywhere
  Have we through a glance ever wanted to meet and then decided not to try?
   Were we by chance afraid to speak and afterward wondered why?
  Have we known each other once before and let each other slip away?
   Will we know each other again once more sometime, someplace, someday?
  Are we looking so hard we just can't see
   that we know each other now?
  Are we trying so hard to find what can be
   that we're missing each other somehow?
Where are you? for I've searched for you by every clock that chimes
Where are you? for I've looked for you so many, many times
  Wherever I go, whatever I do
   it seems I'm always looking for you
  Where are you? Wherever can you be?
   Where are you? Are you looking for me?

Miladene Sundra

The Desk

I was a desk in a country school,
Where children learned "The Golden Rule."

Students who sat upon my cold smooth seat
Were cleanly dressed, and, oh, so neat.

They wrote upon a cold hard slate,
It was ill-advised to e'er be late.

Readin', writin', and 'rithmetic
Were the basic skills that made life tick.

The teacher did those daily chores,
She stoked the fire and swept the floors.

Multi-age groups meant multiple lessons,
It took great energy and late work sessions.

Excellent work was rewarded with banners,
You best dot your "i"s and mind your manners.

Children walked for many a mile,
Their hard work honored with the teacher's smile.

Some who here studied, now, our great land rule,
But, I was their desk in the country school.

Paul C. Hackmann

Pure Blindness

We live in one world, where deep inside we are all one color.
Where deep inside only our human behavior separates us-we're not blind - is it so difficult for us to see the bigotry or have we been taught just to accept it? Thinking it will never end.
These thoughts only decrease the sparks of hope and extinguish the fire in our hearts that hopes to one day put an end to this bigotry and lock it away as an unknown, uneducated period of time, as a heartless memory where we would only look through our eyes and where we were too blind to realize we weren't looking through our souls and just too ignorant to understand why now it may be too late.

Renee T. Robles

Where Are You?

If you ask the Sun
  where is my love?
He will answer: in the rainbow,
  in the sunrise, in the sunset.

If you ask the Wind,
  where is my beloved?
He will reply: in the air that you breath,
  in the storm, in every blade of grass.

If you ask Life,
  where is my passion?
She will answer: within your heart, entwined
  with loving breaths and a keen desire to manifest.

Milagros F. Ramirez

I Know Of A Place

Do you know of a place where you can feel safe
Where no one can harm you at all
Where evil and death breathe not a breath
And you're deaf to their beckoning call

Do you know of a place where you'll never go hungry
Where pestilence dares not to stay
Where you're never too hot, too cold, or unloved
'Cause the sun shines upon you all day

Do you know of a place where a heart beats so strong
That it fills you with life all the time
Where life, love, and care will always be there
And you'll never be subject to crime

Do you know of a place where heaven is known
And the angels look down from the sky
And bid you good night, good life, and sleep tight
While the moon and the stars shine up high

Do you know of a place where the world is at peace
And all people are filled with great charm
Just think of that place and I'll guarantee
You'll be back in your own mother's arms

Tyrone Girod, Jr.

A Dream

A dream could be a place
where no one else can go
Locked up safe inside your mind
for no one else to know.

A dream is kept inside your heart
for no one else to feel
It could be just a fantasy
or it could be something real.

There are different types of dreams you dream
maybe some more than the others
But have you stopped to realize
we were dreams dreamt by our mothers?

Kristen Doyle

Sea Treasures

Morning dew on pearly shells,
Which passers-by quickly sell.
Some, shaped into nifty combs,
Were probably previous homes.
Shells not surfaced...on the ocean floor,
Remain as homes for crabs and more.

Until the waters let loose its grasp with fury,
We wait for sea treasures, to collect in a hurry.
Children pick the shore clean; put them in a cup,
Just about the time the sun comes up.
Another day's tide, this cycle is due,
As Mother nature's witness, this story is true.

Todd Laubacher

Flickering Candle

I lit the candle on the table,
While feeling the chill of winters gloom.
The flame seemed to cast a dreamy mood,
As its warmth slowly filled the room.

It flickered and dimmed with the slightest breeze,
My cat and I snuggled in my easy chair.
I began to ponder in my mind,
Just what was this, that was occurring here?

The shadows danced upon the walls,
Stretched their fingers across the ceiling.
As I lazily watched them dance,
I nodded, welcoming this warm and cozy feeling.

The many forms and shapes were mine to imagine,
So close, I became part of their game.
Till I—like this little candle,
Was consumed by its own flame.

Margaret Skyles

Alone We Stand Together

Alone in the night she sits in the rain
while her friends are inside ignoring her pain
she cries by herself for no one to hear
Her life is soon gone with one final tear
As she proceeds to pull the trigger fowl
A voice in the distance releases a howl
don't end your life you have so much to give
she falls to her knees, a moment to live
A hand from his doom comes out of the night
Let me help you my dear, she shivers with fright
whoever you are just please go away
No I shall not, she hears with dismay
I'll be here with you, I won't leave your side
from me your thoughts of death, you simply can't hide
even if death is what you do choose
We'll leave this world together, for you, my life I will lose

Thomas Sliney

Grandpa's Grave

Magical tombstones all in a row,
When I come to the grave site of someone I know.
Placing a flower off to his side.
Looking up in amazement to see his bride.
I stand up from a prayer and shockingly see,
Lying on his name plate, a pile of debris.
I sweep it off to the side to see his name so true,
Then look up at grandma, who looks so bitterly blue.
Driving away, I still can see,
The flag at his grave site waving at me.
A father, my grandpa, and a loving friend,
This man and my grandma will soon be together again.

Sandra Meddock

Sweet Silhouette

They say you feel better now and things for you are good
While I reflect the many times before me you have stood

But now in front of all of us you lay at final rest
As if you're lost so deep in sleep hands folded on your chest

Your face has lost its color, but it clearly shows the love
They say you're floating on a cloud somewhere high up above

You'll never know how much I wish to be with you right now
In many years, my final rest, the only way known how

That with you I could be again
Forever reuniting two long lost friends

Until this time when again we shall meet
There in the clouds your silhouette is so sweet

Keri Ann Rimbaugh

Waco

The winds whipped the flames in Waco
While the children were still inside.
Did the little ones cry to their mothers
As the flames grew hot and they died?

When winds whipped the flames in Waco
Did the children cry out in their fear
Though remembering what they had been taught-
That their angels would always be near?

While winds whipped the flames in Waco.
Did their mothers hug them tight
And tell each of their loved ones
Soon things will be all right?

Did the children have time to wonder
Why they were kept inside
When the winds whipped the flames in Waco
If God was still at their side?

Marjorie Punches von Pohle

A Bit Of Magnificence

As I view the magnificence of my Creator's handiwork
while walking my favorite path, the whiteness
of billowing cloud tops catch my eye.
Beneath this fluffy delight, low on the horizon,
remains the gray flatness out of which treacherous
storms evolved the night before.
The clouds linger in their loveliness almost with a promise
to return and then, they disappear.
My mind absorbs this breathtaking scene, knowing that I
shall never witness its exactness again.

Mary Beth Nelson

Sonnets Before The Monastery

Don't go trying to chisel into my heart
to find a warm and well lighted place.
I still tend pyres to Kali in the dark
and, however slowly, cremate any trace
of a woman in search of love's tenderness.
Let me hood my head and retire completely.
Your noblesse cannot bend me, yet I am remiss
for here you've detained me. Don't sweetly
beseech me come, return to the world.
I am not yet willing to be reborn...
dancing with death, broken heart unfurled,
safe within my soul's night. It is easy to mourn.
Rather would I cast my heart to the goddess's flame
than to place it in your trust for love's refrain.

Sandra Collins

That Special Someone

Although my friends come and go, my guy stays near,
Whispering those special words I long to hear.
I feel so secure when we cuddle at night,
To see us together is a precious sight.

He wants what's best for me, urges me to do more,
He gives me my strength, more than ever before.
It's hard to find the words to say how I feel,
I know the love between us is very real.

He loves me, I know it-I know it for sure,
It's been quite awhile, he forgot about her.
I treat him with respect, I do what I can,
But I make some mistakes, I am only human.

I get upset when something goes astray,
But when his arm's around me, it calms the day.
I may shed a tear but I don't mean to cry,
I guess I'm afraid he'll someday say good-bye.

It's just all in my head, I shouldn't have doubts,
We love each other-that's what life's all about.
Our lives are better, we've only just begun,
I know in my heart, he's that special someone.

Kristi Rudd

The Mind Of The Universe

The mind of the universe that speaks through me
Whispers love to all creation be it a man, flower, or bee.
The mind of the universe that speaks
only love through mankind, does give us
A knowing that we are truly divine
The mind of the universe even blesses as
we speak, under our feet, the sod.

The mind of the universe that gives
This much love to all creation must
truly be called God.

Vance Ross, Jr.

The Altar

In the providence of the Almighty, only a few there be
Who can climb some lofty mountain, cross th' uncharted sea;
Carve some face from marble, paint a Sistine wall;
Few there be of any age, sometimes no one at all.
Yet out of silent yesterdays, a life can find its star,
Against unnumbered throngs who pass
Alone, it dreams afar.
For Moses saw his burning bush, and Paul his shining light
And Jesus, from His raised cross
Exchanged the wrong for right.
And you, whoever you may be are touched with God's own hand.
Within your soul the spirit burns, brought by His angel band.
Then carve and paint and hew and touch, for genius finds a way
On some new altar you have built to offer beauty for today.

William S. Boice

Winter Twilight

Old woman.
Hands twisted from wiping
each child's tears.
Face carved with laughter
of countless days.
Sunlight races across your face
Flickering through each crease and valley
Ancient eyes, sight burned by that sun.
Wispy dreams dance around you
Music and sobs.
Pain and caresses.
Old woman, lace your fingers with mine.
Old woman, you are me.

Erin Riddell

Two Kinds Of People

It's fun to be around happy people,
Who get a kick out of life.
They always seem to make a big joke,
Out of all their trouble and strife.

Life is so much easier for them,
and they're never without friend.
In a group they shine like a sparkling gem,
and kindness shows in the message they send.

Then there are those with a foreboding gloom,
and a perpetual frown on their face.
They spread a wet blanket all over the room,
the disease of unkindness their case.

They don't seem to realize how happy they'd be,
If they'd only say things real nice,
To stop their being so ornery,
and before opening their mouth, think twice.

Kenneth C. McAfee

A Bequest, A Request

Curse not, my children this dame, emaciated and old,
Who has left behind no estate, trove or gold,
I have left no legacy, no mansion save my obsession,
My poetic works reflecting my emotional profligacy, my passion,
These were reared in my mind, you were nurtured in my womb,
To you I bequeath these when I depart towards my tomb,
These are but your foster siblings, the product of my mind,
To every brain child of mine, be mild, be kind,
These epitomize my thoughts, awry, eerie, or bleary,
My dreams idyllic, experiences bright and dreary,
These were my props, when lonely, forlorn and woe begone,
My near ones immersed in the hectic pursuits of their own.
Never did these forsake me whether I was a doyenne or a dilettante,
Pray, let not these be moth-eaten, my friends, confidante,
Treat not these like riffraff, litter, kitsch, chaff or trash,
For my soul, it would be an agony, a whiplash,
Let not these be scarred, marred, mutilated, dismembered,
By the ravages of war, pestilence sheer negligence be devastated,
Pray, throw not my poems on the garbage heap,
Perturb not your mother, in her eternal sleep.

Nilofer Sultana

I Know A Boy Named Patrick

I know a boy named Patrick
Who I love and cherish everyday
He came into my life in a most unexpected way
He walked right in and stole my heart away.
I know a boy named Patrick
who took us to the creek
To high adventures we can't know
'cause we've become too old.
I know a boy named Patrick
who is happy every day
And can beat the pants off everyone
on any Sega game.
I know a boy named Patrick
who climbed a backstop high
And taught us not to be afraid
and accomplish what we play.
I love the way Pat talks to me,
the way he shares his love
I love the way he'll be with me
even though we'll be apart.

Vilma D. Saucedo

Memories Of Grandma

Let me tell you about a lady
Who meant the world to me.
She was all of the things
I'd ever hope to be.
She was kind, gentle, and loving
To everyone she saw.
She had all the qualities it took
To be the world's best grandma.
She read her Bible every day
And prayed to the good Lord above
That He would watch over her family
With His everlasting love.
She was a mother, grandmother, great-grandmother—all three.
But, more important, she was a child of God-
Just like you and me.
She may not be here in body anymore,
But the memories so often have been told.
And I shall see her once again
When we walk those streets of gold.

Linda Brinkley

Easter Surprise

Who wiggles his nose and has a warm heart?
Who thumps and runs before we can start?
His tail is white and his eyes are light blue
And whoever loves him, loves him true.

Jellybeans, baskets and marshmallow treats
Often accompany him while he eats.
Colorful ribbons and soft, green straw
Are used to decorate his bed on the floor.

With large blue eyes he visits each one
Who deserves to receive a gift for fun
So if you've been good and listening too
Then you'll see him Sunday — why Peter, that's who

Katherine Constantinou

Ganani

For you granny,
who walked barefoot
in your land reclaimed
by the pure kind.
You who never knew
what Jergens could do
to your old cracked hands.
You who never saw
the other side of the orb
but could advise on any matter.
For you and all the grannies
who like you, were tossed aside
after they weren't even good for tending.
I wish I had seen you
open your eyes to this world
because then,
I would have cautioned you.

Milissau N. Wilson

A Perfect Circle

With open arms I welcome the day inhaling deeply
its fresh morning dew-knowing I am anew with innocence
and wanting as an infant who sucks in nourishment
and smiles with complete contentment waiting to be
cuddled and loved unconditionally.
Silently I stand in the garden of Life absorbing sights
and sounds letting my senses take command of my being
Smiling within builds to a climax that bursts through
my system - penetrating slowly at first picking up
momentum as it envelops me and I become the source and
the source becomes me as the circle completes my destiny

Patricia A. Molnar

Oh Lovely Maiden

Oh lovely maiden with the flaxen hair
Whom do you seek as you walk there?
Your hair blowing gently in the breeze
As you gaze intently out to Sea

Your flowing gown bathed in pale moonlight
Or has my imagination but taken flight
Do you seek a lover lost at Sea
As the restless waves beckon to thee

What would happen if I called out to thee
This lonely man beside the Sea
As I watch and wait where the waves break free
Would you hear or even see

If you heard would you come to me
Or continue to stare wistfully out to Sea
Oh how long have you tarried there
All these years so lonely and bare

Are you doomed to walk alone
Never to return to your Earthly home
Will you Eternally walk the moonlit shore
And seek a love that is no more?

Ruby Coggins Gordon

A Wife's Love

To my dearest love
Who was sent by God above; I swear.
We have made an extraordinary pair.

The messenger, A simple Dove, the Maker and Creator of this Love
You must have touched his wing; Or caught a gleam of his glistening eye,
Or maybe as he flew you by; He gave you a simple blink; I think.

Your love is a sensation of the wind upon the skin,
During the soft spring day. Or maybe,
It's a thought in a mother, watching her children play.
Or better yet; It's the light of the Sun,
Shining on the blue inlet bay; I surely say.

For I have felt this love deep inside.
Und es nicht tut mir leid;
But instead has given me great pride; I abide.

Thank you my wife.
I pray that God gives us a long life; Together,
But if we should pass; One after the other,
In the near, please have no fear;
For our love is True; And will begin anew.
Our Marriage; I Do!

Richard A. Dawson

Faceless Father

Let us pick from the sea
of generalities
one mossy shoreline rock
and upon that rock
we'll set our gaze
and disavow the city's call
her light-entombing buildings
...merely a young girl's promise

Let us gaze upon the rotted piling
standing bleak and broken
where long ago a pier once stood
leading to water
and docked boats
where now sits a big-bellied gull
mocking time atop her jilted column
eying prey....

(Wonder where they are today
'Louisiana' some say...)

Tom Carey

"Sadness Of A Father"

Feeling sad about the aloofness of a son
Who's father loves him very much
so sad toward the aloofness
of his daughters who never call
Just to say hello and say
How are you dad where is that love
we once shared
As father to son, as father to daughters
Could their growing up have changed them that much
As not to even send a card
Of wishes at holiday time
Oh the hidden tears of a sad sad dad
Who wonders about a time that used to be
Sharing and caring
About children he loved and still loves
The hidden hurt within
The feeling of emptiness
Will he leave this world
Without those last wonderful words of
"We love you Dad."

Ray Rivera

Somebody's Child

A MOMMA weeps for the child
whose life is
devastated by crack/ soap unknown
a shell
A MOMMA weeps for the child
who must dream fractured dreams
writhe in summer's relentless heat
hug himself toward off wintry blasts
A MOMMA weeps for the child
whose empty stomach SCREAMS for nourishment
soul aches for a touch of humanity
LOVE
A MOMMA weeps for HER child
whose future is nowhere / hopeless
and I
weep PRAY for the MOMMA who weeps....

Shirley E. Riley

Oh, Destiny!

Ohhh, Destiny! Why?
Why do you torment me so?
Again, you come a-whispering
about your grand plan for my life.

As before Destiny,
the soft, warm breath of your whisper
has me off and running.
I know not why...nor to where.

Why, Destiny?
Why must I work so hard?
Before, I thought I was working your plan.
But I failed. Painfully failed.

How, Destiny? How?
How am I to achieve those grand accomplishments?
Maybe..if you'd allow me one little peek
At your plan for my life.

I'm tired Destiny. Growing old.
How much time on this earth do I have?
You whisper of generous rewards.
Please Destiny...Please?

William E. Monroe

An Unborn Plea

Don't kill my cry before I come
Why should I die, what have I done?

They say it's a woman's right to make this deadly choice
To kill a baby who can't fight for its unspoken voice

Like many other helpless babes who may not be conceived
I probably won't be saved, not even by this unborn plea

I don't yet have the voice that if I live I'll speak
To help you make the choice so that death will not wreak

But if you let me live someday I will be part
Of the memories I'll give that you'll keep in your heart

Though I'm not yet there I am still alive
If I live I'll give a tear and a baby's cry

Then you'll hold me gently and sing a lullaby
While waiting so contentedly for calm to clear my eyes

I'll give you all the love a baby can ever give
I'll be a gift from above because you let me live

All I ask you to give is the mother that I need
Please let me live, this is my unborn plea

Yvonne Marie Savon

A Love Letter

Dear One: I want to let you know
why you mean so much to me,
You are someone I can talk with 'bout future plans -
No matter how foolish they may be.

That seed of love you planted deep within my heart
so many precious years ago,
Well-you've nurtured it with care and understanding -
What a way to make love grow!

You can make any dismal morning
so bright - so glowing - a sheer delight,
All it takes is your cheerful smile -
to make my day - and, to make my night!

You're built stairways to the stars for me, and me alone,
You've made every dream of mine come true,
so all those little imperfections you might possess -
mean nothing 'cause they're all just part of why
I LOVE YOU.

Rose Shanen Rovins

What To Think When The Time Comes

When I see my dad how will I react?
Will he want to see me after all these years?

I've missed him for
a long time.
He's my father
and will always be.
Will he be the
same or different?
Married?
Kids?
Or all alone without anyone.
Does he miss me?
Will he want
to see me?
Will he remember
his own daughter
that he once loved?
Hope, that's all that's left.

Sharee Mason

"What Shall I Be Doing?"

What shall I be doing, when "the End" comes?
Will I be tired, from writing some story, or poem?
And go lie down on the bed—for a few minutes—
To give my weary bones, and thoughts—a "rest?"

Or will I be out watering the garden?
To make the plants grow fast—seeds I planted
This Spring, (and me just topple over—)
In the yard there—no one to care? ——————-

Or will I be mopping up a bit of grime
From the sparkling linoleum?
And my knee give out—just one more time?!!
And I collapse there in a heap—no one to weep?

—Or get a letter in the mail—-
With such fantastic news!!!
My heart gives out, with "Joy,"
And I breathe deeply—one last time—Sublime!

Or will I go to bed, when I am weary——-
—And say an "Extra" prayer,
For those I care—(and ne'er wake up again?)
—I'm in My Father's —"Care"—(God's Care.)

Pauline Myers Howell

Too Much Concern

Who can decide about the state of one's affairs?
When what's best for A may not be best for B.
If one is really concerned, if one really cares,
one will not help another if the other can help thee.
Just because one says all the right phrases,
one's emotions might end up going in blazes.
Pouring out one's heart too early
might make the other one feel slight or surely.
When one gets burned too many times expressing emotion,
suddenly being shy is the correct notion.
Ironically, being good to someone doesn't seem like the answer.
One feels stripped of feelings just like a go-go dancer.
Maybe one should put on a feelings shield
to attempt to be healed and to successfully wield.

Sean T. North

Who's To Blame?

Who's to blame when you lose a loved one?
Who's to blame when a child has a gun?
Who's to blame when people commit suicide?
Who's to blame when the most important thing is pride?
Who's to blame when children have no one to talk to?
Who's to blame when only God loves you?
Who's to blame when kids get no attention?
Who's to blame when they're not even mentioned?

Molly West

Life II

Life is a mystery which nobody knows
Why it was given to us?
Why it started?
Why we die young, old, or just in between?
Why we celebrate the day we were born?
One thing you should know is there are
Many other mysteries to figure out besides life!

Melissa Stowell

The Way It Was

Come friend and take a walk with me to look at how it used to be. We will walk back in time to what is now known as the past. Today we will visit an ole farmhouse, full of beauty and charm. Some would say it's shabby and worn by the storms of time, but in my mind I do not agree, I know it is just the way it was.

The wooden gate is open wide, the path leads us to the porch. The porch swing is still there, a good place to sit and dream. Open the front door and step inside to see a fireplace filled with logs on the hearth, a tabby cat sleeps and nearby mama's rocker and her bible. The worn shades, the kerosene lamp, all of this just the way it was.

The bedroom still has the feather mattresses you can bury yourself in. They are supported by an iron bed frame, touch in winter and have cold feet. No bathroom inside but there is a tin tub for your bath but that's all. The kitchen is cozy and warm heated by a wood burning cook stove. Water is drawn from a well or a pump and I know that's the way it was.

The flowers are in bloom, there's so much beauty around this house. Taste the homemade goodies and look at the handmade quilts, all different. There's the bench where quality time was spent in teaching family values. They will last a lifetime and we need more of this today wouldn't you say? We'll take this walk again, there's more to see—that will be just the way it was.

Kathleen S. Davis

Drifting

City back street
Winding to country road
Takes me by a river.
All alone
I clear my head.

Rainbow streaks across the sky.
The wind whistles its tune through the trees.
I take a drink,
Lean back
The shadows cover me.

I open my eyes,
Refreshed and uncertain.
Wet my face.
The sun dries it.
'The water's cool.'

Stretching my muscles,
I learn to walk.
Over and over my feet go.
The wind is dying down.
I'm lost.

Leo M. Belanger

The Volunteers Tender Touch

They give themselves in little ways of love
With a kindly hand clasp or a small caress.
Calling cheerily from a hospital door
Words that helps to relieve one's stress
Telling a joke to make you laugh
But that's not all they do by half
They warmly welcome all they meet
To help them when their defense is down
And to give a lift when you are blue.
They think of kindly things to do.
With heart and soul they reach across the barriers of creed
And hear the deep unfathomed cry of human need.
They are the "Angels of Earth"
Whom we often fail to recognize
Until kindly deeds are done
By the patient ones who gives so much
Whose daily toil brings its tender touch.

Laura Stafford

Country Road

I travel on a country road,
to get me to my destination.
The vast trees all brightly painted
with nature's artistry, are draped overhead.
I feel as though I am blissfully happy,
traveling through an endless tunnel of beauty.
There my mind can wander from reality,
for just a moment.
The splendor encircles my whole being.
Then, at that dazzling moment,
I drive out of my dreams, from that place.
My senses return, as a melancholy feeling
overcomes my spirit.
I long to return. The beauty summons me.
I find rest in the thought
that tomorrow, I will head for my destination
again. The country road awaits my return,
to envelop me from life's ravaging stings.

Mary Ann Lefebvre

Walking To Church

The lantern is light with the flame just right
To guide our path

Arrive at church on time... No, not us
For we are enjoying the singing, music and fuss.

The sounds of the dark night are broken by the choir
Singing undirected and unrestrained for an hour.

The congregation is intense in debate
The preacher is waiting and waiting to close the gate.

Our arrival at church is perfectly timed
To slide in the pew as the church bells chime.

The sermon is read, and we dutifully listen
Folding our hands with head bowed for bless'n.

The walk back home is the greatest thing
As crickets join in our song.

Our lantern glows and beams on the path
Making walking to church a pleasure at night.

Luella L. Ganahl

Neighbors

Red or yellow, black or white,
We shouldn't really have to fight
Because of who we are!

We're all very special in a different kinda way
And that should be okay!

Imagine how the world would be
If we were all the same.
It would be kinda plain,
So let's combine ourselves together
And make the world forever!

Anna K. Neal

You're The One...

You're the one that broke me from the seal.
You're the one that gave me love that is real.
You're the one that cared for me when I was ill.
You're the one I love still
You're the one who stole my heart.
You're the one who broke my heart.
You're the kind that comes and goes
You're the kind I love so.

Christan Blackman

For My Daughter Diana On Turning Fifty - A Celebration Of Your Life

When you were born I thought my heart would surely burst with pride
Your father was enchanted too, he kept you by his side!
Your hair was copper colored and your eyes a vivid blue,
And we were so delighted with the miracle of you!

I've watched the stages of your life with interest and with pride
The difficult and happy times you've taken them in stride.
The years have passed and you have grown, my love has not diminished
You're still a miracle to me, your charm is still not finished!

You're versatile and clever, have beauty in your soul
You're gentle, kind and caring, helping others is your goal.
The things you've learned in fifty years amount to quite a sum,
So just relax now and enjoy the fifty yet to come!

Emma Holliday

Friendships

As years go by and you recall,
your fondest memories of all,
They seem to March by in review
Some are old and some are new,
The days of youth and many choices
Sounds of songs bring rejoices,
The feelings of one's first love
Only brought from heavens above,
Feelings of friendships and friendly faces
Exploring new and old places,
Good friends last one's whole life
Through good times, bad times, pain and strife,
As one looks back life's many trails
True friendship never fails

Addie Gollings

Heaven's Gate

Oregon, my heart goes out to those who have never seen
Your mesmerizing waters, your cathedrals of evergreen
From the cliffs along the ocean that beckon sailors from their ships
Down the mighty Columbia River which escorted settlers on their trips
I've never seen a rainbow in any other State
Which compares to the brilliant spectrum here -
I swear it's Heaven's Gate.

Christine Prapas

The Tasks Of Time

Like the flicker of a candle blowing gently with the wind.
Your passage from this life was much too short to end.
You left me on a Father's Day..... it was 1991.
You left me with a memory...a tear..a void...and a son.
He was the very breath of you, the heart and soul and depth
Of you..one life quietly slipped away, another had just begun.

You meet me in my dreams at night, and I awake to find you gone.
But I have chores to finish here, so I'll see you when I'm done.
With God there are no accidents. He touched your shoulder to say
"... COME NOW, YOU ARE TIRED BUT YOU WILL BE OKAY."
He knew had it been left to ME, I would have wanted you to stay.

I realize that with TIME and a little bit of prayer...God will
ease my pain and lift this burden that I bear. TIME purports
to explain to us all that we cannot comprehend. It takes us
back into the past and to the unknown and then, TIME permits
us to perpetuate the dreams that might have been.

So I will take the time to dream, no matter what the cost.
No matter how much time it takes, no dream is ever lost. When
TIME stands trial for my mistakes, it warrants an appeal. For
without the element of TIME, broken hearts would fail to heal.

Carmen Gardner-Wesley

Beyond Time

As we move from life to life
Through death after death
On the face of time-set millennia,
We assume many shapes,
colors, textures, intensities,
defenses, and dimensions.
Finally we meet
disrobed and vulnerable
our inner beings,
which have journeyed from
shelter to shelter,
protected and hidden
by the variety of available containers.
Exposed at last, we see that
in essence
who is in the end,
is the same as
who was in the beginning.

Joy Grau

"Sleep's Far Shore"

A mystery for the heart there is
within every mood and
set behind a veil is the
allure of vision for each
inspiration yet to be written
in its time without history.

Having stood before blue-white waves
intended for the calm of sleep's far shore
And having dreamed there
I know that each moment complete
ebbs that which in reality
passes down through fantasy.

So the moon when full is become clarity
in white. And, in the wake of its pull
though shadowed by the night
shines every aura of dream
like a new-born star
true to its own reflection
within the mood of a moon-lit stream.

Gerard J. Paulauskas

Just For A Day

Last September I met a man, so gallant
Slightly older, wiser, more extravagant
We sat and talked, smiled
Oh, I guess it was an hour, whiled

He seemed so gentle, kind
Made my heart race, out of sync, blind
Love's broken torch he carried
For the girl he almost married

His heart was given to another, he dreamt
She couldn't see what he meant
Another took her fancy, just think
Alone he was that night, on the brink

Another I met also, sought
His lips made promises, I thought
Friends warned me, leave him be
Learned, I did, he's not for me

Oh what a fool, he slipped away
Could not I have kept him, just for a day?
Where is he now? oh Lord above,
The man with whom I feel in love

E. Rebecca Lawson

The Latchkey

He wakes with the birds in the morning,
A breakfast may be overlooked;
He wanders outside for a playmate,
No time for a prayer or a book.

Soon parent speeds off to the job sight,
As little child fends for himself;
Thank God for community sources
Who rescue through neighborhood helps.

He counts to me eight keys about him,
His years merely mounting to five;
I'd like to just keep him and raise him,
And nurture a bit of that drive.

In spite of the longing, the drifting,
In spite of the time spent alone,
Some day he'll become a role model,
With fabulous homes of his own.

Doris Parker

Suicide Is...

A numbing of the heart
a deafening of the soul
an emotionless face
a wounded spirit
a shattered dream
a tragic past
a broken family
an uncertain idea
a selfish decision
a desperate alternative
a way to ease the pain
an irrational solution!

Carolyn A. Miller

Embraced

In the darkness of this room
As you are off to slumber
Feel my arms about you
As could come from no other
My heart will be with you
Until the day of my return.

Glenda McDaniel

Free Diamonds

Everyone needs a diamond.
A diamond as big as the mind can see.
A diamond, as big as the one,
In your own fantasy.

And then!!
A million diamonds, I did see,
Sparkling out across the sea.
The evening sun was slipping low,
As I looked across, this wonder I behold.

If you have never owned a diamond,
This one is free to everyone.
All you need, is the evening sun,
Shining down, upon the ocean so warm.

Some people say, what did God do for me.
Well, for one thing,
I was born, in the land of the free.

A place where I can take the time to behold,
These wonderful miracles, that unfold.
Miracles taken for granted, day by day,
And I pray that God never takes these
diamonds away.

Cathy "Misty" Reeves

Aeonian

...No transitory thing is this
A fleeting feeling is not intense
It does not stir one's inner being
As you Stir mine -
So tremulous!
And made thus only by your love
Which although weakens,
Yet makes strong
So that, all else within the world
Seems good,
And right.
'Naught can be wrong when
Sweetness and gentility
Abound like air in space.
All is clear.
My life is dear.
For in it darling,
You hold a place.

Isabel S. Cooper

"True Love"

We broke up, on account of me,
A future for us, I couldn't see.
My love for you, at the very start,
Engulfed my entire heart.

There was no room for any doubt,
What life together would be all about.
But then you had a roving eye,
You said you loved me, so I wondered
why?

You'd pretend it was all okay,
To carry on in this way.
You had your cake, and ate it too.
But my shoe didn't fit you.

So with a broken heart, I said goodbye,
Friends would ask, and wonder why?
What you really wanted years ago you lost.
And over the years, you paid the cost

Many times since, and we've both grown old
You've always loved me, I've been told.
I lucked out, because of you,
I married my love, and he was true!!!

Eldrus Goetz

A Light

A light I follow
A light it blinds
Where is it taking me?
This light is divine

Directed at only me
Strong and bright
Attracted to it
I don't have the will to fight

It leads down an untraveled path
Lost like never before
If I catch the light
I'll hold it forevermore

If I catch it
I won't be lost anymore
My heart will fly
My heart will soar

A light I follow
A light it blinds
Where is it taking me?
This light is divine

David Reyling

Sent To Me Hope

Show me the way this heartless day
A place where demons dwell time
Lost realms under an autumn moonshine
I listened to the night sounds glorious
A feeling in shadows where only dreamed
Reflection all that had happened learned
Another time come wind candle flame burn
I wonder what great mystery tomorrow
All the love no capture as sorrow
For I cannot afford my love such sadness
I look to the heart nothing there blind
A calloused fear life often to find
'This way' she said 'we will walk
And listen to the night sounds talk
To walk away this sea ridden bed
Riddled with holes sent hearts of the dead
Turned back to the wind wings of red'

Douglas Wayne Coffman

Insidious Tempest

An insidious tempest razes
A planet in the sun,
Consumes vital animation-
Devours like a Hun.

Then, impelled by insanity,
Moves on to virgin earth
Where winds of impropriety
Draw in maiden universe.

To execute fresh ambush,
Boreas dons Zephyr's clothes-
Traps with honeyed verse;
Then consumes with bitter prose.

Jan Olson

What Is A Son?

A Son is love and moments shared
A Smile he gave to show he cared

A Son is memory and skinned knees
and houses that he built in trees

A Son is toys now growing dusty
and old orange cat that he called Rusty

A Son is Christmas and Halloween
and all of the good times in between

A Son is love that fills your heart
A Son is pain when you have to part

A Son is thanks for the times you had
for all the times both good and bad

A Son is the courage to carry on
this was my son, his name was Jon.

Barbara Griffin

Unlearned

Reflected inventory,
Accumulated calluses,
Loveless activities,
Excluded prevenience,
Jaywalking mentality,
Eluded contentment,
Delusional values,
External
gratifications,
Selfish summations,
Precarious existence.

David C. Worrall

A Candlelight Christmas

On Christmas day it is said,
A special child was born,
In a shelter called a stable,
The only place to keep warm.

Had his family come by her street,
She would have welcomed them there,
She didn't have very much,
But comfort she had to give.

So as we sit by the fireplace,
Enjoying the season's cheer,
Somewhere a woman is sitting,
Beside a candle there.

In front of a broken windowpane,
On a blissful Christmas night,
Hoping someone will come by,
And see the candlelight.
Merry Christmas

Debora J. Davis

A Whisper Symphony

Purple days and violet nights,
A swirling vortex of flashing lights,
Dreams of Green and Visions Blue,
A whisper symphony just for you.

Bands of Gold are struck to play
A silver motif of rainbows gray,
Hills of brown and mountains too,
A whisper symphony just for you.

Silently the orchestra rises
In a brief interlude
Just checking to see
If you're in the mood.

Horns of fire and oboes trees,
A violin flowing with the breeze,
A harpsichord to make it true,
A whisper symphony just for you.

Bennie D. Ketron

the funeral

cradled in his earth stained palms
a thrush too young for flight
plunged from nest to slender grass
like summer's windless kite
thin tissues on a toothpick frame
the bud that promised spring
with startled eyes in hollow spheres
a fluff on broken wing
more gently than his nature knew
his silent vigil kept
until the small heart ceased to beat
the boy so softly wept
his prayer to God unanswered
he placed the lifeless bird
within the dark and shallow grave
where songs are never heard
death came as unfamiliar
but parted most profound
for he would long remember
the treasure he had found

Barbara Barnes

Spring

Ah-h-h-h, Spring!
A time for rejoicing.
The bursting forth of new life
from the dormancy of winter.
Spring engulfs us,
and we are caught up —
in a world of new beginnings;
in the dawn of a new season;
in the freshness and warmth of color.
Soft breezes —
that carry the smell of things growing;
the sounds of birds singing,
and of bees humming.
The peck peck of a woodpecker;
the chorus of frogs singing,
and the gurgle of small streams.
The breath of new life;
a fresh start,
to clear away the memory of winter.
Ah-h-h-h, Spring!

Charles G. Buchanan

Times

There was a time of war
A time of peace
A time of love
A time of hate
But when is our time
We don't know
We must find our time where we go
Where we go is an endless journey
Searching for that time of glory
That moment of everlasting glory

John Colonna

Saying Goodbye

A time will come,
A time to run.
The pain is so,
if it would just go.

Trying to hide,
the deep feelings inside.
I know it's hard,
for you have been scared.

There will be a day,
You may look back and say,
Thanks for the memories.
And thanks for the lesson,
or saying goodbye.

Brandi Hamvold

Falling

He's fallen for me,
All over me,
Under me,
Under where I wish for,
Over where I settled,
Between my leggings,
Furrowed brow,
Adrenalized heart,
Before my ham strings,
On top of my quandary,
Above my corner stone,
Winging it on the walkway,
Into the pitfall of my yearning,
Watching my face,
Hoping he hasn't hurt me,
But fallen all the same.

Beatrice Hraca

The Prophets Spoke

Gathered in solemn assembly
a vivid night some time ago
many prophets came from across the land
to pray and lay on hands.

A child was wheeled to the front of
the room there by helping hands,
while wondering hearts held him so dear,
to hear words they could endure.

God's voice clearly came, as the prophets
spoke, "changes will come, wait,
he will minister to my people and me,
these eyes will someday see.

You will see a mind so bright and clear,
a body strong and active,
faith and courage his testimony,
to witness amongst may."

Some changes have come but slow,
though seeds were planted in rich soil,
in the hearts with faith the saints of old
who see it as the prophets told.

Doris M. Lee

Don't Cry Mommy

While silently weeping
A voice calls out to me
Don't cry mommy
I'm alright you see

I've got to go now mommy
The angels wait for me
Everything will be alright
For they have promised me

But if you get all lonely
And in need of me
Just look to the heavens
For that's where I'll be

Walking with the Angels
And looking out for thee
So don't cry mommy
Just be proud of me

Janet Hughes

A Caring Friend

A love might not last
a year or two
but a friend who sticks around
you know is true,
when things are bad
and you're feeling blue
they help with your problems
some old and some new,
they give you advice
they think will do
this a friend
who cares about you.

Jennifer Courchesne

Untitled

The fire's out, the ashes smolder
A trip inside my mind
I feel a tapping on my shoulder
But leave it all behind
This system nurses a life of pain
Every day's a fight
But in the end I leave my stain
Then exit stage right

Glenn Schultz III

Wounded People

We are wounded
Abandoned
Betrayed
Forsaken
Offended
Left to die-alone
So we struggle on
And in our woundedness
We wound others
We hurt
Betray
Offend
All until we can stop
The cycle of pain
And progress to
Inner peace
And calm

Heal the wound

Jennifer L. Thome

O! A Paintbrush!

I have travelled far and wide
Across a great expanse of land
I've mapped in the ocean's tide,
I've tread on desert sand.

I've seen purple snow topped mountains,
Green eucalyptus trees
White magnolia blossoms,
And scarlet maple leaves.

I've seen the golden sun at dawning,
The orange noon at night,
The silver tips of sea gull wings
When those wings were spread in flight.

I took a lot be snap shots
Of things I saw along the way.
Now that I have "Proof positive"
How can you doubt what I say??

Hazel H. Brown

Change

Minutes roll
across time's blank
tablet,
leaving invisible trails.

Their silver essence
never changes
after they have
passed.

They become
battered memories,
only prints of faces
as the years roll along.

But the core remains,
unchanged, like the
old quarter
that just rolled across this table.

Deanne Elizabeth Durrell

I Sense

All around me I Sense great Joyfulness
All around me I Sense great Togetherness
All around me I Sense great Oneness

But

All around me I Sense great Loss
All around me I Sense great Despair
All around me I Sense great Hopelessness

But then

All around me I Sense great Lightness
All around me I Sense great Thoughts
All around me I Sense great, great

Worldness

Gee Gee Moore

I Still Look Into Your Eyes

I still look into your eyes
Although you are not there.
I still feel the pain you gave
When in my heart you made that tear.
I still read the lines from letters
That you once wrote to me.
I still hold the lock in my heart,
For which only you hold a key.
I still sit and dream of you
When you are not here.
I still want you by my side
To wipe away my tears.
I still want the love we had—
The love we once did share.
I still look into your eyes
Although you are not there.

Amber N. Allen

Romantic Eyes

The eyes of romance see and behold
an endearing story not often told
they seek joy for love in whatever
like finding fun in being together

A holding of hands a caress or touch
the little things that mean so much
no tale about land the sea or the sky
compares to the twinkling of the eye

Their story is a sparkling in the sun
retold by moon glow when a day is done
for the eyes of romance are so keen
even the blind say I see what you mean

Elmer B. Olsen

Untitled

In my eye
An endless reflection of you
Hangs on the Iris

The Pupil your student
with every blink
A heartbeat

A tear for your sorrow
A wink when you smile

My eye,
A reflection of the feelings
For the mirror from the image

Joseph Schrock

Feelin' Down

I was feelin' down
and a little blue,
When my thoughts
turned to you.

To Thee, my heavenly Father
I poured out my heart.
You listened with divine mercy,
And consoled me, my every part.

The Lord knows what it is like
to lose a loved one.
So I know his love
will help me to overcome.

Feelin' down is not so bad
when I have God at my side.
Because I know He is there,
All my troubles will subside.

Adeline M. Kramer

Hope

When heart and soul in sorrow meet,
And devils dance around my feet,
When heart cries out and lips stay dumb,
And searching tears begin to come,
When soul cries out in seething strife,
I sometimes wish to end my life.
It's sad but also very true,
That others of us have this wish too.

When bitter tears concrete my brain,
It hurts to feel this endless pain.
I suddenly think "Now this must be
The ultimate problem facing me,
For surely in the morning's light,
The world will be both new and bright."
Then comes the dawn and night must fall,
Again, I wish to end it all.

Avis Marie Barrett

The Angel Of The Ashes

I poke at the sputtering embers of memory
And dream.
Black-shrouded,
Smelling of ashes and musty basements,
She creeps into my dream.
"I'm tired of being a blind mole,
Hiding in your dark cellar,
Hearing your sad cries.
I want to be a butterfly,
Waltzing in orchards,
Drunk on the fragrance of apple blossoms."

Locked in eternal embrace,
We wrestle to a draw.
From haunting eyes
Her flint-hard spirit shines.
And suddenly
My angel of the ashes and I
Become one,
Poised for flight,
Sparkling in the light.

Edith Reese

Sleeping Away Sorrows

I close my eyes
And dream of you
of being in your arms so tender...
so warm
Lust devoured by love
Emotions so strong they rape my heart
Reality is gone, long ripped apart
My soul was captured by your eyes,
I think we should give love another try
Your touch brings on the night
Feelings too strong to ever fight
I open my eyes.........
You're no longer here
Just another dream
I cry one more tear
A new dawn breaking
More sorrows awakening
Another day to live without you
And of holding on to dreams,
that will never come true..........

Amy Loftus

Verses Best Left Unspoken

Verses best left unspoken
  And favors best left undone
Have quickly rendered broken
  A trust that was dearly won.
The deeds I did were sincere,
  And the words I wrote were true,
But none of them, it is clear,
  Were proper to say or do.
I'm grieved that I offended,
  And caused your pain to return,
Grieved I overextended
  The reach of caring concern.
A counselor's vocation
  Draws lines I cannot dispel,
Yet you gained my admiration
  And my fond regards as well.
In my life's disordered strands,
  You've woven a special part;
Though boundaries bind my hands,
  They never can bind my heart.

Craig L. Teed

I'd Like ...

I'd like to slide down an elephant's ear
And hope he wouldn't shed a tear.

I'd like to walk where dandelions stand
And listen quietly to their golden band.

I'd like to sit under a mushroom wide
And see it any toads do there abide.

I'd like to march in a children's band
And sing out loud, "This is my land!"

I'd like to swim in the blue, blue sea
And let the colorful fish nibble at me.

I'd like to go where wild flowers reign
And make, again, a clover chain.

I'd like to feel the breath of joy
As wonders are found by girl and boy.

So let the children out today,
Let them go out to dream and play.

Catherine Shumaker Brinson

The Wall

The wall is all around me,
And I cannot find my soul.
It soon begins to crush me,
And, oh, it feels so cold.
The wall is all around me,
And I feel so trapped within.
The wall is growing stronger,
And it's built with my own sin.
I feel that I can't fight it,
And darkness is all I see.
I feel that I'm trapped inside it
Never to be free.
But suddenly out of nowhere
A light comes shining through,
And I hear a voice saying
"My child, I died for you."
I turn my eyes to Jesus,
And I place my faith in Him.
My freedom He has given me,
And He paid the price for my sins.

Beth Randolph

In The Night

As darkness falls upon me,
and I cannot see the light,
I try to think about you,
but my mind is just a blank.
I close my eyes and hope,
I'll see you in my dreams,
but as I lay there in the night,
I find it hard to sleep.
I watch the shadows on the wall
and imagine I see your face,
but when the room grows lighter,
the image goes away
and as the night turns into day,
all your memories seem to fade away.

Barbara J. Dixon

Hold My Hand

I have a need; a deep down need
And I hope you will understand.
It may not seem important to you
But I need someone to hold my hand.

The human touch is a comforting touch
But I would neither beg nor demand.
Nevertheless, I would feel much better
If someone would hold my hand.

It would be sad, so lonely and sad
With the sifting of the hourglass sand
To face the final hours of life,
If there's no one to hold my hand.

Don't grieve for me, no bitter tears shed,
For I've made my mark on the land.
Just sit with me and speak with love
And for God's sake hold my hand.

Della Frances Adams

As I End

As the ending nears,
And my life flashes
Before my eyes,
A lifetime in one moment,
All my happiness,
All I've done,
When I die,
I leave them to you.

Cynthia M. Feldbauer

The Beauty Out There

My eyes stare out the window
And I know I must beware
That I fully absorb
All the beauty out there

The warmth of the sun
Feels good on my face
As the pleasant gentle wind
Blows my hair out of place

The scent of the flowers
Like perfume in the air
Enhances the sensation
Of all the beauty out there

The rustle of the leaves
In the trees all around
Is like music to one's ears
It's such a pleasant sound

The magnificence of our senses
Comes to my mind
As I drink in nature's beauty
Even though I am blind

Esther Katz

Just A Little Snowflake

I'm just a little snowflake
And if I make it to the ground
There'll be so many there
That I probably won't be found.

I'm just a little snowflake
Slowly drifting to the ground.
I'm not a lot to look at
But there's beauty to be found.

I'm just a little snowflake.
Some hate to see me come.
But if you'll come and join us
You'll have lots of fun.

I'm just a little snowflake
That will melt away next Spring.
So come on out...play with us.
And please, your sleds do bring.

I'm just a little snowflake
I don't mean you any harm.
Before you know it...winter's gone.
And spring brings in the calm.

Addie Dolly Johnson

The Siege

The posterior slap
and infantile cry
fades now into misty smoky hills
nestles down to rest
lapsed into sleep
by a lullaby
of humid spirits
that forget to reawaken us
Relief has come
the siege is lifted...

...for it was the sweet soft embrace
of exhaustion
which is most desired
the drying cool of perspiration
during a final lax grip of hips
cheek touching cheek until an afterglow
of sleep
and the promise of a Mourning kiss

John C. Squier

A Paean To The One I Love

I've seen the beauty of the mountain-top,
And loved the color of the water-drop.
I've known the joy of a winter scene,
And revelled in the summer's green.
I've heard the magic of the desert night,
And was wooed by early morning's light.
I've felt the tumultuous ocean's roar,
And beheld the kingly eagles soar.
I've roamed gracious garden walks,
And gloried in their golden stalks.
Even the heavenly stars at night
Have entranced me by their sight.
But of all the wonders from up above,
None will match my tender love.

Gene Johnson

You

You changed my life
and made me smile
You made living
seem worth while

You brought the sun
into my life
You said you want me
to be your wife

You taught me how
to love again
You are my lover
and my friend

Now I know
that love is true
And it's all
because of you.

Alisha Scoggin

"Turning Point"

If just your touch could light a fire
And melt the ice around my heart
As you have said

And I could lay a table grand
With fine cuisine and rarest wine
And warm your bed

Would just one hour sustain you
Through all the years to come
When love is dead

Eve McDonald

If We Were Our Brothers' Keeper

If we were our brothers' keeper,
And our brother was the same.
We'd be living as our savior,
There would be no need for blame.

We would use the tools he gave us,
And his rules we would obey.
The frustration and the heartaches,
Through his love would pass away.

All the roads of doubt and anger,
Man has built in his despair.
Would be replaced with goodness,
Scenic highways filled with prayer.

There would be no need for violence,
Peace and Joy we would proclaim.
Sisters, brothers through the father,
Living in his Holy Name.

Adlain R. Culver

Nature Or Nurture

I tried with all that's in me.
And searched for all that's left.
Instilled in them curiosity,
And inspiration for them to find.
Planted seeds of fulfillment,
Somewhere in their minds.
I turn around and close my eyes,
But there they will forever be,
Somewhere o'er the earth,
Forever following me.

Heather Evans

God's Love

When I wake up in the morning
and see the sun rise,

I realize just how much
God can change our lives.

If we just let him
He can take the hurt away,

All that we have to do
is humble ourselves and pray.

For the Lord, our God,
loves us very much,

He reaches down from the heavens
and gives us his special touch.

He makes us new and
turns our lives around,

So that we know that
we are heaven bound.

Through Him the sun
will always rise,

Just as He will
always be by our side.

Heather Hart

Untitled

TV makes me laugh sometimes
and sometimes makes me cry.
Telephones make voices clear
when you're flying through the sky.

Radios make music sweet
and night times not so lonely.
Letters come from sweethearts far
to tell you you're their one and only.

Technology makes life so simple
and sometimes makes us lazy.
It cooks for us in just a wink
saves us time from going crazy.

Books and magazines get lost
but aren't too far forgotten.
Reading can be fun sometimes
when the selection on TV is rotten.

But take the time to enjoy the old
the flowers or the trees.
Technology for all it's worth
has Mother Nature on her knees.

Caroline T. Patti

Gathering Time

It's late in the season
And the harvest is white
It's time for the reaping
So join in the fight
Sharpen your prayer sword
While there is still light
Use it wisely to open the gates
To that city of gold
Where Jesus awaits.
We can't grant salvation
You know this is true
But we can reach out
By the things that we do.
So let's keep on praying
And doing our best
Then Jesus our Savior
Will do the rest.

Aritha Thurber

An Evening Conversation

I thank You, God, for times You came
And touched my life today.
I saw your beauty in the sunrise
A radiant display.

A Bluebird came to feed her babe
At feeder outside my door
I felt You say "I will provide"
I need not ask for more.

When decisions I have to make
I feel so much aware
Of Your presence and assurance.
To know You is my prayer.

I saw Your Spirit in my friend
Your love within her smile
As we lingered over coffee I knew
You came to stay awhile.

I know Your presence is always near.
Because You are the same
Today I was aware of You
And knew You when You came.

Elsie Brayman

Anger And Violence

Anger is dangerous
And violence is, too.
Innocent people
Die because of you.

Control your anger
But don't keep it inside;
Count to ten
Until it subsides.

Violence is caused
By anger, you see.
Not because of people
Like you and me.

So put away the weapons
The knives and the guns.
Think about the people they kill,
It could be one of your loved ones.

Chrissy L. Ward

Love Desired

The love I have for him is deeper
and wider than one can imagine.
He is part of me and always will be.
The Father of my children and the
joy of my life.
And for this another chance I plea.
His touch is what I long for -
The warmth of his love I hunger for.
To be held and comforted in his arms
is like a jewel of gold.
Come to me the one I love.
Take me away with wings of love.
Let us give each other the peace we
need.
And stay for us to abide together
as sweet as a dove.

Janet M. Tindel

Barriers

All my songs are sad, dear,
And yours would be too,
If you cared for someone
Who gave no thought to you.

Nights the stars don't shine;
Dark skies meet the day.
I have been so lonesome
Since you went away.

The few things that were ours;
The little joys we knew
Faded like wilted flowers—
As the barriers built and grew.

I stare out the window,
Oft' pace to and fro.
I sulk in the shadows—
And no where do I go.

Yet at dusk I see you;
Hear your sweet voice, too.
But your smile's for another—
Since the barriers grew.

Edward Hamilton Halsall

River

Through hollow caves
Are beneath the ground
There's crashing of waves
With barely a sound

A river unseen
But it was there I know
By the trail of scars
Left some time ago

The river was once in her
But now it is gone
Will it ever return
If so, for how long

How long this time
Will it flow and rage with power
Forcing itself as it turns and winds
Underneath, in, out and over

She can control her waters
When they will live and when they die
If she can control her river
Why can't I control mine

Edward S. Scott

Friends

Friends,
are like the panes
of a window,
They are merely reflections
of our hopes and dreams,
triumphs and disappointments.

When our hearts
long for comfort,
it's the solace of a friend
that we seek.

When laughter requires company,
to our friends do we look.

Every time a smile is shared,
an angel spreads its wings.

Friends,
reflections of ourselves.
Friends,
the down on an angel's wings

Elizabeth A. Cornele

If I Can't Sing Alleluias

When answers to my earnest prayers
Are not what I expected
May your grace so fill this heart of mine
That your higher ways may be accepted

In the loneliness of pain filled hours
That none but you can share
Lord help me know I'm not alone
For you are present there

If weakness ebbs away the strength
My grateful praises to impart,
If I can't sing Alleluias Lord
Then hear them from my heart

Intensify the fellowship
We share in grace divine
Until your thoughts become my own
Your higher ways be mine!

S. B. Grace

Adoptive Mother's Tribute

You
are the missing piece
in the puzzle of my life.
Precious Gift from God
through sacrifice of another,
long awaited child of my heart.

Through you
I am learning
to trust...
In God,
Myself,
The future.
I embrace the challenges of life
with confidence
and hope renewed.
Yesterday's pain forgotten
every time you smile
and call me
Mommy.

Dianne M. Graham

Untitled

I said goodbye, I didn't want to go
are you so blind you cannot see
a love budding on a flowery bed
perfumed with roses smelling yet
of promise of a love so great
will you let it die or drink the wine
of love's sweet fruit another time
will it be me, or someone new?
Oh God let it be me.

Edna Horn

Around This Time Of Year

I seem to get a blindness,
Around this time of year.
With Christmas Trees and Tinsel,
In this season we love so dear.

I seem to really get blinded,
As the Holiday draws nigh.
With bonus, presents and parties,
And Santa and Reindeer that fly.

Why do I get this blindness?
With turkey, cakes and pies.
When something inside whispers.
There is more here than meets the eye.

The greatest gift that I received,
Came "Gift Wrapped" in human skin.
For God came as flesh and dwelt with us,
And yet He knew no sin.

My eyes now see more clearly,
As this Saviour I receive.
That Jesus is the Messiah,
To all who will just believe.

Gene B. Campbell

Day

A new day dawns, as we
arouse from refreshing slumber
As we in habit this sphere's
pilgrimage, we greet it.
Nourished, we anticipate, joy
and great expectations.
Precious time, used to full
potentiality.
Contentment with peace will
triumph.
Never illuding a moment, as we
achieve, our ultimate goal
Ecstatic, with new daily discoveries
Self confidence trust and reliance
in the Master, for eternity.

Ida Mallory

Easter

It's Easter time. It's Easter
And the whole earth praises thee.
Freshly stirred to growth - reborn
The grass, the flower, the tree.

The birds come back to sing.
Spring rains and sun are warm.
And to the animals
The little ones are born.

Now touch our hearts, dear Lord,
That we may also be
Stirred to inward growth -
New faith, new hope in Thee.

Beatrice Fox Peterson

Solace

A silhouette embraces my dream.
As if it were close but yet reserved.
The portrait
becomes reality
as I imagine my existence from afar.
Looking beyond I see
the shadow that fuels my fear.
I searched for tears,
the hollow scream
ruled by far.
The voice of silence,
now been molded.
Only to be found
from courage within,
can my life
yet begin.

Elizabeth Paige VanSickle

After The Darkness

The night wind bore a noble message,
As it whispered past the tree,
Telling all of those who listened,
"This is how the world should be."

And there within the depth of darkness,
While the crickets played along,
The rhythm of the falling raindrops
Lent its echo to the song.

"Reflect on all the fine creations;
Celebrate the moon and stars.
Think about the world of Venus;
Contemplate the world of Mars."

Amid the dark and somber silence,
The message pierced a lonely heart;
And one who sat alone - and listened -
Felt a revolution start.

So when the sunlight filled the morning,
One (who's soul was moved that night)
Gazed enchanted at the splendor,
And sensed the glory of the light.

Donna Lee Ladd

A Free Ireland

Wisdom blackened by conflict,
as peace is forgotten fast.
An outlander prowls Irish land,
stalking like a thief of cats.

A tree lives lengthy in America,
for only true death is by nature's law.
Not burned by the outlander of far,
like the trees were in Ireland's war.

This land of green defines perfection,
so let no other claim definition.
Still alive, but so destroyed.
Celts must trim a deadly thorn.

Yeats, Joyce, O'Conner may agree -
Leave this land of mine in peace.
Then all will dance and bid farewell,
to the outlanders of Ireland's hills.

Celts dream to dream once more.
Upon their land of leprechaun tales.
Dreaming of a rainbow night,
filled with the sound of victory bells.

Carlton Dewayne Pool

Ancient Music

A touch of wind upon my brow
as she sings her ancient music to me,
Many lives she has touched, cooled
and heated but she never stops,
She whispers in the trees
as they sway to her song.
Her music is clear and cannot be heard
except by the chosen,
Many voices she speaks with her breath.

Her song is for the few to hear,
but her breeze is for all,
She touches everything,
and never leaves a trace,
Time has no meaning to her, as we know it.
She is a free spirit on the
land and air roaming where she pleases
asking for nothing,
But then, what could you give her.
Listen with your heart and mind
and hear the Ancient Music.

Gladys Schwinger

Ritual Of The Wood

In the May Day eve
as the suns shadow
moves in the forest,
Along the road
where the moss-rose grows
you, the sacred one,
and I, shall meet.
Only the Green-man
will witness, as I
show to you the blue,
of my scarlet pulse,
which burns, and cools
and promises, you,
Bone-singer will
appreciate how
my bones bend,
and curve,
gently, venerate
at the nighthawks call.

Candace Reinholdt

The Mask

The mask she wears serves her well
As well as masks can hide,
Until she asks so poignantly,
"I wonder what he's doing?"

New Age woman, doing her best
To make the most of fate,
For she is here and he is there,
It all seems so confusing.

Spring rebirths, burning summers,
Cascades of rich, fall colors,
Jagged icicles pierce her heart,
Alone, not of her choosing.

Drops of rain can ruin most masks
If they are made of paper,
Delicate petals blow away,
Crushing, not preserving.

The smiling mask she wears so well
Transcends and makes connections.
Sweetly she whispers over the lines,
"My love, what are you doing?"

Annabelle M. Sherba

Midnight Musings in Southern California

Do you ever stop to wonder
As you lie in bed, awake,
What other folks are thinking
As they wait for the next quake?

Are they really just as fearful?
Or is it just a piece of cake?
Will the next one be THE BIG ONE?
Or-what precious things will break?

Our state is in an uproar-
It cannot pay its bills,
While every day, Rush Limbaugh
Proclaims the country's ills.

Old Mother Earth lies trembling
Beneath the distant hills,
Dear God! Please come and get me!
Where are my sleeping pills?

Hazel M. Caesar

To The Empire State Building

Man-made Alp with peak of chrome,
Beacon light to welcome home
New Yorkers from both near and far,
converging by plane and train and car!

Those who gave up on Idaho,
raising the cry of Eastward-Ho!
From Florida: leaving with no compunction
A state that boasts a Yeehaw Junction;
from California one hears the wail,
"no one mentioned the Richter scale!"

Returnees from Europe's far flung shore
confiding it all was quite a bore;
into the air one throws a hat,
proclaiming New York is where it's at!

With the sky above, and below, the mud...
Empire State, are you a dud,
accepting with equanimity
Twin Peaks of the Port Authority?

Alice Baumel

"Spirit Of Awareness"

I find the world more
Beautiful, with motion, light and
vibrations;

The stars do not only twinkle,
But sparkle with colorful lights
In the sky, that dance and play
before my eyes;

The breeze brushes laughter
Against my face and suddenly I
Burst with glee and joviality:

The hills and valleys show their
Majestic splendor through
Their shadows and depth;

Birds sing their words of peace
And serenity, letting us know that
There's nothing but spirit for
All who wish to see.

Carolyn Norman

Poetry Contest

I know someday I'll win a poetry contest,
Because I have been greatly blest,
By my God way up above,
Who fills my heart with love.

I take my writing by spells,
Only when my heart swells,
With love out of control,
Coming from deep within my soul.

My love is so bountiful,
Loving all things so beautiful.
Sometimes love wells up in me,
Just bursting to get free.

This is why I write poetry,
For all the world to see!

Joy R. King

God Is With You Day And Night

God is with you when the sun shines
because the light leads you in his path.

God is with you when the moon shines
because when it's dark, He gives you
faith to find your way.

God is with you when you're lost because
He finds you a pathway for you to follow.

God is with you throughout the day and
throughout the night so you can find
a way to his heart.

God loves you just the way you are!

Ericka Idler

Losing You

I wrote this poem,
Because you are going.
But I can't let you leave,
Without you knowing.

That you are special,
and I can see.
How very special
You are to me.

You were there when I needed someone.
You helped me out when I was blue.
I had good times, I had bad times.
I didn't know just what I had.

But you showed me, my life was right.
By being there, just making it bright.
So, when you go, I know you'll be,
as special to others, as you are to me.

Charlene A. Potter

Good-Bye

I think of you often
And wonder where you are.
If you look down at us
To see how we all are
And grow sad
'Cause you're not apart
Of our lives anymore.
I regret things,
Like I know you do
Or did at times.
But the biggest thing
I regret is not saying
"Good-bye" to you.

Amanda Bradley

To My Children

I want to say to my children,
before I too shall pass away.
Just how much they comforted me,
each night and passing day.

Your love and your affection,
no way shall ever be forgot.
You gave your love and care so free,
your dedication shall be for naught.

I love each and every one of you,
with a heart that wants to break.
Please keep mamma in your memories,
and me do not forsake.

I need each and every one of you,
much more than you will ever know.
Whether it be night or day,
grass green or winter's snow.

Give to me just half the love,
that I do feel for you.
And I'll be the richest person,
that this whole world ever knew.

Howard E. Ragsdale

How Many?

How many hearts need be broken
Before that one heart dies?
How many harsh words spoken
Before God hears their cries?

How many lives are ruined
By a parent that just leaves?
How many children must suffer
Before the angels grieve?

How many people must go without
Before one sees they're needing?
How many crimes committed
To notice a city's bleeding?

How many loved ones perish
In the heat of anger and passion
When will the human being
Undertake pity and compassion?

How many harsh words spoken
Before all is said and done?
We shouldn't speak in plurals..
The number my friend, is one.

David Lessard

The Eternal Cord

How frail - yet strong that single
cord of life from womb to grave -
woven through success - distress -
with love and hate depraved.
Reality condones what action stirs
The heart - inner struggles -
growing pains from life to dust depart.
Regrets are few that we have passed
this way to prove our worth -
pressures pull the thread so taut
we are innocent victims - are we naught?
Growth beyond our years at times
dictates our strength while peace of
mind we find within arm's length.
From darkness - through light -
to darkness we return -
courageous journey - living hope
our eternal light still burns.

Florence N. Troll

Untitled

I look but cannot find a star
Behind the smog is where they are
But I make a wish anyway
For things to be better someday

Drugs are dealt on city corners
A funeral that's filled with mourners
So many people, so much pain
No wonder we've all gone insane

A burning cross is on the lawn
The KKK has struck at dawn
Pregnant teens roam the US nation
The Cuban sport is immigration

Sexual harassment in the halls at school
A place where girls just aren't cool
And there is cruel and heartless rape
A world from which there's no escape

Families with no place to live
No one has the heart to give
But there's still hope for tomorrow
Love could help to ease our sorrow

Cara Jackson

Gone And Still Remain

Rose petals and the morning dew
Beside my feet lay scattered 'round
Remnants of the past and all that's new
Fill my heart with pain and joys of you.

Carol Zoranovich

The Sun Keeper

And the world we know is crumbling,
beside the angry sky...
And nothing remains but remembrance,
through the spoken words,
of yesterday...
Comes the Blood,
and the screams,
through the window I hear him crying...
The clouds cover the Sun,
and the Sun-thirsty children weep,
for the forgotten one,
left out in the Rain...
You see his poisoned blood,
and run.
But you can not run far enough,
to fill your empty hands...
And my Sorrow brings another day,
and the echo's of yesterday,
Remain...
Within this empty Heart...

Chrissie Brittain

Beyond

Ancient kingdom, concealed unknown,
Bestow truths presently not shown,
Frail, reaching palms your only glass,
Remotely hidden in blue mask;

Faithless, your unpassionate grasp,
Desist deep silence, all that's asked,
Abandon I gravity bounds,
Be awakening in your sounds;

Infinite large or small no jest,
Atom planets perhaps wave's crest,
Lost, weightless isle in seas of time,
Seeking peace in shores, never find.

Deborah Douglass Kosovic

The Nature Of My Homeless Man

You are
blasphemed and braided,
tangled as gnarled tree bark,
and unsung.

Scattered squirrel nuts of
fisted soft paper
tightly grip the Society Pages.

You are
open mouthed, and silent,
snapping like twigs and
crunched crackling autumn leaves.

Winter comes,
you stand strong -
willed
rooted in your cement garden,
and the plink of silver raindrops
fall.

Caroline Todd

My Roots

Mom, you gave me my first
boost up the tree of life.
From there I slowly climbed
the branches of learning.
I listened to worldly
knowledge from the breezes,
as they blew through the leaves
that were surrounding me.
You are forever at
the roots of my success,
standing by in case I
climb too high, too quickly.
Now I see the hazy
sunshine of the future,
light that beckons me to
escape protecting limbs.
Soon I will try my wings,
and fly away from here,
and you will remain by
the tree that holds my nest.

Barbara Hogle Dickerson

Ontogeny

(For Sam, Sharon, And Liat)

When the warm
breath of summer
was cooled by
autumn breezes,

Promising that a
panoply of color
from nature's
sun machines,

Lemon yellow birch,
prune purple ash,
royal red dogwood,
orange brown maple,

Would soon adorn
the land, a small
cry titillated
two astonished souls,

Whose plasma now
flowed as one in
a glorious seedling,
their link to immortality.

Elliott Perlin

A Mother's Love

Silver wings from on high,
Bring to mind with a sigh,
Baby fingers twined in mine,
Oh Lord God, with you he's thine.

Memories swirling through my mind,
Joys and sorrows of a kind,
Mother love will ever be,
The anchor, moving through the sea.

Waves-clouds-country-thoughts abound,
Crashing, churning, burning steel!
I walk upon this bitter ground,
To God my tortured mind appeal.

Leave to me, His love and peace,
To wrap about and so release,
The agonies of losing Skip.
Remaining? Cherished memories
equipped!

A mother's cry, heard up above,
So answered with His love,
The heavenly doors, opened one day,
Mother - Son - together they say,

Anita H. Cole

The Wonder Of Things

Spring is filled with secret promise
Budding dogwood, cherry blossoms
That dance with the wind that sings.

Summer, with sunflowers, apple trees
And wheat, an ocean of gold that waves
As shadows purple beneath the moon.

Autumn, harvest stored in lofts
Treasure for those who labored
Early frost, red berries of bittersweet.

Winter, sleet grumbles in the water spout
Sketches fairy-rings on grass
And most of all a time to dream.

To know I am a woven part of rainbows
For I live with love's expectancy
Heart young, though very old.

From my chair before the window
Listening to the chant of church bells
Rejoice that I am one of those...who
worship.

Guanetta Gordon

Pick The Pebbles

Pick the pebbles from the sand,
count them one by one.
Amuse thyself my pretty child,
now is the time for fun.

Don't hurry to grow up, that
time will come soon enough,
And believe me, my darling,
the going will be very rough.

So play my child, now, while
thy heart is free from fears,
With growing up comes knowledge,
and wisdom will bring tears,

Find joy in knowing little for
that's the nicest kind of fun—
Yes, my child, pick the pebbles,
count them one by one...

Colleen Durrant Brake

I Am Not Born Today

I am not born today
But anyway
I have heard them say
That they throw some away.
I want to be,
I want to see,
What's out there for me.
Don't cut me short,
Don't abort.
Don't stop my being
Without seeing
My love for you,
Because it's so true.
Don't kill me now
Because somehow
You will love me back,
And that's a fact.
At least give it a go,
And I will show
You the happiness will grow.

Charles Strickland

A Drink

Trees surrounded it
but could not contain it,
With long strides it brushed past
or pushed through.

It came upon a pool
of water, which had been scarce,
Many creatures had converged there
wary of enemies, but driven by thirst.

It approached the pool timidly,
Tiptoed up, glanced about,
'fore lowering its head to drink.

Insects buzzed around it
encircling its head
some landing to sap its blood,
And each time it shook
its hide shifting quickly
over the muscle it hid.

Returning to the trees, it settled below
Swinging its long neck and tail about itself
Believing it best to sleep away its cares

Gianfranco Origliato

Untitled

It's cold in here,
Dark and damp.
Loud noises surround
Unhearing ears.
Scream all you want,
You will never be heard.
It's sad in here.
The walls are painted,
Covered with pictures.
These pictures depict loneliness.
Eyes fill with tears.
The sad life of one who is alone.
It's frightening in here.
There is no sense of purpose.
No real sense of meaning.
There is no one to turn to
When fear overcomes you.
It's cold in here,
But you learn to adjust.

Jennifer Hodgdon

The Man

Death is a robber;
but, he won't steal me!
For I know the man,
From Galilee!

When all others have deserted,
He remained true.
When overcome with despair,
He will lead you.

If your heart has been broken,
He provides the thread.
If for love you've been starving,
He provides the bread.

Let him take your hand,
He will remain at your side.
Allow him to embrace your soul,
And he'll forever be your guide.

So when the time comes,
To draw your last breath;
There's no reason to fear,
Your impending earthly death.

Diane M. Lewis

Jamie Is Crying

Jamie is crying
But I don't know why,
So I'll sit quietly by her
And try not to pry.

"My Mommy and Daddy
Aren't in love anymore.
They're filing some papers
To get a divorce."

"Was it something I did
Or something I said?
I have so many questions
Spinning 'round in my head!"

"Do you think that one day
They'll try to explain
How they've stopped loving me, too?
Oh, I can't stand the pain!"

Jamie is crying
Her cheeks streaked with tears.
A nine-year-old girl-child
With a future of fears.

Jillian Napier

In Full Bloom

All roots are interwoven,
But seeds roam ever wide;
Unfurling into wondrous plants,
Flowering with pride.

Growth is sown on surface earth;
And home, where e'er we long.
Our forebears are humanity—
Disparate, sick or strong.

The firmer is your tilling for a
Tree of empathy,
More fruitful will be harvesting
Of mutuality.

Who may say that you must stay
As sproutings from one plot;
When this can "stem" maturity,
While flight and fancy rot!

Jeanette Birnbaum

One Day At A Time

Our days are slowly waning,
But they will never dim;
For they are brighter now
Than when we first began;
Oh! So long ago.
Obstacles have been many,
And hurdles hard to climb,
But, together, we took them,
One day at a time.

Hilda Ferachi

Dare To Dream

One of the worst things that
can happen is this. Someone can
convince you that you don't have
the right to dream.
Without having a dream,
You accomplish nothing!
Because you have nothing to
Strive for.
DARE TO DREAM
DARE to accomplish!
DARE to do something positive
with your life!

James C. Cullen

Healer

Flowing locks of ebony hair
Chasing down my pillow
She rests on the bed
Of my vulnerability
Speaking words of love
A voice not for the ear
Rather for the heart
Calling
Beckoning
Drawing me in
To arms of understanding
She soothes my pain
Calms my fears
Resurrects a spirit
Left for dead

John Wiliker

Class Reunion Limerick

A class reunion was at hand,
Classmates came across the land,
Beautiful hair of gray,
Medicated keeping pains away,
Traveling in a pretentious van.

Making and wearing a name tag,
If not, your acquaintance may lag,
If you hope to be the same,
Your beauty may be lame,
Surely you're not an old bag,

Wearing fancy tux and tie,
Others wonder if a lie,
Your accomplishment just a show?
Of something you want to blow?
With millions all could say.

After the years no one cares.
Long ago friends are theirs,
Reliving those old time events,
In your life makes happy dents,
Just seeing classmates answers prayers.

Charlotte Martin

Angels

Angels white angels light
Circle 'round my room.
They stop and stand by my bed
And take away the gloom.
They circle round and stand so bold
Beside me in the air.
They lift me up and let me down
And watch o'er me with care.
They take my hand and comfort me
All the long night through,
And when I wake from my sleep
I'm healthy, refreshed and new!

Betty Jane Burge

The Search

When can I crush
Clay idols in the heathen dust?
Where can I pour the speckled stars
I lighted with green jungle lust?
Which startled street awaits
My trembling feet,
My questioning ear?
The glass encrusted mystery
I sought is found not here.
I see reflected in the cushioned air
My mystic print,
Once faint, still blurred,
Of smoking truth which lurks within
The amber of another Mind,
In mine, interred.

Erwin E. Bach

Tunnel

Darkness
Closes in.
Traveling
faster and faster.

The unknown lies ahead.

A flicker of light
Appears
in the distance.

As the sunlight fights
to emerge,
Anxiety vanishes...

With the darkness.

Christine Canavan

Token

Alone there crying
Cowered into a corner
From the hammer-like words
Of a man who seemed to adore her

Never once a cruel hand
Those he only used to embrace
To somehow heal
The rage he threw in her face

He expresses his love
As a token of compensation
Her eyes close as he holds her
A token
Of manipulation

Dawn Shatouhy

Why I Love You So Bonnie

It seems to me the Lord above
Created you for me to Love.
From heaven's depths he took a hue.
Created eyes and gave to you.
When I gaze into their blend.
My soul will heavenward ascend.
He gave you hair he must have spun
Like gold beneath a dawning sun.
Two rosy lips with due seem wet.
Your face I never can forget.
That's why — you're all the world to me
And why I love you so — BONNIE.

Don A. Alonso

"Light Reigns"

Black eerie darkness
Creeping yet still
From whence did it come?
Thus where does it go?

Shadowy creatures
Loom ever large
Villains pursuant?
To frighten or slay?

Mysterious white rays
Distantly peer
Exuding of warmth
Be they friend? Or Foe?

Shadowy creatures
Enveloped by darkness
Together seek victory?
Defeated in battle?...Gone!

Mysterious white rays
Metamorphose as light
Lone savage warrior?
Conquering hero?...Light reigns!

Gayle Elaine Snyder

Soul From Spirit

Suppose the love, without the woman?
Day omits the bird-cancelled song.
The night minus star-shine no more.
Poison no flower, absence of poem.
Impending dreams falter and fade.
Look upon soul from spirit.

John M. Groover

A Little Some One

There is a little some one who lives
deep inside of me. He likes to see
everyone happy and also to be free.
He loves to hear a baby laugh and
teases them till they giggle.
To watch them learn to walk the way
they waddle and wiggle.
To see such happy and bright eyes
and when they are sleeping,
to hear their gentle sighs.
This some one deep inside of me
can find happiness in a bright sunny day
or hear the winds blow through the trees
the music that it plays.
The soft bubbling of a stream to watch
Little fish swim.
This some one deep inside of me.
I think a lot of Him

Ernest R. Petruzzi

Untitled

Two pieces with different shapes
different intentions,
different meanings,
concrete and abstract.

Face them in opposite directions
and they move freely.
Face them towards one another...
do they move?

Pieces with such forms do not fit.
They try. You try.
You force.
You want and need them to connect.

After a while you believe,
their images become one.
They take a new form.

Visibly, they are one.
To them, they are still two.
They are individuals.

Or....they forget
and learn to move and function together.

Gail A. Rousseau

"Romantic Is"

Romantic is
Dinner for two,
Sitting in front of a fire place
With the one special to you.
It's candle light and soft music,
His or her tender touch,
An evening of dancing,
Romantic is such,
It's a rose,
A card expressing care,
Holding hands
And just being there.

Romantic is
All these things.
What beautiful awareness
Of being alive it brings!

Barbara Ann Clegg

Champ

Good things
Do not necessarily come
In small packages.
They also come
In big packages.
I know.

I am Tommy.
I am big
And so is my smile.
It is my big thing.
It comes from where
The angels are.
They told me
To do it often.

Come aboard
Everyone.
Smile with me
Big little Tom.
Champion smiler.

Bub-bub-bub-Boo!

Erwin J. Brandl

"In A Moment"

You've said it, I've said it too,
Doctors and lawyers say it to you
And you hear it on the TV all day through.
Until you're black and blue.
How long is a moment
I'd like to know.
How long is a moment.
The clock doesn't show.
Sixty seconds make a minute.
Sixty minutes make an hour.
Twenty four hours make a day.
But how long is a moment,
The clock doesn't say.

Anthony Fillie

I Wonder

I look at the sea and see
dolphins playing,
I wonder,
what are they saying.
Are they talking about me
as I stand near?
I tell them I love them,
but can they hear?
They stayed with me all
through the day,
It was as if they knew I
wanted them to stay.
Day turned to night,
it was time to part,
I'll always have their
friendship deep in my heart.

Christine F. Spangler

Reaching

Take His hand and hold on tight
don't be frightened of all His might
He will lead you though the night
take His hand and follow Him
He will always lead you right
when times are good and going your way
don't let your hand slip away
when things are bad and
He seems far away
just remember to reach out
because by your side He will always be
so good or bad times always hold on tight
because He always lead you right

Agnes Riley

Autumn

Autumn days slip swiftly by
drifting clouds across the moon.
Softly falls the leaves of gold
T'will be winter, way too soon.

The bright yellow golden rod
sways in the eve'time breeze,
Water foams o'er rocks in creeks
It won't be long till winter freeze.

The campers go flying fast
making wheels on highway, sing.
Going south till winter's end
T'will be back, first sign of spring.

Ella M. Lawyer/Waggle

September

S unny days and even rainy,
E very day brings us closer to
P icturesque maples and oak trees.
T hat put on spectacular shows
E ach tree in autumn, beautiful!
M iracle from a higher power
B ringing joy for us all to see
E xciting every mind and soul
R egardless of whatever age.

Doris Vine

Life

Each new life
Each time
You become a wife
Hoping
There will be no strife
Looking
Forward to the bright
Praying
You won't be crying
In the night
Everything
Will be just right
Happiness, is light
Caring your best for what's in sight
Using all you have to give,
With all your might sharing
What you can
For a kiss good-night

Carol A. Contine

Esoteros

Sensuous beauty of spirit and soul
Embodies the union of you and me
Apart; yet together, Ethereal
Your voice reaches, awakening my senses
You whisper my name; I am there
I breathe your name; we are one
We touch—in Essence
In sensuous beauty of spirit and soul.

We meet; we touch; together
Yet closer than touch is the union
Of spirits, bodies and minds
Fulfilling desire's strong passion
As one
We reach the exquisite heart-home
Known only by some chosen few—
Or two.

Ginger Johnson

My Daddy

With hands as strong as iron,
but a heart of gold;
My Daddy.

With a voice as loud as thunder,
but gentle as a lamb;
My Daddy.

With shoulders that could carry the world,
and also a small child;
My Daddy.

With hair of silver gray,
whom youth has not escaped;
My Daddy.

Elizabeth Trongale

You Always

Listen to my dreams
Encourage the steps I take
Hold my hand if I worry
Help me through my mistakes
You always
Give me a smile to help me out
Make me believe when I'm full of doubt
Help me see through eyes that are clear
Your every word I hold so dear
You always
Make me laugh when I want to cry
Help me soar when I'm feeling high
Understand what I am and why
Always there for each day that goes by
Thank you for always being there
No matter the circumstance
Thank you for you always

Julie Arnold

Untitled

Circular pits of desire
Enfolding upon me
Searching for...
Recognition?

I'm drowning, dying
In its emitted browness
Sunken in endless depths
Of uncertainty.

If only death
Were as troublesome
As thought provoked
Restless emotions.

I would have
Embraced it
Sooner.

Arwen Franquez

A Lazy Day in Autumn

Stroll along through rustling trees,
Enjoy the pungent smell of leaves,
Observe, the birds are flocking yonder,
Preparing to fly south, and ponder
Over frosty nights and nippy morns,
How mother nature does adorn
Her foliage with one big splash of red,
Before she puts it all to bed,
Adding orange and remnants of green,
Amber-yellow completes the scene
Against a sky of transparent blue;
So soon, with this she will be through.
It seems the seasons pass so fast.
Now, lie back in the cool, tall grass,
Absorb the warmth of God's pure sun,
And once more, with this great earth, be
one.

Ida Lillian Hobbs

September

Rain again today.
Even flowers cry,
"Help!" The birds are gone.
Streets are rivers now.

Mud collects on shoes.
Closets smell like must.
Halls are dark as tombs.
Light appears in one!

Edna Mae Everitt

To Let—Heart

Heart available Come on board
Enter of your own accord
Outlook good - No lack of space
Previous tenant left no trace
Memoirs of what might have been
faded flowers in a bin.
Joyful visions and steady flow
of hope—Nowhere else to go
Venture in—There's room for you
Heart available—Almost new.

Josephine F. Cerniglia

"Love Letter"

No arrow so sharp,
ever shot from Cupid's bow.
No more intense emotions,
followed right in a row.
The heart beats heavy and longs for one,
who holds the key, who shall become,
the lover to harmonize and unite,
in a single rose, it can happen tonight.
Can it? Oh, can it wait so long?
for the reply will be romantically strong.
Magic moments are coming near,
only if the answer is yes, beloved dear.

Jennifer Schofield

Beholden To The Evergreen Tree

I look out the window to behold stately
Evergreen trees.
Huge branches, like bear paws shake in
The breeze!
Towering o'er two story houses, around
Where others grow all sizes, shapes,
Filling in the lawns, large gapes.

You fit into the Christmas holiday to
brighten the scene.
The cones you bear, grace wreathes
with red bows
Add beauty, with the green.

Evergreen tree, you're no small thing,
but, easily unnoticed when looking
For signs of spring!

Your green, so gradual, starts to show,
is upon us, before we even know!
From the winter, you wake to bring a
brighter green.
To refresh, renew the early spring scene.

Ann M. Hollibush

Two Kinds Of Beauty

Outer beauty is great,
but can cause an ugly fate.
Inner beauty is pure and fine,
and will make your life divine.

Outer beauty is a nice quality,
but isn't always better.
Inner beauty is a blessing,
and should be in those who deserve it.

Outer beauty in me is mild,
even though I wish it were wild.
Inner beauty I definitely possess,
and it's my best quality, I can fess.

Jennifer Martin

"Thank You "God" For Our World"

In this world of our seemingly
everyday strife,
It seems we think we have such
a terrible life.
Oh, if we'd only look at those around us.
At these time's we really should feel
ashamed at the way we fuss.
There are time's it seems things are
hard to bear.
That we feel at times we have more
than our share.
But this dear 'Heavenly Father' of ours-
Who gave us our beautiful tree's and
flowers
Who sends our much needed rain shower's.
"He" gave us wonderful families -
Also wonderful friends who help us in
time of need-
Who stand beside us and are truly
wonderful indeed!

Jeanette Kusi

Autumn Hope

Bare are the trees.
Fallen are the leaves.

Flown are the birds
With their songs.

Faithful are the branches
Holding empty nests.

Song birds will return.
We'll wait. We'll wait.

Come, spring.

Come, spring.

Ina Leland Broe

Untitled

I feel like a raindrop
falling from the sky;
the sky so warm and beautiful
casts its gay light
over the dusty ground.
Just as that drop begins to feel
like a part of that sky;
it throws the drop down.
Plummeting towards the dirt,
it falls helplessly until...
SPLASH! It hits.
Torn apart it lies there
its happiness left behind.
Sadly it sits only to be covered
by the dust strolling along.

Candice White

Shadows

Cherished memories, treasured past
Casting shadows on the glass
Rising with the morning light
Into day and through the night
Thoughts cannot neglected be
They plague my mind with ecstasy
Your presence felt, though you are gone
A special love that lingers on
Protecting as you follow me
A steady force, no one can see.

Betty Jo Wells

A Petal

A petal of a flower
falls
lifelessly to the ground.
This flower once golden bright
as it stood tall in the gleaming
sunlight.
Love and beauty painted its color
with life able to endure
the trials and tribulations
of time.
Now, fallen hopelessly with age
as time has turned against it
taking its hopes and dreams
turning it into
memories.
Memories, as all they may be
can never be misplaced
for the joy, love, and happiness
will be their's to own
forever and ever...

Debra Millican

My Love Is Gone

My love is gone
far, far, away,
You took it;
You stole it;
You broke me.
Now when I see you,
I see the memories,
The dreams,
The love.
When I dream,
You're there.
I wished for you;
Now you're back,
Back in my life,
It could never be the same.
I had my life back on track,
So now you start calling again, Why?
I don't need you anymore,
So now you want me.
Well it's too late, You can't have me
anymore.

Erica Callahan

Livin' Crazy In A Corner

I live in a corner,
feel crazy, crazy
all the time 'cause
I don't got no soul
from anywhere I looked,
which was everywhere
even places locked
'cause I really wanted some
so I could get smilin'
and movin' on in the big
blue green peace-lovin'
part of the world 'cept
I'm havin' an identity crisis anyway
so I'm goin'
nowhere in my mind
even if I am
runnin' a road till it
ain't right
for runnin' no more

Jenny Arcuni

Ascent

Ah, mountains still envelop me,
Filling the nostrils of my mind
With purer breath and memory
Of heights I long had left behind.

Ascending to the hills today
Was more than journeying, I see,
For I am on a higher way.
There is a new expanse in me.

Faith Cornwall

I Wish I Were An Eagle

I wish I were an eagle
Flying across the sky
Swooping to the valleys below
Soaring again way up high.

I wish I were an eagle
Gliding through the air
Winging my way through the heavens
With the greatest of vigor and flair.

I wish I were an eagle
One of God's beautiful creatures, you see
Casting my shadow upon the earth
Up high with no one but God and me.

I wish I were an eagle
The freest spirit of all
Taking in the seasons
Summer, spring, winter, and fall.

I wish I were an eagle
The most gracious of birds you'll find
For nothing could be more soothing
Than being free of all mankind.

Judy H. Jones

A Window's View

Birds.
Flying, soaring, sweeping, flapping
envoys
timed to eternity.
Feathered wind-blown down
they come.
From the east, the west, the north.
Banded beaked vagabonds
beating
paths of longitudes and latitudes.
Singing away
morning's calm, morning's silence.
A window's view,
sepulchral, sequestered, serene.
A prayer said almost
without words
over coffee and flights
to random nowheres.

Edward J. Myers

Outside Poem

Donna always looks outside,
Evening, day or morning,

Empty as the sky may be;
Five billion stars to see,

Although it seems fast in a day,
Lightness comes our way;

Tightly at night;
Exuberance during the day;
Relaxation during the night...

Donna Falter

Wait For Me

The time that's left is not enough,
For death is one we cannot bluff.
You have found a place within my heart,
And now, my love, I fear we'll part.

And so, denial becomes my daily litany
with prayers for you, self-pity, me.
Mortal pain is now a constant threat,
To live without you is my greatest regret.

I seek from deep within, some solace,
My love for you I pray He'll bless.
That life goes on is what I now fear,
So deep in my heart, you are so dear.

I'll not forget the love we shared,
It means so much that we were paired
to be together throughout destiny,
My love, have faith! And wait for me!

Joan Heinkel

Forever Love

A love forever is laid unto thee,
for I have but only one heart, one life.
And that shall forever be yours,
for you are thy chosen one.

I do not wish that you should leave,
for that would surely break my heart.

Shall my life be no longer full?
Nay, my life shall no longer be,
should you go and relieve yourself of me.

JoyAnn M. Taylor

Play Ground

I shall not slide down a slide,
for I will not go down again.
I shall not swing on a swing,
for I will not go back and forth.
I shall not get on a marry go round,
for I will not go in circles.
I shall not build in a sand box,
for I will not have my dreams destroyed.
I'm going to pick up as many feathers
as I can and soar to where I wish to be.
This is my play ground and I can do
anything I want to do!

Don Nelson

Mythmaker

An artist's feelings can't be denied
For there is a poet that lives inside
On every corner of every page
Lies hidden words all encaged

Lines prove mistaken facts
Allowing your ideas to pile up in stacks
Selling the secrets of a heart of gold
Invites myths to be told

Behind every touching, luring stare
Lies heartache and despair
With a force a fool fell
Discovering his heart is not a stone,
But fragile as a shell

Curing his ache he imagines in his mind
Hope, love, and a lover to find
A dagger is under a blanket of lies
Another heart-broken fool dies

David J. Heim

Meditation

One hour alone
for me
I lie on the floor
and shut my eyes
to align my soul
with the body
the pain disappears
through the warmth
of the Holy Spirit
I am free

A magic moment
when time is still
joy overcomes me
filling me with love and peace
I reach out
and touch my soul
to imagine life
without turmoil
only serenity

My meditation begins

June S. Gatewood

On The Mountain Top

I'm happy on the mountain top,
For my Savior set me free,
He left his home in Glory,
To die upon the tree.

He's forgiven all my sins,
And He took them all away,
As far as East is from the West,
And there they are to stay.

I walked alone in the valley,
With my burdens and my woes,
And then I met my Savior,
And all my spirits rose.

He leads me and He guides me,
And my blessings never stop,
As long as I obey His will,
He keeps me on the top,

Edith L. Price

Thanksgiving Prayer

For love, when sometimes won
For sand, and surf, and sun
For birds that gently sing
I thank you, Oh my King.

For laughter, and for tears
For strength to squelch my fears
For grass, and tree, and sod
I thank you, Oh my God.

Florence Pearson

To The Health Care Of The New Millennium

A cosmic toast from heaven
for the next one thousand years.
May all Souls unite in Oneness
of the truth all Nature reveres.

By using our higher intelligence
our Global Peace will increase
as our primitive fears disappear
and War-like acts can then cease.

Clodah G. Summer

The Plight Of The Rich

"Have you no sensitivity, no concern
for the plight of the rich?
Do 'you people' realize how much it costs
in this country to insure four cars!
We're passing a law prescribing a maximum
of two years of welfare!
Up the gangplank and over the rail,
Women and children first!
Step lively, you welfare queens!
You children must realize that in this
'civilized' society we do things
in a smooth, efficient, orderly fashion.
This is America, not Rwanda.
The computer indicates that you have
exactly one hour to complete this maneuver.
Though you starve and die, rest assured
that the latest opinion poll indicates
that this law is politically correct!"

Joseph T. Hopkins

"Humbly"

Please thank God
for what you have
And always bear
in mind;
What you have
you have because
There's a God
who's good and kind.
Although sometimes
He sends some things
Displeasing to us all;
A climb is never
worth much
Until we've had a fall.

Florence Costantino

The Warning

The eagle will fly no more!
For where will he go to soar?
The mountains are scarred and hidden.
The sky is all but forbidden
Where once the proud spirit did fly!
Oh, why, will no one listen and hear
The eagle's screams of hate and fear?

His spirit soul is lost and dying
But he will always keep trying
And even though his end is near
He will forever try to make us hear
All the reasons why we should fear.

Cynthia L. Payne

Gladiator

With one blow I am beaten
as you rise victorious, my
golden locks twisted
in your grasp.
The roar of victory fills my
ears as I lay, shuddering
on the sand at your feet.
The noise of defeat shuffles
around me as I am carried
from the battle ground
still bearing your blade.
The hum of solitude screams
in my mind as I lay
dying in your gaze.

Doreen Beth

Midnight Wanderer

Midnight streets you must roam
Forever trying to find a home
Lost in a world of what could have been
But stuck in a world now full of sin
A jagged road ahead of you
Left behind all that you've been through
No guarantee of seeing tomorrow
Every night is filled with sorrow
Your hunger growing ever stronger
While each day seems to be getting longer
And at night you feel the pain
Of failure, loss, and nothing gained
But where you finally decide to go
Is something only God can know
Or will you find that place in time
Where the birds will sing and the sun will shine
And after the rains, a colorful rainbow
That can only be seen from your world below

Elizabeth Jesson

The Rapture

Today love and goodness go
forth from me, today I am
happy for the truth set me
free.

Today I am blessed that the
Lord touched my soul, today
is the day that the Lord
made me whole.

Today all the angels, joy and
praises sing, today is the day
that God gave me wings.

Craig Pillsbury

Loneliness

Trapped and alone, not a
friend in the world.
One at a time tears
slowly role down my face
each with a significance.
Loneliness, scared, and most
of all trapped! Trapped in
a world which feels like hate.
Happiness to the eye is no longer there.
All one sees now is a box
filled with loneliness and darkness.

Once I make it back
my eyes will no longer
be filled with tears of
darkness but tears of
joy and happiness!

Aimee C. Munsey

Peace Of Mind

We cannot know what lies ahead
From day to passing day
What changes God is planning
In His wise and loving way

We cannot know the reasons
Why our sorrow has to be
Why we must lose the ones we need
And love especially

We cannot know, but we can trust
And faith can help us find
Our way to those tomorrows
That will bring us peace of mind

Dollie R. McKissick

Let Me Be Your Rainbow

I want to be your rainbow
from here to eternity
Fulfilling all your wants and needs
and whatever you ask of me
I want to be all of the colors
that are tried and true
The beautiful shades of a rainbow
that show my love for you
I want to be your best friend
standing by you in gladness and sorrow
And walking by your side
through all of your tomorrows
And if we don't quite see eye to eye
I'll try to understand
Loving and caring for the child within
as only a mother can
In this rainbow I'll be your partner
the one you can trust and look up to
I offer you my affection and love
because I want to be a rainbow for you

Jean L. Egyed

Untitled

A list of words I cannot spell
From my mind to paper fell.
It's not a meager list I must say
For I could rattle off 100's in a day.
The oddity of it all shall be
The weird words I can spell you see.
Dare me to spell a name so odd
And I can, even if it's Scheherazade.
But spelling words like torture and insane,
To do it I must rack my brain.
"Its" is possessive but "it's" is not
That rule I think I've got.
"I" before "e" except after "c"
Of course that's wrong for spelling Heidi.
It's also "ei" when it sounds like "a."
These spelling rules bring me great dismay.
Please save me from this spelling test.
All I can do, is do my best.

Jessica M. Ayrton

Say When

Like a cup of tea,
from the moment of our birth
to the time we take our final breath
we push one another to the very
brim of their cup, always sneaking
in that extra drop for ourselves,
neglecting the needs of others around
us, right to the point our cup overflows
and our friend's is empty... it is time
to say when.

Alysia McLain

The Look

Lonely, desolate, empty
Look out over the city
See the tall buildings
The sheltered, pampered
Beautiful sights
Around one corner, trash, filth
Lonely, desolate, empty
Longing for more than
A cold street to lay their heads
Look deep in their eyes
The same look as in the mirror
Lonely, desolate, empty

Shelby Mae

Reflection

A dream is born
from within a heart
and fed on each days' deeds,
nurtured by aspirations,
blooms when finally is shared.

The beauty of
a life together,
the joining of the souls,
growing, one mind to the other
begins when each has cared.

As years go by
their dreams unfold
and come to realize,
for sharing their lives and love,
better they both have fared.

Emilie M. Davis

To The Man Of My Dreams

Sweet kindness,
Gentle kisses.
These are only a few of the things
That you have given to me.
You have opened my heart
With your sweetness and love.
You have given me someone
Whom I am so proud of.
You have awakened my dreams
And calmed my fears.
You have held my hand
And wiped away my tears.
You have made all my fantasies come true
And have added love into my life.
It is because of you
That I wear a smile on my face.
And it is back to you
That this joy I feel is traced.
You have showed me all of what real love means
For, you are the man of my dreams!

Corinne Spermon

Contentment

Boat dock floating easy, free
Gentle waves rock it and me

Upward glance toward Western sky
Scenic grandeur fills the eye

Silver crescent against deep blue
Iridescent clouds of pinkish hue

Tree frogs cackling in near trees
Meadow sweet lingering on the breeze

Humble house clutched by rocky hill
Air currents tickle each window sill

From windows stream golden light
Spilling toward the darkening night

Porch deck nestled tree top high
Where squirrels play and birds flit by

Distant eerie owlish whooo
Enchanted woods so old, yet new

Ozark hills draw heart strings fast
Nature's spell holds treasures vast

Eternity be like this I pray
When too soon I'm called away

Delores Hinde

Yesterday

The leaves from the trees
Gently flutter to the ground
They bend and twist ever so graceful
Like movements in a ballet.

The clouds in the sky
Maneuver swiftly out of view
Changing as they travel
As clay in the potter's hand.

The sand in the hourglass
Sifts silently through the pore
Quietly passing time
Like days in a year.

So sail your thoughts
Through the mind they quickly ramble
Driven this way and that
To Rest - In Reflection.

Cathy L. Carson

If I Were A Bird

I wish I were a bird so I could fly
Glide on my wings up in the sky
Hover over rooftops, live in the trees
Like butterflies and honeybees.

If I were a bird, I'd like to be a lark
I'd build my nest right in the park
Where people come to relax or to rest
Then I could sing my very best.

I'd find a way to catch one's attention
Sit on a limb and whistle a tune
Not just for once but again and again
So someone would stop to look and listen.

If I could make a hit with somebody
My mission would make my day
I'd be the happiest bird in the park
Because I could sing well, if I were a lark.

Basilisa Lachica Halog

To My Parents

A tribute to my parents,
Has long been overdue,
To thank them for their care,
Their love and patience, too.

My youthful years seemed to be,
Filled with many "Noes"
Don't do this, don't do that,
You know how it goes...

Many times I used to ponder,
I'd sit and sadly sigh,
They told me what I couldn't do,
But never told me "why"..

Now that I am older,
Facts are brought to light,
I'm grateful to my parents,
I know that they were right.

They are no longer with me,
But, they guide me from above,
In my prayers, I speak to them,
And thank them for their love.

Dorothy Vaughan

Epic Eyes

Watching wide, wondrous, waiting;
Glorious green globes
Staring still, shining, sending
Cunning cat codes.

I feel mysterious mind music.
Then they blink.

Epic eyes, elusive, echoing
Timeless thought-tomes;
Rambling runes, rising, recalling
Long-ago lost lives.

I hear Pierian pale panthers.
Then they sleep.

Janice P. Egry

For Vallie

Let the darkness slip away
go towards the light —
Cleanse thy soul;
it's never too late.
Come back and know you've let go
And learned from whence you came
Follow the light and the glittering stars
and be willing to grieve and start anew.
Go on,
and may the angels be with you.
Good luck on your journey my friend —
we will meet once again.
Go with God and bless you —
for thy will be done.
Accept and go towards your guiding light
you will know it in your heart
when you are ready to find it.

Gail A. Grover

To Our Baby-To-Be

In a sweet moment of delight
God willed that you should be.
A tiny life for us to make
And care for lovingly.

We pray to God for wisdom
To teach you to be strong.
To teach you love and gentleness;
To judge what's right and wrong.

We hope that you'll be happy.
Not from material things,
But just because you are alive
And have a heart that sings.

Because the sun so often shines,
Because the breeze is cool,
Because there is a whispering pine
Beside a quiet pool.

Because there is a God in heaven
To guide you from above.
Because you'll always have a place
Of refuge in our love.

Clara J. Keske

A touch of class had Jackie K.

First lady of another day,
Forgiven is Jacqueline O.
Her style and beauty was loved so,
Point of view is running wild,
About that Mother Nature's child.

John Hensley

A Peek At God's Signs

The Bible bold in thoughts foretold,
God's Spirit in the waters lay.
So take a map, and look and see,
His form in James and Hudson Bay.

Christ cried and reigns for God and man,
To give Communion for our day.
A look at Africa will reveal
God formed his head and bread, the way.

God's Bread's a foot for you to wear -
To church, this message to be told.
His love for you will always be,
The reason for this message bold.

DuWayne E. Oakes

Elysium

Earthen souls unite.
Gods splatter their paint
pigments of sorrow
Blacks, Greys, Blues
encapsulating.
Pools of maroon flowing
glistening
The setting sun burning
over the horizon
The damp dark soil
hidden
by the decaying flesh
of thousands
peacefully sleeping
side by side
strangers together
unknowing
one another
forever.
Earthen souls unite.

Jim A. Smith

Angel Of Light

There's an Angel of light beside me,
Guiding each move I make;
A beautiful, bright, singing angel,
Leading onward for my sake.

This wonderful, gracious Angel of light
Never lets the light go out;
Because that light is peace and hope,
It means I can walk about

Whenever I slumber, I dream so sweet,
Of wildflowers, heaven and such;
I awake and feel the Angel of light,
Its Aura I cannot touch.

This angel is a dear, sweet friend,
That I cannot be without;
It's my companion on rainy days,
A cool breeze when there's a drought.

There is no doubt or cause for fear,
I see through the veil of night;
My path is clear and free of strife,
Because of the Angel of Light.

Betty Steeves

God's Witness

God's witness
Has at hand
Eyes, ears
A hand and a pen
A memory full of
Words and a past
Is urged to report
Thoughts and feelings
Accurately and honestly
Holding ego well at bay
To paint with broad strokes
Color and correct
Until the tones and moods
Are just right
To compose music
Which makes the soul swell,
Spirit rise, skin prickle,
To mold clay, shape and join wood, weave cloths,
Make authentic the being of seeing
The seeing of being.

Jack McMillan

The Painter

The faithful Master painter
Has used His brush this fall,
On the delicate painted leaves
For the pleasure of us all.

The yellow, orange and reds
Against the sky of blue,
There are no mis-painted ones
They are all a radiant hue.

When all the leaves have fallen
And are thick upon the ground,
Autumn time is over
A new season will come around.

The Master will keep on painting
As the seasons come and go,
You know the hand of God
Has created and made it so.

Betty Butler

The Beautiful Warrior

You, you precious child,
have dealt with
so much of the pain.
The horror was
horrible then.
Sweet child it was never you!

The war has been over
for a long time.
I am showing you the
beauty of your life now...
You can trust and
believe again.

You are stronger, wiser,
a true survivor.
"Treasures out of the
darkness",
Is what the Bible says.
You are like a beautiful warrior.

BRAVE and FREE.

Dolores M. Miller

Feeding Time

In my golden years my activities
have changed.
I take the time to look and listen
to the birds at closer range.

I hear the scolding sounds
when no food is out
And sweeter chirpings from others
round about.

One of the choicest views I've had
was of a rabbit and a squirrel
sitting side by side, chomping on the
corn they love, like old friends
true and tried.

Birds, squirrels, rabbits, look
up at the window where I watch satisfied
that they are safe, they look
eagerly for the lifting of the latch.

Alice E. Worth

When You Need Him Most

When you need Him most
He is close by your side.
When you need Him most
His love is your guide.
When your sorrow is deep,
Your heart in despair,
You just have to ask
He will always be there.
He will strengthen your faith
If you will only believe.
What a wonderful love
He gives, you receive.
Just open your heart
Let the Saviour come in.
He will keep you from harm
Forgive all your sins.
When you need Him most
He is close by your side.
When you need Him most
His love is your guide.

Hazel Hopkins O'Brien

A Writer's Life

A writer is a fighter
He stays up night and day
With his pencils and his paper
Then doesn't know what to say.

He eats a lot of pencils
Then wonders where they went,
With erasers sticking to his teeth,
His temper almost spent.

His kids are scared to death of him
And think he's plumb went nuts,
While Mama's washing dishes
And countin' broken cups.

He often throws a tantrum
And tears up lots of script
And aggravates his wife so much
She takes an endless trip.

He interrogates the neighbors
And he does it every day
Now they're signing a petition
To have him put away.

Harold W. Hannebaum

Feared End

Walking the shore.
Hearing the waves crash
against the rocks calling
your name.
Filled with fright yet,
destined to join with the sea.
Slowly you immerse yourself
into the terrified water.
Knowing you will not return,
your fear is washed away going
unseen.

Brandy Brush

Silent Pain

Thoughts liquidating through my mind
heart melting from intense pain
devouring leaving nothing but darkness.
Emptiness inside far too long
Remembering no happiness or love
sorrow dominating a forgotten past
unable to bring a future.
Condemned in a world of my creation
trying to find my way out
reaching to no avail.
Images of things to come
randomly invading my dreams
leaving me distraught at night end
devouring my very essence.
Distance becoming shorter between
future demanding response now
entering its twisted dark domain.
Realm of insanity leading you to believe
its reality is safe haven
never there to protect you.

Christopher A. DesBiens

Stop HCP Abuse

Help stop Hcp abuse
Help stop Hcp abuse
Who say I say
Stop Hcp abuse
Stop Hcp abuse
Who say I say
Let's bring it in
Let's bring it in
Happy and blue
With my beautiful Hcp flag
Which represents help
Stop Hcp Abuse
All just for you
Who say I say
Stop HCP Abuse
Stop HCP Abuse

Joanne Adams

Sister Of Mercy

I searched for Beauty, Truth and Love
But only found a trace
For always they eluded me
Until I saw them in your face.
I sought them in all earthly things
And realized only lies
I searched for Beauty, Truth and Love
And found them in your eyes.
I squandered all my nights and days
And thought that I was living
I searched for Beauty, Truth and Love
You found them in your giving.

Evelyn E. Signorello

Lucy

In a spirit of beauty
Her life unfolds
To bring to light
A courage untold.

A wealth of faith
She gathers in
And sends to others
A light within.

The lives she touches
Can bloom with love
A lighted candle
From her Maker, above.

God sent her to earth
With a special gift
A care for others
Their burdens to lift.

A world of loveliness
Joy, and tears
Lucy is there
to comfort and cheer.

Iva Jane Kierum

Fledgling

Hippity Hip
Hippity Hop
Fledgling
On the adjacent roof top
Batting the breeze
With its wing tip
Hooray! Hooray!
Up and away
But wait!
Suspended in air
Not alive?
Ooops! Takes a dive
Down down
Swoops low and long
Chirps its happy song
Flippity Flappity
Somersaults happily
Back strokes sudden gust
Will make it - it must
Wave Ma and Pa - ta ta and FLY

Jacqueline Burks-Shiver

My Boy Curly

My boy Curly
his hair is curly
and curly he did go
he washed his jeans
and hung them up
but iron he did not no
his shoes are worn
his socks are torn
but don't bother him
you know
he loves his mom
and helps her out
but to school
he just won't go

Dorothy C. Taylor

God Still Reigns

Some skeptics say that God is dead,
His reign is over, His work is done.
But I remember what He has said:
"I'll never forsake you" no not one.

God is not dead nor doth He sleep.
He knows my every thought and care.
When I'm happy, and when I weep,
He is there with me to share.

For lilies in the field He cares,
And fishes in the deepest sea.
For birds and fowl up in the air,
Yes I know He watches over me.

Only a fool says there is no God,
When the heavens declare His glory.
The sun and moon and stars and sod,
Each day repeat the wondrous story.

Henry T. Davis Jr.

"Victim"

Why must the victim
hold everything in,
Must pretend it never happened.

Think they are somehow responsible,
when they have done nothing wrong.

When the victims come forward
to tell their story,
No one believes them.

Victims cannot lie,
They can only try to understand.

They want others to understand
what they have been through.
Understand why this happened.

Why others had to do it,
Why must there be victims.

Cheryl L. French

Hold Me Tight

Hold me tight
Hold me in your loving arms all night
Tell me that you will stay
And never go away
How I miss you holding me in your strong
caring arms
Away from life and all its harms
How I miss making love to you all through
the night
The passion in our hearts beating as one
Like the sound of a slow beating drum
Until the first light of dawn has come
Hold me tight and I will always love you
just as much as I do tonight

Deborah Rohlf

Cats! Cats!

Cats! Cats! Everywhere!
Hold on, don't despair.
I'll get rid of those cats
by guarding them with rats.
Oh yes, yes. Those will be gone
as quick as a flash.

Bonny L. Weeks

Short Observation

Watching through the window, you spoke,
"How beautiful is Youth!" True.
And as I watched I knew
There is more than I can view
Of wisdom in your heart...
A depth I doubt that I can know,
But I can share that little part
That I can reach. So,
Let me bare a secret to you alone...
A year has passed; and he is gone,
A youth I knew and loved.
Since then, I'm reticent to love;
If caught up, I lose my wits. Dove
Gray streaks my hair; some say I'm old,
So it is with care I may be bold
Enough to love again...
I have a heart of seventeen.

Helen M. Cunningham

No Difference

Everybody always forgets me
How forgetful can all of them be
Sure, I am shy
but, that is no reason
to pass me by
I am no different
than anyone else
the only thing about me...
Is I keep to myself
So why do people treat
me so differently?

Cinnamon Orzel

A Question

Miles of hallway-
how long they seem.

Her light is on again.
What is it now?
How can I help?
Does she really know
she touched the button?

There she lies, eyes open-
fingers on her button,
no response to me.
Does she see me-
or does she see beyond
me to a place I've
never been?

Her world, where is it,
in the here and now or
where I cannot go?
So how can I help her?
Do you know?

Ginny O'Neil

Hope

Promise of beauty
grown from deep within,
Shines in the innocence
of her eyes.

Pure understanding.
Unblemished experience.
The certainty of fulfillment.
The lover's precious gift.
My child.

Dawn Derman

Pain

Blessed you be, oh Pain!
How would I know
if the silent germ
is eating my flesh every day
and taking my life away?
When the heart is hungry,
when the tooth is angry,
and when the belly
full of air, water or rocks,
cries for help
you ring the bell.
May be your language
is too harsh, too loud, too clear,
but I am sure
if not, I would not hear.
When your voice
is absent or too low
I have no choice
I am dead before I know.

Jose Paulo Gomes

Alone

Without you
I am empty
A soul left to roam
Throughout eternity alone
My life has lost its meaning
For you gave me strength and courage
To face each new day
Now you are gone
And I am left alone
I will never forget you
Or the time we had

Without you
I am empty
I can no longer cry
I am nothing without you
And wait for a time
When we will be together
For the rest of our days

Heidi McPherson

Christ

I believe you walked on water,
I believe you healed the blind.
I believe you cast out demons,
And I'll never change my mind.
I believe you fed five thousand,
I believe you paid the price.
I believe you rose from death,
I have faith and don't think twice.
I believe you wept in the garden,
I believe you know my pain.
I believe you're in my heart,
The truth is clear and plain.
I believe you watch me sleeping,
I believe you see me sin.
I believe I have forgiveness,
And I know I won't give in.
I believe I'm going to heaven,
I believe the sinners will burn.
I believe you're coming to get me,
And I'm waiting for you to return.

Gina Bucy

Awaiting The Storm

I watch and wait —
I breathe the salt-filled air,
watching the sea grass
bow to the waves.
I wait for the sea gulls to land,
and find a treasure in the sand.

The storm clouds gather overhead
as the sea begins to roar.
The sun hides its face, reappears and
vanishes,
as the rain begins to pour.

Finally, there is peace;
there is serenity.
A calm stillness overflowing.
Suddenly - only the wind is blowing.

Denise Howard-Hall

You? (Portrayed)

Accept me for what I am,
I can be anybody
anyone who I please
But I am my only man.
Call me by my name,
not by my color
or my cover
Because the books you see are not
the same.
Can you see, without eyes,
are you better than me?
Are you your own person?
Or are you someone that you despise?
A stereotyper is an unliked kind,
quick to criticize
choosing to categorize
You should learn to free your mind.

Joe Frey

In Your Eyes

In your eyes
I can see:
A summer day,
with winds so mild.
A country side,
a happy child.
A lake reflection,
of a cloudless sky.
A robin's nest,
an eagle's cry.
A misty mountain,
a great blue sea.
In between it,
you and me.

Crystal Wachter

The Time Ahead

Open your eyes and look at me,
I am real.
Perk up your ears and listen to me,
I am real.
Reach out your hand and touch me,
I am real.

I am not an illusion, nor an image
created by time,
I am a child of this world, and the
future of us all.

Debra L. Mills

The Thunder's Roll

In the season of rain I come.
I can sing among the showers,
to rejoice in the meadows of flowers.
I utter my song, my heart knows joy.

I am not faint before the thunder's roll.
I can withstand the lightning strike,
to receive wisdom in its might.
I cry and cry not out within its pain.

I stand on the wave of the storm.
I praise its strength and homing.
Stand up, the dawn is coming,
and I hear my own soft laughter.

Dawn Busche

Inspiration

Many things inspire me,
I cannot name them all,
I can tell you some of them,
But they amount to being small.

Sports always inspires me,
I constantly play to win,
I continually try to play my best,
No matter the sport I'm in.

To learn things motivates my brain,
To keep up with things in school,
I would like to succeed in life and things,
And I don't want to be a fool.

I had no inspiration for this,
Although I thought and thought,
I studied what to write about,
And this poem's what I got.

Justin Baker

Winter Valentine

The silence of the song birds
  I cradle in my heart
As a lazy snowflake briefly eclipses
  a slanting moonbeam's dart,
Making a shadow on a snowdrift
  'ere its gossamer wings depart.
Somewhere deep in the earth
  a seedling sleeps but dreams of spring
And even I, in the winter night,
  feel a cadence only love can bring.

Cyra Grace Renwick

That Smile

When I walked into that shop,
I didn't see you in advance.
Your face made me stop.
I'll never forget that glance.

I began seeing you everywhere.
And even knowing all the while
That life is never fair,
I could not resist that smile.

I know it was meant to be,
Because we couldn't stay apart.
It was becoming clear to me
You were stealing my heart.

We've been together a long time.
We were joined by God above.
I am yours and you are mine.
And the only man I'll ever love.

Cynthia Townsend

The World

The world is a farce
I do believe,
so much a farce
it's hard to conceive
how men and women have survived
for so long,
with nothing to ally them
but flesh and bone.
But someday I pray
(and hope you'll agree)
that people realize
we're but like the trees,
we all have branches and
we all have leaves,
but most importantly,
we all have in common
the first planted seed.

Hasan H. Brown

Our Friendship

You are so special to me,
I don't know how to explain it to you,
You're the greatest friend there could be,
I don't know what I'd do without you.

To me you mean so much,
You're a friend I thought I'd never find,
My feelings have been touched.
You are a definite one of a kind.

I appreciate everything you've done,
When I need you I only have to call,
When I'm with you I have so much fun,
I know you'll never let me fall.

Audrey Jae

Dreams

As I lie here in bed,
I dream of you, way above my head.

If you come to me,
We'll dream by the sea,

With the sweet smell of sea breeze
  in our hair.
We'll walk along the beach without
  a care.

When my dream is over, I'll still be
  lying here thinking of you.
And when you wake you'll be thinking
  of me too.

Emily M. Bell

The Best Of Prizes

A family tree
has many leaves
and branches of all sizes.

It continues to grow,
through the heat and snow,
with plenty of new surprises.

Dates and places
and lots of faces,
more than one realizes.

Family and friends,
are in the end,
the best of this tree's prizes.

Bethany L. Canfield

I Loved You!

As long as I can remember
  I dreamed of loving you,
As long as I had eyes to see
  I wanted to see you,
As long as I had a heart to feel
  I wanted to feel you,
As long as I have hurt
  It's all because of you.

You took my mind
  my heart and soul,
You tossed it away
  so very cold,
You made me hurt
  so many ways,
But I loved you
  For always!

Cheryl Ann Blansett

Summer's End

Once green upon my branch,
I drop gracefully to the earth.

Taking pride in my departure,
As you admire my ember colors.

You smile at me,
As I lay in the path you walk,

Whisking me up,
Hoping to preserve my beauty.

As intended,
I let you willingly.

Trusting...you'll be reminded,
Of your beauty to this earth.

As someone sets you apart,
In their hearts as well.

Never knowing if it's
at summer's end.

Connie A. Capuano

Your Hands

When your hands hold me
I feel comforted and peaceful.
Your hands are like gold,
So untarnishable, so calm,
melting in the heart of passion.
Your hands so soft and gentle
create in me a tenderness
that can only be surpassed
by the love you create in my heart.
Hands shadowed by the shapes
of floating clouds overhead, letting
the warmth of the sun pass through.
Hands that set no barriers to joy
When they gently touch me.
Hands of strength, so strong
you could move a mountain.
Hands that are brave and bold,
Yet, tender enough to hold.
Hands that press me to yourself.
Hands like pure gold in the melting pot.

Arlean Baird

Dreamtime Discovery

The waves, they crash against the shore.
I feel the salt on my skin
The clouds, they cover up the moon.
A storm is moving in.

The rain, it feels cold on my head,
Like an ice pack for a bruise.
The wind, it blows and stings my face,
Like yellow jackets with the blues.

Lightning zig-zags to the ground,
Like an indecisive falling star.
Thunder booms; it feels like an earthquake.
It sounds like an exploding car.

The precipitation and the ocean calm;
The sun appears.
The shore is full of emotions
And large puddles of tears.

I wonder what other things like this
Go on while I sleep.
It does not matter; it's in God's hands,
Like I am, safe as one of his sheep.

Jessi Nelson

Chad

Chad is great, he is kind.
I just can't get him off my mind,

His eyes are bluer than the sky.
I hope the color will never die.

He is tall and thin,
With the cutest grin.

He has little curls in his hair,
They're so blonde, I can't help but stare.

He is nothing more than a friend,
But our friendship will never end.

April Ailing

Mom

I haven't written to you in so long
I know it has been years,
But when I sit and think of you
Sometimes it brings back tears,
For what I would give if you were here
My words could never say,
My thoughts, my heart, my arms miss you
.... I miss our very last day.

Debbie Swecker

My Life

As days grow long and dark
I know winter is here
But I have nothing to do
So I sit and ponder
My mind wanders,
Back to days of youth
Playing in the park,
Chasing fire flies after dark
My High School ball,
Yes we had it all
Marrying my high school sweetheart
Laughing and crying through the years
Children came and went
But how I love the time we spent
That makes precious memories
For the winter of my life

Edna Stone

"Never Again"

I am alone; yet everyone surrounds me.
I laugh alone, I cry alone;
And people still surround me.
I feel so distant from the rest of
the world, the tears I've cried
frozen in place - knowing, soon they
will fall again - waiting for the next
time, it's my heart I have to mend.
What's wrong with me? I often ask,
is it something I can change -
Leave in the past, or am I destined
to be the outcast?
I am alone, this I know, I cannot
cry - or let my feelings show.
No-one cares, the truth be told.
My heart can ache,
My soul can die,
but never again will I cry!

Amber Torres

Weep For You (For Mario)

Ah! to the vengeance of purity
I lift my first in salute
I see in myself - the tears in my eyes
the emptiness of soul
so with purity we are three
I still miss her but I weep for you.

You stood and smiled
In black silk and blue
dark eyes, so full of pain
a thousand sighs,
anything for peace
you walked straight on - your head erect
refusing to look behind you
But I have wept for you.

Through days gone by
and days to pass when time is by
and as the tide recedes and
then in turn floods - and I turn
my thoughts in circles
And I again will weep for you.

Anna Osterholtz

Paper Dolls

When I was little
I liked to play,
With my paper dolls
Almost every day.

I'd run to my room
And close the door,
Take them from hiding
And spread them on the floor.

I'd dress them up
Dance them around,
Talk and laugh with them
Though they couldn't make a sound.

How well I remember
What fun I had,
For the paper dolls
Were like friends to me!

Edythe Rains

In My Mother's Arms

My mother's arms, so far away
I long to be embraced.
While struggling through the day to day,
I feel I'm being paced.
I love you mom, you are my heart
The warmest place to be.
Give me peace, take me away.
I am in pain you see.

Clare Brady (1994)

Does It Matter To You?

What if I told you that
I lost your ring and I broke
your play button on your radio.
And for some strange reason your
tape disappeared.
Would it matter to you?
You take me out for dinner, but
how often do I do that? You tuck me
in at night, but how would I get
home to do that? You send me flowers
for every little thing that happens.
Do you really think I'm worth it
Sometimes, late at night,
I think, do I take you for granted?
And how often do I look
in your eyes and really tell you
that I love you?
Or does it matter to you?

Jillian Hathaway

In Memory Of Halsey

I've never been adrift at sea;
I mean, you see, not literally;
And yet some stories I have read
In which it's said some folks were dead
Except a lighthouse, all aglow,
Would let them know the way to go.

While joined in struggle e'er so long,
To help the throng who suffer wrong,
I'd pondered often how to speak
For poor and weak who justice seek,
And found in Halsey one who, too,
The wrong did rue and love pursue.

Some days were planned so we would meet
At noon, to eat and thoughts repeat.
We stood to witness side by side
'Gainst war, and pride, and genocide.
His insight did my will increase
To walk in peace and never cease.

Claron Brown

My Texas Sunrise

In gray pre-dawn light
I wait for the sun.
Warm still air holds smells of
rose and green, yet carries
sounds of a distant train and
dew drops off tropical leaves
pretending to be rain.

Sunrise orange stirs air to
nudge awake insects, birds
and patio chimes.
Lawn mist webs appear to be
promising a hot Texas day,
as new shade spreads West
to reach and greet just me.

Joyce A. Saldivar

Little Child

Little child,
I never knew you well,
But I know people who loved you,
And always will.

But you'll never hurt,
In the place you live now,
I'm sure you're an angel,
Sitting among the clouds.

You brought joy,
And especially love,
Your family thanks you for that,
I'm sure they do.

You'll never be forgotten,
By people who knew and loved you,
You gave them something special,
Love and togetherness.

So farewell little child,
Watch over your family,
And may you meet in heaven,
God's special paradise.

Jennifer Lynn Gibbs

The Golden Years

As I reflect upon my life,
I really must confess
Amidst this world of war and strife,
There's been a lot of happiness,
Life is bad and life is good,
Yet, I've always understood,
To keep my faith with God above,
Respect my fellow man
Remember always, those you love,
And be the best you can.
In looking back, I'd like to say
That life's been really great
Every day in every way
No need to hesitate.
I'll just go on until the end.
Whenever that may be
Because I know I'll have a friend.
Who thinks the same of me
Don't worry - be happy!

Janet Spiecher

The First Dandelion

Your golden crown,
I saw you there;
Brave dandelion,
Bright and fair.
Proudly standing,
All alone
With understanding
I went on.

Elizabeth Wilkinson-Anderson

Ethel's Shadow

Shadows lurk but without silences
For their pain cries out for ease
Reason heard but could not stop,
The hurt nor seek to please.

Reversing roles found no contentment.
Binding joys that dared to surface
Now shadows cease, for one is taken
And silence comes to take her place.

Goley S. West

Thinking Of You

When I think of you
I smile.
When I talk to you
I laugh.
When I hold you
I'm warm inside.
When I kiss you
I dream.
But, when I look
Into your eyes
I cry.

April Lange

Living

You should never feel old
I still see a twinkle
In your eye
And a wink or two
If life's without tears
It is not living
If life's without laughter
It is not living
If life's without love
It is not living
If life's without a friend
It is not living
So we want to let you know
We are your friends
So life is worth living

Alex W. Agalzoff

The Calling

A year ago
I stood in beauty
High upon stone hills.
Today I come into
Your grace in homage.
Those places I visited
Reside in me.
And when I am alone
Listening to the locust,
Watching the hawk soar,
I am there again.
In the house of heaven
Listening to the melody
Of the wind.

Brad Fortier

Insomnia

In a corner
in a chair
Little girl in
tattered underwear
Sucking thumb
twisting hair
Seeing? With
a frozen stare
I carry the child
Upstairs to bed
To soothe her fears
I kiss her head
House of mirrors
Pangs of past
What shatters life
Like so much glass
Aching bones
No dream relieves
When sleep eludes
The body grieves

Judy Beaudoin

The Ring

When I was young and in my prime,
I thought the universe was mine,
That if I caught the big brass ring,
Then life would bring me everything.

I soon found out that ring of brass
Was nothing more than shattered glass.
Deception made it shine so bright,
Illusion cast its spell by night.

I learned that we must pay our dues,
Take paths that are not ours to choose
Midst fears that we will lose our place,
And ultimately fall from grace.

The only truth is know thyself,
For that is one's enduring wealth,
And rise to stand among your peers
Amid their censure and their cheers.

And if this strength within abides
With constancy, like moonlit tides,
And truth and honor you uphold,
Then yours will be the ring of gold.

Janet F. Kuklin

My Five Senses

My five senses are very dear.
I use my tongue for taste,
And my ears to hear.

I use my five senses very much.
I use my nose to smell,
And my hands for touch.

There's only one more,
that makes everything bright.
They are my eyes,
which I use for sight.

Donna Michelle Pitts

Option One

If I had my way
I would fashion a noisy river,
Not a muted stream
In whose green-glass eye
The moon just sits.

O for an onrushing sluice
Of tumult and foam
That loves a million stars,
All lost in whitened madness!

David Tanenbaum

Wouldn't It?

Wouldn't it be wonderful
If all the world could see
The love God has for all of us
And sent to you and me?
If each of us would care
About our fellowman,
To love and help each other
And do whatever we can,
Wouldn't it be wonderful?
And peaceful, far and near
Because we have the love of God
And He is always here.
The world could be a perfect place
For each of us to see,
If we lived the love of Jesus
As it was meant to be.

Geraldine E. Kilpatrick

"The Heart"

I have a story
I would like to tell.
About a heart that felt,
A heart that fell.
The heart fell in love;
It just happened one day.
The heart didn't know
It would turn out this way.
The heart hoped
That the love would be good.
It hoped and dreamed,
Like any heart would.
But the other heart
Just didn't feel the same.
The heart didn't know what
To do with the flame.
The heart was dying,
And as it faded from view,
It slowly beat one last wish,
And cried forever when it didn't come true.

Danny W. Gunter

Untitled

When two people meet and
if feels so right you think
nothing can tare you apart
I've had this feeling
once but something unexplainable
swept through both of us like a
hurricane and now were apart
not only in our minds
but also in our hearts...

Dixie Miller

Schizoidacide

"He has a gun pressed against my head,
If he fires I know I'll be dead.
Oh my God!
Oh my God!
This madman's going to kill me."
He thought,
As he held the gun to himself.

Adam Lillico

When We Met

I'll always remember.
I'll never forget
The smile on your face
The day that we met.

I'll always remember.
The tears in my eyes,
The kindness in yours,
My happy surprise.

I'll always remember.
My hope was renewed.
The fears that I'd known
Were slowly subdued.

I'll always remember.
I felt much more brave,
Felt more like a queen
And less like a slave.

I'll always remember.
I'll never forget
The joy that you brought
The day that we met.

Jaclyn Lanham

Fine

How are you?
I'm fine,
except I've lost a son.

And your children?
Fine,
except one child now.

And your grandchildren?
They're fine,
except they have no father.

Did you have a good summer?
Fine, and you?
except for the funeral.

Good talking to you.
Good talking to you, too.

Elizabeth Y. Porter

"Soaring Above"

Like as an eagle,
I'm strong within,
Not sayin' I'm better,
But I was born to win,
Keeping my head up,
Until the very end,
Never struck in foolishness,
Known "commonly,
as a "common-sin",
So I walk beyond
other's doubting thoughts,
Believing in faith,
just as the Bible talks,
So God bless you
as I go on my way
Because I'm soaring above
on my special way

John Alonzo Armstrong

"Every Mom Is Special"

Every mom is special
I'm sure we all agree,
But in my heart I know
She surely belongs to me.

Memories I will always cherish
Of days so long ago,
Days of childhood and adolescence
An adult, who will soon be old.

My mother's love is special
There's love for all to see,
I'll love you, Mom, forever;
Thank you for being so good to me.

Carolyn B. Prewitt

Memories Of The Dead

I look in pictures,
I see the love that had been.
But died with her.

Stories they tell about her...
But cannot be true, though there are no falsities.

They have no love for her, only memories of pain, hurt she caused toward the heart

I love her,
Is that enough?

Emily M. Mikles

Where Are You Now?

Though I haven't seen your dear face -
In 25 years -
I always knew -
I could reach you -
At 64 Blvd de Councelle - Paris -
Now that your parents -
No longer live there -
I feel a loss - abandoned -

Where Are You Now?
In that City of Light -
The Arch of Triumph -
The Eiffel Tower -
Wide boulevards -
Chestnut trees - and parks -
"Notre Dame" -
"Sacre Coeur" -
Artist In "Montmarte" -
Wine and song -
Je T'aime Helene, Je T'aime -

Jamie June Barber

The Last

Once there were four,
In days long past.
It is no more,
I am the last.

Brothers by birth,
Friends by choice.
Beckoned from earth,
Silent their voice.

Memories begin.
Memories galore.
Memories again.
Memories of four.

Wounds to endeavor,
Heal not just by time.
Gone now forever,
Those brothers of mine.

Pain yet to endure,
Oh, the years so fast.
Once there were four,
Now I am the last.

Fred F. Dunn

The Militants Against The World

Round and round the earth circles in time-
In God's beautiful world each day
How can militants in their cruel minds
Destroy and kill in such ways?

We are blessed with a perfect land-
Is it hate or greed or power they need?
To blood stain their hateful hands
On the poor, weak or innocent they see?

Life works in mysterious ways.
The good will always flourish and live-
The bad will ever die and fade-
As the militants the world cannot forgive.

For tomorrow and tomorrow and tomorrow-
Their cruelty mounts in place-
All they have left is sorrow-
And a prison cell they must face.

Janet B. Bolivar

Full Moon Passion

Your fragrance stayed impregnated
in each corner of my body,
and all profound impressions,
in every corner of my soul.

The impetuses were disarmed
from our dazzled eyes,
and they stayed suspended
in our slovenly warm bed.

Our lips remained tired
of travelling mountains and valleys,
discovering butterflies,
through the minimum details.

Thirsty for interrogating,
drop by drop I was drinking,
the lava, while it was running,
by your chestnut firmament.

The full moon, and a weeping willow,
were accomplices of your look,
that left us out of breath,
navigating on your pillow.

Guilmo Barrio

Poetry's Patience
for C. M. Hobbs

I drifted down the Danube
in hunting Heine's home.
I wished to wear his wisdom
and write for you a poem.
I meditated Markham
and scaled his skillful slope
but faltered in my footing
and graced no ground of hope.
I search this soul for someone
who holds the whispered words
to volunteer the verses
my conscious cruelly curbs.
A painful paroxysm
when one cannot find free
a friendship wrapped in rhythms
of perfect poetry.

Jessica S. E. Smith

The Telephone Is Ringing

Lord, the telephone is ringing
In the heavens blue
I'm sending you a message
I am coming home to you.

This world is full of troubles
This world is full of woe
I've grown tired and weary
Through the tunnel I must go.

So send me down an angel
To take me by my hand
And lead me on my journey
To that promised land.

I hear the angels singing
And music from afar
I can see a golden ladder
Winding beyond a star.

Lord, the telephone is ringing
In the heavens blue
I'm sending you a message
I am coming home to you!

Agnes Lys Dillard

The Sea Of Life

The highest virtue hidden,
In my love's characteristic ken,
Is my oasis-dream and desire,
Forever it is my whim,
Now time and space have joined as one,
to bring our lives this meaning,
Her arms provide the comfort,
That my soul could not bear leaving,
Though the trees may die and the
earth lose hope,
Her spirit rules her finest treasure,
As her love will ravish my imagination,
Across a sea of life, forever.

James A. Peters

This Old House

This old house still stands
In spite of time and storm
In memories so forlorn
Of a sweet loving Mother
Of a hard-working Father
Of two God-fearing children
Each one reared as Christian
Sharing memories of sadness
Amid moments of gladness
Each sharing times of hardship
In a lasting relationship
With the strength of God's hands
This old house still stands
In memory of long ago.

George P. Hynes

That Bird, This Child

That bird winging south
In the chill gold of November
Suspects nothing.
This child, its mouth
A joyous shape to remember,
Suspects nothing.

This enchanting day —
Beauty knife-sharp, such splendor
Almost wounding.
That field yielding hay,
Those flowers closing for winter
Suspect nothing.

How suspect that here,
Smiling a still grisly smile,
Minus warning,
A part of this dear
Earth — a man — in just this while
Unleashes death.

Eric Foster Rhodes

"The Last Days Of Summer"

A rainbow of promise appears
in the sky.
The seven colors a beautiful
sight for the eye.
God's promise lives on
in our hearts
Lifting our souls and making
memories easier to part.
As we move into the
winters stay.
A warm handclasp by you
and me, will guide our way.

Ada L. McKinney

The Future

The future is held
in the palm of the hand
of each young woman
and each young man.

They carry with them
the seeds for tomorrow,
the chance to touch lives
filled with confusion or sorrow.

To reach out a hand
or to carry the load,
they'll help lead the way
along life's rocky road.

They have the chance
to make the world a better place,
to help put a smile
on a lonely man's face.

So reach out your hand
to a child in need,
it's the cry for tomorrow
we all must heed.

Julie Gazave

Shadow Of Desire

Shadows of the darkness
In the recess of my mind
Can you help me find the reasons
That I myself can't find?

I have a gift of love to give
For who I cannot say
I love him oh so silently
From a distance, so far away

He knows not of my feelings
No encouragement does he give
Do I tell him of the secret
Where in my heart it lives?

Do I really truly love him
Or is it just because he's there?
Someone safe whose in my fantasy
Someone safe in which to care

I still don't have the answers
I know not what to do
Shadows of the darkness
Can you give me just a clue?

Helen R. Kohler

January 2, 1994 4 A.M. Event

In the dark,
In the silence,
Clearly I hear a young woman
Singing.
Turning to the warm form
Next to me, I wonder...
It's not her.
Stumbling down a darkened hallway,
Could it be a son
Whose voice has not changed?
Hesitate by a lost daughter's door.
Could she have come back
In the night? No.

The song is of hope.
The song of dawn's expectations.
In the dark,
In the silence,
Clearly I hear
A young woman singing.

Alix Hellas

A Lot Like A Star

You're a lot like a star
in the sky
Looking down
We're small in size
You know our thoughts
beyond measure
We've got bad points
I'm sure
But we're all human
Aren't we?
So in the looking glass
I reflect you're there
Sparkling us on
No matter what may
prevail us
Hold on to my hand
if you may
Hold my thoughts
for just awhile.

Ellen Finleyson

Horses, Horses

Horses, Horses
in the sky
playing, fighting
way up high

Horses, Horses
in the sand
racing, chasing
on the land

Horses, Horses
in the fire
whirling, twirling
for their sire

Horses, Horses
in the sea
floating, spinning
for me to see

Carla N. Chinn

Flowers

The flowers she planted
in the springtime-
They would die come fall,
But the beauty they shared
while they were there
Made it all worthwhile.

The flowers she sees now-
They live throughout the years,
And she need not toil over them
Like she did down here.

Channing Humphries

By The Guidance Of His Hand

Have you ever heard the voice whispering
in the wind?
It may be the wisdom of our Lord!
By the guidance of his hand, and
by his love
He plants a garden in our hearts.
If you ever feel lost and alone -
just remember;
Listen to the whispering wind.
He'll always be there when you need
a friend,
So take heed and listen to the wind.

Jean C. Bradford

Planting The Dreams Of Operation

Walking in the security of shadows,
in touch with the fragility
of time, forced, by the howling
winds, from corners of safety,
the details of a handkerchief
were sinking into the room,
enjoying a glimpse of leisure.
The wise and elderly
were wandering or jumping
within view of the wrought iron
fence. Into the garden,
the sight of them was flowing to
look at darkened flowers.

Baron Joseph A. Uphoff Jr.

"To Wed"

Speaketh to mine heart
In words of love spoken
Wrestle around me
In hemp leaves of a rope
Yet unmade
Taketh me down
In a bed of thine passion
After a solemn vow
Of wedded words is sworn
Bindeth me now
With the rope tied by thousands
For all a future
To be loved together
And no more alone
To wed of thee to thine.

Dawn Anne Vinson

My Buddy

A little bundle of azure blue,
Into my heart he flew.
With his silvery wings,
A joyful song he sings.

Perched on my shoulder -
He talked to me,
His love he warbled so earnestly,
At times a noisy scolder.

Each day his act grew bolder,
Out of his cage he scampered about,
Nibbling corners off my paper.
Trying to pull another caper.

Into my garden he now resides,
Under the "welcome" sign.
Greeting people forevermore,
My loyal friend -
My Buddy.

Helen Elizabeth Campbell

Undiffused

When I'm at Death's door I know
I will be with Shinto.
Like an old tree stump
Grey with moss,
Not to sit and count my loss,
But feel the rays come shining through
The tops of trees but undiffused
From a sun that's kind,
Smells like sap from a pine.
To feel blessed
Without a touch or caress.

Donald A. Driskell

The Setting Sun

The setting of the sun
is a story yet untold,
It glides across the horizon,
it's a marvel to behold.

Such a warm and pretty sight,
None can truly understand
The magic of the night,
Nor the mystery of the setting sun.

We look across the sombre skies,
And ponder upon our past.
We wonder wherein our future lies,
And wish our joys would forever last.

The golden rays embrace the clouds,
Birds to their nests return.
The weak, the strong, the meek, the proud,
For a calm retreat they yearn.

There is a certain serenity
That's cherished by everyone.
It's the unmatched beauty seen
In the setting of the sun.

Elsa Lewis

The Sounds Of Silence

Meshed within the sounds of silence
Is a vision I behold
It speaks to me of things unuttered
Like a truth inside the fold

It separates the dregs of systems
That encompass on life's way
and within the sounds of silence
I behold a better day

Though the way of silence is so lonely
On the silent path alone
To greet life and its unfolding
Still I find no other home

When the future so uncertain
Looms like a giant in distress
I must remain in silent meditation
To look and find my right address

Grace Ward

Perspective

Who ever said the world
is constantly changing?

Every time I try to change it,
it becomes the same as ever.

The trees and grasses remain
on the same mountains
surrounded by the same plains
(littered by cities)
covered with the same
bulls--t. Yet,

after noticing new growth
in the mountains
it is my perspective
I find skewed.

James Bartoli

Where Are The Angels Now?

Where are the Angels now, I say.
Is mine with me this dreadful day,
Waist deep in blood red foam I wade,
Toward frenzied beach and cannonade.

Does my Angel take me under wing?
As I hear the shells and shrapnel sing,
And I feel the heat from bursting mine,
And taste this salty bloody brine.

Where are the Angels now, I say,
Could it be they all have flown away,
And left us to a personal fate,
Alone and unredeemed this date?

Oh I see the Angels now so clear,
They mill in flocks o'er death and fear,
At work they harvest souls of men,
And lead them from this ghastly sin.

Upon marble stars and marble crosses,
They roost as guards among the losses,
Some follow men when they are gone,
Some follow men as they live on.

Howard L. Kaiser

Reflections Of A Sunrise

As the sun rises in the East and night
is slowly washed away,
The dawn is waiting for the start of
a brand new day.
Birds begin to sing and roosters start
to crow, the ones that still sleep
miss nature's magnificent show.
Stars that shine brightly at night,
Begin to fade in the morning light.
Dew drops glisten on the grass, like
teardrops from heaven when angels pass.
The wind blows softly through the leaves.
A silent wake-up to the trees.
Then as day passes into night, it will
Begin again at dawn's early light.

Jerald Fowler

Loneliness

I am surrounded by the cold,
it chills me to the bone.

The beating heart inside my chest,
lies heavy like a stone.

Silence roars within my ears,
and echoes through my mind.

There is no solace in my plight,
least none that I can find.

I pray each day for death to come,
and free me from this curse.

I live my life in loneliness,
no torture could be worse.

The sadness here enfolds me,
much like a darkened shroud.

There is no sound, save silence,
nought echoes quite so loud.

There is no pain like loneliness,
it carries such a weight.

Dear God, to me be merciful,
and free me from this fate.

Dianne C. McDermott

The Goodness Of The Lord

The goodness of the Lord,
Is so easy to see,
I have known of His great blessings,
I know that He loves me.
I never could have any doubt,
He was always by my side,
When I was filled with fear,
He dried the tears I cried.
I could never thank Him quite enough,
For all He's done for me.
Thoughts of you dear Jesus,
Fills my heart with ecstasy.
How could I ever find a friend,
More loving or more true,
Jesus, my God, my Savior,
I give my love to you.

Betty Muschar

When The Desert Flowers

No love so great as this of ours
It has kept you all these years
And then
We'll meet again in God's tomorrow
When the desert flowers
bloom again.

Along the bridle paths we wondered
Our hearts were full of love
back then
It will be again in God's tomorrow
When the desert flowers bloom again.

I know you've spent a long time waiting
For this day to come again
When the birds and bees are mating
And the desert flowers bloom again.
Along the moonlit trails we'll saunter
Our horses neck to neck we'll reign
And all the love we've
shared will splendor
When the desert flowers bloom again.

Charlotte Kirkland

To My Mother, Aleksandra

You have a heart so filled with love
It simply overflows,
You show such understanding
As you share another's load.

We learned to love each other
As you showed how much you cared;
You give to others what you have,
Even a little is shared.

I loved my father dearly,
But my strength, Mom, comes from you,
If I were half of what you are
Then I'd be OK, too.

These things I wanted to tell you
Before I go away,
To tell you how much I love you -
There's so much I want to say.

And if I go before you do,
I'll prepare for you a bed
With Dad and Ricky and with me.
At last, the words are said.

Bonnie Jean Vaughn

Untitled

Love has no gender,
it has no face
it is not bound by human notions
of proper time or place

Love is a contented calm,
it makes a pulse race
it is the mystical warmth
when two hearts embrace

Jamie Oerichbauer

Tired

I'm tired of being alone
it hurts to much.
I'm tired of the misery,
pain and such.
I'm tired of speaking
when nobody hears.
I'm tired of crying
all my tears.
I'm tired of walking
with nowhere to go.
I'm tired of asking
and nobody knows.
But mostly I'm tired
of being the only one,
that's tired
of being alone.

Jack Moore

Racism

Racism is bad
It only brings war, hatred,
and killing
all you will remember
is the dead
for blood is all around you
you cannot see the
ground
the bombs will bring
so much smoke that
there will be nothing
in the sky
No sunshine.........

And our world will die

Chelsea Luellon Bolton

Today

I have no more life left in me today.
It poured out of your mouth,
somewhere between your breath
and the words you spoke.

I heard you abandon our dreams today.
As I painfully watched,
hopeless words collecting
in puddles at our feet.

I saw our loneliness in your eyes today.
Dark reflections of loss,
drowning in shadowed pools
of lucid blue hurt.

I cannot feel our pain anymore today.
My tired soul frozen,
in the icy flow of
lost hopes for a lifetime.

Bonnie Jo Arends

Only An Acorn

An acorn fell from the tree
It seems like such a waste
It took a whole year to grow
Now lies there so disgraced

Sure not good for human food
Or much else we can see
Only grew for just one thing
To make another tree

Some say the same of children
Dropped from the family tree
Only purpose they would serve
Add to our pedigree

Still, I can't help but wonder
How precious it might be
To save one and share their joy
For
All
Eternity.

John McPhate

Acceptance

A hurt that goes so deep
It seems to have no bottom
An ache that twists and rips
And makes the pain seem endless
A loss so great
It fills a void.

But then it curves upon itself,
And in the ashes bestirs a spark,
And like a Phoenix
It rises from the ashes
To give us strength
To accept the pain,
To fight it through another day.

Eleanor Kerness

No Killing

We didn't want no killing
It was all in fun
We were going to scare him
Because we all had guns
Somehow the joke was awful
'Cause he shot back in fear
and he didn't miss us
Two of us paid dear
Guns, and cars,
Shots in the night
Another kid goes down
Daddies cuss and mothers cry
Another son goes in the ground

Dorothy Stormer Hancock

Untitled

It bellows and moans
Its deafening sound;
Echoes of torture
And chaos.
It screams through
My life at
Outrageous speeds.
Hints of danger
And turmoil
Sound out at
Every turn
Thrilling and chilling
At the same instant -
Passions unearthly reality.

Diane Moler

Yesterdays

When I think of yesterdays,
It's a mix of takes and pays,
It's a road of pick and choose,
It's a life of win and lose,
But if it could change at all,
It would be so hard to call,
Since I relish every minute,
And everyone and thing in it,
That although there's ups and downs,
There's no gains from tears and frowns,
I'd rather think of happy years,
When we played and had no fears
But how quickly time goes by,
Now we sit here side by side,
Still the lovers that we were,
In the springtime of our years
'Twill always keep us young and true,
When I think of yesterdays and reminisce
with you.

Angelo M. Gabriel

Death Took His Valley

Come my Brother, let's sit a spell.
It's good to talk with you today.
I trust that all is going well,
Since you have gone so far away.

"Yes, death took my valley from me
Along with my family and friends.
But look what I shall gain, you see,
With joy unspeakable that never ends.

Yesterday, as I grew weary
In traveling the pathway of life,
I turned aside to a world so dreary
With all its pain and strife.

Resting awhile with family by my side,
Many loved ones and friends came by
With comforting words to stem the tide,
And then the call, 'Be not afraid, it is I.'

Today I'm traveling to the Heavenly way,
And how happy I will be.
Looking forward to that great day
Trusting you, my friends, I'll see."

Clinton E. Riddle

Hugs

Now-a-days the hug is in
It's used with friends or next of kin
It's just a simple little action
But brings a lot of satisfaction.

It says hello - or maybe, "hi"
But it also says a fond goodbye
It's used for almost everything
To lift your spirits and make you sing.

Rewards a win - or - pardon's sin
It heals a rift - or - thanks a gift.
It shows compassion to a friend
And sympathizes without end.

If you haven't hugged your kid today,
Do it now - it's the modern way
To say I'm sorry - or I love you
Or you're forgiven - or love you, too.

In fact, hugs mean so many things
They tug and pull at your heartstrings
So whether you're losing or basking in
glory
A hug is the perfect end to the story.

Betty M. McIntyre

My Treasure

In my yesterday world I found love
Its quality truly precious to me
Placing in my life a brilliance
So radiant for all to see.

To hold on to my gem forever
This destiny was not to be
When buried one cold winter morning
I thought my treasure was lost for me.

Now in my present today world
I'm finding many happy memories
Because his constant little reminders
Are still given lovingly.

I now know I'll carry always
Life's rarest treasure to see
His undying love, I'll keep forever
Creating my most cherished discovery.

Jeannie Wickham

Is There Life After Death?

Death...
It's something that happens
to everyone,

But no one really knows why.

And yet maybe there's
something more to life,

Or maybe it's just all
a lie.

Is there life after death?

I would like to know.
Can anyone tell me the
truth?
Where do people go?

Annie Keen

My Apple Tree

Today I set out an apple tree
I've wanted one for awhile
At my age (78) I must be an optimist
To watch would have made one smile.

I dug and lifted and struggled
And finally set it with care
While there on my knees exhausted
I uttered a silent prayer,

May this effort not be in vain, Lord
Let it grow strong, healthy and tall
Bear fruit, give a safe home for birds
And soon make shade for us all.

Then I rose and thought what a lovely day
As a bird's song filled the air
I'm so blessed to be able to do this
And to show the world I still care.

Aleen Lowder

Lief

The water runs along the creek
In splashes and in trickles

The flowers bloom along its banks
They are short and tall

We walk along its shore
and know we are God's miracles
big and small

Alyvia Sue Bodnovits

Lost Love

The Tears I leave,
Just show my pain.
As the hurt and sorrow,
Come once again.
I thought I found a man,
Who could be true.
Yet he did me wrong
With someone new.
A baby has been born,
From him and another.
Because we split for a short time,
So he found a different lover.
The trust for a man,
Will never be known.
Happiness has been felt
Just being alone.

Jill Maryann Haberek

"Have Faith"

I was muttering in the sand,
just uttering in my heart,
when lo and behold-
what should unfold,
as the sea began to part.

I walked into the midst,
and the walls began to shake.
My knees began to knock,
and my eye shed a tear-
for my heart began to break.

But just as my hand-
was brought to my eye-
in order to wipe a tear,
the LORD above-
took its place,
and said,
"I am here."

John R. Fransen, Jr.

The Mask

He wears a mask.
It covers his soul.
It hides his tears.
Tears of rejection.
The mask is what they see.
Longing to fit in.
Afraid to be himself.
The mask is expensive though,
The cost is freedom.
Is it worth it?
He asks this everyday.
Indefinitely.
To be Loved,
To have a Friend,
To Live;
He wears a mask.

Charles Barnes

"It All Went Through A Hoop"

It all went through a hoop
Lies, deception, kisses and dreams
They jumped through the night before last
They danced about nakedly
They got drunk with frenzy
Lies spun about like a madman
Deception hid behind the bushes
Kisses lit the bonfire
Dreams went away

D. K. Tkac

The Rose

The vivid colors of your kind
Leave prints of beauty in my mind.
The scent from every living rose
Is instinctive pleasure to my nose.

And every man on earth should know
That roses make romances grow,
No other flower comes close
To the magic power of a rose.

So if your love somehow went sour,
There is quick relief within that hour.
A single rose will bring relief,
Its power is so great and beyond belief.

And if someone you loved has died
Or some poor soul has been belied,
And words and tears just won't assuage,
A fresh cut rose will be quite sage.

Humberto Cappas

One More Time

One more time before I die
Let me fly a kite up in the sky
Chase butterflies on a summer's day
Stop and watch some children play.
Smell the lilacs in the Spring
Listen to a robin sing.
Climb a tree as high as I dare
Admire exhibits at a county fair.
Take a ride on a merry-go-round
Plant some young trees in the ground.
Read "Treasure Island" once again
Spend a day with a lifelong friend
Picnic by a quiet lake
Bake someone a birthday cake.
Sit at my window and watch it snow
Walk to where wild flowers grow.
All this, I ask no more
Ere I depart this earthly shore
Then, when my life has cause to cease
I will die in perfect peace.

Charlotte Anderson

"Out Of Waves And Into The Sun"

Carry me wave of destiny
let me move, let me fly,
Raging sea is not my enemy
it's my strongest ally.

Out of waves and into the sun
Faster and faster,
Out of gravity into the sky
Higher and higher,
Let me move through your gate
Let me test my fate,
And fulfill my deepest desires.

Open up doors of sesame
Let me see what's inside,
I invite sea to dance with me
in sunlight.

Sea gulls will sing to me
Dolphins try to fly,
On the waves of destiny
I can reach the sky.

David Crane

Lonely Love

Lonely Love
Let your love last.
A person may be gone,
But true love doesn't pass.

Lonely Love
I'll be there.
You can trust me
If life is unfair.

Lonely Love
What happened to you?
You're only showing feelings
Of looking so blue.

You can't be lonely
Forever my love,
And you can't be in love if you're lonely
So don't be lonely, love...

Francisca Marie Solis

Our Son

Christopher Michael
Is his name,
Isn't he a doll!
Today's his day,
His special day
Today is the day he was born!
Frogs' and snails'
And puppy dog tails'
That is what baby is made of...
Devil or angel
No one can tell,
His actions are that of both...
Look at him laugh,
Look at him cry
Look at him wiggle and twist...
So just for today,
Because it's his day
Let him do whatever he pleases...
His life has just begun!

Carol A. Cummings

The Wheel

An' I who have died
from the business of death
Who scoured the trenches
to find who was left
Who devoured the carnage
for want of a flag
Do now consume
the Celtic Stag
An' so I reign
as Hades new Lord
Surrounded by sculls
speaking never a word
I take whom I will
humanities best
Lured by my wisdom
to feather their nest
An' yet in the Spring
when all come alive
My throne to the Queen
that some do survive

R. Arlin Genzoli

"My Angels"

Oh I hear the Angels coming
Landing softly on the porch
As I peer through the window
I can see their wings fluttering
For I know they are coming
Just to take me home.

The Angels are in the house
And they gently take my hand
I look around the room
Then I feel the soft wind
As I go with the Angels

I look towards the sky
Then I see my husband's face
As he calls my name
I know I'm going home
To be with my husband and our Lord.

Blanche Edwards

Purity In A Twinkling

Suspending over me....
... like clouds on a rainy day,
so effective -
with an arresting need to deliver,
yet unprepared for consequence;
my reminiscing in yesteryear ...
... hovering, as the clouds atop,
embodied with incessant control
of tedious days and drifting nights.

Soon purifying my heart and soul,
moisture - cool rain divine,
as with God's uniformity to earth;
each rain drop caressing separately,
as designated, then enjoined to pacify.

A feeling of purity in a twinkling.

Each tear I cry so individual
and mercifully enshrined in necessity
of this near perfect deliverance
from my very soul. Yet remains ...
... an unaccomplished urge to see you.

Darlene A. Lytle

Stalking The Covers

Loneliness stalks the room;
the book shelf haunts my soul.
Each colorful jacket beckons-
ignoring feelings-my goal!

Every nook and cranny
rekindles a vanquished role.
Denial leads the challenge-
curiosity triggers the toll.

Linguistic symphonies awake
images of soulful treasures.
Intuition pairs with knowledge,
discerning stolen pleasures.

Characters escape the pages,
entwining histories of myths and sages.
Plots weave their threads;
word dances puzzle my head.

Moments roam the pages,
with depths no longer hidden.
Trembles release the mask,
tears course-at-last-unbidden!

Martanne Louthan

Could This Be?

Thin slate sterling silver
Whisper into night
Across a crimson
Force of mind
Could it be the moonlight?

Mineral universe steady state
Calling in the cold
Past the clear
Cliffs of life
Could this be the threshold?

Stormy omen swirling wind
Telling earth beware
Pushing a gray
Hint of death
Could this be a nightmare?

Shining sun cloudless sky
Shadow casting tree
Flying birds
Singing songs
This is the reality.

Lewis I. Chace

Before I Was Born

Before I was born
Life was no heartbreak
Like now.

To live always
Only in the mind
Is tragedy.

Together with the flesh
This thought full of anguish
Might not exist.

Before I was born
Death
I seldom feared.

With even sublime spirit
What I cannot reach
Is unhappiness.

Together with you
The ultimate love
Might not come to me.

Heryn Kim

Reflection

Just hold my hand,
Let me know you understand,
That my heart is breaking,
For the life that's been taken,
So young, so pure, so new,
For a child's love we never knew.

Angels in heaven, their wings so soft,
Came to earth to carry a soul aloft,
I'm sure "God" loved him so,
He just couldn't let him go.

Time heals, they say,
So for now I pray,
That "God" will try to see,
A good mother I could be.

Betty Synowiecki

Visions

Looking into your eyes,
It's not what it seems,
Always asking why,
And full of great dreams.

We're working together,
On a problem or two,
And forgetting to say,
I love you.

No problem is too big,
No problem is too small,
Because being together,
We have it all!

James J. Wiesen

Time Capsule Towards Eternity

A glowing candle in the dark
firefly sparks in the spring
Red lightning slices blue
after winged cardinals sing

Tears caress the whispering foam
of Pacific's eternal tide
Circus mirrors reflect the light
and there's no place to hide

The empty chatter of egos
colliding at high speed
Brutality of maliciousness
not sensing other's need

It's the paradox of humanity
the blows of fate and time
Struggles of good and depravity
the breath of winds on chime

Time capsule towards eternity
the dance of rhythmic rhyme
Time capsule towards eternity
with a hunger most sublime.

L. S. Thompson Greuling

Unborn Dreams In Porphyry

A special place for unborn dreams
exists in fields of porphyry
fragmented bits of thought suppressed
they scamper freely unrepressed.

Aversion to ambition deemed
these massive planes of unborn dreams
to co-exist with thoughtless days
and through our fear are kept at bay.

Unaware their awesome power
hedonistic unbloomed flowers
our time to them unknown yet spent
in waiting for the bless'd event.

From time to time they're neatly plucked
by muted recognition tucked—-
into the earthbound minds of man
when thus recalled and once more scanned.

Ensuring innovative lives
must wake these dull quiescent minds
to rise above the stagnant pools
and suffer not the ways of fools.

Cheryl L. Ahner

Freedom

I leave now
with a springtime reminder of myself.
See my colorful spirit rise to unprecedented heights
as it just in and out and up and down
diving and catching the wind.
My tail strings trace the lines of my journey.

Smiling, no longer masks the turbulence of illness
nor the plummeting depths of pain
that have imprisoned me.
No longer will dark clouds deflate my aspirations.

Now an everlasting rainbow
replaces any traces of threatening storm.
Please let go of my kite strings,
Set me free to soar!

Kathi Wilder

Untitled

You were never any good under pressure
with courage peeled away
exposing raw cowardice
the sweat of fear oozing from the epidermis of panic
freezing reflexes, numbing the brain,
until like a child you abdicate your will.

I cannot watch your spiritual demise
that shuffling gate of dejection
the daunted expression from sleepless nights
your face refusing to defy gravity
negativity your daily mask
and sulking your only act.

The anger of suppression is welling inside of me
feeding on your indifference
kept in check by mysterious forces
whose charms ar daily wearing thin.
I am looking for the threads
that form the bonds of pain
to unite that knot of uncertainty
that binds you and me together.

Sophie Rivera

"At Last"

On the day of Saturday, March 8, 1975, my search had finally ended.

What a happy day it was - for me and all my friends who shared it with me.

I received an unexpected phone call from one of my sisters who I had been searching for - she had received my letter which I really thought she would never get.

How wonderful it all was - hearing her voice after all these years. We talked and laughed as though we knew each other all our lives.

We learned a lot about one another and how we had so much in common.

You wanted to know all about me, how long I was searching, how I found you and everything.

All we could say to one another was - "I don't believe it" and "At last we found one another."

But you thought the most wonderful part of it all was that I cared enough to search for you after all these years of being away from you.

I thanked God for this day and said, "It was finally meant to be for us to be together again."

At last one of my dreams finally did come true.

Pats Green

Spirit Guest

I long for you, my spirit love,
With devotion and anticipation -
Patiently waiting for darkness to fall...
Trusting in predestination.

My love, my heart, my soul is yours
Though worlds and eons divide us -
Oh, Shade of Night, Sweet Fantasy,
Our attraction can't be denied us.

Gentle Guest, take form and shape,
Come, hold me, kiss me, fill me
With the joy of life, the thrill of desire...
Separation's blade would kill me.

Slip beside me as gently as sleep -
In dreams, united, we'll soar on high
To the realm of passion's altered state
Where forever as soul-mates we'll fly.

Kitt Little Turtle

A Vow Of Love

A vow of love I give to you
With diamond rings and precious jewels
With a heart of love and a world of laughter
This, I give this day and all that's after
To a love I treasure and praise
For one
I need not call a name
For I am your husband
And you are my wife
And together we are married for life

A vow of love I give to you
To always be faithful, loving, and true
To be the wife you married this day
To be by your side forever and always
To bear the children, that we share
To love each other
Regardless of the problems, that we might have
And with my heart I pledge to you
To be the wife you can love through and through

Melissa Marie Williams

Highway 19 Hawaii

I have a contact with the sea and sky
with earth and flower and bird and low'ring cloud
as I pass by at dawn, as I pass by.

The fields of cane wave lush and green, wave high;
the wind has whipped a high stalk to a shroud;
I have a contract with the sea and sky.

Cars dance 'round cars, some fast; they whoosh and sigh.
We're entering the gloom, comes thunder loud
As I pass by at dawn, as I pass by.

Eight golden birds serene go winging by;
a giant truck roars past, the driver proud;
I have a contract with the sea and sky.

I cherish storm and sea; cars pass me by;
with patience calm I seem to be endowed
as I pass by at dawn, as I pass by.

It's true, the storm at sea, the fields and I
breed courage 'ere I face the city's crowd:
I have a contact with the sea and sky
as I pass by at dawn, as I pass by.

JLA-Lo Roberts

Blossoms Of Life

It's amazing how we grow,
With grace and with a flow,
Gradually and beautifully,
As He intends it to be,
We are seeds sown in the ground,
And as time passes, we bloom into beautiful flowers,
Each having different colors and petals,
We sway together until the wind passes along with time,
And soon each petal falls, one by one,
And withers away,
Still leaving its beauty and grace behind,
As a new row of buds soon start to bloom.

Shana Sahibzada

Quiet Times

At sunset, he comes walking down the path
With his faithful dog by his side,

It is a quiet and peaceful time
When his thoughts turn to a personal nature,

He pictures a home in the country with gardens,
shade trees and a near-by lake,

His wish is for a loving and caring woman to
share these things with him,

To be his companion-wife for all time
Never to know loneliness again,

But where does he search to find this special
mate, abroad, in the mountains or by the sea?

First, he must look deep into his heart
To seek out the other qualities, that would ensure
a special relationship,

And he has to be willing to contribute and listen
Only then, will he find her

Shirley Lovell

The Heart

The heart is not a toy to be played
with; it is a loving and giving thing to be earned.
The heart can be broken and torn
and cannot be repaired, but it can also
find love and happiness with friends
and loved ones.
The heart can give love and can take
the love others will give; it can learn to
love the way others will show it.
The heart can also give out hate,
the way others will show you; hate is the
next strongest emotion there is.
The best way to get past hate,
is use the strongest emotion which is love,
and love everyone has, even those you hate.

Richard McCluskey

"Restless Nights"

Replace my sadness with happiness; and with comforts, replace my pains
with love, replace my hatred; and replace my losses with gains.

Take away my tears with laughter, and take away my evil with good.
Take me away from confusion and chaos, and let things be understood.

Let me rid myself of gloom and substitute it with cheer.
Let me rid myself of mixed emotions so I can begin to see things clear.

I need to free myself of darkness; and in return, let me see the light,
To free myself from all of the things that keep me up at night.

Nancy E. Lowman

I Smile

The road of life is long and steep,
With mountains to climb for many a mile,
But at the end of the day, I do not weep,
I smile, oh yes, I smile.
God showed me what a smile can do,
It can mend a heart or chase the blues,
God says to smile and I follow through,
I smile, oh yes, I smile.
I smile at all who come my way,
The babies, the young, the old and grey,
And the one's who have walked that long, long mile,
I have nothing to give but a warm, warm smile.
So I smile, oh yes, I smile.
God formed a smile on every face,
In the end that may be our saving grace,
For as fleeting as a smile can be
And where it goes we cannot see,
But in Heaven all our smiles will meet,
As each smile comes to rest at our Master's Feet.
So I smile, oh yes, I smile.

Pearl McNeill

Little Shaggy Brown Bear

High upon my bedroom shelf, there you sit, little shaggy brown bear
With one eye gone, leg hanging loose and barely any hair
One of your ears is torn away, stuffing hanging from your back;
And in that darling, little, red nose there is a great big crack.

I know I can never make it up to you for treating you so rough
How I wish you could have talked back then and said, "Hey look now
that's enough."
And, of course, I know you loved me when I was just a little boy;
You also knew, my little Boo Bear, that you were my favorite toy.

When you were beside me, I never knew what it was to fear.
Because I knew, when I needed you, that you were always near.
And at night we used to cuddle up close and say a little prayer;
I would know when I awakened, I could always find you there.

Now that I am grown, I find it hard to remember back to three-
To the time when I first got you and you seemed so perfect to me.
But I do remember that at once you truly captured my whole heart.
That's how I know to this very day that we will never part.

Margaret M. Abair

Nature's Blessings

I wake to see a clear blue sky
With rays of light; clouds drifting by.

The trees so green on mountains touched with white
Filled with the son's glorious shining light.

All around his touch I see
From meadows green to bluest sea.

Colors given in love for us
Fill our lives with splendor dust to dust.

God's creation for all to enjoy
From oldest man to youngest boy.

While nature all around us grows
His richest blessings he bestows.

Take time to stop enjoy the splendor
Deepest joy your soul will render

Glory and praise to God on high
For all these blessings by and by.

Someday I want to meet the man
Who created this by his own hand.

Whose love for us we can't compare
He only asks his love we share.

Kimberley Shawn Mondry

Operator, Get Me Jesus

I was walking around with my head hanging down
with so many things weighing heavy on my mind.
Strung-out on drugs, and alcohol too,
high as a kite with no hope in sight.
Confusion and disillusion blurred my view.

Then I stopped, and I thought to myself -
Oh Lord, this is so wrong.
Remembering what Mom and Granny would say,
I ran and found a pay phone.
I said, "Operator, get me Jesus and this is collect."
"You don't need me," she said. "You can dial Him direct."
"I don't have a quarter; all I can dial is you. If you
don't call him for me, what on earth will I do?"
"Dial toll free," she said, "1-800-Do Jesus."
"And you can hold up your head,
for He has paid the price for you."

The phone rang once as soon as I dialed.
The line wasn't busy;
there was no wait at all.
"Hello, Jesus. I know it's been a while, but -"
"Say no more," He said. "I'm just so glad you called."

Sonja O. Fambro

The Carpenter

An Off-White Picket Fence,
With Squeaking Crooked Gate,
To Be Restored To Its One-Time
State Of Perfection -
A Carpenter's Delight, Love Taps Undying,
Relying On A Strong And Gentle Hand,
To Mold And Shape With Understanding -
And Make What's Crooked Straight.
How Grateful Are The Words We Say
In Silent Adoration,
For How He's Mending Fences,
For How The Master's Renovation,
Returns A Vessel To Its Proper Place,
A Touch Of Grace To Make It All Brand New -
Old Things Are Passed Away.
Giving Back Our Gratitude -
Perhaps Some New-Born Shrubs And Roses,
To Bless The New-Found Garden Gate,
An Encouragement To Grow -
God's Blessings Overflow.

Randolph Schwarz

Mellowing Tones

Inside the many far off places,
Within this world, my mind races,
Hearing the call of the meadow lark,
Seeing the light of the moon, a star doth spark,
Mellowing tones of the singing,
Hear of the birds on winging,
Seeing the shining of the golden moon on the harvest,
A lingering longing for excitement's gay ring, upon my heart doth
infest,
Knowing all is awaiting for me to find it once more,
Calling unto me to come knock upon its door,
Together with all my many loves of life, to gaily play,
For sweet music of lively living within my heart, to lay,
Peering over the rainbow of life's tender colors to blend,
A better way in the making, once more to defend,
All together in the peacefulness of cheery living,
Love, good times, unto each other are giving,
Paths of life as yet untouched, imperatively waiting for us to
eagerly explore their many places,
Taking us into their worlds of the greatest excitement, so many
mysterious faces.

LaVerne A. Kerkoski

Flickering Shadows

Flickering shadows cover the cement walk
With the touch of the wind, they begin to rock.
As if rehearsing for one of life's plays
They glide across this stage in the late of the day.

Dancing across the top of the golden marigolds,
Picking up speed as the wind becomes bold.
They remain in one spot for just a short while
Then continue their display across the cement tile.

To be free as the shadows that are casting their spell,
Ever moving, their intricate designs never gel.
Free as the breeze that sweeps them along.
Covering life's stage, this is where they belong.

Vicky Ferrasci

The Old Man Of The Horn

There were many weary sailors
With their spirits bent and worn
After dealing with the terror
From the Old Man of the horn

They tell of pandemonium
As men hope the powers that be
Will give them strength, to set their course
And run dead before the sea

As tons of water swamped the deck
The fierce waves were mountain high
Most sails were blown to ribbons
And all hands knew - that they could die

Soon the great hull of the vessel
Gave a painful, labored moan
And the screaming of the rigging
Made each man feel - so alone

The whole crew had suffered through
The Old Man's fury and the freight
Now, they all dream of doldrums boredom
Just to get them through the night

Martie Manwaring

Ascension

Ascension is a question that brings some apprehension.
With this intention, I plan to move to a new dimension.

With only a short time to prepare,
I have no time for despair,

Ascending right out of this place,
Where only the worldly keep pace.

I feel a new place while I journey to inner space,
Space where others have been and even race,

Hoping to find a new goal or two
For keeping life ever fresh and new.

Ascending is part of our grace,
By settling down in a whole new place,

Moving along this newly found ground,
Keeping our love moving around.

Renewing our mind with treasures from the ascended mound,
I quickly perceive that holiness to be found.

But wait, Ascension is now not a question,
But the better part of my greatest intention.

Where only those who are ready will partake
Of a whole new journey for goodness sake.

Valdyne J. Johnson

Come Winter Tho It May

Come winter tho it may
With whipping winds and frozen scenes
Wrapping the world under mantles of snow, ice stung,
Swallowing, whole, spring and summer days
With frosty breaths from the old man's tongue,
I still have summer dreams.

Let rains come tho they may,
Splattering colorless paint drops across dismal streets,
Pouring forth till our corridors are as water-soaked
As ancient Venice, and are followed by stronger
Reinforcement of ice and sleet.

As I stand before the door of fate
And bid the doorman open up the gate,
Tho you unleash furious winter beasts of frigid form,
With hopeful dreams I'll still be warm.

Neal Feld

Of Mothers

Once I stood on the brink of possibilities.
Within me heaven touched the earth.
And I lived with the most wonderful...
Frightening...
Powerful love...

The labor of sweat and blood gave way to the tears of joy -
And now I stand in awe as my joy carries her possibilities.
God has twice blessed me.
For just as you were once within me -
I now see myself in you...
Remembering...the first kick,
The first smile,
The first step,
And now, the first child.

Generation after generation the love multiplies, so -
Know that I love you, my child, with all my being, and
That I will love your child as well.

Karen A. Bowers

Artificial People, Artificial Minds

We're surrounded by artificial people living artificial lives, lives without meaning or rhyme. Always in an electronic wonderland of time. Making promises with words of opposite meanings. Speaking only in half truths, never speaking what's on your mind! You can see it on video waves and hear in on radio waves every day! Living artificial relationships with anyone they meet. Always looking out for number one, it is always "what's in it for me" never for you! Always letting time slip them by without any thought! Never have time for anyone except for themselves and nothing to give. Always looking for the easy way out and the shortest route, never willing to work things out. Artificial people make their own artificial GOD using only what applies to themselves. Then they seek out others like themselves, calling it religion for all. Always speaking the truth for all. What truth is this, theirs or is it ours? Putting drugs inside themselves and feeling fine they say. Artificial highs are what's so hot to the artificial minds. Educated by the assembly line of thought through their lives, all of this for what? Never to see the sunrise over the sandy beach or elk walk amongst the redwoods. Always living in their artificial world! No, artificial people are not like you or me. Is as sad and fearful fact that there are so few of us and so many of them. Let's not lose the faith in the artificial world.

Rojelio Villarreal

Being Together

I walk alone wondering about you,
Wondering if we will ever be together.

I dream of times we might share,
Wondering if they'll come true.

Alone in a room with no windows,
I see nothing but thoughts of me and you.

Together we will make a difference.
Sharing, caring and wanting the same things.

I walk alone no longer.
For you and I will walk together,
You and I will be one.

Roberta Patrykus

Wûrdz

Words are only letters, arranged in a given way.
Words reveal emotion and can steal the heart away.
Words are the basis for the communication of the minds.
But words are only symbols; hieroglyphics; signs.
Words are the only means I have to express what I feel -
But words are inadequate in making feelings real.

E. M. Simkulet

"My Search For A Friend"

I was looking for a friend as I walked down the street.
Would I find laughter, a handshake, or whom will I meet.
As I continued to walk, I looked around.
I heard a beautiful voice, with a soft gentle sound.
Wait! Would you like to speak to me, as I am lonely and also free.
Would like to stop and talk this day?
As we travel down the street along our way.
We talked of our hobbies, art and what we would like to do.
As we continued to walk, I found he was honest and true.
Then he told me his name and I told him mine.
That we would be friends regardless of time.
We praised the beauty of the heavens as we traveled our way.
Promising to meet again, another beautiful day.

Louise L. Bishop

"If.........?"

If we could go back and re-live our days
Would the outcome be yet another maze?

What if we travelled on a brand new route?
And pursued a different challenge and bout?

Would there be less hurt or sadness and pain?
Would colorful bows show brighter in rain?

Would the up moods come to replace the downs?
Would the smiles rush in to push out the frowns?

Would we love again or need to be loved?
Would all our problems be somehow resolved?

Could all hidden doors be opened with our keys?
Would there be any new uncertainties?

Could we make every and all dreams come true?
Or in the process, would we loose a few?

Would there be new ties or would we be free?
Would life be better, could anyone see?

Could or should destiny be seen or changed?
Isn't the future set and pre-arranged?

Without the unknown, would there be a drive?
Without any drive, could we still survive?

F. Alexander Goleh

To Dance With You Again

We danced in the moonlight together,
You and I,
On a velvety green carpet
Warmed by the afternoon sun.
The orchestra, a symphony of
Chirping crickets. The soloist,
A hidden night bird, trilling his sweet song
In a nearby tree.
The lighting, a hundred million stars
Glittering, dazzling the Heavens
And illuminating earth.
We held each other close -
So close, I could feel the beating of your heart.
We kissed, and the discreet moon
Hid behind a cloud, as if
Reluctant to observe our intimacy.
Oh, let us dance again, my love!
Recalling that one night of ecstasy and joy.
Though the wind is cold, and the sky is moonless,
Let us dance just once again.

Patricia Gough Risk

Broken Heart

Broken heart, dreams and happiness are gone -
you are blind - you cannot see what I see -
there is some one near who want the love,
the dreams and happiness, you gave away -
you got nothing in return - from the one you wanted -

Broken heart, let it go - it is not to be, for love
is not given in return - you suffered the
enormous agonies of passion - so you write a
poem from the end backwards - brushing
away the tears that had not yet fallen - but
the hurt of pain is deep -

Broken heart, look up from the pain, for
there is someone near who care -
who would like the pain in you to fade away -
make new dreams come true - and fixed the
broken heart you carry around -

So! please open the door and let her in,
She is love, she will give you peace,
joy and happiness -
........Just give it a chance......

Ruthlean Hunter

"When You Are Old"

Things get bad when you are old,
You are too hot or you are too cold.
Get up in the early hours of dawn,
By the time you are ready the day is gone.

You put on your pants to be ready,
Why won't your legs hold you steady.
You decide to take a short tramp,
And when you come back, "O THAT DARN CRAMP".

You flex your muscles and they hurt.
And all you did was to put on your shirt.
Go to the table to get a bite,
Where did you put your teeth last night.

You plan to meet with the Lads and Lasses,
Now where did you leave your glasses.
You grab for your cane it falls to the floor,
And you curse old age once more.

But I am not as old as you,
And I know what I am going to do,
For I am not one a job to shirk,
So I'll sit here and watch you work.....

Norman I. Rogers

You Are The One

You... You are everything to me
You are like a fruit upon a tree
You make me happy
Very happy baby.

You... You are the one I want to see
You are the one lying close to me
You are where I want you to be
Close to me, close to me.

You... You are the one who can open up my mind
You are the one that treats me kind
You are everything to me
Can't you see? Can't you see?

You... You are the one I want to see
You are the fruit upon the tree
You are lying close to me, close to me.

You... I am glad that you are here
You take away all my fears
I need to hold you tonight
'cause everything feels so right
'cause of you babe, yes you babe.

Mark Anthony Schroettner

To My Dad - Benjamin Harrison - On His 75th Birthday

You are a wonderful Father and a peach of a dad,
You are the best Father a girl ever had,
You have always shown us love and tender care,
There is not a better Father in the world anywhere.
To us, you have no faults, but others will say you do,
I am sure they are human and take nothing away from you.
When our Mother passed and left you home with eight,
Some said you should desert us, but you took your weight,
Like the true loving man you were and you are still,
No one can take that away from you and they never will.
We have never been hungry from a lack of food,
There was always plenty for a very large brood.
We have never been stranded for shelter as some kids were,
You were always in there pitching and you kept things so dear.
You have shown your love for us in so many, many ways,
— Not just for a moment, but for days upon days
We will truly never have another dad like you,
We may search as deep as the ocean and as high as the blue.
— In the entire world, there is truly only one,
God gave him to us, to be the Father of six daughters and four sons!

Marjorie L. Burgess

Who Is Really Steve?

You are near and I feel so loved.
You are: The peace of a Church with a baby asleep in your arms.
The fun of eating cotton candy on a Ferris Wheel.
The pride of each graduate's accomplishments.
The elixir I feel when I remember the night I said:
"Steve, look at the moon." And you looked into my eyes and said: "I am."
The shock on co-workers' faces then they saw us dancing.
The compassion of labor—seven times.
The charm when I lost my shoe in the snow and you retrieved it and knelt in the snow and replaced and stood up and kissed me as the snow fell softly on us.
You are: My Steve, my lover, my one and only yesterday, today and all my tomorrows.
You are: My husband.
You are: My soul-mate.
You are: My eternal love. And I am yours.

Mary Ann Theresa Perito Horan

"When You Are Old"

Things get bad when you are old,
You are too hot or you are too cold.
Get up in the early hours of dawn,
By the time you are ready the day is gone.

You put on your pants to be ready,
Why won't your legs hold you steady.
You decide to take a short tramp,
And when you come back, "O THAT DARN CRAMP".

You flex your muscles and they hurt.
And all you did was to put on your shirt.
Go to the table to get a bite,
Where did you put your teeth last night.

You plan to meet with the Lads and Lasses,
Now where did you leave your glasses.
You grab for your cane it falls to the floor,
And you curse old age once more.

But I am not as old as you,
And I know what I am going to do,
For I am not one a job to shirk,
So I'll sit here and watch you work.....

Norman I. Rogers

The Best Book

Life is like many things but most of all it is like a book,
You buy a book and open it and take a look.
You finish the first chapter and you're all happy and stuff,
The 2nd chapter is a little more rough.
The book goes on and things get a little more tough,
You become frustrated with yourself,
You fight with your parents and siblings,
And then things begin to rock.
Around the 13th chapter you don't know what to do,
So you either follow other people or you become one with yourself.
Half way through you begin to grow up,
Some people say you don't know what to do,
Do you become serious?
And act like you're grown up,
Or do you act like you're young and don't have a clue?
The rest of your book is filled with peace and harmony,
Or simply nothing.
(Or maybe your book ended really quickly.)
Finally your book finishes and you read the words THE END.

Marcle Holler

White Flowers

You were a strength when my mom was dying
You didn't know, but you eased my crying

You said "although sometimes life seems unfair,
It just might be better where we go from there"

That's why when Mom finally did pass away
White were the flowers you sent that day

They were symbolic of a beginning so bright
A celebration of having emerged from the night

Thank you for sharing my grief and my pain
For showing the rainbow through the rain

I'm sad to have lost a friend who cared
I'm happy about all of the thoughts we shared

As you begin this journey, my friend,
Take this white flower because there's no end...

Teri Waxman

In Memory Of My Mother: Faye Matoushek

You brought me here but couldn't stay.
You gave me love, then were called away.
You showed me light when life seemed dim.
A special bond we had, when God chose to take you with him.
Such a wonderful woman, and mother, and friend—
and the love you had for me, had no beginning nor end.
Today I will marry a wonderful man,
I wish you could be here—
but God had another plan.
You see he needed a special person to join him—
in his beautiful Kingdom above.
A very special person like you mom, full of faith, strength, and love.
So although I miss you, I won't shed a tear—
because I know in my mind,
and my heart you'll be here.

Michele Matoushek-Propes

Little Ones

I miss you little ones.
You grew up so fast.
I miss the sweet smiles and the jolly burst of laughter.
Time will not wait, it just goes on.
Now all of my little ones are grown up
And have families of their own.
I can still hear your footsteps, see the smears on the wall.
Oh how you would giggle when creeping down the hall.
We had our good times.
We had a few ups and downs,
But the love we had didn't have to be found,
For it was always in our hearts; we just passed it around.
I hope for your little ones, time will slow down.
For it was so nice to have you around.

Margaret C. Martin

Mother

Having a mother like you is so very wonderful.
You have been there at every waking moment to dry the tears.
You have given to me the wisdom and knowledge that I have gained.
You have listened to me without too much interference.
You are the one and only mother that a child growing up could ever ask for.
Having you as my mother has never left me feeling ashamed of who you are.
Having you as a mother has taught me that the skies the limit when there is something that you want you go for it.
So to you mother I say that you're the greatest and that you're my gem.
Have a wonderful day mom because you have given so many of them to me.

Michele A. Rush

Untitled

Retired? Or full provisioned for a launch
yet to begin? A new space time wherein
the known and trodden paths of ego's win
are lost among the thorns of jowl, paunch
and slower peristalsis. Now a staunch
unwillingness to future is a "sin."
Pater Prometheus unbound begins
at newfound land: rebirth, new sight, a traunch
of riches from God's hand awaits. New sight
brings hope and courage, love, to hold, not harm,
to know, not fail. An inner mirth, not might,
as cassock yields to pink knit short-sleeved charm,
will conquer in the land ahead. The rite
of peace heralds the dawn without alarms.

Susan E. Hughey

Butterfly Of The Wind

I crown thee butterfly of the wind;
You know the meaning of life.
As everyone searches to find it;
You simply float upon it.
It is neither touchable, nor mysterious,
but rather much simpler than that
It is the simplest beauty that is enjoyed,
That is the meaning the true meaning of life
As it is to you my beautiful butterfly
That I have found it
My daisy of daisies, my song bird
of song birds that I hold so dear.
Thank you and may the Lord bless you,
All the days of your Life;
My Beautiful Daughter Jessica Lynn!

Linda A. Patricia Carroll-Simmons

Shadow

From across the room I watch you, a stranger in your eyes.
You recognize nothing in my gaze though I try,
I try to tell you who you are.
The women in my dreams, the ghost that haunts my thoughts.
Yes I know you, but will you ever know me?
How do I share with you these secrets which burden my heart?
How do I share with you my soul?
How can I bridge the gap from strangers to friends,
friends to lovers, and back again?
I want you, I need you, to fulfill this perfect fantasy.
I need you to be mine.
But all you do is sit there, acknowledging nothing,
while I slowly fall in love with your shadow.

Xavier W. Niz

A Day At The Park

Little stabs of memory - sharp as darts.
The girls, beautiful, light as birds, fluttering against my side,
Anxious to be released into the canvas
I, in my maturity, am content to only look at.
They want to feel the gently sloping ground beneath their feet;
The chill of icy water on the skin's bare edge;
To find the adventure promised in winding river and rocky ledge.
They do not see the string I tie around them before I let them go,
But the radiance in their faces and their innocent shouts of fun,
Their coquettish sidelong glances, dark eyes dancing in the sun
Tell me how safe they feel against its invisible gentle tow.
On the bank, I feel what my father must have felt so many years ago,
When, from the bottom of the hill, he watched my brother and I
Careening wildly toward him on our homemade wooden sled,
His joy mingled with pain as old as philosophy.

Barry W. North

The Dunes Of Liepaja

Here I stand, back in Liepaja
Facing the restless Baltic Sea,
High up on the dunes.
An old and weary traveler now,
With American, German and Latvian
Coins jingling in my pocket,
Not seeing the sparsely clad beauties around me.
I stand alone, high up in the dunes
And let the restless wind strike
My weather-beaten and wrinkled face.
Perhaps I should have come back a younger man?
But there was no freedom then!
Perhaps life should have spared me more?
Would the harsh wind have blown gentler then?

Vilnis O. Atrens

Liar

You said you loved me
you said there was no one else
you told me what I wanted to hear
my whole life revolved around you
suddenly, you changed
you no longer did the things you once did
I felt lonely and deserted
you made cold-hearted remarks
you started treating me different
all I did was sit and think about how it used to be
I thought constantly and soon realized what you were doing
you were only playing with my mind; my whole life began to change
you stayed around, pretending to care; I acted like I didn't know,
playing your game now; one night, I went into a fit of rage
going insane as thoughts of you ran through my mind
remembering the day you told me you loved me
thoughts making me more and more angry
your face, I see, bloody
your lifeless body lying on the floor
you no longer have to lie anymore

Regan Atkins

After It's All Said And Done

After it's all said and done
You shall know everything since my life begun
You shall know the sadness and the times that were fun
Since this moment is upon us and the time has come
To give last respects and bid farewell for but one
After it's all said and done
Should it be known that I sometimes sinned
Or should it be known that I was a Christian till the end
Will I be remembered for my acts of kindness
Or will I be remembered by the ones I took for granted
The accomplishments and goals in life that I did succeed
I hope will be presented as well as my good deeds
The dreams that I chased for thousands of miles
I hope will be the subject of discussion for a long, long while
My material possessions were important to some
And to those I wish love, peace, and happiness by the ton
So to all who knew me, my friends and foes,
I wonder what this event will be like and the time it will come
Only the precious hands of time will tell
After it's all said and done

Louis C. Hollins

Yesterday

I saw you by the seashore
You strengthened my heart
Five years ago you left the world
So suddenly

Yesterday I felt an airy embrace
In the midst of my windswept daydreams
You whispered that I must never give in to despair

I saw you as an angel
Wearing robes of water and white gold
Sandals of autumn leaves

With a touch of your hand
My tears ceased to flow

We walked along the waves
The rays of the sun so soothing
And the mist so inviting

Yesterday you returned
To tell me that you still lived
On in my memory
You spoke of unbreakable bonds
Enduring hope yesterday today always

Sarah J. Young

A Grave With A Name

When a loved one passes away,
You will not have time to play.
It is a very serious matter.
When it comes to someone nearby.
You feel the pain and agony,
And you always wonder why it has happened to you.

A feeling swells within,
A feeling of love and hate.
You find out that you have these feelings,
And you cannot control them,
You begin to feel lonesome,
You call out for help.

An empty hollow shell remains,
Of once a dear close loved one.
All you have left is the memories that soon could fade.
Hold on to the dear memories because,
When that goes what is left behind,
A grave with a name.

Michelle K. Cothern

Turn Away

You got your back up against the wall again.
You wonder how long the game of love brings pain.
You know inside love feels right to you.
But I know he doesn't care for you any day.
Oh, So why don't you just Turn Away. Oh, Turn Away.

You're runnin' 'round in search of his affection.
You feel the need to give your love to him.
But when you need him most he's not around.
He's out havin' fun makin' you pay.
Oh, So why don't you just Turn Away. Oh, Turn Away.

Well, I know you're right for me.
Well, I know I'm right for you.
One day we'll fall in love...
In love, Ooh, In love.

How much more pain can one heart take?
Can't you leave, or has it occurred to you?
Do you find truth in all his wronging? Yeah!
You must believe in the words I say.
Oh, So why don't you just Turn Away. Oh, Turn Away.

Kenneth Roy Berry

"Honey"

To others you're not pretty dear -
Your clothes are out of style -
You'll never be a movie star
But I love you as you are -
You wake up in the morning
With a frown upon your face -
And until you get your coffee dear,
Your voice is a disgrace -
Then your growl will turn to purring
And you're funny like a clown -
Then I know that I'm a lucky one to be
Having you around -
The neighbors hear our arguments,
They think it's quite a shame -
It's a pity they can't tell the truth to us -
It's just a game -
At night when you're beside me
I know you'll never need to roam -
Outside - you can be a tiger -
But a kitten here at home.

Virginia Casciaro

A Gift Of Giving

You're so confused, why is this so? Can life be such a stain?
Your heart is pure, your fate is planned, you have so much to gain.

Your life's been blessed with many things, some love, some pain and sorrow
So why give up the knowledge of the fact there is tomorrow?

With all of your experience in dealing with life's problems
Why try and run and hide from life by staying at the bottom?

It's hard to elevate ourselves when we feel incomplete
But not so hard to stand alone when we get on our feet.

We're fortunate that in our lives we've experienced the good and bad
So why find bitterness and sorrow? Feel fortunate and glad.

Your fear of being lonely is understandable indeed
But why feel lonely, sick at heart, when there is such great need?

A need of someone just like you with compassion truth and faith
Would be a blessing from above if you would just relate.

Relate to those less fortunate, who find it hard to cope
Your vast experience with life itself will give them back new hope.

Your heart will sing of happiness, of bliss, and pure content
For on that day you will thank the Lord for all the joy that he as sent.

Ozzella Moore

M.B.

Your passion for music is beyond belief
Your love for softball is so unique
Your concern for humanity is more than you can speak
You show your love in every word you seek
To write in your music with critique.

When you seek out the world to show its approval
You often look for the wisdom, but find much removal
From the critics who don't understand your talents and gifts
But often try to knock you down with their rifts.

They look only at the outward appearance
Instead of looking deep down to your soul and see your clearance,
You came into the music world as a boy
But as you grow older you bring us all so much joy,
As your life continues you'll be a success
With your music, love and maybe a little stress.

With your passion for sports you bring much happiness to yourself
and many children
And with your dedication to humanity you too bring to life still dreams..

You are the one in a million for the world to see, one in a million for all eternity; You're the one thing we can all believe
You are the one man who does not deceive.

L. Kay Akers

My Dance Teacher

You step into my life, when I tumble into yours.
You warm up my spirit, when I need motivation,
You stretch out your hand, when I need your guidance.
You plie to my level, when I need to understand.
You position me, when I am out of line.
You spot me, when I need to flex or straighten up.
You tap my vulnerability, when I need confidence and strength.
You split my sides with laughter, when I need to releve.
You choreograph gracefully, when I do my ballet.
Your inspiration is the poise, timing and music of my life.
This is no jazz ama jazz;
You teach me all these beautiful things!
May a healthy holiday leap your way,
And a Happy New Year dance into your life.

Sharon Fisher

Jesse

You are my special angel, sent to me from Heaven above.
You've filled my heart with music, and a very special love.

You are my first Great Grandchild...a little red-haired,
brown-eyed boy. The first time that I saw you, I held you

close and felt such joy.

Precious little fingers...
touch my cheek with tenderness.
Dancing eyes and a happy smile...reminds me of how much

I have been blessed.

Tiny little bundle of joy...Mommy strapping you in your
car seat. Away you'd go, on down the hill...
until the next time we would meet.

There came a time when you must leave, and move so far
away. I would not see you again, my Dear, for many and many a day.

Seven long years would come and go, before we would meet again.
Then, one day I saw you standing at my door, and tears of joy
did fall...like rain.

You had now grown into young Manhood...so handsome in your
teens. You looked just like I pictured you for so many years,
in my dreams.

May God go with you now, My Dear, and guide you through
the years.

I know that we'll be proud of you, and now...
there'll be no more tears.

Stella Lakey

Matchbox

Strike a match and smell the sulfur,
We know who started this argument,
As it travels toward the wick.
Why are we always fighting?
Closer and closer until...
It makes contact.
God, you make me so furious! Hotter and hotter,
The candle grows hotter.
And my eyes well up with tears
That suddenly run down my cheeks,
As wax drips down the smooth neck of the candle.
Burning everything they touch:
My hands, the table, my heart, the floor.
I reach into the drawer
And look towards the flame.
I must stop that little flame. I pull out my gun,
For it is no longer little.
With my finger on the trigger
And my mouth near the wick, with one quick breath
I extinguish the candle.

Jennifer Butler

My Love, My Life

You are the sun that dries my tears
You are the light to help me fight my fears
When I'm sick you take care of me
Without you I don't know where I'd be
You give me reason to get up in the morning
You can make me smile without warning
I know everybody thinks I don't deserve you
but I'll show them that my feelings are true
They don't remember I stood strong when you were in pain
Or who sheltered you from the rain.
They'll be reminded because I have one more toy
They'll never understand the reason why
but I know it's because you love me,

Sean M. Kibbe

Desperate Freedom

It never ends...Desperate freedom hide not from
your pursuers.
Give a chance to the wanting, needing, and the changing.
Desperate Freedom
long ago you gave your word upon the knocking of death's hand.
Were you afraid then?
Hear your children cry, hear their voices.
To turn away now would be another promise broken.
Desperate Freedom
chances, you know so well, are not free.
But your children are ready to pay the price.
Death's hand is knocking.
Where are you hiding your face today?
Are you hiding it in tomorrow?
Are you gone to the end of
time?

Angela Rena Jessee

Graduation Day

The moment is upon us,
Your time to shine is here.
But how it really happened,
Is still to me unclear.

For to study was not your forte,
Only recess and a lot of play.
You made it to Graduation,
Despite everything I had to say.

So there you stand so straight and tall,
In your cap and gown.
The image that was once a boy,
Has now become a man.

Today is the first day of the rest of your life,
Decisions yours to make.
Leaving your childhood behind you,
And choosing the road you must take.

And that road will sometimes be rocky,
Life is not always fair.
But stop and think and realize,
There's someone who always cares.

Connie Applegate

You're Everything To Me

You're everything to me
You're the breath of my life
The vision in my soul
The heart that beats deep within me
And you'll always be everything to me

Kids grow up and go their way
So till then, I'll hold you so close to me
I dread the day you go away
For yesterday never again can ever be

And as you grow through all your childish ways
I'll live all that's within you
And perhaps inspire something that's already inside of you

When you hurt I feel pain
When you cry, tears I shed not in vain
In years to come, the sweet memories
Will live on in my heart very melancholy

All the heartaches past I've cast aside
And all frustrations, I've swept to the sea
You're my joy, my life, my pride
'Cause you're everything, yes, everything, you're everything to me

Evelyn Woodward

R.I.P.

How can love be dismissed so easily?
Like a child's worn blanket,
once cherished and indispensable-
now cast aside, forgotten.
Inseparable as the
sun and sky,
we soothed each others fears,
shared secrets,
lived dreams.
Now,
you are no more alive in my life
than loved ones gone
to their eternal rest.
You exist only when I think of you,
then fade
into non-existence,
reduced to hazed memories
and yellowed photographs,
in an album rarely opened

Julie Gramza Hultquist

Catch A Road

The dark moved in
like a flowering sword,

making me a recluse
in the chocolate nights
and cherry moons
of a tiffany iceberg,

Where my heart knew not
the bounds
of a lesser choice.

And we trust
the iron and guts
of man's schemes,

And compromise
makes it all work,

At least until
we whimper
at the feet
of the unknown...
made known...

Bruce K. Westphal

Rainbow Man

The Rainbow Man is well named,
Like Mercury his moods may change.
From indigo to raging red.

The arrow straight and to its mark,
The naked truth lites up the dark.

Some caught within the blinding lite,
Run for the safety of the night.

They hide in darkness that's their way,
Convinced that night is really day.

Others stand and bear their fright,
Clothed in knowing, wearing sight.

Both, colors of the rainbow span,
Is there a rainbow in every man???

Is there a color on that wheel,
That knows just how each one can feel.

Accepts the others, and understands,
The many colors of the Rainbow Man.

Henry J. Meyers

House Of Sorrows

House of Sorrows, House of Tears,
Lock away our Anger. Lock away our fears.
Behind your antique walls of stone
We exorcise our evils for them to atone.

House of Sorrows, House of Hate,
We shut away our demons behind your gate.
All the nightmares we ever knew.
We thrust away and hide in you.

House of Sorrows, House of Rage,
In you our malefactors we have encaged
Behind walls of rock and wire and steel,
So in our homes we might safely feel.

House of Sorrows, House of Shame,
Where humans are given number after name.
Digits hiding sometimes horrendous crimes.
Pitiless men doing pitiless times.

House of Sorrows, House of Night,
Where society's castoffs always alight,
Tonight in uniform I'll walk your runs.
Endless night working with Sorrow's sons.

Jimmie A. Stark

Incredibly Tall

The transatlantic
long distance call echoed
"Please don't call me
I don't know if I'll live
I promise I'll get back
perhaps soon."

Your quivering voice
reached through me
like a mocking ventriloquist

The ugly attire
the one I drape myself with
in your image
got loose and fell
I did not look down

Carefully, I stepped out of it
incredibly tall
I swear I almost touched
the moon
and drank the dark night

Aida Ophelia Saldana

Remember

Do you linger in the morning
Long enough to think and pray;
To seek the Saviour's guidance
And protection through the day?
If the body that He gave you
Is full of strength and health,
Do you ever stop to meditate
Upon your source of wealth?
Do you fill the heart He gave you
With the jewels of His word;
Do you ever speak to others
Of the wonders you have heard?
Do you stop to thank Him daily
For the good that's come your way?
Bless us, Gracious Father,
Let us not forget to pray!

Annie Merle Gray Trent

Fifty Years Plus Five

How to really:
Love,
Cry,
Sacrifice,
Give,
Share,
Be Myself!

Who am I, you say?
A unique human being, gracing
Mother Earth, whose history
is written on the very core
of my being.

My life is:
Sacred,
Holy,
Filled with wonder and excitement
for all that life has and will
offer me!

Praise God, For Life!

Cletus M. S. Watson, Franciscan

Three Golden Nuggets

Three golden nuggets a world to be
LOVE, PEACE and HARMONY.
All distance within if we dare,
a life-time of living we all share.
Within reach and without struggle,
three golden nuggets amid the rubble.

All too soon life passes us by,
before saying "Hello" we have
said "Goodbye."
The packages I send no postage due.
Three golden nuggets I send to you.

Agatha Jordan

Winter Is Coming

The autumn breeze in portent clear
Makes known the winter season's near
And from the cold and frozen north
Angry winds will soon roar forth
To challenge all throughout the land
That none before their wrath can stand
But must seek shelter safe from harm
When winter bares his mighty arm
Then he spreads abroad in sheer delight
An ermine robe so clean and white
The evergreens bow with gentle grace
In their lovely gowns of sparkling lace
The world sleeps under a blanket of white
Until spring ends the long winter night.

Florence Bowers

Space Of Time

Walk through your space of time and listen
Many a season have washed ashore.
Memories fill
each grain of sand
remembering
laughter, sorrow and hope.

Rejoice in past harvests,
but embrace
today's spring,
and watch the caterpillar
for time might not unfold the wings
of a butterfly.

Elvira Tramposch

The Game

Oh, the years are long.
Many have past,
I remember their names.
I haven't forgotten the games.

The smell of a new ball.
The sight of a wooden bat.
It brings back the names,
And my love for the game.

The game is for youth.
Youth I have lost.
I still remember their names.
I haven't forgotten the game.

I pray to God in heaven.
That there will be a batter.
A ball that smells of leather.
And a place where youth doesn't matter.

Edward Lewis Morber

The Family Reunion

Good times and laughter
Merriment in the heart
A family reunion is brewin'
Lord, where do we start?

October first, the decided date
For our family to get together
All our relatives to see...
Mary, looks light as a feather.

Uncle Jed's playin' the fiddle
Aunt Lou's bakin' bread
The kids are tired and cryin'
Evaleen get those young 'uns fed.

Clean the house, sweep the porches
How many beds should we fix?
Tommie, Izora and kids are coming
Hope they get here by six.

Smell the coffee, feel the love
Flowing from our hearts
I can't wait to eat
Mama's fried apple tarts!

Elease Boutcher

Tall Tales, Grandpa And Me

The rains came down in buckets full
My grandpa said 'twas true.
What grandpa said I could believe
For I was only two.

Buckets thumped, crashed and bumped
While sailing through the sky.
Grandpa said lightning flashed
So I could see 'em flying by.

Like as not, what grandpa taught
Grandma couldn't see.
Her child not in tall-tale caught
Like Molly's fibber Mc Gee.

Years passed as others did - found
Tears welling in my eyes.
The rain comes down
In buckets full from countless stormy skies.

Grandma said I'd not remember all
My grandpa said to me.
Long ago — feeling safe, while
Sitting on his knee.

Charles G. Harding

Missy

We had someone we loved so,
Missy Andrews had to go.
Though she left our hearts with grief,
Missy Andrews fell asleep.
If you look up to the sky,
You'll see Missy floating by,
With her wings of solid gold,
And her halo that really glows.
She'll wave to us as she goes by,
Somewhere in the big ole sky.

Gustave Walters

Near The Sea

I love to be near the sea,
my bare feet in the sand.
The ocean waves in rhythm flow,
as the water meets the land.
I love to be near the sea,
watching sea gulls flying without a care.
Wishing I could be flying in the air.
I love to be near the sea,
collecting shells that are hard to find.
A design for a necklace comes to mind.
I love to be near the sea,
watching the sunrise and the sunset,
walking near the sea at night,
under a canopy of stars glistening bright.
When I am near the sea,
confusion no longer remains in me.
Finding answers I could not find before.
Answers I find, when I am near the shore.
Answers I find,
When I am near the shore.

Jo Anne Cowan

Father's Son

I watch my father working;
My children watch him too.
I remember early training
When he taught me what to do.

With strong victorian posture
And rarely a spoken word,
I knew by look and gesture
That he loved without reserve.

Hands gently stroke the soft wood
As he fashions it with care.
I'd embrace him if I could
If he, in fact, were there.

He's been gone a long, long time now;
A man of an earlier time.
Still we see him so clearly - how?
Because those hands of his are mine.

Through form inherited and dear,
His legacy's still here.

John Everett

Echoes

I'm not supposed to be here.
Our fates were all arranged.
Bold hearts were lost forever
Betrayed of life and fame.

And though my war is over
The echoes still remain.
From long ago I hear them
When dead men call my name.

Jim Asher

"My Collections"

Looking back to review my life
My feet had traveled many places
I collected numerous things
Packed away in assorted cases
Some were pretty - some were not
Why I kept them - I forgot
So I sorted out these treasures
Thinking maybe I could measure
What was their worth after all these years
I felt my eyes fill up with tears
The most valuable things I find
Are memories, stored in my mind

Eve Luck

sunglasses

with the sun behind
my head-face,
the b-side of
these sunglasses
shows to me myself
as no mirror could ever do.
the smooth skin of
my cheekbone glistens cracked like
deltas or webs.
the white of my eye
shines, lightening-red
by sleepless night-thoughts of loss.
and in the very,
very,
center of the brown-like leaves' ring
is black, like loneliness

johnny masiulewicz

One Last Time

My soul is in anguish
My heart full of pain
To only touch you once again
To feel the warmth of your embrace
My tears roll down
And strike the earth
Does no one feel my sorrow
Can no one see my pain
I lie awake and cry at night
My dreams are filled with you
My love so far away
O' how my heart needs you near
Feel my sorrow
Hear my tears
Come into my arms
Let me hold you one last time

Carl Hartman

Secrets Of The Heart

Secrets of the heart
never fade.
The dreams never cease,
images never disappear.
Unexpectedly, they surprise you.
Secrets of the heart
plague upon your mind,
upon your soul,
like an endless recurring illness.
Will I ever forget?
Will I ever forgive?
Secrets of the heart
plague my mind,
Are the punishment for my crime?

Daniel Ortiz, Jr.

Warmed Heart

Dedicated to my wife Julie
I was so cold
My heart was chilled

Thinking I was ill
It was loneliness that I felt

You came into my life
And became my friend

The loneliness passing
My heart warming

Now more than friends
It warms more and more

As long as you're with me
I won't ever be cold

Not being cold
I will never feel lonely

Thanks to you and your love
I need never have a chilled heart again

Joseph J. Morelli

Letter to Heaven

Though we never met in life
My little girl
We touched once in death
You lay so still
As peaceful as a dove
I held you ever so frail
Oh the tears I shed
Often I think of you
And what could have been
I missed you so much
A pain, I thought
Would never end
Are you happy at rest
Wings all silver lined
When it is to be my time
I shall see you then
So long for now
My darling Quortney Ann

Jeffrey Nagel

Do Not Usurp My Soul (To All Dependents)

I give you
my love...my support...
my understanding...
but do not usurp
my soul

I willingly
share my thoughts...
my dreams...my life...
but do not usurp
my soul

Release me
let me become
lest I wither
like parched grass
blown in the wind

Dorothy Lauer

Fifty-Six And Holding

Got an old Buick and a dog
named Star. We are trying to
learn how to live on nothing.
I guess we're holding our own.

I bought an old straw hat
and a book, that tells you
how to live on nothing.
So things are looking better
and better. I guess we're
holding our own.

The kids moved out and left
me alone, if it weren't for
Star, I would be alone. But
things are looking up. I am
fifty-six and she's three
months old. We are learning
to live on nothing. I guess
you can say we are holding
our own.

Dullie Josephine Phillips

Easter Is An Orgy

Thinly veiled in morning mist,
narcissus turns to Eucharist.
Pressure on bulb,
pulsating, pulsating.
Bulb responds,
pulsating, pulsating,
then swallows itself,
turns cartwheels inside out,
thrusts itself forward into space:
thin green spear
of spring lily bulb
covered all over
with droplets of dew
drawn by the sun's heat
in vibrating hue.
Spring explodes.

Spring isn't birth. Earth's orgasm!
Pregnant all summer,
Fruit in the fall.

Ellen E. Jones

Only A Dandelion

No thought was given,
No bed was made,
No longing preceded my arrival.
Not a moment was wasted,
Dreaming of me,
No plans for my survival.

No thorns have I,
To adorn my sides,
No stems of mine grow tall
No bloom I bare,
Will fill the air,
With a fragrance desired by all.

No rose am I,
Only a dandelion,
No recipient of prize or ribbon.
Just one of many dandelions,
To which no thought
Was ever given.

Belinda Hall

"Happiness"

Skies are always blue, when I'm with you
No cares or worries do I go through,
I see smiles in all God's creations
Happiness abounds in my life's stations.

Reach out to someone in need,
Of greediness and lust you'll be freed.
Help your neighbor and fellow man
When you see a need, give all you can.

Feel piety for those not blessed
With such unbinding happiness
You don't need riches of the world
For wealth at your feet to unfurl

Count your blessing every day
Let love and happiness be your pay
If you possess real love
You'll own the earth and heaven above.

Dorothy Padgett Willis

Not For Us

Immortal is not for us to be
No - Eternal Life is not for such as we
Yet, the essence of life flows on
Though all we know be gone
We, a part of the essence, become
A piece, in fact, of the total sum

Charles K. Santens

The Poet

A poem is a spirit
Not a "rainbow of color"
Or an ethnic presence
Or a creed.
A poet has a spirit with
Thoughts we feel, not fear.
You read the ideas so
Like your own-or so new
And startling you are aghast!
But you think, evaluate and
Grow some every day,
Thanks to a Poet.

Harriet Thorpe-Olson

Without You

The tide comes and goes,
Like life's highs and lows.
I've been here for days.
My life has been in a haze.
I remember how your car crashed.
As each day has passed.
Your car went up in flames,
And, I'm the one everyone blames.
I still remember your touch.
It always meant so much.
Now that you are no longer here,
I think I will disappear.
I will go to some place,
Where no one knows my face.
You were the one person I could believe.
Now because of your death,
I have to leave.
Now without you,
My life here is through.

Jennifer Cavin

Promises Kept

You promised me days filled with
nothing but blue skies.

You promised me the stars at night
would sparkle like diamonds.

You promised me all the joys of life
and never any sorrow.

You promised me everlasting life
so that we would never part.

You promised me your undying love,
and tears fell from my eyes.

Your promises came from the heart,
and you kept every one.

Frances D. M. DeBarry

A Note To Nykina's Lover

Dear Darvin:
Nykina is a symphonic soul-
A tone poem
Composed of lovely things.
Rhythmic with the dance-
Whirling, and flying on angel wings!

Nykina is sensitivity, and joy-
A sanguinary delight,
That the ballet footlights
With China doll glory
Reveal in shining dazzling brights!

Nykina is the goddess of love
Her velvet voice makes her a dove
Saintly, soft spoken, and serene.
(When up above
Her spirit will fly happily supreme!)

So Darvin, dear
Stay always near.
Her dreams have come true
Because of YOU.

Grace K. Smith

Welcome To My Heart

(To Tabitha)
Out of the darkness of Africa
Away from the jungle,
Where beautiful pristine life
kills pristine life
for survival;

Out from the dark chaos
Of Black killing Black;
Away from the
screams of mothers and children:
Where terror
grows an awful
flower in their eyes;

Out of this dark,
god-less, merciless
inferno comes a Dancing Star —
A Star of ineffable Light:
The shining soul
of Tabitha!

Bishop Basil Tellou

Purple Mists

Purple mists
O'er ridges high...
Such majesty
Of blended sky!
My energies expend anew...
This panoramic world
to view...
This truly uncontested hue...
That calls to me,
At trail's end,
On peaceful mountain peaks,
I now long to see again.

Jo Tambo

"It's In Your Hands!"

You are the Spirit
of America, friends,
so don't let our dream
of freedom ever end!
Let your record show
that you have understood
democracy is
a living brotherhood.
Be like the 'Minute
Men' always ready to
defend and protect
the right by what you do.
For it's in your hands—
the Torch of Liberty.....
Our American
Dream to keep all men free!
O, Freedom Fighters,
honor its promise...and
keep its flame burning
brightly across our land.

Jackie Stinson

Child's View

Swaying in the topmost branches
of an Australian pine,
I ecstatically screamed,
"Simply, wonderfully, mine all mine!"
From this great glorious height
I viewed the earth,
which was followed by pondering
of its magnificent birth.
Still at an age when
I knew little or less,
I returned to the ship on the sea
with me in the crow's nest.

Chad Whalen Swanson

Lost

My mind marvels merely meek
My wandering soul, I do seek

The thump of my heart pounds down deep
Fond memories, I strive to keep

Searching through every season
My fright grows as if a lesion

I must find my soul's keeper now
or my heart will burst, I know not how

I believe one day I will know
Where my soul is and I will go

For now I must hold down my pain
So my heart will beat without restraint

Amanda Church

This Quarry

This quarry ... place of mining stone,
Of carving solid earth ...
Began as but a scratch alone
Giving pebbles birth.

Chip on chip throughout long years...
Wide to deep has come
This yawn ... a chasm now appears,
Not stone, nor gravel from.

From here to yon ... near and far ...
Workings great and small;
Stones rearranged ... now useful ... are
Majestic, strong, and tall.

This sprawled-about complexity
So empty 'neath the skies ...
Cast forth that utility
This absence now belies.

Prizes, pieces ... great or slight ...
Puzzle segments these,
As the yieldings from a life ...
Which another sees.

Bud Lipscomb

Remembering

Though years may dim traces
Of distant moments,
I shall still remember
Autumn walks
And a certain smile
Illuminating winter shadows
With promises
Of yet another Spring

Henry Vaugle

October

October - is the tenth month
of each year
When the change of weather
comes
As fall is here with crisp
cool weather that fills
The air and the bright blue
sky and
With the tree's nice bright
colors of the fall season
And also the golden field's
blooming with bumper crops
To harvest before the winter
season comes with the
Abundant crops to feed
the world

Irene M. Larson

Heaven In The Midst

Of starry nights that curtail a view,
Of mountains towering in solitude.
Of swans awakening at the break of light,
Of winds that carry our kites in flight.
Of trees that dance with
the slightest breeze; creating
music within their leaves.
Of flowers that produce a
hue to skies quilted in baby blue.
With all this beauty, I can only find
an enchanted heart and peace of mind.

Donna D. Oswald

We See

There is such merts
of listening,
that happens
in my thoughts
of yesterdays:

Hearing from the deepest
beyond,
not in human realities
with the negatives of
the eye.

But in the hidden man,
with thousand eyes,
that is promised, and
empowered
in the children of obedience.

To that … we listen, we see.

Betty Iverson

'Me And My Place'

I have a place,
of my very own,
though no ones around,
I'm never alone.
Someone is always there,
throughout it all,
she'll always care.
Perfect in every way,
my secret place,
from which I'll never stray.
Best of friends we'll always be,
she'll never leave,
for she is me.
Sitting in a place,
no one can find,
for it's hidden well,
deep within my mind.

Angela Jackson

That Burden Isn't Yours

Are there times you feel the pang
Of pressures mounting high?
You think you must do something
To replace life's drained supply.
The more you fuss the tighter fits
That noose around your neck.
Each day goes by and self-control
Is lost on life's steep trek.

Anxiety compels you
Take action right away!
Found in hasty efforts
Are more reasons for dismay.
"Let me try to fix things!"
You cry in desperate tones.
But deeper sink your footsteps
As your statements turn to groans.

Perhaps so many troubles
Are in essence opening doors
To teach you active waiting
'Cause that burden isn't yours.

Crystal F. Lofton

She Called Me Back

We sat on the lawn
Of the home she was in;
Her folks wouldn't free her:
And it seemed such a sin.

The insane asylum
Seemed no place for her:
She talked with good logic,
And showed much concern.

As I was leaving,
"Good luck," I said,
She called me back
And told me instead.

It's not luck, but success,
And you work for that:
You put yourself in it —
And you get something back.

Then on I went —
With the thought of my friend;
I will cherish her memory
And work to the end.

Beulah G. Braithwaite

Untitled

A girl sits at her window
on a cold, lonely night,
staring at the city lights,
wishing on their brightness.
She keeps her dreams in a box,
and lets them out one by one.
As they slip into her room,
they fill her head and heart,
the visions of happiness
and delight.
Her dreams may not be big,
but they're her own.
And she hopes one day
she can let them out into the world.
There she can work, toil, and plan
to make them all come true.
And when they do,
she'll sit at her window
staring at the city lights,
remembering how far she's come.

Anjanette M. Prentice

Night Flight

A wise old owl flew in front of me,
On a crisp, and clear dark night.
The moon was big, round and full,
It cast an illuminous light.
I've heard tell, he only flies at night,
And that owls grow old and wise.
Go back to roost when it's getting light,
Have huge, big round eyes.
I've seen him once or twice before,
In the stillness of a night.
He swooped down from the hickory tree,
What a wondrous sight!
With his wings so broad and very wide,
He cast a shadow on the ground and,
When he flew back to the hickory tree,
He didn't make a sound.
He never bothers anyone,
He's an astounding sight to see.
This owl who flies about at night,
Likes the right of living free!

Helen Gibbons

"Sweet Endearments"

Tonight the sky is deep blue
On every star I wish for you
I hear the murmur of the breeze
And gaze upon the restless trees
I see each vision loud and clear
It seems to bring my love near
Yet he is so far away
Loneliness echoes all through the day
When night falls I silently pray
That from your lips you will not say
This is but an interlude
Mine is the heart to brood
Then my dear I dare not chance
To think that you would end romance
With mindless words uttered by fools
Who could not reach loves depth of pools
Our love was destined to flourish
Thoughts of your sweet endearments, I
cherish.

Dorothy Gallagher

I See You

I see you as a Bird
On High…

I see you as a person
upon whom I can rely…

I see you as a flower
blooming in Spring…

I see you as my everything
I see you as Sweet Music
everywhere…

I see you as my Dashing
debonair…

I see you as my Summer
winter and fall.

I see you as my love
most of all…

Bernadine E. Benjamin

Water Wonders

Opalescent dewdrops glistening
on tiny petals pure,
mirror beauty in the morning light
never losing its allure.

Old Dog Zeke is scratching fleas,
not knowing that the pain
can disappear most suddenly
by walking in the rain.

Mother on the childbirth bed
feels a miracle so near.
As the water breaks within her,
a new body does appear.

Opalescent droplets glistening
on a tiny baby's brow,
as the church's oldest ritual
brings God's spirit to her now.

EMBRACE THE VISIONARY BEAUTY.
BEHOLD RELIEF FROM PAIN.
GAZE ON NATURAL BODY
FUNCTIONING AND SYMBOLIC
SPIRITUAL GAIN.

Carol M. Gourlay

Heaven's For Angels

Heaven's for angels, she told me
one day.
Up in the sky, is a land where
they play.
And each of us here has our own
special one.
Who watches over us until day
is done.
Now, my angel and I have seen
many years.
He's watched my smiles, he's watched
my tears
And when I am past and my body
is laid
He'll carry me off to the place that
I've prayed
But now while I'm here and
happily so
My angel he watches wherever
I go.

Catherine R. Kozma

The Wizard

"I've grown old", the wizard said.
"Only grey hairs upon my head,
I can't recall the recent past,
But see the future in my glass.

I see men with swords shooting fire,
Men fly over the eagle's aerie.
I see ships that sail beneath the sea,
Carriages without a whippletree.

I see rooms that move up and down,
And stairways move all over town.
Doors that open by no hand,
And wire fences enclose the land.

I hear music, but no one's there.
Boxes with pictures are everywhere.
Men play a game with ball and stick,
To post a missive, a stamp you lick.

When they lay me to my last rest,
With my crystal ball upon my chest,
May I be allowed to return and see,
All things that have been shown to me".

Corey Morlock

A Man Of Substance

Why have a beating heart
Or blood in my veins
If I wasn't meant to live?
Why have dreams, desire,
Or love
If I wasn't meant to give?
Why are there tomorrows
If they have nothing more
To bring?
Why have a voice
If I wasn't meant to sing?
Why should I be timid
When my love is bold?
Why do I have arms
If you weren't meant to hold?
Why should I question
When the answer isn't clear?
Because a man without substance
Will only disappear.

Hal Wright

Did You Stop To Watch The Sun Set?

Did you stop to watch the sun set?
Or did you let it pass you by?
For night has fallen so quickly
Did you stop to wonder why?
Because here, now, in the darkness,
We cannot see eye to eye.
I wish you had been there when the sun set,
To see the tears I cried.

Jonathan Osborne

"Poetry"

Am I not from within your heart,
Or do I just come from your mind?
Does a feeling or idea,
Give you an opinion?
Must I be taught to be loved,
Can I not come from within?
It does not matter if I rhyme,
Or if I am set by rules;
What does matter, is how you see me,
And what you feel when first we meet.

I look at all the struggles that you have,
In reading and writing me;
And wish that I could tell you how to say,
With punctuation for pauses -
As rests do in music;
Or by words such as "lively,"
"Moderate" or "sad" to let you know-
As you know in music,
How to say me like you do with songs.
Then and only then will you really know
me.

Elsa L. Chase

Every Day

Can you reach out and touch it
Or is it no longer there
Can you feel it inside you
Or has it wasted in the air
Has your life just passed you by
And are your memories beginning to fade
Are you looking at the future
For the memories still to be made
Is your life as carefree and simple
As you have made it out to be
Are you as happy now
As you were with me
Has everything been forgotten
Or is a glimmer of love still there
Have you given up the life
And memories that we are meant to share
Can all the hatred be forgotten
And the anger fade away
Are you able to love me still,
Each and every day?

Cindy Lou Wilkinson

Untitled

One hears dishes break,
or waves breaking against the shore
But no one hears a heart that's
breaking
I wish that some one would
listen very quietly
And just perhaps - perhaps beneath
this smiling face
One could hear a small sound
It is my breaking heart

Eleanor Coen

A Question Of Love

Was it just a game of fate?
Or is it still quite worth the wait?

Was it just a time of tease,
Or should my mind still be at ease?

Was it just one of those things,
That often summer romance brings?

Was is something sweet, but yet,
Something I should now forget?

Was it like a prize I'd won,
The game now through, the fun now done?

Was it really all that fine,
Or memories, a trick of the mind?

Was love really in the air,
Or simply "us" together there?

Was it as to him as me,
Or was it sexual casualty?

Was it something good or bad?
On thoughts, should I be glad or sad?

Was it romance I recall,
Or did we really love at all?

Amanda K. C.

Fish Tales

Scorching heat
or pouring rain,
my weary hands
endure the pain.
"Give him some line."
"Let him play,"
just don't let him
get away.
Weary arms,
reeling motion
rocking with the
rolling ocean.
When you feel
your arms are broke,
you finally get him
to the boat.
"The thrill of Victory."
"The agony of Defeat."
The bigger the Bass,
the better we eat.

Diane M. Ammann

The Apple

Edison did not invent!
Our lives are all a lie.
The plundering of what would sell
and what would free deny.

'Twas Tesla and high frequency
did Morgan grumble from the Glade...
At least Westinghouse was more polite
while fortunes for him made.

Since History is so far wrong,
let poetry explain.
The universe is chained to us,
not we who are in chains!

Ellen Sherman

Our Lord Comes

Hark! Listen to the trumpet sound!
Our Lord has come up in the air.
The dead He'll raise first from the ground.
Then we'll all together meet Him there.

Let not this day
Come unaware;
Search the Word
Yourselves prepare
To meet the Lord
Up in the air.
The time is short;
The day is near;
The Lord will shout
We disappear.

The Bridegroom calls His bride away
For the marriage of the Lamb is come.
We're robed in bridal white array
Washed clean from sin by God's own Son.
He loved us so; He set us free;
Now we shall reign with Him eternally.

Evangeline Bushacker

The Barber Pole

Quietly turning in its place
Outside the barber's door
Watched by copper Indian chief
In front of the Cigar store.

Cobble stone brick to pavement
Underfoot has changed
Soft lights above are now the
glare of neon well arranged

Ice man and his horse replaced
City buses fume and sigh
Bustles are Bermuda shorts
News boys no longer cry "wuxtra!"

Hitching posts and trolley tracks
No longer mar the streets
Traffic signals blink instead
As the policeman walks his beat

The barber pole no longer turns
Its colors don't go round
Big Indian Chief's departed
To his Happy Hunting ground

Agnes M. Phillips

True Sharing

Go read to the blind,
See the glow on their face
Don't rush away
It takes only a little of your time.

Take a handicap person for a drive.
Go down around the river,
Where he hears the ripple of the tide
It only takes a little of your time.

Take nourishing food to a shut-in,
Don't leave it and rush away
Their look of gratitude
will be rewarding,
It only takes a little of your time.
God said "What you do for the least
of these, my brother, you have
done it unto me"

Georgia Steenrod

Speak To Thee Their Heart

Speak, you to thee. Let their heart
Overflow with joy. Make me know of
Your many acquaintances. O how many
times has love come your way, and
you let love rule?
You have experimented with the
weak just to see how many hearts you
could break. You, you who can never
mend even a clay hole.
How, oh how, I do wish you could
meet your match...so the two of you
could exchange heart rizmatic blows
and go down fighting. And each one
of you count the other one out.
I could part my lips to speak kindly
of you once more. And just maybe
secretly you could become someone
special to me again. Speak to thee their
heart, love was what you were created
for; let no one rob you of your secret
experiences.

Emmer J. Stevenson

Disappointment

Coursing the body and
penetrating the soul,
It attacks with a vengeance,
Turning warm to cold.

There's an emptiness
one can't escape,
A betrayal of sorts,
A psychological rape.

It's tragic to discover
the twisted lies,
Faith slips away,
Trust slowly dies.

The anguish may last
weeks or years,
No matter the length,
Its result may be tears.

Perhaps the years will
lessen this pain,
Let time pass by quickly,
So I may feel good again.

Gary D. Crotty

Ode To My Cat

Cat and the fiddle jumped over the moon.
Performing this outing was much too soon.
Strings on the fiddle went awry
Cat in a frenzy started to cry.
Cat and the fiddle a duet galore
Lambs in the pasture bleated, "please
no more."

Edna I. Salzman

K. C.

Her love is soft,
Magic to touch.
Her kiss so gentle,
Never too much.
Her eyes so pure,
Candles cannot touch.

J. T. Phantom

Poetry Prayer

Words of wisdom, words of love
Phrases, teaching, all from above

No one say it's all his own
For know it's but to us; a loan

Words of song, words of praises
Asking, thanking, for all our graces

Learn, remember and pass it on
Share with all, for soon is dawn

The day our Father said will come
Good deeds, good thoughts in total sum

Salvation; at the end of life;
To end man's constant strife

David F. Martin

Butter Yellow

The butter yellow rose
Placed in a soft blue vase.
Yes that butter yellow rose,
I could see my mother's face.

She loved the yellow rose
Much more than white or red.
I could not understand,
She fell down stairs, hit her head.

She never did recover
From that sharp blow that day.
I just could not understand,
I loved her so, my mother.

But every time I see a yellow rose
I think of her loving ways.
I know she went home to God.
She loved him all her days.

Bobbie Tait

Fantasy Wish

A little one with flaxen hair,
Playing with the cannon there,
Looks so like you
My heart skips a beat or two...
His smile and clear blue eyes,
Like yours, flash a wise
Answer at my word,
And I'm sure I've heard
Your voice. He is you,
Lithe and quick; a few
Small freckles across his nose.
He is so sure he does
Just what he wants to do...
And as I watch I think too
What I should not, but do,
How I wish to be with you.

Helen M. Shurley

Freedom

Freedom — contagious feeling,
Sensations deep within,
Stretching, growing, spreading,
Overflows its brim.

Freedom — invisible touchstone,
Anticipation of the mind,
Hoping, believing, trusting,
Releasing chains that bind.

Carolyn Spencer

Sister, Sister!

Sister, sister, what do I see?
Please come, go and run with me!
Through the fields we will go
Until the sun no longer shows!

Sister, sister, what do I see?
Someone at the door for you,
No time for fields, what will I do???

Sister, sister, what do I see?
A baby or two on your knee!
Not much time for talk and tea,
They keep you busy, and also me!

Sister, sister, where must you go?
To a country far from here.
But we can visit twice a year.

Sister, sister, what do I see?
Can you now come run with me?
Through the fields we will go,
Until the sun no longer shows....

Donna A. Walker

"Love Thy Neighbor"

American's natives
Proud people all
Attacked by invaders
They stood their ground tall

Onward "Christian" Soldiers
Push them to the wall
They received you as friends
You must make them fall

They must pay for their sins
The heathens' indecorous gall
How dare they show more love
Than the "proclaimers of the Lord's call"

Dirk A. Myers

Gift Divine

I maneuver the curves of life
pushed where head winds blow
Swimming tidal currents
I'm swept beyond my goal
I struggle a rocky summit
often stagger on the edge
then love the Gift Divine
rescues my wavering pledge
The spirit spins a new cloak
repairs a tattered soul
Renewed I sing His praises
My mantle shines spun-gold

When Love amplifies in me
I'm exalted magnified and free

Flori Ignoffo

Untitled

God made our creation
Out of space and time
Then he put us in it
For the theme and rhyme.
Filled us full of reason,
Logic and decision.
Locked us in it tightly.
Left us there to season.
Then he chuckled gently
For he knew that we
Would search diligently
For his key.

Amy Berney

In His Image

God Almighty, in His infinite wisdom
Put a little of Himself
In each of us, His creations.
He fashioned bodies for us
To house the wonderful Spirits we are.
We were created from His love.
What His purpose is we don't know, but
We are here for a purpose.
We may go through many lifetimes,
Many millenniums before
We know why we are here,
What we must do,
Before we leave this earthly plane and
Return for the last time
To the God who made us,
When we've gone full circle,
Back into the Oneness of God.

Dot Bristol

Untitled

Stage a hunger of a poet,
Put his feelings on a mask,
Ask the audience to wear it,
As the uniform applauds.

Now prepare its meal of wisdom,
Put your logic on his plate,
Find the rhyme to soothe your healing,
From the grief he can't relate.

Dave Birg

A Day Of Dread

When serpents threaten all you own,
  rage flashes through your mind.
Crimson blaze and blackened tunnels;
  your jaw begins to grind.
Protection of those dear to you,
  that's all worth striving for.
But don't join the ranks, become a snake;
  don't make yourself the whore.
There are ways to stay above it all;
  your soul they can't defile.
Raise your head, turn your back,
  don't let your ego rile.
The rules, they follow a outrance,
  are dealt without a care.
Truth and light are in your heart;
  it is they who should beware.
The dove, He carries you away,
  safe, secure, and pleased.
A day of dread will come for them,
  He'll bring them to their knees.

Candace Morimoto

Browsing Through Time

Why do we browse through time
Remembering yesteryear?
When we cannot remember yesterday
And the things that were so near.
The tunnels of our memories
To the past they always flow.
To linger on the things we
Cherished oh! So long ago.
Because, as we browse through time
To the twilight of our years
The things that are important
We hold onto and endear.

Betty Jo Scheffer

Dawn

The first appearance of light.
Rays of crimson and gold
pierce the cold darkness,
chasing the night.
With the larks' familiar melody,
Cricket and frog sounds are gone.
Drops of dew race down the window,
In their daily swan song.
Beyond the dew drops
a spider finishes the weave,
on his new spun home
'tween the downspout and eave.
Hummingbirds hover
round honeysuckle vines,
Young sparrows take flight
for the very first time.
As I take it all in,
this conclusion I've drawn:
days are so lucky,
to each have their own Dawn!

Craig A. Van Muyden

Autumn's Approach

Amber hues and vibrant shades
replace the foliage green.
Little creatures collect their stash
for Winter's slumbered dream.

Fresh, cool air and morning fog
blanket o'er the land.
The Equinox of early dusk
is very close at hand.

Halloween and Libra sun
doth stir creative thought.
And universal spirits fly
in hearts where love is sought.

Goldenrod and pumpkin orange
adorn the Autumn hearth,
Orchards bend with ripened fruit
to tantalize the earth

The Harvest Moon does not reek death
but generates new life.
If Fall did not supply the seed
then Spring could not arrive.

Carina L. Florsek

Parting Ways

Ripples on the sea
Rolling rhythmically round
Dance
Like your laughter
Twinkling with light, reflecting
Into my eyes,
Into my soul,
Lifting my spirit.

Your words stir me
Weaving
Wisdom's texture
Into my life.

I am the water over which you shone,
Over which you played your light.
And now I shall roll back out to sea;
Your light and my water parting ways.

And your light will change
As my water too . . .
Neither quite the same
Having once been touched by the other.

Alison Taylor

When Will You Take Time For Me?

I hurried around this morning
Rushing to plan my day
Clean the house—walk the dog—well,
I'll wait till later to pray

Need to do the laundry and some mending
Write some letters—make your tea
Then I heard a gentle voice softly say
"When are you going to take time for me?"

I thought to myself-"Jesus, just a minute
I have this one more thing to do
I'm so busy with my busy life
I can hardly find time for you".

I really need to wash the car
And my tennis lesson is at three
Again I heard a patient voice say
"When will you take time for me?"

Oh, Jesus, Jesus, Lamb of God
You've always had time for me—
Forgive me, and believe that henceforth
I'll always have time for thee.

June Jenner Deckard

The Wise Butterfly

"Who made the pretty flowers?"
Said the butterfly,
As he spread his dainty wings
Floating through the sky.

"There must be a Creator—
Who made the heaven and earth.
How could such lovely objects
Just happen there by choice."

So he lit upon the smaller tree
To observe the world from there,
And watch the other creatures—
Someone made and put them there.

The morning sun was breaking
Sending colors everywhere.
The birds in the tree tops singing,
Their songs echoing in the air.

"Now how could all this beauty—
The lovely things I see,
Come without a creator—
No, "GOD" above made all these."

Evelyn Anderson

End Infinite

The light—
Seen once in your eyes
by me, and for me,
now is extinguished.

Gone is the love.
Forever bruised—-
this heart, tarnished,
holds no chance for mending.

Mountains unconquered—
for my eyes you wanted this.
But without the love,
no place with you will I go.

The light—
I, too, leave it unburning.
No desire, no need,
for the flame once torched together.

Jane Irene Kelly

In The Eyes Of The Old

The eyes of the old look upon me -
Searching for a glimpse of themselves -
A living example of their work -
dreams -
illusions -

The vibrance they once felt
is absorbed by another -
and so too will that being give the
gift of life -
with all its pain
enthusiasm -
A never ending cycle -
A whirlpool of ideas -
of souls -
flowing into one point -

The beginning -
The end -
The light -
The darkness -
GOD.

Julie M. Skiendziel

Dreams

You lay there at night
Seeing hopes and fears
Remembering a bad day
And those times you had so many tears

Some say they're foolish
Not many know what they mean
You can relive a moment or one to come
And some say it's just a dream

But some people know
That they can be a key
A key that opens the door
That you can start to feel free

Christina Siebeneicher

Jewels

Rubies and diamonds,
Silver and gold,
Are very precious,
I've been told.

But, give me, the jewels of:
Teardrops of a friend -
Lilting laughter of an infant,
Tickled under the chin,
Gray or white hair,
Crowning the head of the aged -
The flight of a bird,
As it is uncaged,
The glow in the eyes,
Of one so dearly beloved -

All these are some of the "jewels" given,
From my Father above!

Betty L. Delaney

Thanksgiving

Saddam Hussein,
Saddam Hussein,
Why are you standing
out in the rain,
Looking in on our
Thanksgiving feast?
You don't bother us in the least.

Alice Lincoln Woodruff

Poetry's Child

Poetry's child
Sings ... dances ... clowns around,
when glad
Never wears a frown;
Happy ... grins all day long
Wearing sunshine like a crown.

Poetry's child
Wavers ... stumbles ... feels forlorn,
So saddened
The heart feels torn;
Cries ... mourns that, that is lost
cloaked in darkness full of thorn.

Poetry's child
Rises ... falls ... tries anew,
Begins afresh
Life to renew;
Smiles ... warmed by love again
Robed in memories fond review.

Joan Crawford Hammond

Memories Of Home

An empty old farm house,
sits alone on a hill.
Its windows are broken,
it's lonely and still.

It brings back the seasons,
each passing in time.
The sounds of the farm yard,
are all memories of mine.

I remember the good food,
my mom used to cook.
Fresh from the garden,
and right from her book.

I remember my father,
who could fix anything.
The machinery for welding
our neighbors would bring.

The visions of dreams,
have faded away.
Like nature's reclaiming
at the end of our day.

Judy Quinn

Where's Mother?

Where's Mother?
Sitting quietly in her chair.
Eyes once alert,
now dull and vacant.
Hands once busy,
lie folded in her lap.
A mind that once composed poetry,
has forgotten the words.
A voice once full of song,
no longer speaks at all.
She walks with help.
She eats when fed.
She sleeps when put to bed.
Sometimes she smiles.
Sometimes she's fearful.
Alzheimer's
"A cure" is what I pray.
For it sneaked in,
and slowly stole my mother away.

Della Jean Shipley

"My Old Home"

High up on a hill top
so lonely and old.
Stands the old homestead
with doorway so cold.
The cherry old fire place
is no longer a glow.
Its rooms are all dreary
in the heat and the cold.
The bright flowers have withered
since we moved away.
The birds are all lonely,
no longer will they stay.
I'm so lonely as I pass that way,
with no one to greet me at end of day.
Memories of days of things before,
when we were so happy in days of yore.

Elsie L. Elder

Bouquet

Sweet John William
So pink, soft and new
Little eyes flickering
Skin as kissed by dew
I knew you'd be
resting after your journey
into life, you see,
but I never expected
I too would be
so tired
after catapulting into a new generation

Effie Dell was grandma's name
and with her eyes delphinium blue
Larkspur tall and stately
she resembled the flowers she grew.

Now I am the grandmother.
What kind will I be?
Sweet John William, what do you see?
Perhaps strong and true
a fading dianthus related to you

Dianne L. Linn

Before Requiem

The child,
so still in the circle
of containment,
pain no longer lingering
in the chasm of her hunger,...
she cries not from
the wells of her eyes,
small brown fingers releasing
air to butterflies.

Tiny flowers struggle
free of her shadow,
as love enters
the diminishing circle,
gathering her close
in repose,...

Together, in one,
they feast at the breast
of Mother Earth.

Jeannette Stanton Miller

It's Raining Tonight

On of those slow summer's
soaking kind of rainy nights,
There's some thunder and lightning
but that does not bother me.
I'm kicked-back, sipping fresh
brewed Hazelnut coffee, and
thinking of you.

Rain dances upon the blue and white
beach umbrella I sit under.
This night the sound of the surf
fills my being.

I wonder where you are tonight?
And if you are alone,
or has someone else
taken my place?
But remember I'm saving
the place next to me
for you only.

Gary Carleen Richardson

Corn Fields

Velvety, golden
Soft and swaying
Fields of amber corn

Graceful, dancing,
Tilt their heads
To greet approaching morn

Gae Plambeck

A Song On The Winds Of Time

Gently, gently, do the breezes blow
Softly down the years
Whispering of love and life
Sighing with joy and tears.

A moment here, a moment there
Crystals of the fine
Forever hanging in the air
Rapture caught in time.

Silkenly they wrap around
Holding each secure
Swaying to a hidden tide
Cleansing each on pure.

Every life is in the balance
In spite of all our fears.
Gently, gently, do the breezes blow
Softly down the years.

Brenda A. Grant

Tearfelt Smile

As tearfelt eyes devise a smile
So gentle a moment held in denial
A whisper of skin begins to dry
And softly again the wind will die

The distant caress, at best to give
Rest in thought to forever live
A shivering mood soothes the mind
To find the will can thrill the time

Broad, the view is through a tear
Truth so bold to hold no fear
Passes in time a moodless while
To try to hide the tearfelt smile

J. Andrew Orr

I'd Really Like To See You!

Wanted to send you this greeting.
Something appropriate to say,
How very nice it was to meet you
Almost a year ago today!

And although I can't see you
Not nearly as much as I'd like,
You're always on my mind;
Each day and Every night!

I hope it's not too much
for me to convey right now,
But I'd really like to see you
Someday, Somewhere, Somehow!

This is just a little something
to let you know thus far,
How very, very special
I Really think you are!

Cassandra L. Johnson

Love Never Found Her

The path of love, passing time,
Somewhere she got left behind.
Around a corner, through the thorns,
Her heart beaten, tattered, torn.

Many others finding the end,
She continues around the bend.
Birds fly high, show her the way,
Continue on until the next day.

She fell asleep along the path;
No one ever missed her laugh.
Around her grave, flowers grown,
Just one more who walked alone.

Jennifer L. Peterman

Bittersweet

When you don't have
Somewhere to belong,
Nowhere is as good
A place as any to be.

It's when you finally realize
Where you need to be,
And find you're not there -
You're here

That it hurts so much.

Debbie Arnett

Untitled

Well,
Now that everything is
Straightened out;
And, for me,
There is no doubt.
Every guy I like
Has feelings for me,
But only friends.
Oh, I'm sorry
As they trip over my heart
Then kick it aside.
When will I find someone?
Now, I realize
That I'm not the first,
But, pray tell,
Why the hell
Did you have to kiss me?

Bekah Keesler

Undecided

My teacher said to me, one day,
"Son, what is your ambition?
Have you decided what you'll be,
Have you a goal or mission?"

It put my brain into a whirl,
For I was young, you see,
And all those years 'till I grew up
Seemed an eternity!

I gulped and stammered for awhile
And wondered what to say.
I hadn't planned my future yet
But just lived for today!

And so I smiled at her, and said
"I haven't yet decided,
I'm happy being just a boy."
(No use to try and hide it).

I'm in no hurry to grow up
And turn into a man,
So I'll be happy as I grow
And be the best I can.

Geraldine Lininger

The Willow

I sat for days beneath the willow
speaking in tongues
through leaf roll and swirl,
I did not eat.
I breathed tree dust,
swallowed the sap from my lips,
dug my feet down
and drank from its roots.
The sun lifted
and spoke
a few words
over my face and shoulders
with a heavy, India red
which all night cooled
and slipped into my skin,
comfortable, resting,
along the length of my pulse.

Dana M. DeSensi

Guardians

Guardian Angels
Standing near,
Soothe my heart
And calm my fear.

Lead me towards
The light of day.
Remove the walls
That block my way.

Preserve my strength
So I may fight
The up-hill battle
To a better life.

You've done your job
And done it well.
It was very seldom
That I fell.

But when I did
You were near
To soothe my heart
And calm my fear.

Carol Kleindorfer

Night Wind

Wind was high, moon and
stars out, long dark night
ghostly figure riding about,

Gallop, gallop he did go burning
fire, shoveling coal,

Wailing, wailing against raw
wind trying to repent of his
sin,

Spiritless he rode a crooked trail
twisting turning straight to hell,

Fire! Fire! He did cry, Why? Oh why?
Did I die, without repenting,

Why? Oh Why?

Dorothy Snow

Grandma's Smile

"A mountain of snow covered her head.
Stars shown from her eyes.
Skin so soft. Could it have been..
rose petals in disguise?

Crow's-feet imprinted there. 'Tis true.
But, they were left from smiles.
Her ears were caverns to wisdom
listening to all life's trials.

Her warmth, her love, her lilting laugh
with nature all compare.
Hands, so versatile, remembered best
folded at last as in prayer.

When I retell her tales of old
or smell a fresh baked pie
the ache of loss returns within.
I steal a secret cry.

But. As the sunshine warms the earth
a special ray seeks to atone.
That's Grandma's smile. It seems to say,
"I'm at rest in my heavenly home."

Jane Hale

Just A Dream

Lying on my bed
Starting to fall asleep
feeling kind of weary
My thoughts become deep

Opening my eyes
But only in my dream
Things are much brighter
are they really what they seem?

I'm lying beside you
and you're holding me tight
As you touch my body
you make me feel so right

Kissing me on the lips
I feel the warmth of your love
It's a feeling so special
That I know it's a gift from above.

I open my eyes
and know it wasn't real
no one here to hold me
and no love for me to feel.

Heather Faust

The Country Store Of Yesterday

Away out in the country
Stood a tiny little store,
The man who worked inside,
Ran the store, and much, much more.
Besides all the goods you needed,
If you felt sad and depressed,
He would listen to your troubles,
You went away feeling blessed.
If you needed any money,
As so many people did,
He would reach into his flour sack
Get your money, yes, he did.
You didn't have to sign a note,
Just your word, and your hand,
No one ever forgot to repay him,
That gave him a feeling, oh so grand.
He kept the flour sack by his chair,
Where his Bible he often read
Spent much leisure time in praying
Could sleep in peace, when he went to bed.

Dorothy E. Sheets

Autumn

What other time of year can bring
Such color to the eye
As red, and orange, and shimmery golds
Fall from the brilliant sky?

Autumn fruits are everywhere
How could we do without them?
Pumpkins, apples, pears, and squash
We savor every item.

The time has come for grand state fairs
And harvesting big pumpkins
For jack-o-lanterns, pies, and cakes
And apple-pumpkin muffins.

Halloween keeps up the fun
We all expect to have
With scary costumes, funny masks,
And treats we sometimes "halve."

Our last big fling is in November
When all just love Thanksgiving
The food, the football, all a joy
Autumn's made for living.

Dianna L. Bishop

A Tale Of Love In Capitalistic America

The splendor of a summer's cotton candy,
Sugar air and stickiness-

Ball park type red #4 with blue penzoate,
(Inject with air till frothy)
dripping from my lips
In a Nutrasweet (TM) world-

Why do faceless vendors sell you
For only $1.50?

This is how I love thee, dearest,
For I really love thee not at all.

Christopher Bradley

One And The Same

Hearts afire, brilliant they glow.
Sunkissed mountains, covered with snow.
Is there doubt that we exist?
A part of glory, the top of the list!

The younger ones we dare behold,
Fantasizing the memories-of days untold.

We speak with many voices,
Though we're all the same.
The brilliance of laughter,
The enemy known as pain.

Showers of enigma cross the boundaries,
Where no one is bound, uncovering the
Treasures there to be found.

Star dust to earth dust-sky to ground,
Lie many secrets - not yet with sound.

As passions doorway crumbles and falls,
The truth uncovered, as HEAVEN calls.
THERE! Only one voice remains.
Where we find we're all—ONE AND THE SAME!

Jean Mehan Reynolds

A World Of Thoughts

A world of thoughts,
Surrounds my head.
A world of thoughts,
Dreamt in bed.

A world of thoughts,
Sits near to me.
A world of thoughts,
Will let me be.

A world of thoughts,
Provokes the sky.
A world of thoughts,
Will make me fly.

My world of thoughts,
Is one with me.
It helps me to be,
All the eye can see.

Create a dream
To all you want it to seem
And let your world of thoughts
Surround you.

Cynthia L. Murphy

Autumn Morn

In valley by lake —
swelling stillness:
Cicadae!

Round lake —
pulsating forest:
Cicadae!

Brightness
in lakes darkness —
Rippling! Cicadae!

Ah, breezes —
soothing, swelling,
with sound! Cicadae!

Cloudiness of morn —
lost
in sweeping swells! Cicadae!

Edward Nathan Stenbar

Sorrows

When someone goes away
tears flow down my face
to mark that dreadful day
and have no one to fill her place.

Angel Hallowell

A Recipe To Turn Hate Into Agape Love

Precious Heavenly Father,
Thank you, for your loving son
Who did walk this Planet Earth
To give your light to each one!

Oh, Precious Lord, Your images
Are in trouble far ashore,
And may lose Priceless Freedom,
Our dear Soldiers fought and died for!

Dear Heavenly Father,
How You loved Your only Child,
But His destiny was to
Save the souls of the world gone wild!!

I pray for the Universe,
And hope people shall not hate.
Be alerted; turn from sin,
Run to Jesus, lest it's too late!!!

Dorothy M. Ralston

The Parting

The time has come, I can tell,
That death has on her cast its spell.
I hold her hand within my own,
The heart within me turns to stone.

I see the furrows on her brow,
To smooth them out, I know not how.
I see the pain upon her face,
That I cannot somehow erase.

Her lips move now, no voice I hear,
(The words are oh so very clear),
They mutely say, "I love you".
And I reply "I love you too".

"Oh mother stay" cries out my heart.
"For I can't bear for us to part.
Oh God, oh God, I need her here.
For just one more, just one more year."

But God hears not my tearful prayer,
And takes her soul, I know not where.
And I'm alone, sad and forlorn.
All, all alone, alone I mourn.

Charles J. Ferris

A Hero

The ageless soil surrounds me
The rain has rinsed away my flesh
Nothing but bones remain

I'm shadowed by a willow tree
The grass veils my precious existence
The sun will not allow me to grow

Bring out your shovels and bulldozers
Dig and dig and identify
Send in the archeologist to identify

And remember, think hard try to remember
How great I once was.

Jon Fortney

Galaxy Of A Country

Like the towering lighthouse
That guides the ship across the sea
If it were not for our brave men and women
Where would our country be

We are proud to be Americans
Where we know we are free
Our heritage is and always will be
Honor, courage, and bravery

We stand united, proud and strong
Through many battles we have gone
Our trust in God and our faith
Is what made this country great

Neither snow, storms, or desert sand
Can stop us from defending our land
As Americans, we can honestly say
We love this good ole U.S. of A.

We do not put a question mark
Where a period should be
We just put our trust in God
And have faith in victory

Jo Reagan

Fantasy

Close by, there is a hidden glen,
That is known to one and me -
A place with scent of blossoms,
And a mystic quality.

I only go by moonlight,
When the stars are hung out high-
A million tiny candles,
Atop the midnight sky.

By the pool he's waiting,
Kneeling gracefully to drink-
Such beauty in that moment,
Now, our hearts in rapture link.

We frolic in the shadows,
Then rest, his head upon my knee-
No one near to think it strange,
My unicorn and me:

Barbara Fulton Schindler

I Hope

I hope for this and I hope for
that; my wishes don't ever come
true. I wish and hope for you
to see me but you don't. I hope
for a career that may not come
true, so what can I hope for
if they don't come true?

In school all I can hope for
is to pass and graduate someday.
I hope my life will be better
than it has been.

If I keep hoping and wishing,
they won't come true. All I want
is someone I can trust and who
will love me for who I am.
So I won't have to hope anymore.

April Danforth

The Star Of Bethlehem

There was a Star in Heaven
That shone down from above
And led them to that manger
It was the gift of God's love.

Then others came to see Jesus
And even the wise men three
For on that night of wonders
Was a glorious sight to see.

They brought their Gifts to Jesus
He was born in a lonely stall
And later on the hill of Golgotha
He paid the price for all.

This is why we have Christmas
Of the Manger scene that day
Then have to suffer such pain
What a price Jesus did pay.

That Star still shines in Heaven
Tis the Son of God, the Lamb
The one that went to Calvary
He is the great I AM.

Joe Shelton

To The Graduates

If you will hear that small, still voice
That tries to talk to you,
You'll know without a single doubt
That's "God" a coming through

He'll tell you how to live your life
The things to say and when.
And if you falter on the way
He'll help you start again.

The only thing you need to do,
Is talk to him each day,
Believe in him and listen
To what he has to say.

As long as you are satisfied
With all the things you do
You'll never have a problem
Being satisfied with you.

Florence E. Masterson

Lesson Learned

So I have learned
the benefit of a still mind
in the selfless action
of physical activity

All dramatics
have been shorn away
No glittery dangles
or bangles in each moment

God's grace appears
in my mind's eye,
showing me to myself
as a master of motion commotion
with a hula hoop twirling
round my still body
exhibiting the value
of stillness:

The perfect point
off which activity
spins in complete harmony

Gretchen Yates Lum

Our World

The world is peaceful
The birds are singing in the trees
The flowers are blooming
And the sun is shining over the world
The earth is happy and joyful!
The oceans, lakes and seas are swaying
The deep blue ocean is crystal clear,
There is friendship in the world
The animals are waking up from hibernation
The earth is alive!!

Jordan M. Pujol

"Times Change"

The center of all that's passed
The bringing in of new
A passage between the years
That may be lost to all but you

A changing of the old
To see a better view
Brought upon maturing eyes
A life only understood by few

Memories that you have shared
These may soon be lost
But moving up in years
Sometimes has a cost

But one day you'll remember
Happiness out of the blue
Then your heart will be filled
With what meant so much to you

Ann Kardos

Autumn

A time of change
The children, now older, wiser
More independent
Making their own way
In a new world of their own.

No longer needing Mommy
Forever by their side
Wanting to grow and learn
To be their own person
A time to grow...

The children; to see their faces
Rosy with excitement
It is their first day of school
Their first day of independence.

Their strong little voices,
Mommy it's okay
I can do it myself
Mommy you can go
I'm a big girl now
A time to let go

Diane Howes

The Rose

I come across a
sweet smelling rose, the
beauty so pure like nobody
knows. With the essence
of the falling rain drop
dew, brings me so much
joy as it reminds me of
you.

Cindy J. Matthews

Kelsey Angel

She came into my life when
the cold winds were blowing,
It seemed the day she was
born, God had made it snowing,
We were all so happy, though
we knew it could not last,
And when I think about it, it's
just a memory of the past.
Lots of times I see her, in my
dreams and thoughts,
And sometimes I'm really mad
because it was God who called the shots.
But then I think it's better, that
she is way up there,
In clouds of love, in nanny's arms,
and always in her care.
Now I'm going to start anew and say
this from my heart,
Kelsey, we really love you, and
always have from the start.

Ariane Nickerson

Indian Summer

The loon laughs as
the crescent moon dips
ever so slightly to
halo his sleek black head.
The summer water escapes
into the cold, calm night.

Slipping through the mists,
Mohegan—Spirit who walks,
carefully finds his way
through the corn field stubble,
pauses, then passes
the self sacrificing scarecrow,

Laughs with the loon,
gives good graces to the moon,
Then, covered with the
cold gray skins of morning,
disappears softly into
the leafless land of the living.

Diane L. Hunt

My Mother's Tears

She told me once of tears and pain
The cuts and blood she shed
The fights, the shame, the tears she cried
But now my mother's dead.

He beat her up again last night
It was the last fight she could take
Too much pain and blood she lost
Too bad she'll never wake.

I have no mother; Dad's in jail
No one to take their place
And as my mother dances on clouds
Her tears stream down my face.

Shannon Utt

Silver Mist (Cinquain)

I know
Of silver mist, ____
Falling like transparent
Veils, before the night ___ colorless
And still.

Josephine M. Sharitz

The Best Of Everything

The straighter the road is,
The easier the way.
The best sleep is at night,
After you've worked all day.

The best teachers I know of,
Is your Mom and your Dad.
You feel so much better happy,
Than you do sad.

The best schools you can go too,
Is the Church of your choice.
To worship the savior,
And give ear to His voice.

The best dictionary there is,
Is God's Holy word.
If there's anything better,
Then I haven't heard.

The best home there is,
Is a home filled with love
And that home can be found,
With God up above.

Ben Clements

The Magic Of The Rocking Horse

Gaze into the magical eyes of
The giant rocking horse

Let your heart and soul travel
Into the land of fantasy

Remembering the magic of when
You were young and took a wondrous
Journey on the rocking horse

You traveled to lands of far and near
But no fear was had for the love of
The rocking horse and the magic of
Travel through spring flowers
And rainbows

So climb upon this wondrous horse
And travel once again into the
Fantasy of times gone by and share
Your dreams with the magic of the

Wondrous rocking horse

Elena Gale Hathway Backus

Friends

I've known friends who left when
the going went bad.
I've known friends who left
when I was not rich enough.
I've known friends who left
when I needed someone to lean on.
I've known friends who left
when I was near death.
But, were they friends?
Friends are the ones who are there
through the bad times in your life.
Friends are there,
come rich or poor.
Friends are there
when you need them.
Friends are there when
you are near death.
Friends are there,
no matter what happens in your life.

Jeffrey St. John

On Seeing Photos of Antarctica

What is the tempo of whiteness?
The images come in a rush, more
than seduction,
seduction presupposing anticipation,
hesitation, measured time.
I am taken completely
by this blue-white vastness.

What is the weight of whiteness?
Beneath the floating surface
drags the blackened blue underside
of fathomless grief,
memories of past connection.

Where is the edge of whiteness?
Fog, vaporous clouds, breath stopped
in cooled exhalation, merge
with surfaces of windswept ice. Here
the sacral blank, without horizon.

Caroline G. Banks

Untitled

One by one
The lights extinguish.
Slowly, evenly
Till darkness surrounds.

One by one
The lights extinguish.
No sound,
No movement,
No one around.

One by one
The lights extinguish.
Fear grasps
The mind,
The heart and soul.

One by one
The lights extinguish.

Jill Ciszczon

"Flower Showers"

If I could, I would command
the Olympians to shower your
universe in fragrant rains of
summer flowers.

The clouds would burst with torrents
of perfumed blossoms, a hurricane of
swirling orchids and lilacs in
Neptunian skies.

The mermaids would gather the
floating petals in baskets of conch,
anointing your vanilla skin and raven hair
in the splendors of summer, while you
bathed in a big, blue ocean.

If I could, I would flood your sleeping
room with a sea of dried buds and
branches, Morpheus would have to wade
through roses and honeysuckle to sprinkle
the dream dust, and Neptune would swim
strong through daisies and sassafras to
make love in your fantasies.

Jeffrey D. Norwalk

Untitled

Fire churns underneath
the moon reaching,
swallowing its shadow,

Standing as a soul to the
vulnerable sky briskly gazing,
My eyes brush the blazing,
suffocates the skin reach within,
reach within.....

Ocean cushions below fingertips
of each wave stroke, tame,

Sunset drenched the sky,
sizzled fear tipped flame,

Polishing the soul that gleamed
every hue blossoming, deepening,
silence.

Emilia Schwab

Wild Sculpture

The Guancoste trees are bare;
the rainy season is not yet.

Sticks stand out, one moves;
birders whisper, over there!

We look! We miss!
we study every upright stub.

The elongated cryptic shape shifts,
brown feathers float in the breeze,
a closed eye opens,
the prominent yellow iris gleams,
the decurved bill outlines
the nightjar mouth.

The Costa Rican wonder, the pootoo,
stands upright in the sun.
A living sculpture
for the birders' lifetime list.

Elizabeth Hart Frazier

The Purpose Of Life

What is the purpose of life,
The reason for our existence?
Is life just a test
Of our strength and persistence?

Is life just a time
To think up new things?
Is the purpose of like
To love other beings?

Is life a time
To help one another?
Is life just a chance
To become a father or mother?

When time is ready,
It will answer the questions above.
But until then,
All we can do is love.

Erica Campbell

Me

The sky, the soft winds, the clouds
The rivers, the trees, the love
The words, the sigh, thee
Aye, wish, love, dreams,
Natures scenes,
me.

Everett L. Burgess

Magical World

Come with me as we ride across
the silver melodies of dawn.
Float down its stream
on a raft of calm
and explore the mysteries
with a curious mind.
Seek out the hiding places
in the deep, deep woods
and learn the secrets they imply.
Climb to the top
of the highest tree
and sway with the dancers there.
Observe your own reflection
in the placid lake
and imagine yourself as one
with this magical world.

Jaquie Zimmerman

The Stars In Your Eyes

When I think of how
The stars shone in your eyes
I somehow seem to forget
About all of the lies

I forget about all the tears
And endless heartache
All the un-kept promises
And all I put at stake

Because when I remember the stars
The clouds disappear
No more heartache or pain
And no more tears

I remember when
You looked sincere
When your eyes alone
Calmed all my fears

But the stars don't shine
The storms are raging
There's no more love
But only hating.

Amber Baker

"Footprints"

The moon that lights the sky at night,
The sun that shines the day,
Look down upon the many tracks
As "Footprints" make their way.

A teacher bends a student's mind,
A huckster vends his wares;
A preacher eulogizes death,
A housewife dusts the chairs.

A doctor births a mother's child,
A dentist fills a tooth;
A Senior draws his final breath
Dreaming of his youth.

A farmer reaps the harvest,
A fisherman baits the line;
My children gather 'round me,
Their heritage is mine.

Across each day of history,
Encased in their own time;
These footprints share a common thread,
"Immortal" in my rhyme!

George Z. Peterson

The Forest Pond

Reflections of sky, and trees around
The sun, the moon, the passing clouds
With changing light and shadow's fall
The forest pond our lives reflects

With hopes as high as the sky above
And the towering trees as well
One learns from setting sun and moon
The limits our lives can have

Autumn leaves show their many hues
When winter's call is heard
But cling as they may to life and limb
We know their fate is sealed

When into life a special light may come
To lift one's spirit and bring hope
Passing time should teach us all
To treasure every moment

For shadows will fall across our lives
As day and night exchange
By closing our eyes, a shadow departs
But the forest pond tells all

Fenton Babcock

Draftees: At The Station

The day was bright,
The sun was hot,
We gazed into the glare

The mothers and the fathers
and the girls with long, long hair.

Sister, brothers, kiss and shake,
solemn faces,
simple words,
Then turn and climb the stairs.

Goodbye small son, big son,
grown son, gone son,
How many times we say it.
Come back son, don't go son.
If only we could say it.

June B. Gallagher

Treasures Of Life

I have the treasure of precious love.
The treasure of joy and peace.
I have found the treasure of blessings,
And sunshine that will never cease.

I have found the treasure of raindrops
And the awesome treasure of tears.
I've found the treasure of laughter
That has helped me all through the years.

The golden treasure of friendships
Are like a string of pearls.
The treasure of a baby's smile;
The playing of boys and girls.

The treasure of the ocean beach,
At the setting of the sun.
The glory of another dawn,
A new day has begun.

There are many others more precious than
gold.
All these in the midst of strife.
Ah, yes, I've found these wealthy treasures
In the span that we call life.

Dorothy Anderson

Unlikely Friend

For those who wish, never insight
The unsuspecting are taken in flight
No number to be taken
It is not to be forsaken

Our life we make and plan
We enjoy the labor of our hands
With years behind and ahead
It sleeps beside me in my bed

As family and friends slip away
Cold replaces the warmness of new days
It is quiet now, alone at last
My mind wanders into days gone past

A fear grips me, I make a plea
But tired and weak, I cannot speak
Yes, someone has heard and comes for me
Ah, a friend but I cannot see

With a coldness and chill
But a warmness that guides
It is death that comes for me
My friend in disguise

Jules R. Rousseau

A Place To Belong

The sidewalk is hard
the wind is cold her stomach
Aches of hunger the Darkness
is bold her tears are
of fear her Dirty little
face her torn clothes
not even shoes for her
Cold little toes Mommy's dead
Daddy left her astray people
pass by day after day with
no remorse not even a blink
of sadness "spare change sir
spare change" we pick up the
pace afraid of the hurting we'll
see in her face wondering what
it would be like if we were
in her place only God knows and
by his grace we will all have
a place.

Jaben L. Carter

Lovely Days

The air is sweet and fresh and warm,
The winds have stopped their blowing
The warmth of Spring has come at last;
To the lands of frequent snowing.
The weather of the South has come
And settled in the North.
It will stay for a little while,
And then will travel forth.
"And then will travel forth?" you ask
"But what is left for us?"
Oh that is the secret of the earth:
We are left in Nature's trust.

Helen Vollrath

Taking A Walk

Memories
Reading writing arithmetic
Thoughts running through
Eating charbroil pizza
Walking on a green path

Gee it's warm today

David Doljan

Stormy Days

A furious storm blew up last night;
The winds were cold and biting.
This morning found me tired and drawn.
Left limp from senseless fighting.

Our love, it changes hour by hour
From warmth with balmy breezes
And then, with ne'er a warning sign,
The air between us freezes.

You say you're sorry, and you add
Your day was most frustrating.
You say I did not cause your wrath
But I'm still sore and aching.

In time, the pain will fade away;
We'll love to be together.
We'll laugh and love and play until
Some force affects the weather.

I wish the sun shone every day
And summer last forever.
If only love could be steadfast
And not change like the weather.

Anne Joyce

The Wolf

I hear the call of the wolf
The winter moon shines
Through the frost covered trees
And I know the wolf is there

The primal howl echoes in my mind
The past - the present - the future
Sacred blood burns in his veins
The power of life shines in his eyes

The wolf surrounds me
He stalks the forest in my mind
I feel his icy breath
I hear the beat of his fierce heart

His eyes burn in the night darkness
Drums thunder in my ears
Night chants call to me
Stars are thrown through the clouds

I have seen the wolf - and he has seen me

James M. Probasco

The Spirit Of Christmas

The Spirit of Christmas comes softly.
The word, December, may bring it.
The quiet of a winter night or
A star-filled sky.
The first snowflakes or
A lighted town square,
All red, green and gold.

Softly, softly comes the peace
Of the Christ Child.
"Peace on Earth, Goodwill to Men."
"Joy to the World, the Lord has come."

The joy and peace of Christmas;
When it softly comes,
Is as mysterious and incomprehensible
As God's love for fallen man.
"I have come that they might have life,
And have it more abundantly."

Eva J. Knopp

Tapestry Of Time

A fantasy of fabrics forms
the woven tapestry of time.
A textured tissue, warp and weft,
showing passage by its line.

An infant is all velvet
soft and warm to touch and hold,
A child feels like denim,
roughened knees and cap of gold.

Young men turn to leather,
girls favor cashmere, lace,
with hair like silken waterfalls,
naive, yet old of face.

Then faces age and furrow,
corduroy and crepe de chine,
or damask, parchment, homespun,
and back to silk again.

The footprint of time's passage
on the surface of a face
Is but a hint of that Life's passage
through this brief time and space.

Jan Murra

Wasted Years

"Time and tide waits for no man."
The years of life fly by.
We look back over yesteryears
And ask the question - Why?

Why have we wasted all these years
In sin and selfish gain?
Trying to make important names
Or achieve great honor and fame.

Too busy to think of others
As we quickly go on our way.
Never seeing the sick and hungry
Or those who have no place to stay.

Now we are older. Our steps are slowed.
We stoop with sorrow and pain.
No ambition to put forth effort.
Life is almost gone. What a shame.

Dear God, forgive our selfish greed
And our wasted life of sin.
Just claim us as your child today
So to heaven we will enter in.

Cora L. Fifield

Untitled

Into our minds we roam
Searching for reasons beyond doubt
Shattered hopes and fallen heros
Left us standing alone
We create our dreams
In sleepless visions
Ticking away of hours
Days and nights dancing in our head
To forget our own rainbows
For they no longer exist
Time spends the day
In reflections of its own self
As eternity fades away
Of what once was
Those puppet strings on a heart
Now becomes a toy
To see only the sun
Burn bright at midnight
For those we love
We are destined to destroy

Grant H. Wass

Time To Move On

Leaves dance gently on the trees,
Their shadows flitting too,
Across the weathered building
That brings back thoughts of you.

It seems only yesterday,
My love was so profound.
I stand deep in reflection,
Making no move, no sound.

Then a wisp of wayward hair
Blows softly in my face,
Brings me back from memories
About you and this place.

I glance upward at the sky.
The sun is shining bright.
But I know that all too soon
The day will turn to night.

Remembering you is sweet,
But forward I must go.
I will leave this place of dreams,
Knowing you would want it so.

Arvylla Breshears

Far Away Mountains

The far away mountains are calling,
Their voice grown stronger with time,
Those far away mountains are calling,
And the name they are calling is mine.
I've wandered this earth as a rover,
Chose the vagabond's way as my own,
But now that my journey's near over,
The mountains are calling me home.
Farewell to you, sisters and brothers,
Goodbye to you, family and friends,
Life's book is no different than others,
It closes when Life's story ends.
And thank you, sweet wife, for your kisses,
Your helpfulness through all those years,
Changing life's blows into misses,
Transforming to laughter its tears.
But now all that road lies behind me,
That much of my journey is done.
Up there's where you're going to find me,
My mountains have welcomed me home.

John A. Jordan

The Wind

It hovers so silent and still
Then comes roaring over the hill
Meek, mild, serene and quiet
Then thundering through in a riot

It can be quietly infinitesimal
Disappearing during the evening lull
Or softly stirring the leaves
As it dances through the trees

Or it can be a destructive force
Whipping tendrils from its source
Whirling, churning, terrifying to see
Coming down the mountain or from the sea

We watch the wind dancing on the water
Merrily racing along with hauteur
Or softly stirring ripples down the river
Making one's senses shake and quiver

Dee Thompson

A Parable Of Words

Just a word, I thought when spoken,
There can be no damage done,
Hearts cannot by words be broken,
Battles are not lost or won.

So I heeded not, deceiving,
Other words in spite I said,
While my tongue was cutting, cleaving,
Other souls, in anguish, bled.

I have learned that words can strengthen,
They can speak of hope and love,
Words can shorten, words can lengthen,
Words can gently lift or shove.

I've learned also, words are weapons,
Which no armor can prevail,
They can crucify and torture,
Even as a driven nail.

Brad Dykeman

"In Just One Moment"

There was beauty,
There was grace.
So much honor,
He was the ace.

Fits of rage, the obsession.
The watching, waiting, hoping to see.
His mind just couldn't accept,
Only now her life is free.

From the height of success,
Now lower than low.
How fast a life destroyed.
On the run, such a show.

The viciousness, the lies,
The hatred, the act.
In the swiftness of a second,
Such a ruthless attack.

Now eternally in the mind.
That moment will always play.
Can't forget, can only regret.
O.J. must answer, on his judgment day

John Paul Carinci

Invasion

They come to answer a nation's cry;
These countless hordes of men.
The friendly Yanks, known as GI's
Our hearts go out to them.

They are strangers in a foreign clime,
The fogs are heavy in the air.
To them our English summertime
Is just one long despair.

To us, their tales of home sound grand,
They own so much, can we believe
That every man can own such land
And in such grandeur live?

We laughed at them and loved them.
They stayed in our poor homes.
So different from the stately gems
They had left with never a moan.

Elfrida E. Walker

When

When two people love
they don't love for sex
they don't love for money
they don't love for promises
that each know won't be kept.

When two people love
they don't love for heartache
they don't love for lies
they don't love for emptiness,
for both know it won't last.

When two people love
they don't love for the sake,
of having someone to hold.
It's not for sex, it's not for money.

When two people love it's for the best
Knowing that they, give their hearts
honestly.

When two people love
they're sure it's real
for they have no second thoughts
and they never let go.

Betty Szepessy Zito

Meant For

Her eyes sparkle like fire
  They instill great desire
In Him for Whom
  It is meant.

Entranced by her smile
  We've walked many a mile
Just to be the one for whom
  It was meant.

With a mien so fine
  She's simply divine
For whom God meant
  Her to be.

With a heart full of joy
  She gave us a boy,
John Justin, for whom
  We were meant.

May that heart be glad
  And never be sad
For whom God meant
  Her to be.

John Lee Cotton

Things We Take For Granted

The sun was bright - the flowers sweet,
  The air was crisp and clear;
The things we take for granted,
  As if they were not there.
The seasons change as years go by,
  The days just come and go;
The great wonders of the earth,
  These, we'll never know.
"We don't take things for granted!"
  "We know the things are there!"
But maybe we don't notice them,
  Perhaps we just don't care.
"I never noticed this before,"
  "Wow, look at what I've found!"
Stop taking things for granted,
  Just stop and look around.

Darla Stouffer

A Lover's "Dilemma"

If I had three wishes,
They'd all be for kisses,
From you and no other.
But will three be ample,
Or only a sample,
I'm sure I'll need another!

Pucker up!

Donald R. Wylie

Certain Sleep

It could have been so easy,
They're just there in the drawer,
To take a small handful,
And sleep forevermore.

But, the challenge of every day,
With obligations to meet,
Requires one must be together,
Solely (Soul-ly) on their feet.

Judith Conrow

The Mystery

What does she conceal,
This beautiful oak?
Strong and straight
She stands in the woods.

Who will be chosen
And who will be free
When fall paints her colors
On faces below?

One by one fall a few,
But many remain
Awaiting their fate
'Til the advent of Spring.

So why does the parent
Keep some for so long;
Why not let them all fly,
Let them loose in the wind?

Is she bent on protection,
Holding fast to the old,
Or does she fear lifting
Bare arms to the world?

Edith L. Richards

Patterns Of Life

Dense, dark clouds
  Threaten from above.
   Sudden lightning pierces!
    Rumbling thunder claps!
     The wind whips fiercely!
      Down come the torrents of rain.

Cloud patterns changing
  As in our own lives;
   Dark times of illness
    And sorrow, bring tears;
     Then hope and contentment
      And joy of life again.

Like wispy white swirls
  Of silver-lined mist
   With foamy whipped topping
    On platters of blue,
     A heavenly still life
      Silently decks the sky.

Hilda Hatlen

Parting Gift

A torch of love flares up for us
This bright October day,
The flaming glory of the year,
That lights November's way.

Like an offering on an altar,
All of nature gives full share;
For leaves like jewels are flashing,
Tossed in the haze-blue air.

Now the beeches share their bounty,
With a gift of precious gold;
It's the summer's hoarded sunlight,
So take what the heart can hold.

There's a funeral pyre for summer
Made of blazing maple leaves;
A flinging forth of wonder,
There'll be no more reprieves.

So fill your memory's storehouse
On this October day,
With gifts to warm you in the cold,
That trails November's way.

Eleanor F. McGraw

People

If everyone could see their life
Through another person's eyes
They might feel like they're looking at
A stranger in disguise
They might not even recognize
The person that they see
But if they'd take the time to look inside
Could they tell you from me?
We all are very different
And that's how God had it planned
He put a lot of thought
In his creation called "a man"....
But now that we are people
And we live upon this earth
I wonder if he really thinks
That what he did was worth
The time and thought he gave it
Or if his efforts were in vain
'Cause a lot of people seem to let
Their lives go down the drain.

Connie Brister

"All That I Can Offer"

I can offer to always be by you
Through happiness and pain,
Over all the rocky roads,
In sunshine or in rain.

I can offer to take care of you
When life has brought you down,
You never need to worry,
For, I will always be around.

I can offer what feels best to you
And you need to understand,
That "I" will always be there
When you need a helping hand.

I can offer to "always" be your friend,
In good times and in bad,
And, whether you are happy,
Or even feeling sad.

This is "All that I can offer you"
I hope you know it's true,
Because this offer that I have,
Is meant from me to you.

Jeri Blumenstein

The Barn At Dawn

The day invades the barn loft
through the knot holes in the boards.
And beams of light now strike the wall
that I am facing towards.

These spears of light should not be thrown
I had done my work, and more.
With impending threat of rain
bale lifting was my chore.

Besieged by bales of fresh cut hay
in the moisture of the morning.
Encircled by this fragrant drug
that did not give me warning.

New galaxies of beaded light
now shine in profuse numbers.
But all the magic of this time
is lost on one who slumbers.

John M. Snyder

Moonshine

As he sat and peered
  through the window
You know he had
  true feelings
Feelings as true as yours.
You never thought
  he had pain
Pain as you do.
You never thought
  death could go to him.
The little things
  you loved about him.
You never thought
  he would end.
End quickly.
The way he flew
  and fluttered
But as the moon flows
  the ocean
He will always flow your mind.

Adriane L. Beveridge

"I Found My God"

I did a lot of traveling,
Throughout my youthful years.

I visited many churches,
I shed a million tears.

I was in search of the God I love,
And in a church I thought He'd be.

And tho I went to many,
The sight of Him I did not see.

But now I'm older and wiser,
And go search now, I do not do.

If you only look within yourself,
Then you will find him, too!

You see, God never leaves His children,
And when I took time to see.

I found Him where He'd always been,
Within the heart of me.

Dorothy J. Fordyce

"My Dearest Friend"

Since the day you first did court me
Till we took our wedding vows
And even now since years have past
I've loved you then as now.

It's fun to think of days gone by
The love our hearts have known
To think how little at first we had
But now how much it's grown.

Thanks for being patient
Understanding, kind, and true
On days that we can share together

I'll treasure them all with you.

May God give you wisdom
  And shower His love down, too.
For you are more than someone
  Special,
My dearest friend are You.

Joan C. Mecusker

Time Is At Hand

What time is it? Overtime.
Time is up. Do you have the time?

We cannot hide
On this walk through life.
Many have tried
And it only brings strife.

Time ticks away
Even when the clock runs down.
And we will pay
If we've only been a clown.

Yes, it's good to have fun
But not all the time.
For at the end of life's run
Will our Lord say, "You are mine"?

Time to eat. Bedtime.
Lunch time. Nap time. Show time.
Time for school. Quitting time.
Play time. Study time.

Judith Jean France

Listen Closely

Listen closely I say,
To an unjust so wrong,
And the price we pay,
A citizen dislike rules our throne.
Making love a fight,
The world not our own.
Together we hide,
A nation demands,
Like puppets we twirl,
Upon every command.
Forced to comply,
To please their soul,
We sacrifice our life,
For a record of gold.
Branded thieves we did no wrong.
Together we grieve - our anguish strong.
Mercy from above,
Is what we pray.
Must we deny love?
Listen closely I say.

Debbie K. Adams

The Fish And Me

I went down to the creek,
to bag a fish that lived so deep.

He took my bait and away he swam,
down the creek towards the dam.

The fish hit the end of my line,
then he knew that it was time.

He'll not give up without a fight,
he jerked again with all his might.

He ripped that hook from his face,
and up that creek he did race.

Down into the deepest hole,
went the fish and went my pole.

I gave that fish a wave good-bye,
for I'll be back again to try.

Sooner or later he'll lose the fight,
and I'll take them home with such delight.

I'll mount that fish on the wall,
for he was the biggest fish of them all.

Bobby N. Cole

Too Late?

When are we too old to love,
To be a part of someone's heart,
Embark upon a longed for art?
Never!

When is it too late to say,
I can do it now and start today
From knowledge stored within?
Never!

And keep it up till the task is done
The dream is won and someone says,
"Isn't it too late for that"?
Never!

June Burns

Twenty-Eight Plus One

Will February be long enough
to do all the celebrating
For all the days significant
that we are here relating?

The Groundhog's Day we can't forget
for he foretells the weather.
Winter - Spring - does he really know?
Hope he gets his act together.

On the fourteenth day as everyone knows,
St. Valentine makes his call;
And Cupid shoots his darts around -
our hearts he does enthrall.

George Washington and Abraham Lincoln
were two men of great renown;
We honor them with grateful hearts;
they never let us down.

Let us look forward to the one year in four
when that extra day comes our way.
On the twenty-ninth we'll celebrate
and dub it Leap Year Day.

Evelyn Copple Widner

Hope Without Measure

I walked down the street
To envision the finality of life,
But only this far did I get.
Life is for most of us unending
And even when appearances
Make us believe that it ends,
This is just a mirage of nature.
It encircles us with its tentacles
And prevents us from looking ahead
At the frivolity of life
Lived without hope
Of another timeless existence
Where sun meets moon in an aura
Of brilliant gold.

Elizabeth Morales

Not To Hurry

How we rush to find our lives…running
to grab everything
As if time were ending in a second

Perhaps a second's pause to look around
will show us all that is good

Our mad dash becomes insignificant
Time becomes rich and plentiful
And life shows us perpetual calm
and infinite wonder

Dave Schwan

Saint Patrick's Day

Although it's a day for the Irish
To honor their saint and show pride,
On March seventeen
When we're all wearing green
It's a day that all races, abide.

So regardless of race, or of country
And with no thought of color of skin,
Just follow the scene
And dress up in green
For we all look alike from within.

And remember while wearing the shamrock
To pray that by doing so would
An impossible dream
By sharing the green
Bring the world to complete brotherhood.

Harry F. Yeoman

37

Hands come together over head
To keep the rain out, and you do
Keep out rain, go to bed
Secure and comfortable too.

When stars shine once and the sun steams
You grow-up daisies, hardly—-
Just spray a wreath of dusty cream
With little weaver hands absurdly.

Yet straight forward you stand in place
Regardless if the world approves
A braveness on your aged face
Watching intent, the universe move.

And then where to (daisies) after
Your galaxy runs out of luck,
Do you just explode (minute power)
And leave the universe abrupt.

Beverly Joan Brian

To The Owner Of A Red Setter Hit On Hillham Road Last Friday

I didn't mean
to kill her,
but she flashed
like a lure
before my steel,
toppled in my
rear-view mirror
like a clown.

I held her body—
both of us heaving,
both of us bathed
scarlet—soaked
from her a fading
sigh and shiver.

Alvin Knox

Poetry

Poetry is like music
to me.
It feeds my soul and
sings to me.
Strong and mighty it
must be,
With wings of song to
float in space
Where adventure waits
for me.
No fright to fear
Only time without tears.
A poem that will run
away with me
To a world where all
mankind can live without fear.

A peaceful world is what we want!
A place where all have
hope, love and no tears.
What a wonderful world this would be.

Anne Magnussen

The River Song

Into the waiting azure sea
The river flows so silently
And then flows out again to meet
The little springs that wait to greet

Returning to the clouds on high
It falls in raindrops from the sky
In laughing streams soon to be found
It waters thirsty Earth and Ground

From snow capped Hills it swiftly flows
To Secret Places that it knows
Who knows where it begins and ends
Yet Promise and Hope to us it sends

And so it is with the Life of MAN
Though we know not our allotted Span
We run our course of Life on Earth
And then in Spirit have Rebirth

Though we may 'Change' New Life we'll know
Just like the River's constant Flow
As the River's Song so shall we be
In the River's Song Eternally

Helen Gleason

Nostalgia

Oh! Just to be a child again —
To play some games and smile again —
To hear my mother's voice again —
To be carefree!

But, one gets old — as mothers will
And, in our lives, God does instill
The fact that we must do His will —
Our destiny!

I've learned that I would not erase
The ups and downs I've had to face.
They've merely made me strong. The pace
Was set for me.

May my example be the kind
That ushers in some good to mind,
When others think of me and find
A constancy.

Beatrice White

"Share"

Take a moment this Christmas morn
To remember the animals,
So sad and forlorn-
Sometimes they wish
They had never been born.
As we destroy the forests-
That was their home you know
Like our homeless-
They have nowhere to go.
So they invade our property
Which irritates us so
But what would you do
If you had no place to go?
So share with the animals
Whatever you have had
And up in heaven God will be glad

Grace M. Spencer

The Runaway

What good does it do,
To run away,
To do what you want,
And have the say?

You sit on the street,
Alone and blue,
An odd looking woman,
Is staring down at you.

You hear the sirens,
As they go by,
Then you hang your head,
And begin to cry.

You think to yourself,
There's got to be a way,
To get out of this mess,
And start a brand new day.

Bonnie White

Solitude

In the dark hours of the night,
when all is calm and quiet
when I am left alone,
solitude.
When all that is left besides the dark,
is silence.

Annisa Maria Diaz-Clark

Ceremoniously, Dear

I've learned to pay attention
To sunsets in the sky
The loss of vision taught me this
I've grown tired of random conversations
Leading only to arguments
Being mute has made me see
I've begun to listen for whispered praise
Amidst the confusion of pitied laughter
Growing deaf brings me a voice
I now pause to touch the roses
Ignoring that threat of thorns
Unable to feel but I hear the pain
I believe in the Creator now
The one who opened up my heart
Folding my hands has allowed healing
If in humility I find joy
In living for each new breath
There will come a time
Not far from now
When I will grow wings and sing.

Dana B. Stenholtz

Together As Ivy

The ivy reaches
to the peak of the sky
in a silent climb
guided by the midnight senses.

The vines bend against one another
around and through one another
like fingers tangled
in a sleepless fire.

The strands intertwine freely-
no telling where one ends
and the other begins
like the bend of four knees.

The limbs curve together,
ascending to extinguish their thirst
from the dewy
rays of dawn.

With the tremble of amber
comes the slow trickle of one vine
cascading off the other
in the awakening of autumn.

Derra L. Dubie

Passing Of Time

Once I was born and soon I will pass
To unknown shores unburdened from
my earthly tasks,
As I travel on with no thought of time,
I will surrender memories that once
were mine.
At one time I danced with life in a
fiery rage,
The flame has diminished like it grew
with age.
My back is bent and my hair is grey
The innermost clock does not know
night from day
Fingers are crippled by age and by time.
Today and tomorrow no more will be mine
I will rest in Heaven at my Master's side
In His loving care, forever, I will abide
Wondrous beauty someday I will find
When I cross Jordan with the passing of
time.

Betty Jo Beheler

Heaven

If I had all the words in our language
to use at a moment's command
If I had all the beautiful pictures
of houses, the sea and land,

If I mixed all the glorious sunsets
with all the mysteries of Mars
If I mixed all the beauty of springtime
with the gleam of the moon and stars,

If I had all the colors of the rainbow
described in beautiful words
If I had all the magical music
If I had all the songs of the birds

If I had all the beautiful flowers
colors gold, bronze and green
Red, yellow, purple, and lilac
No lovelier sight has been seen

I could never oh! never describe it
this wonderful home in the sky
If we only trust in the Savior
We shall reach it by and by.

Irene Gipe

It Won't Happen Again

I could tell you that you
took my dreams away.
I could show you that you
control my body.
I could let you see that
my fear controls me.
I could let you feel my
anger towards you.
I could let it all happen
again.
Now I could tell you that
I've grown up.
Now I could show you
that my body listens to me.
Now I could let you see
my beauty.
Now I could let you feel
my strength.
Now I can't let it happen
again.

Cara Melani Bingham

Poverty?

A mite bit o' homin' makes
travelin' okay. Takes out
the pinch o' bein' away
an' suckles the thought
o' when you come back,
picturin' them folk
waitin' by the track.
Grub's all gone, but the
feast is planned. A heap
o' some lovin' an' a soft
warm hand. A fireside talk
while the younguns sleep
right out in the open
where the stars is steep.
Home's all polished with the
moon so big. Bark on the
trees lights up every twig
an' the quiet sets a peace
in yer min' and makes comin'
home feel mighty fine.

Jann Mattson

Wasteland Wanderer

I am the wasteland wanderer,
Trekking the hot deserts of your love
And the wastelands of your heart;
I roam the wilderness;
I'm a prisoner of your love,
Caught in your forever webs,
Like blue Monday;
I sigh;
I am the wasteland wanderer,
In never-never land,
With memories
Piled above the bones of marriage.

June B. Deaton

Untitled

Life's many faces
turn from joyful to fearful,
from moment to moment.
Unexpected and unnoticed
are the signs that lead us
to triumph or defeat.

We wait, we listen.
The treasures sometimes elude us—
treasures passed by
or passed on
to those ready to accept
the challenge.

Living becomes
an exercise in trust.
In doing so,
we dispel our fear.
We energize our vision.
We make memories
for another day.

Beth Feller

Untitled

I sat on the edge of the dock
Turning over water
Fish, nibbling at my feet
The winds, slapping me in the face
Slowly my mind was slipping away
I felt myself drifting
Deep beneath the water
The darkness overcoming
The coldness freezing
I lie on the bottom
And watch her above
Turning over water.

Catherine Pearce

Sinless Hands

Self-righteous bigots proudly stood
To judge, condemn and stone
A hapless woman caught in sin
No care or mercy shown.

They did not know the awful truth;
Her sin's not worse than theirs,
And they will face a Judgement Day
And need a judge who cares.

No sinful hand dares cast a stone,
And Jesus stands alone.
His hands will soon be pierced by nails;
They will not cast a stone.

Irene O. Gulledge

Are You There?

Are you there? Is that you
Twinkling in the night sky?

Is that you, bursting
From the sun's splendor?

Is that your whisper I hear
When the wind blows?

I call you, and I know you hear me.
Your answer is silent,
But I hear you clearly.

Not with the words you used to speak,
But with the love you spoke them in.

When I sigh at the star,
Am dazzled by the sun,
Kiss the breeze that touches my cheek,

I say, "are you there?"
My heart is lighter,
For I know you are here.

Darlene T. List

Spirit Free

Many years I've spent in bondage
Unable to cross the bar
Today my limits are endless
I'm free as the evening star

The anchor has been lifted
The components of planet earth
That kept me here are severed
Slavery since the day of my birth

Many lessons I have mastered
Spiritual growth a necessity
The body served as the temple
For the process of reality

The silver cord has been broken
At last my spirit is free
Do not cry at my leaving
Rejoice and be happy for me

Faylene Otis

Unattended

Who knows what could go wrong.
Unattended,
Like a bird without a song
I try to whistle
But I don't have the heart
Unattended,
Sometimes left behind
Unattended
Too lazy to turn the axe to grind
Unattended
Even a gold digger could not find
What I left behind, unattended.
Hold my breath hoping sometimes in store
Often being patient
Sometimes wanting more
I pray I don't leave you
I pray I don't leave you
I pray I don't leave you
Unattended.

David E. Dinwiddie

Our Greatest Blessing

Amazing love had he for man,
Unmatched courage to take His stand—
Infinite mercy for every soul,
Words of wisdom for young and old.

Spiritual light he came to give,
So that man may know how to live,
He's what God's grace is all about-
Our greatest blessing without a doubt.

He's the resurrection and so He taught
By His blood His church was bought,
He's the foundation and its head,
And to him we must be wed.

He is the author of eternal salvation,
May this we proclaim in every nation-
He was God and became a man,
So then with Him let's take out stand.

James H. Kilpatrick Sr.

On Silver Wings

Let me fly on silver wings
Up high with wind that sings
Catch Rainbow's, where dreams come true
Bathe in sunshine, sky of blue
Touch white clouds with my feet
While Night enters, Daylight retreats
Capture wonders from stars that shine
To see a world, I call mine
I give you all these things
Let love fly on silver wings

Cloyde F. Coffman Jr.

Yesterday

I rode one day on a country road
upon my little pony.
I passed this school that looked
so cool dressed up in moss and ivy.

I looked away across the brook.
I saw this man who had a book.
I ran to him with open arms.
He looked at me with great alarm!

I asked this man with the book
Why this path he had taken.
"I wanted to remember my yesterdays
And find this beautiful maiden."

Beulah Gregory

Death Of Summer

Oh fall, ye tinted leaves of autumn
Tinged and hued by nature's hand
Emissaries of pending winter
Clothing hills and dunes of sand
Parasails, spinning wildly
From the lofty branch on high
Of the towering tree so noble
Reaching upward to the sky.

Brisk and tingling breezes blowing
Showering colors across the land
Painting figures in autumn foliage
Winter's breath is close at hand
Soon the trees will be denuded
Stark and barren, tall they stand
Creaking, moaning, bowing swaying
As if to say, 'they understand'.

Gene Sword

Untitled

Oh had I met you Robert Burns
Upon the bridge of Ayr
Had I known your Highland Mary
With her face so meek and fair
Oh had I met you Robert Burns
Upon the bridge of Ayr

Had I rambled in your cottage
Had I slumbered in your chair
Had we strolled the banks of Afton
Above the haunts of care
Oh had I met you Robert Burns
Upon the bridge of Ayr

Had I known your Highland lasses
With their pearls rich and rare
I would have loved Clarinda
If I was only there
Oh had I met you Robert Burns
Upon the bridge of Ayr

John J. Hoey

View From The Lake

Early mornings standing by the lake
visions of beauty float before my eyes.
The sun brightly beaming upon the water
sending ripples of sheer delight.
Ducks lazily bathing in the warm
sunlight.
Sea gulls gliding effortlessly through
the air.
Descending gracefully upon the water
with care.
Every now and then a soft breeze
Silently caresses my cheek.
Only to seek solace elsewhere.
The lake so tranquil and still
Yet awaits another mornings view.

Constance L. Howard

'We Pledge And We Sing'

Cross your brows and rummage
Through your lay - investitures.
Cross your legs and count
back our cash.
Lengthen, but don't disrupt,
But please refurbish your sash.
We honestly couldn't convey
any of a better stash.
The class is in counter balance;
The counter balance is in conveyance,
And the harmony is in conjunction
Whilst the junctions are uncoerced.

Jennifer Ann Lee

Warzone

You seduced my body...
then took advantage
of it
you beat away
my innocence...
then laughed
you destroyed
part of
my heart...
then turned
and left me
an abandoned
warzone.

Jessica F. Santora

Here Then Gone

Life with you here
Was filled with many dreams
There was never any trouble
Or hate it seems

Tender, loving words
It was you who spoke them
Your caring, sharing, and kindness
Was strong as a stem

You brought out the sun
And tears in every way
Your gentle hands touched the sad
Each and every day

Your memory stays
In each and every heart
When you gave us hugs goodbye
We knew to depart

Bob Randl (10/18/78 - 9/19/93)
Adam Buechel (3/31/79 - 9/19/93)

Heather Hahn

"Life"

Thinking of days gone by, when life was lived and the sun seemed to shine brighter and hearts were happy and love was real. Like a current of wind blowing through you.

A laugh so wonderfully infectious, and full of mischief. It all seemed to keep the world turning. And life was pleasantly full.

And then there was a time of pain and sadness and life was slipping away into an unknown world all of its own.

Yet there remains the glow from the morning sun as it reflects on our very being. Then at night the moon is bright and full and radiates our very souls.

But time does not stand still, and this big beautiful world God made keeps turning and our lives keep rotating around it.

Dorma Lee Johnson

Why Did You Want To Die?

The pain I feel inside,
was not caused by a friend or lover.
The pain I try so hard to hide,
was caused by my older brother.

It wasn't your time to go,
God wanted you to stay.
What was it that got you so low,
that you took your life away?
A little sister I will no longer be,
a big brother I will never have again.
You took it all away from me,
how could you let this happen?

Our hearts are never going to heal,
a smile will never see our face.
Happiness, we no longer feel,
and our lives will always have an empty
space.

You should be with us now, you didn't
have to die.
I just don't know how, and don't know why,
Why did you want to die?

Danielle Apa

Dear Father Bless America

Dear Father, bless America
We bow our heads and pray.
Keep it safe throughout the night
And through each passing day.
Be with him, who heads our land
And guide him with your helping hand.
Our soldier boys who are away.
Bring them home with us to stay.
And let there be no longer war
And no dissent from any shore.
Again dear Father, this we pray.
Always bless the U.S.A.
Where mountains wedge against the sky,
And lakes are blue, and geese fly high.
Prairie lands where cattle graze,
And deserts where the sun's ablaze.
Where forest trees are straight and tall,
And leaves change color in the Fall.
Where the flag is red and white and blue.
Where men are brave, and hearts are true.

Anna Mae Piersma

Earth's Destiny

We're one; we're all. We scorch the land.
We choose; it's our free will.

We take; we plunder the sea and the sand.
We fear not what we kill.

Greed takes hold and alters the mold,
Of nature's perfect plan.

I fear that anything could be sold,
For the profits that drive the man.

We see before us the shocking change;
We must not look away.

Because now is the time to rearrange
Our priorities, if life is to stay.

Ignore no more! Vow to take action!
Harness the power within you.

For each small step brings satisfaction,
And uncovers the true global view.

So do your part with a smiling heart;
This is a very good deed.

The rewards are apparent; I know we're
that smart.
Others will certainly take heed.

Edward L. Squires

Memory Of Mother

Your Mother has gone on,
to be with her Lord.
She's resting in Jesus,
she has earned her reward.

Her love is a memory,
to hold in your heart.
She left it here with you,
when she had to depart.

Her smile that you treasured,
she left that here too.
To cheer and to comfort,
to give strength just to you.

Yes, memory of mother,
is all that remains.
But memory of mother,
is one of life's dearest things.

Ester Ruth Lockard

Good Morning

Growing inside me
We feel pain together

You let me know just how you feel
What you want -
Growing in me,
With me

Keeping my thoughts
Working my mind
Through the night you keep me
Hoping

Steadily growing inside me -
I can't help to feel joy
Can't help
Hoping,

Everything is going to be
just fine -

Once the good morning shows his face

Demene C. Poindexter

Precious Water

Round and round and round
We finally reached and round
Years of wind and weather
Sculptured fantasies from rock
The view across the valley
Gave cause to meditate
Of those who call the valley home
And something of their fate.
The Colorado River winds
As far as eye can reach
And a checkerboard of varied farms
Gave proof to us its worth.
As families fled from "dust bowl" lands
In search of food and haven
The water that would quench the soil
Must have seemed a gift from heaven
If earthen plots could stories tell
Of those whose lives are mystery
Their dreams fulfilled would add to lore
In Valley History.

Beryl Beagle

I Would Never Forget That Night

It all happened on prom night
We got into a big fight
He wouldn't stop drinking
I couldn't stop thinking
I didn't know what to do
I really didn't have a clue
He got in his car
Wanting to go so far
I couldn't get the keys away
And he would not stay
He drove so far out of sight
I couldn't see him under the moonlight
I worried so much
I just needed his touch
But I knew in my heart
Soon we would be apart
When I got home
His mom called me on the phone
She said he died crashing in a tree
In his hand was a picture of me.

Angel Bezio

"Tribute To Dad"

There is no better way to say
"We love you."
In what other way to show
Sweet father, husband,
Friend and brother
We know now where you are to go.

You saw beauty in life
Friendships given in ten fold
"Peace" was in his garden
A joy for all to see.

How we all have flourished,
Like the petals on the rose.
You colored us in kindness,
Laughter and love.

Your memories stay locked forever
Until such time.
Our deepest hearts will drum to a
Peace march.
Then togetherness in the garden of God
We will flower to peace of mind.

James La Manna

Magic Of Time

Time passes us by.
We never know what time is.
It just goes.
Magic is secret.
The secret of time.

Sometimes I feel the,
Secret of magic is the,
Time we spend in,
Our life.

Life is to know,
The magic of time,
Is part of living;
You can't live without it.
Just the thought of time slowly
Goes to fast.
That is why,
The Magic of time,
Is the secret of life.

Francesca Guy

Still We Weep

In this splinter of eternity
  We spend here on earth,
Our emotions and soul
  Determine its worth.
We are born.
  We live, we love,
We laugh, we sing.
  We think, we hurt,
We despair, we grieve.
  We wonder and we dream.
We are happy or sad,
  We are angry or glad.
We give pain or help,
  We give joy or hope.
And still we weep
  When this infinitesimal segment ends:
We step through the final sleep—-
  Into full eternity.

Houstine Cooper

You Can't Go Home Again

I used to love this town so
Well,
When in its borders I did
Dwell.
The love surges as before;
Now that I've returned here
Once more.

It's changed a lot in thirty
Years.
I shed a few nostalgic tears.
In all the people on the
Street
I recognize no one I meet.

It must be true what people
Say,
You can't go back home to stay.
Because you'll find things not
The same
As when you left to seek
Your fame.

Jean Young

Thanksgiving Memories

Tonight we're leaving.
We're going away.
We won't be home on
Thanksgiving Day.

We'll be with our family.
We're going together.
This is a trip
we'll cherish forever.

We're going skiing
as we have before,
and I hope we'll go
much much more.

We like to be together
in these joyous seasons.
We like to be together
for many reasons.

After a week
we'll be coming home.
Do you want to know why?
That's where we belong.

Julie S. Riley

Untitled

I have a grandson named Derrell
What a lad, very rare,
Spent most of his life
In a wheel chair,
He's in the hospital now
The end is very near,
Surrounded by loved ones very dear
Last night he had a vision
What a dream!
Heaven's gates opened wide
Just to him it seemed,
It's all over folks, I must go
I love you all, I want you to know,
So take away the medicine
Unhook this machine,
Can you imagine such a thing?
Yes, I can, I heard Him sing.

Alfred A. Cullipher

"Well, Now What?"

Well, now what?
What a "mess" you are in!
No way out can you see.
What a "mess!" My, oh, me!

Well, now what?
Do you just sit and cry?
What is it you can do?
Well-lll—you could sit and "stew!"

Well, now what?
You just can't "stew" and cry!
Do something constructive;
Before it's destructive!

Well, now what?
Act fast now! Do not wait!
Call on Christ! He will help!
Under His Blood, be kept!

Well, now what?
Be saved now! Don't delay!
By Christ's Hand, now be led
You, He died for - and -bled!

Helen Geneva Frazier

Forever Friends

Will we ever discover
What entwines us together
An unexplainable force
From a knowingly unknown source

If ever there was an end
We would still be friends
Always cherishing each other's love
As well as the love from up above

Otherwise life would be incomplete
Full of void and defeat
Never knowing what to do
Life would certainly be cold and blue

Therefore, there is you and there is me
And forever friends we will be
Hand in hand and heart to heart
There is no greater force that could tear us apart

Brenda Lowe

Regrets

I thought I knew
What to do,
But when I did,
I didn't.

I tried to do
The best I could,
But soon I saw
I couldn't.

I asked you to
Help me out,
But you said
You wouldn't.

I tried again
Myself to do,
Although I knew,
I shouldn't.

And finally,
The way it went,
How I wish
I hadn't.

Cissi Lundgren

My Love - My Life

Long before I ever knew
What to look for in a man,
God chose you just for me
As part of his divine plan.

Yes, God sent you to me,
For I was there all the time.
He knew just what I needed
For a love of yours is hard to find.

You came, a look, a touch
Was all it took for me,
You filled my heart completely
And made my love a reality.

Forbidden fruit is the sweetest
Or so it would seem,
But God can see beyond
The man-made earthly dream.

So much more than I expected
When I looked around to find,
God's timing is always perfect
He made you forever mine.

God never makes a mistake
He knew right from the start,
As my husband you were all I needed.
Darling, I love you with all my heart.

Jackie Allen

This Girl, My Wife, Norene

I met this girl who was to change my life
When I decided to make her my wife
She makes my days so calm and serene
This girl, my wife, Norene

When things go wrong and I get blue
There is only one thing I have to do
I go home and on her, I lean
This girl, my wife, Norene

And at the end of a long hard day
When things didn't always go her way
The gleam in her eyes could still be seen
This girl, my wife, Norene

I love her with all my heart
Never, do I want us to part
These things, she knows I mean
This girl, my wife, Norene

John Lynch

I Thought I Heard A Whisper

I thought I heard a
whisper blow and the voice
I heard was nothing compared
to the voice that I heard.

I though I heard a whisper
Blow and I heard it again.

The whisper in my ear, it's gotten
Louder and louder and I
couldn't take it any longer

I thought I heard a whisper
blow but my mind was all up
in the air.
But I still can hear that voice
coming to me from the above.
I thought I heard a whisper
blow sometime I still can hear
the voice talking to me
while I wait for the answer

Fannie Fields

Blanket

...and sometimes
when I feel lonely
I'll climb into bed
and wrap a blanket
around myself

it reminds me
of being in his arms,
where I won't be
anymore

it gives me
comfort and reassurance,
now that
I have none

and it makes me
feel loved,
although I'm not

Christine Zemalkowski

"Passion"

Reflections of a midnight hour,
when our bodies entwined as one;
Moments of unending pleasure,
until we saw the rising sun.

I feel so moved; as we, Lay
side by side, breathless.
Pleasures so shared, but we,
do not stop at one;
Hard for us to unfold,
When we know time has come.

Clearly do you stay, in my
thoughts throughout the day;
While memories of the night,
still shimmer, in the heat
of the sun's hot rays.

Dodie Soto

Lease Renewed

With delight in renewal returning
when spring has at last begun,
our winter-worn bodies are yearning
to soak up the sumptuous sun.

No matter if bodies are aging,
we remain glad tenants of living—
even with blizzards raging,
retain a mood of thanksgiving.

Yes, we thank every season that showers
us with gifts for a limited goal,
though conscious of onrushing hours
that take their expected toll.

But, on days of uncommon perfection
at spring's long-awaited rebirth,
we glory in resurrection
and renew our lease on this earth.

Anne Marx

Light In The Dark

Oh what sins the darkness shadows
Weeping faces, drawn, sallow.
Come into the dark to find me
Bring the light and walk beside me
Save me from this horror-zone
Take my hand and lead me home
And when night finds you I'll be morning
Bringing love and light and glory.

Bronwen Pretorius

Shadows

In my evening of tomorrow
when the day is almost done,
I look o'er the great horizon,
and I see the setting sun.

In the mornings of my lifetime
Many suns did rise and set,
And the shadows of life's evening
Walk where life and love have met.

I can see the many faces
of loved ones, who are gone,
The memories I most cherish
Come at night when day is done.

Then I sit and ponder,
o'er life's vast domain,
For I know on some tomorrow
I'll be with them once again.

Helen A. Wailes

Through The Looking Glass

What do you see,
When you look in your mirror?
Just a face that has no meaning,
Or do you see
The image of God in it.

Do you love your neighbor
And do good whenever you can.
Are you too busy to,
Lend a helping hand,
To a stranger along the way.

Do you visit the lonely,
Or give someone a cheery smile.
Are you always complaining,
About the gloomy weather,
Or do you bring sunshine along the way?

Take another look in your mirror.
If you don't like what you see,
Then it's time to change your image.
It's all up to you,
So change if for the better.

Annie E. Helbig

Just Once

I cannot forget what you did
when you lured me
into your office
after class that night,
making me kiss you
and touch you
again and again.

One night, for a price
you cannot let go.

Now that you're desperate
and told her about "us"
she is angry
and you are leaving.
But look-
I am not here
waiting for you.

What I now have from you
is really enough for me.

Donna M. Moriconi

A Mortal Man

If this were truly a perfect world
Where all good things could be
There would be no place for a mortal man
An imperfect man like me
I would be scorned or ridiculed
Forever banned from grace
People would treat me with utter contempt
And look on me with distaste
But I'm not unhappy - I know in my heart
That one small fact is true
However good or bad I am
I'm no better nor worse than you
So now I can see - in retrospect
That perfection can never be
A perfect world isn't possible
As long as there's you and me
So I'll just have to accept the fact
That I am a mortal man
And try to live by the golden rule
And be the best I can

Hal Whaley

Bag Lady

She lay there by the corner,
Where she had come each day,
To sell her many baubles,
For what little they would pay.

Her clothes were old and dirty,
She had smudges on her brow,
The lines along her cheeks,
Had softened up somehow.

No one really knew her,
Or how she came to be,
Living in a hobo jungle,
Her only friend was me.

She never asked for riches,
Just wanted to get by,
Beans were good enough for supper,
Beneath an open sky.

Now she has a special corner,
Where she is standing proud,
Hawking to the angels,
From a big white cloud.

Diane L. Kortes

The Truth

Down by the boat house at the lake.
Where there's nothing but love to make.
I feel like a prisoner on fire
waiting desperately
denied sentencing forever
I search my heart relentlessly
to figure our what I'm
supposed to be.
Empty rooms, crowded by the past.
Here I am stranger to a smile.
Trying to fight the tears, missing
by a mile.
In this life, this world of insanity.
With love so over looked and obscured.
I've never felt this way.
But I never had anyone like you.
I'm at your mercy, when you call my name.
Take me through this fire, this raging wall
of flames.
Only you can break these chains.

Eileen Monroe

Homeward Bound

My goal is to do the best I can
wherever I may be,
To do what God has chosen —
especially for me,
When someone needs a helping hand
Or just someone to talk to —
As God would have me to do.
To be a friend
to tell them about God,
and His love.
His acceptance to attain
home in heaven above.
When I fail - I turn to God
to help me get on the right track.
In prayer and repentance
that I may — get right back.
Love holds all things together.
Just look around,
and have the assurance
when we're Homeward Bound.

Fern Gardiner Smith

Dreams

I whisper my dreams to a shadow unseen,
while holding my pillow good and tight.
There was magic in the air, that night.
Dreams are only dreams, that dreamers
dare dreams, but oh how I wish they were
exactly what they seem.

Cora Hoxtell

Night Quiet

In late night quiet,
While relaxing in my chair—
My mind drifts in silence
To find things hidden there.

Thoughts about my family,
Memories of childhood home,
Dreams of exotic places—
In my chair, I dwell alone.

In peaceful quiet of the night
All is still and tranquil bound,
No phones, no city noises—
Peaceful silence is the sound.

A time to shirk my duties,
A time to talk with God and pray
For all the wrong in our big world
To be all right one day.

So when you're tired and restless—
Or sometimes feeling blue,
Relax in a favorite easy chair
With Night Quiet to comfort you.

Betty Arlene Turnipseed

Good Listener

I'd hang
to your shoulders
when you feel
most life crying
and sing
"never fear,
my Van Gogh ear
will let you fill
and throw it all away."

Jeremy Shubrook

The Sound Of Mind

The inner voice speaks
while you're in tune with nature.
It directs with clarity,
into dreams fulfilled.

Pause you must, from busy times
to encounter mind's calm ways.
Ideas thrive like showers of rain,
then blossom into reality.

The mind hints your directed ways,
then whispers you homeward.
On arrival the voice raises
with countless visions to follow.

You feel connected
to worlds on high
as your unswerving mind
influences the day.

(c) 1994 Kether Communications

Lay By My Side

Lay by my side, and love me.
Whisper, sweet things, so softly.
Lay by my side, and love me.
till the sunrise, in the misty morning.
Lay by me, lay by me, and tell me
that you're my one and only love.
Lay by my side, and kiss me
Oh, so soft, and tender.
Tell me true, that you do really, love me.
More, and more, then you can say.
Lay by me, and give me another reason
for living.
Lay by me, and give me all the love that
you can give.
Lay by my side, and kiss me.
Lay by my side, and be mine.

Jamey L. Zevan

A Patch Of Country

A "PATCH OF COUNTRY" calls to mind
The many patches you can find.
As you look out across the field,
You see the myriad colors yield
The brilliancy that's true and bright,
And sunshine brings the hues to sight.

A patch of sunlight, patch of green,
A patch of sorrel, yellow, clean,
Send out the call to you and me
To see the beauty all so free.
Let's pray a prayer of thankfulness
To God for all that we possess.

James A. Stoddard

The River

I once saw a river
Whose banks were of sand-
It was a beautiful river,
In a beautiful land.

Yet, as I looked at its beauty
I wondered where it went,
And, if it did its duty
Wherever it was sent.

Because there is a force
Behind everything on earth
And, all of nature we endorse
While wondering about our worth...

Adeline Thompson

Like Snow And Ice

You are the snow
White, tender, soft and rich
You appear once in a while
Falling gently over people and things
Giving them a
Magic touch of waited happiness.

I am the ice
Strong, tough and transparent
I travel around many places
Watching endless faces
Claiming traces
Of inspiring freshness

But now that you're gone
There is something deeply precious
That even nature can't deny
We both melt in a
Single crystal drop of water.

Alvaro Pereira

My Friend, Sam

He's a kind and thoughtful fellow,
Who is always just the same.
He treats everyone decent
And Sam is his name.

I feel so very fortunate
That he likes me just as I am.
He's one of life's treasures
Even though he is just plain Sam.

When I am in deep trouble
And everything seems to go wrong.
Sam's always ready and willing
To lend a helping hand that is strong.

He always wears a cheerful grin
And it truly is a joy,
To be in his presence
'Cause he's such a good old boy.

He says that his pet philosophy is;
"I am just what I am".
And I am really proud
To call him, "MY FRIEND, SAM."

Byron C. Casey

The Only Sting Of Satan

Satan's just a big black bee
Who's stinger's been removed
By God, who came to earth as man
For all the world to be approved.

He was the only righteous One
Who could or would perform this act,
Because to do it right and do it well
Was to do it perfect and exact.

He endured until the bitter end,
Till all the stinger was extracted,
God meant business from the very start,
And since that day Satan has reacted.

All that evil Devil can do now
Is buzz around and be a pest,
For with the sting of death removed
The Christian mind can be at rest.

Eternal life is now a surety,
A bee can sting but once, not twice,
God died disguised as His own Son,
Our blessed Savior, Jesus Christ.

Christy Cumbie

A Special Somebody

Who is this special somebody?
Why do I cherish thee?
Why do I love,
Why do I cry,
Why do I get teased?
How do I know this person?
Does this person know me?
Is this person my relative?
Do I love thee?
This person is my grandmother,
The only one I have.
I am her granddaughter,
The only one she has.
I wish to spend many nights with thee.
I wish to spend a birthday.
Or a holiday with thee.
To spend a lovely summer day,
To dance around and play,
to hug and kiss and say I love you.
Every single day.

Amy Cheung

Why!

Oh, the senseless waste!
Why would anyone
want to do that
to themselves?
Slowly destroying
all that they have
to live for.
Piece by piece,
ruining their life
and shattering the world
that they have created,
that they are
the center of,
by erasing themselves
from their loved ones lives.
Oh, Why!

Jeffrey Warren Janisch

Dreamless

Night's slumber came, and you were there
Wind's gentle fingers in your hair.
God's parodied by form and face
You stood there in that dreamer's place.

Your friends were there; so many came
So freely used that cherished name!
Unseen, I longed to enter, too,
That privileged space surrounding you.

My will was shorn like Samson's hair,
Dream and Delilah - disabling pair!
No power to move; no voice to call
Held as I was in dreamer's thrall.

Like darts, my thoughts propelled to you
And made you turn - myself to view.
Yes, viewed me there, but didn't say
A word to me - just turned away.

Awake next morn, in pain I cried,
Last shred of hope within me died.
I knew awake it couldn't be
But hoped in dreams you could love me.

Carrol L. Wanner

An Endless Love

They loved each other endlessly
with a love one rarely knows,
but they kept their love in secrecy
for their fathers were deadly foes.
The men were to embark in a six-year war
then the couple would have to be apart
until they came upon a plan
to run away together after dark.
They planned to meet by a tall Oak tree
that stood in the glow of the moon,
she knew if the plan was to succeed
he would have to arrive there soon.
Worried, she went and looked for him
not knowing what she'd find,
Then she saw him lying in his blood,
one of her father's men shot him from behind.
But years and years have passed since then
some still ask, did the young woman die?
But it is told at the tree on a clear calm night
you can still hear the faint sounds of a
woman's cry.

Jessica Belcher

Astrid Le Fleur' Of Belgium

My lovely friend, Astrid
With blue eyes so bright.
Who sparkles day and night,
Any dark room she enters-
Astrid, brings in the light.

Diamond rings on her fingers,
Glitter polish on her toes.
Emeralds on her ears-
Pearls around her neck,
Bracelets of silver and gold.

Her limousine is of petal pink,
Coats and shawls are made of mink.
Her curly blonde hair glistens,
Like the rays of the sun,
Astrid is a bundle of fun.

Right from the start
Astrid gave from her heart.
Spends money on lavish things.
Her perfume smells like sweet,
Flowers, that bloom in spring.

Carolyn Joan Ragno

My Mother The Unsung Heroine

She was a vibrant woman
With pride in her eyes
When death came
It caught her by surprise.
1939. Ma Douce France
Struggle under enemy rule
We live in sufferance
Life is hard and cruel.
Third of June 1940
Forever she left her home
Fighting for sweet Liberty
Unknowing her time had come.
This proud woman
Was my mother
Every time I can
I remember her
And her smiling eyes.
All my life she has been
My beacon, my light
And of France, another Unsung Heroine.

Christiane Dalrymple

Ron's Dream

You went away and left me
with your "Dream."
And there were many heartaches
in between.
Now the winds of time
have slowly passed.
The "Dream" we shared was
never meant to last.
You slipped away silently
into the night
Leaving me alone to make
things right.
Now, you are gone.
The "Dream" is mine.

Jean Dawe-Hayes

My Inspiration

I've never known anyone as pure as you
With your eyes of baby Blue.
You make me feel sixteen,
With a look I've never seen.
I'm not one of one, but one of two,
Yet I feel that doesn't matter to you,
As time goes by.
I wonder if this is all a lie,
I feel close to you yet so far away
I learn to love you from day to day
I don't believe in fate
Maybe it's not too late

Amy JoAnne Evans 2/26/93

Dying Soul

Can my heart now beat
Without my life blood
My life love
Ripped from my womb
Torn fresh from my soul
The life I once carried
Love
So shortly known
Created from the merging
Of two making one whole
Dead a piece of my soul
Love that is renewed
A mistake that is unwronged
Should I fight for my love
The blood of my soul
The man who makes me whole
Or shall I just die slow

Clare Russell

Virgin Mary

Queen of Heaven;
Woman of many faces;
How easy the task,
Submitting your will
Totally to the Lord.
God asked, "Will you?"
You replied, "Yes."
Simple yet difficult.
Because you were humble
And yielding,
You spend eternity with God.
Adored by all the world,
You guide
Trusting souls to your son, Jesus.

Elaine H. Stevens

It's Thank Heaven Day

I wish I could make the
world sing in tune again
I would spread peace and
love all over the world
I would wipe away all the
tears and make the world laugh again
Jesus gave us the key to be happy
contented life, but we seem
to have lost it.
Friendship and love is always in style
we must love one another
This is our only hope in our
world today
Lucky stars will shine
in heaven above tonight
Because it's thank heaven day .

Elva M. Hull

If The President Lived In Your Town

If the president lived in your town
Would streets be littered with mass?
If your boss was in view of you
Would you pluck aside his cash?

If a friend was listening in
Would you satirize her truth?
If your lover was away
Would you forget his faith in you?

If your neighbor lost his sight
Would you help him cross the street?
...If your mother gave you life
Would you health her heart to beat?

If you had one day to live
Who would you forgive?
The footprints you have pained
Mark the wealth within your name.

Cynthia Renee

Titled 5000

Crystallized harmony and the
(wrinkled purple faced)
woman screams out.
Cane in her back
suspended to admit sanction
Called out to play by the moon.
Sing songs of god and worship him
(along with Mary Jane and Mr. Jack)
Touched by firewands of death
due to misdeeds of her right hand
all for the sake of (boredom)
(wrinkled purple faced)
old woman —
Master of serpents
and Tamer of the snake.
Wise old woman —
run away to the land of
dappled bedfellows.

Heidi Spitzig

Jeffrey

You are the Jewel of my love,
You are the Eye of my life.
You were First in my heart,
who will be Forever true.
You are a Radiant beam,
Who Eternally glows,
Year after year.

Christine Ward

The Sweet Bird

Early one morning as I was
Yawning, I saw the sweet bird fly

The bird had flown, the bird had
Gone in the twinkling of an eye.

Early that morning I stood idly
By, I lost sight of the sweet
Bird's flight, in the twinkling
of an eye.

Forever gone, forever flown
As sweet birds do fly. Gone
forever, to return never; to
where sweet birds fly, as
did my youth in the
twinkling of an eye.

James Anderson

Jesus, Jesus

Jesus is my guide
Yes Jesus is always
with me by my side
For I ask him to always
be my guide
I can do nothing without
Jesus by my side.
For He leadeth me far and wide
as He Jesus is always
at my side
As Jesus within my
heart which is inside

Buna Bennefield

Confusion

Two different worlds
yet similar in certain ways
confusion,
leading me into a dark hole of madness
taking the sunshine away

As I flee to safety
from this enclosed darkness
Which way do I go? Confusion
I can't see behind or in front of me
the road is dark and unclear.

The daisies are dying
the birds have all stopped singing
Where did the sun go? Confusion
Who do I turn to now?
Why won't this ache in my heart go away?

April Smith

Epitome

I have seen a trail of death:
twist on through the nightly news;
leaving spaces in the park;
zone out pieces of the dark;
turn the language that we use

into hushed and burning breath;
pushing everyone to fear
loving, laughing, all of life;
till the mention of a knife
causes cursing that we hear;

nearly never getting dressed,
beating every single breast.

Frank S. Farello

Perspective

We mortals live but in a flash,
yet want our life to mean so much.
A shame today has such import,
tomorrow it will be but smoke.

We live and sweat and toil along,
through headache, heartache; work for gain.
It means so much, we must succeed,
but future views it as a joke.

We cannot bankroll Joy or Fame,
Their Value will not stay for sure.
Don't live today for tomorrow's Pleasure,
or like the vine you'll grow and choke.

Remember as you push and prod,
today's Reward is found today.
Tomorrow's Joy will be made *then*,
our Pleasure is earned stroke by stroke.

Fred Wenger

Picture This

With a touch, of the brush,
You are, cherished so,
You form, is highlighted,
As the colors, unfold,

There is, a blend, of affection,
With every, amiable stroke,
You are a genius, of a gem,
Almost ready, to be cloaked,

The scene, is of essence,
With such a graphic, design,
That intrigues, the soul,
With this compliment, in mind,

I admire you, like a picasso,
To me, you are, a work of art,
You are treasured, like a rembrandt,
And lovingly protected, with all of my heart,

My love, is displayed on canvas,
With your portrait, there in,
Surrounded by, the frame of happiness,
That I pray, will never end.

Freddie Fugate

The Master Painter

With his hand he paints a sunset
With colors pure and bright
And formations ever changing,
It truly is a lovely sight.

When the artist paints a springtime
The trees are veiled in green.
Some are painted pink or white
And on hills wild flowers are seen.

The landscape changes in autumn.
Then in winter he mantles the fields
With white to warm the seeds below,
So in harvest the grain it yields.

'Tis a beautiful world of wonders,
It's all as my Father planned,
For He is the master painter
And the changes are His to command.

Most precious of all His paintings,
Most gracious of all His art,
Is the image of His being
That He painted on my heart.

Elnora Wilson

Untitled

Confusion hits; it sinks in.
You feel hopeless,
When reality comes,
Don't push stop; wake up.
Don't stop reading,
Or it will come back.
Let me stay in the music, in the movie.
Let me stay in my dreams,
Even in my nightmares.
Just as long as I'm not here.
Just as long as reality is dismissed.
Let me especially stay in my dreams.
Let me stay in the book, in the story.
Let me stay in the dark,
Don't turn on the light.

When reality comes,
When destiny arrives.
When reality comes.
Please, pass me by.

Gretchen Luther

The Friendship

Underneath earth's black soil
You find rock rejected.
Polish it and a jewel you
See unexpected.

Friendship is like a jewel too
Years will make it shine.
Nothing else I value more
Than the friends of mine.

Sisterhood and brotherhood
And the friendship does
Humanities string of pearls,
Helping love for us.

Often after years go by
We will then realize,
How important are the friends
Faithful, loving, nice.

Underneath earth's dark soil
We should jewels find,
Building lasting good will, love,
And friendship to mankind

Aini Tossavainen

Poppies

Little golden glowing poppy.
You grew wild only in California
On the hill sides, road banks and sand
in little clusters.
In morning you came out of your bud
each little petal one by one.

The wind shimmering your golden petals
and glittering by sun.
You're showing your beauty to everyone.
You are there all day long.

Then you fold your petals back into bud.
Your day work done.
You last 4 to 5 days then the wind blows
your petals away one by one.

Luther Burbank, said you are a mystery
Of the land and made by God's hand.
No artist can get your glitter and gold that's
made by wind and sun.
The state flower of California you have won.

Esther L. Pohlman

"The Unhappy Heart"

To give up on something,
you like most to do,
that you've been,
honest with, good and true.
No heed, for the hurt,
you shuffle on ahead,
thoughtlessness,
separates, and fills you,
full of dread.

The impassiveness,
that, can let you go,
hurts more than, you can know,
A legend of integrity,
through the years,
then travel through,
the valley of tears.

The uselessness, that follows,
makes you feel, empty and hollow,
the hurt is, to the core,
heart aching, and very sore.

Geraldine McDonough

Fourth Of July

It's the fourth of July,
You see flags flying high,
A tribute to a wonderful land.

See fireworks in the sky,
See the parade go by,
And watch the marching band.

Soldiers and sailors march with zest,
Medals shining on their chest,
Their valor saved this land.

Cars, horses and even goats,
Pull the lovely, flowery floats,
Was there anything ever so grand?

The sound of guns are in the past,
And we pray that it will last,
Never forced to make a stand.

It's the fourth of July,
And we fly our flags high,
Cause we love our wonderful land.

Eli Tueche, Jr.

What A Boy

When you have a baby boy,
You see many things.
The cute baseball cap,
A football and a soccer ball.
And occasionally a racket,
A paddle or cue.
The toys reflect repair or destruction
Will he fix or tare apart?
Those building blocks,
Or maybe some tools.
The book and some papers,
Will he be a writer?
Or just add up the books.
You want to be proud,
What ever he chooses.
A pat on the back,
A hug or two.
Just show him you care,
And always tell them the truth.

Beverly DiSanti

The End Of A Rainbow

There is no such sight
You will ever see
As beautiful as a rainbow
Many colors in its spectrum.

Each has its own beauty
As the sun filters through
Green and red and golden hue
All are so beautiful.

One shade alone cannot compare.
You need all others to enhance
All humanity to view
The arch takes its stance.

No matter all the beauty
It has a beginning and an end
But never undermine
Both ends are as beautiful
As is the rainbow.
This is life and then comes another rainbow.

Cara Caron

"The Same Path"

Until you're on the same path,
  You will never understand.
Until you follow Jesus,
  To the promised land.

Until you walk the narrow,
  Looking only straight ahead.
And seeking God in prayer
  On your knees beside the bed.

Until you feel His heavy heart
  Inside your very own,
And feel the indignation
  That He suffered all alone.

And until you wrestle forces
  Of a world that is unseen,
You cannot share the glory
  Of our soon and coming King.

Elise O'Neill

Plato's Cave

Come out of Plato's cave
you wonders of the earth!
Confront your shadow Gods.
Convince them of your worth.

Enlightened minds see truth,
the spark from which we came,
and knowing only that for sure
can wrestle in His name.

Just risk a turn around and see
the real world pass you by
and drop the chains that hold you from
your vision of the sky.

You're deep inside the shadow world
of false reality.
Now listen to the truth within
and let it set you free.

Jean Franse

Dying Love

Your love brought tears
Your smiles brought laughter
Your love brought tears
That she could never understand

She loved you so much
She loved you with fear
She loved you forever
Until you brought her tears

She came to your side
She came without grief
She came with her love
She could no longer keep

She cried in her bed
For love was not there
Your love was gone
Right into the air

Your love was lost
It was no longer there
Your love had no meaning
No meaning to spare

Autumn Newbern

Lonely

It's the longest we've been apart.
You're very much in my heart.
I miss you so much,
I'd die for your touch.

It's not easy, yet I know it's
something I must do.
I can't wait 'til I am
back with you.

You've been through a lot,
but you've supported me, no matter what.
You have made me proud.
"I LOVE YOU," I will shout out loud.

When I return to you,
it will be for forever.
Wherever I go,
we will go together.

Anne V. Brady

Futuristic Dreams

Timing seems unreal.
Yet perfection shows.
Seeing it so clear.
Neutral living knows.

Smelling scents untold.
Futuristic dreams.
Thoughts in night behold.
The truth is how it seems.

Memories now are late.
Writing, feeling, lost.
Truth will hesitate.
Get the point across.

Hearts will never lie.
Dreams tell of the past.
Memories deny.
Lunatics unmasked.

Living behind the shadows.
In night and morning dawn.
Crying only shows.
The past in mind is gone.

Jennie Nies

The Old Man

The old man told me
That his life
had gone by
Oh so fast

Now it's time for me
to put it all together
But it's
Oh so vast

Where we used to go
and think it over
Learn about the stars and sun
Now I hope that I never
forget the things
that were said and done

Eric E. Hatch

Why Not Me

Alone on the beach
With my feet in the sand
Dreaming of him beside me
hand in hand

This I know will never be
So let the tide take my thoughts
out to sea
Setting me free
From this love that's killing me

I will never love another
I won't even try

When it's time for my curtain to fold
If he could only see into my soul

Beside the break engraved on
my heart will be
Why not me!

Carolyn Seery Dickert

Fall

I ambled around outside this morn
While waiting delivery of the paper.
There's a peaceful calm before the dawn,
I'm engulfed in quiet splendor.
A furry squirrel scampers up the tree,
A bird glides gracefully down to the lawn.
No neighbors stirring, can I see.
I paused, the air was fresh and clean.
Then quickly, a cool breeze sends a chill.
Soon the sun will rise once more.
The wonders of Nature, what a thrill.
Another glance before I go indoor.
From the lake, a lone duck's call.
A Thankful Prayer, and Welcome Fall.

Geraldean B. Roy

What Do You Mean To Me

I can never tell how much
you mean to me but what you mean
to me is an eternity of love and
companionship.

What you mean to me is someone
I can count on to be there when I
need companionship or just need to talk.

What you mean to me is someone
I can love. I love you and you love me.
I want you to know I will always love you.

Andrea Byrd

Untitled

You've lit up my life
You've removed that knife
You told me you wouldn't lie
I feel as if
I don't even need to ask why.
I feel as if I am a flower
And you are the rain giving me a shower.
I've opened my petals and my heart
I've let my colors show
Now, I'm situated and ready to go
You lit the match; the fire burned in a flash
No one has yet put it out
With a splash
Someone said we're a perfect match;
to you I want to attach
And all I hope is that it will last.

dedicated to Nick Freese

Jennifer Wise

The Forces Of Love

A feeling so powerful,
yet so gentle,
is in my grasp

A force so strong,
its power can hold me back,
From everything.
But itself.

Love is a feeling so powerful,
So forceful,
You cannot escape it.
But it can escape you.
And that strengthens its force
of grief, and sorrow.

Yet, when it lasts,
You are overcome with joy,
But that's love.
A force of nature.

Dicla Levi

Untitled

I find it hard to say I'm sorry
You find it hard to just forget
Can we go back in time
To the day when we first met

There are times when I find myself
Feeling lost and all alone
Is this real or am I imagining things
I cannot believe you're really gone

There's a pain inside my heart
Whenever I think your name
Was it meant to be from the start
Or have I been playing a fool's game

Here I stand on the edge of the curb
Holding my heart inside my hands
As I watch time go by
Riding the wind above the desert sands

John Keeling

No One Lives Alone

You say it's your life.
You can do as you please.
Yes, that is very true.
But please don't forget,
how you were nurtured and loved,
when you were very young.
Your life touches many;
family, friends and neighbors.
No one really lives alone.
The good and the bad;
what you do,
what you don't,
affect more than you will ever know.

Joellen Yeray Schutz

Grandpa Made The Cradle

He measured, sawed, and sanded
With a twinkle in his eyes
He would make the grandest cradle
One that money could not buy
It would have a lovely canopy
To shade the newborns' eyes
Its gentle rocking motion
Would soothe the babies' cries
It would last for generations
The babies all would feel his love
It would be a gift to them from pop-pop
To those cherubs from above
With the passing years, the dream was fulfilled
As each grandchild in turn was laid
In the grandest cradle ever fashioned
The cradle that grandpa made.

Irene Pataki Krupp

Feelings Of Love

It was just like it came from nowhere...
You were there, and suddenly at that
moment I knew what I'd been missing.
Your voice was so kind it calmed my
nerves immediately. You looked at
me in a way that made me feel as if
I was floating on top of a big fluffy
cloud. I shook with happiness. Yet I
still can't seem to get you off of my
mind. Could it possibly be. I'm not sure,
I don't know what has come over me.
It was like I was hit with a ton of
bricks that fell from above. Maybe
time will tell, who knows what is
still ahead yet to happen. All I can do
is wait.

Juanita Hamner McKleroy

A Shell

When you see a shell laying on the sand,
You don't often think of the life it had.
This shell was really a mollusk's home,
It covered this animal just like a dome.
As it saw and crawled and lived its life,
The shell that covered it protected it from strife.
And then one day when it washed ashore,
Its life just ended like the closing of a door.
But this mollusk left behind its beauty rare,
And if a child picked it up, it is theirs to share.
So let us too be like this shell,
Let the life we live of our good deeds tell.
And then when we, too, finally come to rest,
Our light will still shine if we've done our best.

Agnes Brasher

As The Light Shimmers

As the light shimmers across the lake,
waves caress the shores from the sail's wake.
The water gurgling at my feet,
the sand between my toes, such a treat.
Being at the lake is such a thrill,
when everything is so very still.
I can be so carefree.
All I have to do is be me.
As the light shimmers across the lake.

Erin L. Smith

The Palm Trees

Stately and tall they stood by the sea side
Waving and dipping their fronds with the tide.
Only slightly did they dip with the gentle breeze,
But bowing low when the earth really sneezed.

In the time of a storm you could hear the fronds drop.
They hit the ground with an angry "plop".
In time of the hurricane they bent very low.
The wind swept them around to break up the row.

Then when the winds ceased they stood quiet and still,
Down the street, in the yards, and on the dune hills.
Waving gently again with the nice caress
Giving to all people and to God their best.

Dorothy Goodwin

Open Your Heart

It's a short life that we live,
We all have so much to give.
Why not stand up and show we care,
Let the whole world know we're there.
The guns are at our own back door,
Our kids are having their own war.
The bombs are killing people far away,
So many children die every day.
Get rid of the hunger, guns, and drugs,
Let's give these kids food, love, and hugs.
It's a rough world we brought them into,
Let's join together and see what we can do.
One person can start the whole motion,
If we stand united it will cross the ocean.
No one needs to suffer so in this age,
Please let us turn the page.
I hold my hand out in hope and love,
And pray for help from God above.

Joanne A. Vogelsong

One

No one lives alone and no one dies alone,
We are one body of humanity united with the world,
We are member's one of another,
Joined together in every moment of time,
If one member suffers all suffer,
If one rejoices all rejoice, for we are one.

The human family and created order are one,
The physical and spiritual are one,
I cannot say of the air, "I have no need of you,"
Or of the land, water and trees, "I have no need of you,"
Plants and animals, sky and sea,
All are part of you and me, for we are one.

The physical spiritual balance is in us,
This makes living in the world special,
Our decisions make a difference to God and the world,
We create and destroy, relate and fracture,
We are in the world, and the world is in us,
We are in God and God is in us, for we are one.

James R. Jacobson

The Question

As Mother Earth swings on its destined orbit;
We give a hail to man for his brief ride on it.
To be or not to be, that is the question;
Give the Word to Man, will he learn from it?
God has offered it all for one great reason;
While the big man plays his games of treason.
As Man tries to mold iron to clay;
The Word continues with us day by day.
Who's fooling who, might be the question;
As nations prepare for the battle, Armageddon.
Time has elapsed, now 'tis about over;
The harvest is ripe, who was the grower?
Who was the host down here on Earth?
Who allowed us a chance through human birth?
How can I plant the seed as I go along;
Cultivate it and help make it strong?
What's lost if I throw Christ to the wind;
Follow the World, get entangled in sin?
As I sit here pondering what to say;
The tares grow thicker day by day.

George Rhoads

We... The Inhabitants... Of The Planet Earth

We maim_
We kill_
We love_
We hate_

What kind of beings are we mortals?
Living but a brief span
In this temporary place!

I know no answer to this search,
Except to say that long ago
Christ found us worthy
To be saved_
By dying on a Cross Himself.

Surely we must, somehow, bear
Some responsibility_somewhere_
In His unique Divine Plan
Of gaining Heaven!

Evelyn H. Vondran

/

?/A
+/-
N/S
M/F
Y/Y

There are no right questions/And there are no wrong answers
Imperfect is the mirror/Reflecting backward shadows
Comforted by constant stars/We cringe at wind's defiance
But all is in balance/Despite the moment changing
For I remain myself/In a family of strangers

H/L
Y/N
E/W
W/B
S/G

As storms give way to calm / And then to storms again
As life and death exchange / Their cries and tears in vain
The mystery solved today / Unravels all too soon
When words at midnight clear / Are puzzles by next noon
I become the fulcrum / Bring harmony from pain

C. Thomas Howes

Life

Life begin with many seeds.
We must nurture an supply them with special needs.
Like plants and flowers we watch them grow, multiply,
and bare much fruit.
We abused it and misused it like an old suit.

Life, we look back and wonder, where did we go wrong? Yet correction
can be made an life again can become strong.
Life can be sweet in every way. Choices are made,
voices are heard and our character is shown every day.

Seeds must be planted with plenty of morals, watered with fresh love.
We must fertilize the mind with a higher being above.
Life can be full of fun, with a ray of faith and hope that
shines like the bright sun.

Life can be long and life can be short.
Decisions can be made in life on how we want to take part.
Like the flowers and the plants that must wither and die.
We are sadden with our hearts and we cry.

Live life fully every day.
Be kind to people and watch what you say.
Pray each day to keep a clean heart.
Life can be like the beginning seeds, always looking for a new start.

Bernice Gilmore

We Only Have Today...While Today Is Still Here

We think we have tomorrow...next week, next month, next year;
We only have today...while today is still here.

Who knows, with a second, what the next one will bring...
who knows when a moment will not stop to cling.

Fate can be a stranger, a stranger stalks the night...
Fate may decide, for us, a tomorrow is not in sight.

This time is the right time to beat with our drum...
Next time is the wrong time...if a next time doesn't come.

We think we have tomorrow...next week, next month, next year;
We only have today...while today is still here.

Gloria Hoffman

Shells

Perusing unclaimed shells,
We strode the unmarked sand.
I glanced upon your closing hand.

You stood so poised,
Among the rising dew.
You were among the few.

Cradling forgotten shelters of the sea,
You arranged and planned their new plight,
Uniquely different each in their own right.

Raging crests filled the vast basin,
Enveloping the shells' extravagant beauty.
Why is the earth angry and moody?

Fear not the untamed spirits, you proclaimed.
As your voice rose up among the rattle,
Commanding the bountiful cliffs to concede their battle.

Your hand is now open and I now believe,
Crossing its texture I find comfort and I'm relieved.
To destroy all that's created by
Housing the dreams and tales of one of God's creatures,
You lose sight of God's majesty and all its features.

Dawne E. Fiore

God Gives Life So We Can Give

We're so busy in our grown up talk.
We tell our children to take a walk.
Dad's away all day or maybe for weeks.
Mom is so tired, she hardly speaks.
Children want and need attention, but are alone.
They have to find out on their own.
Unanswered questions, they cry and pout.
They don't know what life is all about.
They sit there watching T.V.
They wonder, is this what life should be?
Children need to be taught right and wrong.
They need to hear a good bedtime song.
They need to be hugged and cuddled.
Left alone, their lives are muddled.
Our children need our love, hugs and time.
Anything less may lead to a life of crime.
Our children need love and correction.
Balanced training can lead to perfection.
God is the one who makes this connection.
Jesus rose so we can have resurrection.

Al Thomas

The Tracks

The railroad tracks stretch on and on as rail by rail we walk. Together. Hand in hand we face the miles that stretch into eternity. The track curves and twists but never changes its endless formation of rock and steel. Although we stumble and trip sometimes, we lean upon each other. As the miles stretch on behind us we begin to look to the setting sun. We see the twists and turns and blockages of the track. And we begin to look inside ourselves and into each other for strength. We also look behind us at all the slips we've made. And we begin to figure out exactly what the meaning of all these trials is. However by the time that we really understand-the train is on its way.

Hidden by a blind curve or the sweetest lavender, we can only hear its rumblings as it makes its way to us. Ever moving faster, our destiny becomes real. Facing that light, all desire to run leaves us. And we stand. With no fear in our eyes but only dreams in our hearts. And the train moves on; with only an echo of its never changing rhythm.

Carla D. Hartzog

Spoil Sports

It was Nineteen Ninety Four tough times you see
we were going down the road the dog and me

Out comes the neighbor with something wrapped in foil
he says give this to the dog before it spoils

We were home in two skips and a hop
I threw them there Vittles wright in the pot

There we were, me and Huck
licking our chops we were in luck

When almost done, I popped off the cover
I looked at the mutt, and thought you ain't my brother

Then I went soft, for this meal was thrifty
so me and my dog, we went fifty fifty

James P. Hennessey

"Loved Ones"... Dedicated to My Beloved Family

When we were just three little tykes
We were not endowed with wealth,
But, oh, how happy we all were
For we were blessed with love and health.

As time passed on and we all grew,
Many things began to change.
Our Mom grew ill but father still
Was strong and gave us strength.

Mom was gentle, sweet and kind.
Though weak of body, was strong of mind.
Our sadness or sorrow she could not bear
Nonetheless, whenever needed was always there.

Father was quiet, docile, and yet strong
Gave us advice, softly, and was rarely wrong.
He walked through life so straight and tall,
We believed he was the greatest father of them all.

Though they have been gone for many years
Our loving memories of them still bring tears.
We continue to speak of them again and again,
For in our hearts they will forever remain.

Gina McWeeney

A Mother's Tears

A beautiful little 5 year old comes walking down an aisle.
Wearing a frilly yellow dress she flashes Mom, a smile.

A tiny cardboard mortar hat is balanced on her head.
At her pre-school graduation a mother's tears are shed.

Then suddenly — I'm here once more as a long aisle, she walks down.
It's her high school graduation and she wears a cap and gown.

Then that beautiful, young lady send's a soft, shy smile to me.
I wonder where the years have gone as a mothers tears flow free.

A young adult she has become, as four more years flew past.
It's her college graduation now but it would not be her last.

Once more decked out in cap and gown my heart's full of love and pride
Once more, a smile is sent my way once more, this mother cried.

Now a gracious lady looks at me with a cheerful wave and smile
Again she's earned the privilege to walk this commencement aisle.

As she receives the symbolic hood this time, for her Masters Degree.
A mother's eyes filled with tears and this is what she sees.

A beautiful little five year old comes walking down an aisle.
Wearing a frilly yellow dress she flashes Mom, a smile.

Dorothy M. Ariola

Untitled

Your voice is like a soft caress
Weaving a pattern around me
Your touch is the softest, sweetest thing that has ever touched me
In a crowded room I know I can turn around and you'll be watching me
Like I'm the only woman in the room
This warms me faster than any fire or coat
Since I know when we get home
You will show me how much you love me
And I know that even years from now
You will love me
I think that I have always loved you
Just as you've always loved me
I am the luckiest woman alive to have you for a husband
Thank you for loving me the way you do

Barbara Leavell

Bad Parting

Have you ever attended the death of one living?
What a sorrow to feel if you do!
For the sadness you know! - Lingers ever so slow!
As the memories - to each other are given.
I saw tear's in the eye's of the one's who have tried!
In their own way - to hold back!
Their feelings! 'Cause in haste! - Things are said!, and one's
Feeling's are read! But no true "love"! -
Just emotional - "dealings"
When a child must depart - for bad reason!
Like a death - a bad feeling! - remains,
In the homes, and the live's of the loved
one's - who've tried - to love! And confide!
But in vain! They have cried! - only now
To be - some small "memory" stealing!
And the meeting will end - with a "prayer"!
For each "sin"!, and a "prayer"! For the heart's!
That need healing! There is only one way - to hold children
Today - that's with eyes opened wide, ears to hear, not much pride,
and the "good book", that hold's all the wisdom!

Charlene P. Dukes

"Child Of My Heart"

My child, what are you doing today
What are your thoughts, your hopes, your dreams
It's been too long since we talked and laughed
It's been years, it seems.

My child, do you think of me today
Do you miss the times we shared
Do you know in your heart that I need to hear
Your voice, saying that you care.

What have you done since last we met
Have all of your dreams come true
I have the need to know these things
To share in what happens for you.

My child, please don't keep me out of your life
Please remember my love for you
You were the reason I lived long ago
In the days when you loved me too.

Oh, child of my heart that I held to my side
And whispered sweet nothings to
How I so long to hold you close by me once more
I miss you my child, I miss you.

Delores Wilson Reece

The Straw That Broke The Camel's Back

Gosh, that camel looks so big and so strong.
What could cause something to go wrong?
I have this to say, cause I kept track, 'twas
the straw that broke the camel's back.

I'm a lot like the camel in a way.
A lot of harm can come in just one day.
I saw you out sometimes just about two.
This time, I'm telling you that we are through.

You looked like the bird that ate the canary.
I want this over, I don't want to tarry.
You said, but I just saw him that one time.
How many times have I heard that old line?

Yes, me and that old camel are alike.
I'm tired of your lies, so just take a hike.
You played with my heart until it was raw.
Baby, what it finally took was a straw.

Freda Everhart

"A Heart Divided"

A heart divided, split in two,
What is one supposed to do?

My love for the both of them I do share
When really to each one it's quite unfair.

It has not been easy that I had to choose
Which one will win and the other one lose.

I wish one could know what I feel inside,
The countless tears that I have cried.

It has all been in the name of love,
The situation which I thought much of.

Consuming almost my every thought
Conflicting sides within me fought.

Two men who love me so
To which depth they say I will never know.

To them both meaning so much,
My life they both have deeply touched.

Only until now has it come down to this,
One I will be with, the other I'll miss.

In my heart to always each one have a special place,
Nothing ever will be able them from it erase.

Carol Neumann

He's Bigger Than Us All

His crippled little body distorted from disease;
What others took for granted he could not do with ease.

His eyes were not wide open. A squint was always there.
And though his mouth drooped somewhat he had a smile to share.

With arms he couldn't straighten he reached in love to all.
His crippled little body was only four feet tall.

His body bent and crooked, his chin down on his chest - - -
Though in a crowd, so little, seemed bigger than the rest.

He didn't ask for pity, but did the best he could.
He never gave up easy though many surely would.

Oh God, forgive my grumbling when I complain and squall.
This child, while maimed in body, was bigger than us all!

Carol Gipson

Travel Agent

Grandmother's train rolled out of the station,
wheezes lingering for awhile.

Odors of "White Shoulders" perfume and diesel fuel
clung to my hair and clothes.
I couldn't shake the mismatch of smells from my nostrils
any easier than I could let go of Grandma and her last train.

Her journey will bring her to Grandpa again;
that's all she wants, not too much to ask for.

By this time tomorrow she'll be gone from this world — dead,
people will say — thanks to "the plan."

She asked my help for a road map to heaven, begging through
her eyes the need in her heart. I understood.
Together we drew the map and with each mile drawn Grandma's
stooped shoulders lifted, heavy need replaced by lighter hope and peace.

That she trusted I would understand and help squeezes a
perplexing delight in my heart, every now and then. Wonder
what that would look like on an EKG...

My love to you both, Grandma and Grandpa.
I'll know when it's done — I'll feel your smiles.

Brenda C. Nelson

Where Grow The Lilacs

Where grow the Lilacs when the sun is gone?
What says the heart when all the tears are shed?
After the battles of the soul are won,
From Victory's cries come echoes which have led
The conqueror to a realm so far from home
His promise to return is empty ploy,
A fleeing leprechaun, an errant gnome
Who has not cared for either peace or joy.
Why then should search for Lilacs by a stream
Go far beyond the fragrant wooded glen
In outreach for a vagrant passing dream
To capture or to charm the souls of men.
I would these wandering steps not obey
If Lilac blooms, which always fade, would stay.

Dorothy E. Wilkins

Pathway of Love

Dreams come and dreams go
What the future holds,
No one knows
Life is so confusing with all it's emotional roller coasters
No wonder I want to be closer
Closer to someone and see what's inside
Make them see they have nothing to hide
Life may end today or tomorrow
Hopefully I will have a pathway to follow
A road to lead me to love...

A love that shall never die.

Jody Umlor

The Scarecrow

Tell me, Scarecrow, tell me true...
What will you do when your work is through?
Out in the field, day after day,
Waving to all who come your way.

All the crows stay up in the trees
When your sleeves flap in the breeze.
With raucous chatter they call caw-caw!
They don't know you're just made of straw.

Where will you go, Scarecrow
After the crop is picked row-by-row?
You may go tap dancing down the lane
With the wind at your back, in a driving rain.

Faster and faster, no need to wait
To round the bend and meet your fate.
Imagine, Scarecrow, what a sight you'll be
Resting in the arms of the sour apple tree!

Clara B. Hopping

Urban Night - Lures Of A City

Young boy, thirteen or a bit more,
what're you standing on that corner for
past two a.m. on a saturday night,
little behind shaking in pants ... so tight,
anxiously eyeing the passing cars
filled with people, who've just left the bars...
batting your lashes and wriggling those hips,
making soft sucking motions with puckered lips.
Does your momma know you're here,
and that you're already high on beer?
Perhaps a "reefer" or some "speed"
make you feel like a man, indeed.
A man to help momma pay the bills...
enable her to buy those pills
she needs to make her sleep at night,
while your little behind's shaking in pants ... so tight!

Eveline G. Chowrashi

Mystery, Mr. Wind

Mr. Wind, blow the waves ashore.
What's your secret, mystery wind?
Blow across the waves to me,
Gentle Mr. Wind,
Be kind to your friend.
The sailboat glides to and fro,
Mr. Wind is its play fellow.
The birds fly high and swoop so low,
The leaves shake on the tree,
You blow on each, Mr. Wind.
The baby birds cling to their nests,
When Mr. Wind blows mightily.
The rippling of the fields of wheat, repeat and repeat.
Blow wisps of hair across a baby's face,
Where'd you come from and where do you go, mystery wind?
No matter how hard you blow Mr. Wind,
My anchor holds.
You are a mystery no longer,
I have found out the mystery of Mr. Wind.

Anna Holobach

Upon Reflection

Life has many surprises, as it surely seems.
When a young person needs you, and sweetens all your dreams:
With loving kindness and love that you share,
It brings peace and contentment to men everywhere.

God sent this young person to brighten our life,
And now she is grown, someone's lovely new wife.
We now welcome the one who is like a dear son,
Now our joy and our happiness has really begun.

A tiny new babe to add to our bliss, such a sweet
little boy to cuddle and kiss.
Baby smiles and laughter add to our joy, when we
behold this dear little boy.

What more could one ask for, when all's said and done?
They are not our own children, but our hearts they have won.
Their tiny new baby is our pride and joy,
Like a grandson to us, is this dear little boy.

June Briner

Can You Love The Me I Am

Will you love me in the morning when my breath smells bad,
When my hair is a mess and I'm bathrobe clad?
Can your love over come my nasty old habits,
My toy stuffed dogs, my cats, and rabbits?

I need to know if you can love the me I am
When the me I am is not the me you know.

When we are together I am the best I can be,
But early in the morning I am a different me.
How will you feel when we have our first fight,
Will you still love me after that night.

I need to know if you can love the me I am
When the me I am is not that me you know.

What about when I am old and gray,
Tell me then what will you say?
Will you take the bad with the good?
Tell me now if you think you could.

I need to know if you can love the me I am
When the me I am is not the me you know.

Could you love me day after day,
In 50 years will you feel the same way?

Deborah Anthony

My Pal

There are times a man feels down and out,
When everything is wrong;
The hours are fill'd with darkest thoughts,
Which make the day seem long.

This is the time he needs a friend,
A comrade tried and true;
It's not chance friendship that he needs,
But a pal to pull him through.

Someone who's known him gay or sad,
In his struggles from day to day;
Who knows just what his feelings are,
And what to do or say.

A comrade who will back him, when
He's lost that host of friends;
Yes that one true Pal, his Mother,
Is with him to the end.

Aura W. Coleman

Iconoclast

Iconoclast — instincts quietly lie
When humans on torture racks
softly cry,
While in stark clay, "Moulders" ply

The bellicose mind to expand the trap,
Round free souls deep in miry heap
That drains life's tree from vibrant sap,
Till old leaves fall, and wild winds reap.

Phantasy, ruling false emotions bright
—Wafting, amid mystic clouds' spectral hues,
And gliding silently into shadows of night—
Vanishes forever in vaporous dews.

The placid mind, sanctified by universal order,
Knows tranquillity's hand in final account
Of humankind's clash with rampant disorder,
Astride somber years march to the ultimate count.

Left asunder, spirits borne to lifeless ways
Descend darkened valleys of no reprise;
Far from morning sun's turgid haze
Lie infinity's aeons cross cosmos' rise.

Alex V. Christoff

Twenty-One

Hallelujah, I thought this day would never come
When I could come and go at ease
I'll run and play and work some too
I'll watch TV and swim in the pool
Heaven has arrived early for me.

It feels so good to be so free
Not a soul to chew on me
No little siblings to raid my room
All this space to call my own.
Free at last to read and be alone.

What is that noise I hear
Maybe a mouse - nothing to fear
I'd feel much better if someone were near
Time passes slowly when alone
I need a live-in to share my home

Oh, please, Dear God, I pray
For someone good to come my way
To share my chores, and comfort me
It was not meant for me to live alone
But free at last to carry on.

Archie R. Kaze

The Two Left Turns

Glory be the day
When I realize my purpose
of how I arrived to here,
From the path misled with two left turns
Toward simple life so clear

I do not attempt the subtle moves
From the sanctioned bliss of your jail,
I grant your hopes, your dreams, and other half-truths
And remedy for your ail.

You are blind to my nocturnal awakenings,
Of restless wonder and what might have been,
Only to arise at 6:50 a.m.
That repetitiously traps me again.

I should not be here
To serve you supper and solace
And tidy your house unkempt,
But rest in the arms of an unknown other
To eat breakfast of peaceful contempt.

Brian Christopher Swansboro

I Would Be Nothing

Would that I were blind
When I see the smirk of criticism on your face
Or the tears that cloud the eyes.
Would that I were deaf
When the cry of hunger is heard
Or ugly words are spoken.
Would that I not smell
When death bears its ugly face
And cancer eats the flesh.
Would that I not feel
When broken, bent and twisted
In pain I walk alone.

Would I be rich, or poor?
For now I would not see the sun go down.
Or hear the laughter, and smell the rose,
Nor would I feel a loving caress
For only emptiness would be mine.

The bad it comes with all the good
For without all this I would be nothing.

Adelia Arias

Secret Place

Where I go when harsh words tear at my heart.
Where I go when things are falling apart.

A place to go when nothing goes right.
A place to go and spend the night.

Where the wind knows my every secret.
Where peace and I first met.

The place that I can fulfill my every dream.
The place that no one else has seen.

Where I can show my other side.
Where I have nothing to hide.

A place to let myself go.
A place that no one knows.

Where I go to remember when....
Where I go when I'm losing him.

The place where my fantasies begin.
The place where silence is my only friend.

All the secrets and dreams that it has held.
I know they are safe, for the wind will never tell.
When I grow old and finally parish,
No one will ever know of the place I cherished.

Brandi Hungerford

Last Goodbye

How can I explain the pain that is rushing through my head,
When I still cannot believe that a close loved one is dead.

I am so confused right now that it's impossible to find,
The answers to all the questions that are burning in my mind.

I have lost more than a teacher, I have lost a friend,
Whenever I needed a hand, she had one to lend.

With her around, the world we see had so much more to gain,
But now that she is gone there seems no way to stop this pain

Her spirit now is everywhere so in a way she did not die,
But you always feel, like you never got to say your last
goodbye.

Jacob Fenton

No Turning Back

Stars shine brightest
When the day is darkest.
No matter how much we sway
The truth shall have its way.

Tanks will roll
But liberty shan't fall
Canons will roar
But the dove shall soar
The sling will swing
But the Olive branch shall sing.

Oppressors shall freedom fight
And exhibit cowardly might:
Dusk to dawn curfews; freedom for a select few.
Censorship of the press; dissenting views repressed.
Intolerance canonized
Persecution idolized.

Tyranny shall glow
And blood will flow
But the dream shall live on
Until freedom is won.

Dibussi Tande

Some "Before" Thoughts

When the last card has been written, and the last carol has been sung;
When we wrap the last present, and we "think" we are all done;
Whatever happened to, "it's better to give than to receive?"
O, "The joy and the blessings as when we first believed!
Have we lost our "zest and zeal"?
Are we still "in love with Christ?"
Do we thank him for the blessings and our everlasting life?
It is time we "Redo our thinking,"
It is time we "look above",
To realize "the true meaning of Christmas,"
Why our saviour "chose to come to earth."
He opened up the way to heaven, the Father has a great salvation plan,
Let's "look up to Jesus" and stop this "man's in humanity to man".
Let's stop and say, "thank you Jesus for
All you will do, are doing and have done."
Even so; come quickly, Lord Jesus, to take us - to our heavenly home.
For we know these promises are written in "your word,"
The dead in Christ first shall rise and we who remain will be caught
Up to meet Jesus in the air; so shall we ever be with you Lord,"
Won't it be glorious when we get there?

Eva Betty Lea McCracken

New Beginning

Do you know what you'll be doin'
When you fall in love with me?
Do you realize the meaning,
Cause the kids and me make three?
There's a lot of love to give here,
If you're sure that you can see,
The only trap that you will find here,
Is the one thing that'll set you free.
I will have your little baby, if that is what's to be.
And I'll take what comes tomorrow, lovin' you for lovin' me.
I'll be your lover if you want me, I'll be your wife if that comes too
Promise always that you'll love me, for my darlin' I love you.
When my life with you is over,
And I have to start again,
I'll remember how you loved me,
And how you truly were my friend.
I can start a love with friendship
Watch it grow and let it be.
Treasure all the tender moments,
Loving you for loving me.

Janie Minton

The Hypocrite

Though his guiding light's obscured,
Whenever queried to relate
His ideology, he'll state
Profound remarks, somewhat demurred.

First in nearly every case
To proclaim what is wrong or right—
Pontificating sermons, trite,
Convinced that he's been blessed with grace.

Divided is his school of thought—
Each side contrived for pers'nal gain.
His piety he has to feign
Lest all regard his being, naught.

A Jekyll and a Mister Hyde
On matters postulating truth;
His malady is false, forsooth
The hypocrite, in life, has died.

Adolph Haven Connard III

Why

Dear God, I need to know the answer to something troubling me
Why did the train hit three people who were very dear to me?
Two babies, young and innocent, one was yet unborn
It also took the Mother, leaving the Daddy here to mourn

Our grief was overwhelming as we tried to reason why
That all the good and decent people always seemed to die
Why not the bad and evil people who've done nothing good at all
To better lives around them, but laugh at our downfall

There wasn't time to love them or read them stories through
There wasn't time to rock or tell them about your
Couldn't you have waited longer before you took them away?
Perhaps it would have been harder to have loved them more each day

I guess you needed the babies for angels and the Mama for their care
The one's who were left behind had a heavy cross to bear
Our hearts were almost broken and the tracks were deep and wide
Where we plodded through our sorrow and realized you were by our side

As time went by, the load seemed lighter
We looked behind to view
And saw the trail was faint, the foot prints lighter
For Lord, you carried us through.

Frances E. Neiman

The Yearner

I yearn to go back to the country again — land of the prairie farms
Where nostalgic memories haunt me with their everlasting charms.
There's an antediluvian farmhouse with a feather bed upstairs
That sinks way down deep as you say your evening prayers.
And a rustic red barn with a loft for play
Where you swing on Tarzan's rope o'er the ever-soft hay.
The dilapidated grain shed is chock-full of corn,
Where Grandpa fetches animal food every single morn.
The winding, dusty lane with wildflowers on each side
Make gentians, goldenrods and daisies a source of nature's pride.
Aunt Jennie bakes the best cakes that ever you could eat
And the freshly butchered hog makes yummy, yummy meat.
As evening time approaches and the cows meander home
The sheep, goats, ducks and chicks no more today will roam.
Lullaby time is nearing — all quiet, golden and clear
With only sounds of a creaking windmill and an eery hoot owl near —
Reminds me it's time for sleep now, off to a magic land
And dream delightful dreams to the tune of an Angel band.
Three-fourths of a century has passed now, and the farmhouse burned away,
But the most magnificent memories are still alive in me today!

Jean Hayden

Somewhere Beyond

I miss her so, I want to go
where she is now.
Try as I might, I lose the fight,
Each day I awake with heavy heart,
For it's so hard to be apart.
A friendship unsurpassed
A love forever to last.

Oh, yes, I miss her so,
My heart cries out why can't I go
To that somewhere just beyond.
She would not want me to be sad,
She is happy and for that I am glad.

Her ways were tender, a gentle soul
A smile to make the whole room glow.
Like a rosebud, she blossomed to full bloom
Her very presence could light up a room.
Oh, yes, she was a special gift
There will be no other,
Don't you know
She was my Mother!

Betty J. Douglass

Cyprus Swamp In May

They cannot build a golf course here
Where tannined waters mirror swollen boles
sprung from sunken roots.
Where haunting cypress pillars tower to the sun

The sprawling mall will not intrude
On pair of turtles, toy tanks
idling on a half-drowned log,
Nor on a weathered, waiting scow
munching in the mocha sludge.

The blare of traffic can't be heard
Where in the mist the purple heron stilts
among a gossip of coned cypress knees
And gator's throaty love songs croak
through sensual odors of wet earth.

Abandoned rice fields mutely speak
Of man's long labor with the earth
savaged by rampant nature's desolation,
Stirring the breeze of some remembered hope
that this lush cypress Eden will at last endure.

Barbara Steadman

Miles Across The Horizon

Miles across the horizon
where the grass stops and the desert prevails
lives Esperanza Guadalupe Garza.
In her small hot kitchen
with sweat on her brow
and baking powder on her sunflower yellow dress.
She works and kneads the dough
she will mold into lightly toasted empanadas.
They will expel an aroma of temptation.
She will sell these empanadas for pesos
on the dirty crowded streets
of the busy mercado in Ciudad Delicias.
The money she will use to buy her card
the size of her palm.
A card she will use to cross the bridge
that holds back the dirt that runs with liberty
but for now the Senorita, sore yet filled with hope,
lives and works miles across the horizon.

Jennifer Villanueva

To An Old Friend

A friend is like an open fire
Where you stretch and warm your heart,
Bask in the glow of shared memories and mutual feelings.
Years apart are spanned in a moment's time,
Like an old slipper remembers the shape of the foot,
A word, a smile and minds move to recall.

Now that you are gone, old friend,
I have, etched firmly in my heart,
Those times when we sat and drank deeply
From the cup of our friendship.
As a man can hold a love for another,
So held we in those days of yore.

With closed eyes I see that wonderful smile,
And the twinkle of those blue Irish eyes,
Feel the clasp of your hand
On my shoulder, and hear you say,
"Hang in there, John boy,
I'll be seeing you."

John Shelton Cate

I'll Animate; Through Time

It's a lover in me, that controls my soul.
Wherever she is she makes my rainbow spills;

If I could just grasp the feelings, that seems
to be real.

I could see through the animation up there
on the hill.

If you could just hold me, in that mysterious
phase; that would be showing me how good of
days.

Floyd Kimbro

A Message From Heaven

When the snowflakes fall upon the ground,
We know our Lord is all around.

He created this earth for us to protect it,
not knowing one day we would fail to respect it.

If someday he decides he will retire,
He might just turn those snowflakes into fire.
He sends us the rain, the sun, and the snow,
to nurture this land until it is our time to go.

He needs us to help him take care of this world.
We should not expect him to take care of it all.

Frances Di Lallo

Untitled

It was always you in my corner
Whether I smiled or cried or panted for attention
It was always you in my corner
When I stole and when I lied or reached for higher goals
It was always you in my corner
When I searched or retreated and some things needed a push
It was always you in my corner

No other mother
Could birth me so gallantly
Or watch my growth more cautiously
No other mother
Could reserve her fear and
Stretch her hand to help consistently
No other mother
Could struggle through tears
And difficult hours and
Reign victoriously time after time
And even in momentary defeat ... survive.

No other mother was like you in my corner.

Carelese Purdie

Judgement Day

Midst deafening crashes of thunder
Which tore the very sky asunder
With blazing shafts of fierce white lightning
An horrendous sight most frightening.
To late now for sinful man to pray
'Twas the awesome dawn of judgement day.
The earth, sea and sky were greatly awed
By the tremendous voice of the Lord,
He grasped time in the palm of His hand
As though it was a mere grain of sand
While the great vastness of outer space
Vanished instantly from earth's embrace.
Then all graves gave up their waiting dead
And each soul meekly stood with bowed head.
Saints and sinners with great fear trembled
Before God's golden throne assembled.
The Lord stretched forth His arms above
Touching His great handiwork with love
And mankind no longer fearing strife.
Joyfully entered Eternal Life.

Ida R. May

Beyond

Long, long gone for many a night
While people close to you get up tight,
For you have drifted from their sight
To have you back again would be delight.

They have spread their wings and taken flight
For they have traveled into another light,
Any whimpering we make surely is not right
Now they have gone, a fairer land in their sight.

Much broader thoughts and ways
Will now comfort and fill their days,
Out of sight, still close at hand
We at times feel their closeness as they stand.

We feel a presence rare
For which they come and share,
To help us along life's way
Traveling on earth, as we stay.

Dr. George A. Wood Jr., MAC.D., Ph.D

Wild Stallions

You enter a magical dream state,
While still achieving full consciousness,
Then, you see them ride,
Just beyond the horizon,
Down from the mountains of steel,
Hypnotizing,
Mystifying,
Surging forth, from a billowing, churning dust storm,
The wild stallions take your breath away,
Unbelievable beauty born out of nature,
Afraid to took away for fear they may vanish,
Against a fiery, yellow-red-orange sky,
They run freely,
Powered by the wind,
Thunderbolts from hooves vibrate the ground below,
Trampled grass bent over with pure muscle force,
Nature is one with power in their hearts,
It gives them the one and only natural strength,
If dream is a necessity,
Then the wild stallions rule the world!

Candace Nicole Kearney

A Tree Learns

In the morning I hear the wind rising over the open hill
Whistling softly as a gallant hunter
Breathing around my leafless form and suddenly it's winter.
And I clinch my limbs and tremble and repeat idiotic notes
of courage to myself
Then make brisk gestures of command as I nod my branches to the
wind and it nods back as before.
The wind became a champion in my eyes as it has been a winner
for many years
In a marvelous match played a hundred times over the fairways
of the fields
A match each detail of which it changed about untiringly
Sometimes it won with almost laughable ease
Sometimes it came up magnificently from behind.
As I seriously look at its whirly form
I feel the chill of the breeze that covers my branches
I feel it down to the bottom of my trunk. A tree learns early
though
To sway with the wind by studying its style year after year
To utilize them for a valuable benefit
Without offending the majesty of its pride.

Giovanna

God Is A Beautiful Artist

God is a beautiful Artist, and he's perfect too!
Who else but God can do all of the things he can do?
He can touch a tree and turn the leaves to green,
He can paint a butterfly so lovely to be see,
God can stretch out his hand to make a storm pass by-
He then paints a beautiful Rainbow in the sky.

God can caress a leaf and it will unfold,
With the autumn colors of yellow, red and gold.
What an enchanting beauty to behold!
God can place a smile on a child's face, where there was a frown
He knows that a smile is just a frown turned up side down.
Our God is perfect, there's nothing he cannot do!

He can ease a troubled heart, and bring happiness to you.
Let us thank him for his loving care that he gives to us each day
May we say a prayer that he will guide us in the straight and
narrow way,
While through this world we travel on this rough and rocky way.

Alice Francine Mathis Boska

The Couch Potato Cat

I'm a Couch Potato Cat - not a cat in the Hat
Who ever heard of a cat like that

I like adventure and I'm outgoing too
I'm far superior to those cats in the zoo

I ride with John Wayne plus Roy and Dale
I catch outlaws and throw them in Jail

I save the damsel in distress
I do it all without having to get dressed

My heart is pure and my life serene
Why I've even been a feline Marine

I'm a master sleuth, I solve all the Crimes
and I get the job done in one hour's time

I sail the mighty oceans and the river Nile
and I do it all with a switch of the Dial

I live a world of "Let's Pretend"
a world which never has to End

I'm just a Couch Potato Cat
and I for one like it like that

Joe McClintock

Thoughts From The Heart

This poem is written for a special little girl
Who from the time she was born had her daddy's heart in a whirl.
Forever in our thoughts and words his memory will linger
And no one will ever forget how you had him wrapped around
your finger.
He would've given you anything under the sun because many
people have two or three daughters, but your daddy only had one.
If you watched him closely while he talked and saw that smile
and laugh was all he could do, anyone who knew your daddy, Emily,
would know he was talking about you.
You may no remember a lot about him, but we're all here to
let you know that he will always be with you every day and
night as you grow.
As long as you remember his name and try to remember him too,
Emily you'll always have a daddy, he'll always be with you.
I've never seen a father and daughter as close as you and he
Never forget, the last thing he heard from you was, "I love
you too daddy."

Christina Ellis

Who Am I To Pray To You

Who am I to pray to you? I am not one of your dutiful sheep who has followed you all the days of my life. I have constantly wondered off, an annoying stray causing you grief. Who am I to pray to you? You are the King of Kings! And I am so pitifully unworthy of all your precious gifts of mercy...forgiveness, love, and life. Who am I to even lift up my eyes towards you? When I am so caked in sin that I don't even want to look at myself. I have nothing to offer you...that you would want. Many times I have bargained to change my ways. But never found the strength inside myself to do it. What is wrong with me? I know what will happen. Like any little lamb if you do not stay with your shepherd then you're a feast for the wolves. Well now the wolves are upon me, and like any frightened little lamb I cry out to you. But as the wolf's grip cuts off my cry... In the silence I wonder... Why would you come? Who am I to pray to you?

Denise Richardson

A Portrait Of Mom And Dad

He came upon a lonely maid
Who lost her husband I'm afraid.
With fiddle and bow he played a tune
The likes could only make her swoon.

A stately man with eyes of brown
Had hair to match with no balding crown.
With shoulders back and standing tall
A stetson hat would top it all.

The maiden stood not five feet high,
But her hair would grow down to her thigh.
She'd roll it up into a bun
As down their path a life was spun.

She would cry some tears as she laughed with him.
The love they knew grew never dim.
As time passed on and children came
The bond between them stayed the same.

When children fought and her nerves would shatter
She would leave with a scream, but never batter.
Then he'd soon be heading down her trail,
And hand in hand love could not fail.

Eulalia M. Greene

The Class Of 1959

Laverne, I know you knew us all.
Who pranced your High School's herod halls,
In nineteen fifty nine we knew,
We'd change the world, we Okie few.
Armed with goals we Tiger fans
Graduated with a wealth of plans.
Our motto, "Hitch your wagon to a star",
Would guide us long and guide us far.
Bathed in eagerness of unlike kind...
Marched forth the Class of 1959,
Where, like most other teens,
We hung our futures on our dreams.
How successful have you been
My classmates from away back then?
Has your wagon of dreams come true?
Has your star been good to you?
A star, I have found my destiny...
Among the authors of poetry.
And among treasured memories of mine,
The Class of 1959.

Janice N. Chapman

"For Your 15th Wedding Anniversary"

A true friend is hard to find,
Who will love with heart and mind.
But, you two are precious indeed,
Who are always ready to help someone in need.

May your marriage last 75 years,
And have few, if any heart-aches or tears.
May your love be as a shining light
Helping others have a marriage that's bright!

May God's blessings be upon you as one!
May you never feel that you are alone.
May you have joy that comes from our Lord!
May you always be of one accord.

I've loved you, both, from the start,
And this love is really from my heart.
I'm glad I'm kin to y'all in two ways,
And for this, I give God the praise!

Dora L. Harville

Humanity?

Sometimes I think we're of a Master soul
Whose fragments live in mortal forms awhile
Before at last returning to the whole
To ever be recycled sans defile.

As every glist'ning raindrop that we see,
No matter how afar from any shore,
Is destined to rejoin the mother sea
Before return in pristine beauty more.

Such precious gifts are passed on true and sure
Though human bearers falter, thrive or fail
To reappear in future forms as pure
Until they too concede each earthly veil.

So mortal and immortal lives co-dwell
In peace or strife 'til tells the parting knell.

Hunter McRae Hancock

My Hero

Why can't I be more like you? To be so caring to be so true.
Why can't I be more like you? To be so smart and funny too.
But you are you and I am me. Why I can't be like you I just don't see.
For you are the one which I look to when troubles head my way.
And you are the one which I go to when I've had a very bad day.
Your thoughts and your friendship mean so much to me,
For I am young and unexperienced I wish to be more like thee.
I solution for every problem you have hidden up your sleeve.
And you taught me to look beyond the surface,
For appearances often deceive
You are not perfect you said so yourself one day
Of course you have flaws, but to me you're perfect in every way
You are my hero and you always will be.
Life has many different views which you helped me better see.
So when I grow up I wish to be like thee.
To be a hero to some confused kid, like you were a hero to me.

Donna Sayed

My Mother

My Mother with hair of brown,
Would look beautiful dressed in a gown.

My Mother with eyes of green,
Has the prettiest eyes you have ever seen.

My Mother has a zest for life,
Her Angel Food cakes we cut with a knife.

My Mother says your blessings count,
Will one day Heaven mount.

My Mother is the best Grandma around,
Not a better one could be found.

My Mother loves to walk and swim,
At Buhl Park and Farmer Jim.

My Mother enjoys working in her yard,
When occasions arise she sends a card.

My Mother feeds God's birds,
Their beauty is beyond words.

My Mother buys her Grandsons clothes and toys,
She makes them happy young boys.

My Mother has been a wonderful Mother,
We would never trade her for any other!

Bonnie L. Goodwin

Families

I wonder whose idea was families, and
Why friends rate second best
I wonder why families are placed on pedestals
When they frequently fail the test
They say blood is thicker than water
And family must always come first
While husbands and wives
Who often divorce
Must promise "for better or worse"
Some family members earn their place
They're loving, giving, loyal and kind
Others, you see them coming
And wish that you were blind
Why can't we choose the people
Who get to call us kin
Why must we stay connected to
The ones who do us in
I love my family, please believe
With their real and imagined sins
But I wish I could have chosen them
As carefully as I chose my friends

Josie Teal

One Day

One day you'll look around and say to yourself
Why is today different from yesterday?
The music is playing,
The sun is shining,
And the birds are singing.
What makes today any different?

It's because after one day and one day
You've become older from those yesterdays.
You've lived each day as though there'd be a tomorrow.
Tomorrow finally becomes today
And today becomes yesterday.
What once was is no more
And it never will be.
That's what makes today different from yesterday.

Yesterday's people and plans are gone.
Today is here but different.
Today is lived
Expecting it to be the same as yesterday.
Now you hear and now you see but all things today are different.
Will you live this day expecting tomorrow to be the same or different?

James E. Price

Growing Up

I watch as you do your own thing; I pray you can face what it may bring
You're not a child anymore ... I can't tell you how to live-
but look at your life, what a mess!
You think you know it all, if your way is right,
why are you in such pain?
There are many things that you don't know
I've been here longer and had more time to grow.
You say growing up is hard to do
It isn't easy for anyone ... I'm still growing too
The way you are going about it is wrong -
All of those drugs and guns won't make you strong!
Can't you see there is no easy way
growing up is what life is all about.
The ground you are walking on will crack and wash to the sea!
You say your friends and drugs are on top,
their brains are weak and drugs will make you rot!
Do you have one friend who would care if you were
hungry or have clothes to wear?
The time will come when you will see
Your friends are not what you thought they would be!

Wendy Centers

Caught Up...

When the last days, on the earth, are spent,
Will I, be caught up, then,
To kneel beneath my Savior's feet,
And know Him, as my friend?

Will He gently lead and guide me back,
To my home, that I once knew?
And will I answer, with a humble heart,
That I did as I was sent to do?

Will I review the sacrifices made,
And the tests of my earthly stay?
Will I have shown, like Abraham,
My willingness to obey?

I'll try to be caught up in the scriptures,
The sacrament prayers I will hear.
I'll try to be caught up in the Temple,
As I kneel reverently in prayer.

Am I caught up.... in the world around,
Or am I caught up in the Lord?
Someday, I will...be proven,
By my actions, my deeds, and my words.

Gwen H. Hall

Do You Remember.......

Warm sand and hot sun, waves and beach ball fun
Wind-filled jib and taut sails
Speeding smoothly through the iridescent sea-green water.
Balmy days and cool nights beside the fire flames
From the sun-bleached, wind-carved logs,
Remnants of life, their one last gift of beauty light.

Crunchy snow and sled-filled slopes
With friends who laughed and dared the mogul mounds.
Hot cocoa, steamy snow clothes and firelight
Scented wood and crackling logs
As we sipped and loved.
Like the flames, then embers into ash
An enduring all-season love was not to last...
Do you remember....?

Diane Pencin Perample

"Wings"

Wings of silver, wings of gold
Wings of angels' faith unfold
Wings of honor for a deed well done
Wings of time span the days one by one

Wings of bravery, wings of flight
Wings of Orville and Wilbur Wright
Wings to hover, wings of a sail
Wings of the strong, or wings of the frail

Wings of butterflies, wings of a dove
Wings of peace, wings of love
Wings of jets that soar the blue
Wings of eagles, strong and true

Wings of defeat and wings of praise
Wings that flutter through the days
Wings that protect us against all foe
Wings that stay and wings that go.

Wings to carry us home at last
Wings that wipe out all the past
Wings strong, wings that never bend
Wings of life, beginning to end

Belva Hoops

Magic Together

As I lay in bed, holding my pillow,
wishing it was you by my side.
Wondering what are you doing?
When you could be here with
the one who loves you and wants you.
Don't stand out there in the cold,
when your baby, here, can keep you warm.
I'm waiting for you —
ready whenever you are.
Just give me one kiss one night.
Then you and I will know we're
"Magic Together."

Jeannie Ng

THE INVISIBLE WEAVER

HE, WHOM you cannot see, is THE MOST SILENT WEAVER,
With a golden needle placed on a diamond lever,
And silver thread between HIS dexterous fingers,
Weaves silently, a perfect pattern of my life.

HE sees blemishes and numerous tangled strands
With many a rugged knot, which HE carefully tends.
And then blending all colors in one radiant glow
Removes tenderly, the impurities of my life.

HE, constantly assures me of HIS Holy Presence
With complete protection and safe guidance.
And now and then, HE looks at me, because
In HIS hands, hangs the tapestry of my life.

HE proudly displays HIS most magnificent art
with compassion, gently saying: "We are not apart."
And to exhibit HIS prime masterpiece, HE
Discreetly opens wide the curtain of my life.

HE, then towards HIMSELF affectionately, turns my face
with redeeming love and mercy, patience and saving grace.
And after collecting all the elements of HIS creativity,
Breathes in me most graciously, the fullness of my life.

Daisy Marion Hamesh-Das

My Atlanta Family And Cockateel Harry

Jason, Jason, Master of his zoo,
With a whipping tail iguana and a turtle, too,
A Prince of kindergarten, best learner of all,
So glad to be with his peers this fall.

Caroline, a moppet breezy and tall,
Tuned into talent, one above all,
Gifted in classes, swift on her feet,
A blonde Shirley Temple, sweet to meet.

Sarah, a sylph attuned to art,
Song in the clarinet, love in her heart,
Arms full of books, a reader keen,
Athena on the throne, a will serene.

Annette, the Mom, beloved by us all,
A Hillary Lady, a philanthropy doll.
Handsome Dad Jim, a baritone great,
A corporate giant, a mighty saint.

At my "Good-bye, Harry" in early dawn
Sarah's cockateel trilled "Tweet" that sad morn.
Then he picked a fuzzy feather off his cage floor
And dropped it at the door for me to see.

Erma Gross-Haley

All My Heart

With all my heart, I care for others
With all my heart, I give to others
But all my heart is not for others
For all my heart I give to you
I do many things with my heart, but not as
much as I do for you
I may care for others, but I care more for you
I may give to others, but more I give to you
No one steals my heart as you do
No one bids more for my heart than you
Your eyes flatter me
Your arms comfort me
Your smile warms me
Your body moves for me
Never has a man done so much for me
That's why all my heart, I give to you
It dances, and it sings for you
It laughs, and it rings for you
It has never been so joyous for a single soul
Thus, all my heart I give to you

Deborah Mendoza

Love Can Be

With pain in chest instead of heart
With all the wish from life depart
But life goes on day in, day out
With little voice, I wish to shout... little words

With every day in life's cruel wheel
With little hope, myself to kill
But life goes on day in, day out
With little voice, I wish to shout... little words

With time, I've loved and love in pain
With falling tears like crystal rain
But life goes on day in, day out
With little voice, I wish to shout... little words

With tears softly rolling by eyes of red
With each passing second, I wish I were dead
But life goes on day in, day out
With little voice, I wish to shout... little words

James W. Arnold

The Four Seasons Of Life

The four seasons of life have more to do
With attitudes ... than with age.

They have more to do
With choices and circumstances ... than the vernal equinox.

The summer sun of harsh words can scorch a soul
Causing it to wither and waste away
For young and old alike.

The death of a loved one in the autumn may be taken
By accident, by the cruel hand of others, or by disease
Whatever the age.

A child can suffer the blasts
Of chilling winter winds of abuse
As can one of middle or later years.

But the vigor of regeneration that comes in the spring
Can bring renewed life from the Heavenly Source
To any person.

The weathering of all the seasons of life can bring
Strength and growth that no one season can accomplish.

Donna Babcock-Brown

January

January: Month of lengthening days
with cold that nips our noses,
and maybe a snowflake or two,
with bits of greenness here and there
to tell us of the coming spring.
With days of soft blue skies,
and days of gray and misty rain.

January, namesake of Janus
two faced,
Cheering us with sunshine one day
and pelting us with rain and
snow the next!

Jean Seestadt

I Love You

Wow! You got the touch... Your exciting soul is dripping with love... Listen to my songs. Inside my body and singing for you, is my need for you... I sing when we touch. (DO you know... my songs are lonely and love-struck? I need your soul and mystic body.) When my hot body finally found you, I wanted to touch you. My pretty songs were oozing with love. Your alluring soul grabbed me... then my soul woke up. My body jumped with joy. Then you opened up and touched me... "It's those love songs from heaven"...Wow! Love is my lure and love is my key. Your soul and exciting touch, broke my armor. "You got me." My body overflows with songs of desire. Your songs are my proof of love. Your heavenly soul, unlocked my body and now I'm free. You and your magic touch... Unlocked my soul songs....so touch my body with fire...I Love You...

Bill Fox

"Mother's Roses"

With pride she pruned and picked them.
With love she loved and pampered each stem...

Mother's roses to which I can still recall..
The fragrance of each and every one of them all...

They lie pressed in a Bible yet...
For they are all I have of my mother's roses left.

Oh what I'd give to just one more time see...
The love in her eyes when she would say to me,

Baby go take a picture of my roses today...
They are so lovely, what am I to say.

Pink, yellow, white and red....
They bloomed for my mother, but not since she's dead.

The garden so gently tilled and cared.
Is left unattended for mother is not there.

Fran Cook

The Dreaded Image

Who is the stranger I see everyday?
Who is the wanderer gone astray?
who is the person who stands in my way?

I stare at the glass of pain.
Why does it have to be the same?
I must pull myself together or I will go insane.

Can I not live my life alone,
In this place I call home?

I stare at the glass and see my face
And think of how to get out of this place.
Away from the stranger bearing my face.

Daniel A. Fodale

Cherished Embrace

You became my friend, from the start
with love to lend, from your heart.

You drew me near, and made me whole,
I embrace you dear, for filling my soul.

I carve your name, on my spirit
you feel the same, and I love to hear it.

You are my wife, who reflects the sea
The love of my life, that will always be.

With this love, I will never retire
Like the flying dove, soaring higher and higher.

The miracle we face, to make us strong,
is the inner embrace of where we belong.

But if the passion subsides, and our love yields or seizes,
Let us never say goodbye and try to pick up the pieces.

David Fowler

The Golden Years

As we enter into the golden years
with our loved one close at hand
The dreams that we worked for throughout
our whole life withstood the sifting sand

For some these dreams have come to a halt
through death or a marriage that failed
We must learn to forgive and let go of the past
and tackle new goals unveiled

Share the love that's still in your heart
with another in need of a friend
The joy you reap from helping someone
will release your pain from within

Renew yourself with the talents
God blessed you with at birth
Fill your life with a yearning passion
and you'll improve your own self-worth

It's a confident feeling to accomplish new skills
your ego becomes overbearing
You realize you're growing and still able to learn
with the help of God's love and His caring

Betty Jean Wallace

Just Do Your Thing

A sitting duck you better not be, try to use your sensibility,
With perfectionist style, live like a King, JUST DO YOUR THING.
Put pedal pushers on, have no quid pro quo, no stalking horse will you be - NO - NO.
Use stick-to-it-ive-ness when you flap your wings, JUST DO YOUR THING.
With statuesque make a melody, make another trip to Tin Pan Alley,
With hemidemisemiquaver time you sing, JUST DO YOUR THING.
On your whirligig no willy-nilly, for you would never be that silly,
Silver-tongued your speech you bring, JUST DO YOUR THING.
No wild goose chase to hunt a golden egg, be well-to-do, do not beg.
You may wear a necklace made to ring, JUST DO YOUR THING.
An octogenarian may be your life, bur no whipper-snapper, no such strife.
With selectivity you eat your ling, JUST DO YOUR THING.
With no will-o-the wisp and your nomenclature ready, your stability will be so steady,
You will glad tidings to everyone bring, JUST DO YOUR THING.

Fay Paris

Summer Shower

Nature washed the world last night,
With softest showers from out the west,
And then when morning came
I marvelled at it, newly blest.

She'd washed each tiny blade of grass,
And every thirsty tree,
The showers were tossed against the hills
And 'cross the twinkling sea.

The soft white rose a cleaner white,
The deep red rose more red,
Since Nature washed its fragrant face,
And put them all to bed.

There's not a bird, there's not a bee
That does not raise its voice in praise of Thee.

Andy Marshall

Empty Playground

The swing sways
with the help of the wind
The cold, brisk winter air
chills us all
The streets stand still
as the last door is closed
Leaving the land to its own noises
which will be left unheard
Millions locked tight
with solitude to explore- only beyond the door
While the chains of the swing creak,
as the wind blows through
the empty playground once more

Brett Clark

The Marriage

As I say I do
With visions of you
As we stand before the priest
It was meant to be
When we say our speech
No one else but you and me
As I kiss your lips
Nothing will be missed
As we walk hand and hand
There will never be another man
As we face the world as one
We shall never come undone
For the plans that we made
Comes upon us this one judgement day
For the hopes and fears, that stands before us
Will change to tender pure trust
And the world we now see us
As our wedding day ends by dusk

Jodi Marie Pocai

Nothing For Me

I watched and waited for you to return
When you did not come I was concerned
I sat in silence and make not a peep
You made a promise that you didn't keep

I waited longer and watched some more,
for all you had to do was knock on the door.
You ran and hid in the presence of fear,
you didn't know you could still come near.

I quit waiting and watching that day
Why I still care I will not say
You were all I had can't you see
After you left there was nothing for me.

Ellen Simpson

Young Eagles

Young eagles ready to take to the sky—
with wings spread wide, they are eager to fly.
They've watched old eagles do it with ease.
They've strengthened their wings and are ready to seize
the next current of air that passes by.
Destiny urges the fledglings to try.

Young eagles taking that long leap they must—
leaving the aerie and all that they trust—
find the courage and strength they need is there
holding them up as they take to the air.
Old eagles teach them all they should know.
They'll ride air currents and see far below.

Tied to the earth they will no longer be
for all young eagles were meant to be free.
They'll fly to the heavens and back once more
and travel where they've never been before.
When weary they will return to the nest.
The aerie is waiting to give them rest.

Florilla Sorensen

Misunderstood

In a marriage full of uncertainty and no esteem
with wounds not allowed the time to heal
one year blends into another too numerous to mention
in a world with all its moments of imperfection.

Wedded to a direct and calculating stranger
cold as the Arctic unsettled - unchanging . . .
wronged by him is a truth that's disturbing,
no fondness left, only a silence to contend with.

In a relationship of indifference beyond repair
expectations are unrealistic for happiness to share
his love for her was never filled with tenderness . . .
and to understand false-heartedness is pointless.

Hopelessness is a very threatening situation
She is seeking answers to many bare questions
little time left for sadness and regrets . . .
her new approach is to rise above the clouds.

Inwardly, she's coming to terms with self . . .
determined to continue recognizing her worth
with a consciousness to abandon the sinful hurts,
and from a sacred reservoir to draw from with hope.

Eva Widawski

Footsteps Of Yesterday

Footsteps of yesterday the places we once walked
words floating through the air
of the things that we once talked
the cities and towns we both knew
in our life that we passed through
are now distant memories
of all the things, so dear to me
Footsteps of yesterday from the dreams that we once shared
the love that grew between
two hearts that really cared
a friendship that grew to be the best
then couldn't pass the final test
these things now distant memories
of all the things, so dear to me
Footsteps of yesterday from two lives that grew as one
and all those things we didn't do
that for now are left undone
our dreams now scattered by the wind
how I need to be with you again
as I think of those memories and all the things, you mean to me.

Jim McDermott

The Masquerade

The day you first smiled at me
With your funny, toothy amazing grin
Were you making fun for all to see
A hapless person with twice told chagrin
Which role was I fated to play on stage
Loser, winner, martyr, joker or clown
What pronouncement from you, the knowing sage
Time for the audience to sigh and to frown
The final scene has not been acted out
The protagonists are being well seen
Let the world ring its theme with a loud shout
The tangle-one day merry, next day mean
Will destiny make me a sad clown
The parade of a fool around the town.

Antoinette Adelquist Bell

Midnight's Moonlight

I'm looking back on yesteryears, in days gone by...
wonderin' where it all went wrong, and wonderin' why.
I can't look you in the eye, so I'll run and hide...
Still searchin' for the truth you know, still askin' why.

And I'm wondering, Yes I'm wondering
Is it all a lie??? Ohhh... and I wonder why.

I pay the ticket taker and I find my seat
Lean back a notch or two and put up my feet
I ponder the tale they'll tell, is it all 'bout me
I wait and I wonder, is it just a dream???

And I'm wondering, Yes I'm still wondering
Is it all a dream??? Is it all 'bout me???

A cold wind blows as I find my way home
Midnight's moonlight washes the streets I roam
In the beginning it was all so clear to me
I wonder now, is this how it's meant to be???

You lead and I'll follow - I've no where to go
You lead and I'll follow - it's all your show
It's all your show now 'cause I don't know how
You lead and I'll follow - wont you show me now?

Christina M. Wilson

War

Why is there war?
Why do we fight?
Is it secure?
Is it right?

Do we like to lie?
Do we like to choose?
Are we suppose to die?
Are we suppose to lose?
Do we do it for fun?
Do we do it for rights?
When you shoot the gun, where are the lights?

Should we do it?
Should we not?
Will we quit? Will we stop?
Should we want peace?
Should we want love?
Should we want ease from above?

If we let it stop, what then?
Will it start from the top, or will it end?
We won't know until we try, or we can wait till we all die?

Cassandra Marie Jenkins

'Tis Thanksgiving

"'Tis Thanksgiving Day," the turkey said,
"Won't you come and gobble with me...?"
I replied...before the turkey died...
"I'd be delighted to dine with thee..."
"But you must get dressed... to be my
guest." To sit at my table with me...
Oh! My! Oh! My! Did that turkey get dressed.
What a beautiful sight to see...
I said: "Thank you God, for this wonderful
bird"...as the turkey passed by me...
I must confess... The turkey got stuffed...
I made a glutton of me...
There were mashed potatoes..."M——M——
gravy" ...Home made biscuits, cranberry sauce,
Orders of every kind... and ...
Of course..."My guest"... "The turkey..."
We both got stuffed...till...
There was no room left for the pies...
Happy Thanksgiving.....

Florence Mae Mick

She Is A Goddess

She is to me a Goddess-I now a foot stool for her love-As she would listen attentively to soothe the beast within, soon we are to meet. Hopefully to meet in silence-Yet the room will echo to my heart beat-While my flesh trembles-All rational utterance ceases-As a numbness overshadows my euphoria.

Seeing only her endowments of beauty alone and radiant-I savor the ache in my loins- Be gentle for you are alive to love-Whisper, be amorous and find bliss. My body soon quakes at your sight that my tongue is severed to speak-Yet my thoughts still aflame with desire-The magic of love do I seek-Blinded by love and never to hear cascading rivers in my veins-Soon burning out of control. My heart Reaching out to a celestial moon-Forsake me not as I would wither as sallow grass in the turn of the season-I lay before your feet the world of life my love-You have captured my attention, my melody in life.

George L. Johansen

A Captain's Family

Old Captain living in a car I wonder how old you are?
Wrinkled, weather worn of face, still square-shouldered as you walk with style and grace.
Your knees are bent and your ancient beard grows askew.
Those eyes - those eyes show all the wisdom that is in you.
Baggy pants, tattered coat, that threadbare Captain's hat long ago have seen their day of use;
Yet, they do not detract from you in that old abandoned car, your home at the waters edge where you stare day after day watching the gulls devour their prey.
And, when the frozen waters roar no more, you share your breath with them as if an offering to those long dead, asleep on the ocean floor.

While others, pass you by each day —
The sea birds, your last remaining friends will love you until the very end.

When your proud heart gives out one day, I wonder?
Will another Captain take your place to stand on the shore with food in hand as a tribute to those asleep on the ocean's floor?

Elaine Meli

And It Came To Pass

I searched and searched to find a place to receive care in my older years;
Failing health and fragile bones brought worry and silent tears.
I wanted to be in a nursing home of a very special kind,
A place designed for life's changing needs and conducive to peace of mind.

I constantly prayed for the best direction, wondering if what I wanted was right,
Even tried to choose alternative ways, yet no solution was ever in sight.
And it came to pass as I waited alone for something to happen for me
Thanks be to God and the help of others, I came to RRCC.

The presence of contentment was felt from the start, like a wonderful dream come true,
Morale was lifted, doubts shifted, to the garden-like Center that's new.
Departments and staff faithfully work for the good of each resident here,
Because of this place and its dedicated people,
aging is much easier to bear.

Josephine C. Garnett

Paint My Finger Blue

I ask God to paint my finger blue.
Years of happiness in your company
Being able to place on my mind
Reflections of such great joy
At having married you, creating five blessed angels
To honor God for His gifts unequalled
And for the abundances of life unending
Made me full of praise for Him.
God is great! God is good! And I thank Him!
You have since died.
My angels have met with five great tragedies,
Leaving me in life alone.
The land has grown hollow with thirst.
My joys have all turned to sadness.
The glorious gifts are no more.
My humble praises go out still to God
But I, Job, am weakened.
I will wait upon God to renew me.
Only for now, I ask Him to paint my finger blue.

Glenn F. Girdham

The Rose

Oh Beautiful flower of delight.
Yes, always a perfect pose.
You seem to blossom, with such ease.
Your fight to survive no one knows.

Oh Flower, Lovers, Poets and Artists chose.
Yes, radiant survivor of the night.
Your soft petals offer rest for bees.
Yes, you were there in the garden, when Jesus arose.

Oh Flower, never once do you seem to doze.
Husbands or Lovers, know of your way to make things right.
Your way to say "Forgive me please;"
When your sweet fragrance hits the nose.

The Rose, oh flower of wondrous sight!
One of nature's prettiest bows.
Yet your velvet flower is such a tease.
Your prickly thorns make lots of foes.

Oh beautiful flower of delight.
Yes, always a perfect pose.
You seem to blossom with such ease.
Yet you fight to survive; I know.

Cecile A. Thomas

Our Friendship

Many friendships are like plates of glass
yet ours is made to last
Like glass, friendships tend to shatter
With ours nothing seems to matter
As though ours was made of brass,
We could withstand any task.
I know not how you came into my life, yet I do know why
You bring joy into my heart and you don't even try
So I'm glad to say you and I shall never part
We are reassuring friends forever more
My heart will always be your open door.
Never forget those times we shared
We survived through good and bad
You were even there when I was scared
Many yet so few have friendships like ours
Our friendship is like an endless tower
As each day progresses it grows stronger and stronger
We are friends till the end, you and I
No matter how far our journeys may take us
We shall never have to say good-bye.

Brenna Helen Adams

Disharmony

I see you have your crystal ball in front of you...
you are ready... your eyes reflect the world.
I see the reflection in your crystal ball,
your drummer has his hand over your ears, and you can't hear me.
He has lost his desire to create his own beat.
His skins are stretched and worn.
My drum beats wildly as I dance in the wind.
The pulse at my throat betrays me, but you don't see.
Your sheet music is a ditto,
and you don't notice when the world skips my beat.
You are speaking, telling me what to do,
what I know and what I want... and my drum beats louder.
The rhythm of rage makes me dance around you
as you tear apart my music;
try to squelch my desire to create.
As you drone on I watch your crystal ball
shattering shards of frustration
as you try to control my volume.
You close your eyes to me, and my drum beats freely...
I crescendo, upsetting the silence of your world.

Jennifer De Jesus-Jankowski

Will This Come True

Wake up America before it's too late
You are slowly ruining everything that made this country great
Liberal politicians emigrants, and special interest groups
Are working to take over the government of the United States
Turning this country into a socialist state

With legitimate and bastard births
While whites are going the abortion route
Hoping to control the majority vote, by the year 2008
If this comes true
This country will just become another nation failure

Wake up singles, review your life
Get you a good man or woman and start a married life
Sinful living has replaced our family groups
Which was once our greatest strength
We must repent and change our ways

The rise and fall of the Roman Empire
Will be nothing to compare
To the rise and fall of the United States
Which will shake the world
And cause many problems around the earth

Edgar H. Kleckley

Earth

If you listen very carefully while everyone's asleep
You can hear the planet sing to you and fell her rhythm deep.

She sings a song of matter; of energy and time
As she revolves in space she sings an endless rhyme.

She sings of caves and coal and earth,
Of badgers, worms and dust,
Of flint ores and magic tales
Of goblins and of rust.

She sings of ancient cultures, of heroes and their deeds,
And her delight when sensing the delicate growing seeds.

And if you listen carefully while everyone's asleep
You can hear Earth softly whimper and echo in the deep
And catch her softly whisper as she rolls along:
"Isn't anybody left who can hear a planets' song?"

Enid Vien

My Mirrors

In the mirrors to my soul,
You can see my childhood,
life experiences.
You may see sadness or anger
but it's usually laughter.
You can see my strengths, my values,
and my fears.
You can see my love for humanity,
and my passion for life.
You can see my role as mother,
as daughter, as sister,
and as friend.
You can see honesty, sincerity, sensuality,
and determination.
In the mirrors to my soul.
You can see my love for you.

Christine Sanchez

"Commandments Of Life"

For every good thing in life - we must pay the price
You cannot imagine the true shock of a calamity
Until it happens in your own family.
'If only I should have' must be said and done
Before not after the breath is no more.
Money that comes by easy - never seems to last
It slips out of your fingers, twice as fast.
Wars on earth will never cease
As long as humanity rules the peace.
Year after year we hope for that lucky day.
All at once we find we're old and grey
It's then we realize it could not be
For it's hopeless to fight your destiny.

John Sica

I Wonder

Sometimes I sit and wonder where my life is going.
Why does it go so slowly?
I dream at night and wonder, is this reality?
And when I'm awake, is it a formality?
I wonder if it'll get better for me.
Life is so hard to me, can't you see?
Life's only borrowed time.
People could care less if my life is worth a dime
I live my life day to day, wishing there was
Some other way, some answer to this
sadness, to stop my inner madness
that's clouding my mind.
Only if I can find the one thing to
make me end this sorrow, to live
my life not just for today but also for tomorrow

Andrea Blaine

Through Ronnie's Eyes

Thief by day, murderer by night
You crept into my soul and took away my life.
No way to hide, no way to fight.
No cure to be found only death with plight
Destined to fail-your liner, your lungs.
No drug or hope for the pain that comes.
Bid me farewell, she'd no more tears,
I'll be at peace now without any fears.
My family, my friends, around me please gather;
Your love will guide me through the life here after.
My memory will ease you through your grief.
Forget me not - do not weep.
Remember my laughter.
My love please don't forget
In my heart you'll always be forgiving all regret.
I'm ready to go, their arms are open wide.
Through the gates I'll travel,
Into peace on the other side.

Beth Greena Wald

"To A Child"

Read this my child, if your heart within you cries.
You do not understand, the whys and where, the trouble lies.
No matter who you are, you came from God 'tis true.
And as I now care, He much more cares, and He will comfort you.
You are a special angel! You are never mean!
If you act that way 'tis true, you've done an awful thing!
You are a heritage of the Lord. Your parents are blessed by you.
Though many never know or show it, by the unkind things they do.
If you have been told you're special, loved and precious, too,
If you have felt the love of songs, and hands caressing you.
If you have known the safety, when you cuddle down at night
God's Angels would watch over you, and things would be alright.
If you have been taught the love of God. How we all should live.
You would know the joy it brings, as you love, and to others give.
If you've never known this kindness, and you have a tearful heart.
Turn to your loving Saviour. It's not too late to start.
Love Him all you know of. Do what He asks of you.
For you can be a CHILD of GOD. Blessed in all you do.
Then, as you grow older, you'll find HAPPINESS comes from LOVE.
And beauty in the knowing, CHRIST, smiles down from up above.

Jerry Lloyd Radebaugh

Mother Time

Mother Time, it is a shame you've slept your life away,
You haven't helped Father Time to keep the time of day.
Wouldn't you think that Father Time needs a nice long rest?
He has been faithful and done his level best,
To keep the time as perfect as it can be,
But you are sleeping very late, my dear, dear lady.

Just sleep on Mother Time, you are having your way.
You've slept already, thousands of years, they say.
You haven't shown any willingness before,
To carry any part of Father Time's timely chore.
So nestle there in your flowery bed of ease,
No need for you to wake-up now, it's just too late to please.

Father Time needed your help many centuries ago,
But selfishly you slept and never made a show.
Father Time still has the strength to do the job quite well,
He doesn't need your help now, as far as one can tell.
Sleep on sleepy lady, Father Time will win this game,
It's too late for you to creep in now and try to win the fame.

Etta J. Strickland

The Piper's Quest

I am perched and ready to hold
You in search of the gates of gold.
I'll grasp the lonely and the weak
I'll wreck your life and make you weep.

I'll coax you in, just enter my chamber
Once you begin you'll be no stranger.
I'll help you reform and fill up your head
A new God is born, but the rose is dead.

Others will come to play with you
They'll see what you've done and know what to do.
Your skill is theirs once it's learned
Not much compares as the feathers burns.

When we marry, the tables will tilt
I'll make you carry your stone of guilt.
I'm ready today, I'll make you see
Just come my way and I'll set you free.

Jennifer R. Olofsson

Father's Day Thank You

When I asked you for your daughter's hand
You knew not of the things I'd planned.
Would I love her all through her life?
Care for her through wealth or strife?
Would I love her with kindness fair?
Take her burdens for myself to bear?
After these many years I hope you see
The same things your daughter saw in me.

A companion that loves her every step,
Ready to wipe each tear she's wept.
Someone to share her thoughts and ways.
Someone to kneel with when she prays.
No wealth, no possession, or all earth's gold
Could ever match what I now hold.
So I thank you for what you gave to me.
Your daughter's hand through eternity.

Gary M. Homan

The Touch Of A Mother's Hand

The loving touch of a Mother's hand is what makes a house a home;
You know there's always a place for you there,
no matter how far you roam.
No place on earth can offer the feeling of safety her arms can give;
The memories you'll have of her loving touch will stay with you
as long as you live.

The loving touch of a Mother's hand can heal pain deep in your soul;
When you're feeling broken and torn apart, her touch can make
you whole.
You may travel this wide world over from mountain to shifting sand;
Never finding a thing that will compare to the loving touch
of a Mother's hand.

Delores A. Shepherd

You've Been My Everything

You've been my best friend and love,
You've been my strength to face a new day,
You've been my passion throughout the night,
You've been the happiness that's fulfilled my life,
You've been the one that I have chosen to love, honor and cherish,
You've been the one who has always finished my every thought,
You've been the shoulder in which to cry on,
You've been the support of all my hopes and dreams,
You've been the one who has taught me what love really means,
You've been the memories that I hold closest to my heart,
You've been my heart and soul and all that I am,
You've been my one and only love,
You've been my everything...

Cindy L. Cierpisz

Old Man Praying

In my senescence, I praise Thee, O God.
You saw the chatting young nurse who held the mirror
for me "...so we can shave." Reflected there, I saw
my thin beak nose, rheumy eyes, and cracked skin
like a dry dusty cowhide. But the smiling young lady
said I looked "just great." How she lied.
Dear Jesus, You know how she really lied.

O Lord, I refused my tray.

Jesus, they sent a young doctor in to me, poking around,
trying to hit a vein, his needling raising a bunch of
domed bruises up and down my hands and arms. Ole Charlie
in the next bed began to scream. It was not like him
to yell like that. But his bed was all made up and empty!
O God, I was screaming, screaming and hoarsely screaming...

Then in these still quiet hours before dawn, I thank Thee
O Creator for Janice, and for our home. Where is she now,
how many children did we raise, what are their names, what is the
date? Where am I? Why?

In my senescence, I praise Thee O...O...o...o... ... ...

Dewey A. Nelson

Teens

Do you remember your teens? That one person in your dreams
You thought about constantly, did they care for you, honestly?
You tried to bump into them, accidently, be where they went,
frequently. Act surprised they'd appear, pretend you didn't want
them near.

You'd go through mood swings, wishing you had wings,
so that you could leave, never return, hating your parents and their
concern.

One day to your surprise, you're an adult, you realize,
and life is serious, and very tough, the world is very rough.
Now suddenly, you're in charge, alone, making decisions on your own.
Mother and Dad not there to advise, now YOU have to organize
your thoughts and plans, make YOUR choices, ignoring all other voices.

We have all been in your shoes, sometimes you win, sometimes you
lose. When you ARE knocked down, and are lying on the ground,
Not knowing what to do, remember others DO love you.

Audrey Hutton

Walking In Your Footsteps

Many years have passed since your exit from this world.
You were only 39, your accomplishments, numerous.
Your legacy, your "Lei of Love," the joys of your era
Wove securely around me, your girl-child, so precious.

Growing up, I connected with your love for things Hawaiian.
The land, the sea, my fields of joy,
The music, the dance, my pride, my trophy,
The people, our family, my source of love power.

A positive attitude, an unending sacrifice, I was reminded,
Were part of your strong athletic philosophy.
You, fearless leader, coach, teacher, organizer of activities,
Directed me toward participation in the human experience and
secured for me a meaningful plan in the game of life.

Mom said, your quest for knowledge was a passionate one,
Always striving for the summit, dedicated, determined.
Encouraged by this, I soared toward scholastic and athletic heights.

Now, as I take my place in society, I am ever grateful, Dad,
That your spiritual presence and influence
Guided me to this season in my life.
My heart swells with warmth and pride and love for you.

Josephine Cosma Blair

Scarlet Finch

He sits and rests on branches high,
with scarlet feathers on breast lie.

The sun comes up and spreads its light,
for the Scarlet Finch to take to flight.

An early riser, this tiny bird,
he's very persistent to spread his word,

For all mankind to wake and see,
what a beautiful day, today could be.

The morning hours pass quickly by,
the sun has risen straight up in the sky.

The Finch is quiet for it's time to rest,
with his family and friends all close in the nest.

The sun is now setting, the air has cooled down,
now there are Finches from everywhere to be found.

Back with their songs and their stories to tell,
of a beautiful day, that ended so well.

Chris McBee

"Closed For Repair"

The next time you come to my door
You'll see a sign posted there
The doors will be locked because you see
You forgot to leave the key.
Since the day you walked away
No ones been able to get inside.
There's a lot of work left to do
Yes, even after all this time.
I had to leave the attic til the end
This is the hardest place to mend
This is where precious memories are stored.
The doormat needs to be replaced
It was walked on too many times
It's time to open doors and windows wide
So a beam of sunshine can shine inside.
You left without saying good-bye
After all the times I stood by you.
So unless you're coming back to stay, good-bye is what
I wait to hear you say. Until that day the sign will read
"This Heart Closed For Repair."

Cindy J. O'Connell

Farewell

It was a Heavenly drama on that day
When Jesus opened His arms to say,
"Come, I have a better way
than to linger and suffer the earthly way."
So, in His omniscient, omnipotent way
summoned the families - those who care -
For this farewell . . . they must be there.
The conversation was caring, "everyday"
My brother, always ready with something to say
Just rested in their presence and love:
So like the love of the Father, above.
In a few moments he became very tired.
A loved one - so greatly admired.
Took his last breath
And entered into his earthly death.
Is this not the way to view our life here?
Use our talents well and work with cheer.
Work, share as he did - - live a good life
And give it back willingly - away from strife?

Eva Staveley

Memories Of Andy

Your feelings all you hide
You keep them locked inside.
The little boy inside of you
Was hidden behind all the things you do.
I know you're in a better place
But all I can think of is your smiling face.
It wasn't your fault and I shouldn't be mad
And what I can think of is what you had.
Just one red light
And the last time you said goodnight.
Now everyone's sad and feels much pain
I can't stop the tears falling like rain.
All the fun times we had we'll have no more
I wish you were alive and waiting at my door.
You were always a comfort with your eyes shining bright
But now I see you in a whole different light.
I will hold all these feelings down deep
And my memories of Andy I will keep.

Julie Johnson

Men of Christie Street

Go downtown Manhattan to Christie
By the street, sitting or standing you'll see
Folks, all in the same state of mind
Try body and soul to bind

Like the snail, they carry their all on their back
One has a Phi Beta Kappa key around his neck
A silent reminder of his glorious past
And a brown bag containing his repast.

These folks once wore white collars
Professionals that influenced matters
They dined in rich banquet halls
It was them, and no one else

Up the ladder, following their ego drive
Nothing was important except I
Then with the change, to Bacchus they sought refuge
Who now by Christie stand as living refuse

The door step replaces the brass bed
Behold a quarter for morsel they beg
The Corporate executive that wore dark suit
Now perfumes the corner and asks for soup.

Callixtus E. Ita

Love

O love is a feeling that makes a person strive
To crank out one of the Best Poems of 1995;
Love is what made Lassie the farm dog run back
to the farmhouse to alert little Timmy's farm family
whenever little Timmy fell into a dangerous farm pit;
Love is a feeling that will not go away, like a
fungus in your armpit;
So the bottom line is that there will always be
lovers
Wishing to express their love in an heirloom
quality book with imported French marbleized covers;
Which, at $49.95 a pop multiplied by 3,000 poets
Works out to gross literary revenues of roughly
$150,000, so it's
A good bet that whoever thought up the idea of
publishing this book
Doesn't care whether this last line rhymes.

Dave Barry

Dead Of Rwanda

We have never met
and yet, I sense
your spirit lingers
'round untimely grave.
Bulldozer scooping,
shoving its slaves
into the dry sod,
where seed and weed
refused to grow.
Human souls lie
like broken down cars
waiting to die.
You were a brother.
Perhaps a friend
or mother with child
clinging to breasts,
long dried-up wells of
withering flesh.

I shall not forget
You were human.

Barbara A. Cadogan

Autumn Relic

Fed from the strums of virgins' lips I exhale the
ash of an innocent's pyre and call the requiem my
atmosphere, watching the dead fade to crimson.

Lunatic woman exploding from a dark belfry with her
hysterical hair slashing azure like electric chords
of bronze, tightening the sky, killing an hour.

I leave my apartment so that apocalypse angels
do not forget me, to seek with these fat eyes
wounded brick and path, lost old man pipes,
kindergarten collages: In truth, I seek the
security of attic cobwebs.

I dance with childhood friends whose voices have
grown wooden, sing of acorn theories that stay
mysterious beneath the orange static of leaves,

and I bathe with them in the fire of this
rotation's hallmark, extending the dynasty
yet another year with a flock of blazing arrows,

our hungry embraces like war bows,
feeding the arbalests with the memory
of summer kisses.

Eric Noel Perez

In This House

Dear One, we are still growing old together in this house,
You in the spirit, I in the flesh.
The flush of youth no longer gives spring to my step,
But my heart feels young at the thought of your love.

When I put the coffee on each morning (a job you used to do)
In our remodelled kitchen, all white and new,
I recall your saying, "You've waited long enough.
Have anything you want."
It has everything I want, except you!

In the luxurious whirl bath for my arthritis pain,
I lean back, look at clouds, or listen to the rain,
Remembering, "It's only for you," you said, not wavering a minute.
Then you took only one shower in it.

Here I am, using every room in this house
We built to grow old in together.
Your soul and mine are entwined here forever
In this house. Is it really just a place to live?

Mary Meyer Leineweber

Comparison

Like a stiff, stuck in Casablanca, a
desperate stand of heath, clinging to a
wuthering height... as woeful as a

double suicide, that a Grace of minutes
could have spared... an untimely death

of ships, passing so tragically close,
only to sail, on, to oblivion, forgetfulness...

Till some beggar-cum-king unlock with a ring
of silver on stone the Sword's promise of spring:

The hope of a moth battering the flame,
that when this cross is carried home,

there rises, phoenix-like,
the butterfly, that will only light

on her.

Richard Paul

Melting, Down South

A sensual burning
Etching a brand
Is languidly creeping
Down the length of my spine.
From afar,
The moan of a train
Spouting its smokey blues,
And entrancing my awareness
As slowly I focus,
On the view outside my window.
The beauty of silence,
Of ice clinging wetly
Creating sharp appendages
Within a blinding blanket of light.
Which well serves intensity
And, the smoldering below
That in a brief lapse of time,
Will become the searing blaze,
We know...
As summer.

Dorothy Brooks

Reunion of Spirit

By chance on a moment, I sense an old friend. I cross a dimension, to
breathe in your pen. My place of existence, a plane of the mind, that
lives in the passion, of thoughts set to rhyme. As almost by magic,
the spark of your art, this eve bears my presence, from out of the
dark. Like far away echoes, like something you know, like something
familiar, from so long ago. You're still as a baby, escaped by my name.
Remember we sang in the clouds and the rain?
Now you lie tearstruck, in a world where I'm naught, but lost
lonely shadows, of yesterday's thoughts.
Out where you left me, is out where I've been, just where we were
setting a dream to the wind. Our deja-vu dances with tears in your
eyes, I call from the safety, you cry from the lines. How strange I
should surface, just now as you've drawn, from something inside you,
that's sad you've been gone. And I'm saddened mostly, to see you so
lost, when the friend you need most, is the friend you forgot.
Ourselves as a soul, long ago made a deal, this night it is
honored, by something you feel. I'm something created, come back to
you now, to throw you a line, if you don't want to drown. I make you
feel traces, and longing of love. How sad you should hurt from the
coo of a dove. Such quiet reunion, we share here tonight, just so you
remember, the cause and the fight. From a world in a silence, where
a part of you froze, and a part of you ventured, I want you to know.
I'm safe and protected, you're seeing me through. I'm what you're
defending, the innocent you....

Ron Busbee

My Youth

My youth was not wasted.....
I squeezed every drop
from its ravaged rind.

From nurtured seedling to shadowing the field of dreams
this bastard hybrid grew boldly outside his grove of peers
Roots tapping tender psyche during a torrent of envious rain
and branches blithely challenging the glare of admonition.

His ringed protrusion grew hard enough to endure the endless climb
of fearless hands, anxious hearts and the plume of a satanic sign
Latent bloom still bearing fruit bore the green of an ancient limb
yet canopied anima from her tantrums and culture's hideous whim.

Now I deposit this hollowed husk
in the memory bank
only to be withdrawn
when faced with destined poverty.

Forgetting the ache of craving
that idyllic innocence inflicts
I habitually chew the exalted remnants
of provincial recollection.

Daniel G. Baker

Counterpoint

In the stillness of the night
The face of winter faintly smiles
Breathes out through pursing lips
An icy whisper.
My rhododendron tells me this
Closing in upon itself
As broad leaves curl and tightly roll
Composing shapes in foliage gone dry and weak.
It measures changing moments
Waiting silently and patient.
With rounded shoulders shielding me from gusting winds
I hang my head
I read my fingertips, cold nose and ears, the vapor of my breath
And hurry as I can in bulky layers of wool,
Long trailing scarf, high shearling boots.
Adaptively we meet the cold, the two of us
We manage to survive the biting frost
But one of us is playing at charades
The other in surrender bows to winter.

Harriot Mishkoff

Voyage Into Vastness

A sliver of the moon, silver,
The sum of the sun, gold
One visits me at night, hither,
The other during day-time, bold.

Yet the two, one hot, one kind,
Cross the sky, without each other,
The moon is really confined, entwined,
With our blue earth, her mother.

All pace, embrace, in space,
With the sun, center-stage,
Earth and moon, orbiting in haste, grace,
Our solar system, God's celestial cage.

Where are we going—the destination?
We're not traveling space, just spanning time.
Not journeying together, our lives, a hesitation,
Like unraveling lace, Dust abandoning mine.

John C. Flores

Winter Song

The crystal stars lean earthward on their beams,
Timeless in beauty, silent as a thought,
Caressing each heart who walks the night and dreams
Beyond the trying trifles day has brought.

Music like a woman charms the sense,
And humor soothes the ruffled vanity;
And hearthside company grants strong defense
Against the cold of inhumanity.

Faith is a faery flower winterborn
Blooming through evil like an edelweiss,
Bursting in glory in the snowy morn,
Radiant emblem on her shield of ice.

Love is a warming wine, winning our wills,
A perfect rose, a song, a feast, a wraith,
Whose magic raises cities on the hills,
And still remains intangible as faith.

Clyde Beakley

Front Page

They tamped me under in Nanking
a crying compost heap.
I sunbathed
bloated, rotting, stinking
in a blue Pacific paradise.
I exercised
running from caves and bunkers
eaten alive by fire.
I showered
before they stuffed me into the ovens.
I rested as I starved
too weak to move.
The bombs smashed my atoms
integrating me instantly
one with the world.

And now they toss me overboard
with the garbage
food for rats and gulls.
I have lived a thousand deaths.
The last one should be easy.

Grace Hyland

Dreaming Time

My soul doth fly thru volumed air
Among expanse of eagled wing,
I soar above the fragment cloud
And joyfully a song of freedom sing.

I fly beyond the reach of mortals
Travel on a shooting star,
See below the moonlit mountains
Crystal shining, reaching far.

Starburst of a diamond cluster
Meets the mountains of the moon,
Oh! The moon and moonlight madness
Ladles light with a silvered spoon.

Pouring light upon the oceans,
Stretching paths across the seas
And gazing into reflective waters
Moon sees herself and looks at me.

Farewell moon for this dreaming time,
When you return for your dappling hours,
I shall fly again to meet you
To dance among the myriad of stars.

Rose Mary Hooper

In the Pond

The moonshine smears over restless, purling water
and conceals with reflection the murky below with
a panoply of spoon-dip flashes
that smack my eyes to distraction.
And ugly me, waiting for the sun to arrive
to ripen my skin into motion,
towards an illuminated pond,
where the commotion of dry-fractured earth
is smoothed calm into a sandy bottom,
stretched like fresh skin.
And I see the once abrasive grass
now pacified under the recompense
of water-pressure immense,
touching like thick, healthy air,
green and heady.
And everything flows with methodic gentleness,
as if politely greeting
the wake of a passing life
with a watery wave of hello and good-bye.

Christopher W. Hanson

Twilight Reverie

Twilight trimmed her golden lantern
and in it's golden light I walked with
the sunset on the hill.
The world was hushed cradled in the arms
of evening dusk,
where deep, purple shadows watched the velvet
night creep slowly o'er the misty hill.
Flecks of sun dazzled the twilight sky
marbled by the fading blue.
Tall spruces stood like sentinels, stark and
still against flamboyant skies.
As leaflets danced in the frosty chill
and whirled to music of the wind to make muffled
music of a mist veiled stream.
Then through the azure tinted sky a high
crescendo rose and fell, as night travellers
sang a sad adieu and disappeared in silhouettes,
consumed by a crimson, billowing sky.

Anne Kaye

Visions Of Kate

With wonder I stare in the dawn of day,
At the phantom posing in the narrow doorway,
Beloved Kate from a faraway land,
A secret utopia on golden sand.

I seek to touch her lovely face,
Love knowing no bounds, transcending space,
Yet she eludes and guards the key,
To the mystery door between her and me.

So warming the taste of her sabbath feast.
An offering of love to even the least,
The shabby stranger with bright sad eyes,
Surely and angel in mortal disguise.

Her perfume trails boldly and captures my nose,
I smell the fragrance of a wild red rose,
Time standing still in the moment rare,
Suspends my phantom in anointed air.

Beyond the purple mountain tall,
I hear her laughter and tender call,
The torch flaming brightly on benevolent fate,
I imprison forever sweet visions of Kate.

Jean Manning

On Silence

In the darling morning of acquiescent queer silence
Before dawn, foreign stars wink, occasional crescent moon
Lingers while the strange silence of morning
Is broken by sudden stove pipe quirking noise
Jostling thoughts of yesterday's fibrous meaning.

While new day yearnings roam with uncertain kindness
Out of the abyss of nothingness
Into realities so sure and demanding
Only the azure sun arising
Over the earth shaken Bay Bridge beckons truth
While Alcatraz signals its presence.

As ships galore steal their way to other ports
Blasting fog horns pierce the silence
In the crepuscular morning dimness
Of yet another day of lethargic bliss
In Sausalito town, so sleepy
Arise, with a gentle kiss!

Christopher R. Jennings

Mourning Sky

The mourning sky got me
before you did

Yellowing-red on motionless bodies
I am burning from the inside out

Perhaps a day too far
too clear:
I have found too many wrinkles
in yesterday's pristine sheets

Rolling toward their implications
finding you and I in separate
corners of the bed

I feel sick

That same spider's shadow
drifts across our moving sky
as it spins another web between us

This time, I leave before it finishes.

Elisabeth Richards

Never Had No Daddy

Never had no daddy.

Crack mad crazy momma
Bit off all them toes & fingers
Of little baby me.

So here I sit, lookin' out
At 9th & Florida 14 years later —
Mean world drivin' by or
Standin' 'round doorways,
Makin' thin shadows
Under store signs after dark.
"Hey Momma! You're Special Here!"
Over "BIG RED'S CAJUN BAR-B-Q"
In red & white & blue.

You know I can't write & it's hard
To type with the edges of my hands.
& I wonder.

Did she chew 'em up & swallow
Or spit 'em out.

And if she spit —
Where'd she put 'em?

Michael J. McCune

Graffiti on Linen

Black paint on grayed walls wiped
Crimson with anger aerosol the tale of a stuttered
Journey stumbled down an unlettered path,
Wanton destruction the key to futile frustration.

The book of tomorrow is penned on backward
Postcards mailed by overnight express,
Relating the sounds mouthed delicately forward
With ink dipped by an ancient hand.

Woven white colored with strident marks
Whorl-swirl the artist's lonely plea,
Telegraphed to stars winking and blinking
Throughout the forget-me-not sky of a darkened moon.

Whether a sounded symbol sprayed on concrete
Or toed on a sanded shore, both are imprinted
By the micropores of time, addressed to locate
Soul, route backroad home, anywhere.

Marie Scott

An Eddy of Thought

Writers rummage round the memory bin,
Dowsing for dreams, with their bag lady shrew
Dribbling, drivelings, barking at them,
For things they did and things they did not do.

Let 'em kneel before Mnemosyne now,
In livid choler for the muse to view;
Perhaps it all comes back to her somehow,
The things she did and things she did not do.

Declare that he should full of wonder be,
To languish forever in lawful woe;
In solitary berth beneath the sea,
Angling for answers young men yearn to know?

Can't remember how to season his eggs,
How much milk to put in his cereal;
Could it be because he's steeped in old age,
Could it be because he is ethereal?

Mayhaps he's caught in an eddy of thought,
That some deem as right and others deem naught.

O. E. (Mickey) Perkins Jr.

The Hand Of Love

I took the hand of innocence and led
her along the path of maturity, I stole
The sparkle that once shone in her eyes,
and replaced it with lies. I walked with
her on beaches long, I trespassed into
her heart with a lonely song. I spoke
words that were sweet, sweet to
hear, yet, sour in taste, their foundations
weak.

The stars that spied us in the night,
followed us into the daylight, we could
now walk, they made us run. And I
was only the shadow of a candle, blowing
in the wind, that failed to ignite. One man's
loss is another man's gain, that
hand I held knew only pain. Unseen
wounds only bleed on the inside, that
hand I once held, I wish with her I could
hide.

Seamus Gorrell

Reflection

Listen, there was no time to play with my toys.
I was a rock slide - pushing, plummeting, building
momentum - faster and faster as I slid down
the mountain to the valley of mid-life.
Oh, I sniffed the scentless sage and
glimpsed the treeless forest and
the dying ember of a flickering fire, yes,
I watched them bury the old people - strangers, my grandparents, and
I knew there was a war someplace - someone fighting for something and
babies doing drugs, yes,
I read the blank pages and
heard the roaring lion silenced with an animal cracker and
I saw the setting sun sinking slowly behind
a young girl creeping to the nursing home, yes,
I was a boulder - bouncing, bumping, tumbling,
rushing, racing to get to that valley.

Listen, my toys are broken, gone, obsolete, and
who will teach me to play with the new ones?

Earline Brunt

Blue Fins Versus Pinstriped Vikings

The thunder of my sigh
is cast out of
moments where I was in pain
from such endless laughter.
Sleep was a punishment, an interruption
in those years we fumbled through.
The noise we gathered
when told to lower,
were screams of trust
each child wants to play with
from that, I've learned
about those who dazzle us
with the perfume of an acquaintance,
and the few who wear
the true scent of a friend

Michael Craig Berg

The Old Cathedral

Icons of massive masonry,
surrendering to rot and rust,
once sharing days of pomp and pageantry
are now clothed in layered dust.

Embraced by sculptured walls
saints and angels, in sightless wonder,
guard memories which graced the halls
that modern minds now ponder.

Fingers poised o'er silent flute,
mandolins cradled on their knee,
cherubim and seraphim, quite mute,
join in mad medieval cacophony.

Carillons rouse doves from vaulted beam
hewn from giant oak destined to last;
ever-burning holy candles gleam,
mixing present with a shadowed past.

Oh, hallowed place I hear your call
luring me to enter and adore;
as through the centuries you beckoned one and all
to glean the treasures hid behind your door.

Connie Hess

Old Waterway

This waterway of long forgotten memory
Is flanked by narrow measured strips
Of densely cultivated fields
Which precious silt revived with certainty.
At places, sand compacted desert hills
Sweep down within the water's reach -
And villages, flat roofed, were planned
By architects a thousand years gone passed
With life still lived in undetected change.
Ill-humored camels, sure of foot,
Plod slow the unmarked desert routes
And single sailed feluccas carry fast
When northward bound -
Perhaps to join a Pharaoh's golden barque
To where the pyramids stand firm.
The sunset brings the patterned palms
And minarets against a red-gold sky -
In all this time the face worn Sphinx
Looks east across the Nile
To wait the sunrise for eternity.

Joan Boyes

Distant Drums

I hear the beat of distant drums, deep
within my heart. It stirs my deepest
fears, within my very soul. It brings
out past memories that lies within my
brain, I can hear the beat of the drums,
stir taught's long forgotten.

The drums beat on I am eight again not and
only child. I can feel the rain, I see,
faces pass me by. My hand stretch out hear
take my hand feel my pain, hear my cries,
share my joys, stay and talk to me a while,
I am your child.

The drums beat on, and still no one
hear's my cries, so time moves on,
and so did I. So distant drums beat on.
but I will survive, for I am me.
Myself and I.

Eulanhie Anderson

Love And Peace

LOVE comes in all sizes
Big, little, short and tall
And that is not all
It is human
And speaks many languages.

It comes together sometimes in the oddest places;
A church, picnic, convention or school
LOVE has no particular place, time or rule.

It comes together for various reasons;
Loneliness, friendship, kinship
Or hoping for PEACE!

LOVE, like a river
Goes upstream and downstream
Flowing from you to me
And from me to you.

Over the hills and valleys
The highways and airways
LOVE is what we need for unity
LOVE and PEACE, let it be everywhere!

Nola P. Richmond

The Call Of The Cold Wind

There it is again - the call of the cold wind.
Just now I noticed its long wooden digits
Poking and scratching on my window.
Her tongue is ice and licks at my ears.
The bidding is ancient-familiar yet foreign.
I can understand only her gestures and
facial expressions.
"Wake up, the hour is come,
Leave the salt sea of your womb.
Dance in the cold night wind with me.
I will surround you, batter you,
Your feet will tingle and go numb.
But you will see the cold fog from your breath
As you shout in triumph
Not over the cold but over the warmth,
And feel the sting of blood as you clench your fist.
My long fingers can but tap on the glass from outside.
It takes a warrior fist to break it."

George E. Schmauch Jr.

Spring Was So Long Ago

Autumn approaches on silent, damp feet
Leaving summer's green face far, far behind.
Spring was so long ago, magic and sweet.

Youth's memories cling, each one sealed and signed.
Bittersweet this death-in-life state of mind.
Autumn approaches on silent, damp feet.

Winter, flaunting pale hunger, will complete
Life's thin vapor; love is harder to find.
Spring was so long ago, magic and sweet.

Laughter rode the hills on spring's fragrant breath.
Youth and the robin sang free, to unwind.
Autumn approaches on silent, damp feet.

Death sniffs at autumn's heels; will not retreat.
He throws a bone: Indian summer is blind.
Spring was so long ago, magic and sweet.

And you, my soul, will walk a golden street,
Singing in the chains of Fate, not unkind.
Autumn approaches on silent, damp feet.
Spring was so long ago, magic and sweet.

Louise Wilkerson Conn

Coral Reef

The coral castle rises sheer from bottom sand's pure white,
Its lofty turrets reaching near the azure surface light.
Stone fingers standing, interlac'd and lock'd in placid prayer —
Both temple and a trysting place for creatures in its care.

Elkhorn coral's shadows soar o'er convoluted boulders
A-jumbled on the ocean floor, bedecked with lichen shoulders.
Sea fans test the current's gage, defending sacred spaces —
Sheltered lees in pristine cage of ocean's warm embraces.

Trumpet fishes standing tall, tails straining to the sky,
Mute relays for sweet seraphs call to angel fishes shy.
Placid goatfish grazing low, in fields of grass and stone —
A brief bucolic cameo adorning Neptune's throne.

Brilliant, dainty wrasses flash their chevrons blue and gold,
Darting swift to guard their cache, as sunbeams they enfold.
Squads of soldier fish enrolled by sergeant majors bright,
Wheeling, leading charges bold against intruders might.

Kaleidoscope of color found in ocean's depths of blue,
Encircling the ramparts 'round the castle's varied hue.
Enchantment in Elysian Fields, in Eden's wat'ry earth —
The coral, in renewal, yields the promise of its birth.

George W. Crampton

The Promise

I hear it's whisper in the gentleness
of one illicit autumn twilight,
while it's deception goes unfelt
upon the hand of a warm evening breeze.

It lies within that place unseen
between ending life and beginning death;
a shadow beyond a rising copper sphere
while holding a vise on an unfettered soul.

I am desperate to scream, "Persephone!
How could you, you childish wretch!"
But fall instead upon quivering knees,
dropping chin on chest in supplication.

It will come with a biting cold tongue
and a sharp stinging lash; whipping us
like a mother possessed in subduing
the innocent spirit of her child.

V. L. Steward

One Summer

This wispy rye grass, I remember,
standing in the sun in swoon,
its virgin green sheltering,
beneath the swaying fullness,
a young heron, which had flown
the nest too soon.
I remember well the drops of dew
at dawn, that glittered like
a bridal wreath upon
and made the grasses softly bend.
At summer's end, when golden ripe
the rye grass swayed
and dragonflies forsook it for
a winter's resting place,
its seeds traveled far, gently
gliding, graceful, with the breeze.
Their ease filled me with envy.
Now in the winter of my years
and earth bound, I remember.

Erika M. Bruesewitz

Night Sounds: A Sonnet To Spring

Like a silver drum the timeless moon rolls by;
Star-spangled bands of clouds march to its beat.
Soon rosy dawn must leave her bed of sky,
Come trailing sheets of sunlight at her feet.
Spring lilacs drown the warm night air with scent,
As if to question every passing breeze;
And nod their purple heads in royal assent
To whispered answers blown from poplar trees.
The telephone wires hum hymns to soothe the dark;
Car wheels cough gravel hoarsely in their track;
A haunting, wind-lost voice calls from the park;
The whistle from a train comes echoing back.
Night sounds of spring through open windows creep,
To prick the outer edges of our sleep.

Valerie J. Palmer

Eight Months

He hiccoughs upside-down
Sucking a short tentacle.
I am only a wall which moves,
Shrinking his inland sea,
And noises off. He shakes
A minute fist at a future of sharks.

Does gravity come with breath?
Kicking his heels and my ribs
In a squirming headstand
Like a sea-horse colt
In pastures of kelp
He doesn't seem to mind:
Up, down, it's all one.

Yet after the great tides
Beach him with weed and wrack
On shores of fearful air,
You can bet he will yell displeasure
Held up by those same heels
Like a pink wet bat
In the midwife's giant hands.

Elizabeth Cartwright-Hignett

I Love You, Son

He stood on his Appalachian porch, so alone, it seemed
that day in those sun-kissed mountains of my birth.
I, his first born son, was going back to L.A.
He longed so to go with me to start a new life
in a paradise he'd never seen, and never would.
How I've wished we had established a better relationship,
said the things our hearts cried out to express
across a confounding generation gap.
But, we mountain men of soil and toil were never demonstrative.
The next time I saw him, as eloquent in death as in life,
he was prepared for interment amid the maples,
beneath an Appalachian tombstone.
After that I returned to L.A. no more.
A million times I've repeated since that day, I love you, Dad.
Like father, like son:
My own eldest son slipped away some twenty years ago
into the wilds of Los Angeles.
The silent refrains of an aching heart never ends:
I love you, Son.

Arthur Byrd Adams

In The Courtyard

In the courtyard
bricks are slow to warm
on a morning washed with gray.

Inside, a dowager robed in silk
Leans to lift a porcelain cup,
Inhales the scent of tea—

Outside the gates
the streets wind close—
choked with cattle, full of grace

the people, rapt
and bent in haste,
tread cobblestones and dung.

In the window of an alley shop
desperate roses grow
rising from their browned leaves
to lean against the light.

Phebe E. Davidson

Comes Autumn

This crystal day, this Magritte sky
These crisping leaves soon doomed to die
This tonic air ripe-redolent
With fragrant vine and apple scent

In the dappled darkness of the wood
The loosening leaf bids farewell to the bud
That bore it in it green ascendancy
Now brittle in its sere fragility

Clinging once with sap-surge urgency
It downward floats fulfilling verdure's destiny
Feeding the fulsome ever avid earth
Whose waiting womb brings buoyant Spring's rebirth

The waning warmth of the sultry sun
Feeds false hopes that cold won't come
The silent sapient earth knows well
And needs no calendar to tell
The crimsoning leaves — Prepare to fall,
Sojourners here, as are we all

Vivian Schulte

The Return

You came to my house in the wasteland,
to my desolate abode of the moorland,
to the lonely land where beneath a sullen sky
the creeping mists bring in perpetual rains
dripping from the rotted guttering and eaves,
blowing in through the broken window panes
uncurtained and uncared for in the fitful gusts of wind.
Time was when these rooms drab and drear
did resound to the sounds of life
and were sanctuaries of warmth and cheer,
but of late when looking out across my sunless world
stretching away unending to the grey horizon
I saw you coming back again,
back along the old familiar path, the pathway of return.
And now this bleak and desolate ruin becomes once more a sanctuary,
rising to spurn the creepi2ng oblivion of time,
these crumbling walls become gallant halls,
of porticos and turret towers, of moat and keep and leafy bowers
until beneath a clearing sky it rises a fortressed castle,
serene, secure, upon a summer-scented heather moor.

R. J. Matheson

The Stronghold

He knew no miracles, that boy born last
With far to go and everything to prove.
But once, when he was ten and lonely in
The house which older brothers left silent,
A dog with dark imploring eyes came out
Of nowhere, came softly on tentative paws
And stayed all winter, faithful to the boy,
His friend. And then he was summarily
Convicted in the sudden death of two
White leghorn hens, his fate by some unnamed
Avenger sealed. The poison killed slowly,
Eclipsed a week in which the boy stood by,
Reeling before the ghastly spectacle
Of suffering, knowing no tongue to sway
The distant God who let it be. His wounds
Were deep. They would endure beyond the loss
And, veiled, unhealed behind a mask of grim
Sufficiency, live on inside the man
Who all his days in search of life's meaning,
Found none, and never believed in miracles.

Grace Roberson Hicks

For My Daughter Diana On Turning Fifty -
A Celebration Of Your Life

When you were born I thought my heart would surely burst with pride
Your father was enchanted too, he kept you by his side!
Your hair was copper colored and your eyes a vivid blue,
And we were so delighted with the miracle of you!

I've watched the stages of your life with interest and with pride
The difficult and happy times you've taken them in stride.
The years have passed and you have grown, my love has not diminished
You're still a miracle to me, your charm is still not finished!

You're versatile and clever, have beauty in your soul
You're gentle, kind and caring, helping others is your goal.
The things you've learned in fifty years amount to quite a sum,
So just relax now and enjoy the fifty yet to come!

Emma Holliday

Homeless

She trod the streets and allies
In worn out shoes and clothes,
In search of bits and pieces
Of this and that - who knows?

At night she sleeps in doorways
Away from prying eyes,
And wind, and dust, and snide remarks
And moisture from the skies.

At dawn the world is new, again,
Back to her daily beat,
Her worldly goods all wrapped inside
Her bed roll, nice and neat.

A coffee break, a crust of bread,
Her meals are scanty fare,
Respite in a shady park,
And off again, — to nowhere.

Robert E. Harbison

"Seasons"

To everything there is a season,
It has been often said.
The chapters of your life must end,
Though you know not what's ahead.

But there's something of which
You can be assured,
That there's nothing coming to you
That cannot be endured.

As one season blends into another,
Who knows exactly when it ends?
For as that season's ending,
Another is ready to begin.

Just as one door is closing,
Another is ajar.
As opportunity's unfolding,
You can travel far!

To everything there is a season,
Don't waste life with regret.
Make these seasons of your life
The best to come just yet!

Linda Fuller

Speedy Spider

An inspiration of life
Above the doorway clinging to the awning of my house. I saw an inspiration of life before my eyes. Speedy spider I called her, so full of energy, so full of life. As I looked above my head and, as the days went by, I saw speedy spider spinning away, making her web, no matter what rain or shine, night or day she spun away making her web. Sometimes the wind or rain would blow her, Web away, as I awoke
and looked out my door, I felt a sense of sadness as I saw her Web no more, but no wait just as quickly as the night come there she was speedy spider spinning away, a new Web, stronger Web, yes speedy spider had spun away a better built, stronger well constructed, a different style for a different just for one moment, someone or something always teaches us just how much life we have, we share or just how much we give, by simple thought or just by sight, we learn never to give up, we must fight, fight, fight, whatever the problem, it doesn't matter how high we can always stand tall with new Ideas and better beginning. For whatever the reason we must remember never To give up and always remember speedy spider spinning away.

Samuel Flores

Is Summer Ending? Can It Be?

Is summer ending? Can it be? We now await the coming of winter, the season that seems to last so much longer than the others.
And spring was but a sweet dream. We have seen life in full bloom with all the green trees, leaves, and grass and we have seen a profusion of flowers in rainbow colors. Is summer ending? Can it be? The hot humid air, and bodies sweating, the barbecue, the pool party, the old swimming hole and summer beaches. Is summer already passing? Can it be? For vacation time is over and Labor Day is gone. Back to school go the kids. Where has it gone, so fast? Is summer already passing? Can it be? The wild berries have been picked and the fairs have come to each county. The cool air of autumn is starting to put bumps on our skin in the early morn. Sweaters and jackets are replacing summer T-shirts and shorts.
Is summer ending? Can it be? The leaves of the trees have begun to turn color, and the blooming flowers have dried and withered as the cold wind from Canada begins to blow. One cuddles in blankets at evening dusk and early morning's dawn.
Is summer ending? Can it be?
As one might say, summer comes and
summer goes - it is a fleeting as a breeze.

Raymond N. Chaput Jr.

My Saviour's Love

Not in heart or in life
Not in any daily task of old.
Nor in any service of which I perform
Will my saviour's love be left untold.
But in the humblest way of faith
Shall I have an awareness of my saviour's love.
Lest my weary heart should go astray
And miss the love light from above.
My saviour's love is a daily comfort
As from this earthly shore I look with joy.
My life is filled with a spiritual love
Of which this world shall never destroy.
Thus in every daily through and deed
My saviour's love has filled my soul.
And in love he left to me
Faith and hope which shall never grow old.

John C. Carter, Jr.

Caretaking

One stall, two stalls, three stalls or more
There's not a day that we get bored
To one, then to the other
Just waiting on the traveller's little old mother
Moping and sweeping, we do our best
Thinking the men's room, it's in a mess
Starting over again and again
As if the day did already begin
Just sitting around sometimes I'm dreaming
But silence has left with no time to sit
It's back to work, I heard the traveler screaming
Oh yes, you're right, it's back to cleaning.

Perry E. Bradley

Autumn

The goldenrod that heralds fall -
Where does it hide in spring
When dandelions cloak the earth?
There is a time for everything.
Child-wide eyes inspect the world.
Old eyes have already seen it.
But age can still be childlike -
Depends on the spark within it.
God gives and shepherds life,
Enjoyment is there this minute.
Something new is hidden where
The sunlight lets life begin it.
We save the yellow flowers paint
And call it goldenrod,
And all the gold of autumn
In winter, rests beneath the sod.

Paul E. White

"The Elusive"

I slipped quietly through the grasses
With butterfly net raised high,
And quickly, as lightning flashes,
I made a desperate try.

But the fragile little butterfly
Had sensed my selfish plan,
Eluded the confining net.
I failed before I began.

I tried to capture love.
Its beauty whet my desire.
I cleverly set the trap;
This is would require.

I would imprison love,
And keep it close to me.
But this elusive creature,
Too, must soar high and free.

Jeanne Magee Robb

Faces

To each their own,
Young and old etched in time.
Hollow shells of fighting men,
Words in a poem—out of rhyme.
Tangled webs of human masse,
faces in the wind.
Ghostly shapes of hope forlorn,
Traces of what might have been.
Tears flow from hollow eyes,
A memory thinks of home.
Of July days and carefree ways,
The fields they did roam.
Time will cure the troddened soul,
Re-linquish all doubts with-in.
Light returns to hollow eyes,
And faces in the wind.

Donald L. Biesecker Jr.

In The Meadow

I began long ago beneath the mists and the dew.
I became a tiny stream that washed the furry feet of fern
And felt the tremors of young trout that grew and
played in my water.
Long legged bugs skated on my surface, and nails
Carried their glistening shells up my wet banks.
I heard the children come into the meadow; they knelt
Beside me and saw their faces mirrored upon me. And
Sometimes let me run over their young feet - caressing
Small toes and causing laughter.
I wind by the gentians as blue as the sky and
I hear the lark singing close by -
As I hurry along - growing wider - listening to
my own babbling song.
There's an excitement within my depths - I spread out
Past the reeds and lake,
On, on I rush until I am a river!

Valerie LePire Carpenter

"Beyond"

Am I envious of those who've gone beyond
They who know why the sun will dawn
They that have met the maker face-to-face
And know why each star hangs in space

Thompson Buchanan

Fall In Krakow

Icy tears from heaven fall so slowly;
Silently dancing upon each invisible
finger of air.

Fresh snows come early this late October afternoon.
Dim streets are deathly: hollow with a ghostly
cry from an empty child long since past.

Gray winds whisk through winter trees
as the snow (the pure innocent snow!) covers
the leaves turned blood-red from the grasp
of autumn.
Time veneers too, the wretched past, but not the
memory or the agony. Like snows in Spring,
dead leaves seem never to dull.

Softly, so softly a snowflake falls to the ground.
And peace for a moment with nary a sound, but the
crashing call of crystals echoing the alleys
of Krakow,
Whispering for remembrance.

William T. Smith

Schwarzwaldalp Reflection

Torrents of trees spill down the hills,
And bell-tunes sprinkle the air,
While crowds of clouds foretell of chills
Warning to hikers: "take care"!

Waterfalls foam their milky way,
Channeled alongside grasses,
Where cows with full-globed udders sway
Sidling the mountain passes.

Rising air currents pierced by peaks,
Frustrate the camera's view,
Consigning photographs one seeks
To memories that accrue.

Muriel W. Alexander

Empty Skies Over Peleliu

(In Memory of Howard B. Hayes, U.S. Marine Corps)
Take me to the place where your soul died
As sand grew red with your young blood.
Where last your footsteps touched the earth
And heart gave all. For God, For Country,
-For The Corps-

As wind carried your last words to me,
Heaven threw stars upon the verdant soil.
That I would know, as I prayed and see
The void. The wretched emptiness of sky.
-Without you here-

To take my hand once more
Cease my tears in falling
-With your embrace-

J. C. Smith

The Warrior

Don't speak to me of a long-forgotten youth
When hope still lingered in your smile,
and you walked with impatience.

When life wasn't planned and predictions
didn't always come true.
And dreams cascaded down your soul
like a woman's hair upon her shoulders.

When loneliness wasn't permanent, trust not forbidden;
women not temporary, control not an issue.
And you dared to reveal your despair.

A soul scorched and scarred—battles over and won.
Did someone forget to tell you that the war was over?

And you wonder why I'm scared.

Shauna Mackintosh

Pain Of Loneliness

The pain, the emptiness,
When a loved one has gone -
Passed on to another world,
Never to return again.

The feeling of loneliness,
Overwhelms you while you sit alone.
The feeling of loneliness,
Overwhelming even in a crowd.

A smile comes to your face
When you think of your close friend,
Who you loved so dearly,
In a much better place.
But the pain still remains.

Amy Ayers

Biographies of Poets

ABBASI, FEROZA
[p.] A. Majid Kazi and Noornisa Kazi; [m.] A.S. Abbasi; [ch.] Robert Aboud and Ahmed Rez; [ed.] St. Mary's Convent High School, Kinnard College, Lahore (Pakistan); [occ.] Homemaker; [hon.] Roll of Honors (Junior College), Top 3% graduates, Kinnard College, Second prize Essay Competition Junior College; [oth. writ.] Published at age 14 poems in local newspaper writing competition (Essay on Economics), Editor's Choice-National Library of Poetry; [pers.] I grew up in a milieu of intellectual curiosity and political awakening in Pakistan. This has greatly influenced some of my poetry living in difficult corners of the world has enabled me to garner a veritable treasure of life experiences that I draw from for my writings. Reading provides food for thought...and isn't poetry the caviar. [a.] Rancho Palos Verdes, CA.

ADAMS, BRENNA HELEN
[b.] September 6, 1975, Palm Springs, CA; [p.] Bruce Adams and Dayle Carnahan; [ed.] Yucca Valley High School, Sky High School; [hon.] Letters of Commendation, Honor Roll; [oth. writ.] "Love No Longer Exist in the World" published in National Library of Poetry Tears of Fire and "Our Friendship" written to Colleen Chastity Esping in junior year book. Also had "Love No Longer Exist in the World" on Sounds of Poetry; [pers.] If people could take the time and listen to their hearts and believe in themselves the world would be a much better place. Life is to wonderful to waste its beauty. [a.] Little Rock, AR.

ADAMS, GERALD H.
[b.] May 25, 1935, Georgetown, Guyana; [p.] Julia and Joseph Adams (deceased); [m.] Terri, October 21, 1989; [ch.] Gerald, Eric, Ronald and Steven; [ed.] Cambridge Academy, Morris High School, Manhattan State Hospital School of Nursing, St. John's University, New York University; [occ.] Retired; [memb.] American Nurses Association, President Linden Blvd. Block Association; [hon.] Manhattan State Hospital's 25 Year Service award/World of Poetry, Golden Poet and certificate of merit awards; [oth. writ.] Four poems published in World of Poetry Anthologies; [pers.] I count my blessings and try to help those who are less fortunate than myself. My writings has been greatly influenced by my exposure to Shakespeare and Alexander Pope, under instruction from Robert Pinkerton, Principal of Cambridge Academy. [a.] New York, NY.

ADAMS, LINDA
[b.] October 2, 1963, Glendale, CA; [p.] Robert and Marilyn Adams; [ed.] Los Angeles Valley College; [occ.] Soldier, US Army; [memb.] Toastmaster's International; [hon.] Honorable Mention, SWA Contest 1st, 2nd and 2 honorable mentions, Polytechnic H.S.; [oth. writ.] Published in The Plaza, NCASA, Gauntlet, Gotta Write Litmas, A Question of Balance Distinguished Poets of America; [pers.] We, as writers, can change the world. Know who you are and what you want to accomplish. [a.] Ft. Lewis, WA.

ADELMAN, ROBIN FERN
[pen.] Robin Fern Love; [b.] July 31, 1959, Philadelphia; [p.] Marlene Bressler (deceased) and Mr. Leon Love; [m.] Ira Samuel, August 9, 1994; [ch.] Louis, Craig, and Sheri Adelman; [ed.] Northeast High School, Temple University, Charles Morris Price School of Journalism; [occ.] Library Assistant; coder/editor, freelance writer; [memb.] World of Poetry, Humane Society-Kennedy Center, Lincoln Center, Jeanes Hospital, National Museum of American Jewish History, Reform Congregation Keneseth Isreal Sisterhood, Smithsonian Associates, Michael Crawford International Fan Association, Allied Jewish Appeal, Staff Association of the Free Library of Philadelphia; [hon.] Who's Who in the East, 23rd Edition; Who's Who 46 Ed., Who's Who of Emerging Leaders in America, Our Western World's Greatest Poems 1983, Our 20th Century's Greatest Poems 1982; [oth. writ.] Author of Poems - Our Western World's Greatest Poems, our 20th Century's Greatest Poems, Today's Greatest Poems, The National Library of Poetry, and other numerous projects in progress; [pers.] I owe a great debt to my inspirations in life, my dear late grandmother and mother; they instilled in me my sense of artistry in work, and integrity in life, for which I'll forever be grateful. I must also mention my dear husband, Ira, who is a constant source of strength, support, and loving kindness. [a.] Philadelphia, PA.

ADESSO, MARTHA
[pen.] Elizabeth Alexander; [b.] September 1, 1931, Port Jefferson, NY; [p.] May and Alex Alexander; [m.] Anthony G., March 5, 1949; [ch.] Marthia, Nannette, Diane, Susan and Deborah; [ed.] After Manual Training High School, Lamb's Business School, Suffolk County Community College; [occ.] Quilter; [memb.] Suffolk County Homemaker's Council, Bayport Heritage Association, The Association of American Indian Affairs, Inc., Cherokee National Historical Society; [oth. writ.] Published poems in SCC College's "Evolution"; [pers.] Have respect for nature and environment.

AGALZOFF, ALEX W.
[pen.] AWA; [b.] May 1, 1916, Earlimart, CA; [p.] William and Mary Agalzoff; [m.] Sarah A., July 4, 1941; [ch.] Jim, Manya, Peter, Barbara Agalzoff; [ed.] Grade School Utah State School, Lincoln High School, Aircraft Mechanic & Inspector School, Douglas Aircraft Flite Line Inspector; [memb.] Retired Carpenter in 1981 local 1065, Cherry Growers Association since 1949; [oth. writ.] 80 more writings poems, and writings local paper; [pers.] When I write God is by my side, the words just flow in I have written some in 30 minutes.

AGOZZINO, MARIE
[pen.] Rayrme; [b.] Raritan, NJ; [p.] Joseph and Graziella Agozzino; [ed.] Bridgewater-Raritan High School WEst Art Institute of Fort Lauderdale; [occ.] Specialty and Theatrical Clothing/Accessory Designer for the Music and Entertainment Industry; [memb.] National Association for Female Executives (NAFE) and American Association of University Women (AAUW), The National Library of Poetry; [hon.] College honor roll student, The National Library of Poetry Editor's Choice award for "Drink Me With Your Eyes"; honorable merits in Fashion, Dance, Art and Music. Judges' Recognition Award of Excellence in Student Art Exhibition, Personal Profile written in County Newspaper; [oth. writ.] "Drink Me With Your Eyes" appeared in The Coming of Dawn 1993. Other poems/songs appeared in local literature publications; [pers.] Life is a dream, a mystical and magical moonlight...As sacred as the Indian Wind. The Divine Love...A path to fulfillment, a secret that allures you, an enchanted melody that captures your soul, and leads your heart to dance...Close your eyes, Open your mind, Escape the chains of disbelief. Take the hand of the child within you, and let the Adventure begin...[a.] Paritan, NJ.

AKERS, MISTY GAIL
[b.] June 9, 1954, Portland, OR; [p.] Arnold and Marlene Parker; [m.] Divorced; [ch.] Brandy D. Akers; [ed.] 9th grade; [occ.] Writer; [memb.] Middle Eastern Dance and Culture Association Inc., American TaeKwonDo Association, Jazzercise Dance Fitness Inc., and Fitness Club; [hon.] Awards and honors in dance, first degree black belt with trophies, plaques and medals; awards for writing and athletic ability; [oth. writ.] Several poems published currently working on a book of poems for publication; [pers.] Education does not guarantee success but imagination does and filthy rich are those few blessed with both. [a.] Lebanon, OR.

ALBRO, RUTH E.
[b.] July 16, 1946, Jamestown, NY; [p.] Howard and Mildred Albro; [ed.] 9th grade; [occ.] Custodian at Ithaca College; [memb.] Church of Christ; [hon.] Certificates from Eddie Lou Cole, Poet Place, one poem put in the World of Poetry book; [oth. writ.] True Love, Someone to Love, 3 Small Countries of Western Europe, A Good Life, Childhood Days, Distant Drums, Can I Still Love You (want to make it into a song); [pers.] I love to write poems, I've always loved them. My brother use to say, "Ruthie" and her wacky poems. [a.] Brooktondale, NY.

ALDRIDGE, MARY LEE
[pen.] The Black Rose; [b.] April 4, 1943, Winston-Salem, NC; [p.] Mr. and Mrs. Miles Kennedy; [ch.] Kirny LeVarro Gwynn and Joshua Abishai Gwynn (grandson); [ed.] Winston Salem State University; [oth. writ.] 1st book-The Gift of Courage, 2nd-Five Senses and A Brain; several poems published in the Winston Salem Chronicle; one poem published in the 'Old Gold and Black' newspaper of Wake Forest University; an article for the Winston Salem State University. [a.] Winston-Salem, NC.

ALFORD, LAURA JEAN
[pen.] Laura Hudson Alford; [b.] May 8, 1972, Salem, ARK; [p.] Kenneth and Doris Brown; [m.] Gregory K., February 11, 1994; [ed.] West Plains High School; [occ.] Tester and Team Leader Eaton Corp., West Plains, MO; [memb.] First Baptist Church, local charities; [oth. writ.] Echoes of Yesterday, Dusting Off Dreams, and Today's Great Poems; [pers.] I would like to thank all of my friends and family for their support in my writings, they have been my greatest influence. [a.] West Plains, MO.

ALFORD, REX E.
[b.] December 6, 1937, Hollywood, CA; [p.] Harold and Betty Alford (deceased); [m.] Sandra Ellen, July 29, 1972; [ch.] Darisse Lynn, Scott Paige; [ed.] Hollywood High School, LaSalle University; [occ.] Retired; [memb.] American Society for Quality Control, American Society of Mechanical Engineers, Registered Professional Engineer - State of California - past member National Society of Professional Engineers; [oth. writ.] Poetry published in National Library of Poetry "Dance On The Horizon" many poems written for personal enjoyment; [pers.] Any poetic talent that may be mine is owed to my late mother Betty, but most especially to my beloved grandmother, "Ginny". [a.] Houston, TX.

ALLEN, MARY F.
[b.] July 2, 1941, Old Protestant Hospital; [p.] Mrs M.E. Allen and Late Mr. Allen; [ed.] David Lipscomb Elementary School, Franklin High School, David Lipscomb College; [occ.] Worked at McDonald's also volunteer at William Medical Center on Mondays; [memb.] International Society of Poets, Williamson Co. Arts Council, former World of Poetry organization; [hon.] Won 6 awards of poetry - World of Poetry 1987-92, winner of poetry of merit International Society of Poets 1994, Who's Who in Poetry; [oth. writ.] I've had 8 poems published by four publishers. Great Lakes Poetry Press, World of Poetry, Sparrowgrass Poetry Press and Quill Press; [pers.] It is my express hope that these poems will be of encouragement to seek to use their talents for the betterment of humanity and glory of God! [a.] Brentwood, TN.

ALLEN, RICHARD
[pen.] Richard Allen; [b.] December 10, 1952, Cleveland, OH; [p.] Jerry J. Rosenthal (deceased); [ed.] Ottawa University, Cuyahoga Community College, Adelphia University, Mesa Community College; [occ.] Work for Motorola, Inc.; [memb.] Czech Stamp Society, Toastmasters International, Psi Beta (National Honor Society for Psychology); [hon.] Honor Roll-spring 1990, winter-94; [oth. writ.] Poems published in various newspapers and books on poetry; [pers.] I always try to keep learning about life. I am a romantic and write poems to people I care about and love. I also write as a form of crying, so the emotions are never lost. [a.] Mesa, AZ.

ALLISON, ROBERT STEVE JR.
[b.] March 20, 1950, Atchison, KS; [p.] Mary Edith Wheeler Allison and the Late Robert Steve Allison Sr; [ed.] Stamps School of Music, Porterville High, Porterville Community College; [memb.] Porterville Church of Christ, Ex-President of The Mineral Kings, Barbershop Chorus, Society for the Preservation and Encouragement of Barbershop Quartet singing in America, Inc.; [hon.] Total of 6 awards by The World of Poetry; nominated twice for the "Hosscar Awards" at Porterville Barn Theater, made three records in my life and sung and recorded with famous gospel groups; [oth. writ.] Had one poem published in local newspaper. As well as one poem published in one book; another poem in another book; [pers.] In my writing, I feel I mostly strive to reflect qualities like both the beauty and power of the written word. I also mostly strive to bring about needed and/or desirable change in the lives of people including if not especially, in my own life. I have been greatly influenced by the song lyrics of John Lennon, Paul McCartney and Paul Simon. [a.] Porterville, CA.

ALVAREZ, KIRA
[b.] February 3, 1982, Chicago; [ed.] Morgan Park Academy; [memb.] Interlochen Arts Camp alumni; [hon.] Winner of several violin and piano competitions; [oth. writ.] Poem published in "A Question of Balance". [a.] Chicago, IL.

ALVAREZ-BABIN, CARMEN MARIA
[b.] September 20, 1917, San Jose, Costa Rica; [p.] Felix Alvarez, Agripine R. Alvarez; [m.] Ralph D. Babin, December 18, 1950; [ch.] Felix - Paul Babin; [ed.] Sophie B. Wright, HS, New Orleans; LSU Baton Rouge - Newcomb-Tulane, NO NY City UBA; [occ.] Retired from teaching - NYC; [memb.] Literary Clubs in early schools. Current: Cerrantes Soc Poets House - Poetry and Writers - AAUW Smithsonian - Women in the Arts - MVS of Nat His Asso; Democratic Party; [hon.] Awarded Honors in obtaining my US Citizenship (NU, LA 1945), Small Awards in Reading and Spelling while learning english; Golden Poet: 1990-1991; World of Poetry anthology; [oth. writ.] Long Narrative Poem in NYC journal - many pages of short stories (finished), two unfinished novels, essays, and poetry - eng and spanish (finished); [pers.] A deep desire for harmony, peace, brotherhood, fellowship in the world!; [a.] New York, NY

AMMANN, DIANE
[b.] January 18, 1956, Cheverly, MD; [p.] Clyde E. (Pat) and Ada V. Ammann; [ed.] 1974 graduate Chopticon High, currently enrolled in Children's Literature Institute; [hon.] Certificate of Merit 1986 World of Poetry, Golden Poet Award, World of Poetry 1988; [oth. writ.] The Deer published 1982 "Our Twentieth Century's Greatest Poems" World of Poetry Press, People published 1989 "The Golden Treasury of Great Poems, World of Poetry. [a.] Leonardtown, MD.

AMSDEN, JEFFERY GRANT
[b.] September 13, 1961, Elkhart, IN; [p.] Robert and Elizabeth (mother deceased); [ed.] Elkhart Area College; [occ.] Chef; [memb.] International Society of Poets, Elks Lodge #798, North American Tae Kwon Do Association, Professional Karate Commission; [hon.] Outstanding Achievement Award (North American Taw Kwon Do), Certificate of Excellence (Sarasota Herald Tribune), International Poet of Merit Award 1994; [oth. writ.] Currently in the process of writing two novels and will continued poetry on a daily basis; [pers.] Write it Down, Write it Down. Your brain is like a computer hound. It remembers the voices and hears the sound. I don't know why I started so late but I'm glad I started, I think it's great. So if you think of something good and hear the sound treat yourself good, and write it down.

ANDERSON, BENNY
[b.] October 13, 1953, Sweden; [p.] Heine and Britta Anderson; [m.] Kyoko, 1982; [ch.] Ecka and Mitchika; [ed.] College of Fine Art in Stockholm; [occ.] Artist; [memb.] Trade Union of Swedish Artist, Holy Spirit Association of the Unification of World Christianity, International Society of Poets; [hon.] Award of artistic excellence (painting) Manhattan Arts International, Editors Choice Award, Golden Poet Award 1991-92, 3 award of Merit - W.O.P. and 1 poem on Sound of Poetry; [oth. writ.] Included in several spiritual magazines (in Sweden and USA), poems in 3 anthology books, published limited edition collection of poems; Awakening World; [pers.] I believe art as a source of uplifting inspiration and healing on the human soul, keep the vision of hope. [a.] Bogota, NJ.

ANDERSON, DOROTHY
[pen.] Aunt Dolly; [b.] June 20, 1914, Rodeo, CA; [p.] H.W. and M.M. and Lindsey; [m.] Carl O. Anderson, December 7, 1933; [ch.] Joy C. Kinsey, Faye L. DiGiordano, David E. Anderson; [ed.] 8th grade; [occ.] Retired; [hon.] 1994 Editor's Choice award in The National Library of Poetry contest; [oth. writ.] Weekly column of poetry and short stories in The Village Pioneer. Poem in The Desert Sun; Grancare's Newsletter; Church bulletins; [pers.] My love is life is to be happy and make others happy too. Laughter is the best medicine there is. [a.] Haywood, CA.

ANDERSON, EULANKIE
[b.] January 10, 1941, Trinidad; [p.] Errol and Beryl Rosemin; [m.] Leo, December 18, 1971; [ch.] Patricia, Sherry, Richard, Roxam and Dexter; [ed.] St. Roses High and St. Joseph College; [occ.] Self employed - Catering; [memb.] Trinidad Red Cross Society; [hon.] Red Cross Senior Cadet Honors list, and several awards, Senior Class Poetry awards; [oth. writ.] Several school plays and poems; [pers.] I am a realist I have learned to deal with reality and to reject the impracticality of mankind. This way when you expect nothing you are never disappointed, and to look at things as they really exist without any idealization. [a.] Brooklyn, NY.

ANDERSON, MICHELLE L.
[b.] March 31, 1973, Evergreen Park, IL; [p.] William and Barbara Anderson; [ed.] North High School, Phoenix College; [occ.] Student; [memb.] Endometriosis Association; [hon.] Dean's List; [oth. writ.] Several poems published with the World of Poetry, local magazines, and school literary journals; [pers.] I have created my own world with pen and paper, and in turn discovered a world full of opportunity. [a.] Phoenix, AZ.

ANDREWS, DAVID PHYLLEP
[pen.] Phyllep Andrews; [b.] February 27, 1965, Philadelphia, PA; [p.] Ernest and Estella Andrews; [ch.] Robynique Andrews; [ed.] Murrell Dobbins Area Tech High School; [occ.] Incarcerated in Bexar County Jail; oth. writ.] I have written many poems, some which were lost during my active addiction. Someday I will published all of my poems and let the world know who I am. My poetry is my escape from drugs, and might be someone else's too; [pers.] My writing deal with reality through my eyes and those who are no longer a part of my life. To the many friends and family (including my wife) this is my way of saying I love you and I'm sorry please forgive me and return your love to me.

ANGELLE, PAULA MARIE
[pen.] Shorty; [b.] August 16, 1963, Lafayette, LA; [p.] Lenell Mary Brown Angelle and Joseph Clifton Angelle; [ed.] Opelousas High, T.H. Harris Voc. Tech; [occ.] Computer Specialist; [oth. writ.] Getting Together, Why Is This, This Lady, Lenell's Last Stand, Dedication, My Sister, As Long As, A Friend, Tray, I'm Free, How Do I Miss Thee, Friendship, "The Test"; [pers.] I love my sister, "Jackie" and I'm lucky to have her. I love my friend "Wyonne" because she held my mother's hand as she died. She will forever be my true friend. [a.] Houston, TX.

ANTHONY, DEBORAH
[b.] October 14, 1958, Washington, DC; [p.] Robert and Delree Staats; [m.] Wade Anthony, May 27, 1977; [ch.] James, Jacob and William; [ed.] Pratt High School, Pratt Community College; [occ.] Housewife; [memb.] First Southern Baptist Church, Pratt Community Concert Association; [hon.] Golden Poet, 1990-1991; award of merit from World of Poetry 1990; [oth. writ.] Poem published in National Library

of Poetry "Whispers In The Wind" and "At Day's End"; [pers.] God created every one of us as incredibly special, unique individuals. He gave us each the ability to do something specific no other human being can do in the way that we can. The greatest success we can have in life is to use the talents God has given us to fulfill His purposes. [a.] Pratt, KS.

APPELDORN, GREGORY T.
[b.] May 30, 1968, Clanton, AL; [p.] John L. Robinson and Geraldine Appeldorn; [ed.] High school (Lamberton, MN) and Utah State University; [occ.] Student; [memb.] Alpha Tau Omiga Fraternity, National Youth Sports Coaches Association, Cancer Center for Detection and Prevention, Christ the King Lutheran Church, Center for Abused and Exploited Children, The American Business and Professional Guild; [hon.] Editor's Choice Award for At Day's End The National Library of Poetry 1994; Recognized by the International Society of Poets-Washington DC 1994; [oth. writ.] Figments of Your Imagination: The First Book; [pers.] Dusk of a summer night. Cooling down - outside. Heating up - inside. Wanting to tear at the flesh, draw blood and scream. Pain is a natural part of life and love. Kindly, yet forcefully, give me the orgasm that was given me 26 years ago. That day the light pierced my eyes and the air opened my mind to accept things to come without prejudiced opinion. My poetry is for you. [a.] Draper, UT.

ARCUNI, JENNIFER
[b.] May 1, 1994, New York City; [ed.] Hamilton College; [occ.] Getting out of bed by noon; [hon.] Sound of Poetry for "Pumpkins"; [oth. writ.] 'Spotted Moonstones' and various untitled poems were my contribution to Hamilton's Red Weather magazine; [pers.] The idea of poetry as a performance art seems to be dictating much of my current writing. [a.] Redding, CT.

ARENDS, BONNIE JO
[b.] November 8, 1963, Chatham, NJ; [p.] John Arends and Jan Hyde; [ed.] Chatham High School, Morris County College; [occ.] Clerical; [oth. writ.] Previously published in "A Far Off Place" anthology; [pers.] I have recently discovered that I can express some of my hidden emotions and fears through poetry. I hope this will allow others who read my work to identify and realize they are not alone with their anxieties and ghosts. We all need to remember that this life is not a rehearsal, each thing we do is forever. [a.] East Hanover, NJ.

ARMSTRONG, JACK THOMAS
[pen.] Jack T. Armstrong; [b.] August 31, 1967, Detroit; [p.] Marion E. and Dolores L. Armstrong; [ed.] Wayne County Community College; [occ.] Poet, Salesman; [memb.] International Society of Poets; [hon.] I have received the editor's choice awards for outstanding achievement in poetry presented by The National Library of Poetry in 1993 and 1994; [oth. writ.] Published in Dance on the Horizon winter 1993, poemable; also in Days End summer 1994, poem Midnight Blue, and also on cassette, The Sound of Poetry. Musical introduction by The English Chamber Orchestra. Readings by nationally renowned speaker Ira Westreich; [pers.] I was born in Detroit and have always enjoyed the city to it's highest and it's fullest with everything. [a.] Belleville, MI.

ARMSTRONG, JOHN ALONZO
[b.] Harbor City; [p.] Mr. and Mrs. Clarence Armstrong; [m.] Divorced; [ch.] David A. Armstrong and Rose A. Armstrong; [ed.] Henry Clay Jr. High School, Alian Leroy Locke High School, Portland State University, L.A. Harbor College; [occ.] Singer/songwriter/poet/computer operator; [memb.] West Angeles Church of God in Christ; [hon.] Honorable discharged U.S. Army published in "Tears of Fire", "Dark Side of the Moon", A.S.O. Top 100 songwriting lyrics '93 awarded Lyrics Writing Excellence; [oth. writ.] From Platinum Records, Toronto CAN (Cathy Summers), awarded "Editor's Choice award" also ASO's Top new songwriters of the 90's; [pers.] Believe in yourself regardless of what other people say or do, and don't forget to pray. (Peace). [a.] Gardena, CA.

AUSTIN, BARBARA
[pen.] B. Austin; [b.] May 24, 1979, Mercy Hospital, Cadillac; [p.] Lew and April Austin; [ed.] Cadillac High School; [memb.] CHS Drama Club, Choir, Honors English, Tae Kwon Do Federation; [hon.] Academic letter, 5th gup - Tae Kwon Do; [oth. writ.] Poems, short stories; [pers.] It doesn't matter what you look like, it matters who are inside. [a.] Cadillac, MI.

AYERS, SARAH
[b.] April 25, 1956, Winston-Salem, NC; [p.] Evelyn and Mel Jones (both deceased); [m.] Divorced, February 14, 1975; [ch.] Will Ayers IV; [ed.] Forsyth Tech (GED); [occ.] Personal Executive Assistant and previous Airline Reservations Agent; [hon.] I've had recognition throughout my life from teachers, newspapers and journals for my writing ability while at Piedmont Airlines, won the Valentine's Day 1983 poetry contest; [oth. writ.] In the Reservations Dept, several letters to the Greensboro News and Record and various poems in my own collection, published in spiritual newsletters and school newspapers and "Proofrock" literary arts journal; [pers.] My best writing comes when I don't try. Usually, if I am very sad or very happy, the words flow to me. The best thoughts come when I cease to think. [a.] Greensboro, NC.

BABCOCK, FENTON
[b.] May 30, 1926, Aberdeen, WA; [p.] Thorpe and Mabel Spencer Babcock;' [p.] Elizabeth Vorwerk Babcock, October 8, 1950; [ch.] Ann Babcock Walters; [ed.] Yale University; [occ.] Director, National Leadership Forum on Global Challenges; [memb.] Association of Former Intelligence Officers, National Arbor Day Foundation, Fairfax Racquet Club, Smithsonian Institution; [hon.] Intelligence Medal of Merit, Career Intelligence Medal; [oth. writ.] Articles for "Studies in Intelligence", poem entitled "Nature's Way" in the National Library of Poetry volume A Far Off Place; [pers.] I like to think that my poetry honors the literary, artistic, and musical talents of my late parents, and the worldly realism of my supportive wife, in its focus on nature's lessons for mankind, as observed at "Shadow Ridge". [a.] Oakton, VA.

BAIRD, ARLEAN
[pen.] Arlean Baird; [b.] May 22, 1926, Lac QuiParle, CO; [p.] Rose and Axel Hedberg; [m.] Divorced; [ch.] Kay and Michael; [ed.] Dawson High, Certificate in Design (Floral); [occ.] Retired; [memb.] Presbyterian lifetime member in Christian Education; [hon.] Several poems published in local papers, one chosen for S.D.A. Conference, several merit awards, several golden poet awards, blue ribbon awards in floral design; [oth. writ.] Thoughts of Music, Inspirational Thoughts, many articles for Creative Writing; [pers.] Poetry is an expression of words not spoken, memories wrapped in gold. [a.] Marshall, MN.

BAKER, BETTY
[pen.] Betty Baker; [b.] Westchester, OH; [p.] Lucian and Nova Jackson; [m.] Harold; [ch.] Troy, Sherri, Mary (grandchildren-Miranda, Lindsey, Derek) (sister-Juanita Jackson and brother Ralph Jackson); [ed.] Norwood High, WCCC Career Center; [occ.] Baker's Equip Repair (own business), clerical - operator of Independent Cleaning Service; [memb.] Landmark Baptist Temple, Day Business Association, Words and Things, "The Warren Poetry and Playwright Society"; [hon.] Editor's Choice Award from The National Library of Poetry 1994 poem, "Today A Special Babe Was Born"; [oth. writ.] Poems published in newspapers - submitted to Reader's Digest - Modern Maturity Mirabella - "Today A Special Babe Was Born" - Edge of Twilight. [a.] So. Lebanon, OH.

BAKER, LINDSEY
[b.] July 8, 1975, New Orleans, LA; [p.] Charles and Brenda Baker, Jr.; [ed.] St. Mary's Dominican High School, University of Southwestern Louisiana; [occ.] Student; [memb.] USL Marching Band, Newman Club, Alpha Lambda Delta, USL Honors Program; [hon.] National Honor Society, Senior High Honor Band, St. Louise de Marillac Award, Who's Who Among American High School Students; [oth. writ.] "Daddy Come Home" published in high school literary magazine; [pers.] Look towards the future. That's where your opportunities are. [a.] Harvey, LA.

BALANDRAN, STELLA V.
[b.] May 16, 1932, New York City; [p.] Stella Ginorio and Rafael Garcia; [m.] Ricardo, April 13, 1974; [ch.] Charles, Hank and Emil Varona; [ed.] 4 years college - certified paralegal, certified mediator specializing in Administrative Law; [occ.] Author and vocalist; [memb.] American Society of Composers, Authors and Publishers (ASCAP); [hon.] Finalist of the NY OTI Festival in 1986 and 1987, in numerous Spanish festivals as composer and vocalist, poems published in poetry, various anthologies; [oth. writ.] Songs; [pers.] I like to write on the ills and injustices that affect society but because I know the most powerful tool for the good is love, I also write of love.

BANKS, VERA
[pen.] VAJ, Vera Arline Johnson; [b.] May 4, 1911, Spokane, WA; [p.] Esther and William Johnson; [ch.] Three; [ed.] High school trade school; [occ.] Retired; [hon.] American Cancer Society, Election Inspector, Child House Court; [pers.] Love is blind, color is skin deep. Let us live in harmony and forgiveness. A poem combines all the loose ends of life for all to enjoy. [a.] Los Angeles, CA.

BARANCYK, JANICE
[b.] September 1, 1949, Gary, IN; [p.] William and Rose Marie; [ed.] University of Missouri; [occ.] Assistant Bursar, Columbia College-Chicago; [memb.] Protection of the Virgin Mary Orthodox Church (Russian); [hon.] Golden Poet; [oth. writ.] World of Poetry Anthology; [pers.] We are here to help each other. [a.] Crown Point, IN.

BARBER, JUNE D.
[pen.] Jamie June Barber; [b.] January 2, 1930, Paterson, NJ; [p.] Roy and Lucille Barber; [ed.] Grammar, high school, college but no degree; [occ.] Tape Librarian Computer; [memb.] Bronte Society, Haworth England, Holocaust Memorial Museum (Wash., DC); [pers.] What ever you want to do with your life do not falter just go to it.

BARBER, LINDA MARLENE
[pen.] Mrs. Linda M. Davis-Barber; [b.] May 20, 1948, Columbus, OH; [p.] Inglis and Martha Davis; [m.] Steven William Barber, January 9, 19 71; [ch.] Vicki Lynn Barber and Christine Michelle Barber; [ed.] Columbus North High School, Ohio State University; [occ.] Homemaker; [memb.] Future Secretaries of America, French Club, National Honor Society, Temporary Red Cross volunteer, Westerville Art League; [hon.] 3 awards voted me by comrades of Dale Carnegie course, several awards for Pastel drawings-Ohio State Fair Fine Arts, and Westerville ARt League Spring Show; high school graduate with honors; [oth. writ.] My poems are not frequent. But when I write my best I am under deep motivation. Sole publications belong to The National Library of Poetry; [pers.] Interpretive poetry was the one kind I could never understand in school. Having to study it made me hate poetry. I regained my appreciation when I wrote my first tribute to a deceased friend in interpretive style of my own. [a.] Westerville, OH.

BARKSDALE, JANET
[b.] April 15, 1984, Brunswick, GA; [p.] Jeffrey and Jennifer Barksdale; [ed.] Deerfield-Windsor Lower School, West Town Elementary; [hon.] High honors (all A's) 1-4th grade, Young Georgia Author school winner, Outstanding Achievement Certificate for Iowa Tests of Basic Skills in Reading and Math, medal for Spelling Bee; [oth. writ.] "The Leprechaun", "School Is Out", "Our Class", "Fun", Springtime" and "A Real Rabbit" published in the Albany Herald; [pers.] I like to put words and ideas together that have meaning and that rhyme. [a.] Albany, GA.

BARNARD, KEVIN
[pen.] KB; [b.] September 21, 1972, Medford, NH; [p.] Richard and Patricia Erickson; [ed.] Westfield State College, Hull High; [occ.] Copy Editor/Page Designer, Anderson Independent Mail; [hon.] Publication in A Break in the Clouds; Outstanding Poets of 1994, Editor's Choice Awards for both works; [oth. writ.] The Man I Long To Be Loneliness, above mentioned anthologies respectively; [pers.] My writing is an extension of myself, it is an attempt to put into words the emotions, feelings and experiences which have affected me the course of my life. [a.] Anderson, SC.

BARNES, AMY K.
[pen.] Amy Sculley Barnes; [b.] November 2,1 973, Jacksonville, FL; [p.] Jerry and Sharon Sculley; [m.] Dale Lee Barnes, September 4, 1993; [hon.] Editor's Choice award and recognized to be among the top 3% of all entries judged by The National Library of Poetry; [oth. writ.] "This Porcelain Rose" in The National Library of Poetry anthology At Days End. Collection of poetry in a personal library; [pers.] My poetry is a way to express myself to those around me. I owe a great deal to my English teachers who encouraged me. Also, I BIG thanks to my family for all the support they have given me through everything. So this is dedicated to my family - I love each and every one of you. [a.] Norfolk, VA.

BARNEY, JEAN L.
[pen.] Jean L. Barney; [b.] June 22, 1958, Somerville; [p.] John and Carol Castignoli; [m.] Divorced/single; [ch.] Jacob, Christopher, Jeffrey, and Russell Barney; [ed.] Somerville H. S., Bunker Hill Community College, Actors Workshop in Boston; [occ.] Exec. Secretary; [oth. writ.] I'm presently editing my first manuscript and I'm putting together a collection of my poetry together. My goal is to find someone interested in my material for publication by next year. There are some ideas that I will be working on in the future; [pers.] I hope that I can inspire someone else, the way that I have been inspired. [a.] Somerville, MA.

BARRETT, AVIS MARIE
[b.] November 16, 1927, Houston, TX; [p.] Hugh Byron and Mattie Davis McGann; [m.] Deceased, February 14, 1947; [ch.] Laura Ann White Vickers, Donald Lee Barrett; [ed.] John H. Reagan High School, Massey Business College, University of Houston and The Limbaugh Institute for Advanced Conservative Studies; [occ.] Investor-retired from Texaco, Inc.; [memb.] Memorial Drive United Methodist Church, Clayton Library Genealogical Society, Texaco Retiree's Club, National (and Texas) Republican Committees; [hon.] My son and daughter; [oth. writ.] Frequent contributor to "Sound-Off" in Houston Post, several poems published in Houston newspapers; [pers.] I like humor and surprises. Greatly influenced by O. Henry and Emily Dickinson. I love football and handsome quarterbacks and Rush Limbaugh. As Shakespeare said, "I do not suffer fools gladly." [a.] Houston, TX.

BARRIO, GUILMO
[pen.] Guilmo Barrio; [b.] April6, 1939, Concepcion-Chile; [p.] Cayo Barrio Aragon and Raquel Salazar; [m.] Ana Maria Barrio, June 20, 1970; [ch.] Guilmo Alejandro, Ruben Daniel, Paulo Cesar and Zoraida Raquel; [ed.] Salesian High School, University of Concepcion, Chile; DePaul University, Chicago, IL; Dominican Development Foundation, Santo Domingo, Dominican Republic; [occ.] Vice President "Crespo & Associates, Lawrence, MA; principle at "World Commerce Resources" Brookline, MA; [memb.] Occupational Advisory Council at Northern Essex Community College, Board member of Chilean Society of Boston, Past President Board of Directors International Institute, Lawrence, MA; [hon.] St. Augustine award, Merrimack College, North Andover, MA; Community Unsung Hero award, Bradford College, Bradford, MA; Special Lawrencian award, Bread and Roses Heritage Committee and Newspaper The Eagle-Tribune; [oth. writ.] "21 Popular Poems and an Unfinished song"; "Universal Health Care in America;" "1492/1992 Five Centuries of a Tragic Encounter;" "Foreign Americans - Migrant Farm Workers Struggles;" Anguish" poem published in the Anthology Tears of Fire; [pers.] Life is too short to be little. We must think big, to be big. Big in happiness, in accomplishments, in income, in quality of life, in friends, and in respect to others. Respect to the property of others equals peace. [a.] Lawrence, MA.

BARSON, KELLY RUMLER
[b.] May 11, 1970, Jackson, MI; [p.] Richard and Linda Rumler; [m.] Larry, August 12, 1989; [ch.] Alexander, Maxwell and Sylvia; [ed.] Lumen Christi High School; [memb.] Michigan Steam Engine and Thresher's Club; [oth. writ.] "Everything is One Way and The Other" published in 1991 in "Our World's Most Treasured Poems" pg. 420; [pers.] Even when things seem bleak, the sun will rise tomorrow and with it comes hope. [a.] Jackson, MI.

BATTLES, MERRY
[ch.] Hallae Grace; [occ.] Massage Therapy, Japanese Accupressure (17 years); [oth. writ.] I am an artist who wishes to combine art with my poetry. Autobiographical writing about my "True Life Adventures"; [pers.] My greatest joy in life is to learn about the spiritual, so that is reflected in my work. [a.] West Palm Beach, FL.

BAXTER, LUKE N.
[b.] September 12, 1915, Van Buren, AR; [p.] Nora Mae (Welch) Baxter and Lorren Baxter; [m.] deceased; [ch.] Robt. Lee Baxter, Donald Gene Baxter; [ed.] Tulsa Central High School class of 1993; [occ.] REtired; [memb.] Gardena Valley Art Association; [hon.] 5 special mention, 30 honorable mention, adopted by Gardena Valley Art Association as their very own "Golden Poet". Published monthly in "The Palette", Charles Bodet, editor, Cynthia Helzer, asst. editor; [oth. writ.] Published in more than 2 dozen books with prestigious titles; [pers.] Within the galaxy of thought lies a gem of poetic expression.

BEAUDOIN, JUDY
[pen.] Judy B., Judy Hall; [b.] March 15, 1954, McMinnville, TN, [p.] Lowell and Lillian Hall; [m.] John R., February 22,1985; [ed.] Still learning; [occ.] Philosopher, poet, musician, essayist, humorist, unemployed; [hon.] Having my poems published in 3 of the books put out by the National Library of Poetry. That was really an honor to me; [oth. writ.] "Songs for Friends and Lovers" - a collection of poems from the early 1970's. Essays on the Human Condition and Personal Religious Insights; folk songs, gospel songs, various other poems and a children's book currently in progress; [pers.] I love to write. It would be nice to make some money from my writings but I'm realistic. Most artists aren't really famous until after they're dead. So I'll just keep on writing until I'm dead and hope my heirs don't dump my writings in the trash. [a.] Meridian, ID.

BECK, MYRTLE V.
[pen.] Virginia Marlowe; [b.] August 29, 1912, Baltimore; [p.] John and Pearl Latchford; [m.] Ernest W. (deceased), April 17, 1937; [ch.] 3 sons; [ed.] 9th junior high; [occ.] Homemaker; [hon.] Acknowledgement of two other poems namely (Mama) and (Papa), 2 other poems.

BECK, RICHARD L.
[b.] April 26, 1953, Toledo, OH; [m.] Angela; [ch.] Aaron, Nathan, Adam, Grace and Heath; [ed.] Yes, [occ.] Writer, lecturer; [memb.] Yes; [hon.] Yes; [oth. writ.] Many; [pers.] The art of expression is the key to unlocking one's heart. Freeing them from the captivity of their past. [a.] Warsaw, IN.

BECKER, MARLA JANE
[pen.] Randee Sky; [b.] Eldon and Marieta Wambsganss; [ed.] Topeka West High School, University of Kansas; [occ.] Writer/poet; [hon.] American Red Cross service award; [oth. writ.] Leviticus Strip (novel), Books of Poetry: The Night Guardian, The Spanish Man Cuts Grass, Celebrations of Seasons in Kansas, Fire in the Forest; [pers.] I like to highlight the Native American culture in a positive note. They are worthy of our respect and admiration. [a.] Cottonwood Falls, KS.

BEDINGFIELD, DEBORAH
[b.] February 23, 1959, Cornwall, ONT; [p.] Dries and Gerry Slykhuis; [m.] John Wesley; [ch.] Dries, Deirdre, Dustin; [ed.] O.D. High School; [occ.] Poet, housewife and mother of three; [memb.] Tri County Writers, Valley Writer's, Bells Letters; [hon.] Best Poems of 1995, truly an honor; Chapel Recording Monthly award; [oth. writ.] River of Dreams, Poems of America, American Poetry Anthology, Chapel Recording, local newspapers; [pers.] All my work in done with encouragement from my husband, inspiration from my children, and in memory of my dad. [a.] Long Sault, ONT. CAN.

BEEMAN, LOREEN
[pen.] Emmy; [b.] August 20, 1941, Superior; [p.] Lawrence and Dorothy Schrieffer; [m.] Elmer, October 17, 1959; [ch.] 2 sons, 2 daughters and 3 grandchildren; [ed.] Superior Senior High, Superior Community College, Lakeshore Tech College, Medical Dental College, Milwaukee Surgical Nursing; [occ.] Therapeutic Cook (Rocky Knoll Health Facility); [memb.] Nord-Rare disease disorders, Progressive Supranuclear Palsy Association, AARP, Future Nurses Association, Campers of America; [hon.] Dean's list, honorable mention award Sparrowgrass Poetry; [oth. writ.] 2 poems published by Voices of America, one poem published World of Poetry, a published poet in the midst, article by the Rocky Rambler (Rocky Knoll paper); [pers.] Follow your instincts, heart and feelings, and you can do anything you strive for. If you want it bad enough. Go for it. [a.] Plymouth, WS.

BEHELER, BETTY JO
[b.] January 8, 1949, Kingston, SC; [p.] Mr. and Mrs. Andrew J. Casselman; [m.] Walter Ray, November 8, 1976; [ed.] Brunswick Technical College; [occ.] Licensed Practical Nurse; [oth. writ.] "Nature at Play" in Echoes of Yesterday 1994. [a.] Wilmington, NC.

BEHRENS, JUSTIN
[b.] August 30, 1974, Ottumwa, IA; [oth. writ.] A poem in Echoes of Yesterday. Pages and pages of other work, none published; [pers.] The less people understand you, the more they want to. [a.] Ottumwa, IA.

BELCHER, STEVE
[b.] March 4, 1971, Port Jervis, NY; [p.] James and Rose Belcher; [ed.] Port Jervis High School; [memb.] International Society of Poets; [hon.] Who's Who Among American High School Students, Editor's Choice award, Poet of Merit; [oth. writ.] Poem published in "The Coming of Dawn" - National Library of Poetry. Book of Poetry soon to be published; Sometimes you have to look on the darkside of life, so you don't take the good things for granted. Locked doors are hardest to open when they're hidden behind the truth. [a.] Montague, NJ.

BELIVEAU, JUDITH
[pen.] Judith Beliveau; [b.] January 29, 1926, Lima, OH; [p.] Nathalie and Earle Bean; [m.] Divorced; [ch.] Peter, Mark, Melissa Beliveau; [ed.] Convent to the Sacred Heart High School, C.W. Post; [occ.] Retired Librarian; [memb.] Our Mother of Sorrows Catholic Church; [hon.] First place (of 2,000) Essay Contest, Chamber of Commerce award for poem called, "The Annunciation" which was published; [oth. writ.] Short stories; [pers.] I try to write poetry from a spiritual point of view - not necessarily religious - from the study of mankind past and present and from nature also other poets. [a.] Tucson, AZ.

BELL, CAROL M.
[b.] November 3, 1952, San Antonio, TX; [occ.] Professional waitress; [memb.] International Society of Poets; [hon.] 12 awards of merit, 2 honorable mentions - Golden Poet; 1988 and 1989 International Poet of Merit 1993; [oth. writ.] Poems published in anthologies 1988-89, 1990-91, 1995; [pers.] "Beyond the gate" dedicated to Paul G. Yommer, and Lori J. Uttecht, without whom life would have been a boring journey. I thank you. [a.] Weirton, W.VA.

BELL, LENORA M.
[b.] March 4, 1958, Mullens, WV; [p.] Robert and Shirley Keaton; [ch.] Carl, August 16, 1991; [ch.] Anita Lynn and Marion and Nicole; [ed.] Sophia High in 1975, University of Arkansas; [occ.] Housewife; [memb.] International Society of Poets; [hon.] Won the accomplishment of merit award for "The Clown" in 1992, won the accomplishment of merit award for "The Gift of Spring" 1994, won first place in essay contest sponsored by UALR Student Union; [oth. writ.] The Clown, A Tear, The Stranger, Scream of a Whisper, The Gift of Spring, and over 100 others not yet published; [pers.] My writing is also my therapy. Most of my inspiration comes from actual experiences and always from the care of who I am. I thank my God and my family for loving me, especially my husband Carl. [a.] Conway, AR.

BELONIE, SHANNON BRAY
[pen.] Shannon Bray; [b.] November 11, 1975, Houston, TX; [p.] Bob and Wanda Belonie; [m.] Soon-Scarlet Ann Cates, June 3, 1995; [ed.] Clinton High School, Petit Jean Technical College; [occ.] Clinton Recycling Plant - Assistant Director; [memb.] Clinton High Band, Clinton Choirs, American Collegiate Wind Bands, The Church of the Almighty God; [hon.] John Philip Sousa award, Music Honor student, Garden Club Art award, Band Parent award, and Scholarship; [oth. writ.] Race of Worries; [pers.] Have no worries, write what you feel and live to make a difference, leave the rest to God. [a.] Clinton, AR.

BENNETT, GARY WAYNE
[b.] December 8, 1967, Memphis, TN; [p.] Mary Louise Bennett; [m.] Jennifer Lynn Bennett, June 29, 1991; [ed.] Sheffield High, attended Memphis State University; [hon.] Winner of American Civil Liberties Union Poetry Contest; [pers.] I dedicate my message of peace to my Mom who found peace in June 1988. [a.] Memphis, TN.

BERGER, RUTH O'NEILL
[pen.] Ruth O'Neill Berger; [b.] September 8, 1918, Sioux City, IA; [p.] Ruby and Edgar O'Neill; [m.] Frank, November 28, 1940; [ch.] Dennie Michael and Stephen Glenn; [ed.] Alumna of Briar Cliff College; [occ.] Retired was co-owner of business; [memb.] Children's Home Society, Willow Glen Association; [hon.] Typing Speed Pres. of Spanish Club in High School, Pres. of Art Club, and Class Treasurer in College, National Honorary Society, won scholarship to Drake University; [oth. writ.] X-mas nostalgia, Heros Parenting, Best of Times and other articles plus many editorials and many poems; [pers.] Writing keeps my mind alert and I like to assist or benefit others to pursue their goals. I am stimulated by various issues and peoples and hope I can inspire others. [a.] San Jose, CA.

BERRY, KENNETH ROY
[pen.] Kenneth Roy Berry; [b.] January 30, 1967, Greenbrae, CA; [p.] Pearl and Lee Roy Berry; [ed.] San Francisco State University; [occ.] Clerical/ Kenscape Landscaping/musician/singer; [memb.] American Federation of Musicians 1993/94; [hon.] 1985 Outstanding Achievement award in the Fine Arts (Music), from Marin Education Foundation Fund, Who's Who Among American High School Students 1984/85 (Music/Scholastic Achievement); [oth. writ.] Forthcoming 1st CD Project entitled Kenneth Roy 1995, with 11 original songs, featuring "Home Again", "Turn Away" and "Don't Run From Me"; poem - "I Better Have a Beer" for Western Poetry Association, Colorado Springs, CO; [pers.] "Special Thanks to Mom and Dad!", "Family and Friends". [a.] Cotati, CA.

BERRY, SHERLENE
[b.] September 22, 1941, Utah; [p.] Rorick and Elma Harmon; [m.] Bill, September 19, 1986; [ch.] Jon Tingey, Wayne Tingey and Toni LaBrage; [occ.] Office Manager; [oth. writ.] Windows published "Outstanding Poets of 1994", Trust published "Dance on the Horizon", The Flower and Separation published in "The Prolific Writer's Journal", Solitude published 1995 "Treasured Poems of America"; [pers.] I write the words God puts in my heart with the hope that those who read them may feel a glimmer of his hope. [a.] Chandler, AZ.

BEVERIDGE, ADRIANE
[b.] March 2, 1975, Sharon, PA; [p.] Carole Beveridge; [ed.] Dulany High School, Essex Community College, Robert's Hair Institute; [occ.] Stone Mill Bakery; [memb.] Minstrels, Chamber Choir, Voice Class; [hon.] Citizenship award, International Competition of Singing, Being a good friend to others is my highest achievement; [oth. writ.] I have always enjoyed writing, it's the best way for myself to tell my feelings the right way; [pers.] To fly like a bird and see through two eyes. [a.] Lutherville, MD.

BEZIO, ANGEL
[b.] June 27, 1976, Greenfield, MA; [p.] Bonnie Oleary and Nelson Bezio; [ed.] R.C. Mahar Regional High, Salem State College; [occ.] Student. [a.] Orange, MA.

BIGGERS, JACQUELINE
[pen.] Jackie Biggers; [b.] January 14, 1976; [p.] Carolyn and Jackson Biggers; [ed.] Churchill High, Southwestern University; [occ.] Student; [hon.] Orchestra and Educational; [pers.] Don't forget to look at nature, God may be trying to tell you something. [a.] San Antonio, TX.

BILLHEIMER, CLARENCE E.
[b.] November 22, 1948, Canton, OH; [p.] Nancy J. and Samuel P.; [m.] Patsy Mae, December 22, 1979; [ed.] High school, some college, 3 years Bible school at Tennessee Temple, 2 years business college; [occ.] Work for federal government; [memb.] Heritage Baptist Church; [hon.] High honors at Tennessee TEmple; Outstanding progress at Canton Business College; Editor's Choice award from National Library of Poetry; [oth. writ.] "On Running" in Na-

tional Library of Poetry anthology <u>DAnce on the Horizon</u>; currently attempting to write a novel entitled <u>Miracle Baby</u>. Have a self-published poetry book; [pers.] I owe the rebirth of my poetic talent to my pastor who commented on how my talent could be used for God; I try to incorporate much of my faith into my writing. [a.] Columbus, OH.

BILLINGS, BEULAH
[pen.] Boots; [b.] April 28, 1920, Mississippi; [p.] George and Alice Berryhill; [m.] Sam, June 16, 1940; [ch.] Vivian, Beverly, (grand-Lori, Christine, Cynthia, Brian and Charlotte); (great grands-Amanda, Brian, Raeann, Kyle and Brandon); [ed.] 1 year college; [occ.] Retired homemaker; [oth. writ.] Many poems mostly of family, friends and nature; [pers.] A little kindness never hurt anyone. Smiles are like rainbows, they make people happy. [a.] Sun City, AZ.

BIRG, DAVE
[b.] October 8, 1970, Russia; [p.] Michael and Elizabeth Birg; [oth. writ.] "Treasured Poems of America", "Echoes of Yesterday" (some of my poems will be published in these books; [pers.] Poetry is my world. It is everything, I am. My true passion, my real love. [a.] Des Plaines, IL.

BISHOP, BETTY WEBSTER
[b.] August 10, 1925, Hambleton, WV; [p.] Hugh and Eunice Webster; [m.] Buck, June 11, 1942; [ch.] Reg, Rod, Rim and Rylie; [ed.] Tidioute PA, High School; [occ.] Housewife; [memb.] Christian and Missionary Alliance Church, J.O.Y. Class, Sunshine Club, regular contributor to "Where Eagles Fly" and "Sharing and Caring"; [hon.] 3rd Place in National Poetry Contest: Encore in "Where Eagles Fly" in Who's Who in Poetry; Editor's Choice award, 2 golden poet awards; [oth. writ.] Published Christian reader: Reader's Digest: Doll World; local paper, Reminisce; several anthologies and books of poems, a book of dolls, pictures and corresponding captions, waiting to be published; [pers.] My Christian faith, my husband, children, grandchildren, friends and dolls have been my inspiration and continue to be my source of joy. [a.] Hampton, FL.

BISHOP, LOUISE L.
[b.] September 12, 1914; [p.] Expired; [m.] November 27, 1965, Expired; [ed.] 9th grade; [occ.] Nurses' Aid.

BISHOP II, PAUL V.
[b.] March 2, 1979, Richland County; [p.] Paul and Susan Bishop; [ed.] 8th grade promotion, 10 grade student; [occ.] Student; [memb.] Bass Master's Boys "O" Club, "400 Club of Baseball, Latin Club; [hon.] Academic Excellence, Honor Roll, Baseball, Basketball, Golf, Swimming, Future, Problem Solving.

BLACK, H. BLANDENAH
[b.] March 29, 1933, Chicago, IL; [p.] Hazel and Edward Hayes; [m.] James R. Black, Jr., December 19, 1954; [ch.] James III, Rev. Brigitte, Geoffrey and Gregory Black; [ed.] Wilberforce University, Central State University, University of Indiana, DuSable High School; [occ.] Retired Educator; [memb.] AFT, NIABSE, Alpha Kappa Alpha Society, Indiana Retirement Association, First A.M.E. Church; [hon.] I.U. Dons Distinguished Service, State of Indiana; P.R.I.D.E. Committee nomination Reader's Digest 1992 Heroes in Education Recognition award Williams School; [oth. writ.] Mandela A. Clarion Call, Jesse, Martin, Our Astronaut, Children, Children Our Greatest Resource, Dr . Dan, Me, Marvin Gaye, The Sea, The Sun, 2000 and Beyond; [pers.] Educational Philosophy - All children can learn. Basic philosophy - I come this way but once, let me do all the good I can. [a.] Gary, IN.

BLACK, VERNELL
[b.] Columbia, SC; [p.] Manuel and Pauline Coughman; [m.] Marion, March 10, 1959; [ch.] Anthony Black; [ed.] High school graduate, 2 years college; [occ.] Retired; [memb.] Astara, International Society of Poets, North Main Crime Watchers Comm., Foster Parents Association of South Carolina; [hon.] Honorary letters from President Jimmy Carter, Poets of Merit awards, editor's choice award; [oth. writ.] Autumn, published by
The National Library of Poetry 1994, Winter's Rebirth - a winner at the 1994 Symposium in Washington DC, many others not yet published; [pers.] Poetry is a great inspiration to me. I strive to project beautiful thoughts in my poems, by staying close to God, and putting him first in my life. I try to reflect the goodness of God in all of my poetry. [a.] Columbia, SC.

BLACKLEDGE, RAMONA Q.
[b.] September 20, 1952, Mississippi; [m.] Joe A. Blackledge, June 20, 1980; [ch.] John Patrick, Jessica Lauren; [occ.] Elected official, Jones County Tax Assessor-Collector; [oth. writ.] Poem published in "Coming of Dawn", National Library of Poetry; certificate of merit, lyric competition, American Song Festival, honorable mention, 1985 Music City Song Festival, poem published in IAAO Assessment Journal July/Aug. 1994; [pers.] Sing and make music in your heart to the Lord, always giving thanks to God the Father for everything, in the name of our Lord Jesus Christ. (NIV Eph.5:19-20). [a.] Laurel, MS.

BALCKMAN, CHRISTAN
[b.] May 19, 1981, B'hama, AL; [p.] William M. Blackman Jr. and Cindy B. Jones; [ed.] Rudd Jr. High School; [oth. writ.] Have been published in "The Anthology of Poetry by Young Americans" and "River of Dreams"; [pers.] I just want to thank my 5th grade teacher Mrs. Witmire for getting me started in writing poems. [a.] B'ham, AL.

BLAIR, JOSEPHINE COSMA
[b.] January 26, 1942, Puunene, HI; [p.] Manuel and Beatrice Cosma; [m.] David D., August 6, 1988; [ch.] Michael Kahala, James Haleoka-Lena, Ilima Marcel, Greig, [ed.] Hana Elem., Lahainaluna High, Maunaolu Jr. College, Byu, HI; [occ.] Grade 2 teacher, Princess Nahi'Ena'Ena Elem.; [memb.] NEA, HSTA; [oth. writ.] Newspaper article, "Pekelo Does Hana Proud", published in the Hana News; "Tita's Lament" in the book, the space between; several family eulogies; [pers.] It is important to keep alive the legacy of our ancestors, for through their love and devotion we are what we are today. Each one of us will have a chance to create our own legacy. [a.] Lahaina, Maui, HI.

BLAKELY, VAL
[b.] January 18, 1969, San Jose; [p.] Sue and Jack Blakely; [ed.] Silver Creek High School, DeAnza College, California State University-Hayward; [occ.] Environmental Coordinator; [memb.] The National Audubon Society, The Nature Conservancy; [oth. writ.] Several poems published in other anthologies, write short stories, screenplays and picture books; [pers.] I strive to make a difference which I feel is the key to success. [a.] San Jose,a CA.

BLANSETT, CHERYL ANN
[b.] October 25, 1974, Fredericksburg, VA; [p.] Myrna and Elmer Todd; [m.] Charles, August 31, 1991; [ch.] Michael Blansett; [ed.] Spotsylvania High, Strayer College; [occ.] Waitress; [oth. writ.] Poem published in The World of Poetry Anthology; [pers.] I want people to feel the real side of life not just the kindness of people but how many can hurt you if your not very careful. [a.] Spotsylvania, VA.

BLEEM, CATHERINE BERRA
[pen.] "Any Old Mouse"; [b.] November 24, 1935, Herrin, IL; [p.] Ren and Teresa Berra; [m.] John James, December 27, 1956; [ch.] Jeanice, Kaiser, John Ren, Dr. Bernard, James, Dr. Renold; [ed.] DePasul Hospital School of Nursing; [occ.] Grade school teacher's aide volunteer; [memb.] R.S.V.P., St. Boniface Church, St. Clement's Hospital Auxiliary; [hon.] Volunteer awards, newspaper awards, recipe awards, poems published; [oth. writ.] Genealogical (3 books); newspaper (column), recipes (Better Homes and Gardens); [pers.] The challenge is to develop optimism. This internal vision has empowered me to accept happiness, love and peace without looking for a reason. [a.] Walsh, IL.

BLENNER, JEN
[pen.] June Martain; [b.] February 22, 1981, Fair Lawn, NJ; [p.] Cindy and Cary Blenner; [ed.] Memorial Middle School; [occ.] Babysitter; [memb.] Girl Scouts, Dancing, Flash Club, and Chorus; [hon.] Care award; [pers.] I wish for happiness throughout the world. [a.] Fair Lawn, NJ.

BLOOM, BARBARA ANN
[b.] June 7, 1943, Baltimore, MD; [p.] Bessie Kuhrmann and Charles Fennell; [m.] Leonard, Esq., June 15, 1969; [ch.] Rachel Glick and grandson Ryan David Glick; [ed.] Dundalk Sr. High School, Towson State, Peabody Institute of Johns Hopkins University, Balto Hebrew University; [occ.] Homemaker, writer, singer, volunteer community worker; [memb.] Beth Tfilor Sisterhood, Chizuk Amuno Sisterhood, Sinai Auxiliary life member of Hadassahm Golda Meir Honor Society, International Society of Poets, Opera Guild; [hon.] World of Poetry Golden Poet award 1989, Gold Medal of Honor Award 1992, International Poet of Merit award 1993, Hadassah membership achievement awards; [oth. writ.] Poems published in "Blue Book" of the 1976 Third World Congress of Poets, in Owings Mills Times and Great Poems of the Western World Vol. II, Whispers in the Wind by the National Library of Congress, also letters to the editor, and Op-Ed published articles in local newspapers and magazines; [pers.] The only truth is the truth that brings peace, all else is a lie. [a.] Baltimore, MD.

BOCOOK, SHERRY LYNN
[b.] September 1,m 1977, Roanoke, VA; [p.] Jackie L.; [ed.] James River High School; [occ.] Student - fulltime; [memb.] Future Business Leaders of America, Future Farmers of America, Future Homemakers of America, International Society of Poetry; [oth. writ.] Poem published in anthologies <u>Tears of Fire</u> and <u>Darkside of the Moon</u>; [pers.] My writing reflects life in general, sadness, anger, hate, love, and the goodness of friendships. My poem "Doubts" is dedicated to my mother and a very special friend. [a.] Buchanan, VA.

BOLAR, JOHN P.
[pen.] John P. Bolar; [b.] February 5, 1910, Cristobal, C.Zone; [p.] James and Ethel Bolar; [m.] Willene York; [ed.] Marine Eng.; [occ.] Retired; [memb.] American Legion, Veterans of Foreign Wars, Oilers Firemen and Watertenders Union, U.S. Navy WWII; [hon.] WWII Vet Pacific Camp, South Pac. Asiatic, American Campaign, incl. medals for service and WWII victory medal; [oth. writ.] Poems unpublished Quenched Flame, Fuzzy Wuzzy Joe to a Landlubber, Fool In Paradise, Perfidia; [pers.] Born in Canal Zone during Const. bounced on Pres. Teddy Roosevelt's knee when 4 years of age. Cruised around world over 40 times in merchant marine since 1927. [a.] Stockton, CA.

BOLTON, CHELSEA LUELLON
[b.] May 10, 1982, Houston, TX; [p.] Wade and Lois Bolton; [ed.] Nova Middle School; [occ.] Student; [memb.] Girl Scouts of America; [hon.] Certificate of Recognition, Ft. Lauderdale Museum of Art, First place Creative Writing, Broward County FAir 1992 and 1993; Editor's Choice Award, National Library of Poetry 1994; [oth. writ.] Poem entitled HOPE, published in National Library of Poetry, 1994; [pers.] My writings are to let people know what is possible in the future. [a.] Davie, FL.

BOND, JUDITH A.
[pen.] Judi Bond; [b.] September 19, 1954, Toronto; [p.] Marie Vince and Doug Finbow; [m.] Elizabeth J., April 21, 1987; [ed.] Community College, Communication Diploma; [occ.] Vice President Corporate Communications; [memb.] The Myalgic Encephalomyelitis Association; [oth. writ.] Published in River of Dreams 1994, finalist Stephen Leacock poetry awards; [pers.] Lesbian/feminist political and social interpretations. [a.] Paisley, ONT., CAN.

BONINE, VIVIAN WAY
[b.] September 28, 1912, Texas; [p.] Mitchell Way and Jennie Ellison Way; [m.] 1. Morris Small and 2. Arvel Earl Bonine; [ch.] two daughters and four grandchildren and seven great grandchildren; [ed.] Texas Woman's University, West Texas State University; [occ.] Retired motion picture film technician; [memb.] International Alliance of Theatrical and Stage Employees; National Federation of State Poetry Societies; Poetry Society of Texas; South Dakota State Poetry Society, CA State Poetry Society, CA Federation of Chaparral Poets; [hon.] Received Poet Laureates from college English class 1935; United Poets Laureates International 1975; City of Rosemead, CA 1992, Doctor of Arts and Letters (ALD) from Great China Arts College; Hong Kong 1970; [oth. writ.] Over 1,250 poems published in newspapers, magazines and anthologies in U.S. and several foreign countries, including Canada, England, Italy, Taiwan, India and the Philippines; [pers.] My poems have been published over a span of 60 years, but I consider being appointed "Official Poet Laureate of the City of Rosemead" by the Rosemead City Council, a group of business men and women representing a city of over 52,000 population, to be the highest of all my honors in the field of poetry. [a.] Rosemead, CA.

BONNETT, SHAWN J.H.
[b.] September 29, 1956, Temple, TX; [p.] Patricia S. and William E. Jenkins; [m.] James H., August 12, 1989; [ch.] Kelly C. Hines and Kathleen E. Hines; [ed.] Sam Houston University, Medical Assistant/ Laboratory Tech Vocational Training, Correspondence Training with Institute of Children's Literature; [occ.] F/T Clinical Laboratory Assistant for a pediatric practice; [memb.] St. James Episcopal Church, Daughters of the King, various spiritual fellowship groups; [hon.] Editor's Choice awardee in 1994 "National Library of Poetry", "Day's End" Anthology "Tender Spirits", several talent contest awards for Stand-up comedy, songwriting, musical competition (flute); [oth. writ.] Poet's Corner school newspapers/newsletters elementary college; writing various articles/brochures for church council retreats/activities, etc.; [pers.] Writing has always been a catharsis for me, in that what I can't express verbally, the written words release the inhibitions of expression. I strive always for emotional and spiritual uplift- ment for myself and others. [a.] Alexandria, VA.

BORCHER, BETTY
[b.] August 15, 1929, Springdale, ARK; [p.] Otto and Josephine Nelson; [m.] John, August 23, 1946; [ch.] Steven and Shelley; [ed.] Alhambra High School; [occ.] Retired formerly Interior Designer; [memb.] P.E.O., Order of Eastern Star, ASID until retired; [oth. writ.] Poems and reflectors about nature and spiritual thoughts; [pers.] Our connection to each other and the universe is a beautiful experience. I seek to write about these experiences. [a.] Tehachapi, CA.

BOTHA, KATIE
[b.] South Africa; [p.] Adrian and Joe de la Rey; [ch.] Kobus and Adrey; [ed.] Teacher's diploma, Advanced education in Dianetics and Scientology; [occ.] Scientology minister; [memb.] International Society of Poets, International Association of Scientology, Founding Scientology member; [hon.] Editor's Choice awards; [oth. writ.] Published in various anthologies, a series of 12 poems on Africa, a scrapbook with 40 of my poems - a hit; [pers.] The artists dream of a new civilization and they create a future - with world peace. My inner gratitude to L.R. Hubbard, whom I knew personally, for all his gifts to mankind. [a.] Clearwater, FL.

BOUCHER, ELIZABETH ANNE
[pen.] Anne Porter Boucher; [b.] February 24, 1915, Fall River, MA; [occ.] Retired; [memb.] International Woman of the Year, Cambridge, ENG; National Woman of the Year Raleigh, SC; International Society of Poets; [hon.] International Who's Who of Professional and Business Women, 2,000 Notable American Women; [pers.] My deepest thanks to you for what you have done for me and my poetry. I am proved to be a member of your grand profession. You have done do much for me. [a.] Blackstone, MA.

BOWERMAN, CRAIG
[pen.] Bud Mann; [b.] August 29, 1960, Lansing, MI; [p.] Darlene Sawyer and W. Bowerman; [ch.] Robbin, Joey and Shannon; [ed.] Holt Senior High, GED; [occ.] Self-Craig Painting and Drywall Service; [memb.] Ex VP Lansing Chapter Flint Eagles M/C, President Rebel Eagles M/C, Amvets, Biker Association; [hon.] Honorable discharge USMC, Editor Choice award (In The Desert Sun), Good Conduct Medal; [oth. writ.] Life (published in Desert Sun), In The Ghetto (published in A Far Off Place), Perspectives of a Modern Day Man (unpublished); [pers.] Working on a new book of poems right now. A lot of my poems are my feeling on situations in life. I've been writing since I was 8 years old and owe it all to my Aunt Sharon Lutz. [a.] Lansing, MI.

BOWERS, KAREN A.
[pen.] Emma Pendragon; [b.] February 15, 1954, Bonham, TX; [p.] Kenneth and Ednafae Bowers; [ed.] Proviso West High School; [occ.] Travel Industry; [memb.] International Library of Poets; [hon.] 3 Editor's Choice awards from The National Library of Poetry; [oth. writ.] A collection of poems "Chi Reality (just some poems) published Carol Chesick; [pers.] "Of Mothers" was written by request and with inspiration from a soon to be first time grandmother, Marilyn Weglarz. And because I love my mother and daddy. Inspiration is a joy to be shared. [a.] Forest Park, IL.

BOWERS, LORRIE K.
[b.] March 11, 1964, Latrobe, PA; [p.] James R. and Evelyn G. Bowers; [ed.] Richland High, Cambria-Rowe Business College; [occ.] Bookkeeping and Tax Service; [memb.] Westmont Baptist Church; [oth. writ.] A short story published in a local paper and a poem in The Coming of Dawn. I hope to become an author of children's books; [pers.] I am physically challenged-walk with two wooden canes-but I don't let that stop me from doing things. I just have to do somethings differently. If people remember to look to the Lord first, surviving the mountains and valleys of life won't be impossible. I can do all things through Christ which strengthens me. (Php. 4:13). [a.] Johnstown, PA.

BOYELLE, MARSHA L.
[ed.] BA Blue Mountain College, Mississppi County Community College; [occ.] RN-Consultant; [memb.] Memphis Case Managers Association, Arkansas Nurses Association, American Nurses Association; [hon.] Who's Who in Executive Women 1992-93, Who's Who of Women 1992-93; [oth. writ.] "Friendship" published, "Just Yesterday", published; [pers.] Each of us has tasks we must achieve in this life. Along the path we receive strength and courage from our fellow readers. If my words can touch a heart or create a small shaft of light. That will add a small touch of clarify to the prism of life. I have accomplished this task. [a.] Blytherille, ARK.

BRADFORD, ELLEN E.
[pen.] Ellen E. Bradford; [b.] October 30, 1962, Phila; [p.] Jean and Spencer; [ed.] Lower Merion High School; [occ.] Red Cross Volunteer at Town and Country Hospital; [memb.] Red Cross Auxiliary of PA, Osteopathic Medical Association, Lutheran Church of Our Saviour, International Society of Poets; [hon.] Star award for dedicated service (Red Cross volunteer) has served 2400 hours+; [pers.] Member of Lutheran Church of our Saviour, teaches Sunday School, member of Bell Choir. Enjoys bowling with the Super Stars League Poems published in church, community and hospital newsletters and in previous National Library of Poets. [a.] Tampa, FL.

BRADLEY, PERRY E.
[per.] Perry Winkle; [b.] January 16, 1947, Zanesville; [p.] D.H. and G.E. Bradley; [m.] Beverly Kay (2nd), May 10, 1985; [ch.] Michelle, Heather, Misty, Greg and Terry Henderson; [ed.] 1966 American School of Chicago, IL, and Maysville High School; [occ.] Former Steelworker O.F.A.C.; [memb.] VVA Chapter 42 (Walt Davis); [hon.] (Editor's Choice award), The National Library of Poetry 1994, poem: Dedicate Your Life, published through Sparrowgrass Poetry Forum entitled: Through The Mind's Eye 1994;

[oth. writ.] Poems unpublished: Who Help's, Bird Talk, Whiskey, Wine and Beer, just to name a few; [pers.] Mostly inspirational poems I write but sometimes I do write poems that have humor and I like to write poems about people I used to work with. [a.] Zanesville, OH.

BRADY, HENRY G.
[pen.] Henry O'Grady; [m.] Divorced; [ed.] Florida State University; [occ.] Retired professor; [memb.] Episcopal Church, Air Force Association charter member, Air Force Education Federation; [hon.] Thirty awards and citations for Combat Services, WWII and Korean War , USAF, Fellowship, Doctoral Studies, F.S.W.; [oth. writ.] Articles in Adult Learning Psychology and Research in Educational Journals. Poems in various publications; [pers.] Major interests are philosophy, psychology, international relations, sailing, swimming. [a.] Clearwater, FL.

BRAIDOTTI, REGINA
[b.] June 12, 1978, Philadelphia, PA; [p.] Ermino and Christina Braidotti; [ed.] Padua Academy; [occ.] Student; [memb.] National Geographic Society; [hon.] National Honor Society, Tantalizing Stories' Society; [oth. writ.] Stories and poems published in various literary magazines; [pers.] I offer my heartfelt thanks to Peter Roget. [a.] West Chester, PA.

BRAY, PHILLIP ALEXANDER MARTIN
[pen.] Alexander Martin; [b.] January 16, 1960, Batavia; [p.] John William and Alberta Bremiller Bray; [ed.] Attica Central High; [occ.] Black and White Photographic paper Product Tester; [memb.] Alternate Imaginations; The Gay Alliance of the Genesee Valley, Attica Landmark Preservation Society, Attica Historical Society, In Touch International; [hon.] Honor society; [oth. writ.] The Princes of Trilon, Poems of Cedar Court; [pers.] I write poems that reflect my view of things as I preconceive or imagine them to be. My preconceptions are often very inaccurate leading to a second poem. [a.] Batavia, NY.

BRAYMAN, ELSIE
[b.] June 27, 1911, Walton, WV; [p.] William and Stella Walker; [m.] Herbert Aldrich Brayman, October 8, 1932; [ch.] Joyce Jacobs, Janet Miggo, and Marilyn Reese; [ed.] Pierpont High School; [occ.] Retired, a homemaker, artist and writer; [memb.] Austinburg First United Church of Christ, Lake Shore Artists Guild, Ashtabula Writer's Guild; [hon.] Various artistic awards for my paintings over the past 26 years; [oth. writ.] I have written short stories and articles, some of which have been published. At the present time I am writing an autobiography; [pers.] I have enjoyed writing poetry since my teenage years and find it a very fulfilling experience. My hope is that my poems will reflect the appreciation I feel for God's blessings in my life and they will help others find the true joy of living. [a.] Jefferson, OH.

BREWER, JOAN M.
[b.] July 25, 1945, Detroit, MI; [p.] The Late Leroy and Marie Brewer; [ed.] Some college; [occ.] Banker; [memb.] Scholarship Committee member and Missionary of True Love Baptist Church; [hon.] A poem published in Edge of Twilight, fall 1994; [pers.] Continued encouragement from my Pastor, and trusting in the Lord. I am inspired to continue my writing. I want to encourage others through my words of comfort and faith, that they can accomplish anything. [a.] Detroit, MI.

BRINKLEY, LINDA
[b.] January 7, 1952, Newport, AR; [p.] Claude and Maxine Burris; [m.] John, May 28, 1993; [ch.] Dustin and Kacey, John, Jonah and Joel (step); [ed.] Newport High School; [occ.] Domestic Engineer; [hon.] Publication of a poem in high school. Most recently I had a poem published in the anthology "At Day's End" and received an Editor's Choice award; [oth. writ.] "There Is a God" and "I Have A Friend" and numerous unpublished works; [pers.] I believe you can tell alot about a person by the words that he or she may write, so I try to reveal my inner self through my poetry, especially my strong belief in God. [a.] Bradford, AR.

BRINKMAN, KAREN
[pen.] Karen (Olson) Brinkman; [b.] December 14, 1940, Britton, SD; [p.] Alice and Dwight (deceased) Olson; [m.] Divorced; [ch.] Kelly, Traci, Kari, and Glennell; [ed.] Langford High, Criminal Law from SDSU; [occ.] Former National Institute of Health Employee; [memb.] Former NRA member, Equal Employment Opportunity and Burns Irt. Security; [hon.] First Policewoman in Mobridge, SD; [oth. writ.] Previously written for The National Library of Poetry, also like to write country/western song lyrics, as a hobby; [pers.] I have travelled through many states in the U.S. I like to write about the picturesque beauty in each individual state. Scenery is poetic in itself. [a.] Republic, WA.

BRITTAIN, LINDA CRANE
[b.] November 12, 1940, Montpelier, ID; [p.] Jack R. and Jennie S. Crane; [m.] James A., August 12, 1961; [ch.] Tracy B. Acevedo, Travis J. Brittain; [ed.] Master and 60 in English; [occ.] Teacher in junior high school; [oth. writ.] Several poems published in local papers; [pers.] An obituary never fully expresses the loss one feels. I felt a need to say good-bye to Ulva with a poem. [a.] West Valley City, UT.

BROCK, MARTHA
[m.] Clarence L. Brock; [ch.] Byron, Kaye, Heather, Beth; [ed.] Masters in Education; [occ.] Retired after 17 years of teaching; [memb.] ISP, MRA, IRA; [hon.] Semi-finalist at ISP Conference contest 1994; [oth. writ.] Publication of Rainbow Riches 1994, a collection of poems. Published in previous editions of the National Library of Poetry, local newspapers and school papers; [pers.] I try to restore to adults some of what they saw, as children, in the world around them.

BROEKHUIZEN, VICTORIA J.
[b.] January 24, 1971, Audurn, NY; [p.] Sally and Gerald Broekhuizen; [ed.] Cato Meridian Central Schools, Baldwinsville Central and Academics Schools; [occ.] Office Services Secretary; [oth. writ.] "Baby", "Wedding", "Marriage", untitled "50th Anniversary" (all published in your anthologies; [pers.] You can create a poem as long as you remember the things that are important to you especially those you love. [a.] Baldwinsville, NY.

BROMLEY, MATT
[b.] February 5, 1975, Las Vegas, NV; [p.] Tom and Cora Bromley; [memb.] Art Club Vice President; [hon.] Who's Who, several poetic publications, and numerous art awards; [oth. writ.] Other poems I have recently published include: Whispering Garden, Victims of Our Own Predatory, A War of Isolation, and Showdown. I also like to write short stories about those things which only appear in our dreams; [pers.] A tamed heart is a heart torn apart. This time that we see, we see the seed of a tree, and that is the power left to thee...[a.] Roswell, NM.

BROWN, COLLIN E.
[b.] October 14, 1946, Helen and Woodrow Brown; [m.] Mary Mamber G. Brown, August 14, 1993; [ch.] Jim, Mat, Tim, Lisa, Mark; [ed.] High school and tech schools; [occ.] Maintenance Planner; [memb.] Crane Cert. Asst; [oth. writ.] Several unpublished poems; [pers.] In this world today we often become to busy to enjoy the most important things in life. Ironically we will find that there things are free. [a.] Westminster, MD.

BROWN, HASAN H.
[b.] December 11, 1947, K.C., MO; [p.] Fred and Mildred Brown; [ch.] Keisha and Hasan II; [ed.] BA and MFA, U.C.L.A.; [occ.] Businessman, Real Estate Investments; [oth. writ.] Several poems published in community newsletters and National Library of Poetry Anthology series; [pers.] My poetry covers a wide variety of subjects and themes. I try to experiment with a variety of styles and formats when writing. [a.] Los Angles, CA.

BROWN, MYRANDA SUSANNE
[pen.] Myransa Susanne; [b.] May 28, 1977; [p.] Thomas William and Terri Bernice Brown; [ed.] Fort Calhoun Elementary and Fort Calhoun High School; [occ.] Cashier at Bakers; [memb.] FHA (Future Homemakers of America), Spanish Club, MCC (Medical Careers Club), Boys Club of America; [hon.] Secretary of MCC, Junior Councilor of the Week for the Henry Orgams Boys Club Day Camp, Outstanding member of the month of July for Henry Boys Club, lettered in choir three years and the 1993 Editor's Choices award from The National Library of Poetry; [oth. writ.] In general I write a lot. The one that has achieved an award was Wishes From the Heart. In 1993, that received the Editor's Choice Award; [pers.] Writing poems are the keys to my emotions and feelings. When I feel that I'm going go crazy or that I can't go on sit down and write what I'm feeling on paper. It's a great escape. [a.] Ft. Calhoun, NE.

BROWNING, CLARA JANE
[pen.] C.J. Browning; [b.] October 26, 1921, Calexico, CA; [p.] Archie and Irene Dick; [m.] George, November 6, 1945, [ch.] Frances and Tom; [ed.] University of Oregon, U.S. Navy Corps WWII; [occ.] Retired, writer; [memb.] Oregon Coast Council for the Arts, Red Octopus Theater, AARP, OPB member, National Ed. Association, Charter member of WIMSA (Women in Military Service to America); [hon.] NDEA Grant in Spanish -College, Pi Delta Pi French; Sigma Delta Pi; [oth. writ.] "Generation Gap Travel", in Travel News International; in progress co-author "Thoughtful Courtship", "Down East Tales", "Triple D's" World of Poetry; [pers.] Writing in general, and poetry in particular, focuses and clarifies individual thoughts and emotions. [a.] Toledo, OR.

BRUSS, MARY
[b.] April 16, 1919, Chicago, IL; [p.] Albert and Sue Murolo; [m.] Hillard Bruss, November 27, 1952 (deceased); [ed.] Six years Keyboard Harmony, Naprapathic College; [occ.] Retired; [memb.] AARP, St. John Bosco Catholic Church; [oth. writ.] I Promise You, So Many Reminders, Whatever That Means, Sometimes There's A Longing, The Statue of Liberty, Chicago's The Best in the World; [pers.] I put all my poetry to music I play the organ. My favorite hobby is composing music to my lyrics. [a.] Chicago, IL.

BRYAN, JULIE MICHELLE
[b.] May 23, 1979, Ft. Lauderdale, FL; [p.] Donna B. Cianfrani and Matthew Cianfrani (stepfather); [ed.] Cardinal Gibbons High School; [occ.] Student; [hon.] Honor roll and many athletic achievements; [oth. writ.] "What Matters?" and "An Unknown Soul of Season" have been published as of now; [pers.] I believe that a person's heart, soul, and mind is much more important than their appearance. [a.] Lighthouse Point, FL.

BRYANT, FLORENCE
[pen.] Florence Bryant; [b.] April 21, 1906, Texas; [p.] Dr. Joseph and Eva Wright Ponder; [m.] Deceased, May 14, 1924; [ch.] John Edward Bradley, Barbara June Bryant (MacDonald); [ed.] High school graduate; [occ.] State of California Notary Public, and medical and legal secretary out of home; [memb.] National Notary Association; [oth. writ.] In process of writing short stories and 5 books: "Life of Dr. Joe", "The Three Muscateers" (re my two children and me), and "Our Little Animal Friends" et al; [pers.] Nothing is impossible. There is no such word as "can't" - rather it is "I shall try". Over seeming insurmountable odds, my children and I have overcome multitudes of obstacles. My son spent 3 years in the European theatre during World War II, came back in a hospital ship - yet he finished Boston University in 2 years and under a scholarship from B.U. graduated from USC in Los Angeles as an Architect. His homes are all over northern, southern California, State of Washington, Oregon and Texas. My daughter is blind (since 1989) but she never gives up and makes everyone happy. [a.] Hayward, CA.

BRYANT, VICKI E.
[b.] october 9, 1970, Grand Junction, CO; [p.] Norman and Sybil Bryant; [ed.] Brighton High School, Community College of Aurora; [occ.] Assembly Clerk for publishing company; [memb.] Student Government, Shared Governance Committee for Community College of Aurora, Tutor for the D.A.R.E. project; [hon.] Phi Theta Kappa, Partnership award from the D.A.R.E. outreach program; [oth. writ.] "Virgin", "Dream Walk" both published by National Library of Poetry in 1994; [pers.] I believe that if everyone experienced love once and own a box of crayons the world would be a better place. [a.] Commerce City, CO.

BUCKLEY, JAMES M.
[b.] June 19, 1912, Jamaica Plain, MA; [p.] Arthur and Catherine Buckley; [m.] Marilyn L., September 11, 1976; [ch.] James M. Buckley, Jr., Bradford Reed, Carolyn Souza; [ed.] Boston College, Boston University; [occ.] Retired from Director of Adult Education; [pers.] Violinist and songwriter (over 150). [a.] New Bedford, MA.

BUONO, FRANCO
[b.] January 8, 1911, New York City; [p.] Mathew Buono and Rosina Spinelli; [m.] Mary Savino, October 25, 1962; [ed.] College, Literature University; [occ.] Retired; [memb.] Union Della Legion D'Oro Academic in Roma, Italy for many years of merit. Faithful to Institution; [hon.] Certificate of award, merit, achievement, golden poet award; [pers.] Son of Italian immigrants. After my experiences as a child in New York where I was born, adolescence in Italy 1920 and my subsequent tests in the WWII era of Benito Mussolini, I returned to my native land when I began to suffer per nostalgia in 1962. I have an innately charming philosophy of live in reaching my projects and dreams and events in excitement. I remain rooted where I stand or move shuddering my soul. [a.] Auburn, NY.

BUR, JESSICA L.
[b.] March 16, 1974, Michigan; [p.] Michael and Susan Valade-Bur; [ed.] Walled Lake Central; [occ.] Daycare Assistant and writer; [oth. writ.] "I Do" in Tears of Fire; [pers.] All my love, Jason Remner. May we always stay as we are happy and together. Mom and Dad - I love you both very much! Danita-you're the best sister. [a.] Wixom, MI.

BURGOYNE, ROGER D.
[b.] June 12, 1926, Montpelier, ID; [p.] Sidney E. Burgoyne and Beatrice Holmes; [m.] Charlotte Tillotson Burgoyne, August 30, 1946; [ch.] Mary, Kathleen, Roger, Margaret, Janet, Sylvia, Eric, 39 grandchildren and 3 great grand;p [ed.] Montpelie High, Utah State University, University of Utah, Arizona State University, private music and vocal studies; [occ.] Legal Consultant to lawyers; Retired lawyer and personal counselor; [memb.] Former Judge, 3 Term Prosecuting Attorney, Amateur Musician, Opera Singer and Performer; [oth. writ.] Numerous poems, verses and essays as a hobby, many used in greeting cards; [pers.] A really great poem should convey the emotions and feelings associated with the message being conveyed and these should be expressed in a beautiful arrangement of words, this latter being as important as the former. [a.] Tempe, AZ.

BURKS-SHIVER, JACQUELINE
[pen.] Jacqueline Burks-Shiver; [b.] July 3, 1929, New York City; [p.] Leslie Burks and Lorena Eaton; [m.] Deceased; [ch.] Karen, Pena and 3 grandchildren-Anton, Brandon and Curtis; [ed.] AAS New York Tech College, Pace University, Lehman College; [occ.] Retiree-NY Telephone; [memb.] Broadcast Music Inc.; [hon.] National Dean's List, Cash award from Ny Poetry Press; [oth. writ.] Poetry in McCalls Christmas issue 1975, former Professional Lyricist and songwriter with over 30 published; [pers.] Have written 2 poetry chap books - and hope they will both be published and become great successes.

BURNEO, JAMES
[b.] May 21, 1933, Flint, MI; [p.] William and Mary Burneo; [m.] Beth, March 29, 1990; [ed.] University of Arizona and Holly Names College; [occ.] Poet; [pers.] I try to find sacredness in everyday experience and express that feeling in my poetry. [a.] Crockett, CA.

BURRIS, SHERIN R.L.
[b.] October 10, 1969, Coshocton, Memorial; [p.] Mr. and Mrs. Earl P. Burris; [ed.] Riverview District High, Coshocton County Joint Vocational, Hocking Technical College; [occ.] Employee of "Akro" for the corporation Collins and Aikman; [memb.] Coshocton Nazarene Church, National and International Wildlife Federation; [oth. writ.] "Fever For A Cold" by The National Library of Poetry for 1994 publication in "The River of Dreams", "Live Dying" by Riverwind for the 1992 publication. [a.] Coshocton, OH.

BUSCETTO, SALLY
[b.] June 21, 1926, Rochester, NY; [p.] Anthony and Anna Matina; [m.] John, October 23, 1944; [ch.] Linda and Richard Buscetto and Marie White; [ed.] Benjamin Franklin High School; [occ.] Posting on the computer in a business office; [oth. writ.] Several poems published in local newspaper; [pers.] I hope in my writing I have encouraged and given hope to many, and we all work toward a quality life. [a.] Rochester, NY.

BUTLER, REBECCA BATTS DR.
[pen.] Dr. Rebecca Batts Butler; [b.] November 29, 1910, Norfolk, VA; [p.] William and Gussie Batts; [m.] Ellis L. Williams; [ed.] Temple University; [occ.] REtired; [memb.] National Sorority Phi Delta Kappa, National Educational Association, Societas Doctor, National Association of Negro Business and Professional Women, National Association University Women; [hon.] Received over 50 awards, citations and appointments; [oth. writ.] Outstanding Blacks in South Jersey, Problems of Beginning Teachers, Portraits of Black Role Models, two plays-Children of Mant Lands and What Africa Gave to America, book My Thoughts, I Write a book of poems; [pers.] Preparation, persistence and prayer are the ingredients for achieving one's goals. [a.] Cherry Hill, NJ.

BUTCHER, FINN LEON
[b.] May 28, 1952, Aarhuy, DK; [ed.] School of Commerce; [occ.] Freelance photographer; [a.] Aaryus C., Denmark.

BYERS, MARY WYATT
[b.] October 30, 1952, Hanover County, VA; [p.] Frederick and Clara Wyatt; [m.] Williams Byers, Jr., September 3, 1983; [ch.] Anita Elizabeth, William Walker III; [ed.] Norfolk State University; [occ.] Special Education Teacher; [memb.] Mt. Olivet Baptist Church, Sigma Gamma Rho Sorority; [hon.] Several poems received recognition in the World of Poetry contests; [oth. writ.] Play "At the Foot of the Cross" (copyright 1991) numerous poems for church-related events (anniversaries, funerals) - several poems for the World of Poetry contests; [pers.] If I can lift someone's spirit or touch another's life through poetry, then my living shall not be in vain. [a.] Charlottesville, VA.

BYTHER, PATRICIA
[b.] August 20, 1954, Hanover, MD; [p.] William and Elizabeth Bouchat; [m.] James, May 28, 1994; [ed.] Michelle Bouchat Hudson; [ed.] Howard High School, some courses of Baltimore Community College; [occ.] Volunteer and homemaker; [memb.] Maine State Museum Associate, International Society of Poets; [oth. writ.] A poem published in "The Darkside of the

Moon"; [pers.] I thank Jesus for my talent and for the inspiration to write poetry. If in my lifetime, I am able to spread love, peace, happiness, then I have achieved my goal in life. Only then have I been successful. [a.] Winslow, ME.

CABRAL, PAULINA C.
[pen.] Paulina de la Cruz; [b.] June 22, 1919, Philippines; [p.] Segundo Cruz and Mansi Silvestre; [m.] Fidel Cabral, 1948 (deceased); [ch.] Connie, Dionicio, Rey and Cesar; [occ.] Retired; [oth. writ.] Several short stories in Tagalog (the national language of the Philippines) and some essays and short poems published by Ramon Roces Publications before and after World War II; [pers.] Came to the United States in 1974 to be with my daughter Connie, who was then working at the Philippine Consulate General in New York. Now, as life goes on in wonderful ways, I try my best to adjust to the inevitable changes that I encounter all the way. [a.] Teaneck, NJ.

CALABRESE, JASON
[pen.] J. Cal; [b.] June 14, 1971, Waterbury, CT; [p.] William and Carole Calabrese; [ed.] Holy Cross High School, Southern Connecticut State University, University of Connecticut; [occ.] Proprietor, Nite Club, freshman Basketball Coach Kaynor Technical High School; [memb.] Connecticut High School Coaches Association; [hon.] Dean's list, National Citizens Scholarship Foundation of America; [oth. wrfit.] Always on the Horizon, Dark Side of the Moon; [pers.] Don't let people discourage you from reaching your dreams, because they are just discouraged they didn't have what it took to reach theirs. [a.] Waterbury, CT.

CALDWELL, MARTHA
[b.] August 18, 1917, Manchester, IA; [p.] Frank and Brownie Caldwell; [ch.] None but lots of nieces and nephews; [ed.] Kansas State University, Columbia University and Parsons School of Design; [occ.] Retired University of Vermont Professor; [memb.] AARP, Costume Society of Anerica, United Methodist Church, Women in the Military Service, various others; [hon.] My greatest honor is just being alive in this fantastic universe. Also, being chosen to teach at Ege Univ.; [oth. writ.] Other verses, some short articles on textile and costume history, "Letters Home" from abroad; [pers.] Old age, in spite of itself, can be a time of expanding inspiration and creativity. We must find a way to bring all of mankind together in harmony with nature! [a.] Winfield, KS

CAMPBELL, ERICA MARIE
[b.] St. Louise, MO; [p.] DAniel J. (Joe) and Constance T. (Connie) Campbell; [efd.] Holman Middle School; [occ.] 6th grade student; [memb.] First Christian Church of Florissant; [hjon.] Honor roll student, selected as a '93-'94 student council representative, nominated and selected as a '92-'93 school newspaper reporter, appointed as a '93-'94 student council representative and earned designation of honor roll student since '92 eligibility; [oth. writ.] Crime Doesn't Pay, Dance on the Horizon; Flood of 1993, Echoes of Yesterday; [pers.] Kids can do anything if they try.

CANDELMO, ANTHONY JOHN
[b.] February 6, 1943, NJ; [m.] Martha B., August 4, 1973; [ch.] Jessica Lynne, Andrea Barnett; [ed.] Villanova University, Rutgers University, Montclair State, Goeth Institute Germany; [occ.] German teacher-Parsippany Hills High School; [memb.] AATG, NEA, NJEA, NRA; [hon.] Who's Who Among American High School Teachers, 2nd degree Black Belt Tae Kwon Do; [pers.] You win a few - you lose a few, and some get rained out - do the best you can with what you've got. [a.] Parsippany, NJ.

CAPOZZA, DAVID
[pen.] Max; [b.] October 9, 1979, New London, CT; [p.] Ronald and Karen Capozza; [occ.] Freshman at East Lyme High School; [memb.] Amnesty International, Key Club, Ecology Club, Cultural Awareness Club, Cross-Country, Peers Reaching Out, Prevention Players, Math League, Hospital volunteer and altar server; [hon.] New England Science Teacher's award, honor roll, misc. writing awards; [oth. writ.] "Cherish"; [pers.] I find it important to express that many people are deprived of their rights on the basis of race, origin, beliefs, etc. I feel as if everyone should play apart in working for world peace. It doesn't start with someone else but with you. Special thanks to Jeff, Nyssa, Mr. Sdao, Anik, Jim, Keri, Debby, Jen and my parents for believing in me even when I didn't. [a.] East Lyme, CT.

CAPUANO, CONCETTA A.
[pen.] Connie; [b.] October 26, 1936, Rochester, NY; [p.] Deceased; [m.] George A., December 21, 1953; [ch.] Deborahann, Franl; [ed.] Grammer, high school, nursing; [occ.] Antiques; [memb.] St. Paul's Women's Solidarity; [hon.] Two editor choice awards from the National Library of Poetry, a honorable mention, in the Iliad Press Cader Publishing Inc.; [oth. writ.] Several poems published in the National Library of Poetry, and Iliad Press; [pers.] Raised in foster homes most of my childhood, I grew to have deep inner feelings, I love to read and I am always inspired by children, animals, and nature. [a.] Kenmore, NY.

CARDWELL, EVELYN HEATH
[b.] November 1, 1937, North Holston, VA; [p.] Bill and Annie Heath; [m.] Elmer (deceased); [ch.] Noonie, Betty (Christie, Brian, Jamie) Mike, Deb, Steve, Lisa (Trevor), Wayne, Jeannie (Joy) Jim, Karen (Chelsey), Michael; [oth. writ.] Gospel songs, children's stories and poems; [pers.] Take ordinary days as special days... for special days are few and far between... the ordinaries are what makes life have meaning...[a.] Saltville, VA.

CARLSON, AARON MICHAEL
[pen.] Obad Ephriam and Emllik; [b.] August 31, 1972, Minneapolis, MN; [p.] Richard and Gaile Carlson; [ed.] Robbinsdale Cooper High School, School of Communication Arts; [occ.] Student, part-time computer operatr at Abbott-Northwestern Hospital and model for Personality Plus; [oth. writ.] 22 seconds published in "A Far of Place" by the wonderful National Library of Poetry; [pers.] To all of societies slaves. The time is coming. You will know the truth and the truth will set you free. [a.] New Hope, MN.

CARR, BARBARA
[ed.] BA English/Psychology; MS Counseling and Guidance; Training: Institute of Children's Literature - writing for children.; [occ.] Travel Agent; [memb.] Las Amigas de Las Lomas (auxiliary to Crippled Children's Guild of Orthopaedic Hospital, Los Angeles; [hon.] Pi Lambda Theta - Education Honorary - awarded at time of receiving master's degree; [a.] Rolling Hills Est., CA.

CARR, TARA M.
[pen.] T. Milam Coats; [b.] October 2, 1976, Turzana, CA; [p.] Jackson and Sandra Carr; [ed.] St. Helena High School; [occ.] Student; [oth. writ.] "My World", Dark Side of the Moon; [pers.] I feel privileged to have my poetry published in this book. I write for the love of it. I enjoy of writing poetry and novels, and what will come out of my work will be what I feel inside. [a.] St. Helena, CA.

CARRISON, JENNIFER LYNN
[b.] April 16, 1974, Enid, OK; [p.] Dennis R. or E. Yvonne Carrison; [ed.] Ralston High School; [occ.] Hy-Vee, Non-foods/video; [hon.] Student of the Week for 4 years in a row, perfect attendance for 3 years in a row, special Ed volunteer and nurses aide, perfect German student three years in a row, 2nd place in job seeking skills, 4th place in nursing asst skills through HOSA; [oth. writ.] Poem titled "Rain", merit and honorable mention, "My Mother", honorable mention; [pers.] To achieve your dreams, remember your ABC's. [a.] Omaha, NB.

CARROLL, MARJRIE J.
[b.] August 10. 1949, Emmorton, VA; [p.] Harvey and Frances Gribble; [m.] Roy N. Carroll, April 17, 1982; [ch.] Kevin Lee, David Nelson, Jennifer Lynn, Kristi Saun Brown; [ed.] Thomas Edison High School, adult education centers, real estate appraisal school; [occ.] Retired, homemaker, crafter; [mem.] Ladie Rescue Squad Aux; [hon.] APA Poet of Merit award, 1st place Craters ribbon in county fair; [oth. writ.] "The Days of Yesteryear", published 10/90 (My Own Book of Poems), Best New Poets of 1989, several poems published in local newspapers, contest, publishing companies, and 9th grade school newspaper; [pers.] I strive to reflect the true essence of life, the bitter and the sweet in my writings. I truly believe without the bitter, we would take the sweet for granted. [a.] Callao, VA.

CARTER, JOHN C. JR
[b.] december 24, 1928, Port Neches, TX; [p.] John Sr. and Lillian Carter; [ch.] Terry Lynn Sanders; [ed.] Poland High School; [occ.] Retired, Riceland Foods, ordained Pentacostal minister; [hon.] Continental Wrestling Federation, Jonesboro, AK, promoter of wrestling matches for Special Olympics, Arkansas Childrens Hospital and other organizations; [pers.] As I stated, I am an ordained minister. I strive from day to day to be a shining light for our Lord. I have also done ministerial work over the years in hospitals, jails, and prisons throughout the country. [a.] Jonesboro, AK.

CARTER, PRISCILLA L.
[p.] Alice and James Aitken; [m.] deceased; [ch.] Steven, Richard, Susan; [ed.] Lesley College; [occ.] Teacher, counselor, adult evening course instructor, author illustrator of "Mirror Mirror on the Wall" childrens books series; [oth. writ.] Other poems accepted by National Library of Poetry; [pers.] From all adversity there becomes an open door, a challenge for courage and optimism, a learned growth, a thought process toward change. From all joy one reaps the rapture and wonderment reassuring that is all worthwhile. This is captured especially in the eyes and spirit of children, for they are the "springtime" rejuvenation in the evolution of life's beauty. [a.] Reading, MA.

CARTONI, RICHARD THOMAS

[b.] June 27, 1967, Fairfield, Ca; [p.] Richard Thomas Cartoni Sr. and Jill Ann Taylor; [m.] Nickie Lynn Villamor-Cartoni, October 26, 1986; [ch.] Brianna Geselle Cartoni; [ed.] Evergreen Valley College, Los Altos High School, Jarvis E. Bishop Elementary School; [occ.] Full time student; [hon.] Grand Prize winner, National Library of Poetry 1994 Open Poetry Contest, Editor's Choice award 1994; [oth. writ.] Short story and several poems published in annual literary magazine Leaf by Leaf, and poem "Adrift" published in the National Library f Poetry's anthology A Far Off Place; [pers.] I believe that writing poetry is an exploration of the soul, which begins with a faint flicker of comtemplation, and endfs in an inferno of personal nsight. [a.] San Jose, CA.

CASAVANT, HELEN L.

[b.] July 11, 1923, Boston; [p.] Mabel DeVilliae and Daniel Beaudro; [m.] Robert K., September 19, 1941; [ch.] Robert Kent Jr., Beth Virginia; [ed.] High school; [occ.] Retired; [memb.] National Goldwing Road Riders Association, Local Chapter N of Gwrra, South Shore Antique Auto Club, South Shore Antique Auto Foundation, Model A Restores Club of MA; [hon.] All honors and rewards were for volunteer work; [oth. writ.] Almost all my poems have been published in the newspaper; [pers.] Plant a seed of kindness and watch it grow. Store the seeds of love then toss them gently about. Each seed makes more beauty until a full garden grows then life is ours to enjoy. [a.] Wrentham, MA.

CASCIARO, VIRGINIA

[b.] August 1, 1923, Hattisville; [m.] Michael, January 26, 1946; [ch.] Daniel; [ed.] High school; [occ.] Housewife; [memb.] Church; [hon.] A few award certificates from "World of Poetry"; [oth. writ.] I have now published poems of my own. It is hobby for me - I just enjoy writing poetry; [pers.] It is a great pleasure to have someone else read my poems besides myself. [a.] Harrisville, NY.

CASSIDY, SEAN IAN

[b.] April 12, 1977, Mongtomery, NY; [p.] Veronica and Neil Cassidy; [ed.] Monsignor Donovan High School; [occ.] Bus Boy, Southern House Point Pleasant; [memb.] MSSA, Surf Club; [hon.] Editor Choice award, International Society of Poets; [oth. writ.] Over 250 poems, a few short essays, a few short stories; [pers.] Sometimes life doesn't move quick enough for you, that's why you have to step on the pedal. [a.] Brick, NJ.

CASTILLO, PATRICIA

[pen.] Pat Hill-Castillo; [b.] June 20, 1963, Germany; [p.] Paul and Annemarie Hill; [m.] Carlos; [ch.] 1 son; [ed.] Friebl Institute at the University of Erlanger-Nuremberg; [occ.] Foreign Correspondent; [memb.] Several visits of Isreal, one as a volunteer in a Moshav, one as a volunteer in the Isreali Army; [oth. writ.] Poems and prosa about Holocaust, Isreal and the Middle East (one poem published by The National Library of Poetry); [pers.] Strongly influenced by Charles Beaudelaire and Jean-Arthur Rimbaud, French poets of the 19th century as well as by Lord Byron, British poet of same era. [a.] El Paso, TX.

CASTON, LEONARD JR.

[b.] September 25, 1968, New Orleans, LA; [p.] Mr. and Mrs. Lenoard Caston, Sr.; [m.] Valencia L., September 10, 1994; [ch.] Bianca; [ed.] University of Maryland-College Park; [occ.] Paralegal; [memb.] National Capital Paralegal Association, Notary Public of the State of Maryland, National Black Paralegal Association; [pers.] Treasure a gift, because your life is one. [a.] Forestville, MD.

CAVALERI, NICHOLAS

[b.] January 2, 1934, Italy; [p.] Vincenzina and Francesco Cavaleri; [m.] Theresa, September 2, 1956; [ch.] Antoniette, Vincenzina, Francesco, Dominick, Michael and Anthony; [ed.] Magistrate (State College) Locri, Italy; served in the US Army 1953-55 in Korea, honorably discharged as a sargeant; [occ.] Restaurant owner; [memb.] Italian Community Center, Albany, VFW Post 1019; [hon.] Merit diploma, International Diploma of Honor; [oth. writ.] Poems in local newspaper (Times Union), 3 poems published by World of Poetry (1991) and Treasured Poems of America (1994); [pers.] Respect friendship, it is thed substance of life. [a.] Albany, NY.

CELSO, MATTHEW

[b.] December 21, 1973, Dallas; [p.] Joseph and Kathy Celso; [occ.] Offices Assistant at Green Thumb Lawn Care; [pers.] I would like to dedicate this to my Mom, Dad and sister Melissa. I Love you all. Russell, Gene and Melissa at work, thanks for the abuse. Al-inspiration, this ones for you, Ilan (cousin E) Baskin the mie was a joke. MB forever- and hello to the Green Thumb crew. [a.] Plano, TX.

CHAINEY, MARTHA L.

[b.] January 13, 1937, Lynn, MA; [p.] Alexander and Mabel Warden; [m.] Deceased, September 1, 1956; [ch.] Cindy, Hale, Michael Chainey, Darlene Renfrow, Lisa Hardage; [ed.] 2 years college; [occ.] Legal secretary; [memb.] AARP, ASMBA, RCIA, CFC, DCCCD; [hon.] High school honor student two years junior college GPA 3.7, received 3 outstanding performance awards at work, received Editor's Choice award August '94; [oth. writ.] Still working on my novel; [pers.] I am a strong "prolife" advocate and have deep faith that God is in control and I trust in his goodness, compassion, and most importantly his unconditional love for all his beautiful creation. [a.] DeSoto, TX.

CHAPUT, RAYMOND N. JR.

[pen.] The Captain of the World; [b.] November 7, 1941, Willimantic, CT; [p.] Raymond Sr. and Doris Chaput; [ch.] Laura Lee Bradley; [ed.] Windham Regional Tech, St. Mary's, Poetry course at E.O. Smith a Stores CT; [occ.] Housekeeper; [memb.] The World of Poetry, The International Society of Poets; [hon.] Best New Poet of '87 and other Silver '87 and Gold '89, The International Merit Award 1993 and other-In The Desert Sun, did radio station in '93; [oth. writ.] April Love, When Autumn Comes, The Captain of the World, Man of Goldm Summer Ending, etc; [pers.] Today becomes tomorrow, tomorrow becomes today and today tomorrow will soon be today and tomorrow yesterday gone by today's. [a.] Willimantic, CT.

CHASE, ELSA L.

[b.] April 2, 1949, Camden, NJ; [p.] Ervin H. and Marcella D. Chase; [ed.] High school and technical school for drafting; [occ.] Machine Operator, Assembler and Order Packer; [memb.] Lifetime in The International Society of Poets; [hon.] Editor's Awards for poems published by The National Library of Poetry; [oth. writ.] Sam, Blake, Mother, Crystal Hall, Invisible Dreams, Jim (all poems published in bookd by The National Library of Poetry; [pers.] Working on first book of poems to be published along with fathers poems and short stories. Believe in the "Dance of Light" in all of us. [a.] Camden, NJ.

CHEVALIER, MARY SMITHHART

[pen.] Mary S. Chevalier; [b.] November 3, 1929, TX; [p.] Bertha Cox/Auzy Smithhart -both deceased; [m.] Robert Aubrey, June 28, 1946; [ch.] Robert David, Alice Denise, Donna Lynn, Stephen Daniel; [ed.] Joaquin High School, Panola Junior College School of Nursing; [occ.] Homemaker-licensed vocational nurse (ret); [memb.] First Presbyterian Church, former and officer in Daughters of the Republic of Texas; [hon.] Valedictorian 1946 of Joaquin High School class - many nursing awards over a period of 15 years, certificate of merit award (6), honorable mentions (7), Golden Poet awards (5), Gold Medal of Honor 1992, Who's Who in Poetry for 1990, Silver Poet 1990; [oth. writ.] Published in W.O.P.'s "The Great American Anthology" 1988, published article in Rodale's Organic Gardening 1986, published in 1994 NLP's Anthology "Outstanding Poets of 1994" -selected for "The Sound of Poetry" tape; [pers.] Writing poetry is my own personal outlet for the highs or lows. My verse is simple and comes from my heart. It is usually about my family or familiar things. I kept my poems in a folder for years before I let others see them. How surprised I was one day to learn that both my oldest grandchildren were aspiring poets. [a.] Joaquin, TX.

CHI, THOMAS RICHARD

[pen.] Hobbes; [b.] March 10, 1974, Kapiolani Hosp.; [p.] Garret R. and Mira Chi; [ed.] Mililani High School, Leeward Community College; [occ.] Shift manager, Taco Bell; [oth. writ.] One poem to be published in Dark Side of the Moon and two in After The Storm. One poem to be published by Quill Books; [pers.] Stay in school! (Not...) Do whatever is best for you, don't let anyone take control of you!!! Live for tomorrow and not for today. Why ask why! [a.] Mililani, HI.

CHIRIGOS, LISA

[pen.] L.C. Sherwood; [b.] February 8, 1967, IL; [m.] 1989; [ch.] 2 sons; [oth. writ.] Poetry, short stories, working on a novel published with National Library of Poetry; [pers.] My writings vary from one extreme to the next, but it all comes from my heart and soul. It has been my escape my way to show feelings thus the variations. I have been writing for more than 13 years. [a.] Houston, TX.

CHOATE, LAUNICE J.

[pen.] Launice J. Choate; [b.] November 24, 1922, Lexington; [p.] Clifford and Electa Jowers; [m.] Morris (deceased), September 30, 1939; [ch.] Barbara Joyce, Brenda Jean and Betty Jennifer; [ed.] 2 years college; [occ.] Assistant Director of Senior Center; [memb.] Business and Professional Women's Club, Eastern Star, First Baptist Church; [hon.] Honor student in college, Woman of the Year BPW, poems used for church bulletings; [oth. writ.] Just "Poetry" besides a few articles for newspapers; [pers.] My life is dedicated to serving my Lord and Saviour Jesus Christ and this means "family" comes next, then friends and those who need a helping hand. [a.] Lexington, IN.

CHOUDHURY, ALPA
[b.] September 3, 1981, New York, NY; [p.] Aswini Kumar and Neeruj Choudhury; [ed.] St James School, The Melrose; [occ.] Student; [hon.] Editor's Choice Award, National Library of Poetry; [oth. writ.] Several poems in other National Library of Poetry books, Putnam Poets, and Sparrowgrass Poetry Forum Inc; [pers.] Writing poems giving me the chance to say things that I feel in a different way. [a.] Carmel, NY.

CHOWDHURY, JERRY
[b.] July 12, 1938, India; [p.] Azhar and Malina Chaudhri; [m.] Sara Chowdhury, August 8, 1965; [ch.] Jasmine, Cyrus; [ed.] Studied mechanical am nd aerospace engineering in Germany and Canada, licensed professional engineer since 1977; [occ.] Senior engineering specialist; [memb.] National Society of Professional Engineers, Association of Professional Engineers of Ontario, American Society of Mechanical Engineers, American Institute of Aeronauticsd ands Astronautics, American Society for Quality Control, Arizona Society of Professional Engineers, International Society of Poets life member; [hon.] International Poetr of Merit Award, cash award for entry at ISP 1994 contest, many awards for composition, recitation and drama; [oth. writ.] Writing poetry has been a hobbhy since early youth, some published in college magazines, received cash award for contest entry at ISP Convention, selected for "Dark Side of the Moon", technical articles and many contributions to engineering proposals and process descriptions; [pers.] With love, peace, and harmony, we need to live together with all peoples on this planet, understanding with respect for each other's cultures and customs,. For the education of our children we must go for a paradigm shift with emphasis on environment protection. We must learn to love the green lanet, our home. [a.] Mesa, AZ.

CHRISTIE, PHILOMENA
[b.] July 12, 1908, Milwaukee, WI; [hon.] Poetry editors choioces and published; [pers.] Philomena Christie finds the last season of life (86 years, 64 years of marriage) a grateful symbol of God's generosity. Children 2, grandchildren 4, great-grandchildren 4, a fulfillment of continued mores and culture. Reading or writing of poetry a gratifying interest. [a.] MIlwaukee, WI.

CHRISTOFF, ALEX, V.
[b.] Rochester, NY; [p.] Vangel and Helen Christoff (deceased); [m.] Barbara Christoff; [occ.] Wildlife preservationist; [memb.] International Society of Poets, American Legion; [oth. writ.] Published in several anthologies; [pers.] Virtue is illumined from a reflection of the luminous person; evil, emergent monument from the subterranean soul, cl;asps its own brethren., While good suffuses from the universal order, such that, between body and soul lies harmony's keep. [a.] Springwater, NY.

CHURCH, AMANDA
[b.] August 18, 1978; [p.] Robert and Lorrain Church; [ed.] Loyalton High School; [occ.] Student; [memb.] Future Business Leaders of America, 4H, Friday Night Live, Plumas Sierra Literacy Council, Hugh O'Brian Youth Foundation, Block L Athletic Club, CSF; [hon.] Scgolar Athlete 5 times, JV Basketball MVP, 1st Senior Showmanship Swine, Best of Show Photography, N Section California JV Shot Put champ; [oth. writ.] One poem published in At Day's End, many other poems jonored by the Young Writers' Association, won 3rd place in the In Praise of Poertry contest; [pers.] My mind creates my artistic writings unexpectedly and I just put a pen in hand and flow. I always say "write when you are in the mood for your best artworks of literature. [a.] Sattley, CA.

CHVATAL, DONALD P.
[b.] May 14, 1940, Iowa; [ch.] Janet, Judith, Jennifer, Jessica, Joy, [ed.] St. Johns University, MSLS, University of Illinois; [memb.] American Library Assn;

CIMARRUSTI, MARIANNA
[pen.] Angelica; [b.] March 5, 1947; [p.] Frank and Angelina Neverka; [m.] David Cimarrusti, October 15, 1966; [ch.] Jacqueline, Carolyn, James; [ed.] Deerfield High School, floral desing course; [occ.] Flower shop employee; [memb.] Ministry of care to elderly at church parish, catachist for special religious education for disabled at church parish; [oth. writ.] Several poems published in St. Marys Church parish; [pers.] My spiritual prayer poems come from my spiritual experiences. I reflect on the goodness and love bestowed on mankind. The passion for life, and the thread of love pulls us together. [a.] Lake Bluff , IL.

CLARK, CAROLYN A.
[Pen.] Carolyn Abbott; [b.] July 20, 1963, Blountstown; [p.] Jessie J. and Helen J. Abbott; [m.] Darryl W. Clark, June 21, 1981; [ch.] Darryl W. Clark, II; [oth. writ.] Ribbons to My Heart, Heaven Help US All, Music Man; [pers.] Dedicated to my family with all of my love. This makes two for (twooser!) Love You!; [a.] Winter Haven, FL

CLARK, OLIVE I.
[b.] April 2, 1917, Stratford, WI; [ed.] University of Wisconsin, McCormick Seminary; [occ.] Retired teacher; [memb.] Local church organizations; [hon.] Outstanding service awards from several local civic organizations in Waynesboro, VA; [oth. writ.] I have previously had several professional articles published in different publications. Poetry has however been a more recent endeavor, mostly since 1992; [pers.] Since my retirement, I am finding much satisfaction in writing as I feel inspired to do so. I find it an excellent avenue of expression of thought as well as a ministry when shared with others.

CLARK, TOM
[b.] November 8, 19769, Cambridge; [ed.] Emerson College; [a.] Belmont MA.

CLAUSEN, VIOLET V.
[b.] August 1, 1920, Sargent, NE; [p.] Ben and Della Russell; [ch.] Rodney, Carol, Lyle; [ed.] Sargent High, 6 weeks summer school at Kearney; [occ.] Grandmothering; [memb.] VFW Auxiliary; [oth. writ.] My Memoirs and a poem published in the New American Poetry Anthology; [pers.] I try to include in my writings that God is our source. [a.] Stapleton, NE.

CLAYTON, ROBERT
[b.] December 1, 1929, Sidney, OH.

CLERIN, CLAUDETTE LAURE
[pen.] Claudette Aubert; [b.] May 31, 1921, Marseille, France; [p.] Andre' and Elizabeth Excoffon; [m.] L. Roland Clerin (divorced); [ch.] David, Peter, Andre, Esther and grandchildren; [ed.] Lycee Longchamp in Marseille; [occ.] Retired; [oth. writ.] Songs unpublished for which I wrote both words and music in French and English; [pers.] I have been greatly influenced by my uncle Philippe greatly influenced by my Uncle Philippe Excoffon in Marseille who wrote "Madame De Lavalliere" in verses of twelve feet (Alexandrins) He was awarded for it the French honor (Prix Jean Aicard). My parents loved poetry and I studied, many wonderful poets both in French and in English. My mother wrote poetry and a book. [a.] Miami, FL.

COBB, JESSIE S.
[b.] October 2, 1912, Orlando, FL; [p.] Mr. and Mrs. James Samuel Evans; [m.] Wiltie Delmus Vogt, December 29, 1929; [ch.] Virginia Carlisle, William Delmus Vogt; [occ.] Retired; [memb.] Holden Heights Chamber of Commerce, Lucerne Baptist Church, Pat Roberson Coalition; [hon.] Three ribbon swimming Australian Crawl back stroke-free stroke; [oth. writ.] Poetry, local paper and church paper; [pers.] I strive to reflect my life and thoughts on paper as to the creation of God's holy spirit working in my uttermost being, me heart, mind and soul. [a.] Orlando, FL.

CODY, BARBARA LEE
[pen.] Barbara Lee Cody; [b.] September 28, 1925, Pigua, OH; [p.] Deceased; [m.] George F., July 8, 1969; [ch.] 5 stepchildren; [ed.] High school; [occ.] Housewife; [memb.] Englewood Methodist Church; [oth. writ.] A small collection of unpublished poems inspired by high school English teacher; [pers.] Next to God look at the world through the eyes of little children. [a.] Englewood, IL.

COEN, ELEANOR BYRNE
[p.] Edward and Ella Byrne; [m.] Thomas F., 1950; [ch.] Thomas, Mary, Joseph, Theresa, Larry and Christopher; [pers.] A teacher in school told us that we affect everyone we meet - either good or bad - hope, my affect is good. [a.] Newton, MA.

COFFMAN, HEATHER LYNN
[b.] April 20, 1971, Klamath Falls, OR; [p.] Lynn and Shirley Coffman; [ed.] DAyton High, Tongue Point, Job Corps, Clastslop Community College; [occ.] Baker's Assistant; [memb.] International Society of Poets; [oth. writ.] Published in Rain Magazine and The Coming of Dawn by The National Library of Poetry; [pers.] I thank my parents and my sister Michelle. They are my inspiration in life and in everything I do, by reminding me there is always hope and tomorrow is new! [a.] Medford, OR.

COHEN, MARGIE
[b.] December 15, 1948, Denver, CO; [p.] Ed and Jane Murray; [m.] Larry, September 10, 1970; [ch.] Jeremy; [ed.] Denver University; [occ.] Sales Manager-U.S. West; [hon.] World of Poetry-Honorable Mention Certificate "Arrival" and "Dreams", World of Poetry Award of Merit "Another Chance", World of Poetry Golden Poet Award "ARrival", Who's Who in Poetry; [oth. writ.] Selected works for our World's Best Poets-"Arrival" and "My Mother", Archive of the Arts-Feelings of the Past "A Tie of Loyalty", Poetic Voices of America"Arrival", "A Passing Dream", "Bond of Love", Mile High Poetry-Helcion "Dreams", National Library of Poetry Outstanding Poets of 1994 - "Another Chance," Today's Great Poems-"Arrival"; [pers.] My poems all contain deep feelings about humanity, family and personal goals. [a.] Englewood, CO.

COHEN, MARTIN A.
[b.] January 1, 1968, Rome, NY; [ed.] Columbia University, Penn State University, Hamilton College; [occ.] Student, Cardozo Law School, Yeshiva University; [hon.] Kappa Delta Pi, 1993 and 1993 Palis Cohanne Award, 1989 Wallace Bradley Johnson Playwriting Prize. [a.] Rockville Centre, NY.

COLE, ANITA H.
[pen.] Anita H. Cole; [b.] November 4, 1924, Lebanon, NH; [p.] Leonard and Doris Hart; [m.] Richard A., May 29, 1943; [ch.] Dennis Richard and Stephen Leonard; [ed.] South High School, Fitchburg State Teachers, Flitchburg Hospital School of Nursing; [occ.] Retired-Administrative, Mental Health Agency; [memb.] St. Francis Episcopal Church, church lecturer, past president The Listening Ear, past president Marlboro Westboro Mental Health Association, board member Trinity Mental Health Association; [hon.] for 10 years of management/founding of first hotline in the Northeast "The Listening Ear", Valley Forge honor certificate for "Letter to the Editor", Freedom Foundation awards - 3 years in a row for working for the dignity of mankind, literacy certificate helping Americans to read; [oth. writ.] Several published poems - area newspapers - college magazine - audio cassettes - "Golden Treasury of Great Poems", articles in area newspapers - National Library of Poetry book; [pers.] It once occurred to me that I was somebody's daughter; then somebody's wife; then somebody's mother, but never me. Then, through my son's sacrifice of his life for his country I realized I had a responsibility as a person to become 'somebody' in love - in song - in memory. [a.] Princeton, MA.

COLEMAN, AURA W.
[b.] April 7, 1907, Dover, ME; [p.] Will and Edith Coleman; [m.] Ida Hills, April 18, 1931; [ch.] Ronald Hills Coleman and Robert Will Coleman; [ed.] Kennebunk High School, Bates College, Harvard graduate study; [occ.] Retired, Education 43 years; [memb.] Past president Rotary Club, past master Masonic Lodge, Past president N.E. Association Superintendent of Schools; [hon.] Participated in a study tour of the German Education system in West Germany sponsored by the US Department of Education. Talk on the ungraded elementary schools at The American Association of School Association; [oth. writ.] Many articles and perio; [pers.] "Reflections" - So much to do, so little done; so much unfinished, that's begun; my work from dawn to setting sun, makes serious thought, a foolish pun.

COLEMAN, RUTH
[b.] February 27, 1933, Oak Park, IL; [p.] Ruth and Ruben Coleman; [ed.] BS and master's degree; [occ.] Retired; [memb.] Sinsinawa Dominican Sister; [oth. writ.] Awesome Autumn; [pers.] I am impressed with nature and words seem to flow easily when I am touched.

COMBS, ADDIE
[b.] September 1, 1916, Breathitt Co, KY; [p.] Thomas and Laura Francis; [m.] Cecil; [ch.] Wilma Combs Rice, Glen Kash Combs; [ed.] BS degree, taught school 29 years. [a.] Campton, KY.

CONANT, DONNA D.
[b.] August 21, 1939, Compton, CA; [p.] Virginia and Bernard Oswalt; [ch.] Richard Jensen, Wendy White; [ed.] BA, MArt, MMOR in English; [occ.] Teacher; [memb.] SDA Church, SBTA, Coordinator of International Togetherness Day, Salvation Army board member, Women's Auxiliary Salvation Army; [hon.] Cadremember CA Literature Project; [oth. writ.] "I Can't Jump" Guide Magazine, "Double Miracle" Guide Magazine, various poems, stories, newspaper articles; [pers.] The world can be a better place because of the personal impact of individuals who care and who express their caring in creative ways. [a.] Highland, CA.

CONANT, RALPH
[b.] December 17, 1944, Jacksonville, FL; [p.] Gilman and Kathryn Conant; [m.] Divorced; [ch.] W.W.C.; [oth. writ.] This One is For You, John Denver, Just A Feeling, A Brush With The Sands, Working Beauty.

COOK, CURTIS A.
[b.] June 9, 1916, Newport, KY; [p.] Manuel and Zorah Cook; [m.] Dolore L. (deceased), July 20, 1939; [ch.] Kenneth A. Cook; [ed.] Newport Public High; [occ.] Retired; [memb.] Fort Thomas Retired Mens Club, St. John United Church of Christ; [hon.] Kentucky Colonel by former Gov. Ford, named in Who's Who in Kentucky 1967, played violin in high school orchestra, sang in Cincinnati May Festival Chorus 2 years; [oth. writ.] "Tennessee Maneuvers", "Reflections of Our Religious Lives" and other personal poems not published; [pers.] All youth school stay in school and get as much education as possible. Parents will early notice talents of children. Finance them and have children develop them, then when greater opportunities come in later life they'll be ready and reap the rewards. [a.] Fort Thomas, KY.

COOK, LOIS E.
[b.] February 21, 1935, Bham, AL; [p.] Samual and Minnie Springer; [m.] Robert D., May 23, 1962; [ch.] Aaron Scott and Donna Ann; [occ.] Relianvce Electric Co; [memb.] International Society of Poets, Chestnut Mtn Baptist Church; [hon.] Several poet of merit awards, several Editor's Choice awards, two golden poet awards; [oth. writ.] Two novels, unpublished, one completed book of poems as yet unpublished, several songs. Two have been published some poems published in the local paper; [pers.] I try to write about what is happening in the world we live in. I write about love and hope it will help make someone stop and think, about how they can help to make it better. [a.] Gainesville, GA.

COOK, SANDRA BERGEN
[b.] January 29, 1960, Miami, FL; [p.] Judd and Elouise Bergen; [m.] Todd William, May 15, 1993; [ch.] First child due Dec. 1, 1994; [ed.] Southwest Senior High, Miami Dade Community College-South; [occ.] Homemaker, Orchid hobbyist with husband; [memb.] South Dade Amateur Orchid Society; [hon.] Dean's List, awards of merit for English Literature and Composition, Editor's Choice award; [oth. writ.] Oh Blessed Sleep - published in forthcoming. "At Days End" by National Library of Poetry; [pers.] I would like to thank my husband for giving me the courage and confidence to finally go ahead with my writing. [a.] Miami, FL.

COOK SR., LARRY W.
[b.] February 20, 1952, Aiken, SC; [p.] Gertrude Price; [m.] May 25, 1976/divorced; [ch.] Larry W. Cook Jr., Kristie N. Cook and Jason M. Cook; [ed.] 1 1/2 years college, Richmond Academy High School, Aiken Tech College; [occ.] Unemployed; [memb.] National Rehabilitation Association, Dixie Youth Baseball; [hon.] Dean's List; [oth. writ.] The poem-Women-puiblished by you in 1994; [pers.] My poems are based on personal experiences and the people I know. They are my way of expressing feelings I otherwise could not express. [a.] Warrenville, SC.

COOPER, ISABEL S.
[pen.] Isabel S. Cooper; [b.] New York, NY; [ed.] State University of New York at Purchase, Queens College; [occ.] Sculptor, Free-lance writer, art historian; [memb.] College Art Association of America, National League of American Pen Women, New York Artists Wquity; [hon.] Listed in Encyclopedia of Living Artists in America, 5th edition 1990, page 88; Thesis in archives of the Library and Research Center, of the National Museum of Women in the Arts, Wash., DC, awards for stone sculpture; [oth. writ.] Several articles published in Westchester Art News. Essay published in Village Views. Poems published in Wind in the Night Sky. In The Desert Sun, and Outstanding Poets of 1994; [pers.] In both my sculpture and my writings, I strive to express the universal themes of the joys and sufferings of life. [a.] Rye Brook, NY.

CORNELIUS, VIRGINIA A.
[b.] November 8, 1928, Waukesha, WI; [oth. writ.] Children's stories for children's hospitals. Christmas stories for children's hospital - published in local newspaper - poem untitled National Library of Poetry. "Wind in the Night Sky" - poem National Library of Poetry "In The Desert Sun".

CORNWELL, MELVIN G.
[b.] March 19, 1929, Sterling, UT; [p.] George and Elda Cornwell; [m.] Joy M. Marley Jones, November 10, 1951; [ch.] Kathleen and Michael M.; [ed.] College GED, US Army, 8 years of formal schooling; [occ.] Retired; [memb.] Veteran of Foreign Wars, American Legion and The Retired Enlisted Association; [hon.] Military Legion of Merit, Purple Heart and 9 others; [oth. writ.] Have written many but only one published; [pers.] Sentiment and fantasy play a great part in my poems. But real life is always the bottom line. [a.] Mt. Pleasant, UT.

CORY, LINDA MARLENE
[b.] August 20, 1960, IL; [p.] Donald and Teresa Cory; [occ.] Teacher; [memb.] Christian Children's Fund; [pers.] Dedicated to my Father, who inspired a love for music in me, that influenced my interest in poetry, as both reveal rhythm and beauty. [a.] Barrington, IL.

CONSTANTINI, ALICE
[b.] February 19, 1923, New York, NY; [p.] Louis A, and Marion Herman Berg; [m.] Divorced; [ch.] J. Peter, Franklin David, and Thomas Jeffrey Constantini; [ed.] Hunter College of The City of New York, American University, Montclair State College, and City College School of Architecture; [occ.] Painter and Fabric Collagist from Murals to Miniatures; [hon.] Phi Beta Kappa, Sigma Tau Delta (National Writer's Fraternity), many art awards and shows; [oth. writ.] Some poetry published in small (now defunct) literary quarterlies, early planning of a first novel. [a.] New York, NY.

COUGHLIN, MARY M.
[b.] June 30, 1908, Detroit, MI; [p.] William and Martha McCarthy; [m.] George F. Coughlin, June 27, 1953; [ed.] BA Marygrove College 1931, Detroit, MI, MA Wayne State Univ, 1940, Detroit, MI, Teacher's Life Cert of MI and numerous courses in the field of art education; [memb.] I was invited to become a member of the Beta Sigma Phi Fellowship upon earning an MA (1940) - An active member of many art associations in MI and Florida over the years. Presently a sponsoring member of the Charlotte County Art Guild of Punta Gorda, FL and the Guild Century Club - A life member of the MI Assoc of Retired School Personnel - member of the Char-Sota Assoc (The Flor Chap of MARSP) - Member of the Republican Legion of Merit (1992) - An active member in a number of church groups; [hon.] The Veterans of Foreign Wars presented me with their prestigious American Citizenship medal upon my retirement from the Detroit School System. My name is engraved on it. - One of my most cherished honors was being invited to become a Charter Lifetime Member of the Int'l Society of Poets in 1993. I was presented with a beautiful American flag as a member of the 1992 Presidential Task Force. Each star is embroidered. - I have received numerous awards and ribbons as a member of many art assoc. in MI and FL; [oth. writ.] Poems were accepted for publication by the World of Poetry of Sacramento, CA in their book entitled Selected Works of Our World's Best Poets and poems were accepted for publication by the American Poetry Assoc of Santa Cruz, CA to be included in their book entitled American Poetry Anthology Vol X. Poems have been published in many anthologies by the National Library of Poetry and in three of their special books entitled The Best Poems of the 90's, Distinguished Poets of America and Outstanding Poets of 1994. Those invited to submit poems for these books are rated among the top 2% by the judges of the National Library of Poetry. Many articles have been published on the subject of child guidance over the years; [pers.] Throughout my entire life time I have loved the beauties of nature whether it might be the ever changing cloud-filled sky by day or the star-studded sky by night. In my poetry I try to encourage others to notice the beauties of the world about them, to smile readily, to count their blessings and to share their God-given gifts with others. Above all I try to show gratefulness to God for His goodness. Such things, I believe, lead to true happiness, which is what I wish most of all for myself and for those I love; [a.] Port Charlotte, FL

COURTNEY, L. MARTIN II
[b.] December 7, 1917, NY, NY; [p.] L. Martin and Flossie M. Courtney; [m.] Madelyn T., December 28, 1985; [ch.] L. Martin Courtney III, John Robert Randolph, Madelyn B. Goble; [ed.] 3 years college plus several special courses; [occ.] Retired; [memb.] Chairman Advisory Board Foster Grandparents, Retired Senior Volunteers board member, Chaplain Ohio State Council of Senior Citizens, Secty Northwest Ohio Gerontological Association, Chmn Anti-Crime Program, Advisor Cmte Adult Day Care Program, President Trustees Advisory Board Transportation, Disabled American Veterans; [hon.] One of Toledo's ten outstanding yound men 1952; [oth. writ.] Poem Yank Magazine, poetry, short story and columns Army newspapers WWII; poetry post war in Toledo Blade and Pittsburgh Post Gazette newspapers; University Toledo Poetry contest; article for Model R.R. magazine; recently completed children's story - not published yet; [pers.] What have I done for God today! What can I do; what am I willing to do? [a.] La Canada Flintridge, CA.

COVALT, GINGER YATES
[b.] July 3, 1943, Hawaii; [p.] F. Gordon and Annabelle J. Yates; [m.] Wendell, March 24, 1992; [ch.] Erika and Leif Bradly Cobain; [ed.] University of Nevada Las Vegas, Colombia University, Cornell University, post graduate studies in Yoga Fundeu Suddha Peeth, India; [occ.] Dental Hygiene; [memb.] League of Women Voters, American Dental Hygiene Association; [hon.] Competitor and metalist in rough water ocean swimming competitions, Editor's Choice award 1994; [pers.] In my journey to realize and be life's truth writing poetry crystalizes my ever expanding awareness. Sometimes to see and often to mark a transforming shift. [a.] Redondo Beach, CA.

COWAN, FRANK B.
[b.] February 27, 1979, Atlanta, GA; [p.] Michae and Janet Gowan; [ed.] in 10th grade; [hon.] Presidential Academic Award; [oth. writ.] Article published in local paper; [pers.] When the opportunity arises take it, don't wait.

COWAN, JAMES M.
[pen.] The Traveler; [b.] February 17, 1948, Chickasha, OK; [p.] David and Marie Cowan; [m.] Loretta, November 22, 1992; [ch.] Carry, Michael, Candace, Terri Jean and Jeff; [ed.] 13; [occ.] 13 & 13 Ranch in HI; [memb.] Military Order of Purple Heart, Disabled American Vets, Veterans of Foreign Wars, AMVETS; [hon.] Silver Star (3) Purple Hearts - 7 Bronze stars, 2 air medals army recommendation; [oth. writ.] The Spirit Song, Lightning; [pers.] There is no place I would rather be; than where I am now. [a.] Kamuela, HI.

COX, VERNON
[pen.] Mrs. George J. Doyle; [b.] August 23, 1908, Tennesee; [p.] Walter H. Cox and Annie Mae Bennett; [m.] George J. Doyle, June 17, 1934 (divorced 1947); [ch.] Mary Karin, Walter Edward, William Allen, Dennis Lee; [ed.] High school, U.C. Berkeley, UCLA, Cal State, LA City College; [occ.] Retired; [memb.] Honor roll, drama and glee club, Methodist church choir, PTA, horseback club, Sierra Club, AAUW, NSA; [hon.] Third place horseback riding, numerous ribbons for cooking and sewing; [oth. writ.] Several magazines articles, newspaper columnist and society editor, one poem published in England, numerous poetry awards; [pers.] I am very philosophical and people-oriented. I have little patience with crybabies and moochers. The world owes you nothing-few exceptions. A man has a right to be born free. A baby has a right to be born to two loving parents. If you want something, go for it! Don't waste time nor things. Find your own guidelines. Work and play. Fun rejuvenates and helps maintain emotional equilibrium. [a.] hacienda heights, CA.

CRAWFORD-MARTIN, REGINA
[b.] August 16, 1967, Wheeling, WV; [p.] I. Gene and Valeria A. Crawford; [m.] Garr W., August 31, 1991; [ch.] Tyra M. Byrd and Akilah R. Martin; [ed.] Central State University; [occ.] Systems Engineer; [memb.] Easter Seal Association; [hon.] Who's Who Among American High School Students, United States Achievement Academy, All-American Year Book, Presidential Academic Fitness Award; [oth. writ.] Untitled poem published in Dance on the Horizon (1993), Rags to Riches A Trilogy Part 1 published in Echoes of Yesterday 1994. [a.] Garland, TX.

CRISS, RAVEN DOUGLAS
[b.] June 1, Norfolk, VA; [p.] John and Joice Foreman; [ch.] Melinda-Catherine; [ed.] Chariko Regional-Vocational High School, Community College of Rhode Island 1993; [memb.] Society of Young Victims, National Council for Missing or Exploited Children; [hon.] Bronze medal, National VICA Competition - prepared Speech American Poetry Anthology, 1982; [oth. writ.] "LIke the Wind" published in The American Poetry Anthology. I'm currently working on my second book of original poetry, the first "Flight of a Raven", having been released in July 1994; [pers.] Life is not as harsh as black or white, it is the subtleties of gray that make it worth living. Because I love you Jeff, thanks for all of your "blind" faith in me. Rob - you are all there is, and someday you will understand why. [a.] West Kingston, RI.

CRONEN, NATASHA
[b.] October 15, 1994, MN; [p.] Betty and Jerry Cronen; [ed.] High school; [occ.] Student; [memb.] FFA, 4-H, Church Youth Group, Peer Helpers; [hon.] FFA, Treasurer-Star Greenhand - Scholarship, 4-H Ambassador; church youth group - president; [oth. writ.] "Flight" and "Never Coming Back" both published in the National Library of Poetry. [a.] Montevideo, MN.

CRUZ, JOHN B.
[b.] March 22, 1917, Guam; [p.] Antonio and Nicholas G. Cruz; [m.] Margaret E. Henry, August 4, 1947; [ch.] Marsha Ann, John Joseph and Valerie A. Cruz; [ed.] 7th grade attended eveing classes in order to get my diploma and then to college for 2 years; [occ.] Retired; [memb.] Legion of Mary, Third Order of Mary; [hon.] Golden Poetry award by "World of Poetry" at the 3-day convention at Anaheim, CA in Aueust of 1988; [oth. writ.] Letters to the Editor, Wash. DC Daily News 1954, Sat. Eve. Post 1956, letter to President Reagan with a reply commending him with the ability to have the other nations help us at "Desert Storm" 1991; [pers.] Since my younger days I always have this deep compassion to help my fellow man both mentally and physically whenever I can. I always look for goodness in other people. [a.] Sprine Valley, CA.

CRUZ, KEVIN
[b.] Januarey 13, 1973, LaJolla, CA; [p.] Joe and Cheri Cruz; [ed.] California State University-Fullerton; [memb.] Phi Kappa Tau Fraternity, Gamma Omicron chapter; [oth. writ.] Untitled previously published in A Question of Balance. My current interest lie within short stories and evolving my writing skills; [pers.] Life is a matter of the heart. It's an opportunity to contribute and create. Destruction is all too easy. [a.] Fullerton, CA.

CRUZ, PATSY IZURA
[pen.] Izura; [b.] October 14, 1936, Oakland, CA; [p.] Lorenzo and Edna Wade (dec); [m.] Robert Cruz, October 28, 1978; [ch.] Seven children; [ed.] High school, 1-1/2 years college, journalism workshop; [occ.] Activity director for the elderly and social service; [memb.] Eastern Star, Togetherness Social Club, volunteer at Jefferson Park; [hon.] World of

Poetry, Golden Poet 1992,. Great Poems of Our Time, The National Library of Poetry, New York 1991,tv coverage; [oth. writ.] "Did You Say Hello Today", "Yes, I Can" Sammy Davis Jr, "My Bum, MY Hippie and I"; [pers.] I write because I am happy, I write because I am free but most of all I need to be me. I dedicate my influence of writing with life, to myself for being by self. [a.] Oakland CA.

CULLEN, JAMES C.
[b.] January 10, 1963, Hartford, CT; [p.] Elizabeth A. Doyle and Thomas M. Cullen; [ed.] Conard High School; [occ.] Clerk; [hon.] The National Library of Poetry, Editor's Choice Award; [oth. writ.] I have had only one other poem published. It's titled, "Letting Go"; [a.] West Hartford, CT.

CUMBIE, CHRISTY
[b.] March 26, 1941, Belleville, IL; [m.] Jim Cumbie, July 29, 1967; [ch.] Cecelia, Dennis, Randy, granddaughter, Halley; [ed.] Waco High School, Paris Junior College, various courses for further continuing adult education; [occ.] Christian poet, Meals on Wheels volunteer; [memb.] Highland Park Presbyterian Church; [oth. writ.] Poewms published in six anthologies, two newsleters, private publications, personal publication and distribution of chap book; [pers.] I am proud of my talent, but my pride is in my God for giving me such a beautiful way to work for HIm: leading lost souls to their eternal resting place. This is exciting to me every day as I speak from my heart on paper, in rhyme. We all need help, we all need support, we al need love; and we all have God, but we don't al know it yet. [a.] Dallas, TX.

CUNNINGHAM, MELISSA E.
[b.] February 2, 1977, Lochport, NY; [p.] Lewie and Patsy Cunningham; [ed.] High school, nursing student; [oth. writ.] One poem published in The Desert Sun; [a.] Lochport, NY.

CURCIO, KAREN
[b.] May 3, 1939, Oregon; [m.] Philip, February 8, 1958; [ch.] Diane DeLorme, Steve Curcio; [ed.] Mclaughlin Union HIgh; [occ.] Retired insurance representative; [memb.] Lake County Humane Society, Humane Society of U.S., National Wildlife Federation, Defenders of Wildlife, Humane Farming Assoc., EnvironmentalDefense Fund; [hon.] Editor's Choice Award, The National Library of Poetry 1994, High School Honnor Society, editor of high school paper; [oth. writ.] Small stories in environmental and animal defenders publications and magazines; [pers.] I beleive no issue is more important to the future of wildlife and our environment than to protect and preserve the wildlife and environment. [a.] Two Harbors, MN.

CURRY, MICHELE
[b.] February 7, 1963, Toronto; [p.] Catherine MacDonald and Ronald G. Curry; [m.] Andy Higgins; [ch.] Jasmes Paul, Christopher David, Catherine Margaret; [ed.] Durham College; [memb.] Canadian Autrhors Association; [pers.] I want to live an echo's life, that hangs upon the air, to haunt the average thinker, and cause the soul some prayer. [a.] Boewmanville, Ontario.

DAVIS, ADRIENNE
[b.] July 14, Philadelphia; [p.] Kenneth F. and Ethel F. David; [ed.] New Mexico State University; [occ.] Writer, Boening Support Services. [a.] Seattle, WA.

DAVIS, EMILIE M.
[ed.] Colorado State University; [pers.] To Aunt Edie for teaching me to love poetry and to my husband, Eric, for loving me and believing in me; thank you.

DAVIS, FLOYD E. II
[pen.] Floyd E. Davis II; [b.] April 17, 1928, Cleburne, TX; [p.] Floyd E. and Anna L. Davis; [m.] Joann Davis, May 26, 1979; [ch.] Cynthia Dawn, Mark Alan, Robert Adale, Stephen Floyd; [ed.] Texas Christian University; [occ.] Retired Railroad; [memb.] NRA/ILA, AARP, Goodsam Camper, North American Hunting Club, National Library of Poetry, United Methodist Church; [hon.] Golden Poet Award from 1987-1993, Editor's Choice award 1994, honorable discharge US Army WWII, 10 years as Scout and Cub Master, concert violin with Institute of Educational Music; [oth. writ.] Epic poem of the Aleutian Campaign, short stories, book length exhortation "Towers of Babel" songs, words and music. Two poems published in World of Poetry Anthology; [pers.] I write poetry with a moral quote: We see our faults more clearly in others. [a.] Arlington, TX.

DAVIS, LOIS KAHL
[pen.] Lois Kahl Davis; [b.] November 21, 1909, Burr, NE; [p.] Gustave Julius Kahl; [m.] Lois Ethel Bassett, June 19, 1941; [ch.] Jacquelyn Lois Hinson, Dr. Edward Hale Davis, Daniel Lon Davis; [ed.] Bryan Memorial Hospital, Wesleyann and Nebraska University; [occ.] Retired taught Rockford Country school; [memb.] Austin Poetry Society, Poetry Society of Texas lifemember, First Cumberland Presbyterian Church, Chancel choir, Care Givers, Love in Action; [hon.] Took many 1st, 2nd and 3rd place awards in the Austin Poetry Societies monthly contests and in their annual award contests; [oth. writ.] A book: The White Dove Divine, contributed to Anthology "Poetry classical and contemporary"; The American Statesman, Missionary Messenger, Austin visitor and Cumberland Presbyterian Magazine; [pers.] Did private duty nursing for several years and was a school nurse in the Lincoln Nebr. schools for nine years. Did hospital nursing in San Antonio, and in Austin. Then worked for Dr. Wilborn, a pediatrician. [a.] Austin, TX.

DAVIS, ROBBIE
[b.] November 5, 1949, Montgomery, AL; [p.] Edwin and Robbie McLaughlin; [m.] Au "Butch", November 28, 1969; [ch.] Katherine Leigh Davis and Kelli Lynn Davis; [ed.] Terry Parker High School; [occ.] Rural Mail Carrier; [oth. writ.] Other unpublished writings; [pers.] Life is but a step in time - live it one day at a time - feeling it with love, hope and faith. [a.] Jacksonville, FL.

DEAN, HUBERT E.
[b.] February 9, 1912, London, Eng.; [p.] Edward H. and Edith S. Dean; [m.] Marguerite K., November 6, 1965; [ch.] Peter, Anthony, Philip Dean; Robert King; Susan Eberle; [ed.] Woodhouse Grove School, Yorks Eng.; Imperial College of Science and Technology; [occ.] Author; [memb.] Imperial College Gliding Club, Imperial College "22" Club, RAF Club, RAF Yacht Club, British Officers Club of New England, Rotary Club of Branford, CT; [hon.] Air Force Cross (RAF) for test flying Legion of Merit (Officer Class) U.S.A. for joint air weapons development work in WWII; [oth. writ.] Druids' Circle Forward firing weapons development as senior RAF test pilot and combat instructor in N. Africa and Normandy. Northwest Pub. Inc. late 1994 Essays: e.g. The Sea & The Air; The Anatomy of Comparison. Poems: Yesterday's Hurricane. [a.] Indian Harbor Beach, FL.

DEARDUFF, HELEN M.
[pen.] Duffy; [b.] January 1, 1920, New Castle, IN; [p.] Both deceased; [ed.] Public school in Harford City; [occ.] Retired; [memb.] Volunteer work at hospital and sang for 21 years with Singing Secretary been to 3 conventions; [hon.] Won poetry contest as top awards; [oth. writ.] I enjoyed stringing these beads for you. Some are silver, some are gold. Some are black and some are blue. Treat them with tender care and I'll guarantee you'll have them for your grandchildren to see.

DEARSON, JEAN L.
[pen.] Patter by Pixe; [b.] North Carolina; [p.] Mary Stevens and Walter Spruill; [m.] 1945; [ch.] Jerry Dearson; [ed.] High school, business training and art school; [occ.] Retired; [hon.] For scripts for television and stage - World of Poetry; [oth. writ.] For edited local paper, plays for school; [pers.] Am an avid nature lover. Love the good music of the big band era, love to dance and have done some modeling. Love children, animals and people. [a.] Apple Valley, CA.

DEAVER, FRANCES
[pen.] Frances Roberson Deaver; [b.] August 18, 1927, Cleveland, GA; [p.] Carl and Willie Jane Freeman; [m.] Cecil, June 18, 1984; [ch.] Michael David Roberson and Carol Childress (stepdaughter); [ed.] Cleveland High School, Massey Business College; [occ.] Retired; [memb.] Parkway Baptist Church, WBCCI, Airstream Club; [oth. writ.] Book of Poetry "Valley of the Clouds"; [pers.] I try to convey to others my love for Christ for He is the one that inspires me to write. [a.] Jonesboro, GA.

DELEURME, RITA E.
[b.] October 31, 1965, Kelowna, BC; [p.] Roger and Irene Deleurme; [ch.] Edward Tricoteus, Rita-Marie Tricoteux; [ed.] Okanagan University College; [occ.] Special Needs worker and student; [oth. writ.] Published in Anthology entitled "A Far Off Place". Have poems published in local newspapers and magazines. I also write and do art for children's books; [pers.] I dedicate my work to my deceased sister Edith who has been a fountain of encouragement. My late father, Roger, my 2 children, and my best friend Peter C.

DESBIENS, CHRISTOPHER A.
[pen.] Mad Poet; [b.] June 21, 1970, Los Angeles, CA; [m.] Mother of Gina: Penny Dean; [ch.] Gina Kay DesBiens; [occ.] Cook-Bartender; [hon.] Golden Poet Award 1988-94, 2 honorable mentions 1988 and 1990, 2 achievement awards 1989 and 1991; [oth. writ.] Published in several other variety poetry books; [pers.] To live a life full of love, to protect and care for my daughter, to find my heart and soul again in truth. [a.] Tucson, AZ.

DESPATHY, JAMIE
[b.] July 8, 1976, Putnam, CT; [p.] Gerald Despathy and Wanda Linton; [ed.] Plainfield High School; [occ.] CVS Pharmacy full-time; [hon.] Being published for two poems, Norwich Bulletin profile for my accomplishments in poetry; [oth. writ.] "Beaches"

published in A Break in the Clouds and The Space Between "What Is My Destination" also published in The Space Between. Many other poems written, but not published; [pers.] Just on the spirit of the moment, one sentence comes to mind. I grab a pen and paper and it just flows. It releases feelings and thoughts I never knew existed. [a.] Wauregan, CT.

DEUTSCH, LAWRENCE IRA
[b.] June 17, 1939, Brooklyn, NY; [p.] Meyer and Lillian Deutsch; [m.] Karol W., December 31, 1987; [ch.] Jason Lester, Sharlette Lester; [ed.] Brooklyn College, Calvary Bible College and Seminary, Cornerstone University; [occ.] Messianic Rabbi Congregation Beth Ha'Shem; [memb.] Songwriters Club of America, Messianic Jewish Alliance of America, American Association of Christian Counselor; [hon.] International Silver Poets Award, International Golden Poets Award, Hall of Fame, World of Poetry, Who's Who World Poetry, Who's Who in Religion; [oth. writ.] Satan's Lair, Your Treasured Love, Love's Sweet Melody, The Mystery of the Cloth, New American Poetry Anthology, To The Messiah With Love - an original songbook, Messianic; [pers.] You should like what you believe, and believe what you live. [a.] Deer Park, TX.

DIAZ-CLARK, ANNISA MARIA
[b.] June 22, 1978, Greenbre, CA; [p.] Mary Louise Diaz-Clark; [ed.] San Rafael High School; [occ.] Student; [memb.] San Rafael Key Club, P.E.A.C.E. Club, FNL Club, St. Rapheal Church, Varsity Softball and Volleyball, J.V. Basketball; [hon.] Scholar Athlete award, James B. Davidson lifetime honor roll, Math Honors student; [oth. writ.] Why? Echoes of Yesterday. Other poems and short stories - unpublished; [pers.] A teacher and friend once told me: "Friendships are necessities, not luxuries". I've found that these words are very true because for me, my friends are like air and I can't live without them. I love you guys. [a.] San Rafael, CA.

DICKSON, DOROTHY
[b.] March 21, 1911, Cameron; [p.] Delbert and Ida Lewis; [m.] Leo (deceased), June 21, 1933; [ch.] Lang, Jay, Phil and Sharon; [ed.] Haverling High, Geneseo State Teacher's College; [occ.] Retired school teacher 25 years; [memb.] Risingville Meth Church, Past matron Cameron Mills OES, AARP, NYSTR Teachers Association, Stew Co. Past Matron Association; [hon.] Poems published by "The National Library of Poets", being remembered as a "favorite teacher" by past students; [oth. writ.] Have been writing poems for some 40 years but only published by National Library of Poetry; [pers.] Poetry is a release of emotions left, put on paper causing less tears to flow. [a.] Cameron Mills, NY.

DICKSON, RUBY JEAN
[pen.] Ruby Jones; [b.] March 31, 1943, Texarkana, TX; [p.] Elmer Jones and Nellie Sanders; [m.] Russell, August 24, 1994; [ch.] Bridgette, Edward, Stephanie, Byron, Charles, Blenda, Wanda, Ricky, Russell Jr. Lewis; [ed.] Dunbar High, Pikes Peaks Junior College; [occ.] Housewife and writer; [oth. writ.] Several books published in the National Baptist Publishing Board's Catalogue; [pers.] My purpose for writing is to comfort and encourage believers and to reach unbelievers. [a.] Texarkana, AR.

DILE, GEORGE MICHAEL
[pen.] George Michael Dile; [b.] February 3, 1947, OH; [p.] Bernard and Joan Dile; [m.] Yvonne T., June 28, 1980; [ch.] Noel T. Dile, Muffin; [ed.] Antelope Valley High School, Antelope Valley College, CA State University of Long Beach, Los Angeles Harbor College; [occ.] Singer, songwriter, arranger, creative writer; [memb.] International Society of Poets/Honorary Charter member, Veterans of Foreign Wars, San Pedro Post, Rolling Hills Covenant Church choir member; [hon.] Graduated from CA State University of Long Beach on the Dean's honor list, Golden Poet award 1990 and 1991 from World of Poetry; [oth. writ.] Several poems published, several songs copyrighted. I am currently working on a book called "The Silent Forest" and hope to have it published soon; [pers.] C.S. Lewis said, "Let the (mental) pictures tell their own moral. For the moral inherent in them will arise from whatever spiritual roots you have succeeded in striking during the whole course of your life." I would have to agree. [a.] San Pedro, CA.

DILWORTH, FLORENCE CHISHOLM
[b.] July 26, 1950, Littlefork, MN; [p.] Colin and Helene Chisholm; [m.] Special Love-Lee Harvey; [ch.] Christianne, Andrea, George; [ed.] Bachelor of Science; [occ.] Dispatcher/Jailer/Koochiching County Sheriffs Dept; [memb.] American Heart Association, American Red Cross, Friends Against Abuse (Domestic Violence Group); [pers.] I am fortunate enough to have found love and peace through family and friends. [a.] International Falls, MN.

DIOTTAUIANO, MARGARET
[pen.] Margie Diottauiano; [b.] June 4, 1955, Poughkeepsie; [p.] Margaret and John Diottauiano (deceased); [m.] Joel Medina (fiancee); [ch.] Zacharius Samothrakis; [ed.] Early childhood; [occ.] Teacher; [memb.] Salesian Missionary United Way, St. Jude Children's Research Hospital, Muscular Dystrophy; [hon.] "A Gift From God" honorable mention, World of Poetry, National Library of Poetry. Love is Growing - World of Poetry, Reach Within Yourself - Golden Poet World of Poetry "The Beauty of Life" National Library of Poetry, Peace by the Sea - NLP; [oth. writ.] A Child's Dream - NLP, Don't Run from a Dream - World of Poetry, Mother May You Rest in Peace NLP, poems aired on Oldies 97.7; [pers.] I was inspired to write poetry when I awoke one morning at 3:00 a.m. from a dream I had about mom who died March 2, 1972. Since then I've been writing poetry on many subjects. I feel blessed. [a.] Poughkeepsie, NY.

DITMER, ARNOLD
[pen.] Arnold Ditmer; [b.] January 3, 1916, Potedame, O.; [p.] Edward H. and Mary Ditmer; [m.] Ruby Ferm Pearson, June 22, 1940; [ch.] Allen, Gary, Michael; [ed.] High school and St. Clair College; [occ.] Retired; [memb.] Mason 50 years; [oth. writ.] Pirates of Passion, Mated medallions. The story of an adopted son searching for his real mother. The agent who read it did not read all of it because of another he adored was prematurely chosen.

DIXON, NICHOLE
[pen.] Nichole Dixon; [b.] May 4, 1980, Bellflower, CA; [p.] Robert and Melissa Dixon; [ed.] Bellflower High School; [pers.] Living in "Young America" isn't easy, and racism doesn't make it any easier. The outside shouldn't matter when we're all the same on the inside. [a.] Bellflower, CA.

DOERSAM, RAYMOND G.
[b.] January 23, 1915, Rochester, NY; [p.] Raymond and Lillian (deceased); [m.] Doris Holley, 1943; [ch.] Mark and Dawn; [ed.] Rochester Institute of Technology, Cornell University and University of Rochester; [occ.] Retired college and university food service director; [memb.] Audabon Society, North Port Allamanda Garden Club, Bat Conservation International; [pers.] To learn the world a little better than I found it. [a.] North Port, FL.

DONALDSON, JAMES A.
[b.] June 14, 1935, Belfast (UK); [p.] James and Nan Donaldson; [m.] Marrianne C. Salceies-Donaldson, October 13, 1991; [ch.] Timothy, Roger, and Damon (stepson); [ed.] Bangor Grammar. Co. Down Queen's University, Belfast Open University (UK); [occ.] Retired; [hon.] Imperial Service Order (UK); [pers.] Certain Irish poets and T.S. Eliot give me the greatest pleasure. Poems work best for me when, like good paintings, they evoke personal feelings and memories. [a.] Albuquerque, NM.

DONLEA, DONNA
[pen.] Robert V. Brown; [b.] January 7, 1929, Muncie, IN; [p.] Manuel and Grace Brown; [b.] Marna Lois, March 24, 1949; [ch.] Wayne Alan Brown, Debera Darlene Barker, Faunette June Brant, Donna Jean Donlea; [occ.] Deceased; [memb.] Masons F&AM Faternal Order of the Scottish Rite, McCormick View Chapel Church, Brown Brothers Quartett from 1948- 66; [pers.] This poem was submitted by Donna Donlea for her father Robert V. Brown. The poem was written for Marna L. Brown as an anniversary gift. Mr. Brown died on September 29, 1993, after 44 years of marriage. "All things are possible through God". [a.] Muncie, IN.

DOUGLAS, OPAL J.
[pen.] Opal; [hon.] Lots of honors; [pers.] My reason for writing stories, songs, poems is people. Mostly little children. It is food to my heart and soul. [a.] Boise, ID.

DOZE, ROWENA
[pen.] Rowena Doze, [b.] July 7, 1964, Great Bend, KS; [p.] Bob and Florence Doze; [m.] Significant other - Rob Clark; [ch.] David, Chris, Ryan (Rob's); [ed.] Associate Degree; [occ.] COTA and Rehabilitation Coordinator for Hearthstone Nursing Center; [memb.] AOTA, KOTA, Beta Sigma Phi; [hon.] Golden Poet in 1990 and poem published in 1991. [a.] St. John, KS.

DRACOPOULOS, LILI
[pen.] Lulu; [b.] January 19, 1924, Chio, Greece; [p.] Anna and Kosta Abazzi; [m.] John, December 30, 1945; [ch.] 4; [ed.] High school; [occ.] Retired; [memb.] Philoftohos Church Club; [oth. writ.] Other poetry, stories unpublished; [pers.] God did not put love in our hearts to stay. Love only grows as we give it away. [a.] Dallas, TX.

DRAGON, NORMA
[b.] Ashtabula, OH; [p.] Arne and Mayme Lackson (deceased); [m.] Andrew, July 8, 1977; [ch.] David, Faith, Craig, 10 grandchildren, step-Cheryl, Debbie, Jackie, Lori, Mark; [ed.] Harbor High; [occ.] cur-

rently unemployed; [memb.] Bethany Lutheran Church; [hon.] Editor's Choice award, "Dave", won limerick contest on local radio station; [oth. writ.] 7 poems published in 1994. Several to be published in 1995. Several poems published in local newspaper; [pers.] I have a good sense of humor and try to express it in my poems. Also, my faith in God, which gets me through everyday, inspired me greatly. [a.] Ashtabula, OH.

DRANCHEK, MARK S.
[pen.] Mark S. Dranchek; [b.] June 20, 1953, Mechanicsburg, PA; [p.] John and Mary; [ed.] Shippensburg State College; [occ.] Marine Industry; [memb.] International Society of Poets; [hon.] Ednin H. Sponsellor Memorial award - highest college award for honors in philosophy and religion, Editor's Choice award in "A Far Off Place" and "At Days End"; [pers.] When man has reached his lifelong goal, and gained the knowledge of his soul, He'll laugh, and to himself he'll say, "I could have done this yesterday." [a.] Sunrise, FL.

DRAPER, CORENE LUEDECKE
[b.] July 5, 1924, Eldorado, TX; [p.] John H. and Lizzie O. Luedecke; [m.] George W., Sr., December 12, 1942; [ch.] George W. Draper, Jr., Mary Ann Draper Elliott, Candi Kay Draper Homer; [ed.] Eldorado High School; [occ.] Homemaker; [memb.] Presbyterian Church, Women's Hospital Auxiliary; [hon.] Poem published in Wind in the Night Sky, a collection of poetry; [oth. writ.] Numerous other poems written for family and friends; [pers.] Poetry is my way to express the beauty of my innermost thoughts and feelings. [a.] Eldorado, TX.

DRINNON, JANIS BOLTON
[b.] July 28, 1922, Pineville, KY; [p.] Clyde Herman and Violet Hendrickson Bolton; [m.] Kenneth C., June 13, 1948; [ch.] Dena Drinnon Foulk; [ed.] Middlesboro, KY High School, Lincoln Memorial University, Newspaper Institute of America; [occ.] Homemaker; [memb.] New Hopewell Baptist Church; [pers.] Have always enjoyed the finer things of life and nature, especially those that are spiritually uplifting and bring beauty to the soul. Have never been much for organizations--preferring to be a doer rather than a participant. I was an only child and very close to my mother. When she passed away in 1970, it was very difficult for me to give her up. Then, one afternoon as I visited with my mother-in-law, she said, "Just imagine that your mother has gone on a long trip." This seemed to help me in my acceptance. Later, when my father-in-law passed away in 1977, I wanted to say something helpful to her. I really hadn't planned to write a poem, I just started writing things that I thought might comfort her, while at the same time thinking of my mother's trip. My poem, "When Our Purpose Here Is Done", just seemed to evolve. [a.] Knoxville, TN.

DRISCOLL, LOIS I.
[b.] February 27, 1927, Delogah, OK; [m.] James F.; [ch.] Joann Schultz, Joyce Roberts, Jerry Reale; [ed.] Registered Nurse, Bachelor of Science; [occ.] Retired; [oth. writ.] Struggles and Strife Toward Heaven, Granny's Mirror.

DUBANRY, JOSEPH
[pen.] Aaron Sirsoyd; [b.] December 12, 1947; [p.] Joseph and Katherine; [ch.] Karen Teresa, Gary Raymond, Aaron Joseph; [occ.] Driver; [memb.] International Society of Poets; [pers.] Yesterday is just our mind's, today is just our time, tomorrow holds the future, blind. The clock ticks for us all.

DUKE, JAMES H. JR.
[b.] January 8, 1934, M'Boes, IL; [p.] Father deceased - mother Mabel L. Haney; [m.] Pauline (Stark) Duke, December 2, 1956; [ch.] Cynthia Jane (Duke) Reichrath and Stephen Edward Duke; [ed.] Murphysboro Township High School, S.J.U.C., Southern IL College of the Bible, Southern Baptist Theological Seminary; [occ.] Director of Special Ministries; [memb.] Southern Baptist Convention, The Illinois and Baptist State Association, The Elm St. Baptist Church, the Songwriters Club of America; [hon.] Beverly Enterprises presented a plaque for my volunteer service. Square Deal presented a bronze plaque for 20 years of dedicated employment; [oth. writ.] For 13 years published a newsletter names - Jailtalk. Have had two songs published The Wonder of God's Grace and When I Met the Savior; [pers.] The mind was given by God. We must train and use our mind in ways that glorify him and bring honor to his holy name. [a.] Murphysboro, IL.

DUKES, CHARLENE POLLARD
[pen.] CD; [b.] October 16, 1952, Brunswick, GA; [p.] Rev. C.A. and Ruby Martin; [ch.] John Allen, Angela Darlene, Ronnie William, Christopher Allen; [ed.] Ribault High - Trojans FJC; [occ.] Self employed - artist; [memb.] Sarah Brady Handgun, World of Poetry - National Parks, Rainbow Record Co., Cross and Sword Mission; [hon.] Honorable mention past 3 years World of Poetry - LCAA; [oth. writ.] Singer - songwriter musician - since childhood; [pers.] Handmaiden to Jesus Christ follower to same. [a.] White Springs, FL.

DUMITRESCU, CLEOPATRA
[pen.] Cleo Laszlo; [b.] March 14, 1953, Romania; [p.] Pia and Victor Ciulei; [ch.] Christina; [ed.] Queens College of CUNY, Empire Technical School, The New School for Social Research; [occ.] D.P. Manager for Jewelry Co. in New York; [memb.] The Smithsonian Associates, American Museum of Natural History, International Society of Poets; [hon.] Editor's Choice awards for 1993-94 by The National Library of Poetry, Certificate of poetic achievement by the Amherst Society and the poetry center, awards of merit certificates by The World of Poetry; [pers.] Poems published by The National Library of Poetry, Iliad Press; the Amherst Society; Creative Arts and Science, The Poetry Center; "From Far Away...My Love" Bi-lingual (English-Romanian) Book of poems published by Tipocart Brasovia in 1994; [pers.] They say that when faith runs deep the spirit of man returns to home to the stars on the soft wings of the wind. [a.] Woodside, NY.

DUNAGAN, MICHELE
[b.] July 22, 1976, Somerset, KY; [p.] Ronald and Charlotte Dunagan; [ed.] Southwestern High School, Somerset Community College; [oth. writ.] 2 poems untitled and mysteries in anthology by Sparrowgrass Poetry Forum and The Next Generation in the Space Between; [pers.] Poetry and writing let me communicate how I feel much more than when I say it out loud. [a.] Bronston, KY.

DUNCAN, NATALIE INEZ
[b.] April 12, 1977, Heber Springs; [p.] Sandra Sample and Ken Duncan; [ed.] Quitman High School; [occ.] Janitor for Quitman High School, student; [memb.] Students Against Drunk Driving, Future Business Leaders of America, Student Council, First Presbyterian Church, VFW Post 7514 Ladies Auxiliary, International Order of Rainbow for Girls; [hon.] Arkansas State Miss Service for the International Order of Rainbow for Girls, Grand Cross of Colors; [oth. writ.] Poem in school paper and county paper, article in Prism Light, "The Eagle" in At Days End, several unpublished poetry; [pers.] Don't let other people discourage you. You can do anything if you believe in yourself. I try to write my poetry to make people aware of the many problems these days. I hope my writings will reach the right people. [a.] Quitman, AR.

DUNCAN, TEDD
[pen.] Steel Wolf; [b.] January 30, 1978, Portland, OR; [p.] Linda Blackmore; [ed.] 10th grade; [occ.] Roofer; [hon.] Editor's Choice award; [oth. writ.] Warning, published in The Desert Sun; [pers.] "Don't fear the Unknown". [a.] Longmont, CO.

DUNLAP, HELEN ELIZABETH
[pen.] Helen Brown Dunlap; [b.] August 23, 1937, Wellston, OH; [p.] Coleman A. and Margie Brown; [m.] Jerry David, June 16, 1985; [ch.] Timothy A. Voght, Margie Renee Voght and Kaye E. Hembree; [ed.] Jeffersonville High School, I.B.M. Data Processing, Montgomery Co. Police Academy; [occ.] Domestic Engineer; [memb.] Calvary Baptist Church; [hon.] The Editor's Choice award for Outstanding Achievement in poetry presented by The National Library of Poetry, 1994; [oth. writ.] Published in the Calvary Baptist Church paper "The Voice of Calvary" was a tribute. I wrote especially for my dad Reverend C.A. Brown for his 60 years in the ministry. The poems "Daddy", "Where Daddy Lives" and "Why Do We Wait" have also been published in "The Voice of Calvary". The poem, "Daddy" also published in "The Space Between" The National Library of Poetry; [pers.] I always pray before I write each poem and ask God to help me write it, because without God I am nothing. Everything I write is from the heart. Each poem I write I consider to be a gift to the reader. I have always believed when you give a gift it should be from the heart or don't give it at all! [a.] Richmond, IN.

DWYER, MARGARET ANN
[pen.] Margaret Ann Rees-Manley; [b.] January 25, 1936, Mountain Ash, South Wales, UK; [p.] William Charles and Dwynwen Manley; [m.] Charles William, February 21, 1959; [ch.] Karen Keturah Ann and Curtis Duane William Charles (grandchildren Rhiannon Nicole and Joshua Ryan; [ed.] In Great Britian graduated April 1951 with honors; [occ.] Homemaker, poet, retired from Women's Royal Air Force; [memb.] The King's Harvest Foursquare Church, Praise and Worship Tenant, Foursome Women International, International Society of Poets, AARP; [hon.] The World of Poetry, 1987 honorable mention award of merit, 1988 Golden Poet award, 1989 Silver Poet Award, 1990 Silver Poet award, 1992 Golden Poet award; [oth. writ.] "Poem Helping Hands" published in "New American Poetry Anthology - World of Poetry Press. Other's as of yet not published that hopefully will be in book form in

future; [pers.] It is time for the United States and world wide nations to return to their basics. Let us mean it, when we say - as on our currently "In God We Trust". Put God back in our families and classrooms again. Restore America to the place of greatness our foundling fathers labored in God and through God to place her and in God we trust and shall overcome. [a.] Terre Haute, IN.

DYKEMAN, BRAD
[pen.] B. Dykeman; [b.] December 14, 1937, Columbia, MO; [p.] Lewis and Margueriete Dykeman; [m.] Helen, May 23, 1994; [ch.] Joel, Chris, Chuck, Kyle and Kayla; [ed.] Galesburg Senior High, University of Illinois-Chamaign Urbana; [occ.] Robotics welder and tech; [memb.] Friends of the Heritage Arts, VP; The River Prairie Minstrels, Acoustic Music Guild; [hon.] 1 album "Our Brand of Country", 1 45rpm single, "Bring Back Yesterday and Mister Music Man" on G/P Label; [oth. writ.] One finished manuscript "Because He Cared" The Life of Christ in poetry. Two other manuscripts in the works "On Wings of Thought" and "Bits and Pieces" of a sheltered life; [pers.] My high school English teacher told me, "Never quit writing". The love of God and of Christ have always been an integral part of my life. [a.] Moline, IL.

EARLS, DEBRINA
[pen.] Debrina Peek; [b.] September 10, 1956, Sacramento, CA; [p.] Forrest and Marian Peek; [m.[Michael J. Earls, September 3, 1991; [ch.] No human kids, I have five lovely fur-people, my dogs, Sandra, Bully, Bear, Jack and Sam; [ed.] Lincoln High School, Lincoln, CA, graduate 1974 (honors student), life member CA Scholarship Federation, head songleader, Bank of America Scholarship (foreign languages), Sierra College, Rocklin, CA-Dean's List, 75/76; [occ.] Accountant-state of California; [memb.] World of Poetry Society, International Society of Poets, Sparrowgrass Poetry Forum, National Library of Poetry; [hon.] Published in Who's Who in Poetry 1991, Golden Poet Awards for 1989, 1990, 1991 and 1992, Outstanding Poet Award from International Society of Poets for 1993, Editor's Choice Award from National Library of Poetry for 1994; [oth.writ.] Poems published in World of Poetry anthology Great Poems of the Western World, World Treasury of Golden Poems, and Outstanding Poets of 1994 by National Library of Poetry, also in Who's Who in Poetry 1991; [pers.] Always try to be happy because God really does love us all. Keep romance alive in your life, we all need earthly love too. Hug your dog daily. [a.] Sacramento, CA.

ECHELSON, MARTHA R.
[pen.] Marty Duncan Echelson; [b.] March 17, 1921, Sweetwater, TX; [p.] Ina and Ray Duncan; [m.] George Echelson, January 15, 1944; [ch.] George Duncan and Ray Douglas, 49 years old and he is a miracle; [ed.] Nazarath College in Kentucky (fell on wet steps, had to give up nursing etc.); [occ.] I'm 73 and take care of "Doug" my retarded son; [memb.] Eastern Star, Veteran organizations was in the WAAC before my dad became very ill, Little Theatre in Panama; [hon.] Singer with many bands on 14 Army posts and in Aruba, NA, been in plays in Aruba and Panama, lived overseas 40 years; [I'm a poet and an artist, over 2,000 paintings, give as gifts, my family wouldn't let me sell them.

EDGAR, KELLY
[b.] February 22, 1979, Marietta, OH; [p.] Vicka and Jeffrey Edgar; [ed.] Frontier High; [occ.] Student; [memb.] Newport United Methodist Church; [hon.] Honor Society, State Science Fair (superior), United States Achievement Academy yearbook; [oth. writ.] One poem published in the National Library of Poetry; [pers.] I have been significantly influenced and encouraged by my grandmother since my early childhood. [a.] Newport, OH.

EDWARDS, MALON
[b.] December 11, 1975, Chicago, IL; [p.] Lloyd and Minnie Clark; [ed.] Thornwood High School, University of Illinois at Urbana, Champaign; [occ.] Student; [pers.] Poetry involves emotions that bring out pure words of truth. [a.] South Holland, IL.

EDWIN, SABEEN ANN
[b.] September 23,1980, New York; [p.] Ernest and Rita Edwin; [sib.] Yasmin Edwin; [ed.] Studying in 9th grade; [occ.] Student at Townsend Harris High School at Queens College; [hon.] Poetry contest at St. Nicholas of Glentine School, 1990-4 th grade, won 3rd place, 1991-5th grade, won 1st place, 1993- 7th grade, won 2nd place; [oth.writ.] 1994, poetry published in Dance On The Horizon by the National Library of Poetry; [pers.] I like to write poetry, because I can express myself without speaking. It is easier to show your feelings on paper. [a.] Jamacia, NY.

EFFINGER, LYNN
[b.] October 7, 1964, West Chester, PA; [ed.] Dowingtown Area High School; [occ.] Administrative Assistant; [memb.] Chester Do Art Association, P.E.T.A.; [hon.] Business Student, Business English, Honorable Mentions (drawing, watercolor); [oth.writ.] Previous poems published by the National Library of Poetry; [pers.] Ususally, poems for me are a way to express thoughts or deep emotion. [a.] Chester Springs, PA.

EGYED, JEAN LOUISE
[pen.] Jean L. Egyed; [b.] April 17, 1941, San Jose, CA; [p.] Ethel and Emil Egyed; [m.] Horace LaFuse (widow), 1980 to 1989; [ch.] None, but helped rear 28 children through the years; [ed.] 12 years, Hotel Motel Management, 2 years writing and now Animal Science through I.C.S., also foster care; [occ.] Writing and volunteer work; [memb.] A member of the First Baptist Church, the National Library of Poetry, Poetry Academy and Hollywood Artists Records Company; [hon.] National Pen Award, two Golden Poet Awards, several awards of merit; [oth.writ.] I'm working on a novel, 7 poems published in books of poetry, one song through Rainbow Records, three songs through Hollywood Artists; [pers.] I enjoy writing about nature, romance. It is my intention to put the biggest part of my poems to music. I am still hoping to hear one of my songs on the radio or National TV.; [a.] Westwood, CA.

ELLIOTT, STACY DIANE
[b.] August 25,1974, Willard, OH; [p.] Brenda Thornsberry; [ed.] Knott County Central High School, University of Louisville; [occ.] Student; [memb.] Golden Key National Honor Society, Phi Eta Sigma (Freshman Honor Society), member of University of Louisville's College of Arts and Sciences Honors Program; [hon.] Golden Key National Honor Society, Phi Eta Sigma; [oth.writ.] Poetry and essays published in local hometown newspaper, poem published in anthology; [pers.] My poetry is part of myself. Sharing my work is like sharing an intimate part of my soul that noone else ever sees. [a.] Fairdale, KY.

ELLIS, CHRISTEL B.
[b.] October 28, 1929, Waterville, ME; [p.] Ruth Goodwin Basford and Wallace Basford; [m.] Gilbert Randall Ellis, Sr., January 28, 1953; [ch.] Wallissa, Randy, Pamela, Norman, Vicent, Roger, Melanie, Valerie, Evangeline, Joseph and David; [ed.] Crosby High School, Belfast, Maine; [occ.] Minister, mother, housewife; [memb.] Maine Society of Poets, United Amateur Press Association, Salamanca Cong. of Jehovah's Witnesses; [hon.] U.A.P.A. Literary Award, National Library of Poetry Critics Award 1993-1994, lifetime membership Maine Society of Poets; [oth.writ.] Ideals Magazine, several anthologies of poetry, U.A.P.A. publications, periodicals, National Library of Poetry, Best of Maine Poets anthology; [pers.] I write about the pictures, the hopes, the love that Jehovah God gives me in my heart. I love people, places and the beautiful things of earth. I am thankful to Him for my gift of words. [a.] Cattaraugus, NY.

EMERY, MARY LEVET
[b.] March 6, 1906, California; [p.] B.F. Levet; [m.] Earle B.Emery, August 8, 1925; [ch.] Earle Jr., Edward, Marilyn and Les Alan; [ed.] High school; [occ.] Widow, housewife; [memb.] Los Angeles Woman's Symphony Orchestra, no longer in existance; [hon.] Blue ribbons, oil painting, sculpturing; [oth.writ.] One short story, cash award; [pers.] I love poetry and feel that my poems are a gift from God. [a.] California, CA.

ENGBERG-MALUVAC, ROBIN
[pen.] R.L. Engberg; [b.] November 18, 1965, Indiana; [p.] Jean Engberg; [m.] Bryon Maluvac. September 25, 1993; [occ.] Administrative assistant; [memb.] International Society of Poets, Center for Marine Conservation; [hon.]Received Editor's Choice awards from The National Library of Poetry, World Of Poetry's Golden and Silver Poet awards; [pers.] The best day of my life is the day I got married. Bryon, thank you for being my husband. [a.] Chesterton, IN.

ENGEL, LESLIE
[b.] August 6, 1963, New York, NY; [p.] Roger and Judith Engel; [ed.] University of Colorado; [occ.] Marketing; [hon.] Colorado Scholars award, Outstanding Poets of 1994, 2 Editor's Choice awards, The Sounds of Poetry, Best Poems of 1995; [oth. writ.] Staff writer for The Denver Post, former writer editor of feature business articles for bi-monthly and monthly publications, former senior editor/writer monthly trade publication, short stories and poetry; [a.] Forest hills, NY.

ENGLES, JUNE
[b.] August 3, 1959, New York; [p.] Francis and Miriam Engles; [m.] Talib I. Muhammad, June 29, 1991; [ed.] James Monroe High, City College NY; [occ.] Retired; [memb.] Detective Endowment Assn., Guardians, Harlem Hospital Dance and Youth Center, Gospel Hall Church; [oth. writ.] Two poems in anthology, "Drew", "Sorrows of Tomorrow"; [pers.] For my male mentors: my late father, my teacher, Prof Visitacion, and my husband.

ENSOR, BONITA L.
[pen.] bb ensor; [b.] February 20. 1941, Macomb, IL; [p.] Gilbert and Dora Layton; [ed.] Paris American High School, The George Washington University; [occ.] Retired from CIa, presently working on my first novel and assisting on my parents' book; [memb.] Romance Writers of America, Central Intelligence Retirees Association, Defenders of Wildlife; [hon.] CIA Retirement Medallion for Honorable Service; [oth. writ.] Fifteen-page chapbook "Saga of an American Family Abroad", small book of poetry published in 1981 titled "Night Thoughts at Dawn" and "Finally Free", poem published in 1994; [pers.] My writing is greatly influenced by a multicultural upbringing in five foreign countries and a tiny island in the Pacific reflecting numerous culture shocks and subsequent development of a "lone wolf" attitude. I strive to present the universality of all people, cultures, and philosophies in my writing. [a.] Easton, MD.

EPSTEIN, RUTH PERETZ
[b.] Poland; [p.] J. Abraham and Leonora Peretz; [m.] Harry Epstein (deceased); [ch.] Nelly (deceased); [ed.] Polish high school, American high school, school for pattern designing for dresses; [occ.] Former assistant designer; [memb.] Miami Beach Zimra Chorus and Symphonette; [hon.] Received acting award and prize from Miami Beach Community College, congratulatory letter from President Carter for article on peace treaty between Israel and Egypt; [pers.] My aim is to serve mankind and be a guiding light for the younger generation by publishing my autobiography and describing the hardships, tragedies, and triumphs that I faced during World War II in Russia. [a.] Allentown, PA.

ERNST, PAUL F.
[b.] September 4, 1924, Reading OH; [p.] Joseph and Charlotte Ernst; [m.] Divorced; [ch.] Vincent, Marlene, Frederick, Malcolm, Eric; [ed.] SS Peter and Paul Elem., Roger Bacon High, Xavier Univ; [occ.] Retired; [memb.] American Legion, Clyde Trivett Society; [hon.] Numerous insurance company sales awards, twice Tri-State Salesman of the Year; [oth. writ.] Philosophic, not published; [pers.] To be a good salesman, you must be like a contented donkey. Keep moving, keep going, and the load will follow. [a.] Cincinnati, OH.

ERRINGTON, REBECCA M.
[pen.] Becki Errington; [b.] March 20, 1978, Providence; [p.] Timothy and Susan Errington; [ed.] East Providence High; [occ.] Student; [memb.] EPHS Speech and Debate Team, EPHS Tennis Team, EPHS Concert Band, GSRI; [hon.] Debate honors, Outstanding Musician, flute recognition, karate achievements; [oth. writ.] "Where Dreams Begin", and a personal collection; [pers.] Anything is possible If you can dream it, you can make it reality. Know what you want, and always keep it in focus. [a.] Riverside, RI.

ERVIN, LINDA LEE
[b.][September 19, 1964, Paducah, LY; [p.] Donald and Linda Throgmorton; [hon.] Editor's Choice award, National Library of Poetry 1993, 1994, Accomplishment of Merit; [oth. writ.] I have many writings yet to be published; [pers.] I like to write about things that others can identify with. If they can't then perhaps I can take them places they have never been. [a.] Boaz, KY

ESSAK, REBECCA
[b.] February 5, 1971, Skokie, IL; [p.] Robert and Judy Essak; [ed.] DePaul University; [occ.] Teacher; [hon.] Kappa Delta Pi, Dean's List, Golden Key National Honor Society, honored in The National Dean's List, [oth. writ.] poem printed in Echoes of Yesterday; [pers.] You get from the world what you give to the world. May the material, judgmental world fade away as open hearts and minds blossom in gardens all around. [a.] Chicago, IL.

EVANS, AMY JOANNE
[b.] June 13, 1970, DeKalb, IL; [p.] Jack Evans and Diane Mongeau; [ch.] Kyle Stuart Mattis; [ed.] High school; [occ.] Creative calligraphy, assistant production and warehouse supervisor; [hon.] Stock car racing awards, vocal; awards and tapes; [oth. writ.] Many poems about friendship and love the way I see them to be; [pers.] Life is too short to settle for less than what you want out of it. The poem in this book is the first poem I have written in 6 years. It was inspired by someone very special. [a.] DeKalb, IL.

EVASEW, MICHELLE
[b.] September 26, 1978, Phoenixville, PA; [p.] Kenneth and Margaret Evasew; [ed.] Upper Merion Area High School; [occ.] Student; [hon.] National Honor Society, Distinguished Honors; [oth. writ.] "A Single Step" poem published by local newspaper; [pers.] Never take love for granted. [a.] King of Prussia, PA.

EVERS, GENE
[pen.] Gene Alexander Evers; [b.] March 26,1951, Manhattan; [p.] Lee Evers and Pauline Stein; [ed.] Hicksville High School, College graduate, nursing program; [occ.] Script writer, children's stories, lyrics; [memb.] International Poets Society nominee; [hon.] Dean's List; [oth. writ.] Poetry, soon to be completed movie script, lyrics; [pers.] Influenced by ancient philosophy of the Greeks and by Herman Melville, Rosseau, and Willa Cather. Philosophy and literature is the road to God, and freedom of the spirit. [a.] Bethpage, NY.

FALKER, MARGARET BRUNEA
[b.] September 16, 1961, Batavia; [p.] William and Irene Brunea; [m.] Alan Thomas, August 20, 1994; [ch.] Mark Allen, Duane Thomas Falker (daughter inlaws Nancy Ann, Stephanie Shannon); [ed.] Corfu Elementary, Pembroke Central School; [occ.] CNA-owners of A.T.F. furniture store; [hon.] The National Library of Poetry published my first poem "Country Girl" in Dance on the Horizon. I am honored to have won Editor's Choice award 1994. I have been greatly influenced by Walt Whitman ever since I was young. I am so honored to be a part of the best poems of 1995; [oth. writ.] Several other poems; [pers.] I would like to thank my mom and dad, my brothers Bob, Rick and Larry and my sister Rose for being supportive of me and my greatest inspiration my love, Al. Thank you, "Pooper" for the house on the river. Thanks to Diane, Joyce and to Tina for bringing Olivia into my life; [pers.] Always listen to your inner voice, for it is always right. [a.] Batavia, NY.

FALTER, DONNA
[pen.] Dee or Mouth; [b.] January 22, 1979, Newton Wellsley Hospital; [p.] Ann and Stephen Falter; [ed.] Tri-County, Franklin, MA; [occ.] Student w/part-time job working w/kids; [hon.] Lipsinc contest 4th place, bowling, trophy, baseball trophy and the award of my artistic talent writing poems; [pers.] I just wanted to thank my peers and family members for believing in me and my writing. [a.] N. Attleboro, MA.

FAMBRO, SONJA O.
[b.] Bainbridge, GA; [p.] Delois Miller and Wilman Grimsley; [m.] Oscar Lewis Fambro; [ch.] Tamila Nachoen Fambro and Terria G. Fambro-Parker; [ed.] Bethel School, Clark College, Albany State College, Univ. of North Florida, Univ. of West Florida, Norfolk State University, Old Dominion Univ., Jacksonville Univ. [memb.] St. John Missionary Baptist Church, The Sanctuary Choir; [hon.] Received Dean's list certificate and graduated Cum Laude from Albany State College, received Editor's Choice award from The National Library of Poetry; [oth. writ.] "Foolish, Bold Prejudice" (a poem published in At Day's End), lyrics, several poems and essays which I am collecting for my first book, and "Believer In Love" which was sung by the Harrison Brothers; [pers.] This poem is dedicated to my mother and my grandmother (Dr. Grace S. Moore) who taught me that nothing is impossible when you have faith in God. [a.] Orange Park, FL.

FARRAR, JUANITA
[b.] February 22, 1934, Scott, AR; [p.] Ruthie Mae Knox; [m.] Albert Author Farrar, April 21, 1951; [ch.] Remona, Janice, and Alexander; [ed.] Junior College, Drake and Chicago State University, Community Colleges in St. Louis and Kansas City, MO; [occ.] Postal Clerk; [memb.] International Society of Poets and Nashville Songwriters Association International, Citizens for Modern Transit, St. Louis Zoo Friends; [hon.] Hollywood Song Jubilee: Certificate of Achievement 1990-91, World of Poetry; merit certificate 1990, and Golden Poet 1991; [oth. writ.] "Forever-my Valentine", "Rimes of Appreciation", "Scholar of Reasoning", "My Intermost Thoughts", "My Inner Nature" and "By What Means"; [pers.] Love: The world's greatest experience. I try to get my message across with positive suggestions. My need for affection is my motivator. [a.] St. Louis, MO.

FARROW, ANNA M.
[pen.] Anna M. Farrow; [b.] August 28, 1928, 1932, Lancaster, OH; [p.] Walter and Viola Wagner; [m.] Deceased; [ch.] Two; [ed.] High school, various college courses, Ohio University; [occ.] Retired; [memb.] Emmuel Lutheran Church, Bremen Historical Society, volunteer at local Lutheran Food Pantry, belong to writing group, Stonecroft Bible Study group; [oth. writ.] Poem published by National Library of Poetry 1994; [pers.] I began writing at an advanced age. I believe the knowledged that I have gleened from the ups and downs of my life have contributed to my writings. [a.] Bremen, OH.

FELDBAUER, CYNTHIA M.
[b.] September 15, 1962, Pittsburgh, PA; [pers.] Life is so full of expressions. As I go through life's experience. I write in the hopes that someone else understands and can relate to my pain and triumphs and share a common thread. [a.] N. Homestead, PA.

FENTON, JACOB
[b.] May 23, 1979; [ch.] Siblings-Garrett and Candice; [ed.] High school; [memb.] DECA, The National Honor Society, Speech and Debate Team; [hon.]

Various academic achievement awards, 2nd degree brown belt in Tae Kwon Do; [oth. writ.] "For Everyone's Sake" published in River of Dreams; [pers.] Good judgment comes from experience, experience comes from bad judgment. Your memory will live forever Mrs. Crawford.

FERRARO, NANCY

[b.] December 25, 1944, Greensboro, NC; [p.] Richard J. and B. Delores Longest Ferraro; [ch.] Paul Richard Geisert; [occ.] Legal secretary; [memb.] Orange County Sexual Assault Network, Orange County Society for the Prevention of Cruelty to Animals; [hon.] OSCAN 1989 Volunteer of the Year; 1993 Editor's Choice award, 1994 Editor's Choice award both from The National Library of Poetry; [oth. writ.] In The Desert Sun, A Far Off Place; anthologies published by The National Library of Poetry; [pers.] You love who you love! Success, fame and fortune are all illusion. What is real is the feelings and love people share and the acceptance of the humanness and frailities in all of us. [a.] Tustin, CA.

FIEBB, S. LYNN

[b.] May 5, 1956, Bridgeport; [m.] Divorced; [ch.] Melanie, Shawn, Kimberly; [ed.] JHS '75, Mattuck-CHHA; [occ.] CHHA; [oth. writ.] Write songs in my book; [pers.] Writing poems comes without any effort. Finding it easier to deal with feelings a way to say how I feel and for others to know me.

FIFIELD, CORA L.

[b.] January 5, 1910, Nebraska; [p.] Walter and Della Hoggatt; [m.] Sheldon, January 1942; [ch.] Sheldon Bud Fifield and Bobbie Louise Moen; [occ.] Retired; [memb.] Echo Mountain Baptist Church; [hon.] Enjoy oil painting and teach a small class in oil painting; [oth. writ.] Many other poems; three religious hymns which are copyrighted also three other songs entitled: "O Glorious Day", "Babies Lullaby" and "Luna Honeymoon"; [pers.] My life has been greatly influenced by good Christian parents. My goal is to live a clean, healthy, happy life. I live peaceably with others around me and am helpful to those in need. I enjoy writing poems, reading, music and oil painting. [a.] Phoenix, AZ.

FINLEY, JEAN B.

[b.] May 15, 1922, Des Plaines, IL; [p.] Maud Gridley and Edward H. Budlong; [m.] George R. Jr., September 6, 1942; [ch.] Mark Allen Finley, Carol Jean Finley Thielman and 6 grandchildren; [ed.] 2 years college but never stopped learning; [memb.] Bookkeeper and housewife in own business - jewelry store; [hon.] World of Poetry award; [oth. writ.] Short stories unpublished and mystery novel in progress; [pers.] Love to read, play the organ, write, paint (oils, pastel, acrylic) needlework and travel. All if the above! Hate to cook!

FIORE, DAWNE E.

[b.] July 22, 1966, Poughkeepsie, NY; [p.] Marilyn and John Fiore, Sr.; [ed.] BS/MS in Physical Therapy; [memb.] APTA-NC Physical Therapy Chapter Association, USPRIG; [hon.] Published in wedding and anniversary invitations, Golden Poet award; [oth. writ.] Several poems published; [pers.] I feel my gift of prose and verse come from my parents artistic influence and divine inspiration to view life and nature's gift for mankind to reflect. [a.] Durham, NC.

FISH, AIMEE JO

[b.] July 7, 1974, Cloquet, MN; [p.] Mike and Bonnie Fish; [hon.] Editor's Choice award, National Library of Poetry; [oth. writ.] "Poems and Prayers from the Ark" and National Library of Poetry: "In The Desert Sun"; [pers.] I hope people read my poetry as an inspiration. God can guide you through anything. He has gifted me with poetic abilities to express myself. [a.] Carlton, MN.

FLETCHER, RONNIE J.

[pen.] Ronnie J. Boyanton; [b.] November 17, 1952, TN; [p.] Walter Boyanton and Jean McNeil; [m.] Archie, December 11, 1993; [ch.] Sidney and Dawn Marlborough; [ed.] San Diego Mesa College; [occ.] Citibank Recovery Test Center; [memb.] Army National Guard; [hon.] Army Achievement Meritorious Service Enlisted Excellence, National Coin of Honor; [oth. writ.] Echoes of Yesterday, Ignorance Breeds Death; [pers.] When something touches your life, it touches your heart. Now you handle life's changing tides depend on your preception of each situation. Relax. [a.] Kansas City, MO.

FLORES, SAMUEL

[pen.] Sam; [b.] May 22, 1957, Chicago, IL; [p.] Felix E. and Mona E. Flores; [m.] Bertha, December 15, 1990; [ed.] Harrison High, University of Illinois Circle Campus, Notary Public; [occ.] Self employed - Services Flores; [memb.] Jehovah's Witness; [hon.] Editor's Choice award presented by the National Library of Poetry; [hon.] Dog owner award (Baby) 1994, German Sheperd (Best Disciplined); [oth. writ.] Poem published in The National Library of Poetry "A Far Off Place"; [pers.] The truth is the best way to answer any question - If you want the right answer speak with the truth, it's the best way to live. [a.] Chicago, IL.

FLORSEK, CARINA L.

[pen.] Carina L. Florsek; [b.] October 6, 1964, St. Louis; [p.] R. Thomas and Helen Florsek; [m.] Fiancee-Gregory Vrouvas; [ed.] Wheatridge High School, Warren Technical School; [occ.] Offset Press operator; [memb.] Ava Art Guild, St. Anthony's Catholic Church; [oth. writ.] Numerous poems, 2 of which were published in anthologies and numerous songs; [pers.] Man should look for the good in life and not dwell so much on adversities, and don't be afraid to try. Thanks Mom and Dad for the creativity you've passed along to your children. Thanks Greg for your encouragement. [a.] High Ridge, MO.

FLYNN, BILL

[b.] May 8, 1953, Phillipsburgh, NJ; [p.] Mr. and Mrs. John Flynn; [ed.] Wildwood Catholic High School; [occ.] Self employed; [hon.] 1994 Flora Ellis award for community service, 3rd degree Black Belt USA Goju Karate; [oth. writ.] Author of "Meditations of a Christian Martial Artist" freelance writer; [pers.] Wisdom is given to us at birth. Knowledge is up to ourselves to gather. [a.] Stratton, ME.

FODALE, DANIEL A.

[b.] January 20, 1974, Warren, MI; [p.] Tony and Ruth Fodale; [ed.] Notre Dame High School, Michigan State University, Macomb College; [occ.] Student; [hon.] Finals in two contest; [oth. writ.] Several poems including a continuing set. [a.] Fraser, MI.

FOLEY, NANCY

[pen.] NF; [b.] March 17, 1937, Flint, MI; [p.] Charles Berston and Rosalee Smith; [m.] Patrick Foley, September 2, 1957; [ch.] Ryan, Douglas and Kurt Foley; [ed.] High school; [occ.] At leisure; [oth. writ.] Many poems and several short stories about my children's childhood; [pers.] I live one day at a time. I try to follow the teachings of Jesus. I live and let live. [a.] Flint, MI.

FORMUSA, WILLIAM J.

[pen.] Bill Formusa; [b.] December 26, 1921, Chicago; [p.] Marie and John; [m.] Divorced; [ch.] Lynne Elizabeth; [ed.] Illinois College of Commerce; [occ.] Retired - Mgr. Credit Collections - Michael Reese Hospital; [memb.] VFW -9284; [hon.] Golden Poet award 1990 and 1991; [oth. writ.] If I Were Younger, Getting Older, Divorce, Bingo Bill, My Shadow, Where Did All My Money Go; [pers.] Poetry allows man to open up his heart and be judged by his critics in a most sensitive way. A perilous undertaking and yet rewarding. [a.] Elk Grove Village, IL.

FORSYTHE, BRANDON H.

[b.] November 2, 1973, Camden, NJ; [p.] Tom and Creda Forsythe; [ed.] Stephen F. Austin State University, Collin County Community College. [a.] Plano, TX

FORTIER, BRAD

[b.] November 14, 1970, Milwaukee, WI; [p.] Donald and Lonanne Fortier; [ed.] Notre Dame High School, University of Milwaukee; [occ.] Laborer; [memb.] United States Aikido Federation, Midwest Aikido Federation; [oth. writ.] A host of unpublished fiction and poetry; [pers.] When we see with the eyes of the heart, the world becomes such a precious thing. [a.] Milwaukee, WI.

FORTNEY, JONATHAN ROBERT

[pen.] Jon; [b.] February 25, 1973, Holland, MI; [p.] James Fortney and Patricia Walsh; [ed.] Hope College, Forest Hills Central High School; [occ.] Student. [a.] Holland, MI.

FOSTER, TERESA L.

[b.] November 29, 1962, Arlington, VA; [m.] Lance V., April 30, 1988; [ch.] Brandon James, Cameron Austin, Ashlynn Marie; [ed.] Clarke County High School; [occ.] Homemaker; [oth. writ.] Previous poetry published in The National Library of Poetry; [pers.] This poem was written in memory of and dedication to my daughter, Lauryn Amber, who died on March 20, 1993 at 9 1/2 months of age. [a.] Woodbridge, VA.

FOWLER, DAVID P.

[pen.] Devin Altman C. Leary; [b.] January 14, 1968, Pasedena, CA; [p.] Phil and Mary Fowler; [m.] Angela, March 18, 1989; [ed.] Sexton High, Lansing Community College; [occ.] Building Technician; [pers.] Compelled from my heart and mind for everyone's own wellness of being, especially the benevolence of women. [a.] Lansing, MI.

FOWLER, RAYMOND H. JR.

[b.] September 8, 1934, Baltimore, MD; [p.] Raymond Sr., and Hazel L. Fowler; [m.] Betty L. (Main), December 5, 1969; [ch.] Robert Keith, Donald Wayne and E. Lynn Fielder; [ed.] BS-Business Administration, Certificate=Executive Development; [occ.] Sr. Staff Assistant; [memb.] Optimist Club of Randallstown; [hon.] Optimist International, Westinghouse Electric Corporation Community Service award; [oth. writ.] Previous poem "Teddy" published by The National Library of Poetry; [pers.] I attempt to write my poetry in simple, rhyming language for all to enjoy. [a.] Owings Mills, MD.

FOX, WILLARD R.
[pen.] Bill Fox; [b.] June 24, 1933, Cincinnati, OH; [p.] Ronald and Mildred; [ed.] California State-LA; [occ.] Musician; [memb.] ASCAP; [oth. writ.] Many songs; [pers.] The best is yet to come. [a.] Los Angeles, CA.

FRANKLIN, JANET MARIE
[pen.] Janet M. Franklin; [b.] June 2, 1923, Philadelphia, PA; [p.] Ralph and Gertrude Schafenacker; [m.] William A., June 5, 1948; [ch.] William R., Michael C., Trudy Breur, Marianne Smith and Janet Bagnall; [ed.] Doylestown High School, Lansdale School of Business; [occ.] Wife, mother, grandmother; [memb.] Church, Women's Club; [oth. writ.] "Solitude" in At Day's End; [pers.] Writing poetry helps me to express myself in a positive way and, at the same time, gives me a sense of confidence and accomplishment. [a.] Warminster, PA.

FRASER, GAIL A.
[pen.] Susan Rose, tabby cat; [m.] March 7, 1920, Pleasant Grove, MN; [p.] William anf Minnie Falancer; [m.] Late Charles, July 28, 1943; [ch.] William Butran, Lance Gimbe and Carla Marie; [ed.] Greenway High, Itasca Community College, College of St. Scholastica, Lindenwood College; [occ.] Retired Medical Laboratory Technologist, Lab Supervisor; [memb.] American Society of Clinical Pathologists, Emeritus, Clallam County Genealogical Society; [hon.] Scholastic and athletic awards, Mrs. NM 1955 literary award and horticultural sweepstakes award; [oth. writ.] Article in MLO Medical Laboratory Observer, unpublished Susan Rose poems, unpublished book, You Can Live Longer, various newspaper articles, newsletter editor; [pers.] The poems for/by Susan Rose, tabby cat, began with poetic letters to her master, while away and to her beau cat Prince, with ensuing encouragement to publish them. [a.] Sequim, WA.

FRAZELL, KAREN
[b.] June 7, 1961, Springfield, OH; [p.] Sam and Lorraine Terry; [m.] Steve Alan, October 10, 1992; [ed.] Tecmseh High School, Barbizon Model in school nurse aide training; [occ.] General Merchandise Clerk, Meiser; [memb.] Church of God Plain City; [hon.] Hall of Fame, Employee of the Month at Meiser's, Golden Poet 1991, World of Poetry, award of merit certificates, World of Poetry, Certificate of Baptism, Nurse Aide Certificate; [oth. writ.] Song lyrics; [pers.] I want to be a light of hope to reach lost, lonely, hurting souls with the message of love, peace, kindness and with a personal relationship with the Lord, Jesus Christ, as the road to personal and eternal salvation. [a.] Plain City, OH.

FRENCH, CHRISTINE
[b.] June 26, Rhode Island; [ch.] Two daughters; [ed.] Business college and art school (Johnson & Wales and Rhode Island School of Design); [occ.] Primarily writer of seminars and presenter of the seminars; [hon.] Much of my work has been published for which I received many awards; [oth. writ.] My writings include poetry, articles on food and wine, seminars on building self-esteem, values and judgments - how they work and do not, and how we establish relationships; [pers.] Our days are numbered but never limited. [a.] Newark, DE.

FRENCH, JOYICE
[pen.] Shelby Mae; [b.] October 1, 1960, Hillsdale, MI; [p.] Paul and Virginia French; [ed.] Camden-Frnotier High School, Adrian College; [occ.] Finance Director. [a.] Jackson, MI.

FRY, KRISTIN
[b.] February 18, 1981, El Paso, TX; [p.] William D. Fry and Flora Gaither; [ed.] Bassett Middle School; [occ.] Sitting around writing; [hon.] Honorable mention in Art contest, two publications by the National Library of Poetry; "Tears of Fire" and "Dark Side of the Moon"; [oth. writ.] Tons of unpublished short stories, short novels, and poems; [pers.] I enjoy expressing the world's sick, sometimes disturbing insanity in my writing. Basically, because it comes naturally to me. [a.] El Paso, TX.

FUGATE, FREDDIE L.
[b.] February 12, 1954, Tazewell, TN; [p.] John and Thelma Fugate; [occ.] Private Security Investigations; [oth. writ.] Several poems not published as yet, plus one song; [pers.] It is my intent to poetically present, the beauty, of writing that only the mind can invent. [a.] Brooklyn, NY.

FUHLENDORF, CHARLENE
[b.] July 27, 1949, Turlock, CA; [p.] Mickey and ImaJean Martins; [m.] Michael E., November 9, 1974; [ch.] Erik and Allan Fuhlendorf; [ed.] Grace M. Davis High School, Valley Commercial College, Modesto Junior College; [occ.] Homemaker; [memb.] The Ladies Sewing Circle, Grace Lutheran Church; [hon.] 2nd class musician award, Clarinet; [oth. writ.] "My Cat's Clothes", published in The National Library of Poetry's "The Space Between"; [pers.] Each person can find within himself a small morsel of greatness, if only you believe. For we are created in God's image. [a.] Modesto, CA.

FULCE, SUZETTE
[b.] September 30, 1958, San Francisco, CA; [p.] Louise Lewis and Wille Cannon; [m.] Terence D., March 17, 1984; [ch.] Rashod Abdul Fulce; [ed.] Libert Eylau High School, Texarkana College, El Centro College; [occ.] Preschool teacher, certified nursing assistant; [memb.] National Association for Female Executives, International Society of Poets, Sam's Warehouse Club, Bible Way Christian Assembly, Ushers Board; [hon.] Volunteer award - Project Up-lift, Liberty Elementary School, Liberty Eylau Punctual Attendance award; [oth. writ.] The Space Between, The National Library of Poetry; [pers.] I love reading the word of God. The word of God will keep you. I love writing. [a.] Texasarkana, TX.

FULLER, LINDA MARLAINE
[b.] April 20, 1950, Orangeville; [p.] Daniel and Isabel Little; [m.] John Douglas Turnbull, common-law; [ch.] Sherry-Lynn, Dwayne, Trevor (grandchildren-Jessie, Andrew, Michael); [ed.] Orangeville District High School, Humber College; [occ.] Disabled Homemaker and home tutor; [memb.] March of Dimes Funding, Cancer Funding, Westminister United Church; [hon.] 5 years foster parenting, Foster Parent of the Year, volunteer award (1,5,10 years); [oth. writ.] If All the Gold and Silver (A Far Off Place), Awaiting response from Porcupine Quill, Germantion Magazine and Country Women; [pers.] I strive to meet new and existing challenges. I enjoy making and teaching crafts to physically and mentally challenged adults. I have been greatly influenced by the early children's series "Little House", Green Gables, Little Women. [a.] Orangeville, ONT.

FUSCO, DIANE M.
[m.] Paul S. Fusco; [ch.] Paul L. Fusco killed in a car accident 12/3/88. I write poetry in his memory; [occ.] Index Clerk in the Livingston County Clerk's Office; [hon.] Editor's Choice award presented by The National Library of Poetry in 1993 and 1994; [oth. writ.] "Remember Me" published in the Coming of Dawn in 1993 and "Forever Twenty-two" published in The Space Between in 1994. [a.] Livonia, NY.

GABRIEL, A.M. GABE
[pen.] A.M. "Gabe" Gabriel; [b.] May 7, 1929, Chicago Hts., IL; [p.] Rose and Angelo Gabriele; [m.] Mary Ann, August 26, 1950; [ch.] Tarey, Michael, Timothy; [ed.] Bloom Township High School, Valparaiso University, Southwest University; [occ.] Executive, Miles Inc.; [memb.] Career Quest Chairman 1993-1995; Tech Prep Chairman 1992-1994, Goodwill Business Advisory Board, Family Foundations Advisory Board, United Way Site Coordinator 1992, GAC-GAC Advisory Board, Summer Academy Founder and Chairman, Teachers Academy Founder; [hon.] Point of Light-President Bush 1991, Eleven Who Care Award 1990 WQED Channel 11TV, Creativity Man of the Year 1991, ASTD; Allegheny County Commissioner's Award 1992, Day of Caring United Way Initiator; [oth. writ.] Poems, speeches (110 in 1993), Testimony and requests of government for systemic changes in the educational system, church-sponsored prisoner newsletter (monthly); [pers.] My chief aim in life is to help people and to give back a portion of what was given to me. I cam from humble beginnings and realize the difficulty associated with a poor person trying to get an education and progress. My trust is in the Lord. [a.] Pittsburgh, PA.

GARCIA, RICHARD A.
[pen.] Dick Garcia; [b.] April 26, 1938, Honolulu, HI; [p.] Mrs. Rose Skelton; [ed.] High school; [occ.] Artist and freelance photographer; [pers.] I practice positive metaphysics. The use of thought for creating positive reality for one's self. For positive thinking has worked very well for me and I try to influence others through my works and deeds. [a.] Honolulu, HI.

GARDINER, JOHN F.
[p.] William and Margaret Gardiner; [m.] Diane; [ed.] B.S., M.A. and Ed.D.; [occ.] Superintendent of Schools; [memb.] Macomb County Association of School Administrators, Mich. Association of School Boards, MI Association of School Administrators, past president Gast Detroit Historical Society, Veteran of Foreign Wars; [hon.] School named to my honor, citizen of the year award for restoring an 1872 schoolhouse; [oth. writ.] Short story published, four articles published in magazines, poems published in local papers and journals; [pers.] I feel a strong need

to share my sensitivity of human nature and the world that surrounds us with others through the medium of poetry. [a.] Eastpointe, MI.

GARDNER-WESLEY, CARMEN
[b.] April 6, 1950, Chanute AFB IL; [p.] M/Sgt. and Mrs. Jack Gardner; [ch.] Damien and Christopher; [ed.] Schulte High School, California State, Indiana State; [occ.] Professor of Sociology (NY Tech State College); [memb.] Advocate for Humanitarian efforts and women's social issues; [oth. writ.] Presently pursuing completion of 2 books: one book of poetry, one book on societal issues for my psychology and sociology students; [pers.] Inside each poem I write, is the hidden message of someone special in my life. [a.] Terre Haute, IN.

GARNER, TONY STEVEN
[b.] June 23, 1958, Tampa, FL; [p.] Ocie Mae and Thomas Garner; [ed.] High school grad., Day Adult High; [memb.] Tampa Chapter S.T.O.P. Inc., Mrs. Freddie Jean Cusscaux Sr. President; [hon.] Golden Poet award (from World of Poetry; Poet Extraordinare) Volunteer of the Year from Social Services Day Care Program; [oth. writ.] Several 1988 and 1990 poems published in World of Poetry as well in Mental Health Access House Newsletter. Those were years of Golden Poet honors. [a.] Tampa, FL.

GARRETT, KATHY
[pen.] Staria Kay; [b.] October 17, 1954; [m.] Divorced; [ch.] Joseph W. and Wayne B. Ashley; [ed.] Draughn's Business College - Vocational School at Tilghman; [occ.] Custodial and some classes still; [memb.] Saleian Mission Rochelle NY, Eureka Baptist Church; [hon.] Got published in book, donated songs and sold one; [oth. writ.] The World's Most Cherished poems; [pers.] The words in my heart will open words out of others heart. [a.] Paducah, KY.

GAUTHER, JOANNE
[b.] June 24, 1979, Virden, Monitoba; [p.] Ray and Huguette Gauthier; [ed.] Archbishop M.C. O'Neill High School; [pers.] Music is the key that unlocks the magic in my writing. Michael Jackson is my biggest inspiration. [a.] Regina, SASK.

GERHAUSER, STEPHEN JR.
[b.] May 8, 1971, Spokane, WA; [p.] Steve and Annette Gerhauser; [m.] Lori, February 29, 1992; [ch.] Loren Ann Gerhauser; [ed.] Selah High School; [occ.] U.S. Coast Guard; [memb.] The International Church (San Francisco); [oth. writ.] "Moonbeam" published in "A Space Between" National Library of Poetry; [pers.] Personal thanks to the brothers and sisters in the International Church of Christ for their love and showing me the true way. God Bless San Francisco. [a.] Alameda, CA.

GIBBONS, HELEN CLARK
[b.] April 12, 1938, New Milford; [p.] Morris D. and Frances W. Clark; [m.] Edwin, June 15, 1957; [ch.] Betsey, Cynthia, Edwin II, Samantha, Beverly and Michael)grandchildren-Gregory, Joseph, Amber, Tyler and Zachary; [ed.] Woodbury Public School, Woodbury High School; [occ.] Para-Educator, part-time clerk; [hon.] Appeared "Good Morning America" and on "Positively Connecticut", modeled for a book titled "This Is Farmer" written and illustrated by Nancy Tafuri from Roxbury, CT; [oth. writ.] Two other poems selected one for Days End another for Echoes of Yesterday. Another published in another Poetry Anthology. Editor's Choice award for "Gift of Beauty" in Day's End. Two poems selected for taping to music by National Library of Poetry; [pers.] Go through life knowing that there is someone out there just a little bit better than you. Success comes from working at something and doing it little but better each time. [a.] Woodbury, CT.

GILDERSLEEVE, HELEN
[b.] October 23, 1924, Arizona; [p.] Lisle Gaylord and Irene Hailings; [m.] Harry Dale, September 20, 1944; [ch.] Linda Bayley-Kate Matthews-Philip Gildersleeve-Donna Walley; [ed.] Compton High, Compton Junior College; [occ.] Writing-Genealogy-Antiques-Dolls-Music; [memb.] NSDAR-NSCDXVII-Antique Club-American Legion Auxiliary-Doll Club; [hon.] Music Festival awards: four honorable mentions - one finalist; [oth. writ.] Book-1990 "Gaylords and Gildersleeves and Some Lateral Branches". Number of poems and lyrics in CA and NE newspapers. Two theme songs for politicians; [pers.] I believe every person should have this thought when questions arise: "Do The Right Thing". I try very hard to keep this as my personal creed. [a.] O'Neill, NE.

GIPSON, CAROL
[b.] october 20, 1943, Huntington, W.VA; [p.] Willis and Effie Tackett; [m.] Samuel E. Sr., November 20, 1993; [ch.] 7 beautiful children (combined families); [ed.] The University of the State of New York; [occ.] Critical Care, Hospital Supervisor at Saline Memorial Hospital; [memb.] International Society of Poets, American Heart Association; [oth. writ.] Many poems including Expressions of Love, published in 1993 by The National Library of Poetry; [pers.] Mt goal: To do some small part toward healing the hurt, the pain of man. [a.] Benton, AR.

GIRDHAM, GLENN F.
[b.] July 9, 1944, Wauseon, OH; [p.] Glenwood Girdham and Belva Paxson Girdham; [m.] Divorced; [ch.] Matthew John, Joline Angela; [ed.] Morenci High School, United States Military Intelligence School; [occ.] Businessman, writer, financial consultant; [hon.] Editor's Choice award and Poet of Merit award in 1994; [oth. writ.] Over 150 poems and over 150 short stories; [pers.] Where my mind wanders, I tend to become involved in the dimensions and routes that carry me to the determination to pick up a pen and write. There is no time of day that can prevent expressions. [a.] Morenci, MI.

GIROD, TYRONE JR.
[b.] February 15, 1978, Baton Rouge; [p.] Tyrone and Martha Girod; [ed.] Bishop Sullivan Catholic High School; [occ.] Student; [hon.] First place in Louisiana in the Young Author's contest. Published in "Young Author's Anthology", published in "River of Dreams"; [oth. writ.] Many poems written for personal enjoyment of others; [pers.] No one reaches their destination without inspiration. Thank you for your love and inspiration, Daddy and Mommie. I love you. [a.] Baton Rouge, LA.

GIVENS, IJAAZ L.
[pen.] Jaaz; [b.] November 29, 1948, NYC; [p.] Deceased; [m.] Charles E., November 29, 1977; [ch.] Umlayla Givens, Jaliyl Clemons, LaTif Bowen; [ed.] Mid High School, Vista Action Volunteer, Peer/Outreach/Counselor, Berk Business School; [occ.] Human Resource Consultant and Peer Counselor; [hon.] The National Library of Poetry, International Society of Poets "Mothers Helping Mothers"award, Vista/Action Volunteer, services of America award; [oth. writ.] "Questions, Mortal Thoughts", [pers.] I know that you believe that you understand what you think I said, but I'm sure you'll realized, that what you think you heard, is not at all what I meant". [a.] Brooklyn, NY.

GLINSKI, FRANK ZDZISLAW
[b.] 1928, Wyrzysk, Poland; [m.] Eugenia Pilc, 1950; [ch.] Lech, Evon; [ed.] Educated in Poland, Germany, Rutgers University; [occ.]Management; [hon.] Editor's Choice Award 1993, Honorable Diploma for Poetry 1994, President's Award for Literary Excellence; [oth. writ.] Numerous poems and cassettes published in English and Polish;

GLOCK, MILTON F.V. SR.
[b.] July 7, 1918, Baltimore, MD; [p.] Katherine Elizabeth Erker Glock and George Adam Glock, Sr.; [m.] Elizabeth Shackelton, September 26, 1942; [ch.] Milton F.V. Jr., (Fred), Elizabeth Mabel Binker Glock Hughes (Binker); [ed.] Washington College, Wayne University, Vanderbilt University; [occ.] Retired Chemist; [memb.] American Chemical Society, Masonic Order, St. Luke's Episcopal Church; [hon.] Honorable Order of Kentucky Colonels, past-chairman, Louisville section, American Chemical Society; [oth. writ.] "The Chemist Holmes", Investigations, "5:30 Appointment (The Worth)", private printing, "Sounds of Georgia", In The Desert Sun 1994, The National Library of Poetry, many poems and sketches not submitted for publication; [peers.] The frequent trips from Louisville, KY to Atlanta GA have a strange effect on me. I always think of the terrible conditions the Civil War soldiers faced. It is poetic country for me. [a.] Middletown, KY.

GLOMB, PENNY WEEKS
[pen.] Penny Weeks; [b.] September 9, 1937, Erie, PA; [p.] Marjorie Donavan and Harry Linet Weeks; [ch.] Christopher, Kevin; [ed.] St. Agnes Academy, University of St. Thomas; [occ.] Medical/clerical; [hon.] Juried poet, 1991 HOuston Poetry Fest; [oth. writ.] Published 1994 National Library f Poetry Songs on the Horizon, 1991 Houston Poetry Fest anthology; [pers.] Poetry is the last freedom. [a.] Houston, TX.

GOARD, CYNTHIA R.
[b.] December 18, 1978, Charleston, [p.] Iria J. Goard; [ed.] East Bank High School; [memb.] East Bank High School Flag Corp, East Bank High School Band, Bethel Baptist Church; [hon.] 6th grade Presidential Award, 4 awards in elementary and jr high band, 1st and 2nd place Spelling Bee, high school Flag Corp member; [oth. writ.] Own personal collection of poetry.

GOLLIHER, RUBY
[b.] March 17, 1912, Albion OK; [p.] Thomas J. and Hattie Napier; [m.] Three husbands (deceased), 1st marriage March 2, 1929; [ch.] Raye Nell, Derral, Levon, Doyle Albert Lee Jr (Brewers); [ed.] High school, various courses at San Diego State College; [occ.] Retired, Retired Seniors Volunteer; [oth. writ.] Small book of poetry called"Show Me the Way", "Listen to the Desert", "Scram--Scrab--Scrabble", a booklet; [pers.] My poetry comes from the heart and soul, and is dedicated to the ignorance and love of all ages. [a.] Camp Verde, AZ.

GOOD, MARGARET
[pen.] Margaret Brown Good; [b.] February 4, 1933, New Mexico; [p.] Claude and Bertha Brown; [m.] Paul W. Good, March 16, 1962; [ch.] Dena Sue Roberts, Edward F. Good, Steven W. Good; [ed.] Harding College, 2 years; [occ.] Inventory clerk; [memb.] Duneland Rock Club, Church of Christ; [oth. writ.] High school anthology, sermons in poetry anthology, National Library of Poetry Today's Great Poems anthology; [pers.] I like to write poetry specifically for particular occasions and religious poems. [a.] Griffith, IN.

GOODWIN, BONNIE L.
[b.] April 9, 1950, Masury; [p.] John and thelma McLean; [m.] Gary Goodwin, JUne 30, 1973; [ch.] John Gary Goodwin, Gary Goodwin; [ed.] Hubbard High School, Columbus Business University; [occ.] Personnel; [memb.] PTO; [hon.] Editor's Choice Award, Spelling Bee; [oth.,. writ.] "Calendar Babies", "What I Wish For You", "Seasons of Love", "My Gary"; [pers.] "What I Wish For You" was dedicated to wishing the best for all people everywhere. [a.] Wapakoneta, OH.

GOODWIN, JOHN S.
[b.] May 29, 1904; [p.] Alanzo and Mary; [m.] Inez (deceased), August 4, 1928; [ch.] Donald , LOuis; [ed.] CMU, MSU, U of M; [occ.] Retired; [memb.] Honorary State Farmer, Soil Conservation and Environment, Farm Bureau, State Teacher's Association; [a.] Mt. Pleasant, MI.

GORDON, GUANETTA STEWART
[pen.] Guanetta Gordon; [b.] October 4, 1905, K.C., MO; [p.] Samuel L. and Minnie Anna Stewart; [m.] Lynell F. Gordon, July 15, 1924; [ch.] Stewart L. Gordon, Krista Sharon; [ed.] Baker University; University of Kansas, Horner Institute of Fine Arts; [occ.] Retired, author; [memb.] The National League of American Pen Women, International Academy of Poetry, National Federation of State Poetry Societies; The Kansas Authors Club; World Academy of Arts and Culture, World Congress of Poets, Arizona State Poetry Society; [hon.] World Hon. Doctor of Literature, Academy of Arts and Culture, Alumni Citation, Baker University; [oth. writ.] Numerous books, poems and articles published; [pers.] Life is mostly what you make of it. There is a mystic force from which anyone can draw to use for his advancement and to surmount adverse circumstances, something of the infinite which springs from the spirit and fills the heart. [a.] Sun City, AZ.

GORDON, JOAN L.
[b.] August 19, 1905, Jackson, MS; [p.] Robert Lee and Florence McAllister; [m.] Dr. Asa Hines (deceased), June 2, 1935; [ch.] Robert Asa Gordon, Frank Edmund Gordon; {ed.] Jackson State University, Columbia University, University of Pennsylvania; [occ.] Retired professor; [memb.] Georgia Poetry Society, American Sociological Association; [a.] Savannah, GA.

GORMAN, SHIRLEY ANNE
[b.] March 9, 1940, Cave Springs, MO; [p.] Herbert and Frances Gorman; [ed.] Central High, Mid-America Business College; [occ.] Registered author poet; [memb.] Boulevard Baptist Church, Chancel Choir, Transitions PSR Clubhouse, American Bell Association Int. Inc, National Authors Registry,INt. Society of Authors; [hon.] Two Accomplishment of Merit awards, 1 award of merit, 3 Editor's Choice awards, 4 Honorable Mentions, 2 President's Award for Literary Excellence; [oth. writ.] Childrens' book, 450 poems, numerous short stories and essays; [pers.] Much of my writing is aimed at the juvenile market. I spend time caring for my pets, Amos, Buttercup, Smoky, Pumpkin, Yoshi. Enjoy photography. [a.] Springfield, MO.

GOSTIAUX, SHANNON
[b.] August 7, 1977, Pontiac, MI; [p.] Richard and Cindy Gostiaux; [ed.] Laper East High School, Lapeer County Vocation Technical Center; [occ.] Dietary aide; [memb.] American Legion Auxiliary, HOSA, DECA; [hon.] Student of the Month 1991, Editor's Choice Award; [oth. writ.] Poem entitled "Friend" published by The National Library of Poetry; [pers.] No matter what life's cards try to deal you, remember you've always got friends to help you through your trials. [a.] Lapeer, MI.

GOTLIB, GABRIELLE
[b.] November 11, 1980, Brooklyn, NY; [p.] Lia Ratsutsky and Ilya Gotlib; [ed.] Adelphi Academy; [occ.] Student; [hon.] Honor Roll; [oth. writ.] Poems published in school newspaper, poem published in "At Days's End+; [pers.] In my poems I try to express my feelings and thoughts. I've been greatly influenced by my family and friends. [a.] Brooklyn, NY.

GRAHAM, JESSICA A.
[b.] June 9, 1969, Honolulu, HI; [p.] Edward L. and Alice C. Graham; [ed.] Stephen F. Austin State University; [occ.] Administrative Assistant to the Executive Director at Houston Ballet; [memb.] Women In Communication, Inc.; American Rivers; [hon.] "Who's Who In Poetry"; Women In Communications, Inc., Board of Directors; [oth. writ.] "Goodbye", "Why Do I Love You?". [a.] Alvin, TX.

GRANT, BARBARA B.
[b.] July 25, 1931, Greenville, SC; [p.] Alvin O. and Louvenia Anderson; [m.] Chester E., July 3, 1951; [ch.] Kay, Anna, Donna; [occ.] REtired. [a.] Greenville, SC.

GRANT, BRENDA A.
[pen.] Brenda Hopper, Brenda A. Bischoff; [b.] Vircennes, IN; [p.] Carl J. and Roberta Winkler Hopper; [m.] W. Scott, November 18, 1984; [ch.] Boys and girls; [ed.] 18 years; [occ.] Writer/poet; [memb.] Circle of Janus, Broad Ripple Poetry Club, Indiana Poetry Society, Indianapolis Urantia Study Group, Hoosier Environmental Council; [hon.] High school and college honor societies; [oth. writ.] Over 30 poems published in various publications, presently working on non-fiction book; [pers.] I believe in people and I love life. No one ever promised that life would be easy. However, depending on one's attitude, it can be a whole lot of fun. [a.] Indianapolis, IN.

GRANT, LOLA E.
[pen.] L E G at end of poem; [b.] August 23, 1905, Areola, IL; [p.] Fred and Ethel Black Ehrhart; [ch.] Shirley and Charlene; [ed.] University of Illinois; [occ.] Retired teacher; [oth. writ.] Memories, More Memories, One Family History, Poems and Verses of Sense and Nonsense. [a.] Urbana, IL.

GREBINER, TIMOTHY WILLIAM
[b.] October 23, 1969, Pittsburgh, PA; [memb.] Member of human race for past 25 years; [hon.] Guest Speaker (poet), Muse for Mothers in Pittsburgh, several poems published in various reviews and collections; [oth. writ.] Self-published a book of poetry entitled "Prayers in the Temple of the Dawn"; [pers.] Live hard, live fast. Love once, die young. [a.] Pittsburgh, PA.

GREEN, PENNY M.
[b.] February 7, 1969, Plant City, FL; [p.] Earl and Virgie Green, sister-Kathy D. Green; [ed.] Plant City High; [occ.] Rural Carrier Association for U.S. Post Office; [oth. writ.] Untitled poem in Dance on the Horizon, many unpublished poems; [pers.] My writing is my way of expressing my ideas and feelings when I can't get them across any other way. [a.] Crystal Springs, FL.

GREENAWALD, BETH
[b.] June 3, 1969, Pittsburgh; [p.] John and Margaret Karns; [m.] David, Sr., July 20, 1991; [ch.] David M. Greenawald, Jr.; [ed.] University of Pittsburgh; [occ.] Professional Photo Lab Color Analyst; [memb.] Phi Kappa Theta fraternity, Sigma Sigma Sigma Sorority; [hon.] Editor's Choice award, National Library of Poetry; [oth. writ.] Hold Me Strong (A Far Off Place, 1994), several poems written since high school; [pers.] Thanks for the recognition - what a boost for my self-esteem. Thank You Again. [a.] Pittsburgh, PA.

GREGORY, BEULAH
[b.] August 22, 1938, Chavis; [p.] Clifford and Lucille Gilliland; [m.] Fred H. Gregory (deceased), November 20, 1957; [ch.] 2 girls and 2 boys; [ed.] Cocke Co. High School; [hon.] I received the Silver and Gold Poet award; [oth. writ.] Poems; [pers.] I like to make others people happy, think of their happiness first. I am a Christian, serving Christ is my life. I'll always put him first. [a.] Newport, TN.

GREY, STEPHEN
[b.] June 21, 1991, Sask., CAN; [ed.] High school (Canadian); [oth. writ.] 3 act plays published and produced in Canada, U.S. and England, editorial writing (Canadian Newspapers); [pers.] In my opinion, poetry is the only "language" combining the mind, heart and soul to express thoughts, feelings and sincerity. [a.] Fort Lauderdale, FL.

GRIFFIN, BARBARA
[b.] January 8, 1926, Oyster Bay, NY; [p.] Rose and Arthur Brown; [m.] John, November 27, 1949; [ch.] Joy, Laurel, Jon, Scott and Melissa; [ed.] High school; [occ.] Retired-former nursing assistant; [oth. writ.] Ride the Lonely Country - Western 1975, A Vision - A Verse poetry. Important American Poets and Songwriters of 1949-1948 - The Space Between; [pers.] What is a son - poem dedication to Jon Bruce Griffin. December 1958-march 1993 Jon, you will walk forever through the corridors of my heart. I love you. Mom.

GRIGGS, STANLEY EVANS
[b.] June 11, 1925, Colorado, OH; [p.] Benjamin H. and Mary E. Griggs; [m.] Cleo Dott (Thoma), June 15, 1947; [ch.] James David Evans and Tanya Devans; [ed.] Central High, Ohio Wesleyan Capital Univer-

sity, Ohio State University, Kingsway Bible College; [occ.] Pastor and Founder of Open Gate Ministries and Chaplain of Fellowship of Praise Ministry; [hon.] Excellence in Teaching award, Instructor Magazine 67-68, Honorary Doctor of Divinity, Kingsway Bible College; [oth. writ.] Poems published in local newspapers, some engraved in stone at Sunset Cemetery, hundreds of unpublished poems and books. Poem published in The National Library of Poetry Anthology, Echoes of Yesterday; [pers.] My poems and writings are my ministry for they all come from His heart to my heart...to your heart. [a.] Columbus, OH.

GRINDEL, PATRICIA
[b.] August 28, 1947, Flint, MI; [p.] Frank and Irene Karner; [ed.] Clio High School; [oth. writ.] This verse "Karen" was written for her funeral. She was my youngest sister, and killed in a car accident in 1993; [pers.] I am both legally blind and deaf. My husband died of a heart attack just before our silver anniversary and I have been writing since.

GUGLIELMETTI, MARCI
[b.] August 19, 1977, SLC, UT; [p.] Kjeld Guglielmetti/ Ann Douglas; [ed.] Senior in high school; [occ.] Student; [oth. writ.] A poem published in "In The Desert Sun", by the National Library of Poetry (untitled); [pers.] As I grow, my poetry grows with me. As I feel, the words spell out its meaning. I only have to listen to the voice of my heart.

GUNTER, DANNY W.
[b.] January 21, 19 70, Kansas City; [p.] Earl W. Guner and Vernetta R. Lungstrum; [ed.] Turner High School; [occ.] Inventory Control Fleming Foods; [oth. writ.] It Doesn't Matter published in The Space Between. [a.] Independence, MO.

GURNEY, GEORGE ROBERT
[b.] October 23, 1933, Seneca, KS; [p.] Datha Alice and Charles Marion Gurney, Sr. - sister-Shirley Joyce Gurney; [m.] June 21, 1953; [ed.] 12th grade, National School of Aeronautics, numerous training classes by TWA; [occ.] TWA medically retired; [memb.] Immanuel Lutheran Church, Fraternal Communicator at Church, Cancer Support Group "Make Today Count"; [hon.] Numerous awards by employer, Cancer Bike-A-Thon two years, two Editor's Choice awards from National Poets Society, semifinalist award at International Society of Poets 1994; [oth. writ.] Numerous poems in local newspaper, many poems for "Cancer Support Group" and friends, poem published in Hospice Shareletter, copyright on book of poems ("Thoughts of A Daydreamer"; [pers.] Motto "Expect a Miracle - Miracles do happen". [a.] Wentzville, MD.

GUSTAFSON, AMY FOLEY
[b.] Michigan; [m.] Harry, 1984; [ch.] Parker and Scott; [ed.] Michigan State University, Rosary College, Northwestern University; [occ.] Retired 1992- V.P. couture retail chain; [memb.] Gamma Alpha Chi-Advertising, honorary/Theta Sigma Phi-journalism honorary, International Society of Poets, International Society of Authors and Artists, Lyric Opera of Chicago; [hon.] International Poet of Merit - International Society of Poets, several other merit awards; [oth. writ.] Published in over twenty poetry anthologies, incl. Iliad Press, National Library of Poetry, Watermark Press, The Amherst Society, Creative Arts and Sciences Enterprises, etc.; [pers.] I need the words tumbling quietly, cascading between, below the clean white lines. Breaking the silence, that last barrier where, we hide behind the front of each other. [a.] Glenview, Chicago, IL.

GUTSCH, DORIE
[b.] July 12, 1979, Elmbrook, WI; [p.] Patricia and Paul Gutsch; [ed.] Waukesha North High School; [occ.] Student; [pers.] Enhance Peace! [a.] Waukesha, WI.

GUY, FRANCESCA
[b.] April 8, 1962, Hartford, CT; [p.] Rudy and Bea Cross; [m.] Frank W., February 12, 1992; [ch.] Rachael, Matthew, Victoria, Michael, Amanda; [ed.] Manchester High School; [occ.] Feli-baker; [memb.] Girl Scouts; [oth. writ.] Poem published in "Dark Side of Moon"; [pers.] I find personal satisfaction and spiritual growth through my writing. [a.] Mesquite, TX.

HACKMANN, PAUL C.
[b.] April 13, 1937, Postville, IA; [p.] Mildred and Reuben Hackmann; [m.] A. Judith Unruh-Hackmann, January 30, 1960; [ch.] 1st Lt. Jonathan D. Hackmann and 2nd Lt. Ian I. hackmann; [ed.] Bethel College, Fresno State University, University of California-Davis; [occ.] Teacher; [memb.] Fairfield Suisun Teachers Association, CTA, NEA, Solano County Reading Association, First Baptist Church Choir of Vacaville, CA; [hon.] Citizenship award, Teacher in Our Community Honor; [oth. writ.] Several poems published in previous anthologies of the National Library of Poetry; [pers.] I enjoy writing poetry about nature or human relationships. [a.] Winters, CA.

HAEFELE, MARK J.
[pen.] Mark H. Ferris; [b.] September 27, 1971, Modesto, CA; [p.] Jimmie D. and Joyce C.; [ed.] River City High School, Consumer River Junior College; [memb.] Audobon Society, Celebration Christian Center; [oth. writ.] Some poems published in other publications; [pers.] "Work without hope draws nectar in a sieve, and hope without an object cannot live."-Coleridge. Coleridge was right. [a.] West Sacramento, CA.

HALL, DANIEL
[b.] Houston, TX; [hon.] Previous publication in The Space Between; [oth. writ.] I also compose short stories, scripts and have started two novels; [pers.] I feel that life is simply a situation in which we must endure in order to excel to the next level of existence, which in fact may not exist at all. Thus, we must endure and overcome the obstacles that life throws in our path and also learn to love them. [a.] Las Vegas, NV.

HALOG, BASILISA LACHIEA
[pen.] Bess Halog; [b.] April 15, 1920, Rosario, La Union, Philippines; [p.] Gregorio V. Lackica and Natalia G. Orduna; [m.] Leonardo D.,October 27, 1957; [ch.] Leonardo A. Halog; [ed.] National Teachers College; [occ.] Retired Postal Clerk; [memb.] FPEA of San Francisco, FCSF, FAASTAR, Holy Rosary Sodality, Golden Gate Senior Services, World of Poetry, Poetry Academy, The National Library of Poetry; [hon.] 7 Golden Poet awards, 14 awards of merit certificates, Special Achievement award, Dedication to service award, honorary charter membership award; [oth. writ.] Several poems published in the Postmark, the official monthly publication of S.F., USPS; also in the Philippine News of SF and in 10 World of Poetry books; [pers.] Do unto others as you would like others to do unto you. [a.] San Francisco, CA.

HAMBY, OLIVER NEWTON
[pen.] O. Hamby; [b.] December 13, 1914, Hiwassee, NC; [p.] J. Quincy and Lillie Nelson Hamby; [m.] Mary Butler, August 20, 1939; [ch.] Stanley Oliver Hamby, Eloise Hamby Harris; [ed.] Ducktown TN High School, Maryville College, Columbia Theological Seminary; [occ.] Retired since 1/31/81; [memb.] Presbyterian Church in America and Evangel. Presbyterian, Maryville College Literary Society, The Lions Club and Rotary Club; [hon.] Alabama Rural Minister of the Year 1964, Distinguished Service Award, Service awards from Teen Crusade, Bachman Memorial School Association; [oth. writ.] A weekly column (sermon) in The Screen County, GA, News for 10 years and other special articles, other poems but never published; [pers.] God has not left us in ignorance, superstition and dread of the unseen, spiritual realities about us, but has revealed to us all that we need to know: about Himself, ourselves and the world in which we live, in His Holy World. [a.] Hueytown, Al.

HAMILTON, CLOVER D.
[b.] April 1, 1953, California; [p.] Rev. John and Ruby Green; [m.] Maurice Cornell, March 28, 1972; [ch.] Kawhone' Dana Hamilton; [ed.] George Washington High School, California State, University Dominquez Hills; [occ.] Staff Assistant; County of LA Dept of Mental Health; [memb.] NCNW, AGK Choir, American Poetry Society; [hon.] Golden Poet 1990-1991; [oth. writ.] Various poetic, etc., writings relating to life's themes; [pers.] I have a need/desire to pass on to anyone willing to lend an ear, that there is love where it was thought there was none...there is hope when not seen, that good things will come (in time) out of bad and that overall life is worth living...is wonderful...but, be must make it all these things. It's achievable. [a.] Inglewood, CA.

HANCOCK, HUNTER MCRAE
[b.] December 22, 1910, Mayfield, KY; [p.] Samuel and Ruth Hancock; [m.] Christine Maddox, September 7, 1935; [ch.] Hunter Maddox Hancock; [ed.] High school; [occ.] Biology Professor (ret); [memb.] Sigma Xi Research Sec. KY and J.P. Historical Secs and others; [hon.] Biol, Sta. named in honor; [oth. writ.] Articles, letters and other verses in historical journals, newspapers and encyclopedia; [pers.] Although an admirer of more modern poetry, I remain highly appreciative of and loyal to the more classical discipline, rhyme schemes and forms of expressions. [a.] Murray, KY.

HARBISON, ROBERT EDWIN
[b.] August 8, 1920, Palo Verde, AZ; [p.] Lios and Joseph Harbison; [m.] Fay, August 16, 1947; [ed.] Orange Coast Community College; [occ.] Retired; [memb.] Lions International, American Solar Energy Society, International Solar Energy Society; [pers.] Peace in the world can be attained if we can educate our children to respect their contemporaries and forgive and forget any and all transgressions any ancestor may have committed against our forefathers. That was then -this is now. Let's learn to live together.

HARRELL, LINDA BYNUM

[b.] August 6, 1945, Cairo, Ochocknee, GA; [p.] Richard A. Bynum and Irene Rich Bynum Exum; [m.] Deceased (May 4, 1963); [ch.] Johnny Harrell Jr. and Debra Harrell Mixon; [ed.] GED; [occ.] Waitress; [oth. writ.] Poem-"My Little Boy" in book Echoes of Yesterday; [pers.] I've always dreamed one day my poems will be on plaques so the whole world could see clear to my heart of the people I love. [a.] Orlando, FL.

HART, HEATHER L.
[pen.] David Homer and Heather Hart; [b.] November 16, 1969, Pittsburgh, PA; [p.] Linda and Darrell Hart; [ed.] California University of PA; [occ.] Graduate student; [memb.] Delta Phi Epsilon Sorority, Anthropology Club; [hon.] Pi Kappa Delta; [oth. writ.] Poem published in The National Library of Poetry Anthology; [pers.] I write about things that touch my life. I am influenced by contemporary and classic poets; especially Elizabeth Barret Browning. "One Earth, One Chance". [a.] Belle Vernon, PA.

HARTNETT, MICHAEL W.
[b.] February 16, 1971, Utica, NY; [p.] William and Grace Hartnett; [ed.] Ithaca College, University of Rochester; [oth. writ.] Tears of Fire, National Library of Poetry. [a.] Rome, NY.

HASSELL, SUSAN
[pen.] Susan Hassell; [b.] August 15, 1979, Naples, FL; [p.] Jeff and Laura Lee Hassell; [occ.] Student; [pers.] Live your dream. [a.] Naples, FL.

HEDAYATI, JEANETTE
[b.] Washington, DC; [p.] Hilda an Louis Robbin; [m.] Vahid. [a.] Graham, TX.

HEGER, LORI J.
[pen.] X; [b.] March 19, 1958, Sioux City, IA; [p.] Jan and Paul Patterson; [m.] Marty, May 1, 1993; [ed.] North High School, University of South Dakota; [occ.] Receptionist; [memb.] Briar Cliff College, Writer's Club; [oth. writ.] Published in A Space Between.

HELENA, KORKUS
[b.] September 6, 1959, Aye (Belgium); [p.] Julianna and Francois; [m.] Balbin Julius, July 12, 1993; [ed.] Linguistics, philosophy, anthropology, slavistic; [oth. writ.] Poems and novels not yet published. [a.] New York, NY.

HENDERSON, VADA MAE
[b.] April 27, 1942, Marshall, CO; [p.] John and Bonnie Butler; [m.] Deceased William Owen, May 4, 1959; [ch.] Randy, Ronda, Zelda, becky and 6 grandchildren; [ed.] 8th grade, Aurora School; [occ.] Farm wife; [oth. writ.] Poems published in Dance on the Horizon, and also famous poets society, some pieces in Benton paper; [pers.] I like to write funny poems but most of the time I do true ones the one from my heart. Some make you happy some make you cry. I have written them from a little girl of 7 years old. [a.] Hardin, KY.

HERMELIN, MARGIE GALE SCARATO
[pen.] Margie Gale; [b.] November 1, 1926, St. Louis, MO; [p.] Elvira and Roy Scarato; [m.] Victor M., March 18, 1979; [ch.] Cindy Miano, Chris Fragale and Dawn Walters; [ed.] Roosevelt High; [occ.] Retired, Vocalist now with the St. Louis Show Stoppers; [memb.] AMC Players - Women's Varsity Club - Older Women's League, Shaare Emeth Sisterhood Judevine Center for Austin; [oth. writ.] "Love is Showing" published in The National Library of Poetry 1993 Editors Choice Award; [pers.] I hope my poems can show the true meaning of love not only for an individual but for mankind. [a.] Chesterfield, MO.

HERVEY, STEPHEN
[b.] May 18, 1959, Cambridge, England; [p.] Roosevelt and Violet Hervey; [m.] Sarah, December 27, 1992; [ed.] Lock Haven State College, Virginia Commonwealth University; [occ.] Steel Metal Mechanic; [memb.] Worldwide Church of God, Spokesman Club; [hon.] Athletic awards in football, and all marine wrestling Editor's Choice award in poetry; [oth. writ.] Various other romantic and spiritual poems and songs; [pers.] To be really high involves drawing near to the one who is the Most High. [a.] Newport News, VA.

HIGGINS, E. CHIPMAN
[pen.] E. Chipman Higgins; [b.] March 21, 1925, New York, NY; [p.] Ronald and Marjorie Higgins; [m.] Barbara, July 22, 1950; [ch.] Marjorie Evans, Bard Higgins, Neal Walters, Ronald Higgins; [ed.] U.S. Naval Academy, Purdue University; [occ.] Legislative Assistant; [memb.] The Modern Poetry Association, U.S. Navy League National Director, Treasurer-USS Bowfin Submarine Museum; [hon.] Legion of Merit U.S. Navy; [oth. writ.] Contributor U.S. Navy Supply Corps "Newsletter" poetry and articles over 25 years; [pers.] Most significant poetry examines technology's impact upon mankind. [a.] Honolulu, HI.

HILLSBERRY, SUSAN
[b.] June 17, 1943, Walla Walla, WA; [p.] Mr. and Mrs. C. Watkins; [m.] Ron, March 26, 1970; [ch.] Dale, Donna, Dean, Daniel, Becke; [occ.] Medical Technologist, author; [pers.] I endeavor to stimulate thought and inspiration. My love for children and writing go hand in hand. By esteeming our children, we give them permission to esteem themselves and others. [a.] Glenpool, OK.

HOBBS, IDA LILLIAN
[pen.] Ida Lou; [b.] December 20, 1917, Owosso, MI; [p.] Etta and Elmer Johnson (both deceased) birth father-John Neff Askew; [m.] Walter E. (deceased), April 17, 1942; [ed.] Lansing Eastern High School, Eastern Michigan University, Michigan State University, University of Denver, Colorado State University, University of Maryland; [occ.] Retired; [memb.] National Education Association, NACCA, AARP, American Lung Association, Alpha Delta Kappa; [hon.] Alpha Delta Kappa International Honorary Sorority for Teachers, delegate to Adk. International Convention, VP and Pres. ADK Theta chapter, Chaplain, Historian; [oth. writ.] Poems for senior citizen's newsletters (teen-age years, high school paper, Easterner; and Lansing State Journal; [pers.] I trust in the Lord, believing that things happen for a reason. I strive to think positive, don't ever give up. You won't know if you can do something unless you try. [a.] Holt, MI.

HODGES, JAMES
[pen.] Eagle Swanson; [b.] May 8, 1975, Reidsville, NC; [p.] Donald and Rachel Hodges; [ed.] Rockingham County Senior High; [occ.] Machine Operator; [hon.] Journalism award in high school; [oth. writ.] One poem published in an anthology Echoes of Yesterday; [pers.] Be true to your heart. Mountains will crumble. Rivers will part. [a.] Reidsville, NC.

HOFFMAN, GLORIA
[pen.] Gloria Hoffman; [b.] February 8, 1933, Norfolk, VA; [p.] Maxwell L. Levy/Jessie Mashbitz Levy; [m.] FRank Katz Hoffman, September 18, 1954 (deceased); [ch.] Daniel Lewis, L. Stephen, Victoria Anne and Jonathan Maxwell (deceased); [ed.] University of Wisconsin; [occ.] Founder/President Creative Concepts in Communications, LTD and Peoplehood Products and Properties; [memb.] Menorah Med. Center Auxiliary, Brandeis University Women, Shalom Geriatric Center, Friends of Art/Nelson Gallery, New Reform Temple, National Council of Jewish Women, Guild-MO Repertory Theater; [hon.] The World Who's Who of Women, Who's Who in U.S. Women, The Directory of Distinguished Americans (5th edition), The International Register of Profiles, International Leaders in Achievement, Who's Who in Finance and Industry, Who's Who in the World; [oth. writ.] "I Belong To Me -Each person's right to be a somebody special" (self-help book), "Sammy Sluggert Slugs Drugs" (rhymed, illustrated read-aloud to children ages 3-6; [pers.] Grief needs comic relief, life needs levity; smiles need smiling; laughs need laughing; cries need crying; feelings need feeling; feelings need sharing. We are real...and so are our feelings. [a.] Kansas City, MO.

HOGUE, ALINE
[pen.] Aline Frier; [b.] October 8, 1926, Florida; [p.] Joel and Rosa Peacock, deceased; [m.] Clarence, January 4, 1987; [ch.] Ronald, Kenneth, Wade and Carol Frier; [ed.] Turkey Creek High School; [occ.] Homemaker, Avon sales representative; [memb.] Baptist Church, Burchwood Temple; [pers.] I like to write about the beautiful things of nature like trees, mountains, flowers. I want things to console people when losing a love one. They all want me to write.

HOLLIDAY, EMMA
[pen.] Emma Holliday; [b.] September 26, 1923, Attica, IN; [p.] William T. and Frances Reese; [m.] William Holliday, June 1965; [ch.] Diana Conn, Philip McBride, Janice Brown; [ed.] High School grad; [occ.] Retired from Factory, homemaker; [memb.] Richmond Miniature Club, A.I.M. (Indiana Miniaturists); [oth. writ.] "Memories" in the Space Between, "Invisible Ties" and "Bus Stope Reverie" both unpublished; [pers.] I was widowed very young so my 3 children became doubly precious to me and each year of their lives is a celebration of love for me. I've written each of them a poem to try and express this. [a.] Richmond, IN.

HOLLINS, LOUIS CURTIS
[pen.] Twilight/Paris Kennedy Buchanan; [b.] January 16, 1970, Hollowdale, MS; [p.] Earleen Hollins and L.C. Reid; [ed.] Gentry High School; [occ.] Model, singer, rapper, entrepreneur, lecturer, author, poet, designer, actor, humanitarian; [memb.] Ebenezzar Baptist Church; [hon.] Honor roll, highest average in English, literary acclaim from Governor Kirk Fordice of MS and President Bill Clinton Literary acclaim and praise from several critics in NYC; [oth. writ.] Various poems and short stories. Freelance articles and several novels and biographies; [pers.] I

would like me writing to be useless a guide or tool to benefit all people of all races in times of sadness and in times of joy. I hope my writing is the key to happiness and the answer to the problem. [a.] Indianola, MS.

HONSON, MARION
[b.] November 26, 1924, Alabama; [p.] Mary and Frank Little; [m.] Stanley (deceased), February 13, 1969; [ch.] One stepson; [ed.] Rosenwall Elementary School; [occ.] Retired; [memb.] Andrew Jackson Senior Ctr., Emaculate Conception Church; [oth. writ.] Mrs. Hinson started writing during the summer of 1993 at The Andrew Jackson Senior Center in the one day per week poetry classes; [pers.] Ms. Honson was inspired to write this poem after thinking about the injustice she had experienced living in a multicultural community in the Bronx, NY.

HOPKINS, JOSEPH T.
[b.] October 5, 1916; [p.] Joseph and Elizabeth Hopkins; [m.] Mary Hopkins Teacher, April 30, 1983; [ch.] Joseph, William, James Atty and Sheila Atty; [ed.] Hamilton College, Albany Law School, American Bar Association; [occ.] Retired; [oth. writ.] "Five, Nine and Seven" received World of Poetry, Golden Poem award, 1989. National Library of Poetry - in Whispers in the Wind "The Spirit of '92". [a.] Port Orange, FL.

HOPPER, RUBY
[pen.] Sammie Jones; [b.] May 21, 1950, Harrison, AR; [p.] Rev. and Ethel (Bethany) Eddings; [m.] Aldred, August 1, 1970; [ed.] Harrison High School, Berean Bible College; [occ.] Ordained minister, author, housewife; [memb.] National Association of Radio and Telecommunication Engineers, Inc., FCC Volunteer Examiner for Amateur Radio; [hon.] Appreciation award from American Red Cross, Outstanding Achievement award from American Radio Relay League for Emergency Communication during storm 04/87; [oth. writ.] Echoes of Yesterday published my poem, "Progress" in 1994. [a.] Hollister, MO.

HOUCHEN, LILLIAN
[b.] Platte, SD'; [p.] John and Lillian (Baer) Hugg; [m.] William E., June 10, 1961; [ed.] Studies include Art (Watercolor, Oil and China Painting), Writing and Business; [pers.] After a lifelong interest in art, music, poetry and rockhounding and no longer being tied to the 8.00-5.00 grind, I hope to devote more time to painting and to writing, putting down on paper my musings as they occur before they have fled. [a.] Carson, CA.

HOWARD, CONSTANCE SETITIA
[pen.] Setitia; [b.] May 28, 1931, NYC; [p.] Edward and Helen Cohen (deceased), [m.] Samuel T. Howard, (deceased), September 20, 1951; [ch.] Frederick Howard; [ed.] Washington Irving High School, "School for Art Studies"; [occ.] Artist, poet; [memb.] Cancer organization, Heart organization; [hon.] I have won awards in painting and drawing only; [oth. writ.] Southern Comfort, The Reawakening, View From The Lake, Musings on Country Life, A Place For Me, Friends, One Sunday Day, Echoes of Sunday, Buster the Paddle, Holding My Hand; [pers.] Writing to me is a collection of feelings that is best expressed by putting the pen to paper, or brush to canvas. [a.] Albuquerque, NM.

HOWARD, ZELMA LOUISE
[pen.] Z. Louise Howard; [b.] January 9, 1935, Leadwood, MO; [p.] Jessie and S.P. Watson; [m.] David A.; [ch.] 2 daughters, 2 sons, 2 stepchildren, 9 grandchildren; [ed.] High school, some college, licensed professional; [occ.] Retired - Auto worker, now work in health care for ages; [hon.] Poem chosen last spring to be published in River of Dreams book; [oth. writ.] Called Tribute to Auto Workers; [pers.] My inspiration is my love for my family. I write only what my heart wants to say. [a.] Ballwin, MO.

HOWELL, ROBERTA E.
[b.] April 13, 1917, Due West, SC; [p.] Robert and Susie Morton Ellis; [m.] Andrew Rendall, June 14, 1942; [ch.] Rendall Lorre, Robert Emil, Andrea Suzette Hollins; [ed.] Lincoln High, Barber Scotia Jr. College, Johnson C. Smith University, University of Michigan, N.C. Central University; [occ.] Retired Librarian; [memb.] American Association of University Women, Delta Sigma Thets Sorority, Elder-Timothy Darling Presbyterian Church, VP of Area Congregations in Ministry; [hon.] Alpha Kappa Sigma Honorary Scholastic Society; certificate in music - rating "Superior" in Piano, award of merit certificate from World of Poetry 1989; [oth. writ.] Two poems published in Great Poems of the Western World; a book of unpublished poems, shorty story. [a.] Oxford, NC.

HOWES, C. THOMAS
[b.] November 19, 1928, Syracuse, NY; [p.] William Kenneth and Ruth T. Howes; [m.] Ruth P., June 5, 1981; [ch.] Lisa A. Yewdall, Lindsey M. Mucciold (step-Rick Pesto, Karen Coder, Christopher Pesto and Elaine Fisher); [ed.] Syracuse University; [occ.] Retired - 40 years Communications, Aerospace and Transportation Industries; [memb.] A Society of Concern; [pers.] Try to read and write between the lines of daily life. [a.] Havertown, PA.

HUDYNA, MARILEE JANE
[b.] September 23, 1960. Calgary; [p.] Walter and Kay Leskiw (step); [m.] Jerry, February 12, 1983; [ch.] Jerry John Walter, Jason Bill Adam; [ed.] Grade 10; [occ.] Full-time art work, housewife; [pers.] I hope to show other white native they can do it and how I love my children and am slow with work in school. [a.] El Monton, ALB.

HUGLEY, BETTY J.
[b.] July 21, 1933, Sherrill, ARK; [p.] Sue B. Owens and Johnny Parker; [ch.] John Davis, Michael Davis, Kenneth Davis and Glen Davis; [ed.] Miller High School. Wayne County Community College; [occ.] Unemployment Insurance Analyst; [memb.] Emma V. Kelly Temple of Elks #650, International Society of Poets; [oth. writ.] Published book of poems, titled, "Solace, Past and Present"; [pers.] Each day, life provides a new experience, from which I hope to grow. [a.] Detroit, MI.

HUISINGH, MELINDA
[b.] February 28, 1969, San Jose, CA; [ed.] San Jose State University, Revere Academy of Jewelry Arts; [occ.] Self-employed designer and fabricator of fine jewelry; [memb.] International Society of Poets; [pers.] We all have the fire, and we all have the choice to make it our friend, the fire of life, or to make it our foe, the fire of destruction. This makes all the difference in the world. [a.] San Jose, CA.

HULL, SANDRA
[b.] April 10, 1978, Albia, IA; [p.] Tom and Edith Hull; [ed.] Hoarce Mann Elementary School, Evans Jr. High, Ottumwa High School; [occ.] Student; [memb.] Ottumwa Baptist Temple, Highland Hotshots 4-H Club, Wapello County 4-H Council, SADD; [hon.] Various 4-H and school awards, academic letter; [oth. writ.] Several newspaper articles published locally, poem published In The Desert Sun; [pers.] After high school I plan to attend college and pursue a career in business/accounting I plan to continue writing in my spare time. [a.] Ottumwa, IA.

HUNT, ELEANOR
[pen.] Stephanie Shaw; [b.] January 16, 1943, Belfry, KY; [p.] Guy and Lucy Varney Lowe; [m.] John M., September 6, 1972; [ch.] Karen, Timothy, Lenore and Brenda; [ed.] GED, preparing for college credits; [occ.] Domestics; [oth. writ.] Poem published by The National Library of Poetry; [pers.] I strive to convey pleasurable writings I have been greatly inspired by my family friends and God to pursue further writings. [a.] Lexington. KY.

HUNTINGTON, ALFRED
[pen.] Al Hunt; [b.] January 17, 1957, Atlanta, GA; [p.] Sarah Huntington; [ed.] Henry McNeal Turner High, Clark College; [occ.] DeKalb County Employee; [memb.] Praise Connection Magazine staff - a religious publication; [hon.] Received several awards for short fiction; [oth. writ.] Several poems published in "Poetic Voices of America", by Sparrowgrass Poetry Forum; [pers.] Writing creatively has always been my love. I strive to reflect concern of mankind through my writing. [a.] Clarkston, GA.

HUTCHINS, SHARLEEN C.
[b.] January 28, 1961, Monroe, WA; [p.] Patsy Danbof and John Hutchins; [ch.] Sonja Shambaugh, Christopher Peterson; [ed.] Snohomish High school; [occ.] Retail sales manage, Floor Decor; [hon.] Commanding officers accommodation choice award, The NLP; [oth. writ.] "Dance on the Horizon", The NLP; "Dusting Off Dreams" Quill Books; "Listen With Your Heart" Quill books; [pers.] In my present and professional life, I practice what I believe in, if everyone works together to reach a goal it will be reached. My life experiences and faith have greatly influenced my writing. [a.] Snohomish, WA.

HUTCHISON, MARILYN
[b.] August 12, 1954, Waynoka, OK; [p.] C. Joan and L.W. (Bud) Hutchison; [ed.] Wesley School of Nursing; [occ.] Registered Nurse; [pers.] I strive to reflect the vastness of life with an open mind and appreciation. At other times I merely want to express and share the essence of everyday life experiences. I have been greatly influenced by life in rural America, strong family ties, and the privilege of practicing nursing. [a.] Emporia, KS.

HUTTON, AUDREY JEAN
[b.] February 19, 1935, Hampton, England; [p.] George and Florence Cullen; [m.] Russell L., January 31, 1953; [ch.] Barry and Rory; [ed.] High school in England, Citizens Police Academy; [occ.] Apartment Property Manager; [memb.] Tustin Effective Apartment Managers (TEA); [pers.] I try to write from my feelings. Usually from personal experiences. I try to see the good in others. [a.] Tustin, CA.

HUTTON, MARY
[b.] October 24, 1914, Beaumont, CA; [ed.] Eagle Rock High School, variety college experiences; [pers.] Two teachers instilled a love of reading and creating poetry in Mary: Josephine Miles and C.F. MacIntyre. Although traces of their influences are evident in her later work. Mary now speaks her own language which combines elements from the world of surprises. Some with foreknowledge may be disappointed, but the rest of us will relish each surprise. Mary passed award the 6th of May 1994, and we who survive miss her, but this collection can serve to soften the loss.

HYMER, GEORGE A.
[memb.] International Society of Poetry; [oth. writ.] occasional submissions to local and regional newspapers '93 and '94 publications of National Library of Poetry. [a.] Brewster, WA.

IRISH, DIANA
[b.] May 24, 11950, Grand Rapids, MI; [p.] June and Robert Newman; [m.] Harvey, November 22, 19687; [ch.] Timothy, Jamy, Corey, Windy, Robert, Wayne Shellie; [ed.] 12th grade; [occ.] Native American programmer, porcelain doll maker; [memb.] Women Diversity, Grand Valley American Indian Lodge, Southern Poet Association, New England Writers, Dorr Doll Club, [hon.] Numerous awards for dolls, programs, poetry; [oth. writ.] Published in 17 different anthologies, lodge paper and intertribal paper, wrote 3 books;

IRVING, FAITH T.
[b.] September 13, 1941, Honolulu, HI; [p.] Noboru and Yoshiko Sasaki (deceased); [m.] Divorced; [ed.] McKinley High School, Cannon's School of Business; [occ.] Secretary; [memb.] Olivet Baptist Church; [hon.] Territorial Spelling Bee runner-up 1955, 4th place 1988 Free Bonus Poetry Contest, Golden Poet award 1989, Silver Poet Award 1990, Editor's Choice award 1993, 1994; [oth. writ.] Two poems published Mckinley High School Daily Pinion, 1989 World Treasury of Great Poems, Vol II, a select number printed in State Dept of Labor newsletter, Outstanding Poets of 1994; [pers.] There is so much beauty all around us if only we would take the time to enjoy and appreciate all the creations of wonder set before us. God has always been my main source of inspiration in my poetic efforts. [a.] Honolulu, HI.

ISAACS, RICK
[b.] September 18, 1958, St. Louis; [p.] George A. and Mary L, Isaacs; [ed.] Mercy High School; [occ.] Sears; [oth. writ.] "The Sun" published in Whispers in the Wind; [a.] St. Louis, MO.

IVERSON, BETTY
[pen.] Ingie; [b.] February 21, 1932, Pendleton, OR; [p.] Jim and Marie Ingram; [m.] Earl (Buzz) Iverson, February 27, 1949; [ch.] Doug-Bruce and Jamee; [ed.] Pendleton High School; [occ.] Sales clerk; [memb.] Hillyard Baptist Church, alumni Elijah House Restoration of Families; [hon.] Jesus Christ; [pers.] Writing is a working of the deeper thought and intents of the heart level. Writings seem to arise from that place, of experiences of people and events, or of things in this present nature. [a.] Spokane, WA.

IZUKAMMA, AKWURUOHA LUI OBASI
[pen.] Lui Akwuruoha; [b.] August 23, 1958, Obowu, Imo State, Nigeria; [p.] Raphael and Rufina Akwuruoha; [ed.] Community Sec. High School, Alvan Ikoku College of Education, University of Calabar; [occ.] Free-lance writer, poet; [memb.] Association of Nigerian Theatre Artists, International Society of Poets, Shakespeare Festival of Dallas, The Smithsonian Institute; [hon.] International Poet of Merit awards 1993, 1994, Editor's Choice awards 1993, 1994, graduating honor student, Dept of Theatre Arts, University of Calabar; [oth. writ.] Unpublished collection of poems and short stories, art and theatre reviews; [pers.] Writing is a creative endeavor and a purgation of emotion. I strive to achieve a common bond between me, my writings and my readers. Once this is done, I am free and free indeed!

JACKSON, ANGELA
[b.] July 30, 1978, Lancaster, CA; [p.] Jeri and Stever Jackson; [ed.] 11th grade currently; [occ.] Babysitting; [oth. writ.] Many poems, none have been published; [pers.] my poems are the way I express my thoughts and feelings, otherwise, I'm not able to explain them. [a.] Lancaster, CA.

JACKSON, JOHN W. JR.
[pen.] The Poet, Shakespeare II; [b.] August 27, 1958, Fortord, CA; [p.] John and Lavonne Jackson; [m.] Yi Song-cha, October 27, 1978; [ed.] GED, 12 years military; [occ.] Food Service Management, Chef, locksmith; [memb.] International Society of Poets, National Rifle Association; [hon.] The first poem that was entered into a world wide contest, made into the top ten, too many to list; [oth. writ.] This Ole House, The Sweetness of Love, What You Seek, My Thinking Tree, The Shrunken Face, Freedom and over 180 more; [pers.] Poetry is read with the heart, not the mind. Poetry is read with the heart, not the eyes, Poetry this of the heart, not the mind. [a.] Sacramento, CA.

JACKSON, SHIRLEY
[pen.] Shirley Jackson; [b.] November 17, 1937, Independence, MI; [p.] A.W. and Juanita Plumb; [m.] Donald R., June 17, 1955; [ch.] Kevin M. Jackson, Jane Whitmore, David E. Jackson and Jill Barlow; [occ.] Central High School; [occ.] Homemaker; [memb.] First Assembly of God in Siloam Springs; [hon.] Three editor's choice, poems published in newspapers, used on bookmarks, by churches and mortuaries; [oth. writ.] Published book of poetry "From Our Porch Swing". Published poem in "Wind in the Night Sky" and "Outstanding Poets of 1994"; [pers.] My aim with the writing is to life someone's spirits. While honoring God and portraying my innermost feelings so that others may know me better. [a.] Summers, AR.

JACOBSON, JAMES R.
[pen.] Jim Jacobson; [b.] January 19, 1925; [p.] Oscar Jacobson; [m.] Lucille, August 28, 1948; [ch.] nancy, Randy, David and Kim; [ed.] School of Theology; [occ.] retired; [memb.] Rotary, Lions; [hon.] National Athlete Honor Society and National Honor Society; [oth. writ.] Articles- The Christian Home, two parenting books, magazine and newspaper articles; [pers.] I strive to express the inter=relations of all life and quality relationships in families. [a.] Peoria, AZ.

JAMES, MARY PITTMAN
[b.] March 8, 1937; [p.] The late Dunaway and Hilda Pittman; [m.] Billy Y., JUne 24, 1960; [ch.] Gleen Bradem, Gary James and Staci Hensley; [occ.] South Central Bell; [hon.] Publications with the NLP, Baptist Record and a song recorded by "Rainbow Records"; [pers.] It is my hope that the words written here many inspire many to know the one who gives them, a loving heavenly father. [a.] Petal, MS.

JANES, WILLIAM L. JR.
[b.] July 16, 1964, Janesville, WI; [p.] Mr. and Mrs. William L. Janes, Jr.; [ed.] Park College of VA, University of MD, high school grad; [occ.] U.S. Army Drill Sergeant; [memb.] American Red Cross Lifeguard and First Aid Instructor, Christian Children's Foundation, The Tomb of the Unknown Soldier Guard; [hon.] American Red Cross blood donor, Tomb of the Unknown Soldier Identification badge; [oth. writ.] Poem "The Preservation" published in prior anthology; [pers.] "He is no fool, who relinquishes what he cannot loose in order to gain what he cannot keep". Jim Elliott 1956. [a.] Ft. Leonardwood. MO

JANANIN, MILANA
[b.] August 31, 1948, Blanca, Slovenia; [p.] Milan and Stefania Jananin; [ed.] Faculty of Philosophy; [occ.] University teacher; [memb.] Croatian Society of University, Teachers of English, Croatian Society of Applied Linguistics, Croatian Society of Translators; [hon.] 1993 and 1994 Editor's Choice award; [pers.] Croatia forever! [a.] Sutjeskina Polanag, Zagreb, Croatia.

JEAN-FRANCOIS, MARIE CATHELINE
[b.] July 30, 1974, Brooklyn, NY; [p.] Phinelie and Jeveille Jean-Francois; [ed.] The Mary Louis Academy, Hofstra University; [occ.] Full-time student; [memb.] International Society of Poets; [hon.] Dean's List at Hofstra; Editor's Choice award; [oth. writ.] One poem published in The Best Poems of the 90's along in several other anthologies published by NLP. Another poem published in Outstanding Poets of 1994; [pers.] In my poetry, I try to attack real issues and problems we all face and portray them through positive light. [a.] Hollis, NY.

JEFFRE, SUSAN E.
[pen.] Susan Estelle Caldwell Jeffre; [b.] November 2, 1947, Cincinnati, OH; [p.] Paul L. and Justin Jeffre; [ed.] Regina High School; [occ.] Accounting Clerk; [oth. writ.] "Lies"; [pers.] I consider it a gift to be touched by ones own expression I am. [a.] Cincinnati, OH.

JENKINS, CASSANDRA MARIE
[pen.] Casey; [b.] November 17, 1978, Raveena, OH; [p.] Debra and Robert Foit; [ed.] Southeast High School; [hon.] Two Young Authors Awards; [oth. writ.] The Oceans Sacrifice and Deceased Love. Published in two different National Library of Poetry books. And many others not published; [pers.] I write poems mostly for other people to read and enjoy. [a.] Deerfield, OH.

JENKINS JR., ALFRED J.
[ed.] University of Maryland's Asian and European Division, Northern Virginia Community College; [occ.] Sargeant in U.S. Army, Computer Software Analyst; [memb.] Church; [pers.] Works are inspiring, insightful, and romantic as they illustrate his Christian values in today's setting. Alfred is a refreshing new poet with substance, and he writes beautiful song lyrics.

JETER, TERRY A.
[b.] January 18, 1954, Coatesville, PA; [p.] Sidney and Lillian Smith; [m.] Michael Dennis, August 28, 1982; [ch.] Michael, Christopher, April; [ed.] Conestoga Senior High School, Kutztown State College, National Education Center; [occ.] Housewife; [oth. writ.] Compilation of approximately 60 unpublished poe,s. Also book written called "To Hell and Back Again" (unpublished) autobiography; [pers.] Writing gives me an enjoyment and fulfills every aspect of my daily life. [a.] Highland, CA.

JETT, LINDA L.
[b.] January 4, 1948, Akron, OH; [p.] Robert Cadwell and Charlene Kilmire; [m.] Russell H., December 19, 1987; [ch.] Rhonda and Beth Lamb; [ed.] College part-time; [occ.] Customer Service Rep for a distribution center; [hon.] (2) Editor's Choice, (5) honorable mentions, professional reading cassette of my poem, article in local papers; [oth. writ.] Death, Put Your Hand in My Hand, Across the Years, More Than Just A Memory, Take It Away, In My Eyes, Love, Hello My Friend, I Never Wanted, The Ring on His Finger, Am I Just There, A Special Prayer, Tonight Will Be Ours, Then All I Need to Do; [pers.] My dream is to get a complete book of my poetry published. I have been writing for 15 years. Just within the past two years have let them be read by anyone. Now they are getting published a few at a time. [a.] Wood Dale, IL.

JOHNSON, AMY MARA
[b.] March 31, 1978, Chicago, IL; [p.] Daniel Johnson; [ed.] Grand Junction High School; [memb.] GJHS Young Democrats; [hon.] Grand Junction Noon Optimist, Student of the Month; [oth. writ.] One poem published in "The Space Between" by the NLP; [pers.] Everything I have ever written has been about my constant struggle in life: love and hardship. It reflects my character well. [a.] Grand Junction, CO.

JOHNSON, DON F.
[b.] August 1, 1919, North Ogden, UT; [p.] Clarence F. and Annie B. Johnson; [m.] Jeanne K., November 24, 1970; [ch.] Claire Geertje, Gail, Rebecca, Dawn, Sylvia, Sonja Leanne; [ed.] University of Idaho, Brigham Young University, Utah State University, Arizona State University, University of Arizona; [occ.] Retired; [memb.] Past-NASP, Utah Association of School Psychologists, Arizona Association of School Psychologists; [hon.] Lambda Delta Sigma, Dean's List; [oth. writ.] Weekly column in the Eastern Arizona Courier; [pers.] Each act we do in influences others. We ought, therefore to consider well the things, we do so that our influence is positive rather than negative. [a.] Salt Lake City, UT.

JOHNSON, GENE
[pen.] SDWJ; [b.] May 28, 1948, Longview, TX; [p.] Alvin and Adell Johnson; [m.] Sharon, June 6, 1992; [ch.] Ericka and Brandon; [ed.] University of California-Berkeley; [occ.] Writer; [memb.] African American Business Fellowship Group -LA; [oth. writ.] University of Texas at Arlington, newspaper, Campaign speeches for various candidates; [pers.] I would like for my work to not only touch my reader's hearts, but to also move them to another level of understanding causing them to re-direct their actions. [a.] Monroe, LA.

JOHNSON, GENE
[b.] July 18, 1922; [pers.] When Pearl Harbor was attacked, Gene Johnson was working in Panama. He returned to the United States and at age 21 won his wings as a Marine Corps fighter pilot. Later he was selected to fly in a squadron that was assigned the F7F Tigercat. This squadron was the first in the history of the Navy or Marine Corps to fly a twin-engine fighter plane. Three of Pappy Boyington's Black Sheep pilots were also in the squadron. At age 29, Gene volunteered to serve for three years in the Korean War. He attained the rank of Major. When active in tennis, he won three state titles; he did some parachute jumping; he is a former member of Mensa; he completed seven years of college. Gene is a retired high school English teacher. [a.] Riverside, CA.

JOHNSON, JANEY
[b.] November 12, 1942, Russel Co., VA; [p.] Boyce and Viola Franks; [m.] William M., Jr., June 25, 1974; [ch.] Davette Dee, Devon J.; [ed.] Johnsville High School; [occ.] Domestic Engineer; [hon.] Ribbons for paintings; [oth. writ.] My Grandmother Miss B. - An Old Apple Orchard- To My Sister - Cherokee Grandmother - Living Windows - A Misty Day - Moms Cold Cream - Boxes - The Critters Path - The Farm; [pers.] Expressing feelings of beauty, memory and a desire to create with poetry and paintings has been a wonderful gift to me. [a.] Mt. Gilead, OH.

JOHNSON, JUNE ANN
[b.] Long Island City, NY; [p.] Beatrice and Winston Marshall; [m.] Percival Jr., (deceased), June 6, 1953; [ch.] Karl S. Johnson and Blair V. Johnson; [ed.] Jamaica High School, N.Y. State University; [occ.] Tour Guide at Bushnell Theater; [memb.] Hartford Jazz Society, Wadsworth Atheneum, Church of The Good Shepherd (Cestry) and Colt Circle (SEC); [hon.] 1994's Outstanding Poets, many colors of a woman pub. (Uptown Girl), award from Mt. Sinai Hosp. 6 years volunteer service; [oth. writ.] Essence Magazine (no strings 1983) Catalyst Mag Atlanta, GA (The Church Ladies) 1994, Complete Woman Mac (Rosie) 1992, Hells Doorway and Your World National Lib. of Poetry; [pers.] Poetry and music is food for the soul and the heart it would be like starving to be without both. Live, laugh and love and be happy. [a.] Hartford, CT.

JOHNSON, LISA ELAINE
[pen.] Ms. L.E. Johnson; [b.] September 19, Washington, DC; [p.] Clarence and Fannie Johnson; [ed.] Howard University, Duke Ellington School of the Performing Arts; [occ.] Teacher of Performing Arts - Paul Junior High School; [hon.] "Who's Who Among Poets" cum laude - BFA Howard University; [oth. writ.] Poetry printed in "Our World's Most Treasured Poems", "World Treasury of Great Poems Vol. II", "World Treasury of Golden Poems"; [pers.] I am blessed to have such wonderful parents - Clarence and Fannie Johnson. I owe them all my creativity and love. [a.] Washington, DC.

JOHNSON, MARY OAKLEY
[pen.] Mary Bullock; [b.] October 31, 1933, Chapel Hill, TN; [p.] Robbie and Herman Bullock; [m.] Deceased, June 10, 1972; [ch.] Alan, Jenny Lynne and Annie Oakley; [ed.] High school and some college; [occ.] Retired legal and medical secretary; [hon.] Worked 12 years in TN State Government - Lt. Governor and State Senators; [oth. writ.] Books and poems but none published; [pers.] Descendant of William the Conqueror, 1st king of England, Martin Luther, founder of Protestantism and Moses, author of first five books of our Bible. I was born on Halloween same day Martin Luther nailed his 95 thesis to church door in Germany. [a.] Nashville, TN.

JOHNSON, TESHA
[b.] September 16, 1954, Port Huenume; [p.] William and Elizabeth Johnson; [ed.] Channel Island High School, California State University of Northridge; [occ.] Claims Supervisor; [memb.] Class with Class, Channel Islands Reunion Committee Class of '72, and Old Timers Committee of Oxnard; [hon.] Essay on making American beautiful 1970; [pers.] My poetry come from the heart, life experiences is the best lesson one could share with an individual. God has blessed me with this talent. Influence by Richard Wright and Langston Hughes. [a.] Oxnard, CA.

JOHNSON, WILLIAM E.
[pen.] Bill Johnson; [b.] January 16, 1930, New Jersey; [p.] Jean M. Johnson; [m.] Esther B., April 11, 1954; [ch.] Bill Jr., Ann-Renee' Johnson; [ed.] 2 years college; [occ.] Carpenter Civil Service; [memb.] DAV, NCOA, AARP; [hon.] Marriage date to Esther Barrios and two children Bill Jr. and Renee and three grandchildren Brooke, Skye and Connor William; [oth. writ.] 3 previous poetry printings "1992 A Question of Balance", 1993 "The Coming of Dawn", 1994 "Outstanding Poets"; [pers.] My best ideas for writings come from my family. [a.] Barstow, CA.

JOLE, DANA
[b.] October 26, 1948, San Diego; [m.] Karron, January 1, 1970; [ch.] Patricia, Richard, Dawn and Ryan; [ed.] St. Augustine High School, University of San Diego; [occ.] Supervisor of Quality Standards; [memb.] American Society for Quality Control, USD Alumni Association, Communication Studies Society; [hon.] High school honor roll, Scripps Outstanding Senior award - University of San Diego; [oth. writ.] Various poems and short stories published in college anthology, articles for local newspapers; [pers.] My family provides me with the inspiration and focus for my writing. They really are the best part of me. [a.] Santee, CA.

JONES, CHARLES D.
[pen.] Little Jake; [b.] May 31, 1936, Glenwood, NM; [p.] Charley and Elizabeth Jones; [m.] Dorothy, December 25, 1955; [ch.] Timothy, Lynden, Kristy; [ed.] Highland High; [occ.] Retired - Dept. of Defense, 32 years New Mexico Air National Guard; [hon.] 1st place - Creative Arts and Science Contest - Editor's Preference award Creative Arts and Science - recorded work on "The Sound of Poetry" NLP, selected for publication in "Best Poems of 1995" NLP; [oth. writ.] Published in local newsletters and several anthologies of poetry nationally. Unpublished manuscript of "Western" (not cowboy) poetry; [pers.] Committed to the preservation of the "western" style of verse, story and song. Greatly influenced by the writings of Louis L'Amour. [a.] Edgewood, NM.

JONES, CLARENCE DAVID
[pen.] Clarence David; [b.] November 16, 1952, Nashville, TN; [p.] Mr. and Mrs. Shannon Jones, Jr.; [m.] Janet S., June 18, 1977; [ch.] David D. Jones and

Heather A. JOnes; [ed.] Peabody College, Vanderbilt University; [occ.] Information Specialist, AOD Prevention Fairfax City Schools; [memb.] Fellowship of Christian Athletes, American Counselor Association, United States Air Force Reserves; [hon.] Golden Eagle Award, Commendation for Professional Excellence-FCPS; [oth. writ.] Several poems published in different newspapers; [pers.] We need to reflect on our own lives and learn to live in peace, for with all of natures differences, it has learn to live in harmony, we should learn from nature, its all we have left. [a.] Waldorf, MD.

JONES, JAMES G.
[b.] June 14, 1941, Livingston, TX; [p.] Liddie and Ray Lacy; [m.] Lois F., March 6, 1976; [ed.] 3rd grade - class for mentally retarded (had form of dyslexia and a learning disability); [occ.] Disabled; [oth. writ.] Thought's in Your Book, The Coming of Dawn. One horror book unpublished and about a dozen poems unpublished; [pers.] God has given me a very special talent. I would like to share that talent with all poem lovers. [a.] Quitman, TX.

JONES, OLGA
[b.] January 7, 1936, Clyde, Alberta, CAN; [p.] Michael and Annie Koochin; [m.] Harold, December 18, 1953; [ch.] Christopher, Robert and Jeffrey; [ed.] Burnaby North High School; [occ.] Agent in Performing Arts; [pers.] I find my writing is a result of a catharsis in my life. [a.] North Vancouver, B.C., CAN.

JOYCE, ELIZABETH
[b.] March 16, 1942, Hackensack, NJ; [p.] Walter Edwin and Priscilla H. Reich; [ch.] Walter Vance Van Inwegen and Dr. Jeffrey Richard Van Inwegen; [ed.] Bergen Community College, Thomas Edison State College, Ridgewood High School; [occ.] Therapist/ Counselor; [memb.] Spiritual Frontier Fellowship, Association of Research and Enlightenment, American Association for Ethical Hypnosis, New Jersey Metaphysical Society; [hon.] Dean's List; [oth. writ.] Spiritual Frontiers Summer 1993, Monthly column, "Metaphysical Corner" in the Pike County Courier, New Jersey Metaphysical Society Publication, New York Hospital Health News; [pers.] I like to associate our feelings toward nature with feelings within our hearts. My writing focuses on human integrity, love and honor. My influence has been the poems of Stephen Crain. [a.] Mahwah, NJ.

KADEN, SARA
[b.] June 23, 1979, Hannibal, MO; [p.] Melvin and Janice Kaden; [ed.] Monroe City High School; [occ.] Student; [memb.] Softball team, Art club, Spanish Club; [hon.] Honor Roll, Presidential Academic Fitness award; [oth. writ.] Another poem previously published by National Library of Poetry. [a.] Palmyra, MO.

KANNMACHER, CRYSTAL
[pen.] Chris Kannmacher; [b.] July 18, 1941, Clark County, IL; [p.] Fay and Vern Nicholson; [m.] Jon W., March 12, 1960; [ch.] Lisa, Jon, Jamie and Tracey; [ed.] Martinsville High; [oth. writ.] Poem published by National Library of Poetry in "Dance on the Horizon"; [pers.] My writings are from compassion and love I have felt for others. Most have come to me through prayer to God about the loved one.

KARDOS, ANN
[b.] October 10, 1979, Cuy. Falls; [p.] Jim and Jan Kardos; [ed.] Cuyahoga Falls High School; [occ.] Student; [memb.] Rotary Club, Key Club; [hon.] Presidential Academic Fitness Award, Editor's Choice Award, Rotary Scholar; [oth. writ.] Poem published in "In the Desert Sun" by National Library of Poetry. [a.] Cuyahoga Falls, OH.

KASSEL, LAURA
[pen.] Kaszie; [b.] January 25, 1980, Santa Clara; [p.] Randall and Rose Ann; [ed.] Blossom Valley Elementary, Bernal Intermediate and St. Francis High School; [occ.] Student; [memb.] Dance Team, Joy=Youth Group; [hon.] Honor Roll 3 years in Young Authors Four; [oth. writ.] Tears of Fire, church bulletins, Young Authors fair books; [pers.] Life's precious, play hard; don't turn around. [a.] San Jose, CA.

KAUFERBERG, RICHARD
[b.] July 8, 1948, Tracy, MN; [p.] William and Alvina Kauferberg; [ed.] Heather Jo, Brooke Caroline, Laura Elizabeth, Sondra Lynn; [ed.] Walnut Grove High School; [occ.] Auto parts counterman; [oth. writ.] The Hand That Feeds You from The National Library of Poetry "Whispers in the Wind".

KAUFMAN, PETER H.
[b.] June 12, 1928, Chicago, IL; [p.] Daniel, Mary Louise; [ch.] Daniel, Peter, Mark; [ed.] Yale University, University of Southern CA; [occ.] Writer; [hon.] Pi Sigma Alpha; [hon.] Technical Manuels, Procedures, Short stories. [a.] Oceanside, CA.

KAYGANICH, NICHOLAS J.
[b.] November 15, 1923, Dearborn, MI; [p.] Milan and Romana; [m.] May 16, 1953; [ch.] David, Daniel, and Daria; [ed.] Fordson High School, Cleveland Institute of Electronics; [occ.] Retired Telephone Tech; [memb.] International Society of Poets, Orthodox Christian Laity, St. Clement Orthodox Sunday School Staff; [hon.] 3rd place oil painting Michigan Bell Employees Art show 1989; [oth. writ.] Poem-Dance on the Horizon 1994, article-Young Life Magazine 1983; [pers.] A hope for a peaceful world. [a.] Dearborn, MI.

KAZE, ARCHIE R.
[pen.] Rou-Nel; [b.] April 22, 1919, KY; [p.] Thomas and Maude Robinson; [m.] James Philip, January 5, 1946; [ch.] Joyce Anne Quesenberry and Rhonda Jean Kaze; [ed.] High school, business college at Bowling Green Business University; [occ.] Retired; [pers.] I like touching people in poetry.

KEARNEY, CANDACE NICOLE
[b.] November 1, 1975, New York City, NY; [p.] Carolyn and James E. Kearney; [ed.] Herricks High School, Long Island, NY; Junior at Penn State Univ, Major - Political Science/Pre-law; [memb.] American Horseback Riding Assoc, Young Republicans; [hon.] Youth Effectiveness; Outstanding Achievement from Hempstead Town Supervisor; Proclamation of Achievement from County Executive; Achievement Award in Nat'l Night Out Against Crime; Creative Writing Award from the Kennedy Center of Performing Arts; Certificate of Merit - Graduation from the county executive and New York State Senator and Assemblyman from NY State; Community Service Award Youth Council; Music Award Class of '92; Many ribbons won in horse back (hunter/jumper class) riding competition. An accomplished equestrian trophies won in jumping 3 feet 6 inches gates; [oth. writ.] Poems published in Opus - a local publication; [a.] Herricks, NY

KEEN, ANNIE
[pen.] Skitiboo; [b.] July 20, 1983, Nurnburg, Germany; [p.] Ipo and Bill Keen; [ed.] Rosebourough Elementary and Mt. Dora Middle School; [occ.] Student; [memb.] Girl Talk Book club; [hon.] Award from the president for over 95% average on CTBS Test and for making straight A's of my school year; [oth. writ.] Wrote a poetry about how the Cheeta got its spots; [pers.] If you put your mind to it you can do it. [a.] Mt. Dora, FL.

KELLEHER, FRANCES B.
[b.] January 18, 1920, Minot, ND; [p.] Walter and Agnes Olsen; [m.] Cornelius, June 10, 1939; [ch.] Joe, Pat, Tim, Mike, Colleen; [ed.] High school, Teacher's College; [occ.] Homemaker, grandmother to 9 grandchildren and 1 great grand child; [oth. writ.] Many poems for friends, family and special occasions; [pers.] I try to find something good in every person I meet, and I always do. By the Golden Rule, is the only way to live. [a.] Los Gatos, CA.

KENDRICK, MICHAEL WARD
[b.] September 3, 1938, Port Arthur, TX; [p.] Woodrow and Helen Kendrick; [ch.] Michael II, Donna, Carrie, April, Shannon; [ed.] Thomas Jefferson High School; [occ.] Songwriter; [memb.] BMI; [hon.] Several honorable mention awards for songwriting; [oth. writ.] Poems published by two publishers, over 100 songs written and copyrighted; [pers.] To write a song or poem and to be able to touch someone and make them feel what you are feeling is one of God's greatest gifts. [a.] Groves, TX.

KENNEDY, DARROW
[b.] February 8, 1948, Chicago; [p.] Lana, July 29, 1994; [ch.] Tiffany, Daniel and Markel; [ed.] Crane Tech and Columbia College; [occ.] Xerox; [memb.] Marathon Productions, American Federation of Musicians; [oth. writ.] Wrote 2 songs for a play "Cry For Help"; [pers.] If music makes the world go around - then poetry makes my love come down. I love it so I write it. [a.] Broadview, IL.

KENT, ISABEL A.
[b.] August 1, 1933, DeGraff, MN; [p.] Henry and Gladys Hughes; [m.] Stanley J., June 11, 1955; [ch.] Steven, Coleen, Tim, Kevin, Shannon and Shawn (twins); [ed.] High school and 2 years of college; [occ.] Retired; [memb.] St. Lawrence Catholic Church and Guild, former World of Poetry and National Library of Poetry; [hon.] 1989-92 Golden Poet awards, 1990-92 Who's Who in Poetry, numerous honorable mentions for poetry; [oth. writ.] 7 poems published in World of Poetry anthologies, 2 published in National Library of Poetry; [pers.] My poetry is my heart and soul reflected by my beliefs and concepts imprinted on paper. [a.] Perham, MN.

KESERICA, SONJA ANN
[b.] December 18, 1969, Chicago, IL; [p.] FRank and Mara Keserica; [ed.] Fairfax High School, Santa Monica College; [occ.] Receptionist, Kenneth Leventhal and Co.; [pers.] My writings are based on personal experiences that have had a profound and moving emotional impact in my life. [a.] West Hollywood, CA.

KIDER, KAREN LEE
[b.] May 18, 1944, Bronx, NY; [p.] Elsie and Abraham Kider; [m.] Marvin Bernard, September 8, 1962; [ch.] Hope, Craig, Eric, Bonnie, Glen, Melissa (grandson-Adam Hillel Sherman); [occ.] Memories - National Library of Poetry; [pers.] I love to write poetry that reflects my personal feelings I'm proud of my family and their accomplishments. My husband is my best friend and we share a like that is filled with love. I believe each day is a gift and that love and laughter is the key to happiness. [a.] Wantagh, NY.

KIDWELL, GWENDOLENE
[pen.] Gwendolene Kidwell; [b.] June 23, 1972, Bulawayo, Rhodesia; [p.] David and Audry Kidwell; [ed.] Pickens High School, Reinhardt College; [memb.] Phi Theta Kappa; [hon.] Dean's List, The National Dean's List; [oth. writ.] Poems - Within and "Shared Perfection"; [pers.] Two things I will always remember: God is not the author of confusion, and Proverbs 3:5 Trust in the Lord with all your heart and lean not on your own understanding. [a.] Jasper, GA.

KIENER, BETTY J.
[b.] July 26, 1922, Burr Oak, OH; [p.] Pansie Hines Clark; [m.] Robert L., April 10, 1942; [ch.] Jeffrey, James, Judith, Bobbi, Paul, Anthony; [occ.] Wife-homemaker-mother-grandmother; [oth. writ.] Poetry and prose, preserved and scattered through my many scrapbooks; [pers.] I write because I must - to express my personal feelings, experienced through these many years. [a.] Columbus, OH.

KILGORE, DAWN M.
[b.] December 28, 1966, NC; [p.] John and Betty Van Arnum; [m.] Brian T., October 2, 1993; [ed.] St. Pete Junior College; [occ.] Student; [memb.] Christ Our Redeemer Lutheran Church; [oth. writ.] Other poem, some published; [pers.] My concern for other people, animals, and or treatment of the earth inspire me to write. [a.] Tampa, FL.

KING, JOY R.
[pen.] Tara Southerly; [b.] August 5, 1939, Memphis, TN; [p.] Roy and Margaret Rainey; [m.] Guy R.; [ch.] Lonnie King and Cheryl King Ramsey also 3 grandchildren; [ed.] Whitehaven High School; [occ.] Happy housewife-retired medical secretary; [memb.] Oak Grove Baptist Church, Homemakers Club and International Society of Poets; [hon.] 3 Editor's Choice awards, 2 selected for "Sound of Poetry" cassette tape of poems by NLP; [oth. writ.] Sunday Afternoon published in In The Desert Sun, 4th of July in "Tears of Fire", Chelsey in "DAnce on the Horizon", Beautiful Earth in "Treasured Poems of America 1994", several poems in church bulletin; [pers.] I'm striving to get all the love in my heart out and down on paper before I ever depart this wonderful earth. [a.] Paducah, KY.

KING, ROBIN SUZANNE
[b.] June 16, 1960, Lom Poc, CA: [p.] Mona Egan; [ch.] Jacquelyn Colleen King; [ed.] 2 years college, CA Corrections Academy, Rural Fire Fighter Academy; [occ.] Retired Correctional Officer; [hon.] Numerous trophies and awards for horsemanship and marksmanship; [oth. writ.] Published in poetry in Lone Star Magazine, Writers Exchange, Western Horseman, Perceptions and several anthologies; [pers.] My life is like a poem write from the heart. Search your mind for the words. Then take my pen in hand and edit. [a.] SAn Juan Bautista, CA.

KIRKLAND, CHARLOTTE
[pen.] Char; [b.] March 25, 1926, MO; [p.] Lucy and Charly Hart; [m.] Ruffer B., May 12, 1946; [ch.] Pam, Holly, Benjamin and Charlene; [ed.] C.E.D. - 12th; [occ.] Retired; [hon.] Poetry; [oth. writ.] Sea to Shining Sea. [a.] Orange, CA.

KITTS, SHERRY DIANE CREASY
[b.] January 18, 1965, Bluefield, W.VA; [p.] Mr. and Mrs. Anthony Sheets; [m.] Danny Joe, March 13, 1984; [ch.] Daniel Joseph and KayLyn Nicole Kitts; [ed.] Pocahontas High School; [occ.] Songwriter, writing for South Ryder Band; [memb.] Lakeshore Pres. Church; [hon.] Editor Choice award for "Little Angel", several recording contracts; [oth. writ.] Published in "Tears of Fire"; [pers.] I hope to comfort someone in pain or to make someone think about their actions, such as someone being abused or someone who is abusing. I put alot of my own personal experiences into my poetry. [a.] Denver, NC.

KLEINE, MICHELLE
[b.] October 25, 1970, Pomona, CA; [ed.] Chaffey High, Saddleback Community College; [pers.] To be happy, try to be good to other people, and to hope to fall in love. [a.] Dana Point, CA.

KLESCHUK, MIRANDA
[b.] January 4, 1981, Portland, OR; [p.] Mike and Kathy Kleschuk; [ed.] Middle school; [occ.] Student and entrepreneur; [memb.] National Geographic Society, Yearbook Committee, Former Campfire of America; [hon.] Placed second in local district writing contest; [oth. writ.] Black-footed Ferret poem published by National Geographic World 1992 - Super Cat published by National Library of Poetry in an poetry anthology called Dark Side of the Moon; [pers.] I see poetry as a thing of beauty. I have been inspired by all of natures creatures and enjoy writing about them. [a.] Aloha, OR.

KNOPP, EVA J.
[pen.] Eve Grey; [b.] July 13, 1935, Spencer, WVA; [p.] R.J. and Lura Davis Grady; [m.] Charles T., December 6, 1952 (divorced); [ch.] Charles Thompson, Robert Chadwick (deceased), Deborah Lynn, Daniel Lee; [ed.] Spencer High, Arch Moore Vo Tech, CETA; [occ.] Secretary, Baptist Hospital; [memb.] Southern Baptist Church; [hon.] Three awards from "The World of Poetry"; [oth. writ.] Poem published in "Selected Works of Our World's Best Poets" 1992, play "Poor Little Rich Girl" 1948 acted by school class - many unpublished poems and stories, articles; [pers.] I have loved literature and writing since age 10. I owe this to teachers and my mother's family, "Davis" who came from Wales originally and among whom were many writers. I hope to devote full time to writing in the next few years. [a.] Madison, TN.

KOBLENTZ, BONNI
[pen.] Bonni Koblentz; [b.] May 26, 1951, Topeka, KS; [p.] Roy and Nina Villarreal;[m.] Mark, August 10, 1985; [ch.] Cole and Cade Kisner; [ed.] High school, Massage Therapy schools and workshops; [occ.] Entrepreneur and owner - Certified Massage Therapist; [memb.] American Orthopedic Society for Sports Medicine, American Oriental Body Workers of America, Better Business Bureau; [hon.] World of Poetry 1988 - Golden Poet award and honorable mention for Insomnia and publication 1989 and Golden Poet award and honorable mention for Missing Keys, 1990 Golden Poet award, publication and honorable mention for Honey, What I Want For Christmas and publication. Golden Poet award, honorable mention and publication for The Greatest Life, honorable mention 1988 and publication for Decisions - honorable mention and publication for That Special Treatment, honorable mention and publication for Summer in the Street; [oth. writ.] Publication, Quill books in 1992 "Friends" 1994 "Editor's Choice award" and publication for National Library of Poetry for A List to Santa and over 500 other writings in poetry, since childhood. [a.] Redondo Beach, CA.

KORTES, DIANE L.
[b.] October 16, 1950, Butte, MT; [p.] Trygve Bakken and Martha Willing; [m.] Toivo (Sonny); [ch.] Thomas E. and wife Tara J. Adamson; [occ.] Disabled (homemaker); [hon.] 2 golden poet, 1 silver award, 3 honorable mentions from World of Poetry, also poems in 2 books from World of Poetry. Five poems published in The Montana Poet. One poem is now in the State of Montana Archives; [pers.] My poetry is the expression of how I feel inside at that given moment. Therefore each and every poem is a part of me and who I am, or rather, a piece that combines with others to make a whole person. [a.] Winnemucca, NV.

KOVILIC, MARYANN
[b.] March 22, 1956, Chicago, IL; [p.] Petar (Bajica) and Ivana Martinovic; [m.] Nikola, November 23, 1974; [ch.] Radovan (Rodney) and Danilo (Danny); [ed.] Nazerath Academy, Elmhurst College; [occ.] Executive Officer; [memb.] International Society of Poets; [oth. writ.] Published in The National Library of Poetry "The Space Between"; [pers.] Poetry is such a wonderful form of expression to convey ones experiences, emotions and viewpoints which otherwise might remain silent and only known to the beholder.

KRANNING, DORA SILVIA
[b.] March 2, 1946, Zurich, Switzerland; [p.] Anna and Walter Kranning; [ed.] College in Switzerland; [occ.] Dance Instructor at USC and Glendale College; [oth. writ.] Articles publisher in local Swiss newspapers, article in Women in Theatre magazine; [pers.] Poetry as all art forms expresses the depth of human emotion. [a.] Burbank, CA.

KREMINS, KATHLEEN A.
[b.] May 23, 1959, Newark, NJ; [p.] John and Margaret Lahey; [ed.] College of St. Elizabeth; [occ.] English teacher, Mendham High School; [memb.] National Council for Teachers of English; [hon.] SEED (Seeking Educational Equity and Diversity) project leader; [oth.w rit.] Several poems published in college literary magazine, "Linear Measurement" in the National Library of Poetry Anthology, In The Desert Sun (1994); two articles published in Women's Fastpitch; [pers.] In planting the seeds of our diverse voices, we create the inevitable flowering of a common understanding and language for all. [a.] Chester Township, NJ.

KRONER, LUCILLE M.
[b.] August 8, Bolla, MO; [p.] Theodore W. and Virginia Kroner; [ed.] Santa Monica City College, UCLA; [occ.] Retired; [memb.] Santa Monica First Christian Church, Elder and Choir member; [hon.]

Approx. 100+ poetry awards; [oth. writ.] Four poetry books in work, awards from many other poetry companies; [pers.] Let us circle our way in the purpose for world peace and love. [a.] L.A., CA.

KRUPP, IRENE PALAKI
[pen.] Rene; [b.] January 12, 1924, Lorain, OH; [p.] Michael and Margaret Pataki; [m.] Gene O., September 28, 1946; [ch.] Renee, Rebecca, Carole, Karen Laurel, Gene O.; [ed.] M.B. Johnson School of Nursing, taught school and directed an art gallery; [occ.] Retired, on-call grandmother; [memb.] Christian Womens Association, Business Womens Association, Community Congregational Church; [hon.] Poem published in National Magazine for New Expectant Mothers, won tv award for poetry; [oth. writ.] Teaching on Neonatology; [pers.] Through poetry I attempt to shed light on the days of my life. May those who need the lines feel the joy and sometimes pain that help me express my love of God, of man, and nature. [a.] Ft. Myers, FL.

KRUSE, JOAN
[b.] October 8, 1956, Geneva, IL; [p.] Rev. Milton and Evelyn Whitney; [m.] Frank E., April 12, 1980; [ch.] Peter M. VanHorn, Timothy M. and Karel J. Kruse; [ed.] Pearl City High School, Highland Community College; [occ.] restaurant Worker; [memb.] St. John's Lutheran Church, Christian Education staff; [hon.] Cake decorating awards 1979-Cherry Vale Mall and 1993 Valley Bakers Association, 1994 Editor's Choice award, the NLP; [oth. writ.] Two poems published by The NLP; [pers.] This poem was written about my Grandma Clark. She was a big influence in my life and I loved her very much. [a.] Pearl City, IL.

KUKLIN, JANET F.
[pen.] Janet F. Kuklin; [b.] April 1, 1933, Bronx, NY; [p.] Irving and Belle Hertz; [m.] Arlen J., November 28, 1965; [ch.] Julie Elizabeth and Lawrence David Kuklin; [ed.] Los Angeles High School, University of California at Los Angeles; [occ.] Retired Executive Secretary; [oth. writ.] I have been selected for publication in the anthology, Edge of Twilight; [pers.] Since childhood, my writings have been mostly introspective, questioning morality influenced by ever-changing social issues, how we perceive life around us and questioning the very essence of being. [a.] Los Angeles, CA.

KUNTZE, DANA KARIN TANNER
[pen.] Dana Tanner Kunze; [b.] July 30, 1961, Westwood, CA; [p.] Trieve and Barbara Tanner; [m.] John, August 6, 1988; [ch.] None - 2 cats; [ed.] PPSC, San Jose State University, U.C. Davis; [occ.] Student and (volunteer) personal counselor; [hon.] Honor Society 1989 and 1990, San Jose State - Outstanding Internship Work 1984 U.C. Davis, Outstanding Achievement Award, German 1981, Foothill Junior College; [oth. writ.] "Beckoning" - Full Moon Publications 1994, "The Dream" Once Upon A World 1994, "Endless Summer" Amber, Seashell Press, "Fairytale", "Misfortune" and "Moments"; [pers.] Most of my poetry reflects my love of life, romance, and the endless opportunities life has to offer if we have the courage to make our dreams come true. [a.] Menlo Park, CA.

LAMANNA, JAMES M.
[b.] January 7, 1947, Bronxville; [p.] Phil and Margaret; [ed.] Eastchester High, Bulova School of Watchmaking; [occ.] Employee of Town of Eastchester (laborer); [memb.] V.F.W. of Eastchester, VVA of Westchester County; [hon.] A merit award from former poet society from California, Loyalty of Service of V.V.A. 1994; [oth. writ.] Poems and songs of Vietnam; [pers.] Writings in any form derive from the heart and soul of creations. Each individual is different in their own right, enter to our senses to be enjoyed by all or most.

LACKAS, ROSEANNA NAPOLITANO
[b.] October 1, 1948, NYC; [p.] Philip and Anna Napolitano; [m.] Alan L., June 15, 1984; [ed.] St. Patrick's Cathedral High School; [occ.] Housewife; [hon.] Certificate of Merit, honorable mention and golden poet award for "My Man My Everything"; [oth. writ.] "My Man My Everything" published in Great Poems of the Western World Vol. II by World of Poetry, CA; [pers.] If one genuinely likes people then life offers many rewarding pleasures. My writings are inspired by people and life situations. I strive to touch the hearts of mankind. [a.] Bowie, MD.

LADD, DONNA LEE
[b.] October 31, 1959, Louisville, KY; [p.] Leslie and Geneva Ladd; [ed.] Iroquois High School, University of Louisville; [occ.] Grade 5 teacher, Frayser Elementary School; [memb.] Kappa Delta Pi; [hon.] BS El Ed,. awarded with high honors; [oth. writ.] A personal collection of unpublished poetry and poems published in various anthologies; [pers.] In a world where there are so many problems, I find it important to focus on the joy and beauty that is also present. [a.] Louisville, KY.

LAKE, RUTH E. DUFFINA
[pen.] Ruth E. Duffina; [b.] December 1, 1948; [p.] Charles and Mary White; [ch.] Melissa, Claudette, Holly; [ed.] Foxcroft Academy, Northeast Inst. Tech; [memb.] VFW Post #168, American Legion #6, Lady of the Moose Chapter 1149; [hon.] World of Poetry 1990, Golden Poet-Creation of the Fire Flower, Silver Poet award-Creation of the Fire Flower, The American Poetry Association 1990; [oth. writ.] 1981-1983 Dexter Gazzette, poems - Sunrise At Sebasticook, The First Snowfall, Christmas; The American Poetry Association, Season of The Wind, Hearts of Fire 1983, 1984 Words of Praise, 1989 Publisher's Choice, 1994-The Bingo Bugle Carousel Publishing Co "I Think I'll Call"; [pers.] Innovation shimmers from inspiration's energy as souls introproject while striving to achieve their dreams.

LAND, TERESSA MAY
[b.] May 10, 1954, Baltimore, MD; [p.] John and Mary Groce; [m.] Wayne M., February 14, 1989; [ch.] Racheal Marie, Stanley Joseph, Timothy Lee; [ed.] Southern High; [occ.] Certified Nurse Assistance; [oth. writ.] Stranger Pass Through; [pers.] I write what I see and feel that's deep inside where I have been and where I am going. Thanks to my husband. [a.] Norfolk, VA.

LANE, MICHAEL
[pen.] A.A.P., An American Poet; [b.] September 27, 1966, Bronx; [p.] Irene Black and Martin Lane; [m.] Lori;[ch.] Victoria and Samantha; [ed.] Christopher Columbus High School; [occ.] Carpenter/truck driver/father; [hon.] Received several awards of merit mostly for "The Incredible Flight"; [oth. writ.] "Within the Heart", published in Dance on the Horizon; [pers.] The Incredible Flight is a very important poem to me. It's my way of ensuring the legacy of the 7 astronauts who vanished before my eyes. "I stood and cried with a nation that day" we must never forget what they and their families have sacrificed. "The pen has become a link to my soul". [a.] Margate, FL.

LANGWORTHY, MABEL
[b.] January 24, 1935, MI; [p.] Herbert and Melissa (Davis), Mowrey (deceased); [m.] Mortris, January 31, 1953; [ch.] Morris Jr. and wife Deb, Jeanne, Shelly and husband Rob, Teresa and husband Ken, Kenneth and Tracy, five grandchildren; [ed.] Mesick and Grant High schools; [occ.] Housewife; [memb.] The International Society of Poets; [hon.] Editor's Choice award, Top 3% and selection for Sound of Poetry, all for poem "To a Novice Seeker" published in "Dance on the Horizon" by the National Library of Poetry 1994; [oth. writ.] Semi-finalist at 1994 ISP convention in WA DC for poem, "Today's Doorway". Various poetry, as yet unpublished; [pers.] As far back as I can remember, I've had a fascination with the sound of words and the feelings they seemed to have the power, to command. May I be granted the power to use my words wisely. [a.] LeRoy, MI.

LANHAM, JACLYN ANN
[pen.] Darian Wolff; [b.] September 30, 1977, Canton; [ed.] Jackson High School; [occ.] Secretary of Ohio Pro Plan; [memb.] Quill and Scroll (National Journalism Society); [hon.] Received numerous Superior ratings at Music conventions, solo and ensemble contest on flute and french horn. Received superior ratings on many science projects; [oth. writ.] Poems published in local newspapers and high school magazine, Dreamscope" and "Where Dreams Begin" (book); [pers.] Quite often I have wandered if a man can reach his goals with money in his pockets, but poverty in his soul" - Jackie Lanham, I dedicate this poem to my special friend Ron Luikart. [a.] Massilion, OH.

LANIER, D'DEE
[m.] March 19, 19923, Cumberland, MD; [p.] Virgil and Laura Ruppenthal; [m.] Sidney, April 19, 1941; [ch.] Sidney, Jr., Andria Lanier, Marvin Lanier; [ed.] Sam Houston State College; [occ.] Retired teacher; [memb.] Baptist Church; [hon.] Delta Kappa Phi, Alpha Kyl, Kappa Delta Chi; [pers.] Children's lives that I taught in Special Education who were not dumb but special. I feel a teacher is called (like a preacher) to teach mentally disturbed and emotional children in Special Ed.

LANOSZ, CANSADA R.
[pen.] Candi Oswald; [b.] November 14, 1960; [p.] Carl and Joanna Oswald; [m.] Anthony, March 22, 1994; [ch.] Ruthann Marie and Carl Anthony; [ed.] Robert E. Peary High School; [occ.] Computer Attendant; [memb.] Maryland Romance Writers, Lisbon United Methodist Church, I.O.J.D.; [hon.] Honorable mention from The World of Poetry contest; [oth. writ.] Printed in church newsletter; [pers.] "Angels...don;t leave home without them". [a.] Woodbine, MD.

LARKIN, GEORGE
[b.] December 9, 1930, Sherman, TX; [p.] George Sr. and Opal Larkin; [m.] Lee Rodgers, November 2, 1956; [ch.] Rodger Alan and Lisa Darcelle; [ed.] University of North Texas; [occ.] Retired; [memb.]

St. Philip Presby Church, VFW; [hon.] Honorable Recogn., World's Greatest Poets - J. Campbel Ed.; [oth. writ.] Several other poems - 3 published 1992 World's Greatest Poets (Aftermath, An Afternoon Walk, The Game); [pers.] Aim-to complete a volume of poems for publication. Phil - Relating life to nature, i.e., aging with seasons. As perhaps, God intended. [a.] Hurst, TX.

LARSON, CLAUDINE WHITAKER
[b.] February 18, 1930, Kannapolis, NC; [p.] Claude and Elva Whitaker; [m.] Frank L. (deceased), July 3, 1964; [ed.] Cannon High School, St. Andrews Presbyterian College; [occ.] Retired elementary teacher; [memb.] Delta Kappa Gamma, AARP, United Methodist Church Music Director in Grenora - Farm Bureau; [hon.] Delta Kappa Gamma scholarship; [oth. writ.] Poem published by you: book of children's stories published (The Twin's Surprise and other stories) another book is being published now - an essay and poem published in Education Magazine - poem published in Farm Bureau Magazine; [pers.] My deceased husband, Frank was my greatest inspiration for writing, also the many students I've taught. [a.] Grenora, ND.

LATIMER, JAMES
[b.] September 26, 1904, Virgin Isles; [p.] Mr. and Mrs. William Latimer; [ed.] New York University, Teacher's College, University of London England; [occ.] Retired but writing; [memb.] Alumnus NYU, International House; [hon.] Seven medals for service in Royal Canadian Medics Corps in WWII in England. [a.] Canadian, Ottuwa.

LAUER, DOROTHY
[pen.] Dorothy Lauer; [b.] March 5, 1923, Seattle, WA; [m.] Robert, February 8, 1946; [ch.] David and John Lauer, Barbara Carrigan and 7 grandchildren; [ed.] Broadway High School, Seattle Pasadena City College, California State; [occ.] Writer; [memb.] St. Andrew's Episcopal Church, The honor society of Phi Kappa Phi; [hon.] Honor Society 1940, AA-English and Spanish honors, Administrative honors for outstanding scholarship - Pasadena City College; [oth. writ.] Book tracing unity in writings of Dame Rebecca West completed, four collections of poetry in process. Poem 'Danger at Dusk' published in Dance on the Horizon/poem "Meticulous" published in The Dark Side of the Moon; [pers.] My poetry captures a lifetime of images and observations. The spectrum is broad, including people, places, events, nature, feelings, ideas...It is a pastiche of memories. [a.] Tokeland, WA.

LAUER, WILLIAM
[pen.] Will Lauren; [b.] January 18, 1948, Hazleton, PA; [p.] William and Edna Lauer; [m.] Deborah Gorzen Lauer; [ch.] Alexandra, Lindsay, Jonathan, Jude and Brian; [ed.] Hazleton State Hospital School of Nursing; [occ.] Registered Nurse specializing in Psychiatry; [memb.] American Nurses Association, South Carolina Writers Workshop; [hon.] Was president of the Student Nurses Association while in nursing school, was an associate editor of Harbor Lites Literary Magazine at Harbor College; [oth. writ.] Literary Neophyte with several short stories, poems and a novella just submitted for publication Who Hopes For A Sympathetic Ear; [pers.] Served as a combat medic with 27th marines in Viet Nam, I believe we are all helpless and hopeless creatures, and in total control of our destiny. (But don't know it). [a.] Irmo, SC.

LAURENT, HILLARY
[b.] August 25, 1979, GreenBay, WI; [p.] Debbie Laurent and Allen Laurent; [ch.] Cat named Bill; [ed.] St. Mary's School, Kaukauna High School; [occ.] Student; [memb.] Forensics, Cheerleading; [hon.] Several Forensics awards and ribbons, one award for exceptional performance in Reader's and Writer's Workshop, an English academic excellence award, high honor roll; [oth. writ.] A novel (not yet published) several short stories and poems. A poem "Darkness" which was published in "Dance on the Horizon"; [pers.] I love the thrill of seeing my thoughts on paper and the happiness that comes along with getting my work read. [a.] Kaukauna, WI.

LAUTERBACH, L. JOSEPH
[b.] May 7, 1921, Minnesota; [p.] Deceased; [m.] September 3, 1949; [ch.] 5; [ed.] University of Minnesota; [occ.] Retired; [oth. writ.] "My Lord, My God", published in "A Far Off Place"; [pers.] My aspirations are not monumental, my accomplishments of no real substance. But I feel good about myself, comfortable with my faith in God, and live one day at a time in peace and harmony with my fellow man. [a.] Horning, MN.

LAVENDER, CHERYL A.
[b.] December 18, 1953, Louisiana; [p.] James D. and Wanda Jean Radcliffe; [m.] John A., December 19, 1971; [ch.] Holly Katheryn, Kylee Michelle, Samuel Glenn; [occ.] Poet, mother and wife; [pers.] I seek only to glorify my Lord who died to set me free. I write for him. I write because of Him. [a.] Fairview, TN.

LAWLER, BROWNIE
[b.] June 13, 1926, Plantersville; [p.] Joe Wheeler and Inez Caldwell; [m.] Freddie L., July 26, 1946; [ch.] Mrs. Randy Palmer (Trevette), David Lawler and Walter Lawler; [occ.] Housewife; [memb.] Glendale Baptist Church; [hon.] Greatest honor: 3 children, 7 great grandchildren, best husband in the world; [oth. writ.] Several poems published in other books; [pers.] Writing is a personal outlet, the one thing that is done for myself. Seems my writings reflects on God's great gift of people and how nature can bring everything together. [a.] Greenville, MS.

LAWTON, ROBERT C.
[b.] February 24, 1905, Pittsburgh, PA; [p.] George and Adeline Lawton; [m.] Hazel Haws Lawton, July 12, 1933, [ch.] Adeline Elizabeth and Robert Clark Lawton, Jr.; [occ.] Retired; [oth. writ.] Land of the Midnight Sun (Tears of Fire). [a.] Waxahachie, TX.

LeDOUX, VIENTA GRUBBS
[b.] November 16, 1976, Kentucky; [p.] James and Theresa Grubbs; [m.] William Everett LeDoux, Jr.; [m.] August 5, 1994; [ed.] High school; [occ.] Domestic engineer and student; [pers.] I want to thank my husband, Bill, for loving me and keeping me here long enough to write and hopefully inspire others. It's a gift I hope I truly possess. [a.] Greenville, SC.

LEE, FELICIA RENEE
[pen.] Aura de Violetta; [b.] August 1, 1975, Muskogee; [p.] Virginia Elaine Johnson; [ed.] American School of Correspondence, High school graduate; [occ.] Cook/dishwater/artist/model and writer; [hon.] Editor's Choice award for poetry, poem published in Quill books, contracts to get books published; [oth. writ.] The Accused, Prisoner, Life As is: On the Serious Tip: One Intellectual's Point of View, Chocolate or Vanilla, Remember When and To The Point; [pers.] If it weren't for the great Jehovah God in the heavens, I wouldn't be blessed with the great talents that I have. I will continue to strive to successful in whatever I do. [a.] Muskogee, OK.

LEE, JENNIFER A.
[pen.] Jenners; [b.] April 14, 1971, Los Angeles, CA; [p.] Mr. and Mrs. John H. Lee; [ed.] Happily amongst the family - traditions of better real estate; [memb.] AHP, ISP; [hon.] "Newest" member of International Society of Poets; [pers.] Studying - classics. [a.] Thousand Oaks, CA.

LEE-JOHNSON, DORMA
[pen.] Lee-Dallas; [b.] August 23, 1924, Beckham County, OK; [p.] W.P. and Lucinda Dallas; [m.] Lonnie (deceased) 1987, April 22, 1946; [ch.] Danny Kim, Peggy Diane; [ed.] Dale Carnegie, Bible course, High school diploma; [occ.] Homemaker, owner - operator-small cattle ranch; [memb.] United Methodist Church, UME Women's Circle, past pres and sec. treas. of ESA-Sorority, past pres of American Legion; [hon.] Now serving as educational director of ESA Sorority - have served for past 5 years; [pers.] I enjoy life like to read - good movies - walk - dance- play bridge - dinner with friends, worship at church, visit my children and grandchildren, love God and love your children. [a.] Elk City, OK.

LEE SHENG TIN, RUFFINA
[b.] June 21, 1958, St. James, Trinidad; [p.] Mrs. Zilla Hosein-Kahn and the late Mr. Yussaf Hosein; [m.] David John Lee Sheng Tin, August 4, 1979; [ch.] Siblings-Steve and Robert Hosein, Carol Yasmin Ramdin, Leza and Lilah Ali, Anthony, Alland and Cindy Khan; [occ.] Teacher, Maharishi's Transcendental Meditation, Executive Secretary, Diplomatic Mission; [memb.] Founding member-Maharishi Vedic University, Maharishi Institute of Management, Trinidad and Tobago, International Meditation Society; [oth. writ.] Poetry-"Creation Fire" a Cafra Anthology of Caribbean Women's Poetry, 1990, published by Sister Vision; "A Break in the Clouds", the National Library of Poetry, 1993; [pers.] My poem "Sri" is dedicated to my beloved husband, David, for his lifelong support and love, and for honoring me as his Devi. [a.] Trinidad & Tobago, WI.

LEICY, WINIFRED HESSER
[b.] June 12, 1908, Massillon, OH; [p.] Fred and Grace Hesser; [m.] Herbert William, July 15, 1934; [ch.] Linda Leicy Hope; [ed.] Morent Union College; [occ.] Housewife; [memb.] Convenant Presbyterian Church, Woman's Club of Steubenville, Woman's Club Chorus, Tri-State Symphonetto (piano), Alpha Xi Delta Alum. Sorority; [hon.] 60 year member Woman's Club of Steubenville, 60 years plus pin from A=D Sorority; [oth. writ.] Lots of poetry - just for family and friends, none ever published; [pers.] I believe in the Golden Rule. If we live our faith and treat everyone accordingly, we shall succeed in being happy. [a.] Steubenville, OH.

LEIGHTON, RICHARD H.
[b.] Eastport, ME; [p.] Frank E. and Alberta M. Leighton; [m.] Sheila D., September 6, 1958; [ch.] Terri, Nanci, Richard Jr., and Frank; [ed.] University of Harford; [occ.] Marketing Consultant; [memb.] International Society of Poets, American Legion; [hon.] Who's Who in American Colleges and Universities; 1959 Editor's Choice award National Library of Poetry, Top Ten Finalist at ISP Convention 1994; [oth. writ.] The Door, The River (published future in National Library of Poetry), My Journey, The Fiddler, The Ocean (to be published in future National Library of Poetry), The Calling of the Sea, Annie Knott, Passion To Love, My Pledge, The Knight; [pers.] My poetry consists of personal experiences and observations, natural beauty plays a major role in my developing them. Also, my mother's having read poetry, to me as a young child influenced my interest in the subject. [a.] Guilford, CT.

LESSARD, DAVID
[pen.] David Lessard; [b.] September 14, 1941, MA; [p.] Noam and Gladys Lessard; [m.] Linda Darnell, October 4, 1987; [ch.] Bethany, Shannon, Devin, Wes, Linda, Lillian and Dancia; [occ.] GED High school, VT Community College, Glendale Community College, CA College for Health Sciences; [occ.] Respiratory Therapist; [memb.] National Board for Respiratory Care, American Association for Respiratory Care, AZ Society of Respiratory Care; [hon.] Editor's Choice award for "Requiem (For The Living)" published in The Coming of Dawn 1993; [oth. writ.] Several poems published in "Poetic Voices of America". Articles published in Advance Magazine relating to respiratory care, local paper articles published; [pers.] My mother had a great influence on me in regard to my interest in literature. My poetic "leanings" are fostered by such poets as Frost, Dickinson, and Edna St. Vincent Millay. [a.] Payson, AZ.

LEVI, DICLA
[b.] October 9, 1983, Los Angeles, CA; [p.] Ezra and Yonu Levi; [ed.] Beverly Vista, Maimonides, Beverly Hills Studios, Hillel Hebrew Academy; [occ.] Student; [oth. writ.] Poem published in an anthology - Dark Side of the Moon; [pers.] I have been writing since the age of 8. When I write I just let myself go, and enjoy myself thoroughly. I love to write, and to see my work published. [a.] Beverly Hills, CA.

LEVY, MAURICE
[b.] August 15, 1993, Chicago, IL; [p.] Eugene and Jean Levy; [m.] Loris Rissman, September 11, 1955; [ch.] Adren Levy (MD), Andrea Levy (MD) and James Levy; [ed.] University of Illinois, University of Georgia; [occ.] Associate Dean and Professor of Pediatrics; [memb.] Phi Delta Kappa Professional Society, Association for American Medical Colleges, American Heart Association; [hon.] Phi Kappa Phi Honor Society, Kappa Delta Pi honor fraternity; Gold certificate for Outstanding Scientific Exhibit in area of Learning Values at American Academy of Pediatrics, American Academy of Family Physicians award for Outstanding Scientific Exhibit at American Medical Association conference, Gold award from AHA for outstanding service in advancing heart program and stimulating public support to fight against disease of heart and circulation; [oth. writ.] 2 books, 50+ progressional articles, 10 audiovisual programs, 4 poems; [pers.] My poetry is totally different from my professional publications. In my poetry, I try to reflect the world as I see it. [a.] Augusta, GA.

LEWEIL, ROXANN PHILLIPS
[pen.] Roxann/Asher; [b.] December 1, 1942, New Orleans; [p.] Alphese and Winfield Phillips; [m.] Sgt. George W., September 14, 1963; [ch.] George W. Jr., and Sheilia M. Lewiel and Ronald Collins; [ed.] Galileo High School, City College of S.F., U.S. Army, NCR School of Registrys, ARt Institute of S.F.; [occ.] Retired/foster mother of 300 children; [memb.] O.E.S. 5th degree, Founder International House of Prayer; [hon.] As the best Paraprofessional 1&2 in elementary education, best non-profit foster mother in our area; [oth. writ.] Unpublished manuscripts, short stories, poems, recipe books, information pamphlets; [pers.] If we give nothing in the present, the future will be without, love someone daily. [a.] San Francisco, CA.

LEWIS, MICHAEL
[b.] February 24, 1949, Kansas City, KS; [p.] Paul and Margaret Lewis; [m.] Laura, November 26, 1993; [ch.] Timothy, Lehi, Twyla, Joshua; [occ.] Wood Moulding Salesman; [oth. writ.] Book of Poetry "Voices of the Heart"; [pers.] I try to put into words the emotions and feelings we all feel in interpersonal relationships, but often have trouble expressing. [a.] Sacramento, CA.

LEWIS, THURSTON JOHN
[b.] April 27, 1917, LeFlore Co., OK; [p.] William Terrell and Lethal Lewis; [ed.] Henderson State University; [occ.] Seafarer (retired); [memb.] Seafarers International Union, 2nd Baptist Church of Arkahelphia, AARP #4441, Board of Directors Central Arkansas Development Council, Clark County Literary Council (tutor); [oth. writ.] "Poems" by Thurston John Lewis Caleb Jones in WWII; [pers.] The greatest good for the greatest number of people. [a.] Arkadelphia, AR.

LINARES, KELLY
[b.] Havana, Cuba; [ed.] Barry University, Nova University, Kensington University, American International University; [occ.] Teacher; [memb.] The Academy of American Poets, The International Society of Poets; [hon.] Honorable mention 0 Iliad Press, Certificate of Poetic Achievement-The Amherst Society, Poet of Merit award-International Society of Poets; [oth. writ.] Several poems published in local newspapers, published a book in Spanish poetry, entitled "Noches de Vigilia"; [pers.] My poetry blossoms from the innermost of my soul. [a.] Miami, FL.

LINDER, MARY JANE
[pen.] Mary Jane Linder; [b.] September 23, 1921, CA; [p.] Fred and Margaret Anderson; [m.] William (deceased), February 3, 1947; [ch.] 3 daughters; [ed.] California Registered Nurse, B.S. Science - MA in Counseling; [occ.] School nurse; [memb.] Professional School Nurse Association, Poetry Society, Writers Guild, Catholic Society of Charities; [hon.] Nursing services; [oth. writ.] Short stories; [pers.] Poetry is a wonderful artistic expression form - my Irish ancestry, I believe influences the tone of my poetry. [a.] La Canada, Flintridge, CA.

LITTLE, TRUDA M.
[b.] September 10, 1927, Kentucky; [m.] Ralph C. Little, December 27, 1986; [ch.] 5 girls and 2 boys; [occ.] Housewife; [oth. writ.] I love to write poems have been writing since the year 50. It's something I enjoy very much; [pers.] I was born at Pikesville KY, married my first husband, he was a coal miner from Kentucky. To us were born 7 children. [a.] Supply, NC.

LITTLE-TURTLE, KITT
[b.] Quinnetissett, CT; [p.] of Native American ancestry; [ed.] Tourtellotte Memorial High School, University of Connecticut, Worcester Art Museum; [occ.] Free lance artist and writer; [memb.] Nipmuck Indian Council, New England Antiquities Research Association, Native American Models and several local associations; [hon.] Listed in 1994 edition, Reference Encyclopedia of the American Indian (Who's Who section), numerous awards and prizes for poetry, writing and art-work; [oth. writ.] Articles published in Chrysalis Magazine, Dog World, Shaman's Drum, Spirit of Change and frequently appearing in Native American publications; [pers.] Drawing from my heritage I attempt to share the concept of nature and spirit as one. At home both in the woodlands and on the streets I am a "wild Indian" and a nature loving pacifist at the same time. I want to write poetry that all people can identify with, enjoy...and perhaps learn from. Aquene (peace). [a.] Douglas, MA.

LLEW-WILLIAMS, PAUL
[b.] March 12, 1958, Hamilton, ONT, CAN; [p.] Barrie and Evelyn Williams; [ch.] Emily and Sarah; [ed.] University of Windsor-Teachers College, University of Western ONT; [occ.] Music Teacher-Peel Board of Ed., Brampton-Composer; [memb.] ONT Teachers Association; [hon.] 2 band scores published On Sale across Canada; [oth. writ.] Many songs, lyrics; [pers.] I look to the present and the future for inspiration. These are the parts of our lives we can transform. [a.] Orangeville, ONT., CAN.

LLOYD, DENISE S.
[pen.] Sabrina Burton; [b.] Kingston, NY; [p.] Helen and Bynum Burton; [m.] Divorced; [ch.] Sean Cornell, Heather Kamilah; [ed.] Essex County College; [occ.] Human Resources Asst; [hon.] The NLP Editor's Choice award 1994; [oth. writ.] Poem published in AT Day's End, a compilation of poetry by The NLP, other poems not yet published; [pers.] I dedicate this poem to my "better half" - I Love You. [a.] Newark, NJ.

LODER, ADRIAN
[b.] September 14, 1979, Lincoln, NE; [p.] William A. and Janette H. Loder; [ed.] High school; [occ.] Student; [memb.] National Forensics League; [hon.] High honor roll, finalist in NLP's North American Open Poetry Contest; [oth. writ.] Much unpublished material including novels, poetry,etc.; [pers.] My poetry, as well as my prose, strives to illustrate the importance of the individual over society, and how, in the presence of no absolute morals, society presents absolute morals and rules for convenience. My poetry, etc., also reflects emotion. [a.] Danville, PA.

LOFTON, CRYSTAL FAITH
[b.] March 20, 1968, Ft. Collins, CO; [p.] Sharon and Zane Lofton; [ed.] Sunnydale Academy, Union College, OK City Community College, OK Christian Community University of Science and Arts; [occ.] Children's Hospital of OK; [memb.] Project BRUSH OK City Zoo/OK Wildlife Federation, World Wildlife Fund, Center for Marine Conservation; [hon.] Excellence in History - 1987 The National Dean's List, Award of Merit 1989-90, two poems published in "Our World's Favorite Poems" by National Library

of Poetry; [pers.] I write about inspiring aspects of life as I experience them. Greatly influencing me is my Mom and Aunt who read stories to me when I was a child. [a.] Okla City, OK.

LOIGNON, KIMBERLY
[b.] December 22, 1963, S.F., CA; [p.] Judith Loignon Reid and Frederick B. Watson; [ed.] High school, 1982 ICS Day Care Management 1993; [occ.] Custodian West Charleston Baptist Day Care and Preschool, part-time work at Little Caesars Pizza; [hon.] Inventor of the "Bottle Buddy" letter on file with U.S. Patent Office; [oth. writ.] Children's stories (not published) "Otis Goes To School", "Mr. Big and Mr. Small", "Otis and the Magic World", and "Paper Elves"; [pers.] My boss looked at my pants leg the other day, noticing the bleach spots, she said, "What are you? a custodian?" It was a joke, but clothes don't make me a better person. I am who I am. [a.] Las Vegas, NV.

LONG, GEORGE
[pen.] Palmetto Pete; [b.] October 13, 1914, Culeman; [p.] George Long Sr.; [m.] Maxie F., May 6, 1941; [ch.] Carol Harwell and Mr. Terry Long; [ed.] Foley High School, Auburn University; [occ.] Retired Veterinarian; [hon.] Was Southern Miss Dixie 1961; [oth. writ.] Several humera articles published in Orlando newspaper.

LONG, JANE MARIE
[b.] July 28, 1945, Minneapolis, MN; [p.] Bud (deceased) and Ruby Long; [ed.] Lakewood Senior High School, Northern Technical School of Business; [occ.] Official Court Reported for Probate Court; [memb.] Hope Presbyterian Church, Hennepin County District Court Reporters Association, Minnesota Court Reporters Association, National Court Reporters Association; [hon.] Shorthand and typing awards in high school, Underwood award of merit as Outstanding Business Education Student for 1963, Band letters (3 years); [oth. writ.] Three contemporary gospel songs published on record and cassette on Rainbow Records label, first published poem "In My Father's House" published in River of Dreams by National Library of Poetry; over a hundred unpublished poems; many skits and plays for church groups; [pers.] Being a court reported had given me an extensive background of material to write about with poetry of life experiences; I play the piano, organ and alto sax, have had 3 1/2 years of ballroom dance training; 6 years of voice lessons as a coloratura soprano (5 octave voice), I've written three songs and plan to write more. Poetry and music lift the heart and give my life meaning. I am thrilled to be able to share my words and music to inspire others. [a.] Edina, MN.

LOONAN, JUANITA
[b.] August 6, 1954, Nevada, IA; [p.] Raleigh and Lois Rumbaugh; [m.] James Daniel, July 13, 1974; [ch.] Jamie Danielle Loonan and Brice Joseph Loonan; [ed.] Ballard High School; [occ.] Cook, mother and housewife; [memb.] Methodist Church, OID Settler Committee; [hon.] Being published in "Dance on the Horizon" by National Library of Congress; [oth. writ.] Published in National Library of Congress "Dance in the Horizon". Also for my own enjoyment and to bring comfort to a friend who's going through a tough time; [pers.] I write about things that touch my life, be it a friend, a loved one, a gorgeous fall day or a day of quiet reflection - for these are what really matter in my life. [a.] Maxwell, IA.

LOVELAND, CATHY
[b.] January 9, 1975, Riverside, CA; [ed.] University of Redlands; [occ.] Student; [hon.] Golden Poet award, Golden State awards in History and Government, Silver Sands awards for music; [pers.] Perfection is impossible, but enlightenment isn't.

LOWE, BETTY SUE
[pen.] Liz Beth; [b.] June 8, 1936, Kentucky; [p.] Fay and Omar Blacketer; [m.] Divorced, 7/31/54-1/30/83; [ch.] Deborah Fay, Joseph, Victoria, Elle and Cornwell, William Raymond Lowe; [ed.] Valley High School, Ahrens Trade Finishing School, Glendale Community College; [occ.] Retired - private tutor; [memb.] National Honor Society, Phi-Theta-Kappa, World of Poetry, Ball Room Dance Society, Den mother, Brownies Girl Scouts of America; [hon.] Top Honors High school and college for academics, KY State Spelling Champion Scholarships to three universities; [oth. writ.] Doctor Perfectos Treatise, Perfecting Perfection, Over there acknowledged by past president Bush, Survival used by AA many poems, short stories and essays; [pers.] I believe that God is The Wind Beneath My Wings and it is this trust that motivates me to keep on trying no matter what obstacles try to keep me down. [a.] Glendale, AZ.

LOWERY, IRMA CATHERINE
[b.] May 25, 1942, Peterman, AL; [p.] George Lee and Fay Chandler; [m.] Paul, April 17, 1987; [ch.] Angelia Baggett, Mellony Nelson, grandchildren-Sara Salter, Bart Nelson, Cody and Corel Nelson; [ed.] Monroe Co. High; [occ.] Homemaker, Poultry Producer and cattle; [memb.] Ella Wall Research Club, National Poultry and Egg Association; [oth. writ.] Memories, published in Edge of Twilight, Twilights final curtain call, published in Dark Side of the Moon. Slower Times, a poem dedicated to the memory of my grandparents, published in a family newspaper; [pers.] My love of nature has inspired the majority of my poetry. My feelings and love of all God's creations are expressed through poems. [a.] Forest Home, AL.

LUCAS, M. ELIZABETH
[b.] July 20, 1914, Columbia, SC; [p.] George and Marie Lucas; [ed.] Columbia High School, Columbia College, Federal School of Art, University of SC; [occ.] Retired; [memb.] American Legion, Cedar Creek Baptist Church, Women's Memorial (Women in Military Services for America), AARP-Southeast Mineralogical Society; [hon.] Gem and Minerals awards, SC State Fair awards, American Bantam Association awards; [oth. writ.] "When the Ink Flowed" book of containing 106 poems, Off Press Sept 1994; [pers.] Simple words I share. I write what I care about my thoughts and dreams are expressed Imagination, observation and thoughts, I pass on. [a.] Columbia, SC.

LUCE
[b.] July 28, 1947, New York City; [ed.] University of AZ; [occ.] Director, Performance Workshop; [oth. writ.] Written, directed and produced one woman theatre piece titled: "Photographs Without a Camera"; [pers.] Living in a foreign country and speaking a foreign language has sharpened my sense of communication: I feel my words more as I search for the right ones. [a.] Woodland Hills, CA.

LUM, GRETCHEN YATES
[b.] June 10, 1945, Honolulu, HI; [p.] Mr. and Mrs. F.O. Yates; [m.] Philip Wayne (divorced), May 31, 1967; [ch.] Jadine A. Lum; [ed.] California College of Arts and Crafts; [occ.] Artist and Poet; [memb.] Ridgefield Artist Guild, Aldrich Museum of Contemporary Art; [hon.] Merit award- Golden Poems of The Western World-Washington 1989, Editor's Choice award-National Library of Poetry; [oth. writ.] Recordings The Sound of Poetry - National Library of Poetry, Visions, NLP Poet Series, Rare Objects of Art Poetic Highlights; [pers.] Poetry for me is an ever expansion of my experience within the reflections of my inner self. Yoga and meditation has a great influence. [a.] Kapaan, HI.

LUPTON, MARY HOSMER
[pen.] Mary Hosmer Lupton; [b.] January 2, 1914, Olympia, WA; [p.] Kenneth Winthrop Hosmer and Mary Louise Wheller; [m.] 1-Keith Brahe-Wiley, October 12, 1940 and 2) Thomas George Lupton, November 27, 1965; [ch.] Sarah Wiley Guise, Victoria Brahe-Wiley, Andrew Henshaw Lupton; [ed.] At. Anne's School, Gunston Hall Junior College, University of VA; [occ.] Writer and painter; [memb.] VA Society of Mayflower Descendants, Albermarle Chapter NSDAR, Nature Conservancy, New England Historic Genealogical Society; [hon.] Listed in Who's Who of American Women, and/or Who's Who in the South and Southwest since 1974-75, winner of Mary Rawlings 1990; [oth. writ.] Short stories published in "little magazines"; historical articles published in Albermarle County Historical Society Magazine book reviews in local and Richmond VA newspapers.

LUSIGNAN, CARMEN
[pen.] Carmen Rosales; [b.] January 21, 1972, Gulfport, MS; [p.] Robert and Ruth Rosales; [m.] Michael Anthony, March 20, 1993; [ed.] Delgado Community College, International Correspondence School - legal secretary course; [memb.] Junior Girl Scout Leader, Registrar of the Girl Scout Overseas Lone Troop Committee, Daisy Girl Scout Co-Leader; [hon.] Phi Theta Kappa International Honor Society, Senior Class President high school 1990, Girl Scout silver award, The National Dean's List; [oth. writ.] A poem published in "Echoes of Yesterday" by The NLP, "The Sound of Poetry" cassette released by the NLP; [pers.] After all worldly possessions are lost and acquired over lifetimes, the written word shall always endure.

MACLEOD, KENNETH I.E.
[b.] November 17, 1912, Scotland; [p.] Kenneth and Christina; [m.] Jean, April 25, 1935; [ch.] Deidre Jean, Sandra, Kenneth and Aymer; [ed.] MD. Ed. University Scotland, M.P.H. University of Michigan; [occ.] Retired; [memb.] American Association of Science, American P.H. Association, Mass. Medical Society; [oth.writ.] "The Crisis in Authority", (Vantage Press), "High Endeavor" and "The Ranker"; [pers.] I believe that religion is the most the problematic force in human affair, not race. I believe that man is destroying is Rabtat the planet earth, because of greed.

MADER, KYLA MICHELE
[pen.] Kellae Wolfe; [b.] February 4, 1978, Whittier, Pres; [p.] Dawn and Charlie Mader; [ed.] Currently a junior at Whittier High School and ICS Animal Care Specialist program; [occ.] Student; [memb.] Ducks

Unlimited, Sierra Club, Friends of Animals and the Wolf Education and Research Center; [hon.] 2nd place International Poetry Contest, Editor's Choice Award, 2 published poems, newspaper article; [oth.writ.] My House-short story, poems-"Tracks of the Wolf", "The Coming of Darkness", "Untitled Lesson", "Locked Without a Key" and "Nature's Majesty"; [pers.] Listen to the creatures. Hear them with your heart, see them with your soul, for they are God's creatures. Protect them with your whole. [a.] Whittier, CA.

MAKLA, ALICE
[b.] July 25, 1934, Brooklyn, NY; [p.] Amy and Michael Makla; [ed.] Adelphi Academy, academic degree; [occ.] Licensed Real Estate Salesperson, Brooklyn, NY.; [memb.] Licensed Sales Association PA., Paradise Valley Assembly of God, Cresco, PA; [oth.writ.] A Great Day, Wanted That Child; [pers.] I'm influenced by the words of God, since the world is mixed up. [a.] Brooklyn, NY.

MALLORY, IDA
[pen.] Aida; [b.] New York City; [ch.] 2 girls; [ed.] Washington Irving Coed and Syracuse Conservatory of Music, 4 years of Voice Metropolitan School of Arts; [occ.] Singing homemaker; [hon.] Elvis Presley award and poetry; [oth.writ.] "Life" and "Philosophy", cat story-mine whitey; [pers.] Appeared in opera and toured in "Carmen". [a.] Syracuse, NY.

MALONE, PH.D., LAURENCE A.
[b.] December 4, 1911, Cleveland; [p.] Cornelius and Grace; [m.] Nettie Allen Thomas; [ed.] John Carroll, Columbia; [occ.] Retired; [hon.] Many awards for Outstanding Achievements.; [oth. writ.] Knight had Knighted Waltz, Order of St. John; several books.

MAMUNES, TERESA A.
[b.] October 14, 1925; [p.] William and Teresa Chobot; [m.] Anthony Mamunes, September 23, 1950; [ch.] Antony Peter, Teresa Athena and Christopher William; [ed.] Windham High and attended University of Connecticut; [occ.] Retired; [pers.] I have always had a positive approach to life and have tried to convey this in word and deed. I also endeavor to reflect this in my writing. [a.] Storrs, CT.

MARIO, LUIS
[b.] March 28, 1935; [p.] Natividad and Felino Gonzalez; [m.] Magda Gonzalez, July 15, 1976; [ch.] Jose and Felino Gonzalez (previous marriage); [ed.] Municipal School Valdes Rodriguez, Havana accomplished literary studies specializing in poetry; [occ.] Journalist, Managing Editor of Diario Las Americas, (Miami, FL.), Professor of Journalism, University of Miami; [memb.] Culture and Peace in Spain and Germany, Miami Poetic Academy, Inter-American Editor (Buenos Aires, Argentina); [hon.] Namec Cuban National Poet by 43 orginizations in Exile, Honorary Degree North American Spanish Language Academy, first prize in the category of Lyric Poetry by Association of Cuban Educators in Exile, Fiambrere de Plata (Silver Basket_ from the Ateneo Casablanca, Cordoba, Spain; [oth_writ.] Published ten books, A Cuban Poet 1971, From My Sundays 1973, And A Poem Is Born 1975, Fugitive of Misfortune 1978, This Woman...1983, Poetry and Poets 1984, 70 Poets 1986, The Same Woman 1989, Science and Art of Castilian Verse 1991, Cuba in My Verses 1993, hundreds of articles and poems in several national and international publications. [a.] Miami, FL.

MARKEE, ALESHA
[b.] March 23, 1978, Spokane; [p.] Mr. and Mrs. Markee; [ed.] Attending Mead Senior High School, major in Art and English; [occ.] Child Care Worker; [hon.] Awarded 1st place for best poem by junior high student in 1992, published in The Space Between in 1994; [pers.] I've always believed if you live your life behind a mask, you'll cover your future. That is why writing defines me. I love you Corey Mitchum. [a.] Mead, WA.

MARMOLEJO, LEONARD ACUNA DE
[b.] January 11, 1936, Colombia, South America; [p.] Nicolas Acuna and Anunciacion Varela; [m.] Leoncio Marmolejo; [ch.] Luz Helena, Gloria Milena, Diego Fernando and Jaime Leoncio, 3 grandchildren, Jennife Andrea Braun, Jason Kenneth Braun and Jacqueline Mary Iannone; [ed.] Graduated as a teacher from Normal Nacional De Cali, in Colombia, graduated in Social Sciences from State University of New York, studied art at the Conservatory of arts and music in California, Colombia and studied art at SUNY, Farmingdale; [occ.] Retired, now writing my 3rd book of poems, a novel and finishing a book on short stories; [memb.] Suburban Art League, Independent Art Society, Islip Art Museum, Nassau County Museum of Art, member of Latino American Writers Institute; [hon.] 1st award for the short story "El Dolor Del Artista" in Colombia, S.A., have had numerous art exhibits through Long Island and Manhattan, some of my works have been sold in Channel 21 for benefits, other paintings are in permanent exhibit at libraries and private collections, was designated representative of the Society of Humanistic Psychology for South America and the Caribbean for the year 1980, founded and owned a private school, Liceo Eugenio Pacelli, in the city of Cali, Colombia, in 1990, received the diploma for"Who Is Who In Latino U.S.A. Ira Levy Memorial Award; [oth.writ.] I am a special columnist for Spanish Language newspapers edited in New York, "El Heraldo Colombiano", "La Republica", Palpitar Hispano", the name of my column is "Transparencies", collaborated in the book "Colombianos En New York" (1988), my literary works have been published in other newspapers such as "El Bohemio News", I am now publishing my second book "Brindis Por Un Poem" which will be out in September 1994, I have a poem published in the anthology Dance on The Horizon, by The National Library of Poetry 1994, poem titled "Invitation"; [per.] I think that poetry is the soul of the people, and therefore it should carry a noble and altruistic message. [a.] Levittown, NY.

MARQUIS, DANIELLE
[b.] November 10, 1980, Newport, VT; [p.] Venise and Richard Sevigny; [ed.] Kindergarten -8th grade St. John's Academy, 9th grade Seton High School; [[occ.] Student; [memb.] S.A.D.D., chorus and Empathy; [hon.] Math, English, Social Science and Computer Awards; [oth.writ.] "Life" published in The Desert Sun, "Dream Day" published in The Day's End; [pers.] I wish to thank everyone I know for giving me the love and encouragement I needed. [a.] Cadyville, NY.

MARSHALL, RUTH V.
[b.] May 6, 1916, Dallastown, PA; [p.] William and Mary Fry; [m.] Robert T. Marshall; [ch.] Gary, Ronny, Lynn, Rita and Holly; [ed.] Nine Years at Dallastown Public School, high school equivalency diploma (at 75), 27 college credits (Lancaster Bible); [occ.] Retired; [memb.] Red Lion Bible Church, York Co. Conservation Society, Daughters of Union, Veterans of Civil War; [hon.] 1st woman to serve on Dallastown Borough Council, listed as Broadcaster in first edition of Who's Who of America Women-1958-59; [oth.writ.] Who"s Who in the East (1961) (Marqus), 1989 in The Golden Treasury of Great Poems-1991, in Who's Who In Poetry vol III, 1994 Dance On The Horizon; [pers.] Public speaker. Key to success = insist. [a.] Dallastown, PA.

MARSHALL, SHANNON
[b.] August 27, 1977, Wareham; [p.] Pamela and Gerald Marshall; [ed.] Senior at Wareham High School, two summers at Upward Bound; [occ.] Student; [memb.] Upward Bound, Foreign Language Club, A/V Club, Amnesty International; [hon.] Publication in three separate book by The National Library of Poetry, spotlighted for work in the Standard Times and Wareham Courier, being in Upward Bound; [oth.writ.] Publishings in school yearbook and school literary magazine, many that have never been acknowledged; [pers.] I want to thank the Lord for giving me a gift., my family, best friend Anika Bartie, I dedicate this publication to my Godson, Deon T. Santos Jr., sisters, Heather and Arielle Marshall and much love to Upward Bound. [a.] W. Wareham, MA.

MARTIN, ALTA M.
[b.] April 28, 1907, Clinton, CO., MO; [P.] Hugh Elbert and Mary Ann Shannon; [m.] Hugh C., Martin (deceased), June 5, 1927; [ch.] Margaret Frost and Madelyn Everett; [ed.] High school; [occ.] Retired from Medical Clinic, receptionist, Plattsburg, MO., and retired Deputy Collector Clinic; [memb.] P.T.A., B.P.W. Club and Democratic Women's Club; [hon.] Golden Poet Award, plaques and cassette, 4th place, Sacramento California, World of Poetry; [oth.writ.] Published in Young At Heart magazine, O.A.T.S. magazine, St. Joseph News Press, St. Joseph, MO.; [pers.] Writing poetry for 40 years, published 2 poetry books and book titled "My Memoirs-The Good Times". Have written poems for birthdays, births and weddings and Christmas.

MARTIN, LAURA BELLE
[b.] November 15, 1915, Jackson Co, MN; [p.] Eugene Wellington Martin, Mary Hanson Martin; [ed.] Renville Teachers Training 1935, Mankato State U 1968, Taught rural schools; [occ.] Retired. Previously a real estate and farmland manager; Pres of Renville Farms and feedlots, Sec Hist Renville Preservation, Sec Renville Town and Country Boosters, Publicity Chr for both organizations, Mem of Am Legion Aux; [hon.] Listed in Who's Who of the Midwest, Who's Who of America, Who's Who of the World. Int'l Who's Who of Intellectuals, five Thousand Personalities of the World, Int'l book of Honor; [oth. writ.] Poetry, articles for the Renville Museum; [pers.] Success comes to those who have a goal they wish to attain. Nothing much will be accomplished without effort; [a.] Holden, MO

MARTIN, MARGARET C.
[b.] July 27, 1933, Hickory Grove, SC; [p.] James and Mary Wylie; [m.] Arthur Martin, March 6, 1955; [ch.] Bonita Louann, Regina Sue and Matilda Kaye; [ed.] Blacksburg High School, Blacksburg, SC; [occ.] Housewife; [oth.writ.] A poem, "I Love You My Dear" was published by the National Library of Poetry in The Coming of Dawn, 1993, received Editor's Choice Award, also received Editor's Choice Award in 1994 for poem "In My World" published by National Library of Poetry, The Space Between, "Dear Bridget" will be published in the spring of 1995 in the publication of Journey of The Mind, the poem "Little Ones" will be published in the special edition, Best Poems of 1995, has written three children's books, waiting to be published, the poem, "Little Ones", was written for my three daughters, who will always be my special little girls, no matter what age. I love you.

MARTINEZ, RUTH H.
[pen.] Sister Martinez; [b.] October 28, 1917, Waldon, AR; [p.] John and Willie Harris; [m.] Lupe T. Martinez, November 23, 1955; [ch.] Joseph T. Martinez; [ed.] 10th grade; [occ.] Housewife; [oth.writ.] I have lots of poems. I have some lovely art works in beautiful painting and about 65 quilts Id. We call to the hospital to pray and help the sick. [a.] Kingman, AZ.

MASCITTI, MICHAEL
[b.] October 3, 1968, New York; [p.] Patricia and Beri Mascutti; [ed.] BA in History and Religion from Hunter College, enrolled in Masters Program at New School for Social Research; [occ.] Student/deposit clerk; [memb.] Church of Euthanasia; [hon.] Dean's List, scholarship for the New School; [oth.writ.] "Return to Nothing" published in Dance on The Horizon, "A Tribute to Lobo" unpublished and tons of other stuff; [pers.] All things stem from and lead to chaos. Thanks to: the goddess, her lover, M. Moorcork, Trica, Marye, Mithras, friends, family, P. Steele, Rose McDowell, Death in June, current 93, 6 comm, A. LaVey, B. Rice, Fire and Ice, wine, eel, sharks, lobsters (2 claws), Romulans, (sand) Klingons, Lyrans, Wadd, the imagination, the memory, Bloody Sphincter, remember; adapt and proceed, there is no birth without blood. [a.] Sunnyside, NY.

MASSEY, VICKIE
[pen.] Victoria Lynn; [b.] September 3, 1964, Lebanon, TN; [p.] Donnie and Christine Brown; [m.] Dwayne Massey, June 16, 1984; [ch.] Morgan Leigh and Whitney Deigh; [ed.] Macon County High, Volunteer State Community College; [occ.] Computer Programmer and Business Consultant; [hon.] Who's Who Among American High School Students, Who's Who Among American Junior College Students, Summa Cum Laude graduate; [oth.writ.] "A Winter Snow" published in At Day's End by The National Library of Poetry; [pers.] My writings will probably reflect personal experiences. I look for positive motivations in my life. [a.] Hermitage, TN.

MARTLOCK SR., J.W. (Ph.D.)
[b.] June 23, 1943, Dallas, TX; [p.] E.L. and Marie Matlock Sr. [m.] Glenda Faye Matlock, September 4, 1962; [ch.] Johnnie W. Jr. and Joe S. Matlock; [ed.] Doctor of Philosophy in Theology; [occ.] Senior Pastor, Central Full Gospel Fellowship, Inc.; [oth.writ.] "His Name Is Wonderful" (The National Library of Poetry), "Be Fruitful and Multiply" (Vantage Press, Inc.); [pers.] Matthew 6:33 is to me the one most important scripture in the Word of God. I was the reason I was what I was, God is the reason I am what I am. [a.] Fort Worth, TX.

MATTHEWS, LAUREL MAE
[b.] St. Louis, MO; [m.] Ellsworth Matthews; [ch.] Christina Smith, Karen Beck and Kim Wallace; [ed.] AB, Washington University, St. Louis, MO.; [hon.] Phi Beta Kappa, Pi Epsilon Delta, (drama honorary); [oth.writ.] Recorded songs, "Somewhere Beyond The Stars", "Be My Brother", numerous others, poem published "The Rose"; [pers.] Let us be a "pillar of fire" in the earth, a "temple of the living God". [a.] Emigrant, MT.

MAY, IDA R.
[b.] August 31, 1911, Brooklyn; [p.] Ida and Bertram McPherson; [m.] Lionel L. May (deceased); [ch.] Lillian D. Banks and Donald R. May; [ed.] Girl's High, Brooklyn College of the City of New York; [occ.] Art teacher, now retired; [hon.] Awarded scholarship to the National Academy of Art and Design; [oth.writ.] Several poems published by The National Library of Poetry; [pers.] Have traveled extensively and enjoyed every minute. Now living in a little town on Eastern Long Island. [a.] Blue Point, NY.

MAYBERRY, MILDRED E.
[b.] April 4, 1931, Oakland, CA; [p.] Deceased; [m.] Divorced; [ed.] 12th grade, 2 years college; [occ.] Retired; [memb.] International Society of Poets (1994); [hon.] Editor's Choice Awards for "Dismay 1993" and Poverty Gift 1994"; [oth.writ.] "Dismay" (poem), "Poverty A Gift", poem published; [pers.] Eventually everything passes regardless of difficult times. Never give up hope, apply faith to hope. It will see you through. [a.] Castro Valley, CA.

McAFEE, KENNETH C.
[pen.] Ken McAfee; [b.] August 12, 1910, Flint, MI; [p.] John and Elizabeth McAfee; [m.] Marie Joyce, December 26, 1986; [ed.] Michigan State University, Battle Creek College-1933; [occ.] Retired; [memb.] Battle Creek Country Club, Scottish Society of S.W. Michigan, Macfie Clan Society of North America, Navy League, St. Thomas Episcopal Church, National Rife Association, M.S.U. Alumni Association, Rotary Club, A.A.R.P., Sigma Alpha Epsilon Fraternity, American Legion, retired Commander-USNR, retired Vice President-Sheriff Goslin Co.; [hon.] Bishops Cross-Episcopal Church, Paul Harris Fellow, Red Rose Citation - Rotary Club and miscellaneous military awards; [oth.writ.] Poems published in "A Golden Treasure" by Joseph Roussor, "How To Become An Irritation" in Dance On The Horizon, National Library of Poetry, Caroline Sullivan, Editor 1994; [a.] Battle Creek, MI.

McDERMOTT, DIANNE C.
[b.] July 1, 1948, Elkhart, IN; [p.] Tina B. and Charles E. Hawk; [m.] John E. McDermott, July 6, 1970; [ch.] John Charles, Mary Elizabeth, Sarah Lynn and JoAnn Rose-Evin; [ed.] Graduate of Elkhart Central High School, class of 1967; [occ.] Factory Worker; [oth.writ.] Several other poems, unpublished; [pers.] There is none so rich as he who possesses the love of family and friends and the beauty of poetry and music. [a.] Edwardsburg, MI.

McDONALD, HATTIE
[p.] Mr. and Mrs. McMillian; [m.] A.G. McDonald, December 1963, (deceased); [ed.] High school; [occ.] Retired cafeteria worker; [memb.] First Baptist Church Missionary Worker, AARP, Senior Choir; [pers.] I strive to reflect what God reveals to my mind. Words God gave me. [a.] Fayetteville, NC.

McDOWELL, BARBARA
[pen.] Barbara McDowell; [b.] October 28, 1925, Kingston, Ontario Canada; [p.] Margaret and Wray; [m.] Donald McDowell, January 26, 1952; [ch.] Brenda Lee McDowell; [ed.] Toronto Teacher's College; [occ.] Housewife; [memb.] Canadian Antique Collectors Association, Bayview Golf and Country Club, Kingston Yacht Club, Kingston Golf and Country Club, Ontario Association of Superannuated Women Teachers; [hon.] Superannuated Teacher's of Ontario District 23, Lion's Club Music Festival 2nd place, 82% marks 1975, Lion's Club Music Festival-2nd place-87 1/2 % marks, 1976, Professional Sales Person Course (1989) Certificate, Cullen Country Barns; [oth.writ.] "Beauty", poem published by The National of Poetry (1994); [pers.] I try to put into words the beauty of God's work and creations which we can see or hear. [a.] North York, Ontario Canada.

McHENRY, MARTHA K. JOHNSON
[b.] Austin, TX; [p.] Leonard and Leora Earls Johnson; [ed.] B.S. Degree-Tillotson College, M.A. Degree-S.F. State University, Doctorate in Literature-World University; [occ.] Retired public school educator-forty years in Texas and California; [memb.] (Golden), Zeta Phi Beta Sorority, (Life) National Association for the Advancement of Colored People (Life) American Association of University Women, National Council of Negro Women, S.F. State Alumni Association, (member) California Retired Teachers Association and Commonwealth Club of California; [hon.] Academic Advancement Award, Black Authors Award from Delta Sigma Sorority and Zeta of the Year; [oth.writ.] Published, Golden Book of Poems, Living Poems For Today, Time To Read-short stories for children; [pers.] It is my desire to help the world become a better place through my writing. [a.] San Francisco, CA.

McINTOSH, TAMIKA ZANICE
[b.] June 21, 1972, Philadelphia, PA; [p.] Jacqueline Laura Tatam and John Tatam; Stanley Robert Warren, Robena Lawry; [ed.] Burlington County Vocational and Technical High School; Essey County College; [hon.] National Honor Society; Who's Who Among American High School Students; Vocational Talented and Gifted; Perfect Attendance Award; [oth.writ.] Goodbye For Now published by the Nat'l Library of Poetry; [pers.] I don't want to be known or remembered as an advocate for any cause other than that of humanity. I write in order to tell my story and hopefully others can relate and find love, hope, and faith; [a.] Irvington, NJ

McINTYRE, DONALD M.
[b.] January 19, 1940, Winnipeg, Manitoba Canada; [ed.] B.A. (Philosophy) 1963, St. John's College, Camarillo, California, M.A. (English), 1968, Loyola University of Los Angeles, Los Angeles, California; [hon.] Winner of Golden Poet Award, 1985-1992, from World of Poetry; [oth.writ.] Published in numerous anthologies by World of Poetry; [pers.] The art of poetry, as expressed by this author in his writings, is

an illustration of modern philosophical existential theories coupled with the psychological technique of stream of consciousness. [a.] Santa Barbara, CA.

McLELLAND, EVA
[pen.] Koni Wildflower; [b.] May 4, 1916, Laurel Hill, FL; [p.] William and Dora Edward; [ed.] Shellhorn High and several home study courses, including a writing course-also a journalism course; [occ.] Retired from government service with State Department and Air Force requiring extensive foreign travel; [memb.] Historical Society, National Arbor Day Foundation and several environmental organizations; [hon.] Presidential Legion of Merit Medallion and pin, many certificates of appreciation, name to be next to Ronald Reagan on Special Freedom monument in process now, honored by National Library of Poetry recognition of my poetic achievements, also by International Society of Poetry; [oth.writ.] Published in two National Library of Poetry anthologies, several articles published in local newspapers, now working on a book, the adventures of my life; [pers.] I strive to reflect the beauty and goodness of nature, and show the best, as well as the worst in mankind. [a.] Troy, AL.

McMICHAEL, LYNN
[b.] March 30, 1962, Gothenburg, NE; [p.] Meryl and Sharon McMichael; [m.] Single; [ch.] Gavin Ambrose, age 7; [ed.] Mid Plains Community College School of Practical Nursing; [occ.] L.P.N. and Shift Manager of McDonalds; [hon.] Mid Plains Community College, President's Honor Roll September 1989 and March 1990, Dean's Honor Roll September 1990, 100% Award of Excellence for retention in Dean Vaughn System of Medical Terminology April 1989; [oth.writ.] Poetry published in 1991 by Sparrowgrass Poetry Forum, 1994 by National Library of Poetry, various times locally, currently writing my first Science fiction novel; [pers.] "Beyond The Gate" is about my great grandma, who died at age 96. Her husband had died many years previous and both her sons died in the service. At the time this piece was written, all 5 daughters were still living. [a.] Gothenburg, NE.

McWEENEY, GINA
[b.] Waterbury, CT; [p.] Vincent and Vita DiBattista; [m.] Charles F. McWeeney; [ch.] Cregg McWeeney and Charlene McWeeney Burdacki; [occ.] Executive Vice President and Chief Administrative Officer; [memb.] Association of Iron and Steel Engineers; [hon.] Honored in 1992 at the Annual Women In; [pers.] I find an inner peace when writing poetry. I like to convey this experience through my writings. [a.] Watertown, CT.

McWHORTER, GEORGE T.
[b.] May 10, 1931, Washington, DC; [p.] George and Nell; [ed.] St. Albans School for Boys (Washington, DC.), B.A. (Florida Southern College), B.M., (Eastman School of Music), M.M. (University of Michigan), A.M.L.S. (University of Michigan); occ.] Curator, rare books and Professor, University of Louisville Library; [memb.] Sons of American Revolution, Sons of Confederate Veterans, Military Order of Stars and Bars, Scottish Rite of Freemasonry, Actors and Equity Association, American Guild of Musical Artists, American Guild of Variety Artists; [hon.] N.S.A.L. (National Society of Artists and Letters, 1948-50, U.S. Fulbright (1959 Paris), Distinguished Service Citation (1953, U.S. Army), Distinguished Citizen of Louisville (1972), K.C.C.H. (32 degree Mason), Who's Who in S.E. (1994), Jefferson Davis Achievement Award, Who's Who (1995); [oth.writ.] Arthur Rackham (1972), The Seafarer (1975), Burroughs Dictionary (University Press of America 1987), Remembering Barry Bingham (1990), Edgar Rice Burroughs Memorial Collection Catalog (1991), Arthur Rackham Memorial Collection Catalog (1994), Burroughs Bulletin (editor), Sun Rising (TV Doc); [pers.] "Ars Longa Vita Brevis" (art is long, life is short). [a.] Louisville, KY.

MEALING, RONALD W.
[b.] June 18, 1937, Sydney, Australia; [p.] William George (deceased) and Vira Thelma; [m.] Kathleen Anne, February 1966, divorced 1987; [ch.] John Joseph, Suzanne Louise, Donna Therese and Michelle Linda, grandchildren Joshua Mark; [ed.] Christian Brothers High School, Australian Society of Accountants; [occ.] Freelance writer and motion picture (animation) producer; [memb.] Nashville Area Chamber of Commerce, Civil Air Patrol (USAF Auxiliary); [hon.] Reserve Forces Medal, (long service), Royal Regiment of Australian Artillery, Editors Choice Award 1994, National Library of Poetry, 1993\94 North American open poetry competition; [oth.writ.] "On Cost and Such Things" 1965 (Circa), "Adventures in The Lost Kingdom of Radish", December 1984 (publication Australia) "Why Should It Be?" (Dance On The Horizon 1994), "Where Will The Children Go?" (Dark Side Of The Moon 1995). [a.] Nashville, TN.

MECUSKER, JOAN C.
[b.] April 27, 1954, Eau Claire, WI; [p.] Earl and Alyce Myers; [m.] Bud (Walter) Mecusker Jr., October 20, 1973; [ch.] Wendi D. Mecusker; [ed.] Elk Mound High School, Elk Mound, Wisconsin, Indianhead Technical College, New Richmond, WI; [occ.] Dairy farm; [memb.] Christian Missionary Alliance Church, Menomonie, WI; [hon.] Received Golden Poet Award and many honorable mentions from the World of Poetry, International Society of Poets, poem included in Best Poems of 1994; [oth.writ.] A home business resulting in "Heart to Heart" greeting cards for all occasions, as well as matted and framed original poetry, poetry written for relatives and sympathy cards for encouragement, "Silent Was The Night", the birth of Christ to the resurrection in poetry form; [pers.] I write to bring encouragement and hope to the reader. My personal relationship with God is many times the source of my values and I hope to point those who are hurting to the only one I feel truly understands their pain. [a.] Menomonie, WI.

MENDOZA, DEBORAH
[pen.] Deborah Mendoza; [b.] August 26, 1980; [p.] Angel A. and Maria U. Mendoza; [ed.] W.C. Bryant Elementary, Bingham Middle Magnet, Metropolitan Advanced Technical High School; [occ.] Student; [hon.] Editor's Choice Award presented by The National Library of Poetry; [oth.writ.] Single poem published in Tears of Fire by The National Library of Poetry. [a.] Kansas City, MO.

MERRITT, V.R.
[pen.] A. P. Ashley; [b.] March 4, 1952, Afton, WY; [p.] Rand and Jean Merritt; [m.] Karen D. Merritt (Reddick), September 23, 1972; [ch.] Brandy, Christopher, Jonathon, Cassandra and Andrew; [ed.] High school graduate, Star Valley High; [occ.] Automotive Technician, Butler Ford and Acura, Ashland, OR.; [oth.writ.] "Morning", "Treasured Poems of America" winter 1994, "Sensations of Love", "I Wonder", "A Stone", American Poetry Annual, 1993, "Thoughts", Whisper In The Wind; [pers.] "To The Poet" reflects my feelings toward poetry. I write what I feel and hope that someone else may get a smile or a tear from it. [a.] Medford, OR.

MERRYWEATHER, JOYCE JOHNSON
[b.] October 18, 1920, Utah; [p.] E.M. and Rosella Jolley; [m.] C.R. Johnson, deceased, now married to Max B. Merryweather, June 2, 1990; [ch.] Rosalie J. Smith, Glade Raymond Johnson, Janell J. Lawrence, Jeffrey J. Johnson and Julie Ann J. Ferguson; [ed.] Provo High School and Brigham Young University, majored in Business and Social Work; [occ.] Retired; [memb.] Lions Club, BYU emeritus Club, LDS Church, Disabled American Veterans Auxiliary, Utah State Legislator Delegate, Utah County Women's Legislative Council, Orem Women's Club, National Retired Federation Association, Orem Senior Citizens, Dance Club, lifetime member of International Society of Poets; [hon.] Semi-finalist at the Washington, DC International Society poetry contest for three years, 1992, 1993 and 1994, won 2nd place at poetry contest in San Francisco, won Editor's Choice Award from National Library of Poetry, appointed to Advisory Panel of International Society of Poets, published in the Library of Congress, Outstanding Poets of 1994; [oth.writ.] Veterans poetry as my husband still has schapel in leg from WW II, have written stories, plays and poetry off and on all of my life for family, friends, church and all organizations that I belong to, I have had some of my work published and have received various awards and honors for them, I am for sure going to publish a book of my poetry soon; [pers.] I believe in serving my fellow man and that all humans are children of God and are to be treated with dignity and respect. I serve my church and family. My jewels are my children, my 35 grandchildren and my 8 great grandchildren. [a.] Orem, UT.

MEUER, NORMA SHIPPY
[pen.] Norma Shippy Meuer; [b.] November 8, 1910, Guide Rock, NE; [p.] Ada Baker and John Van Horn; [m.] Fred Meuer (deceased); [ch.] James Shippy and Evelyn Habersat; [ed.] Book of life, 84 years, Stillwater High School, Stillwater, MN; [occ.] Retired, 20 years as volunteer teacher at several county parks, county park volunteer and teacher of Language of Music using the harmonica as an instrument; [oth.writ.] Poems, published locally; [pers.] Each day is a gift, its worth beyond measure, each year is a void to be filled with treasure. The hours are minutes to live and to learn. Use it all wisely, they never return.

MEYERS, HENRY J.
[b.] August 5, 1925, New York, NY; [p.] Edward and Leah; [m.] Divorced; [ch.] Stephen and Roger Meyers; [ed.] B.S. Long Island University, M.D. California College of Med. U.S.C.; [occ.] Physician; [pers.] My writings serve as a diary to the events in my life, past and present.

MICK, FLORENCE M.
[pen.] Mark in Time; [b.] September 23, 1929, Tioga Co., PA; [p.] Charles Johnson (deceased) and Iva Lapoint; [m.] Joseph R. Mick Sr. (deceased), February 7, 1956; [ch.] Joann, Susan, and Lena Mick

(deceased at age 19); [ed.] High school and several Christian Workers Teacher's courses; [occ.] Retired, I do some teaching in Diven and Parley Colburn Elementary Schools, Chemung Co., NY; [memb.] I have vested rights in the state of New York with 14 years; [hon.] 2 Golden Poets Awards, World of Poetry, Ruby and Emerald Poet with I.S.P., I won two scholarships in art and awards as a camp counselor, thanks for publishing several of my poems; [oth.writ.] I have written some songs and 5 children's books, plus I have 14 books of poems to be published; [pers.] Most of my works are going to charity and Junvile Diabetes, undetectable birth defects and babies born with Aids. My last book goes to help burn victims. I write under Mark In Time, as I want to make a mark that count. [a.] Elmira, NY.

MILLARD, CHARLES A.
[b.] 1934, Chicago; [p.] Deceased; [m.] Darlene, 28 years; [ch.] George (25) and Michele (28); [pers.] Charles is SS retirement, with progressive chronic MS for the last 35 years, writing for the last 30. He now studies Philosophy, Physics and Psychology. Other interests now are Ancient Roman History, Ancient Hebrew and Egyptian Hieroglyphics. He also paints, putting faces to some of his writing. Some of his other works are, "Cobwebs of Time" a 90's version of the Hunchback of N.D. "Winter Of Part 1" a love poem and "Always Part II" "Life" a poetic philosophical observation. "The Darkness" looking inside manic depression, people who have M.D. all ask the same question after reading it "how did you find darkness" not even my"God" can. Honors and awards, 1994 President's Award for literary excellence from the N.R.A. and Honorable Mention for "Death of Winter, Birth of Spring". Certificate of Poetic Achievement from the Amherst Society. My writing is not meant to be entertaining, but more thought provoking and I fine writing, painting, etc. an altered state of consciousness and the need to express our subconscious feelings. In so doing I "paint" what I "hear" and "write" what I "see". With philosophy the study of "thinking" and psychology the examination of that thinking, now I am almost 60, I would like to live long enough to really learn how to "paint" and "write".

MILLER, DOLORES
[b.] February 16, 1951, Philadelphia, PA; [p.] Michael and Peg Steinberg; [m.] Lawrence Miller, February 3, 1973; [ch.] Lawrence Michael and Michelle; [ed.] Roxbourgh High, Holy Family College, Bucks Community College, [occ.] Owner of Uniform and Baby Clothes store; [memb.] MADD, American Cancer Society, Special Olympics Founders Circle, Child Help USA; [hon.] It is a honor for a number of my poems to be published by The National Library of Poetry; [oth.writ.] Poems and writings published in Ghost Writers and Not Alone Anymore, Inc., and Ebbing Tide and Write To Heal; [pers.] In my writing I strive to reflect the strength in the human spirit to overcome obstacles and the beauty of nature and God's love. [a.] Richboro, PA.

MILLER, DOROTHY J.
[b.] August 2, 1926, Ada H (Palmer), PA; [p.] Bertha E., Snyder; [ch.] nancy, Sharon and Andrew; [ed.] High school; [occ.] Retired; [memb.] Hour of Power, Eagles Club, Cystic Fibrosis Foundation; [hon.] Received employee of the month and also employee of the year at my previous job; [oth.writ.] Poem published in Wind In The Night Sky and in Our World's Favorite Poems, Who's Who In Poetry; [pers.] I want to convey that family is very important in our lives and to have faith.[a.] Liverpool, NY.

MILLER, MICHAEL JOHN
[pen.] Poe; [b.] September 10, 1968, Gardena, CT; [p.] Linda L. and Walter G. Miller; [ed.] Graduated North Torrance High School with a B average, certified as an electronic techinican at S.C.R.O.C.; [occ.] Bouncer; [memb.] A member of the National Society of Poetry; [hon.] Award of Merit for the poem "Change", an Editor's Choice Award, Golden Poet of 1991, Award of Merit for "The Sound of Hope", Award of Merit for "Friendship"; [oth.writ.] My poem "Friendship" is in the book Selected Work of Our World's Best Poets, my poem "Keepers of The Lights" in in Our World's Favorite Poems and my poem "The Stars Of Love" is in the book Outstanding Poets of 1994; [pers.] If we all help each other the way God helps us, we will all be fine. [a.] Wildomar, CA.

MILLICAN, DEBRA A.
[pen.] Alec; [b.] December 28, 1955, Sherman, TX; [p.] Mr. and Mrs. Kenneth Mauldin; [ed.] 12th and two years of Creative Writing and 1 year of computers; [occ.] Bartender at my father's club, The Mi-Wuk; [oth.writ.] "My Room of Play", "Spirit The Wind", "The Door" and "Illusions" all published in 1994; [pers.] This is to my father, whom after reading my poems, ask me if I had copied them from a book. I love you dad, Alece. [a.] Fort Smith, AR.

MILLWATER, MARION
[pen.] Marion Millwater; [b.] December 6, 1918, Plainfield, NJ; [p.] Marguerite and Reginald Ralli; [m.] Harold Millwater, May 30, 1936; [ch.] Shirley and Sandra; [ed.] High school and Drake Business College, Rutger's Real Estate Seminar with a highest mark of "Distinguished"; [occ.] Housewife; [memb.] Westfield Board of Realtors, Elks Club, Watchung Bowman, Ladies Auxiliary of Rescue Squad and the AARp # 1182 in Cape May Courthouse.

MINNINGER, DANIEL R.
[pen.] Ross Daniels; [b.] August 11, 1964, Pottstown, PA; [p.] Hazel and William Minninger; [ed.] Graduated Boyertown Area Senior High School (class of 1982), 2 years college, 1 plus numerous courses in the Air Force; [occ.] Texas Department of Health; [memb.] Hemlock Society; [hon.] U.S. Air Force commendation medal (twice), U.S Air Force achievement medal; [oth.writ.] "The One" published in The Space Between, 1994, numerous unpublished poems; [pers.] Live all your dreams to the fullest, for we never know when or where our road will come to an end. [a.] Austin, TX.

MINOR, PAMELA SHANNON
[pen.] Tweety or just Shannon; [b.] May 11, 1975, Sun Valley, CA; [p.] Pamela G. and step-dad Bill Heist; [ed.] High school graduate, currently attending college; [occ.] Teacher's assistant at Winnetka Elementary School; [hon.] Editor's Choice Award from National Library of Poetry and Honorable Mention from the PTSA for musical accomplishment; [oth.writ.] Four other poems previously published in National Library of Poetry anthologies; [pers.] I try my best at all I do and I try to always remember that you can not get what you want unless you go after it yourself and earn it. [a.] Reseda, CA.

MINTON, JANIE
[b.] March 10, 1952, Michigan; [p.] Porter and Virginia Dowler; [m.] Kenny Minton, November 13, 1993; [ed.] Otsego High School graduate; [occ.] Craftsman; [memb.] NRA member, National Poet's Society member since 1978; [hon.] Achievement Awards in poetry, awards for best of state in poetry entry at the state fair; [oth.writ.] "What Goes Around" published in At Day's End, "Dreams", published in A Far Off Place, published article in Woman's World magazine, published article in Reader's Digest, wrote poems for Hallmark Cards; [pers.] Living and let living may be a lost cause if a friend is lost in the process. Don't be afraid to reach out to people. Even if it's only in a poem. A lot of people like you for what you can do, but a good friend likes you for who you are. [a.] Elizabeth City, NC.

MIRANDA, FRANK
[pen.] Nathan T. Sharpe; [b.] May 11, 1955, Yuma, AZ; [p.] Rudolfo and Frances; [m.] Brenda Lee Miranda, December 3, 1988; [ch.] Samantha Ann; [ed.] High school, Yuma Union High, college-Arizona Western; [occ.] Airlines; [oth.writ.] "Journey of A Soul", poetry, "Circle of Being" philosophy, "Imagine-The Circle Complete"; [pers.] Mankind is on the verge of his next step... into his evolution, not only in the physical, rather what more important... spiritually. Our time.. is ..now. [a.] Orange, CA.

MIROSEVIC, IVAN
[pen.] Ive Meros; [b.] October 30, 1938, Velaluka; [p.] Petar and Maria Croatia Mirosevic; [m.] Karenza; [ch.] Melaina and Mireille; [ed.] Technician School, Department of Naval, Architecture and Marine Engineering in Port of Split Croatia; [occ.] Engineer Specialist in Modular Ship Design and Construction; [memb.] The Society of Naval Architects and Marine Engineers New York since 1970, Society of Plastic Engineers Dangerous Good Marine Surveyor; [oth.writ.] Several technical papers, poems in English and Croatian Language; [pers.] Study astronomy to be inspired for writing poetry. [a.] El Carson, CA.

MITCHELL, ALLEN
[b.] January 1, 1945, Elizabethtown, TN; [ch.] Sean, Heather and Matthew; [ed.] Unaka High School, ICS Engineering; [occ.] Electrical construction engineer; [memb.] Midway Macedonia Baptist Church; [oth.writ.] "The Day I Died", published by the National Library of Poetry in their book A Break In The Clouds 1993, "Words" published by the National Library of Poetry in Outstanding Poets of 1994. [a.] Carrollton, GA.

MITCHELL, PAMELA LOU
[pen.] Pamela Sears Mitchell; [b.] December 27, 1951, Hominy, OK; [p.] Edmond Sears and H. Louise Lackey; [m.] Robert W. Mitchell, October 7, 1972; [ed.] Derby Senior High School, Derby, KS; [occ.] Handicapped, housewife; [memb.] West Haysville Baptist Church; [hon.] Editor's Choice Award 1994 by the National Library of Poetry; [oth.writ.] My poem "Harmonized Bliss" was in the National Library of Poetry book Dance On The Horizon 1994; [pers.] My inspiration comes from my faith, my husband and very loving but pushy friends. I try to show in my poems that God (for me) is everywhere and everything. [a.] Wichita, KS.

MITCHELL, SHANNON EILEEN
[b.] March 26, 1978, Tarzana; [p.] Lori and Wayne Mitchell; [ed.] High school, 3 years; [occ.] Student; [memb.] I am a drum major in my high school band; [hon.] I have several awards in baton twirling and music; [oth.writ.] Other poems, 1 published in River of Dreams; [pers.] My poems are dedicated to the poetic person in the reader. [a.] Granada Hills, CA.

MITCHELL, TIMOTHY M.
[b.] October 22, 1963, Omaha, NE; [p.] Charles Thomas (deceased) and Florence Marie Lutwitze; [ed.] Omaha Cathedral High School, St. John's (MN) University, Creighton University, University of NE-Omaha (B.G.S., M.A.-English), SUNY-Albany (in progress M.L.S.); [occ.] Graduate student, libraries volunteer, employee of the Research Foundation via SUNYA Film and Television Documentation Center; [hon.] Phi Kappa Phi, Alpha Sigma Lambda, Golden Key; [oth.writ.] "Grandfather's Farm" (1993 Winter) "Fallen Petals" (1994 Summer) both in National Library of Poetry anthologies, The Shaping of Real Time, A Study of Chapters 24, 25, 26, in "The Log from the Sea Of Cortez" - John Steinbeck Library, Archives (Salinas, CA). [a.] Omaha, NE.

MIZE, PATRICIA P.
[b.] January 7, 1940, Birmingham, AL; [p.] Luther and Jewell Pilkington; [m.] Joseph A. Mize, September 3, 1955; [ch.[Terri A. Mize Shugart and Lisa J. Mize Templin; [ed.] Gardendale High; [occ.] Housewife; [memb.] 1st Baptist Church of Gardendale; [oth.writ.] Several poems unpublished; [pers.] My wish is that my poems would be an inspiration to others to seek and find Jesus Christ. [a.] Gardendale, AL.

MODGLIN SR., WILLIAM HENRY
[pen.] William Henry Modglin Sr.; [b.] July 29, 1939, Muncie, IN; [p.] Henry and Estella Modglin; [m.] Gail I. Modglin, December 25, 1991; [ch.] William, Micheal, James, Terri, Sherri and Anita; [ed.] Graduate of Muncie Central, Muncie, Indiana; [occ.] Police Officer, Ball Memorial Hospital, Muncie, IN; [memb.] Mason, Muncie 433, Ancient Accepted Scottish Rite, Valley of Indianapolis, IN., Murat Temple A.A.O.N.M.S. of Indianapolis, IN; [hon.] U.S. Navy 1957 until 1966; [oth.writ.] "The Moon", "The Darkness", "The Sun"-Raindrops", "This Day", "Anger Hurts", "By Yourself", "Taps", "Quiet Dream", "Rainbow", "In The Garden", "Outdoor Living"; [pers.] My poems are a gift to who ever will take the time to read. [a.] Muncie, IN.

MOECKEL, DEBI HENSLEY
[b.] October 19, 1955, Hazard, KY; [p.] Paul and Ernestine Hensley; [m.] Richard Moeckel, December 13, 1986; [ed.] Hazard High School, University of Kentucky; [occ.] Freelance writer, Cert. Image Consultant; [memb.] Charter lifetime member of the International Society of Poets, member of the Inter Society of Authors and Artists; [hon.] Semi-finalist winner, Inter Society of Poets, 1993 Poet Of The Year; [oth.writ.] Had several poems published in various anthologies; [pers.] Attributes inspiration to the love and support from family and friends. [a.] Palm Harbor, FL.

MOENTER, TRACI
[b.] October 5, 1979, St. Rita's, Lima, OH; [p.] F. David and Diane Moenter; [ed.] Delphos St. John's Elementary and I'm currently a freshman at Delphos St. John's High School; [memb.] The Dancer by Gina, 4-H, Precious Moments Birthday Club, Scholastic Bowl; [hon.] Ohio Music Education Association; [oth.writ.] Remembering and Missing You; [pers.] Dedicated to St. John's class of '98. I have one sister 13 years old. [a.] Delphos, OH.

MOFFETT, EMILY B.
[b.] August 27, 1935, Orlando, FL; [p.] Edward L. and Margaret C. Bridges; [m.] Kenneth D. Moffett, October 27, 1956; [ch.] Mirella C., Natalie DeHaven, Teresa Duane; [ed.] National Cathedral-D.C., Penn Hall, PA 12th grade, Junior College, Secretarial D.C., Orange Memorial Hospital (Lab Tech), Orlando, FL; [occ.] Housewife, genealogist, would be writer; [memb.] DAR, Colonial Dames of XVII Century, Washington Family Dames of Magna Charter, editor church paper; [oth.writ.] Poetry, short story, poetry in process of publishing; [pers.] "Cheris God's gifts". [a.] Milton, FL.

MOHR, BRANDY
[b.] January 5, 1980; [p.] Judy and Vincent Mohr; [ed.] K-8 (just went into 9th) at Brockport Central School; [occ.] Freshman in high school; [hon.] High honor student; [oth.writ.] Several unpublished poems and short stories; [pers.] You should tell people how you feel about them today because there might not be a chance to tomorrow. [a.] Spencerport, NY.

MOLER, DIANE
[b.] December 2, 1970, Hinsdale, IL; [p.] Peter and Karen Moler; [ed.] College of DuPage (AA), Southern Illinois University, BS in Administration of Justice and BA in Psychology; [occ.] Residential Mental Health Counselor and student; [memb.] PETA (People For The Ethical Treatment of Animals), PSA (Psychology Students Association), SIU Skydivers, Habitat for Humanity; [oth.writ.] Many others but few published; [pers.] I write from the heart. My emotions direct my writing. Friends and family influence me also. [a.] Naperville, IL.

MOLINE, MARY
[pers.] Mary Moline has achieved a rare standard of excellence as a mother, author, sculptor, poet and publisher. She is one of ten children of Italian immigrants. She was born in West Virginia. She studied sociology at West Virginia University and philosophy at John's Hopkins University in Maryland and screenwriting at U.C.L.A. Mary is the author of sixteen books, twelve have been published. She is the creator of a highly successful series of porcelain dolls which she manufactured in Europe. She is the founder and president of two corporations and the holder of several patents. She is considered a world authority on Norman Rockwell's art. Her doll series is based on the characters in Rockwell's illustrations. She has attained international recognition for the outstanding accomplishments of her career. Most important to Mary is her undying devotion to the children of Appalachian families in Western Pennsylvania. Her poetic folk tales are laced with the passions and experiences of her life. [a.] Gold River, CA.

MONROE, WILLIAM E.
[b.] December 20, 1937, Orlando, FL; [oth.writ.] "Snapshots" poetry and short stories, "When Doctors Won't Help" (non-fiction) and a novel in process; [pers.] The greatest tests of my creativity are a lack of interest from others in my work and contentment with competing aspects of my life, which too often slides into complacency. [a.] Orlando, FL.

MOORE, GEE GEE
[pen.] Gee Gee Moore; [b.] December 24, 1952, Charlotte; [p.] Gonnie M. Murray; [ch.] Marice M. Brown; [ed.] Kinston High School, Lenior Community College, Shaw University; [occ.] Ass. of baby sitting; [memb.] International Black Writers, Charlotte, International Writers Global Inc., YWCA; [hon.] National Library of Poetry, Ceder Poetry, Iliad Press, YWCA, National Society of Poets, Charlotte Observer, Arts and Science Council; [oth.writ.] National Library of Poetry, Ceder Poetry, Iliad Press, YWCA, National Society of Poets, Charlotte Observer, Arts and Science Council; [pers.] I write poems to let people read what they see in them. People see, hear, feel what they have forgotten years ago. People and children read what they understand in life. This to me is what I write to understand. [a.] Charlotte, NC.

MOORE, OZZELLA
[b.] May 10, 1938, Wisconsin; [p.] Victor and Antoinette Lauren; [ch.] Timothy and Rebecca (twins age 27); [ed.] Graduate J.E. Murphy High, Hurley, Wis., (elective studies) Junior College, Ca. Math, Writing, Developmentally Handicapped disorders; [occ.] Free-lance writer, specialty documents and research; [memb.] Southside Church of Christ, V.F.W. Auxiliary, AARP; [hon.] State first place winner, publisher\writer V.F.W. newsletter 1993-94; [oth.writ.] National Library of Poetry 1991, 1992, 1993, 1994, Community Resource Directory, Life Planning Approach, Letter of Intent, Basic Needs Assessments, based on depression, stress and behavior disorders, (workbooks); [pers.] Giving up is a useless waste of energy. Reach out and make a difference. Smile, it takes a lot less effort than a frown and a lot more satisfying. [a.] Rogers, AR.

MOORE, QUENITTIE
[b.] February 17, 1931, Wake County; [p.] Otis and Mirdie Evans; [m.] Wallace Moore, April 15, 1953; [ch.] Gloria, Mirdie, Wallace Jr., Wanessia and Herman Moore; [ed.] Mill Grove High, North Carolina Central University, Durham Technical Community College; [occ.] Asst. Funeral Director, Notary Public; [memb.] Chestnut Grove Baptist Church, president of senior choir, vice president of program committee; [hon.] Editor's Choice Award, "One Mom Against Drunk Drivers" published in Wind In The Night Sky; [oth.writ.] Several other poems published in the Carolina Times newspaper, poems and manuscript, no previous publications; [pers.] Thank God for my knowledge to write and my family members for their support. A special thanks to Auset Bakhufu (better known) as Janet Barbour and Charlotte Timberlake Hayliyer for your patience and assurance. Special thanks to my sister-in-law, Earlene Moore. [a.] Durham, NC.

MORABITO, MARY M.
[pen.] Mary Matosiah Morabito; [b.] July 23, 1929, Milwaukee, WI; [p.] Hatcher Matosiah and Sophie Sadachiah; m.] Dominic Don Morabito, March 20, 1951 and June 17, 1951; [ch.] David, Stella, Lucille and Mary Dominique; [ed.] R.N. LA County General School of Nursing also AA from ELAJC and PCC and nearly BS from Cal State CA; [occ.] Retired, RN caregiver to disabled adult daughter; [hon.] Writer's

book award, narrative epic poem of Robert Peavy's discovery of North Pole placed in archives (National Archives) by Peavy's daughter Marie Peavy Stafford; [oth.writ.] Ararat -a decade of American writings, anthology AGBUNY 1969, also American poets, Paris AGBU 1976; [pers.] I believe all knowledge is one and that the present categorization and contradictory breakdown of thinking will resolve itself, as "psychology" may include again the Lord. [a.] Temple City, CA.

MORALES, ELIZABETH
[b.] September 14, 1941, Puerto Rico; [p.] Felix and Julia Morales; [ed.] MS in Elementary Education, Long Island University; [occ.] Teacher, remedial reading, grades 1-4, Spanish, grades 1-4; [memb.] Sisters of St. John the Baptist; [hon.] Award of Merit Certificates for poems "A Hymn To The Sun" and "Autumn Breezes" (World of Poetry) Golden Poet 1991 certificate (World of Poetry), Editor's Choice Award (National Library of Poetry); [oth.writ.] Collection of unpublished poetry, Journey of Life I, II, III, Spanish poems, Viajedevida I; [pers.] I believe that life is a journey and enjoy writing my "journey experiences". [a.] Staten Island, NY.

MORBER, EDWARD L.
[b.] January 6, 1949, Murphysboro, IL; [p.] Clarence and Catheryn Morber; [m.] Deborah S., Gale, June 8, 1974; [ch.] Heath, Paul and Scott; [ed.] Gorham High School, Gorham, IL; [occ.] Plumber; [memb.] Veterans of Foreign Wars, American Legion, St. Elizabeth Catholic Church, Plumbers and Pipefitters Local # 160; [oth.writ.] Freckle Face Boy; [pers.] The fans have never deserted baseball, but baseball has deserted the fans! [a.] Ava, IL.

MORGAN, JANE
[b.] December 3, 1953, Brawley, CA; [p.] Sam and Helen M. Ray; [m.] John Reece Morgan Jr., October 6, 1973; [ch.] Justin Lee and Michelle Renee' Morgan; [ed.] High school-1972, graduated from Orange High School, Orange, California; [occ.] Homemaker and writer of poetry; [memb.] Longview Newcomers Club, Mobberly Baptist Church; [hon.] 1st published poem in book Edge of Twilight; [oth.writ.] Many other writings but none published yet; [pers.] pers.] Being a descendant of the poet, James Whitcomb Riley, my family says that's where my talent for writing comes from. I don't really care where it came from, I just love writing it. I believe poetry is a part of my soul and is reflected in each one I write. [a.] Longview, TX.

MORRIS, IDA TOTH
[b.] July 5, 1923, Detroit, MI; [p.] Geza and Margaret Toth; [m.] James C. Morris (deceased), June 14, 1946; [ch.] Ray Morris; [ed.] Western High School, Detroit, MI., Maryville College, Maryville, TN; [occ.] Former taught Creative Writing at Maryville College and Texas State, founder of Media Matters, a writing consulting service in Harlingen, TX and Women's Editor of Valley Morning Star; [memb.] Vice president Writer's Association of Blount County (TN), vice president Christian Writers League, chairperson, Valley Women's Politician Caucus, member All Valley Literary Society, member Valley By-Liners, president Blount County (TN) Humane Society; [hon.] Named in 1977 Who's Who In American Women, Personalities of The South, Southern Poetry Association, Dictionary of International Biography; [oth.writ.] Article in National Observer, columnist for Valley Morning Star, The News World (NYC), THe Daily TImes (Maryville, TN), and Brownsville Herald (TX), contributor to book "Roots By The River" which received highest award by the Texas Historical Society; [pers.] I think it's a terrible shame that anyone may pass through an entire lifetime without leaving some written personal record of having been on earth. Spoken words evaporate in the air that surrounds us. What we have written remains forever. [a.] Maryville, TN.

MORRISON, ARTHUR R.
[pen.] Arthur R. Morrison; [b.] April 4, 1931, Bayonne, NJ; [p.] John S. Sr. and Mable M.; [m.] Marjorie L., October 2, 1976; [ch.] Sharon Lynn, Patricia, Arthur R., Leonard A., Brian Paul and David Arron; [ed.] Patterson Junior High, Patterson, Patterson High, Baltimore, MD, Leadership School U.S. Air Force, Korea, Sgt.; [occ.] Retired, security field; [memb.] Disabled American Veterans # 33, American Legion, Post # 75, Arizona Grand Lodge of Maryland, Masons 30 years, Song Writers Association, Nashville, Arizona's Song Writers, Phoenix, AZ, Korea War Veterans, Phoenix, AZ, Commodore Computer Club, AZ, Top Records, AM41086; [hon.] Editor's Choice Award, "When A Writer Dies" 1989, Editor's Choice Award, "Color Blind" 1994, Honorable Discharged 4 years, Editor's Choice Award, National Library of Poetry, 1989 and 1994, 32 poems published; [oth.writ.] Bio., John S. Morrison WWI, WWII, State and National magazines, 50,000 circulation, Disabled American Veterans, 1986, Recall, Mayor Johnson, Editorial, Paradise Valley newspaper 1993, circulation 35, 000, I have had 6 poems put to music, series of Western short stories; [pers.] My wife Marjorie has been my inspiration for my writings. Without her love and understanding, I feel my writings would not be possible. I write about life, as I see it as I have live it. Sometimes funny, sometimes sad. As I have traveled down life's road. [a.] Phoenix, AZ.

MUJA, KATHLEEN
[b.] June 24, 1965, Denver; [p.] Thomas R. and Bridget C. Cramer; [ch.] Thomas C. Muja; [ed.] East High School graduate, BSBA University of Denver; [occ.] Labor and Employment Specialist II; [memb.] Vice president, Network Colorado, ADI board member, IAPES member, Denver Jaycees member; [hon.] Member of Sterling Who's Who; [oth.writ.] 8 published poems, news articles for club newspapers; [pers.] Life is too short to dwell in darkness. [a.] Denver, CO.

MUNDY, SHIRLY J.
[pen.] Susanne Southwood; [b.] June 20, 1930, Indiana; [p.] Clyde and Helen Keeler; [m.] William Mundy, June 10, 1950; [ch.] Vanonna Mundy Shillings; [ed.] Cloverdale High School, Business-DePaul University; [occ.] Retired; [memb.] First Baptist Church, Scleroderma Foundation, International Society of Poets; [hon.] From Old National Trails for work done with handicapped youth 1990, 1991, 1992, 1993, 1994; [pers.] In my paintings and poems I strive to glorify the Lord for all the gifts He has given me.

MUNOZ, BONNIE MORRIS
[b.] June 1, 1931, Pampa, TX; [p.] Claude Morris and Winnie Myers; [m.] Pedro J. Munoz, January 1, 1948 (widow 1979); [ch.] Seven daughters, 3 sons; [ed.] A & M Consolidated High School at College Station Texas, some college credits; [occ.] Grandmother and poet; [memb.] Woman's Department Greater El Paso Chamber of Commerce, Woman's Charra. Association Juarez, International Society of Poets, Bermudez Inc. National Social and Charity Group, Juarez Chih Mex.; [hon.] Silver Poet 1985, Silver Poet 1992, Golden Poet 1991, Golden Poet 1993; [oth.writ.] "Widow" World of Poetry 1983, Hope" Anthology of Contemporary Poetry 1987, "The Eagles Us" World's Most Beloved Poets 1991, "Memory of Pedro Munoz" World's Gold and Silver Poets. "Conquistadors" Our World;s Favorite Gold and Silver Poems 1993; [pers.] My poetry has helped me cope with grief, sorrow, love, anger and to express to my very large family my love, morals, memories and expectations. I like poetry that is melodic. [a.] El Paso, TX.

MUNRO, DINA G.
[pen.] JD; [b.] November 16, 1965, Martinez, CA; [p.] Calvin and Virginia Stone; [ch.] Amanda, Amber and Corey Munro; [ed.] Graduated Stylemasters College of Hair Designing in 1987, received my GED June 1994, volunteer work with coast and headstart; [occ.] Parent, homemaker, volunteer; [memb.] 1984 donated blood to the American Red Cross, 1986 volunteered for the emergency support shelter, 1992 volunteered for Columbia Olympic Aids Task Force, 1993 parent of child enrolled in lower Columbia Head Start, member of policy council, center officer, co-producer of TV show Parent-Talk, selection committee for the headstart community out reach program; [hon.] National Library of Poetry's Editor's Choice Award, 1987 Sebatians Cellophane Award, 1993 headstart parent volunteer recognition award; [oth.writ.] Have three manuscripts about completed, (1) For The Love of Poetry, (2) Poetry From The Heart, (3) Hallow Whispers Within My Soul, poems published in anthologies At Day's End and After The Storm, Tower Records wants "When It Love You Crave" to record as a song and The Rock Band, "Da Meinge" has taken 3, Pipers Dream, Going Toward The Water and When It's Love; [pers.] Upon the boundaries within your dreams you'll fine those who disbelieve. Cautious, of the draggers thrown up in your way. Try to hold your footing as you stagger upon the negativity of those within the grips of living out their dreams. Only to fall short upon their own insecurities, that tripped them up and made them fall upon their knees. Anger flares for those of you who has the strength and courage to fly upon the eagle's wings, right into the horizon of their dreams. [a.] Longview, VA.

MURPHY, JOYCE L.
[b.] May 20, 1938, El Centro, CA; [p.] Alvin and Helen Hicks; [m.] Divorced; [ch.] Larry, Kerry, Randy and Jeanette (all married), 8 grandchildren; [ed.] High school, GED, several college classes in English/writing; [occ.] Disabled due to chronic fatigue/ Epsteen Barr; [oth.writ.] Several poems published in anthologies; [pers.] I have been writing for a little over 1 1/2 years. It has been a new gift of God after some deep healing following abandonment and divorce from my husband of 34 years. During the 5 years of recovery, I worked as a mental health aide in a Christian Therapy Program in a hospital in Buena Park, CA until disabled. The desire of my heart has been and is to minister God's love, comfort and healing to His hurting people. I am a born again Christian and pray that my writings (over 225 poems) will minister to others I am writing my autobiography as a testimonial. [a.] Yucaipa, CA.

MURPHY, REGINALD
[b.] August 25, 1951, P.E.I., Canada; [p.] Stephen and Frances Murphy; [ch.] Christine and Raymond; [ed.] BA 1975 Montclair State College, Montclair, NJ; [occ.] Philosopher/ school custodian; [pers.] Love is all that really matters. [a.] Belleville, NJ.

MYERS, EDWARD J.
[pen.] E.J. Myers; [b.] June 26, 1943, Virginia; [p.] Dewey C. and Goldia B. Myers; [ch.] Jennifer Dawn; [ed.] Hillsville (VA) High, Patrick Henry College; [occ.] Self-employed (business); [hon.] Various newspaper writing awards, life member National Poetry Society; [oth.writ.] Newspapers, outdoor magazines, presently completing final draft to first novel, a Western Poetry published in The Writer and other little magazines; [pers.] Although most of my published material has been non-fiction, my first love has always been poetry. I especially like the works od T.S. Eliot. [a.] Martinsville, VA.

NACHT, MICHELLE
[b.] December 20, 1994, New Brunswick, NJ; [p.] Beverly Trabilsy and Richard Nacht; [ch.] I'll have 5 when I get older (my wish); [ed.] Still in high school, freshman; [hon.] Just my poems being published from this contest; [oth.writ.] A lot of other poems, one published in Echoes Of Yesterday; [pers.] Brian, I love you. Thanks for everything. It's ok to cry! Love isn't love until you give it away. [a.] East Brunswick, NJ.

NAGY, JESSICA
[b.] February 6, 1979, Bridgeport, CT; [p.] William and Michelle Nagy; [ed.] Currently attending St. Joseph High School in Trumbull, CT, graduated St. Mark School in Stratford, CT; [occ.] Part time cashier; [memb.] Junior Achievement school clubs, Wildlife Club, Ecology Club, Spanish Club; [hon.] Duns Scotus Scholar Award, Spanish Honors, Biology Honors; [oth.writ.] A published poem in a newspaper, a published poem in Wind In The Night Sky, and many unpublished works. [a.] Bridgeport, CT.

NASH, RUSS
[b.] February 25, 1921, Minneapolis, MN; [p.] Maurice W. and Elsie E. Nash; [m.] Ruth Cole Nash, February 1, 1944; [ch.] Andrew Nash and Pamela S. Saur; [ed.] B.A. English, University of Minneapolis 1943, M.A., Columbia University 1948; [occ.] Associate Prof. Sociology Emeritus, University of Dubuque, Executive Producer "The Question Box" at TCI Community Access TV, Arts contributor Juliens Journal; [memb.] Dubuque County Fine Arts Society, Dubuque Chapter NAACP, IA Citizens For the Arts, Dubuque Writers Guild; [hon.] Poems in "Lyrical Iowa", "Against The Grain", "Galley 1991", "The Lead Rush Review", "Song of Myself"; [pers.] I feel that the arts are the most effective means for achieving intercultural sharing and understanding. [a.] Dubuque, IA.

NASON, TRACY
[pen.] Tracy Nason; [b.] October 24, 1979, Portland, ME; [p.] Ralph P. and Susan O. Nason Jr.: [ed.] Freshman at Deering High School; [memb.] Book club, Deering High Debate, yearbook; [oth.writ.] "Cove's Tide"; [pers.] I'm not stopping till I reach the top! Go for your dreams, the sky's the limit. [a.] Portland, ME.

NEAL, PATRICIA A.
[b.] August 12,1946, Detroit, MI; [p.] Bernard and Dorothy Friend; [m.] Divorced; [ch.] Renee E.H. DeBell, John J.H. Neal and Alexis R. DeBell (granddaughter); [ed.] Associate Degree Nursing, Associate Degree Science; [occ.] Registered Nurse working in Infection Control, Education and Administration; [memb.] A.p.I.C., Golden Poets, Marquis Who's Who, Amway Distributor; [hon.] Who's Who In American Nursing, Who's Who of Exceptional Professionals, Golden Poet Award, poem published in World Treasury of Golden Poems; [oth.writ.] Numerous poems and children's stories; [pers.] God put me on this earth to help others. It is not always in a physical way such as nursing. Sometimes just a word of comfort or reassurances is all that is needed. May I be all that God would have me be. [a.] Port Huron, MI.

NEIBERT, SHARON
[pen.] Sharon Moulton; [b.] July 22, 1962, Chester, PA; [p.] Robert J. and Kathryn Moulton; [ch.] Joseph Bennett; [ed.] Chester High School and Delaware County Institute of Training; [occ.] Private duty Nurse's Aide; [memb.] Upland Terrace Homes Resident Organization, Upland Baptist Church, Upland A.C. Boosters; [hon.] Editor's Choice Award for Outstanding Achievement in poetry, highest overall class average; [oth.writ.] A poem published in Dance On The Horizon from the National Library of Poetry; [pers.] I strive to reflect on subjects that effect all of mankind. In my writing I try to put myself in someone else's shoes. I have been influenced to write about things that have happened to me or someone in my family. [a.] Upland, PA.

NELON, CLYDE
[b.] August 27, 1916, Uree, NC, Rutherford County; [p.] W.J. and Dovie R. Nelon; [m.] Mary Kathryn Seagle, August 18, 1936; [ch.] Alexander E. Nelon, 3 grandchildren, 3 great grandsons; [ed.] A.B. Degree, University of North Carolina, 1940; [occ.] Retired; [memb.] All Saints Anglican Church in America, Arden, NC; [hon.] First State Secretary for state of North Carolina Future Teachers of America Clubs, 1939-1940, elected and served on Vestry many times in several Episcopal Churches; [oth.writ.] Parish reporter for National Church publication "Ecclesia" Angelican Church in America 1988-1993; [pers.] Enjoy simple things in life. I live on family estate in the country outside the city limits. [a.] Hendersonville, NC.

NELSON, DEWEY A. (MD)
[pen.] Dewey A. Nelson; [b.] December 2, 1927, Eldorado, AR; [p.] Herman Eugene and Pearl, Estelle (Shirley) Nelson; [m.] Jem Nolt Nelson, October 7, 1951; [ch.] Allen, Stephen, Jean, John and Daniel; [ed.] B.S. Cornell University 1948, MD Cornell University 1951, Res. Bellevue Hospital 1951-1952, 1954-1957, Chief Neurol, Med Center Delaware 1951-1983, Hon Sr. 1983, Associate Clinical Prof Neurology Thomas Jefferson Med Center Philadelphia 1971-1979, Prof. Neruol 1975; [occ.] Neurologist and Educator; [memb.] New Castle County Medical Society, American Medical Association, Philadelphia Neurol Society, Fell. American Neuro Physiological Society, Fell. American Academy Neurol, Ruling Elder Red Clay Creek Presbyterian Church; [hon.] Teogle foundation scholar 1946-1951, bronze hope chest award, National MS Society 1960, plaque med advisory MS Society 1979, bronze star US Army Korea 1954, UN Service Medal, Korea Service Medal 1954; [oth.writ.] 70 articles Neurology, medical periodicals, textbooks, poetry to magazines and newspapers (4 pieces); [pers.] My experience with life, death, science, joy and suffering makes me believe that scientific writing and poetry are one. That is, one tries to trim away fat and penetrate far into the marrow-hoping to expose a modicum of compassion. [a.] Wilmington, DE.

NELSON, MARY BETH
[b.] December 19, 1927, El Paso, TX; [p.] Marshall and Ruby Dupree; [m.] Walter A "Cotton" Nelson; [ch.] Janis Dudley, Michael Nelson, Sharon Martin and Jill Christal; [ed.] Lubbock High School, Bachelors work at Southwestern University in Georgetown, TX and Texas Tech in Lubbock, Master's Degree from West Texas A&M University in Canyon, TX; [occ.] Retired elementary teacher and free lance writer; [oth.writ.] Daily devotional and other inspiration writings which have been published in several religious publications, published journalistic articles, writings for children, song writing. [a.] Clarendon, TX.

NELSON, SHARON DIANE
[pen.] S. Nelson -McPherson; [b.] California; [p.] Russell E. Nelson and Betty L. Hamblen; [ch.] Shaun A. and Michelle D. McPherson; [ed.] LAHC, WCC, AVCC, CSUN; [occ.] Human services; [memb.] Whatcom County Crisis Services, International Society of Poets; [hon.] President's Honors, Dean's List (AVCC, LAHC), 1994 Editor's Choice Award, National Library of Poetry; [oth.writ.] Local and college newspapers, curriculum reports, poem published in At Day's End; [pers.] Poetry writing began 30 years ago during the Viet Nam war. Subjects range from birth to death, landscape to sea, love to heartbreak and politics to art. [a.] Bellingham, WA.

NEMEC, CYNTHIA
[b.] November 28, 1957, Bay City, TX; [p.] Edward and Bernice; [m.] Vincent Nemec, June 6, 1981; [ch.] Stephanie (age 9) and Thomas (age 5); [ed.] BAT from Sam Houston State University, Learning Resources Endorsement from University of Houston at Clear Lake; [occ.] Librarian at Cherry Elementary; [memb.] Alpha Delta Kappa, Texas Library Association, Texas Classroom Teachers Association, Secretary of Holy Cross School Board; [hon.] Cum Laude at SHSU, Dean's List at SHSU; [oth.writ.] Published a booklet entitled "A New Beginning" also won an Editor's Choice for publication The Coming of Dawn, poetry business-costume designed prints; [pers.] I write with my heart. I believe I am a channel of God's wonderful love and I try to reflect that in my writing. [a.] Bay City, TX.

NEMEC, NORMA J.
[b.] Cresco, IA; [p.] Bessie and Kenneth Shaw (both deceased); [sib.] Elizabeth Joyce Kirkland and Daisy Wright (Dallas, TX), David K. Shaw (Waterloo, IA); [ed.] St. Mary's High School, Waterloo, IA, Iowa State Teacher's College, Cedar Falls, IA; [occ.] Executive Secretary, San Bernardino City Unified School District, San Bernardino, CA: [memb.] Our Lady of the Rosary Cathedral, life member, Beta Sigma Phi Sorority, National Association of Female Executives, San Bernardino Emblem Club # 178 and NARFE; [hon.] Several outstanding performance and

sustained superior performance awards, Outstanding Administrator of the Year in the Military Airlift Command; [oth.writ.] Several articles for local newspapers, "Clouds" in Tears of Fire, and "My Sun, My Mon, My Stars" in At Day's End both published by the National Library of Poetry; [pers.] Blessings of a special love, peace, joy and spirituality give me inspiration to achieve goals and objectives. [a.] San Bernardino, CA.

NETTLES, T. HAROLD
[pen.] Tiger; [b.] March 25, 1959, Guliford County, NC; [p.] Thomas L. and Radie V. Nettles; [m.] Single; [ed.] Dudley High School, GSO, NC, N.C., A & T State University, GSC, NC; occ.] Transport department, Guliford County Schools; [memb.] International Society of Poets, the Wu Shu Li Association; [hon.] Award, St. Stephens United Church of Christ; [oth.writ.] Several poems published in church paper, several in books from the National Library of Poetry, recognize Guliford County Schools and news and record; [pers.] I write from what's inside of my heart and what God inspires me to say. [a.] Greensboro, NC.

NEWELL, SALLY
[b.] March 7, 1960, St Mary's, PA; [p.] Van and Clara Newell; [ed.] Harborcreek High School; [occ.] Secretary/GECAC, Erie, PA; [hon.] Publication in the National Library of Poetry's At Day's End; [oth.writ.] Have written numerous amount of poems, have done some brochures for my work place and friends; [pers.] Would be interested in writing for greeting card companies, along with designing my own cards, posters, etc. Some day hope to hear the words to music. [a.] Erie, PA.

NEWMAN, FREDERICK J.
[b.] August 15, 1955, St. Stephen, CA; [p.] Everett and Virginia Newman; [m.] Eileen Newman, August 27, 1973; [ch.] Frederick James II, Jeremy Andrew and Daniel Everett; [ed.] Wheeler High School, North Stonington, CT, Woodland High School, Woodland, ME; [occ.] Finishing room operator pulp and paper mill; [oth.writ.] World of Poetry, "Peace In The Land" 1991, the National Library of Poetry, "Old Morning Sun" 1993, "Reasons" 1993, "Final Stand" 1993, five books completed (not published as yet, 2 tapes not published); [pers.] The art of poetry must bring some kind of feeling to the listener, if not it is just not poetry. [a.] Princeton, MA.

NEWMAN, SANDRA
[b.] June 21, 1963, Canada; [p.] Joyce and Clarence Muir; [m.] Jack Newman, March 8, 1986, [ch.] Wenell (14), Shelly (12), Randy (10), Saydee (4) and Domnick (2); [ed.] Finished high school, went on to business school one year course; [occ.] Housewife; [hon.] Editor's Choice Award, the National Library of Poetry; [oth.writ.] The National Library of Poetry Coming of Dawn 1993, "Tiny Little Guy"; [pers.] I live for my kids and my outlook on life includes them. [a.] West Jordan, UT.

NEWSOME, SCOTT WESLEY
[b.] July 14, 1973, Marietta, GA; [m.] Michelle Lynn Newsome, April 10, 1994; [ch.] Fred Brown; [pers.] Until apathy is removed from the mind there can be no life to live, only the repetition of mistakes. Made in the past forever. [a.] Powder Springs, GA.

NGUYEN, LY DAI
[pen.] Mac Ly Tao; [b.] October 7, 1939, Saigon, Viet Nam; [p.] Hoc Dai Nguyen and Cangthi Nguyen; [m.] Dung Thi Tran, April 1, 1966; [ch.] Larry Linh, Thuong Long, Kieu Diem and Tuong Lan Nguyen; [ed.] Petrus Truong Vinh Ky High School, Saigon, Viet Nam, Vietnamese National Military Academy (VNMA) Dalat, Viet Nam; [occ.] Writer, OMD, instructor of Tai Chi and Yoga; [memb.] Vietnamese Overseas, P.E.N./Southwester USA Center (committee of writers in prison), Vietnamese -America Arts and Letters Association (VAALA), Vietnamese American Buddhist Center for charitable services, Bao Quang (committee of social and cultural), International Society of Poets; [hon.] Special award of Nguoi Viet newspaper's writers' contest on poems, studies research relating to at Dau Lunar Year (1945) Famine, city Westminster Insignia for Tai Chi instructor's volunteer in senior citizen center; [oth.writ.] Meditations Zen poems written in communist's training camps (1975-84), portrait of the prisoner of conscience, several poems, literature articles published in local newspapers and magazines in Little Saigon, capital of Vietnamese's refugee; [pers.] I try to convey in my writing the ideal of struggle for the human rights in Viet Nam. I have been very much affected by the sufferings of oppressed people in our present time. [a.] Santa Ana, Orange County, CA.

NGUYEN, THANH
[pen.] Thanh Nguyen, Troi-Dong, Nguoi-Xu-Thai; [b.] August 25, 1947, Vietnam; [p.] Thuoc and Sol; [m.] Minh-Chau, April 1985; [ch.] Hoang-Yen (daughter) and Hoang-Dan (son); [ed.] MBA University of Tennessee 1978, MA in Economics 1972, Law Degree, Law in Saigon VN 1970, Nguyen Trai High School 1964; [occ.] Chief Accountant, CFO Title Guaranty Company, Houston, TX; [memb.] Who's Who In America South and Southwest since 1992, Who's Who In The World since 1993; [oth.writ.] Que Huong Men Yeu 1989 (poetry) Tho Troi-Dong 1993. [a.] Houston, TX.

NIERMAN, MARJORY
[b.] August 15, 1936, Fairplay, CO; [p.] Warren and Bernadean Yarroll; [m.] Leon K. Nierman, March 18, 1956, [ch.] Sharon Thompson, Darlene Beaman and Steve Nierman, grandchildren, Amy, Kelly, Terri, Emily and Erica, [ed.] Some college completed still pursuing education; [occ.] Writer, student, wife, mother, grandmother; [memb.] Resurrection Lutheran Church; [hon.] Listed in Who's Who Of American Women, award for Best Thespian, award for first place in debate in state; [oth.writ.] Poetry, short stories, published in The Space Between, Dream International Quarterly, also working on a science fiction novel, another published short story, "The Other Side of Fear'; [pers.] Have faith in God, respect others, do the best you can at whatever you attempt, love and appreciate family. [a.] Houston, TX.

NORTH, SEAN T.
[b.] August 19, 1967, Ann Arbor, MI; [p.] Thomas North and Jane White; [ed.] AAS (accounting), Macomb Community College, BBA (marketing) Walsh College; [occ.] Professional assistant; [hon.] Accomplishment of merit, "Soul Search" Creative Arts and Science Enterprise; [oth.writ.] "Temporary Pleasure", At Day's End and "Is TV For Me", Echoes of Yesterday, the National Library of Poetry; [pers.] Worry about what you can change and don't worry about what you cannot change. [a.] Clinton Township, MI.

NORWALK, LUCILLE A.
[pen.] Lucy Lawn; [b.] September 16, 1917, Martin, OH; [p.] Henry and Emma Wilkins; [m.] Clinton O. Norwalk, June 29, 1940; [ch.] Keith Alan (dentist), David Lee (barber and G.M worker), Thomas Kent (Minister); [ed.] Elementary and high school, business seminars, etc., was secretary for 25 years and later reporter and columnist, now semi-retired; [occ.] Columnist, Exponent Weekly, Oak Harbor, OH; [memb.] St. John's United Church of Christ, teacher, St. John's Sunday School, Women's Fellowship, President Ruthenians, Happy Hobby Garden Club, County Democratic Executive and Central Auxiliary, Master-Geona Grange, Grange Club, new member, Legion Auxiliary, Maumee Bay Church Women; [hon.] Federation Woman of the Year, Mrs. Ottawa County-three times, Woman of the Year-United Way, etc., poetic awards; [oth.writ.] Plays, programs, news articles, Geona Views, etc.; [pers.] "Keeping busy and doing for others is one of the secrets to a full and happy life".

NOTT, BRANDISHEA
[Pen.] Brandishia Christian; [b.] October 20, 1978, Hollywood, CA; [p.] Carla Nott; [ed.] Puyallup High School; [oth. writ.] My sister, Chantille Ward, and I are writting poems for a book we play to publish together in the future; [pers.] I write poems from other people's point of view to give the reader a sense of being or feeling what others might in that situation; [a.] Puyallup, WA

NOYES, PATRICIA
[pen.] Tryssa; [b.] August 27, 1975, Seoul, South Korea; [p.] Patrick S. and Chi N. Noyes; [occ.] Mobile subscriber, Equipment Network Switching Systems Operator; [pers.] I want my works to reflect my uniqueness and originality. Even now, being in the Army, I strive to retain my individuality. [a.] Las Vegas, NV.

NUNEZ, HENRY J.
[b.] August 6, 1950, Dominican Republic; [m.] Diane, September 7, 1974; [ch.] Corey Jean and Stacy Ann; [ed.] George Washington High School; [occ.] Coordinator, Con Edison Company; [hon.] Bronze star, Viet Nam Service Medal, Golden Poet; [oth.writ.] Several poems published by the National Library of Poetry; [pers.] I feel very fortunate that the Lord has bestowed upon me the gift of expressing myself through poetry. [a.] New York, NY.

O'BRIEN, LAWRENCE EDWARD
[b.] May 4, 1964, Ludington, MI; [p.] Edward J. O'Brien and Ruth A. Ferenz; [ch.] Matthew G. (June 26, 1990) and Lawrence E. O'Brien II (December 31, 1983); [ed.]
Ludington High, U.S. Navy Technical Schools (electronics); [occ.] Single parent, writer, author temporary position at (PCA) Packaging Corporation of America; [oth.writ.] "The Race Into Eternity" (unpublished), working on children's books and poetry; [pers.] I try to keep a positive attitude toward life and to my new found abilities. I would also like to help all those children to keep a positive attitude to life and their abilities. [a.] Ludington, MI.

O'DAY, BERNARD W.
[pen.] Bernard W. O'Day, Colchester, VT; [p.] John F. O'Day and Albina Delorge; [m.] Addie Rashaw, August 26, 1950; [ch.] Cheryl Anne, Michael John, Kevin James and Mark Alan; [ed.] Burlington High School; [occ.] Supervisor Industrial Photographer, General Electric Co. 38 years retired; [memb.] Lite n Lens Camera Club (founder), Vermont Macintosh User's Group, AARP and the American-French Genealogical Society, past-Knights of Columbus, General Electric Activities Association, Cliffside Country Club, Christ the King Parents Association, S. Burlington Boys Baseball Association, S. Burlington Adult Education Program, Photographic Society of America, Professional Photographers of America; [hon.] BHS Alumni Association Award for the highest standing in the Merchandising and Sales Curriculum, 12 merit awards (program presentations in chapter and national conventions) from PP of A, 6 service awards-GEAA, 6 service award from PSA, Certificate of Merit as founder and for 25 years service to the Lite n Lens Camera Club; [oth.writ.] Poem published in local newspaper, editor of and essays for 6 high school reunion booklets, articles for VMUG newsletter, technical paper for PP of A Journal and engineering articles on industrial photography and general reporting for GE plant newspaper; [pers.] A "moment", a "lifetime" an "event" may become the basis for a poem, but it is the selection of appropriate thoughts and words, and the effect of poetic construction that determines their significance ever after! I find the effort to be very rewarding and this is why I try. [a.] Williston, VT.

OAKES, OWEN
[pen.] Owen Oakes; [b.] May 3,1960, Bangor, ME; [p.] Lawrence and Ethel Oakes; [m.] Nancy A. Oakes, June 22, 1985; [ch.] Kristen Marie; [ed.] Brewer High School; [occ.] Salesman; [memb.] International Society of Poets; [oth.writ.] Many other poems. [a.] Levant, ME.

OBINZE, E.N.D.
[pers.] Born into a Nigerian teaching family. Graduate of the British Open University and the University of Sussex, England. Honors in International Relations. A poet, script-writer for songs. Previous careers, school teacher. civil servant, cash controller at Harrods of London. Charter lifetime member of the International Society of Poets. Previous membership, Fellow of the Business Management Association, London. Interests, classical songs and music, writing, gardening, badminton. My personal life and my writings mirror my belief that peace among people and nations should be the principle for humanity. My writings are inspired by my desire to project my inner self.

ODOM, FRANCES LUNN
[b.] September 8, 1926, Darlington, SC; [p.] William Dossie and Laura M. Lunn; [m.] Cephas H. Odom, September 17, 1949; [ch.] William Freddie, Larry Cephas, Laura Ann, Mary Elizabeth and Carol Ruth; [ed.] St. John's High School Adult Education, diploma at age sixty three; [occ.] Retired; [memb.] Swift Creek Baptist Church, Disabled American Veteran Auxiliary; [hon.] State Adult Achievement Award 1990; [oth.writ.] Several poems published in newspaper, D.A.V. newsletter and some entered in poetry competitions have been published; [pers.] Poetry is a source of peace when it has been used to help a loved one. It is also a way to express feelings and thoughts on all subjects and can be humorous or serious. [a.] Hartsville, SC.

ODOMS, CLAIRE WARRING
[pen.] Claire W. Odoms; [b.] August 4, 1973, Hartford, CT; [p.] Richard and Gene Odoms; [ed.] Bloomfield High School, Central Connecticut State University, Capital Community Technical College; [occ.] Student; [memb.] Jack-n-Jill of America, Inc.; [hon.] Bloomfield High School Journalism Award 1990, University of Connecticut -Day of Pride 1991; [oth.writ.] Several unpublished poems; [pers.] "Maybe if you wish hard enough and live long enough, anything's possible". [a.] Bloomfield, CT.

ODORIZZI, C.M. (MRS.)
[pen.] DeeDe; [b.] August 17, 1909, Hutley, WI; [p.] John and Nora Colenso; [m.] Chas. M. Odorizzi; [ch.] Carol Rae Dillman, Linda Lee Rudolph and Terri LaTshaw; [ed.] B.A. in teaching, Masters, University of Wisconsin, University of Delaware, University of Texas, Wake Forest; [occ.] Writing, children's books; [memb.] United Methodist Church, teacher-Marquette, MI., founded Sunnyhill School for the Retarded, Stepping Stone School for Down Syndrome children; [hon.] Who's Who in Education, Alpha Delta Kappa, Distinguished Woman of Florida, Outstanding Woman of Naples, FL; [oth.writ.] Poetry, Chicago Tribune, Ideals Magazine, book of poems.

OGLETREE, JOE
[b.] March 5, 1956, Augusta, GA; [p.] Verne and Marjorie Ogletree; [m.] Belva Ogletree; [ch.] Jonathan and Joshua Ogletree; [ed.] Thomson High School; [occ.] Operator at Thiele Kaolin, Wrens, GA; [oth.writ.] Poem published in Where Dreams Begin; [pers.] I enjoy reflecting on the simple pleasures of everyday living. [a.] Thomson, GA.

OH, CHOO H.
[pen.] Christian; [b.] July 3, 1970, Seoul, Korea; [p.] Dr. and Mrs. Paul S. Oh; [m.] Ji Yon Kim; [ed.] Northside High, Penn State University, George Mason University, Averett College; [memb.] Society of Automotive Sales Professionals; [hon.] Sigma Pi Alpha, Golden Key, National Honor Society; [oth.writ.] Several poems published in the Penn State Literary magazine, "The Forum"; [pers.] Ji Yon, you have been my inspiration for the last two years that we've been together. May it continue to inspire and propel me to greater heights. [a.] Fairfax, VA.

OLAH, LISA
[b.] July 19, 1979; [p.] Richard and Peggy Olah; [ed.] K-9, currently a sophomore-Rib Lake High School; [occ.] High school student; [oth.writ.] With Darkness... Comes Memories. [a.] Westboro, WI.

OLESON, MILDRED V.
[b.] November 10, 1922, Waltham, MA; [p.] Harold and Minnie Arey; [m.] George E. Oleson, October 7, 1944; [ch.] John-deceased, Jean and Nancy; [ed.] High school diploma; [occ.] Retired; [memb.] St. Paul Lutheran Church, M.E.S.H.-Cooperative Extension, Community Concerts Association; [hon.] Editor's top 3% Choice Award, National Library of Poetry, semi-finalist, International Society of Poets 1994, plaque for 30 years of teaching Sunday School, Lutheran Church; [oth.writ.] Articles for church programs, have put some songs to music; [pers.] I have always enjoyed the beauty of nature, but as I grow older, I'm learning to relax and with God's help I'm able to put my thoughts into poetry. [a.] Berlin, NH.

OLSEN, MARIE FUHRIMAN
[b.] October 19, 1925, Utah; [p.] Norman and Elva Fuhriman; [m.] Blaine Alma Olsen, January 15, 1948; [ch.] Maxine, Norman, Jay, Brian, Ronald, Elva Lee, Sheldon and Leah; [ed.] Bachelor's (social work), Masters (Gerontology), Utah State University, Logna, Cache County, Utah; [occ.] Housewife; [memb.] The National League of American Pen Woman, Inc., the Utah State Poetry Society; [oth.writ.] "Room For Only The Living", "Summer Farm House", "My Teeth In The Drawer", magazine articles, "Young Mother Hubbard", "They Said IT Couldn't Be Done", "The Day I Rode The Train Free", "No Xmas Gifts For Mother", "This Only Happens To Others"; [pers.] Do good and leave behind you a monument of virtue that time can never destroy. [a.] Providence, UT.

OLSON, HARRIET THORPE
[b.] August 30, 1971, Dickinson, ND; [p.] Olaf and Clara (D.) Thorpe; [m.] Alvin B. Olson, June 13, 1946; [ed.] Dickinson Public Schools-kindergarten thru 12, N.D.S.U.-Fargo, ND, University of Minnesota, B.S.-1940, Music, Northwestern University-M.A. 1955, Reading and Counciling and Guidance George Williams College, Chicago American University, Washington, DC; [occ.] Retired teacher, doing volunteer work for several agencies; [memb.] Order of Eastern Star, V.F.W. Auxiliary, Rebekah, Delta Kappa Gamma, Untied Methodist Church, RSVP, Scandavian Ethnic Festivals, AARP, SARTA, Silver Haired Assembly, Delta Kappa Gamma, Stark County Council on Aging, International Society of Poets, Region VIII, Council on Aging; [pers.] To never be responsible for a child's hurt and to try to be of some good each day.

OLSSON, S. INGEMAR C.
[b.] August 10, 1943, Gothenburg; [p.] Conrad and Gunhild Olsson; [m.] Dr. Deborah A. Uimbrell, June 15, 1991; [ed.] Royal Naval Academy, Sweden Military Staff College, Stockholm University of Gothenburg; [occ.] Cruise counselor; [memb.] Republican Senatorial Inner Circle, Major, Royal Swedish Marines Reserves; [hon.] UN Medal twice, '79,'80, Jordan Tourism Medal 1985, U.S. Republican Senatorial Medal of Freedom 1994, lifetime honorary member of "Le Clefs d'oor", siege, Paris, France; [oth.writ.] 1976, 1994, reporter, editor and correspondent for "Today" (1 DAG) Swedish Daily newspaper, "Esteem" inter-national shipping magazine and US Africa magazine and several other publications; [pers.] Wrote the first poems in 1994. [a.] Bellaire, TX.

ORTIZ, SHANNON
[b.] June 8, 1977, Iveson, AZ: [p.] Salvador Ortiz and Sandra Roe; [ed.] Canyon Del Ora High School, expected to graduate December 1994; [occ.] Cashier, food server, Peco's Bill's Texas BBQ Restaurant; [oth.writ.] One poem published in The Desert Sun, a book from the National Library of Poetry; [pers.] I have been greatly influenced by life itself as opposed to death by suicide. [a.] Oracle, AZ.

OUTERBRIDGE, KEISHA ANGELA NICKCOLE
[b.] April 27, 1974, Paget, Bermuda; [p.] Tammie Bremar and Leon Saunders; [ed.] Dickey Hill Elementary in Baltimore, MD,. Bermuda Institute, Bermuda High and now Coppin State College in Baltimore, MD; [occ.] Student at Coppin State College (sophomore); [oth.writ.] Recently had a poem published by the National Library of Poetry entitled "Oh God Why Me"; [pers.] In dedication to my biological father, Royston Mitchell Howes. [a.] Baltimore, MD.

PADDIO-JOHNSON, EUNICE A.
[pen.] Pat; [b.] June 25, 1928, Crowley; [p.] Ce'cile Chesle and Henry Paddio; [m.] Widow of John D. Johnson, Sr.; [ch.] Deidre, Clarence, Henry, Bertrand and Ce'cile; [ed.] BS Grambling, MA-UCLA, MS Cornell, Ph.D. progressive, further study LSU University of MN., SUNY-A, NCCC; [occ.] Minister, trainer and free lance writer; [memb.] Turner Chapel AME Church, National Education Association, Delta Sigma Theta Sorority, AARP, St. helena Parish Tourist Commission, St. Helena Parish Recreation and Parks Commissions, Esther Grand Chapter OES, etc.; [hon.] Humanitarian and Trail Blazer of the Year, Black and Gold Award, community header of the year, Lovie Garrison Henry Rainbow Award; [oth.writ.] Pat's First Book of Poetry and Prose, St. Helena and others, Louisiana Poets, Creative Career Exploration Program, etc.; [pers.] Helping others gives one the freedom to live and love. [a.] Greensburg, LA.

PAGE, WENDY L.
[b.] September 26, 1955, Roswell, NM; [p.] Robert and Bonolyn Page; [ed.] Georgetown High, Georgetown, MA, Post-graduate, Medical Assistant program; [occ.] Residential counselor for developmentally disabled adults and homemaker; [memb.] World of Poetry, American Poetry Association, National Library of Poetry; Island Pond Baptist Church (N.H.), C.W.A.; [hon.] Honors 1990 and 1991, poems "Perplexity", "Impossible Wishing", "Seeking", Golden Poet 1990 poem "Perplexity", National Library of Poetry 1992 top ten poems "The Sound of Poetry" cassette for poem "Seeking", "Seeking" also put to music/song; [oth.writ.] Published poems/4 books, "Perplexity", "Brown Eyed Susan", "Who Are You Sir", "Your Windows", "Flower Smile", "Love Under Northern Light's", "Seeking", "You", "Token Memories", "Impossible Wishing" published in World of Poetry anthology 1990, Our World's Favorite Gold and Silver Poems 1991, National Library of Poetry's, The Best Poems of The 90's, 1992, and Our World's Favorite Poems, Who's Who In Poetry as well as several other unpublished poems; [pers.] I write from my heart, personal experiences and observations. A special thank you to Danny, who will always have a special place in my heart and who first inspired my writing as a teen, I love you. I am thankful for may family, dear friends, "commonplace" things, nature and her awesomeness and try not to take any for granted. I see life and it's trials "refining", kindness passed on and not repaid, I strive to reflect these in my writing. A special thank you to you Lord... for without me ye can do nothing. John 15:5c. [a.] Kingston, NH.

PARKER, JOAN S.
[p.] John Grace Smith; [m.] Chuck; [ch.] Kim Litscher and Kevin Arnold; [ed.] High school, Culpeper Co. High; [occ.] Prof operator local bank; [pers.] I find personal experiences and nature are my easiest subjects and most rewarding. [a.] Culpeper, VA.

PARKER, MAZELL
[pen.] Zetta; [p.] Willie and Lillian Jones; [ch.] Garry D. Ridgle and Kenneth Parker; [ed.] Bachelor of Arts, Dominguez Hills, University, Carson, California; [occ.] Social worker Department of Children Services, Los Angeles County, Los Angeles, CA; [memb.] Bethel AME Church; [oth.writ.] 1 poem published, several poems not published. [a.] Los Angeles, CA.

PARRISH, DAVID J.
[pen.] David J. Parrish; [b.] July 28, 1956, San Diego, CA; [p.] Judy R. and Jan G. Parrish; [ed.] Punahou School, U.S.C. Cinema School; [occ.] Firefighter, Honolulu Fire Department; [oth.writ.] Screenplays, short stories, poetry, nothing sold, nothing published...yet; [pers.] I hope to make a contribution to 20th century thought. [a.] Honolulu, HI.

PASCAL, GIANNI
[pen.] Paul Pascal; [b.] October 21, 1900, Switzerland; [p.] Emanuele and Lucia Gianini; [ed.] University of Lyon, France, degrees in Physics, Mathematics and Engineering; [occ.] Retired, Engineer-Aeronautic Lockheed Aircraft and Bechtel Corp; [memb.] California Society of Engineering; [oth.writ.] Published 12 books (poetry) "The Soul That Lets The Light Go Free", "Thoughts Volume I,II, III, IV, and V", "Letter To My Son", "Letter To My Daughter", "New York Library" and other poems, "The Four Seasons", autobiography "Born To Win", "Twentieth Century", several poems published in local newspapers; [pers.] Through a lifelong interest in philosophy, poetry has found its full expression-now at age 94 it is in full bloom. My purpose in writing prose is to give through my experience a unique interpretation of life. [a.] Beverly Hills, CA.

PASSMORE, R. DEAN
[b.] January 24, 1949, Chicago; [p.] Chas. H. and Irene R. Passmore; [ed.] B.A., M.F.A., University of Eastern Florida at Tampa; [occ.] Poet; [memb.] American Legion, Chicago Council on Foreign Relations, National Authors Registry, The Literary Network; [oth.writ.] Published poems, "Cycle" "Near and Far", "Spin", "Whisper"; [pers.] Change and experimentation are the life the lifeblood of the individual as well as all of mankind.

PATEL-DAS, PURUSHOTTAMDAS B.
[pen.] Das; [b.] July 1, 1929, Uttersanda, Gujarat India; [p.] Father-Bhailaghia Govindghai Patel and (mother) Diwaligen Bhailalbhai Patel; [m.] Ansuya alias Hansa, May 11, 1947; [ch.[Kiran, Kaushik Deepak and Kamlesh; [ed.] Matriculation examination, passed in 1947; [occ.] Retired businessman; [memb.] Founder of the Land Records Department class III Government Servants' Association, Gujarat State India; [hon.] Obtained little amount of cash prizes from leading magazines in India, Editor's Choice Award for Outstanding Achievement in poetry presented by the National Library of Poetry in the year 1993 and 1994 for 5 poems, invited to join International Society of Poets 1992,93, 94, poems "Words and Blood" and "Flame" published in my own handwritings in the Senior Citizens News, Harrisburg with photostat (copies) of above said awards, my brief introduction and photographs, poem "Affection" accepted for publication by them; [oth.writ.] Several social ex religious articles, narratives, essays, numerous poems, biography of my 3 1/2 year old grandson Kunjal etc., published in leading newspapers and literary magazines in India, documentary film script entitled "Riddhi-Siddhi) on land reforms for Gujarat State Government India; [pers.] Little knowledge of English, but my grandson Anish has been my inspiration for writing poems in English language. Artistic manuscript in my own handwritings in 247 pages entitled "Child" a collection of 58 poems in Gujarati and English with 94 pictures and one social novel entitled "When Got Flower..Found In Ash". Scheduled to be published during my visit to India. [a.] Harrisburg, PA.

PATENTE, MICHELLE SUZETTE
[pen.] Magrait; [p.] Rose and Robert Marcel; [ed.] George Washington High, the Jay Dash School of Dance (certificate of teaching), the Community College of Philadelphia (Associates Degree in Library Science); [occ.] Story writer and performing artist; [memb.] Twenty five year member of Nichiren Shoshu of America, a Buddhist organization for value creation and human revolution; [hon.] Royalties are for drug and alcohol rehabilitation in America, especially street alcoholism, prison system reconstruction, child prostitution and teenage runaways; [oth.writ.] "Quidipem" (poetry), nine lyric myths, "Jesefca" and other stories (selected stories) "Umbrians Poetica" an extensive work of poetry over a 16 year span written in poverty, "My Father Was A Frenchman" (an extensive book of short stories); [pers.] I continue to live my work, classical literature and the victorian poets are my pastimes. My cellist and I use the Bach studies for our performances, at which time I read to an audience and she accompanies me on her musical cello'., at that time, John Sebastian's presence can be deeply felt and the audience forms a beautiful soul of its own. [a.] Philadelphia, PA.

PATRICK, KATHY L.
[b.] May 19, 1950, Renick, MO; [p.] Louise Nelson and Lee Kindell; [ch.} David and Sean Patrick; [hon.] "So Tell Me Child", Editor's Choice Award 1994; [pers.] "Milvano" was written about a special friend from Il Pescatore's Ristorante in Oakland, California. [a.] Oakland, CA.

PATRYKUS, ROBERTA
[pen.] Bobbie; [b.] June 16, 1953, Chicago; [p.] Maryann and John Schimpf; [m.] Michael, June 21, 1972; [ch.] David Michael and Jason Robert; [ed.] Grammar, high school, beauty diploma, food service and sanitation licenses, child care diploma, cake decorating; [occ.] Receiving and sales associate and housewife, [hon.] Employee of month, cake decoration awards, baking award and publications, my two sons and husband my best awards; [oth.writ.] 2 publications in your poem book and also cook books; [pers.] My writings are what I feel about real life, my family and my friends. I feel these make people see the real meaning of life. [a.] Lake Zurich, IL.

PATTERSON, ROY
[b.] April 26, 1926, Ironwood, MI; [p.] Donald and Helmi Patterson; [m.] Elaine Patterson, August 28, 1948; [ch.] David R. and Thomas D. Patterson; [ed.] B.S. University of Michigan, M.D. University of Michigan; [occ.] Professor of Medicine, Northwestern University Medical School; [memb.] Master,

American College of Physicians, Royal College of Medicine; [hon.] Ernest S. Bagley, Professorship of Medicine.[a.] Wilmette, IL.

PAULAUSKAS, GERALD J.
[pen.] J.J. Paul; [b.] March 24, 1958, New Haven, CT; [p.] Barbara and George; [m.] Myong K. Paulauskas, August 3, 1983; [ch.] David (10) and Thomas (7); [ed.] High school graduate, Hamden, Connecticut; [occ.] Postal employee; [oth.writ.] Three published works in the National Library of Poetry's anthology, untitled, re: thoughts inspired, published in Tears of Fire, "At Love's Bequest" published in Dance On Horizon and "A Touch of April" published in At Day's End; [pers.] Each soul possesses a unique light. The closer a soul comes to truth the greater illumination of this light experienced. Spiritual truth is the gift of God to all whom might aspire to more than the world would teach. Let us each study therefore the perfect light of God's love. [a.] Lancaster, CA.

PAULUN, CARL L.
[b.] August 14, 1937; [m.] Grace M. Paulun; [hon.] Editor's Choice Award by the National Library of Poetry; [oth.writ.] Current book of prose and poetry, "Let's Be Friends" published by Vantage Press, "Thank God It's Friday" and other song poems made into songs; [pers.] Use the talent that God has already given you before you ask for any more talent. [a.] New Philadelphia, PA.

PAYNTER, KAREN L.
[b.] February 1, 1950, Michigan; [p.] Sidney and MaryEllen Apley; [m.] Ralph A. Paynter, April 27, 1968; [ch.] Paul E. and Anita M. [pers.] "My First Grandchild" was written in memory of my granddaughter Kendra Lynn Paynter. [a.] Roseville, MI.

PEAVEY, ANNABELLE (LEWIS)
[b.] August 19, 1909, Florida, NY; [p.] George and Flora Lewis; [m.] Lloyd W. Peavey, September 5, 1931; [ch.] Lewis William, George D. and James R.; [ed.] B.S. Syracuse University, M.S. New Platz, NY; [occ.] Retired teacher, Goshen NY Central School. [a.] Middletown, NY.

PENFOLD, CHASTITY RENEE
[b.] July 1, 1972, Buffalo, NY; [p.] Neil and Deborah Ann Wilson Penfold; [ed.] West Valley Central School, graduated in June of 1990; [occ.] Certified Nursing Assistant at Fiddler's Green Manor Nursing Home in Springville, New York; [oth.writ.] Poem "Colours" published in the Springville Journal and Hamburg Sun Circa 1987, poem "Vexation" soon to be published in the National Library of Poetry's anthology Echoes of Yesterday, poem, "Distilling Memory" published in the forthcoming anthology "And Time Stood Still" from the National Poetry Association, I have been writing for 11 years and have two books including illustrations near completion; [oth.writ.] My influence as an artist and a poet include Sylvia Plath, Anne Sexton and the music, lyrics, artwork of Kurt Cobain. [a.] Springville, NY.

PEREZ, NESTOR L.
[b.] October 16, 1950, Mayaguez; [p.] Eudo and Ana Perez; [m.] Neida Perez, December 1975; [ch.] Christopher, Roxie and Jennifer Perez; [ed.] Ph.D. in Metallurgical Engineering, University of Idaho; [occ.] Professor, University of Puerto Rico, Mayaguez Campus; [memb.] American Society for Metals; [hon.] First prize winner Engineering Division, 29th Conference, Idaho Academy of Science, Moscow, Idaho 1988, first prize trophy, band category, talent show, Puerto Rico; [oth.writ.] Many poems and songs for my own jazz rock band called Rotsen Prez, Puerto Rico, Mayaguez area; [pers.] During my silent moments, my mind can hush tranquility to shamble my thoughts and create ideas. This is a true phenomenon that amazingly puts on the alert for providing the audience with the best of me. [a.] Mayaguez, PR.

PERRY, CLAY
[pen.] Clay Perry; [b.] July 18, 1912, Smysson County, KY; [p.] Lester and Addie Perry; [m.] Wilma Fritz Perry, June 25, 1933; [ch.] Edward C. Perry Jr. and Ruth Ann Garverich; [ed.] Graduated from Mt. Zion High School 1931; [occ.] Retired from General Electric Company; [memb.] Member of Gospel Baptist Church, Galion Hospital Auxiliary; [hon.] Played on high school champion basketball team and baseball team, won honors and awards in track meets; [oth.writ.] I sold my first song lyrics in 1936 to Asheo Sizemore of the Grand Old Opera in Nashville, Tennessee, in 1970 my poem "I Live In Faith" was set to music and copyrighted and sung in many churches and also by the Gospel Singing Spicer Family; [pers.] My poems and songs are mostly religious. I thank my Heavenly Father for this wonderful gift. He has given me and also the National Library of Poetry for making a dream come true. [a.] Galion, OH.

PETERS, JAMES A.
[pen.] Peter De Bergerac; [b.] May 15, 1964, Brooklyn, NY; [p.] James G. and Leonore A. Peters; [m.] Single; [ed.] High School of Art and Design, NY, Kingsborough Community College, Brooklyn, NY; [hon.] Graduation with honors, Phi Theta Kappa 1993 from Kingsborough Community College, honors student, Dean's List, National Dean's List, Outstanding Student and graduate from a two year college award; [pers.] My writing is best described as a violin playing beautiful music by itself, only to transform itself into a dove, encircling above the head of the listener, then suddenly piercing the heart and soul of the listener as a lightning bolt. [a.] Brooklyn, NY.

PETERSON, BEATRICE FOX
[b.] November 9, 1909, Maine; [p.] Florence and Herman Fox; [m.] Harry Peterson, December 18, 1936; [ch.] Cynthia Kelley and Harry Peterson; [ed.] Russell Sage College, Troy, NY, Hunter College, New York City; [occ.] Retired; [memb.] Thrasher Memorial Methodist Church, United Methodist Women, Vinton Historical Society, Thursday Morning Music Club, National Geographic Society, AARP; [hon.] Special honors in Psychology, Russell Sage College, Troy, NY; [oth.writ.] Poems in Thrasher Church publications, poems in Virginia Originals 1982, 1990, published by U.M.W. of Virginia Conference; [pers.] "Do unto others as ye would that men should do unto you" is a concept even small children understand. If we could all live by this rule we might find peace in our time. [a.] Vinton, VA.

PETRUZZI, ERNEST R.
[pen.] ERP; [b.] June 2, 1927, Brockway, PA; [p.] Angeline and Nestie Petruzzi; [m.] Phyllis; [ch.] Ernest, Ricky, Mark, Jeannine and Michelle; [ed.] High school, Brockway, PA., attended Pitt University and University of West Virginia; [occ.] Retired as supervisor U.S. Steel Corp.; [oth.writ.] Have compiled a complete book of my poems for my wife, my children and each of my brothers and sisters containing verses I've written for them on their birthdays and special occasions and other favorite of mine; [pers.] I have always felt time flies too swiftly to worry about what tomorrow may bring or to have regrets about past experiences. Here and now we should enjoy the beauty of the present and God's hand in our life. My way of expressing this philosophy is my poetry. [a.] Pittsburgh (Bethel Park), PA.

PHELAN, THOMAS A.
[b.] January 20, 1928,, New York City; [m.] Ann (deceased); [ch.] Tommy, Theresa, Barbara and William; [ed.] Bergen Community College, Fairleigh Dickinson University, Thomas A. Edison College, Creative Writing, Humanities; [occ.] Private Det., karate instructor, prod/director dinner theatre; [memb.] Acc. Amer. Poets, Bergen Poets, Det.End Association; [hon.] Author's Award by N.J. Institute of Tech., Poetry Gold Medal of Honor, Achievement Award by Lodi, N.J. Board of Education, featured in On Books Column of New York Times; [oth.writ.] Published book of poetry "A Point Beyond Silence", unpublished "A Place of Shadows" plus 5 others, novel being edited, 3 screenplays, 2 plays for dinner theatre, published in literary magazine and newspapers throughout country and in Ireland. [a.] Bergenfield, NJ.

PHILLIPS, D. JOSEPHINE
[pen.] Josephine Phillips; [b.] July 19, 1937, Brevard, NC; [p.] Russeles and Elizabeth Banks; [ch.] LeLand, Michelle, Everette and Delno; [ed.] 3 years college; [occ.] Writing and painting; [memb.] RVA; [oth.writ.] The Candle and Rocking Horse, book; [pers.] I love to paint with oils, I love to write poetry and songs, also love my family and friends. A firm believer in God. [a.] Hendersonville, NC.

PHILLIPS, JULIA M.
[b.] October 31, 1917, Burgaw, NC; [p.] Mr. and Mrs. T.T. Murphy; [m.] Theodore D. Phillips (deceased), August 15, 1965; [ch.] (step) Mary Phillips Royce and Ted Phillips; [ed.] High school, Burgaw 1934, 2 year teaching certificate, East Carolina Teacher's College, AB Degree, East Caroline College, M.A. East Caroline University and University of Texas; [occ.] Retired teacher after 39 years in 5 states; [memb.] North Carolina Retired School Personnel, Alpha Delta Kappa, Fidelis Delta President and Leg. Ch. (15 years), NCRSP Dist, 14 of North Carolina Ed. Association, Carteret Writers Friend of Ft Macon, Careret Historian; [hon.] 1st place Carteret Writers poetry contest 1992, publishing first novel 1972, "Probably Tomorrow", 1st place poetry award 1992 Carteret Writers; [oth.writ.] Novel, "Probably Tomorrow" published 1972, articles in North Carolina Education magazine and local paper, Carteret News Times.

PICKLES, MICHELLE
[pen.] Chelle Lynn; [b.] August 28, 1977, Mt. Vernon, IL; [p.] Charles Pickles and Patricia Burgess; [ed.] Centralia High School (Go Orphans); [memb.] FCA, GAAC, NIKE, Drama Club, International Society of Poets; [hon.] 2 poems published by the National Library of Poetry, Editor's Choice Award for Outstanding Achievement in poetry; [oth.writ.] Several poems that are not published, but I have another one which is untitled that is in the book called

In The Desert Sun by National Library of Poetry; [pers.] I had a friend who passed away awhile back, who love to write poems just as much as I do and I know if she were able to submit a poem she had written it would be in this book next to mine. [a.] Centralia, IL.

PICKNELL, DIANA
[b.] February 23, 1955, Seattle, WA; [p.] Clyde and Jean Ries; [ed.] Lutheran Bible Institute, 1977 (Seattle, WA), South Kitsap High School, 1973 (Port Orchard, WA); [occ.] Legal Technician, Merit Systems Protection Board; [memb.] Lifetime member International Society of Poets; [hon.] International Poet of Merit Award, 1994 (ISP); [oth.writ.] The Space Between, National Library of Poetry 1994 anthology, The Sound of Poetry, National Library of Poetry 1994 audio tape. [a.] Seattle, WA.

PIERSON, HELEN BOWERS
[pen.] Helen Bowers Pierson; [b.] March 10, 1913, West Unity; [p.] Frank and Ella May Bowers; [m.] Floyd Pierson, December 21, 1929; [ch.} Ralph D. Pierson, (Michigan) and Carol J. Stantz (Ohio); [ed.] West Unity School; [occ.] Housewife; [memb.] United Methodist Church.

PIERSON, MANDA
[b.] April 1, 1979, PA; [p.] Lance and Sherry Lopez, Lew Pierson - real father; [ed.] Sophmore at BHS; [oth. writ.] I have had two of my poems published by the Nat'l Library of Poetry, which I'm very proud of; [pers.] I think poetry is a way of life; if you don't like poetry, you don't like life; [a.] Buffalo, NY

PINO, RICK
[b.] April 7, 1975, Syossett, NY; [p.] Ines Gaudro; [ed.] West Deptford High School, Westville, NJ; [occ.] Secondary Education, History student at Seton Hall University; [memb.] Layout Editor for Renaissance Seton Hall's literary magazine, Seton Hall's choir; [pers.] I would like to dedicate this poem to all my close friends, past and present, who have helped me to maintain my innocence of youth. [a.] Mantua, NJ.

PIROLLI, ALBERT M.
[pen.] Albert M. Pirolli; [b.] August 28, 1931, Philadelphia, PA; [p.] Albert J. and Anna Pirolli; [m.] Julia, September 4, 1954; [ch.] Albert, Anna Marie, Daniel, Bernadette and Francine; [ed.] Bucks County Community College, Temple University; [occ.] Retired Law Enforcement Officer; [memb.] Fraternal Order of Police, PA, Sports Hall of Fame member, Executive Director of Philadelphia All Star football game; [hon.] Have received eight awards for outstanding artist, plaques for outstanding football coach (high school); [oth.writ.] Have had articles published in newspapers and magazines, currently writing a book; [pers.] This ia s thought that is in every parent's mind and I hope this will give them the courage to say it. [a.] Richboro, PA.

PLAMBECK, GAE
[b.] July 21, 1942, Dodge City, KS; [p.] Max and Helen Bainter; [m.] Charles Plambeck, July 24, 1964; [ch.] Cassandra Rachelle born in Tokyo, Japan in 1966; [ed.] 1 year at Pasadena City College in Pasadena, CA: [occ.] Housewife and world traveler and have lived in Japan and Saudi Arabia; [hon.] I am short on secular education and honors but feel I am more than compensated by my knowledge and love of God's word and His creation which is the inspiration for my poetry, poem "Cornfields" awarded Honorable Mention and Golden Poet trophy for 1992 from World of Poetry; [oth.writ.] Several poems published in local newspapers and in various poetry anthologies, poem "Gypsy", Acadia Poetry anthology, "Twilight", "Athena" anthology Other Side of The Mirror, poem "Sunset", Echoes of Yesterday, poem "Rainbow; [pers.] In my poetry, I strive to bring recognition and honor not to myself, but to God, from who I received my talents, by writing of the beauties of His creation (Romans 1:20). [a.] Grove, OK.

PLAYER, GALE L.
[b.] June 30, 1935, Rochester, NY; [p.] Berton and Erma Patterson; [m.] Divorced; [ch.] Joanne, Jeanne, Jacquelyn and James (all married); [ed.] Spencerport Central School (Spencerport, NY), attended Rochester Business Institute (Rochester, NY), Moody Bible Institute (Chicago, IL), certificate; [occ.] Department Secretary and Administrative Assistant, SUNY College at Brockport, NY; [memb.] For many years I studied music at the Eastman School of Music (Rochester, NY) and have been a church organist since 1965, I am also very active in church work (singles ministry and occasionally teach Sunday School); [hon.] Dean's List (RBI), Alpha Phi Iota (Honor Society/RBI), Adele Catlin Secretarial Award (SUNY Brockport, 1988), Editor's Choice Award for poem "Power To Kill", At Day's End (National Library of Poetry, 1994); [oth.writ.] Have written numerous articles, short items and poetry for various magazines and newspapers; [pers.] Due to work commitments, I do not have the time I would like to in order to follow my first love...that of writing. As I near my retirement, I hope to become more involved. [a.] Spencerport, NY.

PNIEWSKI, GARY THOMAS
[b.] December 24, 1947, Cleveland, OH; [p.] Al and Bridget Pniewski; [m.] Delores Pniewski, June 20, 1987; [ch.] Jennifer Lynn and Patrick Allen; [ed.] Benedictine High School, Cuya Hoga Community College; [occ.] Retired Columbus Ohio Police Department; [memb.] International Freelance Photographers Organization, Police and Fire Retirees of Ohio; [hon.] Accomplishment of merit -creative arts and science (1994); [oth.writ.] The National Library of Poetry, Tears of Fire, "Fly Away" (1993), creative arts and science (Fire From Within), "World Of Tribes" (1994); [pers.] Poetry stirs the inner spirit unleashing the beast in all of us, traveling segmented journeys through the mind. [a.] Welch, WV.

POETE, SHAUNA
[pen.] Poet L. Luchiano, Tessa Baden; [b.] December 19, 1979, California; [p.] Leonar Fajardo; [ed.] Attending Taft High School; [hon.] National Junior Honor Society; [oth.writ.] "I Sit Beside Myself", "I'm Rich", "I Stroll Against The Wind", "Age of A Rose"; [pers.] I want to send special thanks to my mommy Leonar and I love you. [a.] Canoga Park, CA.

POHLMAN, ESTHER L.
[pen.] LaFaye Pohlman; [b.] 1900, Santa Rosa, CA; [p.] Robert and Pauline Mills; [m.] William C. Pohlman, August 7, 1932; [ch.] John S., Ruth L. and Katherine L.; [ed.] Genera; [occ.] Retired; [memb.] Co-chairman of American Women Volunteers 1942-1946, Trustee for local Union 560, Delegate to Central Labor, Chairman for sick at Weimar Sanitarium; [hon.] Untied States Treasury Department, in behalf of the war finance program a citation March 29, 1946; [oth.writ.] In the World of Poetry, 3 poems in one book and 1 in another 1989, 1990, 1991, 1992. [a.] Sparks, NV.

POLOWCZYK, LUCAS
[b.] March 18, 1975, Poland; [p.] Teresa and Grzeyorz Polowczyk; [ed.] Studying in Marymount Manhattan College; [occ.] Student; [oth.writ.] Local publications; [pers.] In genesis is sealed the flame of union lovers seek. Let silence in to find. [a.] New York, NY.

POOL, CARLTON DEWAYNE
[pen.] Byron Cei Wilde; [b.] August 22, 1953, El Paso, TX; [p.] Alvis and Iona Pool; [m.] Caroline Hawk; [ch.] Rosalyn, Daniel, Dawna and Devon; [ed.] Alaska High School, years of traveling in stage productions and meeting wonderful people from this planet of ours; [occ.] Stage Director of a touring show (family); [hon.] Over the years, I have had the honor in working with many known entertainers, actors, etc., it has enriched my life in understanding friendship; [oth.writ.] "Lady-Child" which is published in your edition of Echoes of Yesterday, "Lady-Child" was my first poem to be seen by any publication; [pers.] It is ny view that one must do their best or the world will suffer. This planet of ours requires all of us for continuation on a positive note. [a.] El Paso, TX.

PORTER, BEULAH M.
[pen.] Beulah Langston Porter; [b.] August 26, 1905, Bridgpoet, Wise Co., TX; [p.] Henry S. Langston and Rachel A.; [m.] Harold W. Porter (deceased), August 28, 1928; [ch.] Clifford Charles and Nola Faye; [ed.] Public schools of Texas; [occ.] Widow-retired, mother, grandmother, great grandmother; [hon.] 2 trophies, one Silver Poet Award 1989, for Beulah Langston Porter, one Golden Poet Award 1988, 2 other Golden Poet plaques for 1989 and 1991, 9 certificates of merit and one International Society of Poets for Beulah Porter 1993-1994; [oth.writ.] A collection of poetry from 1940 to present time; [pers.] I believe in doing the very best I can do, in every phase of my life. [a.] Spokane, WA.

PORTER, KERRY
[b.] January 26, 1977, Athens; [p.] Kenneth and Debra Porter; [pers.] It amazes me how one line of poetry can tell a story, reveal secrets and simply live, unaware of it's own complexity. Dedicated to Matthew Anderson. [a.] Athens, AL.

PORTER, MARTHA
[pen.] Martha Porter; [b.] May 9, 1922, Shelby County, TX; [p.] Dan and Kizzie Pollard (deceased); [m.] W. Claude Porter (deceased), October 11, 1940; [ch.] Sherry Porter Baxley; [ed.] High school; [occ.] Retired; [memb.] Nominated for membership in International Society of Poets.

PRETORIUS, BRONWEN
[b.] March 11, 1975, South Africa; [p.] Wendy and Andre Pretorius; [ed.] Durban Girls College and Durban Girls High School, South Africa; [occ.] Working in family fashion design business; [oth.writ.] Other published and competition level poetry; [pers.] It seems that poetry has become my lifeblood. What an honor to share it with other poets and all the great people in the promised land of America. [a.] Montclair, NJ.

PRITCHARD, PEARL C.
[b.] July 28, 1908, Branson, MO; [p.] Lewis and Emma Sellers; [m.] Archie A. Pritchard (deceased), January 16, 1936; [ch.] Allen Thomas and William A. Pritchard; [ed.] Topeka Kansas High School, attended four colleges and one university, degree from the College of Love and Care for Others; [occ.] Author; [memb.] Past activities include working in philanthropic groups such as, American Red Cross, visiting in prisons and nursing homes, active in Christian Women's groups; [oth.writ.] Poetic Pearls volume 1; [pers.] Life motto, "Only one life, and will soon be past, only what is done for Christ will last". Author is 86 years old and blind. [a.] Upland, CA.

PROUDFOOT, RICHARD L.
[b.] April 29, 1952, Addison, MI; [p.] Homer and Bernice Proudfoot; [m.] Melissa, June 11, 1992; [ch.] Chad, Brad, Scott, Elmer, Brodrick and Breanne; [ed.] Addison High, Siena Heights; [occ.] Telecommunications Consultant; [oth.writ.] One other published poem; [pers.] I try and keep things simple because the simple things in life are the best things in life. [a.] Manitou Beach, MI.

PUCEK, TAMIE
[b.] February 28, 1960, Richmond, TX; [p.] Marie and Elhart Pucek; [ed.] Lamar Consolidated High School, Rosenberg, Texas; [occ.] Bookkeeper, hoping to have a writing career; [hon.] Editor's Choice Award for 1993 and 1994 from the National Library of Poetry; [oth.writ.] I have written over 30 original poems, a children's book (unpublished), one short story (unpublished), one poem "Empty Shell" published in The Desert Sun and one poem "Adam" in Dance On The Horizon all anthologies by the National Library of Poetry; [pers.] My writing comes from feelings of all kinds. When I write a poem, I'm usually inspired by something or someone. My other writing is an idea which comes from imagination. [a.] Richmond, TX.

PULVER, JOHN R.
[pen.] J; [b.] November 2, 1955, Kokomo, IN; [p.] Ada Hensler and Edward Pulver; [ch.] Joel, Stacy and Tommy; [ed.] Haworth High, Kokomo, IN; [occ.] K-Mart Fashions, Westland, MI; [hon.] The highest honor I have received is that "Lynn" will always be by my side "I Love You"; [oth.writ.] Several poems have been published, I am in the process of writing a book to share my feelings of life, love and pain with others; [pers.] I wish to share with all that poetry is more than words and lines. I hope that all can understand it's a way of self expression that can make a losing man win. [a.] Flat Rock, MI.

PURVIANCE, DEBORAH LUM
[b.] October 18, 1948, Vicksburg, MS; [p.] Mr. and Mrs. William D. Lum;[m.] Hollis L. Purviance, January 21, 1979; [ch.] William Lum, Mary Elizabeth and Martha-Ker Brady; [ed.] Port Gibson High School, Hinds Junior College, Delta State College; [occ.] Event coordinator, historian, homemaker; [memb.] Angique Bowie Knife Association, 1800' Spring Festival Committee, First Families of Mississippi, Daughters of the American Revolution; [oth.writ.] Newspaper articles; [pers.] Creative talents should be given every opportunity to flourish. [a.] Port Gibson, MS.

QUIETSTORM, JEAN-PAILIPPE
[b.] February 12, 1959, Baltimore, MD; [p.] Barbara McCormick and William Tyler Reap; [ed.] National University, Criminal Justice/forensic; [occ.] Freelance; [memb.] International Society of Poets, The American Poetry Society; [hon.] Editor's Choice Award 1993 and 1994, International Society of Poets Award, certificate of poetic achievement. [a.] Payson, AZ.

RABSON, HERMAN N. (HON.)
[b.] September 12, 1909, Cleveland, OH; [p.] Abraham and Mary Rabinowitz; [m.] Helen Wolper Rabson, March 18, 1939; [ch.] Edward A. Rabson, wife Gloria, grandchildren, Lauren and triplets Lindsay, Jaclyn and Jaimee; [ed.] Franklin K. Lane High School, Brooklyn, NY, Columbia University (pre-law N.Y.C.), Brooklyn Law School (St. Lawrence University); [occ.] U.S. Administrative Law Judge, U.S. Coast Guard-retired 1982, NY State Hearing Officer-resigned, Specialty Maritime Law, Lawyer (State of New York) retired; [memb.] Admitted to practice law, state of New York-1932, Supreme Court of the United States-1962, U.S. Court of Appeals 2nd Circuit, U.S. District Courts (S.D. and E.D. of New York), American Bar Association (retired), N.Y County Bar Association (retired); [hon.] President high school Alumni Association 1929-30, member of board of directors Home For The Aged, various offices I.O.O.F., member of board of directors Home of Old Israel (N.Y.C.), [oth.writ.] Legal editor (Courting the Law Showman's Trade review), entertainment field of law, Echoes of Yesterday, National Library of Poetry, "Sunset Dreams"; [pers.] My wife and I have taught our son, wife and grandchildren "to love and cherish the laws of the Lord and that He will always love and cherish them". [a.] Forest Hills, NY.

RADEBAUGH, GERALDINE MARGARETTE
[pen.] Jenny Lloyd Radebaugh; [b.] May 1, 1927, Henryetta, OK; [p.] John Henry and Margaret Lloyd; [m.] Theon Leroy Radebaugh, March 24, 1946; [ch.] Johnny Phillip, Jenny Lynn, Timothy Leroy and David Roger; [ed.] St. Michael's of Henryetta, self educated carpentry (including building of own home and son's thru F.H.A.; [occ.] Christian, mother, grandmother and carpenter; [memb.] Church of Christ, American Citizen for God and Country; [hon.] President of senior class, Bible School teacher (all ages), Ladies Bible class teacher; [oth.writ.] Poems printed in the newspaper and bulletins, a tract printed in 1983, poems written for others to give to their loved ones, etc.; [pers.] Any and all the talents I have been blessed with through-out my life I give the credit to the Master and loving people who have gone on and to those who still remain. [a.] Henryetta, OK.

RAGNO, CAROLYN JOAN
[pen.] Shining Star; [b.] August 12, 1940, Newark, NJ; [p.] Albert and Antionette Ragno; [ed.] Franklin Morrell High School, Irvington, NJ, N.Y.U., New York, Pace College-N.Y., National School Aeronautics, Kansas City, MO, Institute of Applied Science and Criminology, Chicago, IL; [occ.] Concert accomplished pianist, Police Fiction K-9 Mystery Writer (freelance), and Mounted Police Mystery Writer; [memb.] Police and fire clubs; [hon.] Distinguished medal and award from the FBI (Gold Medal), Legion of Honor for Police, Sheriff and FBI (medal), Medal of Merit from National Chief of Police, K-9 Humanitarian Award and Medal of Honor (for all my work with Police K-9's); [oth.writ.] I write fiction K-9 mystery's for police departments and mounted police (Newark Police Department) in USA, I write poems about PTL, and their K-9's and I gained National recognition on April 21, 1994 in the town newspaper, I'm in Who's Who In American Law Enforcement and nominated for 10 consecutive years, I am in all the state libraries in USA and Library of Congress, Washington, DC, I also write songs (love); [pers.] For the past 6 years I have been entertaining K-9 Police Departments. I feature real K-9 and M.P. and myself as Lieutenant Carol as the main characters. I employ a unique literary device of writing in the voice of both characters. I write from the dog and horse point of view and mine. That's what makes it interesting. I make posters, signs, blankets for dogs and horses and send then care packages full of toys and treats. I love bringing a smile to everyone I meet especially to the Police Department. [a.] Irvington, NJ.

RAMIREZ, MILAGROS F.
[b.] February 26, 1919, Mayaguez, PR; [m.] Widow, September 6, 1941; [ch.] Mildred L. Lopez and Jose' A. Ramirez; [ed.]Mayaguez High School-1938, Colegio La Milagrosa, Secretarial Sciences-1940; [occ.] Retired from Gulf Oil Corp in San Juan where I worked for 25 years; [memb.] Ex-president San Juan Chapter PSI 1966, Ex-president Women of Unity 1961-1985, Ex-1st Lady Lodge Genesis -101-1978, Editor bulletin La Hija del Caribe 1992-1995; [hon.] Gulf Petroleum S.A. for outstanding performance as executive secretary 1977, Gulf Petroleum S.A traditions of service award 1982, Unity San Juan, PR 1961-1985, award for 24 years of services, club Hija del Caribe 1993 for the editing of bulletin; [oth.writ.] Lectures delivered to secretaries, invocations, toasts, etc.; [pers.] My message to everyone is that there is no age gap to put into good use the blessings the Father has bestowed upon us. [a.] San Juan, PR.

RAMOS, AMANDA
[b.] July 25, 1981, Frankfort, Germany; [p.] Jeanette Vahsholtz and Ron Ramos; [ed.] At Abilene Middle School, went to Enterprise Elementary; [occ.] Student; [memb.] Smoky Hill Girl Scouts; [hon.] Jessie Carl Citizenship Award, Enterprise Elementary, D.A.R.E. essay contest; [pers.] Always remember peace, love, recycle and be groovy. [a.] Abilene, KS.

RAMPTON, KATHLEEN
[b.] September 14, 1948, Brigham City, UT; [ed.] B.A. English, California State College, Sonoma; [occ.] Accountant, manager manufacturing company; [memb.] International Society of Poets; [hon.] Graduated with honors from California State College, Sonoma; [oth.writ.] I have a poem being published in your anthology Dark Side of The Moon, in winter 1994; [pers.] My writing reflects my love of the Northern California countryside in which I live, it also reflects my gratitude toward those individuals who have encouraged me to be the poet I am. [a.] Santa Rosa, CA.

RANDALL, MICHAEL PAUL
[pen.] Mykee; [b.] March 14, 1952, Sidney, OH; [p.] Pauline and Paul Randall; [m.] Divorced; [ch.] Mica Allen and Emily Ann; [ed.] High school: [occ.] Polisher at the Stolle Corporation, Sidney, Ohio [hon.] 1994 poet book; [oth.writ.] Oh Here Is Me Sometimes Sometimes, I Think Of Only Sue, Oh How Long, Remember When; [pers.] Many of times it seems that life just isn't fair and I am glad I have

special friend to turn to so all my writing and poems is dedicated to her, thanks Sue for being there. [a.] Jackson Center, OH.

RAYMOND, VIRGINIA
[b.] November 11, 1932, Bristol, NH; [p.] Mr. and Mrs. Samuel R. Clow; [m.] Roy Raymond (deceased), February 26, 1949; [ch.] Alan, Stephen, Bonnie, Rodney, Roy Jr., Linda and Cathy; [ed.] Took courses in nursing, I attended Claremont Schools for many years I worked in nursing homes and private duty; [occ.] I care for my son Rodney who is quaudplegic here at home and 2 grandsons James and Jared; [oth.writ.] You will be publishing my first poem "God Is Love" this winter, it will be also on a cassette with 8 other poems; [pers.] My family have always been # 1 to me then nursing. I love music and reading and for years I have written poems. My goal is to publish a book of poetry. [a.] Claremont, NH.

REBER, ROBERT
[pen.] Bob Reber; [b.] September 17, 1965, Alpena, MI; [p.] Marrianne and Richard Reber; [ed.] BSBA-Aquinas College; [occ.] Sales representative, Sentry Insurance; [oth.writ.] "Storms Inside of My Head", a collection of thoughts in prose, "Soul Psalms" a collection of thoughts in prose, "Dream Dances of Souls" a novel; [pers.] Images of the higher-deeper self are found in thoughts and emotions. The true blessing to be celebrated in life. [a.] Fond du Lac, WI.

REED, MARYLIN
[pen.] Mariam St. Marie; [b.] November 27, 1947, NY; [ch.] Lisa, Shelly and Erek; [ed.] M.S. Human Resource Management, B.A. Public Admin./Government, Certified Organization Development Specialist; [occ.] Staff Analyst for New York City; [hon.] Magna Cum Laude; [oth.writ.] Unpublished mystery, "A Case of Strange Alliances", various articles in "Real Estate Weekly" trade publication, several poems published in local newspapers. [a.] New York, NY.

REESE, EDITH
[b.] February 11, 1923, Princeton, WV; [p.] Katherine and Clarence Norris; [m.] The Rev. Dr. H. Lawrence Reese, May 16, 1953; [ch.] Anita Elizabeth Sinclair and Mark Andrew Reese; [ed.] B.A., The George Washington University, 4 year scholarship, teacher certification, Shimer College, degrees in French, Literature and Mathematics; [occ.] English and math tutor, 12 years editor and technical writer; [memb.] Delta Zeta, Alpha Lambda Delta, Peace Fellowship, Adult Children of Alcoholics; [hon.] Phi Beta Kappa; [oth.writ.] "The Eye of The Spider" published by National Library of Poetry, poems and articles in local papers, for me, poetry is a lifeline; [pers.] I am on a perpetual quest for self-knowledge and transformation. [a.] Nigara Falls, NY.

REESE, SHARON E.
[b.] August 24, 1938, New York City; [oth.writ.] "Grandpa's Visit" a poem; [pers.] I pray we all wake up in time to change this world to one of love and stop destroying our earth. [a.] Deerfield Beach, FL.

REID, BARBARA R.
[b.] December 5, 1927, Moreauville, LA; [p.] W.A. and Elnora Rozas; [m.] Deceased, August 13, 1950; [ch.] Katherine, Monica, Maxwell and Toni; [ed.] B.S. Degree N.S.U., Natchitoches, LA, Master's Degree in Administration and supervision from University of Southern Miss; [occ.] Retired school teacher and supervisor; [memb.] Southern Poetry Association; [hon.] Placement in several poetry contests; [pers.] I am influenced by all the people I have loved.[a.] Cottonport, LA.

REINICKER, CHARLOTTE EICHFIELD
[pen.] Mikki; [b.] December 22, 1937, Camden, NJ; [p.] Anna and Henry J. Enichfeld; [m.] James L. Reinicker, September 6, 1958; [ch.] James L. Jr., Dawn Lizbeth, Michael Lisa, Andrew L. and Tobitha-Lin; [ed.] Moore College of Art and Design Camden County Community College, Haddonfield Memorial High School; [occ.] Homemaker, etc; [memb.] Lutheran Church; [oth.writ.] Poems published in the Garden Isle (local newspaper) and the Lihue Lutheran Aloha newsletter, and in 1994's Dance On The Horizon; [pers.] By some of my writings I hope to bring deeper thought and awareness, and hopefully favorable reaction to mankinds' relationship with our Heavenly Father and His magnificent creation, our earth. Most of my writings concern our relationship with a loving Father God.

RENY, SCARLET DEE
[pen.] Sacarlet Red; [b.] February 25, 1977, Hanover, NH; [p.] Elyce and Garry Reny Sr.; [ed.] Junior in West High School enrolled in Manchester School of Technology taking child care; [occ.] Hostess at McDonald's Restaurant; [memb.] Future Homemakers of America, I hold the office of Public Relations, I have held the offices of Vice President and Treasurer; [hon.] Honor Roll, Greatest Effort, Most Improvement Awards; [oth.writ.] Short stories and I'm currently writing a book, I write some songs.

REYES, JANELL MARIE
[b.] June 22, 1965, San Diego; [p.] Thomas Keller and Karen Penner; [m.] Michael Reyes, October 8, 1985; [ch.] Carolina (9) and Joshua Reyes (4); [ed.] M.A. History at CSU, Fresno; [occ.,] History instructor at College of Sequoias and Fresno City College; [memb.] Tokalon, Civil War Re-enactment Society, Fresno County Historical Society; [pers.] History for me is nothing less than a rollercoaster on rails of passion. [a.] Tulare, CA.

REYLING, DAVID A.
[b.] April 6, 1973, McLeansboro, IL; [p.] Fred Reyling and Donna Grady, [ed.] High school graduate; [occ.] Active duty military; [memb.] Non-commissioned Officers Association; [hon.] AF Achievement Medal; [oth.writ.] "Sugar On The Knife" published in Echoes Of Yesterday; [pers.] Believe in yourself before believing in others, for others to believe in you, you must believe in yourself. [a.] Maxwell AFB, AL.

RHOADS, GEORGE
[b.] February 22, 1931, Wabash, IN; [p.] Norman and Hazel Rhoads; [m.] Peggy, December 16, 1950; [ch.] Colleen, Randy, Richard and David; [ed.] High school plus several courses at Taylor University; [occ.] Ex Cop and Production Control Sal, General Motors, retired; [memb.] National Library of Poetry, National Rife Association, Baptist; [hon.] Editor's Choice Award, National Library of Poetry 1994; [oth.writ.] Field and Stream; [pers.] I dedicate these poems to my son Randy who was killed in 1990 in a welding accident. I must plant more seed. [a.] Wabash, IN.

RICE, CHARLOTTE SPAHN
[b.] May 10, 1926, Canton, IL; [p.] Bessie Prose and George Spahn; [m.] Rollin H. Rice, September 2, 1951; [ch.] Sylvia Jean and Sidney Rollin; [ed.] R.N. graduate of Cottage Hospital School of Nursing, Galesburg, IL, B.S.N. -Knox College, Galesburg, IL; [occ.] Retired; [memb.] B & PW (Business and Professional Women-25 years; [hon.] National Honor Society high school, Carney Award, highest honors, nursing school, academic scholarship, Knox College, Golden Poet-1991; [oth.writ.] My legacy to our children, letters to the editor; [pers.] It's important to find time in which to live, celebrate the holidays, birthdays and anniversaries, develop creative talents, pursue hobbies and time to bring gladness into the lives of others. Don't spend all your time making a living. [a.] Toulon, IL.

RICHARDS, ANN
[b.] March 29, 1936, West Virginia; [ch.] One married son, two granddaughters; [ed.] Some college in areas of interest; [occ.] Work; [memb.] International Society of Poets and Mid-Willamette Valley Arts Council; [oth.writ.] Poem "My Son" published in The Space Between; [pers.] Poetry, to me is an expression of emotions and opinions that comes from the heart. [a.] Monmouth, OR.

RICHARDS, EDITH L.
[b.] September 24, 1920, Omaha, NE; [m.] Deceased; [ch.] Diane, Jim and Terri; [ed.] BA University of Alabama in Huntsville, one year graduate work Montevallo, Alabama School of Music; [occ.] Organist, music director-St. Matthews Episcopal Church, Madison, AL; [memb.] American Guild of Organists, Organ Historical Society; [hon.] Dean's List, graduate of the year, music department, UAH; [pers.] I have always wanted to write, but somehow never got started.[a.] Huntsville, AL.

RICHARDSON, DENISE ANN
[pen.] Denise Joanou; [b.] December 14, 1964, Louisville, KY; [p.] Mr. and Mrs. Richard W. Satterly; [m.] Divorced and happy; [ch.] Sara Ann Richardson; [ed.] Jeffersontown High School; [occ.] Full time mother, part time writer; [memb.] Jeffersontown PTA; [hon.] 1993 Editor's Choice Award for Outstanding Achievement in poetry, presented by the National Library of Poetry; [oth.writ.] "Pale As The Moon" is in Whispers in The Wind by the National Library of Poetry 1993; [pers.] I am working on my first horror novel. I hope you will be hearing from me soon. [a.] Louisville, KY.

RICHMOND, NOLA (NAIMA) P.
[b.] August 20, 1932, Millen, GA; [ch.] Rowena, Gwen, Pamela and Brian, grandchildren, Damon, Karla, Adeya, Kashana and Gerard; [ed.] David T. Howard, Atlanta,GA K-12, graduate with honors, University of Minnesota-Human Service certificate with distinction; [occ.] Minneapolis Public Schools as an Educational Assistant; [memb.] Interests-sewing, I designed a dress of African Heritage that is in the Minnesota Historical Society's Archive Department, I was recognized as one of the Upper Midwest's persons in the Fashion, Mode and Makers of 1994 through the Minnesota Historical Society, I like the theater and jazz; [oth.writ.] My poetry is published in the National Library of Poetry, two Editor's Choice Awards, Arcadia Poetry Press and Sparrowgrass Poetry Forum, Minnesota Women's Press, Insight

News, North News, also Famous Poets of Society. I have read my poetry at the Minnesota Science Museum, Minnesota Historical Society, Your Place or Mine, Oak Park Neighborhood Center, Phyllis Wheatly Community Center, Summer Library, Northeast Middle School and Audubon Elementary School and KFAI Radio Station. I have conducted a poetry workshop for Girl Scout Troop # 6213 and a workshop for women's group, Kofi. I am a recipient for the 1994 Twin Cities NOW, "Anita Hill Peace and Justice Award". [a.] Minneapolis, MN.

RICHTER, CAROLYN J.
[b.] April 5, 1963, Floresville, TX; [p.] Salvadar and Margie Urrabazo; [m.] Donald J. Richter, September 28, 1985; [ch.] Shanna Lynee Richter; [ed.] Texas Lutheran College, Southwest Texas State University; [occ.] Spanish Teacher, Segiun High School; [memb.] Member of the Stockdale Spanish Speaking Church of Christ; [oth.writ.] "Little Red Bird", "Little Blue Bird" (children's short story, not yet published), several poems (not published), one poem "If I Could Turn Back Time", published; [pers.] Writing poems enables me to express what I cannot express verbally. [a.] Stockdale, TX.

RIDGEWAY, VALERIE JEANNE
[b.] June 8, 1957, Elberton, GA; [p.] Doris and Jack Ridgeway; [m.] David Lynn Martin; [ch.] Sandi Jeanne, John Christopher, Daniel Lee and Kristopher Miles; [occ.] Business owner and manager; [oth.writ.] "My Guardian Angel" published in Echoes of Yesterday, children's stories, lyrics and poetry, a novel "The True Burn", short stories, ballads and plays, seminar booklets, greeting cards; [pers.] Share with me your life, even if it is only a small portion. I in turn will deliver to the world the moment. [a.] Elberton, GA.

RIDLEN, LILLIAN HEIGLE
[b.] November 15, 1946, New Orleans; [p.] Joseph Manuel and Lillian Mae; [m.] Theriot Hegile, Larry Vinson Ridlen, December 28, 1968; [ch.] Larry V. Jr., Kenneth C. and Jennifer C.; [ed.] Graduate Orleans Practical Nursing Program 1969, Real Estate course, River Parish Vo tech, 1986, TIPS Trainer, certified 1987; [occ.] Rosary marker/crafter; [memb.] International Society of Poets; [hon.] My personal biography is in Who's Who In The South and Southwest, Who's Who of American Women and Who's Who in The World (current editions), Who's Who of Female Executives and Who's Who in Advertising, Who's Who of Emerging Leaders in America, Who's Who of Women Executives International, Who's Who of Professional and Business Women and Two Thousand Notable American Women, I have also received two award for outstanding lyric writing; [oth.writ.] A Sampling of Southern Cooking 1985, a home study course in bartending 1989, composer, lyricist Tony's Song for artist Wayne Presley 1990, poems included in the anthologies by Poetry Press, the Poetry Center, Quill Books, The Amherst Society, Iliad Press, Sparrowgrass Poetry Forum and the National Library of Poetry, a poem "Prayer For Overeaters Anonymous" and a Christian rap song for a Garyville, LA Baptist Church; [pers.] I see poetry as a picture painted on an open page. Painted with thought, feeling, imagination, memory, emotion and insight. I strive to make my poems understandable to all who may read them. [a.] LaPlace, LA.

RIEDEL, JACQUELINE
[b.] July 3, 1980, Arizona; [p.] Fred and Julie Riedel; [ed.] Currently in 9th grade South Mountain High School; [memb.] National Junior Honor Society; [hon.] Scholastic merit (straight A's) superior rating at solo and ensemble, and 1st place in softball tournament; [oth.writ.] "What If"; [pers.] I like poetry because of the emotion it shows and how it moves people. I hope my poetry moves people as much as it moved me. [a.] Avondale, AZ.

RILEY, JULIE S.
[b.] January 10, 1983, McComb, MS; [p.] Susan Lightsey and Joey Riley; [ed.] 6th grade; [occ.] Student; [memb.] Monticello Baptist Church; [hon.] Class favorite, class beauty, homecoming maid, poem published in The Coming of Dawn; [oth.writ.] "A Day At The Beach", "Our World". [a.] Monticello, MS.

RIMBAUGH, KERI ANN
[pen.] "Raymond"; [b.] November 1, 1977, LaPorte, IN; [p.] James and Bunnie Rimbaugh; [ed.] Currently enrolled as a junior at LaPorte High School; [memb.] National Honor Society, Spanish Club; [oth.writ.] Several poems including, "Strength By Weakness" which was published in the National Library of Poetry's, The River of Dreams and "Nowhere Bound" published in my high school magazine Reflections; [pers.] If you write about what you love, you soon begin to love to write. I love to experience life, and I thank my parents for that opportunity. Thanks to Ross, Rita, Matt, Big Mike, Nancy, Harley and Tony for all being an important part of my heart. [a.] Stillwell, IN.

RISK, PATRICIA GOUGH
[pen.] Patricia Gough Risk; [b.] April 1, 1920, London, UK; [p.] Harold and Daisy Gilbert; [m.] 1st-Patrick Gough and 2nd Viv Risk, June 1, 1940 and July 18, 1987; [ch.] Sally Ramer, Margaret Saucedo, Annie Van Dalsem and Patrick Gough Jr.; [ed.] Educated in England, 12 years; [occ.] Retired; [memb.] Saint Mary's Catholic Church, Gilroy, CA., The Grange, Society of American Poets, National Heart Foundation, Gilroy Senior Citizens Club; [hon.] Editor's Choice Award by the National Library of Poetry, for my poem "Anchors of Life"; [oth.writ.] Poems published in Poetry Center's 1993 anthology, Space Between, "Feelings", anthology "Sisters" also Feelings Magazine and Poet's Pen Magazine and anthology, a novel published in December 1993, "The Labrinthine Ways", I am currently writing a second novel; [pers.] I love to write novels and poetry and strive in my poems anyway to stress the beauty of nature and the glory of God's wonderful world. [a.] Gilroy, CA.

RITTGERS, DAISY
[pen.] Daisy Rittgers; [b.] November 28, 1907, Westervelt; [p.] David and Estella Sands; [m.] Carl Rittgers (deceased), March 4, 1933; [ed.] Degree in Education, taught 42 years in Shelby County Schools, sub-teacher for 10 years, taught my last class in 1975; [occ.] Retired teacher; [memb.] Golden Nineties Poetry Club, Women of The Moose of Shelbybille, Methodist Women of Clarksburg, Retired Teachers of Illinois; [hon.] I am an artist, I have won many awards for my work in town and country art shows, I have many Honorable Mentions and Editor's Choice for my poetry; [oth.writ.] "Window In My Soul", "When Its Sunset In The Valley", "Myself", "Listen With Your Heart", "Time", "The Crucifixion"; [pers.] I write when I'm happy, I write when I'm sad, I write to make the world a better place and that through my eyes others will see beauty in the world that God made. [a.] Shelbyville, IL.

RIVERA, RAY
[b.] New York City; [m.] Julia Ewasow, June 14, 1992; [ch.] Three; [occ.] Band leader-composer, singer, guitarist; [memb.] ASCAP-Local 802; [hon.] Grammy nominee for album "Let Me Hear Some Jazz", Universal Leadership Foundation Award for past achievements of excellence, Outstanding Leadership and Humanitarian Services to the community, state and nation, 1990 World of Poetry Award of Merit for poem "Free America".

ROBARDEY, RUSSELL GEORGE
[b.] September 29, 1974, Arizona; [p.] Jayne and Norman Vanderwall; [m.] Rachel Anne Robardey, July 16, 1993; [ch.] 2 daughters (deceased) and child on the way; [ed.] Some college; [occ.] Varies, write in free time; [oth.writ.] "The Rose" and various poems; [pers.] All this just makes my ego bigger. [a.] Mesa, AZ.

ROBB, JEANNE MAGEE
[b.] April 30, 1926, Silverton, OR; [p.] Louis W. and Lillian Magee; [m.] E. Clark Robb, December 30, 1947; [ch.] Becky Robb Hicks, Phillip, Paul, Peter and John Robb; [ed.] B.A., Calvin College, Grand Rapids, MI., M.Ed., University of Arizona, Tucson, AZ; [occ.] Marriage and Family Therapist; [memb.] American Association for Marriage and Family Therapy, American Association of Christian Counselors, licenses, State of Oregon, licensed Marriage and Family Therapist, state of California, licensed Marriage Family Child Counselor; [oth.writ.] Poems written throughout my adult life as mother of five, participant in community affairs, Marriage and Family Therapist, and pastor's wife, song lyrics and writing for church periodicals; [pers.] Most of my poems were written as the result of reflections in-and-about my personal and professional life, with little thought given to publication. They are expressions of my faith and statements of my vision and convictions about the "good life" of faith. [a.] Salem, OR.

ROBERTS, MARGARET (MICKIE) ROWE
[pen.] Mickie Roberts; [b.] January 30, 1927, Clarksburg, WV; [p.] Orion A. and Lottie V. Rowe; [m.] Richard D. Roberts, September 23, 1950; [ch.] None, we love our two puppies, old border terrier Daisy Sue a 12 year old and old border collie Maggie Lou a 3 year old; [ed.] Poca High School, Poca, WV, attended Morris Harvey College, Marshall University and Huntington School of Business; [occ.] Housewife, retired after 37 1/2 years teaching elementary and working in accounting; [memb.] Beverly Hills United Methodist Church, United Methodist Women, Hospice of Huntington, Contact of Huntington Tri-state Literacy Council; [hon.] United Methodist "Teacher of The Year" 1988, Huntington District; [oth.writ.] Only what I have submitted to the National Library of Poetry, I did however, have memorials in the form of verse printed in the Putnam Democrat, Winfield, WV; [pers.] I love God, He is number 1 in my life. I love life and treasure each day. I love people and I love and enjoy working with children. I love

nature, all of God's creation and I love writing about God's great love for all people everywhere. [a.] Huntington, WV.

ROBERTS, NELLIE MINGUS
[b.] August 16, 1921, Kentucky; [p.] James and Fannie Mingus; [m.] James C. Roberts, June 13, 1942; [ch.] Wanda Berlaine, Brenda Carol, Hayward Stewart and Dale Lee; [occ.] Housebound for years; [memb.] None except my name is on the book of life in heaven; [hon.] Four Golden Awards; [oth.writ.] Fourteen poems published in the World of Poetry books and in local newspaper; [pers.] I just want my life to reflect the love of Jesus. Had one of my way is in my gospel poems. [a.] Leitchfield, KY.

ROBERTS, PAUL G.
[pen.] Free Bird; [b.] January 7, 1960, Koblenz, Germany; [p.] Martha and Charles Roberts; [m.] Elizabeth, August 4, 1989; [ch.] Brande Sjasti; [ed.] ASC Degree, general studies Central Texas College; [occ.] Controller Observer Central Americas; [hon.] National Library of Poetry Best Poet; [oth.writ.] Songwriting, "I Know You're Going To Leave Me"; [pers.] "Help those who cannot help themselves. Your own reward will not be measured by material means". [a.[] APO, AA.

ROBINSON, CARMEN MIRANDA
[pen.] Miranda; [b.] September 24, 1950, Albert Lea, MN; [p.] Mr. and Mrs. Pete Miranda; [ch.[Russell; [ed.] Central High School, San Diego City College; [occ.] Tele-operator; [hon.] Two Editor's Choice Awards from the National Library of Poetry; [oth.writ.] Poems published in Whispers In The Wind, At Day's End, and Dusting Off Dreams as well as others; [pers.] Poetry has been my therapy in bad times an expression on how I feel and see the world. [a.] Stoughton, WI.

ROBINSON, VELMA
[pers.] Velma Green Robinson was born in Alabama in 1914, She was a school teacher for many years until her retirement and is an active member of the Baptist Church. The author has been married to James Leroy Robinson since 1934 and they currently reside in Decatur, Alabama. She is a member of NRTA and AARP. She has published various poems in collections such as A View From The Edge by the National Library of Poetry, the American Poetry Anthology and Images. Mrs. Robinson had received the Amherst Society Certificate of Poetic Achievement and a Certificate of Merit from Talent and Associated Companies. In addition, the author has had seven of her songs recorded and three poems on tape, a member of International Society of Poets and Artist, has had a short story in the International Press, published in Best Poets of The 90's and Distinguished Poets of America, National Library of Poetry, American Annual and received Merit of Achievement from Creative Arts and Science.

ROBLES, RENEE TERESA
[pen.] Renee Robles; [b.] May 7, 1979, Oxnard, CA; [p.] Paul and Kathy Robles; [ed.] Blackstock Junior High School, Hueneme High School; [oth.writ.] Poetry, "Feelings", "If Ever", "Love", "Life", "Hatred", "Darkness", "Knowledge", "Always", "Apologies", "Pain", "Lost Friendship", "troubles", "Tears", "Memories", "Changes", "Why", "In Time", "Don't Go" and many more; [pers.] Never be deprived of your soul, for your soul is the one thing that is true and will never deceive you. So believe in yourself, do as you believe and your questions will be answered and your dreams will be fulfilled. [a.] Oxnard, CA.

ROCHELEAU, SABRINA
[b.] May 9, 1976, Wilmington; [p.] Minta W. Stroud; [ed.] High Point Central High School, currently a freshman at North Carolina State University; [occ.] Student; [hon.] National Honor Society, Vocational Honor Society, Beta Club, school, local and regional winner of state writing contest; [oth.writ.] 3 poems published in my high school' s literary magazine, 1 poem published in At Day's End, 1 poem published in After The Storm, 100 poems stored in my computer's memory banks; [pers.] Things that are perceived to be real are real in their consequences. I know longer fear lies, my new enemy hides behind the truth. [a.] High Point, NC.

RODRIGUEZ, OSCAR E.
[b.] December 9, 1938, San Juan, PR; [p.] Oscar Rodriguez and Julia M. Jusimo; [ch.] Albert, Michelle, Omar and Lisa; [ed.] University of Puerto Rico-BA, University of Chicago-MA; [occ.] Professor of English, Humacao University College; [memb.] Modern Language Association; [hon.] Magna Cum Laude, Outstanding Educators of America 1972, The International Poet of Merit Award 1994; [oth.writ.] 34 articles on Human Sexuality, "Secret Love", At Day's End, "A University Theatre", Surco, a magazine of the arts, several newspaper articles; [pers.] Poetry as an existential experience expresses the whole gamut of human thoughts, actions and emotions. [a.] Humacao, PR.

ROGAHN, MICHELLE D.
[b.] October 7, 1956, Abilene, TX; [p.] George and Lenora Cohrac; [m.] Dennis M. Rogahn, October 12,1990; [ch.] Luauna, Nicole and Andrew; [occ.] Own my own housecleaning service "Maids To Perfection"; [memb.] Haven Baptist Church; [hon.] Received an International Poet of Merit Award in 1992, was 1 of the 100 winners in 1992; [oth.writ.] I do occasional poetry writing for our church bulletin, am currently working on a book of poetry entitled "My Thoughts Exactly"; [pers.] My husband is the strongest inspiration I have for my poetry, by allowing me to be and express myself as I am. [a.] Madison, AL.

ROJAS, DAVID
[b.] August 21, 1967, E. Patchogue, NY; [oth.writ.] Personal compilation of short writings entitled "NonAffectatiousments"; [pers.] Outstratizationalizmentation. [a.] Denver, CO.

ROMINE, DEBRA D.
[b.] March 17, 1954, Umatilla, OR; [p.] Evelyn and Howard Addison; [m.] Larry J. Romine, February 14, 1975; [ch.] Kala'tchay and Zachary; [ed.] Continuing and ongoing; [occ.] Homeschooling parent, homemaker, poet; [memb.] Human race, family; [hon.] Editor's Choice, National Library of Poetry, The Coming of Dawn; [oth.writ.] "It Should Take A Least A Week", untitled (thank you thought), both published in National Library of Poetry anthologies, The Coming of Dawn and Desert Sun; [pers.] Please correspond with comments regarding my poetry and others that I might learn and broaden my views. All poetic forms are interesting. [a.] LaGrande, OR.

ROOD, STEVE A.
[b.] August 16, 1943, Hartford, CT; [p.] Betty and J. L. Rush Sr.; [ch.] Shane Rood; [ed.] West Rome High, Floyd College, Berry College; [occ.] Service officer, manager, Georgia Department Veterans Service; [memb.] American Legion, Disabled American Veterans, V.F.W.; [hon.] Leadership Georgia Program; [pers.] I met a woman that made me want to write poetry, November 8. She changed my life. [a.] Rome, GA.

ROSI, MILDRED F.
[pen.] Mildred F. Rosi; [b.] December 27, 1916, New York City; [p.] Anne and Frank Manniello; [m.] James L. Rosi, December 24, 1978; [ch.] 5; [ed.] Academy of St. Vincent, New York University, Coleman College, Traphagen School of Design, Mandle School for Med. Asst.; [occ.] Retired; [memb.] Cert. Medical Assistant AAMA, Arizona State Poets and Writers, Church Choir; [hon.] Won Roosevelt Medal for best poem by a child, was in Bronx Home News, received Bauseh Lomb Medal for medical secretariat, was artist of the month in Pelham, NY for my paintings, I am an artist in oils, starred in many plays for different theaters of our town NY, NJ and Arizona; [oth.writ.] Wrote "Beautiful Hawaii" (just lyrics), Harry Mann wrote music, Lani McIntire featured it in Hotel Lexington's Green Room for 3 years before he died, this was in 1942-43-44, was elected on "Songs For Sale", Jan Murray on 2 songs; [pers.] I am a staunch believer in all the arts, I believe in the beauty of earth that God has created and all His living creatures, both animal and humans. I believe God is our Creator and we all must journey thru life till our turn comes to die. [a.] Chandler, AZ.

ROSS, YVONNE M.
[b.] Paris, France; [p.] Germaine and Roger Merau; [m.] Densil L. Ross, December 15, 1946; [ch.] Bertrand, Suzanne and Roger, grandchildren, John, Danielle, Jan and Erica; [ed.] Ecoledes Filles, Draviel, France, Ecolede Commerce Juvisy, France (2 years), business and languages (Tri-Lang. Secr.) A.S. University of New York, Albany; [occ.] Retired Nurse and Health Information Manager; [memb.] The International Women's Writing Guild, International Poetry Association, National New York and Southeastern HIMA, VVA Chapter 315, V.F.W. Post # 9217, Balle of Normandy Association, Canada-American Association, Clearwater Association, Nature Conservancy Association, Club France; [hon.] I have a few all due to the encouragement of the English Department at Sullivan County Community College, especially Mrs. Cloumnan, Mr. Kantor and Mr. Pizano; [oth.writ.] "The Prisoner" (true story), a children's book (just sent out), a number of poems (French and English) and short story; [pers.] I came to the US as a war bride WWII, 2nd boat March 1946. I love people, their trial and tribulations. I admire the courage and wisdom of everyday ordinary hardworking people wherever I am, at home or traveling abroad. I love the children, the launa, the llora and even stormy weather. I strive to understand this so complex world of ours. [a.] Ferndale, NY.

ROSS JR., VANCE
[b.] April 30, 1950, Baltimore; [p.] Vance and Mary Helen Ross; [m.] Adrienne H. Ross, August 17, 1992; [ch.] Vance Angelo Ross; [ed.] University of Baltimore, Georgia State University; [occ.] Sales

marketing self employed business owner; [oth.writ.] Poem, "God Is Me"; [pers.] I am pursuing a Doctorate Degree in Metaphysical Religious Science. "Love is the thread that connects all beings". [a.] Atlanta, GA.

ROY, GERALDEAN EDNA
[pen.] Geraldean B. Roy; [b.] August 14, 1927, Samsonville, NY; [p.] Otis and Wilma Barringer, 1 of 12 children; [m.] Francis W. Roy, April 20, 1950; [ch.] Cynthia, Steven, Patricia and Henry; [ed.] Ellenville High School, New York 1943, some community college courses, Indian River, Ft. Pierce; [occ.] Retired; [memb.] President-Takewood Park Property Owners Association, Ft. Pierce, FL. 1993-1994, Florida Lakewatch; [hon.] St. Lucie Co. Soroptimist "Woman of The Year" 1984, World of Poetry, Golden Poet 1988, University of Florida's Extension Homemakers' Public Relations, 3rd state 1985, American Legion Auxiliary 1993 and 1994; [oth.writ.] Appreciation for program on American Flags Educational programs, Constitution, Famous American Women, stories about trips through U.S., historical places and scenic place, publications local newspaper, monthly 50 plus, previous poems-National Poetry; [pers.] I like to share my writings on family, God, country and nature. "Work for a better world through faith, love, respect, responsibility, education and dedication". [a.] Ft. Pierce (Lakewood Park), FL.

RUCKER, KAREN L.
[b.] March 22, 1953, Elliott County, KY; [p.] Willis and Mabel Rucker; [ed.] High school graduate-Huntington High School, Chillicothe, Ohio; [occ.] Factory worker, Mead Corp., (Chilpaco Mill); [pers.] I am thankful for the freedom to worship God, our Creator and the privilege of being a citizen of the United States of America. [a.] Chillicothe, OH.

RUNGE, LONI
[b.] Sioux Falls, SD; [p.] Darell and Rico Rungo; [ed.] I am an eight grader at St. Mary's School; [hon.] Champion and reserve champion and several 1st at horse shows around us; [pers.] I get most of my ideas for poems by my surroundings and personal experiences of the world around me. [a.] Hartford, SD.

RUNYON, THEODORE HENRY
[pen.] Ted Runyon; [b.] November 8, 1919, Newark, NJ; [p.] Theodore W.S. and Martha C.; [m.] Mildred Carolyn, May 10, 1946; [ch.] Susan, Ted, Bill and Dan; [ed.] Graduate Brown Military Academy, University of California, Berkley Engineer, George Washington University BS, Foreign Affairs, Southwestern College A.S., Real Estate, graduate Command and Gen. Staff College U.S. Army, graduate Air Command Gen. Staff College USAF, graduate Nato DEF College Paris, graduate National War College Washington,DC; [occ.] Real Estate Broker (the Prudential Cal Reality), and Community Colleges of California instructor; [memb.] The Resurrection Lutheran Church past president, past president U.S. Navy Lg., past president the Retired Officers Association, member R.E. Certificate Inst. California, member California Education Association; [hon.] Legion of merit x 3, Dist. Flying Cross, Air Medal x 7, Purple Heart, Theatre Combat ribbons, Command Pilot, Master Missile Man, First U.S. Commander Atomic, Guided Missile Wing (Matador) in Germany, Europe; [oth.writ.] Real estate columns Coronado Journal, honor thesis National War Coll 1963, "Military in Space Whats To Be Done", poems published in local newspapers; [pers.] Poetry like beautiful music is a touchstone to peace and happiness. [a.] Coronado, CA.

RUPERT, RUTH C.
[b.] September 5, 1926, Oakmont, PA; [p.] Charles C. and Rose M. Rupert; [ed.] 1 thru 12 grades, Oakmont, PA Public Schools; [occ.] Retired from AT&T; [memb.] Life member Telephone Pioneers of America; [hon.] From World of Poetry, award of Merit Certificate 1988, Golden Poet Awards 1988 and 1991, Silver Poet Awards 1989 and 1990. [a.] Oakmont, PA.

RUSH, MICHELE A.
[b.] December 26, 1965, Norristown; [p.] Barbara and Domenic Cemini; [p.] Thomas Rush, February 14, 1987; [ch.] Danielle Nicole, Adam Thomas and Sara Ashley; [ed.] Methacton High School; [hon.] 7th Edition 2000 Notable Woman, 13th Edition of Who's Who In The World; [oth.writ.] "Living With Acholic", "What's Happening To Our Children", "Never Expected You", all published through National Library of Poetry; [pers.] I have found that my mother has influenced the better part of me to her I say thank-you. [a.] Collegeville, PA.

RUSSELL, MARK
[pen.] The Pentecostal Poet; [b.] November 7, 1969, Chicago, IL; [p.] Willie and Blanche; [m.] Nina Marie, July 22, 1991; [ch.] Marquis-3 years, Willie III-2 years; [ed.] College in process, Mesa Community College; [occ.] Protective Service officer, Motorola Security; [memb.] Member of Gethsemane Park Apostolic Church, the Pentecostal Assemblies of the World-P.A.W., P.Y.P.U., Pentecostal Young People's Union; [hon.] To be able to bless other ears with God's magnificent words of communication; [oth.writ.] Write poems for church functions, special occasions, dedications, also write christian songs, trying to get book published; [pers.] Never let your diligence die in your search for life's purpose. [a.] Mesa, AZ.

RUSSELL, RHONDA SAMMONS
[b.] May 19, 1942, Ada, OK; [p.] Dr. J.R. and Vina Sammons; [m.] Joel Reed Russell, April 2, 1989; [ch.] Christopher Russell; [ed.] Northwest Classen High School, University of Oklahoma, Golden Gate Baptist Theological Seminary; [occ.] Piano teacher, Minister of Music, Artistic Director Solano Children's Chorus; [memb.] California Music Teachers Association, Music Teachers National Association, Tau Beta Sigma life member; [hon.] 1st recipient California Singing Churchwoman Scholarship, Outstanding Bandsman-O.U., Arty Award nominee for Musical Director, Dean's List 1984-1985, Who's Who Among American Colleges and Universities 1984-1985; [oth.writ.] Poems, songs and choral compositions, "My Mentor" published 1994; [pers.] I have and will continue to touch many lives through musical performances, but the printed word can last and continue to touch lives long after the writer is gone. [a.] Vacaville, CA.

SACAUSKIS, MARY A. (MRS MICHAEL A.)
[pen.] Mary A.Sacauskis; [b.] July 12, 1925, Willard, WI; [p.] Mr. and Mrs. John Rozich; [m.] Michael A. Sacauskis, August 20, 1960; [ch.] Mary Jo Andreu (Mrs. Bruce Andreu) and Michael J. Sacauskis; [ed.] Finished high school, Art Institute of Chicago (no degree); [occ.] Retired housewife and caretaker of husband who is a victim of Alzheimer Disease and the inspiration of my first published poem in The Desert Sun; [memb.] Sunnyvale Art Club, Santa Clara Water Color Society; [oth.writ.] Various and sundry poetry and Spiritual Meditations, all for personal edification, except for "To My Husband" published in The Desert Sun; [pers.] I thank God for the blessings of creativity and imagination. The world would be a dreary place without these gifts however they are expressed.

SALDANA, AIDA OPHELIA
[b.] April 2, 1946, Mexico City; [p.] Ignacio and Irene Saldana; [ch.] Luis and Perla; [ed.] Bachelor Degree in Fine Arts and Communication at Colombia College; [occ.] Hair designer; [hon.] The National Library of Poetry; [oth.writ.] Short stories; [pers.]] I want to be a citizen of the world and love always. I want to live in harmony with nature, animals and humankind, but most of all I do not want to have dreams, I want to make them come true. [a.] Chicago, IL.

SALYER, SHIRLEY
[b.] January 21, 1940, Scott, CA; [p.] Willard and Lucille Dingus; [m.] Floyd J. Salyer, May 23, 1959; [ch.] Donna Lawson and Veronica Boges; [ed.] High school graduate of Nickelsville Elementary and High School; [occ.] Housewife and farmer; [memb.] Free-will Baptist Church; [hon.] Judge's Editor's Choice Award for poem published in At Day's End; [oth.writ.] "A Daughter's Memory"; [pers.] I feel an excitement of making lines rhyme, especially if they relate to people close home. [a.] Nickelsville, VA.

SAMPLES, MARTHA
[pen.] Martha Samples; [b.] May 21, 1930, Springfield, KY; [p.] Ivan and Effie Boblitt; [m.] Selbert Samples, February 8, 1947; [ch.] Sharon, Gary, Brian and Chris; [ed.] Ahrens Trade High School; [occ.] Housewife; [memb.] Hillsdale Baptist Church and Senior Citizens Association; [oth.writ.] Other inspirational poems; [pers.] I feel that I owe what talent I have to God. [a.] Louisville, KY.

SANTOS, STEVE
[b.] March 27, 1965, Hondo, TX; [p.] Antonio L. Santos and Evangelina M. Guedea; [ed.] Milby High School, International Correspondence School-Locksmith, TV-VCR; [occ.] Locksmith, North Forest Ind School District; [oth.writ.] "A Love So True", " As Rare As A Pearl", other poems which have not been published; [pers.] I praise the Lord that I have been blessed to be able to write down that which is deeply embedded in my heart. [a.] Houston, TX.

SANTOS, THERESA ANN
[pen.] Terry; [b.] November 29, 1972, Hyannis, MA; [p.] JoAnn and Ferdinand F. Santos; [ed.] Dennis Yarmouth Regional High School; [occ.] Clerk; [memb.] Dennis Yarmouth High Chorus, Dennis Yarmouth High School marching and concert band; [hon.] Dennis Yarmouth High Academic All Star team, college scholarship; [oth.writ.] Two poems published by the National Library of Poetry; [pers.] My family will always be special to me. They are my true inspiration. Thank you and never forget that I love all of you more than you'll ever know. [a.] Yarmouthport, MA.

SAWYER, LESLIE I.
[pen.] Leslie Nunamker Sawyer; [b.] November 6, 1959, Portsmouth; [p.] Walter and Ruby Nunamaker; [m.] Divorced; [ch.] Margaret Eloise Sawyer; [ed.] Woodrow Wilson High School; [occ.] Self employed; [hon.] High school journalism, high school talent shows, chorus; [oth.writ.] Music, poem published last year in At Day's End; [pers.] "That's okay". [a.] Portsmouth, VA.

SAWYER, TUNJI
[b.] June 22, 1975, Baltimore, MD; [p.] Samuel and Angela Sawyer; [ed.] Baltimore City College, high school-Baltimore, MD, Morgan State University, sophomore, Baltimore, MD; [occ.] Full time student, assistant to the Director of Student Activities, Morgan State University; [memb.] Sweet Prospect Baptist Church-member, The Sable Quill Literary Journal, Morgan State University; [hon.] The National Dean's List 1993-1994, "Silence" published by the National Library of Poetry; [oth.writ.] "Silence" published by the National Library of Poetry, The Edge of Twilight, "The Season of Matchless Love" a poem of Josephine Baker, "We Real Cool Now" and "Non-smoking Please"; [pers.] Even if you have already seen, love it, hated it, believe in it or lost faith in it, it is still worth writing about. [a.] Baltimore, MD.

SCHEFFER, BETTY JO
[b.] February 20, 1933, Laurel, MA; [m.] Auburn Lee Scheffer, July 18, 1961; [ch.] Peggy Jo Turner, Chester L. Woods, Tamara Tracy and Sandy Monteleone; [ed.] College of The Mainland; [occ.] Retired, Micro-computer Specialist; [memb.] Phi Theta Kappa Alumni Association; [hon.] Phi Theta Kappa; [oth.writ.] Several poems published in college newspaper and in the 1989 American Poetry Anthology; [pers.] Whatever successes I have achieved in life I attribute to the support of my loving husband. [a.] League City, TX.

SCHLEPP, NEIL B.
[pen.] N.B. Schlepp; [b.] March 11, 1958, Bowdle, SD; [p.] Vic and Doris Schlepp; [m.] Bernadette Schlepp, May 19, 1979; [ch.] Luke and Amanda; [ed.] Black Hills State University, Spearfish, SD, Bowdle High School, SD; [occ.] Police officer, Spearfish SD Police Department; [memb.] Fraternal Order of Police, SD Peace Officers, National DARE Officers, SD DARE Officers, Knights of Columbus; [hon.] World of Poetry, Golden Poet Award, Silver Poet Award, Award of Merit, National Library of Poetry Editor's Choice Award 1993 and 1994, "Friend of Education Award" in 1991 and 1994, "Exceptional Duty Award"; [oth.writ.] Poems published in American Anthology of Midwest Poetry, American Poetry Anthology, Poetic Voices of America, Treasured Poems of America, Whispers In The Wind, At Day's End; [pers.] Inspired by the works of Kahlil Gibran and Shakesphere. [a.] Spearfish, SD.

SCHREIBER, LISA
[b.] November 6, 1980, Fredericksburg, VA: [p.] Mr. and Mrs. Kenneth Schreiber; [ed.] Student at Stafford Senior High School, Stafford, VA; [occ.] Student; [oth.writ.] Previous work published in The Space Between; [pers.] I believe that what you have is God's gift to you and what you do with what you have is your gift to God. My poetry is my gift to God. [a.] Falmouth, VA.

SCHROAT, BRYAN ADAM
[b.] March 11, 1969, Encino, CA: [p.] Ronald and Jean Schroat; [hon.] Editor's Choice Award for Outstanding Achievement in poetry, National Library of Poetry 1994, thank you; [oth.writ.] "Just For You", A Far Off Place; [pers.] I am influenced by every person I meet, see or read about. I would like to thank my family, friends, former lovers also God for creating women. [a.] Simi Valley, CA.

SCHULTZ III, GLENN A.
[b.] January 29, 1971, Oroville, CA; [p.] Charlene (deceased) and Glenn Schultz II; [m.] Delphine Schultz, May 7, 1994; [ch.] Expecting; [ed.] High school diploma; [occ.] Mason; [memb.] Active member of the Kingdom Hall of Jehovah's Witnesses; [pers.] I believe that putting at title in my poems limits its interpretation. When people read my work I want them to interpret it according to how it makes them feel. [a.] Valparaiso, IN.

SCHWAB, EMILIA
[b.] January 27, 1974, Edmonds, WA; [p.] Rick Bart and Mayvis Schwab; [ed.] Seattle Central C.C. University of Washington, Hillcrest Lutheran Academy in Fergus Falls, MN; [occ.] Assistant manager of clothing store Clothestime in Seattle, obtaining interior decorating and business degree, I love theater the most at Seattle Central; [oth.writ.] Stocks of unpublished poems that are sacred to my heart; [pers.] I once read that sharing your poetry is like walking naked in the street, then I checked to make sure my clothes were on, but on a stage in a theater it is much harder to strip yourself emotionally with no pen to comfort my body as my only instrument. If I couldn't write, I'd explode. [a.] Bothell, WA.

SCHWAN, DAVE
[pen.] Dave Schwan; [b.] August 22, 1956, East Chicago, IN; [p.] Mr. and Mrs. Paul Schwan; [ed.] B.S. Ball State University, Munice, IN., Highland High School, Highland, IN, 1974; [occ.] Broadcaster, news anchor; [memb.] American Federation of T.V. and Radio Artists/ILL News Broadcasters Association; [oth.writ.] "A Getaway To Keep Going" (novella), various poems, articles; [pers.] I like my writings or poems to bring images or situations into readers' minds. If I stimulate their imaginations, I've succeeded. [a.] Chicago, IL.

SCHWARZ, AMY E.
[b.] August 21, 1968, Janesville, WI; [p.] Alan D. Schwarz; [ch.] Nichole and Elizabeth Schwarz; [a.] Milton, WI.

SCOTT, EDWARD J.
[b.] February 7, 1972, NH; [p.] Mr. and Mrs John J. Scott; [m.] Single; [ed.] High school graduate; [occ.] U.S. Army as a heavy construction equipment mechanic; [memb.] Member of Poets' Guild editor of my company newsletter; [hon.] Editor's Choice Award awarded by the National Library of Poetry in 1994; [oth.writ.] "A Sparrow's Tale" published by Sparrowgrass Poetry Forum, "Strength" also a poem published by the National Library of Poetry, I also still have other poems with certain publishers which have not yet been published; [pers.] I am published but not yet well-known. My next goal is to publish my first book of poems called "101 Treasures Taken From The Heart". It is a collection of 101 poems I have written in the past few years. I would love for the world to be able to share with me what I have shared with the world. [a.] Sanford, ME.

SEDELMAIER, NORMAN W.
[b.] March 26, 1938, Michigan; [p.] Nora Criss and Robert Taylor; [ch.] Lee Ann, Lynn, Rosann, Dylan and Conn; [ed.] Grand Lodge Mi-High, 2 years Lansing Community College, honors student, Dean's List etc.; [occ.] Artist camera person, Millbrook Printing Company; [memb.] None, but I have plans, I paint every week-end when I'm not writing, I wrote my first poem to explain a mural-big mistake (never published); [hon.] Numerous awards all in art (painting) executed a native American mural for Lansing Community College, all in art (visual); [oth.writ.] I am the complete novice, I hated English loved literature, I write poetry nearly everyday now, I think about 70 poems or so this year; [pers.] To resonate the human condition in beauty, clarity and truth (and write half as well as Emily Dickinson). [a.] Grand Lodge, MI.

SEOH, ROY M.
[pen.] Roy M. Seoh; [b.] February 22, 1924, Koje; [ed.] Ph.D. University of Washington; [occ.] Retired (professor); [oth.writ.] Numerous academic papers in English, Japanese, Chinese and Korean on East Asian philosophical thoughts. [a.] Irvine, CA.

SERVICE, REGINA NOELL
[pen.] Reg Noell; [b.] May 24, 1918, Baltimore, MD; [m.] William F. Noell (40 years), December 15, 1934, later married a short time to G. Service (deceased 11 years); [ch.] Joyce, Barbara, Therese, Anne, Tim and Gregory; [ed.] High school, many courses Catonsville Community College and Towson State; [occ.] Costume maker for the Little Theater at Charlestown Clowning All Around, guitarist in band called "Charles Tones"; [memb.] Church Guild, past member of Catonsville Women's Club, past member of St. Mark Mothers Club, retired Ladies Auxiliary of St. Martin; [hon.] Very few, but I'm not finished yet, being honored with a "Geri Award" and Senior Citizen Hall of Fame, October 20, 1994; [oth.writ.] Many writings, poems mostly spiritual, a few children's stories, still in my desk drawer; [pers.] My goal is to make sad people smile... my favorite word is enthusiasm and my desire is to please God. [a.] Baltimore, MD.

SHADEED, JENNIFER
[b.] August 25, 1976, Danbury, CT; [p.] David and Joan Shadeed; [ed.] Port St. Lucie High ; [occ.] Going to college at the University of Central Florida; [oth.writ.] Have poems published in the high school literary magazine, and poems published for the National Library of Poetry. [a.] Port St. Lucie, FL.

SHANNON, NETTA
[b.] September 4, 1943, Anniston, AL; [p.] Harold and Adreene Wainscott; [m.] Charles Shannon, November 28, 1964; [ch.] Tim, Kim and Keith, grandchildren, Dylan, Trevor, Garrett and Hunter; [ed.] Graduate high school, S.R> Butler, Huntsville, AL, college-Murray University, Murray, KY 2 1/2/ years; [occ.] Housewife; [memb.] Wooley Springs Baptist Church; [hon.] Semi-finalist National Library of Poetry contest 1994; [oth.writ.] Poem, "Gift of Love", Library of Poetry in Echoes of Yesterday; [pers.] My goal is to help others face everyday problems and to give encouragement and hope to all who read my writings. I thank God for allowing me to use my talent. [a.] Ardmore, AL.

SHARITZ, JOSEPHINE M.

[pen.] Josephine M. Sharitz; [b.] June 29, 1912, Atlanta, GA; [p.] Deceased; [m.] Lt. Thorold J. Scharitz (April 5, 1932, deceased in World War II, Nunberg, Germany), December 28, 1952; [ch.] Lt. Charles J. Sharitz, Dorothy Sharitz Ward and Josephine; [ed.] Graduated from Florida State University, studied several years at University of Miami and at Barry University in Miami Shores, Florida, took course in History of Chinese Art at Skidmore, also other studies elsewhere; [occ.] Retired Art Consultant from Dade County Schools, Miami, Florida, now a painter; [memb.] In teacher professional organizations in Florida while teaching there; [hon.] People like my poems and paintings, I spend hours on my poetry, it is a part of me also love to paint, has an article and picture in the Miami Herald about my work with children I taught in schools in Dade County, Miami, Florida; [oth.writ.] Three poems published in literary magazine at Florida State University "Talaria" published fall of 1947, Sanquins-Destiny, Silver - Solitude, voted into Vivian Laraimore Rader Poetry Group, Miami, Florida, poem "Remember Me" published in World Anthology of Love Poems" in 1983; [pers.] I love all the arts, enjoy painting and love writing poetry and short stories. I enjoy people and nature. [a.] Atlanta, GA.

SHATOUHY, DAWN LEIGH

[pen.] Dawny Bear; [b.] April 15, 1971, Pennsylvania; [p.] Dr. Joseph and Melody Shatouhy; [occ.] Secretary; [oth.writ.] "I Stand Alone".

SHATTUCK, DANIEL M.

[pen.] Daniel M. Shattuck; [b.] July 15, 1968, Holyoke, MA; [p.] Chester and Jean Shattuck; [m.] Single; [ed.] 1.5 years of college in theatre and communications Holyoke Community College; [occ.] Painting contractor also operator phone company; [memb.] Several environmental groups, humane efforts groups and many animal activist groups, who all serve to better the world we live in; [hon.] American Legion Award 1986, most improved student, certified hockey coach, several entry level management certificates; [oth.writ.] A book of poems, short stories and a manuscript titled "The Ultimate Religion", till in the works at this time; [pers.] Life to me is truly most rewarding when one finds pleasure in the art of giving oneself without the expectations to receive. [a.] East Hampton, MA.

SHEETS, DOROTHY E.

[pen.] Dorothy E. Sheets; [b.] September 13, 1921, Vinton, OH; [p.] Francis and Elizabeth Cardwell; [m.] Deceased, December 14, 1940; [ch.] Donna, Doris and Patricia; [ed.] High school; [occ.] Caregiver for my father who is 94 years old; [memb.] AARP; [oth.writ.] "The Player Plant"; [pers.] This poem is a true story about a little country store. I worked 2 1/2 years at Holzer Medical Center in Pediatrics. [a.] Gallipolis, OH.

SHEPHERD, DELORES A.

[pen.] Delores A. Shepherd; [b.] February 2, 1938, Middletown, OH; [p.] Frank and Martha Berry (both deceased); [m.] Robert B. Shepherd, July 1, 1978; [ch.] Diedri, Jeff, Denise, Bobby, Bernice, Kaye, Barbara, Bill and Shirley; [ed.] Monroe High School, Monroe, OH; [occ.] Homemaker, amateur poet; [oth.writ.] 1 poem previously published by National Library of Poetry, another published by Quill Books, Harlingen, TX, one published in newsletter of Al-Anon; [pers.] Nearly all my poetry is about an experience of my own or someone very close to me. My friends tell me that is when I truly bare my heart. [a.] Tampa, FL.

SHEPHERD, SHARON

[b.] March 13, 1946, Atascadero, CA: [p.] James and Louise McDowell; [ch.] Jeffery Blair; [ed.] Burbank High, California State University at Long Beach, Los Valley College, Orange Coast Community College; [occ.] Starving poet; [oth.writ.] Essays and poems in the Library of Congress incorporated by the defense team in the FCC vs Smothers Brothers/CBS license revocation hearings, one poem published in the anthology Echoes of Yesterday, and incorporated onto an audio-tape; [pers.] As a poet/writer I'm particularly drawn to the "concrete" form, choosing the interplay of words to convey a specific feeling thereby creating a mental flow and hopefully ending in the construction of a visual spatial piece of work, EE Cummings, Jack Kerouac and Leonard Cohen have been extremely influential on me. [a.] Carpinteria, CA.

SHERIFF, REBECCA LINER

[b.] September 25, 1947, Concord, NC; [p.] Paul Liner and Alene Watts; [ed.] BBA Georgia State University, CPA: [occ.] Corporate Controller (CPA) Chase Instruments Corp; [memb.] GSU Alumni, Phi Theta Kappa Alumni, GSCPA's, AICPA, Ousley Methodist; [hon.] Who's Who in Georgia, Who's Who in Executive and Professional Women, Honorable Mention World of Poetry contest; [oth.writ.] "Disappointment", Echoes of Yesterday, "Ode To My Father" poetry in American Heritage. [a.] Decatur, GA.

SHERMAN, ELLEN

[b.]June 12, 1954, Atlantic City, NJ; [p.] Adopted by Helen and Ed; [ch.] Jim and Cassie; [occ.] Freelance writer, journalist; [memb.] International Tesla Society; [hon.] My friends all think I'm a genius; [oth.writ.] Over 100 poems written, numerous published in literary magazines, unsold screenplay, published articles in the Woodstock Times, The Fayette Citizen, currently working on a new screenplay; [pers.] My three poetical influences are Bob Dylan, Paul Simon and Bill Shakespere. [a.] Peachtree City, GA.

SHERWOOD-DANIEL, TERI

[pen.] Teri Sherwood-Daniel; [b.] June 8, 1957, Silver Creek, NY; [m.] Timothy Daniel, June 12, 1982; [ch.] 2 daughters 17 and 14; [ed.] Gowanda Central School, Gowanda, NY, 1976 graduate, 33 credit hours in psychology; [occ.] Self employed writer; [oth.writ.] "The Mystical Clearing" children's books, poetry and song lyrics; [pers.] To the children, savor every moment of time. Always have a dream of the future, for the future will always be ahead of you, waiting with open arms. [a.] Perrysburg, NY.

SHIELDS, SUSAN B.

[b.] September 9, 1947, Spartanburg, SC; [p.] Will H. and Faye Ballenger; [m.] Kenneth, March 27, 1976; [occ.] Furniture sales; [a.] Greenwood, SC.

SHORES, WILLIAM W.

[b.] April 1, 1942, Wetumka, OK; [p.] William A. and Rosebud Shores; [m.] Divorced; [ch.] William Christopher, Melissa Rana, Kathleen Pearlette, Dude Earnest and Shelly Dee; [ed.] Nashoba High School, Oklahoma State "GED"; [occ.] Retired "Sr. Tech" state of Oklahoma employee; [memb.] Church of Christ, life member International Society of Poets, National English Trumpeter Club, National Pigeon Association, Oklahoma Pigeon Association, life member American Quarter Horse Association, life member American Angus Association; [hon.] NPA Master Breeder, NPA All Breed Master Judge, NETC Outstanding Breeder Award, President of NETC, past sectary treasurer of NETC, past Church of Christ song leader; [oth.writ.] I have written several articles over the years in magazines that are published worldwide, such as APJ, Pigeon Review and Clinton Daily News, a local newspaper; [pers.] I take pride in my poetry work, because it comes from my heart. I have never nor will I ever take learning lessons on the proper way to write poetry. I do not like the unreal things of life. [a.] Nashoba, OK.

SIDDEN, PEGGY RUTH CLEMENTS

[pen.] Peggy C. Sidden; [b.] November 1, 1938, Hatch, NM; [p.] Arthur Lee and Corinne Vest Clements; [m.] Bobby Joe Sidden, October 16, 1976; [ch.] None by this marriage, Deborah Romero, Rebekah Calloway, Elizabeth Schoenfelder and Jay Jefferies; [ed.] 2 year college equivalent (secretarial); [occ.] Disabled, retired; [memb.] Tides support group for depressives and manic depressives, member of the Mental health Association Board of Directors, Lena C. Godwin Award for courage, speaker at annual banquet 1994; [hon.] "The Ebb and Flow of Life with Manic Depression" standing ovation, speaker for United Way meetings representing Mental Health Association; [oth.writ.] Numerous newspaper articles, most well known written on manic depressive illness, numerous poems, have written autobiography (unpublished); [pers.] Be creative, God likes talent, too. [a.] King, NC.

SIDES, JAMES G.

[b.] March 2, 1970, Houston, TX; [p.] Jerry and Sylvia Sides; [m.] Heather Lynn Sides, August 7, 1993; [ed.] BBA Marketing/management from the University of Houston; [occ.] Assistant underwriter; [pers.] It is the evil who want to rule the world, the good who want to change it, out but it is the apathetic who destroy it.

SIMM, LINDSAY

[b.] March 26, 1981, Houston, TX; [p.] Susan M. and Archie Simm; [occ.] Intermediate School student; [memb.] Spanish Club, National Junior Honors Society; [hon.] Grade awards, National Junior Honors Society Award, band awards; [oth.writ.] "Barrier" in In The Desert Sun, a short story in Creative Kids magazine; [pers.] I enjoy writing and I write whenever I have free time and I am in the mood. I also enjoy playing my flute and I am in my school's band. [a.] Spring, TX.

SIMMONS, JANICE HALSELL

[pen.] Janice Halsell Simmons; [b.] October 9, 1944, Magnolia, MS; [p.] Lillie James and William Halsell; [m.] McKenzie Simmons, October 19, 1975; [ch.] Timothy, McKinley, Christopher, Nicole, Donese and Terrellesa; [ed.] Eva Gordon High School, Southern University, Straight Business College; [occ.] Retired; [memb.] Cain AME Church, Parents Teacher's Association, Reader's Guild; [hon.] World of Poetry 1985, 88 and 90 Honorable Mentions, World of Poetry Golden Poet Awards, 1985, 1986,

1987, 1988, 1989 and 1990; [oth.writ.] Our World's Most Cherished Poems, John Campbell, publisher, poem-"For The Good Of Mankind"; [pers.] To possess a talent is God's special gift to me. To share that talent is my contribution to mankind. [a.] Bakersfield, CA.

SIMOES, ANTONIO
[b.] February 11, 1940, MA; [p.] Elisa and Antonio; [ch.] Ann, Christine, Jean, Paul; [ed.] EdD Columbia Univ; MA Columbia Univ; BS Boston College; [occ.] Dean - Fairfield Univ - Fairfield, CT; [memb.] NABE/ASCD-AERA; [hon.] Fulbright Phi Delta Kappa; [oth. writ.] 2 books, 25 articles; [pers.] Peace; [a.] Fairfield, CT

SIMPSON, JAMIE
[pen.] Jamie Simpson; [b.] October 12, 1974, Haverhill, MA; [p.] Karen and Gary Simpson; [ed.] Coe-Brown Northwood Academy; [occ.] Stockperson, Wal-Mart, Portsmouth, NH; [hon.] Graduation with honors; [pers.] Writing is my outlet. In the words I write I can be open and honest about everything without fear of being judged. It is in my writing where I can be myself. [a.] Barrington, NH.

SLINEY, THOMAS
[pen.] Tom Slayer; [b.] July 17, 1973; [m.] Not married; [pers.] Life is a long process which must be endured. Never think that you are alone because whether you know it or not there is always someone who watches over you. Don't give up. [a.] Bronx, NY.

SLOAN, BERNICE
[b.] November 25, 1941, SC; [p.] Granville and Bertha Buchanan; [m.] David Sloan, August 3, 1957; [ch.] Eddie Sloan and Barbara Harvell; [occ.] Lab technician, Milliken Company; [memb.] Faith Independent Baptist Church, Junior High Girls Sunday School Class Teacher; [pers.] I trust that my poetry gives hope to the hopeless and encourages the downhearted and lets them know that there is someone who cares for them. [a.] Marietta, SC.

SMELTZER, SUSAN
[b.] September 13, 1941, Sapulpa, OK; [p.] Mr. and Mrs. F.C. Smeltzer; [m.] Dr. Philip S. Snyder, July 14, 1973, [ed.] Tulsa University (Tulsa, OK), Sapulpa High School (Sapulpa, OK), Western State College (Gunnison, CO), Oklahoma City University (Oklahoma City, OK), University of Southern California (Los Angeles, CA), Akademie For Musik (Vienna, Austria); [occ.] Professional pianist, teacher, organist; [memb.] Tuesday Musical Club, National Guild of Piano Teachers, Sigma Alpha Iota; [hon.] Winner of over 21 competitions as a pianist, over 50 poems, poetry, booklet, Fulbright Grant to Vienna, Austria, have reviews in the New York Times and other New York magazines for Carnegie Recital Hall debut, Brahms-Saal, debut (Vienna, Austria) highly successful, over 47 honors and awards in the U.S. and Europe; [oth.writ.] (Pianist, strings, composition, poetry and art) set a world record, peace efforts, poetry booklet, "Selected Orchestrations of Poetic Expressions" contributions to numerous magazines and books; [pers.] It is my hope that my creative efforts will be an inspiration for peace. My insight was influenced especially by romanticism in music, lyrical poets and humanity. [a.] Houston, TX.

SMITH, ANDREA M.
[b.] May 7, 1979, Kentucky; [p.] William and Jana Smith; [ed.] Collins Lane Elementary, Bondurant Middle School, Western Hills High School; [occ.] Sophomore in high school; [memb.] National Beta Club currently in Drama Club, SADD (Student Against Drunk Driving), and TLC at my high school; [hon.] Straight A's and B's, National Merit Awards in math and science; [pers.] I absolutely love writing poetry. It's a great way of expressing how you feel about anything in life. [a.] Frankfort, KY.

SMITH, CORNELIA
[b.] February 3, 1974, Washington, DC; [p.] Stuart and Editha Smith; [ed.] University of Maryland; [occ.] Student of psychology; [oth.writ.] 60 other poems, one published i Potomac Review and others in the process of being published; [pers.] As long as you harm none, do what you want-Wiccan Reed. [a.] Potomac, MD.

SMITH, DORIS WILMA DUNN
[b.] August 21, 1933, Greensboro, NC; [p.] David Harry and Wilma Kerns Dunn; [m.] Ralph Ray Smith, June 1, 1957; [ch.] A. Glenn Smith, Harriet L. Smith Berenbrock, Marcus R. Smith; [ed.] BS Flora MacDonald College-1955, MAT, University of California-Irvine 1973, Ph.D., University of California-BH 1980; [occ.] Mathematics' instructor, Long Beach Unified Schools; [memb.] NEA, CTA, TALB, NCTA, GSA, IWWG, Toastmasters International, AAUW, NAFE, Covenant Pres. Church and the Hummel Collectors Club; [hon.] EI Dupont de Nemours Fellowship, Personalities of America, W/W American Women, W/W in the West, Five Thousand Personalities of the World; [oth.writ.] Several poems published together with my books, A Limb of Your Tree and Science, Math and You; [pers.] Poetry is the vehicle I have found to truly get my inner most thoughts on paper. [a.] Anaheim, CA.

SMTIH, ETTA JEAN
[pen.] E. J. Smith; [b.] February 3, 1946, Rockwood, TN; [ed.] B.S. Liberal studies; [occ.] Systems Analyst; [hon.] Phi Kappa Phi, Thomas Burnett Swan Poetry Award 1991; [oth.writ.] Poems published in local newspaper, Revelry '91, Edge Of Twilight, Poetic Voices of America, self published "Poems From A Mid-Life Crisis"; [pers.] I write what I feel so that others will know they are not alone. [a.] Orlando, FL.

SMITH, FREN GARDINER
[pen.] Fern Gardiner Smith; [b.] April 13, 1931, Sparta, IL; [p.] Otis and Elsie Gardiner; [m.] Francis I.G. Smith, November 30, 1991; [ch.] 4 children, 9 grandchildren and 2 great granddaughters; [ed.] High school graduate with some college courses; [occ.] Disabled, retirement; [memb.] Fairview Baptist Church, Rebekkahs-Monday Club and SenioR Citizen Club; [hon.] Starting Honorable Mentions, 1989 thru 1992 Golden Poet Awards, won spelling bee contest to go to state, won blue ribbon at local fair and second at another showing for oil paintings, started painting in 1992; [oth.writ.] "Respect For My Parents", "Life Eternal", "My Vision", "Bless, Praise and Glory", "Be Faithful", "Nevertire", "My Blueprint"; [pers.] Ancestor wrote poetry-Julia Gardiner Tyler for her husband President Tyler. My favorite scripture "I can do all things through Christ which strengtheneth me". Phil. 4:13. [a.] Tilden, IL.

SMITH, HERBERT H.
[pen.] Herbert H. Smith; [b.] February 15, 1928, Letcher Co., KY; [p.] Hewey and Leona Smith; [m.] Florence Ison Smith, February 5, 1949; [ch.] 8 children, 17 grandchildren; [ed.] 2 years high school; [occ.] Retired coal miner; [memb.] Masonic Lodge, April 21, 1950, Shriner's September 18, 1965; [oth.writ.] Several other poems. [a.] Whitesburg, KY.

SMITH, JESSICA S. E.
[pers.] For Cathy, my sun, my shadow. My confidence, my poetry. My hero, my best friend.

SMITH, LORENA A.
[pen.] Lorena Smith; [b.] January 29, 1955, York, PA; [p.] Donald Niel and Dorothy Louise Lloyd; [ed.] Hialeah High class of 1972, Hialeah Miami Lakes night school; [occ.] Retail, floor supervisor; [hon.] Editor's Choice Award for "The Lord Be With You", National Library of Poetry 1993; [oth.writ.] "My Prayer" published in anthology titled In The Desert Sun 1994; [pers.] This poem is in memory of my brother who was killed in Vietnam. If you believe in "peace" and practice "peace" there will be no need for "war". [a.] Hialeah, FL.

SMITH, MELANIE JANE
[b.] January 5, 1959, Louisville, KY; [p.] Harold and Elizabeth Smith; [ed.] Linden Hall School, Lititz, PA; [occ.] Volunteer Christian Health Center; [memb.] Our Savior Lutheran Church.

SMITH, SANDRA R.
[b.] November 29, 1941, Salisbury, MD; [ed.] Associate in Science (Northern Virginia Community College), Institute of Children's Literature (Conn); [occ.] Electric power industry specialist (Federal Government); [memb.] Society of Literary Friends, Ashton, MD, American Legion; [oth.writ.] "Never Knowing" in A Far Off Place, National Library of Poetry; [pers.] i seek to evoke a shared remembrance with my writing. [a.] Silver Spring, MD.

SNYDER, JEANNE M.
[b.] February 7, 1959, Elmhurst, IL; [p.] Kenneth and Mercedes Snyder; [ed.] High school graduate, some college, Bilingual in Spanish and English, always learning; [occ.] Jacklynne of many trades; [hon.] Golden Poet Awards for 1986, 1987, 1988, 1989, 1990, 1992 with World of Poetry, 15 Merit Awards, conversion of poem "This Void" into song on record album called "Hallelluah" through Rainbow Records Company, Honorary Charter membership for 1993 Outstanding Achievement in poetry, International Society of Poets, Editor's Choice Award by National Library of Poetry, 1993, inclusion in World of Poetry's Who's Who In Poetry, volume II and III, included in book A View From The Edge with the National Library of Poetry, in Outstanding Poets of 1994; [pers.] There is no wealth more precious than health. Your harvest is ready in due season. Everything good for all as in love, is truly possible. [a.] Campbell, CA.

SORGE, MAXINE K.
[pen.] Max or Maxi; [b.] Altoona, PA; [p.] Allen and Elsie M. Kennedy; [m.] Roland H. Sorge (deceased), April 6, 1947; [ch.] Alan Paul (39 years), Lynn Wayne (10 1/2 years), Gary Lee (34 years) all deceased, Tammy Dawn; [ed.] High school; [memb.] ASA 80's Photography Club, Alto Art Guild; [hon.]

Numerous awards in art and photography including 1985 Photographer of the Year, had a painting take 1st place in the state May of 1993, same painting published in North Light magazine spring of 1994; [oth.writ.] Approximately 117 poems, 3 short stories and 1 song, poem "Ode To A Library" published in National Library of Poetry's 1994 anthology At Day's End, Editorial on Abortion published in local newspaper; [pers.] Life is such a challenge! Each day is like a blank sheet of paper. I alone determine the outcome. With my beautiful daughter,my terrific son-in-law and the memories of my 3 sons, how can I not write? [a.] Altoona, PA.

SORIA JR., ANTONIO
[pen.] Northside Poet; [b.] September 10, 1974, Houston, TX; [p.] Antonio and Maria Soria; [ed.] A graduate from Sam Houston High School; [occ.] College; [memb.] Thanks to those true friends for being there, love you. Follow me to somewhere else, where all the eyes are closed, where the pen in hand represents so much strength; [hon.] Poetry Best Writer's Award 1994, I remember winning the quietness of a crowd in a school talent show, I would give up my life to reach an emotion that would inspire me to write a great poem; [oth.writ.] "Lonely Days" was published and I have about 1,000 more and wish to get some of those published; [pers.] Mom I'm taking the whole Northside for a ride on these little shoulders. Only Galveston realizes my greatness, for when I'm in her under tow always wants to take me to her heart. I'll see you at the waves. [a.] Houston, TX.

SORENSEN, LISA RENEE
[b.] November 25, 1980, San Jose, CA; [p.] Martha and Eric Sorensen; [ed.] Centennial Middle School, 4.0 average, plan to go to Colorado University, triple major; [occ.] Babysitting and odd jobs; [memb.] Student Council at Centennial Middle School, soccer player, drama performer; [hon.] Honor Roll, Principle's Honor Roll, President Academic Fitness Award, sports awards; [oth.writ.] Many other poems and stories for mostly school, 3 poems for National Library of Poetry; [pers.] "Life can be taken away just as quickly as it was given, so use it wisely". [a.] Boulder, CO.

SOWERS, JOSEPH W.
[b.] August 30,1974, Boynton Beach, FL; [p.] William and Diana Sowers; [ed.] Atlanta High School, Florida Atlantic University; [occ.] College student; [oth.writ.] Many personal poems and writings; [pers.] Searching for fulfillment in and of ourselves is to put on a ludicrous and empty show. Put aside your fears, anxieties and worldly doubts. Open the essential Book-the Bible. Open your heart and your mind. I challenge that those who don't believe the Bible have never opened their hearts, opened their minds and read it. [a.] Delray Beach, FL.

SPENCER, GRACE M.
[b.] February 3, 1898, Cuba, MO; [p.] Mrs. and Mr. W. F. Mitchell; [m.] William F. Spencer, November 9, 1949; [ed.] Two years college, first 20 years was cosmetic buyer at Stix Baer and Fuller, St,Louis, MO; [occ.] Retired, was lingerie buyer, large department store for 25 years.

SPIKER, T. D.
[b.] November 12, 1970, Martinsburg, WV; [ed.] Berkeley Springs (WV) High School, Shepherd College; [memb.] Shepherd College Alumni Association; [hon.] Catherine C. Fix essay contest-1990, Dean's List-1993, the National Dean's List 1989-91, Cum Laude" college graduate 1993, North American Open poetry contest, semi finalist 1993, Who's Who Among American High School Students 1987-89; [oth.writ.] Various work in West Virginia Senior High magazine-1989, Bohemian Bridge magazine 1993-94, Whisper In The Wind 1993; [pers.] "Logic" wouldn't be a word if we all possessed it. [a.] Hedgesville, WV.

SPRAGUE, PAMELA M.
[b.] March 24, 1960, Pittsfield, MA: [p.] Francis Sprague and Barbara Dowsey; [ed.] Gateway Regional High School; [occ.] Volunteer work at a Rape Crisis Center in area and a visiting friend to an elder person; [hon.] 3 Silver Poet Awards out of California; [oth.writ.] I have a total of 167 poems as of September 1994, I also have a few children's stories, I am currently working on a children's book, it is a bout a little boy and his imaginary friend, who is a pumpkin; [pers.] I started writing at the age of ten. Was pretty much a loner back then, but my words expressed all that I was feeling. Strangely enough Elvis Presley was my inspiration on a lot of them. I would usually be listening to his music when a poem would come to mind. Someday soon all read them and fall in love too. [a.] Lee, MA.

SPROUSE, MILDRED C.
[b.] April 11, 1910, Carrollton, MO; [p.] William and Sarah J. Harden; [m.] Charles Robert Sprouse, December 6, 1941; [ch.] C. Jane Sprouse; [ed.] High school, business college; [memb.] Professional Writers League of Long Beach, Women's Club of Seal Beach, Creative Writing Chairman of above, Methodist Church, 50 year membership Girl Scouts; [hon.] Seal Beach Woman of the Year 1987, ten years junior coordinator; [oth.writ.] Published a book of poetry 1983. [a.] Seal Beach, CA.

SQUIRES, EDWARD L.
[b.] August 19, 1955, Los Angeles, CA; [p.] Janice Juckel; ed.] U.C.L.A., B.A. Psychology and teaching credential; [occ.] Elementary teacher; [memb.] Agouva Hills Spectrum Club; [hon.] Published poet, (1994) At Day's End, National Library of Poetry, Dean's List, UCLA; [pers.] A global awakening to the clear and present dangers confronting our planet must transcend our egocentrism if we are to live in harmony with nature.

STAFFORD, LAURA
[pen.] Smiley or Rixie; [b.] December 29, Bayside; [p.] William Wesley Rix; [m.] Jessie Irene MacArthur; [ch.] Iris, Joyce, Erma, Allison and Brenda; [ed.] Business, art, musician, volunteer, homemaker; [occ.] I paint, taught art at schools also privately; [memb.] M.S. Society and Hospice Cancer volunteer, A.C.W. Church Women, 6 years on Diosces A.N. Board, member or Womens Institute; [hon.] 2 certificates as a Golden Poet, certificate and pins for teaching art and playing music; [oth.writ.] Many poems in West Prince Arts Council, also short story about a dog we owned, published in anthologies; [pers.] I believe in leaving something behind so that others will remember you, and some poetry can change your whole life and way of thinking. [a.] Summerside P.E.I., Canada.

STAMATIOU, KIKI
[pen.] Kyriakh; [b.] July 4, 1969, Kalamazoo, MI; [p.] Toula and Odysseus Stamatiou; [ed.] Mattawan High School, Mattawan, MI, high school diploma conferred June 1988, KVCC, Kalamazoo, MI, Associate Degree of Arts conferred August 1990, Western Michigan University, Kalamazoo, MI, Bachelor's Degree of Arts conferred August 1992; [occ.] Writer, I also adapt novels into screenplays; [memb.[Songwriter's Club of America, National Authors Registry, International Society of Poets, International Society of Authors and Artist, National Poetry Association, Kalamazoo County Historical Society, Michigan Historical Society; [hon.] Recognition award for making top 1% and Editor's Preference of Excellence Award by Creative Arts and Science Enterprises, Poet of Merit Award August 1994 from International Society of Poets, poem "Glimmer" and "Drug" were rated outstanding by Poetry International; [oth.writ.] Poem "Ode To The Ancient One" appears in anthology The Space Between, Summer 1994 edition, published by National Library of Poetry, 3 poems appear in anthology Somewhere Between Night and Day, Fall 1994 edition, published by Twilight Press, poem "Conualece" will appear in anthology After The Storm, Summer 1995 edition, by National Library of Poetry; [pers.] Soft milky feathers from a pristine dove lie frozen against serenaded chords and electric chills run down marshy spines, there he goes down yesterday's river filled with candy gems. There he races to find his luscious pot of gold. [a.] Kalamazoo, MI.

STAMATOVIC, VUKICA (VICKY)
[b.] June 10, 1975, New Jersey; [p.] Julka Stamatovic; [ed.] Grover Cleveland High School; [occ.] Secretary Dr. Dana Jackola, Ridgewood, NY; [pers.] My mother was a great influence on my poetry, she taught me to always write what I feel and love. [a.] Ridgewood, NY.

STANFORD-COX, MARLENE
[pen.] Marlene Sanford-Cox; [p.] Robert and Selma Stanford; [m.] Jack Benjamin Cox, August 4, 1957; [ch.] Teresa, Daniel, Roxanne, Susan and Anne Marie; [ed.] BFA, Art History and painting; [occ.] Visual Artist-watercolor; [memb.] Crosslake Art Club, Duluth Art Institute, Nisswa Women's Club; [hon.] Grant to teach, acceptance of art into jured shows, mentor grant (45 years ago), 1st place poster contest American Legion, Editor's Choice Award, National Library of Poetry, In The Desert Sun 1994; [oth.writ.] Short stories, poetry, research papers in art and art history; [pers.] I look for parallels in design concepts used in pottery, weaving and borders by native Americans. All designs come from nature and are similar in pre-historic cultures that were separated by thousands of miles. I believe that there is a common thread that weaves its way through all cultures and somehow ties us all together. In researching these early designs, the most compelling thought was that the artists who made them were keepers of the land. They had high regard and great reverence for all of nature and the earth. In some small way, I am attempting to bring awareness and appreciation to these people who came before us. We can learn from their ways of harmony with the earth. [a.] Nisswa, MN.

STANLEY, MYRTLE CRAIG
[b.] October 10, 1908, Clinton, TN; [p.] George and Mary Ellis Craig; [m.] The late Gordon M. Stanley, November 18, 1949; [ed.] Graduated Powell High School, attended University of Tennessee; [occ.]

Retired; [memb.] Former member Delta Kappa Gamma; [hon.] I have taught Sunday School classes in the Baptist Church, I have spoken to small groups in the Presbyterian Church; [oth.writ.] A few short stories and letters to the Editors on current issues, I have some booklets for children but none have been published; [pers.] "Give to the world the best that you have and the best will come back to you".

STANS, ROSARIA ANGELA
[pen.] Sarina Sue Stans; [b.] April 26, 1915, East, NY; [p.] John and Mary Luciano; [m.] Louis Stans, deceased, July 17, 1944; [ch.] Maria Hunt and Louis J. Stans; [ed.] 3 years Girl Commercial High, 6 months Hefley's Business School; [occ.] Retired; [hon.] World of Poetry (Eddie Lou Cole); [oth.writ.] "In Gratitude" and others not published; [pers.] My 7th grade teacher told me to keep writing, so I have. [a.] Sacramento, CA.

STARK, JIMMIE A.
[b.] December 28, 1959, Neodesha, KS; [p.] Leslie E. and Addie M. Stark; [m.] Kathleen Siobhan (Tobin) Stark, October 31, 1991; [ed.] Evie (KS) High School, Pittsburgh State University, U.S. Army Military Police School; [occ.] Corrections officer; [memb.] Kansas Association of Public Employees; [hon.] Honorable discharge U.S. Armed Forces; [oth.writ.} Various professional and union related material, published poetry National Library of Poetry publication Edge of Twilight; [pers.] Mankind is constantly questing for meaning among the great and the awesome. Rather they should seek the Divinity among the commonplace and the mundane. There they will find the fingerprint of God. [a.] Hutchinson, KS.

STEELE, TRACY
[b.] June 18, 1976, Pensacola; [memb.] Mural Club in West Columbia High School, Art Society at North Augusta High School, Film Society (homemade organization of several friend in Columbia); [hon.] 2nd place in S.C. State Fair, 3 dimensional art, 2nd place in an archery tournament in Thompson, GA: [oth.writ.] Myself and 3 other students wrote, directed, produced and acted in a school play called "Another Way Out" '91-'92, a large volume of unpublished poems; [pers.] My writings generally reflects my life style at the time it is written, there fore I can hardly dislike any of them, all of them being a part of my life and view of life. [a.] N. Augusta, SC.

STEEVES, BETTY
[pen.] Nana; [b.] July 13, 1937, Johnson City, TN; [m.] Divorced; [ch.] Stanley Clinton and Robert Pierino; [ed.] Mt. Vernon High, currently enrolled in The Institute of Children's Literature; [occ.] Town clerk, Shenandoah, VA; [oth.writ.] One poem published in Echoes of Yesterday, one poem to be published in The Best Poems of 1995, various poems unpublished; [pers.] If I can help just one person through my writing, I will die a happy woman. [a.] Shenandoah, VA.

STEVENS, LAURIE
[pen.] Baby Marx; [b.] December 11, 1961, Boothbay Harbor; [p.] Charles and Priscilla Stevens; [m.] Richard Marx, February 14, 1992; [ch.] Chrudel, Amy, Michael, Meagan, Janie, Emily, Nia and Vina; [ed.] Grades 1-12, 5 years college, 5 years correspondence school, 2 years NRI, 3 years NACSS; [occ.] Travel consultant; [memb.] Arts Council Cooperation, United States Humane Society; [hon.] National Honor Society, graduated from NRI with high honors; [oth.writ.] "Believe In You", "You"; [pers.] Be who you are, don't try to be someone else. [a.] Boothbay Region, ME.

STEVENSON, DONALD R.
[pen.] Steven Dray; [b.] April 19, 1916, East Walden, NY; [p.] Ohin Stevenson and Phoebe Ward; [m.] Aleath Lindsay Baird-deceased, May 27, 1945; [ch.[Michael Ward Stevenson; [ed.] High school, writing course; [occ.] Retired, was warehouseman, later salesman for company; [hon.] 4 Golden Poet Awards from World of Poetry; [oth.writ.] Autobiography for writing course; [pers.] Am 78, seen many facets of life, never in service, could not pass physical, never knew a father's love. Mother died 1920 of TB, I find poetry to be second to music as a universal language. [a.] Williston, FL.

STEVENSON, JACK
[pen.] O. Shaw-Christian Fellows; [b.] December 5, 1921, Titusville, PA; [p.] Maurice D. and Esther E. Stevenson; [m.] Irene I. (April 28, 1942), December 6, 1942 (first marriage -wife deceased); [ch.] James and Anita Kaye (first marriage), Bonnie, Dale and Jay (2nd marriage), Jeffery Dean-passed away at 10 months (Cerebral Palsy); [ed.] High school, post grad (in 2 schools), trade school, turned down scholarship to Ryder College for lack of funds; [occ.[Maintenance Department at Ell-Con National Co.; [memb.] Church of God, AARP, National Committee to Preserve S.S. and Medicare; [hon.] Merit Awards from World of Poetry and National Library of Poetry; [oth.writ.] Novel (fiction) title "Ken and Ben-Not What You'd Think", short stories and anecdotes, over 100 poems; [pers.] May what flows from my pen depict the grace of God and my life reflect His glory; [a.] Greenville, SC.

STEVERSON, VEROCGA
[pen.] Verocga; [b.] December 6, 1976, Fort Belvoir, VA; [p.] Verocga Steverson; [occ.] Student at Virginia Polytechnic University; [memb.] National Honor Society, TC Channel 49 Club, basketball, softball, volleyball, bowling; [hon.] National Honor Society, 4 year scholarship to Virginia Tech.

STEWART, BRYANT DRAYTON
[b.] December 30,1915, South Orange, NJ; [p.} Stewart F. and Valeda Johnson Bryant; [m.] Matiko Iio Bryant, August 15, 1981; [ch.} David, Kendall, Burgess (2nd marriage), Nina, Tanya and Marina (1st marriage); [ed.] Deep Springs College, California 1932-34, Stanford University, California 1936, BA, Columbia University, New York 1938 MA; [occ.] Consultant on Planning and Housing Community Development; [memb.] National Association of Housing, Sorra Club, local and state officer National Duties, Philadelphia Rehabilitation Plan, Corporation Sec.,; [hon.] Phi Beta Kappa 1936, Magna Cum Lauda, Stanford 1936, poetry prize, Stanford 1936, in school's oratorical contests,League of Nations National essay contests; [oth.writ.] Magazine, newspapers, policies and programs on community development of many aspects, especially in housing, poetry positive since 11 years of age; [pers.] The future of the human race depends on rapid improvements in awareness of realistic, dangers, destructiveness of all people and expansion of success of positive in communities and cultures. [a.] Philadelphia, PA.

STODDARD, JAMES A.
[pen.] Jim, Jimmy; [b.] January 28, 1922, Nyack, NY; [p.] Jason E. Stoddard and Alice S.S.; [m.] Margaret M. Stoddard, August 26, 1947; [ch.] Alice M. Stoddard (RN), Carey J., David A., Robert E. Stoddard, PA-C; [ed.] High school, college, B.A. 1 year toward MA., US Army training, Europe WWII, Spanish Language Institute, Boy Scouts of America training, 12 years Scoutmaster; [occ.] Active retirement from Missionary work in Guatemala, CA. supt. building and grounds, Huehue Academy one activity of many, 38 years; [memb.] The American Legion, Smithsonian Institute, National Rife Association of America, Poetry CLub, BMV, Bradenton; [hon.] Various US Army Medals WWII, 50th year-Normandy Campaign Medal, the Gold Jubilee of Operation OverLord Medal; [oth.writ.] Many other poems written over the years; [pers.] During my trips to Africa, Europe, Central and South America and throughout the USA, I've seen many "Patches" of all kinds of things. All is beautiful ... thus the short poem on a "Patch of Country". I have 21 plus books of poems such as Browning, Mr. and Mrs, Bryon Tennyson,Wordsworth, etc. I love poetry, I like to write poems. [a.] Bradenton, FL.

STONE, KATRINE F.
[b.] September 22, 1911, Minneapolis, MN; [p.] Mr. and Mrs. Henry N. Stone; [ed.] College trained Army Nurse; [occ.] Retired Army Nurse; [memb.] Retired Army Nurse Corp. Association, retired Army Officer Association, International Society of Poets, Women in Military Service for America; [hon.] Army commendation ribbon, World War II Campaign Ribbons, numerous awards from International Society of Poets 1989, 1990, 1991; [oth.writ.] Book of poems published 1946 (September Interlude); [pers.] Poetry comes from the heart of man and the soul of God. [a.] Thomson, GA.

STONE, PHYLLIS FAIRCLOTH
[b.] February 26, 1931, Onaway, MI; [p.] Ernest E. (former state representative) and Edna Eldridge Faircloth; [m.] Jerry M. Stone, 1950; [ch.] Jalon, Kim, Jerry, Manley II, grandchildren, Jeffrey Neuman, April and Shawn Wagner; [ed.] Onaway High School, B.S.-Eastern Michigan University, M.A.-Western Michigan University; [occ.] Public school instructor of English, Literature, music and reading (35 years) now retired; [memb.] Student Council-high school, Retired Teacher's Association, International Society of Poets; [hon.,] Music award-high school, Editor's Choice Award, National Library of Poetry; [oth.writ.] Copyrights to 26 songs, 100 poems; [pers.] Poetry is the expression of the soul of a free nation. I am deeply grateful to be able to contribute to the soul of America. [a.] Onaway, MI.

STONE, SANDRA WALLRAVEN
[pen.] Sandra Wallraven Stone; [b.] June 17, 1939, Springer, Ok; [p.] Homer Elps and Hortense Culpepper Wallraven; [m.] Leo Aldon Stone (2nd), June 2, 1962; [ch.] Lisa Sherilyn Talley, Roland Aldon Stone, Tony Ray Willson and Danny Lee Stone; [ed.] Lee Elementary, Oklahoma City, Capitol Hill Junior and Senior High, Oklahoma City, Amarillo College, Amarillo, Texas, life itself; [occ.] Housewife and curatorial volunteer (Reno County Museum); [memb.] Democratic Party, Reno County (KS) Historical Society, Partridge (KS) Community Church; [hon.] 2

Editor's Choice Awards, National Library of Poetry, 5 Honorable Mentions (2 for same poem), World of Poetry; [oth.writ.] "Dear Washington D.C.", "Amarillo (TX) Advocate" 1972, Through The Past V.A. postcards, Reno County Historical Society "Legacy", poem in Poems That Will Live Forever, Whispers In The Wind and The Space Between, columns in newspaper supplement "Neighbors" (The Hutchinson News), and books of poems, books of short stories and Science Fiction, novels given to family and friends; [pers.] Everything in nature serves a purpose, nothing is wasted in the long run. People are the same even if all you can do is smile and give encouragement, you are important and must feel good about your place in the pattern. [a.] Hutchinson, KS.

STOUFFER, DARLA JEAN

[b.] April 14, 1972, Latrobe, PA; [p.] Louis and Judith Pasquale (deceased); [m.] Larry Stouffer, June 24, 1989; [ch.] Brittany Alexis and Katelyn Marie; [ed.] Greater Latrobe Area High School; [memb.] National Honor Society, Vision Committee Care Teams; [hon.] National Honor Society; [oth.writ.] Several unsubmitted poems, songs and children's books, a poem entitled "Love Is Not Perfect" in Echoes of Yesterday; [pers.] I write what comes from within. All of my work is based on life experiences as seen through my eyes. [a.] Derry, PA.

STOUT, VIOLET DARLENE

[pen.] Violet D. Stout; [b.] January 16, 1934, Old County Jail, Susanville, CA; [p.] Violet L. Ellsworth and Lawrence M. Wood; [ch.] Deborah L., Rozlah M., Wade P., Terri E., Monte C. and Karen L. (twins), Teresa R. and Jody D.; [ed.] Lassen Union High School graduate 1952; [occ.] Advocate, poet; [hon.] Who's Who in Poetry 1986, Poet Laureate of Lassen County from 1991 till present, Golden Poet Award August 24, 1985, public (open house) birthday party (60 years), 2 namesakes; [oth.writ.] Several publishings in World of Poetry Press, American Poetry Association, Great Lakes Poetry Press, Lassen County Times, Lassen Advocate; [pers.] "One may gain knowledge readily, but must have wisdom to disperse it". [a.] Susanvill, CA.

STRADER, LORI JEAN

[b.] August 24, 1977, Gulfport; [p.] Christine and Eugene Strader; [ed.] Gulfport High School, senior year incomplete; [occ.] Student; [oth.writ.] Several recreational works not yet published; [pers.] I don't write to be recognized, I write to express my thoughts more clearly to myself and others, nothing more. [a.] Gulfport, MS.

STRICKLAND, CHARLES

[pen.] Shawn Wesley; [b.] March 9, 1951, Columbus, OH; [p.] Charles and Cleo Strickland; [m.] Patricia Strickland, October 29, 1976; [ch.] Monica Strickland; [ed.] Centerburg High School, Devry Institute of Technology; [occ.] Computer programer; [hon.] National Honor Society, Centerburg High School, Presidential Honor Society, Devry Institute of Technology; [oth.writ.] Several poems to be published in "Today Great Poem", by the Famous Poets Society of Hollywood, California, one poem to be published in Echoes of Yesterday; [pers.] I love writing poetry. [a.] Centerbury, OH.

STRICKLAND, ETTA JERNIGAN

[b.] December 7, 1915, Johnston County, Dunn, NC; [p.] Millard and Arrel Barefoot Jernigan; [m.] Charles Allen Strickland, November 19, 1933; [ch.] Delilah B. and Jacquelyn Strickland; [ed.] Meadow High School, selected college courses; [occ.] Retired; [memb.] Order of the Eastern Star, Sardis Presbyterian Church, Elder and Clerk of the Session; [hon.] Several trophies and plaques in church and poetry works; [oth.writ.] Poems published in several anthology books, church newsletters, public readings; [pers.] I endeavor to write poems with Christian influence and poems that are morally uplifting. [a.] Linden, NC.

STRICKLAND, MARJORIE H.

[pen.] Marj Strickland, Marjorie Lund; [b.] December 12,1 926, Eagar, AZ; [p.] Vermnon and Lillian Hamblin; [m.] Dewey L. Strickland, July 5, 1976 (our second); [ed.] Round Valley High, Northland Pioneer College, Creative Writing; [occ.] Retired; [memb.] Women's Relief Society, Church of Jesus Christ of LDS; [oth.writ.] Short story in local newspaper, several poems in a booklet published by a local church group; [pers.] I have been memorizing and writing poetry since early childhood. I write about the small town in the white mountains where I live. I have written several poems about Arizona. My favorite hobbies are camping, fishing and rock collecting. I am a devote Christian and have written several poems on religious subjects, including some patterned after the Psalms of David. [a.] Eagar, AZ.

STRINGER, JOHN C.

[b.] August 15, 1965, Columbus, MS (AFB); [p.] Leonora and James A. Stringer (deceased); [m.] Deborah P. Stringer, July 15, 1994; [ch.] Expecting our first child (girl), December 25, 1994; [ed.] Finished high school 1983, top 15% of class; [occ.] Head of security for popular night club; [hon.] Golden Poet of the Year Award, 1987, 1988, 1989, Outstanding Young Men of America 1988; [oth.writ.] Several poems published in many books and anthologies from 1987-present; [pers.] I write about events and people close to my heart. I think we're all searching for true love and now that I've found it in my wife, I'll never want or need for anything ever again. Thanks Debbie. [a.] Jackson, MS.

SUNDQUIST, CARL V.

[b.] March 30, 1931, Brainerd, MN; [p.] Clarence and Mary Sunquist; [m.] Alice, June 28, 1952; [ch.] Edward Charles and Laura Jean Corosu; [ed.] Washington High School; [occ.] Retired (B.N. Railroad); [memb.] Assemblies of God Church, Church Board member, Wycliffe Bible Translators, Minnesota State Sheriffs Association; [hon.] Christian Service Award from Assemblies of God Church, Crosby, MN, Wycliffe Bible Translators 5 year service award; [oth.writ.] The Great American Goat, Jesus, Anchor of Our Soul, Call To Worship, Flow Holy Spirit; [pers.] I try to express what God has given to me in my writing and hope it may be a blessing to others as it has been to me and may God have all the glory. [a.] Brainerd, MN.

SUTHERLAND, OLLIE

[b.] May 11, 1918, Texas; [m.] Ernest Sutherland (died June 1991), February 18, 1940; [ch.] Sharon, Charles and Keith, 6 grandchildren, 2 great grandchildren; [ed.] High school Texas, B.S. Texas State University, Denton, TX, graduated honors, University of N.M. Albuquerque; [occ.] Retired teacher; [memb.] Albuquerque Association of Educational Retirees, N.M.E.A. Outreach, W.P.S. Baptist Church; [hon.] Editor's Choice Award, National Library of Poetry; [oth.writ.] Published poetry collection in Thanatos Magazine, Spring 1993, three poems in National Library of Poetry anthologies, several poems published in school newspapers and in Strong-Thorn Mortuary Newsletters; [pers.] I lost my husband as the result of an automobile accident. Writing poetry serves as therapy as I heal from the traumatic loss. We had been married for 51 years. [a.] Albuquerque, NM.

SUTTON, CHRISTINA

[b.] April 20, 1980, Chicago, IL; [p.] Katherine and Steven Sutton; [sib.] Scott Sutton; [ed.] Freshman in John Fitzgerald Kennedy High School; [hon.] Editor's Choice Award, John Robert Powers Modeling graduate, publication of poetry in Dance On The Horizon and After The Storm; [oth.writ.] I have many other writings that I am trying to get published and I believe in the future they will be; [pers.] In my poetry, stands my deepest feelings and emotions about life. When I was a child I enjoyed reading the work of Robert Frost in my school reading books. [a.] Chicago, IL.

SWEENEY, THOMAS J.

[pen.] Darby O'Toole; [b.] January 21,1934, Poughkeepsie, NY; [p.] Deceased; [m.] Mary A. (Hellard) Sweeney (deceased), July 25, 1959; [ch.] Patricia O'Hanlon, Kathleen Chapman, Richard and William Sweeney, 4 granddaughters; [ed.] Poughkeepsie High School, class of 1951; [occ.] Retired Regional Loss Prevention Manager; [memb.] AARP, Knights of Columbus, former professional memberships, American Society of Industrial Security, Connecticut Narcotic Enforcement Officers Association, National Association of Chiefs of Police; [hon.] Previously awarded two Editor's Choice Awards by the National Library of Poetry, have been cited for outstanding volunteer efforts over 6 years by the Dutchess County Tourism Promotion Agency, in the Spring of 1994, was cited as the initial recipient of the volunteer of the year award; [oth.writ.] "Sense and Nonsense", Treasured Poems of America, Winter 1991, "We Fall For Autumn, or In Autumn We Fall" Treasured Poems of America, Fall 19911, "Wit-A-Sarcasm", Poetic Voices in America, Spring 1992, "Power Plants", A Question of Balance, Fall 1992, "The Bosox Lament", Distinguished Poet's of America, 1993, 'The Flavor is Dutchess", Dutchess COunt (NY) 1993-94 Travel Guide, "The Tone of Things" (originally scheduled to appear in Outstanding Poets-1994), (now scheduled for A Far Off Place); [pers.] While occasionally motivated to write a poem of serious theme of substance, I generally write light hearted verses depicting friends, relatives, acquaintances or situations, as observers thru the eyes of an irrepressible rascal. [a.] Poughkeepsie, NY.

SWORD, GENE

[pen.] Eneg Drows; [b.] April 1, 1928, Pikeville, KY; [p.] Everett and Ocie Sword; [m.] Rose Marie (Hughes) Sword, March 29, 1975; [ch.] Joan, Janine, Eugenia, Eugene and Jamie; [ed.] Scott High School, Blackstone School of Law, University of Maryland, Texas A & M and Houston Community College; [occ.] Sales and small businessman; [oth.writ.] Numerous poems, short stories and technical writings; [pers.] Poetry is an outward way of expressing the inward person. Natural occurrences impress me most. [a.] Livingston, TX.

TAINTER, KERRIE HOLTON
[pen.] Kerrie S. Holton (maiden name); [b.] June 8, 1965, New Orleans; [p.] Margaret Reeves and Don Holton; [m.] Richard M. Tainter, August 29, 1994; [ed.] Isidore Newman School (New Orleans), The John's Hopkin University, B.S. E.E. (Baltimore), Tulane University, M. English (New Orleans), Mayo Graduate School Ph > D. (Rochester); [occ.] Graduate student; [memb.] IEEE, IEEE Engineering in Medicine and Biology Society, Alpha Eta Mu Beta, Sigma Xi; [hon.] Mayo Graduate School Fellowship, Sigma Xi Research grant, N. American poetry contest finalist (Winter 1994, Summer 1995); [oth.writ.] EMBS Magazine Student Edition, "Student Corner", several poems also published by National Library of Poetry. [a.] Rochester, MN.

TAMBO, JOSEPHINE
[pen.] Jo Tambo; [b.] June 23, 1933, Long Island, NY; [p.] William Tambo, December 23, 1956; [ch.] Craig (29)-wife Kimberly, Andrea, grandson Shawn; [ed.] 56 MSU BA, speech and language pathology, certificate of clinical, graduate from Michigan State University 1956, Cum Laude; [occ.] Speech pathologist, private practice and for Easter Seals; [memb.] American Speech Language, Hearing Association; [hon.] Phi Kappa Phi, National Ed Honor Society, CEU Awards; [oth.writ.] Several poems published in two previous editions of National Library of Poetry; [pers.] I enjoy being able to poetically express my expressions of life's emotions and experiences. As I improve, I hope others may enjoy them and relate to them as I do.

TANENBAUM, DAVID E.
[m.] Lillian Bendroff; [ch.] Clifford H. and Richard L. Tanenbaum; [ed.] Southern High School, Philadelphia, PA, graduate schools of social work, Boston University, University of Pennsylvania (doctoral program); [occ.] Professor, consultant in social work, University of Illinois, Boston College (now retired from teaching); [memb.] National Association of Social Workers, Massachusetts Academy of Psychiatric Social Work, Keneseth Israel Congregation, Alliance for the Mentally Ill of Pennsylvania, NASW Diplomate in Clinical Social Work; [hon.] Fulbright Award (1963-64) as scholar to lecture and teach at the University of Tampere, Finland. [oth.writ.] "Crescendo" an early poem published by the Reconstructionist Foundation, a large number of essays and prose-poems in sundry professional journals devoted to advocacy and research; [pers.] I enjoy writing poetry because of its enduring qualities. Like science, it provides one way of communicating realty. Attitudes, feelings and values reflect both similarities and differences among persons and societies in respect to various aspects of living, such as regard for life, responsibility, loyalty, freedom to change and an identity with harmonious multicultural relationships. Of considerable meaning to the poet is the integration of people, cultures and ideas for sustaining an environment that can nourish creative effort. [a.] Huntingdon Valley, PA.

TARVER, REGINALD D.
[pen.] Reggie; [b.] September 15, 1959, Washington, DC; [p.] Marion and David Tarver; [m.] Felicia Anne, June 8, 1991; [ch.] Osie and Reginald II; [ed.] BBA, Computer Information Systems Science, University of The District of Columbia (Fall 1994); [occ.] Technical Consultant, Automated Concepts, Inc.; [memb.] Isle of Patmas Baptist Church, Deacon (in training), IPBC Males chorus; [hon.] Honors Program nominee for English Literature and Advanced Writings, UDC: [oth.writ.] Various writings old and new to be published in the future; [pers.] I write about everything within my environment. Internal and external, carpal and spiritual, everything is of significance. [a.] Washington, DC.

TAYLOR, GAIL E.
[b.] May 1, 1958, Kitt Hospital; [p.] Mr. and Mrs, Wesley and Grace Taylor; [m.] Single; [ed.] Gerrittsrtun, Pleasant View, Lenape Elementary Schools, Ford City High and Lenape Tech (diploma and certificate) graduate 1977; [occ.] Industrial Center in Kittanning doing assembly line work; [memb.] A.R.C. Association, Retarded Citizens Committee, its a activity group and a couple Bible studies; [hon.] Certifications in American Tae Kwondo Association, pig calling contest (got a pink ribbon for 6th place), certificate in first aide course and bowling contest, I was also in the Women's Pool League for 3 years and got a trophy; [oth.writ.] I'm in the Industrial Newsletter, a lot of my poems were placed in the newsletter; [pers.] When writing poems words seem to pot in my mind cause I put my heart and feelings into it. Maybe someday I would love to have my own books published in the future. [a.] Kittanning, PA.

TAYLOR, JOYANN MARIE
[b.] December 2, 1974, Eau Claire, WI; [p.] Raymond C. Taylor and Mary K,. Bala; [ed.] Forest Lake Senior High, Lakewood Community College, Institute of Children's Literature; [occ.] Student, factory; [memb.] People To People International; [hon.] People to People Student Ambassador to Russia, 1992; [oth.writ.] Previous publications in National Library of Poetry anthologies; [pers.] With hard work, patience and support, anyone can achieve anything they set their mind to. [a.] Forest Lake, MN.

TAYLOR, LINDA G.
[pen.] Shannon Christie; [b.] September 17, 1952, Pittsburgh; [p.] Mr. and Mrs. Harry P. Muders; [m.] Samuel J. Taylor, August 18, 1973; [ch.] Ashley Lynn; [ed.] Quaker Valley High School (1970), Robert Morris College (1972), Operating Room Tech School (1977-USN), Pharmacy Technician School (1981-USN); [occ.] Pharmacy Technician; [memb.] National Author Registry, Association of Pharmacy Technicians, Celiac Sprue Foundation; [hon.] Accomplished of merit "In That One Moment", Creative Arts and Science Enterprise, Editor's Choice Award 1993 Where Dreams Begin, National Library of Poetry, "Farmer's Thanksgiving Prayer" 1994, Editor Choice Award, National Library of Poetry; [oth.writ.] "Mountains", "Dreamer", "All About You', Memories 1993, "Pen Etched Memories", "Death of Dreams", "In Answer To The Vampire's Requiem", "In That One Moment", "Little Miracles", "Old Blue Jeans", "That Dark Entity" 1994; [pers.] If you write what you know about or believe in it it is sure to be understood. [a.] Honolulu, HI.

TAYLOR, SEAN M.
[b.] February 2, 1971, Bellevue, WA; [p.] Jim and Sandy Taylor; [ed.] Sammamish High School, Bellevue Community School, University of Idaho; [occ.] Student of Psychology, University of Idaho; [memb.] Ritual Advisor, E-Dah-Ho Chapter, Order of DeMolay, Moscow Idaho; [hon.] DeMolay Chevalier, Bellevue Washington; [oth.writ.] Appeared in Fagere (literary Digest, University of Idaho), 2 anthologies, one by the National Library of Poetry, and one anthology done by Sparrowgrass Poetry. [a.] Bellevue, WA.

TEAL, JOSIE
[b.] August 15, 1936, Houston, TX; [p.] Walter R. and Viola W. Haller; [m.] Dr. James S. Teal, August 7, 1960; [ch.] James S. Teal II (USN-27 years old); [ed.] Jack Yates High School, Wiley College, Texas Southern University, San Francisco State College AB, MA Degrees; [occ.] Head Counselor, Ben Franklin M.S., San Francisco, CA; [memb.] Delta Sigma Theta Sorority, Alpha Delta Kappa, International Society for Women Educators, California Association for Counseling and Development, Jones Memorial United Methodist Church, International Kajukenbo Association; [hon.] Numerous awards from church, community and professional organizations for my 34 years of working with youth; [oth.writ.] "Black History Is No Mystery", "Touch Someone"; [pers.] I write as a result of my life's experiences. Joy, humor, frustration and pain all motivate me to write. [a.] San Francisco, CA.

TEED, CRAIG L.
[pen.] Craig L. Teed; [b.] October 9, 1947, Birmingham, AL;[p.] Reginald and Mary Sue Teed; [m.] Shirley Jean Love, January 6, 1973; [ed.] McAdory High, University of Montevallo, University of Alabama, Emory University (Candler School of Theology); [occ.] Community residence counselor, McLean Hospital, Belmont, MA; [memb.] International Society of Poets, Massachusetts Humane Society, Phi Alpha Theta, History Honor Society; [hon.] D.A.R > History Award, Hallie Farmer History Award; [oth.writ.] Numerous unpublished poems, I'm currently publishing a major poetic work entitled "With Songs On My Lips, A Modern Rubaiyat; [pers.] I believe that there is a close connecting between poetry and music, and that both flow from that beauty which is the highest attribute of both God and man. [a.] Somerville, MA.

TEITELBAUM, PHYLLIS LEAH
[b.] May 2, 1928, Brooklyn, NY; [p.] Oscar and Regina Abrams; [m.] Irving Teitelbaum, divorced; [ch.] Shifra and Ozer Teitelbaum; [ed.] Brooklyn College, Long Island University and New York University; [occ.] Retired teacher; [oth.writ.] Poem published in The Edge of Twilight, others not yet published but in the works; [pers.] If we take every adversity and problem as a lesson to be learned our spirits will survive and grow in a positive way. Edna St. Vincent Millay was the poet who touched me most. [a.] Brooklyn, NY.

THACKER, AGNES
[pen.] AG; [oth.writ.] Also published in The Space Between; [pers.] My name is Agnes Thacker. I live in Stuart, Florida. I sign my poems AG, a shortened form of my first name. I was inspired to write many of my poems at the time of my son's death and thereafter. Many of my poems ask questions, seeking answers from God and deal with the deepest feelings and emotions man could experience. Occasionally, I paint with oils when the mood arises. Scenic paintings are my specialty. I am a make-up artist for many of the major cosmetic companies. I am a REIKI HEALER and promote the belief in healing all parts of self BODY-MIND-SPIRIT.

THOMAS, AFLRED A.
[pen.] Al Thomas; [b.] April 23, 1942, Birmingham, al; [p.] Levine; [m.] Divorced; [ch.] Chrism (30 years), Lima (22 years) and Jiff (20); [ed.] G.E.D.-high school Sprindail Elementary Pinson Elementary, Trussville High and Tarrant High; [occ.] Checker at dock, Rockaway Express, truckline; [memb.] I.S.P., Mt. Paran Church of God, (4 locations, North, Central, West and East), Teamster's Union; [hon.] Honorable Mention, Golden Poet, Poet of Merit, Editor's Choice, safety awards at work, an award for a poem I wrote and published for work, quality award; [oth.writ.] 1 poem in over 20 anthologies in past 2 years from 2 different publishing companies, National Library of poetry and Sparrowgrass, about 6 newsletters, one in each, I'm also on about 6 or 8 tapes, 1 complete album; [pers.] I'm inspired to write by many sources, God is my ultimate inspiration. Divorce was hard on me, but I was raised to know God loves and cares for me. [a.] Norcross, GA.

THOMAS, CECILE A.
[pen.] Cecile A. Thomas; [b.] June 15, 1957, Springfield, MA: [m.] Daniel A. Thomas, June 25, 1983; [ed.] Bethel High School, Bethel, CT, Olivet Nazarene College, Kankakee, IL, Naugutuck Adult Education, Naugutuck, CT; [occ.] Inspirational Speaker, singer, songwriter; [hon.] Recipient of 2 V.F.W. 1973 local awards, Bethel, CT, writing; [oth.writ.] Several poems published in international newsletters, published in two local newspapers, recently published in Echoes of Yesterday, anthology and the sound of poetry anthology tape; [pers.] I thank God for His open arms and open doors. I also am so glad my husband believed in me even before I did. [a.] Waterbury, CT.

THOMAS, GLORIA E.
[b.] April 6, 1939, Chicago, IL; [p.] Donald and Verlie Cambric; [m.] Marvin Bryant Thomas Sr., May 15, 1958; [ch.] Bridgette, Charles, Tonia, Marvin Jr. and Sheila (all write); [ed.] Harvard College of Automation, diploma in Computer Programing in 1970; [occ.] Supervisor of District Operations, main post office, Chicago, IL; [memb.] International Society of Poets, National Urban League, National Association of Supervisors; [oth.writ.] Written since grade school, in 4th or 5th grade, the teacher would bring sweets each week for the best poems, I would always win, my popularity increased with those wanting some of the treats; [pers.] I believe in people thinking for themselves, education is nice, but many people think it makes them intelligent. I've tried to instill in my children and grandchildren they must use their own minds, not depend on others to think for them. [a.] Country Club Hills, IL.

THOMAS, MAXINE TAYLOR;
[pen.] Maxine Taylor Thomas; [b.] April 13, 1925, Utah; [p.] Kimball and Emily Jensen; [m.] The late James L. Taylor, May 14, 1944; [ch.] Myron, Howard, Ron, Merigold, Randy and Connie; [ed.] Graduate of Duchesne High School, took several classes at University of Utah; [occ.] Retired from Duchesne County as County Treasurer for 23 years; [memb.] Member of Church of Jesus Christ of Later Day Saints; [oth.writ.] "We Are Not Alone", "The Message", "Dear Howard", all published in National Library of Poetry, "The Lazy Days of Summer" and "Peace" waiting to be published; [pers.] Now married to Elmer Thomas, have time now to write poetry when inspired. Hope some of the messages touch other lives for good. [a.] Duchesne, UT.

THOMAS, SEAN C.
[b.] April 18, 1975, New Hyde Park, NY; [p.] John and Mary Ann Thomas; [ed.] New Hyde Park Memorial High School, Martin Lutherville College; [occ.] Student and sophomore English major with a concentration in writing; [memb.] National Honor Society; [hon.] National Library of Poetry's Editor's Choice Award, New Hyde Park Memorial High School English Department Award, second annual North Shore Young Author;s Conference, World Hunger essay contest, Browning Society Poetry contest; [oth.writ.] "The Watcher", "A Note in Passing", "A Mother's Wish", "The Loft's", "Celtic Dream"; [pers.] My writing has always been my way of finding my own place in a world so consumed in conformity. [a.] Purchase, NY.

THOMPSON, ADELINE
[pen.] Addie; [b.] September 1, 1927, Hawley, TX; [p.] Jim and Erna Boyd; [m.] W.D. Thompson, May 3, 1946; [ch.] Gwynn, Linda, Patsy, Michael and Steven; [ed.] High school; [occ.] Housewife; [memb.] Republican Task Force, The 700 Club, Living Word Outreach Church; [oth.writ.] Poems I've never tried to get them published before; [pers.] I usually write about my own experiences or what I see around me. I am a very distant relative of Edgar Allan Poe. [a.] Houston, TX.

THOMPSON, ELIZABETH ANNE
[b.] February 25, 1979, Akron, OH; [p.] Lyle Jr. and Cynthia Thompson; [ed.] Graduated from Holderness Central School, currently a sophomore at Plymouth Regional High School; [occ.] Student; [memb.] Student Council, yearbook, French Club; [hon.] High honors in academic achievement, Presidential Academic Fitness Award, varsity x-country running, varsity tennis; [oth.writ.] Other poems published through the National Library of Poetry; [pers.] This poem is dedicated to you. Thanks for being there for me, you're the best. [a.] Holderness, NH.

THOMPSON, STEPHEN ALEXANDER
[b.] February 14, 1975; [memb.] International Society of Poets, lifetime member; [hon.] The International Poet of Merit Award in 1994, the National Library of Poetry's Editor's Choice Award in 1994; [oth.writ.] "Nights In The Rain", published by Pacific Rim in Quest of A Dream, "Looking For The Wind" published by National Library of Poetry in A Far Off Place", "The Crimson Field" in the ISP 1994 audio compilation the sound of poetry; [pers.] Poetry is not just something I do. It is not just putting words together. It is not even close to being just a form of writing, at least not for me. It is my life and deepest thoughts in an organized manner. [a.] Jamesville, WI.

THOMSON, RICHARD J.
[b.] December 20, 1930, Phoenix, AZ; [p.] Richard and Nancy Thomson; [m.] Wilda M. Thomson, June 14, 1963; [ch.] Nancy Grace and Mary Ruth; [ed.] Phoenix Union High, Grand Canyon College, B.A., Southwestern B.T.S., BD, University of Houston, East Texas Baptist, Texas A & I, Bee County, Arizona State University; [occ.] Real Estate Agent; [memb.] First Baptist Church, National Association of Realtors, AARP; [hon.] The Most Prominent Educators of Texas (1983), 2 paintings hang in Texas Retirement System building in Austin, Texas, GCC Canyon Trails (1953) dedicated to 8 other students and me; [oth.writ.] Eight poems published, two unpublished books of poetry; [pers.] A Christian philosophy of glorifying God and love towards others. [a.] George West, TX.

TIKALSKY, SARAH
[pen.] Sarah L. Tikalsky; [b.] July 19, 1977, New Prague, MN; [p.] Richard and Jeanne Tikalsky; [ed.] I am a high school senior in New Prague; [memb.] Holy Trinity Lutheran Church; [oth.writ.] One poem published in The Darkside of The Moon; [pers.] The teachers that offered me the greatest encouragement in my writings are, Mr. William Bergevin, Mrs. Elaine Bruchman and especially Mrs. Valerie Drummerhausen. [a.] New PRague, MN.

TOOKER, GRANT CALVIN
[pen.] Cal Tooker; [b.] August 1, 1924, SD; [p.] Grant and Elizabeth Tooker; [ed.] Master of Science in Library Science/USC; [occ.] Retiree; [oth.writ.] "The Hoar Frost", "Peace", "O God"; [pers.] Upon entering this planet's orb I was a preacher's kid, last born child of Rev. Grant and Elizabeth Tooker. The family farmhouse, my birthplace was located smack-dab in the middle of the Dakota prairies. Being a "P.K." and sporting the names of two presidents-what were my odds? Despite them, the rural environment, dirt and gravel roads, the "dust-bowl", swarms of grasshoppers, kerosene lamps, cow-chips for the kitchen stove, outdoor plumbins (?), 40 degree weather and a one room schoolhouse all provided a miscellany of experiences. Now, after a lifetime as a "P.K.", WWII G.I., professional librarian and a retiree, I am ready to start my life. Becoming a novice writer with the pen name of Cal Tooker is becoming an exciting and rewarding mode for discovering aspects of me that I didn't believe existed. [a.] Whittier, CA.

TOOMEY, LILLIAN
[pen.] Lil Toomey; [b.] January 11, 1943, Owosso, MI; [p.] Warren and Lorena Morgan; [m.] David Toomey, November 5, 1960; [ch.] Robin Toomey (Criner) and Timothy Toomey; [ed.] Byron High School and Lansing Community College graduate (honors); [occ.] Supervisor for Senior Companion Program-Lansing, MI; [memb.] International Society of Authors and Artists, Owosso Wesleyan Church, MI Association of Foster Grandparent/Senior Companion Program; [hon.] "My Childhood Home" (Honorable Mention and The Presidents Awards), "In The Beginning God Created " (Editor's Challenge Award), "Stacy and The Squirrel" (accomplishment of merit), "Victorian Charm", (Honorable Mention-1994, Longfellow Awards Program); [pers.] I love to paint pictures with words, and I hope my words will inspire and bring happiness to others as well as growth. [a.] Owosso, MI.

TOSSAVAINEN, ANINI
[b.] July 21, 1927, Finland; [ch.] Aino, Leila, Tuula and Eric, 3 grandchildren; [ed.] Business college; [occ.] Retired; [memb.] Finnish Brotherhood and Sisterhood, Finnish Home Association, Finnish Ski Club and Lutheran Church of the Cross; [hon.] Golden Poet Awards and Honorary Awards; [oth.writ.] Book of poems "Muistojen Mailta" Finnish language. Also monthly articles Finnish language, Finnish newspaper and often poems. [a.] Berkeley, CA.

TRACY, PATRICIA ROSE
[pen.] Patti Rose Patsy; [b.] February 10, 1945, Markhan, IL; [p.] Edward and Lillian Bishop; [m.]

Neil Micheal Tracy, September 2, 1972; [ch.] Terry Allen, age 21; [occ.] Poet-writing lyric's and housewife; [memb.] None so far, but still hopeful; [hon.] I am new at this, but who knows; [oth.writ.] One book is still in the making, another book is called "Dusting Off Dreams", and also one is River of Dreams and now Best Poets of 1995, and I am working on a record to be recorded; [pers.] I try to reflect my feelings and hopes in the poems I write. My wish is that others will find renewed strength and know there is a new tomorrow waiting to make of it whatever they choose. "Show love now". Don't wait till its too late. [a.] Wausau, WI.

TRAMPOSCH, ELVIRA

[b.] January 6, 1936, Germany; [p.] Elfriede and Heinrich Sehlhoff; [m.[Ernst Tramposch, September 24, 1966; [ch.] Debbie, Ernst, Robert and Steven, grandchildren, Elaine, Jason and Alexandra; [ed.] High school, college courses; [occ.] Homemaker; [memb.] Thirteen-WNET, Lutheran Church, Iroquois Indian Museum; [hon.] Volunteering awards; [oth.writ.] German poems, as a young teen from growing up times in Germany, since living in the U.S. poems in English on different subjects; [pers.] "The emotions of a thought brings forth the unfolding word that leads the hand to write". [a.] Franklin Square, NY.

TRASGA, AQUINO T.

[pen.] Ike, G.A. Star; [b.] March 7, 1947, Philippines; [p.] Vicente and Ignacia Tubola Trasga; [m.] Regina Calacsan Trasga, April 27, 1985; [ed.] Bagumbayan Primary School, Tigbauan Elementary School, Tigbauan High School, West Visayas State College, Philippine Normal College, De Vry Institute of Technology; [occ.] Pathology Assistant; [memb.] International Society of Poets, Fatima Prayer Community, Circulo Tigbaueno of the Midwest; [hon.] High school Valedictorian, Magna Cum Laude, Seato Scholarship Award, Rotary Award for Scholarship, PNC-DEC Scholarship for special education (teaching the visually impaired), 1991 Core member of the year award from Fatima Prayer Community, Dean's List; [oth.writ.] Several poems published in college paper and in our FPC newsletter; [pers.] "With God's help, nothing is impossible". [a.] Aurora, IL.

TUAZON, TRACY

[b.] September 18, 1979, Oxnard; [p.] Edwin and Teresa Tuazon; [ed.] Channel Islands High School, I'm a freshman there; [occ.] A student from Channel Islands High School; [memb.] I'm in different clubs like Key Club, band, CSF and Asian American Clubs in high school; [hon.] I received for outstanding literature and another award; [oth.writ.] I have poetry writings in my book I keep whenever I'm bored; [pers.] I express my feelings to poetry how love and friendship are important to me. [a.] Oxnard, CA.

TUCKNESS, THERESE MARIE

[pen.] Therese Marie Tuckness; [b.] January 15, 1959, Wayne, MI; [p.] Dave and Jackei (step-mom), Allbee; [m.] David John Tuckness, January 15, 1978, renewal January 16, 1994; [ch.] Rhonda Mae Tuckness, senior at Reynolds High School; [ed.] Western Business College, Portland, Oregon, graduate; [occ.] U.S. Bank, Columbia Center, Gresham, Oregon; [memb.] Pastor's wife in Glenwood, WA, Baptist Church, Teen Leader and flutist, also a volunteer at Mt. Hood Medical Center, Gresham, OR; [hon.] Perfect attendance and Honor Roll in college (3.52 GPA), Golden Poet since 1989 till 1993, P.S.I. Award 1985 and award for being a volunteer; [oth.writ.] Short stories, music, many other poems, all unpublished as yet; [pers.] I thank my Lord Jesus for impressing in my heart and life all the poems that are written since 1980. [a.] Troutdate, OR.

TURNER, EDITH COX

[b.] February 8, 1903, Guide, NC; [p.] George and Sina Smity Lewis Cox; [m.] Marcus S. Turner, December 10, 1930; [ch.] Dr. John C., Jean Sins Nell and Marcus all college graduates; [ed.] High school and one year college, taught school 9 years before married; [occ.] Retired but attending organizations f which I am a member; [memb.] American Legion Auxiliary Woman's Club, Eastern Star, past president of Methodist Women Circle, was state Chaplain of Eastern Star; [oth.writ.] Had poems published in local newspaper, was voted outstanding senior citizen in county and third runner up in state; [pers.] I have a plaque that the bank presented to me stating that I was Outstanding Citizen. [a.] Lake Junaluska, NC.

UMLOR, JODY ANN

[pen.] Jodeci; [b.] September 1, 1975, Michigan; [p.] JoAnn and Marvin Umlor; [ed.] St. Anthony's Grade School and Kenowa Hills High School; [occ.] Bookkeeper; [hon.] Awards in dance, singing and own personal honors; [oth.writ.] Poem called "Never Forget" published in Dance On The Horizon; [pers.] Don't be scared to reach for the stars because one day you may catch one and believe me, its the best feeling ever. [a.] Grand Rapids, MI.

UPHOFF JR., BARON JOSEPH A. (CAPT.)

[b.] March 15, 1950, Colorado Springs; [p.] Melva C. and Joseph A. Uphoff; [m.] Never married; [ed.] Dr. of Divinity, Universal Life Church 1993, Hon. Professor of Mathematics, A.I.C.R., 1993, Nidan (black belt), World Alliance of Martial Artists, CA 1994; [occ.] Surrealist; [memb.] The Institute of Martial Arts, Poetry West, Colorado Springs Fine Arts Center, Fraternal Order of Eagles, First United Methodist Church, American Numismatic Association; [hon.] Knight, Corps. Diplomatique, Sovereign Military Order of the Knights Templar of Jerusalem 1994, Certificate of Merit of Distinguished Services to Metamathematics and Surrealism, I.B.C. 1991, Medal of Honor, Distinguished Lifelong Achievements, A.B.I. 1993; [oth.writ.] "The Talisman Dreaming" 1987, "The Unified Field" 1988, "Vector Keys for Analytical Labanotation" 1994, "Tense Keys for Analytical Labanotation" 1994; [pers.] The photograph of a poem resides most clearly in the uncomprehending mind where the foreign alphabet acquires true impact as a pattern and shapes of drawing. [a.] Colorado Springs, CO.

UTTERBACK, ALMEDA LOU

[pen.] Almeda Lou Utterback; [b.] June 22, 1939, Aldrich, MO; [p.] Alta Meda and Oren Witt; [m.] Norman Frank Utterback, June 17, 1950; [ch.] Franklin Darell and Katherine Ann Utterback; [ed.] Bolivar MO grade school, Bolivar MO High School; [occ.] Homemaker, poetry writer; [memb.] Temple Baptist Church Discipleship training union, Sunday School class, Women's Missionary Union, member of Temple Baptist Church, Springfield, MO; [hon.] Many awards, have poems published in books Outstanding Poets of 1994, award of merit for California Earthquake, Editor's Choice Award for Outstanding Achievement in poetry; [oth.writ.] Newspapers, poem about the great flood of 1993 in Springfield, MO., poem about the tornado of Springfield, MO, "House On The Hill", "Mother's Old Rocking Chair", published; [pers.] I want to dedicate this poem to the Reverend Don Combs, wife Diane, children, Jeremy, Jessica, Jimmy Combs and friends of Temple Baptist Church for the support and love that they bestow upon me. [a.] Springfield, MO.

VAHLBERG, DAVE

[b.] April 15, 1953, Emmett, ID; [p.] Barry and Ruth Vahlberg; [m.] Kristi Vahlberg, September 13, 1985; [ch.] Brenda Ann, Cassandra Lynn and Amberly Dawn; [ed.] Emmett High, Boise State University; [occ.] Quality Control Safety Supervisor; [memb.] Volunteer CPR/First Aid instructor for the American Red Cross; [oth.writ.} An unpublished book of poetry; [pers.] The strength of love and the human spirit is an integral theme of my poetry. [a.] Boise, ID.

VALLECORSA, LUCRETIA GRACE

[b.] March 25, 1981, Albuquerque, NM; [p.] Marius and Peggy Vallecorsa; [ed.] Paradise Christian School; [occ.] 9th grade student; [pers.] The poem is of Joseph Christian, my nephew born June 15, 1992. [a.] Albuquerque, NM.

VAN BUSKIRK, CHRISTA

[b.] August 16, 1977, Norwalk, CT; [p.] Linda and David Van Buskirk; [ed.] Currently a high school senior at Norwalk High School, Norwalk, CT; [occ.] Student; [memb.] National Honor Society, French CLub, school newspaper, United States Tennis Association; [hon.] Who's Who Among American High School Students (2 years), National French contest winner (1992) and poems published in National Library of Poetry, Best Poets Honors (1995), (1993-1994); [oth.writ.] An article I wrote published in my school newspaper on the new school-based health center, my article was printed on the cover page; [pers.] I always strive to do my best in all that I do. I always try to be myself, work hard, give 100% and I know that in the end I will succeed. [a.] Norwalk, CT.

VANCIL, NORMA L.

[pen.] Jenna Victor; [b.] June 12, 1920, Hoquiam, WA; [m.] Wayne H. Vancil; [occ.] Home person; [hon.] Poetry, Honorable Mention, poems published in newspaper and Great Poems of the Western World III; [oth.writ.] Biography, stories; [pers.] From the land and nature comes a commitment for us to respect all the seasons and their beauty. [a.] Yelm, WA.

VAN KUIKEN, JEROME

[b.] April 8, 1974, The Philippines; [p.] Rev. and Mrs. Jerry Van Kuiken; [ed.] Mount Carmel High School, Kentucky Mountain Bible College; [occ.] Bible college student; [memb.] KMBC Student Council member. President of the class of 1996; [hon.] Who's Who Among American High School Students; [oth.writ.] Poems included in various publications including the National Library of Poetry's 1993 anthology, I am presently working on a children's fantasy book; [pers.] My life and poetry derive meaning from my relationships with Jesus Christ. [a.] Vancleve, KY.

VANGA, BOZSI F.
[pen.] Bozsi F. Vanga; [b.] October 10, 1945, Kapuvar; [p.] Deceased; [m.] Deceased; [ch.] 2 daughters, 26 and 27; [ed.] College and Divinity Self Realization, arts, poetry, sci-fi uniting ; [memb.] Leukemia Foundation, The Eastern European News; [hon.] Many untiring poetry and the arts, service community and the elderly; [oth.writ.] Many, many competitions; [pers.] I strive to reflect the best I possibly can on human nature such as it is, to reflect the truth and to perhaps give joy to my fellow beings by so doing. [a.] Cromwell, IN.

VARNELL, OLA
[b.] May 14, 1914, Arkansas; [p.] Seymora and Isabella Green; [m.] Clovis J. Varnell, November 29, 1930; [ch.] James B. Varnell; [ed.] 12 grade, some college, C.P.A., Clovis James Varnell Jr., 12 grade; [occ.] Police officer, SRG; [memb.] Olive Street Baptist Church; [hon.] Trophy, Golden Poet Award 1988, World of Poetry in Convention Center in Anaheim, CA; [oth.writ.] Award of Merit Certificate, poem "Four Seasons" 1987-1988, poem "Precious Love" won my trophy, Golden Poet Award-1989, "Gloomy Days" 1989, Silver Poet 1990; [pers.] As I think in my heart I want to help someone with my poems. Poem printed "Life" in Archive of the Arts, Biloxi, MS, (Reflections of Being) Tital.

VERRILL, MARY
[b.] June 4, 1956, Eau Claire, WI; [m.] Kent Verrill; [ch.] Two children; [ed.] M.A. in English, University of Wisconsin-Madison, B.A. Viterbo College; [occ.] Writer, editor, musician; [memb.] The Loft, Minneapolis, MN, Women Against Military Madness (WAMM); [hon.] Neighborhood News Service Awards 1988, 1989, 1990 for various journalistic articles, Minneapolis-St. Paul; [oth.writ.] Short stories and essays (some published),poetry, some in Grounds for Peace, (WAMM, 1975); [pers.] I believe in the power of the written word and hope to use it wisely. [a.] St. Paul, MN.

VERSOCKI JR., MICHAEL A.
[b.] April 16, 1972; [p.] Mike and Sue Versocki; [ed.] Freeport High School, Nassau Community College, S.U.N.Y. Old Westbury; [occ.] Student; [memb.] South Nassau Christian Church; [hon.] One of my poems was published in The Space Between titled "Casual Thoughts"; [oth.writ.] Various poems, lyrics and short stories; [pers.] When I write, the things I write must mean something to me. If it doesn't then they are just words. [a.] Freeport, NY.

VIGENSKI, RICK
[b.] July 30, 1954, Chelsea, MA; [p.] Ralph and Sheila Sullvian Vigenski; [m.] Joanne Vigenski, August 5, 1972; [ch.] Melissa Serene, Aaron Patrick and Elizabeth Maureen; [ed.] AAS Media Advertising Arts, Tidewater Community College, Fine Arts major, Old Dominion University; [occ.] Free lance graphic designer, landscaper and writer; [memb.] Tidewater Society of Communicating Arts, Tidewater Astronomical Society, Norfolk Botanical Garden Club, Friends of the Zoo, Virginia Zoological Park; [hon.] Summa Cum Laude Association, graduate of TCC, Dean's List at ODU, finalist in several poetry competitions locally and nationally; [occ.] Student publication, short stories, Shady Characters and A Dog's Life, Scrivener published poems, "Pleasure Hunt" and "Burial At Sea" and an op ed piece in the Virginia Pilot and Ledger Star; [pers.] Thanks to all who have helped me along the way, especially my family and my teachers, as well as those who have fixed me when I have broken. My debts and gratitude remain forever. [a.] Norfolk, VA.

VILLANUEVA, JENNIFER
[b.] July 20, 1977, San Antonio, TX; [ed.] John Jay High School; [memb.] Society of English Scholars, Parnassus, John Jay Literary magazine Senior Editor; [hon.] Sandra Cisneros Special Award 1994, Ides of March/Palo Alto College; [oth.writ.] Several poems published in Parnassus; [pers.] "Adelante no mas" (Forward only). [a.] San Antonio, TX.

VILLARREAL, ROJELIO
[b.] November 15, 1958, Fabons, TX; [p.] Rojelio and Grace Villarreal; [m.] Lori; [ed.] BS from University of Maryland; [occ.] Systems Administrator at Franklin Square Hospital Center. [a.] Reisterstown, MD.

VINSON, DAWN ANNE
[b.] August 8, 1966, Albuquerque, NM; [p.] Barbara A. Phillips; [m.] Brian Edward Vinson, August 1, 1992; [ch.] Christopher Lee; [ed.] Los Alamos High School, Capps College, U.S. Army; [occ.] Artist, crafter, writer; [memb.] Friends of Partick Henry, National Preservation Society, NRA, Republican Party, CBN Partner, Life Outreach Partner; [hon.] Several 1st, 2nd, 3rd place ribbons as a crafter; [oth.writ.] Dark Side of The Moon, several newspaper articles, Poetic Voices of America; [pers.] Jesus Christ has been my inspiration all my life. All I do is for His glory and by His love. I love British literature and also oddly enough, was influenced by the work of Edgar Allan Poe. [a.] Barboursville, VA.

VOGELSONG, JOANNE A.
[b.] May 15, 1951, Bath, NY; [p.] Marge and Don Starkweather and Jim Morehouse; [m.] Gary L. Vogelsong, November 17, 1979; [ch.] Bill, Matt, Joy, Rachel and Jodi, grandchild-Jade; [ed.] Corning East High; [occ.] Writer, homemaker; [memb.] Plain Congregational Church, National Arts Council; [hon.] Poet of Merit Award; [oth.writ.] Poems published in previous anthologies; [pers.] My husband is a great influence and my children all offer such great encouragement. I am currently working on a book and hope to see it published soon. [a.] Bowling Green, OH.

VYDELINGUM, NADARAJEN A. (PH.D.)
[pen.] Raju Ameerdana; [b.] June 1, 1945, Mauritius; [p.] Souba and Mareeaya Vyedlingum; [m.] Rosemary Vydelingum, Ed.D., November 6, 1971; [ch.[Naomi Natalie (16 years) and Eric Ydelingum (14 years); [ed.] B.Sc. with honors, Cell Biology, MSc Biochemistry, Ph.d. Clinical Biochemistry, University of London, UK; [occ.] Health Scientist Administrator, National Institute of Health, lecturer, John Hopkins University; [memb.] Chartered member Institute of Biology UK, American Society for Biological Chemistry, American Cancer Society, American Diabetes Society, Biochemical Society (UK), Council of Biology Editors, American Medical Writers Association; [hon.] Principal investigator NIH Award 1985-88, PI-American Diabetes Award 1982-1984, PI-Research Fellow American Heart 1979-1981, Who's Who in Science and Engineering, American Men and Women of Science 1992, In The East (1992); [oth.writ.] Author, peer reviewed scientific papers, book reviewer for Science books, Boston University, Editor of scientific reviews for NIH grants, reviewer for several scientific journals and books; [pers.] Poetry, like music is food for the soul, the rhythmic sound holds our attention while our search for deeper meaning challenges our intellect. [a.] Rockville, MD.

WADE, ANDREIA CATHERINE
[b.] July 26, 1951, Santa Paula, CA; [p.] Andrew and Elcie White Wade; m.] Divorced; [ch.] Larry Stevens, Donna Stevens Fitch, Rebecca and R. Jasen Stevens; [ed.] Fillmore High School, Ventura Junior College; [occ.] Cosmetics manager, Wal-Mart, Extraordinaire Models; [memb.] Starlight Foundations, Operations U.S.A. Childrens Miracle Network, T.M.T.A., Teacher of Children's Acting and Modeling; [hon.] Editor's Choice Award, National Library of Poetry, Models Guild; [oth.writ.] Published school papers, local and state newspapers, children's stories, poetry and musical lyrics; [pers.] In my writings I always strive to improve my efforts, to be worthy of those kind souls that inspire and comfort me. [a.] Bakersfield, CA.

WALKER, BILLY L.
[pen.] Billy L. Walker; [b.] April 17, 1928, Marshall Co., KY; [p.] Bennie and Jennie; [m.] Betty, August 30, 1947; [ch.] Mike, Pat, Neica and Marty; [ed.] Calvert High, Murray St. U., Paducah Junior College, ITI Chicago, IL; [occ.] Retired chemist; [memb.] National Geo. Society, charter member of the Planetary Society, Vaughn's Chapel C.P. Church; [oth.writ.] Several poems published in newspapers and magazines, Coming of Dawn, short ways and stories; [pers.] I enjoy writing and sharing my work with other people. [a.] Possum Trot, KY.

WALKER, CYNTHIA
[pen.] Cynny Jones; [b.] August 18, 1969, New York; [ed.] English major at Hunter College; [hon.] Certificate of Achievement for 1st place short story (1993), contest, Editor's Choice Award for Outstanding Achievement in poetry (1993), the International Poet of Merit Award (1994); [oth.writ.] "Dehlila's Disease", "Hope Village", "The Haunting of Harold", "Mercy Killing"; [pers.] Dedicated to Valory Christian Jones, Victoria Grace Jones, Coleman Kieth Jones and Sadie Hayes. Thank you for your inspiration. [a.] Jamaica, NY.

WALKER, DONNA A.
[b.] October 25, 1943, Benton Harbor, MI; [p.] James and Anna Carollo; [m.] Wayne, May 2, 1970; [ch.] Michelle, Vincent, Anthony and Amy-Marie; [ed.] Benton Harbor High, Lake Michigan College; [occ.] Licensed Practical Nurse and Home Health Respite worker; [hon.] World of Poetry, Silver Poet; [oth.writ.] "Knight In Blue Armor", and "Round About", published in World of Poetry; [pers.] I believe that poetry about family is like a snapshot taken of them, and is a way to "remember when". [a.] Portage, IN.

WALL, LUCILLE SMALLWOOD
[pen.] Lucille Smallwood Wall; [b.] March 25, 1914, Murrayville, GA, Hall Co.; [p.] Clayton and Mary Smallwood; [m.] Crawford L. Wall, May 8, 1932; [ch.] William C. Wall; [ed.] High school, 1 year college, N.M Western, graduate of Famous Artists School in Conn; [occ.] Retired teacher, artist, writer; [memb.] Relief Society of Church of Jesus Christ of L.D.S., adult teacher and other jobs in church; [hon.] Salutatorian high school, Martin Institute, 100%

award for perfect spelling in Brooke Co. WV Elementary School, basketball award in high school, volunteer senior citizens, Pagosa Springs, CO., bus driver 5 years; [oth.writ.] Several sport stories, Acoma Indian piece published and 3 manuscripts not published, one 70,000 word story of Civil War and my great grandmother called "Chaff In The Storm" (GA story), one narrative of the Biblical Abraham called Nomad Princes and another Western novel Chiricohus Grass; [pers.] Not what we give but what we share, for the gift without the giver is bare, who gives Himself with his alms feeds three, Himself his hungering neighbor and me. [a.] Dell City, TX.

WALLACE, BETTY JEAN
[b.] June 15, 1937, Columbus, IN; [p.] Henritta and Thomas J. Wycoff; [ch.] 8 children, 15 grandchildren; [ed.] Columbus High, approved University of Beauty Culture, PCDI-Bookkeeping and accounting home study course; [occ.] Deli service; [oth.writ.] A poem for the National Library of Poetry contest; [pers.] My poetry comes from living life. [a.] Seymour, IN.

WALTRIP, LOUISE
[b.] January 31, 1958, Palo Alto, CA; [p.] George and Man Sau Wong; [m.] Dennis F. Waltrip, November 11, 1978; [ch.] Charity Ruth and Aaron Timothy; [ed.] Yerba Buena High School and Evergreen Valley College; [occ.] Word processing operator; [hon.] Employee of the Year 1991-1992; [oth.writ.] Numerous published and unpublished poems and short stories; [pers.] Life holds unexpected miracles. Be patient, and these miracles will unfold before your very eyes. [a.] San Jose, CA.

WANGLER, BOB
[pen.] Bob Wangler; [b.] march 29, 1916, Royal Oak, MI; [p.] Albert and Johanna Wangler; [m.] Catherine Wangler (deceased), November 25, 1950; [ch.] Frank and Richard Wangler; [ed.] One year Wayne University, Royal Oak Senior High School; [occ.] Retired meter reader; [oth.writ.] Several hundred letters to the editor, various newspapers; [pers.] There has to be those who recognize God as the Divine Source of all beauty on earth, and who feel compelled to record their impressions of it in poetry and song. [a.] Lemon Grove, CA.

WARD, CHRISTINE
[b.] January 28, 1976, Cleveland; [p.] David and Melinda Ward; [ed.] Lutheran West High School, Cuyahoga Community College; [occ.] Student; [hon.] Perfect attendance, band, honor and merit roll, Who's Who Among American High School Students; [oth.writ.] Poem previously published by the National Library of Poetry; [pers.] "We love Him because He first loved us". John 4:19. [a.] Strongsville, OH.

WARD, KATHRYN
[pen.] Katie Ward; [b.] Duluth, MN; [m.] Glen M. (Hap) Harold Jr., December 27, 1957; [ed.] Northrop Collegiate School, Cornell College, University of Minnesota; [occ.] Technical Writer, editor, technical illustrator, manage my own communications company-Katie's Rhetoric Service; [memb.] Mensa; [oth.writ.] Published dog magazine "Animal Crackers"; [pers.] I try to express in verse, what most animal lovers feel about their pets but cannot put into words and to mirror the heart and soul of their canine companions. [a.] Bloomington, MN.

WARNER, RUTH
[b.] October 6, 1923, Toledo, OH; [p.] Pearl and David Edwards; [m.] Neal E. Warner, October 27, 1945; [ch.] Craig Warner; [ed.] Woodward High School, Stautzenberger Sec. School; [occ.] Housewife (former secretary); [memb.] The International Society of Poets, International Society of Authors and Artists, the National Authors Registry; [hon.] 2 Editor's Choice Awards from National Library of Poetry, 2 Honorable Mention Certificates and 2 1994 President's Awards from Iliad Press, 2 1994 President's Awards Certificates from the National Author's Registry; [oth.writ.] "The Long Road Back" published in Odysses, "Her Rag Dolls" published in Outstanding Poets of 1994, "Fragile Images" published in Whispers In The Wind, "Fragile Flower" published in The Space Between, "Zest For Living" published in Treasured Poems of America, Fall 1994, "The Separation" published in Pen Etched Memories"; [pers.] Many real life experiences form the background for my poetry. Trials and tribulations of friends also supply good material. [a.] Northwood, OH.

WASHINGTON, NICOLE
[b.] December 15, 1975, Brooklyn, NY; [p.] Cathaleen Washington; [Clara Barton High School for the Health Professions, spent 1 1/2 semester at Kingsborough Community College, transferred to York College; [occ.] Full time student; [memb.] Member of the Church of Christ in South Jamaica, New York; [hon.] Volunteer service award; [oth.writ.] I have one poem that is published in an anthology called The Edge of Twilight; [pers.] I will continue to use the many talents that the Lord has blessed me with. Matthew 25:14-30. [a.] Jamaica Queens, NY.

WASS, GRANT H.
[b.] August 24, 1959, Northridge, CA; [p.] Mr. and Mrs. E. H. Wass; [m.] Patricia Wass, July 12, 1993; [ch.] Shane David, Shianne Erin and Sky Glenn; [ed.] Simi Valley High School, Simi Valley Adult Ed. and the many lessons learned and still learning from the vast choices that life offers me; [occ.] To shine some light into the dark mind of society with my words; [oth.writ.] Just what I keep in my journals at home; [pers.] To live and deal with these insane times of reality, one must keep a true heart. The sun does shine beyond rainbows. [a.] Palmdale, CA.

WATERS, VIRGINIA DEAN
[p.] Deceased; [m.] Deceased; [ch.] 7, 4 girls and 3 boys.

WATKINS, AETHENA C.
[b.] August 19, 1981, West Covina, CA; [p.] Richard and Denise Watkins; [ed.] 7th grade; [occ.] Student at Fulton Middle School, Fountain Valley, CA; [hon.[Inducted into the International Poets Society, August 1994, numerous creative writing awards since 3rd grade; [oth.writ.] "What Is Beautiful" published 1994, book title A Far Off Place; [pers.] I want to be a model. I love children and want to work with "special children" when I grow up. [a.] Fountain Valley, CA.

WATKINS, OPAL E.
[b.] September 5, 1922, Fountain Hills, AR; [ch.] 4 girls and 1 boy; [ed.] 12th grad, 1 year at Charles Beauty School, diploma in 1959, diploma from Institute of Children Literature, February 24, 1993; [occ.] Retired beautician; [hon.] Who's Who in Poetry and Golden Poet of 1989, Golden Poet of 1990 from Golden World of Poetry; [oth.writ.] Poe published in Diet Journal. [a.] Crossett, AR.

WATTS, MARY BAKER
[pen.] Mary Sarah; [b.] June 16, 1922, Michigan; [p.] Edwin and Elizabeth Sarah; [m.] Earl T. Watts (2nd husband), 1961; [ch.] Dale, Edwin, Steve, Donald, Terry, Gary, Kenneth and Ronnie; [ed.] High school; [occ.] Volunteer at the Saint Agnes Hospital, 5 years; [memb.] St. Agnes Guild, life member, Fresno, California Chamber of Commerce of Fresno, volunteer, before my volunteer work I was a housewife; [hon.] Nominated volunteer of the year, had picture made with Mayor of Fresno, dressed dolls for underprivileged children, hand dressed, picture in local news, wrote poems and stories for church paper, recited my poems for church; [oth.writ.] Poem called "You Showed Your Love Too Late", published in the American Anthology and the poem "You Can't Measure Love" in the anthology Hearts on Fire, signed by John Frost; [pers.] I have written poems since age seven. I have many poems and stories. I was a very sick and abused child, lost both parents to suicide when very young. Michigan Children's Aide raised me. [a.] Marquette, MI.

WAXMAN, TERI
[b.] December 25, 1957, Little Rock, AR; [ed.] B.S. in Accounting at University of Missouri, St. Louis; [occ.] CPA; [pers.] This poem was written to a dear friend who passed on, he was very helpful to my sister and I when our mom died. [a.] St. Louis, MO.

WEAVER, GRACE MARGARET
[b.] September 4, 1909, Philadelphia, PA; [p.] James Henry (Harry) and Beaulah Grace Davis Weaver; [m.[Single; [ed.] Normal School (Glassboro, NJ), several summers at Temple University, Philadelphia, B.A., Morningside College, Sioux City, Iowa, THM, Cliff school of Theology-Denver, CO; [occ.] Retired minister, United Methodist Church, one of the first women to be ordained elder; [memb.] Several choirs and choral groups, leader of a bell choir, pianist; [pers.] Poem being submitted "A Piece of Bread" one of a group of communion poems, this do, Wine-Fruit of the Grape, Arise to Neuness of Life, Remember, Come to the Fountain. [a.] Salem, OR.

WEBSTER, JODIE MARLINDA
[b.] September 5, 1980; [p.] Vicky and Vernon Webster; [ed.] Student at Grant Co. High School; [oth.writ.] Another poem which is being published in an anthology titled The Dark Side of The Moon; [pers.] Poetry is like a rainy day, cool and soothing I have been greatly influenced by the great alternative rock singers, and to you I say Rock On Beavis. [a.] Dry Ridge, KY.

WEISKOPF, WANDA
[b.] August 2, 1921, Missouri; [p.] Elmer and Stella Connell; [m.] Herbert Weiskopf, July 10, 1943; [ch.] Douglas Weiskopf and Marta Weiskopf Hampel; [ed.] Graduated from high school, Jefferson City, MO, studied at St. Louis Institute of Music, Los Angeles Conservatory of Music, studied voice privately with such teacher as Madame Vetta Karst and Rosa Raisa; [occ.] Retired opera and concert singer; [memb.] Los Angeles Chapter of the National Writers Club, National Association of Teachers of Singing, Los Angeles Chapter, Emeritus; [hon.] A number of prize winning poems, World of Poetry; [oth.writ.]

"All Is Not Winter" (collected poems, published by Encore Publishers, Portland, OR) L.A. My Way (12 poems in collection of stories and poems, Excellence Enterprises, publishers, "On The Wings of Song" (my life with the Maestro), an autobiographical memoir-Excellence Enterprises; [pers.] Life is very beautiful-we must cherish and make the most of it. [a.] Burbank, CA.

WELBORN, YVONNE
[pen.] Yvonne Dufek-Hogue Welborn; [b.] January 19, 1950, Ypsilanti, MI; [p.] Louis and Josephine Dufek; [ch.] James II and Jesse Welborn; [ed.] Graduate from Belleville High in 1968, certificates from word processing I and II, computer, bookkeeping and accounting; [occ.] Meijer Associate in Grocery Department, Belleville, MI; [hon.] Editor's Choice Award presented to me by the National Library of Poetry 1994; [oth.writ.] Poem published in The Space Between, one of my father's published in the Ypsilanti Press in 1978; [pers.] My hope is to have a book of my poetry published within the next few years. I have also written several stories none been published. My poetry is expressions from my heart and mind written by my hand. [a.] Ypsilanti, MI.

WELCH, SHARON K.
[b.] August 4, 1941, IN; [m.] Bob Welch, June 24, 1972; [ch.] Steve and Mark Cosgrove and Greg Welch, 2 grandchildren; [occ.] Housewife; [memb.] International Society of Poets Advisory Board member; [hon.] Selected writer for Chapel Recording, song-My Prayer, several merit of awards from National Library of Poetry, Outstanding Poets of 1994; [oth.writ.] Break In The Clouds, A New Beginning, Outstanding Poets of 1994, Looking Back Famous Poets Anthology, Saying Goodbye, Tears of Fire, Going Home, At Day's End, Your Choice, National Library of Poetry; [pers.] This poem is dedicated to my son Greg and his faithful dog Dino. The best friend man could ever have. [a.] Indianapolis, IN.

WELDIN, NYLAH
[pen.] LaunaLee; [b.] May 23, 1936, Glendale, CA; [p.] Norman and Grace Holt; [m.[David Weldin, May 5, 1979; [ch.[John Thomas, Christine Howard, Ethan Collins; [ed.] Roseville High, California, Spokane Falls College, Spokane Community College; [occ.] Artist, poet; [hon.] Boy Scout Leader, Den Mother, Honor Roll, President's List in college; [oth.writ.] Other poems, novel, unfinished; [pers.] I have learned in my search for truth and beauty that if you take care of the small things in life, the big things will take care of themselves. [a.] Cheney, WA.

WESTABY, EVE
[b.] September 8, 1926, Chicago, IL; [p.] Emily and Joseph; [m.] Dale; [ch.] Six children, thirteen grandchildren and one great grandchild; [ed.] I am a true believer in education, all my life I have been taking classes and will continue to do so for as long as I can; [occ.] Acue pressurest; [memb.] A long time member of Christian Womens, also a member of local groups, my church membership is very important to me; [hon.] I have been honored throughout my life, have received many awards, teaching children in church has been my own personal honor, the children have awarded me over and over, it has been an honor giving birth to my own children, I am very proud of them; [oth.writ.] The first poem I ever wrote, "Infinity" was printed in the book Dance On The Horizon, I have had several articles printed in our local newspapers; [pers.] My husband always supports everything I do. He believes in me and constantly tells me how proud he is of my accomplishments. Our love for each other grows stronger every day. We know God is blessing us and we always thank Him, we love Him. [a.] Weston, WI.

WESTCOTT, ROBBIN KAY
[b.] June 10, 1958, Kellogg, ID; [p.] John and Mary Donaldson, Bessie Messersmith; [m.] Gary Westcott Sr., April 18, 1975; [ch.] Gary Jr. and Jeremy Westcott; [ed.] 1975 graduate of Abraham Lincoln High; [occ.] Manager of a small trucking company I and my husband own; [hon.] I have received 2 merits of awards for poetry and was given the honor to write a poem for a speech for the graduation of the 5th grade students at Krett Elementary; [oth.writ.] 1 poem published in Our World's Most Treasured Poems; [pers.] I like to write about things with meaning and I like to write about things in my life and I like to try to get the reader to be able to visualize my writing. My favorite poet is Alice E. Chase. [a.] Council Bluffs, IA.

WESTMORELAND, JOHN WHITE
[b.] December 11, 1960, Lowrance Hospital; [p.] Eugene and Opal Westmoreland; [ed.] Bachelor's and Associate Degrees; [occ.] Tutor, commentator and poet; [hon.] Men's Bible Class Accompanist, appointed Secretary of Coddle Creek Democratic Precinct, elected member of National Beta Club, Mooresville, North Carolina; [oth.writ.] Hodgenville Kentucky, Drury's Publishing, Louisville, Kentucky, These Days, Charlotte, NC, The Charlotte Observer, Mooresville, NC, Mooresville Tribune, Minot North Dakota and Harlingen Texas, Quill Books; [pers.] "It is of interest to me that my birth date is on the third Sunday of Advent in 1960. The pediatrician had predicted an eventful Saturday, December 10. Yet, I came along on Sunday, December 11-just in time for services".

WHALEY, KRYSTAL L.
[b.] May 26, 1980, Georgia; [p.] Nan and Joe Whaley; [ed.] Sevier County High School; [occ.] School, freshman; [memb.] S.C.H.S-band, drama club, Elizabeth Williams Senior Dance Troupe; [oth.writ.] "Love", A Far Off Place, "Picture Blue", 8th grade literary book; [pers.] People say teenagers are too wild and uncontrollable, but I say that they are just creative in their own way. [a.] Sevierville, TN.

WHEELER, RANDALL D.
[b.] October 13, 1957, Salem, IN; [p.] Anita E. Hedrick; [m.] Never married; [ed.] Eastern High School, Pekin, IN, NRI, Washington, DC, LSSC Saulte Ste, MI, U.S.A.F. training; [occ.] Burger King; [memb.] Calvary Baptist Church, Disabled American Veterans; [oth.writ.] Satan and miscellaneous poems, and short stories; [pers.] I believe the Bible. [a.] Laurel, MT.

WHITE, BEATRICE
[b.]April 21, 1917, Keeseville, NY; [p.] Isaac and Minnie (Abare) La Mountzin; [m.] Donald R. White, April 18, 1938; [ch.] Eugene, Carol (deceased in 1953), Gail and Susan; [ed.] Elementary (St. John's), high school (Keeseville); [occ.] Widow and housekeeper; [memb.] Catholic Daughters of the Americas, Altar Rosary Society, Knights of Columbus Auxiliary, Keeseville Senior Citizens Club and Plattsburgh Senior Citizens Council, Anderson Falls Heritage Society, Marine Corps League Auxiliary and V.F.W. Auxiliary; [hon.] Award for highest average in 2 years of high school, French at grammar school graduation, award for highest average in commercial course at high school graduation, award for composition on "Transportation Problems and Solutions" by radio station WEAV Plattsburg, NY and honored at community dinner sponsored by Anderson Falls Heritage Club, a narration on taps of "My Gift" by Ira Westreich; [oth.writ.] A poem, "My Gift" published by the National Library of Poetry in their 1994 anthology of poetry, though I have written poetry, essays, journals, philosophical thoughts, etc., most of my life, this is my second attempt for publication, thanks to the National Library of Poetry; [pers.] Inspirational thoughts must be written immediately. Other writing takes more time and effort, but I enjoy it all. [a.] Keeseville, NY.

WHITE, CANDICE
[pen.] Candice White; [b.] February 17, 1979, Salem, OR; [p.] Thomas and Lois White; [ed.] Currently attending South Salem High School; [oth.writ.] I currently have many un-published poems; [pers.] My poems are simply my thoughts, feelings and heart speaking to me. If you listen carefully, you'd be surprised what is being said, it's pure poetry. [a.] Salem, OR.

WHITE, PATTY
[pen.] P.J. White; [b.] May 10, 1948, Silsbee, TX; [p.] Tom and Marie Tennison; [m.] Bob White, August 6, 1979; [ch.] Darin Ashley; [ed.] Silsbee High School and Lamar University of Beaumont, TX; [occ.] Poet, songwriter; [memb.] International Society of Poets, lifetime member, First United Methodist Church Choir in Jasper, TX; [hon.] In two previous National Library of Poetry contests, I have won one Editor's Choice Award, and both poems were chosen to be recorded on "The Sound of Poetry" cassettes; [oth.writ.] Numerous poems, some entered in other current contests, one published in a local newspaper; [pers.] Family, faith and friendships are all very important to me for a rewarding life. I wrote the poem for this book for my parents so they will always remember how much I appreciate them and thank them for the wonderful job they did raising my brother and sisters and me. I feel very fortunate to have turned out so much like them. [a.] Sam Rayburn, TX.

WHITE, PAUL ERSKINE
[pen.] PW; [b.] March 5, 1907, Huntington, WV; [p.] Orilas G. and Lena Madden White; [m.] Mary E. White (deceased 1988), September 5, 1942; [ch.] Craig C. and Greg G. [ed.] Bachelor Science Bethany College West Virginia, 1928; [occ.] Retired January 1, 1994 from OUE Bookstore 1975-1991, previous Bethany College 1952-1975; [memb.] National Cambridge Glass Collectors, Bethany, WV Christian Church, Republican Party, human race; [hon.] None to talk about, I have many gold and silver certificates; [oth.writ.] Since 1921, 1988 Poetry Face to Face, Mary and Paul TX August 11, 1980, 1989 Vol 2 Poet Face to Face M&P, Tx, 1991 Nat Trail and Old 40 in Verse and Pictures, 1910-1991, No. Missing; [a.] Belmont, OH.

WHITE-EPSTEIN, GLORIA M.
[b.] April 7, 1936, Fitchburg, MA; [p.] Leon J. and Louise M. (Therrien) White Sr.; [m.] David I. Epstein

(ph.D.), August 7, 1992; [ed.] M.A. in History from Northeastern University, Boston, MA; [occ.] Clerk II, U Mass/Dartmouth, North Dartmouth, MA; [memb.] Dramatist Guild, NY Playwrights Platform, Boston, MA, International Society of Poets and American Poetry Society; [hon.] B.S. in History, Cum Laude, Northeastern University, Boston, MA, American Poetry Association; [oth.writ.] Plays, "The Dutchess" and "Double Image" produced Lyric Stage, Boston, MA, poetry published, The National Library of Poetry; [pers.] "Organization is the key to success, but to succeed at anything I look within myself". [a.] Wareham, MA.

WIDAWSKI, EVA
[b.] June 10, 1926; [p.] Miladay Bernard Winkler; [m.] Sam Widawski, August 16, 1952; [ch.] Margie, Lana, Gail and Saul; [ed.] Sam and J are holocaust survivors; [occ.] Homemaker; [hon.] Golden Poet 1990, Award of Merit Certificate 1991 and 1992, Editor's Choice Award 1994, honored as a Golden Poet for 1991; [oth. writ.] About Our Forefathers; [pers.] My poems are biographic a legacy...about the concerns for those that will question after we are no longer here; [a.] Los Angeles, CA

WIDNER, EVELYN COPPLE
[b.] January 4, 1911, Jefferson County, IL; [p.] Birthel and Mayme (Dickinson) Copple; [m.] Eldon L. Widner, November 7, 1980; [ed.] Centralia High School, Centralia, IL, B.A. Degree, Monmouth College, Monmouth, IL, other additional credits for special K-14, teaching and supervising instructional materials; [occ.] Retired, former schoolteacher and learn center director, (Media Specialist); [memb.] NRTA, IRTA, Tri-County Retired Teachers Association, Delta Kappa Gamma, Professional Society International, International Society of Poets, Jacksonville Area Genealogical and Historical Society, Central Christian Church, Jacksonville, IL; [hon.] Teacher Emeritus, Galesburg, IL, high honor student in high school, Editor's Choice Award from National Library of Poetry, International Poet of Merit Award from International Society of Poets 1993, poems published in National Library of Poetry anthologies, poems read on cassette "Sound of Poetry"; [oth.writ.] I have written many poems for anniversaries, birthdays, various occasions and celebrations, also my school days, travels, the seasons, etc., for many years I have composed my own Christmas greetings in the form of acrostics, some have been published in newsletters, bulletins, the National Library of Poetry and Impressions cassettes, several are now copyrighted and ready for publication; [pers.] I continue to enjoy expressing my thoughts and feelings in poetry. It helps to fulfill my desire to promote love, peace and understanding throughout our beautiful world. My greatest and deepest hope is that my poems will be an inspiration to anyone who reads them. All these things will always be important in my life. [a.] Jacksonville, IL.

WILBORN, LINDESY M.
[b.] August 31, 1977, Mishawaka, IN; [p.] Wayne E. and Kandie L. Wilborn; [ed.] Currently senior at Penn High School, plan to attend IUSB after I graduate; [occ.] Work at pet store called FOr Pet's Sake; [memb.] PHS Advanced Women's Choir; [hon.] Valedictorian of 8th grade class, Honor Roll; [oth.writ.] Poem "The Prisoner" published in Dark Side Of The Moon, several poems published in school literary magazines and newspapers; [pers.] My dream of success will never be diminished so long as interest such as this is shown. I'll never forget those who helped me along the way. Someday I wish to reward them. [a.] Mishawaka, IN.

WILDER, KATHLEEN ANN
[pen.] Kathi Wilder; [b.] September 14, 1942, Albert Lea; [p.] Louis and Kathryn Warmka; [m.] Norbert Wilder, June 24, 1964; [ch.] Philip Leon, Paul Louis, Patrick Lee and Jeffrey John; [ed.] 2 1/2 years college of St. Benedict, St. Joseph, MN; [occ.] Media clerk at Brookside Middle School; [memb.] St. Theodore's Catholic Church, Knights of Columbus Auxiliary; [hon.] Honored for fostering children for 20 years, honored for 20 years of working with Boy Scouts; [pers.] This poem was written in loving memory of a co-worker, Bob Robertson, who taught at Brookside School in Albert Lea, MN. He fought a gallant fight against cancer and was an inspiration to all. [a.] Albert Lea, MN.

WILKES, CAROLYN
[b.] September 10, 1949, Jeff Davis; [p.] George and Allene Thompson; [m.] William E. Wilkes, September 30, 1989; [ch.] Denise, Donnie and Angie Smith. [ed.] Jeff Davis High, Southern Georgia College; [occ.] Cutting room sewing factory; [memb.] American Heart Association; [hon.] 1 year college in Genealogy of the Elderly; [oth.writ.] Several poems published in local newspaper, 2 poems published in the books Tears of Fire and one in Dark Side of The Moon; [pers.] I love to write about people, loved ones, people that have lost loved ones. I hope to help them in some little way and ease some of their heartache. [a.] Lumber City, GA.

WILKINS, DOROTHY
[b.] March 20, 1919, Isabel, SD; [p.] Jessie and Ernest Sevrens; [m.] Glenn E. Wilkins, March 15, 1942; [ch.] Carole, Nancy and Ellen; [ed.] High school and college; [pers.] My mother, a teacher loved books and poetry and greatly encouraged her family in those areas. [a.] Del Rey, CA.

WILKINSON, MARGUERITE I.
[pen.] Marguerite I. Wilkinson; [b.] December 12, 1922, Pasadena, CA; [p.] Robert A. and Margaret I. Roberts; [m.] Vernon R. Wilkinson, December 6, 1943; [ch.] Dr. Mitchell Ray Wilkinson, [ed.] Pasadena Junior College; [occ.] Rancher and homemaker; [memb.] United Methodist Women, Read and Review Book Club of Odessa, Texas, Farm Bureau of Texas, Riverside and Landowners Protection Coalition, Inc; [hon.] Honorees in the 1988 Texas Family Land Heritage Honors ceremony in the Capitol, Austin, Texas; [oth.writ.] "The V Bar Journal", "The V Bar Update", "Poetry's Musings", all unpublished; [pers.] Since early childhood I have thought of Spring as a time of awakening -- the visible display of promises kept, rebirth and eternal life. [a.] San Angelo, TX.

WILLETT, EDWARD F.
[pen.] Edward F. Willett; [b.] August 25, 1933, Maple Rapids, MI; [p.] Frank James and Eleanor Emily; [m.] Elizabeth Ann (deceased), July 18, 1958; [ch.] James Edward (7-18-59), and SFC James E. Willett-El Paso, Texas, Army; [memb.] Lansing Michigan Jaycees 1962-1969, Lansing YMCA Mystic Lake Union Committee-secretary 5 years; [hon.] Jaycee of the Month, October 1962, Outstanding New Jaycee 1963; [pers.] Expressions from the pen are never lost! [a.] Perry, MI.

WILLIAMS, DANNY
[b.] DC; [p.] George and Carlisle Williams; [m.] Single; [ed.] University of District of Columbia (two years); [occ.] Word Processor, work in a theatre workshop; [memb.] The Mary Wilson International Fan Club (USA); [oth.writ.] "The Proposal" in Dark Side of The Moon, "Sunday With Mary Wilson" in Mary Wilson newsletter, "A Song For You" and "In The Night" in t-shirts (promotion), other articles for newspaper and books; [pers.] "Writing is a way to express those emotions, especially if you are shy, and it is good therapy". [a.] Brooklyn, NY.

WILLIAMS, JAMES EARL BREWER
[b.] November 15, 1942, Memphis, TN; [p.] J.T. and Alma L. Brewer; [m.] Hanne Klos Williams, June 29, 1987; [ch.] Rita J., LaTonya M., Paul M., Jamie E., Jayson L., and Christopher D.; [ed.] BS-Chemistry, BS-Computer Science, AA-Business, many U.S. Army schools; [occ.] Battalion S-4 officer/log management, Spec-0346 (GS-12); [memb.] Bush Grove Baptist Church, American Red Cross, United Kenpo Karate Association, 3rd D-Black Belt; [hon.] Retired military (Army) 20 years, Honorable Awards, Army Commendation Medal with 4 oak leaf cluster, National Defense Service Medal, Master Parachute Badge, Meritorious Service Medal, Vietnam Cross of Gallantry w/palm, Vietnam Service Medal with 3 bronze star, good conduct medal with 5 awards, Who's Who in Poetry III, several awards for outstanding achievement in poetry 1989, 1990, 1991, 1992.

WILLIAMS, LOLETIA C.
[b.] October 8, 1959, Wichita, KS; [p.] Mr. and Mrs. Henry L. Williams Jr.; [ed.] B.S. Liberal Arts-Social Sciences, Kansas State University, Manhattan, Kansas; [occ.] Police Specialist-Investigations Division; [memb.] Alpha Kappa Alpha Sorority Inc.; [hon.] I have been extremely honored to learn one of my poems is to be published by the National Library of Poetry, the name of the poem is "Heartfelt Dreams"; [pers.] I have been so fortunate in my life to have a wonderful family who has always encouraged me to grow spiritually and appreciate myself. This poetry is another way of echoing the sentiments listed above. [a.] Everett, WA.

WILLIAMS, MELISSA MARIE
[pen.] Marie; [b.] January 30, 1976; [p.] Marilyn Staidum and Lawyer Williams JR.; [ed.] Senior at Terrebonne High School; [memb.] Key Club, President of Church Youth Organization, Journalism, National Honor Society; [hon.] Who's Who Among American High School Students, published poem in the National Library of Poetry, A Question of Balance, Honor Roll, nominated for Girls/Boys State; [oth.writ.] Articles in school newspaper called Mirror; [pers.] Believing in something greater than your self, can only be done through strength. [a.] Houma, LA.

WILLIAMS, SHAREL
[pen.] Sharel White; [b.] March 7, 1968, Houston, TX; [p.] Linda Kay Corbin; [ch.] Talyna Renee, Celia Adeline and Katrina Mara; [occ.] Mother; [hon.] Editor's Choice Award; [oth.writ.] "Sweet Celia" in A Far Off Place; [pers.] I hope that someday those with the authority will stop discriminating against the poor, for we have rights too, and hope someday to have my kidnapped daughter, Celia back. [a.] Ehrenberg, AZ.

WILLIAMS, W. G.
[b.] 23 years old; [p.] Leo C. and Jenner Rae Williams; [pers.] Most of my writings are from my life's fears, thoughts and questions. The rest are my views of the unknown or things unable to express views of their own. Read deep into the words, for I spare not nor waste a single letter that has less meaning. If I am lost, waste no tears, emotions run your mind aimlessly and you'll never understand the reason I'm gone. Ignorance is found by those who seek from eyes, ears and preconceptions. Options are endless and with an open mind you'll always find an answer with no discrepancies. In time everything can and will be answered . A reason why we are born, live and die. As a child I remember, remembering blackness. Was there light before the blackness? I will one day know. [a.] Jacksonville, FL.

WILLIAMSON, BARBARA J.
[pen.] B.J. Brackin; [b.] September 5, 1959, PA: [p.] James and Dorothy Brackin; [m.] John S. Williamson, November 1, 1988; [ch.] Joshua Campbell, Justin David and Amy Elizabeth; [ed.] The University of Alabama, Pennsylvania State University; [occ.] Poet and homemaker; [memb.] The Yorklyn Center for Creative Arts, the Hockessin United Methodist Church; [hon.] Honorable Mention in the University of Alabama in Huntsville art contest 1988, Dean's List, National Honor Society; [oth.writ.] Poetry published in the Axis and the Shadows literary magazines, poetry book To Trust Once More, ready for publication, short stories; [pers.] My poetry is a form of communication which hopefully enables others to understand the complexities of life. [a.] Wilmington, DE.

WILLMORE, REBECCA
[b.] January 2, 1980; [p.] Mike and Claudia Willmore; [ed.] Leonardtown High School; [occ.] Student at Leonardtown High School; [hon.] Honor Roll, poems have been recognized in front of school; [oth.writ.] "Free", "Mama's Pot Surprise", "Hear Him, See Me, Listen", A Little Bit of Heaven", etc.; [pers.] I cannot take full credit for my poetry. It is only He who speaks through me to glorify Him. My parents have been there for me since day one and God has been there before that and ever since. [a.] Leonardtown, MD.

WILSON, BERNICE W.
[b.] March 26, 1941, Hamilton, GA; [p.] Clarence and Ruby Williams; [m.] Divorced; [ch.] Michael E. Wilson; [ed.] Some college, Blayton Business College; [occ.] Administrative Assistant; [memb.] National Authors Registry, the International Society of Poets; [hon.] Accomplishment of merit from Creative Arts and Science Ent., Honorable Mention from Iliad Press, Editor's Choice Award, National Library of Poetry and Editor's Choice Quarterly Award, Verses magazine and NAR; [oth.writ.] "I Love You", "A Tree That's Bare", "Shadows in The Night", "When I Was Little", "Spring", "Passing of Life", "You Are My Life" and "Lonely", I have written other poems that have not been published, I am also in the process of writing lyrics for songs; [pers.] My writing is a way of expressing how I perceive life and the world in which I live. [a.] Smyrna, GA.

WILSON, CHRISTINA M.
[b.] February 23, 1971, Brooklyn, NY; [p.] Barbara A. Stuart and John J. Errico; [ed.] Santa Luces Community High School, Community College of the Air Force, Community College of Southern NV; [occ.] Full time student and full time office clerk; [memb.] Art Club, Community College of Southern Nevada, and the Candlebox Fan Club of course, staff writer for CCSN news magazine, "Reflections"; [hon.] Florida Academic Scholar, AMN (month February 1991), AMN (quarter January -March 1991); [oth.writ.] Sci-fi, active adventure stories (none published yet), countless poems and songs (again none published); [pers.] There is no more powerful force in the universe except that of words and songs. It touches every person in every part of the world in every culture. Its meaning is so regular and I give my life to it. [a.] Las Vegas, NV.

WILSON, ELVA MAE
[b.] June 13, 1922, Windham, MT; [p.] Hattie L. Eighmey and Herbert H. Benjamin; [m.] Richard Wilson (deceased), September 26, 1970; [ch.] Kathleen Marie Painter, Billie June Hodges, Vincent L. Aiken Jr., Roger L. Aiken and Esther Eileen Bair; [ed.] West High School, Denver Colorado Business Administration Olympic College, Bremerton, WA; [occ.] Retired grandmother of five, great grandmother of three, gardening outside, houseplants inside; [memb.] The Heritage Foundation, the Smithsonian Institution, National Geographic Society, National Rife Association, NRA, ILA, V.F.W. Auxiliary, National Park Trust, United Seniors Association, Christian Coalition, Grass roots political worker, Political Advisory member; [hon.] Five Golden Poet Awards, five award of Merit Certificates from World of Poetry, Honorary Charter membership for Outstanding Achievement in Poetry by International Society of Poets; [oth.writ.] Poetry in Christmas cards and letters, birthday, get well, sympathy and anniversary cards; [pers.] I believe God blessed me with the ability to write poetry. Do unto others as you would have them do unto you. [a.] Bremerton, WA.

WILSON, JOHN D.
[b.] September 8, 1957, Boston; [p.] William H. and Joan H. Wilson; [m.] Karen B. Beer, June 1, 1991; [ed.] Colorado State University, University of California, Davis; [occ.] Software consultant; [memb.] United State Chess Federation, American Contract Bridge League, United States Badminton Association; [hon.] USCF Advanced Life Master, ACBL Club Master; [pers.] A poem must reflect the anguish and hope in one's heart if it is to be a testimony of life. Thank you, Sally Ann. [a.] Los Angeles, CA.

WILSON, MARGARET J.
[pen.] M.J. Wilson; [b.] October 20, 1917, Radford, VA; [p.] Florence and Robert L. Jenkins; [m.] Felix C. Wilson JR. (deceased); [ch.] Four daughters; [ed.] High school and 1 year college; [occ.] Secretary until retirement, retired painter.

WILSON, MILISSAU
[b.] December 5, 1967, Mozambique; [p.] Fabiao and Teresa Nuvunga; [m.] Stephen Wilson, July 14, 1990; [ch.] Daniela Vanise Wilson; [ed.] College; [occ.] Student, Miami Dade Community College; [oth.writ.] Several unpublished poems; [pers.] My writing reflects my past experiences, my life in the USA, the problems affecting the society.

WILSON, STEPHANIE D.
[b.] August 3, 1964, Oklahoma City, OK; [p.] Willie A. and Wilma J. Wilson; [ed.] Grandview Senior High and Longview College; [occ.] Free-lance artist; [hon.] Certificate of award, girls varsity track, Flags Corps, Phi Beta Sigma's Little Sisters Sweethearts, Editor's Choice Award 1994; [oth.writ.] "You Were Like A Rose", "Truth Or A Lie For Love", "Blue Moon", "Coming of Age", "Desire", "Beautiful Love of You", "The Pawn and The Poet", "Doubtness", "The Red Side Show" and many more; [pers.] Through my heart, God's love flows, without the Lord Almighty, I am unable to create. I am a woman of soul. [a.] Grandview, MO.

WILSON, THERESA VICTORIA
[pen.] Tessie; [b.] September 18, 1947, Washington,DC; [p.] Thomas L. Wilson and Mary Lynn Wilson (deceased); [oth.writ.] "Carpal Tunnel Syndrome"; [pers.] The poems I write are heartfelt expressions from my personal experiences. "All gifts are from God, and with God all things are possible". [a.] Washington, DC.

WINGFIELD, MARVIN B.
[b.] October 26, 1907, MO; [p.] William Austin and Sarah Elizabeth Johnson Wingfield; [ed.] High school, some business college; [pers.] Done much reading in philosophy history, literature, religion. Would like to leave twenty words to posterity. [a.] Sedalia, MO.

WISE, PAULA SHANAYE
[b.] October 16, 1979, Hammond, IN; [p.] Paul and Genevieve Wise; [ed.] Freshman at Wirt High School, Gary, IN; [memb.] Member of yearbook staff at William A. Wirt High School-dark room technician and layout designer; [hon.] National Junior Honor Society-3.5 GPA; [oth.writ.] Poem "Rise" published in The Space Between, "Rise" recently published in Make-A-Wish Foundation newsletter, won 1st place in an essay contest, "What It Takes To Be A Secretary"; [pers.] I think the public enjoys teen writers because we have a distinct perspective on life. Also, poetry opens doors for self-expression and that is the best thing that you can give a person, the opportunity to express their thoughts. [a.] Gary, IN.

WITHEE, BEVERLY
[b.] December 26, 1967, St. Thomas, Virgin Island; [p.] David Frederick and Pamela Brackett Whitee Sr.; [ed.] Oliver Perry Walker Senior High School, University of New Orleans, Delgado Community College; [occ.] Rehabilitation Technician, Administrative Assistant; [memb.] International Society of Poets, Symphony Chorus of New Orleans, Concert Choir of New Orleans, Aurora United Methodist Church; [hon.] World of Poetry, Golden Poet (1992), the National Library of Poetry, Editor's Choice Awards (1993) and (1994), published poems in two anthologies, Whispers In The Wind (1993) and Outstanding Poets of 1994 (1994); [pers.] In the world of famous poets, my greatest inspiration is Helen Steiner Rice. Her works encourage me to write forever, or for as long as God allows. [a.] Harvey, LA.

WITMAN, CHERLY
[b.] December 16, 1971; [occ.] Loan Operation Specialist; [pers.] There is nothing in the world like writing. Your characters are in your control and they can be and do all that you can only dream for your own life, and for every time you fail in love your characters succeed. It is the best of two worlds, real and imaginary. [a.] East Earl, PA.

WODE, GLORIA MARGARET (CLINEDINST)
[b.] October 23, 1922, Elizabeth, NJ; [p.] Charles Edward and Margaret (Retzel) Clinedinst; [m.] Claude Raymond Wode Sr., April 11, 1942; [ch.] Gloria Claudette Lamb, Kathleen Margaret Maerkel, Carole Lynn Stout, Claude Raymond Wode, Jr., Robert John Wode and Dorothy Jean Tomlinson, 17 grandchildren, 8 great-grandchildren; [ed.] High school; [occ.] Retired, the author has been writing for over 25 years, but just started submitting her works into contests; [memb.] Creative Arts and Science Enterprises, Painted Post, New York, International Society of Authors and Artists, Painted Post, NY, Quill Books, Harlingen, TX, National Library of Poetry, Owings Mills, Maryland, International Society of Poets, Owings Mills, Maryland, World of Poetry , Sacramento, CA; [hon.] World of Poetry -Golden Trophies 1991 and 1992, 1 Golden Poet plaque 1991, Who's Who plaque, 2 Commemorative Certificates, 6 Certificates of Merit, 1 Golden Certificate and given the title of Golden Poet 1991-1992, the Editor-in-Chief, Charles J. Palmer, of Creative Arts and Science Enterprises awarded her an "Accomplishment of Merit' with an upraised gold seal for her poem "My Plea", he also congratulated her on her fine work; [oth.writ.] All our anthologies of literary works and biography will be in circulation world-wide. Books placements in Asia, Africa, Europe, Australia, South America, Antarctica and of course North America. Our book also goes to libraries, colleges, schools, hospitals and we always send complimentary copies to our Armed Forces serving overseas. "Let's Go, He Awaits Your Call", Great Poems of Our Times, anthology-published by Jeffrey Franz 1993, "Mother's Love Unending" and "A Poem of Deep Thought", World of Poetry, anthology -"Our Worlds Most Treasured Poems, John Campbell, Editor and Publisher 1991, "Early Morn" published in "All My Tomorrows", anthology -Quill Books, Shirley J. Mikkelson, Publisher 1993, Gloria is one of 273 poets out of 1800 submissions that have been published in "All My Tomorrows" anthology. Gloria is expecting to receive five more publications in the next six weeks. Four of her poems have been published on cassette tapes called "Sound of Poetry" by National Library of Poetry.

WOODS, ASHLEY J.
[b.] England; [ch.] Karen, Duane, Darren and Jay; [ed.] 1994 graduate of La Roche College, (non-traditional student); [occ.] Accountant/Political Activist; [memb.] The human race; [hon.] Dean's List, Honors student; [oth.writ.] Political views published in local papers. Poetry published in La Roche Literary magazine. [a.] Pittsburgh, PA.

WOODS, LAURA SIMPSON
[b.] January 20, 1937, Louisville, KY; [p.] Millage Lee and Julia McGee Simpson (both deceased); [ch.] Germaine Denise Woods; [ed.] Sylvania F. Williams and F.P. Richare Elementary Schools, Booker T. Washington High School, Dillard University, LSUNO, IUSE, University of Louisville; [occ.] Retired elementary school teacher (34 years); [memb.] NRTA, KRTA, Brown Memorial, C.M.E. Church, Delta Sigma Theta Sorority (inactive), JCTRA, AARP, Shawnee Gardens' Tenants Association, Dillard University Alumni Association; [hon.] Honor student-4 years Dillard University, Cum Laude '58 graduate, Dillard University, Who's Who Among Colleges and Universities-58, PTA life membership-1992, Distinguished Service Award, Brown Memorial C.M.E. Church 1986, 1992, 1993, JCPS Outstanding Staff Award 1992, 1993, Who's Who Among Teachers in America 1992, 1993, Honorary Citizen, N.O. LA, 1993, Spirit of Louisville Award 1993, Clifford Turner Freedom Award-1992; [oth.writ.] "Sunrise" IN The Desert Sun, National Library of Poetry, "Sometimes", Dark Side of The Moon, National Library of Poetry, "Me", Best Poems of 1995, National Library of Poetry, an unpublished collection of poems "My Love For You", Apropos February 1995; [pers.] I believe that I am an instrument in this cycle of life to assist wherever I am needed with God's help, His will be done. [a.] Louisville, KY.

WOODWARD, EVELYN
[b.] November 23, 1940, Rockville, CT; [p.] Henry and Catherine Gonder; [m.] Raymond Woodward, August 6, 1958; [ch.] Richard, Donna, Dennis, Robert and Catherine; [ed.] Only GED and a writer's course; [occ.] Food handler; [oth.writ.] I only have two other poems published, but I hope to have other poems and some short stories and a novel published, I hope to have the poems to be song lyrics someday; [pers.] When I learned I was to have my youngest child, someone told me "a child is a gift from God". He gave my husband and me five gifts. She was the one at age 5 months old who inspired this poem, but it's my feelings for all five children. We also have 4 grandchildren, we hit the jackpot!

WOOLDRIDGE, JUDITH J.
[pen.] Judith Wooldridge; [b.] January 8, 1938, Humboldt, KS; [p.] Gerald and Emma Yockey; [m.] Gilbert Wooldridge, February 11, 1957; [ch.] Brenda Ann and Kimberly Kay; [ed.] I attended Humboldt Elementary and high school in Humboldt, Kansas; [occ.] Wife, mother, grandmother and Chapter Paraprofessional at Garfield School, Coffeyville, KS; [memb.] Emmanul Baptist Church, Women's International Bowling Congress, U.S.D. 445 and life member of P.T.A.; [hon.] Golden Poet Award 1989, Award of Merit, Silver Poet 1990 and Who's Who in Poetry 1990 for World of Poetry, Bowler of the Year 1984 and Mrs. Congeniality 1993, Editor's Choice Award 1994; [oth.writ.] Several poems, the poem "My Rock Flowers" which was published in 1989 in Golden Poets, I also have published "I, We, They and Them" in the Tears of Fire; [pers.] I strive to reflect the inner love and spirit I have for my family, the children I work with and my fellowman. Thank you for letting me express myself. [a.] Coffeyville, KS.

WORCESTER, R.J.
[b.] December 19, 1919, Goodyear, AZ; [p.] Herbert and Phoebe M.; [m.] Catherine H., June 4, 1944; [ch.] Elizabeth Ann and Robert James; [ed.] B.S.E.E., University of Arizona Tucson 1945, post grad. work in Electronics and Nuclear Physics; [occ.] Retired; [memb.] National Society Professional Engineers, Knights of Columbus, American Society Mechanical Engineers; [hon.] Outstanding contribution award N.S.P.E.; [oth.writ.] Various technical and political articles; [pers.] Life is fun when you follow God's lead. [a.] Chatsworth, CA.

WORTHINGTON JR., SAMUEL WHEELER
[pen.] Sam Worthington; [b.]May 7, 1907, Baltimore, MD; [p.] Sam and Lucy O. Worthington; [m.] Mary Pegram Wilson Worthington, January 8, 1955; [ch.] S.W. Worthington III and Mary George Worthington; [ed.] Wilson North Carolina High School and University of North Carolina, A.B. Degree 1928; [occ.] Retired but still active peanut and cattle farmer; [memb.] St. Thos Episcopal Church, Windsor, NC, choir member; [hon.] President Bertie County Farm Bureau 10 years, chairman East Carolina Layman's Association 2 years in 60's; [oth.writ.] Unpublished jingles to wife, hospital nurse and own children, newspaper articles regarding problems of agriculture and other solution; [pers.] Praise god for my wonderful satisfying life in this great outdoors and the endless challenges of the farm, no regrets whatsoever. [a.] Windsor, NC.

WRIGHT, CARMEN
[pen.] Carmen Wright; [b.] October 3, 1962, Wiesbaden, West Germany; [p.] Jesse and Gisela Wright; [sib.] Sherrie Wright Mitchell; [m.] Single; [ed.] Bachelors in Psychology Associates in Humanities, graduated from Virginia Commonwealth University and Danville Community College; [occ.] Artistic Designer Consultant; [memb.] International society of Poets, Fairview United Methodist of Danville; [hon.] Semi-finalist in 2 International Society of Poets competitions also was awarded the Golden Poet and the Silver Poet Awards in a national competition previously, several newspaper and magazine article features done in Danville (hometown) and Richmond, Virginia; [oth.writ.} Throughout high school and college I have had my poetry published in gifted creative writer's magazines entitled "The Oddessey" and various church and college newsletters; [pers.] Writing poetry enriches my life, by allowing my artistic nature freedom and spontaneity, I've experienced both pondering of beauty and added depth to my spirit. Poetry is one of the richest arts one can experience. [a.] Glen Allen, VA.

WRIGHT, HAL
[b.] September 11, 1966, Grand Rapids, MI; [p.] Ed and Rose Wright; [m.] Single; [ed.] BA, Liberal Arts with English major, Aquinas College, Godwin Heights High School; [occ.] Supervisor, Camer Center retail store and mini lab; [memb.] St. Jude League; [hon.] Dean's List (four years), Magna Cum Laude, American Legion Award (high school), National Honor Society (high school), Merit Awards for Science, Journalism, Art and Citizenship (high school); [oth.writ.] Poems published in Aquinas College publications, (Student Sampler, Visions and Revisions), poem published in "Grand Rapids College Review"; [pers.] Writing poetry is one thing I truly love. I hope to continue without diluting the joy and integrity of my work, and I hope to find an audience. [a.] Grand Rapids, MI.

WRIGHT, MARGARET EVANS
[b.] April 3, 1935, Charlottesville, VA; [p.] VeLena and William Clarence Evans; [m.] Jim Wright (divorced), August 25, 1956; [ch.] Jeff, Chad and Scott Wright, Lori Wright Taylor; [ed.] Tahlequah Senior High School, Tahlequah, OK, B.S. Degree, Northeastern State University, Teaching Certification, NSU, M.Ed., NSU, Tahlequah, OK; [occ.] Retired, former secretary, teacher and checker; [memb.] AAUW (Association of American University Women), Delta Sigma Epsilon Social Sorority (recording secretary), NSU Square Dance Club, Grace Baptist Church; [hon.] Winner of local poetry contest 1952, senior class poet of graduating class 1953, Golden Poet Award 1988, Golden Poet Award 1989, Who's Who in Poetry 1990; [oth.writ.] Several poems in newspa-

pers, Christmas and Easter cantatas (composed music and words to these and many other songs); [pers.] I love to write poetry and set the words to music. I have played violin, clarinet and organ, but my favorite thing to do is sit at my piano and compose music and lyrics. [a.] Cleveland, OK.

WRIGHT, OPAL L.
[pen.] Lou Wright; [b.] March 2, 1914, Longview, TX; [p.] Frank and Evey Nichols (deceased); [m.] John P. Wright, APril 11, 1942; [ch.] 3 boys and 1 girl all married, 7 grandchildren and 6 great grandchildren; [ed.] B.S. in Education with 5 teaching fields; [occ.] Retired after 30 years in a classroom (writing); [memb.] Order of Eastern Star (50 years), T.R.O.A., Retired Officers' Association of Service Personnel, R.W.A., Romance Writers of America and Tyler Rose Chapter; [hon.] Editor's Choice Award from the National Library of Poetry 1994; [oth.writ.] News and magazine articles and short stories; [pers.] It is my desire to so live my life that it will bring honor to my God, my parents and my country and bring sorrow to none. [a.] Tyler, TX.

WRIGHT, WILBUR HAROLD
[b.] March 1, 1918, Rochester, NY; [p.] Edward John and Rosetta Standbrook Wright; [m.] Florence Stoll Wright-1919-1991, Lucille Hammil Wright, November 21, 1992; [ch.] Carol Jo Wright, Susan W. Kenney, Janet W. Bailey and Judith H. Minor; [ed.] West High School (Rochester), A.B. University of Rochester, Ed.M., Ed.D. Harvard University; [occ.] Professor Emeritus, State University of NY Geneseo, Educational Consultant, photographer; [memb.] Presbyterian Church, Torch Club International, Heritage Society, SUNY Geneseo; [hon.] Phi Beta Kappa, Phi Delta Kappa, Standard Bearer, Fulbright-Hayes Lecturer or Education and Consultant on University Administration at the University of Tehran, Iran, NY Elderhostel 12 year, Leadership Award, SUNY Geneseo Foundation Meritorious Service Award; [oth.writ.] "The Turning" Where Dreams Begin, the National Library of Poetry 1993; [pers.] Poetry has served as a means of expressing personal thoughts and feelings in rhythmical language. There is added pleasure in fitting words within a metrical form and setting them to music. [a.] Geneseo, NY.

WYATT SR., ROBERT H.
[pen.] Daighn (Dane) Werner; [b.] October 13, 1921, Springfield, IL; [p.] Ed and Virginia Wyatt (deceased); [m.] Marianne Bouvier Wyatt, June 25, 1988; [ch.] From previous marriage, Robert II, Rhonda and Randall; [ed.] Graduated high school earned promotions in field of pipeline, refinery construction over world, worked much of career foreign, was in Libya when Americans bombed Tri-Poli, Benghazl 1986; [occ.] Retired, play golf (14 HDCP), take cruises and travel in 1936 5th wheel RV as member of Good Sam Club; [memb.] None at present, former member of N.A.C.E. (National Association Corposion Engineers), Honorary member of Fort Mtr. Co. Auto Club (S.A.A.C.), due to affiliation with Carroll Shelby, CO.; [hon.] Cited in WWII for two President Unit Citations in PT Squadron, honorary member Boystown, NE, because of donations, was written up during WWII in Saturday Evening Post in series, "Cloak and Dragger" based on O.S.S. Operations in European Theater with Dough Fairbanks Jr., as Commanding Officer; [oth.writ.] Have (23) manuscripts awaiting re-write of 760-1100 pages each, published book "Sicilian Episode" on part true story during time spent in WWII on Pt. Patrols, 30-50 poems being complied for possible book form; [pers.] I have tried to always keep in mind when writing that a child might read my works and I wouldn't want him/her to be embarrassed by the contents. Was foreman over program building Shelby GT 350/500's and Cobra Race/Sports Cars. [a.] Mandeville, LA.

YERGAN, JAMES F.
[b.] 1946, Cleveland, OH; [hon.] Honorably discharged from U.S. Marine Corps; [oth.writ.] Previous work published in A Break In The Clouds 1993, Treasured Poems of America, Fall 1993, currently completing his own book due soon; [pers.] Enjoys writing of lost loves, Viet-Nam and the Civil War. [a.] Lagrange, OH.

YOUNG, GWEN M.
[b.] July 14, 1957, Newport News, VA; [p.] Judy and Theodore Miller; [m.] Derris S. Young, May 2, 1985; [ch.] Shannon Jessie and Shasta Autumn Young; [ed.] Roger's Senior High and A.V. Junior College; [memb.] I'm in the choir at the Christian Life Assembly in Techachapi; [oth.writ.] I've had two other poems published, I hope to someday have a book of poems published; [pers.] My goal in life is to be inspired by the Lord to write poetry that will melt the hardest of hearts and lead people to the Lord. All that I have is a gift from the Lord and I hope to share this gift with others. [a.] Techachapi, CA.

YOUNG, TONY D.
[b.] January 9, 1949, Detroit, MI; [p.] Evelyn A. Rogers and Robert D. Young; [m.] Carolyn D. Young, May 24, 1983; [ch.] Dawn Ulanj-Kenyata, Tony D. Young Jr.; [ed.] High school graduate, Eastern High School 1967, Detroit, MI; [occ.] Laborer, Chrysler Corp Eldon Axle; [memb.] UAW Local 961; [hon.] Vietnam Service Award; [oth.writ.] Unpublished short stories, "The FLy", "The Man in The Apartment 2-5", "The Flagpole", "Waiting For The Boogy Man", "Shocked", "A Hole In The Wall"; [pers.] Always give thanks to the Almighty Jehovah for all the good that happens in your life. [a.] Detroit, MI.

ZAK, CHRISTINA
[pen.] Christina Zak; [b.] January 25, 1959, Port Lavaca, TX; [p.] Jerry and Pauline Zak; [ch.] Natasha and John; [ed.] AAS Restaurant Mgmt. and Culinary Arts; [occ.] Retired yacht detailer; [oth.writ.] "My Gift", "Life" published in Tears of Fire", dedicated to Natasha and John, "I Watched", dedicated to my dad, many more waiting for the right break, also working on 2 children's books; [pers.] My world of writing is inspired by the laughter of my children and their unconditional love, but with my pen and paper we can create a world of ours, alone. [a.] Port Lavaca, TX.

ZHORAY, GEORGIANNA
[b.] January 25, 1961, Staten Island; [p.} Wanda Helen Barbach and John Stephen Zhoray Sr.; [ch.] Misty and Corky, 2 cats that are the kids I never had; [ed.] Katharine Gibbs Business School; [occ.] Legal Secretary, Wall Street law firm; [memb.] International Society of Poets (Administrative panel member), World Wildlife Fund, National Wildlife Foundation; [hon.] Editor's Choice Award, National Library of Poetry, Golden Poet Award, 3 Awards of Merit and Who's Who status all World of Poetry Society; [oth.writ.] "The Struggle Within", "Partners", "A Dream", "No More Heroes" and "Never Again"; [pers.] Writing poetry has been a release for me, to me it is not difficult at all, merely something I enjoy immensely but something I cannot do on command. [a.] Staten Island, NY.

ZESCHKE, MERLE R.
[b.] December 29, 1929, Chicago, IL; [p.] Esther and Elmer Zeschke; [m.] Barbara J. Zeschke, March 21, 1959; [ch.] Lori Anne and Steven Mitchell; [ed.] Lakeview High School, Chicago, IL., University of Illinois, B.S., Ed.M., Ed.S.; [occ.] Retired school administrator and teacher; [memb.] National Education Association, Illinois Education Association, Illinois Coaches Association, Illinois Counselors Association, memberships have lapsed since retirement; [hon.] Honor Roll while attending the University of Illinois , Alpha Chapter of Kappa Delta Pi; [oth.writ.] Several poems published in local newspapers, also poem published in an anthology titled River of Dreams by the National Library of Poetry; [pers.] I do not strive to emulate antiquity, but rather try to address the real issues confronting society today and stimulate innovative thinking. [a.] Sedona, AZ.

ZIEMBA, STEPHANIE L.
[pen.] Steph; [b.] October 12, 1978, Harrisburg, PA: [p.] Stanley C. and Beverly D. Ziemba; [sib.] Christopher M. Ziemba, 82nd Airborn (Army); [ed.] Freshman, Cedar Cliff High School; [occ.] Student; [oth.writ.] "Alone", Dark Side of The Moon; [pers.] I write to express what's in my soul. I dedicate this to the heart. [a.] Camp Hill, PA.

Index of Poets

Index

A

Abair, Margaret M. 369
Abbasi, Feroza 39
Abbott, Carolyn 73
Abrams, Alice L. 56
Adam, Monique 115
Adams, Arthur Byrd 431
Adams, Brenna Helen 422
Adams, Cleveland 25
Adams, Debbie K. 394
Adams, Della Frances 342
Adams, Frances 65
Adams, Joanne 356
Adams, Linda 112
Adamski, Corrinne 56
Adamson, Alta I. 37
Adelman, Robin Fern 276
Adesso, Martha 165
Agalzoff, Alex W. 360
Agozzino, Marie 124
Agrio, Pablo J. 115
Ahner, Cheryl L. 367
Ahram, Mamoun 142
Ailing, April 359
Ake, Vilma Jean 118
Akers, L. Kay 375
Akers, Misty Gail 277
Akwuruoha, Lui O. 231
Albright, Lora 163
Albro, Ruth E. 121
Alcorn, James D. 200
Alcorn, Sam J. 156
Alden, Martha 113
Aldrich-Krachinski, Stephanie 142
Aldridge, Mary Lee 267
Aldridge, Shelby Jean 305
Alexander, Anita 71
Alexander, Muriel W. 434
Alford, Laura J. 316
Alford, Rex E. 279
Allen, Amber N. 341
Allen III, John D. 189
Allen, Jackie 400
Allen, Leoma Cardwell 133
Allen, Louise 153
Allen, Richard 137
Allison Jr., Robert Steve 296
Alons, Nichole Lynne 249
Alonso, Don A. 349
Alvarez, Kira 229
Alvarez-Babin, Carmen Maria 56
Alvino, Lori-Ann 291
Amanda K. C. 382
Amman, Brenda 48
Ammann, Diane M. 382
Amsden, Jeffery Grant 91
Anderson, Charlotte 366
Anderson, Dorothy 391
Anderson, Eulanhie 430
Anderson, Evelyn 385
Anderson, Glen R. 79
Anderson, James 404
Anderson, John E. 203
Anderson, Linda Hansen 148
Anderson, Michelle L. 145
Andersson, Benny 39
Andre, Zadie L. 238
Andrea, Marie C. 236
Andrews, David Phyllep 52
Andrews, Tiffany 300
Angell, Deborah E. 180
Angell, Raymond H. 318
Angelle, Paula Marie 263
Anthony, Deborah 411
Apa, Danielle 398
Appeldorn, Gregory T. 65
Apperson, Alice 63
Applegate, Connie 376
Archbold, Judy 92
Arciszewski, Tiffany 221
Arcuni, Jenny 351
Arends, Bonnie Jo 364
Arias, Adelia 412
Ariola, Dorothy M. 409
Arlotta-Cupo, Madeline 121
Armstrong, Jack T. 34
Armstrong, John Alonzo 361
Arnett, Debbie 386
Arnold, Bill 47
Arnold, James W. 418
Arnold, Julie 350
Arns, James R. 84
Asbury, Mary 322
Ash, Maribelle Cooper 234
Asher, Jim 378
Atherton, Norma 232
Atkins, Regan 374
Atrens, Vilnis O. 374
Austin, Barbara 55
Aversa, Umberto A. 218
Ayers, Amy 434
Ayers, Catherine M. 36
Ayers, Sarah 98
Ayrton, Jessica M. 353

B

Babcock, Fenton 391
Babcock-Brown, Donna 418
Babin, Jason 62
Bach, Erwin E. 349
Backus, Elena Gale Hathway 390
Bacon, Marcella Anna 164
Bader, Beth 29
Bailey, Jermaine C. 189
Bailey Jr., Carl Emanual 49
Bailey, Lonnie 138
Bailey, Melissa 111
Bailey-Jones, Shirley 217
Baird, Arlean 358
Baisden, Pam 166
Baker, Amber 391
Baker, Betty 66
Baker, Daniel G. 427
Baker, Judith A. 171
Baker, Julie M. 80
Baker, Justin 358
Baker, Lindsey N. 152
Baker, Lisa 237
Baker, Paula C. 327
Balandran, Stella V. 222
Baldys, Mary Marcy 237
Ballard, Frances E. 175
Balmain, Theran 272
Banks, Caroline G. 390
Bao, Bianca Yongrong 69
Barancyk, Janice 80
Barber, Jamie June 361
Barber, Mattie Belle 166
Barber, Robert D. 248
Barksdale, Janet 44
Barling, Marilyn Louise 220
Barnard, Kevin 317
Barnes, Amy Sculley 30
Barnes, Charles 366
Barnes, Jan 57
Barnett, N. Edith 231
Barney, Jean L. 53
Barnhart, Hazel A. 74
Barrett, Avis Marie 342
Barretto, Lisa Ann Noelani Brown 113
Barrick, Marletta 126
Barrio, Guilmo 362
Barron, Mary J. DePrez 96
Barrow, Pete 236
Barrow, Theresa 226
Barry, Dave 425
Barson, Kelly Rumler 228
Barto, Anne M. 169
Bartoli, James 363
Barton, Doris 34
Battles, Heather 62
Battles, Merry 149
Baumel, Alice 346
Bauzys, Ona 118
Baxter, Luke N. 242
Beagle, Beryl 399
Beakley, Clyde 427
Beasley, Mary 285
Beaudoin, Judy 360
Beaver, Diana 50
Beck, Craig 73
Beck, Myrtle V. 273
Beck, Richard 301
Becker, Maureen 314
Becker-Wiech, Cheryl L. 36
Beeman, Loreen E. 139
Beers, Connie L. 45
Beheler, Betty Jo 396
Behrendt, Lisa Anne 225
Behrens, Justin 24
Belanger, Leo M. 337
Belcher, Jessica 403
Belcher, Steve 148
Beliveau, Judith 48
Bell, Antoinette Adelquist 421
Bell, Carol M. 215
Bell, Dianna 16
Bell, Emily M. 358
Bell, Lenora M. 250
Belle, Karen 224
Bellot, Frances E. 176
Belonie, Shannon Bray 109
Bench, Shirley J. 276
Bendio, Lenee 128
Benedict, Pamela C. 114
Benedict, Renee 237
Benjamin, Bernadine E. 381
Bennefield, Buna 404
Bennett, Gary 91
Bennett, Tina 248
Bennin, Violet 99
Benoit, Deanna J. 28
Bentley, Angela Lothridge 174
Berg, Michael Craig 429
Berger, Ruth O'Neill 296
Bergren, Ada Jones 197
Berman, Lillian 139
Bernand, William G., Sr. 126
Bernardy, Diane M. 75
Berney, Amy 384
Berry, Kenneth Roy 375
Berry, Sherlene 236
Beth, Doreen 353
Bevacqua, Kathleen 245
Beveridge, Adriane L. 394
Bezio, Angel 399
Bienfang, Judith 89
Biesecker Jr., Donald L. 434
Biggers, Jackie 190
Billheimer, Clarence E. 201
Billings, Boots 9
Billings, C. S. 293
Billos, Rachel 163
Binder, Nancy R. 326
Bingham, Alexander D. 203
Bingham, Cara Melani 396
Birg, Dave 384
Birnbaum, Jeanette 348
Bischoff, Arley M. 58
Bishop, Dianna L. 387
Bishop, Louise L. 371
Black, H. Blandenah 306
Black, Ruth A. 303
Black, Vernell 164
Blackhall, Donna L. 8
Blackledge, Ramona Q. 331
Blackman, Christan 338
Blade, Melinda K. 225
Blaine, Andrea 423
Blair, Josephine Cosma 424
Blaisdell, Kathleen 130
Blake, Evelyn Kimball 192
Blakely, Val 120
Blakey, Louise 151
Blakley, Melva 245
Bland, Shawn M. 225
Blansett, Cheryl Ann 358
Blanton, Betty 29
Bleem, Catherine Berra 91
Blenner, Jen 215
Blokh, David 42
Bloom, Barbara 194
Bloom, Thomas R. 230
Bloss, Gerald 89
Blumenstein, Jeri 394
Bock, Kathleen 226
Bocook, Sherry 137
Bodnovits, Alyvia Sue 365
Boggus, Regina 218
Boice, William S. 334
Bolar, John Philip 23
Bole, Helen 72
Bolivar, Janet B. 361
Bolton, Chelsea Luellon 364
Bolton, J. H. 283
Bond, Judith A. 42
Bonine, Vivian Way 233
Bonnett, Shawn H. 167
Bonnette, Susan 103
Bonyea, Tonya Hall 101
Boone, Jacki J. 202
Boorse, Christina 199
Booth, Sylvia 261
Boquecosa, Rolando L. 293
Borcher, Betty 172
Boska, Alice Francine Mathis 415
Botha, Katie 250
Botti, Ernest A. 92

Bouchard, Tricia 114
Boucher, Anne Porter 7
Bouley, Armand N. 52
Bourree, Felix 10
Boutcher, Elease 378
Bove, Wade J. 119
Bowden, Billy 4
Bower, James M. E. 32
Bowers, Florence 377
Bowers, Harry W. 183
Bowers, Karen A. 371
Bowers, Karen Denise 319
Bowers, Lorrie K. 123
Bowker, Robert S. 241
Boyd, Marsha Jean 319
Boyer, Helen Mowery 177
Boyer Sr., Kenneth C. 139
Boyes, Joan 430
Boyle, Phebe Anne 241
Brackin, B. J. 113
Braddock, Josephine T. 169
Bradford, Jean C. 363
Bradley, Amanda 346
Bradley, Christopher 387
Bradley, Perry E. 313
Brady, Anne V. 405
Brady, Clare 359
Braidotti, Regina 143
Braithwaite, Beulah G. 381
Brake, Colleen Durrant 347
Brakel, Marion 113
Brandl, Erwin J. 349
Brasher, Agnes 406
Brault, Meggan S. 150
Bray, Phillip Alexander Martin 308
Brayman, Elsie 344
Brent, Evelyn J. 64
Breshears, Arvylla 392
Brewer, Joan M. 180
Brian, Beverly Joan 395
Bridwell, Kimberly 147
Briggs, Rae Ann Michelle 307
Brinck, Vera E. 128
Briner, June 411
Brings, Kelly 243
Brinkley, Linda 335
Brinkman, Karen Olson 119
Brinkman, Mary M. 290
Brinson, Catherine Shumaker 342
Brister, Connie 394
Bristol, Dot 384
Britt, Alton D. 54
Brittain, Chrissie 347
Brittain, Linda C. 144
Britton, Melissa 269
Brizzi, Jillann 79
Broad, Janet I. 60
Brock, Gene 214
Brock, Martha W. 243
Brodfuehrer, Kristie 276
Broe, Ina Leland 351
Broekhuizen, Victoria J. 218
Brogan, Josette Reboul 115
Bromley, Matt 297
Brooks, Dorothy 426
Brooks, Suzanne Moffat 111
Broughton, Nilsa 131
Brown, Brian 31
Brown, Claron 359
Brown, Collin E. 85
Brown, Corinne 82
Brown, Dorothy I. 10
Brown, E. Talley 162
Brown, Gloristine 71
Brown, Hasan H. 358
Brown, Hazel H. 341
Brown, Kenneth Kurtiland 134
Brown, Kristi Danielle 314
Brown, Lisa 243
Brown, Martha E. 136
Brown, Mary 147
Brown, Rebekah S. 220
Brown, Robert V. 23
Brown, Sheila 216
Brown, Vicki 267
Brownback, Lloyd F. 101
Browning, Clarajane 170
Browning, Ellen 213
Browning, Mary 302
Brownley, Galoris 21
Broyles, LaNise 329
Brubaker, Lucille 240
Bruce, Charlotte 36
Bruce, Deborah Ann 178
Bruesewitz, Erika M. 431
Brumage, Kathleen R. 228
Bruni, Laura 262
Brunt, Earline 429
Brush, Brandy 356
Bruss, Mary 133
Bruton, P. J. 284
Bruun, Victoria 109
Bryan, Julie Michelle 79
Bryant, Drayton S. 212
Bryant, Florence 36
Bryant, Thelma 328
Bryant, Vicki E. 249
Buchanan, Lorraine F. 247
Buchanan, R. Kay 102
Buchanan, Thompson 434
Buchmiller, Stanley F. 272
Buchner, Linda Corkins 297
Buckley, James M. 191
Bucy, Gina 357
Bullock, Mary 139
Bumgarner, Erika 61
Bunger, Melanie 221
Buono, Franco 31
Bur, Jessica L. 81
Burbridge, Julie Anne 34
Burchett, Gayle 74
Burford, Jo 77
Burge, Betty Jane 349
Burgess, Everett L. 390
Burgess, Marjorie L. 372
Burgoyne, Roger D. 295
Burkam, George R. 62
Burke, Dennis A. 52
Burks-Shiver, Jacqueline 356
Burleigh, Giovanna 64
Burlingame, Mary G. 246
Burmeister, Mike 268
Burneo, Jim 67
Burns, Ethna M. 186
Burns, June 395
Burns, Phyllis 157
Burrell, Andrea 25
Burris, Sherin R. L. 313
Burton, Diane 196
Busbee, Ron 426
Buscetto, Sally 293
Busche, Dawn 358
Bush, Virgiinia Stonestreet 305
Bushacker, Evangeline 383
Bustamante-Just, Carmen 38
Buster, Scott 238
Butler, Betty 355
Butler, Dr. Rebecca Batts 324
Butler, Ethel S. 7
Butler, Jennifer 376
Butt, Nancy A. 111
Butts, Harry E. 80
Buyansky, Nicole J. 299
Byers, Mary Wyatt 258
Byers, Robert 102
Byers, Stanley 107
Byers, Winifred 245
Bynum, Barbara K. 173
Byrd, Andrea 406
Byther, Patricia 143

C

Cabral, Paulina C. 220
Cacciola, Erasmia 9
Cadogan, Barbara A. 426
Caesar, Hazel M. 346
Cahill, Catherine A. 203
Cain, Dorothy 176
Calabrese, Jason 38
Calandra, Albert J. 197
Caldwell, Martha M. 216
Caldwell, R. F. 221
Calhoun, Courtney Sherrod 57
Calhoun III, John C. 9
Callahan, Erica 351
Camacho, Henry 11
Cammarata, Rose 142
Campbell, Erica 390
Campbell, Gene B. 345
Campbell, Helen Elizabeth 363
Campbell, Joyce L. 60
Campbell, Kate 96
Campbell, Wilma Lee 327
Campbell, Wood M. 162
Canales, Michelle 264
Canavan, Christine 349
Canfield, Bethany L. 358
Cannon, James A., Jr. 171
Capozza, David 90
Cappas, Humberto 366
Capuano, Connie A. 358
Cardassi, Phyllis J. 161
Cardwell, Evelyn H. 32
Carey, Tom 335
Carinci, John Paul 393
Carlile, Martha Hale 246
Carlson, Aaron 15
Carm, Jane Winkler O. 66
Carmeline 265
Caron, Cara 405
Carpenter, Arden K. 189
Carpenter, Valerie LePire 434
Carr, Barbara 11
Carr, Martha J. 156
Carr, Michele 93
Carr, Tara M. 216
Carranza, Efren P. 92
Carreira, Natalie 323
Carriker, Wilda Louise 224
Carrillo, Eleanor 75
Carrion, Monica 219
Carrison, Jennifer Lynn 82
Carroll, Marjorie J. 115
Carroll-Simmons, Linda A. Patricia 374
Carson, Cathy L. 354
Carter, Herbert Lathan 51
Carter, Jaben L. 391
Carter, Priscilla L. 144
Cartoni, Richard Thomas 275
Cartwright, Winifred A. 252
Cartwright-Hignett, Elizabeth 431
Casarez Jr., Robert 120
Casavant, Helen L. 207
Casciaro, Virginia 375
Case, David 90
Casey, Byron C. 402
Cass, Carmelita T. 67
Cassidy, Sean Ian 227
Castelino, Nicole Barbara 154
Castillo, Melinda L. 130
Caston Jr., Leonard 325
Cate, John Shelton 414
Cates, Minnie E. 241
Causseaux, Rae Nell 235
Cavaleri, Nicholas 299
Cavin, Jennifer 379
Celso, Matthew A. 254
Centeno, Jesse 30
Centers, Wendy 417
Cepeda, Maria Lyn 131
Cerepak, Julia Lee 173
Cerniglia, Josephine F. 351
Cesler, Susan 238
Chace, Lewis I. 367
Chainey, Martha L. 298
Champine, Janice J. 28
Chan, Charlene D. 17
Chang, Yih-Chau 296
Chapman, Janice N. 416
Chapman, Mary Elizabeth 103
Charles, Leah Jeannine 128
Chase, Elsa L. 382
Chase, Ervin H. 26
Chaussée, Sandi 228
Cherry, Sharon Reisch 239
Cheung, Amy 402
Chevalier, Mary S. 131
Chi, Thomas R. 241
Chiaravalloti, Theresa 110
Chinn, Carla N. 363
Chirigos, Lisa 275
Chitty, Peyton W. 261
Chludzinski, Frank C. 175
Cho, Caroline 64
Cholst, Sheldon 298
Chou, Pei-Mei 312
Choudhury, Alpana 177
Chowdhury, Jerry 205
Chowrashi, Eveline G. 410
Christensen, Bonny 51
Christie, Philomena 244
Christoff, Alex V. 411
Chu-Sit, Teresa 267
Chubrich, Sophie 266
Churaman, Dandrea 33
Church, Amanda 380
Chvatal, Donald P. 35
Cierpisz, Cindy L. 424
Cimarrusti, Marianna 152
Ciszczon, Jill 390
Clark, Bobby 37
Clark, Brett 420
Clark, Lori L. 309

Clark, Olive I. 309
Clark, Tom 330
Clausen, Violet V. 264
Clay, Curtis, Jr. 14
Clayton, Robert P. 127
Clegg, Barbara Ann 349
Clements, Ben 390
Clerin, Claudette L. 69
Climaco, Gregorio Cesar Israel 84
Clinkscale Jr., Vaudry B. 256
Cobain, Ginger 77
Cobb, Jessie S. 192
Cody, Barbara Lee 177
Coen, Eleanor 382
Coffey-Watkins, Mary 247
Coffman, Douglas Wayne 340
Coffman, Heather Lynn 58
Coffman Jr., Cloyde F. 397
Coffman, Sherri A. 288
Coggiano, Jean 37
Cogill, KyraLea 321
Cohen, Margie 237
Cohen, Martin 243
Cohen, Martin A. 236
Cohen, Sandi L. 238
Cole, Anita H. 347
Cole, Bobby N. 395
Coleman, Aura W. 411
Coleman, Kimberly 240
Coleman, Ruth 134
Collins, Misty Dawn 255
Collins, Pamela Lynn 295
Collins, Sandra 333
Colonna, John 340
Combs, Addie 207
Conan, Zoila 283
Conant, Donna D. 193
Conant, Ralph G. 277
Condra, Angela 28
Conn, Louise Wilkerson 430
Connard III, Adolph Haven 413
Conner, Leland L. 331
Conrad, Christie 60
Conrow, Judith 393
Conroy, Joan E. 36
Constantinou, Katherine 335
Contine, Carol A. 350
Conway, Alan 22
Conway, Carolyn 78
Cook, Curtis A. 78
Cook, Fran 419
Cook, Lois E. 257
Cook, Sandra Bergen 122
Cook Sr., Larry W. 150
Cooley, Marilyn B. 254
Coomes, Geraldine Sawyer 40
Cooper, Houstine 399
Cooper, Isabel S. 339
Cooper, Kelly Jo 142
Cordell, Maureen 219
Cordova, Denice L. Glover 59
Cordova, J. Austin 233
Corn, Joanie 32
Cornele, Elizabeth A. 344
Cornelius, Virginia 150
Cornett, Doris 6
Cornwall, Faith 352
Cornwall, Marketa 222
Cornwell, Melvin G. 294
Corrigan, Marlene 238
Cory, Linda Marlene 227
Costa, Misty 325
Costantini, Alice 192
Costantino, Florence 353
Cothern, Michelle K. 375
Cottom, Yuriko Bayu 301
Cotton, John Lee 393
Coughlin, Mary M. 234
Courchesne, Jennifer 341
Courtney II, L. Martin 306
Cover, Berniece 77
Cowan, Frank B. 65
Cowan, James M. 41
Cowan, Jo Anne 378
Cowne, Michael E. 307
Cox, George 176
Cox, Myrtle 122
Cox, Richard E. 133
Cox, Vernon 295
Crampton, George W. 430
Crane, David 366
Crawford, Desiree 91
Crawford-Martin, ReGina 98
Crews, Pamela L. 146
Crispin, Charles Don 60
Criss, Raven Douglas 158
Croft, Jean 34
Cron, Sandy 127
Cronen, Natasha 269
Crosby, Roland L. 110
Crotty, Gary D. 383
Crow, Linda I. 135
Crowe, Mary Anne 112
Cruise, Peggy 225
Crume, Eunice 37
Cruz, John B. 201
Cruz, Kevin 254
Cruzan, Pat 244
Cullen, James C. 348
Cullipher, Alfred A. 399
Culver, Adlain R. 343
Cumbie, Christy 402
Cummings, Carol A. 366
Cunningham, Helen M. 357
Cunningham, Melissa 311
Cunningham, Pamella A. 128
Curcio, Karen 165
Current, Sandra 313
Curry, Lillian C. 238
Curry, Michele 95
Curtis, Kris 106
Custer, Carolyn Jean 191
Custer, Estelle 56

D

Dabney, Paula A. 132
Daliege, Mark T. 288
Dalrymple, Christiane 403
Danforth, April 388
Daniels, Anthony J. 56
Daniels, Ross 53
Danko, John P. 195
Dante, Joseph Raphael 52
Darlington, Barbara L. 212
Darrington-Rule, Eva 110
Daugherty, Linda K. 99
Daughtry, Florence 80
Daulton, Fred 71
Davalos, Pauline 166
David, Kenneth D. 299
Davidson, Phebe E. 431
Davidson, Rock 286
Davis, Adrienne 6
Davis, Debora J. 340
Davis, Emilie M. 354
Davis, Floyd E. II 27
Davis, Jennifer A. 200
Davis Jr., Henry T. 356
Davis, Kathleen S. 337
Davis, Kevin 291
Davis, Lois Kahl 147
Davis, Louise 310
Davis, Marie 289
Davis, Michael B. 309
Davis, Mike A. 279
Davis, Patricia 107
Davis, Ray 123
Davis, Robbie 216
Davis, Todd 169
Davis, Yvonne G. Engel 220
Davison, Donna D. 182
Dawe-Hayes, Jean 403
Dawson, Richard A. 335
Day, Sandra K. 94
De Baun, Irene P. 180
de Gaona, Rafaela 278
De Jesus-Jankowski, Jennifer 422
De Marmolejo, Leonora Acuna 303
de Paula, Henrique 61
Dean, Hubert W. 93
DeAngelis, Marjorie A. 105
Dearduff, Helen M. 50
Deason, Jean 11
Deaton, June B. 397
Deaver, Frances Roberson 9
DeBarry, Frances D. M. 380
Debry, Meredith 315
Dechant, Sandy 135
Deckard, June Jenner 385
Decker, Cassandra N. 54
Delaney, Betty L. 385
Deleurme, Rita E. 106
Delgado, Cynthia H. 19
DeMille, Ronald 230
DeMovic, Robert A. 156
Denning, Julius L. 18
Dennis, Nicole M. 288
Dennison, Clarence N. 199
Depew, Nicole 262
DePorres, Mari 282
DePuy, Patricia G. 324
Derman, Dawn 357
DesBiens, Christopher A. 356
DeSensi, Dana M. 387
DeServio, Natasha 141
Despathy, Jamie L. 70
Deutsch, Lawrence I. 120
Devine, Anne 200
Devine, John 203
Devot, Lisa 316
Di Lallo, Frances 414
Diaz-Clark, Annisa Maria 396
Dick, Clara S. 171
Dickerson, Barbara Hogle 347
Dickert, Carolyn Seery 406
Dickson, Dorothy 12
Dickson, Ruby Jones 230
Diem, Richard A. 103
Dile, George Michael 199
Dillard, Agnes Lys 362
Dilworth, Florence 192
Dingman, Rhonda T. 240
Dinwiddie, David E. 397
DiPaola, Mary 160
DiSanti, Beverly 405
Ditmer, Arnold 75
Dixon, Barbara J. 342
Dixon, Nichole 294
D'lanor 314
Dobias, Agnes M. 35
Dockstader, Harvey Joseph 171
Dodd, James W. 51
Dodge, Debora 42
Dodrill, Davan James 56
Doersam, Raymond G. 149
Dolan, Brian 200
Dolega, Ramona Therese 223
Doljan, David 391
Dolny, Roman 112
Donaldson, James A. 188
Donnelly, Virginia H. 318
Doombadfe, Amebi 172
Doombadze, Amelie 180
Dorrbecker, Robin O. 226
Doss, Julia Lee 40
Doucet, Kathie Guidry 232
Douglas, Gwen 48
Douglas, Rebecca 251
Douglass, Betty J. 413
Douville, Eugene 179
Downey, E. Corey 95
Downs, Shirley 118
Doyle, Edith 40
Doyle, John M. 76
Doyle, Kristen 332
Doze, Rowena 321
Drach, Mary 94
Dracopoulos, Lili 244
Dragon, Norma 150
Drake, Robyn 282
Dranchek, Mark S. 131
Draper, Corene Luedecke 31
Drappo, Marion C. 164
Drew, Lynne M. 151
Driggers, Barbara 208
Drinnon, Janis B. 179
Drinnon, Suzanne 169
Driscoll, Lois 260
Driskell, Donald A. 363
Drummond, Pat 261
Dryden, William 95
Dubie, Derra L. 396
Duff, Bertha 27
Duke, James H., Jr. 67
Dukes, Charlene P. 409
Dull, Diane B. 182
Dunagan, Michele Marie 100
Duncan, Denise 182
Duncan, Muriel S. 147
Duncan, Natalie 158
Duncan, Patricia 219
Duncan, Theodore W. 98
Duncan-Echelson, Martha 112
Dunlap, Helen Brown 19
Dunn, Fred F. 361
Dunn, Helen D. 59
Duong, Linh 310
Durham, Katherine 217
Durrell, Deanne Elizabeth 341
DuVall, John Willard 205
Dwyer, Margaret Ann 127
Dykeman, Brad 393
Dykman, Shirley 246

Dylik, Joe 90

E

Eagan, Marilynn J. 223
Eagleton, E. Lucile 271
Earls, Mary L. 107
East, Victoria H. 117
Ebaugh, Frances Carnahan 190
Eckart, Mollie 320
Edgar, Kelly 226
Edgar, Rita May 313
Edwards, Kelley J. 121
Edwards, Malon 304
Edwin, Sabeen 268
Effinger, Lynn 254
Egry, Janice P. 354
Egyed, Jean L. 353
Eibach, Jennifer 19
Ekonomidis, Patricia 114
Elam, Molly 168
Elder, Elsie L. 386
Elder, Melissa 313
Eldridge, Kimberly 219
Elias, E. L. 263
Elliott, Connie S. 23
Elliott, Eugenia L. 185
Elliott, Mrs. John M. 179
Elliott, Stacy Diane 284
Ellis, Charlie E. 178
Ellis, Christel B. 209
Ellis, Christina 415
Ellis, Melanie M. 108
Elvin, Kenneth A. 286
Emery, Mary Levet 314
Emly, Karri 121
Endicott, Marie F. 272
Engberg-Maluvac, Robin 239
Engel, Leslie 143
Engles, June N. 182
English, Norman R. 127
Ens, G. George 154
Ensor, BB 69
Epstein, Ruth Peretz 140
Erby, Deborah H. 204
Erney, Robert 310
Ernst, Kathryn Burns 118
Ernst, Paul F. 106
Errington, Becki 296
Ervin, Linda Lee 237
Eshuis, Rita G. 224
Esposito, Lisa Smith 256
Essak, Rebecca 299
Eulalia 416
Evans, Amy JoAnne 403
Evans, Fern M. 15
Evans, Heather 343
Evans, I. J. 143
Evans, Nancy Lee 287
Evans, Nellie L. 279
Evasew, Michelle 106
Everett, John 378
Everhart, Freda 409
Everitt, Edna Mae 350
Evers, Gene 26
Everson, Richard 221
Ewings, Mary H. 323

F

Falker, Margaret Brunea 215
Falter, Donna 352
Fambro, Sonja O. 370
Fancher, Michele D. 130
Fanning, Martha Jeanne 307
Fanuiel, Miriam Y. 322
Farello, Frank S. 404
Farrar, Juanita 83
Farrow, Anna M. 90
Faust, Heather 387
Feece, Dianna 177
Feld, Neal 371
Feldbauer, Cynthia M. 342
Felker, Virginia F. 328
Feller, Beth 397
Feller, Maxine Sue 157
Fenton, Jacob 412
Fenton, Theresa 299
Ferachi, Hilda 348
Ferguson, D. 231
Fernandez-Douglas, Joan 14
Ferraro, Nancy 243
Ferrasci, Vicky 370
Ferris, Charles J. 388
Ferris-Dunn, Lynn 232
Fical, Kim R. 291
Fielder, Marilyn 133
Fields, Fannie 400
fields, lynn alyson 148
Fields, Samuel Preston 253
Fierros, Ruth V. 282
Fife, Margaret A. 114
Fifield, Cora L. 392
Fillie, Anthony 350
Fillinger, Jan 4
Finlay, Linda D. 124
Finley, Jean B. 86
Finleyson, Ellen 363
Finney, Scott W. 317
Fiore, Dawne E. 408
Fish, Aimee Jo 51
Fisher, Sari J. 108
Fisher, Sharon 375
Fiskaali, Audrie M. 81
Fitzgerald, Ann L. 22
Fitzgerald, Erin 213
Flesher, Theresa 94
Fletcher, James C. 206
Fletcher, Ronnie J. 286
Flores, John C. 210, 427
Florsek, Carina L. 384
Flynn, Bill 41
Fodale, Daniel A. 419
Fogg, Mary L. 231
Foland, Eleanor 185
Foley, Nancy 140
Forcier, P. Marguerite 122
Ford, Doye 89
Ford, Louis James 278
Fordyce, Dorothy J. 394
Forland, Amber 201
Formusa, William J. 117
Forrester, Annie Ruth 37
Forshey, Jennifer 85
Fortier, Brad 360
Fortney, Jon 388
Foss, Marcella C. Lester 324
Foster, Donna Kaye Hooper 85
Foster, Mary Jane 239
Foster, Teresa 225
Fourroux, Gloria Spitzfaden 47
Fowler, David 419
Fowler, Jerald 364
Fowler, Mary A. 332
Fowler, Raymond H., Jr. 137
Fox, Bill 419
Fox, Frances Juanice 57
France, Judith Jean 394
Frances, Anna 209
Frank, Maxine Graham 233
Franklin, Janet M. 213
Franquez, Arwen 350
Franse, Jean 405
Fransen, John R., Jr. 366
Fraser, Gail 220
Fraser, Terez 227
Frazell, Karen 113
Frazier, Elizabeth Hart 390
Frazier, Helen Geneva 400
Fredline, Brenda Sue 76
Freeburn, James H. 28
Freeny, Akilah 186
Fremon, Mori 145
French, Cheryl L. 356
French, Christine 82
Fretz, Ginny 176
Frey, Joe 357
Frey, M. L. 129
Fridh, Melvin 233
Frier, Alini 77
Frimand, Martha Merriken 304
Froemming, Hazel 59
Frohlich, Dawn 13
Fry, Kristin 112
Fry, Mary A. 306
Frye, James 45
Fugate, Freddie 404
Fugleberg, Timothy Ole 132
Fuhlendorf, Charlene 175
Fuhs, Marvin 109
Fujii, Terry R. 303
Fulce, Suzette 130
Fulginiti, Samuel S. 217
Fuller, Mabel 143
Fuller, Olen C. 144
Fusco, Diane 46

G

Gabriel, Angelo M. 365
Gail, Patricia A. 158
Gaines, David C. 76
Gajewski, Lillia 101
Gallagher, Dorothy 381
Gallagher, June B. 391
Gallagher, Kevin P. 305
Gamper, Lavina 121
Ganahl, Luella L. 338
Garcia, Richard A. 120
Garcia, Sef 245
Gardiner, George H. 51
Gardiner, John F. 3
Gardner Jr., Marvin B. 104
Gardner-Wesley, Carmen 338
Garland, Tammy 244
Garner, Pearlie Robinson 99
Garner, Tony S. 261
Garnett, Josephine C. 422
Garrett, Bertha 31
Garrett Jr., Grover J. 190
Garrett, Kathy 109
Gary, Kay 244
Gates, Luwonna Rae 284
Gatewood, June S. 352
gatewood, r. e. 300
Gay, Rosie Branch 108
Gazave, Julie 362
Gebhart, Lily 226
Gehr, Colleen A. 174
Geller, Kenneth S. 246
Gennetts, A. 288
Genoway, Robert Galen 220
Gentry, Elsie B. 12
Genzoli, R. Arlin 366
Geralis, Joseph 61
Gerhauser Jr., Stephen 304
Gerlick, Diana 187
Gernert, Todd 320
Gibbons, Helen 381
Gibbs, Jennifer Lynn 360
Giblin, Gloria M. 38
Giblin, Joyce 55
Gilby, Kelly 253
Gildersleeve, Helen 36
Gillenwater, Zeddie 123
Gillespie, Labelle 237
Gillette, Elsie 29
Gilmore, Bernice 408
Gilmore, Frank 211
Gilpatrick, Thelma 108
Ginn, Rebecca 246
Giovanna 415
Giovannetti, Celeste A. 19
Gipe, Irene 396
Gipson, Carol 410
Girdham, Glenn F. 422
Girod, Tyrone, Jr. 332
Gish, Velma Ruppel 217
Giunta, Stacia 290
Givens, Ijaaz L. 207
Gleason, Helen 395
Glinski, Frank Z. 199
Glock Sr., Milton F. V. 233
Goetz, Eldrus 339
Goff, Martha L. 305
Gohm, Kelly 97
Goins, Marquita 222
Goldade, Elisa 195
Golden, Price D. 288
Goleh, F. Alexander 371
Golliher, Ruby 330
Gollings, Addie 338
Gomes, J. Anthony 259
Gomes, Jose Paulo 357
Good, Margaret 328
Goodrich, Margaret L. 161
Goodwin, Bonnie L. 416
Goodwin, Dorothy 407
Gordon, Guanetta 347
Gordon, Lisa 312
Gordon, Ronnie Lee 317
Gordon, Ruby Coggins 335
Gordon-Lee, Janet 206
Gorman, Shirley Anne 228
Gorman, Tony 119
Gorrell, Seamus 429
Gospodarek, Katie 237
Gostiaux, Shannon 244
Gotlib, Miriam 118
Gourlay, Carol M. 381
Gower, Vivian 122
Grabowski, Kim M. 285
Grace, S. B. 344
Graham, Dianne M. 344
Graham, Jessica A. 45

Grainger, Carol Lee 6
Granato, Karen S. 231
Grant, Barbara 13
Grant, Brenda A. 386
Grant, Lola E. 132
Grant, Marie M. 222
Grant, Michael J. 262
Grau, Joy 339
Gravlin, Mary E. 259
Gray, Amber 64
Greathouse, Stacy 122
Grebiner, Timothy W. 229
Green, Dan 17
Green, Fordyce 84
Green, Janet C. 69
Green, Pats 368
Green, Penny M. 247
Greene, Agnes 176
Greenhaw, Elisabelle 173
Greenman, Joel 88
Gregg, Christina 79
Gregor, Muriel M. 284
Gregory, Beulah 397
Greifenstein, B. Margaret 102
Greig, Geraldine Gobi 197
Greuling, L. S. Thompson 367
Grey, Stephen 278
Grider, Carolyn 86
Griffin, Barbara 340
Griffith, Kimberly 263
Griggs, Jesse C. 13
Griggs, Stanley Evans 103
Grijalva, Rick 245
Grimes, Ralph E. 242
Grisa, Karrieann 322
Groeger, Mary Elizabeth 321
Groover, John M. 349
Gross-Haley, Erma 418
Grove, Leah M. 315
Grover, Gail A. 354
Grzyll, Margaret 116
Guenther, Martha 260
Guetz, Marian Fyhrie 270
Guglielmetti, Marci 117
Gulledge, Irene O. 397
Gulley, Rebecca L. 249
Gundunas, Peter 220
Gunter, Danny W. 361
Gunter, Mark A. 128
gurney, george 206
Gustafson, Amy Foley 72
Gute, Richard 96
Guterman, Dorothy C. 7
Guthrie, Grace 194
Guthrie, Tara 317
Gutsch, Dorie 57
Guy, Francesca 399
Guymon, Marvin I. 93

H

Haas, Marie 167
Haberek, Jill Maryann 366
Hackmann, Paul C. 332
Haefele, Mark J. 241
Hager, Christina Marie 183
Hagerty, Dawn M. 50
Hahn, Heather 398
Haines, Sheris 269
Hale, Jane 387
Hall, Belinda 379
Hall, Daniel 84
Hall, George L. 19
Hall, Gwen H. 417
Hall, Sylvia 322
Hallmark, Cheryll 214
Hallowell, Angel 388
Halog, Basilisa Lachica 354
Halpern, Linda Caray 158
Halsall, Edward Hamilton 344
Hamby, Oliver N. 327
Hamesh-Das, Daisy Marion 418
Hamilton, Clover D. 16
Hamilton, Julianne S. 76
Hamlett, Karen E. 218
Hamlin, Norma 219
Hammer, Tressie 134
Hammond, Joan Crawford 385
Hampton, Phillip L. 114
Hamric, Ramona E. 313
Hamrick, Peggy 168
Hamvold, Brandi 340
Hancock, Dorothy Stormer 365
Hancock, Hunter McRae 416
Handler, Dorothy S. 62
Hanelt, Sabrina 166
Haney, Debbie 122
Hannebaum, Harold W. 355
Hansen, Elizabeth 92
Hansen, Floyd 66
Hanson, Christopher W. 428
Hardee, Richard 297
Hardin, Mary Louise S. 219
Hardin, Steven D. L. 259
Harding, Charles G. 378
Harer, Tremayne 121
Harkins, Rose 240
Harlow, Eldora 24
Harold, John W. 23
Harrell, Linda B. 298
Harris, Shannon Dee 323
Harris, Tony 268
Harrison, Elizabeth A. 87
Harrison, Stanley N. 108
Harrison, Terry A. 282
Hart, Heather 343
Hart, Heather Lynn 93
Hart, Vanessa 163
Hartman, Carl 378
Hartman, Edward 183
Hartman, Lois Ijams 224
Hartnett, Michael W. 162
Hartzog, Carla D. 408
Harvey, Richard G., 248
Harville, Dora L. 416
Harwood, Michele 118
Hashberger, Kim 253
Hassell, Susan 300
Hassett, Clinton 204
Hatch, Eric E. 406
Hathaway, Jillian 359
Hatlen, Hilda 393
Hauser, Sherrie 94
Haviland, Eileen M. 40
Hayden, Jean 413
Hayden, Marion M. 230
Hayes, Amanda M. 194
Hayner, Rolande 256
Haynes, Danny 172
Haywood, Phillip W. 236
Heard, Anita 194
Hecht, Jolyn 5
Hedayati, Jeanette 34
Hedin, Dana 39
Heim, David J. 352
Heindselman, Russell 138
Heinkel, Joan 352
Heisey Jr., Edward 73
Heitfield, Heather 33
Heitman, Karen G. 109
Heitmann, Joanna 47
Heitmiller, Donald Edward 76
Helbig, Annie E. 401
Helfrick, Rachel 157
Hellas, Alix 362
Helmer, Rosemary E. 118
Hembree, Chester E. 46
Hemelik, Anthony John 171
Hemphill, Stephanie 155
Hemple, Florence L. 70
Henderson, Vada Mae 330
Hendrix, Sylvia 283
Henkel, Patricia D. 229
Henley, Libbie 216
Henn, Rozel I. 280
Hennessey, James P. 408
Henningsen, Verna 293
Henrich, Christa 85
Henshaw, Ronald E. 274
Hensley, John 354
Herman, Kelly K. 118
Hermelin, Margie Gale 330
Hernandez, Paul F. 148
Herold, Jan F. 182
Herrin, Martha L. 137
Hertlein, Clara Tse 50
Hervey, Stephen 140
Hess, Connie 429
Hess, Dana 207
Hetzel, Joyce Virginia 24
Hickey, Ryan M. 224
Hicks, Angela 38
Hicks, Grace Roberson 432
Higgins, E. Chipman 227
Higgs, Verle Nichols 118
Hill, Gracie Sanderson 45
Hill, L. M. 307
Hill, Robin 168
Hill-Castillo, Pat 331
Hillberry, Fay Ward 80
Hillen, Stephanie 94
Hillsberry, Susan 316
Hinde, Delores 354
Hines, Linda 289
Hire, Jeanne 20
Hishynsky, Zen 153
Hite, Deborah L. 9
Hixon, Donald 24
Hobbs, Heather Ann 196
Hobbs, Ida Lillian 350
Hodgdon, Jennifer 348
Hodges, James 211
Hodges, James D. 58
Hodgins, Toni 157
Hodson, Glenda 191
Hoey, John J. 398
Hoffenbacker, Christina 29
Hoffer, Clarice 63
Hoffman, Gloria 408
Holland, Clara M. 191
Holland, Tom 295
Holler, Marcie 373
Hollibush, Ann M. 351
Holliday, Emma 338, 432
Hollins, Louis C. 374
Holloway, Winnie 292
Holmack, Larry 109
Holmes, Jennie 195
Holmes, Rosie 274
Holobach, Anna 411
Holohan, J. Patricia 256
Homan, Gary M. 424
Honson, Marion 249
Hoogstad, Jean B. 27
Hooper, Merle 307
Hooper, Rose Mary 427
Hoops, Belva 417
Hoover, Bill 212
Hopkins, Annie 13
Hopkins, Joseph T. 353
Hopper, Cheryl 78
Hopper, Ruby 255
Hopping, Clara B. 410
Horan, Mary Ann Theresa Perito 372
Horan, Michael, Jr. 279
Horn, Edna 345
Horoszewski, John 17
Horton, Ray 287
Horvath, Elaine M. 89
Hotchkiss, Joey 65
Houchen, Lillian 230
House, Jamie A. 48
Howard, Constance L. 398
Howard, June R. 192
Howard, Z. Louis 117
Howard-Hall, Denise 357
Howell, Pauline Myers 337
Howell, Roberta E. 97
Howell, Valerie B. 219
Howes, C. Thomas 407
Howes, Diane 389
Hoxtell, Cora 401
Hraca, Beatrice 340
Hric, Joan E. 24
Hromoko, Mary-Ann 125
Hubbard, Calvin E. 190
Hubbard, Rick L. 259
Hubbard, Ruby 274
Hubbert, Karla 237
Huckeba, Martine Hovis 234
Hudson, Claudette L. 196
Hudson, Colleen E. 184
Huffman, Pat 262
Huggard, G. S. 216
Hughes, Janet 341
Hughes, Patricia S. 300
Hughes, Temple Anne 283
Hughesman, Stacey 239
Hughey, Susan E. 373
Hugley, Betty J. 20
Huisingh, Melinda 109
Hull, Elva M. 403
Hull, Sandra 99
Hultquist, Julie Gramza 377
Humble, Steven Hardy 308
Humphries, Bennie J. 193
Humphries, Channing 363
Hungerford, Brandi 412
Hunt, Diane L. 389
Hunt, Eleanor 210
Hunter, Ruthlean 372
Huntington, Alfred L. 176
Hurn, Della 209
Hurst, Ann Marie 58

Husband, Rebecca 281
Hutchins, Sharleen C. 298
Hutchison, Marilyn L. 302
Hutton, Audrey 424
Hutton, Mary 243
Huxford, Colette L. 191
Hyland, Grace 427
Hymer, George A. 202
Hynes, George P. 362

I

Iannicelli, Louis S. 216
Ida, Sharon 108
Idler, Ericka 346
Ignoffo, Flori 384
Iken-Mendler, Dorothy 13
Immings, Shanna L. 124
Ingraham, Shannon 301
Inniss, Richard 262
Irish, Diana 58
Irving, Faith T. 87
Isaacs, Rick 218
Isbitski, Estelle 25
Ita, Callixtus E. 425
Iverson, Betty 381

J

Jackson, Angela 381
Jackson, Cara 347
Jackson Jr., John W 43
Jackson, Kathryn 312
Jackson, Rosemarie 119
Jackson, Shirley 230
Jackson-Flach, Virginia 232
Jacobson, James R. 407
Jacobson, Kelly 237
Jae, Audrey 358
James, Christi 71
James, Mary Pittman 133
James, Ola Margaret 321
Jamison, Michelle P. 239
Janes, William L., Jr. 155
Janisch, Jeffrey Warren 402
Januszewski, Hope 35
Jarrell, Willa Eloise 273
Jean-Francois, Marie-Catheline 257
Jeffre, Susan Estelle Caldwell 265
Jenkins, Cassandra Marie 421
Jenkins Jr., Alfred J. 196
Jennings, Christopher R. 428
Jennings, Kathleen 108
Jennings, Sherilin 158
Jensen, John R. 21
Jensen, Nicole 329
Jessee, Angela Rena 376
Jesson, Elizabeth 353
Jeter, Terry 290
Jett, Linda L. 278
Johansen, George L. 421
Johnson, Addie Dolly 343
Johnson, Amy Mara 29
Johnson, Bill 119
Johnson, Cassandra L. 386
Johnson, Charlotte M. 17
Johnson, Don F. 187
Johnson, Dorma Lee 398
Johnson, Gene 343
Johnson, Ginger 350
Johnson, Janey B. 204
Johnson Jr., Dennis J. 181
Johnson, Julie 425
Johnson, June Ann 34
Johnson, Kodiak E. 103
Johnson, Lisa Elaine 327
Johnson, Lois A. 319
Johnson, Lori D. 98
Johnson, Mary 98
Johnson, Maurine Chlovis 266
Johnson, Michael Curtis 167
Johnson, Nell 224
Johnson, Noel K. 157
Johnson, Ray 260
Johnson Sr., Harry H. 75
Johnson, Tesha 157
Johnson, Valdyne J. 370
Johnson, William R. 220
Johnston, Arthur L. 172
Joiner, Kathleen Moore 234
Jolie, Dana M. 11
Jolly, Bonnie Watson 175
Jonas, Edward Joseph 80
Jones, Calgary B. 193
Jones, Charley 188
Jones, Clarence David 74
Jones, Ellen E. 379
Jones, James G. 184
Jones, James M. 89
Jones, Joan M. 4
Jones, Judy H. 352
Jones, Karen J. 294
Jones, Lambert T. 250
Jones, Leah A. 120
Jones, Linda M. 300
Jones, Margaret 115
Jones, Orovelia Lao 266
Jones, Regina 234
Jones, Will 222
Jones, Winifred 111
Jopp, Linda 295
Jordan, Agatha 377
Jordan, John A. 392
Jorg, Alice Whiteside 72
Joyce, Anne 392
Joyce, Elizabeth 86
Joyce, Tara Leigh 290
Julevich, Mark 103

K

Kachel, Maria Jeanne 253
Kaden, Sara 120
Kaiser, Howard L. 364
Kalanta, Katherine 120
Kallen, Lindsay 325
Kane, Richard M. 243
Kang, Harjinder 23
Kannmacher, Chris 31
Karas, Tracy 308
Kardos, Ann 389
Karpiak, Catherine M. 48
Kasahara, Lena 152
Kassel, Laura 320
Katranis, Evangeline 33
Katz, Esther 343
Kaufenberg, Richard 114
Kaufman, Peter H. 112
Kavaya, Nicholas 280
Kaye, Anne 428
Kayganich, Nicholas J. 130
Kaze, Archie R. 411
Kearney, Candace Nicole 415
Keeling, John 406
Keen, Annie 365
Keesler, Bekah 386
Keith, Frances Snyder 52, 54
Kelleher, Frances B. 65
Keller, Ed 170
Keller, Tawnya 140
Kelley, Jeffrey 171
Kelly, Jane Irene 385
Kelly, Mary C. 143
Kelly, Nansi 282
Kendig, Spencer Knox 114
Kendrick, Michael 223
Kennedy, Darrow 170
Kent, Isabel 46
Kerkoski, LaVerne A. 370
Kern, Janice P. 207
Kerness, Eleanor 365
Kerr, Margaret Harrison 318
Keserica, Sonya Ann 227
Keske, Clara J. 354
Kether Communications, (c) 1994 402
Ketron, Bennie D. 340
Khublall, Vasantha 145
Kibbe, Sean M. 376
Kidd, Steven 231
Kiddoo, Ann 14
Kider, Karen Lee 326
Kidwell, Gwendolene 9
Kidwell, Maureen Marr 241
Kiener, Betty J. 85
Kierum, Iva Jane 356
Kilgore, Dawn M. 17
Kilpatrick, Geraldine E. 360
Kilpatrick Sr., James H. 397
Kim, Heryn 367
Kimbro, Floyd 414
Kimura, Yoshiye 326
Kimzey, Mike 223
Kinder, Esther S. 73
King, Agnes L. 85
King, Elva 206
King, Joy R. 346
King, Robin Suzanne 120
King, Terri 304
King, Trudy 310
King, Vera B. 218
Kirby, Lillian M. 165
Kirchman, Hilda 28
Kirkland, Charlotte 364
Kirkland, James E. 30
Kitts, Sherry 262
Klauer, Kristen 267
Kleckley, Edgar H. 422
Kleckner, Johnnye 90
Kleindorfer, Carol 387
Kleine, Michelle 132
Kleschuk, Miranda 227
Klink, Kimberly 319
Klipfel, Jackie 49
Klippert, Kristina 114
Klotsche, Catherine 41
Knapp, Norma 251
Knight, Kathy 329
Knight, Lila C. 310
Knopp, Eva J. 392
Knowles, Carrie 12
Knowles, J. 253
Knox, Alvin 395
Koblentz, Bunni 199
Kofie, Anthony 87
Kohl, Vicki 167
Kohler, Helen R. 362
Kohn, Danielle Jodie 25
Kohn, Kimberly A. 153
Kohoutek, Charlene W. 10
Kontner, Carin 115
Konz, Mary Margaret 111
Koon, David John 87
Kortes, Diane L. 401
Kosovic, Deborah Douglass 347
Kossman, Miriam R. 107
Kovach, George D. 212
Kovilic, Maryann 261
Kowalski, Melissa 94
Kozlowski, Melissa 104
Kozma, Catherine R. 382
Kraft, Debra 3
Kraft, Susen 232
Kramer, Adeline M. 342
Krannig, Dora Silvia 54
Kraus, Betty E. 58
Kremins, Kathleen A. 270
Krobel, Millie 152
Kroner, Lucille M. 319
Kruger, Bridget 246
Krupp, Irene Pataki 406
Kruse, Joan H. 52
Kruse, LeRoy 222
Kruzich, Melissa 130
Krysiak, Angie 173
Kuklin, Janet F. 360
Kunze, Dana Tanner 187
Kusi, Jeanette 351
Kustra, Richard A. 238
Kuzmitz, Michael 104

L

L., Esther Pohlman 404
La Manna, James 399
La Pointe, Minnie McMahan 120
Lachapelle, Louis J. 316
Lackas, Roseanna Napolitano 277
Lackey, Marian 118
Lada, Crystal 39
Ladd, Donna Lee 345
Laffey, John 3
Lake, Ruth E. Duffina 154
Lakey, Stella 376
LaMay Sr., Edward E. 63
Lamoreaux, Melba Riggs 318
Land, Teressa M. 228
Landers, Latonya 97
Lane, Michael 164
Lang, D. Thomas 86
Lange, April 360
Langley, Sarah 258
Langston, Estelle Jones 75
Langworthy, Mabel 223
Lanham, Jaclyn 361
Lanier, D'dee 66
Lanosz, Cansada R. 19
LaPeer, Charlotte Marie 81
Larkin, George 5
Larson, Claudine W. 179
Larson, Irene M. 380
Larson, Laura 150
Latimer, James 12
Laubacher, Todd 333
Lauer, Dorothy 379
Laurent, Hillary 63

Lauterbach, L. Joseph 273
LaVeglia, Geri 86
Lavender, Cheryl A. 188
Law, Patricia F. 122
Lawhorn, Margaret 233
Lawler, Brownie 78
Lawrence, Joyce 211
Lawrence, Marilyn D. 311
Lawson, Bobby 15
Lawson, E. Rebecca 339
Lawton, Robert C. 156
Lawyer/Waggle, Ella M. 350
Le, Paul 273
Lea, Michael A. 136
Leach, Therlow R. 257
Leavell, Barbara 409
Lebworth, Christina D. 68
LeDeoux, Danielle 8
LeDoux, Dixie J. 172
LeDoux, Vienta 273
Ledsworth, Linda 151
Lee, Doris M. 341
Lee, Felicia Renee 74
Lee, Gary Hayworth 186
Lee, Jennifer Ann 398
Lee, Kerry Jo 265
Lefebvre, Mary Ann 338
Leffew, A. J. 180
Lehmann, Augie M. 66
Leicy, Winifred Hesser 137
Leigh, Damon 91
Leighton, Richard H. 312
Leineweber, Mary Meyer 426
Leiterman, Rose 118
Leitzes, Frederick Jay 92
Leon, Andrea 330
Leonard, Rachel 255
Lepage, Louise 215
Lerch, Truea Margaret 223
LeRoy, Viola G. 308
Lessard, David 346
Levi, Dicla 406
Levin, Paula 218
Levin, Robert 97
Levy, Maurice 326
Lewellyn, Mary J. 219
Lewiel, Roxann 95
Lewis, Alwyn D. 178
Lewis, Diane M. 348
Lewis, Edna E. 208
Lewis, Elsa 363
Lewis Jr., Roy S. 306
Lewis, Martha Champion 229
Lewis, Michael J. 235
Lewis, Ora S. 146
Lewis, Ruth 126
Lewis, Thurston John 165
Leyda, Kendra 97
Liddell-Donald, Odies 298
Lillico, Adam 361
Linares, Nelly 124
Lind, Katherine 107
Linden, Anne Shirley 88
Linder, Mary Jane 263
Lindquist, Hazel F. 26
Lindsay, Candee 184
Lindsay, Irene Hazel Coureges 180
Lindsey, Patricia 291
Lininger, Geraldine 387
Linn, Dianne L. 386
Lipscomb, Bud 380
Lipson, Jonathan D. 177
List, Darlene T. 397
Listro, Kim 287
Little, Barbara 67
Little, Kevin L. 139
Little, Truda M. 282
Llew-Williams, Paul 229
Lloyd, Denise S. 22
Lloyd, Maurece W. 160
Lloyd, William H. 104
Lobel, Dorothy C. 190
Lockard, Ester Ruth 398
Loder, Adrian 45
Lofton, Crystal F. 381
Loftus, Amy 342
Loignon, Kimberly 108
Long, George 186
Long, Jane Marie 175
Long, Tommy 269
Longnecker, Shirley 99
Loonan, Juanita 17
Lopez, Mary L. 226
Lord, Melissa 242
Louthan, Martanne 367
Loveland, Cathy 191
Lovell, Shirley 369
Lowder, Aleen 365
Lowe, Betty Sue 48
Lowe, Brenda 400
Lowery, Irma Catherine 8
Lowery, Michelle 220
Lowman, Nancy E. 369
Lu, Wu-Chi 266
Lucas, Freida 48
Lucas, Gayleen 63
Lucas, M. Elizabeth 125
Luce 232
Luck, Eve 378
Luehmann, Wendy 100
Lukacinsky, Marlene 321
Lum, Gretchen Yates 389
Lund, Trisha Renee 113
Lundgren, Cissi 400
Lupton, Mary Hosmer 310
Lusignan, Carmen 211
Luther, Gretchen 404
Lymeh, Mamie B. 321
Lynch, John 400
Lytle, Darlene A. 367

M

Macbeth, Verna 292
Macdonald, Samantha 105
Mack, Marie J. 142
Mackintosh, Shauna 434
Macleod, Kenneth I. E. 308
Mader, Kyla 123
Madge, Edith 22
Mae, Shelby 353
Maertens, Jeanne Roberts 5
Magnussen, Anne 395
Maid, Prarie 100
Maki, Matt T. 117
Makla, Alice 55
Malfitana, Mary Ellen 270
Mallory, Ida 345
Malone, Laurence A. 318
Malsam, Stacy 252
Mamunes, Teresa A. 271
Mancuso, Peter 224
Manisero, Mary 315
Mann, Bud 22
Manning, Ehren 178
Manning, Jay F. 10
Manning, Jean 428
Manwaring, Martie 370
Maples, Ronald E. 140
Marapao, Herminia P. 39
Marcotte, Pegi 331
Marik, David F. 40
Mario, Luis 100
Mariotti, Celine Rose 5
Markee, A'Lesha 194
Marko, Alice K. 174
Marks, Dawn J. 69
Marks, Janet 59
Marks, Marie 263
Marks, Milli 299
Marks, Rex H. 232
Marotta, Toni Marie 245
Marquis, Danielle 213
Marra, Nicolina 109
Marriage, Lisa N. 258
Marsden, Nicole 308
Marsh, Thelma 146
Marshall, Andy 420
Marshall, Bertha L. 54
Marshall, Ruth V. 162
Marshall, Seth 95
Marshall, Shannon 309
Martel, Ricardo 222
Martin, Alta M. 201
Martin, Charlotte 348
Martin, David F. 383
Martin, Irma J. 181
Martin, Jennifer 351
Martin, Jerry 183
Martin, Laura Lyons 280
Martin, Margaret C. 373
Martin, Robyn D. 96
Martin, Susan Lynn 153
Martin, Valerie Jeanne Ridgeway 236
Martin, William D. 315
Martinez, Ruth H. 98
Martino, Kristin 251
Marx, Anne 400
Mascitti, Michael 165
masiulewicz, johnny 378
Mason, Peggy Jo 94
Mason, Sharee 336
Massey, Vickie 327
Masters, Judy Ann 75
Masterson, Florence E. 389
Mather, Robert W. 227
Matheson, R. J. 432
Mathis, Mary 328
Mathis, Patsy K. 121
Matlock, J. W., Sr. 228
Matney, Lenora M. 322
Matoushek-Propes, Michele 373
Mattax, Mark 266
Matthews, Cindy J. 389
Matthews, Heather 210
Matthews, Laurel Mae 240
Mattson, Jann 396
Maule, Tracey 295
Maurer, April 129
Maxey, Chris 197
May, Ida R. 414
May, Shirley 220
Mayberry, Mildred E. 285
Mayfield, Vera 258
Maynard, Magdalene R. 121
Maynard, Sandra Jean 113
Mays, Delia 57
McAfee, Kenneth C. 334
McAllister, Donnie Vale 209
McAninch, Charles A. 88
McBee, Chris 425
McBride, Mary C. 217
McBroom, Kathy L. 215
McCabe, Sharon Floyd 317
McCafferty, Cara 159
McCain, Jeannette 5
McCauley, Joseph 186
McClintock, Joe 415
McCluskey, Kelly 124
McCluskey, Richard 369
McCollum, Eileen 213
McCracken, Eva Betty Lea 412
McCuen, Dana L. 196
McCune, Michael J. 428
McDaniel, Glenda 339
McDermott, Dianne C. 364
McDermott, Jim 420
McDermott, Sister Laura 135
McDonald, Eve 343
McDonald, Gloria 71
McDonald, Hattie 208
McDonald, Karen 286
McDonald, Mary Peat 104
McDonnell, Rachel Blue 227
McDonough, Geraldine 405
McDonough, Rosemarie 121
McFarland, Karen 223
McFrancis, Donna 35
McGhee, Victoria A. 249
McGillivray, Patricia Middaugh 149
McGraw, Eleanor F. 394
McHenry, Lori 309
McHenry, Marie I. 244
McHenry, Martha K. 321
McIntosh, Tamika 146
McIntyre, Betty M. 365
McIntyre, Donald M. 37
McKee, B. J. 114
McKeen, Nancy 289
McKendall, Robert P. 95
McKenzie, Robert P. 318
McKim, Rosalie M. 150
McKinney, Ada L. 362
McKissick, Dollie R. 353
McKleroy, Juanita Hamner 406
McKnight, Natalie 215
McLain, Alysia 353
McLean, Shari 119
McLelland, Eva 57
McMichael, Lynn 305
McMillan, Jack 355
McNeill, Pearl 369
McPhate, John 365
McPherson, Heidi 357
McTavish, Claire 76
McWeeney, Gina 409
McWhorter, George T. 7
McWilliams, Roy F. 221
Mead, Elaine V. 15
Meadors, Eilene 32
Mealing, Ronald W. 217
Mecusker, Joan C. 394
Meddock, Sandra 333
Medford, Robert E., Jr. 294

Medina, Margaret DiOttaviano 289
Meilahn, Nancy E. 320
Meister, Terri Sue 150
Meli, Elaine 421
Melton, Mary D. 269
Mendoza, Deborah 418
Menser, Tina 217
Mercer, Myrtle 234
Mercorelli, Anthony 178
Merlini, Sandra A. 281
Merritt, V. R. 101
Merryweather, Joyce Johnson 44
Meuer, Norma Shippy 274
Meyer, Jessica 53
Meyer, R. Jane 256
Meyers, Henry J. 377
Mick, Bree 43
Mick, Florence Mae 421
Mickey, Benjamin Franklin 42
Midkiff, Iva 214
Mier, Hope 15
Migimoto, Fumi 75
Mihalik, Bianca 181
Mikles, Emily M. 361
Millard, Charles A. 29
Miller, Carolyn A. 339
Miller, Charles W. 8
Miller, Della 54
Miller, Dixie 361
Miller, Dolores M. 355
Miller, Dorothy J. 72
Miller, Jeannette Stanton 386
Miller, Juli 191
Miller, Marjorie 235
Miller, Martha Ingram 260
Miller, Meredith W. 318
Miller, Michael John 106
Miller, Mike 97
Miller, R. M. 156
Miller, Timothy D. 159
Millican, Debra 351
Mills, Debra L. 357
Mills, Robert A. 160
Milner, Rebecca E. 271
Minler, Karen 159
Minor, Shannon 286
Minton, Janie 413
Miranda, Margaret C. 264
Mirosevic, Ivan 176
Mishkoff, Harriet 427
Mitchell, Allen 71
Mitchell, Andrew 82
Mitchell, Louise 281
Mitchell, Pamela Sears 233
Mitchell, Shannon Eileen 105
Mitchell, Timothy 225
Mitchem, Ruth Ann 298
Mize, Patricia P. 166
Mizell, Roberta Powell Loyd 324
Modglin, William Henry 238
Moeckel, Debi Hensley 93
Moenter, Traci 328
Moffett, Emily B. 84
Mohney, Cathy L. 46
Mohr, Brandy 83
Moler, Diane 365
Moline, Mary 232
Mollick, John J. 16
Molnar, Patricia A. 335
Mondry, Kimberley Shawn 369
Monroe, Eileen 401
Monroe, William E. 336
MontBlanc, Sara 232
Monter, Lillie G. 142
Montgomery, Mary Alice 225
Montz, Lynne 242
Moodie, Sonia 241
Mooers, Cavin T. F. 77
Moore, Aimee R. 10
Moore, April 30
Moore, Gee Gee 341
Moore, Jack 364
Moore, Janice 21
Moore, Jennifer L. 39
Moore, Kristie D. 263
Moore, Naomi C. 268
Moore, Ophelia 325
Moore, Ozzella 375
Moore, Pamela B. 97
Moore, Ruth E. 286
Moores, L. M. 141
Morabito, Mary Matosiah 243
Morales, Elizabeth 395
Morber, Edward Lewis 378
Morelli, Joseph J. 379
Morgan, Helen Kelsey 61
Morgan, Jane 66
Morgan, John 183
Morgan, Phyllis J. 268
Morgan, Trista 226
Morganna 63
Moriconi, Donna M. 401
Morimoto, Candace 384
Morlock, Corey 382
Morris, Ida T. 189
Morris, Kristy Nicole 291
Morris, Nalda 265
Morris-Dillon, Dorothy 174
Morrison, Arthur R. 175
Morrison, Shaunna 155
Moss, Cassandra Fitzkee 13
Moss, Damon 181
Motika, Thomas 169
Mrozinski, Nezera 296
Muello, Mary 112
Muja, Kathleen A. 242
Mull, Verna 295
Mundy, Shirly J. 320
Munoz, Bonnie Morris 18
Munro, Dina G. 198
Munsey, Aimee C. 353
Murff, Reagan 99
Murnaghan, Fran 92
Murphy, Amy R. 30
Murphy, Cynthia L. 388
Murphy, Joyce 20
Murphy, Reginald 164
Murra, Jan 392
Murray, Candice 50
Murray, Mary E. 237
Muschar, Betty 364
Muse, Meeka 100
Musmecci, Marian S. 311
Myer, Candice M. 5
Myers, Anza Lo Presti 183
Myers, Dirk A. 384
Myers, Edward J. 352
Myers, Suzanne 131

N

Nacht, Michelle 105
Nadeau, Lilianne B. 165
Nagel, Jeffrey 379
Nagle, Rose M. 329
Nagy, Jessica 62
Naito, Yukihiro 269
Nakatsuka, Jennifer 189
Napier, Jillian 348
Nash, Kay Renee 224
Nash, Russ 289
Nason, Tracy 256
Navarijo, Mary Jo 218
Neal, Anna K. 338
Neal, Paula Lynette 132
Neibert, Sharon 140
Neiman, Frances E. 413
Nelon, Clyde 60
Nelson, Brenda C. 410
Nelson, Dewey A. 424
Nelson, Don 352
Nelson, Jessi 359
Nelson, Mary Beth 333
Nelson, Sharon 159
Nemec, Cynthia 212
Nemec, Norma J. 146
Nestor, Mary Ellen K. Aduleit 148
Nettles, T. H. 292
Neumann, Carol 410
Newbern, Autumn 405
Newbolds, James A. 78
Newbrey, Rebecca L. 159
Newell, Sally 145
Newman, Frederick J. 82
Newman, Sandra 305
Newsome, Scott Wesley 273
Newton, Peggy 267
Ng, Jeannie 418
Nguyen, Mac Ly Tao - Ly Dai 265
Nguyen, Thanh 234
Nichols, Pamela A. 292
Nicholson, Sheila Love 106
Nickerson, Ariane 389
Nielsen, Joyce K. 70
Nielsen, Shirley 240
Nielson, Mike 296
Nierman, Marjory 309
Nies, Jennie 405
Nieto, Karrie L. 236
Nikkel, Karen 144
Nishioka, Liane M. 261
Nitsch, Keith 147
Niz, Xavier W. 374
Nolf, Mona Broadus 96
Norman, Carolyn 346
Norris, Milidia 329
Norris, Natalie 126, 135
North, Barry W. 374
North, Sean T. 337
Norwalk, Jeffrey D. 390
Norwalk, Lucille A. 277
Nott, Brandishea Christian 196
Nowak, Jane Luciene 200
Nowakowski, Persefanie 129
Noyes, Patricia 141
Nunez, Henry J. 26

O

Oakes, DuWayne E. 355
Oakes, Owen 249
O'Brien, Hazel Hopkins 355
O'Brien, Lawrence E. 262
O'Brien, Martin J. 294
O'Connell, Cindy J. 425
O'Day, Bernard W. 211
O'Dell, Peter R. 97
Odom, Frances Lunn 12
Odoms, Claire W. 12
O'Donnell, Leanora Casey 279
Odorizzi, C. M. 316
Oerichbauer, Jamie 364
Oerly, Ruthenne 217
Offineer, Rita Joyce 156
Ogletree, Joe 64
O'Grady, Henry 178
Oh, Choo H. 205
"Oh" Kelly, Allen L. 61
Okantey, Caroline 195
Olah, Lisa 256
Oldham, Sherry Lee 264
Oleksak, Karl 280
Olender, Wanda J., nurse 277
Oleson, Mildred V. 129
Oliveira, Kristy Armas 106
Olivencia, Magali 123
Olofsson, Jennifer R. 424
Olsen, Elmer B. 341
Olsen, Harold 186
Olsen, Kristine 99
Olsen, Marie Fuhriman 270
Olson, Jack Robert 210
Olson, Jan 340
Olson, Marjorie J. 125
Olsson, S. Ingemar C. 247
O'Neil, Ginny 357
O'Neill, Elise 405
O'Neill, Mary B. 297
O'Neill, Thomas 240
O'Neill, Thomas R. 142
Orender, Betty 202
Origliato, Gianfranco 348
Orr, J. Andrew 386
Orr, Mandy 303
Orti, Lori 129
Ortiz, Daniel, Jr. 378
Ortiz, Shannon 117
Orton, Nell Blanton 290
Orzel, Cinnamon 357
Osborn, Carol 210
Osborne, Jay 45
Osborne, Jonathan 382
Osborne, Winifred J. 260
Osgood, Nethelia 117
Oshiro, Jean H. 72
Osterholtz, Anna 359
Ostfeld, Adrian M. 30
Oswald, Donna D. 380
Otis, Faylene 397
Otis, Kathryn 96
O'Toole, Darby 148
Otto, Teri Ann 229
Ouano, Elisha 210
Outerbridge, Keisha 138
Overbye, Eileen 178
Owen, Doris Jean 73

P

Paddio-Johnson, Eunice 202
Paddock, Stephen B. 110
Paff, William A. 228
Pagac, Stacy 110
Page, Martha C. 265

Page, Wendy L. 275
Pairadee III, Archie R. 85
Pairsh, Marty 270
Paisley, Laurel Joan 163
Palacio, Angela M. 67
Palk, Bufar 42
Palmer, Minnie 281
Palmer, Valerie J. 431
Paolillo, Louise 274
Pape, Moritz E. 234
Pardel, Carmen 68
Paris, Fay 419
Parker, Doris 339
Parker, Jessie L. 21
Parker, Joan S. 53
Parker, Mazell 308
Parker, Roy A. 152
Parks, June 43
Parrish, David J. 197
Partlow, Sara 304
Pascal, Paul 252
Pascucci, Edward A. 179
Passmore, R. Dean 107
Patania, Mary 236
Patel-Das, P. B. 221
Patènte, Michelle Suzette 147
Patrykus, Roberta 371
Patten, Lee 253
Patterson, Elexia Ruth 71
Patterson, Paula 105
Patterson, Roy 259
Patti, Caroline T. 343
Paul, Christopher L. 81
Paul, Richard 426
Paulauskas, Gerard J. 339
Paulun, Carl L. 170
Paverd, Laurence E. 223
Payne, Cynthia L. 353
Paynter, Karen L. 100
Pearce, Catherine 397
Pearce, Glenn Stuart 38
Pearson, Florence 352
Pease, Barbara 210
Peck, Joyce 193
Peek, Debrina 213
Peets, Ronald R. 154
Peiler, Charlotte M. 201
Pellegrin, Kathy Arnold 264
Peltz, Jennifer 9
Pendery, Eric Christopher 42
Pendleton, J. B. 234
Penfold, Chastity R. 68
Peng, Ling Fan 303
Penick, Patricia Florida 103
Perample, Diane Pencin 417
Pereira, Alvaro 402
Perez, Eric Noel 426
Perez Jr., Roman 98
Perez, Julianna 194
Perez, Nestor L. 251
Perkins Jr., O. E. (Mickey) 429
Perkins, Marlyn H. 161
Perlin, Elliott 347
Perras, Patricia A. 110
Perry Sr., Clay 8
Perry, Susie 293
Person, Sharon D. 262
Peterman, Jennifer L. 386
Peters, Elizabeth 187
Peters, James A. 362
Peters, Timothy A. 96
Petersen, Gene 20
Peterson, Beatrice Fox 345
Peterson, George Z. 391
Peterson, Marion M. 116
Peterson, Mary L. 112
Peterson, Richard W. 225
Peterson, Sarah E. 106
Petruzzi, Ernest R. 349
Petsch, Timothy S. 217
Petty, Mary Ellen 120
Phantom, J. T. 383
Phelan, Claire Joseph 55
Phelan, Thomas A. 147
Phillips, Agnes M. 383
Phillips, Dullie Josephine 379
Phillips, Julia M. 22
Phillips, Mary E. 243
Piatt, Mary Jo 150
Piccola, Ruth Ann 233
Pickering, Netta 322
Pickles, Michelle 310
Picknell, Diana 246
Pierce, Shirlene R. 261
Piersma, Anna Mae 398
Pierson, Helen Bowers 27
Pierson, Manda L. 257
Pillsbury, Craig 353
Ping, Shirley 134
Pino, Rick 242
Pionke, James A. 38
Pirolli, Albert M. 15
Pitkin, Shane 145
Pitts, Donna Michelle 360
Plaia, Virginia M. 154
Plambeck, Gae 386
Planz, Lucille 113
Platt, Helen 16
Player, Gale L. 32
Plummer, Randy 248
Pniewski, Gary Thomas 213
Pocai, Jodi Marie 420
Poete, Shauna 323
Poff, Amanda 213
Pohlman, Esther L. 404
Poindexter, Demene C. 399
Polasek, D. 314
Poles, Alessandra A. 16
Pollestad, Betty Lou 88
Polowczyk, Lucas 243
Pomales, Luis 254
Pool, Carlton Dewayne 345
Pool, Lorna L. 258
Pope, Mary Delaney 216
Pope, Nita E. Clemons 276
Porrett, Renee 111
Porter, Beulah Langston 195
Porter, Elizabeth Y. 361
Porter, Grace 91
Porter, Kerry 240
Porter, Lillian H. 239
Porter, Martha P. 101
Porttelo, Caesar 19
Post, Deborah Mae 35
Potter, Charlene A. 346
Powers, Marion Knott 147
Powers, Verna 291
Prapas, Christine 338
Prentice, Anjanette M. 381
Pretorius, Bronwen 400
Prewitt, Carolyn B. 361
Priadka, Michel J. 225
Price, Edith L. 352
Price, James C. 174
Price, James E. 417
Pritchard, Pearl C. 315
Probasco, James M. 392
Profumo, Denise 41
Proudfoot, Richard L. 96
Pucek, Tamie 311
Pujol, Jordan M. 389
Pulver, John 190
Pumroy, Mildred 106
Purdie, Carelese 414
Purdum-Smith, Kathleen 285
Purtle, Barbara 84
Purviance, Deborah Lum 181
Putnam, Elizabeth M. 55

Q

Quietstorm, Jean-Philippe 51
Quinn, Judy 385

R

Rabson, Herman N. 214
Radebaugh, Jerry Lloyd 423
rafferty, sven lars loebler 149
Ragno, Carolyn Joan 403
Ragon, Katrina 227
Ragsdale, Howard E. 346
Rains, Edythe 359
Rajaram, Jayashree 68
Ralph, Beverly A. 30
Ralston, Dorothy M. 388
Ramirez, Milagros F. 332
Ramos, Amanda 74
Rampton, Kathleen 137
Rand, Rolle 110
Randall, Michael Mykee Paul 289
Randolph, Beth 342
Rankin, Moira 328
Rapose, Julie A. 187
Rastrelli, Tina Louise 121
Ray, Audrey L. 174
Raymond, Virginia 115
Rea.., Jesse L. 90
Read, W. A. 105
Reagan, Jo 388
Reber, Robert E. 229
Redfern, Nieves 239
Redfoot, Michell S. 137
Redlin, Betty L. 16
Reece, Crystal Gayle 174
Reece, Delores Wilson 409
Reed, A. H. 266
Reed, Christopher 198
Reed, Danielle N. 41
Reed, Gerald 26
Reed, Marylin 224
Reedy, Carolyn Selvoski 83
Reese, Edith 342
Reese, Lee Fleming 298
Reese, Sarah Porter 115
Reese, Sharon E. 287
Reeves, Cathy "Misty" 339
Reeves, Della 211
Reffert, David C. 4
Reich, Herb 79
Reid, Barbara R. 10
Reidelberger, Pat 132
Reinhart, Steven L. 281
Reinholdt, Candace 345
Reinicker, Charlotte Eichfeld 18
Renee, Cynthia 403
Renwick, Cyra Grace 358
Reny, Scarlet Dee 101
Reyes, Janell Marie 208
Reyling, David 339
Reynolds, Jean Mehan 388
Reynolds, Lee 96
Reynolds, Mary 149
Reynolds, R. W. 167
Rhoads, George 407
Rhodes, Eric Foster 362
Rice, Katina 249
Richards, Ann 62
Richards, Edith L. 393
Richards, Elisabeth 428
Richardson, Denise 415
Richardson, Gary Carleen 386
Richardson, Steven 239
Richfield, Hedy 189
Richie, Tonya 226
Richmond, Steven S. 248
Richter, Billy 87
Richter, Carolyn J. 65
Riddell, Erin 334
Riddle, Clinton E. 365
Ridlen, Lillian Heigle 131
Riedel, Jacqueline 83
Rife, Susan A. 120
Rigsby, Shonda L. 238
Riley, Agnes 350
Riley, Julie S. 399
Riley, Linda 100
Riley, Shirley E. 336
Rimbaugh, Keri Ann 333
Riolo, Michael A. 242
Riper, Trudy Van 169
Rippy, Ruby F. 99
Risk, Patricia Gough 372
Ritchie, Josephine O. 170
Rivera, Ray 336
Rivera, Sophie 368
Robardey, Russell George 117
Roberts, Alice M. 44
Roberts, Alice R. 195
Roberts, Gwendolyn A. 47
Roberts, Howard G. 20
Roberts, JLA-Lo 368
Roberts, Marjorie 219
Roberts, Mickie 311
Roberts, Nellie Mingus 116
Roberts, Paul 163
Roberts, Shirley Stewart 240
Robertson, Debra S. 44
Robertson, Irene E. 32
Robinson, Carmen 30
Robinson, Janice 49
Robinson, Jessica 184
Robinson, Marilyn B. 119
Robinson, Velma 327
Robles, Renee T. 332
Rocheleau, Sabrina 230
Rockwell, Nancy Jo 95
Rodriguez, Margaret 227
Rodriguez, Oscar E. 272
Roe, LaNae M. 94
Rogahn, Michelle D. 222
Rogers, Alice 14
Rogers, Leon, Sr. 235
Rogers, Norman I. 372, 373
Rohlf, Deborah 356

Rojas, David 4
Roldan, Kathy Jimenez 300
Roll, Renee 221
Romine, Debra D. 72
Rood, Steve A. 331
Roosa, Diane 198
Roossien, Virginia 122
Roper, Lisa 228
Rose, Susan 220
Roseberry, Jeannie 172
Rosenberger, Marlon M. 236
Roskoski, Sam 287
Ross, Andrew C. 208
Ross, Vance, Jr. 334
Ross, Yvonne 232
Rossell, Kathy 235
Rountree, Carlton W. 8
Rousseau, Gail A. 349
Rousseau, Jules R. 391
Rovins, Rose Shanen 336
Rowland, Kathy S. 329
Roy, Geraldean B. 406
Roy, Lloyd H. 221
Rubel, Barry 81, 190
Rucker, Karen L. 160
Rud, Lula 283
Rudd, Kristi 334
Ruf, Karin 245
Ruff, Michael 317
Rumford, Elise Bills 180
Runge, Loni 306
Runyon, Ted H. 235
Rupert, Ruth C. 98
Rush, Edna 43
Rush, Michele A. 373
Russell, Clare 403
Russell, Mark 159
Russell, Rhonda 95
Rustenholtz, Robert L., Sr. 264
Ryder, Nona B. 322
Rysanek, Pacita B. 326

S

Sacauskis, Mary 250
Sahibzada, Shana 369
Saldana, Aida Ophelia 377
Saldivar, Joyce A. 359
Salers, Kelli 284
Saling, Joseph H. 76
Saltiban III, Debbie Lynn 88
Salvagno Jr., Louis 302
Salyer, Shirley 234
Salzman, Edna I. 383
Samarzia, Shirley 304
Samples, Martha 139
Sanchez, Christine 423
Sannita, Mary Ann 119
Santens, Charles K. 379
Santiago, Cinsearae 78
Santillo, Stephanie Anne 280
Santora, Jessica F. 398
Santos, Steve 276
Santos, Theresa Ann 287
Santry, Sunny 102
Saucedo, Vilma D. 334
Saunders, Joanne J. 185
Saveley, Barb 53
Savlov, Melissa Z. 134
Savok, Joyce E. 21
Savon, Yvonne Marie 336
Sawyer, Leslie Nunamaker 158
Sawyer, Tunji 293
Sawyers, Erna M. 33
Sayed, Donna 416
Scalise, Christina 82
Scarborough, Lacy 143
Schaffrath Jr., Robert W. 315
Scheffer, Betty Jo 384
Schemenauer, Rosetta Ewing 102
Schifilliti, Sal 301
Schindler, Barbara Fulton 388
Schlepp, N. B. 151
Schlotzhauer, Mary 315
Schmauch Jr., George E. 430
Schmitz, Gina R. 202
Schmitz, Ralph 254
Schmitzer, Donna 60
Schnabel, Elvira C. 170
Schnackenberg, Darlene 25
Schofield, Jennifer 351
Schreiber, Lisa 103
Schrieber, Vicki 250
Schroat, Bryan 184
Schrock, Joseph 341
Schroettner, Mark Anthony 372
Schueller, Tanya R. 161
Schulte, Vivian 432
Schultz III, Glenn 341
Schutz, Joellen Yeray 406
Schwab, Emilia 390
Schwan, Dave 395
Schwarz, Amy 182
Schwarz, Randolph 370
Schwinger, Gladys 345
Scoggin, Alisha 343
Scott, Edward S. 344
Scott, Lynne F. 319
Scott, Marie 429
Scott, Marigold 115
Scott, Rhena Norma 312
Scriven, Norman 285
Scroggins Sr., Charles Everett 81
Sears, Katherine 226
Sebanz, Victoria 231
Sedelmaide, Norm 119
Seestadt, Jean 419
Seideman, Myra 125
Seifert, Heather Noelle 195
Seifrid, Phyllis 141
Senkiw, Irene E. 11
Seoh, Roy M. 165
Service, Regina Noell 104
Sewell, Madeline F. 168
Shadeed, Jennifer 24
Shank, Rose A. 329
Shannon, Netta 260
Shapo, Jacqueline Raznik 203
Sharitz, Josephine M. 389
Sharpe, Nathan T. 116
Shatouhy, Dawn 349
Shattuck, Daniel M. 61
Shaver, Millie 111
Shaver, Ree 135
Shearer, Anna 24
Sheehan, Kevin D. 316
Sheets, Dorothy E. 387
Shelton, Joe 389
Shelton, Katherine 217
Shepherd, Delores A. 424
Shepherd, Sharon 155
Sherba, Annabelle M. 345
Sheridan, Theresa 246
Sheriff, Rebecca Liner 230
Sherman, Ellen 382
Sherman, Helen 36
Sherry, Sharon E. 115
Sherwood-Daniel, Teri 290
Shields, Susan 246
Shipley, Della Jean 385
Shockey, Teri L. 294
Shores, William W. 320
Shubrook, Jeremy 401
Shuler, Shirley 247
Shurley, Helen M. 383
Shurvinton, Kimly 109
Sica, John 423
Sidden, Peggy C. 271
Sides, James G. 73
Siebeneicher, Christina 385
Signaigo, Joseph Augustine 235
Signorello, Evelyn E. 356
Sikes, Delores 182
Silva, Mark 242
Silva, Sergio C. 98
Simkulet, E. M. 371
Simmons, Charron 83
Simmons, Janice Halsell 71
Simmons, P. 154
Simoes, Antonio 44
Simpson, Ellen 420
Simpson, Jamie 203
Simpson, Wanda 160
Sinclair, Sarah M. 280
Sinnette, Marilyn 104
Skiendziel, Julie M. 385
Skinner, Paul 306
Skinner, Virginia 323
Sky, Randee 104
Skyles, Margaret 333
Sliney, Thomas 333
Sloan, Bernice 62
Small, Fred 3
Smeltzer, Susan 145
Smith, Andrea 189
Smith, April 404
Smith, Bud 55
Smith, Chad Michael 33
Smith, Cornelia 187
Smith, Doris Dunn, Ph.D. 49
Smith, Erin L. 407
Smith, Etta Jean 184
Smith, Fern Gardiner 401
Smith, Grace K. 380
Smith, Herbert H. 69
Smith, J. C. 434
Smith, Jessica S. E. 362
Smith, Jim A. 355
Smith, Lorena A. 326
Smith, Melanie 234
Smith, Mia 223
Smith, Nantanit 268
Smith, Sandra R. 240
Smith, Saralyn V. 160
Smith, William T. 434
Smith, Zelma 303
Smyder, Jennifer 10
Snider, Jessica 64
Snow, Dorothy 387
Snowden, Virginia 284
Snyder, Doris 3
Snyder, Eileen G. 177
Snyder, Gayle Elaine 349
Snyder, Jeanne M. 193
Snyder, John M. 394
Soileau, Kenneth 312
Solis, Francisca Marie 366
Solomon, Marvin 309
SookDeo, Neil 163
Sorensen, Florilla 420
Sorensen, Lisa 272
Sorge, Max 164
Sorge-Kokinda, Carol 179
Soto, Dodie 400
Southwell, Phyllis 247
Spangler, Christine F. 350
Spaulding, Midge 226
Spears, Flora 91
Spears, Tiffanny 291
Spencer, Carolyn 383
Spencer, Grace M. 396
Spermon, Corinne 354
Spiecher, Janet 360
Spight, Edwin L. 65
Spiker, T. D. 253
Spillan, Linda 257
Spillers, Shana M. 331
Spiros, Mitchell D. 305
Spitzig, Heidi 403
Sprague, Pamela M. 302
Sprouse, Mildred C. 317
Spurling, Shirley C. 96
Squar, Mara 101
Squier, John C. 343
Squire, Shirley 141
Squires, Edward L. 398
St. John, Jeffrey 390
Stafford, Laura 337
Stahl, Roxie E. 269
Stahley, Mark 233
Stallings, Courtney L. 27
Stallings, Sarah 254
Stamatiou, Kiki 152
Stamatovic, Vicky 167
Stanberry, D. Elaine 324
Standridge, Bill 23
Stanford-Cox, Marlene 103
Stanley, Mary Lee 141
Stanley, Myrtle C. 110
Stans, Sarina Sue 244
Stanton, Lois Katz 302
Stark, Jimmie A. 377
Staska, Elsie J. 69
Staveley, Eva 425
Stead, Burl P. 6
Steadman, Barbara 413
Steadman, Veda Nylene 127
Steele, Tracy 235
Steenrod, Georgia 383
Steeves, Betty 355
Steeves, Marjorie 251
Stenbar, Edward Nathan 388
Stenholtz, Dana B. 396
Stephens, Leigh 116
Stephens, Rachel 292
Stephens, Valerie P. 229
Stephenson, Ruby L. 161
Stepnowski, Frank 74
Stetson, Susan 157
Stevens, Elaine H. 403
Stevens, Laurie 122
Stevenson, Donald B. 196
Stevenson, Emmer J. 383
Stevenson, Jack 204

Stevenson, Mary 100
Steward, Danny R. 35
Steward, V. L. 431
Stewart, Grace Elaine 207
Stewart, Thomas E. 301
Stinson, Jackie 380
Stisser, Betty E. 86
Stoddard, James A. 402
Stokes, Mary Parsons 230
Stoltz, Ann Marie 79
Stolz, Esther 70
Stolzenburg, Eldon L. 181
Stone, Edna 359
Stone, Joy E. 25
Stone, Katrine F. 128
Stone, Phylliss Faircloth 277
Stone, Sandra Wallraven 94
Stonebarger, Katie 167
Stouffer, Darla 393
Stout, Violet D. 107
Stowell, Melissa 337
Strader, Lori Jean 246
Strange, Tensie Lee 297
Strem, George G. 184
Strianese, Jeanette 70
Strickland, Charles 348
Strickland, Etta J. 423
Strickland, Leigh Victoria 325
Strickland, Marj 216
Stringer, John C. 47
Strong, Barbara J. 74
Stroup, Sandra 94
Sturgeon, Hazel 206
Sudziarski, Nancy Lee 102
Sullivan, Lindo M. 138
Sultana, Nilofer 334
Summa Jr., Robert P. 285
Summer, Clodah G. 352
Sundquist, Carl V. 28
Sundra, Miladene 332
Suniga, Killarney H. J. 133
Susanne, Myranda 257
Sutherland, Donna G. 53
Sutherland, Ollie 126
Sutton, Jimmie Nell Bush 59
Swallow, Melissa Chris 296
Swansboro, Brian Christopher 412
Swanson, Bonnie L. 204
Swanson, Chad Whalen 380
Swartwood, Michael 125
Swatling, Carol-Ann 53
Swearingen, Debra A. 88
Swecker, Debbie 359
Sweet, Dahn 22
Sweet, Glenn R. 41
Swick, Debbie Peterman 246
Swift, Chad 6
Swinford, Iva Mae 12
Swisher, Loretta V. 120
Sword, Gene 397
Sykes, Beatrice 201
Synek, M. 275
Synowiecki, Betty 367
Szetela, Debbie 212
Szuromi, Laszlo 144

T

Tabor, Curtis B. 179
Tainter, Kerrie Holton 248
Tait, Bobbie 383
Tambo, Jo 380
Tande, Dibussi 412
Tanenbaum, David 360
Tarbox, Vernon H. 146
Tardiff, Margaret 242
Tarver, Reginald D. 153
Tausch, Susan D. 280
Taylor, Alison 384
Taylor, Ashley E. 205
Taylor, Carrie 83, 177
Taylor, Dorothy C. 356
Taylor, Elaine N. 214
Taylor, Gail E. 77
Taylor, Gene W. 123
Taylor, JoyAnn M. 352
Taylor, Linda G. 324
Taylor, Sean M. 244
Teal, Josie 417
Tearpak, Clara 6
Tebbe, Kerstin 327
Tedder, Mary Rebecca 112
Teed, Craig L. 342
Teichmann, Lucy 162
Teitelbaum, Phyllis 109
Tellou, Basil 380
Terry, Ruth Garms 153
Teuscher, D. R. 255
Thacker, Agnes 55
Thomas, Al 408
Thomas, Cecile A. 422
Thomas, Charlotte B. 188
Thomas, Christina 41
Thomas, Fannie 64
Thomas, Gloria E. 67
Thomas, Maxine Taylor 312
Thomas, Sean C. 258
Thomas, Valeria Jane 247
Thome, Jennifer L. 341
Thompson, Adeline 402
Thompson, Dee 392
Thompson, Linda S. 116
Thompson, Martha 252
Thompson, Patricia L. 296
Thompson, Stephen Alexander 100
Thomson, Richard J. 118
Thorne, Gareth 61
Thorpe-Olson, Harriet 379
Thurber, Aritha 344
Tidwell, Michelle 136
Tiernan, Carol A. S. 43
Tikalsky, Sarah L. 106
Timpanelli-Dempsey, Veronica 229
Tindel, Janet M. 344
Titus, Nicole K. 245
Tkac, D. K. 366
Todd, Caroline 347
Toler, Joy Hope 39
Toles, Lucy Stevens 283
Tomaino, Joseph R. 198
Tooker, G. Calvin 168
Toomey, Lil 302
Torres, Amber 359
Tossavainen, Aini 404
Townsend, Cynthia 358
Tozzi, John F. 205
Tracy, Elizabeth 47
Tracy, Melissa 105
Tracy, Patti Rose 155
Tramell, Tiffany K. 316
Tramposch, Elvira 377
Transou, Larry 270
Trasga, Aquino Tubola 185
Trent, Annie Merle Gray 377
Tretton, Frances-Faith 68
Tribble, Lois Jennison 161
Triebenbach, Lynnae 110
Tripp, Mary Ann 125
Tripp, Tiffany Nicole 311
Troll, Florence N. 346
Trongale, Elizabeth 350
Trudeau, Gloria 82
Trudell, Kay 112
Tschantz, Rose Milligan 97
Tuazon, Tracy 220
Tucker, C. Ray 146
Tucker, Leala Randall 274
Tucker, Nell B. 105
Tuckness, Therese Marie 291
Tueche, Eli, Jr. 405
Tumey, Kristy 223
Turley, Sharon 301
Turner, Edith Cox 44
Turner, Steven Price 107
Turnipseed, Betty Arlene 401
Turtle, Kitt Little 368
Tuttle, Larry L. 169
Tweedie, Valerie J. 325

U

Umbdenstock, Lorraine 297
Umlor, Jody 410
Ungerecht, Theresa A. 100
Uonelli, Elaine M. 34
Uphoff Jr., Baron Joseph A. 363
Urban, Mike 162
Ursu, Mike 94
Utt, Shannon 389
Utterback, Almeda Lou 208

V

Vahlberg, Dave 66
Valdez, Yvette 116
Valentine, Evelyn Sampson 195
Valentine, Richard D. 271
Vallecorsa, Lucretia 112
Van Bibber, Janet 185
Van Every, Phillip 305
Van Kuiken, Jerome 33
Van Muyden, Craig A. 384
Van Nordstrand, Robert A. 101
van Oosbree, R. 307
Van Wyk, Jacob W. 46
Van Zandt, Beverly 203
Vancil, Norma L. 104
VanSickle, Elizabeth Paige 345
VanSlambrouck, Patty 111
Varga, Boske D. 287
Varnell, Ola 111
Vasquez, Richard 101
Vaughan, Dorothy 354
Vaughan, Rita 103
Vaughn, Bonnie Jean 364
Vaugle, Henry 380
Veno, Elsie 206
Verhelle, Mildred 218
Verrill, Mary 243
Versocki, Mike 107
Vien, Enid 423
Vigenski, Rick 104
Villanueva, Jennifer 414
Villarreal, Amy 290
Villarreal, Rojelio 371
Vilsmeyer, Vicki 224
Vine, Doris 350
Vinson, Dawn Anne 363
Virg-In, Alicia 3
Vogelsong, Joanne A. 407
Voget, Antoinette 188
Vollrath, Helen 391
Vomhof, Claire 45
Von Hagel, Pam 224
von Pohle, Marjorie Punches 333
Vondran, Evelyn H. 407
Voytek, Laura L. 105
Vydelingum, Nadarajen A. 318

W

Wachter, Crystal 357
Wackler, Joe 209
Wade, Andreia Catherine 198
Waeckerle, Leola 127
Wagner, Inez Mahan 204
Wailes, Helen A. 401
Wald, Beth Greena 423
Waldbillig, Marcia 115
Waldo, Heatherlynn 81
Waldrop, Teri L. 263
Walker, Billy L. 5
Walker, Cynthia 27
Walker, Donna A. 384
Walker, Elfrida E. 393
Walker III, Grover C. 205
Walker, Lynda C. 276
Walker, Silvia 113
Walker, Teresa 167
Wall, Lucille Smallwood 267
Wallace, Betty Jean 419
Walsh, N. M. 163
Walter, Wendy 106
Walters, Gustave 378
Walters, Mildred 252
Walters, Wendy 97
Waltrip, Louise 251
Wang, Harry 188
Wangler, Bob 87
Wanner, Carrol L. 402
Ward, Barbara M. 21
Ward, Chrissy L. 344
Ward, Christina M. 18
Ward, Christine 403
Ward, Grace 363
Ward, Joyce 199
Ward, Katie 129
Warner, Ruth 134
Warntjes, Rita 105
Warrenburg, Wanda 275
Washington, Nicole 313
Waskewicz, K. 278
Wass, Grant H. 392
Waters, Virginia D. 159
Watkins, Aethena C. 59
Watkins, B. B. 235
Watkins, Opal E. 107
Watson, Cletus M. S., Franciscan 377
Watson, Lydia R. (Bowers) 245
Watson-Hansen, LanaJo 114
Watters, Cory Jean 202
Watts, Mary Baker 149
Waxman, Teri 373
Waxwood, Vincenne A. 243
Weaver, Grace M. 178

Weaver, Laura L. 264
Weaver, Pamela S. 135
Web, Alice Jeanne 32
Webber, Brent 14
Weber, Glenna 86
Webster, Jodie 35
Weeks, Bonny L. 356
Weeks, Penny 151
Wegge, Barbara J. 26
Weiskopf, Wanda 221
Welborn, Yvonne Dufek-Hogue 122
Welch, Sharon 93
Weldin, Nylah 244
Wells, Betty Jo 351
Wells, Cora 28
Wells, Dennis Michael 79
Wells, Marty H. 244
Wells, Tess 299
Wenger, Fred 404
Werner, Luetta G. 239
Wesley, Summer 279
West, Goley S. 360
West, Molly 337
West, Nancy Fay 109
Westaby, Eve 4
Westcott, Robbin 166
Westerback, Michael A. 160
Westman, Rebecca 96
Westmoreland, John White 7
Westover, Wynn Earl 255
Westphal, Bruce K. 377
Whalen, Jody 200
Whaley, Hal 401
Whaley, Krystal Lee 129
Whattam, Kevin 102
Wheeler, Mary 222
Wheeler, Pat 151
Wheeler, Randall D. 122
Wheeler, Sue 259
White, Beatrice 396
White, Bonnie 396
White, Candice 351
White, Floyd Edward 18
White, Patty 138
White-Epstein, Gloria M. 177
White-Harrison, Mima 252
Whiteaker, Janet F. 197
Whitehead, Betty 183
Whiting, Casey T. 46
Whitlow, Coty Lynn 186
Whitmore, Cleve II 173
Whittington, Katrina 221
Wickham, Jeannie 365
Widawski, Eva 420
Widner, Evelyn Copple 395
Widner, Linda 121
Wiegel, Stephanie M. 108
Wieland, A. J. 260
Wiener, Florence K. 38
Wiesen, James J. 367
Wilborn, Lindsey M. 105
Wilcox, Heather D. 246
Wilcox, Robin 241
Wilder, Kathi 368
Wiliker, John 348
Wilke, Randy J. 126
Wilkes, Carolyn 185
Wilkins, Dorothy E. 410
Wilkinson, Cindy Lou 382
Wilkinson, Heidi 90
Wilkinson, Marguerite I. 293
Wilkinson, Sherrie Isenhart 275
Wilkinson-Anderson, Elizabeth 360
Willett, Edward F. 14
William 242
Williams, Barbara Z. 187
Williams, Dailin Gao 60
Williams, Dale 173
williams, danny 77
Williams, Enid Jo 87
Williams, James E. 27
Williams, LoLetia C. 241
Williams, M. Kaylor 138
Williams, Melissa Marie 368
Williams, Robert M. 219
Williams, Sharel 308
Williams, W. G. 233
Willingham, Rae Ann 266
Willis, Dorothy Padgett 379
Willis, Helen 43
Willis, Linda Ann 278
Willmore, Rebecca 314
Wills, George Roland 70
Wilson, Alice Stewart 124
Wilson, Angela D. 11
Wilson, Bernice W. 68
Wilson, Christina M. 421
Wilson, Elnora 404
Wilson, John D. 7
Wilson, Julie F. 79
Wilson, Margaret J. 272
Wilson, Milissau N. 335
Wilson, Nancy 264
Wilson, Nancy L. 155
Wilson, Sara J. 303
Wilson, Stephanie D. 155
Wilson, Theresa V. 110
Wilson, Trevor 231
Wiman, Mary Jo 231
Wineinger, Peggy 330
Winfield, Catherine 40
Wingfield, Marvin B. 98
Wingham, Erma 198
Wingo, Dorothy Maria 192
Winslett, Ray 136
Winstead, Andrew Cannon 90
Winter, Jason 91
Wise, Jennifer 406
Wise, Paula S. 290
Withee, Beverly 3
Witkowski, Tasha 225
Witman, Cheryl 14
Wode, Gloria Margaret (Clinedinst) 31
Wohlers, Sharon K. 228
Wojtysiak, Loraine 116
Wolc, Natalie 98
Wolf, Lawrence 236
Womack, Kathy 136
Wood Jr., George A. 414
Wood, Lee 255
Wood, Lisa L. 99
Wood, Lorilee J. 102
Woodall, R. Mark 162
Woodruff, Alice Lincoln 385
Woods, Ashley J. 20
Woods, Laura S. 217
Woodward, Evelyn 376
Wooldridge, Judith 209
Worcester, R. J. 239
Worrall, David C. 340
Worth, Alice E. 355
Worthington, Sam 97
Wouten, Danny 70
Wrezinski, ShariLynn 229
Wright, Carmen 193
Wright, Donna M. 18
Wright, Hal 382
Wright, L. H. A. 268
Wright, Laura 125, 238
Wright, Linda 283
Wright, Margaret Evans 102
Wright, Martha Belle 116
Wright, Opal L. 99
Wright, Raymond M. 271
Wright, Vicki Lynn 250
Wright, Wanda 292
Wright, Wilbur Harold 119
Wring, Bo 59
Wyatt Sr., Robert H. 281
Wylie, Donald R. 393

Y

Yakoubian, William K. 227
Yamamura, Shelby H. S. 288
Yanchyshyn, Madelyn 97
Yarbrough, Lily May 95
Yeoman, Harry F. 395
Yergan, J. F. 216
Yerkes, Voni 109
Yesia, Walter M. 136
Young, Gwen M. 50
Young, Jean 399
Young, Sarah J. 374
Young, Tony D. 323
Yu, Willy 144

Z

Zak, Christina 85
Zamora, Mary Lou 279
Zemalkowski, Christine 400
Zeschke, Merle R. 241
Zevan, Jamey L. 402
Ziegler, Karen A. 108
Ziemba, Stephanie L. 228
Zimmerman, Jaquie 391
Zito, Betty Szepessy 393
Zmuda, Nicole 98
Zoranovich, Carol 347